FRANCIS PARKMAN

Francis Parkman

The Oregon Trail
The Conspiracy of Pontiac

THE LIBRARY OF AMERICA

The paper used in this publication meets the
minimum requirements of the American National Standard for
Information Sciences—Permanence of Paper for Printed
Library Materials, ANSI Z39.48—1984.

Distributed to the trade in the United States
and Canada by the Viking Press.

Library of Congress Catalog Number: 90-62264
For cataloging information, see end of Notes.
ISBN 0–940450–54–2

First Printing
The Library of America—53

Manufactured in the United States of America

WILLIAM R. TAYLOR
WROTE THE NOTES FOR THIS VOLUME

Grateful acknowledgment is made to the National Endowment for the Humanities, the Ford Foundation, and the Andrew W. Mellon Foundation for their generous support of this series.

Contents

The Oregon Trail   1

The Conspiracy of Pontiac

    VOLUME I   343

    VOLUME II   613

Chronology   919

Note on the Texts   931

Notes   936

THE OREGON TRAIL

*Sketches of
Prairie and Rocky-Mountain Life*

"Let him who crawls enamor'd of decay,
  Cling to his couch, and sicken years away;
  Heave his thick breath, and shake his palsied head;
  Ours—the fresh turf, and not the feverish bed."

BYRON.

THE
California
&
OREGON TRAIL.

The journey which the following narrative describes was undertaken on the writer's part with a view of studying the manners and character of Indians in their primitive state. Although in the chapters which relate to them, he has only attempted to sketch those features of their wild and picturesque life which fell, in the present instance, under his own eye, yet in doing so he has constantly aimed to leave an impression of their character correct as far as it goes. In justifying his claim to accuracy on this point, it is hardly necessary to advert to the representations given by poets and novelists, which, for the most part, are mere creations of fancy. The Indian is certainly entitled to a high rank among savages, but his good qualities are not those of an Uncas or an Outalissi.

The sketches were originally published in the Knickerbocker Magazine, commencing in February, 1847.

BOSTON, *February* 15, 1849.

Contents.

CHAPTER   PAGE

I. The Frontier, ... 9

II. Breaking the Ice, ... 16

III. Fort Leavenworth, ... 26

IV. 'Jumping Off,' 29

V. 'The Big Blue,'. 39

VI. The Platte and the Desert, ... 55

VII. The Buffalo, ... 67

VIII. Taking French Leave, ... 82

IX. Scenes at Fort Laramie, ... 96

X. The War Parties, ... 110

XI. Scenes at the Camp, ... 130

XII. Ill Luck, ... 147

XIII. Hunting Indians, ... 154

XIV. The Ogillallah Village, ... 176

XV. The Hunting Camp, ... 195

XVI. The Trappers, ... 215

XVII. The Black Hills, ... 224

XVIII. A Mountain Hunt, ... 228

XIX. Passage of the Mountains, ... 239

XX. The Lonely Journey, ... 254

XXI. The Pueblo and Bent's Fort, ... 272

XXII. Tête Rouge, the Volunteer, ... 279

XXIII. Indian Alarms, ... 284

XXIV. The Chase, ... 294

XXV. The Buffalo Camp, ... 303

XXVI. Down the Arkansas, ... 317

XXVII. The Settlements, ... 333

Chapter I.

THE FRONTIER.

"Away, away from men and towns
To the silent wilderness."
SHELLEY.

LAST SPRING, 1846, was a busy season in the city of St. Louis. Not only were emigrants from every part of the country preparing for the journey to Oregon and California, but an unusual number of traders were making ready their wagons and outfits for Santa Fé. Many of the emigrants, especially of those bound for California, were persons of wealth and standing. The hotels were crowded, and the gunsmiths and saddlers were kept constantly at work in providing arms and equipments for the different parties of travellers. Almost every day steamboats were leaving the levee and passing up the Missouri, crowded with passengers on their way to the frontier.

In one of these, the 'Radnor,' since snagged and lost, my friend and relative, Quincy A. Shaw, and myself, left St. Louis on the twenty-eighth of April, on a tour of curiosity and amusement to the Rocky Mountains. The boat was loaded until the water broke alternately over her guards. Her upper-deck was covered with large wagons of a peculiar form, for the Santa Fé trade, and her hold was crammed with goods for the same destination. There were also the equipments and provisions of a party of Oregon emigrants, a band of mules and horses, piles of saddles and harness, and a multitude of nondescript articles, indispensable on the prairies. Almost hidden in this medley one might have seen a small French cart, of the sort very appropriately called a 'mule-killer,' beyond the frontiers, and not far distant a tent, together with a miscellaneous assortment of boxes and barrels. The whole equipage was far from prepossessing in its appearance; yet, such as it was, it was destined to a long and arduous journey, on which the persevering reader will accompany it.

The passengers on board the Radnor corresponded with

her freight. In her cabin were Santa Fé traders, gamblers, speculators, and adventurers of various descriptions, and her steerage was crowded with Oregon emigrants, 'mountain men,' negroes, and a party of Kanzas Indians, who had been on a visit to St. Louis.

Thus laden, the boat struggled upward for seven or eight days against the rapid current of the Missouri, grating upon snags, and hanging for two or three hours at a time upon sand-bars. We entered the mouth of the Missouri in a drizzling rain, but the weather soon became clear, and showed distinctly the broad and turbid river, with its eddies, its sand-bars, its ragged islands and forest-covered shores. The Missouri is constantly changing its course; wearing away its banks on one side, while it forms new ones on the other. Its channel is shifting continually. Islands are formed, and then washed away; and while the old forests on one side are undermined and swept off, a young growth springs up from the new soil upon the other. With all these changes, the water is so charged with mud and sand that it is perfectly opaque, and in a few minutes deposits a sediment an inch thick in the bottom of a tumbler. The river was now high; but when we descended in the autumn it was fallen very low, and all the secrets of its treacherous shallows were exposed to view. It was frightful to see the dead and broken trees, thick-set as a military abattis, firmly imbedded in the sand, and all pointing down stream, ready to impale any unhappy steamboat that at high water should pass over that dangerous ground.

In five or six days we began to see signs of the great western movement that was then taking place. Parties of emigrants, with their tents and wagons, would be encamped on open spots near the bank, on their way to the common rendezvous at Independence. On a rainy day, near sunset, we reached the landing of this place, which is situated some miles from the river, on the extreme frontier of Missouri. The scene was characteristic, for here were represented at one view the most remarkable features of this wild and enterprising region. On the muddy shore stood some thirty or forty dark slavish-looking Spaniards, gazing stupidly out from beneath their broad hats. They were attached to one of the Santa Fé companies, whose wagons were crowded together on the banks above. In the midst of these, crouching over a smouldering fire, was a group of Indians, belonging to a remote Mexican tribe. One or two French hunters from the mountains, with their long hair and buckskin dresses, were looking at the boat; and seated on a log close at hand were three men, with rifles lying across their knees. The foremost of these, a tall, strong figure, with a clear blue eye and an open, intelligent face, might very well represent that race of restless and intrepid pioneers whose axes and rifles have opened a path from the Alleghanies to the western prairies. He was on his way to Oregon, probably a more congenial field to him than any that now remained on this side the great plains.

Early on the next morning we reached Kanzas, about five hundred miles from the mouth of the Missouri. Here we landed, and leaving our equipments in charge of my good friend Colonel Chick, whose log-house was the substitute for a tavern, we set out in a wagon for Westport, where we hoped to procure mules and horses for the journey.

It was a remarkably fresh and beautiful May morning. The rich and luxuriant woods through which the miserable road conducted us, were lighted by the bright sunshine and enlivened by a multitude of birds. We overtook on the way our late fellow-travellers, the Kanzas Indians, who, adorned with all their finery, were proceeding homeward at a round pace; and whatever they might have seemed on board the boat, they made a very striking and picturesque feature in the forest landscape.

Westport was full of Indians, whose little shaggy ponies were tied by dozens along the houses and fences. Sacs and Foxes, with shaved heads and painted faces, Shawanoes and Delawares, fluttering in calico frocks and turbans, Wyandots dressed like white men, and a few wretched Kanzas wrapped in old blankets, were strolling about the streets, or lounging in and out of the shops and houses.

As I stood at the door of the tavern, I saw a remarkable-looking person coming up the street. He had a ruddy face, garnished with the stumps of a bristly red beard and moustache; on one side of his head was a round cap with a knob at the top, such as Scottish laborers sometimes wear: his coat was of a nondescript form, and made of a gray Scotch plaid,

with the fringes hanging all about it; he wore pantaloons of
coarse homespun, and hob-nailed shoes; and to complete his
equipment, a little black pipe was stuck in one corner of his
mouth. In this curious attire, I recognized Captain C. of the
British army, who, with his brother, and Mr. R. an English
gentleman, was bound on a hunting expedition across the
continent. I had seen the captain and his companions at St.
Louis. They had now been for some time at Westport, making
preparations for their departure, and waiting for a reinforcement, since they were too few in number to attempt it alone.
They might, it is true, have joined some of the parties of emigrants who were on the point of setting out for Oregon and
California; but they professed great disinclination to have any
connection with the 'Kentucky fellows.'

The captain now urged it upon us, that we should join
forces and proceed to the mountains in company. Feeling no
greater partiality for the society of the emigrants than they
did, we thought the arrangement an advantageous one, and
consented to it. Our future fellow-travellers had installed
themselves in a little log-house, where we found them all surrounded by saddles, harness, guns, pistols, telescopes, knives,
and in short their complete appointments for the prairie. R.,
who professed a taste for natural history, sat at a table stuffing
a woodpecker; the brother of the captain, who was an Irishman, was splicing a trail rope on the floor, as he had been an
amateur sailor. The captain pointed out, with much complacency, the different articles of their outfit. 'You see,' said he,
'that we are all old travellers. I am convinced that no party
ever went upon the prairie better provided.' The hunter
whom they had employed, a surly-looking Canadian, named
Sorel, and their muleteer, an American from St. Louis, were
lounging about the building. In a little log stable close at
hand were their horses and mules, selected by the captain,
who was an excellent judge.

The alliance entered into, we left them to complete their
arrangements, while we pushed our own to all convenient
speed. The emigrants for whom our friends professed such
contempt, were encamped on the prairie about eight or ten
miles distant, to the number of a thousand or more, and new
parties were constantly passing out from Independence to

join them. They were in great confusion, holding meetings, passing resolutions, and drawing up regulations, but unable to unite in the choice of leaders to conduct them across the prairie. Being at leisure one day, I rode over to Independence. The town was crowded. A multitude of shops had sprung up to furnish the emigrants and Santa Fé traders with necessaries for their journey; and there was an incessant hammering and banging from a dozen blacksmiths' sheds, where the heavy wagons were being repaired, and the horses and oxen shod. The streets were thronged with men, horses, and mules. While I was in the town, a train of emigrant wagons from Illinois passed through, to join the camp on the prairie, and stopped in the principal street. A multitude of healthy children's faces were peeping out from under the covers of the wagons. Here and there a buxom damsel was seated on horseback, holding over her sunburnt face an old umbrella or a parasol, once gaudy enough, but now miserably faded. The men, very sober-looking countrymen, stood about their oxen; and as I passed I noticed three old fellows, who, with their long whips in their hands, were zealously discussing the doctrine of regeneration. The emigrants, however, are not all of this stamp. Among them are some of the vilest outcasts in the country. I have often perplexed myself to divine the various motives that give impulse to this strange migration; but whatever they may be, whether an insane hope of a better condition in life, or a desire of shaking off restraints of law and society, or mere restlessness, certain it is, that multitudes bitterly repent the journey, and after they have reached the land of promise, are happy enough to escape from it.

In the course of seven or eight days we had brought our preparations near to a close. Meanwhile our friends had completed theirs, and becoming tired of Westport, they told us that they would set out in advance, and wait at the crossing of the Kanzas till we should come up. Accordingly R. and the muleteer went forward with the wagon and tent, while the captain and his brother, together with Sorel, and a trapper named Boisverd, who had joined them, followed with the band of horses. The commencement of the journey was ominous, for the captain was scarcely a mile from Westport, riding along in state at the head of his party, leading his intended buffalo horse by a rope, when a tremendous thunder-storm came on, and drenched them all to the skin. They hurried on to reach the place about seven miles off, where R. was to have had the camp in readiness to receive them. But this prudent person, when he saw the storm approaching, had selected a sheltered glade in the woods, where he pitched his tent, and was sipping a comfortable cup of coffee while the captain galloped for miles beyond through the rain to look for him. At length the storm cleared away, and the sharp-eyed trapper succeeded in discovering his tent: R. had by this time finished his coffee, and was seated on a buffalo-robe smoking his pipe. The captain was one of the most easy-tempered men in existence, so he bore his ill-luck with great composure, shared the dregs of the coffee with his brother, and laid down to sleep in his wet clothes.

We ourselves had our share of the deluge. We were leading a pair of mules to Kanzas when the storm broke. Such sharp and incessant flashes of lightning, such stunning and continuous thunder, I had never known before. The woods were completely obscured by the diagonal sheets of rain that fell with a heavy roar, and rose in spray from the ground; and the streams rose so rapidly that we could hardly ford them. At length, looming through the rain, we saw the log-house of Colonel Chick, who received us with his usual bland hospitality; while his wife, who, though a little soured and stiffened by too frequent attendance on camp-meetings, was not behind him in hospitable feeling, supplied us with the means of repairing our drenched and bedraggled condition. The storm clearing away at about sunset, opened a noble prospect from the porch of the colonel's house, which stands upon a high hill. The sun streamed from the breaking clouds upon the swift and angry Missouri, and on the immense expanse of luxuriant forest that stretched from its banks back to the distant bluffs.

Returning on the next day to Westport, we received a message from the captain, who had ridden back to deliver it in person, but finding that we were in Kanzas, had intrusted it with an acquaintance of his named Vogel, who kept a small grocery and liquor shop. Whisky by the way circulates more freely in Westport than is altogether safe in a place where every man carries a loaded pistol in his pocket. As we passed this establishment, we saw Vogel's broad German face and knavish-looking eyes thrust from his door. He said he had something to tell us, and invited us to take a dram. Neither his liquor nor his message were very palatable. The captain had returned to give us notice that R., who assumed the direction of his party, had determined upon another route from that agreed upon between us; and instead of taking the course of the traders, to pass northward by Fort Leavenworth, and follow the path marked out by the dragoons in their expedition of last summer. To adopt such a plan without consulting us, we looked upon as a very high-handed proceeding; but suppressing our dissatisfaction as well as we could, we made up our minds to join them at Fort Leavenworth, where they were to wait for us.

Accordingly, our preparation being now complete, we attempted one fine morning to commence our journey. The first step was an unfortunate one. No sooner were our animals put in harness, than the shaft-mule reared and plunged, burst ropes and straps, and nearly flung the cart into the Missouri. Finding her wholly uncontrollable, we exchanged her for another, with which we were furnished by our friend Mr. Boone of Westport, a grandson of Daniel Boone, the pioneer. This foretaste of prairie experience was very soon followed by another. Westport was scarcely out of sight, when we encountered a deep muddy gully, of a species that afterward became but too familiar to us; and here for the space of an hour or more the cart stuck fast.

Chapter II.

BREAKING THE ICE.

"Though sluggards deem it but a foolish chase,
    And marvel men should quit their easy chair,
The weary way and long long league to trace;—
    Oh there is sweetness in the *prairie* air,
And life that bloated ease can never hope to share."
                                        CHILDE HAROLD.

BOTH SHAW and myself were tolerably inured to the vicissitudes of travelling. We had experienced them under various forms, and a birch canoe was as familiar to us as a steamboat. The restlessness, the love of wilds and hatred of cities, natural perhaps in early years to every unperverted son of Adam, was not our only motive for undertaking the present journey. My companion hoped to shake off the effects of a disorder that had impaired a constitution originally hardy and robust; and I was anxious to pursue some inquiries relative to the character and usages of the remote Indian nations, being already familiar with many of the border tribes.

Emerging from the mud-hole where we last took leave of the reader, we pursued our way for some time along the narrow track, in the checkered sunshine and shadow of the woods, till at length, issuing forth into the broad light, we left behind us the farthest outskirts of that great forest, that once spread unbroken from the western plains to the shore of the Atlantic. Looking over an intervening belt of shrubbery, we saw the green, ocean-like expanse of prairie, stretching swell over swell to the horizon.

It was a mild, calm spring day; a day when one is more disposed to musing and reverie than to action, and the softest part of his nature is apt to gain the ascendency. I rode in advance of the party, as we passed through the shrubbery, and as a nook of green grass offered a strong temptation, I dismounted and lay down there. All the trees and saplings were in flower, or budding into fresh leaf; the red clusters of the maple-blossoms and the rich flowers of the Indian apple were there in profusion; and I was half inclined to regret leaving behind the land of gardens, for the rude and stern scenes of the prairie and the mountains.

Meanwhile the party came in sight from out of the bushes. Foremost rode Henry Chatillon, our guide and hunter, a fine athletic figure, mounted on a hardy gray Wyandot pony. He wore a white blanket-coat, a broad hat of felt, moccasons, and pantaloons of deer-skin, ornamented along the seams with rows of long fringes. His knife was stuck in his belt; his bullet-pouch and powder-horn hung at his side, and his rifle lay before him, resting against the high pommel of his saddle, which, like all his equipments, had seen hard service, and was much the worse for wear. Shaw followed close, mounted on a little sorrel horse, and leading a larger animal by a rope. His outfit, which resembled mine, had been provided with a view to use rather than ornament. It consisted of a plain, black Spanish saddle, with holsters of heavy pistols, a blanket rolled up behind it, and the trail-rope attached to his horse's neck hanging coiled in front. He carried a double-barrelled smooth-bore, while I boasted a rifle of some fifteen pounds weight. At that time our attire, though far from elegant, bore some marks of civilization, and offered a very favorable contrast to the inimitable shabbiness of our appearance on the return journey. A red flannel shirt, belted around the waist like a frock, then constituted our upper garment; moccasons had supplanted our failing boots; and the remaining essential portion of our attire consisted of an extraordinary article, manufactured by a squaw out of smoked buckskin. Our muleteer, Delorier, brought up the rear with his cart, wading ankle-deep in the mud, alternately puffing at his pipe, and ejaculating in his prairie patois: *"Sacre enfant de garce!"* as one of the mules would seem to recoil before some abyss of unusual profundity. The cart was of the kind that one may see by scores around the market-place in Montreal, and had a white covering to protect the articles within. These were our provisions and a tent, with ammunition, blankets, and presents for the Indians.

We were in all four men with eight animals; for besides the spare horses led by Shaw and myself, an additional mule was driven along with us as a reserve in case of accident.

After this summing up of our forces, it may not be amiss to glance at the characters of the two men who accompanied us.

Delorier was a Canadian, with all the characteristics of the true Jean Baptiste. Neither fatigue, exposure, nor hard labor could ever impair his cheerfulness and gayety, or his obsequious politeness to his *bourgeois*; and when night came, he would sit down by the fire, smoke his pipe, and tell stories with the utmost contentment. In fact the prairie was his congenial element. Henry Chatillon was of a different stamp. When we were at St. Louis, several of the gentlemen of the Fur Company had kindly offered to procure for us a hunter and guide suited for our purposes, and on coming one afternoon to the office, we found there a tall and exceedingly well-dressed man, with a face so open and frank that it attracted our notice at once. We were surprised at being told that it was he who wished to guide us to the mountains. He was born in a little French town near St. Louis, and from the age of fifteen years had been constantly in the neighborhood of the Rocky Mountains, employed for the most part by the Company, to supply their forts with buffalo meat. As a hunter, he had but one rival in the whole region, a man named Cimoneau, with whom, to the honor of both of them, he was on terms of the closest friendship. He had arrived at St. Louis the day before, from the mountains, where he had remained for four years; and he now only asked to go and spend a day with his mother, before setting out on another expedition. His age was about thirty; he was six feet high, and very powerfully and gracefully moulded. The prairies had been his school; he could neither read nor write, but he had a natural refinement and delicacy of mind, such as is very rarely found even in women. His manly face was a perfect mirror of uprightness, simplicity, and kindness of heart; he had, moreover, a keen perception of character, and a tact that would preserve him from flagrant error in any society. Henry had not the restless energy of an Anglo-American. He was content to take things as he found them; and his chief fault arose from an excess of easy generosity, impelling him to give away too profusely ever to thrive in the world. Yet it was commonly remarked of him, that whatever he might choose to do with what belonged to himself, the property of others was always safe in his hands. His bravery was as much celebrated in the mountains as his skill in hunting; but it is characteristic of him that in a country where the rifle is the chief arbiter between man and man, Henry was very seldom involved in quarrels. Once or twice, indeed, his quiet good nature had been mistaken and presumed upon, but the consequences of the error were so formidable, that no one was ever known to repeat it. No better evidence of the intrepidity of his temper could be wished, than the common report that he had killed more than thirty grizzly bears. He was a proof of what unaided nature will sometimes do. I have never, in the city or in the wilderness, met a better man than my noble and true-hearted friend, Henry Chatillon.

We were soon free of the woods and bushes, and fairly upon the broad prairie. Now and then a Shawanoe passed us, riding his little shaggy pony at a 'lope;' his calico shirt, his gaudy sash, and the gay handkerchief bound around his snaky hair, fluttering in the wind. At noon we stopped to rest not far from a little creek, replete with frogs and young turtles. There had been an Indian encampment at the place, and the framework of their lodges still remained, enabling us very easily to gain a shelter from the sun, by merely spreading one or two blankets over them. Thus shaded, we sat upon our saddles, and Shaw for the first time lighted his favorite Indian pipe; while Delorier was squatted over a hot bed of coals, shading his eyes with one hand, and holding a little stick in the other, with which he regulated the hissing contents of the frying-pan. The horses were turned to feed among the scattered bushes of a low oozy meadow. A drowsy spring-like sultriness pervaded the air, and the voices of ten thousand young frogs and insects, just awakened into life, rose in varied chorus from the creek and the meadows.

Scarcely were we seated when a visitor approached. This was an old Kanzas Indian; a man of distinction, if one might judge from his dress. His head was shaved and painted red, and from the tuft of hair remaining on the crown dangled several eagle's feathers, and the tails of two or three rattle-snakes. His cheeks, too, were daubed with vermillion; his ears were adorned with green glass pendants; a collar of grizzly bears' claws surrounded his neck, and several large necklaces of wampum hung on his breast. Having shaken us by the hand with a cordial grunt of salutation, the old man, dropping his red blanket from his shoulders, sat down cross-legged on the ground. In the absence of liquor, we offered him a cup of sweetened water, at which he ejaculated 'Good!' and was beginning to tell us how great a man he was, and how many Pawnees he had killed, when suddenly a motley concourse appeared wading across the creek toward us. They filed past in rapid succession, men, women and children: some were on horseback, some on foot, but all were alike squalid and wretched. Old squaws, mounted astride of shaggy, meagre little ponies, with perhaps one or two snake-eyed children seated behind them, clinging to their tattered blankets; tall lank young men on foot, with bows and arrows in their hands; and girls whose native ugliness not all the charms of glass beads and scarlet cloth could disguise, made up the procession; although here and there was a man who, like our visitor, seemed to hold some rank in this respectable community. They were the dregs of the Kanzas nation, who, while their betters were gone to hunt the buffalo, had left the village on a begging expedition to Westport.

When this ragamuffin horde had passed, we caught our horses, saddled, harnessed, and resumed our journey. Fording the creek, the low roofs of a number of rude buildings appeared, rising from a cluster of groves and woods on the left; and riding up through a long lane, amid a profusion of wild roses and early spring flowers, we found the log-church and schoolhouses belonging to the Methodist Shawanoe Mission. The Indians were on the point of gathering to a religious meeting. Some scores of them, tall men in half-civilized dress, were seated on wooden benches under the trees; while their horses were tied to the sheds and fences. Their chief, Parks, a remarkably large and athletic man, was just arrived from Westport, where he owns a trading establishment. Beside this, he has a fine farm and a considerable number of slaves. Indeed the Shawanoes have made greater progress in agriculture than any other tribe on the Missouri frontier; and both in appearance and in character form a marked contrast to our late acquaintance, the Kanzas.

A few hours' ride brought us to the banks of the river

Kanzas. Traversing the woods that lined it, and ploughing through the deep sand, we encamped not far from the bank, at the Lower Delaware crossing. Our tent was erected for the first time, on a meadow close to the woods, and the camp preparations being complete, we began to think of supper. An old Delaware woman, of some three hundred pounds weight, sat in the porch of a little log-house, close to the water, and a very pretty half-breed girl was engaged, under her superintendence, in feeding a large flock of turkeys that were fluttering and gobbling about the door. But no offers of money, or even of tobacco, could induce her to part with one of her favorites: so I took my rifle, to see if the woods or the river could furnish us any thing. A multitude of quails were plaintively whistling in the woods and meadows; but nothing appropriate to the rifle was to be seen, except three buzzards, seated on the spectral limbs of an old dead sycamore, that thrust itself out over the river from the dense sunny wall of fresh foliage. Their ugly heads were drawn down between their shoulders, and they seemed to luxuriate in the soft sunshine that was pouring from the west. As they offered no epicurean temptations, I refrained from disturbing their enjoyment; but contented myself with admiring the calm beauty of the sunset, for the river, eddying swiftly in deep purple shadows between the impending woods, formed a wild but tranquillizing scene.

When I returned to the camp, I found Shaw and an old Indian seated on the ground in close conference, passing the pipe between them. The old man was explaining that he loved the whites, and had an especial partiality for tobacco. Delorier was arranging upon the ground our service of tin cups and plates; and as other viands were not to be had, he set before us a repast of biscuit and bacon, and a large pot of coffee. Unsheathing our knives, we attacked it, disposed of the greater part, and tossed the residue to the Indian. Meanwhile our horses, now hobbled for the first time, stood among the trees, with their fore-legs tied together, in great disgust and astonishment. They seemed by no means to relish this foretaste of what was before them. Mine, in particular, had conceived a mortal aversion to the prairie life. One of them, christened Hendrick, an animal whose strength and hardihood were his only merits, and who yielded to nothing but the cogent arguments of the whip, looked toward us with an indignant countenance, as if he meditated avenging his wrongs with a kick. The other, Pontiac, a good horse, though of plebeian lineage, stood with his head drooping and his mane hanging about his eyes, with the grieved and sulky air of a lubberly boy sent off to school. Poor Pontiac! his forebodings were but too just; for when I last heard from him, he was under the lash of an Ogillallah brave, on a war party against the Crows.

As it grew dark, and the voices of the whippoorwills succeeded the whistle of the quails, we removed our saddles to the tent, to serve as pillows, spread our blankets upon the ground, and prepared to bivouac for the first time that season. Each man selected the place in the tent which he was to occupy for the journey. To Delorier, however, was assigned the cart, into which he could creep in wet weather, and find a much better shelter than his *bourgeois* enjoyed in the tent.

The river Kanzas at this point forms the boundary line between the country of the Shawanoes and that of the Delawares. We crossed it on the following day, rafting over our horses and equipage with much difficulty, and unlading our cart in order to make our way up the steep ascent on the farther bank. It was a Sunday morning; warm, tranquil and bright; and a perfect stillness reigned over the rough inclosures and neglected fields of the Delawares, except the ceaseless hum and chirrupping of myriads of insects. Now and then an Indian rode past on his way to the meeting-house, or through the dilapidated entrance of some shattered log-house, an old woman might be discerned, enjoying all the luxury of idleness. There was no village bell, for the Delawares have none; and yet upon that forlorn and rude settlement was the same spirit of Sabbath repose and tranquillity as in some little New England village among the mountains of New Hampshire, or the Vermont woods.

Having at present no leisure for such reflections, we pursued our journey. A military road led from this point to Fort Leavenworth, and for many miles the farms and cabins of the Delawares were scattered at short intervals on either hand. The little rude structures of logs, erected usually on the borders of a tract of woods, made a picturesque feature in the landscape. But the scenery needed no foreign aid. Nature had done enough for it; and the alternation of rich green prairies and groves that stood in clusters, or lined the banks of the numerous little streams, had all the softened and polished beauty of a region that has been for centuries under the hand of man. At that early season, too, it was in the height of its freshness and luxuriance. The woods were flushed with the red buds of the maple; there were frequent flowering shrubs unknown in the east; and the green swells of the prairie were thickly studded with blossoms.

Encamping near a spring, by the side of a hill, we resumed our journey in the morning, and early in the afternoon had arrived within a few miles of Fort Leavenworth. The road crossed a stream densely bordered with trees, and running in the bottom of a deep woody hollow. We were about to descend into it, when a wild and confused procession appeared, passing through the water below, and coming up the steep ascent toward us. We stopped to let them pass. They were Delawares, just returned from a hunting expedition. All, both men and women, were mounted on horseback, and drove along with them a considerable number of pack-mules, laden with the furs they had taken, together with the buffalo-robes, kettles, and other articles of their travelling equipment, which, as well as their clothing and their weapons, had a worn and dingy aspect, as if they had seen hard service of late. At the rear of the party was an old man, who, as he came up, stopped his horse to speak to us. He rode a little tough shaggy pony, with mane and tail well knotted with burs, and a rusty Spanish bit in its mouth, to which, by way of reins, was attached a string of raw hide. His saddle, robbed probably from a Mexican, had no covering, being merely a tree of the Spanish form, with a piece of grisly bear's skin laid over it, a pair of rude wooden stirrups attached, and in the absence of girth, a thong of hide passing around the horse's belly. The rider's dark features and keen snaky eye were unequivocally Indian. He wore a buckskin frock, which, like his fringed leggings, was well polished and blackened by grease and long service; and an old handkerchief was tied around his head. Resting on the saddle before him, lay his rifle; a weapon in the use of which the Delawares are skilful, though, from its weight, the distant prairie Indians are too lazy to carry it.

'Who's your chief?' he immediately inquired.

Henry Chatillon pointed to us. The old Delaware fixed his eyes intently upon us for a moment, and then sententiously remarked:

'No good! Too young!' With this flattering comment he left us, and rode after his people.

This tribe, the Delawares, once the peaceful allies of William Penn, the tributaries of the conquering Iroquois, are now the most adventurous and dreaded warriors upon the prairies. They make war upon remote tribes, the very names of which were unknown to their fathers in their ancient seats in Pennsylvania; and they push these new quarrels with true Indian rancor, sending out their little war-parties as far as the Rocky Mountains, and into the Mexican territories. Their neighbors and former confederates, the Shawanoes, who are tolerable farmers, are in a prosperous condition; but the Delawares dwindle every year, from the number of men lost in their warlike expeditions.

Soon after leaving this party, we saw, stretching on the right, the forests that follow the course of the Missouri, and the deep woody channel through which at this point it runs. At a distance in front were the white barracks of Fort Leavenworth, just visible through the trees upon an eminence above a bend of the river. A wide green meadow, as level as a lake, lay between us and the Missouri, and upon this, close to a line of trees that bordered a little brook, stood the tent of the Captain and his companions, with their horses feeding around it; but they themselves were invisible. Wright, their muleteer, was there, seated on the tongue of the wagon, repairing his harness. Boisverd stood cleaning his rifle at the door of the tent, and Sorel lounged idly about. On closer examination, however, we discovered the Captain's brother, Jack, sitting in the tent, at his old occupation of splicing trail-ropes. He welcomed us in his broad Irish brogue, and said that his brother was fishing in the river, and R—— gone to the garrison. They returned before sunset. Meanwhile we erected our own tent not far off, and after supper, a council was held, in which it was resolved to remain one day at Fort

Leavenworth, and on the next to bid a final adieu to the frontier; or in the phraseology of the region, to 'jump off.' Our deliberations were conducted by the ruddy light from a distant swell of the prairie, where the long dry grass of last summer was on fire.

Chapter III.

FORT LEAVENWORTH.

"I've wandered wide and wandered far,
　　But never have I met,
　In all this lovely western land,
　　A spot more lovely yet."

BRYANT.

O<small>N THE NEXT MORNING</small> we rode to Fort Leavenworth. Colonel, now General Kearney, to whom I had had the honor of an introduction when at St. Louis, was just arrived, and received us at his quarters with the high-bred courtesy habitual to him. Fort Leavenworth is in fact no fort, being without defensive works, except two block-houses. No rumors of war had as yet disturbed its tranquillity. In the square grassy area, surrounded by barracks and the quarters of the officers, the men were passing and repassing, or lounging among the trees; although not many weeks afterwards it presented a different scene; for here the very offscourings of the frontier were congregated, to be marshalled for the expedition against Santa Fé.

Passing through the garrison, we rode toward the Kickapoo village, five or six miles beyond. The path, a rather dubious and uncertain one, led us along the ridge of high bluffs that border the Missouri; and by looking to the right or to the left, we could enjoy a strange contrast of opposite scenery. On the left stretched the prairie, rising into swells and undulations, thickly sprinkled with groves, or gracefully expanding into wide grassy basins, of miles in extent; while its curvatures, swelling against the horizon, were often surmounted by lines of sunny woods; a scene to which the freshness of the season and the peculiar mellowness of the atmosphere gave additional softness. Below us, on the right, was a tract of ragged and broken woods. We could look down on the summits of the trees, some living and some dead; some erect, others leaning at every angle, and others still piled in masses together by the passage of a hurricane. Beyond their extreme verge, the turbid waters of the Missouri were discernible through the boughs, rolling powerfully along at the foot of the woody declivities on its farther bank.

The path soon after led inland; and as we crossed an open meadow, we saw a cluster of buildings on a rising ground before us, with a crowd of people surrounding them. They were the storehouse, cottage, and stables of the Kickapoo trader's establishment. Just at that moment, as it chanced, he was beset with half the Indians of the settlement. They had tied their wretched, neglected little ponies by dozens along the fences and out-houses, and were either lounging about the place, or crowding into the trading-house. Here were faces of various colors; red, green, white, and black, curiously intermingled and disposed over the visage in a variety of patterns. Calico shirts, red and blue blankets, brass ear-rings, wampum necklaces, appeared in profusion. The trader was a blue-eyed, open-faced man, who neither in his manners nor his appearance betrayed any of the roughness of the frontier; though just at present he was obliged to keep a lynx eye on his suspicious customers, who, men and women, were climbing on his counter, and seating themselves among his boxes and bales.

The village itself was not far off, and sufficiently illustrated the condition of its unfortunate and self-abandoned occupants. Fancy to yourself a little swift stream, working its devious way down a woody valley; sometimes wholly hidden under logs and fallen trees, sometimes issuing forth and spreading into a broad, clear pool; and on its banks in little nooks cleared away among the trees, miniature log-houses, in utter ruin and neglect. A labyrinth of narrow, obstructed paths connected these habitations one with another. Sometimes we met a stray calf, a pig or a pony, belonging to some of the villagers, who usually lay in the sun in front of their dwellings, and looked on us with cold, suspicious eyes as we approached. Farther on, in place of the log-huts of the Kickapoos, we found the pukwi lodges of their neighbors, the Pottawattamies, whose condition seemed no better than theirs.

Growing tired at last, and exhausted by the excessive heat and sultriness of the day, we returned to our friend, the trader. By this time the crowd around him had dispersed, and left him at leisure. He invited us to his cottage, a little white-and-green building, in the style of the old French settlements; and ushered us into a neat, well-furnished room. The blinds were closed, and the heat and glare of the sun excluded: the room was as cool as a cavern. It was neatly carpeted too, and furnished in a manner that we hardly expected on the frontier. The sofas, chairs, tables, and a well-filled book-case, would not have disgraced an eastern city; though there were one or two little tokens that indicated the rather questionable civilization of the region. A pistol loaded and capped, lay on the mantel-piece; and through the glass of the book-case, peeping above the works of John Milton, glittered the handle of a very mischievous-looking knife.

Our host went out, and returned with iced water, glasses, and a bottle of excellent claret; a refreshment most welcome in the extreme heat of the day; and soon after appeared a merry, laughing woman, who must have been, a year or two before, a very rich and luxuriant specimen of creole beauty. She came to say that lunch was ready in the next room. Our hostess evidently lived on the sunny side of life, and troubled herself with none of its cares. She sat down and entertained us while we were at table with anecdotes of fishing-parties, frolics, and the officers at the fort. Taking leave at length of the hospitable trader and his friend, we rode back to the garrison.

Shaw passed on to the camp, while I remained to call upon Colonel Kearney. I found him still at table. There sat our friend the Captain, in the same remarkable habiliments in which we saw him at Westport; the black pipe, however, being for the present laid aside. He dangled his little cap in his hand, and talked of steeple-chases, touching occasionally upon his anticipated exploits in buffalo-hunting. There, too, was R——, somewhat more elegantly attired. For the last time, we tasted the luxuries of civilization, and drank adieus to it in wine good enough to make us almost regret the leave-taking. Then, mounting, we rode together to the camp, where every thing was in readiness for departure on the morrow.

Chapter IV.

'JUMPING OFF.'

'We forded the river and clomb the high hill,
Never our steeds for a day stood still;
Whether we lay in the cave or the shed,
Our sleep fell soft on the hardest bed;
Whether we couched in our rough capôte,
On the rougher plank of our gliding boat,
Or stretched on the sand, or our saddles spread
As a pillow beneath the resting head,
   Fresh we woke upon the morrow;
All our thoughts and words had scope,
We had health and we had hope,
   Toil and travel, but no sorrow.'
                SIEGE OF CORINTH.

THE READER need not be told that John Bull never leaves home without encumbering himself with the greatest possible load of luggage. Our companions were no exception to the rule. They had a wagon drawn by six mules, and crammed with provisions for six months, besides ammunition enough for a regiment; spare rifles and fowling-pieces, ropes and harness; personal baggage, and a miscellaneous assortment of articles, which produced infinite embarrassment on the journey. They had also decorated their persons with telescopes and portable compasses, and carried English double-barrelled rifles of sixteen to the pound calibre, slung to their saddles in dragoon fashion.

By sunrise on the twenty-third of May we had breakfasted; the tents were levelled, the animals saddled and harnessed, and all was prepared. *'Avance donc! get up!'* cried Delorier from his seat in front of the cart. Wright, our friends' muleteer, after some swearing and lashing, got his insubordinate train in motion, and then the whole party filed from the ground. Thus we bade a long adieu to bed and board, and the principles of Blackstone's Commentaries. The day was a most auspicious one; and yet Shaw and I felt certain misgivings, which in the sequel proved but too well founded. We had just

29

learned that though R—— had taken it upon him to adopt this course without consulting us, not a single man in the party was acquainted with it; and the absurdity of our friend's high-handed measure very soon became manifest. His plan was to strike the trail of several companies of dragoons, who last summer had made an expedition under Colonel Kearney to Fort Laramie, and by this means to reach the grand trail of the Oregon emigrants up the Platte.

We rode for an hour or two, when a familiar cluster of buildings appeared on a little hill. 'Hallo!' shouted the Kickapoo trader from over his fence, 'where are you going?' A few rather emphatic exclamations might have been heard among us, when we found that we had gone miles out of our way, and were not advanced an inch toward the Rocky Mountains. So we turned in the direction the trader indicated; and with the sun for a guide, began to trace a 'bee-line' across the prairies. We struggled through copses and lines of wood; we waded brooks and pools of water; we traversed prairies as green as an emerald, expanding before us for mile after mile; wider and more wild than the wastes Mazeppa rode over:

> 'Man nor brute,
> Nor dint of hoof, nor print of foot,
> Lay in the wild luxuriant soil;
> No sign of travel; none of toil;
> The very air was mute.'

Riding in advance, as we passed over one of these great plains, we looked back and saw the line of scattered horsemen stretching for a mile or more; and far in the rear, against the horizon, the white wagons creeping slowly along. 'Here we are at last!' shouted the Captain. And in truth we had struck upon the traces of a large body of horse. We turned joyfully and followed this new course, with tempers somewhat improved; and toward sunset encamped on a high swell of the prairie, at the foot of which a lazy stream soaked along through clumps of rank grass. It was getting dark. We turned the horses loose to feed. 'Drive down the tent-pickets hard,' said Henry Chatillon, 'it is going to blow.' We did so, and secured the tent as well as we could; for the sky had changed totally, and a fresh damp smell in the wind warned us that a stormy night was likely to succeed the hot clear day. The prairie also wore a new aspect, and its vast swells had grown black and sombre under the shadow of the clouds. The thunder soon began to growl at a distance. Picketing and hobbling the horses among the rich grass at the foot of the slope, where we encamped, we gained a shelter just as the rain began to fall; and sat at the opening of the tent, watching the proceedings of the Captain. In defiance of the rain, he was stalking among the horses, wrapped in an old Scotch plaid. An extreme solicitude tormented him, lest some of his favorites should escape, or some accident should befall them; and he cast an anxious eye toward three wolves who were sneaking along over the dreary surface of the plain, as if he dreaded some hostile demonstration on their part.

On the next morning we had gone but a mile or two, when we came to an extensive belt of woods, through the midst of which ran a stream, wide, deep, and of an appearance particularly muddy and treacherous. Delorier was in advance with his cart; he jerked his pipe from his mouth, lashed his mules, and poured forth a volley of Canadian ejaculations. In plunged the cart, but midway it stuck fast. Delorier leaped out knee-deep in water, and by dint of *sacres* and a vigorous application of the whip, he urged the mules out of the slough. Then approached the long team and heavy wagon of our friends; but it paused on the brink.

'Now my advice is—,' began the Captain, who had been anxiously contemplating the muddy gulf.

'Drive on!' cried R——.

But Wright, the muleteer, apparently had not as yet decided the point in his own mind; and he sat still in his seat on one of the shaft-mules, whistling in a low contemplative strain to himself.

'My advice is,' resumed the Captain, 'that we unload; for I'll bet any man five pounds that if we try to go through, we shall stick fast.'

'By the powers, we shall stick fast!' echoed Jack, the Captain's brother, shaking his large head with an air of firm conviction.

'Drive on! drive on!' cried R—— petulantly.

'Well,' observed the Captain, turning to us as we sat looking on, much edified by this by-play among our confederates, 'I can only give my advice, and if people won't be reasonable, why they won't, that's all!'

Meanwhile, Wright had apparently made up his mind; for he suddenly began to shout forth a volley of oaths and curses, that, compared with the French imprecations of Delorier, sounded like the roaring of heavy cannon after the popping and sputtering of a bunch of Chinese crackers. At the same time, he discharged a shower of blows upon his mules, who hastily dived into the mud, and drew the wagon lumbering after them. For a moment the issue was dubious. Wright writhed about in his saddle, and swore and lashed like a madman; but who can count on a team of half-broken mules? At the most critical point, when all should have been harmony and combined effort, the perverse brutes fell into lamentable disorder, and huddled together in confusion on the farther bank. There was the wagon up to the hub in mud, and visibly settling every instant. There was nothing for it but to unload; then to dig away the mud from before the wheels with a spade, and lay a causeway of bushes and branches. This agreeable labor accomplished, the wagon at length emerged; but if I mention that some interruption of this sort occurred at least four or five times a day for a fortnight, the reader will understand that our progress towards the Platte was not without its obstacles.

We travelled six or seven miles farther, and 'nooned' near a brook. On the point of resuming our journey, when the horses were all driven down to water, my homesick charger Pontiac made a sudden leap across, and set off at a round trot for the settlements. I mounted my remaining horse, and started in pursuit. Making a circuit, I headed the runaway, hoping to drive him back to camp; but he instantly broke into a gallop, made a wide tour on the prairie, and got past me again. I tried this plan repeatedly, with the same result: Pontiac was evidently disgusted with the prairie; so I abandoned it, and tried another, trotting along gently behind him, in hopes that I might quietly get near enough to seize the trail-rope which was fastened to his neck, and dragged about a dozen feet behind him. The chase grew interesting. For mile after mile I followed the rascal, with the utmost care not to alarm him, and gradually got nearer, until at length old Hendrick's nose was fairly brushed by the whisking tail of the unsuspecting Pontiac. Without drawing rein, I slid softly to the ground; but my long heavy rifle encumbered me, and the low sound it made in striking the horn of the saddle startled him; he pricked up his ears, and sprang off at a run. 'My friend,' thought I, remounting, 'do that again, and I will shoot you!'

Fort Leavenworth was about forty miles distant, and thither I determined to follow him. I made up my mind to spend a solitary and supperless night, and then set out again in the morning. One hope, however, remained. The creek where the wagon had stuck was just before us; Pontiac might be thirsty with his run, and stop there to drink. I kept as near to him as possible, taking every precaution not to alarm him again; and the result proved as I had hoped; for he walked deliberately among the trees, and stooped down to the water. I alighted, dragged old Hendrick through the mud, and with a feeling of infinite satisfaction picked up the slimy trail-rope, and twisted it three times round my hand. 'Now let me see you get away again!' I thought, as I remounted. But Pontiac was exceedingly reluctant to turn back; Hendrick too, who had evidently flattered himself with vain hopes, showed the utmost repugnance, and grumbled in a manner peculiar to himself at being compelled to face about. A smart cut of the whip restored his cheerfulness; and dragging the recovered truant behind, I set out in search of the camp. An hour or two elapsed, when, near sunset, I saw the tents, standing on a rich swell of the prairie, beyond a line of woods, while the bands of horses were feeding in a low meadow close at hand. There sat Jack C——, cross-legged, in the sun, splicing a trail-rope, and the rest were lying on the grass, smoking and telling stories. That night we enjoyed a serenade from the wolves, more lively than any with which they had yet favored us; and in the morning one of the musicians appeared, not many rods from the tents, quietly seated among the horses, looking at us with a pair of large gray eyes; but perceiving a rifle levelled at him, he leaped up and made off in hot haste.

I pass by the following day or two of our journey, for

nothing occurred worthy of record. Should any one of my readers ever be impelled to visit the prairies, and should he choose the route of the Platte, (the best, perhaps, that can be adopted,) I can assure him that he need not think to enter at once upon the paradise of his imagination. A dreary preliminary, protracted crossing of the threshold, awaits him before he finds himself fairly upon the verge of the 'great American desert;' those barren wastes, the haunts of the buffalo and the Indian, where the very shadow of civilization lies a hundred leagues behind him. The intervening country, the wide and fertile belt that extends for several hundred miles beyond the extreme frontier, will probably answer tolerably well to his preconceived ideas of the prairie; for this it is from which picturesque tourists, painters, poets and novelists, who have seldom penetrated farther, have derived their conceptions of the whole region. If he has a painter's eye, he may find his period of probation not wholly void of interest. The scenery, though tame, is graceful and pleasing. Here are level plains, too wide for the eye to measure; green undulations, like motionless swells of the ocean; abundance of streams, followed through all their windings by lines of woods and scattered groves. But let him be as enthusiastic as he may, he will find enough to damp his ardor. His wagons will stick in the mud; his horses will break loose; harness will give way, and axle-trees prove unsound. His bed will be a soft one, consisting often of black mud, of the richest consistency. As for food, he must content himself with biscuit and salt provisions; for strange as it may seem, this tract of country produces very little game. As he advances, indeed, he will see, mouldering in the grass by his path, the vast antlers of the elk, and farther on, the whitened skulls of the buffalo, once swarming over this now deserted region. Perhaps, like us, he may journey for a fortnight, and see not so much as the hoof-print of a deer; in the spring, not even a prairie-hen is to be had.

Yet, to compensate him for this unlooked-for deficiency of game he will find himself beset with 'varmints' innumerable. The wolves will entertain him with a concerto at night, and skulk around him by day, just beyond rifle-shot; his horse will step into badger-holes; from every marsh and mudpuddle will arise the bellowing, croaking and trilling of legions of frogs, infinitely various in color, shape and dimensions. A profusion of snakes will glide away from under his horse's feet, or quietly visit him in his tent at night; while the pertinacious humming of unnumbered mosquitoes will banish sleep from his eyelids. When thirsty with a long ride in the scorching sun over some boundless reach of prairie, he comes at length to a pool of water, and alights to drink, he discovers a troop of young tadpoles sporting in the bottom of his cup. Add to this, that all the morning the sun beats upon him with a sultry, penetrating heat, and that, with provoking regularity, at about four o'clock in the afternoon, a thunder-storm rises and drenches him to the skin. Such being the charms of this favored region, the reader will easily conceive the extent of our gratification at learning that for a week we had been journeying on the wrong track! How this agreeable discovery was made I will presently explain.

One day, after a protracted morning's ride, we stopped to rest at noon upon the open prairie. No trees were in sight; but close at hand, a little dribbling brook was twisting from side to side through a hollow; now forming holes of stagnant water, and now gliding over the mud in a scarcely perceptible current, among a growth of sickly bushes, and great clumps of tall rank grass. The day was excessively hot and oppressive. The horses and mules were rolling on the prairie to refresh themselves, or feeding among the bushes in the hollow. We had dined; and Delorier, puffing at his pipe, knelt on the grass, scrubbing our service of tin-plate. Shaw lay in the shade, under the cart, to rest for awhile, before the word should be given to 'catch up.' Henry Chatillon, before lying down, was looking about for signs of snakes, the only living things that he feared, and uttering various ejaculations of disgust, at finding several suspicious-looking holes close to the cart. I sat leaning against the wheel in a scanty strip of shade, making a pair of hobbles to replace those which my contumacious steed Pontiac had broken the night before. The camp of our friends, a rod or two distant, presented the same scene of lazy tranquillity.

'Hallo!' cried Henry, looking up from his inspection of the snake-holes, 'here comes the old Captain!'

The Captain approached, and stood for a moment contemplating us in silence.

'I say, Parkman,' he began, 'look at Shaw there, asleep under the cart, with the tar dripping off the hub of the wheel on his shoulder!'

At this Shaw got up, with his eyes half opened, and feeling the part indicated, he found his hand glued fast to his red flannel shirt.

'He 'll look well, when he gets among the squaws, won't he!' observed the Captain, with a grin.

He then crawled under the cart, and began to tell stories, of which his stock was inexhaustible. Yet every moment he would glance nervously at the horses. At last he jumped up in great excitement. 'See that horse! There—that fellow just walking over the hill! By Jove! he's off. It 's your big horse, Shaw; no it isn't, it 's Jack's. Jack! Jack! hallo, Jack!' Jack, thus invoked, jumped up and stared vacantly at us.

'Go and catch your horse, if you don't want to lose him!' roared the Captain.

Jack instantly set off at a run, through the grass, his broad pantaloons flapping about his feet. The Captain gazed anxiously till he saw that the horse was caught; then he sat down, with a countenance of thoughtfulness and care.

'I tell you what it is,' he said, 'this will never do at all. We shall lose every horse in the band some day or other, and then a pretty plight we should be in! Now I am convinced that the only way for us is to have every man in the camp stand horse-guard in rotation whenever we stop. Supposing a hundred Pawnees should jump up out of that ravine, all yelling and flapping their buffalo robes, in the way they do? Why in two minutes, not a hoof would be in sight.' We reminded the Captain that a hundred Pawnees would probably demolish the horse-guard, if he were to resist their depredations.

'At any rate,' pursued the Captain, evading the point, 'our whole system is wrong; I'm convinced of it; it is totally unmilitary. Why the way we travel, strung out over the prairie for a mile, an enemy might attack the foremost men, and cut them off before the rest could come up.'

'We are not in an enemy's country yet,' said Shaw; 'when we are, we'll travel together.'

'Then,' said the Captain, 'we might be attacked in camp. We've no sentinels; we camp in disorder; no precautions at all to guard against surprise. My own convictions are, that we ought to camp in a hollow-square, with the fires in the centre; and have sentinels, and a regular password appointed for every night. Beside, there should be videttes, riding in advance, to find a place for the camp and give warning of an enemy. These are my convictions. I don't want to dictate to any man. I give advice to the best of my judgment, that's all; and then let people do as they please.'

We intimated that perhaps it would be as well to postpone such burdensome precautions until there should be some actual need of them; but he shook his head dubiously. The Captain's sense of military propriety had been severely shocked by what he considered the irregular proceedings of the party; and this was not the first time he had expressed himself upon the subject. But his convictions seldom produced any practical results. In the present case, he contented himself, as usual, with enlarging on the importance of his suggestions, and wondering that they were not adopted. But his plan of sending out videttes seemed particularly dear to him; and as no one else was disposed to second his views on this point, he took it into his head to ride forward that afternoon, himself.

'Come, Parkman,' said he, 'will you go with me?'

We set out together, and rode a mile or two in advance. The Captain, in the course of twenty years' service in the British army, had seen something of life; one extensive side of it, at least, he had enjoyed the best opportunities for studying; and being naturally a pleasant fellow, he was a very entertaining companion. He cracked jokes and told stories for an hour or two; until looking back, we saw the prairie behind us stretching away to the horizon, without a horseman or a wagon in sight.

'Now,' said the Captain, 'I think the videttes had better stop till the main body comes up.'

I was of the same opinion. There was a thick growth of woods just before us, with a stream running through them. Having crossed this, we found on the other side a fine level meadow, half encircled by the trees; and fastening our horses to some bushes, we sat down on the grass; while, with an old stump of a tree for a target, I began to display the superiority of the renowned rifle of the backwoods over the foreign innovation borne by the Captain. At length voices could be heard in the distance, behind the trees.

'There they come!' said the Captain; 'let's go and see how they get through the creek.'

We mounted and rode to the bank of the stream, where the trail crossed it. It ran in a deep hollow, full of trees: as we looked down, we saw a confused crowd of horsemen riding through the water; and among the dingy habiliments of our party, glittered the uniforms of four dragoons.

Shaw came whipping his horse up the bank, in advance of the rest, with a somewhat indignant countenance. The first word he spoke was a blessing fervently invoked on the head of R——, who was riding, with a crest-fallen air, in the rear. Thanks to the ingenious devices of this gentleman, we had missed the track entirely, and wandered, not toward the Platte, but to the village of the Iowa Indians. This we learned from the dragoons, who had lately deserted from Fort Leavenworth. They told us that our best plan now was to keep to the northward until we should strike the trail formed by several parties of Oregon emigrants, who had that season set out from St. Joseph's in Missouri.

In extremely bad temper, we encamped on this ill-starred spot; while the deserters, whose case admitted of no delay, rode rapidly forward. On the day following, striking the St. Joseph's trail, we turned our horses' heads toward Fort Laramie, then about seven hundred miles to the westward.

Chapter V.

THE 'BIG BLUE.'

"A man so various, that he seemed to be
Not one, but all mankind's epitome,
Stiff in opinions, always in the wrong,
Was every thing by starts, and nothing long,
But in the space of one revolving moon,
Was gamester, chemist, fiddler, and buffoon."

DRYDEN.

THE GREAT MEDLEY of Oregon and California emigrants, at their camps around Independence, had heard reports that several additional parties were on the point of setting out from St. Joseph's, farther to the northward. The prevailing impression was, that these were Mormons, twenty-three hundred in number; and a great alarm was excited in consequence. The people of Illinois and Missouri, who composed by far the greater part of the emigrants, have never been on the best terms with the 'Latter Day Saints;' and it is notorious throughout the country how much blood has been spilt in their feuds, even far within the limits of the settlements. No one could predict what would be the result, when large armed bodies of these fanatics should encounter the most impetuous and reckless of their old enemies on the broad prairie, far beyond the reach of law or military force. The women and children at Independence raised a great outcry; the men themselves were seriously alarmed; and, as I learned, they sent to Colonel Kearney, requesting an escort of dragoons as far as the Platte. This was refused; and as the sequel proved, there was no occasion for it. The St. Joseph's emigrants were as good Christians and as zealous Mormon-haters as the rest; and the very few families of the 'Saints' who passed out this season by the route of the Platte, remained behind until the great tide of emigration had gone by; standing in quite as much awe of the 'gentiles' as the latter did of them.

We were now, as I before mentioned, upon this St. Joseph's trail. It was evident, by the traces, that large parties were a few days in advance of us; and as we too supposed them to be Mormons, we had some apprehension of interruption.

The journey was somewhat monotonous. One day we rode on for hours, without seeing a tree or a bush: before, behind, and on either side, stretched the vast expanse, rolling in a succession of graceful swells, covered with the unbroken carpet of fresh green grass. Here and there a crow, or a raven, or a turkey-buzzard, relieved the uniformity.

'What shall we do to-night for wood and water?' we began to ask of each other; for the sun was within an hour of setting. At length a dark green speck appeared, far off on the right; it was the top of a tree, peering over a swell of the prairie; and leaving the trail, we made all haste toward it. It proved to be the vanguard of a cluster of bushes and low trees, that surrounded some pools of water in an extensive hollow; so we encamped on the rising ground near it.

Shaw and I were sitting in the tent, when Delorier thrust his brown face and old felt hat into the opening, and dilating his eyes to their utmost extent, announced supper. There were the tin cups and the iron spoons, arranged in military order on the grass, and the coffee-pot predominant in the midst. The meal was soon dispatched; but Henry Chatillon still sat cross-legged, dallying with the remnant of his coffee, the beverage in universal use upon the prairie, and an especial favorite with him. He preferred it in its virgin flavor, unimpaired by sugar or cream; and on the present occasion it met his entire approval, being exceedingly strong, or as he expressed it, 'right black.'

It was a rich and gorgeous sunset—an American sunset; and the ruddy glow of the sky was reflected from some extensive pools of water among the shadowy copses in the meadow below.

'I must have a bath to-night,' said Shaw. 'How is it, Delorier? Any chance for a swim down there?'

'Ah! I cannot tell; just as you please, Monsieur,' replied Delorier, shrugging his shoulders, perplexed by his ignorance of English, and extremely anxious to conform in all respects to the opinions and wishes of his *bourgeois*.

'Look at his moccason,' said I. It had evidently been lately immersed in a profound abyss of black mud.

'Come,' said Shaw; 'at any rate we can see for ourselves.'

We set out together; and as we approached the bushes, which were at some distance, we found the ground becoming rather treacherous. We could only get along by stepping upon large clumps of tall rank grass, with fathomless gulfs between, like innumerable little quaking islands in an ocean of mud, where a false step would have involved our boots in a catastrophe like that which had befallen Delorier's moccasons. The thing looked desperate: we separated, so as to search in different directions, Shaw going off to the right, while I kept straight forward. At last I came to the edge of the bushes: they were young water-willows, covered with their caterpillar-like blossoms, but intervening between them and the last grass clump was a black and deep slough, over which, by a vigorous exertion, I contrived to jump. Then I shouldered my way through the willows, trampling them down by main force, till I came to a wide stream of water, three inches deep, languidly creeping along over a bottom of sleek mud. My arrival produced a great commotion. A huge green bull-frog uttered an indignant croak, and jumped off the bank with a loud splash: his webbed feet twinkled above the surface, as he jerked them energetically upward, and I could see him ensconcing himself in the unresisting slime at the bottom, whence several large air bubbles struggled lazily to the top. Some little spotted frogs instantly followed the patriarch's example; and then three turtles, not larger than a dollar, tumbled themselves off a broad 'lily pod,' where they had been reposing. At the same time a snake, gayly striped with black and yellow, glided out from the bank, and writhed across to the other side; and a small stagnant pool into which my foot had inadvertently pushed a stone was instantly alive with a congregation of black tadpoles.

'Any chance for a bath, where you are?' called out Shaw, from a distance.

The answer was not encouraging. I retreated through the willows, and rejoining my companion, we proceeded to push our researches in company. Not far on the right, a rising ground, covered with trees and bushes, seemed to sink down abruptly to the water, and give hope of better success; so toward this we directed our steps. When we reached the place we found it no easy matter to get along between the hill and the water, impeded as we were by a growth of stiff, obstinate young birch trees, laced together by grape-vines. In the twilight, we now and then, to support ourselves, snatched at the touch-me-not stem of some ancient sweet-brier. Shaw, who was in advance, suddenly uttered a somewhat emphatic monosyllable; and looking up, I saw him with one hand grasping a sapling, and one foot immersed in the water, from which he had forgotten to withdraw it, his whole attention being engaged in contemplating the movements of a water-snake, about five feet long, curiously checkered with black and green, who was deliberately swimming across the pool. There being no stick or stone at hand to pelt him with, we looked at him for a time in silent disgust; and then pushed forward. Our perseverance was at last rewarded; for several rods farther on, we emerged upon a little level grassy nook among the brushwood, and by an extraordinary dispensation of fortune, the weeds and floating sticks, which elsewhere covered the pool, seemed to have drawn apart, and left a few yards of clear water just in front of this favored spot. We sounded it with a stick; it was four feet deep: we lifted a specimen in our closed hands; it seemed reasonably transparent, so we decided that the time for action was arrived. But our ablutions were suddenly interrupted by ten thousand punctures, like poi-soned needles, and the humming of myriads of overgrown musquitoes, rising in all directions from their native mud and slime and swarming to the feast. We were fain to beat a retreat with all possible speed.

We made toward the tents, much refreshed by the bath, which the heat of the weather, joined to our prejudices, had rendered very desirable.

'What's the matter with the Captain? look at him!' said Shaw. The Captain stood alone on the prairie, swinging his hat violently around his head, and lifting first one foot and then the other, without moving from the spot. First he looked down to the ground with an air of supreme abhor-rence; then he gazed upward with a perplexed and indignant countenance, as if trying to trace the flight of an unseen en-emy. We called to know what was the matter; but he replied only by execrations directed against some unknown object.

We approached, when our ears were saluted by a droning sound, as if twenty bee-hives had been overturned at once. The air above was full of large black insects, in a state of great commotion, and multitudes were flying about just above the tops of the grass-blades.

'Don't be afraid,' called the Captain, observing us recoil. 'The brutes won't sting.'

At this I knocked one down with my hat, and discovered him to be no other than a 'dor-bug;' and looking closer, we found the ground thickly perforated with their holes.

We took a hasty leave of this flourishing colony, and walking up the rising ground to the tents, found Delorier's fire still glowing brightly. We sat down around it, and Shaw began to expatiate on the admirable facilities for bathing that we had discovered, and recommended the Captain by all means to go down there before breakfast in the morning. The Captain was in the act of remarking that he couldn't have believed it possible, when he suddenly interrupted himself, and clapped his hand to his cheek, exclaiming that 'those infernal humbugs were at him again.' In fact, we began to hear sounds as if bullets were humming over our heads. In a moment something rapped me sharply on the forehead, then upon the neck, and immediately I felt an indefinite number of sharp wiry claws in active motion, as if their owner were bent on pushing his explorations farther. I seized him, and dropped him into the fire. Our party speedily broke up, and we adjourned to our respective tents, where closing the opening fast, we hoped to be exempt from invasion. But all precaution was fruitless. The dor-bugs hummed through the tent, and marched over our faces until daylight; when, opening our blankets, we found several dozen clinging there with the utmost tenacity. The first object that met our eyes in the morning was Delorier, who seemed to be apostrophizing his frying-pan, which he held by the handle, at arm's length. It appeared that he had left it at night by the fire; and the bottom was now covered with dor-bugs, firmly imbedded. Multitudes beside, curiously parched and shrivelled, lay scattered among the ashes.

The horses and mules were turned loose to feed. We had just taken our seats at breakfast, or rather reclined in the classic mode, when an exclamation from Henry Chatillon, and a shout of alarm from the Captain, gave warning of some casualty, and looking up, we saw the whole band of animals, twenty-three in number, filing off for the settlements, the incorrigible Pontiac at their head, jumping along with hobbled feet, at a gait much more rapid than graceful. Three or four of us ran to cut them off, dashing as best we might through the tall grass, which was glittering with myriads of dew drops. After a race of a mile or more, Shaw caught a horse. Tying the trail-rope by way of bridle round the animal's jaw, and leaping upon his back, he got in advance of the remaining fugitives, while we, soon bringing them together, drove them in a crowd up to the tents, where each man caught and saddled his own. Then were heard lamentations and curses; for half the horses had broke their hobbles, and many were seriously galled by attempting to run in fetters.

It was late that morning before we were on the march; and early in the afternoon we were compelled to encamp, for a thunder-gust came up and suddenly enveloped us in whirling sheets of rain. With much ado, we pitched our tents amid the tempest, and all night long the thunder bellowed and growled over our heads. In the morning, light peaceful showers succeeded the cataracts of rain, that had been drenching us through the canvas of our tents. About noon, when there were some treacherous indications of fair weather, we got in motion again.

Not a breath of air stirred, over the free and open prairie: the clouds were like light piles of cotton; and where the blue sky was visible, it wore a hazy and languid aspect. The sun beat down upon us with a sultry penetrating heat almost insupportable, and as our party crept slowly along over the interminable level, the horses hung their heads as they waded fetlock deep through the mud, and the men slouched into the easiest position upon the saddle. At last, toward evening, the old familiar black heads of thunder-clouds rose fast above the horizon, and the same deep muttering of distant thunder that had become the ordinary accompaniment of our afternoon's journey began to roll hoarsely over the prairie. Only a few minutes elapsed before the whole sky was densely shrouded, and the prairie and some clusters of woods in front assumed a purple hue beneath the inky shadows. Suddenly from the densest fold of the cloud the flash leaped out, quivering again and again down to the edge of the prairie; and at the same instant came the sharp burst and the long rolling peal of the thunder. A cool wind, filled with the smell of rain, just then overtook us, levelling the tall grass by the side of the path.

'Come on; we must ride for it!' shouted Shaw, rushing past at full speed, his led horse snorting at his side. The whole party broke into full gallop, and made for the trees in front. Passing these, we found beyond them a meadow which they half inclosed. We rode pell-mell upon the ground, leaped from horseback, tore off our saddles; and in a moment each man was kneeling at his horse's feet. The hobbles were adjusted, and the animals turned loose; then, as the wagons came wheeling rapidly to the spot, we seized upon the tent-poles, and just as the storm broke, we were prepared to receive it. It came upon us almost with the darkness of night: the trees which were close at hand, were completely shrouded by the roaring torrents of rain.

We were sitting in the tent, when Delorier, with his broad felt hat hanging about his ears, and his shoulders glistening with rain, thrust in his head.

'Voulez vous du souper, tout de suite? I can make fire, sous la charette—I b'lieve so—I try.'

'Never mind supper, man; come in out of the rain.'

Delorier accordingly crouched in the entrance, for modesty would not permit him to intrude farther.

Our tent was none of the best defence against such a cataract. The rain could not enter bodily, but it beat through the canvas in a fine drizzle, that wetted us just as effectually. We sat upon our saddles with faces of the utmost surliness, while the water dropped from the vizors of our caps, and trickled down our cheeks. My india-rubber cloak conducted twenty little rapid streamlets to the ground; and Shaw's blanket coat was saturated like a sponge. But what most concerned us, was the sight of several puddles of water rapidly accumulating; one, in particular, that was gathering around the tent-pole, threatened to overspread the whole area within the tent, holding forth but an indifferent promise of a comfortable night's rest. Toward sunset, however, the storm ceased as suddenly as it began. A bright streak of clear red sky appeared above the western verge of the prairie, the horizontal rays of the sinking sun streamed through it, and glittered in a thousand prismatic colors upon the dripping groves and the prostrate grass. The pools in the tent dwindled and sunk into the saturated soil.

But all our hopes were delusive. Scarcely had night set in, when the tumult broke forth anew. The thunder here is not like the tame thunder of the Atlantic coast. Bursting with a terrific crash directly above our heads, it roared over the boundless waste of prairie, seeming to roll around the whole circle of the firmament with a peculiar and awful reverberation. The lightning flashed all night, playing with its livid glare upon the neighboring trees, revealing the vast expanse of the plain, and then leaving us shut in as if by a palpable wall of darkness.

It did not disturb us much. Now and then a peal awakened us, and made us conscious of the electric battle that was raging, and of the floods that dashed upon the stanch canvas over our heads. We lay upon india-rubber cloths, placed between our blankets and the soil. For a while, they excluded the water to admiration; but when at length it accumulated and began to run over the edges, they served equally well to retain it, so that toward the end of the night we were unconsciously reposing in small pools of rain.

On finally awaking in the morning the prospect was not a cheerful one. The rain no longer poured in torrents; but it pattered with a quiet pertinacity upon the strained and saturated canvas. We disengaged ourselves from our blankets, every fibre of which glistened with little bead-like drops of water, and looked out in the vain hope of discovering some token of fair weather. The clouds, in lead-colored volumes, rested upon the dismal verge of the prairie, or hung sluggishly overhead, while the earth wore an aspect no more attractive than the heavens, exhibiting nothing but pools of water, grass beaten down, and mud well trampled by our mules and horses. Our companions' tent, with an air of forlorn and passive misery, and their wagons in like manner, drenched and wobegone, stood not far off. The Captain was just returning from his morning's inspection of the horses.

He stalked through the mist and rain, with his plaid around his shoulders, his little pipe, dingy as an antiquarian relic, projecting from beneath his moustache, and his brother Jack at his heels.

'Good morning, Captain.'

'Good morning to your honors,' said the Captain, affecting the Hibernian accent; but at that instant, as he stooped to enter the tent, he tripped upon the cords at the entrance, and pitched forward against the guns which were strapped around the pole in the centre.

'You are nice men, you are!' said he, after an ejaculation not necessary to be recorded, 'to set a man-trap before your door every morning to catch your visitors.'

Then he sat down upon Henry Chatillon's saddle. We tossed a piece of Buffalo robe to Jack, who was looking about in some embarrassment. He spread it on the ground, and took his seat, with a stolid countenance, at his brother's side.

'Exhilarating weather, Captain.'

'Oh, delightful, delightful!' replied the Captain; 'I knew it would be so; so much for starting yesterday at noon! I knew how it would turn out; and I said so at the time.'

'You said just the contrary to us. We were in no hurry, and only moved because you insisted on it.'

'Gentlemen,' said the Captain, taking his pipe from his mouth with an air of extreme gravity, 'it was no plan of mine. There's a man among us who is determined to have every thing his own way. You may express your opinion; but don't expect him to listen. You may be as reasonable as you like; oh, it all goes for nothing! That man is resolved to rule the roast, and he'll set his face against any plan that he didn't think of himself.'

The Captain puffed for awhile at his pipe, as if meditating upon his grievances; then he began again.

'For twenty years I have been in the British army; and in all that time I never had half so much dissension, and quarrelling, and nonsense, as since I have been on this cursed prairie. He's the most uncomfortable man I ever met.'

'Yes;' said Jack, 'and don't you know, Bill, how he drank up all the coffee last night, and put the rest by for himself till the morning!'

'He pretends to know every thing,' resumed the Captain; 'nobody must give orders but he! It's, oh! we must do this; and, oh! we must do that; and the tent must be pitched here, and the horses must be picketed there; for nobody knows as well as he does.'

We were a little surprised at this disclosure of domestic dissensions among our allies, for though we knew of their existence, we were not aware of their extent. The persecuted Captain seeming wholly at a loss as to the course of conduct that he should pursue, we recommended him to adopt prompt and energetic measures; but all his military experience had failed to teach him the indispensable lesson, to be 'hard' when the emergency requires it.

'For twenty years,' he repeated, 'I have been in the British army, and in that time I have been intimately acquainted with some two hundred officers, young and old, and I never yet quarrelled with any man. Oh, "any thing for a quiet life!" that's my maxim.'

We intimated that the prairie was hardly the place to enjoy a quiet life, but that, in the present circumstances, the best thing he could do toward securing his wished-for tranquillity, was immediately to put a period to the nuisance that disturbed it. But again the Captain's easy good-nature recoiled from the task. The somewhat vigorous measures necessary to gain the desired result were utterly repugnant to him; he preferred to pocket his grievances, still retaining the privilege of grumbling about them. 'Oh, any thing for a quiet life!' he said again, circling back to his favorite maxim.

But to glance at the previous history of our transatlantic confederates. The Captain had sold his commission, and was living in bachelor ease and dignity in his paternal halls, near Dublin. He hunted, fished, rode steeple-chases, ran races, and talked of his former exploits. He was surrounded with the trophies of his rod and gun; the walls were plentifully garnished, he told us, with moose-horns and deer-horns, bearskins and fox-tails; for the Captain's double-barrelled rifle had seen service in Canada and Jamaica; he had killed salmon in Nova Scotia, and trout, by his own account, in all the streams of the three kingdoms. But in an evil hour a seductive stranger came from London; no less a person than R——;

who, among other multitudinous wanderings, had once been upon the western prairies, and naturally enough, was anxious to visit them again. The Captain's imagination was inflamed by the pictures of a hunter's paradise that his guest held forth; he conceived an ambition to add to his other trophies the horns of a buffalo, and the claws of a grizzly bear; so he and R—— struck a league to travel in company. Jack followed his brother, as a matter of course. Two weeks on board of the Atlantic steamer brought them to Boston; in two weeks more of hard travelling they reached St. Louis, from which a ride of six days carried them to the frontier; and here we found them, in the full tide of preparation for their journey.

We had been throughout on terms of intimacy with the Captain, but R——, the motive-power of our companions' branch of the expedition, was scarcely known to us. His voice, indeed, might be heard incessantly; but at camp he remained chiefly within the tent, and on the road he either rode by himself, or else remained in close conversation with his friend Wright, the muleteer. As the Captain left the tent that morning, I observed R—— standing by the fire, and having nothing else to do, I determined to ascertain, if possible, what manner of man he was. He had a book under his arm, but just at present he was engrossed in actively superintending the operations of Sorel, the hunter, who was cooking some corn-bread over the coals for breakfast. R—— was a well-formed and rather good-looking man, some thirty years old; considerably younger than the Captain. He wore a beard and moustache of the oakum complexion, and his attire was altogether more elegant than one ordinarily sees on the prairie. He wore his cap on one side of his head; his checked shirt, open in front, was in very neat order, considering the circumstances, and his blue pantaloons, of the John Bull cut, might once have figured in Bond-street.

'Turn over that cake, man! turn it over quick! Don't you see it burning?'

'It ain't half done,' growled Sorel, in the amiable tone of a whipped bull-dog.

'It is. Turn it over, I tell you!'

Sorel, a strong, sullen-looking Canadian, who, from having spent his life among the wildest and most remote of the

Indian tribes, had imbibed much of their dark vindictive spirit, looked ferociously up, as if he longed to leap upon his *bourgeois* and throttle him; but he obeyed the order, coming from so experienced an artist.

'It was a good idea of yours,' said I, seating myself on the tongue of the wagon, 'to bring Indian meal with you.'

'Yes, yes,' said R——, 'it's good bread for the prairie— good bread for the prairie. I tell you that's burning again.'

Here he stooped down, and unsheathing the silver-mounted hunting-knife in his belt, began to perform the part of cook himself; at the same time requesting me to hold for a moment the book under his arm, which interfered with the exercise of these important functions. I opened it; it was 'Macaulay's Lays;' and I made some remark, expressing my admiration of the work.

'Yes, yes; a pretty good thing. Macaulay can do better than that, though. I know him very well. I have travelled with him. Where was it we met first—at Damascus? No, no; it was in Italy.'

'So,' said I, 'you have been over the same ground with your countryman, the author of "Eothen?" There has been some discussion in America as to who he is. I have heard Milnes's name mentioned.'

'Milnes? Oh, no, no, no; not at all. It was Kinglake; Kinglake's the man. I know him very well; that is, I have seen him.'

Here Jack C——, who stood by, interposed a remark (a thing not common with him), observing that he thought the weather would become fair before twelve o'clock.

'It's going to rain all day,' said R——, 'and clear up in the middle of the night.'

Just then, the clouds began to dissipate in a very unequivocal manner; but Jack, not caring to defend his point against so authoritative a declaration, walked away whistling, and we resumed our conversation.

'Borrow, the author of "The Bible in Spain," I presume you know him, too?'

'Oh, certainly; I know all those men. By the way, they told me that one of your American writers, Judge Story, had died lately. I edited some of his works in London; not without faults, though.'

Here followed an erudite commentary on certain points of law, in which he particularly animadverted on the errors into which he considered that the Judge had been betrayed. At length, having touched successively on an infinite variety of topics, I found that I had the happiness of discovering a man equally competent to enlighten me upon them all, equally an authority on matters of science or literature, philosophy or fashion. The part I bore in the conversation was by no means a prominent one; it was only necessary to set him going, and when he had run long enough upon one topic, to divert him to another, and lead him on to pour out his heaps of treasure in succession.

'What has that fellow been saying to you?' said Shaw, as I returned to the tent. 'I have heard nothing but his talking for the last half-hour.'

R—— had none of the peculiar traits of the ordinary 'British snob;' his absurdities were all his own, belonging to no particular nation or clime. He was possessed with an active devil, that had driven him over land and sea, to no great purpose, as it seemed; for although he had the usual complement of eyes and ears, the avenues between these organs and his brain appeared remarkably narrow and untrodden. His energy was much more conspicuous than his wisdom; but his predominant characteristic was a magnanimous ambition to exercise on all occasions an awful rule and supremacy, and this propensity equally displayed itself, as the reader will have observed, whether the matter in question was the baking of a hoe-cake or a point of international law. When such diverse elements as he and the easy-tempered Captain came in contact, no wonder some commotion ensued; R—— rode rough-shod, from morning till night, over his military ally.

At noon the sky was clear, and we set out, trailing through mud and slime six inches deep. That night we were spared the customary infliction of the shower-bath.

On the next afternoon we were moving slowly along, not far from a patch of woods which lay on the right. Jack C—— rode a little in advance;

'The livelong day he had not spoke;'

when suddenly he faced about, pointed to the woods, and roared out to his brother:

'Oh, Bill! here's a cow!'

The Captain instantly galloped forward, and he and Jack made a vain attempt to capture the prize; but the cow, with a well-grounded distrust of their intentions, took refuge among the trees. R—— joined them, and they soon drove her out. We watched their evolutions as they galloped around her, trying in vain to noose her with their trail-ropes, which they had converted into *lariettes* for the occasion. At length they resorted to milder measures, and the cow was driven along with the party. Soon after, the usual thunder-storm came up, the wind blowing with such fury that the streams of rain flew almost horizontally along the prairie, roaring like a cataract. The horses turned tail to the storm, and stood hanging their heads, bearing the infliction with an air of meekness and resignation; while we drew our heads between our shoulders, and crouched forward, so as to make our backs serve as a pent-house for the rest of our persons. Meanwhile, the cow, taking advantage of the tumult, ran off, to the great discomfiture of the Captain, who seemed to consider her as his own especial prize, since she had been discovered by Jack. In defiance of the storm, he pulled his cap tight over his brows, jerked a huge buffalo-pistol from his holster, and set out at full speed after her. This was the last we saw of them for some time, the mist and rain making an impenetrable veil; but at length we heard the Captain's shout, and saw him looming through the tempest, the picture of a Hibernian cavalier, with his cocked pistol held aloft for safety's sake, and a countenance of anxiety and excitement. The cow trotted before him, but exhibited evident signs of an intention to run off again, and the Captain was roaring to us to head her. But the rain had got in behind our coat collars, and was travelling over our necks in numerous little streamlets, and being afraid to move our heads, for fear of admitting more, we sat stiff and immovable, looking at the Captain askance, and laughing at his frantic movements. At last, the cow made a sudden plunge and ran off; the Captain grasped his pistol firmly, spurred his horse, and galloped after, with evident designs of mischief. In a moment we heard the faint report, deadened by the rain,

and then the conqueror and his victim reappeared, the latter shot through the body, and quite helpless. Not long after, the storm moderated, and we advanced again. The cow walked painfully along under the charge of Jack, to whom the Captain had committed her, while he himself rode forward in his old capacity of vidette. We were approaching a long line of trees, that followed a stream stretching across our path, far in front, when we beheld the vidette galloping toward us, apparently much excited, but with a broad grin on his face.

'Let that cow drop behind!' he shouted to us; 'here's her owners!'

And in fact, as we approached the line of trees, a large white object, like a tent, was visible behind them. On approaching, however, we found, instead of the expected Mormon camp, nothing but the lonely prairie, and a large white rock standing by the path. The cow, therefore, resumed her place in our procession. She walked on until we encamped, when R——, firmly approaching with his enormous English double-barrelled rifle, calmly and deliberately took aim at her heart, and discharged into it first one bullet and then the other. She was then butchered on the most approved principles of woodcraft, and furnished a very welcome item to our somewhat limited bill of fare.

In a day or two more we reached the river called the 'Big Blue.' By titles equally elegant, almost all the streams of this region are designated. We had struggled through ditches and little brooks all that morning; but on traversing the dense woods that lined the banks of the Blue, we found that more formidable difficulties awaited us, for the stream, swollen by the rains, was wide, deep and rapid.

No sooner were we on the spot, than R—— had flung off his clothes, and was swimming across, or splashing through the shallows, with the end of a rope between his teeth. We all looked on in admiration, wondering what might be the design of this energetic preparation; but soon we heard him shouting: 'Give that rope a turn round that stump! You, Sorel; do you hear? Look sharp, now Boisverd! Come over to this side, some of you, and help me!' The men to whom these orders were directed paid not the least attention to them, though they were poured out without pause or intermission.

Henry Chatillon directed the work, and it proceeded quietly and rapidly. R——'s sharp brattling voice might have been heard incessantly; and he was leaping about with the utmost activity, multiplying himself, after the manner of great commanders, as if his universal presence and supervision were of the last necessity. His commands were rather amusingly inconsistent; for when he saw that the men would not do as he told them, he wisely accommodated himself to circumstances, and with the utmost vehemence ordered them to do precisely that which they were at the time engaged upon, no doubt recollecting the story of Mahomet and the refractory mountain. Shaw smiled significantly; R—— observed it, and approaching with a countenance of lofty indignation, began to vapour a little, but was instantly reduced to silence.

The raft was at length complete. We piled our goods upon it, with the exception of our guns, which each man chose to retain in his own keeping. Sorel, Boisverd, Wright and Delorier took their stations at the four corners, to hold it together, and swim across with it; and in a moment more, all our earthly possessions were floating on the turbid waters of the Big Blue. We sat on the bank, anxiously watching the result, until we saw the raft safe landed in a little cove far down on the opposite bank. The empty wagons were easily passed across; and then, each man mounting a horse, we rode through the stream, the stray animals following of their own accord.

Chapter VI.

THE PLATTE AND THE DESERT.

"Seest thou yon dreary plain, forlorn and wild,
The seat of desolation?"
PARADISE LOST.

"Here have we war for war, and blood for blood."
KING JOHN.

WE WERE NOW arrived at the close of our solitary journeyings along the St. Joseph's Trail. On the evening of
the twenty-third of May we encamped near its junction with
the old legitimate trail of the Oregon emigrants. We had ridden long that afternoon, trying in vain to find wood and water, until at length we saw the sunset sky reflected from a pool
encircled by bushes and a rock or two. The water lay in the
bottom of a hollow, the smooth prairie gracefully rising in
ocean-like swells on every side. We pitched our tents by it; not
however before the keen eye of Henry Chatillon had discerned some unusual object upon the faintly defined outline
of the distant swell. But in the moist, hazy atmosphere of the
evening, nothing could be clearly distinguished. As we lay
around the fire after supper, a low and distant sound, strange
enough amid the loneliness of the prairie, reached our ears—
peals of laughter, and the faint voices of men and women. For
eight days we had not encountered a human being, and this
singular warning of their vicinity had an effect extremely wild
and impressive.

About dark a sallow-faced fellow descended the hill on
horseback, and splashing through the pool, rode up to the
tents. He was enveloped in a huge cloak, and his broad felt-
hat was weeping about his ears with the drizzling moisture
of the evening. Another followed, a stout, square-built,
intelligent-looking man, who announced himself as leader of
an emigrant party, encamped a mile in advance of us. About
twenty wagons, he said, were with him; the rest of his party
were on the other side of the Big Blue, waiting for a woman

who was in the pains of child-birth, and quarrelling mean-while among themselves.

These were the first emigrants that we had overtaken, al-though we had found abundant and melancholy traces of their progress throughout the whole course of the journey. Sometimes we passed the grave of one who had sickened and died on the way. The earth was usually torn up, and covered thickly with wolf-tracks. Some had escaped this violation. One morning, a piece of plank, standing upright on the sum-mit of a grassy hill, attracted our notice, and riding up to it, we found the following words very roughly traced upon it, apparently by a red-hot piece of iron:

MARY ELLIS.

DIED MAY 7th, 1845.

AGED TWO MONTHS.

Such tokens were of common occurrence. Nothing could speak more for the hardihood, or rather infatuation, of the adventurers, or the sufferings that await them upon the journey.

We were late in breaking up our camp on the following morning, and scarcely had we ridden a mile when we saw, far in advance of us, drawn against the horizon, a line of objects stretching at regular intervals along the level edge of the prairie. An intervening swell soon hid them from sight, until, ascending it a quarter of an hour after, we saw close before us the emigrant caravan, with its heavy white wagons creeping on in their slow procession, and a large drove of cattle following behind. Half a dozen yellow-visaged Missou-rians, mounted on horseback, were cursing and shouting among them; their lank angular proportions, enveloped in brown homespun, evidently cut and adjusted by the hands of a domestic female tailor. As we approached, they greeted us with the polished salutation: 'How are ye, boys? Are ye for Oregon or California?'

As we pushed rapidly past the wagons, children's faces were thrust out from the white coverings to look at us; while the care-worn, thin-featured matron, or the buxom girl, seated in front, suspended the knitting on which most of them were engaged to stare at us with wondering curiosity. By the side of each wagon stalked the proprietor, urging on his patient oxen, who shouldered heavily along, inch by inch, on their interminable journey. It was easy to see that fear and dissension prevailed among them; some of the men—but these, with one exception, were bachelors—looked wistfully upon us as we rode lightly and swiftly past, and then impatiently at their own lumbering wagons and heavy-gaited oxen. Others were unwilling to advance at all, until the party they had left behind should have rejoined them. Many were murmuring against the leader they had chosen, and wished to depose him; and this discontent was fomented by some ambitious spirits, who had hopes of succeeding in his place. The women were divided between regrets for the homes they had left and apprehension of the deserts and the savages before them.

We soon left them far behind, and fondly hoped that we had taken a final leave; but unluckily our companions' wagon stuck so long in a deep muddy ditch, that before it was extricated the van of the emigrant caravan appeared again, descending a ridge close at hand. Wagon after wagon plunged through the mud; and as it was nearly noon, and the place promised shade and water, we saw with much gratification that they were resolved to encamp. Soon the wagons were wheeled into a circle; the cattle were grazing over the meadow, and the men, with sour, sullen faces, were looking about for wood and water. They seemed to meet with but indifferent success. As we left the ground, I saw a tall slouching fellow, with the nasal accent of 'down east,' contemplating the contents of his tin cup, which he had just filled with water.

'Look here, you,' said he; 'it's chock full of animals!'

The cup, as he held it out, exhibited in fact an extraordinary variety and profusion of animal and vegetable life.

Riding up the little hill, and looking back on the meadow, we could easily see that all was not right in the camp of the emigrants. The men were crowded together, and an angry discussion seemed to be going forward. R—— was missing from his wonted place in the line, and the Captain told us that he had remained behind to get his horse shod by a blacksmith who was attached to the emigrant party. Something whispered in our ears that mischief was on foot; we kept on, however, and coming soon to a stream of tolerable water, we stopped to rest and dine. Still the absentee lingered behind. At last, at the distance of a mile, he and his horse suddenly appeared, sharply defined against the sky on the summit of a hill; and close behind, a huge white object rose slowly into view.

'What is that blockhead bringing with him now?'

A moment dispelled the mystery. Slowly and solemnly, one behind the other, four long trains of oxen and four emigrant wagons rolled over the crest of the declivity and gravely descended, while R—— rode in state in the van. It seems, that during the process of shoeing the horse, the smothered dissensions among the emigrants suddenly broke into open rupture. Some insisted on pushing forward, some on remaining where they were, and some on going back. Kearsley, their captain, threw up his command in disgust. 'And now, boys,' said he, 'if any of you are for going ahead, just you come along with me.'

Four wagons, with ten men, one woman and one small child, made up the force of the 'go-ahead' faction, and R——, with his usual proclivity toward mischief, invited them to join our party. Fear of the Indians—for I can conceive of no other motive—must have induced him to court so burdensome an alliance. As may well be conceived, these repeated instances of high-handed dealing sufficiently exasperated us. In this case, indeed, the men who joined us were all that could be desired; rude indeed in manners, but frank, manly and intelligent. To tell them we could not travel with them was of course out of the question. I merely reminded Kearsley that if his oxen could not keep up with our mules he must expect to be left behind, as we could not consent to be farther delayed on the journey; but he immediately replied, that his oxen '*should* keep up; and if they couldn't, why he allowed he'd find out how to make 'em!' Having also availed myself of what satisfaction could be derived from giving R—— to understand my opinion of his conduct, I returned to our own side of the camp.

On the next day, as it chanced, our English companions broke the axle-tree of their wagon, and down came the whole cumbrous machine lumbering into the bed of a brook! Here was a day's work cut out for us. Meanwhile, our emigrant associates kept on their way, and so vigorously did they urge forward their powerful oxen, that, with the broken axle-tree and other calamities, it was full a week before we overtook them; when at length we discovered them, one afternoon, crawling quietly along the sandy brink of the Platte. But meanwhile various incidents occurred to ourselves.

It was probable that at this stage of our journey the Pawnees would attempt to rob us. We began therefore to stand guard in turn, dividing the night into three watches, and appointing two men for each. Delorier and I held guard together. We did not march with military precision to and fro before the tents: our discipline was by no means so stringent and rigid. We wrapped ourselves in our blankets, and sat down by the fire; and Delorier, combining his culinary functions with his duties as sentinel, employed himself in boiling the head of an antelope for our morning's repast. Yet we were models of vigilance in comparison with some of the party; for the ordinary practice of the guard was to establish himself in the most comfortable posture he could; lay his rifle on the ground, and enveloping his nose in his blanket, meditate on his mistress, or whatever subject best pleased him. This is all well enough when among Indians, who do not habitually proceed further in their hostility than robbing travellers of their horses and mules, though, indeed, a Pawnee's forbearance is not always to be trusted; but in certain regions farther to the west, the guard must beware how he exposes his person to the light of the fire, lest perchance some keen-eyed skulking marksman should let fly a bullet or an arrow from amid the darkness.

Among various tales that circulated around our camp-fire was a rather curious one, told by Boisverd, and not inappropriate here. Boisverd was trapping with several companions on the skirts of the Blackfoot country. The man on guard, well-knowing that it behooved him to put forth his utmost precaution, kept aloof from the fire-light, and sat watching intently on all sides. At length he was aware of a dark, crouching figure, stealing noiselessly into the circle of the light. He hastily cocked his rifle, but the sharp click of the lock caught the ear of Blackfoot, whose senses were all on the alert. Raising his arrow, already fitted to the string, he shot it in the direction of the sound. So sure was his aim, that he drove it through the throat of the unfortunate guard, and then, with a loud yell, bounded from the camp.

As I looked at the partner of my watch, puffing and blowing over his fire, it occurred to me that he might not prove the most efficient auxiliary in time of trouble.

'Delorier,' said I, 'would you run away if the Pawnees should fire at us?'

'Ah! oui, oui, Monsieur!' he replied very decisively.

I did not doubt the fact, but was a little surprised at the frankness of the confession.

At this instant a most whimsical variety of voices—barks, howls, yelps and whines—all mingled as it were together, sounded from the prairie, not far off, as if a whole conclave of wolves of every age and sex were assembled there. Delorier looked up from his work with a laugh, and began to imitate this curious medley of sounds with a most ludicrous accuracy. At this they were repeated with redoubled emphasis, the musician being apparently indignant at the successful efforts of a rival. They all proceeded from the throat of one little wolf, not larger than a spaniel, seated by himself at some distance. He was of the species called the prairie-wolf; a grim-visaged, but harmless little brute, whose worst propensity is creeping among horses and gnawing the ropes of raw-hide by which they are picketed around the camp. But other beasts roam the prairies, far more formidable in aspect and in character. These are the large white and gray wolves, whose deep howl we heard at intervals from far and near.

At last I fell into a doze, and awaking from it, found Delorier fast asleep. Scandalized by this breach of discipline, I was about to stimulate his vigilance by stirring him with the stock of my rifle; but compassion prevailing, I determined to let him sleep awhile, and then arouse him, and administer a suitable reproof for such a forgetfulness of duty. Now and then I walked the rounds among the silent horses, to see that all was right. The night was chill, damp, and dark, the dank grass bending under the icy dew-drops. At the distance of a rod or two the tents were invisible, and nothing could be seen but the obscure figures of the horses, deeply breathing, and restlessly starting as they slept, or still slowly champing the grass. Far off, beyond the black outline of the prairie, there was a ruddy light, gradually increasing, like the glow of a conflagration; until at length the broad disk of the moon, blood-red, and vastly magnified by the vapors, rose slowly upon the darkness, flecked by one or two little clouds, and as the light poured over the gloomy plain, a fierce and stern howl, close at hand, seemed to greet it as an unwelcome intruder. There was something impressive and awful in the place and the hour; for I and the beasts were all that had consciousness for many a league around.

Some days elapsed, and brought us near the Platte. Two men on horseback approached us one morning, and we watched them with the curiosity and interest that, upon the solitude of the plains, such an encounter always excites. They were evidently whites, from their mode of riding, though, contrary to the usage of that region, neither of them carried a rifle.

'Fools!' remarked Henry Chatillon, 'to ride that way on the prairie; Pawnee find them—then they catch it!'

Pawnee *had* found them, and they had come very near 'catching it;' indeed, nothing saved them from trouble but the approach of our party. Shaw and I knew one of them; a man named Turner, whom we had seen at Westport. He and his companion belonged to an emigrant party encamped a few miles in advance, and had returned to look for some stray oxen, leaving their rifles, with characteristic rashness or ignorance, behind them. Their neglect had nearly cost them dear; for just before we came up, half a dozen Indians approached, and seeing them apparently defenceless, one of the rascals seized the bridle of Turner's fine horse, and ordered him to dismount. Turner was wholly unarmed; but the other jerked a little revolving pistol out of his pocket, at which the Pawnee recoiled; and just then some of our men appearing in the distance, the whole party whipped their rugged little horses, and made off. In no way daunted, Turner foolishly persisted in going forward.

Long after leaving him, and late that afternoon, in the midst of a gloomy and barren prairie, we came suddenly upon the great Pawnee trail, leading from their villages on the Platte, to their war and hunting grounds to the southward. Here every summer pass the motley concourse; thousands of savages, men, women, and children, horses and mules, laden with their weapons and implements, and an innumerable multitude of unruly wolfish dogs, who have not acquired the civilized accomplishment of barking, but howl like their wild cousins of the prairie.

The permanent winter villages of the Pawnees, stand on the lower Platte, but throughout the summer the greater part of the inhabitants are wandering over the plains, a treacherous, cowardly banditti, who by a thousand acts of pillage and murder, have deserved summary chastisement at the hands of government. Last year a Dahcotah warrior performed a signal exploit at one of these villages. He approached it alone, in the middle of a dark night, and clambering up the outside of one of the lodges, which are in the form of a half-sphere, he looked in at the round hole made at the top for the escape of smoke. The dusky light from the smouldering embers showed him the forms of the sleeping inmates; and dropping lightly through the opening, he unsheathed his knife, and stirring the fire, coolly selected his victims. One by one, he stabbed and scalped them; when a child suddenly awoke and screamed. He rushed from the lodge, yelled a Sioux war-cry, shouted his name in triumph and defiance, and in a moment had darted out upon the dark prairie, leaving the whole village behind him in a tumult, with the howling and baying of dogs, the screams of women, and the yells of the enraged warriors.

Our friend Kearsley, as we learned on rejoining him, signalized himself by a less bloody achievement. He and his men were good woodsmen, and well skilled in the use of the rifle; but found themselves wholly out of their element on the prairie. None of them had ever seen a buffalo; and they had very vague conceptions of his nature and appearance. On the day after they reached the Platte, looking towards a distant swell, they beheld a multitude of little black specks in motion upon its surface.

'Take your rifles, boys,' said Kearsley, 'and we'll have fresh meat for supper.' This inducement was quite sufficient. The ten men left their wagons, and set out in hot haste, some on horseback and some on foot, in pursuit of the supposed buffalo. Meanwhile a high grassy ridge shut the game from view; but mounting it after half an hour's running and riding, they found themselves suddenly confronted by about thirty mounted Pawnees! The amazement and consternation were mutual. Having nothing but their bows and arrows, the Indians thought their hour was come, and the fate that they were no doubt conscious of richly deserving, about to overtake them. So they began, one and all, to shout forth the most cordial salutations of friendship, running up with extreme earnestness to shake hands with the Missourians, who were as much rejoiced as they were to escape the expected conflict.

A low undulating line of sand-hills bounded the horizon before us. That day we rode ten consecutive hours, and it was dusk before we entered the hollows and gorges of these gloomy little hills. At length we gained the summit, and the long-expected valley of the Platte lay before us. We all drew rein, and, gathering in a knot on the crest of the hill, sat joyfully looking down upon the prospect. It was right welcome; strange too, and striking to the imagination, and yet it had not one picturesque or beautiful feature; nor had it any of the features of grandeur, other than its vast extent, its solitude and its wildness. For league after league, a plain as level as a frozen lake, was outspread beneath us; here and there the Platte, divided into a dozen thread-like sluices, was traversing it, and an occasional clump of wood, rising in the midst like a shadowy island, relieved the monotony of the waste. No living thing was moving throughout the vast landscape, except the lizards that darted over the sand and through the rank grass and prickly pear, just at our feet. And yet stern and wild associations gave a singular interest to the view; for here each man lives by the strength of his arm and the valor of his heart. Here society is reduced to its original elements, the whole fabric of art and conventionality is struck rudely to pieces, and men find themselves suddenly brought back to the wants and resources of their original natures.

We had passed the more toilsome and monotonous part of the journey; but four hundred miles still intervened between us and Fort Laramie; and to reach that point cost us the travel of three additional weeks. During the whole of this time, we were passing up the centre of a long narrow sandy plain, reaching like an outstretched belt, nearly to the Rocky Mountains. Two lines of sand-hills, broken often into the wildest and most fantastic forms, flanked the valley at the distance of a mile or two on the right and left; while beyond them lay a barren, trackless waste—'The Great American Desert'—extending for hundreds of miles to the Arkansas on the one side, and the Missouri on the other. Before us and behind us, the level monotony of the plain was unbroken as far as the eye could reach. Sometimes it glared in the sun, an expanse of hot, bare sand; sometimes it was veiled by long coarse grass. Huge skulls and whitening bones of buffalo were scattered every where; the ground was tracked by myriads of them, and often covered with the circular indentations where the bulls had wallowed in the hot weather. From every gorge and ravine, opening from the hills, descended deep, well-worn paths, where the buffalo issue twice a day in regular procession down to drink in the Platte. The river itself runs through the midst, a thin sheet of rapid, turbid water, half a mile wide, and scarce two feet deep. Its low banks, for the most part, without a bush or a tree, are of loose sand, with which the stream is so charged that it grates on the teeth in drinking. The naked landscape is of itself, dreary and monotonous enough; and yet the wild beasts and wild men that frequent the valley of the Platte, make it a scene of interest and excitement to the traveller. Of those who have journeyed there, scarce one, perhaps, fails to look back with fond regret to his horse and his rifle.

Early in the morning after we reached the Platte, a long procession of squalid savages approached our camp. Each was on foot, leading his horse by a rope of bull-hides. His attire consisted merely of a scanty cincture, and an old buffalo robe, tattered and begrimed by use, which hung over his shoulders. His head was close shaven, except a ridge of hair reaching over the crown from the centre of the forehead, very much like the long bristles on the back of a hyena, and he carried his bow and arrows in his hand, while his meagre little horse was laden with dried buffalo meat, the produce of his hunting. Such were the first specimens that we met—and very indifferent ones they were—of the genuine savages of the prairie.

They were the Pawnees whom Kearsley had encountered the day before, and belonged to a large hunting party, known to be ranging the prairie in the vicinity. They strode rapidly past, within a furlong of our tents, not pausing or looking towards us, after the manner of Indians when meditating mischief, or conscious of ill desert. I went out and met them; and had an amicable conference with the chief, presenting him with half a pound of tobacco, at which unmerited bounty he expressed much gratification. These fellows, or some of their companions, had committed a dastardly outrage upon an emigrant party in advance of us. Two men, out on horseback at a distance, were seized by them, but lashing their horses, they broke loose and fled. At this the Pawnees raised the yell and shot at them, transfixing the hindermost through the back with several arrows, while his companion galloped away and brought in the news to his party. The panic-stricken emigrants remained for several days in camp, not daring even to send out in quest of the dead body.

The reader will recollect Turner, the man whose narrow escape was mentioned not long since. We heard that the men whom the entreaties of his wife induced to go in search of him, found him leisurely driving along his recovered oxen, and whistling in utter contempt of the Pawnee nation. His party was encamped within two miles of us; but we passed them that morning, while the men were driving in the oxen, and the women packing their domestic utensils and their numerous offspring in the spacious patriarchal wagons. As we looked back, we saw their caravan, dragging its slow length along the plain; wearily toiling on its way, to found new empires in the West.

Our New-England climate is mild and equable compared with that of the Platte. This very morning, for instance, was close and sultry, the sun rising with a faint oppressive heat; when suddenly darkness gathered in the west, and a furious blast of sleet and hail drove full in our faces, icy cold, and urged with such demoniac vehemence that it felt like a storm of needles. It was curious to see the horses; they faced about in extreme displeasure, holding their tails like whipped dogs,

and shivering as the angry gusts, howling louder than a concert of wolves, swept over us. Wright's long train of mules
came sweeping round before the storm, like a flight of brown
snow-birds driven by a winter tempest. Thus we all remained
stationary for some minutes, crouching close to our horses'
necks, much too surly to speak, though once the Captain
looked up from between the collars of his coat, his face
blood-red, and the muscles of his mouth contracted by the
cold into a most ludicrous grin of agony. He grumbled something that sounded like a curse, directed, as we believed,
against the unhappy hour when he had first thought of leaving home. The thing was too good to last long; and the instant the puffs of wind subsided we erected our tents, and
remained in camp for the rest of a gloomy and lowering day.
The emigrants also encamped near at hand. We being first on
the ground, had appropriated all the wood within reach; so
that our fire alone blazed cheerily. Around it soon gathered a
group of uncouth figures, shivering in the drizzling rain.
Conspicuous among them were two or three of the half-
savage men who spend their reckless lives in trapping among
the Rocky Mountains, or in trading for the Fur Company in
the Indian villages. They were all of Canadian extraction;
their hard, weather-beaten faces and bushy moustaches
looked out from beneath the hoods of their white capotes
with a bad and brutish expression, as if their owner might be
the willing agent of any villany. And such in fact is the character of many of these men.

On the day following we overtook Kearsley's wagons, and
thenceforward, for a week or two, we were fellow-travellers.
One good effect, at least, resulted from the alliance; it materially diminished the serious fatigues of standing guard; for the
party being now more numerous, there were longer intervals
between each man's turns of duty.

Chapter VII.

THE BUFFALO.

"Twice twenty leagues
Beyond remotest smoke of hunter's camp,
Roams the majestic brute, in herds that shake
The earth with thundering steps."

BRYANT.

FOUR DAYS on the Platte, and yet no buffalo! Last year's signs of them were provokingly abundant; and wood being extremely scarce, we found an admirable substitute in the *bois de vache*, which burns exactly like peat, producing no unpleasant effects. The wagons one morning had left the camp; Shaw and I were already on horseback, but Henry Chatillon still sat cross-legged by the dead embers of the fire, playing pensively with the lock of his rifle, while his sturdy Wyandot pony stood quietly behind him, looking over his head. At last he got up, patted the neck of the pony (whom, from an exaggerated appreciation of his merits, he had christened 'Five Hundred Dollar'), and then mounted, with a melancholy air.

'What is it, Henry?'

'Ah, I feel lonesome; I never been here before; but I see away yonder over the buttes, and down there on the prairie, black—all black with buffalo!'

In the afternoon, he and I left the party in search of an antelope; until at the distance of a mile or two on the right, the tall white wagons and the little black specks of horsemen were just visible, so slowly advancing that they seemed motionless; and far on the left rose the broken line of scorched, desolate sand-hills. The vast plain waved with tall rank grass, that swept our horses' bellies; it swayed to and fro in billows with the light breeze, and far and near antelope and wolves were moving through it, the hairy backs of the latter alternately appearing and disappearing as they bounded awkwardly along; while the antelope, with the simple curiosity peculiar to them, would often approach us closely, their little

67

horns and white throats just visible above the grass tops, as they gazed eagerly at us with their round black eyes.

I dismounted, and amused myself with firing at the wolves. Henry attentively scrutinized the surrounding landscape; at length he gave a shout, and called on me to mount again, pointing in the direction of the sand-hills. A mile and a half from us, two minute black specks slowly traversed the face of one of the bare glaring declivities, and disappeared behind the summit. 'Let us go!' cried Henry, belaboring the sides of 'Five Hundred Dollar;' and I following in his wake, we galloped rapidly through the rank grass toward the base of the hills.

From one of their openings descended a deep ravine, widening as it issued on the prairie. We entered it, and galloping up, in a moment were surrounded by the bleak sand-hills. Half of their steep sides were bare; the rest were scantily clothed with clumps of grass, and various uncouth plants, conspicuous among which appeared the reptile-like prickly-pear. They were gashed with numberless ravines; and as the sky had suddenly darkened, and a cold gusty wind arisen, the strange shrubs and the dreary hills looked doubly wild and desolate. But Henry's face was all eagerness. He tore off a little hair from the piece of buffalo-robe under his saddle, and threw it up, to show the course of the wind. It blew directly before us. The game were therefore to windward, and it was necessary to make our best speed to get round them.

We scrambled from this ravine, and galloping away through the hollows, soon found another, winding like a snake among the hills, and so deep that it completely concealed us. We rode up the bottom of it, glancing through the shrubbery at its edge, till Henry abruptly jerked his rein, and slid out of his saddle. Full a quarter of a mile distant, on the outline of the farthest hill, a long procession of buffalo were walking, in Indian file, with the utmost gravity and deliberation; then more appeared, clambering from a hollow not far off, and ascending, one behind the other, the grassy slope of another hill; then a shaggy head and a pair of short broken horns appeared issuing out of a ravine close at hand, and with a slow, stately step, one by one, the enormous brutes came into view, taking their way across the valley, wholly unconscious

of an enemy. In a moment Henry was worming his way, lying
flat on the ground, through grass and prickly-pears, toward
his unsuspecting victims. He had with him both my rifle and
his own. He was soon out of sight, and still the buffalo kept
issuing into the valley. For a long time all was silent; I sat
holding his horse, and wondering what he was about, when
suddenly, in rapid succession, came the sharp reports of the
two rifles, and the whole line of buffalo, quickening their pace
into a clumsy trot, gradually disappeared over the ridge of the
hill. Henry rose to his feet, and stood looking after them.

'You have missed them,' said I.

'Yes,' said Henry; 'let us go.' He descended into the ravine,
loaded the rifles, and mounted his horse.

We rode up the hill after the buffalo. The herd was out of
sight when we reached the top, but lying on the grass, not far
off, was one quite lifeless, and another violently struggling in
the death agony.

'You see I miss him!' remarked Henry. He had fired from a
distance of more than a hundred and fifty yards, and both
balls had passed through the lungs; the true mark in shooting
buffalo.

The darkness increased, and a driving storm came on. Tying our horses to the horns of the victims, Henry began the
bloody work of dissection, slashing away with the science of a
connoisseur, while I vainly endeavored to imitate him. Old
Hendrick recoiled with horror and indignation when I endeavored to tie the meat to the strings of raw hide, always
carried for this purpose, dangling at the back of the saddle.
After some difficulty we overcame his scruples; and heavily
burdened with the more eligible portions of the buffalo, we
set out on our return. Scarcely had we emerged from the labyrinth of gorges and ravines, and issued upon the open prairie, when the prickling sleet came driving, gust upon gust,
directly in our faces. It was strangely dark, though wanting
still an hour of sunset. The freezing storm soon penetrated to
the skin, but the uneasy trot of our heavy-gaited horses kept
us warm enough, as we forced them unwillingly in the teeth
of the sleet and rain, by the powerful suasion of our Indian
whips. The prairie in this place was hard and level. A flourishing colony of prairie-dogs had burrowed into it in every

direction, and the little mounds of fresh earth around their holes were about as numerous as the hills in a corn-field; but not a yelp was to be heard; not the nose of a single citizen was visible; all had retired to the depths of their burrows, and we envied them their dry and comfortable habitations. An hour's hard riding showed us our tent dimly looming through the storm, one side puffed out by the force of the wind, and the other collapsed in proportion, while the disconsolate horses stood shivering close around, and the wind kept up a dismal whistling in the boughs of three old half-dead trees above. Shaw, like a patriarch, sat on his saddle in the entrance, with a pipe in his mouth, and his arms folded, contemplating, with cool satisfaction, the piles of meat that we flung on the ground before him. A dark and dreary night succeeded; but the sun rose, with a heat so sultry and languid that the Captain excused himself on that account from waylaying an old buffalo bull, who with stupid gravity was walking over the prairie to drink at the river. So much for the climate of the Platte!

But it was not the weather alone that had produced this sudden abatement of the sportsman-like zeal which the Captain had always professed. He had been out on the afternoon before, together with several members of his party; but their hunting was attended with no other result than the loss of one of their best horses, severely injured by Sorel, in vainly chasing a wounded bull. The Captain, whose ideas of hard riding were all derived from transatlantic sources, expressed the utmost amazement at the feats of Sorel, who went leaping ravines, and dashing at full speed up and down the sides of precipitous hills, lashing his horse with the recklessness of a Rocky Mountain rider. Unfortunately for the poor animal, he was the property of R——, against whom Sorel entertained an unbounded aversion. The Captain himself, it seemed, had also attempted to 'run' a buffalo, but though a good and practised horseman, he had soon given over the attempt, being astonished and utterly disgusted at the nature of the ground he was required to ride over.

Nothing unusual occurred on that day; but on the following morning, Henry Chatillon, looking over the ocean-like expanse, saw near the foot of the distant hills something that looked like a band of buffalo. He was not sure, he said, but at all events, if they were buffalo, there was a fine chance for a race. Shaw and I at once determined to try the speed of our horses.

'Come, Captain; we'll see which can ride hardest, a Yankee or an Irishman.'

But the Captain maintained a grave and austere countenance. He mounted his led horse, however, though very slowly; and we set out at a trot. The game appeared about three miles distant. As we proceeded, the Captain made various remarks of doubt and indecision; and at length declared he would have nothing to do with such a break neck business; protesting that he had ridden plenty of steeple-chases in his day, but he never knew what riding was till he found himself behind a band of buffalo day before yesterday. 'I am convinced,' said the Captain, 'that "running" is out of the question.* Take my advice now, and don't attempt it. It's dangerous, and of no use at all.'

'Then why did you come out with us? What do you mean to do?'

'I shall "approach," ' replied the Captain.

'You don't mean to "approach" with your pistols, do you? We have all of us left our rifles in the wagons.'

The Captain seemed staggered at this suggestion. In his characteristic indecision, at setting out, pistols, rifles, 'running' and 'approaching' were mingled in an inextricable medley in his brain. He trotted on in silence between us for a while; but at length he dropped behind, and slowly walked his horse back to rejoin the party. Shaw and I kept on; when lo! as we advanced, the band of buffalo were transformed into certain clumps of tall bushes, dotting the prairie for a considerable distance. At this ludicrous termination of our chase, we followed the example of our late ally, and turned back toward the party. We were skirting the brink of a deep ravine, when we saw Henry and the broad-chested pony coming toward us at a gallop.

*The method of hunting called 'running,' consists in attacking the buffalo on horseback and shooting him with bullets or arrows when at full speed. In 'approaching' the hunter conceals himself, and crawls on the ground towards the game, or lies in wait to kill them.

'Here's old Papin and Frederic, down from Fort Laramie!' shouted Henry, long before he came up. We had for some days expected this encounter. Papin was the *bourgeois* of Fort Laramie. He had come down the river with the buffalo-robes and the beaver, the produce of the last winter's trading. I had among our baggage a letter which I wished to commit to their hands; so requesting Henry to detain the boats if he could until my return, I set out after the wagons. They were about four miles in advance. In half an hour I overtook them, got the letter, trotted back upon the trail, and looking carefully, as I rode, saw a patch of broken, storm-blasted trees, and moving near them, some little black specks like men and horses. Arriving at the place, I found a strange assembly. The boats, eleven in number, deep-laden with the skins, hugged close to the shore, to escape being borne down by the swift current. The rowers, swarthy ignoble Mexicans, turned their brutish faces upward to look, as I reached the bank. Papin sat in the middle of one of the boats upon the canvas covering that protected the robes. He was a stout, robust fellow, with a little gray eye, that had a peculiarly sly twinkle. 'Frederic,' also, stretched his tall raw-boned proportions close by the *bourgeois*, and 'mountain men' completed the group; some lounging in the boats, some strolling on shore; some attired in gayly-painted buffalo robes, like Indian dandies; some with hair saturated with red paint, and beplastered with glue to their temples; and one bedaubed with vermilion upon the forehead and each cheek. They were a mongrel race; yet the French blood seemed to predominate: in a few, indeed, might be seen the black snaky eye of the Indian half-breed, and one and all, they seemed to aim at assimilating themselves to their savage associates.

I shook hands with the *bourgeois*, and delivered the letter: then the boats swung round into the stream and floated away. They had reason for haste, for already the voyage from Fort Laramie had occupied a full month, and the river was growing daily more shallow. Fifty times a day the boats had been aground: indeed, those who navigate the Platte invariably spend half their time upon sand-bars. Two of these boats, the property of private traders, afterwards separating from the rest, got hopelessly involved in the shallows, not very far from the Pawnee villages, and were soon surrounded by a swarm of the inhabitants. They carried off every thing that they considered valuable, including most of the robes; and amused themselves by tying up the men left on guard, and soundly whipping them with sticks.

We encamped that night upon the bank of the river. Among the emigrants there was an overgrown boy, some eighteen years old, with a head as round and about as large as a pumpkin, and fever-and-ague fits had dyed his face of a corresponding color. He wore an old white hat, tied under his chin with a handkerchief: his body was short and stout, but his legs of disproportioned and appalling length. I observed him at sunset, breasting the hill with gigantic strides, and standing against the sky on the summit, like a colossal pair of tongs. In a moment after, we heard him screaming frantically behind the ridge, and nothing doubting that he was in the clutches of Indians or grizzly bears, some of the party caught up their rifles and ran to the rescue. His outcries, however, proved but an ebullition of joyous excitement; he had chased two little wolf pups to their burrow, and he was on his knees, grubbing away like a dog at the mouth of the hole, to get at them.

Before morning he caused more serious disquiet in the camp. It was his turn to hold the middle-guard; but no sooner was he called up, than he coolly arranged a pair of saddle-bags under a wagon, laid his head upon them, closed his eyes, opened his mouth, and fell asleep. The guard on our side of the camp, thinking it no part of his duty to look after the cattle of the emigrants, contented himself with watching our own horses and mules; the wolves, he said, were unusually noisy; but still no mischief was anticipated until the sun rose, and not a hoof or horn was in sight! The cattle were gone! While Tom was quietly slumbering, the wolves had driven them away.

Then we reaped the fruits of R——'s precious plan of travelling in company with emigrants. To leave them in their distress was not to be thought of, and we felt bound to wait until the cattle could be searched for, and, if possible, recovered. But the reader may be curious to know what punishment awaited the faithless Tom. By the wholesome law of the prairie, he who falls asleep on guard is condemned to walk all day, leading his horse by the bridle, and we found much fault with our companions for not enforcing such a sentence on the offender. Nevertheless, had he been of our own party, I have no doubt that he would in like manner have escaped scot-free. But the emigrants went farther than mere forbearance: they decreed that since Tom couldn't stand guard without falling asleep, he shouldn't stand guard at all, and henceforward his slumbers were unbroken. Establishing such a premium on drowsiness could have no very beneficial effect upon the vigilance of our sentinels; for it is far from agreeable, after riding from sunrise to sunset, to feel your slumbers interrupted by the butt of a rifle nudging your side, and a sleepy voice growling in your ear that you must get up, to shiver and freeze for three weary hours at midnight.

'Buffalo! buffalo!' It was but a grim old bull, roaming the prairie by himself in misanthropic seclusion; but there might be more behind the hills. Dreading the monotony and languor of the camp, Shaw and I saddled our horses, buckled our holsters in their places, and set out with Henry Chatillon in search of the game. Henry, not intending to take part in the chase, but merely conducting us, carried his rifle with him, while we left ours behind as incumbrances. We rode for some five or six miles, and saw no living thing but wolves, snakes, and prairie-dogs.

'This won't do at all,' said Shaw.

'What won't do?'

'There's no wood about here to make a litter for the wounded man: I have an idea that one of us will need something of the sort before the day is over.'

There was some foundation for such an apprehension, for the ground was none of the best for a race, and grew worse continually as we proceeded; indeed it soon became desperately bad, consisting of abrupt hills and deep hollows, cut by frequent ravines not easy to pass. At length, a mile in advance, we saw a band of bulls. Some were scattered grazing over a green declivity, while the rest were crowded more densely together in the wide hollow below. Making a circuit, to keep out of sight, we rode toward them, until we ascended a hill, within a furlong of them, beyond which nothing intervened that could possibly screen us from their view. We dismounted behind the ridge just out of sight, drew our saddle-girths, examined our pistols, and mounting again, rode over the hill, and descended at a canter toward them, bending close to our horses' necks. Instantly they took the alarm; those on the hill descended; those below gathered into a mass, and the whole got in motion, shouldering each other along at a clumsy gallop. We followed, spurring our horses to full speed; and as the herd rushed, crowding and trampling in terror through an opening in the hills, we were close at their heels, half suffocated by the clouds of dust. But as we drew near, their alarm and speed increased; our horses showed signs of the utmost fear, bounding violently aside as we approached, and refusing to enter among the herd. The buffalo now broke into several small bodies, scampering over the hills in different directions, and I lost sight of Shaw; neither of us knew where the other had gone. Old Pontiac ran like a frantic elephant up hill and down hill, his ponderous hoofs striking the prairie like sledge-hammers. He showed a curious mixture of eagerness and terror, straining to overtake the panic-stricken herd, but constantly recoiling in dismay as we drew near. The fugitives, indeed, offered no very attractive spectacle, with their enormous size and weight, their shaggy manes and the tattered remnants of their last winter's hair covering their backs in irregular shreds and patches, and flying off in the wind as they ran. At length I urged my horse close behind a bull, and after trying in vain, by blows and spurring, to bring him alongside, I shot a bullet into the buffalo from this disadvantageous position. At the report, Pontiac swerved so much that I was again thrown a little behind the game. The bullet entering too much in the rear, failed to disable the bull, for a buffalo requires to be shot at particular points, or he will certainly escape. The herd ran up a hill, and I followed in pursuit. As Pontiac rushed headlong down on the other side, I saw Shaw and Henry descending the hollow on the right, at a leisurely gallop; and in front, the buffalo were just disappearing behind the crest of the next hill, their short tails erect, and their hoofs twinkling through a cloud of dust.

At that moment, I heard Shaw and Henry shouting to me; but the muscles of a stronger arm than mine could not have checked at once the furious course of Pontiac, whose mouth was as insensible as leather. Added to this, I rode him that morning with a common snaffle, having the day before, for the benefit of my other horse, unbuckled from my bridle the curb which I ordinarily used. A stronger and hardier brute never trod the prairie; but the novel sight of the buffalo filled him with terror, and when at full speed he was almost incontrollable. Gaining the top of the ridge, I saw nothing of the buffalo; they had all vanished amid the intricacies of the hills and hollows. Reloading my pistols, in the best way I could, I galloped on until I saw them again scuttling along at the base of the hill, their panic somewhat abated. Down went old Pontiac among them, scattering them to the right and left, and then we had another long chase. About a dozen bulls were before us, scouring over the hills, rushing down the declivities with tremendous weight and impetuosity, and then laboring with a weary gallop upward. Still Pontiac, in spite of spurring and beating, would not close with them. One bull at length fell a little behind the rest, and by dint of much effort, I urged my horse within six or eight yards of his side. His back was darkened with sweat: he was panting heavily, while his tongue lolled out a foot from his jaws. Gradually I came up abreast of him, urging Pontiac with leg and rein nearer to his side, when suddenly he did what buffalo in such circumstances will always do; he slackened his gallop, and turning toward us, with an aspect of mingled rage and distress, lowered his huge shaggy head for a charge. Pontiac, with a snort, leaped aside in terror, nearly throwing me to the ground, as I was wholly unprepared for such an evolution. I raised my pistol in a passion to strike him on the head, but thinking better of it, fired the bullet after the bull, who had resumed his flight; then drew rein, and determined to rejoin my companions. It was high time. The breath blew hard from Pontiac's nostrils, and the sweat rolled in big drops down his sides; I myself felt as if drenched in warm water. Pledging myself (and I redeemed the pledge) to take my revenge at a future opportunity, I looked round for some indications to show me where I was, and what course I ought to pursue; I might as well have looked for landmarks in the midst of the ocean. How many miles I had run, or in what direction, I had no idea; and around me the prairie was rolling in steep swells and pitches, without a single distinctive feature to guide me. I had a little compass hung at my neck; and ignorant that the Platte at this point diverged considerably from its easterly course, I thought that by keeping to the northward I should certainly reach it. So I turned and rode about two hours in that direction. The prairie changed as I advanced, softening away into easier undulations, but nothing like the Platte appeared, nor any sign of a human being; the same wild endless expanse lay around me still; and to all appearance I was as far from my object as ever. I began now to consider myself in danger of being lost; and therefore, reining in my horse, summoned the scanty share of woodcraft that I possessed (if that term be applicable upon the prairie) to extricate me. Looking round, it occurred to me that the buffalo might prove my best guides. I soon found one of the paths made by them in their passage to the river; it ran nearly at right angles to my course; but turning my horse's head in the direction it indicated, his freer gait and erected ears assured me that I was right.

But in the mean time my ride had been by no means a solitary one. The whole face of the country was dotted far and wide with countless hundreds of buffalo. They trooped along in files and columns, bulls, cows and calves, on the green faces of the declivities in front. They scrambled away over the hills to the right and left; and far off, the pale blue swells in the extreme distance were dotted with innumerable specks. Sometimes I surprised shaggy old bulls grazing alone, or sleeping behind the ridges I ascended. They would leap up at my approach, stare stupidly at me through their tangled manes, and then gallop heavily away. The antelope were very numerous; and as they are always bold when in the neighborhood of buffalo, they would approach quite near to look at me, gazing intently with their great round eyes, then suddenly leap aside, and stretch lightly away over the prairie, as swiftly as a racehorse. Squalid, ruffian-like wolves sneaked through the hollows and sandy ravines. Several times I passed through villages of prairie-dogs, who sat, each at the mouth of his burrow, holding his paws before him in a supplicating attitude, and yelping away most vehemently, energetically whisking his little tail with every squeaking cry he uttered. Prairie-dogs are not fastidious in their choice of companions; various long, checkered snakes were sunning themselves in the midst of the village, and demure little gray owls, with a large white ring around each eye, were perched side by side with the rightful inhabitants. The prairie teemed with life. Again and again I looked toward the crowded hill-sides, and was sure I saw horsemen; and riding near, with a mixture of hope and dread, for Indians were abroad, I found them transformed into a group of buffalo. There was nothing in human shape amid all this vast congregation of brute forms.

When I turned down the buffalo path, the prairie seemed changed; only a wolf or two glided past at intervals, like conscious felons, never looking to the right or left. Being now free from anxiety, I was at leisure to observe minutely the objects around me; and here, for the first time, I noticed insects wholly different from any of the varieties found farther to the eastward. Gaudy butterflies fluttered about my horse's head; strangely formed beetles, glittering with metallic lustre, were crawling upon plants that I had never seen before; multitudes of lizards, too, were darting like lightning over the sand.

I had run to a great distance from the river. It cost me a long ride on the buffalo path, before I saw, from the ridge of a sand-hill, the pale surface of the Platte glistening in the midst of its desert valleys, and the faint outline of the hills beyond waving along the sky. From where I stood, not a tree nor a bush nor a living thing was visible throughout the whole extent of the sun-scorched landscape. In half an hour I came upon the trail, not far from the river; and seeing that the party had not yet passed, I turned eastward to meet them, old Pontiac's long swinging trot again assuring me that I was right in doing so. Having been slightly ill on leaving camp in the morning, six or seven hours of rough riding had fatigued me extremely. I soon stopped, therefore; flung my saddle on the ground, and with my head resting on it, and my horse's trail-rope tied loosely to my arm, lay waiting the arrival of the party, speculating meanwhile on the extent of the injuries Pontiac had received. At length the white wagon coverings rose from the verge of the plain. By a singular coincidence, almost at the same moment two horsemen appeared coming down from the hills. They were Shaw and Henry, who had searched for me awhile in the morning, but well knowing the futility of the attempt in such a broken country, had placed themselves on the top of the highest hill they could find, and picketing their horses near them, as a signal to me, had laid down and fallen asleep. The stray cattle had been recovered, as the emigrants told us, about noon. Before sunset, we pushed forward eight miles farther.

'JUNE 7, 1846.—Four men are missing; R——, Sorel, and two emigrants. They set out this morning after buffalo, and have not yet made their appearance; whether killed or lost, we cannot tell.'

I find the above in my note-book, and well remember the council held on the occasion. Our fire was the scene of it; for the palpable superiority of Henry Chatillon's experience and skill made him the resort of the whole camp upon every question of difficulty. He was moulding bullets at the fire, when the Captain drew near, with a perturbed and care-worn expression of countenance, faithfully reflected on the heavy features of Jack, who followed close behind. Then emigrants came straggling from their wagons towards the common centre; various suggestions were made, to account for the absence of the four men; and one or two of the emigrants declared, that when out after the cattle, they had seen Indians dogging them, and crawling like wolves along the ridges of the hills. At this the Captain slowly shook his head with double gravity, and solemnly remarked:
'It's a serious thing to be travelling through this cursed wilderness;' an opinion in which Jack immediately expressed a thorough coincidence. Henry would not commit himself by declaring any positive opinion:
'Maybe he only follow the buffalo too far; maybe Indian kill him; maybe he got lost; I cannot tell!'
With this the auditors were obliged to rest content; the emigrants, not in the least alarmed, though curious to know what had become of their comrades, walked back to their wagons, and the Captain betook himself pensively to his tent. Shaw and I followed his example.
'It will be a bad thing for our plans,' said he as we entered,

'if these fellows don't get back safe. The Captain is as helpless on the prairie as a child. We shall have to take him and his brother in tow; they will hang on us like lead.'

'The prairie is a strange place,' said I. 'A month ago I should have thought it rather a startling affair to have an acquaintance ride out in the morning and lose his scalp before night, but here it seems the most natural thing in the world; not that I believe that R—— has lost his yet.'

If a man is constitutionally liable to nervous apprehensions, a tour on the distant prairies would prove the best prescription; for though when in the neighborhood of the Rocky Mountains he may at times find himself placed in circumstances of some danger, I believe that few ever breathe that reckless atmosphere without becoming almost indifferent to any evil chance that may befall themselves or their friends.

Shaw had a propensity for luxurious indulgence. He spread his blanket with the utmost accuracy on the ground, picked up the sticks and stones that he thought might interfere with his comfort, adjusted his saddle to serve as a pillow, and composed himself for his night's rest. I had the first guard that evening; so, taking my rifle, I went out of the tent. It was perfectly dark. A brisk wind blew down from the hills, and the sparks from the fire were streaming over the prairie. One of the emigrants, named Morton, was my companion; and laying our rifles on the grass, we sat down together by the fire. Morton was a Kentuckian, an athletic fellow, with a fine intelligent face, and in his manners and conversation he showed the essential characteristics of a gentleman. Our conversation turned on the pioneers of his gallant native state. The three hours of our watch dragged away at last, and we went to call up the relief.

R——'s guard succeeded mine. He was absent; but the Captain, anxious lest the camp should be left defenceless, had volunteered to stand in his place; so I went to wake him up. There was no occasion for it, for the Captain had been awake since nightfall. A fire was blazing outside of the tent, and by the light which struck through the canvas, I saw him and Jack lying on their backs, with their eyes wide open. The Captain responded instantly to my call; he jumped up, seized the double-barrelled rifle, and came out of the tent with an air of solemn determination, as if about to devote himself to the safety of the party. I went and lay down, not doubting that for the next three hours our slumbers would be guarded with sufficient vigilance.

Chapter VIII.

TAKING FRENCH LEAVE.

"Parting is such sweet sorrow!"
ROMEO AND JULIET.

ON THE EIGHTH of June, at eleven o'clock, we reached the South Fork of the Platte, at the usual fording-place. For league upon league the desert uniformity of the prospect was almost unbroken; the hills were dotted with little tufts of shrivelled grass, but betwixt these the white sand was glaring in the sun; and the channel of the river, almost on a level with the plain, was but one great sand-bed, about half a mile wide. It was covered with water, but so scantily that the bottom was scarcely hidden; for, wide as it is, the average depth of the Platte does not at this point exceed a foot and a half. Stopping near its bank, we gathered *bois de vache*, and made a meal of buffalo-meat. Far off, on the other side, was a green meadow, where we could see the white tents and wagons of an emigrant camp; and just opposite to us we could discern a group of men and animals at the water's edge. Four or five horsemen soon entered the river, and in ten minutes had waded across and clambered up the loose sand-bank. They were ill-looking fellows, thin and swarthy, with care-worn anxious faces, and lips rigidly compressed. They had good cause for anxiety; it was three days since they first encamped here, and on the night of their arrival they had lost one hundred and twenty-three of their best cattle, driven off by the wolves, through the neglect of the man on guard. This discouraging and alarming calamity was not the first that had overtaken them. Since leaving the settlements, they had met with nothing but misfortune. Some of their party had died; one man had been killed by the Pawnees; and about a week before, they had been plundered by the Dahcotahs of all their best horses, the wretched animals on which our visitors were mounted being the only ones that were left. They had encamped, they told us, near sunset, by the side of the Platte, and their oxen were scattered over the meadow, while the

82

band of horses were feeding a little farther off. Suddenly the ridges of the hills were alive with a swarm of mounted Indians, at least six hundred in number, who, with a tremendous yell, came pouring down toward the camp, rushing up within a few rods, to the great terror of the emigrants; but suddenly wheeling, they swept around the band of horses, and in five minutes had disappeared with their prey through the openings of the hills.

As these emigrants were telling their story, we saw four other men approaching. They proved to be R—— and his companions, who had encountered no mischance of any kind, but had only wandered too far in pursuit of the game. They said they had seen no Indians, but only 'millions of buffalo;' and both R—— and Sorel had meat dangling behind their saddles.

The emigrants re-crossed the river, and we prepared to follow. First the heavy ox-wagons plunged down the bank, and dragged slowly over the sand-beds; sometimes the hoofs of the oxen were scarcely wetted by the thin sheet of water; and the next moment the river would be boiling against their sides, and eddying fiercely around the wheels. Inch by inch they receded from the shore, dwindling every moment, until at length they seemed to be floating far out in the very middle of the river. A more critical experiment awaited us; for our little mule-cart was but ill-fitted for the passage of so swift a stream. We watched it with anxiety till it seemed to be a little motionless white speck in the midst of the waters; and it *was* motionless, for it had stuck fast in a quicksand. The little mules were losing their footing, the wheels were sinking deeper and deeper, and the water began to rise through the bottom and drench the goods within. All of us who had remained on the hither bank galloped to the rescue; the men jumped into the water, adding their strength to that of the mules, until by much effort the cart was extricated, and conveyed in safety across.

As we gained the other bank, a rough group of men surrounded us. They were not robust, nor large of frame, yet they had an aspect of hardy endurance. Finding at home no scope for their fiery energies, they had betaken themselves to the prairie; and in them seemed to be revived, with redoubled force, that fierce spirit which impelled their ancestors, scarce more lawless than themselves, from the German forests, to inundate Europe, and break to pieces the Roman empire. A fortnight afterward, this unfortunate party passed Fort Laramie, while we were there. Not one of their missing oxen had been recovered, though they had remained encamped a week in search of them; and they had been compelled to abandon a great part of their baggage and provisions, and yoke cows and heifers to their wagons to carry them forward upon their journey, the most toilsome and hazardous part of which lay still before them.

It is worth noticing, that on the Platte one may sometimes see the shattered wrecks of ancient claw-footed tables, well waxed and rubbed, or massive bureaus of carved oak. These, many of them no doubt the relics of ancestral prosperity in the colonial time, must have encountered strange vicissitudes. Imported, perhaps, originally from England; then, with the declining fortunes of their owners, borne across the Alleghanies to the remote wilderness of Ohio or Kentucky; then to Illinois or Missouri; and now at last fondly stowed away in the family wagon for the interminable journey to Oregon. But the stern privations of the way are little anticipated. The cherished relic is soon flung out to scorch and crack upon the hot prairie.

We resumed our journey; but we had gone scarcely a mile, when R—— called out from the rear:

'We'll 'camp here.'

'Why do you want to 'camp? Look at the sun. It is not three o'clock yet.'

'We'll 'camp here!'

This was the only reply vouchsafed. Delorier was in advance with his cart. Seeing the mule-wagon wheeling from the track, he began to turn his own team in the same direction.

'Go on, Delorier;' and the little cart advanced again. As we rode on, we soon heard the wagon of our confederates creaking and jolting on behind us, and the driver, Wright, discharging a furious volley of oaths against his mules; no doubt venting upon them the wrath which he dared not direct against a more appropriate object.

Something of this sort had frequently occurred. Our English friend was by no means partial to us, and we thought we discovered in his conduct a deliberate intention to thwart and annoy us, especially by retarding the movements of the party which he knew that we, being Yankees, were anxious to quicken. Therefore he would insist on encamping at all unseasonable hours, saying that fifteen miles was a sufficient day's journey. Finding our wishes systematically disregarded, we took the direction of affairs into our own hands. Keeping always in advance, to the inexpressible indignation of R——, we encamped at what time and place we thought proper, not much caring whether the rest chose to follow or not. They always did so, however, pitching their tent near ours, with sullen and wrathful countenances.

Travelling together on these agreeable terms did not suit our tastes; for some time we had meditated a separation. The connection with this party had cost us various delays and inconveniences; and the glaring want of courtesy and good sense displayed by their virtual leader did not dispose us to bear these annoyances with much patience. We resolved to leave camp early in the morning, and push forward as rapidly as possible for Fort Laramie, which we hoped to reach, by hard travelling, in four or five days. The Captain soon trotted up between us, and we explained our intentions.

'A very extraordinary proceeding, upon my word!' he remarked. Then he began to enlarge upon the enormity of the design. The most prominent impression in his mind evidently was, that we were acting a base and treacherous part in deserting his party, in what he considered a very dangerous stage of the journey. To palliate the atrocity of our conduct, we ventured to suggest that we were only four in number, while his party still included sixteen men; and as, moreover, we were to go forward and they were to follow, at least a full proportion of the perils he apprehended would fall upon us. But the austerity of the Captain's features would not relax. 'A very extraordinary proceeding, gentlemen!' and repeating this, he rode off to confer with his principal.

By good luck, we found a meadow of fresh grass, and a large pool of rain-water in the midst of it. We encamped here at sunset. Plenty of buffalo skulls were lying around, bleaching in the sun; and sprinkled thickly among the grass was a great variety of strange flowers. I had nothing else to do, and so gathering a handful, I sat down on a buffalo-skull to study them. Although the offspring of a wilderness, their texture was frail and delicate, and their colors extremely rich: pure white, dark blue, and a transparent crimson. One travelling in this country seldom has leisure to think of any thing but the stern features of the scenery and its accompaniments, or the practical details of each day's journey. Like them, he and his thoughts grow hard and rough. But now these flowers suddenly awakened a train of associations as alien to the rude scene around me as they were themselves; and for the moment my thoughts went back to New England. A throng of fair and well-remembered faces rose, vividly as life, before me. 'There are good things,' thought I, 'in the savage life, but what can it offer to replace those powerful and ennobling influences that can reach unimpaired over more than three thousand miles of mountains, forests, and deserts?'

Before sunrise on the next morning, our tent was down; we harnessed our best horses to the cart and left the camp. But first we shook hands with our friends the emigrants, who sincerely wished us a safe journey, though some others of the party might easily have been consoled had we encountered an Indian war-party on the way. The Captain and his brother were standing on the top of a hill, wrapped in their plaids, like spirits of the mist, keeping an anxious eye on the band of horses below. We waved adieu to them as we rode off the ground. The Captain replied with a salutation of the utmost dignity, which Jack tried to imitate; but being little practised in the gestures of polite society, his effort was not a very successful one.

In five minutes we had gained the foot of the hills, but here we came to a stop. Old Hendrick was in the shafts, and being the very incarnation of perverse and brutish obstinacy, he utterly refused to move. Delorier lashed and swore till he was tired, but Hendrick stood like a rock, grumbling to himself and looking askance at his enemy, until he saw a favorable opportunity to take his revenge, when he struck out under the shaft with such cool malignity of intention that Delorier only escaped the blow by a sudden skip into the air, such as no one but a Frenchman could achieve. Shaw and he then joined forces, and lashed on both sides at once. The brute stood still for a while till he could bear it no longer, when all at once he began to kick and plunge till he threatened the utter demolition of the cart and harness. We glanced back at the camp, which was in full sight. Our companions, inspired by emulation, were levelling their tents and driving in their cattle and horses.

'Take the horse out,' said I.

I took the saddle from Pontiac and put it upon Hendrick; the former was harnessed to the cart in an instant. '*Avance donc!*' cried Delorier. Pontiac strode up the hill, twitching the little cart after him as if it were a feather's weight; and though, as we gained the top, we saw the wagons of our deserted comrades just getting into motion, we had little fear that they could overtake us. Leaving the trail, we struck directly across the country, and took the shortest cut to reach the main stream of the Platte. A deep ravine suddenly intercepted us. We skirted its sides until we found them less abrupt, and then plunged through the best way we could. Passing behind the sandy ravines called 'Ash Hollow,' we stopped for a short nooning at the side of a pool of rainwater; but soon resumed our journey, and some hours before sunset were descending the ravines and gorges opening downward upon the Platte to the west of Ash Hollow. Our horses waded to the fetlock in sand; the sun scorched like fire, and the air swarmed with sand-flies and musquitoes.

At last we gained the Platte. Following it for about five miles, we saw, just as the sun was sinking, a great meadow, dotted with hundreds of cattle, and beyond them an emigrant encampment. A party of about a dozen came out to meet us, looking upon us at first with cold and suspicious faces. Seeing four men, different in appearance and equipment from themselves, emerging from the hills, they had taken us for the van of the much-dreaded Mormons, whom they were very apprehensive of encountering. We made known our true character, and then they greeted us cordially. They expressed much surprise that so small a party should venture to traverse that region, though in fact such attempts are not unfrequently made by trappers and Indian traders. We rode with them to their camp. The wagons, some fifty in number, with here and there a tent intervening, were arranged as usual in a circle; in the area within the best horses were picketed, and the whole circumference was glowing with the dusky light of the fires, displaying the forms of the women and children who were crowded around them. This patriarchal scene was curious and striking enough; but we made our escape from the place with all possible dispatch, being tormented by the intrusive curiosity of the men, who crowded around us. Yankee curiosity was nothing to theirs. They demanded our names, where we came from, where we were going, and what was our business. The last query was particularly embarrassing; since travelling in that country, or indeed any where, from any other motive than gain, was an idea of which they took no cognizance. Yet they were fine-looking fellows, with an air of frankness, generosity, and even courtesy, having come from one of the least barbarous of the frontier counties.

We passed about a mile beyond them, and encamped. Being too few in number to stand guard without excessive fatigue, we extinguished our fire, lest it should attract the notice of wandering Indians; and picketing our horses close around us, slept undisturbed till morning. For three days we travelled without interruption, and on the evening of the third encamped by the well-known spring on Scott's Bluff.

Henry Chatillon and I rode out in the morning, and descending the western side of the Bluff, were crossing the plain beyond. Something that seemed to me a file of buffalo came into view, descending the hills several miles before us. But Henry reined in his horse, and keenly peering across the prairie with a better and more practised eye, soon discovered its real nature. 'Indians!' he said. 'Old Smoke's lodges, I b'lieve. Come! let us go! Wah! get up, now, "Five Hundred Dollar!"' And laying on the lash with good will, he galloped forward, and I rode by his side. Not long after, a black speck became visible on the prairie, full two miles off. It grew larger and larger; it assumed the form of a man and horse; and soon we could discern a naked Indian, careering at full gallop toward us. When within a furlong he wheeled his horse in a wide circle, and made him describe various mystic figures upon the prairie; and Henry immediately compelled 'Five Hundred Dollar' to execute similar evolutions. 'It *is* Old

Smoke's village,' said he, interpreting these signals; 'didn't I say so?'

As the Indian approached we stopped to wait for him, when suddenly he vanished, sinking, as it were, into the earth. He had come upon one of the deep ravines that every where intersect these prairies. In an instant the rough head of his horse stretched upward from the edge, and the rider and steed came scrambling out, and bounded up to us; a sudden jerk of the rein brought the wild panting horse to a full stop. Then followed the needful formality of shaking hands. I forget our visitor's name. He was a young fellow, of no note in his nation; yet in his person and equipments he was a good specimen of a Dahcotah warrior in his ordinary travelling dress. Like most of his people, he was nearly six feet high; lithely and gracefully, yet strongly proportioned; and with a skin singularly clear and delicate. He wore no paint; his head was bare; and his long hair was gathered in a clump behind, to the top of which was attached transversely, both by way of ornament and of talisman, the mystic whistle, made of the wing-bone of the war-eagle, and endowed with various magic virtues. From the back of his head descended a line of glittering brass plates, tapering from the size of a doubloon to that of a half dime, a cumbrous ornament, in high vogue among the Dahcotahs, and for which they pay the traders a most extravagant price; his chest and arms were naked, the buffalo robe, worn over them when at rest, had fallen about his waist, and was confined there by a belt. This, with the gay moccasons on his feet, completed his attire. For arms he carried a quiver of dog-skin at his back, and a rude but powerful bow in his hand. His horse had no bridle; a cord of hair, lashed around his jaw, served in place of one. The saddle was of most singular construction; it was made of wood covered with raw hide, and both pommel and cantle rose perpendicularly full eighteen inches, so that the warrior was wedged firmly in his seat, whence nothing could dislodge him but the bursting of the girths.

Advancing with our new companion, we found more of his people, seated in a circle on the top of a hill; while a rude procession came straggling down the neighboring hollow, men, women, and children, with horses dragging the lodge-poles behind them. All that morning, as we moved forward, tall savages were stalking silently about us. At noon, we reached Horse Creek; and as we waded through the shallow water, we saw a wild and striking scene. The main body of the Indians had arrived before us. On the farther bank, stood a large and strong man, nearly naked, holding a white horse by a long cord and eyeing us as we approached. This was the chief, whom Henry called 'Old Smoke.' Just behind him, his youngest and favorite squaw sat astride of a fine mule: it was covered with caparisons of whitened skins, garnished with blue and white beads, and fringed with little ornaments of metal that tinkled with every movement of the animal. The girl had a light clear complexion, enlivened by a spot of vermilion on each cheek; she smiled, not to say grinned, upon us, showing two gleaming rows of white teeth. In her hand, she carried the tall lance of her unchivalrous lord, fluttering with feathers; his round white shield hung at the side of her mule; and his pipe was slung at her back. Her dress was a tunic of deer-skin, made beautifully white by means of a species of clay found on the prairie, and ornamented with beads, arrayed in figures more gay than tasteful, and with long fringes at all the seams. Not far from the chief, stood a group of stately figures, their white buffalo robes thrown over their shoulders, gazing coldly upon us; and in the rear, for several acres, the ground was covered with a temporary encampment; men, women, and children swarmed like bees; hundreds of dogs, of all sizes and colors, ran restlessly about; and close at hand, the wide shallow stream was alive with boys, girls and young squaws, splashing, screaming, and laughing in the water. At the same time a long train of emigrant wagons were crossing the creek, and dragging on in their slow, heavy procession, passed the encampment of the people whom they and their descendants, in the space of a century, are to sweep from the face of the earth.

The encampment itself was merely a temporary one during the heat of the day. None of the lodges were erected; but their heavy leather coverings, and the long poles used to support them, were scattered every where around, among weapons, domestic utensils, and the rude harness of mules and horses. The squaws of each lazy warrior had made him a shelter from the sun, by stretching a few buffalo-robes, or the corner of a lodge-covering upon poles; and here he sat in the shade, with a favorite young squaw, perhaps, at his side, glittering with all imaginable trinkets. Before him stood the insignia of his rank, as a warrior, his white shield of bull-hide, his medicine bag, his bow and quiver, his lance and his pipe, raised aloft on a tripod of three poles. Except the dogs, the most active and noisy tenants of the camp were the old women, ugly as Macbeth's witches, with their hair streaming loose in the wind, and nothing but the tattered fragment of an old buffalo-robe to hide their shrivelled wiry limbs. The day of their favoritism passed two generations ago; now the heaviest labors of the camp devolved upon them; they were to harness the horses, pitch the lodges, dress the buffalo-robes, and bring in meat for the hunters. With the cracked voices of these hags, the clamor of dogs, the shouting and laughing of children and girls, and the listless tranquillity of the warriors, the whole scene had an effect too lively and picturesque ever to be forgotten.

We stopped not far from the Indian camp, and having invited some of the chiefs and warriors to dinner, placed before them a sumptuous repast of biscuit and coffee. Squatted in a half circle on the ground, they soon disposed of it. As we rode forward on the afternoon journey, several of our late guests accompanied us. Among the rest was a huge bloated savage, of more than three hundred pounds' weight, christened *Le Cochon*, in consideration of his preposterous dimensions, and certain corresponding traits of his character. 'The Hog' bestrode a little white pony, scarce able to bear up under the enormous burden, though, by way of keeping up the necessary stimulus, the rider kept both feet in constant motion, playing alternately against his ribs. The old man was not a chief; he never had ambition enough to become one; he was not a warrior nor a hunter, for he was too fat and lazy; but he was the richest man in the whole village. Riches among the Dahcotahs consist in horses, and of these 'The Hog' had accumulated more than thirty. He had already ten times as many as he wanted, yet still his appetite for horses was insatiable. Trotting up to me, he shook me by the hand, and gave me to understand that he was a very devoted friend; and then he began a series of most earnest signs and gesticulations, his oily countenance radiant with smiles, and his little eyes peeping out with a cunning twinkle from between the masses of flesh that almost obscured them. Knowing nothing at that time of the sign-language of the Indians, I could only guess at his meaning. So I called on Henry to explain it.

'The Hog,' it seems, was anxious to conclude a matrimonial bargain. He said he had a very pretty daughter in his lodge, whom he would give me, if I would give him my horse. These flattering overtures I chose to reject; at which 'The Hog,' still laughing with undiminished good humor, gathered his robe about his shoulders, and rode away.

Where we encamped that night, an arm of the Platte ran between high bluffs; it was turbid and swift as heretofore, but trees were growing on its crumbling banks, and there was a nook of grass between the water and the hill. Just before entering this place, we saw the emigrants encamping at two or three miles' distance on the right; while the whole Indian rabble were pouring down the neighboring hill in hope of the same sort of entertainment which they had experienced from us. In the savage landscape before our camp, nothing but the rushing of the Platte broke the silence. Through the ragged boughs of the trees, dilapidated and half dead, we saw the sun setting in crimson behind the peaks of the Black Hills; the restless bosom of the river was suffused with red; our white tent was tinged with it, and the sterile bluffs, up to the rocks that crowned them, partook of the same fiery hue. It soon passed away; no light remained, but that from our fire, blazing high among the dusky trees and bushes. We lay around it wrapped in our blankets, smoking and conversing until a late hour, and then withdrew to our tent.

We crossed a sun-scorched plain on the next morning; the line of old cotton-wood trees that fringed the bank of the Platte forming its extreme verge. Nestled apparently close beneath them, we could discern in the distance something like a building. As we came nearer, it assumed form and dimensions, and proved to be a rough structure of logs. It was a little trading fort, belonging to two private traders; and originally intended, like all the forts of the country, to form a hollow square, with rooms for lodging and storage opening upon the area within. Only two sides of it had been completed; the place was now as ill-fitted for the purposes of defence as any of those little log-houses, which upon our constantly-shifting frontier have been so often successfully maintained against overwhelming odds of Indians. Two lodges were pitched close to the fort; the sun beat scorching upon the logs; no living thing was stirring except one old squaw, who thrust her round head from the opening of the nearest lodge, and three or four stout young pups, who were peeping with looks of eager inquiry from under the covering. In a moment a door opened, and a little, swarthy, black-eyed Frenchman came out. His dress was rather singular; his black curling hair was parted in the middle of his head, and fell below his shoulders; he wore a tight frock of smoked deer-skin, very gayly ornamented with figures worked in dyed porcupine-quills. His moccasons and leggins were also gaudily adorned in the same manner; and the latter had in addition a line of long fringes, reaching down the seams. The small frame of Richard, for by this name Henry made him known to us, was in the highest degree athletic and vigorous. There was no superfluity, and indeed there seldom is among the active white men of this country, but every limb was compact and hard; every sinew had its full tone and elasticity, and the whole man wore an air of mingled hardihood and buoyancy.

Richard committed our horses to a Navaho slave, a mean-looking fellow, taken prisoner on the Mexican frontier; and relieving us of our rifles with ready politeness, led the way into the principal apartment of his establishment. This was a room ten feet square. The walls and floor were of black mud, and the roof of rough timber; there was a huge fireplace made of four flat rocks, picked up on the prairie. An Indian bow and otter-skin quiver, several gaudy articles of Rocky Mountain finery, an Indian medicine-bag, and a pipe and tobacco-pouch, garnished the walls, and rifles rested in a corner. There was no furniture except a sort of rough settle, covered with buffalo-robes, upon which lolled a tall half-breed, with his hair glued in masses upon each temple, and saturated with vermilion. Two or three more 'mountain men' sat cross-legged on the floor. Their attire was not unlike that of Richard himself; but the most striking figure of the group was a naked Indian boy of sixteen, with a handsome face, and light, active proportions, who sat in an easy posture in the corner near the door. Not one of his limbs moved the breadth of a hair; his eye was fixed immovably, not on any person present, but, as it appeared, on the projecting corner of the fireplace opposite to him.

On these prairies the custom of smoking with friends is seldom omitted, whether among Indians or whites. The pipe, therefore, was taken from the wall, and its great red bowl crammed with the tobacco and *shongsasha*, mixed in suitable proportions. Then it passed round the circle, each man inhaling a few whiffs and handing it to his neighbor. Having spent half an hour here, we took our leave; first inviting our new friends to drink a cup of coffee with us at our camp a mile farther up the river.

By this time, as the reader may conceive, we had grown rather shabby; our clothes had burst into rags and tatters; and what was worse, we had very little means of renovation. Fort Laramie was but seven miles before us. Being totally averse to appearing in such a plight among any society that could boast an approximation to the civilized, we soon stopped by the river to make our toilet in the best way we could. We hung up small looking-glasses against the trees and shaved, an operation neglected for six weeks; we performed our ablutions in the Platte, though the utility of such a proceeding was questionable, the water looking exactly like a cup of chocolate, and the banks consisting of the softest and richest yellow mud, so that we were obliged, as a preliminary, to build a causeway of stout branches and twigs. Having also put on radiant moccasons, procured from a squaw of Richard's establishment, and made what other improvements our narrow circumstances allowed, we took our seats on the grass with a feeling of greatly increased respectability, to await the arrival of our guests. They came; the banquet was concluded, and the pipe smoked. Bidding them adieu, we turned our horses' heads toward the fort.

An hour elapsed. The barren hills closed across our front, and we could see no farther; until having surmounted them, a rapid stream appeared at the foot of the descent, running into the Platte; beyond was a green meadow, dotted with bushes, and in the midst of these, at the point where the two rivers joined, were the low clay walls of a fort. This was not Fort Laramie, but another post of less recent date, which having sunk before its successful competitor, was now deserted and ruinous. A moment after, the hills seeming to draw apart as we advanced, disclosed Fort Laramie itself, its high bastions and perpendicular walls of clay crowning an eminence on the left beyond the stream, while behind stretched a line of arid and desolate ridges, and behind these again, towering aloft seven thousand feet, arose the grim Black Hills.

We tried to ford Laramie creek at a point nearly opposite the fort, but the stream, swollen with the rains in the mountains, was too rapid. We passed up along its bank to find a better crossing place. Men gathered on the wall to look at us. 'There's Bordeaux!' called Henry, his face brightening as he recognized his acquaintance; 'him there with the spy-glass; and there's old Vaskiss, and Tucker, and May; and by George! there's Cimoneau!' This Cimoneau was Henry's fast friend, and the only man in the country who could rival him in hunting.

We soon found a ford. Henry led the way, the pony approaching the bank with a countenance of cool indifference, bracing his feet and sliding into the stream with the most unmoved composure:

> 'At the first plunge the horse sunk low,
> And the water broke o'er the saddle-bow.'

We followed; the water boiled against our saddles, but our horses bore us easily through. The unfortunate little mules came near going down with the current, cart and all; and we watched them with some solicitude scrambling over the loose round stones at the bottom, and bracing stoutly against the stream. All landed safely at last; we crossed a little plain, descended a hollow, and riding up a steep bank, found ourselves before the gateway of Fort Laramie, under the impending blockhouse erected above it to defend the entrance.

Chapter IX.

SCENES AT FORT LARAMIE.

" 'Tis true they are a lawless brood,
But rough in form, nor mild in mood."
THE BRIDE OF ABYDOS.

LOOKING BACK, after the expiration of a year, upon Fort Laramie and its inmates, they seem less like a reality than like some fanciful picture of the olden time; so different was the scene from any which this tamer side of the world can present. Tall Indians, enveloped in their white buffalo-robes, were striding across the area or reclining at full length on the low roofs of the buildings which inclosed it. Numerous squaws, gayly bedizened, sat grouped in front of the apartments they occupied; their mongrel offspring, restless and vociferous, rambled in every direction through the fort; and the trappers, traders and *engagés* of the establishment were busy at their labor or their amusements.

We were met at the gate, but by no means cordially welcomed. Indeed, we seemed objects of some distrust and suspicion, until Henry Chatillon explained that we were not traders, and we, in confirmation, handed to the *bourgeois* a letter of introduction from his principals. He took it, turned it upside down, and tried hard to read it; but his literary attainments not being adequate to the task, he applied for relief to the clerk, a sleek, smiling Frenchman, named Montalon. The letter read, Bordeaux (the *bourgeois*) seemed gradually to awaken to a sense of what was expected of him. Though not deficient in hospitable intentions, he was wholly unaccustomed to act as master of ceremonies. Discarding all formalities of reception, he did not honor us with a single word, but walked swiftly across the area, while we followed in some admiration to a railing and a flight of steps opposite the entrance. He signed to us that we had better fasten our horses to the railing; then he walked up the steps, tramped along a rude balcony, and kicking open a door, displayed a large room, rather more elaborately finished than a barn. For furniture it had a rough bedstead, but no bed; two chairs, a chest of drawers, a tin-pail to hold water, and a board to cut tobacco upon. A brass crucifix hung on the wall, and close at hand a recent scalp, with hair full a yard long, was suspended from a nail. I shall again have occasion to mention this dismal trophy, its history being connected with that of our subsequent proceedings.

This apartment, the best in Fort Laramie, was that usually occupied by the legitimate *bourgeois*, Papin; in whose absence the command devolved upon Bordeaux. The latter, a stout, bluff little fellow, much inflated by a sense of his new authority, began to roar for buffalo-robes. These being brought and spread upon the floor, formed our beds; much better ones than we had of late been accustomed to. Our arrangements made, we stepped out to the balcony to take a more leisurely survey of the long looked-for haven at which we had arrived at last. Beneath us was the square area surrounded by little rooms, or rather cells, which opened upon it. These were devoted to various purposes, but served chiefly for the accommodation of the men employed at the fort, or of the equally numerous squaws whom they were allowed to maintain in it. Opposite to us rose the blockhouse above the gateway; it was adorned with a figure which even now haunts my memory; a horse at full speed, daubed upon the boards with red paint, and exhibiting a degree of skill which might rival that displayed by the Indians in executing similar designs upon their robes and lodges. A busy scene was enacting in the area. The wagons of Vaskiss, an old trader, were about to set out for a remote post in the mountains, and the Canadians were going through their preparations with all possible bustle, while here and there an Indian stood looking on with imperturbable gravity.

Fort Laramie is one of the posts established by the 'American Fur Company,' who well-nigh monopolize the Indian trade of this whole region. Here their officials rule with an absolute sway; the arm of the United States has little force; for when we were there, the extreme outposts of her troops were about seven hundred miles to the eastward. The little fort is built of bricks dried in the sun, and externally is of an oblong form, with bastions of clay, in the form of ordinary blockhouses, at two of the corners. The walls are about fifteen feet high, and surmounted by a slender palisade. The roofs of the apartments within, which are built close against the walls, serve the purpose of a banquette. Within, the fort is divided by a partition; on one side is the square area, surrounded by the store-rooms, offices, and apartments of the inmates; on the other is the *corral*, a narrow place, encompassed by the high clay walls, where at night, or in presence of dangerous Indians, the horses and mules of the fort are crowded for safe keeping. The main entrance has two gates, with an arched passage intervening. A little square window, quite high above the ground, opens laterally from an adjoining chamber into this passage; so that when the inner gate is closed and barred, a person without may still hold communication with those within, through this narrow aperture. This obviates the necessity of admitting suspicious Indians, for purposes of trading, into the body of the fort; for when danger is apprehended, the inner gate is shut fast, and all traffic is carried on by means of the little window. This precaution, though highly necessary at some of the Company's posts, is now seldom resorted to at Fort Laramie; where, though men are frequently killed in its neighborhood, no apprehensions are now entertained of any general designs of hostility from the Indians.

We did not long enjoy our new quarters undisturbed. The door was silently pushed open, and two eyeballs and a visage as black as night looked in upon us; then a red arm and shoulder intruded themselves, and a tall Indian, gliding in, shook us by the hand, grunted his salutation, and sat down on the floor. Others followed, with faces of the natural hue; and letting fall their heavy robes from their shoulders, they took their seats, quite at ease, in a semicircle before us. The pipe was now to be lighted and passed round from one to another; and this was the only entertainment that at present they expected from us. These visitors were fathers, brothers, or other relatives of the squaws in the fort, where they were permitted to remain, loitering about in perfect idleness. All those who smoked with us were men of standing and repute. Two or three others dropped in also; young fellows who neither by their years nor their exploits were entitled to rank with the old men and warriors, and who, abashed in the presence of their superiors, stood aloof, never withdrawing their eyes from us. Their cheeks were adorned with vermilion, their ears with pendants of shell, and their necks with beads. Never yet having signalized themselves as hunters, or performed the honorable exploit of killing a man, they were held in slight esteem, and were diffident and bashful in proportion. Certain formidable inconveniences attended this influx of visitors. They were bent on inspecting every thing in the room; our equipments and our dress alike underwent their scrutiny; for though the contrary has been carelessly asserted, few beings have more curiosity than Indians in regard to subjects within their ordinary range of thought. As to other matters, indeed, they seem utterly indifferent. They will not trouble themselves to inquire into what they cannot comprehend, but are quite contented to place their hands over their mouths in token of wonder, and exclaim that it is 'great medicine.' With this comprehensive solution, an Indian never is at a loss. He never launches forth into speculation and conjecture; his reason moves in its beaten track. His soul is dormant; and no exertions of the missionaries, Jesuit or Puritan, of the old world or of the new, have as yet availed to rouse it.

As we were looking, at sunset, from the wall, upon the wild and desolate plains that surround the fort, we observed a cluster of strange objects, like scaffolds, rising in the distance against the red western sky. They bore aloft some singular-looking burdens; and at their foot glimmered something white like bones. This was the place of sepulture of some Dahcotah chiefs, whose remains their people are fond of placing in the vicinity of the fort, in the hope that they may thus be protected from violation at the hands of their enemies. Yet it has happened more than once, and quite recently, that war parties of the Crow Indians, ranging through the country, have thrown the bodies from the scaffolds, and broken them to pieces, amid the yells of the Dahcotahs, who remained pent up in the fort, too few to defend the honored relics from insult. The white objects upon the ground were buffalo-skulls, arranged in the mystic circle, commonly seen at Indian places of sepulture upon the prairie.

We soon discovered, in the twilight, a band of fifty or sixty horses approaching the fort. These were the animals belonging to the establishment; who having been sent out to feed, under the care of armed guards, in the meadows below, were now being driven into the *corral* for the night. A little gate opened into this inclosure: by the side of it stood one of the guards, an old Canadian, with gray bushy eyebrows, and a dragoon-pistol stuck into his belt; while his comrade, mounted on horseback, his rifle laid across the saddle in front of him, and his long hair blowing before his swarthy face, rode at the rear of the disorderly troop, urging them up the ascent. In a moment the narrow *corral* was thronged with the half-wild horses, kicking, biting, and crowding restlessly together.

The discordant jingling of a bell, rung by a Canadian in the area, summoned us to supper. This sumptuous repast was served on a rough table in one of the lower apartments of the fort, and consisted of cakes of bread and dried buffalo meat— an excellent thing for strengthening the teeth. At this meal were seated the *bourgeois* and superior dignitaries of the establishment, among whom Henry Chatillon was worthily included. No sooner was it finished, than the table was spread a second time, (the luxury of bread being now, however, omitted,) for the benefit of certain hunters and trappers of an inferior standing; while the ordinary Canadian *engagés* were regaled on dried meat in one of their lodging rooms. By way of illustrating the domestic economy of Fort Laramie, it may not be amiss to introduce in this place a story current among the men when we were there.

There was an old man named Pierre, whose duty it was to bring the meat from the store-room for the men. Old Pierre, in the kindness of his heart, used to select the fattest and the best pieces for his companions. This did not long escape the keen-eyed *bourgeois*, who was greatly disturbed at such improvidence, and cast about for some means to stop it. At last he hit on a plan that exactly suited him. At the side of the meat-room, and separated from it by a clay partition, was another apartment, used for the storage of furs. It had no other communication with the fort, except through a square hole in the partition; and of course it was perfectly dark. One evening the *bourgeois*, watching for a moment when no one observed him, dodged into the meat-room, clambered through the hole, and ensconced himself among the furs and buffalo-robes. Soon after, old Pierre came in with his lantern; and, muttering to himself, began to pull over the bales of meat, and select the best pieces, as usual. But suddenly a hollow and sepulchral voice proceeded from the inner apartment:— 'Pierre! Pierre! Let that fat meat alone! Take nothing but lean!' Pierre dropped his lantern, and bolted out into the fort, screaming, in an agony of terror, that the devil was in the store-room; but tripping on the threshold, he pitched over upon the gravel, and lay senseless, stunned by the fall. The Canadians ran out to the rescue. Some lifted the unlucky Pierre; and others, making an extempore crucifix out of two sticks, were proceeding to attack the devil in his strong-hold, when the *bourgeois*, with a crest-fallen countenance, appeared at the door. To add to the *bourgeois's* mortification, he was obliged to explain the whole stratagem to Pierre, in order to bring the latter to his senses.

We were sitting, on the following morning, in the passage-way between the gates, conversing with the traders Vaskiss and May. These two men, together with our sleek friend, the clerk Montalon, were, I believe, the only persons then in the fort who could read and write. May was telling a curious story about the traveller Catlin, when an ugly, diminutive Indian, wretchedly mounted, came up at a gallop, and rode past us into the fort. On being questioned, he said that Smoke's village was close at hand. Accordingly only a few minutes elapsed before the hills beyond the river were covered with a disorderly swarm of savages, on horseback and on foot. May finished his story; and by that time the whole array had descended to Laramie Creek, and commenced crossing it in a mass. I walked down to the bank. The stream is wide, and was then between three and four feet deep, with a very swift current. For several rods the water was alive with dogs, horses, and Indians. The long poles used in erecting the lodges are carried by the horses, being fastened by the heavier end, two or three on each side, to a rude sort of pack-saddle, while the other end drags on the ground. About a foot behind the horse, a kind of large basket or pannier is suspended between the poles, and firmly lashed in its place. On the back of the horse are piled various articles of luggage; the basket also is well filled with domestic utensils, or, quite as often, with a litter of puppies, a brood of small children, or a super-annuated old man. Numbers of these curious vehicles, called, in the bastard language of the country, *travaux*, were now splashing together through the stream. Among them swam countless dogs, often burdened with miniature *travaux*; and dashing forward on horseback through the throng came the superbly-formed warriors, the slender figure of some lynx-eyed boy clinging fast behind them. The women sat perched on the pack-saddles, adding not a little to the load of the already overburdened horses. The confusion was prodigious. The dogs yelled and howled in chorus; the puppies in the *travaux* set up a dismal whine as the water invaded their comfortable retreat; the little black-eyed children, from one year of age upward, clung fast with both hands to the edge of their basket, and looked over in alarm at the water rushing so near them, sputtering and making wry mouths as it splashed against their faces. Some of the dogs, encumbered by their load, were carried down by the current, yelping piteously; and the old squaws would rush into the water, seize their favorites by the neck, and drag them out. As each horse gained the bank, he scrambled up as he could. Stray horses and colts came among the rest, often breaking away at full speed through the crowd, followed by the old hags, scream-ing, after their fashion, on all occasions of excitement. Buxom young squaws, blooming in all the charms of vermilion, stood here and there on the bank, holding aloft their master's lance, as a signal to collect the scattered portions of his household. In a few moments the crowd melted away; each family, with its horses and equipage, filing off to the plain at the rear of the fort; and here, in the space of half an hour, arose sixty or seventy of their tapering lodges. Their horses were feeding by hundreds over the surrounding prairie, and their dogs were roaming every where. The fort was full of men, and the chil-dren were whooping and yelling incessantly under the walls.

These new-comers were scarcely arrived, when Bordeaux was running across the fort, shouting to his squaw to bring him his spy-glass. The obedient Marie, the very model of a squaw, produced the instrument, and Bordeaux hurried with it up to the wall. Pointing it to the eastward, he exclaimed, with an oath, that the families were coming. But a few moments elapsed before the heavy caravan of the emigrant wagons could be seen, steadily advancing from the hills. They gained the river, and without turning or pausing plunged in; they passed through, and slowly ascending the opposing bank, kept directly on their way past the fort and the Indian village, until, gaining a spot a quarter of a mile distant, they wheeled into a circle. For some time our tranquillity was undisturbed. The emigrants were preparing their encampment; but no sooner was this accomplished, than Fort Laramie was fairly taken by storm. A crowd of broad-brimmed hats, thin visages, and staring eyes, appeared suddenly at the gate. Tall awkward men, in brown homespun; women with cadaverous faces and long lank figures, came thronging in together, and, as if inspired by the very demon of curiosity, ransacked every nook and corner of the fort. Dismayed at this invasion, we withdrew in all speed to our chamber, vainly hoping that it might prove an inviolable sanctuary. The emigrants prosecuted their investigations with untiring vigor. They penetrated the rooms, or rather dens, inhabited by the astonished squaws. They explored the apartments of the men, and even that of Marie and the *bourgeois*. At last a numerous deputation appeared at our door, but were immediately expelled. Being totally devoid of any sense of delicacy or propriety, they seemed resolved to search every mystery to the bottom.

Having at length satisfied their curiosity, they next proceeded to business. The men occupied themselves in procuring supplies for their onward journey; either buying them with money, or giving in exchange superfluous articles of their own.

The emigrants felt a violent prejudice against the French Indians, as they called the trappers and traders. They thought, and with some justice, that these men bore them no good will. Many of them were firmly persuaded that the French were instigating the Indians to attack and cut them off. On visiting the encampment we were at once struck with the extraordinary perplexity and indecision that prevailed among the emigrants. They seemed like men totally out of their element; bewildered and amazed, like a troop of schoolboys lost in the woods. It was impossible to be long among them without being conscious of the high and bold spirit with which most of them were animated. But the *forest* is the home of the backwoodsman. On the remote prairie he is totally at a loss. He differs as much from the genuine 'mountain-man,' the wild prairie hunter, as a Canadian voyageur, paddling his canoe on the rapids of the Ottawa, differs from an American sailor among the storms of Cape Horn. Still my companion and I were somewhat at a loss to account for this perturbed state of mind. It could not be cowardice: these men were of the same stock with the volunteers of Monterey and Buena Vista. Yet for the most part, they were the rudest and most ignorant of the frontier population; they knew absolutely nothing of the country and its inhabitants; they had already experienced much misfortune, and apprehended more; they had seen nothing of mankind, and had never put their own resources to the test.

A full proportion of suspicion fell upon us. Being strangers, we were looked upon as enemies. Having occasion for a supply of lead and a few other necessary articles, we used to go over to the emigrant camps to obtain them. After some hesitation, some dubious glances, and fumbling of the hands in the pockets, the terms would be agreed upon, the price tendered, and the emigrant would go off to bring the article in question. After waiting until our patience gave out, we would go in search of him, and find him seated on the tongue of his wagon.

'Well, stranger,' he would observe, as he saw us approach, 'I reckon I won't trade!'

Some friend of his had followed him from the scene of the bargain, and suggested in his ear that clearly we meant to cheat him, and he had better have nothing to do with us.

This timorous mood of the emigrants was doubly unfortunate, as it exposed them to real danger. Assume, in the presence of Indians, a bold bearing, self-confident yet vigilant, and you will find them tolerably safe neighbors. But your safety depends on the respect and fear you are able to inspire. If you betray timidity or indecision, you convert them from that moment into insidious and dangerous enemies. The Dahcotah saw clearly enough the perturbation of the emigrants, and instantly availed themselves of it. They became extremely insolent and exacting in their demands. It has become an established custom with them to go to the camp of every party, as it arrives in succession at the fort, and demand a feast. Smoke's village had come with this express design, having made several days' journey with no other object than that of enjoying a cup of coffee and two or three biscuits. So the 'feast' was demanded, and the emigrants dared not refuse it.

One evening, about sunset, the village was deserted. We met old men, warriors, squaws, and children in gay attire, trooping off to the encampment, with faces of anticipation; and, arriving here, they seated themselves in a semicircle. Smoke occupied the centre, with his warriors on either hand; the young men and boys next succeeded, and the squaws and children formed the horns of the crescent. The biscuit and coffee were most promptly dispatched, the emigrants staring open-mouthed at their savage guests. With each emigrant party that arrived at Fort Laramie this scene was renewed; and every day the Indians grew more rapacious and presumptuous. One evening, they broke to pieces, out of mere wantonness, the cups from which they had been feasted; and this so exasperated the emigrants, that many of them seized their rifles and could scarcely be restrained from firing on the insolent mob of Indians. Before we left the country this dangerous spirit on the part of the Dahcotah had mounted to a yet higher pitch. They began openly to threaten the emigrants with destruction, and actually fired upon one or two parties of whites. A military force and military law are urgently called for in that perilous region; and unless troops are speedily stationed at Fort Laramie, or elsewhere in the neighborhood, both the emigrants and other travellers will be exposed to most imminent risks.

The Ogillallah, the Brulé, and the other western bands of the Dahcotah, are thorough savages, unchanged by any contact with civilization. Not one of them can speak an European tongue, or has ever visited an American settlement. Until within a year or two, when the emigrants began to pass through their country on the way to Oregon, they had seen no whites except the handful employed about the Fur Company's posts. They esteemed them a wise people, inferior only to themselves, living in leather lodges, like their own, and subsisting on buffalo. But when the swarm of *Meneaska*, with their oxen and wagons, began to invade them, their astonishment was unbounded. They could scarcely believe that the earth contained such a multitude of white men. Their wonder is now giving way to indignation; and the result, unless vigilantly guarded against, may be lamentable in the extreme.

But to glance at the interior of a lodge. Shaw and I used often to visit them. Indeed we spent most of our evenings in the Indian village; Shaw's assumption of the medical character giving us a fair pretext. As a sample of the rest I will describe one of these visits. The sun had just set, and the horses were driven into the *corral*. The Prairie Cock, a noted beau, came in at the gate with a bevy of young girls, with whom he began a dance in the area, leading them round and round in a circle, while he jerked up from his chest a succession of monotonous sounds, to which they kept time in a rueful chant. Outside the gate, boys and young men were idly frolicking; and close by, looking grimly upon them, stood a warrior in his robe, with his face painted jet-black, in token that he had lately taken a Pawnee scalp. Passing these, the tall dark lodges rose between us and the red western sky. We repaired at once to the lodge of Old Smoke himself. It was by no means better than the others; indeed, it was rather shabby; for in this democratic community the chief never assumes superior state. Smoke sat cross-legged on a buffalo-robe, and his grunt of salutation as we entered, was unusually cordial, out of respect no doubt to Shaw's medical character. Seated around the lodge were several squaws, and an abundance of children. The complaint of Shaw's patients was, for the most part, a severe inflammation of the eyes, occasioned by exposure to the sun, a species of disorder which he treated with some success. He had brought with him a homœopathic medicine-chest, and was, I presume, the first who introduced that harmless system of treatment among the Ogillallah. No sooner had a robe been spread at the head of the lodge for our accommodation, and we had seated ourselves upon it, than a patient made her appearance; the chief's daughter herself, who, to do her justice, was the best-looking girl in the village. Being on excellent terms with the physician, she placed herself readily under his hands, and submitted with a good grace to his applications, laughing in his face during the whole process, for a squaw hardly knows how to smile. This case dispatched, another of a different kind succeeded. A hideous, emaciated old woman sat in the darkest corner of the lodge rocking to and fro with pain, and hiding her eyes from the light by pressing the palms of both hands against her face. At Smoke's command, she came forward, very unwillingly, and exhibited a pair of eyes that had nearly disappeared from excess of inflammation. No sooner had the doctor fastened his gripe upon her, than she set up a dismal moaning, and writhed so in his grasp that he lost all patience, but being resolved to carry his point, he succeeded at last in applying his favorite remedies.

'It is strange,' he said, when the operation was finished, 'that I forgot to bring any Spanish flies with me; we must have something here to answer for a counter-irritant!'

So, in the absence of better, he seized upon a red-hot brand from the fire, and clapped it against the temple of the old squaw, who set up an unearthly howl, at which the rest of the family broke out into a laugh.

During these medical operations, Smoke's eldest squaw entered the lodge, with a sort of stone mallet in her hand. I had observed some time before a litter of well-grown black puppies, comfortably nestled among some buffalo-robes at one side; but this new-comer speedily disturbed their enjoyment; for seizing one of them by the hind paw, she dragged him out, and carrying him to the entrance of the lodge, hammered him on the head till she killed him. Being quite conscious to what this preparation tended, I looked through a hole in the back of the lodge to see the next steps of the process. The squaw, holding the puppy by the legs, was swinging him to and fro through the blaze of a fire; until the hair was singed off. This done, she unsheathed her knife and cut him into small pieces which she dropped into a kettle to boil. In a few moments a large wooden dish was set before us, filled with this delicate preparation. We felt conscious of the honor. A dog-feast is the greatest compliment a Dahcotah can offer to his guest; and knowing that to refuse eating would be an affront, we attacked the little dog, and devoured him before the eyes of his unconscious parent. Smoke in the mean time was preparing his great pipe. It was lighted when we had finished our repast, and we passed it from one to another till the bowl was empty. This done, we took our leave without farther ceremony, knocked at the gate of the fort, and after making ourselves known, were admitted.

One morning, about a week after reaching Fort Laramie, we were holding our customary Indian levee, when a bustle in the area below announced a new arrival; and looking down from our balcony, I saw a familiar red beard and moustache in the gateway. They belonged to the Captain, who with his party had just crossed the stream. We met him on the stairs as he came up, and congratulated him on the safe arrival of himself and his devoted companions. But he remembered our treachery, and was grave and dignified accordingly; a tendency which increased as he observed on our part a disposition to laugh at him. After remaining an hour or two at the fort, he rode away with his friends, and we have heard nothing of him since. As for R——, he kept carefully aloof. It was but too evident that we had the unhappiness to have forfeited the kind regards of our London fellow-traveller.

———————

NOTE.

Somewhat more than a year from this time Shaw happened to be in New York, and coming one morning down the steps of the Astor House, encountered a small newsboy with a bundle of penny papers under his arm, who screamed in his ear, "Another great battle in Mexico!" Shaw bought a paper, and having perused the glorious intelligence, was looking over the remaining columns, when the following paragraph attracted his notice:

ENGLISH TRAVELLING SPORTSMEN.—Among the notable arrivals in town are two English gentlemen, William and John C.——, Esqrs., at the Clinton Hotel, on their return home after an extended Buffalo hunting tour in Oregon and the wild West. Their party crossed the continent in March, 1846, since when our travellers have seen the wonders of our great West, the Sandwich Islands, and the no less agreeable Coast of Western Mexico, California, and Peru. With the real zeal of sportsmen they have pursued adventure whenever it has offered, and returned with not only a correct knowledge of the West, but with many a trophy that shows they have found the grand sport they sought. The account of "Oregon," given by those observing travellers, is most glowing, and though upon a pleasure trip, the advantages to be realized by commercial men have not been overlooked, and they prophecy for that "Western State," a prosperity not exceeded at the east. The fisheries are spoken of as the best in the country, and only equalled by the rare facilities for agriculture. A trip like this now closed is a rare undertaking, but as interesting as rare to those who are capable of a full appreciation of all the wonders that met them in the magnificent region they have traversed.

In some admiration at the heroic light in which Jack and the Captain were here set forth, Shaw pocketed the newspaper, and proceeded to make inquiry after his old fellow-travellers. Jack was out of town, but the Captain was quietly established at his hotel. Except that the red moustache was shorn away, he was in all respects the same man whom we had left upon the South Fork of the Platte. Every recollection of former differences had vanished from his mind, and he greeted his visitor most cordially. "Where is R——?" asked Shaw. "Gone to the devil," hastily replied the Captain, "that is, Jack and I parted from him at Oregon City, and haven't seen him since." He next proceeded to give an account of his journeyings after leaving us at Fort Laramie. No sooner, it seemed, had he done so, than he and Jack began to slaughter the buffalo with unrelenting fury, but when they reached the other side of the South Pass their rifles were laid by as useless, since there were neither Indians nor game to exercise them upon. From this point the journey, as the Captain expressed it, was a great bore. When they reached the mouth of the Columbia, he and Jack sailed for the Sandwich Islands, whence they proceeded to Panama, across the Isthmus, and came by sea to New Orleans.

Shaw and our friend spent the evening together, and when they finally separated at two o'clock in the morning, the Captain's ruddy face was ruddier than ever.

Chapter X.

THE WAR PARTIES.

"By the nine gods he swore it,
And named a trysting day,
And bade his messengers ride forth
East and west and south and north,
To summon his array."
LAYS OF ANCIENT ROME.

THE SUMMER of 1846 was a season of much warlike excitement among all the western bands of the Dahcotah. In 1845 they encountered great reverses. Many war parties had been sent out; some of them had been totally cut off, and others had returned broken and disheartened; so that the whole nation was in mourning. Among the rest, ten warriors had gone to the Snake country, led by the son of a prominent Ogillallah chief, called the Whirlwind. In passing over Laramie Plains they encountered a superior number of their enemies, were surrounded, and killed to a man. Having performed this exploit, the Snakes became alarmed, dreading the resentment of the Dahcotah, and they hastened therefore to signify their wish for peace by sending the scalp of the slain partisan, together with a small parcel of tobacco attached, to his tribesmen and relations. They had employed old Vaskiss, the trader, as their messenger, and the scalp was the same that hung in our room at the fort. But the Whirlwind proved inexorable. Though his character hardly corresponds with his name, he is nevertheless an Indian, and hates the Snakes with his whole soul. Long before the scalp arrived, he had made his preparations for revenge. He sent messengers with presents and tobacco to all the Dahcotah within three hundred miles, proposing a grand combination to chastise the Snakes, and naming a place and time of rendezvous. The plan was readily adopted, and at this moment many villages, probably embracing in the whole five or six thousand souls, were slowly creeping over the prairies and tending toward the common centre at 'La Bonte's Camp,' on the Platte. Here their warlike rites were to be celebrated with more than ordinary solemnity, and a thousand warriors, as it was said, were to set out for the enemy's country. The characteristic result of this preparation will appear in the sequel.

I was greatly rejoiced to hear of it. I had come into the country almost exclusively with a view of observing the Indian character. Having from childhood felt a curiosity on this subject, and having failed completely to gratify it by reading, I resolved to have recourse to observation. I wished to satisfy myself with regard to the position of the Indians among the races of men; the vices and the virtues that have sprung from their innate character and from their modes of life, their government, their superstitions, and their domestic situation. To accomplish my purpose it was necessary to live in the midst of them, and become, as it were, one of them. I proposed to join a village, and make myself an inmate of one of their lodges; and henceforward this narrative, so far as I am concerned, will be chiefly a record of the progress of this design, apparently so easy of accomplishment, and the unexpected impediments that opposed it.

We resolved on no account to miss the rendezvous at 'La Bonte's Camp.' Our plan was to leave Delorier at the fort, in charge of our equipage and the better part of our horses, while we took with us nothing but our weapons and the worst animals we had. In all probability jealousies and quarrels would arise among so many hordes of fierce impulsive savages, congregated together under no common head, and many of them strangers, from remote prairies and mountains. We were bound in common prudence to be cautious how we excited any feeling of cupidity. This was our plan, but unhappily we were not destined to visit 'La Bonte's Camp' in this manner; for one morning a young Indian came to the fort and brought us evil tidings. The new-comer was a dandy of the first water. His ugly face was painted with vermilion; on his head fluttered the tail of a prairie-cock, (a large species of pheasant, not found, as I have heard, eastward of the Rocky Mountains;) in his ears were hung pendants of shell, and a flaming red blanket was wrapped around him. He carried a dragoon-sword in his hand, solely for display, since the knife, the arrow, and the rifle are the arbiters of every prairie fight;

but as no one in this country goes abroad unarmed, the dandy carried a bow and arrows in an otter-skin quiver at his back. In this guise, and bestriding his yellow horse with an air of extreme dignity, 'The Horse,' for that was his name, rode in at the gate, turning neither to the right nor the left, but casting glances askance at the groups of squaws who, with their mongrel progeny, were sitting in the sun before their doors. The evil tidings brought by 'The Horse' were of the following import: The squaw of Henry Chatillon, a woman with whom he had been connected for years by the strongest ties which in that country exist between the sexes, was dangerously ill. She and her children were in the village of the Whirlwind, at the distance of a few days' journey. Henry was anxious to see the woman before she died, and provide for the safety and support of his children, of whom he was extremely fond. To have refused him this would have been gross inhumanity. We abandoned our plan of joining Smoke's village, and of proceeding with it to the rendezvous, and determined to meet The Whirlwind, and go in his company.

I had been slightly ill for several weeks, but on the third night after reaching Fort Laramie a violent pain awoke me, and I found myself attacked by the same disorder that occasioned such heavy losses to the army on the Rio Grande. In a day and a half I was reduced to extreme weakness, so that I could not walk without pain and effort. Having within that time taken six grains of opium, without the least beneficial effect, and having no medical adviser, nor any choice of diet, I resolved to throw myself upon Providence for recovery, using, without regard to the disorder, any portion of strength that might remain to me. So on the twentieth of June we set out from Fort Laramie to meet the Whirlwind's village. Though aided by the high-bowed 'mountain-saddle,' I could scarcely keep my seat on horseback. Before we left the fort we hired another man, a long-haired Canadian, with a face like an owl's, contrasting oddly enough with Delorier's mercurial countenance. This was not the only reinforcement to our party. A vagrant Indian trader, named Reynal, joined us, together with his squaw Margot, and her two nephews, our dandy friend, 'The Horse,' and his younger brother, 'The Hail Storm.' Thus accompanied, we betook ourselves to the prairie, leaving the beaten trail, and passing over the desolate hills that flank the bottoms of Laramie Creek. In all, Indians and whites, we counted eight men and one woman.

Reynal, the trader, the image of sleek and selfish complacency, carried 'The Horse's' dragoon-sword in his hand, delighting apparently in this useless parade; for, from spending half his life among Indians, he had caught not only their habits but their ideas. Margot, a female animal of more than two hundred pounds' weight, was couched in the basket of a *travail*, such as I have before described; besides her ponderous bulk, various domestic utensils were attached to the vehicle, and she was leading by a trail-rope a packhorse, who carried the covering of Reynal's lodge. Delorier walked briskly by the side of the cart, and Raymond came behind, swearing at the spare horses which it was his business to drive. The restless young Indians, their quivers at their backs and their bows in their hands, galloped over the hills, often starting a wolf or an antelope from the thick growth of wild-sage bushes. Shaw and I were in keeping with the rest of the rude cavalcade, having in the absence of other clothing adopted the buckskin attire of the trappers. Henry Chatillon rode in advance of the whole. Thus we passed hill after hill and hollow after hollow, a country arid, broken, and so parched by the sun that none of the plants familiar to our more favored soil would flourish upon it, though there were multitudes of strange medicinal herbs, more especially the absanth, which covered every declivity, and cacti were hanging like reptiles at the edges of every ravine. At length we ascended a high hill, our horses treading upon pebbles of flint, agate, and rough jasper, until, gaining the top, we looked down on the wild bottoms of Laramie Creek, which far below us wound like a writhing snake from side to side of the narrow interval, amid a growth of shattered cotton-wood and ash trees. Lines of tall cliffs, white as chalk, shut in this green strip of woods and meadow-land, into which we descended and encamped for the night. In the morning we passed a wide grassy plain by the river; there was a grove in front, and beneath its shadows the ruins of an old trading fort of logs. The grove bloomed with myriads of wild roses, with their sweet perfume fraught with recollections of home. As we emerged from the trees, a rattlesnake, as large as a man's arm, and more than four feet long, lay coiled on a rock, fiercely rattling and hissing at us; a gray hare, double the size of those of New England, leaped up from the tall ferns; curlew were screaming over our heads, and a whole host of little prairie-dogs sat yelping at us at the mouths of their burrows on the dry plain beyond. Suddenly an antelope leaped up from the wild-sage bushes, gazed eagerly at us, and then erecting his white tail, stretched away like a greyhound. The two Indian boys found a white wolf, as large as a calf, in a hollow, and giving a sharp yell, they galloped after him; but the wolf leaped into the stream and swam across. Then came the crack of a rifle, the bullet whistling harmlessly over his head, as he scrambled up the steep declivity, rattling down stones and earth into the water below. Advancing a little, we beheld, on the farther bank of the stream, a spectacle not common even in that region; for, emerging from among the trees, a herd of some two hundred elk came out upon the meadow, their antlers clattering as they walked forward in a dense throng. Seeing us, they broke into a run, rushing across the opening and disappearing among the trees and scattered groves. On our left was a barren prairie, stretching to the horizon; on our right, a deep gulf, with Laramie Creek at the bottom. We found ourselves at length at the edge of a steep descent; a narrow valley, with long rank grass and scattered trees stretching before us for a mile or more along the course of the stream. Reaching the farther end, we stopped and encamped. An old huge cotton-wood tree spread its branches horizontally over our tent. Laramie Creek, circling before our camp, half inclosed us; it swept along the bottom of a line of tall white cliffs that looked down on us from the farther bank. There were dense copses on our right; the cliffs, too, were half hidden by shrubbery, though behind us a few cotton-wood trees, dotting the green prairie, alone impeded the view, and friend or enemy could be discerned in that direction at a mile's distance. Here we resolved to remain and await the arrival of the Whirlwind, who would certainly pass this way in his progress toward La Bonté's Camp. To go in search of him was not expedient, both on account of the broken and impracticable nature of the country and the uncertainty of his position and movements; besides, our horses were almost worn out, and I was in no condition to travel. We had good grass, good water, tolerable fish from the stream, and plenty of smaller game, such as antelope and deer, though no buffalo. There was one little drawback to our satisfaction; a certain extensive tract of bushes and dried grass, just behind us, which it was by no means advisable to enter, since it sheltered a numerous brood of rattlesnakes. Henry Chatillon again dispatched 'The Horse' to the village, with a message to his squaw that she and her relatives should leave the rest and push on as rapidly as possible to our camp.

Our daily routine soon became as regular as that of a well-ordered household. The weather-beaten old tree was in the centre; our rifles generally rested against its vast trunk, and our saddles were flung on the ground around it; its distorted roots were so twisted as to form one or two convenient arm-chairs, where we could sit in the shade and read or smoke; but meal-times became, on the whole, the most interesting hours of the day, and a bountiful provision was made for them. An antelope or a deer usually swung from a stout bough, and haunches were suspended against the trunk. That camp is daguerreotyped on my memory; the old tree, the white tent, with Shaw sleeping in the shadow of it, and Reynal's miserable lodge close by the bank of the stream. It was a wretched oven-shaped structure, made of begrimed and tattered buffalo-hides stretched over a frame of poles; one side was open, and at the side of the opening hung the powder-horn and bullet-pouch of the owner, together with his long red pipe, and a rich quiver of otter-skin, with a bow and arrows; for Reynal, an Indian in most things but color, chose to hunt buffalo with these primitive weapons. In the darkness of this cavern-like habitation, might be discerned Madame Margot, her overgrown bulk stowed away among her domestic implements, furs, robes, blankets, and painted cases of *par' fléche*, in which dried meat is kept. Here she sat from sunrise to sunset, a bloated impersonation of gluttony and laziness, while her affectionate proprietor was smoking, or begging petty gifts from us, or telling lies concerning his own achievements, or perchance engaged in the more profitable occupation of cooking some preparation of prairie delicacies. Reynal was an adept at this work; he and Delorier have joined forces, and are hard at work together over the fire, while Raymond spreads, by way of table-cloth, a buffalo-hide carefully whitened with pipeclay, on the grass before the tent. Here, with ostentatious display, he arranges the teacups and plates; and then, creeping on all fours, like a dog, he thrusts his head in at the opening of the tent. For a moment we see his round owlish eyes rolling wildly, as if the idea he came to communicate had suddenly escaped him; then collecting his scattered thoughts, as if by an effort, he informs us that supper is ready, and instantly withdraws.

When sunset came, and at that hour the wild and desolate scene would assume a new aspect, the horses were driven in. They had been grazing all day in the neighboring meadow, but now they were picketed close about the camp. As the prairie darkened we sat and conversed around the fire, until becoming drowsy we spread our saddles on the ground, wrapped our blankets around us and lay down. We never placed a guard, having by this time become too indolent; but Henry Chatillon folded his loaded rifle in the same blanket with himself, observing that he always took it to bed with him when he camped in that place. Henry was too bold a man to use such a precaution without good cause. We had a hint now and then that our situation was none of the safest; several Crow war-parties were known to be in the vicinity, and one of them, that passed here some time before, had peeled the bark from a neighboring tree, and engraved upon the white wood certain hieroglyphics, to signify that they had invaded the territories of their enemies, the Dahcotah, and set them at defiance. One morning a thick mist covered the whole country. Shaw and Henry went out to ride, and soon came back with a startling piece of intelligence; they had found within rifle-shot of our camp the recent trail of about thirty horsemen. They could not be whites, and they could not be Dahcotah, since we knew no such parties to be in the neighborhood; therefore they must be Crows. Thanks to that friendly mist, we had escaped a hard battle; they would inevitably have attacked us and our Indian companions had they seen our camp. Whatever doubts we might have entertained, were quite removed a day or two after, by two or three Dahcotah, who came to us with an account of having hidden in a ravine on that very morning, from whence they saw and counted the Crows; they said that they followed them, carefully keeping out of sight, as they passed up Chugwater; that here the Crows discovered five dead bodies of Dahcotah, placed according to the national custom in trees, and flinging them to the ground, they held their guns against them and blew them to atoms.

If our camp were not altogether safe, still it was comfortable enough; at least it was so to Shaw, for I was tormented with illness and vexed by the delay in the accomplishment of my designs. When a respite in my disorder gave me some returning strength, I rode out well armed upon the prairie, or bathed with Shaw in the stream, or waged a petty warfare with the inhabitants of a neighboring prairie-dog village. Around our fire at night we employed ourselves in inveighing against the fickleness and inconstancy of Indians, and execrating the Whirlwind and all his village. At last the thing grew insufferable.

'To-morrow morning,' said I, 'I will start for the fort, and see if I can hear any news there.' Late that evening, when the fire had sunk low, and all the camp were asleep, a loud cry sounded from the darkness. Henry started up, recognized the voice, replied to it, and our dandy friend, 'The Horse,' rode in among us, just returned from his mission to the village. He coolly picketed his mare, without saying a word, sat down by the fire and began to eat, but his imperturbable philosophy was too much for our patience. Where was the village?— about fifty miles south of us; it was moving slowly and would not arrive in less than a week; and where was Henry's squaw?—coming as fast as she could with Mahto-Tatonka, and the rest of her brothers, but she would never reach us, for she was dying, and asking every moment for Henry. Henry's manly face became clouded and downcast; he said that if we were willing he would go in the morning to find her, at which Shaw offered to accompany him.

We saddled our horses at sunrise. Reynal protested vehemently against being left alone, with nobody but the two Canadians and the young Indians, when enemies were in the neighborhood. Disregarding his complaints, we left him, and coming to the mouth of Chugwater, separated, Shaw and Henry turning to the right, up the bank of the stream, while I made for the fort.

Taking leave for a while of my friend and the unfortunate squaw, I will relate by way of episode what I saw and did at Fort Laramie. It was not more than eighteen miles distant, and I reached it in three hours; a shrivelled little figure, wrapped from head to foot in a dingy white Canadian capote, stood in the gateway, holding by a cord of bull's hide, a shaggy wild-horse, which he had lately caught. His sharp prominent features, and his little keen snake-like eyes, looked out from beneath the shadowy hood of the capote, which was drawn over his head exactly like the cowl of a Capuchin friar. His face was extremely thin and like an old piece of leather, and his mouth spread from ear to ear. Extending his long wiry hand, he welcomed me with something more cordial than the ordinary cold salute of an Indian, for we were excellent friends. He had made an exchange of horses to our mutual advantage; and Paul, thinking himself well-treated, had declared every where that the white man had a good heart. He was a Dahcotah from the Missouri, a reputed son of the half-breed interpreter, Pierre Dorion, so often mentioned in Irving's 'Astoria.' He said that he was going to Richard's trading-house to sell his horse to some emigrants, who were encamped there, and asked me to go with him. We forded the stream together, Paul dragging his wild charge behind him. As we passed over the sandy plains beyond, he grew quite communicative. Paul was a cosmopolitan in his way; he had been to the settlements of the whites, and visited in peace and war most of the tribes within the range of a thousand miles. He spoke a jargon of French and another of English, yet nevertheless he was a thorough Indian; and as he told of the bloody deeds of his own people against their enemies, his little eye would glitter with a fierce lustre. He told how the Dahcotah exterminated a village of the Hohays on the Upper Missouri, slaughtering men, women, and children; and how an overwhelming force of them cut off sixteen of the brave Delawares, who fought like wolves to the last, amid the throng of their enemies. He told me also another story, which I did not believe until I had heard it confirmed from so many independent sources that no room was left for doubt. I am tempted to introduce it here.

Six years ago, a fellow named Jim Beckwith, a mongrel of French, American, and negro blood, was trading for the Fur Company, in a very large village of the Crows. Jim Beckwith was last summer at St. Louis. He is a ruffian of the first stamp; bloody and treacherous, without honor or honesty; such at least is the character he bears upon the prairie. Yet in his case all the standard rules of character fail, for though he will stab a man in his sleep, he will also perform most desperate acts of daring; such for instance as the following: While he was in the Crow village, a Blackfoot war-party, between thirty and forty in number, came stealing through the country, killing stragglers and carrying off horses. The Crow warriors got upon their trail and pressed them so closely that they could not escape, at which the Blackfeet, throwing up a semicircular breastwork of logs at the foot of a precipice, coolly awaited their approach. The logs and sticks piled four or five feet high, protected them in front. The Crows might have swept over the breastwork and exterminated their enemies; but though outnumbering them tenfold, they did not dream of storming the little fortification. Such a proceeding would be altogether repugnant to their notions of warfare. Whooping and yelling, and jumping from side to side like devils incarnate, they showered bullets and arrows upon the logs; not a Blackfoot was hurt, but several Crows, in spite of their leaping and dodging were shot down. In this childish manner, the fight went on for an hour or two. Now and then a Crow warrior in an ecstasy of valor and vainglory would scream forth his war-song, boasting himself the bravest and greatest of mankind, and grasping his hatchet, would rush up and strike it upon the breastwork, and then as he retreated to his companions, fall dead under a shower of arrows; yet no combined attack seemed to be dreamed of. The Blackfeet remained secure in their intrenchment. At last Jim Beckwith lost patience;

'You are all fools and old women,' he said to the Crows; 'come with me, if any of you are brave enough, and I will show you how to fight.'

He threw off his trapper's frock of buckskin and stripped

himself naked like the Indians themselves. He left his rifle on the ground, and taking in his hand a small light hatchet, he ran over the prairie to the right, concealed by a hollow from the eyes of the Blackfeet. Then climbing up the rocks, he gained the top of the precipice behind them. Forty or fifty young Crow warriors followed him. By the cries and whoops that rose from below he knew that the Blackfeet were just beneath him; and running forward he leaped down the rock into the midst of them. As he fell he caught one by the long loose hair, and dragging him down tomahawked him; then grasping another by the belt at his waist, he struck him also a stunning blow, and gaining his feet, shouted the Crow war-cry. He swung his hatchet so fiercely around him, that the astonished Blackfeet bore back and gave him room. He might, had he chosen, have leaped over the breastwork and escaped; but this was not necessary, for with devilish yells the Crow warriors came dropping in quick succession over the rock among their enemies. The main body of the Crows, too, answered the cry from the front, and rushed up simulta-neously. The convulsive struggle within the breastwork was frightful; for an instant the Blackfeet fought and yelled like pent-up tigers; but the butchery was soon complete, and the mangled bodies lay piled up together under the precipice. Not a Blackfoot made his escape.

As Paul finished his story we came in sight of Richard's fort. It stood in the middle of the plain; a disorderly crowd of men around it, and an emigrant camp a little in front.

'Now, Paul,' said I, 'where are your Minnicongew lodges?'

'Not come yet,' said Paul, 'may be come to-morrow.'

Two large villages of a band of Dahcotah had come three hundred miles from the Missouri, to join in the war, and they were expected to reach Richard's that morning. There was as yet no sign of their approach; so pushing through a noisy, drunken crowd, I entered an apartment of logs and mud, the largest in the fort: it was full of men of various races and complexions, all more or less drunk. A company of California emigrants, it seemed, had made the discovery at this late day that they had encumbered themselves with too many supplies for their journey. A part therefore they had thrown away or sold at great loss to the traders, but had determined to get rid of their very copious stock of Missouri whisky, by drinking it on the spot. Here were maudlin squaws stretched on piles of buffalo-robes; squalid Mexicans, armed with bows and arrows; Indians sedately drunk; long-haired Canadians and trappers, and American backwoodsmen in brown homespun; the well-beloved pistol and bowie-knife displayed openly at their sides. In the middle of the room a tall, lank man, with a dingy broadcloth coat, was haranguing the company in the style of the stump orator. With one hand he sawed the air, and with the other clutched firmly a brown jug of whisky, which he applied every moment to his lips, forgetting that he had drained the contents long ago. Richard formally introduced me to this personage; who was no less a man than Colonel R——, once the leader of the party. Instantly the Colonel seizing me, in the absence of buttons, by the leather fringes of my frock, began to define his position. His men, he said, had mutinied and deposed him; but still he exercised over them the influence of a superior mind; in all but the name he was yet their chief. As the Colonel spoke, I looked round on the wild assemblage, and could not help thinking that he was but ill qualified to conduct such men across the deserts to California. Conspicuous among the rest stood three tall young men, grandsons of Daniel Boone. They had clearly inherited the adventurous character of that prince of pioneers; but I saw no signs of the quiet and tranquil spirit that so remarkably distinguished him.

Fearful was the fate that months after overtook some of the members of that party. General Kearny, on his late return from California, brought in the account how they were interrupted by the deep snows among the mountains, and maddened by cold and hunger, fed upon each other's flesh!

I got tired of the confusion. 'Come, Paul,' said I, 'we will be off.' Paul sat in the sun, under the wall of the fort. He jumped up, mounted, and we rode toward Fort Laramie. When we reached it, a man came out of the gate with a pack at his back and a rifle on his shoulder; others were gathering about him, shaking him by the hand, as if taking leave. I thought it a strange thing that a man should set out alone and on foot for the prairie. I soon got an explanation. Perrault—this, if I recollect right, was the Canadian's name—had quarrelled with the *bourgeois*, and the fort was too hot to hold him. Bordeaux, inflated with his transient authority, had abused him, and received a blow in return. The men then sprang at each other, and grappled in the middle of the fort. Bordeaux was down in an instant, at the mercy of the incensed Canadian; had not an old Indian, the brother of his squaw, seized hold of his antagonist, he would have fared ill. Perrault broke loose from the old Indian, and both the white men ran to their rooms for their guns; but when Bordeaux, looking from his door, saw the Canadian, gun in hand, standing in the area and calling on him to come out and fight, his heart failed him; he chose to remain where he was. In vain the old Indian, scandalized by his brother-in-law's cowardice, called upon him to go upon the prairie and fight it out in the white man's manner; and Bordeaux's own squaw, equally incensed, screamed to her lord and master that he was a dog and an old woman. It all availed nothing. Bordeaux's prudence got the better of his valor, and he would not stir. Perrault stood showering opprobrious epithets at the recreant *bourgeois*. Growing tired of this, he made up a pack of dried meat, and slinging it at his back, set out alone for Fort Pierre, on the Missouri, a distance of three hundred miles, over a desert country, full of hostile Indians.

I remained in the fort that night. In the morning, as I was coming out from breakfast, conversing with a trader named McCluskey, I saw a strange Indian leaning against the side of the gate. He was a tall, strong man, with heavy features.

'Who is he?' I asked.

'That's the Whirlwind,' said McCluskey. 'He is the fellow that made all this stir about the war. It's always the way with the Sioux; they never stop cutting each other's throats; it's all they are fit for; instead of sitting in their lodges, and getting robes to trade with us in the winter. If this war goes on, we'll make a poor trade of it next season, I reckon.'

And this was the opinion of all the traders, who were vehemently opposed to the war, from the serious injury that it must occasion to their interests. The Whirlwind left his village the day before to make a visit to the fort. His warlike ardor had abated not a little since he first conceived the design of avenging his son's death. The long and complicated preparations for the expedition were too much for his fickle, inconstant disposition. That morning Bordeaux fastened upon him, made him presents, and told him that if he went to war he would destroy his horses and kill no buffalo to trade with the white men; in short, that he was a fool to think of such a thing, and had better make up his mind to sit quietly in his lodge and smoke his pipe, like a wise man. The Whirlwind's purpose was evidently shaken; he had become tired, like a child, of his favorite plan. Bordeaux exultingly predicted that he would not go to war. My philanthropy at that time was no match for my curiosity, and I was vexed at the possibility that after all I might lose the rare opportunity of seeing the formidable ceremonies of war. The Whirlwind, however, had merely thrown the firebrand; the conflagration was become general. All the western bands of the Dahcotah were bent on war; and as I heard from McCluskey, six large villages were already gathered on a little stream, forty miles distant, and were daily calling to the Great Spirit to aid them in their enterprise. McCluskey had just left them, and represented them as on their way to La Bonte's Camp, which they would reach in a week, *unless they should learn that there were no buffalo there*. I did not like this condition, for buffalo this season were rare in the neighborhood. There were also the two Minnicongew villages that I mentioned before; but about noon, an Indian came from Richard's Fort with the news that they were quarrelling, breaking up, and dispersing. So much for the whisky of the emigrants! Finding themselves unable to drink the whole, they had sold the residue to these Indians, and it needed no prophet to fortell the result; a spark dropt into a powder-magazine would not have produced a quicker effect. Instantly the old jealousies and rivalries and smothered feuds that exist in an Indian village broke out into furious quarrels. They forgot the warlike enterprise that had already brought them three hundred miles. They seemed like ungoverned children inflamed with the fiercest passions of men. Several of them were stabbed in the drunken tumult; and in the morning they scattered and moved back toward the Missouri in small parties. I feared that, after all, the long-projected meeting and the ceremonies that were to attend it might never take place, and I should lose so admirable an opportunity of seeing the Indian under his most fearful and characteristic aspect; however in foregoing this, I should avoid a very fair probability of being plundered and stripped, and it might be, stabbed or shot into the bargain. Consoling myself with this reflection, I prepared to carry the news, such as it was, to the camp.

I caught my horse, and to my vexation found he had lost a shoe and broken his tender white hoof against the rocks. Horses are shod at Fort Laramie at the moderate rate of three dollars a foot; so I tied Hendrick to a beam in the *corral*, and summoned Roubidou, the blacksmith. Roubidou, with the hoof between his knees, was at work with hammer and file, and I was inspecting the process, when a strange voice addressed me.

'Two more gone under! Well, there is more of us left yet. Here's Jean Gras and me off to the mountains to-morrow. Our turn will come next, I suppose. It's a hard life, any how!'

I looked up and saw a little man, not much more than five feet high, but of very square and strong proportions. In appearance he was particularly dingy; for his old buckskin frock was black and polished with time and grease, and his belt, knife, pouch and powder-horn appeared to have seen the roughest service. The first joint of each foot was entirely gone, having been frozen off several winters before, and his moccasons were curtailed in proportion. His whole appearance and equipment bespoke the 'free trapper.' He had a round, ruddy face, animated with a spirit of carelessness and gayety not at all in accordance with the words he had just spoken.

' "Two more gone," ' said I; 'what do you mean by that?'

'Oh,' said he, 'the Arapahoes have just killed two of us in the mountains. Old Bull-Tail has come to tell us. They stabbed one behind his back, and shot the other with his own rifle. That's the way we live here! I mean to give up trapping after this year. My squaw says she wants a pacing horse and some red ribbons: I'll make enough beaver to get them for her, and then I'm done! I'll go below and live on a farm.'

'Your bones will dry on the prairie, Rouleau!' said another trapper, who was standing by; a strong, brutal-looking fellow, with a face as surly as a bull-dog's.

Rouleau only laughed, and began to hum a tune and shuffle a dance on his stumps of feet.

'You'll see us, before long, passing up your way,' said the other man.

'Well,' said I, 'stop and take a cup of coffee with us;' and as it was quite late in the afternoon, I prepared to leave the fort at once.

As I rode out, a train of emigrant wagons was passing across the stream. 'Whar are ye goin', stranger?' Thus I was saluted by two or three voices at once.

'About eighteen miles up the creek.'

'It's mighty late to be going that far! Make haste, ye'd better, and keep a bright look-out for Indians!'

I thought the advice too good to be neglected. Fording the stream, I passed at a round trot over the plains beyond. But 'the more haste, the worse speed.' I proved the truth of the proverb by the time I reached the hills three miles from the fort. The trail was faintly marked, and riding forward with more rapidity than caution, I lost sight of it. I kept on in a direct line guided by Laramie Creek, which I could see at intervals darkly glistening in the evening sun, at the bottom of the woody gulf on my right. Half an hour before sunset I came upon its banks. There was something exciting in the wild solitude of the place. An antelope sprang suddenly from the sage-bushes before me. As he leaped gracefully not thirty yards before my horse, I fired, and instantly he spun round and fell. Quite sure of him, I walked my horse toward him, leisurely re-loading my rifle, when to my surprise he sprang up and trotted rapidly away on three legs into the dark recesses of the hills, whither I had no time to follow. Ten minutes after, I was passing along the bottom of a deep valley, and chancing to look behind me, I saw in the dim light that something was following. Supposing it to be a wolf, I slid from my seat and sat down behind my horse to shoot it; but as it came up, I saw by its motions that it was another antelope. It approached within a hundred yards, arched its graceful neck, and gazed intently. I levelled at the white spot on its chest, and was about to fire, when it started off, ran first to one side and then to the other, like a vessel tacking against a wind, and at last stretched away at full speed. Then it stopped again, looked curiously behind it, and trotted up as before; but not so boldly, for it soon paused and stood gazing at me. I fired; it leaped upward and fell upon its tracks. Measuring the distance, I found it two hundred and four paces. When I stood by his side, the antelope turned his expiring eye upward. It was like a beautiful woman's, dark and rich. 'Fortunate that I am in a hurry,' thought I; 'I might be troubled with remorse, if I had time for it.'

Cutting the animal up, not in the most skilful manner, I hung the meat at the back of my saddle, and rode on again. The hills (I could not remember one of them) closed around me. 'It is too late,' thought I, 'to go forward. I will stay here to-night, and look for the path in the morning.' As a last effort, however, I ascended a high hill, from which, to my great satisfaction, I could see Laramie Creek stretching before me, twisting from side to side amid ragged patches of timber; and far off, close beneath the shadows of the trees, the ruins of the old trading-fort were visible. I reached them at twilight. It was far from pleasant, in that uncertain light, to be pushing through the dense trees and shrubbery of the grove beyond. I listened anxiously for the foot-fall of man or beast. Nothing was stirring but one harmless brown bird, chirping among the branches. I was glad when I gained the open prairie once more, where I could see if any thing approached. When I came to the mouth of Chugwater, it was totally dark. Slackening the reins, I let my horse take his own course. He trotted on with unerring instinct, and by nine o'clock was scrambling down the steep descent into the meadows where we were encamped. While I was looking in vain for the light of the fire, Hendrick, with keener perceptions, gave a loud neigh, which was immediately answered in a shrill note from the distance. In a moment I was hailed from the darkness by the voice of Reynal, who had come out, rifle in hand, to see who was approaching.

He, with his squaw, the two Canadians and the Indian boys, were the sole inmates of the camp, Shaw and Henry Chatillon being still absent. At noon of the following day they came back, their horses looking none the better for the journey. Henry seemed dejected. The woman was dead, and his children must henceforward be exposed, without a protector, to the hardships and vicissitudes of Indian life. Even in the midst of his grief he had not forgotten his attachment to his *bourgeois*, for he had procured among his Indian relatives two beautifully ornamented buffalo-robes, which he spread on the ground as a present to us.

Shaw lighted his pipe, and told me in a few words the history of his journey. When I went to the fort they left me, as I mentioned, at the mouth of Chugwater. They followed the course of the little stream all day, traversing a desolate and barren country. Several times they came upon the fresh traces of a large war-party, the same, no doubt, from whom we had so narrowly escaped an attack. At an hour before sunset, without encountering a human being by the way, they came upon the lodges of the squaw and her brothers, who in compliance with Henry's message, had left the Indian village, in order to join us at our camp. The lodges were already pitched, five in number, by the side of the stream. The woman lay in one of them, reduced to a mere skeleton. For some time she had been unable to move or speak. Indeed, nothing had kept her alive but the hope of seeing Henry, to whom she was strongly and faithfully attached. No sooner did he enter the lodge than she revived and conversed with him the greater part of the night. Early in the morning she was lifted into a *travail*, and the whole party set out toward our camp. There were but five warriors; the rest were women and children. The whole were in great alarm at the proximity of the Crow war-party, who would certainly have destroyed them without mercy had they met. They had advanced only a mile or two, when they discerned a horseman, far off, on the edge of the horizon. They all stopped, gathering together in the greatest anxiety, from which they did not recover until long after the horseman disappeared; then they set out again. Henry was riding with Shaw a few rods in advance of the Indians, when Mahto-Tatonka, a younger brother of the woman, hastily called after them. Turning back, they found all the Indians crowded around the *travail* in which the woman was lying. They reached her just in time to hear the death-rattle in her throat. In a moment she lay dead in the basket of the vehicle. A complete stillness succeeded; then the Indians raised in concert their cries of lamentation over the corpse, and among them Shaw clearly distinguished those strange sounds resembling the word 'Halleluyah,' which together with some other accidental coincidences, has given rise to the absurd theory that the Indians are descended from the ten lost tribes of Israel.

The Indian usage required that Henry, as well as the other relatives of the woman, should make valuable presents, to be placed by the side of the body at its last resting-place. Leaving the Indians, he and Shaw set out for the camp and reached it, as we have seen, by hard pushing, at about noon. Having obtained the necessary articles, they immediately returned. It was very late and quite dark when they again reached the lodges. They were all placed in a deep hollow among the dreary hills. Four of them were just visible through the gloom, but the fifth and largest was illuminated by the ruddy blaze of a fire within, glowing through the half-transparent covering of raw-hides. There was a perfect stillness as they approached. The lodges seemed without a tenant. Not a living thing was stirring—there was something awful in the scene. They rode up to the entrance of the lodge, and there was no sound but the tramp of their horses. A squaw came out and took charge of the animals, without speaking a word. Entering, they found the lodge crowded with Indians; a fire was burning in the midst, and the mourners encircled it in a triple row. Room was made for the new-comers at the head of the lodge, a robe spread for them to sit upon, and a pipe lighted and handed to them in perfect silence. Thus they passed the greater part of the night. At times the fire would subside into a heap of embers, until the dark figures seated around it were scarcely visible; then a squaw would drop upon it a piece of buffalo-fat, and a bright flame instantly springing up, would reveal on a sudden the crowd of wild faces, motionless as bronze. The silence continued unbroken. It was a relief to Shaw when daylight returned and he could escape from this house of mourning. He and Henry prepared to return homeward; first, however, they placed the presents they had brought near the body of the squaw, which, most gaudily attired, remained in a sitting posture in one of the lodges. A fine horse was picketed not far off, destined to be killed that morning for the service of her spirit, for the woman was lame, and could not travel on foot over the dismal prairies to the villages of the dead. Food, too, was provided, and household implements, for her use upon this last journey.

Henry left her to the care of her relatives, and came immediately with Shaw to the camp. It was some time before he entirely recovered from his dejection.

Chapter XI.

SCENES AT THE CAMP.

"Fierce are Albania's children; yet they lack
    Not virtues, were those virtues more mature;
Where is the foe that ever saw their back?
    Who can so well the toil of war endure?"
                CHILDE HAROLD.

REYNAL HEARD guns fired one day, at the distance of a mile or two from the camp. He grew nervous instantly. Visions of Crow war-parties began to haunt his imagination; and when we returned, (for we were all absent,) he renewed his complaints about being left alone with the Canadians and the squaw. The day after, the cause of the alarm appeared. Four trappers, one called Moran, another Saraphin, and the others nicknamed 'Rouleau' and 'Jean Gras,' came to our camp and joined us. They it was who fired the guns and disturbed the dreams of our confederate Reynal. They soon encamped by our side. Their rifles, dingy and battered with hard service, rested with ours against the old tree; their strong rude saddles, their buffalo-robes, their traps, and the few rough and simple articles of their travelling equipment, were piled near our tent. Their mountain-horses were turned to graze in the meadow among our own; and the men themselves, no less rough and hardy, used to lie half the day in the shade of our tree, lolling on the grass, lazily smoking, and telling stories of their adventures; and I defy the annals of chivalry to furnish the record of a life more wild and perilous than that of a Rocky Mountain trapper.

With this efficient reinforcement the agitation of Reynal's nerves subsided. He began to conceive a sort of attachment to our old camping ground; yet it was time to change our quarters, since remaining too long on one spot must lead to certain unpleasant results, not to be borne with unless in a case of dire necessity. The grass no longer presented a smooth surface of turf; it was trampled into mud and clay. So we removed to another old tree, larger yet, that grew by the river side at a furlong's distance. Its trunk was full six feet in diameter; on one side it was marked by a party of Indians with various inexplicable hieroglyphics, commemorating some warlike enterprise, and aloft among the branches were the remains of a scaffolding, where dead bodies had once been deposited, after the Indian manner.

'There comes Bull-Bear,' said Henry Chatillon, as we sat on the grass at dinner. Looking up, we saw several horsemen coming over the neighboring hill, and in a moment four stately young men rode up and dismounted. One of them was Bull-Bear, or Mahto-Tatonka, a compound name which he inherited from his father, the most powerful chief in the Ogillallah band. One of his brothers and two other young men accompanied him. We shook hands with the visitors, and when we had finished our meal—for this is the orthodox manner of entertaining Indians, even the best of them—we handed to each a tin cup of coffee and a biscuit, at which they ejaculated from the bottom of their throats, 'How! how!' a monosyllable by which an Indian contrives to express half the emotions that he is susceptible of. Then we lighted the pipe, and passed it to them as they squatted on the ground.

'Where is the village?'

'There,' said Mahto-Tatonka, pointing southward; 'it will come in two days.'

'Will they go to the war?'

'Yes.'

No man is a philanthropist on the prairie. We welcomed this news most cordially, and congratulated ourselves that Bordeaux's interested efforts to divert the Whirlwind from his congenial vocation of bloodshed had failed of success, and that no additional obstacles would interpose between us, and our plan of repairing to the rendezvous at La Bonté's Camp.

For that and several succeeding days, Mahto-Tatonka and his friends remained our guests. They devoured the relics of our meals; they filled the pipe for us, and also helped us to smoke it. Sometimes they stretched themselves side by side in the shade, indulging in raillery and practical jokes, ill becoming the dignity of brave and aspiring warriors, such as two of them in reality were.

Two days dragged away, and on the morning of the third

we hoped confidently to see the Indian village. It did not come; so we rode out to look for it. In place of the eight hundred Indians we expected, we met one solitary savage riding toward us over the prairie, who told us that the Indians had changed their plan, and would not come within three days; still he persisted that they were going to the war. Taking along with us this messenger of evil tidings, we retraced our footsteps to the camp, amusing ourselves by the way with execrating Indian inconstancy. When we came in sight of our little white tent under the big tree, we saw that it no longer stood alone. A huge old lodge was erected close by its side, discolored by rain and storms, rotten with age, with the uncouth figures of horses and men, and outstretched hands that were painted upon it, well nigh obliterated. The long poles which supported this squalid habitation thrust themselves rakishly out from its pointed top, and over its entrance were suspended a 'medicine-pipe' and various other implements of the magic art. While we were yet at a distance, we observed a greatly increased population of various colors and dimensions, swarming around our quiet encampment. Moran, the trapper, having been absent for a day or two, had returned, it seemed, bringing all his family with him. He had taken to himself a wife, for whom he had paid the established price of one horse. This looks cheap at first sight, but in truth the purchase of a squaw is a transaction which no man should enter into without mature deliberation, since it involves not only the payment of the first price, but the formidable burden of feeding and supporting a rapacious horde of the bride's relatives, who hold themselves entitled to feed upon the indiscreet white man. They gather round like leeches, and drain him of all he has.

Moran, like Reynal, had not allied himself to an aristocratic circle. His relatives occupied but a contemptible position in Ogillallah society; for among these wild democrats of the prairie, as among us, there are virtual distinctions of rank and place; though this great advantage they have over us, that wealth has no part in determining such distinctions. Moran's partner was not the most beautiful of her sex, and he had the exceedingly bad taste to array her in an old calico gown, bought from an emigrant woman, instead of the neat and graceful tunic of whitened deer-skin worn ordinarily by the squaws. The moving spirit of the establishment, in more senses than one, was a hideous old hag of eighty. Human imagination never conceived hobgoblin or witch more ugly than she. You could count all her ribs through the wrinkles of the leathery skin that covered them. Her withered face more resembled an old skull than the countenance of a living being, even to the hollow, darkened sockets, at the bottom of which glittered her little black eyes. Her arms had dwindled away into nothing but whip-cord and wire. Her hair, half black, half gray, hung in total neglect nearly to the ground, and her sole garment consisted of the remnant of a discarded buffalo-robe tied round her waist with a string of hide. Yet the old squaw's meagre anatomy was wonderfully strong. She pitched the lodge, packed the horses, and did the hardest labor of the camp. From morning till night she bustled about the lodge, screaming like a screech-owl when any thing displeased her. Then there was her brother, a 'medicine-man,' or magician, equally gaunt and sinewy with herself. His mouth spread from ear to ear, and his appetite, as we had full occasion to learn, was ravenous in proportion. The other inmates of the lodge were a young bride and bridegroom; the latter one of those idle, good-for-nothing fellows who infest an Indian village as well as more civilized communities. He was fit neither for hunting nor for war; and one might infer as much from the stolid unmeaning expression of his face. The happy pair had just entered upon the honeymoon. They would stretch a buffalo-robe upon poles, so as to protect them from the fierce rays of the sun, and spreading beneath this rough canopy a luxuriant couch of furs, would sit affectionately side by side for half the day, though I could not discover that much conversation passed between them. Probably they had nothing to say; for an Indian's supply of topics for conversation is far from being copious. There were half a dozen children, too, playing and whooping about the camp, shooting birds with little bows and arrows, or making miniature lodges of sticks, as children of a different complexion build houses of blocks.

A day passed, and Indians began rapidly to come in. Parties of two or three or more would ride up and silently seat themselves on the grass. The fourth day came at last, when about noon horsemen suddenly appeared into view on the summit of the neighboring ridge. They descended, and behind them followed a wild procession, hurrying in haste and disorder down the hill and over the plain below; horses, mules, and dogs, heavily-burdened *travaux*, mounted warriors, squaws walking amid the throng, and a host of children. For a full half-hour they continued to pour down; and keeping directly to the bend of the stream, within a furlong of us, they soon assembled there, a dark and confused throng, until, as if by magic, a hundred and fifty tall lodges sprung up. On a sudden the lonely plain was transformed into the site of a miniature city. Countless horses were soon grazing over the meadows around us, and the whole prairie was animated by restless figures careering on horseback, or sedately stalking in their long white robes. The Whirlwind was come at last! One question yet remained to be answered: 'Will he go to the war, in order that we, with so respectable an escort, may pass over to the somewhat perilous rendezvous at La Bonte's camp?'

Still this remained in doubt. Characteristic indecision perplexed their councils. Indians cannot act in large bodies. Though their object be of the highest importance, they cannot combine to attain it by a series of connected efforts. King Philip, Pontiac, and Tecumseh, all felt this to their cost. The Ogillallah once had a war-chief who could control them; but he was dead, and now they were left to the sway of their own unsteady impulses.

This Indian village and its inhabitants will hold a prominent place in the rest of the narrative, and perhaps it may not be amiss to glance for an instant at the savage people of which they form a part. The Dahcotah (I prefer this national designation to the unmeaning French name, Sioux) range over a vast territory, from the river St. Peter's to the Rocky Mountains themselves. They are divided into several independent bands, united under no central government, and acknowledging no common head. The same language, usages, and superstitions, form the sole bond between them. They do not unite even in their wars. The bands of the east fight the Ojibwas on the Upper Lakes; those of the west make incessant war upon the Snake Indians in the Rocky Mountains. As the whole people is divided into bands, so each band is divided into villages. Each village has a chief, who is honored and obeyed only so far as his personal qualities may command respect and fear. Sometimes he is a mere nominal chief; sometimes his authority is little short of absolute, and his fame and influence reach even beyond his own village; so that the whole band to which he belongs is ready to acknowledge him as their head. This was, a few years since, the case with the Ogillallah. Courage, address, and enterprise may raise any warrior to the highest honor, especially if he be the son of a former chief, or a member of a numerous family, to support him and avenge his quarrels; but when he has reached the dignity of chief, and the old men and warriors, by a peculiar ceremony, have formally installed him, let it not be imagined that he assumes any of the outward semblances of rank and honor. He knows too well on how frail a tenure he holds his station. He must conciliate his uncertain subjects. Many a man in the village lives better, owns more squaws and more horses, and goes better clad than he. Like the Teutonic chiefs of old, he ingratiates himself with his young men by making them presents, thereby often impoverishing himself. Does he fail in gaining their favor, they will set his authority at naught, and may desert him at any moment; for the usages of his people have provided no sanctions by which he may enforce his authority. Very seldom does it happen, at least among these western bands, that a chief attains to much power, unless he is the head of a numerous family. Frequently the village is principally made up of his relatives and descendants, and the wandering community assumes much of the patriarchal character. A people so loosely united, torn, too, with rankling feuds and jealousies, can have little power or efficiency.

The western Dahcotah have no fixed habitations. Hunting and fighting, they wander incessantly, through summer and winter. Some are following the herds of buffalo over the waste of prairie; others are traversing the Black Hills, thronging, on horseback and on foot, through the dark gulfs and sombre gorges, beneath the vast splintering precipices, and emerging at last upon the 'Parks,' those beautiful but most perilous hunting-grounds. The buffalo supplies them with almost all the necessaries of life; with habitations, food, clothing, and fuel; with strings for their bows, with thread, cordage, and trailropes for their horses, with coverings for their saddles, with vessels to hold water, with boats to cross streams, with glue, and with the means of purchasing all that they desire from the traders. When the buffalo are extinct, they too must dwindle away.

War is the breath of their nostrils. Against most of the neighboring tribes they cherish a deadly, rancorous hatred, transmitted from father to son, and inflamed by constant aggression and retaliation. Many times a year, in every village, the Great Spirit is called upon, fasts are made, the war-parade is celebrated, and the warriors go out by handfuls at a time against the enemy. This fierce and evil spirit awakens their most eager aspirations, and calls forth their greatest energies. It is chiefly this that saves them from lethargy and utter abasement. Without its powerful stimulus they would be like the unwarlike tribes beyond the mountains, who are scattered among the caves and rocks like beasts, living on roots and reptiles. These latter have little of humanity except the form; but the proud and ambitious Dahcotah warrior can sometimes boast of heroic virtues. It is very seldom that distinction and influence are attained among them by any other course than that of arms. Their superstition, however, sometimes gives great power to those among them who pretend to the character of magicians. Their wild hearts, too, can feel the power of oratory, and yield deference to the masters of it.

But to return. Look into our tent, or enter, if you can bear the stifling smoke and the close atmosphere. There, wedged close together, you will see a circle of stout warriors, passing the pipe around, joking, telling stories, and making themselves merry, after their fashion. We were also infested by little copper-colored naked boys and snake-eyed girls. They would come up to us, muttering certain words, which being interpreted conveyed the concise invitation, 'Come and eat.' Then we would rise, cursing the pertinacity of Dahcotah hospitality, which allowed scarcely an hour of rest between sun and sun, and to which we were bound to do honor, unless we would offend our entertainers. This necessity was particularly burdensome to me, as I was scarcely able to walk, from the effects of illness, and was of course poorly qualified to dispose of twenty meals a day. Of these sumptuous banquets, I gave a specimen in a former chapter, where the tragical fate of the little dog was chronicled. So bounteous an entertainment looks like an outgushing of good-will; but doubtless one half at least of our kind hosts, had they met us alone and unarmed on the prairie, would have robbed us of our horses, and perchance have bestowed an arrow upon us beside. Trust not an Indian. Let your rifle be ever in your hand. Wear next your heart the old chivalric motto, 'Semper Paratus.'

One morning we were summoned to the lodge of an old man, in good truth the Nestor of his tribe. We found him half sitting, half reclining on a pile of buffalo-robes; his long hair, jet-black even now, though he had seen some eighty winters, hung on either side of his thin features. Those most conversant with Indians in their homes will scarcely believe me when I affirm that there was dignity in his countenance and mien. His gaunt but symmetrical frame did not more clearly exhibit the wreck of by-gone strength, than did his dark, wasted features, still prominent and commanding, bear the stamp of mental energies. I recalled, as I saw him, the eloquent metaphor of the Iroquois sachem: 'I am an aged hemlock; the winds of an hundred winters have whistled through my branches, and I am dead at the top!' Opposite the patriarch was his nephew, the young aspirant Mahto-Tatonka; and beside these, there were one or two women in the lodge.

The old man's story is peculiar, and singularly illustrative of a superstitious custom that prevails in full force among many of the Indian tribes. He was one of a powerful family, renowned for their warlike exploits. When a very young man, he submitted to the singular rite to which most of the tribe subject themselves before entering upon life. He painted his face black; then seeking out a cavern in a sequestered part of the Black Hills, he lay for several days, fasting, and praying to the Great Spirit. In the dreams and visions produced by his weakened and excited state, he fancied, like all Indians, that he saw supernatural revelations. Again and again the form of an antelope appeared before him. The antelope is the graceful peace-spirit of the Ogillallah; but seldom is it that such a gentle visitor presents itself during the initiatory fasts of their young men. The terrible grizzly bear, the divinity of war, usually appears to fire them with martial ardor and thirst for renown. At length the antelope spoke. He told the young dreamer that he was not to follow the path of war; that a life of peace and tranquillity was marked out for him; that thenceforward he was to guide the people by his counsels, and protect them from the evils of their own feuds and dissensions. Others were to gain renown by fighting the enemy; but greatness of a different kind was in store for him.

The visions beheld during the period of this fast usually determine the whole course of the dreamer's life, for an Indian is bound by iron superstitions. From that time, Le Borgne, which was the only name by which we knew him, abandoned all thoughts of war, and devoted himself to the labors of peace. He told his vision to the people. They honored his commission and respected him in his novel capacity.

A far different man was his brother, Mahto-Tatonka, who had transmitted his names, his features, and many of his characteristic qualities, to his son. He was the father of Henry Chatillon's squaw, a circumstance which proved of some advantage to us, as securing for us the friendship of a family perhaps the most distinguished and powerful in the whole Ogillallah band. Mahto-Tatonka, in his rude way, was a hero. No chief could vie with him in warlike renown, or in power over his people. He had a fearless spirit, and a most impetuous and inflexible resolution. His will was law. He was politic and sagacious, and with true Indian craft he always befriended the whites, well knowing that he might thus reap great advantages for himself and his adherents. When he had resolved on any course of conduct, he would pay to the warriors the empty compliment of calling them together to deliberate upon it, and when their debates were over, he would quietly state his own opinion, which no one ever disputed. The consequences of thwarting his imperious will were too formidable to be encountered. Wo to those who incurred his displeasure! He would strike them or stab them on the spot; and this act, which if attempted by any other chief would instantly have cost him his life, the awe inspired by his name enabled him to repeat again and again with impunity. In a community where, from immemorial time, no man has acknowledged any law but his own will, Mahto-Tatonka, by the force of his dauntless resolution, raised himself to power little short of despotic. His haughty career came at last to an end. He had a host of enemies only waiting for their opportunity of revenge, and our old friend Smoke, in particular, together with all his kinsmen, hated him most cordially. Smoke sat one day in his lodge, in the midst of his own village, when Mahto-Tatonka entered it alone, and approaching the dwelling of his enemy, called on him in a loud voice to come out, if he were a man, and fight. Smoke would not move. At this, Mahto-Tatonka proclaimed him a coward and an old woman, and striding close to the entrance of the lodge, stabbed the chief's best horse, which was picketed there. Smoke was daunted, and even this insult failed to call him forth. Mahto-Tatonka moved haughtily away; all made way for him, but his hour of reckoning was near.

One hot day, five or six years ago, numerous lodges of Smoke's kinsmen were gathered around some of the Fur Company's men, who were trading in various articles with them, whisky among the rest. Mahto-Tatonka was also there with a few of his people. As he lay in his own lodge, a fray arose between his adherents and the kinsmen of his enemy. The war-whoop was raised, bullets and arrows began to fly, and the camp was in confusion. The chief sprang up, and rushing in a fury from the lodge, shouted to the combatants on both sides to cease. Instantly—for the attack was preconcerted—came the reports of two or three guns, and the twanging of a dozen bows, and the savage hero, mortally wounded, pitched forward headlong to the ground. Rouleau was present, and told me the particulars. The tumult became general, and was not quelled until several had fallen on both sides. When we were in the country the feud between the two families was still rankling, and not likely soon to cease.

Thus died Mahto-Tatonka, but he left behind him a goodly army of descendants, to perpetuate his renown and avenge his fate. Besides daughters, he had thirty sons, a number which need not stagger the credulity of those who are best acquainted with Indian usages and practices. We saw many of them, all marked by the same dark complexion, and the same peculiar cast of features. Of these, our visitor, young Mahto-

Tatonka, was the eldest, and some reported him as likely to succeed to his father's honors. Though he appeared not more than twenty-one years old, he had oftener struck the enemy, and stolen more horses and more squaws than any young man in the village. We of the civilized world are not apt to attach much credit to the latter species of exploits; but horse-stealing is well known as an avenue to distinction on the prairies, and the other kind of depredation is esteemed equally meritorious. Not that the act can confer fame from its own intrinsic merits. Any one can steal a squaw, and if he chooses afterward to make an adequate present to her rightful proprietor, the easy husband for the most part rests content, his vengeance falls asleep, and all danger from that quarter is averted. Yet this is esteemed but a pitiful and mean-spirited transaction. The danger is averted, but the glory of the achievement also is lost. Mahto-Tatonka proceeded after a more gallant and dashing fashion. Out of several dozen squaws whom he had stolen, he could boast that he had never paid for one, but snapping his fingers in the face of the injured husband, had defied the extremity of his indignation, and no one yet had dared to lay the finger of violence upon him. He was following close in the footsteps of his father. The young men and the young squaws, each in their way, admired him. The one would always follow him to war, and he was esteemed to have an unrivalled charm in the eyes of the other. Perhaps his impunity may excite some wonder. An arrow shot from a ravine, a stab given in the dark, require no great valor, and are especially suited to the Indian genius; but Mahto-Tatonka had a strong protection. It was not alone his courage and audacious will that enabled him to career so dashingly among his compeers. His enemies did not forget that he was one of thirty warlike brethren, all growing up to manhood. Should they wreak their anger upon him, many keen eyes would be ever upon them, many fierce hearts would thirst for their blood. The avenger would dog their footsteps every where. To kill Mahto-Tatonka would be no better than an act of suicide.

Though he found such favor in the eyes of the fair, he was no dandy. As among us, those of highest worth and breeding are most simple in manner and attire, so our aspiring young friend was indifferent to the gaudy trappings and ornaments of his companions. He was content to rest his chances of success upon his own warlike merits. He never arrayed himself in gaudy blanket and glittering necklaces, but left his statue-like form limbed like an Apollo of bronze, to win its way to favor. His voice was singularly deep and strong. It sounded from his chest like the deep notes of an organ. Yet after all, he was but an Indian. See him as he lies there in the sun before our tent, kicking his heels in the air and cracking jokes with his brother. Does he look like a hero? See him now in the hour of his glory, when at sunset the whole village empties itself to behold him, for to-morrow their favorite young partisan goes out against the enemy. His superb head-dress is adorned with a crest of the war-eagle's feathers, rising in a waving ridge above his brow, and sweeping far behind him. His round white shield hangs at his breast, with feathers radiating from the centre like a star. His quiver is at his back; his tall lance in his hand, the iron point flashing against the declining sun, while the long scalp-locks of his enemies flutter from the shaft. Thus, gorgeous as a champion in his panoply, he rides round and round within the great circle of lodges, balancing with a graceful buoyancy to the free movements of his war-horse, while with a sedate brow he sings his song to the Great Spirit. Young rival warriors look askance at him; vermilion-cheeked girls gaze in admiration, boys whoop and scream in a thrill of delight, and old women yell forth his name and proclaim his praises from lodge to lodge.

Mahto-Tatonka, to come back to him, was the best of all our Indian friends. Hour after hour and day after day, when swarms of savages of every age, sex and degree, beset our camp, he would lie in our tent, his lynx-eye ever open to guard our property from pillage.

The Whirlwind invited us one day to his lodge. The feast was finished and the pipe began to circulate. It was a remarkably large and fine one, and I expressed my admiration of its form and dimensions.

'If the Meneaska likes the pipe,' asked the Whirlwind, 'why does he not keep it?'

Such a pipe among the Ogillallah is valued at the price of a horse. A princely gift, thinks the reader, and worthy of a chieftain and a warrior. The Whirlwind's generosity rose to no such pitch. He gave me the pipe, confidently expecting that I in return should make him a present of equal or superior value. This is the implied condition of every gift among the Indians as among the Orientals, and should it not be complied with, the present is usually reclaimed by the giver. So I arranged upon a gaudy calico handkerchief an assortment of vermilion, tobacco, knives and gunpowder, and summoning the chief to camp, assured him of my friendship, and begged his acceptance of a slight token of it. Ejaculating *how! how!* he folded up the offerings and withdrew to his lodge.

Several days passed, and we and the Indians remained encamped side by side. They could not decide whether or not to go to the war. Toward evening, scores of them would surround our tent, a picturesque group. Late one afternoon a party of them mounted on horseback came suddenly in sight from behind some clumps of bushes that lined the bank of the stream, leading with them a mule, on whose back was a wretched negro, only sustained in his seat by the high pommel and cantle of the Indian saddle. His cheeks were withered and shrunken in the hollow of his jaws; his eyes were unnaturally dilated, and his lips seemed shrivelled and drawn back from his teeth like those of a corpse. When they brought him up before our tent, and lifted him from the saddle, he could not walk or stand, but he crawled a short distance, and with a look of utter misery sat down on the grass. All the children and women came pouring out of the lodges around us, and with screams and cries made a close circle about him, while he sat supporting himself with his hands, and looking from side to side with a vacant stare. The wretch was starving to death! For thirty-three days he had wandered alone on the prairie, without weapon of any kind; without shoes, moccasons, or any other clothing than an old jacket and pantaloons; without intelligence and skill to guide his course, or any knowledge of the productions of the prairie. All this time he had subsisted on crickets and lizards, wild onions, and three eggs which he found in the nest of a prairie dove. He had not seen a human being. Utterly bewildered in the boundless, hopeless desert that stretched around him, offering to his inexperienced eye no mark by which to direct his course, he had walked on in despair, till he could walk no longer, and then crawled on his knees, until the bone was laid bare. He chose the night for his travelling, laying down by day to sleep in the glaring sun, always dreaming, as he said, of the broth and corn-cake he used to eat under his old master's shed in Missouri. Every man in the camp, both white and red, was astonished at his wonderful escape not only from starvation but from the grizzly bears, which abound in that neighborhood, and the wolves which howled around him every night.

Reynal recognized him the moment the Indians brought him in. He had run away from his master about a year before and joined the party of M. Richard, who was then leaving the frontier for the mountains. He had lived with Richard ever since, until in the end of May he with Reynal and several other men went out in search of some stray horses, when he got separated from the rest in a storm, and had never been heard of up to this time. Knowing his inexperience and help-lessness, no one dreamed that he could still be living. The Indians had found him lying exhausted on the ground.

As he sat there, with the Indians gazing silently on him, his haggard face and glazed eye were disgusting to look upon. Delorier made him a bowl of gruel, but he suffered it to re-main untasted before him. At length he languidly raised the spoon to his lips; again he did so, and again; and then his appetite seemed suddenly inflamed into madness, for he seized the bowl, swallowed all its contents in a few seconds, and eagerly demanded meat. This we refused, telling him to wait until morning, but he begged so eagerly that we gave him a small piece, which he devoured, tearing it like a dog. He said he must have more. We told him that his life was in danger if he ate so immoderately at first. He assented, and said he knew he was a fool to do so, but he must have meat. This we absolutely refused, to the great indignation of the senseless squaws, who, when we were not watching him, would slyly bring dried meat and *pommes blanches*, and place them on the ground by his side. Still this was not enough for him. When it grew dark he contrived to creep away between the legs of the horses and crawl over to the Indian village, about a furlong down the stream. Here he fed to his heart's content, and was brought back again in the morning, when

Jean Gras, the trapper, put him on horseback and carried him to the fort. He managed to survive the effects of his insane greediness, and though slightly deranged, when we left this part of the country, he was otherwise in tolerable health, and expressed his firm conviction that nothing could ever kill him.

When the sun was yet an hour high, it was a gay scene in the village. The warriors stalked sedately among the lodges, or along the margin of the streams, or walked out to visit the bands of horses that were feeding over the prairie. Half the village population deserted the close and heated lodges and betook themselves to the water; and here you might see boys and girls, and young squaws, splashing, swimming and diving, beneath the afternoon sun, with merry laughter and screaming. But when the sun was just resting above the broken peaks, and the purple mountains threw their prolonged shadows for miles over the prairie; when our grim old tree, lighted by the horizontal rays, assumed an aspect of peaceful repose, such as one loves after scenes of tumult and excitement; and when the whole landscape, of swelling plains and scattered groves, was softened into a tranquil beauty; then our encampment presented a striking spectacle. Could Salvator Rosa have transferred it to his canvas, it would have added new renown to his pencil. Savage figures surrounded our tent, with quivers at their backs, and guns, lances or tomahawks in their hands. Some sat on horseback, motionless as equestrian statues, their arms crossed on their breasts, their eyes fixed in a steady unwavering gaze upon us. Some stood erect, wrapped from head to foot in their long white robes of buffalo-hide. Some sat together on the grass, holding their shaggy horses by a rope, with their broad dark busts exposed to view as they suffered their robes to fall from their shoulders. Others again stood carelessly among the throng, with nothing to conceal the matchless symmetry of their forms; and I do not exaggerate when I say, that only on the prairie and in the Vatican have I seen such faultless models of the human figure. See that warrior standing by the tree, towering six feet and a half in stature. Your eyes may trace the whole of his graceful and majestic height, and discover no defect or blemish. With his free and noble attitude, with the bow in his hand, and the quiver at his back, he might seem, but for his face, the Pythian Apollo himself. Such a figure rose before the imagination of West, when on first seeing the Belvidere in the Vatican, he exclaimed, 'By God, a Mohawk!'

When the sky darkened and the stars began to appear; when the prairie was involved in gloom, and the horses were driven in and secured around the camp, the crowd began to melt away. Fires gleamed around, duskily revealing the rough trappers and the graceful Indians. One of the families near us would always be gathered about a bright blaze, that displayed the shadowy dimensions of their lodge, and sent its lights far up among the masses of foliage above, gilding the dead and ragged branches. Withered witch-like hags flitted around the blaze; and here for hour after hour sat a circle of children and young girls, laughing and talking, their round merry faces glowing in the ruddy light. We could hear the monotonous notes of the drum from the Indian village, with the chant of the war-song, deadened in the distance, and the long chorus of quavering yells, where the war-dance was going on in the largest lodge. For several nights, too, we could hear wild and mournful cries, rising and dying away like the melancholy voice of a wolf. They came from the sisters and female relatives of Mahto-Tatonka, who were gashing their limbs with knives, and bewailing the death of Henry Chatillon's squaw. The hour would grow late before all retired to rest in the camp. Then the embers of the fires would be glowing dimly, the men would be stretched in their blankets on the ground, and nothing could be heard but the restless motions of the crowded horses.

I recall these scenes with a mixed feeling of pleasure and pain. At this time, I was so reduced by illness that I could seldom walk without reeling like a drunken man, and when I rose from my seat upon the ground the landscape suddenly grew dim before my eyes, the trees and lodges seemed to sway to and fro, and the prairie to rise and fall like the swells of the ocean. Such a state of things is by no means enviable any where. In a country where a man's life may at any moment depend on the strength of his arm, or it may be on the activity of his legs, it is more particularly inconvenient. Medical assistance of course there was none; neither had I the means of pursuing a system of diet; and sleeping on damp ground, with an occasional drenching from a shower, would hardly be recommended as beneficial. I sometimes suffered the extremity of languor and exhaustion, and though at the time I felt no apprehensions of the final result, I have since learned that my situation was a critical one.

Besides other formidable inconveniences, I owe it in a great measure to the remote effects of that unlucky disorder, that from deficient eyesight I am compelled to employ the pen of another in taking down this narrative from my lips; and I have learned very effectually that a violent attack of dysentery on the prairie is a thing too serious for a joke. I tried repose and a very sparing diet. For a long time, with exemplary patience, I lounged about the camp, or at the utmost staggered over to the Indian village, and walked faint and dizzy among the lodges. It would not do; and I bethought me of starvation. During five days I sustained life on one small biscuit a day. At the end of that time I was weaker than before, but the disorder seemed shaken in its strong-hold, and very gradually I began to resume a less rigid diet. No sooner had I done so than the same detested symptoms revisited me; my old enemy resumed his pertinacious assaults, yet not with his former violence or constancy, and though before I regained any fair portion of my ordinary strength weeks had elapsed, and months passed before the disorder left me, yet thanks to old habits of activity, and a merciful Providence, I was able to sustain myself against it.

I used to lie languid and dreamy before our tent, and muse on the past and the future, and when most overcome with lassitude, my eyes turned always toward the distant Black Hills. There is a spirit of energy and vigor in mountains, and they impart it to all who approach their presence. At that time I did not know how many dark superstitions and gloomy legends are associated with those mountains in the minds of the Indians, but I felt an eager desire to penetrate their hidden recesses, to explore the awful chasms and precipices, the black torrents, the silent forests that I fancied were concealed there.

Chapter XII.

ILL-LUCK.

"One touch to her hand, and one word in her ear,
  When they reach'd the hall-door, and the charger stood near;
  So light to the croupe the fair lady he swung,
  So light to the saddle before her he sprung!
  'She is won! we are gone, over bank, bush, and scaur;
  They'll have fleet steeds that follow,' quoth young Lockinvar."

MARMION.

A CANADIAN came from Fort Laramie, and brought a
curious piece of intelligence. A trapper, fresh from the
mountains, had become enamoured of a Missouri damsel belonging to a family who with other emigrants had been for
some days encamped in the neighborhood of the fort. If
bravery be the most potent charm to win the favor of the
fair, then no wooer could be more irresistible than a Rocky
Mountain trapper. In the present instance, the suit was not
urged in vain. The lovers concerted a scheme, which they proceeded to carry into effect with all possible dispatch. The emigrant party left the fort, and on the next succeeding night but
one encamped as usual, and placed a guard. A little after midnight, the enamoured trapper drew near, mounted on a strong
horse, and leading another by the bridle. Fastening both animals to a tree, he stealthily moved towards the wagons, as if
he were approaching a band of buffalo. Eluding the vigilance
of the guard, who were probably half asleep, he met his mistress by appointment at the outskirts of the camp, mounted
her on his spare horse, and made off with her through the
darkness. The sequel of the adventure did not reach our ears,
and we never learned how the imprudent fair one liked an
Indian lodge for a dwelling, and a reckless trapper for a bridegroom.

At length the Whirlwind and his warriors determined to
move. They had resolved after all their preparations not to go
to the rendezvous at La Bonté's camp, but to pass through
the Black Hills and spend a few weeks in hunting the buffalo

on the other side, until they had killed enough to furnish them with a stock of provisions and with hides to make their lodges for the next season. This done, they were to send out a small independent war-party against the enemy. Their final determination left us in some embarrassment. Should we go to La Bonté's camp, it was not impossible that the other villages should prove as vacillating and indecisive as the Whirlwind's, and that no assembly whatever would take place. Our old companion Reynal had conceived a liking for us, or rather for our biscuit and coffee, and for the occasional small presents which we made him. He was very anxious that we should go with the village which he himself intended to accompany. He declared he was certain that no Indians would meet at the rendezvous, and said moreover that it would be easy to convey our cart and baggage through the Black Hills. In saying this, he told as usual an egregious falsehood. Neither he nor any white man with us had ever seen the difficult and obscure defiles, through which the Indians intended to make their way. I passed them afterward, and had much ado to force my distressed horse along the narrow ravines, and through chasms where daylight could scarcely penetrate. Our cart might as easily have been conveyed over the summit of Pike's Peak. Anticipating the difficulties and uncertainties of an attempt to visit the rendezvous, we recalled the old proverb, about 'A bird in the hand,' and decided to follow the village.

Both camps, the Indians' and our own, broke up on the morning of the first of July. I was so weak that the aid of a potent auxiliary, a spoonful of whisky, swallowed at short intervals, alone enabled me to sit my hardy little mare Pauline, through the short journey of that day. For half a mile before us and half a mile behind, the prairie was covered far and wide with the moving throng of savages. The barren, broken plain stretched away to the right and left, and far in front rose the gloomy precipitous ridge of the Black Hills. We pushed forward to the head of the scattered column, passing the burdened *travaux*, the heavily laden pack-horses, the gaunt old women on foot, the gay young squaws on horseback, the restless children running among the crowd, old men striding along in their white buffalo-robes, and groups of young warriors mounted on their best horses. Henry Chatillon, looking backward over the distant prairie, exclaimed suddenly that a horseman was approaching, and in truth we could just discern a small black speck slowly moving over the face of a distant swell, like a fly creeping on a wall. It rapidly grew larger as it approached.

'White man, I b'lieve,' said Henry; 'look how he ride! Indian never ride that way. Yes; he got rifle on the saddle before him.'

The horseman disappeared in a hollow of the prairie, but we soon saw him again, and as he came riding at a gallop toward us through the crowd of Indians, his long hair streaming in the wind behind him, we recognized the ruddy face and old buckskin frock of Jean Gras the trapper. He was just arrived from Fort Laramie, where he had been on a visit, and said he had a message for us. A trader named Bisonette, one of Henry's friends, was lately come from the settlements, and intended to go with a party of men to La Bonte's camp, where, as Jean Gras assured us, ten or twelve villages of Indians would certainly assemble. Bisonette desired that we would cross over and meet him there, and promised that his men should protect our horses and baggage while we went among the Indians. Shaw and I stopped our horses and held a council, and in an evil hour resolved to go.

For the rest of that day's journey our course and that of the Indians was the same. In less than an hour we came to where the high barren prairie terminated, sinking down abruptly in steep descent; and standing on these heights, we saw below us a great level meadow. Laramie Creek bounded it on the left, sweeping along in the shadow of the declivities, and passing with its shallow and rapid current just below us. We sat on horseback, waiting and looking on, while the whole savage array went pouring past us, hurrying down the descent, and spreading themselves over the meadow below. In a few moments the plain was swarming with the moving multitude, some just visible, like specks in the distance, others still passing on, pressing down, and fording the stream with bustle and confusion. On the edge of the heights sat half a dozen of the elder warriors, gravely smoking and looking down with unmoved faces on the wild and striking spectacle.

Up went the lodges in a circle on the margin of the stream.

For the sake of quiet we pitched our tent among some trees at half a mile's distance. In the afternoon we were in the village. The day was a glorious one, and the whole camp seemed lively and animated in sympathy. Groups of children and young girls were laughing gayly on the outside of the lodges. The shields, the lances and the bows were removed from the tall tripods on which they usually hung, before the dwellings of their owners. The warriors were mounting their horses, and one by one riding away over the prairie toward the neighboring hills.

Shaw and I sat on the grass near the lodge of Reynal. An old woman, with true Indian hospitality, brought a bowl of boiled venison and placed it before us. We amused ourselves with watching half a dozen young squaws who were playing together and chasing each other in and out of one of the lodges. Suddenly the wild yell of the war-whoop came pealing from the hills. A crowd of horsemen appeared, rushing down their sides, and riding at full speed toward the village, each warrior's long hair flying behind him in the wind like a ship's streamer. As they approached, the confused throng assumed a regular order, and entering two by two, they circled round the area at full gallop, each warrior singing his war-song as he rode. Some of their dresses were splendid. They wore superb crests of feathers, and close tunics of antelope skins, fringed with the scalp-locks of their enemies; their shields too were often fluttering with the war-eagle's feathers. All had bows and arrows at their backs; some carried long lances, and a few were armed with guns. The White Shield, their partisan, rode in gorgeous attire at their head, mounted on a black-and-white horse. Mahto-Tatonka and his brothers took no part in this parade, for they were in mourning for their sister, and were all sitting in their lodges, their bodies bedaubed from head to foot with white clay, and a lock of hair cut from each of their foreheads.

The warriors circled three times round the village; and as each distinguished champion passed, the old women would scream out his name, in honor of his bravery, and to incite the emulation of the younger warriors. Little urchins, not two years old, followed the warlike pageant with glittering eyes, and looked with eager wonder and admiration at those whose honors were proclaimed by the public voice of the village. Thus early is the lesson of war instilled into the mind of an Indian, and such are the stimulants which excite his thirst for martial renown.

The procession rode out of the village as it had entered it, and in half an hour all the warriors had returned again, drop-ping quietly in, singly or in parties of two or three.

As the sun rose next morning we looked across the meadow, and could see the lodges levelled and the Indians gathering together in preparation to leave the camp. Their course lay to the westward. We turned toward the north with our three men, the four trappers following us, with the Indian family of Moran. We travelled until night. I suffered not a little from pain and weakness. We encamped among some trees by the side of a little brook, and here during the whole of the next day we lay waiting for Bisonette, but no Bisonette appeared. Here also two of our trapper friends left us, and set out for the Rocky Mountains. On the second morning, de-spairing of Bisonette's arrival, we resumed our journey, tra-versing a forlorn and dreary monotony of sun-scorched plains, where no living thing appeared save here and there an antelope flying before us like the wind. When noon came we saw an unwonted and most welcome sight; a rich and luxuri-ant growth of trees, marking the course of a little stream called Horse-shoe Creek. We turned gladly toward it. There were lofty and spreading trees, standing widely asunder, and supporting a thick canopy of leaves, above a surface of rich, tall grass. The stream ran swiftly, as clear as crystal, through the bosom of the wood, sparkling over its bed of white sand, and darkening again as it entered a deep cavern of leaves and boughs. I was thoroughly exhausted, and flung myself on the ground, scarcely able to move. All that afternoon I lay in the shade by the side of the stream, and those bright woods and sparkling waters are associated in my mind with recollections of lassitude and utter prostration. When night came I sat down by the fire, longing, with an intensity of which at this moment I can hardly conceive, for some powerful stimulant.

In the morning, as glorious a sun rose upon us as ever ani-mated that desolate wilderness. We advanced, and soon were surrounded by tall bare hills, overspread from top to bottom with prickly-pears and other cacti, that seemed like clinging reptiles. A plain, flat and hard, and with scarcely the vestige of grass, lay before us, and a line of tall misshapen trees bounded the onward view. There was no sight or sound of man or beast, or any living thing, although behind those trees was the long-looked-for place of rendezvous, where we fondly hoped to have found the Indians congregated by thousands. We looked and listened anxiously. We pushed forward with our best speed, and forced our horses through the trees. There were copses of some extent beyond, with a scanty stream creeping through their midst; and as we pressed through the yielding branches, deer sprang up to the right and left. At length we caught a glimpse of the prairie beyond. Soon we emerged upon it, and saw, not a plain covered with encampments and swarming with life, but a vast unbroken desert stretching away before us league upon league, without a bush or a tree, or any thing that had life. We drew rein and gave to the winds our sentiments concerning the whole aboriginal race of America. Our journey was in vain, and much worse than in vain. For myself, I was vexed and disappointed beyond measure; as I well knew that a slight aggravation of my disorder would render this false step irrevocable, and make it quite impossible to accomplish effectually the design which had led me an arduous journey of between three and four thousand miles. To fortify myself as well as I could against such a contingency, I resolved that I would not under any circumstances attempt to leave the country until my object was completely gained.

And where were the Indians? They were assembled in great numbers at a spot about twenty miles distant, and there at that very moment they were engaged in their warlike ceremonies. The scarcity of buffalo in the vicinity of La Bonte's camp, which would render their supply of provisions scanty and precarious, had probably prevented them from assembling there; but of all this we knew nothing until some weeks after.

Shaw lashed his horse and galloped forward. I, though much more vexed than he, was not strong enough to adopt this convenient vent to my feelings; so I followed at a quiet pace, but in no quiet mood. We rode up to a solitary old tree, which seemed the only place fit for encampment. Half its branches were dead, and the rest were so scantily furnished with leaves that they cast but a meagre and wretched shade, and the old twisted trunk alone furnished sufficient protection from the sun. We threw down our saddles in the strip of shadow that it cast, and sat down upon them. In silent indignation we remained smoking for an hour or more, shifting our saddles with the shifting shadow, for the sun was intolerably hot.

Chapter XIII.

HUNTING INDIANS.

——"I tread,
With fainting steps and slow,
Where wilds immeasurably spread
Seem lengthening as I go."
GOLDSMITH.

A<small>T LAST</small> we had reached La Bonte's camp, toward which our eyes had turned so long. Of all weary hours, those that passed between noon and sunset of the day when we arrived there may bear away the palm of exquisite discomfort. I lay under the tree reflecting on what course to pursue, watching the shadows which seemed never to move, and the sun which remained fixed in the sky, and hoping every moment to see the men and horses of Bisonette emerging from the woods. Shaw and Henry had ridden out on a scouting expedition, and did not return until the sun was setting. There was nothing very cheering in their faces nor in the news they brought.

'We have been ten miles from here,' said Shaw. 'We climbed the highest butte we could find, and could not see a buffalo or Indian; nothing but prairie for twenty miles around us.' Henry's horse was quite disabled by clambering up and down the sides of ravines, and Shaw's was severely fatigued.

After supper that evening, as we sat around the fire, I proposed to Shaw to wait one day longer, in hopes of Bisonette's arrival, and if he should not come, to send Delorier with the cart and baggage back to Fort Laramie, while we ourselves followed the Whirlwind's village, and attempted to overtake it as it passed the mountains. Shaw, not having the same motive for hunting Indians that I had, was averse to the plan; I therefore resolved to go alone. This design I adopted very unwillingly, for I knew that in the present state of my health the attempt would be extremely unpleasant, and as I considered, hazardous. I hoped that Bisonette would appear in the course of the following day, and bring us some information by which to direct our course, and enable me to accomplish my purpose by means less objectionable.

The rifle of Henry Chatillon was necessary for the subsistence of the party in my absence; so I called Raymond, and ordered him to prepare to set out with me. Raymond rolled his eyes vacantly about, but at length, having succeeded in grappling with the idea, he withdrew to his bed under the cart. He was a heavy-moulded fellow, with a broad face, exactly like an owl's, expressing the most impenetrable stupidity and entire self-confidence. As for his good qualities, he had a sort of stubborn fidelity, an insensibility to danger, and a kind of instinct or sagacity, which sometimes led him right, where better heads than his were at a loss. Besides this, he knew very well how to handle a rifle and picket a horse.

Through the following day the sun glared down upon us with a pitiless, penetrating heat. The distant blue prairie seemed quivering under it. The lodge of our Indian associates was baking in the rays, and our rifles, as they leaned against the tree, were too hot for the touch. There was a dead silence through our camp and all around it, unbroken except by the hum of gnats and musquitoes. The men, resting their foreheads on their arms, were sleeping under the cart. The Indians kept close within their lodge, except the newly-married pair, who were seated together under an awning of buffalo-robes, and the old conjurer, who with his hard, emaciated face and gaunt ribs was perched aloft like a turkey-buzzard, among the dead branches of an old tree, constantly on the look-out for enemies. He would have made a capital shot. A rifle bullet, skilfully planted, would have brought him tumbling to the ground. Surely, I thought, there could be no more harm in shooting such a hideous old villain, to see how ugly he would look when he was dead, than in shooting the detestable vulture which he resembled. We dined, and then Shaw saddled his horse.

'I will ride back,' said he, 'to Horse-Shoe Creek, and see if Bisonette is there.'

'I would go with you,' I answered, 'but I must reserve all the strength I have.'

The afternoon dragged away at last. I occupied myself in cleaning my rifle and pistols, and making other preparations for the journey. After supper, Henry Chatillon and I lay by the fire, discussing the properties of that admirable weapon, the rifle, in the use of which he could fairly out-rival Leather-stocking himself.

It was late before I wrapped myself in my blanket, and lay down for the night, with my head on my saddle. Shaw had not returned, but this gave us no uneasiness, for we presumed that he had fallen in with Bisonette, and was spending the night with him. For a day or two past I had gained in strength and health, but about midnight an attack of pain awoke me, and for some hours I felt no inclination to sleep. The moon was quivering on the broad breast of the Platte; nothing could be heard except those low inexplicable sounds, like whisperings and footsteps, which no one who has spent the night alone amid deserts and forests will be at a loss to understand. As I was falling asleep, a familiar voice, shouting from the distance, awoke me again. A rapid step approached the camp, and Shaw on foot, with his gun in his hand, hastily entered.

'Where's your horse?' said I, raising myself on my elbow.

'Lost!' said Shaw. 'Where's Delorier?'

'There,' I replied, pointing to a confused mass of blankets and buffalo robes.

Shaw touched them with the butt of his gun, and up sprang our faithful Canadian.

'Come, Delorier; stir up the fire, and get me something to eat.'

'Where's Bisonette?' asked I.

'The Lord knows; there's nobody at Horse-Shoe Creek.'

Shaw had gone back to the spot where we had encamped two days before, and finding nothing there but the ashes of our fires, he had tied his horse to the tree while he bathed in the stream. Something startled his horse, who broke loose, and for two hours Shaw tried in vain to catch him. Sunset approached, and it was twelve miles to camp. So he abandoned the attempt, and set out on foot to join us. The greater part of his perilous and solitary work was performed in darkness. His moccasons were worn to tatters and his feet severely lacerated. He sat down to eat, however, with the usual equanimity of his temper not at all disturbed by his misfortune, and my last recollection before falling asleep was of Shaw, seated cross-legged before the fire, smoking his pipe. The horse, I may as well mention here, was found the next morning by Henry Chatillon.

When I awoke again there was a fresh damp smell in the air, a gray twilight involved the prairie, and above its eastern verge was a streak of cold red sky. I called to the men, and in a moment a fire was blazing brightly in the dim morning light, and breakfast was getting ready. We sat down together on the grass, to the last civilized meal which Raymond and I were destined to enjoy for some time.

'Now bring in the horses.'

My little mare Pauline was soon standing by the fire. She was a fleet, hardy, and gentle animal, christened after Paul Dorion, from whom I had procured her in exchange for Pontiac. She did not look as if equipped for a morning pleasure ride. In front of the black, high-bowed mountain-saddle, holsters, with heavy pistols, were fastened. A pair of saddle-bags, a blanket tightly rolled, a small parcel of Indian presents tied up in a buffalo-skin, a leather bag of flour, and a smaller one of tea were all secured behind, and a long trail-rope was wound round her neck. Raymond had a strong black mule, equipped in a similar manner. We crammed our powder-horns to the throat, and mounted.

'I will meet you at Fort Laramie on the first of August,' said I to Shaw.

'That is,' replied he, 'if we don't meet before that. I think I shall follow after you in a day or two.'

This in fact he attempted, and he would have succeeded if he had not encountered obstacles against which his resolute spirit was of no avail. Two days after I left him, he sent Delorier to the fort with the cart and baggage, and set out for the mountains with Henry Chatillon; but a tremendous thunder-storm had deluged the prairie, and nearly obliterated not only our trail but that of the Indians themselves. They followed along the base of the mountains, at a loss in which direction to go. They encamped there, and in the morning Shaw found himself poisoned by ivy, in such a manner that it was impossible for him to travel. So they turned back reluctantly toward Fort Laramie. Shaw's limbs were swollen to

double their usual size, and he rode in great pain. They encamped again within twenty miles of the fort, and reached it
early on the following morning. Shaw lay seriously ill for a
week, and remained at the fort till I rejoined him some time
after.

To return to my own story. We shook hands with our
friends, rode out upon the prairie, and clambering the sandy
hollows that were channelled in the sides of the hills, gained
the high plains above. If a curse had been pronounced upon
the land, it could not have worn an aspect of more dreary and
forlorn barrenness. There were abrupt broken hills, deep
hollows and wide plains; but all alike glared with an insupportable whiteness under the burning sun. The country, as if
parched by the heat, had cracked into innumerable fissures
and ravines, that not a little impeded our progress. Their
steep sides were white and raw, and along the bottom we
several times discovered the broad tracks of the terrific grizzly
bear, nowhere more abundant than in this region. The ridges
of the hills were hard as rock, and strewn with pebbles of flint
and coarse red jasper; looking from them, there was nothing
to relieve the desert uniformity of the prospect, save here and
there a pine-tree clinging at the edge of a ravine, and stretching over its rough, shaggy arms. Under the scorching heat,
these melancholy trees diffused their peculiar resinous odor
through the sultry air. There was something in it, as I approached them, that recalled old associations: the pine-clad
mountains of New-England, traversed in days of health and
buoyancy, rose like a reality before my fancy. In passing that
arid waste I was goaded with a morbid thirst produced by my
disorder, and I thought with a longing desire on the crystal
treasure poured in such wasteful profusion from our thousand
hills. Shutting my eyes, I more than half believed that I heard
the deep plunging and gurgling of waters in the bowels of the
shaded rocks. I could see their dark icy glittering far down
amid the crevices, and the cold drops trickling from the long
green mosses.

When noon came, we found a little stream, with a few trees
and bushes; and here we rested for an hour. Then we travelled on, guided by the sun, until, just before sunset, we
reached another stream, called Bitter Cotton-wood Creek. A

thick growth of bushes and old storm-beaten trees grew at intervals along its bank. Near the foot of one of the trees we flung down our saddles, and hobbling our horses, turned them loose to feed. The little stream was clear and swift, and ran musically over its white sands. Small water-birds were splashing in the shallows, and filling the air with their cries and flutterings. The sun was just sinking among gold and crimson clouds behind Mount Laramie. I well remember how I lay upon a log by the margin of the water, and watched the restless motions of the little fish in a deep still nook below. Strange to say, I seemed to have gained strength since the morning, and almost felt a sense of returning health.

We built our fire. Night came, and the wolves began to howl. One deep voice commenced, and it was answered in awful responses from the hills, the plains, and the woods along the stream above and below us. Such sounds need not and do not disturb one's sleep upon the prairie. We picketed the mare and the mule close at our feet, and did not awake until daylight. Then we turned them loose, still hobbled, to feed for an hour before starting. We were getting ready our morning's meal, when Raymond saw an antelope at half a mile's distance, and said he would go and shoot it.

'Your business,' said I, 'is to look after the animals. I am too weak to do much, if any thing happens to them, and you must keep within sight of the camp.'

Raymond promised, and set out with his rifle in his hand. The animals had passed across the stream, and were feeding among the long grass on the other side, much tormented by the attacks of the numerous large green-headed flies. As I watched them, I saw them go down into a hollow, and as several minutes elapsed without their reappearing, I waded through the stream to look after them. To my vexation and alarm I discovered them at a great distance, galloping away at full speed, Pauline in advance, with her hobbles broken, and the mule, still fettered, following with awkward leaps. I fired my rifle and shouted to recall Raymond. In a moment he came running through the stream, with a red handkerchief bound round his head. I pointed to the fugitives, and ordered him to pursue them. Muttering a 'Sacre!' between his teeth, he set out at full speed, still swinging his rifle in his hand. I walked up to the top of a hill, and looking away over the prairie, could just distinguish the runaways, still at full gallop. Returning to the fire, I sat down at the foot of a tree. Wearily and anxiously hour after hour passed away. The old loose bark dangling from the trunk behind me flapped to and fro in the wind, and the mosquitoes kept up their incessant drowsy humming; but other than this, there was no sight nor sound of life throughout the burning landscape. The sun rose higher and higher, until the shadows fell almost perpendicularly, and I knew that it must be noon. It seemed scarcely possible that the animals could be recovered. If they were not, my situation was one of serious difficulty. Shaw, when I left him, had decided to move that morning, but whither he had not determined. To look for him would be a vain attempt. Fort Laramie was forty miles distant, and I could not walk a mile without great effort. Not then having learned the sound philosophy of yielding to disproportionate obstacles, I resolved to continue in any event the pursuit of the Indians. Only one plan occurred to me; this was, to send Raymond to the fort with an order for more horses, while I remained on the spot, awaiting his return, which might take place within three days. But the adoption of this resolution did not wholly allay my anxiety, for it involved both uncertainty and danger. To remain stationary and alone for three days, in a country full of dangerous Indians, was not the most flattering of prospects; and protracted as my Indian hunt must be by such delay, it was not easy to foretell its ultimate result. Revolving these matters, I grew hungry; and as our stock of provisions, except four or five pounds of flour, was by this time exhausted, I left the camp to see what game I could find. Nothing could be seen except four or five large curlew, which, with their loud screaming, were wheeling over my head, and now and then alighting upon the prairie. I shot two of them, and was about returning, when a startling sight caught my eye. A small, dark object, like a human head, suddenly appeared, and vanished among the thick bushes along the stream below. In that country every stranger is a suspected enemy. Instinctively I threw forward the muzzle of my rifle. In a moment the bushes were violently shaken, two heads, but not human heads, protruded, and to my great joy I recognized the downcast, disconsolate countenance of the black mule and the yellow visage of Pauline. Raymond came upon the mule, pale and haggard, complaining of a fiery pain in his chest. I took charge of the animals while he kneeled down by the side of the stream to drink. He had kept the runaways in sight as far as the Side Fork of Laramie Creek, a distance of more than ten miles; and here with great difficulty he had succeeded in catching them. I saw that he was unarmed, and asked him what he had done with his rifle. It had encumbered him in his pursuit, and he had dropped it on the prairie, thinking that he could find it on his return; but in this he had failed. The loss might prove a very formidable one. I was too much rejoiced however at the recovery of the animals to think much about it; and having made some tea for Raymond in a tin vessel which we had brought with us, I told him that I would give him two hours for resting before we set out again. He had eaten nothing that day; but having no appetite, he lay down immediately to sleep. I picketed the animals among the richest grass that I could find, and made fires of green wood to protect them from the flies; then sitting down again by the tree, I watched the slow movements of the sun, begrudging every moment that passed.

The time I had mentioned expired, and I awoke Raymond. We saddled and set out again, but first we went in search of the lost rifle, and in the course of an hour Raymond was fortunate enough to find it. Then we turned westward, and moved over the hills and hollows at a slow pace towards the Black Hills. The heat no longer tormented us, for a cloud was before the sun. Yet that day shall never be marked with white in my calendar. The air began to grow fresh and cool, the distant mountains frowned more gloomily, there was a low muttering of thunder, and dense black masses of cloud rose heavily behind the broken peaks. At first they were gayly fringed with silver by the afternoon sun; but soon the thick blackness overspread the whole sky, and the desert around us was wrapped in deep gloom. I scarcely heeded it at the time, but now I cannot but feel that there was an awful sublimity in the hoarse murmuring of the thunder, in the sombre shadows that involved the mountains and the plain. The storm broke. It came upon us with a zigzag blinding flash, with a terrific crash of thunder, and with a hurricane that howled over the prairie, dashing floods of water against us. Raymond looked round, and cursed the merciless elements. There seemed no shelter near, but we discerned at length a deep ravine gashed in the level prairie, and saw half way down its side an old pine tree, whose rough horizontal boughs formed a sort of pent-house against the tempest. We found a practicable passage, and hastily descending, fastened our animals to some large loose stones at the bottom; then climbing up, we drew our blankets over our heads, and seated ourselves close beneath the old tree. Perhaps I was no competent judge of time, but it seemed to me that we were sitting there a full hour, while around us poured a deluge of rain, through which the rocks on the opposite side of the gulf were barely visible. The first burst of the tempest soon subsided, but the rain poured steadily. At length Raymond grew impatient, and scrambling out of the ravine, he gained the level prairie above.

'What does the weather look like?' asked I, from my seat under the tree.

'It looks bad,' he answered; 'dark all around,' and again he descended and sat down by my side. Some ten minutes elapsed.

'Go up again,' said I, 'and take another look;' and he clambered up the precipice. 'Well, how is it?'

'Just the same, only I see one little bright spot over the top of the mountain.'

The rain by this time had begun to abate; and going down to the bottom of the ravine, we loosened the animals, who were standing up to their knees in water. Leading them up the rocky throat of the ravine, we reached the plain above. 'Am I,' I thought to myself, 'the same man who, a few months since, was seated, a quiet student of belles-lettres, in a cushioned arm-chair by a sea-coal fire?'

All around us was obscurity; but the bright spot above the mountain-tops grew wider and ruddier, until at length the clouds drew apart, and a flood of sunbeams poured down from heaven, streaming along the precipices, and involving them in a thin blue haze, as soft and lovely as that which wraps the Apennines on an evening in spring. Rapidly the clouds were broken and scattered, like routed legions of evil spirits. The plain lay basking in sunbeams around us; a rainbow arched the desert from north to south, and far in front a line of woods seemed inviting us to refreshment and repose. When we reached them, they were glistening with prismatic dew-drops, and enlivened by the songs and flutterings of a hundred birds. Strange winged insects, benumbed by the rain, were clinging to the leaves and the bark of the trees.

Raymond kindled a fire with great difficulty. The animals turned eagerly to feed on the soft rich grass, while I, wrapping myself in my blanket, lay down and gazed on the evening landscape. The mountains, whose stern features had lowered upon us with so gloomy and awful a frown, now seemed lighted up with a serene, benignant smile, and the green waving undulations of the plain were gladdened with the rich sunshine. Wet, ill, and wearied as I was, my spirit grew lighter at the view, and I drew from it an augury of good for my future prospects.

When morning came, Raymond awoke, coughing violently, though I had apparently received no injury. We mounted, crossed the little stream, pushed through the trees, and began our journey over the plain beyond. And now, as we rode slowly along, we looked anxiously on every hand for traces of the Indians, not doubting that the village had passed somewhere in that vicinity; but the scanty shrivelled grass was not more than three or four inches high, and the ground was of such unyielding hardness that a host might have marched over it and left scarcely a trace of its passage. Up hill and down hill, and clambering through ravines, we continued our journey. As we were skirting the foot of a hill, I saw Raymond, who was some rods in advance, suddenly jerking the reins of his mule. Sliding from his seat, and running in a crouching posture up a hollow, he disappeared; and then in an instant I heard the sharp quick crack of his rifle. A wounded antelope came running on three legs over the hill. I lashed Pauline and made after him. My fleet little mare soon brought me by his side, and after leaping and bounding for a few moments in vain, he stood still, as if despairing of escape. His glistening eyes turned up toward my face with so piteous a look, that it was with feelings of infinite compunction that I shot him through the head with a pistol. Raymond skinned and cut him up, and we hung the fore-quarters to our saddles, much rejoiced that our exhausted stock of provisions was renewed in such good time.

Gaining the top of a hill, we could see along the cloudy verge of the prairie before us lines of trees and shadowy groves, that marked the course of Laramie Creek. Some time before noon we reached its banks, and began anxiously to search them for footprints of the Indians. We followed the stream for several miles, now on the shore and now wading in the water, scrutinizing every sand-bar and every muddy bank. So long was the search, that we began to fear that we had left the trail undiscovered behind us. At length I heard Raymond shouting, and saw him jump from his mule to examine some object under the shelving bank. I rode up to his side. It was the clear and palpable impression of an Indian moccason. Encouraged by this, we continued our search, and at last some appearances on a soft surface of earth not far from the shore attracted my eye; and going to examine them, I found half a dozen tracks, some made by men and some by children. Just then Raymond observed across the stream the mouth of a small branch, entering it from the south. He forded the water, rode in at the opening, and in a moment I heard him shouting again; so I passed over and joined him. The little branch had a broad sandy bed, along which the water trickled in a scanty stream; and on either bank the bushes were so close that the view was completely intercepted. I found Raymond stooping over the footprints of three or four horses. Proceeding, we found those of a man, then those of a child, then those of more horses; and at last the bushes on each bank were beaten down and broken, and the sand ploughed up with a multitude of footsteps, and scored across with the furrows made by the lodge-poles that had been dragged through. It was now certain that we had found the trail. I pushed through the bushes, and at a little distance on the prairie beyond found the ashes of an hundred and fifty lodge-fires, with bones and pieces of buffalo-robes scattered around them, and in some instances the pickets to which horses had been secured still standing in the ground. Elated by our success, we selected a convenient tree, and turning the animals loose, prepared to make a meal from the fat haunch of our victim.

Hardship and exposure had thriven with me wonderfully. I had gained both health and strength since leaving La Bonte's camp. Raymond and I made a hearty meal together, in high spirits; for we rashly presumed that having found one end of the trail we should have little difficulty in reaching the other. But when the animals were led in, we found that our old ill-luck had not ceased to follow us close. As I was saddling Pauline, I saw that her eye was as dull as lead, and the hue of her yellow coat visibly darkened. I placed my foot in the stirrup to mount, when instantly she staggered and fell flat on her side. Gaining her feet with an effort, she stood by the fire with a drooping head. Whether she had been bitten by a snake, or poisoned by some noxious plant, or attacked by a sudden disorder, it was hard to say; but at all events, her sickness was sufficiently ill-timed and unfortunate. I succeeded in a second attempt to mount her, and with a slow pace we moved forward on the trail of the Indians. It led us up a hill and over a dreary plain; and here, to our great mortification, the traces almost disappeared, for the ground was hard as adamant; and if its flinty surface had ever retained the dint of a hoof, the marks had been washed away by the deluge of yesterday. An Indian village, in its disorderly march, is scattered over the prairie, often to the width of full half a mile; so that its trail is nowhere clearly marked, and the task of following it is made doubly wearisome and difficult. By good fortune, plenty of large ant-hills, a yard or more in diameter, were scattered over the plain, and these were frequently broken by the footprints of men and horses, and marked by traces of the lodge-poles. The succulent leaves of the prickly pear, also, bruised from the same causes, helped a little to guide us; so, inch by inch, we moved along. Often we lost the trail altogether, and then would recover it again; but late in the afternoon we found ourselves totally at fault. We stood alone, without a clue to guide us. The broken plain expanded for league after league around us, and in front the long dark ridge of mountains was stretching from north to south. Mount Laramie, a little on our right, towered high above the rest, and from a dark valley just beyond one of its lower declivities, we discerned volumes of white smoke, slowly rolling up into the clear air.

'I think,' said Raymond, 'some Indians must be there. Perhaps we had better go.' But this plan was not rashly to be adopted, and we determined still to continue our search after the lost trail. Our good stars prompted us to this decision, for we afterward had reason to believe, from information given us by the Indians, that the smoke was raised as a decoy by a Crow war-party.

Evening was coming on, and there was no wood or water nearer than the foot of the mountains. So thither we turned, directing our course toward the point where Laramie Creek issues forth upon the prairie. When we reached it, the bare tops of the mountains were still brightened with sunshine. The little river was breaking, with a vehement and angry current, from its dark prison. There was something in the near vicinity of the mountains, in the loud surging of the rapids, wonderfully cheering and exhilarating; for although once as familiar as home itself, they had been for months strangers to my experience. There was a rich grass-plot by the river's bank, surrounded by low ridges, which would effectually screen ourselves and our fire from the sight of wandering Indians. Here, among the grass, I observed numerous circles of large stones, which, as Raymond said, were traces of a Dahcotah winter encampment. We lay down, and did not awake till the sun was up. A large rock projected from the shore, and behind it the deep water was slowly eddying round and round. The temptation was irresistible. I threw off my clothes, leaped in, suffered myself to be borne once round with the current, and then, seizing the strong root of a water-plant, drew myself to the shore. The effect was so invigorating and refreshing, that I mistook it for returning health. 'Pauline,' thought I, as I led the little mare up to be saddled, 'only thrive as I do, and you and I will have sport yet among the buffalo beyond these mountains.' But scarcely were we mounted and on our way, before the momentary glow passed. Again I hung as usual in my seat, scarcely able to hold myself erect.

'Look yonder,' said Raymond; 'you see that big hollow there; the Indians must have gone that way, if they went any where about here.'

We reached the gap, which was like a deep notch cut into the mountain-ridge, and here we soon discerned an ant-hill furrowed with the mark of a lodge-pole. This was quite enough; there could be no doubt now. As we rode on, the opening growing narrower, the Indians had been compelled to march in closer order, and the traces became numerous and distinct. The gap terminated in a rocky gateway, leading into a rough passage upward, between two precipitous mountains. Here grass and weeds were bruised to fragments by the throng that had passed through. We moved slowly over the rocks, up the passage; and in this toilsome manner we advanced for an hour or two, bare precipices, hundreds of feet high, shooting up on either hand. Raymond, with his hardy mule, was a few rods before me, when we came to the foot of an ascent steeper than the rest, and which I trusted might prove the highest point of the defile. Pauline strained upward for a few yards, moaning and stumbling, and then came to a dead stop, unable to proceed further. I dismounted, and attempted to lead her; but my own exhausted strength soon gave out; so I loosened the trail-rope from her neck, and tying it round my arm, crawled up on my hands and knees. I gained the top, totally exhausted, the sweat-drops trickling from my forehead. Pauline stood like a statue by my side, her shadow falling upon the scorching rock; and in this shade, for there was no other, I lay for some time, scarcely able to move a limb. All around, the black crags, sharp as needles at the top, stood glowing in the sun, without a tree, or a bush, or a blade of grass, to cover their precipitous sides. The whole scene seemed parched with a pitiless, insufferable heat.

After awhile I could mount again, and we moved on, descending the rocky defile on its western side. Thinking of that morning's journey, it has sometimes seemed to me that there was something ridiculous in my position; a man, armed to the teeth, but wholly unable to fight, and equally so to run away, traversing a dangerous wilderness, on a sick horse. But these thoughts were retrospective, for at the time I was in too grave a mood to entertain a very lively sense of the ludicrous.

Raymond's saddle-girth slipped; and while I proceeded he was stopping behind to repair the mischief. I came to the top of a little declivity, where a most welcome sight greeted my eye; a nook of fresh green grass, nest bed among the cliffs, sunny clumps of bushes on one side, and shaggy old pine-trees leaning forward from the rocks on the other. A shrill, familiar voice saluted me, and recalled me to days of boy-hood; that of the insect called the 'locust' by New-England schoolboys, which was fast clinging among the heated boughs of the old pine-trees. Then, too, as I passed the bushes, the low sound of falling water reached my ear. Pauline turned of her own accord, and pushing through the boughs, we found a black rock, overarched by the cool green canopy. An icy stream was pouring from its side into a wide basin of white sand, from whence it had no visible outlet, but filtered through into the soil below. While I filled a tin cup at the spring, Pauline was eagerly plunging her head deep in the pool. Other visitors had been there before us. All around in the soft soil were the footprints of elk, deer, and the Rocky Mountain sheep; and the grizzly-bear too had left the recent prints of his broad foot, with its frightful array of claws. Among these mountains was his home.

Soon after leaving the spring we found a little grassy plain, encircled by the mountains, and marked, to our great joy, with all the traces of an Indian camp. Raymond's practised eye detected certain signs, by which he recognized the spot where Reynal's lodge had been pitched and his horses pick-eted. I approached, and stood looking at the place. Reynal and I had, I believe, hardly a feeling in common. I disliked the fellow, and it perplexed me a good deal to understand why I should look with so much interest on the ashes of his fire, when between him and me there seemed no other bond of sympathy than the slender and precarious one of a kindred race.

In half an hour from this we were clear of the mountains. There was a plain before us, totally barren and thickly-peopled in many parts with the little prairie-dogs, who sat at the mouths of their burrows and yelped at us as we passed.

The plain, as we thought, was about six miles wide; but it cost us two hours to cross it. Then another mountain-range rose before us, grander and more wild than the last had been. Far out of the dense shubbery that clothed the steeps for a thousand feet shot up black crags, all leaning one way, and shattered by storms and thunder into grim and threatening shapes. As we entered a narrow passage on the trail of the Indians, they impended frightfully on one side, above our heads.

Our course was through dense woods, in the shade and twinkling sunlight of overhanging boughs. I would I could recall to mind all the startling combinations that presented themselves, as winding from side to side of the passage, to avoid its obstructions, we could see, glancing at intervals through the foliage, the awful forms of the gigantic cliffs, that seemed at times to hem us in on the right and on the left, before us and behind! Another scene in a few moments greeted us; a tract of gay and sunny woods, broken into knolls and hollows, enlivened by birds and interspersed with flowers. Among the rest I recognized the mellow whistle of the robin, an old familiar friend, whom I had scarce expected to meet in such a place. Humble-bees too were buzzing heavily about the flowers; and of these a species of larkspur caught my eye, more appropriate, it should seem, to culti-vated gardens than to a remote wilderness. Instantly it re-called a multitude of dormant and delightful recollections.

Leaving behind us this spot and its associations, a sight soon presented itself, characteristic of that warlike region. In an open space, fenced in by high rocks, stood two Indian forts, of a square form, rudely built of sticks and logs. They were somewhat ruinous, having probably been constructed the year before. Each might have contained about twenty men. Perhaps in this gloomy spot some party had been beset by their enemies, and those scowling rocks and blasted trees might not long since have looked down on a conflict, un-chronicled and unknown. Yet if any traces of bloodshed re-mained they were completely hidden by the bushes and tall rank weeds.

Gradually the mountains drew apart, and the passage ex-panded into a plain, where again we found traces of an Indian encampment. There were trees and bushes just before us, and we stopped here for an hour's rest and refreshment. When we had finished our meal, Raymond struck fire, and lighting his pipe, sat down at the foot of a tree to smoke. For some time I observed him puffing away with a face of unusual solemnity. Then slowly taking the pipe from his lips, he looked up and remarked that we had better not go any farther.

'Why not?' asked I.

He said that the country was become very dangerous, that we were entering the range of the Snakes, Arapahoes, and Gros-ventre Blackfeet, and that if any of their wandering parties should meet us, it would cost us our lives; but he added, with a blunt fidelity that nearly reconciled me to his stupidity, that he would go any where I wished. I told him to bring up the animals, and mounting them we proceeded again. I confess that, as we moved forward, the prospect seemed but a dreary and doubtful one. I would have given the world for my ordinary elasticity of body and mind, and for a horse of such strength and spirit as the journey required.

Closer and closer the rocks gathered round us, growing taller and steeper, and pressing more and more upon our path. We entered at length a defile which I never have seen rivalled. The mountain was cracked from top to bottom, and we were creeping along the bottom of the fissure, in dampness and gloom, with the clink of hoofs on the loose shingly rocks, and the hoarse murmuring of a petulant brook which kept us company. Sometimes the water, foaming among the stones, overspread the whole narrow passage; sometimes, withdrawing to one side, it gave us room to pass dry-shod. Looking up, we could see a narrow ribbon of bright blue sky between the dark edges of the opposing cliffs. This did not last long. The passage soon widened, and sunbeams found their way down, flashing upon the black waters. The defile would spread out to many rods in width; bushes, trees and flowers would spring by the side of the brook; the cliffs would be feathered with shrubbery, that clung in every crevice, and fringed with trees, that grew along their sunny edges. Then we would be moving again in the darkness. The passage seemed about four miles long, and before we reached the end of it, the unshod hoofs of our animals were lamentably broken, and their legs cut by the sharp stones. Issuing from the mountain we found another plain. All around it stood a circle of lofty precipices, that seemed the impersonation of Silence and Solitude. Here again the Indians had encamped, as well they might, after passing with their women, children, and horses, through the gulf behind us. In one day we had made a journey which had cost them three to accomplish.

The only outlet to this amphitheatre lay over a hill some two hundred feet high, up which we moved with difficulty. Looking from the top, we saw that at last we were free of the mountains. The prairie spread before us, but so wild and broken that the view was every where obstructed. Far on our left one tall hill swelled up against the sky, on the smooth, pale-green surface of which four slowly moving black specks were discernible. They were evidently buffalo, and we hailed the sight as a good augury; for where the buffalo were, there too the Indians would probably be found. We hoped on that very night to reach the village. We were anxious to do so for a double reason, wishing to bring our wearisome journey to an end, and knowing moreover that though to enter the village in broad daylight would be a perfectly safe experiment, yet to encamp in its vicinity would be dangerous. But as we rode on, the sun was sinking, and soon was within half an hour of the horizon. We ascended a hill and looked round us for a spot for our encampment. The prairie was like a turbulent ocean, suddenly congealed when its waves were at the highest, and it lay half in light and half in shadow, as the rich sunshine, yellow as gold, was pouring over it. The rough bushes of the wild sage were growing every where, its dull pale-green overspreading hill and hollow. Yet a little way before us, a bright verdant line of grass was winding along the plain, and here and there throughout its course water was glistening darkly. We went down to it, kindled a fire, and turned our horses loose to feed. It was a little trickling brook, that for some yards on either bank turned the barren prairie into fertility, and here and there it spread into deep pools, where the beaver had dammed it up.

We placed our last remaining piece of the antelope before a scanty fire, mournfully reflecting on our exhausted stock of provisions. Just then an enormous gray hare, peculiar to these prairies, came jumping along, and seated himself within fifty yards to look at us. I thoughtlessly raised my rifle to shoot him, but Raymond called out to me not to fire for fear the report should reach the ears of the Indians. That night for the first time we considered that the danger to which we were exposed was of a somewhat serious character; and to those who are unacquainted with Indians, it may seem strange that our chief apprehensions arose from the supposed proximity of the people whom we intended to visit. Had any straggling party of these faithful friends caught sight of us from the hill-top, they would probably have returned in the night to plunder us of our horses and perhaps of our scalps. But we were on the prairie, where the *genius loci* is at war with all nervous apprehensions; and I presume that neither Raymond nor I thought twice of the matter that evening.

While he was looking after the animals, I sat by the fire engaged in the novel task of baking bread. The utensils were of the most simple and primitive kind, consisting of two sticks inclining over the bed of coals, one end thrust into the ground while the dough was twisted in a spiral form round the other. Under such circumstances all the epicurean in a man's nature is apt to awaken within him. I revisited in fancy the far distant abodes of good fare, not indeed Frascati's, or the Trois Frères Provençaux, for that were too extreme a flight; but no other than the homely table of my old friend and host, Tom Crawford, of the White Mountains. By a singular revulsion, Tom himself, whom I well remember to have looked upon as the impersonation of all that is wild and backwoodsman-like, now appeared before me as the ministering angel of comfort and good living. Being fatigued and drowsy, I began to doze, and my thoughts, following the same train of association, assumed another form. Half-dreaming, I saw myself surrounded with the mountains of New England, alive with water-falls, their black crags cinctured with milk-white mists. For this reverie I paid a speedy penalty; for the bread was black on one side and soft on the other.

For eight hours Raymond and I, pillowed on our saddles, lay insensible as logs. Pauline's yellow head was stretched over me when I awoke. I got up and examined her. Her feet indeed were bruised and swollen by the accidents of yesterday, but her eye was brighter, her motions livelier, and her mysterious malady had visibly abated. We moved on, hoping within an hour to come in sight of the Indian village; but again disappointment awaited us. The trail disappeared, melting away upon a hard and stony plain. Raymond and I separating, rode from side to side, scrutinizing every yard of ground, until at length I discerned traces of the lodge-poles, passing by the side of a ridge of rocks. We began again to follow them.

'What is that black spot out there on the prairie?'

'It looks like a dead buffalo,' answered Raymond.

We rode out to it, and found it to be the huge carcass of a bull killed by the hunters as they had passed. Tangled hair and scraps of hide were scattered all around, for the wolves had been making merry over it, and had hollowed out the entire carcass. It was covered with myriads of large black crickets, and from its appearance must certainly have lain there for four or five days. The sight was a most disheartening one, and I observed to Raymond that the Indians might still be fifty or sixty miles before us. But he shook his head, and replied that they dared not go so far for fear of their enemies, the Snakes.

Soon after this we lost the trail again, and ascended a neighboring ridge, totally at a loss. Before us lay a plain perfectly flat, spreading on the right and left, without apparent limit, and bounded in front by a long broken line of hills, ten or twelve miles distant. All was open and exposed to view, yet not a buffalo nor an Indian was visible.

'Do you see that!' said Raymond; 'now we had better turn round.'

But as Raymond's *bourgeois* thought otherwise, we descended the hill and began to cross the plain. We had come so far that I knew, perfectly well, neither Pauline's limbs nor my own could carry me back to Fort Laramie. I considered that the lines of expediency and inclination tallied exactly, and that the most prudent course was to keep forward. The ground immediately around us was thickly strewn with the skulls and bones of buffalo, for here a year or two before the Indians had made a 'surround;' yet no living game presented itself. At length, however, an antelope sprang up and gazed at us. We fired together, and by a singular fatality we both missed, although the animal stood, a fair mark, within eighty yards. This ill success might perhaps be charged to our own eagerness, for by this time we had no provision left except a little flour. We could discern several small lakes, or rather extensive pools of water, glistening in the distance. As we approached them, wolves and antelope bounded away through the tall grass that grew in their vicinity, and flocks of large white plover flew screaming over their surface. Having failed of the antelope, Raymond tried his hand at the birds, with the same ill-success. The water also disappointed us. Its muddy margin was so beaten up by the crowd of buffalo that our timorous animals were afraid to approach. So we turned away and moved toward the hills. The rank grass, where it was not trampled down by the buffalo, fairly swept our horses' necks.

Again we found the same execrable barren prairie offering no clue by which to guide our way. As we drew near the hills, an opening appeared, through which the Indians must have gone if they had passed that way at all. Slowly we began to ascend it. I felt the most dreary forebodings of ill-success, when on looking round I could discover neither dent of hoof, not footprint, nor trace of lodge-pole, though the passage was encumbered by the ghastly skulls of buffalo. We heard thunder muttering; a storm was coming on.

As we gained the top of the gap, the prospect beyond began to disclose itself. First, we saw a long dark line of ragged clouds upon the horizon, while above them rose the peak of the Medicine-Bow, the vanguard of the Rocky Mountains; then little by little the plain came into view, a vast green uniformity, forlorn and tenantless, though Laramie Creek glistened in a waving line over its surface, without a bush or a tree upon its banks. As yet, the round projecting shoulder of a hill intercepted a part of the view. I rode in advance, when suddenly I could distinguish a few dark spots on the prairie, along the bank of the stream.

'Buffalo!' said I. Then a sudden hope flashed upon me, and eagerly and anxiously I looked again.

'Horses!' exclaimed Raymond, with a tremendous oath, lashing his mule forward as he spoke. More and more of the plain disclosed itself, and in rapid succession more and more horses appeared, scattered along the river bank, or feeding in bands over the prairie. Then, suddenly standing in a circle by the stream, swarming with their savage inhabitants, we saw rising before us the tall lodges of the Ogillallah. Never did the heart of wanderer more gladden at the sight of home than did mine at the sight of those wild habitations!

Chapter XIV.

THE OGILLALLAH VILLAGE.

"They waste us—ay—like April snow,
    In the warm noon, we shrink away;
And fast they follow, as we go
    Towards the setting day."

                                        BRYANT.

SUCH A NARRATIVE as this is hardly the place for portraying the mental features of the Indians. The same picture, slightly changed in shade and coloring, would serve with very few exceptions for all the tribes that lie north of the Mexican territories. But with this striking similarity in their modes of thought, the tribes of the lake and ocean shores, of the forests and of the plains, differ greatly in their manner of life. Having been domesticated for several weeks among one of the wildest of the wild hordes that roam over the remote prairies, I had extraordinary opportunities of observing them, and I flatter myself that a faithful picture of the scenes that passed daily before my eyes may not be devoid of interest and value. These men were thorough savages. Neither their manners nor their ideas were in the slightest degree modified by contact with civilization. They knew nothing of the power and real character of the white men, and their children would scream in terror at the sight of me. Their religion, their superstitions and their prejudices were the same that had been handed down to them from immemorial time. They fought with the same weapons that their fathers fought with, and wore the same rude garments of skins.

Great changes are at hand in that region. With the stream of emigration to Oregon and California, the buffalo will dwindle away, and the large wandering communities who depend on them for support must be broken and scattered. The Indians will soon be corrupted by the example of the whites, abased by whisky and overawed by military posts; so that within a few years the traveller may pass in tolerable security through their country. Its danger and its charm will have disappeared together.

As soon as Raymond and I discovered the village from the gap in the hills, we were seen in our turn; keen eyes were constantly on the watch. As we rode down upon the plain, the side of the village nearest us was darkened with a crowd of naked figures gathering around the lodges. Several men came forward to meet us. I could distinguish among them the green blanket of the Frenchman Reynal. When we came up the ceremony of shaking hands had to be gone through with in due form, and then all were eager to know what had become of the rest of my party. I satisfied them on this point, and we all moved forward together toward the village.

'You've missed it,' said Reynal; 'if you'd been here day before yesterday, you'd have found the whole prairie over yonder black with buffalo as far as you could see. There were no cows, though; nothing but bulls. We made a "surround" every day till yesterday. See the village there; don't that look like good living?'

In fact I could see, even at that distance, that long cords were stretched from lodge to lodge, over which the meat, cut by the squaws into thin sheets, was hanging to dry in the sun. I noticed too that the village was somewhat smaller than when I had last seen it, and I asked Reynal the cause. He said that old Le Borgne had felt too weak to pass over the mountains, and so had remained behind with all his relations, including Mahto-Tatonka and his brothers. The Whirlwind too had been unwilling to come so far, because, as Reynal said, he was afraid. Only half a dozen lodges had adhered to him, the main-body of the village setting their chief's authority at naught, and taking the course most agreeable to their inclinations.

'What chiefs are there in the village now?' said I.

'Well,' said Reynal, 'there's old Red-Water, and the Eagle-Feather, and the Big Crow, and the Mad Wolf and the Panther, and the White-Shield, and—what's his name?—the half-breed Shienne.'

By this time we were close to the village, and I observed that while the greater part of the lodges were very large and neat in their appearance, there was at one side a cluster of squalid, miserable huts. I looked toward them, and made some remark about their wretched appearance. But I was touching upon delicate ground.

'My squaw's relations live in those lodges,' said Reynal, very warmly, 'and there isn't a better set in the whole village.'

'Are there any chiefs among them?' asked I.

'Chiefs?' said Reynal; 'yes, plenty!'

'What are their names?' I inquired.

'Their names? Why, there's the Arrow-Head. If he isn't a chief he ought to be one. And there's the Hail-Storm. He's nothing but a boy, to be sure; but he's bound to be a chief one of these days!'

Just then we passed between two of the lodges, and entered the great area of the village. Superb, naked figures stood silently gazing on us.

'Where's the Bad Wound's lodge?' said I to Reynal.

'There you've missed it again! The Bad Wound is away with the Whirlwind. If you could have found him here, and gone to live in his lodge, he would have treated you better than any man in the village. But there's the Big Crow's lodge yonder, next to old Red-Water's. He's a good Indian for the whites, and I advise you to go and live with him.'

'Are there many squaws and children in his lodge?' said I.

'No; only one squaw and two or three children. He keeps the rest in a separate lodge by themselves.'

So, still followed by a crowd of Indians, Raymond and I rode up to the entrance of the Big Crow's lodge. A squaw came out immediately and took our horses. I put aside the leather flap that covered the low opening, and stooping, entered the Big Crow's dwelling. There I could see the chief in the dim light, seated at one side, on a pile of buffalo-robes. He greeted me with a guttural 'How, cola!' I requested Reynal to tell him that Raymond and I were come to live with him. The Big Crow gave another low exclamation. If the reader thinks that we were intruding somewhat cavalierly, I beg him to observe that every Indian in the village would have deemed himself honored that white men should give such preference to his hospitality.

The squaw spread a buffalo-robe for us in the guest's place at the head of the lodge. Our saddles were brought in, and scarcely were we seated upon them before the place was thronged with Indians, who came crowding in to see us. The Big Crow produced his pipe and filled it with the mixture of tobacco and *shongsasha*, or red willow bark. Round and round it passed, and a lively conversation went forward. Meanwhile a squaw placed before the two guests a wooden bowl of boiled buffalo-meat, but unhappily this was not the only banquet destined to be inflicted on us. Rapidly, one after another, boys and young squaws thrust their heads in at the opening, to invite us to various feasts in different parts of the village. For half an hour or more we were actively engaged in passing from lodge to lodge, tasting in each of the bowl of meat set before us, and inhaling a whiff or two from our entertainer's pipe. A thunder-storm that had been threatening for some time now began in good earnest. We crossed over to Reynal's lodge, though it hardly deserved this name, for it consisted only of a few old buffalo-robes, supported on poles, and was quite open on one side. Here we sat down, and the Indians gathered round us.

'What is it,' said I, 'that makes the thunder?'

'It's my belief,' said Reynal, 'that it is a big stone rolling over the sky.'

'Very likely,' I replied; 'but I want to know what the Indians think about it.'

So he interpreted my question, which seemed to produce some doubt and debate. There was evidently a difference of opinion. At last old Mene-Seela, or Red-Water, who sat by himself at one side, looked up with his withered face, and said he had always known what the thunder was. 'It was a great black bird; and once he had seen it, in a dream, swooping down from the Black Hills, with its loud roaring wings; and when it flapped them over a lake, they struck lightning from the water.'

'The thunder is bad,' said another old man, who sat muffled in his buffalo-robe; 'he killed my brother last summer.'

Reynal, at my request, asked for an explanation; but the old man remained doggedly silent, and would not look up. Some time after, I learned how the accident occurred. The man who was killed belonged to an association which, among other mystic functions, claimed the exclusive power and privilege of

fighting the thunder. Whenever a storm which they wished to
avert was threatening, the thunder fighters would take their
bows and arrows, their guns, their magic drum, and a sort of
whistle, made out of the wing-bone of the war-eagle. Thus
equipped, they would run out and fire at the rising cloud,
whooping, yelling, whistling and beating their drum, to
frighten it down again. One afternoon, a heavy black cloud
was coming up, and they repaired to the top of a hill, where
they brought all their magic artillery into play against it. But
the undaunted thunder, refusing to be terrified, kept moving
straight onward, and darted out a bright flash which struck
one of the party dead, as he was in the very act of shaking his
long iron-pointed lance against it. The rest scattered and ran
yelling in an ecstasy of superstitious terror back to their
lodges.

The lodge of my host Kongra Tonga, or the Big Crow,
presented a picturesque spectacle that evening. A score or
more of Indians were seated around it in a circle, their dark
naked forms just visible by the dull light of the smouldering
fire in the centre. The pipe glowing brightly in the gloom as it
passed from hand to hand round the lodge. Then a squaw
would drop a piece of buffalo-fat on the dull embers. Instantly a bright glancing flame would leap up, darting its clear
light to the very apex of the tall conical structure, where the
tops of the slender poles that supported its covering of leather
were gathered together. It gilded the features of the Indians,
as with animated gestures they sat around it, telling their endless stories of war and hunting. It displayed rude garments of
skins that hung around the lodge; the bow, quiver and lance,
suspended over the resting-place of the chief, and the rifles
and powder-horns of the two white guests. For a moment all
would be bright as day; then the flames would die away, and
fitful flashes from the embers would illumine the lodge, and
then leave it in darkness. Then all the light would wholly
fade, and the lodge and all within it be involved again in
obscurity.

As I left the lodge next morning, I was saluted by howling
and yelping from all around the village, and half its canine
population rushed forth to the attack. Being as cowardly as
they were clamorous, they kept jumping around me at the

distance of a few yards, only one little cur, about ten inches long, having spirit enough to make a direct assault. He dashed valiantly at the leather tassel which in the Dahcotah fashion was trailing behind the heel of my moccason, and kept his hold, growling and snarling all the while, though every step I made almost jerked him over on his back. As I knew that the eyes of the whole village were on the watch to see if I showed any sign of apprehension, I walked forward without looking to the right or left, surrounded wherever I went by this magic circle of dogs. When I came to Reynal's lodge I sat down by it, on which the dogs dispersed growling to their respective quarters. Only one large white one remained, who kept running about before me and showing his teeth. I called him, but he only growled the more. I looked at him well. He was fat and sleek; just such a dog as I wanted. 'My friend,' thought I, 'you shall pay for this! I will have you eaten this very morning!'

I intended that day to give the Indians a feast, by way of conveying a favorable impression of my character and dignity; and a white dog is the dish which the customs of the Dahcotah prescribe for all occasions of formality and importance. I consulted Reynal; he soon discovered that an old woman in the next lodge was owner of the white dog. I took a gaudy cotton handkerchief, and laying it on the ground, arranged some vermilion, beads, and other trinkets upon it. Then the old squaw was summoned. I pointed to the dog and to the handkerchief. She gave a scream of delight, snatched up the prize and vanished with it into her lodge. For a few more trifles, I engaged the services of two other squaws, each of whom took the white dog by one of his paws, and led him away behind the lodges, while he kept looking up at them with a face of innocent surprise. Having killed him they threw him into a fire to singe; then chopped him up and put him into two large kettles to boil. Meanwhile I told Raymond to fry in buffalo fat what little flour we had left, and also to make a kettle of tea as an additional item of the repast.

The Big Crow's squaw was briskly at work sweeping out the lodge for the approaching festivity. I confided to my host himself the task of inviting the guests, thinking that I might thereby shift from my own shoulders the odium of fancied neglect and oversight.

When feasting is in question, one hour of the day serves an Indian as well as another. My entertainment came off about eleven o'clock. At that hour, Reynal and Raymond walked across the area of the village, to the admiration of the inhabitants, carrying the two kettles of dog meat slung on a pole between them. These they placed in the centre of the lodge, and then went back for the bread and the tea. Meanwhile I had put on a pair of brilliant moccasons, and substituted for my old buck-skin frock a coat which I had brought with me in view of such public occasions. I also made careful use of the razor, an operation which no man will neglect who desires to gain the good opinion of Indians. Thus attired, I seated myself between Reynal and Raymond at the head of the lodge. Only a few minutes elapsed before all the guests had come in and were seated on the ground, wedged together in a close circle around the lodge. Each brought with him a wooden bowl to hold his share of the repast. When all were assembled, two of the officials, called 'soldiers' by the white men, came forward with ladles made of the horn of the Rocky Mountain sheep, and began to distribute the feast, always assigning a double share to the old men and chiefs. The dog vanished with astonishing celerity, and each guest turned his dish bottom upward to show that all was gone. Then the bread was distributed in its turn, and finally the tea. As the soldiers poured it out into the same wooden bowls that had served for the substantial part of the meal, I thought it had a particularly curious and uninviting color.

'Oh!' said Reynal, 'there was not tea enough, so I stirred some soot in the kettle, to make it look strong.'

Fortunately an Indian's palate is not very discriminating. The tea was well sweetened, and that was all they cared for.

Now, the former part of the entertainment being concluded, the time for speech-making was come. The Big Crow produced a flat piece of wood on which he cut up tobacco and *shongsasha*, and mixed them in due proportions. The pipes were filled and passed from hand to hand around the company. Then I began my speech, each sentence being interpreted by Reynal as I went on, and echoed by the whole audience with the usual exclamations of assent and approval. As nearly as I can recollect, it was as follows:

'I had come, I told them, from a country so far distant, that at the rate they travel, they could not reach it in a year.'

'How! how!'

'There the Meneaska were more numerous than the blades of grass on the prairie. The squaws were far more beautiful than any they had ever seen, and all the men were brave warriors.'

'How! how! how!'

Here I was assailed by sharp twinges of conscience, for I fancied I could perceive a fragrance of perfumery in the air, and a vision rose before me of white-kid gloves and silken moustaches with the mild and gentle countenances of numerous fair-haired young men. But I recovered myself and began again.

'While I was living in the Meneaska lodges, I had heard of the Ogillallah, how great and brave a nation they were, how they loved the whites, and how well they could hunt the buffalo and strike their enemies. I resolved to come and see if all that I heard was true.'

'How! how! how! how!'

'As I had come on horseback through the mountains, I had been able to bring them only a very few presents.'

'How!'

'But I had enough tobacco to give them all a small piece. They might smoke it, and see how much better it was than the tobacco which they got from the traders.'

'How! how! how!'

'I had plenty of powder, lead, knives, and tobacco at Fort Laramie. These I was anxious to give them, and if any of them should come to the fort before I went away, I would make them handsome presents.'

'How! how! how! how!'

Raymond then cut up and distributed among them two or three pounds of tobacco, and old Mene-Seela began to make a reply. It was quite long, but the following was the pith of it.

'He had always loved the whites. They were the wisest people on earth. He believed they could do every thing, and he was always glad when any of them came to live in the Ogil-lallah lodges. It was true I had not made them many presents, but the reason of it was plain. It was clear that I liked them, or I never should have come so far to find their village.'

Several other speeches of similar import followed, and then this more serious matter being disposed of, there was an in-terval of smoking, laughing and conversation; but old Mene-Seela suddenly interrupted it with a loud voice:

'Now is a good time,' he said, 'when all the old men and chiefs are here together, to decide what the people shall do. We came over the mountain to make our lodges for next year. Our old ones are good for nothing; they are rotten and worn out. But we have been disappointed. We have killed buffalo bulls enough, but we have found no herds of cows, and the skins of bulls are too thick and heavy for our squaws to make lodges of. There must be plenty of cows about the Medicine Bow Mountain. We ought to go there. To be sure it is farther westward than we have ever been before, and perhaps the Snakes will attack us, for those hunting-grounds belong to them. But we must have new lodges at any rate; our old ones will not serve for another year. We ought not to be afraid of the Snakes. Our warriors are brave, and they are all ready for war. Besides, we have three white men with their rifles to help us.'

I could not help thinking that the old man relied a little too much on the aid of allies, one of whom was a coward, an-other a blockhead, and the third an invalid. This speech pro-duced a good deal of debate. As Reynal did not interpret what was said, I could only judge of the meaning by the fea-tures and gestures of the speakers. At the end of it however the greater number seemed to have fallen in with Mene-Seela's opinion. A short silence followed, and then the old man struck up a discordant chant, which I was told was a song of thanks for the entertainment I had given them.

'Now,' said he, 'let us go and give the white men a chance to breathe.'

So the company all dispersed into the open air, and for some time the old chief was walking round the village, sing-ing his song in praise of the feast, after the usual custom of the nation.

At last the day drew to a close, and as the sun went down the horses came trooping from the surrounding plains to be picketed before the dwellings of their respective masters. Soon within the great circle of lodges appeared another concentric circle of restless horses; and here and there fires were glowing and flickering amid the gloom, on the dusky figures around them. I went over and sat by the lodge of Reynal. The Eagle-Feather, who was a son of Mene-Seela, and brother of my host the Big Crow, was seated there already, and I asked him if the village would move in the morning. He shook his head, and said that nobody could tell, for since old Mahto-Tatonka had died, the people had been like children that did not know their own minds. They were no better than a body without a head. So I, as well as the Indians themselves, fell asleep that night without knowing whether we should set out in the morning toward the country of the Snakes.

At daybreak, however, as I was coming up from the river after my morning's ablutions, I saw that a movement was contemplated. Some of the lodges were reduced to nothing but bare skeletons of poles; the leather covering of others was flapping in the wind as the squaws were pulling it off. One or two chiefs of note had resolved, it seemed, on moving; and so having set their squaws at work, the example was tacitly followed by the rest of the village. One by one the lodges were sinking down in rapid succession, and where the great circle of the village had been only a moment before, nothing now remained but a ring of horses and Indians, crowded in confusion together. The ruins of the lodges were spread over the ground, together with kettles, stone mallets, great ladles of horn, buffalo-robes, and cases of painted hide, filled with dried meat. Squaws bustled about in their busy preparations, the old hags screaming to one another at the stretch of their leathern lungs. The shaggy horses were patiently standing while the lodge-poles were lashed to their sides, and the baggage piled upon their backs. The dogs with their tongues lolling out, lay lazily panting, and waiting for the time of departure. Each warrior sat on the ground by the decaying embers of his fire, unmoved amid all the confusion, while he held in his hand the long trail-rope of his horse.

As their preparations were contemplated, each family

moved off the ground. The crowd was rapidly melting away. I could see them crossing the river, and passing in quick succession along the profile of the hill on the farther bank. When all were gone, I mounted and set out after them, followed by Raymond, and as we gained the summit, the whole village came in view at once, straggling away for a mile or more over the barren plains before us. Every where the iron points of lances were glittering. The sun never shone upon a more strange array. Here were the heavy-laden pack-horses, some wretched old woman leading them, and two or three children clinging to their backs. Here were mules or ponies covered from head to tail with gaudy trappings, and mounted by some gay young squaw, grinning bashfulness and pleasure as the Meneaska looked at her. Boys with miniature bows and arrows were wandering over the plains, little naked children were running along on foot, and numberless dogs were scampering among the feet of the horses. The young braves, gaudy with paint and feathers, were riding in groups among the crowd, and often galloping, two or three at once along the line, to try the speed of their horses. Here and there you might see a rank of sturdy pedestrians stalking along in their white buffalo-robes. These were the dignitaries of the village, the old men and warriors, to whose age and experience that wandering democracy yielded a silent deference. With the rough prairie and the broken hills for its back-ground, the restless scene was striking and picturesque beyond description. Days and weeks made me familiar with it, but never impaired its effect upon my fancy.

As we moved on, the broken column grew yet more scattered and disorderly, until, as we approached the foot of a hill, I saw the old men before mentioned seating themselves in a line upon the ground, in advance of the whole. They lighted a pipe and sat smoking, laughing, and telling stories, while the people, stopping as they successively came up, were soon gathered in a crowd behind them. Then the old men rose, drew their buffalo-robes over their shoulders, and strode on as before. Gaining the top of the hill, we found a very steep declivity before us. There was not a minute's pause. The whole descended in a mass, amid dust and confusion. The horses braced their feet as they slid down, women and children were screaming, dogs yelping as they were trodden upon, while stones and earth went rolling to the bottom. In a few moments I could see the village from the summit, spreading again far and wide over the plain below.

At our encampment that afternoon I was attacked anew by my old disorder. In half an hour the strength that I had been gaining for a week past had vanished again, and I became like a man in a dream. But at sunset I lay down in the Big Crow's lodge and slept, totally unconscious till the morning. The first thing that awakened me was a hoarse flapping over my head, and a sudden light that poured in upon me. The camp was breaking up, and the squaws were moving the covering from the lodge. I arose and shook off my blanket with the feeling of perfect health; but scarcely had I gained my feet when a sense of my helpless condition was once more forced upon me, and I found myself scarcely able to stand. Raymond had brought up Pauline and the mule, and I stooped to raise my saddle from the ground. My strength was quite inadequate to the task. 'You must saddle her,' said I to Raymond, as I sat down again on a pile of buffalo-robes:

"Et hæc etiam fortasse meminisse juvabit,"

I thought, while with a painful effort I raised myself into the saddle. Half an hour after, even the expectation that Virgil's line expressed seemed destined to disappointment. As we were passing over a great plain, surrounded by long broken ridges, I rode slowly in advance of the Indians, with thoughts that wandered far from the time and from the place. Suddenly the sky darkened, and thunder began to mutter. Clouds were rising over the hills, as dreary and dull as the first forebodings of an approaching calamity; and in a moment all around was wrapped in shadow. I looked behind. The Indians had stopped to prepare for the approaching storm, and the dark, dense mass of savages stretched far to the right and left. Since the first attack of my disorder the effects of rain upon me had usually been injurious in the extreme. I had no strength to spare, having at that moment scarcely enough to keep my seat on horseback. Then, for the first time, it pressed upon me as a strong probability that I might never leave those deserts. 'Well,' thought I to myself, 'a prairie makes quick and sharp work. Better to die here, in the saddle to the last, than to stifle in the hot air of a sick chamber; and a thousand times better than to drag out life, as many have done, in the helpless inaction of lingering disease.' So, drawing the buffalo-robe on which I sat, over my head, I waited till the storm should come. It broke at last with a sudden burst of fury, and passing away as rapidly as it came, left the sky clear again. My reflections served me no other purpose than to look back upon as a piece of curious experience; for the rain did not produce the ill effects that I had expected. We encamped within an hour. Having no change of clothes, I contrived to borrow a curious kind of substitute from Reynal; and this done, I went home, that is, to the Big Crow's lodge, to make the entire transfer that was necessary. Half a dozen squaws were in the lodge, and one of them taking my arm held it against her own, while a general laugh and scream of admiration was raised at the contrast in the color of the skin.

Our encampment that afternoon was not far distant from a spur of the Black Hills, whose ridges, bristling with fir trees, rose from the plains a mile or two on our right. That they might move more rapidly toward their proposed hunting-grounds, the Indians determined to leave at this place their stock of dried meat and other superfluous articles. Some left even their lodges, and contented themselves with carrying a few hides to make a shelter from the sun and rain. Half the inhabitants set out in the afternoon, with loaded pack-horses, toward the mountains. Here they suspended the dried meat upon trees, where the wolves and grizzly bears could not get at it. All returned at evening. Some of the young men declared that they had heard the reports of guns among the mountains to the eastward, and many surmises were thrown out as to the origin of these sounds. For my part, I was in hopes that Shaw and Henry Chatillon were coming to join us. I would have welcomed them cordially, for I had no other companions than two brutish white men and five hundred savages. I little suspected that at that very moment my unlucky comrade was lying on a buffalo-robe at Fort Laramie, fevered with ivy poison, and solacing his woes with tobacco and Shakspeare.

As we moved over the plains on the next morning, several

young men were riding about the country as scouts; and at length we began to see them occasionally on the tops of the hills, shaking their robes as a signal that they saw buffalo. Soon after, some bulls came in sight. Horsemen darted away in pursuit, and we could see from the distance that one or two of the buffalo were killed. Raymond suddenly became inspired. I looked at him as he rode by my side; his face had actually grown intelligent!

'This is the country for me!' he said; 'if I could only carry the buffalo that are killed here every month down to St. Louis, I'd make my fortune in one winter. I'd grow as rich as old Papin, or Mackenzie either. I call this the poor man's market. When I'm hungry, I have only got to take my rifle and go out and get better meat than the rich folks down below can get, with all their money. You won't catch me living in St. Louis another winter.'

'No,' said Reynal, 'you had better say that, after you and your Spanish woman almost starved to death there. What a fool you were ever to take her to the settlements.'

'Your Spanish woman?' said I; 'I never heard of her before. Are you married to her?'

'No,' answered Raymond, again looking intelligent; 'the priests don't marry their women, and why should I marry mine?'

This honorable mention of the Mexican clergy introduced the subject of religion, and I found that my two associates, in common with other white men in the country, were as indifferent to their future welfare as men whose lives are in constant peril are apt to be. Raymond had never heard of the Pope. A certain bishop, who lived at Taos or at Santa Fé, embodied his loftiest idea of an ecclesiastical dignitary. Reynal observed that a priest had been at Fort Laramie two years ago, on his way to the Nez Percé mission, and that he had confessed all the men there, and given them absolution. 'I got a good clearing out myself, that time,' said Reynal, 'and I reckon that will do for me till I go down to the settlements again.'

Here he interrupted himself with an oath, and exclaimed: 'Look! look! The "Panther" is running an antelope!'

The Panther, on his black-and-white horse, one of the best

in the village, came at full speed over the hill in hot pursuit of an antelope, that darted away like lightning before him. The attempt was made in mere sport and bravado, for very few are the horses that can for a moment compete in swiftness with this little animal. The antelope ran down the hill toward the main body of the Indians, who were moving over the plain below. Sharp yells were given, and horsemen galloped out to intercept his flight. At this he turned sharply to the left, and scoured away with such incredible speed that he distanced all his pursuers, and even the vaunted horse of the Panther himself. A few moments after, we witnessed a more serious sport. A shaggy buffalo-bull bounded out from a neighboring hollow, and close behind him came a slender Indian boy, riding without stirrups or saddle, and lashing his eager little horse to full speed. Yard after yard he drew closer to his gigantic victim, though the bull, with his short tail erect and his tongue lolling out a foot from his foaming jaws, was straining his unwieldy strength to the utmost. A moment more, and the boy was close alongside of him. It was our friend the Hail-Storm. He dropped the rein on his horse's neck, and jerked an arrow like lightning from the quiver at his shoulder.

'I tell you,' said Reynal, 'that in a year's time that boy will match the best hunter in the village. There, he has given it to him!—and there goes another! You feel well, now, old bull, don't you, with two arrows stuck in your lights? There, he has given him another! Hear how the Hail-Storm yells when he shoots! Yes, jump at him; try it again, old fellow! You may jump all day before you get your horns into that pony!'

The bull sprang again and again at his assailant, but the horse kept dodging with wonderful celerity. At length the bull followed up his attack with a furious rush, and the Hail-Storm was put to flight, the shaggy monster following close behind. The boy clung in his seat like a leech, and secure in the speed of his little pony, looked round toward us and laughed. In a moment he was again alongside of the bull who was now driven to complete desperation. His eyeballs glared through his tangled mane, and the blood flew from his mouth and nostrils. Thus, still battling with each other, the two enemies disappeared over the hill.

Many of the Indians rode at full gallop toward the spot. We

followed at a more moderate pace, and soon saw the bull lying dead on the side of the hill. The Indians were gathered around him, and several knives were already at work. These little instruments were plied with such wonderful address, that the twisted sinews were cut apart, the ponderous bones fell asunder as if by magic, and in a moment the vast carcass was reduced to a heap of bloody ruins. The surrounding group of savages offered no very attractive spectacle to a civilized eye. Some were cracking the huge thigh-bones and devouring the marrow within; others were cutting away pieces of the liver, and other approved morsels, and swallowing them on the spot with the appetite of wolves. The faces of most of them, besmeared with blood from ear to ear, looked grim and horrible enough. My friend the White Shield proffered me a marrow-bone, so skilfully laid open, that all the rich substance within was exposed to view at once. Another Indian held out a large piece of the delicate lining of the paunch; but these courteous offerings I begged leave to decline. I noticed one little boy who was very busy with his knife about the jaws and throat of the buffalo, from which he extracted some morsel of peculiar delicacy. It is but fair to say, that only certain parts of the animal are considered eligible in these extempore banquets. The Indians would look with abhorrence on any one who should partake indiscriminately of the newly-killed carcass.

We encamped that night, and marched westward through the greater part of the following day. On the next morning we again resumed our journey. It was the seventeenth of July, unless my notebook misleads me. At noon we stopped by some pools of rain-water, and in the afternoon again set forward. This double movement was contrary to the usual practice of the Indians, but all were very anxious to reach the hunting-ground, kill the necessary number of buffalo, and retreat as soon as possible from the dangerous neighborhood. I pass by for the present some curious incidents that occurred during these marches and encampments. Late in the afternoon of the last-mentioned day we came upon the banks of a little sandy stream, of which the Indians could not tell the name; for they were very ill acquainted with that part of the country. So parched and arid were the prairies around, that they could not supply grass enough for the horses to feed upon, and we were compelled to move farther and farther up the stream in search of ground for encampment. The country was much wilder than before. The plains were gashed with ravines and broken into hollows and steep declivities, which flanked our course, as, in long scattered array, the Indians advanced up the side of the stream. Mene-Seela consulted an extraordinary oracle to instruct him where the buffalo were to be found. When he with the other chiefs sat down on the grass to smoke and converse, as they often did during the march, the old man picked up one of those enormous black and green crickets, which the Dahcotah call by a name that signifies 'They who point out the buffalo.' The 'Root-Diggers,' a wretched tribe beyond the mountains, turn them to good account by making them into a sort of soup, pronounced by certain unscrupulous trappers to be extremely rich. Holding the bloated insect respectfully between his fingers and thumb, the old Indian looked attentively at him and inquired, 'Tell me, my father, where must we go to-morrow to find the buffalo?' The cricket twisted about his long horns in evident embarrassment. At last he pointed, or seemed to point, then westward. Mene-Seela, dropping him gently on the grass, laughed with great glee, and said that if we went that way in the morning we should be sure to kill plenty of game.

Toward evening we came upon a fresh green meadow, traversed by the stream, and deep-set among tall sterile bluffs. The Indians descended its steep bank; and as I was at the rear, I was one of the last to reach this point. Lances were glittering, feathers fluttering, and the water below me was crowded with men and horses passing through, while the meadow beyond was swarming with the restless crowd of Indians. The sun was just setting, and poured its softened light upon them through an opening in the hills.

I remarked to Reynal, that at last we had found a good 'camping-ground.

'Oh, it is very good,' replied he, ironically, 'especially if there is a Snake war-party about, and they take it into their heads to shoot down at us from the top of these hills. It is no plan of mine, 'camping in such a hole as this!'

The Indians also seemed apprehensive. High up on the top of the tallest bluff, conspicuous in the bright evening sunlight, sat a naked warrior on horseback, looking around, as it seemed, over the neighboring country; and Raymond told me that many of the young men had gone out in different directions as scouts.

The shadows had reached to the very summit of the bluffs before the lodges were erected and the village reduced again to quiet and order. A cry was suddenly raised, and men, women and children came running out with animated faces, and looked eagerly through the opening on the hills by which the stream entered from the westward. I could discern afar off some dark, heavy masses, passing over the sides of a low hill. They disappeared, and then others followed. These were bands of buffalo-cows. The hunting-ground was reached at last, and every thing promised well for the morrow's sport. Being fatigued and exhausted, I went and lay down in Kongra-Tonga's lodge, when Raymond thrust in his head, and called upon me to come and see some sport. A number of Indians were gathered, laughing, along the line of lodges on the western side of the village, and at some distance, I could plainly see in the twilight two huge black monsters stalking, heavily and solemnly, directly toward us. They were buffalo-bulls. The wind blew from them to the village, and such was their blindness and stupidity, that they were advancing upon the enemy without the least consciousness of his presence. Raymond told me that two young men had hidden themselves with guns in a ravine about twenty yards in front of us. The two bulls walked slowly on, heavily swinging from side to side in their peculiar gait of stupid dignity. They approached within four or five rods of the ravine where the Indians lay in ambush. Here at last they seemed conscious that something was wrong, for they both stopped and stood perfectly still, without looking either to the right or to the left. Nothing of them was to be seen but two huge black masses of shaggy mane, with horns, eyes, and nose in the centre, and a pair of hoofs visible at the bottom. At last the more intelligent of them seemed to have concluded that it was time to retire. Very slowly, and with an air of the gravest and most majestic deliberation, he began to turn round, as if he were revolving on a pivot. Little by little his ugly brown side was exposed to view. A white smoke sprang out, as it were from the ground; a sharp report came with it. The old bull gave a very undignified jump, and galloped off. At this his comrade wheeled about with considerable expedition. The other Indian shot at him from the ravine, and then both the bulls were running away at full speed, while half the juvenile population of the village raised a yell and ran after them. The first bull soon stopped, and while the crowd stood looking at him at a respectful distance, he reeled and rolled over on his side. The other, wounded in a less vital part, galloped away to the hills and escaped.

In half an hour it was totally dark. I lay down to sleep, and ill as I was, there was something very animating in the prospect of the general hunt that was to take place on the morrow.

Chapter XV.

THE HUNTING CAMP.

"The Persé owt of Northamberlande,
And a vowe to God mayde he,
That he wolde hunte in the mountayns
Off Chyviat within dayes thre,
In the mauger of doughté Doglés,
And all that ever with him be."

CHEVY CHASE.

LONG BEFORE DAYBREAK the Indians broke up their camp. The women of Mene-Seela's lodge were as usual among the first that were ready for departure, and I found the old man himself sitting by the embers of the decayed fire, over which he was warming his withered fingers, as the morning was very chilly and damp. The preparations for moving were even more confused and disorderly than usual. While some families were leaving the ground the lodges of others were still standing untouched. At this, old Mene-Seela grew impatient, and walking out to the middle of the village stood with his robe wrapped close around him, and harangued the people in a loud, sharp voice. Now, he said, when they were on an enemy's hunting-grounds, was not the time to behave like children; they ought to be more active and united than ever. His speech had some effect. The delinquents took down their lodges and loaded their pack-horses; and when the sun rose, the last of the men, women, and children had left the deserted camp.

This movement was made merely for the purpose of finding a better and safer position. So we advanced only three or four miles up the little stream, before each family assumed its relative place in the great ring of the village, and all around the squaws were actively at work in preparing the camp. But not a single warrior dismounted from his horse. All the men that morning were mounted on inferior animals, leading their best horses by a cord, or confiding them to the care of boys. In small parties they began to leave the ground and ride rapidly away over the plains to the westward. I had taken no food that morning, and not being at all ambitious of farther abstinence, I went into my host's lodge, which his squaws had erected with wonderful celerity, and sat down in the centre, as a gentle hint that I was hungry. A wooden bowl was soon set before me, filled with the nutritious preparation of dried meat, called *pemmican* by the northern voyagers, and *wasna* by the Dahcotah. Taking a handful to break my fast upon, I left the lodge just in time to see the last band of hunters disappear over the ridge of the neighboring hill. I mounted Pauline and galloped in pursuit, riding rather by the balance than by any muscular strength that remained to me. From the top of the hill I could overlook a wide extent of desolate and unbroken prairie, over which, far and near, little parties of naked horsemen were rapidly passing. I soon came up to the nearest, and we had not ridden a mile before all were united into one large and compact body. All was haste and eagerness. Each hunter was whipping on his horse, as if anxious to be the first to reach the game. In such movements among the Indians this is always more or less the case; but it was especially so in the present instance, because the head chief of the village was absent, and there were but few 'soldiers,' a sort of Indian police, who among their other functions usually assume the direction of a buffalo hunt. No man turned to the right hand or to the left. We rode at a swift canter straight forward, up hill and down hill, and through the stiff, obstinate growth of the endless wild sage bushes. For an hour and a half the same red shoulders, the same long black hair rose and fell with the motion of the horses before me. Very little was said, though once I observed an old man severely reproving Raymond for having left his rifle behind him, when there was some probability of encountering an enemy before the day was over. As we galloped across a plain thickly set with sage bushes, the foremost riders vanished suddenly from sight, as if diving into the earth. The arid soil was cracked into a deep ravine. Down we all went in succession and galloped in a line along the bottom, until we found a point where, one by one, the horses could scramble out. Soon after, we came upon a wide shallow stream, and as we rode swiftly over the hard sand-beds and through the thin sheets of rippling water, many of the savage horsemen threw themselves to the ground, knelt on the sand, snatched a hasty draught, and leaping back again to their seats, galloped on again as before.

Meanwhile scouts kept in advance of the party; and now we began to see them on the ridge of the hills, waving their robes in token that buffalo were visible. These however proved to be nothing more than old straggling bulls, feeding upon the neighboring plains, who would stare for a moment at the hostile array and then gallop clumsily off. At length we could discern several of these scouts making their signals to us at once; no longer waving their robes boldly from the top of the hill, but standing lower down, so that they could not be seen from the plains beyond. Game worth pursuing had evidently been discovered. The excited Indians now urged forward their tired horses even more rapidly than before. Pauline, who was still sick and jaded, began to groan heavily; and her yellow sides were darkened with sweat. As we were crowding together over a lower intervening hill, I heard Reynal and Raymond shouting to me from the left; and looking in that direction, I saw them riding away behind a party of about twenty mean-looking Indians. These were the relatives of Reynal's squaw, Margot, who not wishing to take part in the general hunt, were riding towards a distant hollow, where they could discern a small band of buffalo which they meant to appropriate to themselves. I answered to the call by ordering Raymond to turn back and follow me. He reluctantly obeyed, though Reynal, who had relied on his assistance in skinning, cutting up, and carrying to camp the buffalo that he and his party should kill, loudly protested and declared that we should see no sport if we went with the rest of the Indians. Followed by Raymond, I pursued the main body of hunters, while Reynal, in a great rage, whipped his horse over the hill after his ragamuffin relatives. The Indians, still about a hundred in number, rode in a dense body at some distance in advance. They galloped forward, and a cloud of dust was flying in the wind behind them. I could not overtake them until they had stopped on the side of the hill where the scouts were standing. Here, each hunter sprang in haste from the tired animal which he had ridden, and leaped upon the fresh horse that he had brought with him. There was not a saddle or a bridle in the whole party. A piece of buffalo robe girthed over the horse's back, served in the place of the one, and a cord of twisted hair, lashed firmly round his lower jaw, answered for the other. Eagle feathers were dangling from every mane and tail, as insignia of courage and speed. As for the rider, he wore no other clothing than a light cincture at his waist, and a pair of moccasons. He had a heavy whip, with a handle of solid elk-horn, and a lash of knotted bull-hide, fastened to his wrist by an ornamental band. His bow was in his hand, and his quiver of otter or panther skin hung at his shoulder. Thus equipped, some thirty of the hunters galloped away towards the left, in order to make a circuit under cover of the hills, that the buffalo might be assailed on both sides at once. The rest impatiently waited until time enough had elapsed for their companions to reach the required position. Then riding upward in a body, we gained the ridge of the hill, and for the first time came in sight of the buffalo on the plain beyond.

They were a band of cows, four or five hundred in number, who were crowded together near the bank of a wide stream that was soaking across the sand-beds of the valley. This was a large circular basin, sun-scorched and broken, scantily covered with herbage and encompassed with high barren hills, from an opening in which we could see our allies galloping out upon the plain. The wind blew from that direction. The buffalo were aware of their approach, and had begun to move, though very slowly and in a compact mass. I have no farther recollection of seeing the game until we were in the midst of them, for as we descended the hill other objects engrossed my attention. Numerous old bulls were scattered over the plain, and ungallantly deserting their charge at our approach, began to wade and plunge through the treacherous quicksands of the stream, and gallop away towards the hills. One old veteran was struggling behind all the rest with one of his fore-legs, which had been broken by some accident, dangling about uselessly at his side. His appearance, as he went shambling along on three legs, was so ludicrous that I could not help pausing for a moment to look at him. As I came near, he would try to rush upon me, nearly throwing himself down at every awkward attempt. Looking up, I saw the whole body of Indians full an hundred yards in advance. I lashed Pauline in pursuit and reached them but just in time; for as we mingled among them, each hunter, as if by a common impulse, violently struck his horse, each horse sprang forward convulsively, and scattering in the charge in order to assail the entire herd at once, we all rushed headlong upon the buffalo. We were among them in an instant. Amid the trampling and the yells I could see their dark figures running hither and thither through clouds of dust, and the horsemen darting in pursuit. While we were charging on one side, our companions had attacked the bewildered and panic-stricken herd on the other. The uproar and confusion lasted but for a moment. The dust cleared away, and the buffalo could be seen scattering as from a common centre, flying over the plain singly, or in long files and small compact bodies, while behind each followed the Indians, lashing their horses to furious speed, forcing them close upon their prey, and yelling as they launched arrow after arrow into their sides. The large black carcasses were strewn thickly over the ground. Here and there wounded buffalo were standing, their bleeding sides feathered with arrows; and as I rode past them their eyes would glare, they would bristle like gigantic cats, and feebly attempt to rush up and gore my horse.

I left camp that morning with a philosophic resolution. Neither I nor my horse were at that time fit for such sport, and I had determined to remain a quiet spectator; but amid the rush of horses and buffalo, the uproar and the dust, I found it impossible to sit still; and as four or five buffalo ran past me in a line, I drove Pauline in pursuit. We went plunging close at their heels through the water and the quicksands, and clambering the bank, chased them through the wild sage-bushes that covered the rising ground beyond. But neither her native spirit nor the blows of the knotted bull-hide could supply the place of poor Pauline's exhausted strength. We could not gain an inch upon the poor fugitives. At last, however, they came full upon a ravine too wide to leap over; and as this compelled them to turn abruptly to the left, I contrived to get within ten or twelve yards of the hindmost. At this she faced about, bristled angrily, and made a show of charging. I shot at her with a large holster pistol, and hit her somewhere in the neck. Down she tumbled into the ravine, whither her companions had descended before her. I saw their dark backs appearing and disappearing as they galloped along the bottom; then, one by one, they came scrambling out on the other side, and ran off as before, the wounded animal following with unabated speed.

Turning back, I saw Raymond coming on his black mule to meet me; and as we rode over the field together, we counted dozens of carcasses lying on the plain, in the ravines and on the sandy bed of the stream. Far away in the distance, horses and buffalo were still scouring along, with little clouds of dust rising behind them; and over the sides of the hills we could see long files of the frightened animals rapidly ascending. The hunters began to return. The boys, who had held the horses behind the hill, made their appearance, and the work of flaying and cutting up began in earnest all over the field. I noticed my host Kongra Tonga beyond the stream, just alighting by the side of a cow which he had killed. Riding up to him, I found him in the act of drawing out an arrow, which, with the exception of the notch at the end, had entirely disappeared in the animal. I asked him to give it to me, and I still retain it as a proof, though by no means the most striking one that could be offered, of the force and dexterity with which the Indians discharge their arrows.

The hides and meat were piled upon the horses, and the hunters began to leave the ground. Raymond and I, too, getting tired of the scene, set out for the village, riding straight across the intervening desert. There was no path, and as far as I could see, no landmarks sufficient to guide us; but Raymond seemed to have an instinctive perception of the point on the horizon toward which we ought to direct our course. Antelope were bounding on all sides, and as is always the case in the presence of buffalo, they seemed to have lost their natural shyness and timidity. Bands of them would run lightly up the rocky declivities, and stand gazing down upon us from the summit. At length we could distinguish the tall white rocks and the old pine-trees that, as we well remembered, were just above the site of the encampment. Still, we could see nothing of the village itself until, ascending a grassy hill, we found the circle of lodges, dingy with storms and smoke, standing on the plain at our very feet.

I entered the lodge of my host. His squaw instantly brought me food and water, and spread a buffalo-robe for me to lie upon; and being much fatigued, I lay down and fell asleep. In about an hour the entrance of Kongra-Tonga, with his arms smeared with blood to the elbows, awoke me. He sat down in his usual seat, on the left side of the lodge. His squaw gave him a vessel of water for washing, set before him a bowl of boiled meat, and as he was eating, pulled off his bloody moccasons and placed fresh ones on his feet; then out-stretching his limbs, my host composed himself to sleep.

And now the hunters, two or three at a time, began to come rapidly in, and each consigning his horses to the squaws, entered his lodge with the air of a man whose day's work was done. The squaws flung down the load from the burdened horses, and vast piles of meat and hides were soon accumulated before every lodge. By this time it was darkening fast, and the whole village was illumined by the glare of fires blazing all around. All the squaws and children were gathered about the piles of meat, exploring them in search of the dain-tiest portions. Some of these they roasted on sticks before the fires, but often they dispensed with this superfluous opera-tion. Late into the night the fires were still glowing upon the groups of feasters engaged in this savage banquet around them.

Several hunters sat down by the fire in Kongra-Tonga's lodge to talk over the day's exploits. Among the rest, Mene-Seela came in. Though he must have seen full eighty winters, he had taken an active share in the day's sport. He boasted that he had killed two cows that morning, and would have killed a third if the dust had not blinded him so that he had to drop his bow and arrows and press both hands against his eyes to stop the pain. The fire-light fell upon his wrinkled face and shrivelled figure as he sat telling his story with such inim-itable gesticulation that every man in the lodge broke into a laugh.

Old Mene-Seela was one of the few Indians in the village with whom I would have trusted myself alone without suspi-cion, and the only one from whom I should have received a gift or a service without the certainty that it proceeded from an interested motive. He was a great friend to the whites. He liked to be in their society, and was very vain of the favors he had received from them. He told me one afternoon, as we were sitting together in his son's lodge, that he considered the beaver and the whites the wisest people on earth; indeed, he was convinced they were the same; and an incident which had happened to him long before had assured him of this. So he began the following story, and as the pipe passed in turn to him, Reynal availed himself of these interruptions to translate what had preceded. But the old man accompanied his words with such admirable pantomime that translation was hardly necessary.

He said that when he was very young, and had never yet seen a white man, he and three or four of his companions were out on a beaver hunt, and he crawled into a large beaver-lodge, to examine what was there. Sometimes he was creeping on his hands and knees, sometimes he was obliged to swim, and sometimes to lie flat on his face and drag himself along. In this way he crawled a great distance under ground. It was very dark, cold and close, so that at last he was almost suffocated, and fell into a swoon. When he began to recover, he could just distinguish the voices of his companions outside, who had given him up for lost, and were singing his death-song. At first he could see nothing, but soon he discerned something white before him, and at length plainly distinguished three people, entirely white, one man and two women, sitting at the edge of a black pool of water. He became alarmed and thought it high time to retreat. Having succeeded, after great trouble, in reaching daylight again, he went straight to the spot directly above the pool of water where he had seen the three mysterious beings. Here he beat a hole with his war-club in the ground, and sat down to watch. In a moment the nose of an old male beaver appeared at the opening. Mene-Seela instantly seized him and dragged him up, when two other beavers, both females, thrust out their heads, and these he served in the same way. 'These,' continued the old man, 'must have been the three white people whom I saw sitting at the edge of the water.'

Mene-Seela was the grand depositary of the legends and traditions of the village. I succeeded, however, in getting from him only a few fragments. Like all Indians, he was excessively superstitious, and continually saw some reason for withholding his stories. 'It is a bad thing,' he would say, 'to tell the tales in summer. Stay with us till next winter, and I will tell you every thing I know; but now our war-parties are going out, and our young men will be killed if I sit down to tell stories before the frost begins.'

But to leave this digression. We remained encamped on this spot five days, during three of which the hunters were at work incessantly, and immense quantities of meat and hides were brought in. Great alarm, however, prevailed in the village. All were on the alert. The young men were ranging through the country as scouts, and the old men paid careful attention to omens and prodigies, and especially to their dreams. In order to convey to the enemy (who, if they were in the neighborhood, must inevitably have known of our presence,) the impression that we were constantly on the watch, piles of sticks and stones were erected on all the surrounding hills, in such a manner as to appear at a distance like sentinels. Often, even to this hour, that scene will rise before my mind like a visible reality;—the tall white rocks; the old pine-trees on their summits; the sandy stream that ran along their bases and half encircled the village; and the wild-sage bushes, with their dull green hue and their medicinal odor, that covered all the neighboring declivities. Hour after hour the squaws would pass and repass with their vessels of water between the stream and the lodges. For the most part, no one was to be seen in the camp but women and children, two or three superannuated old men, and a few lazy and worthless young ones. These, together with the dogs, now grown fat and good-natured with the abundance in the camp, were its only tenants. Still it presented a busy and bustling scene. In all quarters the meat, hung on cords of hide, was drying in the sun, and around the lodges the squaws, young and old, were laboring on the fresh hides that were stretched upon the ground, scraping the hair from one side and the still adhering flesh from the other, and rubbing into them the brains of the buffalo, in order to render them soft and pliant.

In mercy to myself and my horse, I never went out with the hunters after the first day. Of late, however, I had been gaining strength rapidly, as was always the case upon every respite of my disorder. I was soon able to walk with ease. Raymond and I would go out upon the neighboring prairies to shoot antelope, or sometimes to assail straggling buffalo, on foot; an attempt in which we met with rather indifferent success. To kill a bull with a rifle-ball is a difficult art, in the secret of which I was as yet very imperfectly initiated. As I came out of Kongra-Tonga's lodge one morning, Reynal called to me from the opposite side of the village, and asked me over to breakfast. The breakfast was a substantial one. It consisted of the rich, juicy hump-ribs of a fat cow; a repast absolutely unrivalled. It was roasting before the fire, impaled upon a stout stick, which Reynal took up and planted in the ground before his lodge; when he, with Raymond and myself, taking our seats around it, unsheathed our knives and assailed it with good will. In spite of all medical experience, this solid fare, without bread or salt, seemed to agree with me admirably.

'We shall have strangers here before night,' said Reynal.

'How do you know that?' I asked.

'I dreamed so. I am as good at dreaming as an Indian. There is the Hail-Storm; he dreamed the same thing, and he and his crony, the Rabbit, have gone out on discovery.'

I laughed at Reynal for his credulity, went over to my host's lodge, took down my rifle, walked out a mile or two on the prairie, saw an old bull standing alone, crawled up a ravine, shot him, and saw him escape. Then, quite exhausted and rather ill-humored, I walked back to the village. By a strange coincidence, Reynal's prediction had been verified; for the first persons whom I saw were the two trappers, Rouleau and Saraphin, coming to meet me. These men, as the reader may possibly recollect, had left our party about a fortnight before. They had been trapping for a while among the Black Hills, and were now on their way to the Rocky Mountains, intending in a day or two to set out for the neighboring Medicine Bow. They were not the most elegant or refined of companions, yet they made a very welcome addition to the limited society of the village. For the rest of that day we lay smoking and talking in Reynal's lodge. This indeed was no better than a little hut, made of hides stretched on poles, and entirely open in front. It was well carpeted with soft buffalo-robes, and here we remained, sheltered from the sun, surrounded by various domestic utensils of Madame Margot's household. All was quiet in the village. Though the hunters had not gone out that day, they lay sleeping in their lodges, and most of the women were silently engaged in their heavy tasks. A few young men were playing at a lazy game of ball in the centre of the village; and when they became tired, some girls supplied their place with a more boisterous sport. At a little distance, among the lodges, some children and half-grown squaws were playfully tossing up one of their number in a buffalo-robe, an exact counterpart of the ancient pastime from which Sancho Panza suffered so much. Farther out on the prairie, a host of little naked boys were roaming about, engaged in various rough games, or pursuing birds and ground-squirrels with their bows and arrows; and woe to the unhappy little animals that fell into their merciless, torture-loving hands! A squaw from the next lodge, a notable active housewife, named Weah Washtay, or the Good Woman, brought us a large bowl of *Wasna*, and went into an ecstasy of delight when I presented her with a green glass ring, such as I usually wore with a view to similar occasions.

The sun went down, and half the sky was glowing fiery red, reflected on the little stream as it wound away among the sage-bushes. Some young men left the village, and soon returned, driving in before them all the horses, hundreds in number, and of every size, age and color. The hunters came out, and each securing those that belonged to him, examined their condition, and tied them fast by long cords to stakes driven in front of his lodge. It was half an hour before the bustle subsided and tranquillity was restored again. By this time it was nearly dark. Kettles were hung over the blazing fires, around which the squaws were gathered with their children, laughing and talking merrily. A circle of a different kind was formed in the centre of the village. This was composed of the old men and warriors of repute, who with their white buffalo-robes drawn close around their shoulders, sat together, and as the pipe passed from hand to hand, their conversation had not a particle of the gravity and reserve usually ascribed to Indians. I sat down with them as usual. I had in my hand half a dozen squibs and serpents, which I had made one day when encamped upon Laramie Creek, out of gunpowder and charcoal, and the leaves of 'Fremont's Expedition,' rolled round a stout lead-pencil. I waited till I contrived to get hold of the large piece of burning *bois-de-vache* which the Indians kept by them on the ground for lighting their pipes. With this I lighted all the fireworks at once, and tossed them whizzing and sputtering into the air, over the heads of the company. They all jumped up and ran off with yelps of astonishment and consternation. After a moment or two, they ventured to come back one by one, and some of the boldest, picking up the cases of burnt paper that were scattered about, examined them with eager curiosity to discover their mysterious secret. From that time forward I enjoyed great repute as a 'fire-medicine.'

The camp was filled with the low hum of cheerful voices. There were other sounds, however, of a very different kind, for from a large lodge, lighted up like a gigantic lantern by the blazing fire within, came a chorus of dismal cries and wailings, long drawn out, like the howling of wolves, and a woman, almost naked, was crouching close outside, crying violently, and gashing her legs with a knife till they were covered with blood. Just a year before, a young man belonging to this family had gone out with a war-party and had been slain by the enemy, and his relatives were thus lamenting his loss. Still other sounds might be heard; loud earnest cries often repeated from amid the gloom, at a distance beyond the village. They proceeded from some young men who, being about to set out in a few days on a warlike expedition, were standing at the top of a hill, calling on the Great Spirit to aid them in their enterprise. While I was listening, Rouleau, with a laugh on his careless face, called to me and directed my attention to another quarter. In front of the lodge where Weah Washtay lived another squaw was standing, angrily scolding an old yellow dog, who lay on the ground with his nose resting between his paws, and his eyes turned sleepily up to her face, as if he were pretending to give respectful attention, but resolved to fall asleep as soon as it was all over.

'You ought to be ashamed of yourself!' said the old woman. 'I have fed you well, and taken care of you ever since you were small and blind, and could only crawl about and squeal a little, instead of howling as you do now. When you grew old, I said you were a good dog. You were strong and gentle when the load was put on your back, and you never ran among the feet of the horses when we were all travelling together over the prairie. But you had a bad heart! Whenever a rabbit jumped out of the bushes, you were always the first to run after him and lead away all the other dogs behind you. You ought to have known that it was very dangerous to act so. When you had got far out on the prairie, and no one was near to help you, perhaps a wolf would jump out of the ravine; and then what could you do? You would certainly have been killed, for no dog can fight well with a load on his back. Only three days ago you ran off in that way, and turned over the bag of wooden pins with which I used to fasten up the front of the lodge. Look up there, and you will see that it is all flapping open. And now to-night you have stolen a great piece of fat meat which was roasting before the fire for my children. I tell you, you have a bad heart, and you must die!'

So saying, the squaw went into the lodge, and coming out with a large stone mallet, killed the unfortunate dog at one blow. This speech is worthy of notice, as illustrating a curious characteristic of the Indians; the ascribing intelligence and a power of understanding speech to the inferior animals; to whom, indeed, according to many of their traditions, they are linked in close affinity; and they even claim the honor of a lineal descent from bears, wolves, deer or tortoises.

As it grew late, and the crowded population began to disappear, I too walked across the village to the lodge of my host, Kongra-Tonga. As I entered, I saw him, by the flickering blaze of the fire in the centre, reclining half asleep in his usual place. His couch was by no means an uncomfortable one. It consisted of soft buffalo-robes, laid together on the ground, and a pillow made of whitened deer-skin, stuffed with feathers and ornamented with beads. At his back was a light framework of poles and slender reeds, against which he could lean with ease when in a sitting posture; and at the top of it, just above his head, his bow and quiver were hanging. His squaw, a laughing, broad-faced woman, apparently had not yet completed her domestic arrangements, for she was bustling about the lodge, pulling over the utensils and the bales of dried meats that were ranged carefully around it. Unhappily, she and her partner were not the only tenants of the dwelling; for half a dozen children were scattered about, sleeping in every imaginable posture. My saddle was in its place at the head of the lodge, and a buffalo-robe was spread on the ground before it. Wrapping myself in my blanket, I lay down; but had I not been extremely fatigued, the noise in the next lodge would have prevented my sleeping. There was the monotonous thumping of the Indian drum, mixed with occasional sharp yells, and a chorus chanted by twenty voices. A grand scene of gambling was going forward with all the appropriate formalities. The players were staking on the chance issue of the game their ornaments, their horses, and as the excitement rose, their garments, and even their weapons; for desperate gambling is not confined to the hells of Paris. The men of the plains and the forests no less resort to it as a violent but grateful relief to the tedious monotony of their lives, which alternate between fierce excitement and listless inaction. I fell asleep with the dull notes of the drum still sounding on my ear; but these furious orgies lasted without intermission till daylight. I was soon awakened by one of the children crawling over me, while another larger one was tugging at my blanket and nestling himself in a very disagreeable proximity. I immediately repelled these advances by punching the heads of these miniature savages with a short stick which I always kept by me for the purpose; and as sleeping half the day and eating much more than is good for them makes them extremely restless, this operation usually had to be repeated four or five times in the course of the night. My host himself was the author of another most formidable annoyance. All these Indians, and he among the rest, think themselves bound to the constant performance of certain acts as the condition on which their success in life depends, whether in war, love, hunting, or any other employment. These 'medicines,' as they are called in that country, which are usually communicated in dreams, are often absurd enough. Some Indians will strike the butt of the pipe against the ground every time they smoke; others will insist that every thing they say shall be interpreted by contraries; and Shaw once met an old man who conceived that all would be lost unless he compelled every white man he met to drink a bowl of cold water. My host was particularly fortunate in his allotment. The Great Spirit had told him in a dream that he must sing a certain song in the middle of every night; and regularly at about twelve o'clock his dismal monotonous chanting would awaken me, and I would see him seated bolt upright on his couch, going through his dolorous performance with a most business-like air. There were other voices of the night, still more inharmonious. Twice or thrice, between sunset and dawn, all the dogs in the village, and there were hundreds of them, would bay and yelp in chorus; a most horrible clamor, resembling no sound that I have ever heard, except perhaps the frightful howling of wolves that we used sometimes to hear, long afterward, when descending the Arkansas on the trail of Gen. Kearney's army. The canine uproar is, if possible, more discordant than that of the wolves. Heard at a distance slowly rising on the night, it has a strange unearthly effect, and would fearfully haunt the dreams of a nervous man; but when you are sleeping in the midst of it, the din is outrageous. One long loud howl from the next lodge perhaps begins it, and voice after voice takes up the sound, till it passes around the whole circumference of the village, and the air is filled with confused and discordant cries, at once fierce and mournful. It lasts but for a moment, and then dies away into silence.

Morning came, and Kongra-Tonga, mounting his horse, rode out with the hunters. It may not be amiss to glance at him for an instant in his domestic character of husband and father. Both he and his squaw, like most other Indians, were very fond of their children, whom they indulged to excess, and never punished, except in extreme cases, when they would throw a bowl of cold water over them. Their offspring became sufficiently undutiful and disobedient under this system of education, which tends not a little to foster that wild idea of liberty and utter intolerance of restraint which lie at the very foundation of the Indian character. It would be hard to find a fonder father than Kongra-Tonga. There was one urchin in particular, rather less than two feet high, to whom he was exceedingly attached; and sometimes spreading a buffalo-robe in the lodge, he would seat himself upon it, place his small favorite upright before him, and chant in a low tone some of the words used as an accompaniment to the war-dance. The little fellow, who could just manage to balance himself by stretching out both arms, would lift his feet and turn slowly round and round in time to his father's music, while my host would laugh with delight, and look smiling up into my face to see if I were admiring this precocious perfor-mance of his offspring. In his capacity of husband he was somewhat less exemplary. The squaw who lived in the lodge with him had been his partner for many years. She took good care of his children and his household concerns. He liked her well enough, and as far as I could see, they never quarrelled; but all his warmer affections were reserved for younger and more recent favorites. Of these he had at present only one, who lived in a lodge apart from his own. One day while in his camp, he became displeased with her, pushed her out, threw after her her ornaments, dresses, and every thing she had, and told her to go home to her father. Having consummated this summary divorce, for which he could show good reasons, he came back, seated himself in his usual place, and began to smoke with an air of the utmost tranquillity and self-satisfaction.

I was sitting in the lodge with him on that very afternoon, when I felt some curiosity to learn the history of the numer-ous scars that appeared on his naked body. Of some of them, however, I did not venture to inquire, for I already under-stood their origin. Each of his arms was marked as if deeply gashed with a knife at regular intervals, and there were other scars also, of a different character, on his back and on either breast. They were the traces of those formidable tortures which these Indians, in common with a few other tribes, in-flict upon themselves at certain seasons; in part, it may be, to gain the glory of courage and endurance, but chiefly as an act of self-sacrifice to secure the favor of the Great Spirit. The scars upon the breast and back were produced by running through the flesh strong splints of wood, to which ponderous buffalo-skulls are fastened by cords of hide, and the wretch runs forward with all his strength, assisted by two compan-ions, who take hold of each arm, until the flesh tears apart and the heavy loads are left behind. Others of Kongra-Tonga's scars were the result of accidents; but he had many which he received in war. He was one of the most noted warriors in the village. In the course of his life he had slain, as he boasted to me, fourteen men; and though, like other Indians, he was a great braggart and utterly regardless of truth, yet in this statement common report bore him out. Being much flattered by my inquiries, he told me tale after tale, true or false, of his warlike exploits; and there was one among the rest illustrating the worst features of the Indian character too well for me to omit it. Pointing out of the opening of the lodge toward the Medicine Bow Mountain, not many miles distant, he said that he was there a few summers ago with a war-party of his young men. Here they found two Snake Indians, hunting. They shot one of them with arrows, and chased the other up the side of the mountain till they surrounded him on a level place, and Kongra-Tonga himself jumping forward among the trees, seized him by the arm. Two of his young men then ran up and held him fast while he scalped him alive. They then built a great fire, and cutting the tendons of their captive's wrists and feet, threw him in, and held him down with long poles until he was burnt to death. He garnished his story with a great many descriptive particulars much too revolting to mention. His features were remarkably mild and open, without the fierceness of expression common among these Indians; and as he detailed these devilish cruelties, he looked up into my face with the same air of earnest simplicity which a little child would wear in relating to its mother some anecdote of its youthful experience.

Old Mene-Seela's lodge could offer another illustration of the ferocity of Indian warfare. A bright-eyed active little boy was living there. He had belonged to a village of the Gros-Ventre Blackfeet, a small but bloody and treacherous band, in close alliance with the Arapahoes. About a year before, Kongra-Tonga and a party of warriors had found about twenty lodges of these Indians upon the plains a little to the eastward of our present camp; and surrounding them in the night, they butchered men, women, and children without mercy, preserving only this little boy alive. He was adopted into the old man's family, and was now fast becoming identified with the Ogillallah children, among whom he mingled on equal terms. There was also a Crow warrior in the village, a man of gigantic stature and most symmetrical proportions. Having been taken prisoner many years before and adopted by a squaw in place of a son whom she had lost, he had forgotten his old national antipathies, and was now both in act and inclination an Ogillallah.

It will be remembered that the scheme of the grand warlike combination against the Snake and Crow Indians originated in this village; and though this plan had fallen to the ground, the embers of the martial ardor continued to glow brightly. Eleven young men had prepared themselves to go out against the enemy. The fourth day of our stay in this camp was fixed upon for their departure. At the head of this party was a well-built, active little Indian, called the White Shield, whom I had always noticed for the great neatness of his dress and appearance. His lodge too, though not a large one, was the best in the village, his squaw was one of the prettiest girls, and altogether his dwelling presented a complete model of an Ogillallah domestic establishment. I was often a visitor there, for the White Shield being rather partial to white men, used to invite me to continual feasts at all hours of the day. Once when the substantial part of the entertainment was concluded, and he and I were seated cross-legged on a buffalo-robe smoking together very amicably, he took down his warlike equipments, which were hanging around the lodge, and displayed them with great pride and self-importance. Among the rest was a most superb head-dress of feathers. Taking this from its case, he put it on and stood before me, as if conscious of the gallant air which it gave to his dark face and his vigorous graceful figure. He told me that upon it were the feathers of three war-eagles, equal in value to the same number of good horses. He took up also a shield gayly painted and hung with feathers. The effect of these barbaric ornaments was admirable, for they were arranged with no little skill and taste. His quiver was made of the spotted skin of a small panther, such as are common among the Black Hills, from which the tail and distended claws were still allowed to hang. The White Shield concluded his entertainment in a manner characteristic of an Indian. He begged of me a little powder and ball, for he had a gun as well as bow and arrows; but this I was obliged to refuse, because I had scarcely enough for my own use. Making him, however, a parting present of a paper of vermilion, I left him apparently quite contented.

Unhappily on the next morning the White Shield took cold, and was attacked with a violent inflammation of the throat. Immediately he seemed to lose all spirit, and though before no warrior in the village had borne himself more proudly, he now moped about from lodge to lodge with a forlorn and dejected air. At length he came and sat down, close wrapped in his robe, before the lodge of Reynal, but when he found that neither he nor I knew how to relieve him, he arose and stalked over to one of the medicine-men of the village. This old imposter thumped him for some time with both fists, howled and yelped over him, and beat a drum close to his ear to expel the evil spirit that had taken possession of him. This vigorous treatment failing of the desired effect, the White Shield withdrew to his own lodge, where he lay disconsolate for some hours. Making his appearance once more in the afternoon, he again took his seat on the ground before Reynal's lodge, holding his throat with his hand. For some time he sat perfectly silent with his eyes fixed mournfully on the ground. At last he began to speak in a low tone:

'I am a brave man,' he said; 'all the young men think me a great warrior, and ten of them are ready to go with me to the war. I will go and show them the enemy. Last summer the Snakes killed my brother. I cannot live unless I revenge his death. To-morrow we will set out and I will take their scalps.'

The White Shield, as he expressed this resolution, seemed to have lost all the accustomed fire and spirit of his look, and hung his head as if in a fit of despondency.

As I was sitting that evening at one of the fires, I saw him arrayed in his splendid war-dress, his cheeks painted with vermilion, leading his favorite war-horse to the front of his lodge. He mounted and rode round the village, singing his war-song in a loud hoarse voice amid the shrill acclamations of the women. Then dismounting, he remained for some minutes prostrate upon the ground, as if in an act of supplication. On the following morning I looked in vain for the departure of the warriors. All was quiet in the village until late in the forenoon, when the White Shield issuing from his lodge, came and seated himself in his old place before us. Reynal asked him why he had not gone out to find the enemy?

'I cannot go,' answered the White Shield in a dejected voice. 'I have given my war-arrows to the Meneaska.'

'You have only given him two of your arrows,' said Reynal. 'If you ask him, he will give them back again.'

For some time the White Shield said nothing. At last he spoke in a gloomy tone:

'One of my young men has had bad dreams. The spirits of the dead came and threw stones at him in his sleep.'

If such a dream had actually taken place it might have broken up this or any other war-party, but both Reynal and I were convinced at the time that it was a mere fabrication to excuse his remaining at home.

The White Shield was a warrior of noted prowess. Very probably, he would have received a mortal wound without the show of pain, and endured without flinching the worst tortures that an enemy could inflict upon him. The whole power of an Indian's nature would be summoned to encounter such a trial; every influence of his education from childhood would have prepared him for it; the cause of his suffering would have been visibly and palpably before him, and his spirit would rise to set his enemy at defiance, and gain the highest glory of a warrior by meeting death with fortitude. But when he feels himself attacked by a mysterious evil, before whose insidious assaults his manhood is wasted, and his strength drained away, when he can see no enemy to resist and defy, the boldest warrior falls prostrate at once. He believes that a bad spirit has taken possession of him, or that he is the victim of some charm. When suffering from a protracted disorder, an Indian will often abandon himself to his supposed destiny, pine away and die, the victim of his own imagination. The same effect will often follow from a series of calamities, or a long run of ill-success, and the sufferer has been known to ride into the midst of an enemy's camp, or attack a grizzly bear single-handed, to get rid of a life which he supposed to lie under the doom of misfortune.

Thus after all his fasting, dreaming, and calling upon the Great Spirit, the White Shield's war-party was pitifully broken up.

Chapter XVI.

THE TRAPPERS.

"Ours the wild life, in tumult still to range,
  From toil to rest, and joy in every change;
  The exulting sense, the pulse's maddening play,
  That thrills the wanderer of the trackless way;
  That for itself can woo the approaching fight,
  And turn what some deem danger to delight:
  Come when it will we snatch the life of life;
  When lost, what recks it by disease or strife?"

                                        THE CORSAIR.

IN SPEAKING of the Indians, I have almost forgotten two bold adventurers of another race, the trappers Rouleau and Saraphin. These men were bent on a most hazardous enterprise. A day's journey to the westward was the country over which the Arapahoes are accustomed to range, and for which the two trappers were on the point of setting out. These Arapahoes, of whom Shaw and I afterwards fell in with a large village, are ferocious barbarians, of a most brutal and wolfish aspect; and of late they had declared themselves enemies to the whites, and threatened death to the first who should venture within their territory. The occasion of the declaration was as follows:

In the previous spring, 1845, Col. Kearney left Fort Leavenworth with several companies of dragoons, and marching with extraordinary celerity, reached Fort Laramie, whence he passed along the foot of the mountains to Bent's Fort, and then, turning eastward again, returned to the point from whence he set out. While at Fort Laramie, he sent a part of his command as far westward as Sweetwater, while he himself remained at the fort, and dispatched messages to the surrounding Indians to meet him there in council. Then for the first time the tribes of that vicinity saw the white warriors, and, as might have been expected, they were lost in astonishment at their regular order, their gay attire, the completeness of their martial equipment, and the great size and power of their horses. Among the rest, the Arapahoes came in consid-

erable numbers to the fort. They had lately committed numerous acts of outrage, and Col. Kearney threatened that if they
killed any more white men he would turn loose his dragoons
upon them, and annihilate their whole nation. In the evening,
to add effect to his speech, he ordered a howitzer to be fired
and a rocket to be thrown up. Many of the Arapahoes fell
prostrate on the ground, while others ran away screaming
with amazement and terror. On the following day they withdrew to their mountains, confounded with awe at the appearance of the dragoons, at their big gun which went off twice at
one shot, and the fiery messenger which they had sent up to
the Great Spirit. For many months they remained quiet, and
did no farther mischief. At length, just before we came into
the country, one of them, by an act of the basest treachery,
killed two white men, Boot and May, who were trapping
among the mountains. For this act it was impossible to discover a motive. It seemed to spring from one of those inexplicable impulses which often actuate Indians, and appear no
better than the mere outbreaks of native ferocity. No sooner
was the murder committed than the whole tribe were in extreme consternation. They expected every day that the avenging dragoons would arrive, little thinking that a desert of nine
hundred miles in extent lay between the latter and their
mountain fastnesses. A large deputation of them came to Fort
Laramie, bringing a valuable present of horses, in compensation for the lives of the murdered men. These Bordeaux refused to accept. They then asked him if he would be satisfied
with their delivering up the murderer himself; but he declined
this offer also. The Arapahoes went back more terrified than
ever. Weeks passed away, and still no dragoons appeared. A
result followed which all those best acquainted with Indians
had predicted. They conceived that fear had prevented Bordeaux from accepting their gifts, and that they had nothing to
apprehend from the vengeance of the whites. From terror
they rose to the height of insolence and presumption. They
called the white men cowards and old women; and a friendly
Dahcotah came to Fort Laramie and reported that they were
determined to kill the first of the white dogs whom they
could lay hands on.

Had a military officer, intrusted with suitable powers, been stationed at Fort Laramie, and having accepted the offer of the Arapahoes to deliver up the murderer, had ordered him to be immediately led out and shot, in presence of his tribe, they would have been awed into tranquillity, and much danger and calamity averted; but now the neighborhood of the Medicine Bow Mountain and the region beyond it was a scene of extreme peril. Old Mene-Seela, a true friend of the whites, and many other of the Indians, gathered about the two trappers, and vainly endeavored to turn them from their purpose; but Rouleau and Saraphin only laughed at the danger. On the morning preceding that on which they were to leave the camp, we could all discern faint white columns of smoke rising against the dark base of the Medicine Bow. Scouts were out immediately, and reported that these proceeded from an Arapahoe camp, abandoned only a few hours before. Still the two trappers continued their preparations for departure.

Saraphin was a tall, powerful fellow, with a sullen and sinister countenance. His rifle had very probably drawn other blood than that of buffalo or even Indians. Rouleau had a broad ruddy face, marked with as few traces of thought or of care as a child's. His figure was remarkably square and strong, but the first joints of both his feet were frozen off, and his horse had lately thrown and trampled upon him, by which he had been severely injured in the chest. But nothing could check his inveterate propensity for laughter and gayety. He went all day rolling about the camp on his stumps of feet, talking and singing and frolicking with the Indian women, as they were engaged at their work. In fact Rouleau had an unlucky partiality for squaws. He always had one, whom he must needs bedizen with beads, ribbons, and all the finery of an Indian wardrobe; and though he was of course obliged to leave her behind him during his expeditions, yet this hazardous necessity did not at all trouble him, for his disposition was the very reverse of jealous. If at any time he had not lavished the whole of the precarious profits of his vocation upon his dark favorite, he always devoted the rest to feasting his comrades. If liquor was not to be had—and this was usually the case—strong coffee would be substituted. As the men of that region are by no means remarkable for providence or self-restraint, whatever was set before them on these occasions, however extravagant in price or enormous in quantity, was sure to be disposed of at one sitting. Like other trappers, Rouleau's life was one of contrast and variety. It was only at certain seasons, and for a limited time, that he was absent on his expeditions. For the rest of the year he would be lounging about the fort, or encamped with his friends in its vicinity, lazily hunting or enjoying all the luxury of inaction; but when once in pursuit of the beaver, he was involved in extreme privations and desperate perils. When in the midst of his game and his enemies, hand and foot, eye and ear, are incessantly active. Frequently he must content himself with devouring his evening meal uncooked, lest the light of his fire should attract the eyes of some wandering Indian; and sometimes having made his rude repast, he must leave his fire still blazing, and withdraw to a distance under cover of the darkness, that his disappointed enemy, drawn thither by the light, may find his victim gone, and be unable to trace his footsteps in the gloom. This is the life led by scores of men in the Rocky Mountains and their vicinity. I once met a trapper whose breast was marked with the scars of six bullets and arrows, one of his arms broken by a shot and one of his knees shattered; yet still, with the undaunted mettle of New-England, from which part of the country he had come, he continued to follow his perilous occupation. To some of the children of cities it may seem strange, that men with no object in view should continue to follow a life of such hardship and desperate adventure, yet there is a mysterious, resistless charm in the basilisk eye of danger, and few men perhaps remain long in that wild region without learning to love peril for its own sake, and to laugh carelessly in the face of death.

On the last day of our stay in this camp, the trappers were ready for departure. When in the Black Hills they had caught seven beaver, and they now left their skins in charge of Reynal, to be kept until their return. Their strong, gaunt horses, were equipped with rusty Spanish bits, and rude Mexican saddles, to which wooden stirrups were attached, while a buffalo-robe was rolled up behind them, and a bundle of beaver traps slung at the pommel. These, together with their rifles, their knives, their powder-horns and bullet-pouches, flint and steel and a tin cup, composed their whole travelling equipment. They shook hands with us, and rode away; Saraphin with his grim countenance, like a surly bull-dog's, was in advance; but Rouleau, clambering gayly into his seat, kicked his horse's sides, flourished his whip in the air, and trotted briskly over the prairie, trolling forth a Canadian song at the top of his lungs. Reynal looked after them with his face of brutal selfishness.

'Well,' he said, 'if they are killed, I shall have the beaver. They'll fetch me fifty dollars at the fort, any how.'

This was the last I saw of them.

We had been for five days in the hunting-camp, and the meat, which all this time had hung drying in the sun, was now fit for transportation. Buffalo-hides also had been pro-cured in sufficient quantities for making the next season's lodges; but it remained to provide the long slender poles on which they were to be supported. These were only to be had among the tall pine woods of the Black Hills, and in that direction therefore our next move was to be made. It is wor-thy of notice that amid the general abundance which during this time had prevailed in the camp, there were no instances of individual privation; for although the hide and the tongue of the buffalo belong by exclusive right to the hunter who has killed it, yet any one else is equally entitled to help himself from the rest of the carcass. Thus the weak, the aged, and even the indolent come in for a share of the spoils, and many a helpless old woman, who would otherwise perish from star-vation, is sustained in profuse abundance.

On the twenty-fifth of July, late in the afternoon, the camp broke up, with the usual tumult and confusion, and we were all moving once more, on horseback and on foot, over the plains. We advanced however but a few miles. The old men, who during the whole march had been stoutly striding along on foot in front of the people, now seated themselves in a circle on the ground, while all the families erecting their lodges in the prescribed order around them, formed the usual great circle of the camp; meanwhile these village patriarchs sat smoking and talking. I threw my bridle to Raymond, and sat down as usual along with them. There was none of that re-serve and apparent dignity which an Indian always assumes when in council, or in the presence of white men whom he distrusts. The party, on the contrary, was an extremely merry one, and as in a social circle of a quite different character, 'if there was not much wit, there was at least a great deal of laughter.'

When the first pipe was smoked out, I rose and withdrew to the lodge of my host. Here I was stooping, in the act of taking off my powder-horn and bullet-pouch, when suddenly, and close at hand, pealing loud and shrill, and in right good earnest, came the terrific yell of the war-whoop. Kongra-Tonga's squaw snatched up her youngest child, and ran out of the lodge. I followed, and found the whole village in confusion, resounding with cries and yells. The circle of old men in the centre had vanished. The warriors with glittering eyes came darting, their weapons in their hands, out of the low openings of the lodges, and running with wild yells toward the farther end of the village. Advancing a few rods in that direction, I saw a crowd in furious agitation, while others ran up on every side to add to the confusion. Just then I distinguished the voices of Raymond and Reynal, shouting to me from a distance, and looking back, I saw the latter with his rifle in his hand, standing on the farther bank of a little stream that ran along the outskirts of the camp. He was calling to Raymond and myself to come over and join him, and Raymond, with his usual deliberate gait and stolid countenance, was already moving in that direction.

This was clearly the wisest course, unless we wished to involve ourselves in the fray; so I turned to go, but just then a pair of eyes, gleaming like a snake's, and an aged familiar countenance was thrust from the opening of a neighboring lodge, and out bolted old Mene-Seela, full of fight, clutching his bow and arrows in one hand and his knife in the other. At that instant he tripped and fell sprawling on his face, while his weapons flew scattering away in every direction. The women with loud screams were hurrying with their children in their arms to place them out of danger, and I observed some hastening to prevent mischief, by carrying away all the weapons they could lay hands on. On a rising ground close to the camp stood a line of old women singing a medicine-song to allay the tumult. As I approached the side of the brook, I heard gun-shots behind me, and turning back, I saw that the crowd had separated into two long lines of naked warriors confronting each other at a respectful distance, and yelling and jumping about to dodge the shot of their adversaries, while they discharged bullets and arrows against each other. At the same time certain sharp, humming sounds in the air over my head, like the flight of beetles on a summer evening, warned me that the danger was not wholly confined to the immediate scene of the fray. So wading through the brook, I joined Reynal and Raymond, and we sat down on the grass, in the posture of an armed neutrality, to watch the result.

Happily it may be for ourselves, though quite contrary to our expectation, the disturbance was quelled almost as soon as it had commenced. When I looked again, the combatants were once more mingled together in a mass. Though yells sounded occasionally from the throng, the firing had entirely ceased, and I observed five or six persons moving busily about, as if acting the part of peace-makers. One of the village heralds or criers proclaimed in a loud voice something which my two companions were too much engrossed in their own observations, to translate for me. The crowd began to disperse, though many a deep-set black eye still glittered with an unnatural lustre, as the warriors slowly withdrew to their lodges. This fortunate suppression of the disturbance was owing to a few of the old men, less pugnacious than Mene-Seela, who boldly ran in between the combatants, and aided by some of the 'soldiers,' or Indian police, succeeded in effecting their object.

It seemed very strange to me that although many arrows and bullets were discharged, no one was mortally hurt, and I could only account for this by the fact that both the marksman and the object of his aim were leaping about incessantly during the whole time. By far the greater part of the villagers had joined in the fray, for although there were not more than a dozen guns in the whole camp, I heard at least eight or ten shots fired.

In a quarter of an hour all was comparatively quiet. A large circle of warriors was again seated in the centre of the village, but this time I did not venture to join them, because I could see that the pipe, contrary to the usual order, was passing from the left hand to the right around the circle; a sure sign that a 'medicine-smoke' of reconciliation was going forward, and that a white man would be an unwelcome intruder. When I again entered the still agitated camp it was nearly dark, and mournful cries, howls, and wailings resounded from many female voices. Whether these had any connection with the late disturbance, or were merely lamentations for relatives slain in some former war expeditions, I could not distinctly ascertain.

To inquire too closely into the cause of the quarrel was by no means prudent, and it was not until some time after that I discovered what had given rise to it. Among the Dahcotah there are many associations, or fraternities, connected with the purposes of their superstitions, their warfare, or their social life. There was one called 'The Arrow-Beakers,' now in a great measure disbanded and dispersed. In the village there were however four men belonging to it, distinguished by the peculiar arrangement of their hair, which rose in a high bristling mass above their foreheads, adding greatly to their apparent height, and giving them a most ferocious appearance. The principal among them was the Mad Wolf, a warrior of remarkable size and strength, great courage, and the fierceness of a demon. I had always looked upon him as the most dangerous man in the village; and though he often invited me to feasts, I never entered his lodge unarmed. The Mad Wolf had taken a fancy to a fine horse belonging to another Indian, who was called the Tall Bear; and anxious to get the animal into his possession, he made the owner a present of another horse nearly equal in value. According to the customs of the Dahcotah, the acceptance of this gift involved a sort of obligation to make an equitable return; and the Tall Bear well understood that the other had in view the obtaining of his favorite buffalo-horse. He however accepted the present without a word of thanks, and having picketed the horse before his lodge, he suffered day after day to pass without making the expected return. The Mad Wolf grew impatient and angry; and at last, seeing that his bounty was not likely to produce the desired return, he resolved to reclaim it. So this evening, as soon as the village was encamped, he went to the lodge of the Tall Bear, seized upon the horse that he had

given him, and led him away. At this the Tall Bear broke into
one of those fits of sullen rage not uncommon among the
Indians. He ran up to the unfortunate horse, and gave him
three mortal stabs with his knife. Quick as lightning the Mad
Wolf drew his bow to its utmost tension, and held the arrow
quivering close to the breast of his adversary. The Tall Bear, as
the Indians who were near him said, stood with his bloody
knife in his hand, facing the assailant with the utmost calmness. Some of his friends and relatives, seeing his danger, ran
hastily to his assistance. The remaining three Arrow-Breakers,
on the other hand, came to the aid of their associate. Many of
their friends joined them, the war-cry was raised on a sudden,
and the tumult became general.

The 'soldiers,' who lent their timely aid in putting it down,
are by far the most important executive functionaries in an
Indian village. The office is one of considerable honor, being
confided only to men of courage and repute. They derive
their authority from the old men and chief warriors of the
village, who elect them in councils occasionally convened for
the purpose, and thus can exercise a degree of authority
which no one else in the village would dare to assume. While
very few Ogillallah chiefs could venture without instant jeopardy of their lives to strike or lay hands upon the meanest of
their people, the 'soldiers,' in the discharge of their appropriate functions, have full license to make use of these and similar acts of coercion.

Chapter XVII.

THE BLACK HILLS.

"To sit on rocks, to muse o'er flood and fell,
    To slowly trace the forest's shady scene,
    Where things that own not man's dominion dwell,
    And mortal foot hath ne'er, or rarely been;
    To climb the trackless mountain all unseen,
    With the wild flock that never needs a fold;
    Alone o'er steeps and foaming falls to lean;
    This is not solitude; 'tis but to hold
Converse with Nature's charms, and view her stores unrolled."

CHILDE HAROLD.

WE TRAVELLED EASTWARD for two days, and then the gloomy ridges of the Black Hills rose up before us. The village passed along for some miles beneath their declivities, trailing out to a great length over the arid prairie, or winding at times among small detached hills of distorted shapes. Turning sharply to the left, we entered a wide defile of the mountains, down the bottom of which a brook came winding, lined with tall grass and dense copses, amid which were hidden many beaver dams and lodges. We passed along between two lines of high precipices and rocks, piled in utter disorder one upon another, and with scarcely a tree, a bush, or a clump of grass to veil their nakedness. The restless Indian boys were wandering along their edges and clambering up and down their rugged sides, and sometimes a group of them would stand on the verge of a cliff and look down on the array as it passed in review beneath them. As we advanced, the passage grew more narrow; then it suddenly expanded into a round grassy meadow, completely encompassed by mountains; and here the families stopped as they came up in turn, and the camp rose like magic.

The lodges were hardly erected when, with their usual precipitation, the Indians set about accomplishing the object that had brought them there; that is, the obtaining poles for supporting their new lodges. Half the population, men, women, and boys, mounted their horses and set out for the interior of the mountains. As they rode at full gallop over the shingly rocks and into the dark opening of the defile beyond, I thought I had never read or dreamed of a more strange or picturesque cavalcade. We passed between precipices more than a thousand feet high, sharp and splintering at the tops, their sides beetling over the defile or descending in abrupt declivities, bristling with black fir-trees. On our left they rose close to us like a wall, but on the right a winding brook with a narrow strip of marshy soil intervened. The stream was clogged with old beaver-dams, and spread frequently into wide pools. There were thick bushes and many dead and blasted trees along its course, though frequently nothing remained but stumps cut close to the ground by the beaver, and marked with the sharp chisel-like teeth of those indefatigable laborers. Sometimes we were diving among trees, and then emerging upon open spots, over which, Indian-like, all galloped at full speed. As Pauline bounded over the rocks I felt her saddle-girth slipping, and alighted to draw it tighter; when the whole array swept past me in a moment, the women with their gaudy ornaments tinkling as they rode, the men whooping, and laughing, and lashing forward their horses. Two black-tailed deer bounded away among the rocks; Raymond shot at them from horseback; the sharp report of his rifle was answered by another equally sharp from the opposing cliffs, and then the echoes, leaping in rapid succession from side to side, died away rattling far amid the mountains.

After having ridden in this manner for six or eight miles, the appearance of the scene began to change, and all the declivities around us were covered with forests of tall, slender pine-trees. The Indians began to fall off to the right and left, and dispersed with their hatchets and knives among these woods, to cut the poles which they had come to seek. Soon I was left almost alone; but in the deep stillness of those lonely mountains, the stroke of hatchets and the sound of voices might be heard from far and near.

Reynal, who imitated the Indians in their habits as well as the worst features of their character, had killed buffalo enough to make a lodge for himself and his squaw, and now he was eager to get the poles necessary to complete it. He asked me to let Raymond go with him, and assist in the work. I assented, and the two men immediately entered the thickest part of the wood. Having left my horse in Raymond's keeping, I began to climb the mountain. I was weak and weary, and made slow progress, often pausing to rest, but after an hour had elapsed, I gained a height, whence the little valley out of which I had climbed seemed like a deep, dark gulf, though the inaccessible peak of the mountain was still towering to a much greater distance above. Objects familiar from childhood surrounded me; crags and rocks, a black and sullen brook that gurgled with a hollow voice deep among the crevices, a wood of mossy distorted trees and prostrate trunks flung down by age and storms, scattered among the rocks, or damming the foaming waters of the little brook. The objects were the same, yet they were thrown into a wilder and more startling scene, for the black crags and the savage trees assumed a grim and threatening aspect, and close across the valley the opposing mountain confronted me, rising from the gulf for thousands of feet, with its bare pinnacles and its ragged covering of pines. Yet the scene was not without its milder features. As I ascended, I found frequent little grassy terraces, and there was one of these close at hand, across which the brook was stealing, beneath the shade of scattered trees that seemed artificially planted. Here I made a welcome discovery, no other than a bed of strawberries, with their white flowers and their red fruit, close nestled among the grass by the side of the brook, and I sat down by them, hailing them as old acquaintances; for among those lonely and perilous mountains, they awakened delicious associations of the gardens and peaceful homes of far-distant New-England.

Yet wild as they were, these mountains were thickly peopled. As I climbed farther, I found the broad dusty paths made by the elk, as they filed across the mountain side. The grass on all the terraces was trampled down by deer; there were numerous tracks of wolves, and in some of the rougher and more precipitous parts of the ascent, I found foot-prints different from any that I had ever seen, and which I took to be those of the Rocky Mountain sheep. I sat down upon a rock; there was a perfect stillness. No wind was stirring, and not even an insect could be heard. I recollected the danger of becoming lost in such a place, and therefore I fixed my eye upon one of the tallest pinnacles of the opposite mountain. It rose sheer upright from the woods below, and by an extraordinary freak of nature, sustained aloft on its very summit a large loose rock. Such a landmark could never be mistaken, and feeling once more secure, I began again to move forward. A white wolf jumped up from among some bushes, and leaped clumsily away; but he stopped for a moment, and turned back his keen eye and his grim bristling muzzle. I longed to take his scalp and carry it back with me, as an appropriate trophy of the Black Hills, but before I could fire, he was gone among the rocks. Soon after I heard a rustling sound, with a cracking of twigs at a little distance, and saw moving above the tall bushes the branching antlers of an elk. I was in the midst of a hunter's paradise.

Such are the Black Hills, as I found them in July; but they wear a different garb when winter sets in, when the broad boughs of the fir tree are bent to the ground by the load of snow, and the dark mountains are whitened with it. At that season the mountain-trappers, returned from their autumn expeditions, often build their rude cabins in the midst of these solitudes, and live in abundance and luxury on the game that harbors there. I have heard them relate, how with their tawny mistresses, and perhaps a few young Indian companions, they have spent months in total seclusion. They would dig pitfalls, and set traps for the white wolves, the sables, and the martens, and though through the whole night the awful chorus of the wolves would resound from the frozen mountains around them, yet within their massive walls of logs they would lie in careless ease and comfort before the blazing fire, and in the morning shoot the elk and the deer from their very door.

Chapter XVIII.

A MOUNTAIN HUNT.

"Come, shall we go and kill us venison?
And yet it irks me, the poor dappled fools,
Being native burghers of this desert city,
Should in their own confines, with forked heads,
Have their round haunches gored."

AS YOU LIKE IT.

THE CAMP was full of the newly-cut lodge-poles; some, already prepared, were stacked together, white and glistening, to dry and harden in the sun; others were lying on the ground, and the squaws, the boys, and even some of the warriors, were busily at work peeling off the bark and paring them with their knives to the proper dimensions. Most of the hides obtained at the last camp were dressed and scraped thin enough for use, and many of the squaws were engaged in fitting them together and sewing them with sinews, to form the coverings for the lodges. Men were wandering among the bushes that lined the brook along the margin of the camp, cutting sticks of red willow, or *shongsasha*, the bark of which, mixed with tobacco, they use for smoking. Reynal's squaw was hard at work with her awl and buffalo sinews upon her lodge, while her proprietor, having just finished an enormous breakfast of meat, was smoking a social pipe along with Raymond and myself. He proposed at length that we should go out on a hunt. 'Go to the Big Crow's lodge,' said he, 'and get your rifle. I'll bet the gray Wyandot pony against your mare that we start an elk or a black-tailed deer, or likely as not, a big-horn, before we are two miles out of camp. I'll take my squaw's old yellow horse; you can't whip her more than four miles an hour, but she is as good for the mountains as a mule.'

I mounted the black mule which Raymond usually rode. She was a very fine and powerful animal, gentle and manageable enough by nature; but of late her temper had been soured by misfortune. About a week before, I had chanced to offend some one of the Indians, who out of revenge went secretly into the meadow and gave her a severe stab in the haunch with his knife. The wound, though partially healed, still galled her extremely, and made her even more perverse and obstinate than the rest of her species.

The morning was a glorious one, and I was in better health than I had been at any time for the last two months. Though a strong frame and well compacted sinews had borne me through hitherto, it was long since I had been in a condition to feel the exhilaration of the fresh mountain-wind and the gay sunshine that brightened the crags and trees. We left the little valley and ascended a rocky hollow in the mountain. Very soon we were out of sight of the camp, and of every living thing, man, beast, bird, or insect. I had never before, except on foot, passed over such execrable ground, and I desire never to repeat the experiment. The black mule grew indignant, and even the redoubtable yellow horse stumbled every moment, and kept groaning to himself as he cut his feet and legs among the sharp rocks.

It was a scene of silence and desolation. Little was visible except beetling crags and the bare shingly sides of the mountains, relieved by scarcely a trace of vegetation. At length, however, we came upon a forest tract, and had no sooner done so than we heartily wished ourselves back among the rocks again; for we were on a steep descent, among trees so thick that we could see scarcely a rod in any direction.

If one is anxious to place himself in a situation where the hazardous and the ludicrous are combined in about equal proportions, let him get upon a vicious mule, with a snaffle bit, and try to drive her through the woods down a slope of forty-five degrees. Let him have a long rifle, a buckskin frock with long fringes, and a head of long hair. These latter appendages will be caught every moment and twitched away in small portions by the twigs, which will also whip him smartly across the face, while the large branches above thump him on the head. His mule, if she be a true one, will alternately stop short and dive violently forward, and his positions upon her back will be somewhat diversified and extraordinary. At one time he will clasp her affectionately, to avoid the blow of a bough overhead; at another, he will throw himself back and fling his knee forward against the side of her neck, to keep it from being crushed between the rough bark of a tree and the equally unyielding ribs of the animal herself. Reynal was cursing incessantly during the whole way down. Neither of us had the remotest idea where we were going; and though I have seen rough riding, I shall always retain an evil recollection of that five minutes' scramble.

At last we left our troubles behind us, emerging into the channel of a brook that circled along the foot of the descent; and here, turning joyfully to the left, we rode in luxury and ease over the white pebbles and the rippling water, shaded from the glaring sun by an overarching green transparency. These halcyon moments were of short duration. The friendly brook, turning sharply to one side, went brawling and foaming down the rocky hill into an abyss, which, as far as we could discern, had no bottom; so once more we betook ourselves to the detested woods. When next we came forth from their dancing shadow and sunlight, we found ourselves standing in the broad glare of day, on a high jutting point of the mountain. Before us stretched a long, wide, desert valley, winding away far amid the mountains. No civilized eye but mine had ever looked upon that virgin waste. Reynal was gazing intently; he began to speak at last:

'Many a time, when I was with the Indians, I have been hunting for gold all through the Black Hills. There's plenty of it here; you may be certain of that. I have dreamed about it fifty times, and I never dreamed yet but what it came out true. Look over yonder at those black rocks piled up against that other big rock. Don't it look as if there might be something there? It won't do for a white man to be rummaging too much about these mountains; the Indians say they are full of bad spirits; and I believe myself that it's no good luck to be hunting about here after gold. Well, for all that, I would like to have one of these fellows up here, from down below, to go about with his witch-hazel rod, and I'll guarantee that it would not be long before he would light on a gold-mine. Never mind; we'll let the gold alone for to-day. Look at those trees down below us in the hollow; we'll go down there, and I reckon we'll get a black-tailed deer.'

But Reynal's predictions were not verified. We passed

mountain after mountain, and valley after valley; we explored deep ravines; yet still, to my companion's vexation and evident surprise, no game could be found. So, in the absence of better, we resolved to go out on the plains and look for an antelope. With this view we began to pass down a narrow valley, the bottom of which was covered with the stiff wild-sage bushes and marked with deep paths, made by the buffalo, who, for some inexplicable reason, are accustomed to penetrate, in their long grave processions, deep among the gorges of these sterile mountains.

Reynal's eye was ranging incessantly among the rocks and along the edges of the black precipices, in hopes of discovering the mountain-sheep peering down upon us in fancied security from that giddy elevation. Nothing was visible for some time. At length we both detected something in motion near the foot of one of the mountains, and in a moment afterward a black-tailed deer, with his spreading antlers, stood gazing at us from the top of a rock, and then, slowly turning away, disappeared behind it. In an instant Reynal was out of his saddle, and running toward the spot. I, being too weak to follow, sat holding his horse and waiting the result. I lost sight of him, then heard the report of his rifle deadened among the rocks, and finally saw him reappear, with a surly look, that plainly betrayed his ill success. Again we moved forward down the long valley, when soon after we came full upon what seemed a wide and very shallow ditch, incrusted at the bottom with white clay, dried and cracked in the sun. Under this fair outside, Reynal's eye detected the signs of lurking mischief. He called me to stop, and then alighting, picked up a stone and threw it into the ditch. To my utter amazement it fell with a dull splash, breaking at once through the thin crust, and spattering round the hole a yellowish creamy fluid, into which it sank and disappeared. A stick, five or six feet long, lay on the ground, and with this we sounded the insidious abyss close to its edge. It was just possible to touch the bottom. Places like this are numerous among the Rocky Mountains. The buffalo, in his blind and heedless walk, often plunges into them unawares. Down he sinks; one snort of terror, one convulsive struggle, and the slime calmly flows above his shaggy head, the languid undulations of its sleek and placid surface alone betraying how the powerful monster writhes in his death-throes below.

We found after some trouble a point where we could pass the abyss, and now the valley began to open upon the plains which spread to the horizon before us. On one of their distant swells we discerned three or four black specks, which Reynal pronounced to be buffalo.

'Come,' said he, 'we must get one of them. My squaw wants more sinews to finish her lodge with, and I want some glue myself.'

He immediately put the yellow horse to such a gallop as he was capable of executing, while I set spurs to the mule, who soon far outrun her plebeian rival. When we had galloped a mile or more, a large rabbit, by ill-luck, sprang up just under the feet of the mule, who bounded violently aside in full career. Weakened as I was, I was flung forcibly to the ground, and my rifle falling close to my head, went off with the shock. Its sharp, spiteful report rang for some moments in my ear. Being slightly stunned, I lay for an instant motionless, and Reynal, supposing me to be shot, rode up and began to curse the mule. Soon recovering myself, I arose, picked up the rifle and anxiously examined it. It was badly injured. The stock was cracked, and the main screw broken, so that the lock had to be tied in its place with a string; yet happily it was not rendered totally unserviceable. I wiped it out, reloaded it, and handing it to Reynal, who meanwhile had caught the mule and led her up to me, I mounted again. No sooner had I done so, than the brute began to rear and plunge with extreme violence; but being now well prepared for her, and free from incumbrance, I soon reduced her to submission. Then taking the rifle again from Reynal, we galloped forward as before.

We were now free of the mountains and riding far out on the broad prairie. The buffalo were still some two miles in advance of us. When we came near them, we stopped where a gentle swell of the plain concealed us from their view, and while I held his horse Reynal ran forward with his rifle, till I lost sight of him beyond the rising ground. A few minutes elapsed: I heard the report of his piece, and saw the buffalo running away at full speed on the right, and immediately after, the hunter himself, unsuccessful as before, came up and mounted his horse in excessive ill-humor. He cursed the Black Hills and the buffalo, swore that he was a good hunter, which indeed was true, and that he had never been out before among those mountains without killing two or three deer at least.

We now turned toward the distant encampment. As we rode along, antelope in considerable numbers were flying lightly in all directions over the plain, but not one of them would stand and be shot at. When we reached the foot of the mountain-ridge that lay between us and the village, we were too impatient to take the smooth and circuitous route; so turning short to the left, we drove our wearied animals directly upward among the rocks. Still more antelope were leaping about among these flinty hill-sides. Each of us shot at one, though from a great distance, and each missed his mark. At length we reached the summit of the last ridge. Looking down, we saw the bustling camp in the valley at our feet, and ingloriously descended to it. As we rode among the lodges, the Indians looked in vain for the fresh meat that should have hung behind our saddles, and the squaws uttered various suppressed ejaculations, to the great indignation of Reynal. Our mortification was increased when we rode up to his lodge. Here we saw his young Indian relative, the Hail-Storm, his light graceful figure reclining on the ground in an easy attitude, while with his friend the Rabbit, who sat by his side, he was making an abundant meal from a wooden bowl of *wasna*, which the squaw had placed between them. Near him lay the fresh skin of a female elk, which he had just killed among the mountains, only a mile or two from the camp. No doubt the boy's heart was elated with triumph, but he betrayed no sign of it. He even seemed totally unconscious of our approach, and his handsome face had all the tranquillity of Indian self-control; a self-control which prevents the exhibition of emotion without restraining the emotion itself. It was about two months since I had known the Hail-Storm, and within that time his character had remarkably developed. When I first saw him, he was just emerging from the habits and feelings of the boy into the ambition of the hunter and warrior. He had lately killed his first deer, and this had excited his aspirations after distinction. Since that time he had been continually in search of game, and no young hunter in the village had been so active or so fortunate as he. It will perhaps be remembered how fearlessly he attacked the buffalo-bull, as we were moving toward our camp at the Medicine Bow Mountain. All this success had produced a marked change in his character. As I first remembered him he always shunned the society of the young squaws, and was extremely bashful and sheepish in their presence; but now, in the confidence of his own reputation, he began to assume the airs and the arts of a man of gallantry. He wore his red blanket dashingly over his left shoulder, painted his cheeks every day with vermilion, and hung pendants of shells in his ears. If I observed aright, he met with very good success in his new pursuits; still the Hail-Storm had much to accomplish before he attained the full standing of a warrior. Gallantly as he began to bear himself among the women and girls, he still was timid and abashed in the presence of the chiefs and old men; for he had never yet killed a man, or stricken the dead body of an enemy in battle. I have no doubt that the handsome smooth-faced boy burned with a keen desire to flesh his maiden scalping-knife, and I would not have encamped alone with him without watching his movements with a distrustful eye.

His elder brother, the Horse, was of a different character. He was nothing but a lazy dandy. He knew very well how to hunt, but preferred to live by the hunting of others. He had no appetite for distinction, and the Hail-Storm, though a few years younger than he, already surpassed him in reputation. He had a dark and ugly face, and he passed a great part of his time in adorning it with vermilion, and contemplating it by means of a little pocket looking-glass which I gave him. As for the rest of the day, he divided it between eating and sleeping, and sitting in the sun on the outside of a lodge. Here he would remain for hour after hour, arrayed in all his finery, with an old dragoon's sword in his hand, and evidently flattering himself that he was the centre of attraction to the eyes of the surrounding squaws. Yet he sat looking straight forward with a face of the utmost gravity, as if wrapped in profound meditation, and it was only by the occasional sidelong glances which he shot at his supposed admirers that one could detect the true course of his thoughts.

Both he and his brother may represent a class in the Indian community: neither should the Hail-Storm's friend, the Rabbit, be passed by without notice. The Hail-Storm and he were inseparable: they ate, slept, and hunted together, and shared with one another almost all that they possessed. If there be any thing that deserves to be called romantic in the Indian character, it is to be sought for in friendships such as this, which are quite common among many of the prairie tribes.

Slowly, hour after hour, that weary afternoon dragged away. I lay in Reynal's lodge, overcome by the listless torpor that pervaded the whole encampment. The day's work was finished, or if it were not, the inhabitants had resolved not to finish it at all, and all were dozing quietly within the shelter of the lodges. A profound lethargy, the very spirit of indolence, seemed to have sunk upon the village. Now and then I could hear the low laughter of some girl from within a neighboring lodge, or the small shrill voices of a few restless children, who alone were moving in the deserted area. The spirit of the place infected me; I could not even think consecutively; I was fit only for musing and reverie, when at last, like the rest, I fell asleep.

When evening came, and the fires were lighted round the lodges, a select family circle convened in the neighborhood of Reynal's domicil. It was composed entirely of his squaw's relatives, a mean and ignoble clan, among whom none but the Hail-Storm held forth any promise of future distinction. Even his prospects were rendered not a little dubious by the character of the family, less however from any principle of aristocratic distinction than from the want of powerful supporters to assist him in his undertakings, and help to avenge his quarrels. Raymond and I sat down along with them. There were eight or ten men gathered around the fire, together with about as many women, old and young, some of whom were tolerably good-looking. As the pipe passed round among the men, a lively conversation went forward, more merry than delicate, and at length two or three of the elder women (for the girls were somewhat diffident and bashful) began to assail Raymond with various pungent witticisms. Some of the men took part, and an old squaw concluded by bestowing on him a ludicrous nickname, at which a general laugh followed at his

expense. Raymond grinned and giggled, and made several futile attempts at repartee. Knowing the impolicy and even danger of suffering myself to be placed in a ludicrous light among
the Indians, I maintained a rigid inflexible countenance, and
wholly escaped their sallies.

In the morning I found, to my great disgust, that the camp
was to retain its position for another day. I dreaded its languor and monotony, and to escape it, I set out to explore the
surrounding mountains. I was accompanied by a faithful
friend, my rifle, the only friend indeed on whose prompt assistance in time of trouble I could implicitly rely. Most of the
Indians in the village, it is true, professed good will towards
the whites, but the experience of others and my own observation had taught me the extreme folly of confidence, and the
utter impossibility of foreseeing to what sudden acts the
strange unbridled impulses of an Indian may urge him. When
among this people danger is never so near as when you are
unprepared for it, never so remote as when you are armed
and on the alert to meet it at any moment. Nothing offers so
strong a temptation to their ferocious instincts as the appearance of timidity, weakness, or security.

Many deep and gloomy gorges, choked with trees and
bushes, opened from the sides of the hills, which were shaggy
with forests wherever the rocks permitted vegetation to
spring. A great number of Indians were stalking along the
edges of the woods, and boys were whooping and laughing
on the mountain-sides, practising eye and hand, and indulging their destructive propensities by following birds and small
animals and killing them with their little bows and arrows.
There was one glen, stretching up between steep cliffs far into
the bosom of the mountain. I began to ascend along its bottom, pushing my way onward among the rocks, trees, and
bushes that obstructed it. A slender thread of water trickled
along its centre, which since issuing from the heart of its native rock could scarcely have been warmed or gladdened by a
ray of sunshine. After advancing for some time, I conceived
myself to be entirely alone; but coming to a part of the glen
in a great measure free of trees and undergrowth, I saw at
some distance the black head and red shoulders of an Indian
among the bushes above. The reader need not prepare himself

for a startling adventure, for I have none to relate. The head
and shoulders belonged to Mene-Seela, my best friend in the
village. As I had approached noiselessly with my moccasoned
feet, the old man was quite unconscious of my presence; and
turning to a point where I could gain an unobstructed view
of him, I saw him seated alone, immovable as a statue, among
the rocks and trees. His face was turned upward, and his eyes
seemed riveted on a pine-tree springing from a cleft in the
precipice above. The crest of the pine was swaying to and fro
in the wind, and its long limbs waved slowly up and down, as
if the tree had life. Looking for a while at the old man, I was
satisfied that he was engaged in an act of worship, or prayer,
or communion of some kind with a supernatural being. I
longed to penetrate his thoughts, but I could do nothing
more than conjecture and speculate. I knew that though the
intellect of an Indian can embrace the idea of an all-wise, all-
powerful Spirit, the supreme Ruler of the universe, yet his
mind will not always ascend into communion with a being
that seems to him so vast, remote, and incomprehensible; and
when danger threatens, when his hopes are broken, when the
black wing of sorrow overshadows him, he is prone to turn
for relief to some inferior agency, less removed from the ordinary scope of his faculties. He has a guardian spirit, on whom
he relies for succor and guidance. To him all nature is instinct
with mystic influence. Among those mountains not a wild
beast was prowling, a bird singing, or a leaf fluttering, that
might not tend to direct his destiny, or give warning of what
was in store for him; and he watches the world of nature
around him as the astrologer watches the stars. So closely is
he linked with it, that his guardian-spirit, no unsubstantial
creation of the fancy, is usually embodied in the form of some
living thing; a bear, a wolf, an eagle, or a serpent; and Mene-
Seela, as he gazed intently on the old pine-tree, might believe
it to inshrine the fancied guide and protector of his life.

Whatever was passing in the mind of the old man, it was
no part of sense or of delicacy to disturb him. Silently retracing my footsteps, I descended the glen until I came to a point
where I could climb the steep precipices that shut it in, and
gain the side of the mountain. Looking up, I saw a tall peak
rising among the woods. Something impelled me to climb; I

had not felt for many a day such strength and elasticity of limb. An hour and a half of slow and often intermitted labor brought me to the very summit; and emerging from the dark shadows of the rocks and pines, I stepped forth into the light, and walking along the sunny verge of a precipice, seated myself on its extreme point. Looking between the mountain-peaks to the westward, the pale blue prairie was stretching to the farthest horizon, like a serene and tranquil ocean. The surrounding mountains were in themselves sufficiently striking and impressive, but this contrast gave redoubled effect to their stern features.

Chapter XIX.

PASSAGE OF THE MOUNTAINS.

"Dear Nature is the kindest mother still,
　　Though always changing, in her aspect mild;
From her bare bosom let me take my fill,
　　Her never weaned, though not her favored child.
　　O, she is fairest in her features wild,
When nothing polished dares pollute her path;
　　On me by day and night she ever smiled,
Though I have marked her where none other hath,
And sought her more and more, and loved her best in wrath."
　　　　　　　　　　　　　　　　CHILDE HAROLD.

WHEN I TOOK LEAVE of Shaw at La Bonte's camp, I promised that I would meet him at Fort Laramie on the first of August. That day, according to my reckoning, was now close at hand. It was impossible, at best, to fulfil my engagement exactly, and my meeting with him must have been postponed until many days after the appointed time, had not the plans of the Indians very well coincided with my own. They, too, intended to pass the mountains and move toward the fort. To do so at this point was impossible, because there was no opening; and in order to find a passage we were obliged to go twelve or fourteen miles southward. Late in the afternoon the camp got in motion, defiling back through the mountains along the same narrow passage by which they had entered. I rode in company with three or four young Indians at the rear, and the moving swarm stretched before me, in the ruddy light of sunset, or in the deep shadow of the mountains, far beyond my sight. It was an ill-omened spot they chose to encamp upon. When they were there just a year before, a war-party of ten men, led by the Whirlwind's son, had gone out against the enemy, and not one had ever returned. This was the immediate cause of this season's warlike preparations. I was not a little astonished, when I came to the camp, at the confusion of horrible sounds with which it was filled; howls, shrieks, and wailings were heard from all the women present, many of whom, not content with this exhibition of grief for the loss of their friends and relatives, were gashing their legs deeply with knives. A warrior in the village, who had lost a brother in the expedition, chose another mode of displaying his sorrow. The Indians, who though often rapacious, are utterly devoid of avarice, are accustomed in times of mourning, or on other solemn occasions, to give away the whole of their possessions, and reduce themselves to nakedness and want. The warrior in question led his two best horses into the centre of the village, and gave them away to his friends; upon which, songs and acclamations in praise of his generosity mingled with the cries of the women.

On the next morning we entered once more among the mountains. There was nothing in their appearance either grand or picturesque, though they were desolate to the last degree, being mere piles of black and broken rocks, without trees or vegetation of any kind. As we passed among them along a wide valley, I noticed Raymond riding by the side of a young squaw, to whom he was addressing various insinuating compliments. All the old squaws in the neighborhood watched his proceedings in great admiration, and the girl herself would turn aside her head and laugh. Just then the old mule thought proper to display her vicious pranks; she began to rear and plunge most furiously. Raymond was an excellent rider, and at first he stuck fast in his seat; but the moment after, I saw the mule's hind-legs flourishing in the air, and my unlucky follower pitching head foremost over her ears. There was a burst of screams and laughter from all the women, in which his mistress herself took part, and Raymond was instantly assailed by such a shower of witticisms, that he was glad to ride forward out of hearing.

Not long after, as I rode near him, I heard him shouting to me. He was pointing toward a detached rocky hill that stood in the middle of the valley before us, and from behind it a long file of elk came out at full speed and entered an opening in the side of the mountain. They had scarcely disappeared, when whoops and exclamations came from fifty voices around me. The young men leaped from their horses, flung down their heavy buffalo-robes, and ran at full speed toward the foot of the nearest mountain. Reynal also broke away at a gallop in the same direction, 'Come on! come on!' he called to us. 'Do you see that band of big-horn up yonder? If there's one of them, there's a hundred!'

In fact, near the summit of the mountain, I could see a large number of small white objects, moving rapidly upward among the precipices, while others were filing along its rocky profile. Anxious to see the sport, I galloped forward, and entering a passage in the side of the mountain, ascended among the loose rocks as far as my horse could carry me. Here I fastened her to an old pine-tree that stood alone, scorching in the sun. At that moment Raymond called to me from the right that another band of sheep was close at hand in that direction. I ran up to the top of the opening, which gave me a full view into the rocky gorge beyond; and here I plainly saw some fifty or sixty sheep, almost within rifle-shot, clattering upward among the rocks, and endeavoring, after their usual custom, to reach the highest point. The naked Indians bounded up lightly in pursuit. In a moment the game and hunters disappeared. Nothing could be seen or heard but the occasional report of a gun, more and more distant, reverberating among the rocks.

I turned to descend, and as I did so, I could see the valley below alive with Indians passing rapidly through it, on horseback and on foot. A little farther on, all were stopping as they came up; the camp was preparing, and the lodges rising. I descended to this spot, and soon after Reynal and Raymond returned. They bore between them a sheep which they had pelted to death with stones from the edge of a ravine, along the bottom of which it was attempting to escape. One by one the hunters came dropping in; yet such is the activity of the Rocky Mountain sheep, that although sixty or seventy men were out in pursuit, not more than half a dozen animals were killed. Of these only one was a full grown male. He had a pair of horns twisted like a ram's, the dimensions of which were almost beyond belief. I have seen among the Indians ladles with long handles, capable of containing more than a quart, cut out from such horns.

There is something peculiarly interesting in the character and habits of the mountain sheep, whose chosen retreats are above the region of vegetation and of storms, and who leap among the giddy precipices of their aerial home as actively as the antelope skims over the prairies below.

Through the whole of the next morning we were moving forward, among the hills. On the following day the heights gathered around us, and the passage of the mountains began in earnest. Before the village left its camping-ground, I set forward in company with the Eagle-Feather, a man of powerful frame, but of bad and sinister face. His son, a light-limbed boy, rode with us, and another Indian, named the Panther, was also of the party. Leaving the village out of sight behind us, we rode together up a rocky defile. After a while, however, the Eagle-Feather discovered in the distance some appearance of game, and set off with his son in pursuit of it, while I went forward with the Panther. This was a mere *nom de guerre*; for, like many Indians, he concealed his real name out of some superstitious notion. He was a very noble looking fellow. As he suffered his ornamented buffalo-robe to fall in folds about his loins, his stately and graceful figure was fully displayed; and while he sat his horse in an easy attitude, the long feathers of the prairie-cock fluttering from the crown of his head, he seemed the very model of a wild prairie-rider. He had not the same features with those of other Indians. Unless his handsome face greatly belied him, he was free from the jealousy, suspicion and malignant cunning of his people. For the most part, a civilized white man can discover but very few points of sympathy between his own nature and that of an Indian. With every disposition to do justice to their good qualities, he must be conscious that an impassable gulf lies between him and his red brethren of the prairie. Nay, so alien to himself do they appear, that having breathed for a few months or a few weeks the air of this region, he begins to look upon them as a troublesome and dangerous species of wild beast, and if expedient, he could shoot them with as little compunction as they themselves would experience after performing the same office upon him. Yet, in the countenance of the Panther, I gladly read that there were at least some points of sympathy between him and me. We were excellent friends, and as we rode forward together through rocky passages, deep dells and little barren plains, he occupied himself very zealously in teaching me the Dahcotah language. After a while, we came to a little grassy recess, where some gooseberry-bushes were growing at the foot of a rock: and these offered such temptation to my companion, that he gave over his instruction, and stopped so long to gather the fruit, that before we were in motion again the van of the village came in view. An old woman appeared, leading down her pack-horse among the rocks above. Savage after savage followed, and the little dell was soon crowded with the throng.

That morning's march was one not easily to be forgotten. It led us through a sublime waste, a wilderness of mountains and pine-forests, over which the spirit of loneliness and silence seemed brooding. Above and below, little could be seen but the same dark green foliage. It overspread the valleys, and the mountains were clothed with it, from the black rocks that crowned their summits to the impetuous streams that circled round their base. Scenery like this, it might seem, could have no very cheering effect on the mind of a sick man, (for to-day my disease had again assailed me,) in the midst of a horde of savages; but if the reader has ever wandered, with a true hunter's spirit, among the forests of Maine, or the more picturesque solitudes of the Adirondack Mountains, he will understand how the sombre woods and mountains around me might have awakened any other feelings than those of gloom. In truth, they recalled gladdening recollections of similar scenes in a distant and far different land.

After we had been advancing for several hours, through passages always narrow, often obstructed and difficult, I saw at a little distance on our right a narrow opening between two high, wooded precipices. All within seemed darkness and mystery. In the mood in which I found myself, something strongly impelled me to enter. Passing over the intervening space, I guided my horse through the rocky portal, and as I did so, instinctively drew the covering from my rifle, half expecting that some unknown evil lay in ambush within those dreary recesses. The place was shut in among tall cliffs, and so deeply shadowed by a host of old pine-trees, that though the sun shone bright on the side of the mountain, nothing but a dim twilight could penetrate within. As far as I could see, it had no tenants except a few hawks and owls, who, dismayed at my intrusion, flapped hoarsely away among the shaggy branches. I moved forward, determined to explore the mystery to the bottom, and soon became involved among the pines. The genius of the place exercised a strange influence upon my mind. Its faculties were stimulated into extraordinary activity, and as I passed along, many half-forgotten incidents, and the images of persons and things far distant, rose rapidly before me, with surprising distinctness. In that perilous wilderness, eight hundred miles removed beyond the faintest vestige of civilization, the scenes of another hemisphere, the seat of ancient refinement passed before me, more like a succession of vivid paintings than any mere dreams of the fancy. I saw the church of St. Peter's illumined on the evening of Easter-Day, the whole majestic pile from the cross to the foundation-stone, pencilled in fire, and shedding a radiance, like the serene light of the moon, on the sea of upturned faces below. I saw the peak of Mount Etna towering above its inky mantle of clouds, and lightly curling its wreaths of milk-white smoke against the soft sky, flushed with the Sicilian sunset. I saw also the gloomy vaulted passages and the narrow cells of the Passionist convent, where I once had sojourned for a few days with the fanatical monks, its pale stern inmates, in their robes of black; and the grated window from whence I could look out, a forbidden indulgence, upon the melancholy Coliseum and the crumbling ruins of the Eternal City. The mighty glaciers of the Splugen too, rose before me, gleaming in the sun like polished silver, and those terrible solitudes, the birth-place of the Rhine, where bursting from the bowels of its native mountain it lashes and foams down the rocky abyss into the little valley of Andeer. These recollections, and many more crowded upon me, until remembering that it was hardly wise to remain long in such a place, I mounted again and retraced my steps. Issuing from between the rocks, I saw, a few rods before me, the men, women and children, dogs and horses, still filing slowly across the little glen. A bare round hill rose directly above them. I rode to the top, and from this point I could look down on the savage procession as it passed just beneath my feet, and far on the left I could see its thin and broken line, visible only at intervals, stretching away for miles among the mountains. On the farthest ridge, horsemen were still descending like mere specks in the distance.

I remained on the hill until all had passed, and then descending followed after them. A little farther on I found a very small meadow, set deeply among steep mountains; and here the whole village had encamped. The little spot was crowded with the confused and disorderly host. Some of the lodges were already completely prepared, or the squaws perhaps were busy in drawing the heavy coverings of skin over the bare poles. Others were as yet mere skeletons, while others still, poles, covering and all, lay scattered in complete disorder on the ground among buffalo-robes, bales of meat, domestic utensils, harness and weapons. Squaws were screaming to one another, horses rearing and plunging, dogs yelping, eager to be disburdened of their loads, while the fluttering of feathers and the gleam of barbaric ornaments added liveliness to the scene. The small children ran about amid the crowd, while many of the boys were scrambling among the overhanging rocks, and standing, with their little bows in their hands, looking down upon the restless throng. In contrast with the general confusion, a circle of old men and warriors sat in the midst, smoking in profound indifference and tranquillity. The disorder at length subsided. The horses were driven away to feed along the adjacent valley, and the camp assumed an air of listless repose. It was scarcely past noon; a vast white canopy of smoke from a burning forest to the eastward overhung the place, and partially obscured the rays of the sun; yet the heat was almost insupportable. The lodges stood crowded together without order in the narrow space. Each was a perfect hot-house, within which the lazy proprietor lay sleeping. The camp was silent as death. Nothing stirred except now and then an old woman passing from lodge to lodge. The girls and young men sat together in groups, under the pine-trees upon the surrounding heights. The dogs lay panting on the ground, too lazy even to growl at the white man. At the entrance of the meadow, there was a cold spring among the rocks, completely overshadowed by tall trees and dense undergrowth. In this cool and shady retreat a number of the girls were assembled, sitting together on rocks and fallen logs, discussing the latest gossip of the village, or laughing and throwing water with their hands at the intruding Meneaska. The minutes seemed lengthened into hours. I lay for a long time under a tree, studying the Ogillallah tongue, with the zealous instructions of my friend the Panther. When we were both tired of this, I went and lay down by the side of a deep, clear pool, formed by the water of the spring. A shoal of little fishes of about a pin's length were playing in it, sporting together, as it seemed, very amicably; but on closer observation, I saw that they were engaged in a cannibal warfare among themselves. Now and then a small one would fall a victim, and immediately disappear down the maw of his voracious conqueror. Every moment, however, the tyrant of the pool, a monster about three inches long, with staring goggle eyes, would slowly issue forth with quivering fins and tail from under the shelving bank. The small fry at this would suspend their hostilities, and scatter in a panic at the appearance of overwhelming force.

'Soft-hearted philanthropists,' thought I, 'may sigh long for their peaceful millennium; for from minnows up to men, life is an incessant battle.'

Evening approached at last, the tall mountain-tops around were still gay and bright in sunshine, while our deep glen was completely shadowed. I left the camp, and ascended a neighboring hill, whose rocky summit commanded a wide view over the surrounding wilderness. The sun was still glaring through the stiff pines on the ridge of the western mountain. In a moment he was gone, and as the landscape rapidly darkened, I turned again toward the village. As I descended the hill, the howling of wolves and the barking of foxes, came up out of the dim woods from far and near. The camp was glowing with a multitude of fires, and alive with dusky naked figures, whose tall shadows flitted among the surrounding crags.

I found a circle of smokers seated in their usual place; that is, on the ground before the lodge of a certain warrior, who seemed to be generally known for his social qualities. I sat down to smoke a parting pipe with my savage friends. That day was the first of August, on which I had promised to meet Shaw at Fort Laramie. The Fort was less than two days' journey distant, and that my friend need not suffer anxiety on my account, I resolved to push forward as rapidly as possible to the place of meeting. I went to look after the Hail-Storm, and having found him, I offered him a handful of hawks'-bells and a paper of vermilion, on condition that he would guide me in the morning through the mountains within sight of Laramie Creek.

The Hail-Storm ejaculated 'How!' and accepted the gift. Nothing more was said on either side; the matter was settled, and I lay down to sleep in Kongra-Tonga's lodge.

Long before daylight, Raymond shook me by the shoulder. 'Every thing is ready,' he said.

I went out. The morning was chill, damp, and dark; and the whole camp seemed asleep. The Hail-Storm sat on horseback before the lodge, and my mare Pauline and the mule which Raymond rode were picketed near it. We saddled and made our other arrangements for the journey, but before these were completed the camp began to stir, and the lodge-coverings fluttered and rustled as the squaws pulled them down in preparation for departure. Just as the light began to appear, we left the ground, passing up through a narrow opening among the rocks which led eastward out of the meadow. Gaining the top of this passage, I turned round and sat looking back upon the camp, dimly visible in the gray light of the morning. All was alive with the bustle of preparation. I turned away, half unwilling to take a final leave of my savage associates. We turned to the right, passing among rocks and pine-trees so dark, that for a while we could scarcely see our way. The country in front was wild and broken, half hill, half plain, partly open and partly covered with woods of pine and oak. Barriers of lofty mountains encompassed it; the woods were fresh and cool in the early morning; the peaks of the mountains were wreathed with mist, and sluggish vapors were entangled among the forests upon their sides. At length the black pinnacle of the tallest mountain was tipped with gold by the rising sun. About that time the Hail-Storm, who rode in front, gave a low exclamation. Some large animal leaped up from among the bushes, and an elk, as I thought, his horns thrown back over his neck, darted past us across the open space, and bounded like a mad thing away among the adjoining pines. Raymond was soon out of his saddle, but before he could fire, the animal was full two hundred yards distant. The ball struck its mark, though much too low for mortal effect. The elk however wheeled in his flight, and ran at full speed among the trees, nearly at right angles to his former course. I fired and broke his shoulder; still he moved on, limping down into a neighboring woody hollow, whither the young Indian followed and killed him. When we reached the spot, we discovered him to be no elk, but a black-tailed deer, an animal nearly twice the size of the common deer, and quite unknown in the east. We began to cut him up: the reports of the rifles had reached the ears of the Indians, and before our task was finished several of them came to the spot. Leaving the hide of the deer to the Hail-Storm, we hung as much of the meat as we wanted behind our saddles, left the rest to the Indians, and resumed our journey. Meanwhile the village was on its way, and had gone so far, that to get in advance of it was impossible. Therefore we directed our course so as to strike its line of march at the nearest point. In a short time, through the dark trunks of the pines, we could see the figures of the Indians as they passed. Once more we were among them. They were moving with even more than their usual precipitation, crowded close together in a narrow pass between rocks and old pine-trees. We were on the eastern descent of the mountain, and soon came to a rough and difficult defile, leading down a very steep declivity. The whole swarm poured down together, filling the rocky passage-way like some turbulent mountain-stream. The mountains before us were on fire, and had been so for weeks. The view in front was obscured by a vast dim sea of smoke and vapor, while on either hand the tall cliffs, bearing aloft their crest of pines, thrust their heads boldly through it, and the sharp pinnacles and broken ridges of the mountains beyond them were faintly traceable as through a veil. The scene in itself was most grand and imposing, but with the savage multitude, the armed warriors, the naked children, the gayly apparelled girls, pouring impetuously down the heights, it would have formed a noble subject for a painter, and only the pen of a Scott could have done it justice in description.

We passed over a burnt tract where the ground was hot beneath the horses' feet, and between the blazing sides of two mountains. Before long we had descended to a softer region, where we found a succession of little valleys watered by a stream, along the borders of which grew abundance of wild gooseberries and currants, and the children and many of the men straggled from the line of march to gather them as we passed along. Descending still farther, the view changed rapidly. The burning mountains were behind us, and through the open valleys in front we could see the ocean-like prairie, stretching beyond the sight. After passing through a line of trees that skirted the brook, the Indians filed out upon the plains. I was thirsty and knelt down by the little stream to drink. As I mounted again, I very carelessly left my rifle among the grass, and my thoughts being otherwise absorbed, I rode for some distance before discovering its absence. As the reader may conceive, I lost no time in turning about and galloping back in search of it. Passing the line of Indians, I watched every warrior as he rode by me at a canter, and at length discovered my rifle in the hands of one of them, who, on my approaching to claim it, immediately gave it up. Having no other means of acknowledging the obligation, I took off one of my spurs and gave it to him. He was greatly delighted, looking upon it as a distinguished mark of favor, and immediately held out his foot for me to buckle it on. As soon as I had done so, he struck it with all his force into the side of his horse, who gave a violent leap. The Indian laughed and spurred harder than before. At this the horse shot away like an arrow, amid the screams and laughter of the squaws, and the ejaculations of the men, who exclaimed: 'Washtay!—Good!' at the potent effect of my gift. The Indian had no saddle, and nothing in place of a bridle except a leather string tied round the horse's jaw. The animal was of course wholly uncontrollable, and stretched away at full speed over the prairie, till he and his rider vanished behind a distant swell. I never saw the man again, but I presume no harm came to him. An Indian on horseback has more lives than a cat.

The village encamped on the scorching prairie, close to the foot of the mountains. The heat was most intense and penetrating. The coverings of the lodgings were raised a foot or more from the ground, in order to procure some circulation of air; and Reynal thought proper to lay aside his trapper's dress of buckskin and assume the very scanty costume of an Indian. Thus elegantly attired, he stretched himself in his lodge on a buffalo-robe, alternately cursing the heat and puffing at the pipe which he and I passed between us. There was present also a select circle of Indian friends and relatives. A small boiled puppy was served up as a parting feast, to which was added, by way of dessert, a wooden bowl of gooseberries, from the mountains.

'Look there,' said Reynal, pointing out of the opening of his lodge; 'do you see that line of buttes about fifteen miles off? Well, now do you see that farthest one, with the white speck on the face of it? Do you think you ever saw it before?'

'It looks to me,' said I, 'like the hill that we were 'camped under when we were on Laramie Creek, six or eight weeks ago.'

'You've hit it,' answered Reynal.

'Go, and bring in the animals, Raymond,' said I; 'we'll camp there to-night, and start for the fort in the morning.'

The mare and the mule were soon before the lodge. We saddled them, and in the mean time a number of Indians collected about us. The virtues of Pauline, my strong, fleet, and hardy little mare, were well known in camp, and several of the visitors were mounted upon good horses which they had brought me as presents. I promptly declined their offers, since accepting them would have involved the necessity of transferring poor Pauline into their barbarous hands. We took leave of Reynal, but not of the Indians, who are accustomed to dispense with such superfluous ceremonies. Leaving the camp, we rode straight over the prairie towards the white-faced bluff, whose pale ridges swelled gently against the horizon, like a cloud. An Indian went with us, whose name I forget, though the ugliness of his face and the ghastly width of his mouth dwell vividly in my recollection. The antelope were numerous, but we did not heed them. We rode directly towards our destination, over the arid plains and barren hills; until, late in the afternoon, half spent with heat, thirst, and fatigue, we saw a gladdening sight; the long line of trees and the deep gulf that mark the course of Laramie Creek. Passing through the growth of huge dilapidated old cotton-wood trees that bordered the creek, we rode across to the other side.

The rapid and foaming waters were filled with fish playing and splashing in the shallows. As we gained the farther bank, our horses turned eagerly to drink, and we, kneeling on the sand, followed their example. We had not gone far before the scene began to grow familiar.

'We are getting near home, Raymond,' said I.

There stood the Big Tree under which we had encamped so long; there were the white cliffs that used to look down upon our tent when it stood at the bend of the creek; there was the meadow in which our horses had grazed for weeks, and a little farther on, the prairie-dog village where I had beguiled many a languid hour in persecuting the unfortunate inhabitants.

'We are going to catch it now,' said Raymond, turning his broad, vacant face up toward the sky.

In truth the landscape, the cliffs, and the meadow, the stream and the groves, were darkening fast. Black masses of cloud were swelling up in the south, and the thunder was growling ominously.

'We will 'camp there,' I said, pointing to a dense grove of trees lower down the stream. Raymond and I turned toward it, but the Indian stopped and called earnestly after us. When we demanded what was the matter, he said, that the ghosts of two warriors were always among those trees, and that if we slept there, they would scream and throw stones at us all night, and perhaps steal our horses before morning. Thinking it as well to humor him, we left behind us the haunt of these extraordinary ghosts, and passed on toward Chugwater, riding at full gallop, for the big drops began to patter down. Soon we came in sight of the poplar saplings that grew about the mouth of the little stream. We leaped to the ground, threw off our saddles, turned our horses loose, and drawing our knives began to slash among the bushes to cut twigs and branches for making a shelter against the rain. Bending down the taller saplings as they grew, we piled the young shoots upon them, and thus made a convenient pent-house; but all our labor was useless. The storm scarcely touched us. Half a mile on our right the rain was pouring down like a cataract, and the thunder roared over the prairie like a battery of cannon; while we by good fortune received only a few heavy drops from the skirt of the passing cloud. The weather cleared and the sun set gloriously. Sitting close under our leafy canopy, we proceeded to discuss a substantial meal of *wasna* which Weah-Washtay had given me. The Indian had brought with him his pipe and a bag of *shongsasha*; so before lying down to sleep, we sat for some time smoking together. Previously, however, our wide-mouthed friend had taken the precaution of carefully examining the neighborhood. He reported that eight men, counting them on his fingers, had been encamped there not long before. Bisonette, Paul Dorion, Antoine Le Rouge, Richardson, and four others, whose names he could not tell. All this proved strictly correct. By what instinct he had arrived at such accurate conclusions, I am utterly at a loss to divine.

It was still quite dark when I awoke and called Raymond. The Indian was already gone, having chosen to go on before us to the Fort. Setting out after him, we rode for some time in complete darkness, and when the sun at length rose, glowing like a fiery ball of copper, we were ten miles distant from the Fort. At length, from the broken summit of a tall sandy bluff we could see Fort Laramie, miles before us, standing by the side of the stream like a little gray speck, in the midst of the boundless desolation. I stopped my horse, and sat for a moment looking down upon it. It seemed to me the very centre of comfort and civilization. We were not long in approaching it, for we rode at speed the greater part of the way. Laramie Creek still intervened between us and the friendly walls. Entering the water at the point where we had struck upon the bank, we raised our feet to the saddle behind us, and thus kneeling as it were on horseback, passed dry-shod through the swift current. As we rode up the bank, a number of men appeared in the gateway. Three of them came forward to meet us. In a moment I distinguished Shaw; Henry Chatillon followed with his face of manly simplicity and frankness, and Delorier came last, with a broad grin of welcome. The meeting was not on either side one of mere ceremony. For my own part, the change was a most agreeable one from the society of savages and men little better than savages, to that of my gallant and high-minded companion, and our noble-hearted guide. My appearance was equally gratifying to Shaw, who was beginning to entertain some very uncomfortable surmises concerning me.

Bordeaux greeted me very cordially, and shouted to the cook. This functionary was a new acquisition, having lately come from Fort Pierre with the trading wagons. Whatever skill he might have boasted, he had not the most promising materials to exercise it upon. He set before me, however, a breakfast of biscuit, coffee, and salt pork. It seemed like a new phase of existence, to be seated once more on a bench, with a knife and fork, a plate and tea-cup, and something resembling a table before me. The coffee seemed delicious, and the bread was a most welcome novelty, since for three weeks I had eaten scarcely any thing but meat, and that for the most part without salt. The meal also had the relish of good company, for opposite to me sat Shaw in elegant dishabille. If one is anxious thoroughly to appreciate the value of a congenial companion, he has only to spend a few weeks by himself in an Ogillallah village. And if he can contrive to add to his seclusion, a debilitating and somewhat critical illness, his perceptions upon this subject will be rendered considerably more vivid.

Shaw had been upwards of two weeks at the Fort. I found him established in his old quarters, a large apartment usually occupied by the absent *bourgeois*. In one corner was a soft and luxurious pile of excellent buffalo-robes, and here I lay down. Shaw brought me three books.

'Here,' said he, 'is your Shakespeare and Byron, and here is the Old Testament, which has as much poetry in it as the other two put together.'

I chose the worst of the three, and for the greater part of that day I lay on the buffalo-robes, fairly revelling in the creations of that resplendent genius which has achieved no more signal triumph than that of half beguiling us to forget the pitiful and unmanly character of its possessor.

Chapter XX.

THE LONELY JOURNEY.

"Of antres vast, and deserts idle,
Rough quarries, rocks, and hills whose heads touch heaven."
ОТНЕLLO.

O
N THE DAY of my arrival at Fort Laramie, Shaw and I were lounging on two buffalo-robes in the large apartment hospitably assigned to us; Henry Chatillon also was present, busy about the harness and weapons, which had been brought into the room, and two or three Indians were crouching on the floor, eyeing us with their fixed unwavering gaze.

'I have been well off here,' said Shaw, 'in all respects but one; there is no good *shongsasha* to be had for love or money.'

I gave him a small leather bag containing some of excellent quality, which I had brought from the Black Hills. 'Now, Henry,' said he, 'hand me Papin's chopping-board, or give it to that Indian, and let him cut the mixture; they understand it better than any white man.'

The Indian, without saying a word, mixed the bark and the tobacco in due proportions, filled the pipe, and lighted it. This done, my companion and I proceeded to deliberate on our future course of proceeding; first, however, Shaw acquainted me with some incidents which had occurred at the fort during my absence.

About a week previous, four men had arrived from beyond the mountains; Sublette, Reddick, and two others. Just before reaching the fort, they had met a large party of Indians, chiefly young men. All of them belonged to the village of our old friend Smoke, who, with his whole band of adherents, professed the greatest friendship for the whites. The travellers therefore approached, and began to converse without the least suspicion. Suddenly, however, their bridles were violently seized, and they were ordered to dismount. Instead of complying, they struck their horses with full force, and broke away from the Indians. As they galloped off they heard a yell behind them, mixed with a burst of derisive laughter, and the reports of several guns. None of them were hurt, though Reddick's bridle-rein was cut by a bullet within an inch of his hand. After this taste of Indian hostility, they felt for the moment no disposition to encounter farther risks. They intended to pursue the route southward along the foot of the mountains to Bent's Fort; and as our plans coincided with theirs, they proposed to join forces. Finding, however, that I did not return, they grew impatient of inaction, forgot their late escape, and set out without us, promising to wait our arrival at Bent's Fort. From thence we were to make the long journey to the settlements in company, as the path was not a little dangerous, being infested by hostile Pawnees and Camanches.

We expected, on reaching Bent's Fort, to find there still another reinforcement. A young Kentuckian, of the true Kentucky blood, generous, impetuous, and a gentleman withal, had come out to the mountains with Russel's party of California emigrants. One of his chief objects, as he gave out, was to kill an Indian; an exploit which he afterwards succeeded in achieving, much to the jeopardy of ourselves, and others who had to pass through the country of the dead Pawnee's enraged relatives. Having become disgusted with his emigrant associates, he left them, and had some time before set out with a party of companions for the head of the Arkansas. He sent us previously a letter, intimating that he would wait until we arrived at Bent's Fort, and accompany us thence to the settlements. When however he came to the fort, he found there a party of forty men about to make the homeward journey. He wisely preferred to avail himself of so strong an escort. Mr. Sublette and his companions also set out, in order to overtake this company; so that on reaching Bent's Fort, some six weeks after, we found ourselves deserted by our allies and thrown once more upon our own resources.

But I am anticipating. When, before leaving the settlement, we had made inquiries concerning this part of the country of General Kearney, Mr. Mackenzie, Captain Wyeth, and others well acquainted with it, they had all advised us by no means to attempt this southward journey with fewer than fifteen or twenty men. The danger consists in the chance of encountering Indian war-parties. Sometimes, throughout the whole length of the journey, (a distance of three hundred and fifty miles,) one does not meet a single human being; frequently, however, the route is beset by Arapahoes and other unfriendly tribes; in which case the scalp of the adventurer is in imminent peril. As to the escort of fifteen or twenty men, such a force of whites could at that time scarcely be collected in the whole country; and had the case been otherwise, the expense of securing them, together with the necessary number of horses, would have been extremely heavy. We had resolved, however, upon pursuing this southward course. There were, indeed, two other routes from Fort Laramie; but both of these were less interesting and neither was free from danger. Being unable therefore to procure the fifteen or twenty men recommended, we determined to set out with those we had already in our employ; Henry Chatillon, Delorier and Raymond. The men themselves made no objection, nor would they have made any had the journey been more dangerous; for Henry was without fear, and the other two without thought.

Shaw and I were much better fitted for this mode of travelling than we had been on betaking ourselves to the prairies for the first time a few months before. The daily routine had ceased to be a novelty. All the details of the journey and the camp had become familiar to us. We had seen life under a new aspect; the human biped had been reduced to his primitive condition. We had lived without law to protect, a roof to shelter, or garment of cloth to cover us. One of us at least had been without bread, and without salt to season his food. Our idea of what is indispensable to human existence and enjoyment had been wonderfully curtailed, and a horse, a rifle and a knife seemed to make up the whole of life's necessaries. For these once obtained, together with the skill to use them, all else that is essential would follow in their train, and a host of luxuries besides. One other lesson our short prairie experience had taught us; that of profound contentment in the present, and utter contempt for what the future might bring forth.

These principles established, we prepared to leave Fort Laramie. On the fourth day of August, early in the afternoon, we bade a final adieu to its hospitable gateway. Again Shaw

and I were riding side by side on the prairie. For the first
fifty miles we had companions with us; Troché, a little trapper, and Rouville, a nondescript in the employ of the Fur
Company, who were going to join the trader Bisonette at
his encampment near the head of Horse Creek. We rode
only six or eight miles that afternoon before we came to a
little brook traversing the barren prairie. All along its course
grew copses of young wild-cherry trees, loaded with ripe
fruit, and almost concealing the gliding thread of water with
their dense growth, while on each side rose swells of rich
green grass. Here we encamped; and being much too indolent to pitch our tent, we flung our saddles on the ground,
spread a pair of buffalo-robes, lay down upon them, and began to smoke. Meanwhile, Delorier busied himself with his
hissing frying-pan, and Raymond stood guard over the band
of grazing horses. Delorier had an active assistant in Rouville, who professed great skill in the culinary art, and seizing upon a fork, began to lend his zealous aid in making
ready supper. Indeed, according to his own belief, Rouville
was a man of universal knowledge, and he lost no opportunity to display his manifold accomplishments. He had been a
circus-rider at St. Louis, and once he rode round Fort
Laramie on his head, to the utter bewilderment of all the
Indians. He was also noted as the wit of the fort; and as he
had considerable humor and abundant vivacity, he contributed more that night to the liveliness of the camp than all
the rest of the party put together. At one instant he would
be kneeling by Delorier, instructing him in the true method
of frying antelope-steaks, then he would come and seat himself at our side, dilating upon the orthodox fashion of braid-
ing up a horse's tail, telling apocryphal stories how he had
killed a buffalo-bull with a knife, having first cut off his tail
when at full speed, or relating whimsical anecdotes of the
bourgeois Papin. At last he snatched up a volume of Shakspeare that was lying on the grass, and halted and stumbled
through a line or two to prove that he could read. He went
gambolling about the camp, chattering like some frolick-
some ape; and whatever he was doing at one moment, the
presumption was a sure one that he would not be doing it the
next. His companion Troché sat silently on the grass, not

speaking a word, but keeping a vigilant eye on a very ugly little Utah squaw, of whom he was extremely jealous.

On the next day we travelled farther, crossing the wide sterile basin called 'Goché's Hole.' Towards night we became involved among deep ravines; and being also unable to find water, our journey was protracted to a very late hour. On the next morning we had to pass a long line of bluffs, whose raw sides, wrought upon by rains and storms, were of a ghastly whiteness most oppressive to the sight. As we ascended a gap in these hills, the way was marked by huge footprints, like those of a human giant. They were the track of the grizzly bear; and on the previous day also we had seen abundance of them along the dry channels of the streams we had passed. Immediately after this we were crossing a barren plain, spreading in long and gentle undulations to the horizon. Though the sun was bright, there was a light haze in the atmosphere. The distant hills assumed strange, distorted forms, and the edge of the horizon was continually changing its aspect. Shaw and I were riding together, and Henry Chatillon was alone, a few rods before us; he stopped his horse suddenly, and turning round with the peculiar eager and earnest expression which he always wore when excited, he called us to come forward. We galloped to his side. Henry pointed towards a black speck on the gray swell of the prairie, apparently about a mile off. 'It must be a bear,' said he; 'come, now we shall all have some sport. Better fun to fight him than to fight an old buffalo-bull; grizzly bear so strong and smart.'

So we all galloped forward together, prepared for a hard fight; for these bears, though clumsy in appearance and extremely large, are incredibly fierce and active. The swell of the prairie concealed the black object from our view. Immediately after it appeared again. But now it seemed quite near to us; and as we looked at it in astonishment, it suddenly separated into two parts, each of which took wing and flew away. We stopped our horses and looked round at Henry, whose face exhibited a curious mixture of mirth and mortification. His hawk's eye had been so completely deceived by the peculiar atmosphere, that he had mistaken two large crows at the distance of fifty rods for a grizzly bear a mile off. To the

journey's end Henry never heard the last of the grizzly bear
with wings.

In the afternoon we came to the foot of a considerable hill.
As we ascended it, Rouville began to ask questions concerning our condition and prospects at home, and Shaw was edifying him with a minute account of an imaginary wife and
child, to which he listened with implicit faith. Reaching the
top of the hill, we saw the windings of Horse Creek on the
plains below us, and a little on the left we could distinguish
the camp of Bisonette among the trees and copses along the
course of the stream. Rouville's face assumed just then a most
ludicrously blank expression. We inquired what was the matter; when it appeared that Bisonette had sent him from this
place to Fort Laramie with the sole object of bringing back a
supply of tobacco. Our rattlebrain friend, from the time of his
reaching the fort up to the present moment, had entirely forgotten the object of his journey, and had ridden a dangerous
hundred miles for nothing. Descending to Horse Creek, we
forded it, and on the opposite bank a solitary Indian sat on
horseback under a tree. He said nothing, but turned and led
the way towards the camp. Bisonette had made choice of an
admirable position. The stream, with its thick growth of trees,
inclosed on three sides a wide green meadow, where about
forty Dahcotah lodges were pitched in a circle, and beyond
them half a dozen lodges of the friendly Shienne. Bisonette
himself lived in the Indian manner. Riding up to his lodge,
we found him seated at the head of it, surrounded by various
appliances of comfort not common on the prairie. His squaw
was near him, and rosy children were scrambling about in
printed-calico gowns; Paul Dorion also, with his leathery face
and old white capote, was seated in the lodge, together with
Antoine Le Rouge, a half-breed Pawnee, Sibille, a trader, and
several other white men.

'It will do you no harm,' said Bisonette, 'to stay here with
us for a day or two, before you start for the Pueblo.'

We accepted the invitation, and pitched our tent on a rising
ground above the camp and close to the edge of the trees.
Bisonette soon invited us to a feast, and we suffered abundance of the same sort of attention from his Indian associates.
The reader may possibly recollect that when I joined the

Indian village, beyond the Black Hills, I found that a few families were absent, having declined to pass the mountains along with the rest. The Indians in Bisonette's camp consisted of these very families, and many of them came to me that evening to inquire after their relatives and friends. They were not a little mortified to learn that while they, from their own timidity and indolence, were almost in a starving condition, the rest of the village had provided their lodges for the next season, laid in a great stock of provisions, and were living in abundance and luxury. Bisonette's companions had been sustaining themselves for some time on wild cherries, which the squaws pounded up, stones and all, and spread on buffalo-robes, to dry in the sun; they were then eaten without farther preparation, or used as an ingredient in various delectable compounds.

On the next day, the camp was in commotion with a new arrival. A single Indian had come with his family the whole way from the Arkansas. As he passed among the lodges, he put on an expression of unusual dignity and importance, and gave out that he had brought great news to tell the whites. Soon after the squaws had erected his lodge, he sent his little son to invite all the white men, and all the more distinguished Indians to a feast. The guests arrived and sat wedged together, shoulder to shoulder, within the hot and suffocating lodge. The Stabber, for that was our entertainer's name, had killed an old buffalo bull on his way. This veteran's boiled tripe, tougher than leather, formed the main item of the repast. For the rest, it consisted of wild cherries and grease boiled together in a large copper kettle. The feast was distributed, and for a moment all was silent, strenuous exertion; then each guest, with one or two exceptions, however, turned his wooden dish bottom upward to prove that he had done full justice to his entertainer's hospitality. The Stabber next produced his chopping-board, on which he prepared the mixture for smoking, and filled several pipes, which circulated among the company. This done, he seated himself upright on his couch, and began with much gesticulation to tell his story. I will not repeat his childish jargon. It was so entangled, like the greater part of an Indian's stories, with absurd and contradictory details, that it was almost impossible to disengage from it a single particle of truth. All that we could gather was the following:

He had been on the Arkansas, and there he had seen six great war-parties of whites. He had never believed before that the whole world contained half so many white men. They all had large horses, long knives, and short rifles, and some of them were attired alike in the most splendid war-dresses he had ever seen. From this account it was clear that bodies of dragoons and perhaps also of volunteer cavalry had been passing up the Arkansas. The Stabber had also seen a great many of the white lodges of the Meneaska, drawn by their long-horned buffalo. These could be nothing else than covered ox-wagons used no doubt in transporting stores for the troops. Soon after seeing this, our host had met an Indian who had lately come from among the Camanches. The latter had told him that all the Mexicans had gone out to a great buffalo hunt. That the Americans had hid themselves in a ravine. When the Mexicans had shot away all their arrows, the Americans had fired their guns, raised their war-whoop, rushed out, and killed them all. We could only infer from this, that war had been declared with Mexico, and a battle fought in which the Americans were victorious. When some weeks after, we arrived at the Pueblo, we heard of General Kearney's march up the Arkansas, and of General Taylor's victories at Matamoras.

As the sun was setting that evening a great crowd gathered on the plain by the side of our tent, to try the speed of their horses. These were of every shape, size, and color. Some came from California, some from the States, some from among the mountains, and some from the wild bands of the prairie. They were of every hue, white, black, red and gray, or mottled and clouded with a strange variety of colors. They all had a wild and startled look, very different from the staid and sober aspect of a well-bred city steed. Those most noted for swiftness and spirit were decorated with eagle feathers dangling from their manes and tails. Fifty or sixty Dahcotah were present, wrapped from head to foot in their heavy robes of whitened hide. There were also a considerable number of the Shienne, many of whom wore gaudy Mexican ponchos, swathed around their shoulders, but leaving the right arm bare. Mingled among the crowd of Indians were a number of Canadians, chiefly in the employ of Bisonette. Men, whose home is the wilderness, and who love the camp-fire better than the domestic hearth. They are contented and happy in the midst of hardship, privation, and danger. Their cheerfulness and gayety is irrepressible, and no people on earth understand better how 'to daff the world aside and bid it pass.' Besides these, were two or three half-breeds, a race of rather extraordinary composition, being according to the common saying half Indian, half white man, and half devil. Antoine Le Rouge was the most conspicuous among them, with his loose pantaloons and his fluttering calico shirt. A handkerchief was bound round his head to confine his black snaky hair, and his small eyes twinkled beneath it, with a mischievous lustre. He had a fine cream-colored horse whose speed he must needs try along with the rest. So he threw off the rude high-peaked saddle, and substituting a piece of buffalo-robe, leaped lightly into his seat. The space was cleared, the word was given, and he and his Indian rival darted out like lightning from among the crowd, each stretching forward over his horse's neck and plying his heavy Indian whip with might and main. A moment, and both were lost in the gloom; but Antoine soon came riding back victorious, exultingly patting the neck of his quivering and panting horse.

About midnight, as I lay asleep, wrapped in a buffalo-robe on the ground by the side of our cart, Raymond came up and woke me. Something he said was going forward which I would like to see. Looking down into the camp I saw on the farther side of it, a great number of Indians gathered around a fire, the bright glare of which made them visible through the thick darkness; while from the midst of them proceeded a loud, measured chant which would have killed Paganini outright, broken occasionally by a burst of sharp yells. I gathered the robe around me, for the night was cold, and walked down to the spot. The dark throng of Indians was so dense that they almost intercepted the light of the flame. As I was pushing among them with but little ceremony, a chief interposed himself, and I was given to understand that a white man must not approach the scene of their solemnities too closely. By passing round to the other side where there was a little opening in the crowd, I could see clearly what was going forward, without intruding my unhallowed presence into the inner circle. The society of the 'Strong Hearts' were engaged in one of their dances. The 'Strong Hearts' are a warlike association, comprising men of both the Dahcotah and Shienne nations, and entirely composed, or supposed to be so, of young braves of the highest mettle. Its fundamental principle is the admirable one of never retreating from any enterprise once commenced. All these Indian associations have a tutelary spirit. That of the Strong Hearts is embodied in the fox, an animal which white men would hardly have selected for a similar purpose, though his subtle and cautious character agrees well enough with an Indian's notions of what is honorable in warfare. The dancers were circling round and round the fire, each figure brightly illumined at one moment by the yellow light, and at the next drawn in blackest shadow as it passed between the flame and the spectator. They would imitate with the most ludicrous exactness the motions and the voice of their sly patron the fox. Then a startling yell would be given. Many other warriors would leap into the ring, and with faces upturned toward the starless sky, they would all stamp, and whoop, and brandish their weapons like so many frantic devils.

Until the next afternoon we were still remaining with Bisonette. My companion and I with our three attendants then left his camp for the Pueblo, a distance of three hundred miles, and we supposed the journey would occupy about a fortnight. During this time we all earnestly hoped that we might not meet a single human being, for should we encounter any, they would in all probability be enemies, ferocious robbers and murderers, in whose eyes our rifles would be our only passports. For the first two days nothing worth mentioning took place. On the third morning, however, an untoward incident occurred. We were encamped by the side of a little brook in an extensive hollow of the plain. Delorier was up long before daylight, and before he began to prepare breakfast he turned loose all the horses, as in duty bound. There was a cold mist clinging close to the ground, and by the time the rest of us were awake the animals were invisible. It was only after a long and anxious search that we could discover by their tracks the direction they had taken. They had all set off for Fort Laramie, following the guidance of a mutinous old mule, and though many of them were hobbled, they had travelled three miles before they could be overtaken and driven back.

For the following two or three days, we were passing over an arid desert. The only vegetation was a few tufts of short grass, dried and shrivelled by the heat. There was an abundance of strange insects and reptiles. Huge crickets, black and bottle green, and wingless grasshoppers of the most extravagant dimensions, were tumbling about our horses' feet, and lizards without numbers, were darting like lightning among the tufts of grass. The most curious animal, however, was that commonly called the horned-frog. I caught one of them and consigned him to the care of Delorier, who tied him up in a moccason. About a month after this, I examined the prisoner's condition, and finding him still lively and active, I provided him with a cage of buffalo-hide, which was hung up in the cart. In this manner he arrived safely at the settlements. From thence he travelled the whole way to Boston, packed closely in a trunk, being regaled with fresh air regularly every night. When he reached his destination he was deposited under a glass case, where he sat for some months in great tranquillity and composure, alternately dilating and contracting his white throat to the admiration of his visitors. At length, one morning about the middle of winter, he gave up the ghost. His death was attributed to starvation, a very probable conclusion, since for six months he had taken no food whatever, though the sympathy of his juvenile admirers had tempted his palate with a great variety of delicacies. We found also animals of a somewhat larger growth. The number of prairie dogs was absolutely astounding. Frequently the hard and dry prairie would be thickly covered, for many miles together, with the little mounds which they make around the mouth of their burrows, and small squeaking voices yelping at us, as we passed along. The noses of the inhabitants would be just visible at the mouth of their holes, but no sooner was their curiosity satisfied than they would instantly vanish. Some of the bolder dogs—though in fact they are no dogs at all—but little marmots rather smaller than a rabbit—would sit yelping at us on the top of their mounds, jerking their tails emphatically with every shrill cry they uttered. As the danger drew nearer they would wheel about, toss their heels into the air and dive in a twinkling down into their burrows. Toward sunset, and especially if rain were threatening, the whole community would make their appearance above ground. We would see them gathered in large knots around the burrow of some favorite citizen. There they would all sit erect, their tails spread out on the ground, and their paws hanging down before their white breasts, chattering and squeaking with the utmost vivacity upon some topic of common interest, while the proprietor of the burrow with his head just visible on the top of his mound, would sit looking down with a complacent countenance on the enjoyment of his guests. Meanwhile, others would be running about from burrow to burrow, as if on some errand of the last importance to their subterranean commonwealth. The snakes are apparently the prairie dog's worst enemies, at least I think too well of the latter to suppose that they associate on friendly terms with these slimy intruders, who may be seen at all times basking among their holes, into which they always retreat when disturbed. Small owls, with wise and grave countenances, also make their abode with the prairie dogs, though on what terms they live together I could never ascertain. The manners and customs, the political and domestic economy of these little marmots is worthy of closer attention than one is able to give when pushing by forced marches through their country, with his thoughts engrossed by objects of greater moment.

On the fifth day after leaving Bisonette's camp, we saw, late in the afternoon, what we supposed to be a considerable stream, but on our approaching it, we found to our mortification nothing but a dry bed of sand, into which all the water had sunk and disappeared. We separated, some riding in one direction and some in another, along its course. Still we found no traces of water, not even so much as a wet spot in the sand. The old cotton-wood trees that grew along the bank, lamentably abused by lightning and tempest, were withering with the drought, and on the dead limbs, at the summit of the tallest, half a dozen crows were hoarsely cawing, like birds of evil omen, as they were. We had no alternative but to keep on. There was no water nearer than the South Fork of the Platte, about ten miles distant. We moved forward, angry and silent, over a desert as flat as the outspread ocean.

The sky had been obscured since the morning by thin mists and vapors, but now vast piles of clouds were gathered together in the west. They rose to a great height above the horizon, and looking up toward them, I distinguished one mass darker than the rest, and of a peculiar conical form. I happened to look again, and still could see it as before. At some moments it was dimly seen, at others its outline was sharp and distinct; but while the clouds around it were shifting, changing and dissolving away, it still towered aloft in the midst of them, fixed and immovable. It must, thought I, be the summit of a mountain; and yet its height staggered me. My conclusion was right, however. It was Long's Peak, once believed to be one of the highest of the Rocky Mountain chain, though more recent discoveries have proved the contrary. The thickening gloom soon hid it from view, and we never saw it again, for on the following day, and for some time after, the air was so full of mist that the view of distant objects was entirely intercepted.

It grew very late. Turning from our direct course, we made for the river at its nearest point, though in the utter darkness, it was not easy to direct our way with much precision. Raymond rode on one side and Henry on the other. We could hear each of them shouting that he had come upon a deep ravine. We steered at random between Scylla and Charybdis, and soon after became as it seemed inextricably involved with deep chasms all around us, while the darkness was such that we could not see a rod in any direction. We partially extricated ourselves by scrambling, cart and all, through a shallow ravine. We came next to a steep descent, down which we plunged without well knowing what was at the bottom. There was a great cracking of sticks and dry twigs. Over our heads were certain large shadowy objects; and in front something like the faint gleaming of a dark sheet of water. Raymond ran his horse against a tree; Henry alighted, and feeling on the ground, declared that there was grass enough for the horses. Before taking off his saddle, each man led his own

horses down to the water in the best way he could. Then picketing two or three of the evil-disposed, we turned the rest loose,
and lay down among the dry sticks to sleep. In the morning
we found ourselves close to the South Fork of the Platte, on a
spot surrounded by bushes and rank grass. Compensating ourselves with a hearty breakfast, for the ill-fare of the previous
night, we set forward again on our journey. When only two
or three rods from the camp I saw Shaw stop his mule, level
his gun, and after a long aim fire at some object in the grass.
Delorier next jumped forward, and began to dance about, belaboring the unseen enemy with a whip. Then he stooped
down, and drew out of the grass by the neck an enormous
rattlesnake, with his head completely shattered by Shaw's bullet. As Delorier held him out at arm's length with an exulting
grin, his tail, which still kept slowly writhing about, almost
touched the ground; and the body in the largest part was as
thick as a stout man's arm. He had fourteen rattles, but the
end of his tail was blunted, as if he could once have boasted
of many more. From this time till we reached the Pueblo, we
killed at least four or five of these snakes every day, as they lay
coiled and rattling on the hot sand. Shaw was the Saint
Patrick of the party, and whenever he or any one else killed a
snake he always pulled off his tail and stored it away in his
bullet-pouch, which was soon crammed with an edifying collection of rattles, great and small. Delorier with his whip also
came in for a share of the praise. A day or two after this, he
triumphantly produced a small snake about a span and a half
long, with one infant rattle at the end of his tail.

We forded the South Fork of the Platte. On its farther bank
were the trace of a very large camp of Arapahoes. The ashes
of some three hundred fires were visible among the scattered
trees, together with the remains of sweating lodges, and all
the other appurtenances of a permanent camp. The place
however had been for some months deserted. A few miles
farther on we found more recent signs of Indians; the trail of
two or three lodges, which had evidently passed the day before, where every footprint was perfectly distinct in the dry,
dusty soil. We noticed in particular the track of one moccason,
upon the sole of which its economical proprietor had placed a
large patch. These signs gave us but little uneasiness, as the

number of the warriors scarcely exceeded that of our own party. At noon we rested under the walls of a large fort, built in these solitudes some years since, by M. St. Vrain. It was now abandoned and fast falling into ruin. The walls of unbaked bricks were cracked from top to bottom. Our horses recoiled in terror from the neglected entrance, where the heavy gates were torn from their hinges and flung down. The area within was overgrown with weeds, and the long ranges of apartments once occupied by the motley concourse of traders, Canadians and squaws, were now miserably dilapidated. Twelve miles farther on, near the spot where we encamped, were the remains of still another fort, standing in melancholy desertion and neglect.

Early on the following morning we made a startling discovery. We passed close by a large deserted encampment of Arapahoes. There were about fifty fires still smouldering on the ground, and it was evident from numerous signs that the Indians must have left the place within two hours of our reaching it. Their trail crossed our own, at right angles, and led in the direction of a line of hills, half a mile on our left. There were women and children in the party, which would have greatly diminished the danger of encountering them. Henry Chatillon examined the encampment and the trail with a very professional and business-like air.

'Supposing we had met them, Henry?' said I.

'Why,' said he, 'we hold out our hands to them, and give them all we've got; they take away every thing, and then I believe they no kill us. Perhaps,' added he, looking up with a quiet unchanged face, 'perhaps we no let them rob us. Maybe before they come near, we have a chance to get into a ravine, or under the bank of the river; then, you know, we fight them.'

About noon on that day we reached Cherry Creek. Here was a great abundance of wild-cherries, plums, gooseberries, and currants. The stream, however, like most of the others which we passed, was dried up with the heat, and we had to dig holes in the sand to find water for ourselves and our horses. Two days after, we left the banks of the creek, which we had been following for some time, and began to cross the high dividing ridge which separates the waters of the Platte from those of the Arkansas. The scenery was altogether changed. In place of the burning plains, we were passing now through rough and savage glens, and among hills crowned with a dreary growth of pines. We encamped among these solitudes on the night of the sixteenth of August. A tempest was threatening. The sun went down among volumes of jet-black cloud, edged with a bloody red. But in spite of these portentous signs, we neglected to put up the tent, and being extremely fatigued, lay down on the ground and fell asleep. The storm broke about midnight, and we erected the tent amid darkness and confusion. In the morning all was fair again, and Pike's Peak, white with snow, was towering above the wilderness afar off.

We pushed through an extensive tract of pine woods. Large black-squirrels were leaping among the branches. From the farther edge of this forest we saw the prairie again, hollowed out before us into a vast basin, and about a mile in front we could discern a little black speck moving upon its surface. It could be nothing but a buffalo. Henry primed his rifle afresh and galloped forward. To the left of the animal was a low rocky mound, of which Henry availed himself in making his approach. After a short time we heard the faint report of the rifle. The bull, mortally wounded from a distance of nearly three hundred yards, ran wildly round and round in a circle. Shaw and I then galloped forward, and passing him as he ran, foaming with rage and pain, we discharged our pistols into his side. Once or twice he rushed furiously upon us, but his strength was rapidly exhausted. Down he fell on his knees. For one instant he glared up at his enemies, with burning eyes, through his black tangled mane, and then rolled over on his side. Though gaunt and thin, he was larger and heavier than the largest ox. Foam and blood flew together from his nostrils as he lay bellowing and pawing the ground, tearing up grass and earth with his hoofs. His sides rose and fell like a vast pair of bellows, the blood spouting up in jets from the bullet-holes. Suddenly his glaring eyes became like a lifeless jelly. He lay motionless on the ground. Henry stooped over him, and making an incision with his knife, pronounced the meat too rank and tough for use; so, disappointed in our hopes of an addition to our stock of provisions, we rode away and left the carcass to the wolves.

In the afternoon we saw the mountains rising like a gigantic wall at no great distance on our right. *'Des sauvages! des sauvages!'* exclaimed Delorier, looking round with a frightened face, and pointing with his whip towards the foot of the mountains. In fact, we could see at a distance a number of little black specks, like horsemen in rapid motion. Henry Chatillon, with Shaw and myself, galloped towards them to reconnoitre, when to our amusement we saw the supposed Arapahoes resolved into the black tops of some pine-trees which grew along a ravine. The summits of these pines, just visible above the verge of the prairie, and seeming to move as we ourselves were advancing, looked exactly like a line of horsemen.

We encamped among ravines and hollows, through which a little brook was foaming angrily. Before sunrise in the morning the snow-covered mountains were beautifully tinged with a delicate rose color. A noble spectacle awaited us as we moved forward. Six or eight miles on our right, Pike's Peak and his giant brethren rose out of the level prairie, as if springing from the bed of the ocean. From their summits down to the plain below they were involved in a mantle of clouds, in restless motion, as if urged by strong winds. For one instant some snowy peak, towering in awful solitude, would be disclosed to view. As the clouds broke along the mountain, we could see the dreary forests, the tremendous precipices, the white patches of snow, the gulfs and chasms as black as night, all revealed for an instant, and then disappearing from the view. One could not but recall the stanza of Childe Harold:

> 'Morn dawns, and with it stern Albania's hills,
> Dark Suli's rocks, and Pindus' inland peak,
> Robed half in mist, bedewed with snowy rills,
> Array'd in many a dun and purple streak,
> Arise; and, as the clouds along them break,
> Disclose the dwelling of the mountaineer:
> Here roams the wolf, the eagle whets his beak,
> Birds, beasts of prey, and wilder men appear,
> And gathering storms around convulse the closing year.'

Every line save one of this description was more than verified here. There were no 'dwellings of the mountaineer' among these heights. Fierce savages, restlessly wandering through summer and winter, alone invade them. 'Their hand is against every man, and every man's hand against them.'

On the day after, we had left the mountains at some distance. A black cloud descended upon them, and a tremendous explosion of thunder followed, reverberating among the precipices. In a few moments every thing grew black, and the rain poured down like a cataract. We got under an old cottonwood tree, which stood by the side of a stream, and waited there till the rage of the torrent had passed.

The clouds opened at the point where they first had gathered, and the whole sublime congregation of mountains was bathed at once in warm sunshine. They seemed more like some luxurious vision of eastern romance than like a reality of that wilderness; all were melted together into a soft delicious blue, as voluptuous as the sky of Naples or the transparent sea that washes the sunny cliffs of Capri. On the left the whole sky was still of an inky blackness; but two concentric rainbows stood in brilliant relief against it, while far in front the ragged cloud still streamed before the wind, and the retreating thunder muttered angrily.

Through that afternoon and the next morning we were passing down the banks of the stream, called 'La Fontaine qui Bouille,' from the boiling spring whose waters flow into it. When we stopped at noon, we were within six or eight miles of the Pueblo. Setting out again, we found by the fresh tracks that a horseman had just been out to reconnoitre us; he had circled half round the camp, and then galloped back full speed for the Pueblo. What made him so shy of us we could not conceive. After an hour's ride we reached the edge of a hill, from which a welcome sight greeted us. The Arkansas ran along the valley below, among woods and groves, and closely nestled in the midst of wide corn-fields and green meadows where cattle were grazing, rose the low mud walls of the Pueblo.

Chapter XXI.

THE PUEBLO AND BENT'S FORT.

"It came to pass, that when he did address
　　Himself to quit at length this mountain land,
　Combined marauders half-way barred egress,
　　And wasted far and near with glaive and brand."
　　　　　　　　　　　　　　CHILDE HAROLD.

WE APPROACHED the gate of the Pueblo. It was a wretched species of fort, of most primitive construction, being nothing more than a large square inclosure, surrounded by a wall of mud, miserably cracked and dilapidated. The slender pickets that surmounted it were half broken down, and the gate dangled on its wooden hinges so loosely, that to open or shut it seemed likely to fling it down altogether. Two or three squalid Mexicans, with their broad hats, and their vile faces overgrown with hair, were lounging about the bank of the river in front of it. They disappeared as they saw us approach; and as we rode up to the gate, a light active little figure came out to meet us. It was our old friend Richard. He had come from Fort Laramie on a trading expedition to Taos; but finding when he reached the Pueblo that the war would prevent his going farther, he was quietly waiting till the conquest of the country should allow him to proceed. He seemed to consider himself bound to do the honors of the place. Shaking us warmly by the hand, he led the way into the area.

Here we saw his large Santa Fé wagons standing together. A few squaws and Spanish women, and a few Mexicans, as mean and miserable as the place itself, were lazily sauntering about. Richard conducted us to the state apartment of the Pueblo. A small mud room, very neatly finished, considering the material, and garnished with a crucifix, a looking-glass, a picture of the Virgin, and a rusty horse-pistol. There were no chairs, but instead of them a number of chests and boxes ranged about the room. There was another room beyond, less sumptuously decorated, and here three or four Spanish girls, one of them very pretty, were baking cakes at a mud fireplace in the corner. They brought out a poncho, which they spread upon the floor by way of table-cloth. A supper, which seemed to us luxurious, was soon laid out upon it, and folded buffalo-robes were placed around it to receive the guests. Two or three Americans, beside ourselves, were present. We sat down Turkish fashion, and began to inquire the news. Richard told us that, about three weeks before, General Kearney's army had left Bent's Fort to march against Santa Fé; that when last heard from they were approaching the mountainous defiles that led to the city. One of the Americans produced a dingy newspaper, containing an account of the battles of Palo Alto and Resaca de la Palma. While we were discussing these matters, the doorway was darkened by a tall, shambling fellow, who stood with his hands in his pockets taking a leisurely survey of the premises before he entered. He wore brown homespun pantaloons, much too short for his legs, and a pistol and Bowie knife stuck in his belt. His head and one eye were enveloped in a huge bandage of white linen. Having completed his observations, he came slouching in, and sat down on a chest. Eight or ten more of the same stamp followed, and very coolly arranging themselves about the room, began to stare at the company. Shaw and I looked at each other. We were forcibly reminded of the Oregon emigrants, though these unwelcome visitors had a certain glitter of the eye, and a compression of the lips, which distinguished them from our old acquaintances of the prairie. They began to catechise us at once, inquiring whence we had come, what we meant to do next, and what were our future prospects in life.

The man with the bandaged head had met with an untoward accident a few days before. He was going down to the river to bring water, and was pushing through the young willows which covered the low ground, when he came unawares upon a grizzly bear, which, having just eaten a buffalo-bull, had lain down to sleep off the meal. The bear rose on his hind legs, and gave the intruder such a blow with his paw that he laid his forehead entirely bare, clawed off the front of his scalp, and narrowly missed one of his eyes. Fortunately he was not in a very pugnacious mood, being surfeited with his late meal. The man's companions, who were close behind, raised a shout, and the bear walked away, crushing down the willows in his leisurely retreat.

These men belonged to a party of Mormons, who, out of a well-grounded fear of the other emigrants, had postponed leaving the settlements until all the rest were gone. On account of this delay they did not reach Fort Laramie until it was too late to continue their journey to California. Hearing that there was good land at the head of the Arkansas, they crossed over under the guidance of Richard, and were now preparing to spend the winter at a spot about half a mile from the Pueblo.

When we took leave of Richard, it was near sunset. Passing out of the gate, we could look down the little valley of the Arkansas; a beautiful scene, and doubly so to our eyes, so long accustomed to deserts and mountains. Tall woods lined the river, with green meadows on either hand; and high bluffs, quietly basking in the sunlight, flanked the narrow valley. A Mexican on horseback was driving a herd of cattle toward the gate, and our little white tent, which the men had pitched under a large tree in the meadow, made a very pleasing feature in the scene. When we reached it, we found that Richard had sent a Mexican to bring us an abundant supply of green corn and vegetables, and invite us to help ourselves to whatever we wished from the fields around the Pueblo.

The inhabitants were in daily apprehension of an inroad from more formidable consumers than ourselves. Every year, at the time when the corn begins to ripen, the Arapahoes, to the number of several thousands, come and encamp around the Pueblo. The handful of white men, who are entirely at the mercy of this swarm of barbarians, choose to make a merit of necessity; they come forward very cordially, shake them by the hand, and intimate that the harvest is entirely at their disposal. The Arapahoes take them at their word, help themselves most liberally, and usually turn their horses into the cornfields afterward. They have the foresight, however, to leave enough of the crops untouched to serve as an inducement for planting the fields again for their benefit in the next spring.

The human race in this part of the world is separated into three divisions, arranged in the order of their merits: white men, Indians, and Mexicans; to the latter of whom the honorable title of 'whites' is by no means conceded.

In spite of the warm sunset of that evening the next morning was a dreary and cheerless one. It rained steadily, clouds resting upon the very tree-tops. We crossed the river to visit the Mormon settlement. As we passed through the water, several trappers on horseback entered it from the other side. Their buckskin frocks were soaked through by the rain, and clung fast to their limbs with a most clammy and uncomfortable look. The water was trickling down their faces, and dropping from the ends of their rifles and from the traps which each carried at the pommel of his saddle. Horses and all, they had a most disconsolate and wobegone appearance, which we could not help laughing at, forgetting how often we ourselves had been in a similar plight.

After half an hour's riding, we saw the white wagons of the Mormons drawn up among the trees. Axes were sounding, trees were falling, and log-huts going up along the edge of the woods and upon the adjoining meadow. As we came up the Mormons left their work and seated themselves on the timber around us, when they began earnestly to discuss points of theology, complain of the ill-usage they had received from the 'Gentiles,' and sound a lamentation over the loss of their great temple of Nauvoo. After remaining with them an hour we rode back to our camp, happy that the settlements had been delivered from the presence of such blind and desperate fanatics.

On the morning after this we left the Pueblo for Bent's Fort. The conduct of Raymond had lately been less satisfactory than before, and we had discharged him as soon as we arrived at the former place; so that the party, ourselves included, was now reduced to four. There was some uncertainty as to our future course. The trail between Bent's Fort and the settlements, a distance computed at six hundred miles, was at this time in a dangerous state; for since the passage of General Kearney's army, great numbers of hostile Indians, chiefly Pawnees and Camanches, had gathered about some parts of it. A little after this time they became so numerous and audacious, that scarcely a single party, however large, passed between the fort and the frontier without some token of their hostility. The newspapers of the time sufficiently display this state of things. Many men were killed, and great numbers of horses and mules carried off. Not long since I met with a gentleman, who, during the autumn, came from Santa Fé to Bent's Fort, where he found a party of seventy men, who thought themselves too weak to go down to the settlements alone, and were waiting there for a reinforcement. Though this excessive timidity fully proves the ignorance and credulity of the men, it may also evince the state of alarm which prevailed in the country. When we were there in the month of August, the danger had not become so great. There was nothing very attractive in the neighborhood. We supposed, moreover, that we might wait there half the winter without finding any party to go down with us; for Mr. Sublette and the others whom we had relied upon, had, as Richard told us, already left Bent's Fort. Thus far on our journey Fortune had kindly befriended us. We resolved therefore to take advantage of her gracious mood, and trusting for a continuance of her favors, to set out with Henry and Delorier, and run the gauntlet of the Indians in the best way we could.

Bent's Fort stands on the river, about seventy-five miles below the Pueblo. At noon of the third day we arrived within three or four miles of it, pitched our tent under a tree, hung our looking-glasses against its trunk, and having made our primitive toilet, rode toward the fort. We soon came in sight of it, for it is visible from a considerable distance, standing with its high clay walls in the midst of the scorching plains. It seemed as if a swarm of locusts had invaded the country. The grass for miles around was cropped close by the horses of General Kearney's soldiery. When we came to the fort, we found that not only had the horses eaten up the grass, but their owners had made way with the stores of the little trading post; so that we had great difficulty in procuring the few articles which we required for our homeward journey. The army was gone, the life and bustle passed away, and the fort was a scene of dull and lazy tranquillity. A few invalid officers and soldiers sauntered about the area, which was oppressively hot; for the glaring sun was reflected down upon it from the high white walls around. The proprietors were absent, and we were received by Mr. Holt, who had been left in charge of the fort. He invited us to dinner, where, to our admiration, we found a table laid with a white cloth, with castors in the centre and chairs placed around it. This unwonted repast concluded, we rode back to our camp.

Here, as we lay smoking round the fire after supper, we saw through the dusk three men approaching from the direction of the fort. They rode up and seated themselves near us on the ground. The foremost was a tall, well-formed man, with a face and manner such as inspire confidence at once. He wore a broad hat of felt, slouching and tattered, and the rest of his attire consisted of a frock and leggins of buckskin, rubbed with the yellow clay found among the mountains. At the heel of one of his moccasons was buckled a huge iron spur, with a rowel five or six inches in diameter. His horse, who stood quietly looking over his head, had a rude Mexican saddle, covered with a shaggy bear skin, and furnished with a pair of wooden stirrups of most preposterous size. The next man was a sprightly, active little fellow, about five feet and a quarter high, but very strong and compact. His face was swarthy as a Mexican's, and covered with a close, curly, black beard. An old, greasy, calico handkerchief was tied round his head, and his close buckskin dress was blackened and polished by grease and hard service. The last who came up was a large, strong man, dressed in the coarse homespun of the frontiers, who dragged his long limbs over the ground as if he were too lazy for the effort. He had a sleepy gray eye, a retreating chin, an open mouth and a protruding upper lip, which gave him an air of exquisite indolence and helplessness. He was armed with an old United States yager, which redoubtable weapon, though he could never hit his mark with it, he was accustomed to cherish as the very sovereign of firearms.

The first two men belonged to a party who had just come from California, with a large band of horses, which they had disposed of at Bent's Fort. Munroe, the taller of the two, was from Iowa. He was an excellent fellow, open, warm-hearted and intelligent. Jim Gurney, the short man, was a Boston sailor, who had come in a trading vessel to California, and taken the fancy to return across the continent. The journey had already made him an expert 'mountain-man,' and he pre-sented the extraordinary phenomenon of a sailor who understood how to manage a horse. The third of our visitors, named Ellis, was a Missourian, who had come out with a party of Oregon emigrants, but having got as far as Bridge's Fort, he had fallen home-sick, or as Jim averred, love-sick,— and Ellis was just the man to be balked in a love adventure. He thought proper therefore to join the California men, and return homeward in their company.

They now requested that they might unite with our party, and make the journey to the settlements in company with us. We readily assented, for we liked the appearance of the first two men, and were very glad to gain so efficient a reinforcement. We told them to meet us on the next evening at a spot on the river side, about six miles below the Fort. Having smoked a pipe together, our new allies left us, and we lay down to sleep.

Chapter XXII.

TETE ROUGE, THE VOLUNTEER.

"Ah me! what evils do environ
The man that meddles with cold iron."
HUDIBRAS.

THE NEXT MORNING having directed Delorier to repair with his cart to the place of meeting, we came again to the Fort to make some arrangements for the journey. After completing these we sat down under a sort of porch, to smoke with some Shienne Indians whom we found there. In a few minutes we saw an extraordinary little figure approach us in a military dress. He had a small, round countenance, garnished about the eyes with the kind of wrinkles commonly known as crow's feet, and surmounted by an abundant crop of red curls, with a little cap resting on the top of them. Altogether, he had the look of a man more conversant with mint-juleps and oyster suppers than with the hardships of prairie-service. He came up to us and entreated that we would take him home to the settlements, saying that unless he went with us he should have to stay all winter at the Fort. We liked our petitioner's appearance so little, that we excused ourselves from complying with his request. At this he begged us so hard to take pity on him, looked so disconsolate and told so lamentable a story, that at last we consented, though not without many misgivings.

The rugged Anglo-Saxon of our new recruit's real name proved utterly unmanageable on the lips of our French attendants, and Henry Chatillon, after various abortive attempts to pronounce it, one day coolly christened him Tête Rouge, in honor of his red curls. He had at different times been clerk of a Mississippi steamboat, and agent in a trading establishment at Nauvoo, besides filling various other capacities, in all of which he had seen much more of 'life' than was good for him. In the spring, thinking that a summer's campaign would be an agreeable recreation, he had joined a company of St. Louis volunteers.

'There were three of us,' said Tête Rouge, 'me and Bill Stephens and John Hopkins. We thought we would just go out with the army, and when we had conquered the country, we would get discharged and take our pay, you know, and go down to Mexico. They say there is plenty of fun going on there. Then we could go back to New-Orleans by way of Vera Cruz.'

But Tête Rouge, like many a stouter volunteer, had reckoned without his host. Fighting Mexicans was a less amusing occupation than he had supposed, and his pleasure trip was disagreeably interrupted by brain fever, which attacked him when about half way to Bent's Fort. He jolted along through the rest of the journey in a baggage-wagon. When they came to the Fort he was taken out and left there, together with the rest of the sick. Bent's Fort does not supply the best accommodations for an invalid. Tête Rouge's sick chamber was a little mud room, where he and a companion, attacked by the same disease, were laid together, with nothing but a buffalo-robe between them and the ground. The assistant surgeon's deputy visited them once a day and brought them each a huge dose of calomel, the only medicine, according to his surviving victim, which he was acquainted with.

Tête Rouge woke one morning, and turning to his companion, saw his eyes fixed upon the beams above with the glassy stare of a dead man. At this the unfortunate volunteer lost his senses outright. In spite of the doctor, however, he eventually recovered; though between the brain-fever and the calomel, his mind, originally none of the strongest, was so much shaken that it had not quite recovered its balance when we came to the Fort. In spite of the poor fellow's tragic story, there was something so ludicrous in his appearance, and the whimsical contrast between his military dress and his most unmilitary demeanor, that we could not help smiling at them. We asked him if he had a gun. He said they had taken it from him during his illness, and he had not seen it since; but perhaps, he observed, looking at me with a beseeching air, you will lend me one of your big pistols if we should meet with any Indians. I next inquired if he had a horse; he declared he had a magnificent one, and at Shaw's request, a Mexican led him in for inspection. He exhibited the outline of a good horse, but his eyes were sunk in the sockets, and every one of his ribs could be counted. There were certain marks too about his shoulders, which could be accounted for by the circumstance, that during Tête Rouge's illness, his companions had seized upon the insulted charger, and harnessed him to a cannon along with the draft horses. To Tête Rouge's astonishment we recommended him by all means to exchange the horse, if he could, for a mule. Fortunately the people at the Fort were so anxious to get rid of him that they were willing to make some sacrifice to effect the object, and he succeeded in getting a tolerable mule in exchange for the broken-down steed.

A man soon appeared at the gate, leading in the mule by a cord which he placed in the hands of Tête Rouge, who being somewhat afraid of his new acquisition tried various flatteries and blandishments to induce her to come forward. The mule, knowing that she was expected to advance, stopped short in consequence, and stood fast as a rock, looking straight forward with immovable composure. Being stimulated by a blow from behind she consented to move, and walked nearly to the other side of the Fort before she stopped again. Hearing the bystanders laugh, Tête Rouge plucked up spirit and tugged hard at the rope. The mule jerked backward, spun herself round and made a dash for the gate. Tête Rouge, who clung manfully to the rope, went whisking through the air for a few rods, when he let go and stood with his mouth open, staring after the mule, who galloped away over the prairie. She was soon caught and brought back by a Mexican, who mounted a horse and went in pursuit of her with his lasso.

Having thus displayed his capacities for prairie travelling, Tête proceeded to supply himself with provisions for the journey, and with this view he applied to a quarter-master's assistant who was in the Fort. This official had a face as sour as vinegar, being in a state of chronic indignation because he had been left behind the army. He was as anxious as the rest to get rid of Tête Rouge. So, producing a rusty key, he opened a low door which led to a half subterranean apartment, into which the two disappeared together. After some time they came out again, Tête Rouge greatly embarrassed by a multiplicity of paper parcels containing the different articles of his forty days' rations. They were consigned to the care of Delorier, who about that time passed by with the cart on his way to the appointed place of meeting with Munroe and his companions.

We next urged Tête Rouge to provide himself, if he could, with a gun. He accordingly made earnest appeals to the charity of various persons in the Fort, but totally without success, a circumstance which did not greatly disturb us, since in the event of a skirmish, he would be much more apt to do mischief to himself or his friends than to the enemy. When all these arrangements were completed, we saddled our horses, and were preparing to leave the Fort, when looking round we discovered that our new associate was in fresh trouble. A man was holding the mule for him in the middle of the Fort, while he tried to put the saddle on her back, but she kept stepping sideways and moving round and round in a circle until he was almost in despair. It required some assistance before all his difficulties could be overcome. At length he clambered into the black war-saddle on which he was to have carried terror into the ranks of the Mexicans.

'Get up,' said Tête Rouge, 'come now, go along, will you.'

The mule walked deliberately forward out of the gate. Her recent conduct had inspired him with so much awe, that he never dared to touch her with his whip. We trotted forward toward the place of meeting, but before we had gone far, we saw that Tête Rouge's mule, who perfectly understood her rider, had stopped and was quietly grazing in spite of his protestations, at some distance behind. So getting behind him, we drove him and the contumacious mule before us, until we could see through the twilight the gleaming of a distant fire. Munroe, Jim and Ellis were lying around it; their saddles, packs and weapons were scattered about and their horses picketed near them. Delorier was there too with our little cart. Another fire was soon blazing high. We invited our new allies to take a cup of coffee with us. When both the others had gone over to their side of the camp, Jim Gurney still stood by the blaze, puffing hard at his little black pipe, as short and weather-beaten as himself.

'Well!' he said, 'here are eight of us; we'll call it six—for them two boobies, Ellis over yonder, and that new man of yours, won't count for any thing. We'll get through well enough, never fear for that, unless the Camanches happen to get foul of us.'

Chapter XXIII.

INDIAN ALARMS.

"To all the sensual world proclaim,
One crowded hour of glorious life
Were worth an age without a name."
                                        SCOTT.

W E BEGAN our journey for the frontier settlements on
the twenty-seventh of August, and certainly a more
ragamuffin cavalcade never was seen on the banks of the Upper Arkansas. Of the large and fine horses with which we had
left the frontier in the spring, not one remained: we had supplied their place with the rough breed of the prairie, as hardy
as mules and almost as ugly; we had also with us a number of
the latter detestable animals. In spite of their strength and
hardihood, several of the band were already worn down by
hard service and hard fare, and as none of them were shod,
they were fast becoming foot-sore. Every horse and mule had
a cord of twisted bull-hide coiled around his neck, which by
no means added to the beauty of his appearance. Our saddles
and all our equipments were by this time lamentably worn
and battered, and our weapons had become dull and rusty.
The dress of the riders fully corresponded with the dilapidated furniture of our horses, and of the whole party none
made a more disreputable appearance than my friend and I.
Shaw had for an upper garment an old red flannel shirt, flying
open in front, and belted around him like a frock; while I, in
absence of other clothing, was attired in a time-worn suit of
leather.

Thus, happy and careless as so many beggars, we crept
slowly from day to day along the monotonous banks of the
Arkansas. Tête Rouge gave constant trouble, for he could
never catch his mule, saddle her, or indeed do any thing else
without assistance. Every day he had some new ailment, real
or imaginary, to complain of. At one moment he would be
wobegone and disconsolate, and at the next he would be visited with a violent flow of spirits, to which he could only give

vent by incessant laughing, whistling, and telling stories.
When other resources failed, we used to amuse ourselves by
tormenting him; a fair compensation for the trouble he cost
us. Tête Rouge rather enjoyed being laughed at, for he was an
odd compound of weakness, eccentricity and good-nature.
He made a figure worthy of a painter as he paced along before us, perched on the back of his mule, and enveloped in a
huge buffalo-robe coat, which some charitable person had
given him at the fort. This extraordinary garment, which
would have contained two men of his size, he chose, for some
reason best known to himself, to wear inside out, and he
never took it off, even in the hottest weather. It was fluttering
all over with seams and tatters, and the hide was so old and
rotten that it broke out every day in a new place. Just at the
top of it a large pile of red curls was visible, with his little cap
set jauntily upon one side, to give him a military air. His seat
in the saddle was no less remarkable than his person and
equipment. He pressed one leg close against his mule's side,
and thrust the other out at an angle of forty-five degrees. His
pantaloons were decorated with a military red stripe, of which
he was extremely vain; but being much too short, the whole
length of his boots was usually visible below them. His blanket, loosely rolled up into a large bundle, dangled at the back
of his saddle, where he carried it tied with a string. Four or
five times a day it would fall to the ground. Every few minutes he would drop his pipe, his knife, his flint and steel, or a
piece of tobacco, and have to scramble down to pick them up.
In doing this he would contrive to get in every body's way;
and as the most of the party were by no means remarkable for
a fastidious choice of language, a storm of anathemas would
be showered upon him, half in earnest and half in jest, until
Tête Rouge would declare that there was no comfort in life,
and that he never saw such fellows before.

Only a day or two after leaving Bent's Fort, Henry Chatillon rode forward to hunt, and took Ellis along with him. After they had been some time absent we saw them coming
down the hill, driving three dragoon-horses, which had escaped from their owners on the march, or perhaps had given
out and been abandoned. One of them was in tolerable condition, but the others were much emaciated and severely

bitten by the wolves. Reduced as they were, we carried two of them to the settlements, and Henry exchanged the third with the Arapahoes for an excellent mule.

On the day after, when we had stopped to rest at noon, a long train of Santa Fé wagons came up and trailed slowly past us in their picturesque procession. They belonged to a trader named Magoffin, whose brother, with a number of other men, came over and sat down around us on the grass. The news they brought was not of the most pleasing complexion. According to their accounts, the trail below was in a very dangerous state. They had repeatedly detected Indians prowling at night around their camps; and the large party which had left Bent's Fort a few weeks previous to our own departure had been attacked, and a man named Swan, from Massachusetts, had been killed. His companions had buried the body; but when Magoffin found his grave, which was near a place called 'The Caches,' the Indians had dug up and scalped him, and the wolves had shockingly mangled his remains. As an offset to this intelligence, they gave us the welcome information that the buffalo were numerous at a few days' journey below.

On the next afternoon, as we moved along the bank of the river, we saw the white tops of wagons on the horizon. It was some hours before we met them, when they proved to be a train of clumsy ox-wagons, quite different from the rakish vehicles of the Santa Fé traders, and loaded with government stores for the troops. They all stopped, and the drivers gathered around us in a crowd. I thought that the whole frontier might have been ransacked in vain to furnish men worse fitted to meet the dangers of the prairie. Many of them were mere boys, fresh from the plough, and devoid of knowledge and experience. In respect to the state of the trail, they confirmed all that the Santa Fé men had told us. In passing between the Pawnee Fork and the Caches, their sentinels had fired every night at real or imaginary Indians. They said also that Ewing, a young Kentuckian in the party that had gone down before us, had shot an Indian who was prowling at evening about the camp. Some of them advised us to turn back, and others to hasten forward as fast as we could; but they all seemed in such a state of feverish anxiety, and so little capable of cool judgment, that we attached slight weight to what they said. They next gave us a more definite piece of intelligence; a large village of Arapahoes was encamped on the river below. They represented them to be quite friendly; but some distinction was to be made between a party of thirty men, travelling with oxen, which are of no value in an Indian's eyes, and a mere handful like ourselves, with a tempting band of mules and horses. This story of the Arapahoes therefore caused us some anxiety.

Just after leaving the government wagons, as Shaw and I were riding along a narrow passage between the river-bank and a rough hill that pressed close upon it, we heard Tête Rouge's voice behind us. 'Hallo!' he called out; 'I say, stop the cart just for a minute, will you?'

'What's the matter, Tête?' asked Shaw, as he came riding up to us with a grin of exultation. He had a bottle of molasses in one hand, and a large bundle of hides on the saddle before him, containing, as he triumphantly informed us, sugar, biscuits, coffee and rice. These supplies he had obtained by a stratagem on which he greatly plumed himself, and he was extremely vexed and astonished that we did not fall in with his views of the matter. He had told Coates, the master-wagoner, that the commissary at the fort had given him an order for sick-rations, directed to the master of any government train, which he might meet upon the road. This order he had unfortunately lost, but he hoped that the rations would not be refused on that account, as he was suffering from coarse fare and needed them very much. As soon as he came to camp that night, Tête Rouge repaired to the box at the back of the cart, where Delorier used to keep his culinary apparatus, took possession of a saucepan, and after building a little fire of his own, set to work preparing a meal out of his ill-gotten booty. This done, he seized upon a tin plate and spoon, and sat down under the cart to regale himself. His preliminary repast did not at all prejudice his subsequent exertions at supper; where, in spite of his miniature dimensions, he made a better figure than any of us. Indeed, about this time his appetite grew quite voracious. He began to thrive wonderfully. His small body visibly expanded, and his cheeks, which when we first took him were rather yellow and cadaverous, now dilated in a wonderful manner, and became ruddy in proportion. Tête Rouge, in short, began to appear like another man.

Early in the afternoon of the next day, looking along the edge of the horizon in front, we saw that at one point it was faintly marked with pale indentations, like the teeth of a saw. The lodges of the Arapahoes, rising between us and the sky, caused this singular appearance. It wanted still two or three hours of sunset when we came opposite their camp. There were full two hundred lodges standing in the midst of a grassy meadow at some distance beyond the river, while for a mile around and on either bank of the Arkansas were scattered some fifteen hundred horses and mules, grazing together in bands, or wandering singly about the prairie. The whole were visible at once, for the vast expanse was unbroken by hills, and there was not a tree or a bush to intercept the view.

Here and there walked an Indian, engaged in watching the horses. No sooner did we see them than Tête Rouge begged Delorier to stop the cart and hand him his little military jacket, which was stowed away there. In this he instantly invested himself, having for once laid the old buffalo-coat aside, assumed a most martial posture in the saddle, set his cap over his left eye with an air of defiance, and earnestly entreated that somebody would lend him a gun or a pistol only for half an hour. Being called upon to explain these remarkable proceedings, Tête Rouge observed, that he knew from experience what effect the presence of a military man in his uniform always had upon the mind of an Indian, and he thought the Arapahoes ought to know that there was a soldier in the party.

Meeting Arapahoes here on the Arkansas was a very different thing from meeting the same Indians among their native mountains. There was another circumstance in our favor. General Kearney had seen them a few weeks before, as he came up the river with his army, and renewing his threats of the previous year, he told them that if they ever again touched the hair of a white man's head he would exterminate their nation. This placed them for the time in an admirable frame of mind, and the effect of his menaces had not yet disappeared. I was anxious to see the village and its inhabitants. We thought it also our best policy to visit them openly, as if unsuspicious of any hostile design; and Shaw and I, with Henry Chatillon, prepared to cross the river. The rest of the party meanwhile moved forward as fast as they could, in order to get as far as possible from our suspicious neighbors before night came on.

The Arkansas at this point, and for several hundred miles below, is nothing but a broad sand-bed, over which a few scanty threads of water are swiftly gliding, now and then expanding into wide shallows. At several places, during the autumn, the water sinks into the sand and disappears altogether. At this season, were it not for the numerous quicksands, the river might be forded almost any where without difficulty, though its channel is often a quarter of a mile wide. Our horses jumped down the bank, and wading through the water, or galloping freely over the hard sand-beds, soon reached the other side. Here, as we were pushing through the tall grass, we saw several Indians not far off; one of them waited until we came up, and stood for some moments in perfect silence before us, looking at us askance with his little snake-like eyes. Henry explained by signs what we wanted, and the Indian gathering his buffalo-robe about his shoulders, led the way toward the village without speaking a word.

The language of the Arapahoes is so difficult, and its pronunciation so harsh and guttural, that no white man, it is said, has ever been able to master it. Even Maxwell the trader, who has been most among them, is compelled to resort to the curious sign-language common to most of the prairie tribes. With this Henry Chatillon was perfectly acquainted.

Approaching the village, we found the ground all around it strewn with great piles of waste buffalo-meat in incredible quantities. The lodges were pitched in a very wide circle. They resembled those of the Dahcotah in every thing but cleanliness and neatness. Passing between two of them, we entered the great circular area of the camp, and instantly hundreds of Indians, men, women, and children, came flocking out of their habitations to look at us; at the same time, the dogs all around the village set up a fearful baying. Our Indian guide walked toward the lodge of the chief. Here we dismounted; and loosening the trail-ropes from our horses' necks, held them securely, and sat down before the entrance, with our rifles laid across our laps. The chief came out and shook us by the hand. He was a mean-looking fellow, very tall, thin-visaged, and sinewy, like the rest of the nation, and with scarcely a vestige of clothing. We had not been seated half a minute before a multitude of Indians came crowding around us from every part of the village, and we were shut in by a dense wall of savage faces. Some of the Indians crouched around us on the ground; others again sat behind them; others, stooping, looked over their heads; while many more stood crowded behind, stretching themselves upward, and peering over each other's shoulders, to get a view of us. I looked in vain among this multitude of faces to discover one manly or generous expression; all were wolfish, sinister, and malignant, and their complexions, as well as their features, unlike those of the Dahcotah, were exceedingly bad. The chief, who sat close to the entrance, called to a squaw within the lodge, who soon came out and placed a wooden bowl of meat before us. To our surprise, however, no pipe was offered. Having tasted of the meat as a matter of form, I began to open a bundle of presents, tobacco, knives, vermilion, and other articles which I had brought with me. At this there was a grin on every countenance in the rapacious crowd; their eyes began to glitter, and long thin arms were eagerly stretched toward us on all sides to receive the gifts.

The Arapahoes set great value upon their shields, which they transmit carefully from father to son. I wished to get one of them; and displaying a large piece of scarlet cloth, together with some tobacco and a knife, I offered them to any one who would bring me what I wanted. After some delay a tolerable shield was produced. They were very anxious to know what we meant to do with it, and Henry told them that we were going to fight their enemies the Pawnees. This instantly produced a visible impression in our favor, which was increased by the distribution of the presents. Among these was a large paper of awls, a gift appropriate to the women; and as we were anxious to see the beauties of the Arapahoe village, Henry requested that they might be called to receive them. A warrior gave a shout, as if he were calling a pack of dogs together. The squaws, young and old, hags of eighty and girls of sixteen, came running with screams and laughter out of the lodges; and as the men gave way for them, they gathered round us and stretched out their arms, grinning with delight, their native ugliness considerably enhanced by the excitement of the moment.

Mounting our horses, which during the whole interview we had held close to us, we prepared to leave the Arapahoes. The crowd fell back on each side, and stood looking on. When we were half across the camp an idea occurred to us. The Pawnees were probably in the neighborhood of the Caches; we might tell the Arapahoes of this, and instigate them to send down a war-party and cut them off, while we ourselves could remain behind for a while and hunt the buffalo. At first thought this plan of setting our enemies to destroy one another seemed to us a master-piece of policy; but we immediately recollected that should we meet the Arapahoe warriors on the river below, they might prove quite as dangerous as the Pawnees themselves. So rejecting our plan as soon as it presented itself, we passed out of the village on the farther side. We urged our horses rapidly through the tall grass, which rose to their necks. Several Indians were walking through it at a distance, their heads just visible above its waving surface. It bore a kind of seed, as sweet and nutritious as oats; and our hungry horses, in spite of whip and rein, could not resist the temptation of snatching at this unwonted luxury as we passed along. When about a mile from the village, I turned and looked back over the undulating ocean of grass. The sun was just set; the western sky was all in a glow, and sharply defined against it, on the extreme verge of the plain, stood the numerous lodges of the Arapahoe camp.

Reaching the bank of the river, we followed it for some distance farther, until we discerned through the twilight the white covering of our little cart on the opposite bank. When we reached it we found a considerable number of Indians there before us. Four or five of them were seated in a row upon the ground, looking like so many half-starved vultures. Tête Rouge, in his uniform, was holding a close colloquy with another by the side of the cart. His gesticulations, his attempts at sign-making, and the contortions of his countenance, were most ludicrous; and finding all these of no avail, he tried to make the Indian understand him by repeating English words very loudly and distinctly again and again. The Indian sat with his eye fixed steadily upon him, and in spite of the rigid immobility of his features, it was clear at a glance that he perfectly understood his military companion's character and thoroughly despised him. The exhibition was more amusing than politic, and Tête Rouge was directed to finish what he had to say as soon as possible. Thus rebuked, he crept under the cart and sat down there; Henry Chatillon stopped to look at him in his retirement, and remarked in his quiet manner that an Indian would kill ten such men and laugh all the time.

One by one our visitors arose and stalked away. As the darkness thickened we were saluted by dismal sounds. The wolves are incredibly numerous in this part of the country, and the offal around the Arapahoe camp had drawn such multitudes of them together, that several hundreds were howling in concert in our immediate neighborhood. There was an island in the river, or rather an oasis in the midst of the sands at about the distance of a gun-shot, and here they seemed gathered in the greatest numbers. A horrible discord of low mournful wailings, mingled with ferocious howls, arose from it incessantly for several hours after sunset. We could distinctly see the wolves running about the prairie within a few rods of our fire, or bounding over the sand-beds of the river and splashing through the water. There was not the slightest danger to be feared from them, for they are the greatest cowards on the prairie.

In respect to the human wolves in our neighborhood, we felt much less at our ease. We seldom erected our tent except in bad weather, and that night each man spread his buffalo-robe upon the ground with his loaded rifle laid at his side or clasped in his arms. Our horses were picketed so close around us that one of them repeatedly stepped over me as I lay. We were not in the habit of placing a guard, but every man that night was anxious and watchful; there was little sound sleeping in camp, and some one of the party was on his feet during the greater part of the time. For myself, I lay alternately waking and dozing until midnight. Tête Rouge was reposing close to the river bank, and about this time, when half asleep and half awake, I was conscious that he shifted his position and crept on all fours under the cart. Soon after I fell into a sound sleep, from which I was aroused by a hand shaking me by the shoulder. Looking up, I saw Tête Rouge stooping over me with his face quite pale and his eyes dilated to their utmost expansion.

'What's the matter?' said I.

Tête Rouge declared that as he lay on the river bank, something caught his eye which excited his suspicions. So creeping under the cart for safety's sake, he sat there and watched, when he saw two Indians, wrapped in white robes, creep up the bank, seize upon two horses and lead them off. He looked so frightened and told his story in such a disconnected manner that I did not believe him, and was unwilling to alarm the party. Still it might be true, and in that case the matter required instant attention. There would be no time for examination, and so directing Tête Rouge to show me which way the Indians had gone, I took my rifle, in obedience to a thoughtless impulse, and left the camp. I followed the river back for two or three hundred yards, listening and looking anxiously on every side. In the dark prairie on the right I could discern nothing to excite alarm; and in the dusky bed of the river, a wolf was bounding along in a manner which no Indian could imitate. I returned to the camp, and when within sight of it, saw that the whole party was aroused. Shaw called out to me that he had counted the horses, and that every one of them was in his place. Tête Rouge being examined as to what he had seen, only repeated his former story with many asseverations, and insisted that two horses were certainly carried off. At this Jim Gurney declared that he was crazy; Tête Rouge indignantly denied the charge, on which Jim appealed to us. As we declined to give our judgment on so delicate a matter, the dispute grew hot between Tête Rouge and his accuser, until he was directed to go to bed and not alarm the camp again if he saw the whole Arapahoe village coming.

Chapter XXIV.

THE CHASE.

"Mightiest of all the beasts of chase,
  That roam in woody Caledon,
Crashing the forest in his race,
  The mountain Bull comes thundering on."
                                CADYOW CASTLE.

T HE COUNTRY before us was now thronged with buffalo, and a sketch of the manner of hunting them will not be out of place. There are two methods commonly practised, 'running' and 'approaching.' The chase on horseback, which goes by the name of 'running,' is the more violent and dashing mode of the two. Indeed, of all American wild sports this is the wildest. Once among the buffalo, the hunter, unless long use has made him familiar with the situation, dashes forward in utter recklessness and self-abandonment. He thinks of nothing, cares for nothing but the game; his mind is stimulated to the highest pitch, yet intensely concentrated on one object. In the midst of the flying herd, where the uproar and the dust are thickest, it never wavers for a moment; he drops the rein and abandons his horse to his furious career; he levels his gun, the report sounds faint amid the thunder of the buffalo; and when his wounded enemy leaps in vain fury upon him, his heart thrills with a feeling like the fierce delight of the battlefield. A practised and skilful hunter well mounted, will sometimes kill five or six cows in a single chase, loading his gun again and again as his horse rushes through the tumult. An exploit like this is quite beyond the capacities of a novice. In attacking a small band of buffalo, or in separating a single animal from the herd and assailing it apart from the rest, there is less excitement and less danger. With a bold and well-trained horse the hunter may ride so close to the buffalo that as they gallop side by side he may reach over and touch him with his hand; nor is there much danger in this as long as the buffalo's strength and breath continue unabated; but when he becomes tired and can no longer run with ease, when his tongue lolls out and the foam flies from his jaws, then the hunter had better keep a more respectful distance; the distressed brute may turn upon him at any instant; and especially at the moment when he fires his gun. The wounded buffalo springs at his enemy; the horse leaps violently aside; and then the hunter has need of a tenacious seat in the saddle, for if he is thrown to the ground there is no hope for him. When he sees his attack defeated the buffalo resumes his flight, but if the shot be well directed he soon stops; for a few moments he stands still, then totters and falls heavily upon the prairie.

The chief difficulty in running buffalo, as it seems to me, is that of loading the gun or pistol at full gallop. Many hunters for convenience' sake carry three or four bullets in the mouth; the powder is poured down the muzzle of the piece, the bullet dropped in after it, the stock struck hard upon the pommel of the saddle, and the work is done. The danger of this method is obvious. Should the blow on the pommel fail to send the bullet home, or should the latter in the act of aiming, start from its place and roll toward the muzzle, the gun would probably burst in discharging. Many a shattered hand and worse casualties beside have been the result of such an accident. To obviate it, some hunters make use of a ramrod, usually hung by a string from the neck, but this materially increases the difficulty of loading. The bows and arrows which the Indians use in running buffalo have many advantages over firearms, and even white men occasionally employ them.

The danger of the chase arises not so much from the onset of the wounded animal as from the nature of the ground which the hunter must ride over. The prairie does not always present a smooth, level and uniform surface; very often it is broken with hills and hollows, intersected by ravines, and in the remoter parts studded by the stiff wild-sage bushes. The most formidable obstructions, however, are the burrows of wild animals, wolves, badgers, and particularly prairie dogs, with whose holes the ground for a very great extent is frequently honey-combed. In the blindness of the chase the hunter rushes over it unconscious of danger; his horse, at full career, thrusts his leg deep into one of the burrows; the bone snaps, the rider is hurled forward to the ground and probably killed. Yet accidents in buffalo running happen less frequently than one would suppose; in the recklessness of the chase, the hunter enjoys all the impunity of a drunken man, and may ride in safety over the gullies and declivities, where, should he attempt to pass in his sober senses he would infallibly break his neck.

The method of 'approaching' being practised on foot, has many advantages over that of 'running;' in the former, one neither breaks down his horse nor endangers his own life; instead of yielding to excitement he must be cool, collected and watchful; he must understand the buffalo, observe the features of the country and the course of the wind, and be well skilled moreover in using the rifle. The buffalo are strange animals; sometimes they are so stupid and infatuated that a man may walk up to them in full sight on the open prairie, and even shoot several of their number before the rest will think it necessary to retreat. Again at another moment they will be so shy and wary, that in order to approach them the utmost skill, experience and judgment are necessary. Kit Carson, I believe, stands pre-eminent in running buffalo; in approaching, no man living can bear away the palm from Henry Chatillon.

To resume the story. After Tête Rouge had alarmed the camp, no further disturbance occurred during the night. The Arapahoes did not attempt mischief, or if they did the wakefulness of the party deterred them from effecting their purpose. The next day was one of activity and excitement, for about ten o'clock the man in advance shouted the gladdening cry of *buffalo, buffalo!* and in the hollow of the prairie just below us, a band of bulls were grazing. The temptation was irresistible, and Shaw and I rode down upon them. We were badly mounted on our travelling horses, but by hard lashing we overtook them, and Shaw running alongside of a bull, shot into him both balls of his double-barrelled gun. Looking round as I galloped past, I saw the bull in his mortal fury rushing again and again upon his antagonist, whose horse constantly leaped aside, and avoided the onset. My chase was more protracted, but at length I ran close to the bull and killed him with my pistols. Cutting off the tails of our victims by way of trophy, we rejoined the party in about a quarter of an hour after we left it. Again and again that morning rang out the same welcome cry of *buffalo, buffalo!* Every few moments in the broad meadows along the river, we would see bands of bulls, who, raising their shaggy heads, would gaze in stupid amazement at the approaching horsemen, and then breaking into a clumsy gallop, would file off in a long line across the trail in front, toward the rising prairie on the left. At noon, the whole plain before us was alive with thousands of buffalo, bulls, cows, and calves, all moving rapidly as we drew near; and far-off beyond the river the swelling prairie was darkened with them to the very horizon. The party was in gayer spirits than ever. We stopped for a nooning near a grove of trees by the river side.

'Tongues and hump-ribs to-morrow,' said Shaw, looking with contempt at the venison steaks which Delorier placed before us. Our meal finished, we lay down under a temporary awning to sleep. A shout from Henry Chatillon aroused us, and we saw him standing on the cart-wheel, stretching his tall figure to its full height while he looked toward the prairie beyond the river. Following the direction of his eyes, we could clearly distinguish a large dark object, like the black shadow of a cloud, passing rapidly over swell after swell of the distant plain; behind it followed another of similar appearance though smaller. Its motion was more rapid, and it drew closer and closer to the first. It was the hunters of the Arapahoe camp pursuing a band of buffalo. Shaw and I hastily caught and saddled our best horses, and went plunging through sand and water to the farther bank. We were too late. The hunters had already mingled with the herd, and the work of slaughter was nearly over. When we reached the ground we found it strewn far and near with numberless black carcasses, while the remnants of the herd, scattered in all directions, were flying away in terror, and the Indians still rushing in pursuit. Many of the hunters however remained upon the spot, and among the rest was our yesterday's acquaintance, the chief of the village. He had alighted by the side of a cow, into which he had shot five or six arrows, and his squaw, who had followed him on horseback to the hunt, was giving him a draught of water out of a canteen, purchased or plundered from some volunteer soldier. Re-crossing the river, we over-took the party who were already on their way.

We had scarcely gone a mile when an imposing spectacle presented itself. From the river bank on the right, away over the swelling prairie on the left, and in front as far as we could see, extended one vast host of buffalo. The outskirts of the herd were within a quarter of a mile. In many parts they were crowded so densely together that in the distance their rounded backs presented a surface of uniform blackness; but elsewhere they were more scattered, and from amid the mul-titude rose little columns of dust where the buffalo were roll-ing on the ground. Here and there a great confusion was perceptible, where a battle was going forward among the bulls. We could distinctly see them rushing against each other, and hear the clattering of their horns and their hoarse bellow-ing. Shaw was riding at some distance in advance, with Henry Chatillon: I saw him stop and draw the leather covering from his gun. Indeed, with such a sight before us, but one thing could be thought of. That morning I had used pistols in the chase. I had now a mind to try the virtue of a gun. Delorier had one, and I rode up to the side of the cart; there he sat under the white covering, biting his pipe between his teeth and grinning with excitement.

'Lend me your gun, Delorier,' said I.

'Oui, Monsieur, oui,' said Delorier, tugging with might and main to stop the mule, which seemed obstinately bent on going forward. Then every thing but his moccasons disap-peared as he crawled into the cart and pulled at the gun to extricate it.

'Is it loaded?' I asked.

'Oui, bien chargé, you'll kill, mon bourgeois; yes, you'll kill—c'est un bon fusil.'

I handed him my rifle and rode forward to Shaw.

'Are you ready?' he asked.

'Come on,' said I.

'Keep down that hollow,' said Henry, 'and then they won't see you till you get close to them.'

The hollow was a kind of ravine very wide and shallow; it ran obliquely toward the buffalo, and we rode at a canter along the bottom until it became too shallow; when we bent close to our horses' necks, and then finding that it could no longer conceal us, came out of it and rode directly toward the herd. It was within gunshot; before its outskirts, numerous grizzly old bulls were scattered, holding guard over their females. They glared at us in anger and astonishment, walked toward us a few yards, and then turning slowly round retreated at a trot which afterwards broke into a clumsy gallop. In an instant the main body caught the alarm. The buffalo began to crowd away from the point toward which we were approaching, and a gap was opened in the side of the herd. We entered it, still restraining our excited horses. Every instant the tumult was thickening. The buffalo, pressing together in large bodies, crowded away from us on every hand. In front and on either side we could see dark columns and masses, half hidden by clouds of dust, rushing along in terror and confusion, and hear the tramp and clattering of ten thousand hoofs. That countless multitude of powerful brutes, ignorant of their own strength, were flying in a panic from the approach of two feeble horsemen. To remain quiet longer was impossible.

'Take that band on the left,' said Shaw; 'I'll take these in front.'

He sprang off, and I saw no more of him. A heavy Indian whip was fastened by a band to my wrist; I swung it into the air and lashed my horse's flank with all the strength of my arm. Away she darted, stretching close to the ground. I could see nothing but a cloud of dust before me, but I knew that it concealed a band of many hundreds of buffalo. In a moment I was in the midst of the cloud, half suffocated by the dust and stunned by the trampling of the flying herd; but I was drunk with the chase and cared for nothing but the buffalo. Very soon a long dark mass became visible, looming through the dust; then I could distinguish each bulky carcass, the hoofs flying out beneath, the short tails held rigidly erect. In a moment I was so close that I could have touched them with my gun. Suddenly, to my utter amazement, the hoofs were jerked upward, the tails flourished in the air, and amid a cloud of dust the buffalo seemed to sink into the earth before me. One vivid impression of that instant remains upon my mind. I remember looking down upon the backs of several buffalo dimly visible through the dust. We had run unawares upon a ravine. At that moment I was not the most accurate judge of depth and width, but when I passed it on my return, I found it about twelve feet deep and not quite twice as wide at the bottom. It was impossible to stop; I would have done so gladly if I could; so, half sliding, half plunging, down went the little mare. I believe she came down on her knees in the loose sand at the bottom; I was pitched forward violently against her neck and nearly thrown over her head among the buffalo, who amid dust and confusion came tumbling in all around. The mare was on her feet in an instant and scrambling like a cat up the opposite side. I thought for a moment that she would have fallen back and crushed me, but with a violent effort she clambered out and gained the hard prairie above. Glancing back I saw the huge head of a bull clinging as it were by the forefeet at the edge of the dusty gulf. At length I was fairly among the buffalo. They were less densely crowded than before, and I could see nothing but bulls, who always run at the rear of a herd. As I passed amid them they would lower their heads, and turning as they ran, attempt to gore my horse; but as they were already at full speed there was no force in their onset, and as Pauline ran faster than they, they were always thrown behind her in the effort. I soon began to distinguish cows amid the throng. One just in front of me seemed to my liking, and I pushed close to her side. Dropping the reins I fired, holding the muzzle of the gun within a foot of her shoulder. Quick as lightning she sprang at Pauline; the little mare dodged the attack, and I lost sight of the wounded animal amid the tumultuous crowd. Immediately after, I selected another, and urging forward Pauline, shot into her both pistols in succession. For a while I kept her in view, but in attempting to load my gun, lost sight of her also in the confusion. Believing her to be mortally wounded and unable to keep up with the herd, I checked my horse. The crowd rushed onward. The dust and tumult passed away, and on the prairie, far behind the rest, I saw a solitary buffalo galloping heavily. In a moment I and my victim were running side by side. My firearms were all empty, and I had in my pouch nothing but rifle bullets, too large for the pistols and too small for the gun. I loaded the latter, however, but as often as I levelled it to fire, the little bullets would roll out of the muzzle and the gun returned only a faint report like a squib, as the powder harmlessly exploded. I galloped in front of the buffalo and attempted to turn her back; but her eyes glared, her mane bristled, and lowering her head, she rushed at me with astonishing fierceness and activity. Again and again I rode before her, and again and again she repeated her furious charge. But little Pauline was in her element. She dodged her enemy at every rush, until at length the buffalo stood still, exhausted with her own efforts; she panted, and her tongue hung lolling from her jaws.

Riding to a little distance, I alighted, thinking to gather a handful of dry grass to serve the purpose of wadding, and load the gun at my leisure. No sooner were my feet on the ground than the buffalo came bounding in such a rage toward me that I jumped back again into the saddle with all possible dispatch. After waiting a few minutes more, I made an attempt to ride up and stab her with my knife; but the experiment proved such as no wise man would repeat. At length, bethinking me of the fringes at the seams of my buckskin pantaloons, I jerked off a few of them, and reloading the gun, forced them down the barrel to keep the bullet in its place; then approaching, I shot the wounded buffalo through the heart. Sinking to her knees, she rolled over lifeless on the prairie. To my astonishment, I found that instead of a fat cow I had been slaughtering a stout yearling bull. No longer wondering at the fierceness he had shown, I opened his throat, and cutting out his tongue, tied it at the back of my saddle. My mistake was one which a more experienced eye than mine might easily make in the dust and confusion of such a chase.

Then for the first time I had leisure to look at the scene around me. The prairie in front was darkened with the retreating multitude, and on the other hand the buffalo came filing up in endless unbroken columns from the low plains upon the river. The Arkansas was three or four miles distant. I turned and moved slowly toward it. A long time passed before, far down in the distance, I distinguished the white covering of the cart and the little black specks of horsemen before and behind it. Drawing near, I recognized Shaw's elegant tunic, the red flannel shirt conspicuous far off. I overtook the party, and asked him what success he had met with. He had assailed a fat cow, shot her with two bullets, and mortally wounded her. But neither of us were prepared for the chase that afternoon, and Shaw, like myself, had no spare bullets in his pouch; so he abandoned the disabled animal to Henry Chatillon, who followed, dispatched her with his rifle, and loaded his horse with her meat.

We encamped close to the river. The night was dark, and as we lay down, we could hear mingled with the howlings of wolves the hoarse bellowing of the buffalo, like the ocean beating upon a distant coast.

Chapter XXV.

THE BUFFALO CAMP.

"In pastures measureless as air,
The bison is my noble game."
BRYANT.

NO ONE in the camp was more active than Jim Gurney, and no one half so lazy as Ellis. Between these two there was a great antipathy. Ellis never stirred in the morning until he was compelled to, but Jim was always on his feet before daybreak; and this morning as usual the sound of his voice awakened the party.

"Get up, you booby! up with you now, you're fit for nothing but eating and sleeping. Stop your grumbling and come out of that buffalo-robe or I'll pull it off for you.'

Jim's words were interspersed with numerous expletives, which gave them great additional effect. Ellis drawled out something in a nasal tone from among the folds of his buffalo-robe; then slowly disengaged himself, rose into a sitting posture, stretched his long arms, yawned hideously, and finally raising his tall person erect, stood staring round him to all the four quarters of the horizon. Delorier's fire was soon blazing, and the horses and mules, loosened from their pickets, were feeding on the neighboring meadow. When we sat down to breakfast the prairie was still in the dusky light of morning; and as the sun rose we were mounted and on our way again.

'A white buffalo!' exclaimed Munroe.

'I'll have that fellow,' said Shaw, 'if I run my horse to death after him.'

He threw the cover of his gun to Delorier and galloped out upon the prairie.

'Stop, Mr. Shaw, stop!' called out Henry Chatillon, 'you'll run down your horse for nothing; it's only a white ox.'

But Shaw was already out of hearing. The ox, who had no doubt strayed away from some of the government wagon trains, was standing beneath some low hills which bounded

303

the plain in the distance. Not far from him a band of veritable buffalo bulls were grazing; and startled at Shaw's approach, they all broke into a run, and went scrambling up the hillsides to gain the high prairie above. One of them in his haste and terror involved himself in a fatal catastrophe. Along the foot of the hills was a narrow strip of deep marshy soil, into which the bull plunged and hopelessly entangled himself. We all rode up to the spot. The huge carcass was half sunk in the mud which flowed to his very chin, and his shaggy mane was outspread upon the surface. As we came near the bull began to struggle with convulsive strength; he writhed to and fro, and in the energy of his fright and desperation would lift himself for a moment half out of the slough, while the reluctant mire returned a sucking sound as he strained to drag his limbs from its tenacious depths. We stimulated his exertions by getting behind him and twisting his tail; nothing would do. There was clearly no hope for him. After every effort his heaving sides were more deeply imbedded and the mire almost overflowed his nostrils; he lay still at length, and looking round at us with a furious eye, seemed to resign himself to his fate. Ellis slowly dismounted, and deliberately levelling his boasted yager, shot the old bull through the heart; then he lazily climbed back again to his seat, pluming himself no doubt on having actually killed a buffalo. That day the invincible yager drew blood for the first and last time during the whole journey.

The morning was a bright and gay one, and the air so clear that on the farthest horizon the outline of the pale blue prairie was sharply drawn against the sky. Shaw felt in the mood for hunting; he rode in advance of the party, and before long we saw a file of bulls galloping at full speed upon a vast green swell of the prairie at some distance in front. Shaw came scouring along behind them, arrayed in his red shirt, which looked very well in the distance; he gained fast on the fugitives, and as the foremost bull was disappearing behind the summit of the swell, we saw him in the act of assailing the hindmost; a smoke sprang from the muzzle of his gun, and floated away before the wind like a little white cloud; the bull turned upon him, and just then the rising ground concealed them both from view.

We were moving forward until about noon, when we stopped by the side of the Arkansas. At that moment Shaw appeared riding slowly down the side of a distant hill; his horse was tired and jaded, and when he threw his saddle upon the ground, I observed that the tails of two bulls were dangling behind it. No sooner were the horses turned loose to feed than Henry, asking Munroe to go with him, took his rifle and walked quietly away. Shaw, Tête Rouge and I, sat down by the side of the cart to discuss the dinner which Delorier placed before us; we had scarcely finished when we saw Munroe walking towards us along the river bank. Henry, he said, had killed four fat cows, and had sent him back for horses to bring in the meat. Shaw took a horse for himself and another for Henry, and he and Munroe left the camp together. After a short absence all three of them came back, their horses loaded with the choicest parts of the meat; we kept two of the cows for ourselves and gave the others to Munroe and his companions. Delorier seated himself on the grass before the pile of meat, and worked industriously for some time to cut it into thin broad sheets for drying. This is no easy matter, but Delorier had all the skill of an Indian squaw. Long before night, cords of raw hide were stretched around the camp, and the meat was hung upon them to dry in the sunshine and pure air of the prairie. Our California companions were less successful at the work; but they accomplished it after their own fashion, and their side of the camp was soon garnished in the same manner as our own.

We meant to remain at this place long enough to prepare provisions for our journey to the frontier, which as we supposed might occupy about a month. Had the distance been twice as great and the party ten times as large, the unerring rifle of Henry Chatillon would have supplied meat enough for the whole within two days; we were obliged to remain, however, until it should be dry enough for transportation; so we erected our tent and made the other arrangements for a permanent camp. The California men, who had no such shelter, contented themselves with arranging their packs on the grass around their fire. In the meantime we had nothing to do but amuse ourselves. Our tent was within a rod of the river, if the broad sand-beds, with a scanty stream of water coursing here and there along their surface, deserve to be dignified with the name of river. The vast flat plains on either side were almost on a level with the sand-beds, and they were bounded in the distance by low, monotonous hills, parallel to the course of the Arkansas. All was one expanse of grass; there was no wood in view, except some trees and stunted bushes upon two islands which rose from amid the wet sands of the river. Yet far from being dull and tame this boundless scene was often a wild and animated one; for twice a day, at sunrise and at noon, the buffalo came issuing from the hills, slowly advancing in their grave processions to drink at the river. All our amusements were to be at their expense. Except an elephant, I have seen no animal that can surpass a buffalo bull in size and strength, and the world may be searched in vain to find any thing of a more ugly and ferocious aspect. At first sight of him every feeling of sympathy vanishes; no man who has not experienced it, can understand with what keen relish one inflicts his death wound, with what profound contentment of mind he beholds him fall. The cows are much smaller and of a gentler appearance, as becomes their sex. While in this camp we forebore to attack them, leaving to Henry Chatillon, who could better judge their fatness and good quality, the task of killing such as we wanted for use; but against the bulls we waged an unrelenting war. Thousands of them might be slaughtered without causing any detriment to the species, for their numbers greatly exceed those of the cows; it is the hides of the latter alone which are used for the purpose of commerce and for making the lodges of the Indians; and the destruction among them is therefore altogether disproportioned.

Our horses were tired, and we now usually hunted on foot. The wide, flat sand-beds of the Arkansas, as the reader will remember, lay close by the side of our camp. While we were lying on the grass after dinner, smoking, conversing, or laughing at Tête Rouge, one of us would look up and observe, far out on the plains beyond the river, certain black objects slowly approaching. He would inhale a parting whiff from the pipe, then rising lazily, take his rifle, which leaned against the cart, throw over his shoulder the strap of his pouch and powder-horn, and with his moccasons in his hand, walk quietly across the sand toward the opposite side of the river. This was very easy; for though the sands were about a quarter of a mile wide, the water was nowhere more than two feet deep. The farther bank was about four or five feet high, and quite perpendicular, being cut away by the water in spring. Tall grass grew along its edge. Putting it aside with his hand, and cautiously looking through it, the hunter can discern the huge shaggy back of the buffalo slowly swaying to and fro, as, with his clumsy swinging gait, he advances towards the water. The buffalo have regular paths by which they come down to drink. Seeing at a glance along which of these his intended victim is moving, the hunter crouches under the bank within fifteen or twenty yards, it may be, of the point where the path enters the river. Here he sits down quietly on the sand. Listening intently, he hears the heavy monotonous tread of the approaching bull. The moment after, he sees a motion among the long weeds and grass just at the spot where the path is channelled through the bank. An enormous black head is thrust out, the horns just visible amid the mass of tangled mane. Half sliding, half plunging, down comes the buffalo upon the river-bed below. He steps out in full sight upon the sands. Just before him a runnel of water is gliding, and he bends his head to drink. You may hear the water as it gurgles down his capacious throat. He raises his head, and the drops trickle from his wet beard. He stands with an air of stupid abstraction, unconscious of the lurking danger. Noiselessly the hunter cocks his rifle. As he sits upon the sand, his knee is raised, and his elbow rests upon it, that he may level his heavy weapon with a steadier aim. The stock is at his shoulder; his eye ranges along the barrel. Still he is in no haste to fire. The bull, with slow deliberation, begins his march over the sands to the other side. He advances his foreleg, and exposes to view a small spot, denuded of hair, just behind the point of his shoulder; upon this the hunter brings the sight of his rifle to bear; lightly and delicately his finger presses upon the hair-trigger. Quick as thought the spiteful crack of the rifle responds to his slight touch, and instantly in the middle of the bare spot appears a small red dot. The buffalo shivers; death has overtaken him, he cannot tell from whence; still he does not fall, but walks heavily forward, as if nothing had happened. Yet before he has advanced far out upon the sand, you see him stop; he totters; his knees bend under him, and his head sinks forward to the ground. Then his whole vast bulk sways to one side; he rolls over on the sand, and dies with a scarcely perceptible struggle.

Waylaying the buffalo in this manner, and shooting them as they come to water, is the easiest and laziest method of hunting them. They may also be approached by crawling up ravines, or behind hills, or even over the open prairie. This is often surprisingly easy; but at other times it requires the utmost skill of the most experienced hunter. Henry Chatillon was a man of extraordinary strength and hardihood; but I have seen him return to camp quite exhausted with his efforts, his limbs scratched and wounded, and his buckskin dress stuck full of the thorns of the prickly-pear, among which he had been crawling. Sometimes he would lay flat upon his face, and drag himself along in this position for many rods together.

On the second day of our stay at this place, Henry went out for an afternoon hunt. Shaw and I remained in camp, until, observing some bulls approaching the water upon the other side of the river, we crossed over to attack them. They were so near, however, that before we could get under cover of the bank our appearance as we walked over the sands alarmed them. Turning round before coming within gun-shot, they began to move off to the right in a direction parallel to the river. I climbed up the bank and ran after them. They were walking swiftly, and before I could come within gun-shot distance they slowly wheeled about and faced toward me. Before they had turned far enough to see me I had fallen flat on my face. For a moment they stood and stared at the strange object upon the grass; then turning away, again they walked on as before; and I, rising immediately, ran once more in pursuit. Again they wheeled about, and again I fell prostrate. Repeating this three or four times, I came at length within a hundred yards of the fugitives, and as I saw them turning again I sat down and levelled my rifle. The one in the centre was the largest I had ever seen. I shot him behind the shoulder. His two companions ran off. He attempted to follow, but soon came to a stand, and at length lay down as quietly as an ox chewing the cud. Cautiously approaching him, I saw by his dull and jelly-like eye that he was dead.

When I began the chase, the prairie was almost tenantless; but a great multitude of buffalo had suddenly thronged upon it, and looking up, I saw within fifty rods a heavy, dark column stretching to the right and left as far as I could see. I walked toward them. My approach did not alarm them in the least. The column itself consisted almost entirely of cows and calves, but a great many old bulls were ranging about the prairie on its flank, and as I drew near they faced toward me with such a shaggy and ferocious look that I thought it best to proceed no farther. Indeed I was already within close rifle-shot of the column, and I sat down on the ground to watch their movements. Sometimes the whole would stand still, their heads all facing one way; then they would trot forward, as if by a common impulse, their hoofs and horns clattering together as they moved. I soon began to hear at a distance on the left the sharp reports of a rifle, again and again repeated; and not long after, dull and heavy sounds succeeded, which I recognized as the familiar voice of Shaw's double-barreled gun. When Henry's rifle was at work there was always meat to be brought in. I went back across the river for a horse, and returning, reached the spot where the hunters were standing. The buffalo were visible on the distant prairie. The living had retreated from the ground, but ten or twelve carcasses were scattered in various directions. Henry, knife in hand, was stooping over a dead cow, cutting away the best and fattest of the meat.

When Shaw left me he had walked down for some distance under the river-bank to find another bull. At length he saw the plains covered with the host of buffalo, and soon after heard the crack of Henry's rifle. Ascending the bank, he crawled through the grass, which for a rod or two from the river was very high and rank. He had not crawled far before to his astonishment he saw Henry standing erect upon the prairie, almost surrounded by the buffalo. Henry was in his appropriate element. Nelson, on the deck of the 'Victory,' hardly felt a prouder sense of mastery than he. Quite unconscious that any one was looking at him, he stood at the full height of his tall, strong figure, one hand resting upon his side, and the other arm leaning carelessly on the muzzle of his rifle. His eye was ranging over the singular assemblage around him. Now and then he would select such a cow as suited him, level his rifle, and shoot her dead; then quietly re-loading, he would resume his former position. The buffalo seemed no more to regard his presence than if he were one of themselves; the bulls were bellowing and butting at each other, or else rolling about in the dust. A group of buffalo would gather about the carcass of a dead cow, snuffing at her wounds; and sometimes they would come behind those that had not yet fallen, and endeavor to push them from the spot. Now and then some old bull would face toward Henry with an air of stupid amazement, but none seemed inclined to attack or fly from him. For some time Shaw lay among the grass, looking in surprise at this extraordinary sight; at length he crawled cautiously forward, and spoke in a low voice to Henry, who told him to rise and come on. Still the buffalo showed no sign of fear; they remained gathered about their dead companions. Henry had already killed as many cows as we wanted for use, and Shaw, kneeling behind one of the carcasses, shot five bulls before the rest thought it necessary to disperse.

The frequent stupidity and infatuation of the buffalo seems the more remarkable from the contrast it offers to their wildness and wariness at other times. Henry knew all their peculiarities; he had studied them as a scholar studies his books, and he derived quite as much pleasure from the occupation. The buffalo were a kind of companions to him, and, as he said, he never felt alone when they were about him. He took great pride in his skill in hunting. Henry was one of the most modest of men; yet in the simplicity and frankness of his character, it was quite clear that he looked upon his pre-eminence in this respect as a thing too palpable and well-established ever to be disputed. But whatever may have been his estimate of his own skill, it was rather below than above that which others placed upon it. The only time that I ever saw a shade of scorn darken his face, was when two volunteer soldiers, who had just killed a buffalo for the first time, undertook to instruct him as to the best method of 'approaching.' To borrow an illustration from an opposite side of life, an Eton-boy

might as well have sought to enlighten Porsons on the forma-
tion of a Greek verb, or a Fleet-street shopkeeper to instruct
Chesterfield concerning a point of etiquette. Henry always
seemed to think that he had a sort of prescriptive right to the
buffalo, and to look upon them as something belonging peculiarly to himself. Nothing excited his indignation so much as
any wanton destruction committed among the cows, and in
his view shooting a calf was a cardinal sin.

Henry Chatillon and Tête Rouge were of the same age; that
is, about thirty. Henry was twice as large, and fully six times
as strong as Tête Rouge. Henry's face was roughened by
winds and storms; Tête Rouge's was bloated by sherry-
cobblers and brandy-toddy. Henry talked of Indians and buffalo; Tête Rouge of theatres and oyster-cellars. Henry had led
a life of hardship and privation; Tête Rouge never had a
whim which he would not gratify at the first moment he was
able. Henry moreover was the most disinterested man I ever
saw; while Tête Rouge, though equally good-natured in his
way, cared for nobody but himself. Yet we would not have
lost him on any account; he admirably served the purpose of a
jester in a feudal castle; our camp would have been lifeless
without him. For the past week he had fattened in a most
amazing manner; and, indeed, this was not at all surprising,
since his appetite was most inordinate. He was eating from
morning till night; half the time he would be at work cooking
some private repast for himself, and he paid a visit to the
coffee-pot eight or ten times a day. His rueful and disconsolate face became jovial and rubicund, his eyes stood out like a
lobster's, and his spirits, which before were sunk to the
depths of despondency, were now elated in proportion; all
day he was singing, whistling, laughing, and telling stories.
Being mortally afraid of Jim Gurney, he kept close in the
neighborhood of our tent. As he had seen an abundance of
low dissipated life, and had a considerable fund of humor, his
anecdotes were extremely amusing, especially since he never
hesitated to place himself in a ludicrous point of view, provided he could raise a laugh by doing so. Tête Rouge, however, was sometimes rather troublesome; he had an inveterate
habit of pilfering provisions at all times of the day. He set
ridicule at utter defiance; and being without a particle of self-

respect, he would never have given over his tricks, even if they had drawn upon him the scorn of the whole party. Now and then, indeed, something worse than laughter fell to his share; on these occasions he would exhibit much contrition, but half an hour after we would generally observe him stealing round to the box at the back of the cart, and slyly making off with the provisions which Delorier had laid by for supper. He was very fond of smoking; but having no tobacco of his own, we used to provide him with as much as he wanted, a small piece at a time. At first we gave him half a pound together; but this experiment proved an entire failure, for he invariably lost not only the tobacco, but the knife intrusted to him for cutting it, and a few minutes after he would come to us with many apologies and beg for more.

We had been two days at this camp, and some of the meat was nearly fit for transportation, when a storm came suddenly upon us. About sunset the whole sky grew as black as ink, and the long grass at the river's edge bent and rose mournfully with the first gusts of the approaching hurricane. Munroe and his two companions brought their guns and placed them under cover of our tent. Having no shelter for themselves, they built a fire of driftwood that might have defied a cataract, and wrapped in their buffalo-robes, sat on the ground around it to bide the fury of the storm. Delorier ensconced himself under the cover of the cart. Shaw and I, together with Henry and Tête Rouge, crowded into the little tent; but first of all the dried meat was piled together, and well protected by buffalo-robes pinned firmly to the ground. About nine o'clock the storm broke, amid absolute darkness; it blew a gale, and torrents of rain roared over the boundless expanse of open prairie. Our tent was filled with mist and spray beating through the canvas, and saturating every thing within. We could only distinguish each other at short intervals by the dazzling flash of lightning, which displayed the whole waste around us with its momentary glare. We had our fears for the tent; but for an hour or two it stood fast, until at length the cap gave way before a furious blast; the pole tore through the top, and in an instant we were half suffocated by the cold and dripping folds of the canvas, which fell down upon us. Seizing upon our guns, we placed them erect, in

order to lift the saturated cloth above our heads. In this agreeable situation, involved among wet blankets and buffalo-
robes, we spent several hours of the night, during which the
storm would not abate for a moment, but pelted down above
our heads with merciless fury. Before long the ground beneath us became soaked with moisture, and the water gathered there in a pool two or three inches deep; so that for a
considerable part of the night we were partially immersed in a
cold bath. In spite of all this, Tête Rouge's flow of spirits did
not desert him for an instant; he laughed, whistled, and sang
in defiance of the storm, and that night he paid off the long
arrears of ridicule which he owed us. While we lay in silence,
enduring the infliction with what philosophy we could muster, Tête Rouge, who was intoxicated with animal spirits, was
cracking jokes at our expense by the hour together. At about
three o'clock in the morning, 'preferring the tyranny of the
open night' to such a wretched shelter, we crawled out from
beneath the fallen canvas. The wind had abated, but the rain
fell steadily. The fire of the California men still blazed amid
the darkness, and we joined them as they sat around it. We
made ready some hot coffee by way of refreshment; but when
some of the party sought to replenish their cups, it was found
that Tête Rouge, having disposed of his own share, had privately abstracted the coffee-pot and drank up the rest of the
contents out of the spout.

In the morning, to our great joy, an unclouded sun rose
upon the prairie. We presented rather a laughable appearance,
for the cold and clammy buckskin, saturated with water,
clung fast to our limbs; the light wind and warm sunshine
soon dried them again, and then we were all incased in armor
of intolerable rigidity. Roaming all day over the prairie and
shooting two or three bulls, were scarcely enough to restore
the stiffened leather to its usual pliancy.

Besides Henry Chatillon, Shaw and I were the only hunters
in the party. Munroe this morning made an attempt to run a
buffalo, but his horse could not come up to the game. Shaw
went out with him, and being better mounted soon found
himself in the midst of the herd. Seeing nothing but cows and
calves around him, he checked his horse. An old bull came
galloping on the open prairie at some distance behind, and

turning, Shaw rode across his path, levelling his gun as he passed, and shooting him through the shoulder into the heart. The heavy bullets of Shaw's double-barrelled gun made wild work wherever they struck.

A great flock of buzzards were usually soaring about a few trees that stood on the island just below our camp. Throughout the whole of yesterday we had noticed an eagle among them; to-day he was still there; and Tête Rouge, declaring that he would kill the bird of America, borrowed Delorier's gun and set out on his unpatriotic mission. As might have been expected, the eagle suffered no great harm at his hands. He soon returned, saying that he could not find him, but had shot a buzzard instead. Being required to produce the bird in proof of his assertion, he said he believed that he was not quite dead, but he must be hurt, from the swiftness with which he flew off.

'If you want,' said Tête Rouge, 'I'll go and get one of his feathers; I knocked off plenty of them when I shot him.'

Just opposite our camp, was another island covered with bushes, and behind it was a deep pool of water, while two or three considerable streams coursed over the sand not far off. I was bathing at this place in the afternoon when a white wolf, larger than the largest Newfoundland dog, ran out from behind the point of the island, and galloped leisurely over the sand not half a stone's throw distant. I could plainly see his red eyes and the bristles about his snout; he was an ugly scoundrel, with a bushy tail, large head, and a most repulsive countenance. Having neither rifle to shoot nor stone to pelt him with, I was looking eagerly after some missile for his benefit, when the report of a gun came from the camp, and the ball threw up the sand just beyond him; at this he gave a slight jump, and stretched away so swiftly that he soon dwindled into a mere speck on the distant sand-beds. The number of carcasses that by this time were lying about the prairie all around us, summoned the wolves from every quarter; the spot where Shaw and Henry had hunted together soon became their favorite resort, for here about a dozen dead buffalo were fermenting under the hot sun. I used often to go over the river and watch them at their meal; by lying under the bank it was easy to get a full view of them. Three different

kinds were present; there were the white wolves and the gray
wolves, both extremely large, and besides these the small prairie wolves, not much bigger than spaniels. They would howl
and fight in a crowd around a single carcass, yet they were so
watchful, and their senses so acute, that I never was able to
crawl within a fair shooting distance; whenever I attempted
it, they would all scatter at once and glide silently away
through the tall grass. The air above this spot was always full
of buzzards or black vultures; whenever the wolves left a carcass they would descend upon it, and cover it so densely that
a rifle bullet shot at random among the gormandizing crowd
would generally strike down two or three of them. These
birds would now be sailing by scores just above our camp,
their broad black wings seeming half transparent as they expanded them against the bright sky. The wolves and the buzzards thickened about us with every hour, and two or three
eagles also came into the feast. I killed a bull within rifle-shot
of the camp; that night the wolves made a fearful howling
close at hand, and in the morning the carcass was completely
hollowed out by these voracious feeders.

After we had remained four days at this camp we prepared
to leave it. We had for our own part about five hundred
pounds of dried meat, and the California men had prepared
some three hundred more; this consisted of the fattest and
choicest parts of eight or nine cows, a very small quantity
only being taken from each, and the rest abandoned to the
wolves. The pack animals were laden, the horses were saddled, and the mules harnessed to the cart. Even Tête Rouge
was ready at last, and slowly moving from the ground, we
resumed our journey eastward. When we had advanced about
a mile, Shaw missed a valuable hunting-knife and turned back
in search of it, thinking that he had left it at the camp. He
approached the place cautiously, fearful that Indians might be
lurking about, for a deserted camp is dangerous to return to.
He saw no enemy, but the scene was a wild and dreary one;
the prairie was overshadowed by dull, leaden clouds, for the
day was dark and gloomy. The ashes of the fires were still
smoking by the river side; the grass around them was trampled down by men and horses, and strewn with all the litter
of a camp. Our departure had been a gathering signal to the

birds and beasts of prey; Shaw assured me that literally dozens of wolves were prowling about the smouldering fires, while multitudes were roaming over the prairie around; they all fled as he approached, some running over the sand-beds and some over the grassy plains. The vultures in great clouds were soaring overhead, and the dead bull near the camp was completely blackened by the flock that had alighted upon it; they flapped their broad wings, and stretched upward their crested heads and long skinny necks, fearing to remain, yet reluctant to leave their disgusting feast. As he searched about the fires he saw the wolves seated on the distant hills waiting for his departure. Having looked in vain for his knife, he mounted again, and left the wolves and the vultures to banquet freely upon the carrion of the camp.

Chapter XXVI.

DOWN THE ARKANSAS.

"They quitted not their harness bright,
Neither by day nor yet by night;
  They lay down to rest
  With corslet laced,
Pillowed on buckler cold and hard.
  They carved at the meal
  With gloves of steel,
And they drank the red wine through the helmet barred."
      THE LAY OF THE LAST MINSTREL.

IN THE SUMMER of 1846, the wild and lonely banks of the Upper Arkansas beheld for the first time the passage of an army. General Kearney, on his march to Santa Fé, adopted this route in preference to the old trail of the Cimarron. When we came down, the main body of the troops had already passed on; Price's Missouri regiment, however, was still on the way, having left the frontier much later than the rest; and about this time we began to meet them moving along the trail, one or two companies at a time. No men ever embarked upon a military expedition with a greater love for the work before them than the Missourians; but if discipline and subordination be the criterion of merit, these soldiers were worthless indeed. Yet when their exploits have rung through all America, it would be absurd to deny that they were excellent irregular troops. Their victories were gained in the teeth of every established precedent of warfare; they were owing to a singular combination of military qualities in the men themselves. Without discipline or a spirit of subordination, they knew how to keep their ranks and act as one man. Doniphan's regiment marched through New Mexico more like a band of free companions than like the paid soldiers of a modern government. When General Taylor complimented Doniphan on his success at Sacramento and elsewhere, the Colonel's reply very well illustrates the relations which subsisted between the officers and men of his command:

'I don't know any thing of the manœuvres. The boys kept coming to me, to let them charge; and when I saw a good opportunity, I told them they might go. They were off like a shot, and that's all I know about it.'

The backwoods lawyer was better fitted to conciliate the good-will than to command the obedience of his men. There were many serving under him, who both from character and education could better have held command than he.

At the battle of Sacramento his frontiersmen fought under every possible disadvantage. The Mexicans had chosen their own position; they were drawn up across the valley that led to their native city of Chihuahua; their whole front was covered by intrenchments and defended by batteries of heavy cannon; they outnumbered the invaders five to one. An eagle flew over the Americans, and a deep murmur rose along their lines. The enemy's batteries opened; long they remained under fire, but when at length the word was given, they shouted and ran forward. In one of the divisions, when midway to the enemy a drunken officer ordered a halt; the exasperated men hesitated to obey.

'Forward, boys!' cried a private from the ranks; and the Americans, rushing like tigers upon the enemy, bounded over the breastwork. Four hundred Mexicans were slain upon the spot, and the rest fled, scattering over the plain like sheep. The standards, cannon and baggage were taken, and among the rest a wagon laden with cords, which the Mexicans, in the fulness of their confidence, had made ready for tying the American prisoners.

Doniphan's volunteers, who gained this victory, passed up with the main army; but Price's soldiers whom we now met, were men from the same neighborhood, precisely similar in character, manners and appearance. One forenoon, as we were descending upon a very wide meadow, where we meant to rest for an hour or two, we saw a dark body of horsemen approaching at a distance. In order to find water, we were obliged to turn aside to the river bank, a full half mile from the trail. Here we put up a kind of awning, and spreading buffalo-robes on the ground, Shaw and I sat down to smoke beneath it.

'We are going to catch it now,' said Shaw; 'look at those fellows; there'll be no peace for us here.'

And in good truth about half the volunteers had straggled away from the line of march, and were riding over the meadow toward us.

'How are you?' said the first who came up, alighting from his horse and throwing himself upon the ground. The rest followed close, and a score of them soon gathered about us, some lying at full length and some sitting on horseback. They all belonged to a company raised in St. Louis. There were some ruffian faces among them, and some haggard with debauchery; but on the whole they were extremely good-looking men, superior beyond measure to the ordinary rank and file of an army. Except that they were booted to the knees, they wore their belts and military trappings over the ordinary dress of citizens. Besides their swords and holster pistols, they carried slung from their saddles the excellent Springfield carbines, loaded at the breech. They inquired the character of our party, and were anxious to know the prospect of killing buffalo, and the chance that their horses would stand the journey to Santa Fé. All this was well enough, but a moment after a worse visitation came upon us.

'How are you, strangers? whar are you going and whar are you from?' said a fellow, who came trotting up with an old straw hat on his head. He was dressed in the coarsest brown homespun cloth. His face was rather sallow from fever-and-ague, and his tall figure, though strong and sinewy, was quite thin, and had besides an angular look, which, together with his boorish seat on horseback, gave him an appearance any thing but graceful. Plenty more of the same stamp were close behind him. Their company was raised in one of the frontier counties, and we soon had abundant evidence of their rustic breeding; dozens of them came crowding round, pushing between our first visitors, and staring at us with unabashed faces.

'Are you the captain?' asked one fellow.

'What's your business out here?' asked another.

'Whar do you live when you're at home?' said a third.

'I reckon you're traders,' surmised a fourth; and to crown

the whole, one of them came confidently to my side and inquired in a low voice, 'What's your partner's name?'

As each new comer repeated the same questions, the nuisance became intolerable. Our military visitors were soon disgusted at the concise nature of our replies, and we could overhear them muttering curses against us. While we sat smoking, not in the best imaginable humor, Tête Rouge's tongue was never idle. He never forgot his military character, and during the whole interview he was incessantly busy among his fellow soldiers. At length we placed him on the ground before us, and told him that he might play the part of spokesman for the whole. Tête Rouge was delighted, and we soon had the satisfaction of seeing him talk and gabble at such a rate that the torrent of questions was in a great measure diverted from us. A little while after, to our amazement, we saw a large cannon with four horses come lumbering up behind the crowd; and the driver, who was perched on one of the animals, stretching his neck so as to look over the rest of the men, called out:

'Whar are you from, and what's your business?'

The captain of one of the companies was among our visitors, drawn by the same curiosity that had attracted his men. Unless their faces belied them, not a few in the crowd might with great advantage have changed places with their commander.

'Well, men,' said he, lazily rising from the ground where he had been lounging, 'it's getting late, I reckon we had better be moving.'

'I shan't start yet any how,' said one fellow, who was lying half asleep with his head resting on his arm.

'Don't be in a hurry, captain,' added the lieutenant.

'Well, have it your own way, we'll wait awhile longer,' replied the obsequious commander.

At length however our visitors went straggling away as they had come, and we, to our great relief, were left alone again.

No one can deny the intrepid bravery of these men, their intelligence and the bold frankness of their character, free from all that is mean and sordid. Yet for the moment the extreme roughness of their manners, half inclines one to forget their heroic qualities. Most of them seem without the least perception of delicacy or propriety, though among them individuals may be found in whose manners there is a plain courtesy, while their features bespeak a gallant spirit equal to any enterprise.

No one was more relieved than Delorier by the departure of the volunteers; for dinner was getting colder every moment. He spread a well-whitened buffalo-hide upon the grass, placed in the middle the juicy hump of a fat cow, ranged around it the tin plates and cups, and then acquainted us that all was ready. Tête Rouge, with his usual alacrity on such occasions, was the first to take his seat. In his former capacity of steamboat clerk, he had learned to prefix the honorary *Mister* to every body's name, whether of high or low degree; so Jim Gurney was Mr. Gurney, Henry was Mr. Henry, and even Delorier, for the first time in his life, heard himself addressed as Mr. Delorier. This did not prevent his conceiving a violent enmity against Tête Rouge, who in his futile though praiseworthy attempts to make himself useful, used always to intermeddle with cooking the dinners. Delorier's disposition knew no medium between smiles and sunshine and a downright tornado of wrath; he said nothing to Tête Rouge, but his wrongs rankled in his breast. Tête Rouge had taken his place at dinner; it was his happiest moment; he sat enveloped in the old buffalo-coat, sleeves turned up in preparation for the work, and his short legs crossed on the grass before him; he had a cup of coffee by his side and his knife ready in his hand, and while he looked upon the fat hump ribs, his eyes dilated with anticipation. Delorier sat just opposite to him, and the rest of us by this time had taken our seats.

'How is this, Delorier? You haven't given us bread enough.'

At this Delorier's placid face flew instantly into a paroxysm of contortions. He grinned with wrath, chattered, gesticulated, and hurled forth a volley of incoherent words in broken English at the astonished Tête Rouge. It was just possible to make out that he was accusing him of having stolen and eaten four large cakes which had been laid by for dinner. Tête Rouge, utterly confounded at this sudden attack, stared at

Delorier for a moment in dumb amazement, with mouth and eyes wide open. At last he found speech, and protested that the accusation was false; and that he could not conceive how he had offended Mr. Delorier, or provoked him to use such ungentlemanly expressions. The tempest of words raged with such fury that nothing else could be heard. But Tête Rouge from his greater command of English had a manifest advantage over Delorier, who after sputtering and grimacing for awhile, found his words quite inadequate to the expression of his wrath. He jumped up and vanished, jerking out between his teeth one furious *sacre enfant de garce*, a Canadian title of honor, made doubly emphatic by being usually applied together with a cut of the whip to refractory mules and horses.

The next morning we saw an old buffalo bull escorting his cow with two small calves over the prairie. Close behind came four or five large white wolves, sneaking stealthily through the long meadow-grass, and watching for the moment when one of the children should chance to lag behind his parents. The old bull kept well on his guard, and faced about now and then to keep the prowling ruffians at a distance.

As we approached our nooning-place, we saw five or six buffalo standing at the very summit of a tall bluff. Trotting forward to the spot where we meant to stop, I flung off my saddle and turned my horse loose. By making a circuit under cover of some rising ground, I reached the foot of the bluff unnoticed, and climbed up its steep side. Lying under the brow of the declivity, I prepared to fire at the buffalo, who stood on the flat surface above, not five yards distant. Perhaps I was too hasty, for the gleaming rifle-barrel levelled over the edge caught their notice; they turned and ran. Close as they were, it was impossible to kill them when in that position, and stepping upon the summit, I pursued them over the high arid table-land. It was extremely rugged and broken; a great sandy ravine was channelled through it, with smaller ravines entering on each side, like tributary streams. The buffalo scattered, and I soon lost sight of most of them as they scuttled away through the sandy chasms; a bull and a cow alone kept in view. For a while they ran along the edge of the great ravine, appearing and disappearing as they dived into some chasm and again emerged from it. At last they stretched out upon the broad prairie, a plain nearly flat and almost devoid of verdure, for every short grass-blade was dried and shrivelled by the glaring sun. Now and then the old bull would face toward me; whenever he did so I fell to the ground and lay motionless. In this manner I chased them for about two miles, until at length I heard in front a deep hoarse bellowing. A moment after, a band of about a hundred bulls, before hidden by a slight swell of the plain, came at once into view. The fugitives ran toward them. Instead of mingling with the band, as I expected, they passed directly through, and continued their flight. At this I gave up the chase, and kneeling down, crawled to within gun-shot of the bulls, and with panting breath and trickling brow sat down on the ground to watch them; my presence did not disturb them in the least. They were not feeding, for, indeed, there was nothing to eat; but they seemed to have chosen the parched and scorching desert as the scene of their amusements. Some were rolling on the ground amid a cloud of dust; others, with a hoarse rumbling bellow, were butting their large heads together, while many stood motionless, as if quite inanimate. Except their monstrous growth of tangled grizzly mane, they had no hair; for their old coat had fallen off in the spring, and their new one had not as yet appeared. Sometimes an old bull would step forward, and gaze at me with a grim and stupid countenance; then he would turn and butt his next neighbor; then he would lie down and roll over in the dirt, kicking his hoofs in the air. When satisfied with this amusement, he would jerk his head and shoulders upward, and resting on his forelegs, stare at me in this position, half blinded by his mane, and his face covered with dirt; then up he would spring upon all fours, and shake his dusty sides; turning half round, he would stand with his beard touching the ground, in an attitude of profound abstraction, as if reflecting on his puerile conduct. 'You are too ugly to live,' thought I; and aiming at the ugliest, I shot three of them in succession. The rest were not at all discomposed at this; they kept on bellowing and butting and rolling on the ground as before. Henry Chatillon always cautioned us to keep perfectly quiet in the presence of a wounded buffalo, for any movement is apt to excite him to make an attack; so I sat still upon the ground, loading and firing with as little motion as possible. While I was thus employed, a spectator made his appearance: a little antelope came running up with remarkable gentleness to within fifty yards; and there it stood, its slender neck arched, its small horns thrown back, and its large dark eyes gazing on me with a look of eager curiosity. By the side of the shaggy and brutish monsters before me, it seemed like some lovely young girl wandering near a den of robbers or a nest of bearded pirates. The buffalo looked uglier than ever. 'Here goes for another of you,' thought I, feeling in my pouch for a percussion-cap. Not a percussion-cap was there. My good rifle was useless as an old iron bar. One of the wounded bulls had not yet fallen, and I waited for some time, hoping every moment that his strength would fail him. He still stood firm, looking grimly at me, and disregarding Henry's advice, I rose and walked away. Many of the bulls turned and looked at me, but the wounded brute made no attack. I soon came upon a deep ravine which would give me shelter in case of emergency; so I turned round and threw a stone at the bulls. They received it with the utmost indifference. Feeling myself insulted at their refusal to be frightened, I swung my hat, shouted, and made a show of running toward them; at this they crowded together and galloped off, leaving their dead and wounded upon the field. As I moved towards the camp I saw the last survivor totter and fall dead. My speed in returning was wonderfully quickened by the reflection that the Pawnees were abroad, and that I was defenceless in case of meeting with an enemy. I saw no living thing, however, except two or three squalid old bulls scrambling among the sand-hills that flanked the great ravine. When I reached camp the party were nearly ready for the afternoon move.

We encamped that evening at a short distance from the river bank. About midnight, as we all lay asleep on the ground, the man nearest to me, gently reaching out his hand, touched my shoulder, and cautioned me at the same time not to move. It was bright starlight. Opening my eyes and slightly turning, I saw a large white wolf moving stealthily around the embers of our fire, with his nose close to the ground. Disengaging my hand from the blanket, I drew the cover from my rifle, which lay close at my side; the motion alarmed the wolf, and with long leaps he bounded out of the camp. Jumping up, I fired after him, when he was about thirty yards distant; the melancholy hum of the bullet sounded far away through the night. At the sharp report, so suddenly breaking upon the stillness, all the men sprang up.

'You've killed him,' said one of them.

'No I haven't,' said I; 'there he goes, running along the river.'

'Then there's two of them. Don't you see that one lying out yonder?'

We went out to it, and instead of a dead white wolf, found the bleached skull of a buffalo. I had missed my mark, and what was worse, had grossly violated a standing law of the prairie. When in a dangerous part of the country, it is considered highly imprudent to fire a gun after encamping, lest the report should reach the ears of the Indians.

The horses were saddled in the morning, and the last man had lighted his pipe at the dying ashes of the fire. The beauty of the day enlivened us all. Even Ellis felt its influence, and occasionally made a remark as we rode along, and Jim Gurney told endless stories of his cruisings in the United States service. The buffalo were abundant, and at length a large band of them went running up the hills on the left.

'Do you see them buffalo?' said Ellis, 'now I'll bet any man I'll go and kill one with my yager.'

And leaving his horse to follow on with the party, he strode up the hill after them. Henry looked at us with his peculiar humorous expression, and proposed that we should follow Ellis to see how he would kill a fat cow. As soon as he was out of sight we rode up the hill after him, and waited behind a little ridge till we heard the report of the unfailing yager. Mounting to the top, we saw Ellis clutching his favorite weapon with both hands, and staring after the buffalo, who one and all were galloping off at full speed. As we descended the hill we saw the party straggling along the trail below. When we joined them, another scene of amateur hunting awaited us. I forgot to say that when we met the volunteers, Tête Rouge had obtained a horse from one of them, in exchange for his mule, whom he feared and detested. This horse he christened James. James, though not worth so much

as the mule, was a large and strong animal. Tête Rouge was
very proud of his new acquisition, and suddenly became ambitious to run a buffalo with him. At his request, I lent him
my pistols, though not without great misgivings, since when
Tête Rouge hunted buffalo the pursuer was in more danger
than the pursued. He hung the holsters at his saddle-bow;
and now as we passed along, a band of bulls left their grazing
in the meadow, and galloped in a long file across the trail in
front.

'Now's your chance, Tête; come, let's see you kill a bull.'

Thus urged, the hunter cried, 'get up!' and James, obedient
to the signal, cantered deliberately forward at an abominably
uneasy gait. Tête Rouge, as we contemplated him from behind, made a most remarkable figure. He still wore the old
buffalo-coat; his blanket which was tied in a loose bundle behind his saddle, went jolting from one side to the other, and a
large tin canteen half full of water which hung from his pommel, was jerked about his leg in a manner which greatly embarrassed him.

'Let out your horse, man; lay on your whip!' we called out
to him. The buffalo were getting farther off at every instant.
James being ambitious to mend his pace, tugged hard at the
rein, and one of his rider's boots escaped from the stirrup.

'Woh! I say, woh!' cried Tête Rouge, in great perturbation,
and after much effort James' progress was arrested. The
hunter came trotting back to the party, disgusted with
buffalo-running, and he was received with overwhelming
congratulations.

'Too good a chance to lose,' said Shaw, pointing to another
band of bulls on the left. We lashed our horses and galloped
upon them. Shaw killed one with each barrel of his gun. I
separated another from the herd and shot him. The small bullet of the rifle pistol striking too far back, did not immediately
take effect, and the bull ran on with unabated speed. Again
and again I snapped the remaining pistol at him. I primed it
afresh three or four times, and each time it missed fire, for the
touch-hole was clogged up. Returning it to the holster, I began to load the empty pistol, still galloping by the side of the
bull. By this time he was grown desperate. The foam flew
from his jaws and his tongue lolled out. Before the pistol was

loaded he sprang upon me, and followed up his attack with a furious rush. The only alternative was to run away or be killed. I took to flight, and the bull bristling with fury, pursued me closely. The pistol was soon ready, and then looking back, I saw his head five or six yards behind my horse's tail. To fire at it would be useless, for a bullet flattens against the adamantine skull of a buffalo bull. Inclining my body to the left, I turned my horse in that direction as sharply as his speed would permit. The bull rushing blindly on with great force and weight, did not turn so quickly. As I looked back, his neck and shoulder were exposed to view; turning in the saddle, I shot a bullet through them obliquely into his vitals. He gave over the chase and soon fell to the ground. An English tourist represents a situation like this as one of imminent danger; this is a great mistake; the bull never pursues long, and the horse must be wretched indeed, that cannot keep out of his way for two or three minutes.

We were now come to a part of the country where we were bound in common prudence to use every possible precaution. We mounted guard at night, each man standing in his turn; and no one ever slept without drawing his rifle close to his side or folding it with him in his blanket. One morning our vigilance was stimulated by our finding traces of a large Camanche encampment. Fortunately for us, however, it had been abandoned nearly a week. On the next evening we found the ashes of a recent fire, which gave us at the time some uneasiness. At length we reached the Caches, a place of dangerous repute; and it had a most dangerous appearance, consisting of sand-hills every where broken by ravines and deep chasms. Here we found the grave of Swan, killed at this place, probably by the Pawnees, two or three weeks before. His remains, more than once violated by the Indians and the wolves, were suffered at length to remain undisturbed in their wild burial-place.

For several days we met detached companies of Price's regiment. Horses would often break loose at night from their camps. One afternoon we picked up three of these stragglers quietly grazing along the river. After we came to camp that evening, Jim Gurney brought news that more of them were in sight. It was nearly dark, and a cold, drizzling rain had set in;

but we all turned out, and after an hour's chase nine horses were caught and brought in. One of them was equipped with saddle and bridle; pistols were hanging at the pommel of the saddle, a carbine was slung at its side, and a blanket rolled up behind it. In the morning, glorying in our valuable prize, we resumed our journey, and our cavalcade presented a much more imposing appearance than ever before. We kept on till the afternoon, when, far behind, three horsemen appeared on the horizon. Coming on at a hand-gallop, they soon overtook us, and claimed all the horses as belonging to themselves and others of their company. They were of course given up, very much to the mortification of Ellis and Jim Gurney.

Our own horses now showed signs of fatigue, and we resolved to give them half a day's rest. We stopped at noon at a grassy spot by the river. After dinner Shaw and Henry went out to hunt; and while the men lounged about the camp, I lay down to read in the shadow of the cart. Looking up, I saw a bull grazing alone on the prairie more than a mile distant. I was tired of reading, and taking my rifle I walked toward him. As I came near, I crawled upon the ground until I approached to within a hundred yards; here I sat down upon the grass and waited till he should turn himself into a proper position to receive his death-wound. He was a grim old veteran. His loves and his battles were over for that season, and now, gaunt and war-worn, he had withdrawn from the herd to graze by himself and recruit his exhausted strength. He was miserably emaciated; his mane was all in tatters; his hide was bare and rough as an elephant's and covered with dried patches of the mud in which he had been wallowing. He showed all his ribs whenever he moved. He looked like some grizzly old ruffian grown gray in blood and violence, and scowling on all the world from his misanthropic seclusion. The old savage looked up when I first approached, and gave me a fierce stare; then he fell to grazing again with an air of contemptuous indifference. The moment after, as if suddenly recollecting himself, he threw up his head, faced quickly about, and to my amazement came at a rapid trot directly toward me. I was strongly impelled to get up and run, but this would have been very dangerous. Sitting quite still, I aimed, as he came on, at the thin part of the skull above the nose. After he had passed over about three-quarters of the distance between us, I was on the point of firing, when, to my great satisfaction, he stopped short. I had full opportunity of studying his countenance; his whole front was covered with a huge mass of coarse matted hair, which hung so low that nothing but his two fore-feet were visible beneath it; his short thick horns were blunted and split to the very roots in his various battles, and across his nose and forehead were two or three large white scars, which gave him a grim, and at the same time, a whimsical appearance. It seemed to me that he stood there motionless for a full quarter of an hour, looking at me through the tangled locks of his mane. For my part, I remained as quiet as he, and looked quite as hard; I felt greatly inclined to come to terms with him. 'My friend,' thought I, 'if you'll let me off, I'll let you off.' At length he seemed to have abandoned any hostile design. Very slowly and deliberately he began to turn about; little by little his side came into view, all beplastered with mud. It was a tempting sight. I forgot my prudent intentions, and fired my rifle; a pistol would have served at that distance. Round spun old bull like a top, and away he galloped over the prairie. He ran some distance, and even ascended a considerable hill, before he lay down and died. After shooting another bull among the hills, I went back to camp.

At noon, on the fourteenth of September, a very large Santa Fé caravan came up. The plain was covered with the long files of their white-topped wagons, the close black carriages in which the traders travel and sleep, large droves of animals, and men on horseback and on foot. They all stopped on the meadow near us. Our diminutive cart and handful of men made but an insignificant figure by the side of their wide and bustling camp. Tête Rouge went over to visit them, and soon came back with half a dozen biscuits in one hand, and a bottle of brandy in the other. I inquired where he got them. 'Oh,' said Tête Rouge, 'I know some of the traders. Dr. Dobbs is there besides.' I asked who Dr. Dobbs might be. 'One of our St. Louis doctors,' replied Tête Rouge. For two days past I had been severely attacked by the same disorder which had so greatly reduced my strength when at the mountains; at this time I was suffering not a little from the sudden pain and weakness which it occasioned. Tête Rouge, in answer to my inquiries, declared that Dr. Dobbs was a physician of the first standing. Without at all believing him, I resolved to consult this eminent practitioner. Walking over to the camp, I found him lying sound asleep under one of the wagons. He offered in his own person but an indifferent specimen of his skill, for it was five months since I had seen so cadaverous a face. His hat had fallen off, and his yellow hair was all in disorder; one of his arms supplied the place of a pillow; his pantaloons were wrinkled half way up to his knees, and he was covered with little bits of grass and straw, upon which he had rolled in his uneasy slumber. A Mexican stood near, and I made him a sign that he should touch the doctor. Up sprang the learned Dobbs, and sitting upright, rubbed his eyes and looked about him in great bewilderment. I regretted the necessity of disturbing him, and said I had come to ask professional advice.

'Your system, sir, is in a disordered state,' said he, solemnly, after a short examination.

I inquired what might be the particular species of disorder.

'Evidently a morbid action of the liver,' replied the medical man; 'I will give you a prescription.'

Repairing to the back of one of the covered wagons, he scrambled in; for a moment I could see nothing of him but his boots. At length he produced a box which he had extracted from some dark recess within, and opening it, he presented me with a folded paper of some size. 'What is it?' said I. 'Calomel,' said the doctor.

Under the circumstances I would have taken almost any thing. There was not enough to do me much harm, and it might possibly do good; so at camp that night I took the poison instead of supper.

That camp is worthy of notice. The traders warned us not to follow the main trail along the river, 'unless,' as one of them observed, 'you want to have your throats cut!' The river at this place makes a bend; and a smaller trail, known as 'the Ridge-path,' leads directly across the prairie from point to point, a distance of sixty or seventy miles.

We followed this trail, and after travelling seven or eight miles, we came to a small stream, where we encamped. Our position was not chosen with much forethought or military skill. The water was in a deep hollow, with steep, high banks; on the grassy bottom of this hollow we picketed our horses, while we ourselves encamped upon the barren prairie just above. The opportunity was admirable either for driving off our horses or attacking us. After dark, as Tête Rouge was sitting at supper, we observed him pointing with a face of speechless horror over the shoulder of Henry, who was opposite to him. Aloof amid the darkness appeared a gigantic black apparition, solemnly swaying to and fro as it advanced steadily upon us. Henry, half vexed and half amused, jumped up, spread out his arms, and shouted. The invader was an old buffalo-bull, who, with characteristic stupidity, was walking directly into camp. It cost some shouting and swinging of hats before we could bring him first to a halt and then to a rapid retreat.

That night the moon was full and bright; but as the black clouds chased rapidly over it, we were at one moment in light and at the next in darkness. As the evening advanced, a thunder-storm came up; it struck us with such violence that the tent would have been blown over if we had not interposed the cart to break the force of the wind. At length it subsided to a steady rain. I lay awake through nearly the whole night, listening to its dull patter upon the canvass above. The moisture, which filled the tent and trickled from every thing in it, did not add to the comfort of the situation. About twelve o'clock Shaw went out to stand guard amid the rain and pitch darkness. Munroe, the most vigilant as well as one of the bravest among us, was also on the alert. When about two hours had passed, Shaw came silently in, and touching Henry, called him in a low quick voice to come out. 'What is it?' I asked. 'Indians, I believe,' whispered Shaw; 'but lie still; I'll call you if there's a fight.'

He and Henry went out together. I took the cover from my rifle, put a fresh percussion cap upon it, and then, being in much pain, lay down again. In about five minutes Shaw came in again. 'All right,' he said, as he lay down to sleep. Henry was now standing guard in his place. He told me in the morning the particulars of the alarm. Munroe's watchful eye discovered some dark objects down in the hollow, among the horses, like men creeping on all-fours. Lying flat on their faces, he and Shaw crawled to the edge of the bank, and were soon convinced that what they saw were Indians. Shaw silently withdrew to call Henry, and they all lay watching in the same position. Henry's eye is one of the best on the prairie. He detected after a while the true nature of the moving objects; they were nothing but wolves creeping among the horses.

It is very singular that when picketed near a camp horses seldom show any fear of such an intrusion. The wolves appear to have no other object than that of gnawing the trail-ropes of raw-hide by which the animals are secured. Several times in the course of the journey my horse's trail-rope was bitten in two by these nocturnal visitors.

Chapter XXVII.

THE SETTLEMENTS.

"And some are in a far countree,
    And some all restlessly at home;
But never more, ah never, we
    Shall meet to revel and to roam."
                SIEGE OF CORINTH.

THE NEXT DAY was extremely hot, and we rode from morning till night without seeing a tree, or a bush, or a drop of water. Our horses and mules suffered much more than we, but as sunset approached, they pricked up their ears and mended their pace. Water was not far off. When we came to the descent of the broad shallow valley where it lay, an unlooked-for sight awaited us. The stream glistened at the bottom, and along its banks were pitched a multitude of tents, while hundreds of cattle were feeding over the meadows. Bodies of troops, both horse and foot, and long trains of wagons with men, women, and children, were moving over the opposite ridge and descending the broad declivity in front. These were the Mormon battalion in the service of government, together with a considerable number of Missouri Volunteers. The Mormons were to be paid off in California, and they were allowed to bring with them their families and property. There was something very striking in the half-military, half-patriarchal appearance of these armed fanatics, thus on their way with their wives and children, to found, it might be, a Mormon empire in California. We were much more astonished than pleased at the sight before us. In order to find an unoccupied camping-ground, we were obliged to pass a quarter of a mile up the stream, and here we were soon beset by a swarm of Mormons and Missourians. The United States officer in command of the whole came also to visit us, and remained some time at our camp.

In the morning the country was covered with mist. We were always early risers, but before we were ready, the voices of men driving in the cattle sounded all around us. As we

333

passed above their camp, we saw through the obscurity that the tents were falling, and the ranks rapidly forming; and mingled with the cries of women and children, the rolling of the Mormon drums and the clear blast of their trumpets sounded through the mist.

From that time to the journey's end, we met almost every day long trains of government wagons, laden with stores for the troops, and crawling at a snail's pace towards Santa Fé.

Tête Rouge had a mortal antipathy to danger, but on a foraging expedition one evening, he achieved an adventure more perilous than had yet befallen any man in the party. The night after we left the Ridge-Path we encamped close to the river. At sunset we saw a train of wagons encamping on the trail, about three miles off; and though we saw them distinctly, our little cart, as it afterward proved, entirely escaped their view. For some days Tête Rouge had been longing eagerly after a dram of whisky. So, resolving to improve the present opportunity, he mounted his horse James, slung his canteen over his shoulder, and set forth in search of his favorite liquor. Some hours passed without his returning. We thought that he was lost, or perhaps that some stray Indian had snapped him up. While the rest fell asleep I remained on guard. Late at night a tremulous voice saluted me from the darkness, and Tête Rouge and James soon became visible, advancing toward the camp. Tête Rouge was in much agitation and big with some important tidings. Sitting down on the shaft of the cart, he told the following story.

When he left the camp he had no idea, he said, how late it was. By the time he approached the wagoners it was perfectly dark; and as he saw them all sitting around their fires within the circle of wagons, their guns laid by their sides, he thought he might as well give warning of his approach, in order to prevent a disagreeable mistake. Raising his voice to the highest pitch, he screamed out in prolonged accents, *'camp ahoy!'* This eccentric salutation produced any thing but the desired result. Hearing such hideous sounds proceeding from the outer darkness, the wagoners thought that the whole Pawnee nation were about to break in and take their scalps. Up they sprang staring with terror. Each man snatched his gun; some stood behind the wagons; some threw themselves flat on the

ground, and in an instant twenty cocked muskets were levelled full at the horrified Tête Rouge, who just then began to
be visible through the darkness.

'Thar they come,' cried the master wagoner, 'fire, fire,
shoot that feller.'

'No, no!' screamed Tête Rouge, in an ecstasy of fright;
'don't fire, don't; I'm a friend, I'm an American citizen!'

'You're a friend, be you,' cried a gruff voice from the wagons, 'then what are you yelling out thar for, like a wild Injun.
Come along up here if you're a man.'

'Keep your guns p'inted at him,' added the master wagoner, 'may be he's a decoy, like.'

Tête Rouge in utter bewilderment made his approach, with
the gaping muzzles of the muskets still before his eyes. He
succeeded at last in explaining his character and situation, and
the Missourians admitted him into camp. He got no whisky;
but as he represented himself as a great invalid, and suffering
much from coarse fare, they made up a contribution for him
of rice, biscuit, and sugar from their own rations.

In the morning at breakfast, Tête Rouge once more related
this story. We hardly knew how much of it to believe, though
after some cross-questioning we failed to discover any flaw in
the narrative. Passing by the wagoner's camp, they confirmed
Tête Rouge's account in every particular.

'I wouldn't have been in that feller's place,' said one of
them, 'for the biggest heap of money in Missouri.'

To Tête Rouge's great wrath they expressed a firm conviction that he was crazy. We left them after giving them the
advice not to trouble themselves about war-whoops in future,
since they would be apt to feel an Indian's arrow before they
heard his voice.

A day or two after, we had an adventure of another sort
with a party of wagoners. Henry and I rode forward to hunt.
After that day there was no probability that we should meet
with buffalo, and we were anxious to kill one, for the sake of
fresh meat. They were so wild that we hunted all the morning
in vain, but at noon as we approached Cow Creek we saw a
large band feeding near its margin. Cow Creek is densely
lined with trees which intercept the view beyond, and it runs
as we afterward found at the bottom of a deep trench. We

approached by riding along the bottom of a ravine. When we were near enough, I held the horses while Henry crept toward the buffalo. I saw him take his seat within shooting distance, prepare his rifle and look about to select his victim. The death of a fat cow was certain, when suddenly a great smoke arose from the bed of the Creek with a rattling volley of musketry. A score of long-legged Missourians leaped out from among the trees and ran after the buffalo, who one and all took to their heels and vanished. These fellows had crawled up the bed of the Creek to within a hundred yards of the buffalo. Never was there a fairer chance for a shot. They were good marksmen; all cracked away at once and yet not a buffalo fell. In fact the animal is so tenacious of life that it requires no little knowledge of anatomy to kill it, and it is very seldom that a novice succeeds in his first attempt at approaching. The balked Missourians were excessively mortified, especially when Henry told them that if they had kept quiet he would have killed meat enough in ten minutes to feed their whole party. Our friends, who were at no great distance, hearing such a formidable fusilade, thought the Indians had fired the volley for our benefit. Shaw came galloping on to reconnoitre and learn if we were yet in the land of the living.

At Cow Creek we found the very welcome novelty of ripe grapes and plums which grew there in abundance. At the little Arkansas, not much farther on, we saw the last buffalo, a miserable old bull, roaming over the prairie alone and melancholy.

From this time forward the character of the country was changing every day. We had left behind us the great arid deserts, meagerly covered by the tufted buffalo-grass, with its pale green hue, and its short shrivelled blades. The plains before us were carpeted with rich and verdant herbage sprinkled with flowers. In place of buffalo we found plenty of prairie hens, and we bagged them by dozens without leaving the trail. In three or four days we saw before us the broad woods and the emerald meadows of Council Grove, a scene of striking luxuriance and beauty. It seemed like a new sensation as we rode beneath the resounding arches of these noble woods. The trees were ash, oak, elm, maple and hickory, their mighty limbs deeply overshadowing the path, while enormous grape-vines were entwined among them, purple with fruit. The shouts of our scattered party, and now and then a report of a rifle rang amid the breathing stillness of the forest. We rode forth again with regret into the broad light of the open prairie. Little more than a hundred miles now separated us from the frontier settlements. The whole intervening country was a succession of verdant prairies, rising in broad swells and relieved by trees clustering like an oasis around some spring, or following the course of a stream along some fertile hollow. These are the prairies of the poet and the novelist. We had left danger behind us. Nothing was to be feared from the Indians of this region, the Sacs and Foxes, the Kanzas, and the Osages. We had met with signal good fortune. Although for five months we had been travelling with an insufficient force through a country where we were at any moment liable to depredation, not a single animal had been stolen from us. And our only loss had been one old mule bitten to death by a rattlesnake. Three weeks after we reached the frontier, the Pawnees and the Camanches began a regular series of hostilities on the Arkansas trail, killing men and driving off horses. They attacked, without exception, every party, large or small, that passed during the next six months.

Diamond Spring, Rock Creek, Elder Grove, and other camping places beside, were passed all in quick succession. At Rock Creek we found a train of government provision wagons under the charge of an emaciated old man in his seventy-first year. Some restless American devil had driven him into the wilderness at a time when he should have been seated at his fireside with his grandchildren on his knees. I am convinced that he never returned; he was complaining that night of a disease, the wasting effects of which upon a younger and stronger man, I myself had proved from severe experience. Long ere this no doubt the wolves have howled their moon-light carnival over the old man's attenuated remains.

Not long after we came to a small trail leading to Fort Leavenworth, distant but one day's journey. Tête Rouge here took leave of us. He was anxious to go to the Fort in order to receive payment for his valuable military services. So he and his horse James, after bidding an affectionate farewell, set out together, taking with them as much provision as they could conveniently carry, including a large quantity of brown sugar. On a cheerless rainy evening we came to our last encamping ground. Some pigs belonging to a Shawanoe farmer, were grunting and rooting at the edge of the grove.

'I wonder how fresh pork tastes,' murmured one of the party, and more than one voice murmured in response. The fiat went forth, 'That pig must die,' and a rifle was levelled forthwith at the countenance of the plumpest porker. Just then a wagon train, with some twenty Missourians, came out from among the trees. The marksman suspended his aim, deeming it inexpedient under the circumstances to consummate the deed of blood.

In the morning we made our toilet as well as circumstances would permit, and that is saying but very little. In spite of the dreary rain of yesterday, there never was a brighter and gayer autumnal morning than that on which we returned to the settlements. We were passing through the country of the half-civilized Shawanoes. It was a beautiful alternation of fertile plains and groves, whose foliage was just tinged with the hues of autumn, while close beneath them rested the neat log-houses of the Indian farmers. Every field and meadow bespoke the exuberant fertility of the soil. The maize stood rustling in the wind, matured and dry, its shining yellow ears thrust out between the gaping husks. Squashes and enormous yellow pumpkins lay basking in the sun in the midst of their brown and shrivelled leaves. Robins and blackbirds flew about the fences; and every thing in short betokened our near approach to home and civilization. The forests that border on the Missouri soon rose before us, and we entered the wide tract of shrubbery which forms their outskirts. We had passed the same road on our outward journey in the spring, but its aspect was totally changed. The young wild apple-trees, then flushed with their fragrant blossoms, were now hung thickly with ruddy fruit. Tall grass flourished by the roadside in place of the tender shoots just peeping from the warm and oozy soil. The vines were laden with dark purple grapes, and the slender twigs of the maple, then tasseled with their clusters of small red flowers, now hung out a gorgeous display of leaves stained by the frost with burning crimson. On every side we saw the tokens of maturity and decay where all had before been fresh and beautiful. We entered the forest, and ourselves and our horses were checkered as we passed along, by the bright spots of sunlight that fell between the opening boughs. On either side the dark, rich masses of foliage almost excluded the sun, though here and there its rays could find their way down, striking through the broad leaves and lighting them with a pure transparent green. Squirrels barked at us from the trees; coveys of young partridges ran rustling over the leaves below, and the golden oriole, the blue-jay and the flaming red-bird darted among the shadowy branches. We hailed these sights and sounds of beauty by no means with an unmingled pleasure. Many and powerful as were the attractions which drew us toward the settlements, we looked back even at that moment with an eager longing toward the wilderness of prairies and mountains behind us. For myself I had suffered more that summer from illness than ever before in my life, and yet to this hour I cannot recall those savage scenes and savage men without a strong desire again to visit them.

At length for the first time during about half a year, we saw the roof of a white man's dwelling between the opening trees. A few moments after we were riding over the miserable log-bridge that leads into the centre of Westport. Westport had beheld strange scenes, but a rougher looking troop than ours with our worn equipments and broken-down horses, was never seen even there. We passed the well-remembered tavern, Boone's grocery and old Vogle's dram-shop, and encamped on a meadow beyond. Here we were soon visited by a number of people who came to purchase our horses and equipage. This matter disposed of, we hired a wagon and drove on to Kanzas landing. Here we were again received under the hospitable roof of our old friend Colonel Chick, and seated under his porch, we looked down once more on the eddies of the Missouri.

Delorier made his appearance in the morning, strangely transformed by the assistance of a hat, a coat and a razor. His little log-house was among the woods not far off. It seemed he had meditated giving a ball on the occasion of his return, and had consulted Henry Chatillon, as to whether it would do to invite his *bourgeois*. Henry expressed his entire conviction that we would not take it amiss, and the invitation was now proffered accordingly, Delorier adding as a special inducement that Antoine Lajeunesse was to play the fiddle. We told him we would certainly come, but before the evening arrived, a steamboat which came down from Fort Leavenworth, prevented our being present at the expected festivities. Delorier was on the rock at the landing-place, waiting to take leave of us.

'Adieu! mes bourgeois, adieu! adieu!' he cried out as the boat put off; 'when you go another time to de Rocky Montagnes I will go with you; yes, I will go!'

He accompanied this patronizing assurance by jumping about, swinging his hat, and grinning from ear to ear. As the boat rounded a distant point, the last object that met our eyes was Delorier still lifting his hat and skipping about the rock. We had taken leave of Munroe and Jim Gurney at Westport, and Henry Chatillon went down in the boat with us.

The passage to St. Louis occupied eight days, during about a third of which time we were fast aground on sand-bars. We passed the steamer Amelia crowded with a roaring crew of disbanded volunteers, swearing, drinking, gambling, and fighting. At length one evening we reached the crowded levee of St. Louis. Repairing to the Planters' House, we caused diligent search to be made for our trunks, which after some time were discovered stowed away in the farthest corner of the store-room. In the morning we hardly recognized each other; a frock of broadcloth had supplanted the frock of buckskin; well-fitted pantaloons took the place of the Indian leggins, and polished boots were substituted for the gaudy moccasons.

After we had been several days at St. Louis we heard news of Tête Rouge. He had contrived to reach Fort Leavenworth, where he had found the paymaster and received his money. As a boat was just ready to start for St. Louis, he went on board and engaged his passage. This done, he immediately got drunk on shore, and the boat went off without him. It was some days before another opportunity occurred, and meanwhile the sutler's stores furnished him with abundant means of keeping up his spirits. Another steamboat came at last, the clerk of which happened to be a friend of his, and by the advice of some charitable person on shore, he persuaded Tête Rouge to remain on board, intending to detain him there until the boat should leave the Fort. At first Tête Rouge was well contented with this arrangement, but on applying for a dram, the bar-keeper, at the clerk's instigation, refused to let him have it. Finding them both inflexible in spite of his entreaties, he became desperate and made his escape from the boat. The clerk found him after a long search in one of the barracks; a circle of dragoons stood contemplating him as he lay on the floor, maudlin drunk, and crying dismally. With the help of one of them the clerk pushed him on board, and our informant, who came down in the same boat, declares that he remained in great despondency during the whole passage. As we left St. Louis soon after his arrival, we did not see the worthless, good-natured little vagabond again.

On the evening before our departure, Henry Chatillon came to our rooms at the Planters' House to take leave of us. No one who met him in the streets of St. Louis, would have taken him for a hunter fresh from the Rocky Mountains. He was very neatly and simply dressed in a suit of dark cloth; for although since his sixteenth year he had scarcely been for a month together among the abodes of men, he had a native good taste and a sense of propriety which always led him to pay great attention to his personal appearance. His tall athletic figure with its easy flexible motions appeared to advantage in his present dress; and his fine face, though roughened by a thousand storms, was not at all out of keeping with it. We took leave of him with much regret; and unless his changing features, as he shook us by the hand, belied him, the feeling on his part was no less than on ours.* Shaw had given him a horse at Westport. My rifle, which he had always been

---

*I cannot take leave of the reader without adding a word of the guide who had served us throughout with such zeal and fidelity. Indeed his services had far surpassed the terms of his engagement. Yet whoever had been his employers, or to whatever closeness of intercourse they might have thought fit to admit him, he would never have changed the bearing of quiet respect which he considered due to his *bourgeois*. If sincerity and honor, a boundless generosity of spirit, a delicate regard to the feelings of others, and a nice perception of what was due to them, are the essential characteristics of a gentleman, then Henry Chatillon deserves the title. He could not write his own name, and he had spent his life among savages. In him sprang up spontaneously those qualities which all the refinements of life and intercourse with the highest and best of the better part of mankind, fail to awaken in the brutish nature of

fond of using, as it was an excellent piece, much better than his own, is now in his hands, and perhaps at this moment its sharp voice is startling the echoes of the Rocky Mountains. On the next morning we left town, and after a fortnight of railroads and steamboats we saw once more the familiar features of home.

---

some men. In spite of his bloody calling, Henry was always humane and merciful; he was gentle as a woman, though braver than a lion. He acted aright from the free impulses of his large and generous nature. A certain species of selfishness is essential to the sternness of spirit which bears down opposition and subjects the will of others to its own. Henry's character was of an opposite stamp. His easy good-nature almost amounted to weakness; yet while it unfitted him for any position of command, it secured the esteem and good-will of all those who were not jealous of his skill and reputation.

CONSPIRACY OF PONTIAC

INDIAN WAR

THE CONQUEST OF CANADA.

Vol. I.

Preface

TO THE SIXTH EDITION.

I CHOSE the subject of this book as affording better opportunities than any other portion of American history for portraying forest life and the Indian character; and I have never seen reason to change this opinion. In the nineteen years that have passed since the first edition was published, a considerable amount of additional material has come to light. This has been carefully collected, and is incorporated in the present edition. The most interesting portion of this new material has been supplied by the Bouquet and Haldimand Papers, added some years ago to the manuscript collections of the British Museum. Among them are several hundred letters from officers engaged in the Pontiac war, some official, others personal and familiar, affording very curious illustrations of the events of the day and of the characters of those engaged in them. Among the facts which they bring to light, some are sufficiently startling; as, for example, the proposal of the Commander-in-Chief to infect the hostile tribes with the small-pox, and that of a distinguished subordinate officer to take revenge on the Indians by permitting an unrestricted sale of rum.

The two volumes of the present edition have been made uniform with those of the series "France and England in North America." I hope to continue that series to the period of the extinction of French power on this continent. "The Conspiracy of Pontiac" will then form a sequel; and its introductory chapters will be, in a certain sense, a summary of what has preceded. This will involve some repetition in the beginning of the book, but I have nevertheless thought it best to let it remain as originally written.

BOSTON, 16 September, 1870.

Preface

TO THE FIRST EDITION.

THE CONQUEST of Canada was an event of momentous consequence in American history. It changed the political aspect of the continent, prepared a way for the independence of the British colonies, rescued the vast tracts of the interior from the rule of military despotism, and gave them, eventually, to the keeping of an ordered democracy. Yet to the red natives of the soil its results were wholly disastrous. Could the French have maintained their ground, the ruin of the Indian tribes might long have been postponed; but the victory of Quebec was the signal of their swift decline. Thenceforth they were destined to melt and vanish before the advancing waves of Anglo-American power, which now rolled westward unchecked and unopposed. They saw the danger, and, led by a great and daring champion, struggled fiercely to avert it. The history of that epoch, crowded as it is with scenes of tragic interest, with marvels of suffering and vicissitude, of heroism and endurance, has been, as yet, unwritten, buried in the archives of governments, or among the obscurer records of private adventure. To rescue it from oblivion is the object of the following work. It aims to portray the American forest and the American Indian at the period when both received their final doom.

It is evident that other study than that of the closet is indispensable to success in such an attempt. Habits of early reading had greatly aided to prepare me for the task; but necessary knowledge of a more practical kind has been supplied by the indulgence of a strong natural taste, which, at various intervals, led me to the wild regions of the north and west. Here, by the camp-fire, or in the canoe, I gained familiar acquaintance with the men and scenery of the wilderness. In 1846, I visited various primitive tribes of the Rocky Mountains, and was, for a time, domesticated in a village of the western Dahcotah, on the high plains between Mount Laramie and the range of the Medicine Bow.

The most troublesome part of the task was the collection of

the necessary documents. These consisted of letters, journals, reports, and despatches, scattered among numerous public offices, and private families, in Europe and America. When brought together, they amounted to about three thousand four hundred manuscript pages. Contemporary newspapers, magazines, and pamphlets have also been examined, and careful search made for every book which, directly or indirectly, might throw light upon the subject. I have visited the sites of all the principal events recorded in the narrative, and gathered such local traditions as seemed worthy of confidence.

I am indebted to the liberality of Hon. Lewis Cass for a curious collection of papers relating to the siege of Detroit by the Indians. Other important contributions have been obtained from the state paper offices of London and Paris, from the archives of New York, Pennsylvania, and other states, and from the manuscript collections of several historical societies. The late William L. Stone, Esq., commenced an elaborate biography of Sir William Johnson, which it is much to be lamented he did not live to complete. By the kindness of Mrs. Stone, I was permitted to copy from his extensive collection of documents such portions as would serve the purposes of the following History.

To President Sparks of Harvard University, General Whiting, U. S. A., Brantz Mayer, Esq., of Baltimore, Francis J. Fisher, Esq., of Philadelphia, and Rev. George E. Ellis, of Charlestown, I beg to return a warm acknowledgment for counsel and assistance. Mr. Benjamin Perley Poore and Mr. Henry Stevens procured copies of valuable documents from the archives of Paris and London. Henry R. Schoolcraft, Esq., Dr. Elwyn, of Philadelphia, Dr. O'Callaghan, of Albany, George H. Moore, Esq., of New York, Lyman C. Draper, Esq., of Philadelphia, Judge Law, of Vincennes, and many others, have kindly contributed materials to the work. Nor can I withhold an expression of thanks to the aid so freely rendered in the dull task of proof-reading and correction.

The crude and promiscuous mass of materials presented an aspect by no means inviting. The field of the history was uncultured and unreclaimed, and the labor that awaited me was like that of the border settler, who, before he builds his rugged dwelling, must fell the forest-trees, burn the undergrowth, clear the ground, and hew the fallen trunks to due proportion.

Several obstacles have retarded the progress of the work. Of these, one of the most considerable was the condition of my sight. For about three years, the light of day was insupportable, and every attempt at reading or writing completely debarred. Under these circumstances, the task of sifting the materials and composing the work was begun and finished. The papers were repeatedly read aloud by an amanuensis, copious notes and extracts were made, and the narrative written down from my dictation. This process, though extremely slow and laborious, was not without its advantages; and I am well convinced that the authorities have been even more minutely examined, more scrupulously collated, and more thoroughly digested, than they would have been under ordinary circumstances.

In order to escape the tedious circumlocution, which, from the nature of the subject, could not otherwise have been avoided, the name English is applied, throughout the volume, to the British American colonists, as well as to the people of the mother country. The necessity is somewhat to be regretted, since, even at an early period, clear distinctions were visible between the offshoot and the parent stock.

BOSTON, August 1, 1851.

Contents of Vol. I.

CHAPTER I.

INTRODUCTORY.—INDIAN TRIBES EAST OF THE MISSISSIPPI.

General Characteristics.—Tribal Divisions.—Mode of Government.
—Social Harmony.—The Totem.—Classification of Tribes.—The
Iroquois.—Their Position and Character.—Their Political Organiza-
tion.—Traditions of their Confederacy.—Their Myths and Legends.—
Their Eloquence and Sagacity.—Arts—Agriculture.—Their Dwell-
ings, Villages, and Forts.—Their Winter Life.—The War Path.—
Festivals and Pastimes.—Pride of the Iroquois.—The Hurons or
Wyandots.—Their Customs and Character.—Their Dispersion.—
The Neutral Nation. Its Fate.—The Eries and Andastes.—Triumphs
of the Confederacy.—The Adoption of Prisoners.—The Tuscaroras.—
Superiority of the Iroquois Race.—The Algonquins.—The Lenni
Lenape.—Their changing Fortunes.—The Shawanoes.—The Miamis
and the Illinois.—The Ojibwas, Pottawattamies, and Ottawas.—The
Sacs and Foxes.—The Menomonies and Knisteneaux.—Customs of
the Northern Algonquins.—Their Summer and Winter Life.—
Legends of the Algonquins.—Religious Faith of the Indians.—The
Indian Character.—Its Inconsistencies.—Its Ruling Passions.—Pride.—
Hero-worship.—Coldness, Jealousy, Suspicion.—Self-control.—Intellec-
tual Traits.—Inflexibility.—Generous Qualities 359

CHAPTER II.
1663—1763.
FRANCE AND ENGLAND IN AMERICA.

Contrast of French and English Colonies.—Feudalism in Canada.—
Priests and Monks.—Puritanism and Democracy in New England.—
French Life in Canada.—Military Strength of Canada.—Religious
Zeal.—Missions.—The Jesuits.—Brebeuf and Lallemant.—Martyrdom
of Jogues.—Results of the Missions.—French Explorers.—La Salle.—
His Plan of Discovery.—His Sufferings—His Heroism.—He discovers
the Mouth of the Mississippi.—Louisiana.—France in the West.—
Growth of English Colonies.—Approaching Collision 390

CHAPTER III.
1608—1763.
THE FRENCH, THE ENGLISH, AND THE INDIANS.

Champlain defeats the Iroquois.—The Iroquois Wars.—Misery of Canada.—Expedition of Frontenac.—Success of the French.—French

Influence in the West.—*La Verandrye.*—*The English Fur-trade.*—
Protestant and Romish Missions.—*The English and the Iroquois.*—
Policy of the French.—*The Frenchman in the Wigwam.*—*Coureurs
des Bois.*—*The White Savage.*—*The English Fur-trader.*—*William
Penn and his Eulogists.*—*The Indians and the Quakers.*—*Injustice
of Penn's Successors.*—*The Walking Purchase.*—*Speech of Canassatego.*—*Removal of the Delawares.*—*Intrusion of Settlers.*—*Success of French Intrigues.*—*Father Picquet.*—*Sir William Johnson.*—
Position of Parties .403

CHAPTER IV.
1700–1755.
COLLISION OF THE RIVAL COLONIES.

The Puritan and the Canadian.—*Fort Frederic.*—*Acadia.*—*The
French on the Ohio.*—*Mission of Washington.*—*Trent driven from the
Ohio.*—*Death of Jumonville.*—*Skirmish at the Great Meadows.*—
Alarm of the Indians.—*Congress at Albany.*—*French and English Di-
plomacy.*—*Braddock and Dieskau.*—*Naval Engagement.*—*The War in
Europe and America.*—*Braddock in Virginia.*—*March of his Army.*—
Beaujeu at Fort du Quesne.—*Ambuscade at the Monongahela.*—*Rout
of Braddock.*—*Its Consequences.*—*Acadia, Niagara, and Crown
Point.*—*Battle of Lake George.*—*Prosecution of the War.*—*Oswego*—
Fort William Henry.—*Storming of Ticonderoga.*—*State of Canada.*—
Plans for its Reduction.—*Progress of the English Arms.*—*Wolfe before
Quebec.*—*Assault at Montmorenci.*—*Heroism of Wolfe.*—*The Heights
of Abraham.*—*Battle of Quebec.*—*Death of Wolfe.*—*Death of Mont-
calm.*—*Surrender of Quebec.*—*Fall of Canada* 423

CHAPTER V.
1755–1763.
THE WILDERNESS AND ITS TENANTS AT THE CLOSE OF
THE FRENCH WAR.

Sufferings of the Frontier.—*Treaties with the Western Tribes.*—*Chris-
tian Frederic Post.*—*The Iroquois.*—*The remote Tribes.*—*The Forest.*—
Indian Population.—*Condition of the Tribes.*—*Onondaga.*—*The
Delawares and neighboring Tribes.*—*Their Habits and Condition.*—
The Shawanoes, Miamis, Illinois, and Wyandots.—*English Settle-
ments.*—*Forest Thoroughfares.*—*Fur-traders*—*Their Habits and
Character.*—*The Forest Traveller.*—*The French at the Illinois.*—*Mili-
tary Life in the Forest.*—*The Savage and the European.*—*Hunters and
Trappers.*—*Civilization and Barbarism* 455

CHAPTER VI.
1760.
THE ENGLISH TAKE POSSESSION OF THE WESTERN POSTS.

The victorious Armies at Montreal. —Major Robert Rogers. —His Expedition up the Lakes. —His Meeting with Pontiac. —Ambitious Views of Pontiac. —He befriends the English. —The English take Possession of Detroit. —Of other French Posts. —British Power Predominant in the West .468

CHAPTER VII.
1760–1763.
ANGER OF THE INDIANS. —THE CONSPIRACY.

Discontent of the Tribes. —Impolitic Course of the English. —Disorders of the Fur-trade. —Military Insolence. —Intrusion of Settlers. —French Intrigue. —The Delaware Prophet. —An abortive Plot. —Pontiac's Conspiracy. —Character of Pontiac. —Gloomy Prospects of the Indian Race. —Designs of Pontiac. —His War Messengers. —Tribes engaged in the Conspiracy. —Dissimulation of the Indians. —The War-belt among the Miamis 475

CHAPTER VIII.
1763.
INDIAN PREPARATION.

The Indians as a military People. —Their inefficient Organization. — Their insubordinate Spirit. —Their Improvidence. —Policy of the Indian Leaders. —Difficulties of Forest Warfare. —Defenceless Condition of the Colonies. —The Peace of Paris. —Royal Proclamation. —The War-chief. His Fasts and Vigils. —The War-feast. —The War-dance. —Departure of the Warriors. —The Bursting of the Storm 489

CHAPTER IX.
1763, APRIL.
THE COUNCIL AT THE RIVER ECORCES.

Pontiac musters his Warriors. —They assemble at the River Ecorces. — The Council. —Speech of Pontiac. —Allegory of the Delaware. —The Council dissolves. —Calumet Dance at Detroit. —Plan to surprise the Garrison 495

CHAPTER X.
1763, MAY.
DETROIT.

Strange Phenomenon. —Origin and History of Detroit. —Its Condition in 1763. —Character of its Inhabitants. —French Life at Detroit. —The

*Fort and Garrison.—Pontiac at Isle à la Peche.—Suspicious Conduct of
the Indians.—Catharine, the Ojibwa Girl.—She reveals the Plot.—
Precautions of the Commandant.—A Night of Anxiety* 503

CHAPTER XI.
1763.
TREACHERY OF PONTIAC.

*The Morning of the Council.—Pontiac enters the Fort.—Address and
Courage of the Commandant.—The Plot defeated.—The Chiefs suffered
to escape.—Indian Idea of Honor.—Pontiac again visits the Fort.—
False Alarm.—Pontiac throws off the Mask.—Ferocity of his Warriors.—
The Ottawas cross the River.—Fate of Davers and Robertson.—General
Attack.—A Truce.—Major Campbell's Embassy.—He is made Prisoner
by Pontiac* .513

CHAPTER XII.
1763.
PONTIAC AT THE SIEGE OF DETROIT.

*The Christian Wyandots join Pontiac.—Peril of the Garrison.—Indian
Courage.—The English threatened with Famine.—Pontiac's Council
with the French.—His Speech.—He exacts Provision from the French.
—He appoints Commissaries.—He issues Promissory Notes.—His
Acuteness and Sagacity.—His Authority over his Followers.—His
Magnanimity.* .527

CHAPTER XIII.
1763.
ROUT OF CUYLER'S DETACHMENT.— FATE OF THE
FOREST GARRISONS.

*Re-enforcement sent to Detroit.—Attack on the Schooner.—Relief at
Hand.—Disappointment of the Garrison.—Escape of Prisoners.—
Cuyler's Defeat.—Indian Debauch.—Fate of the Captives.—Capture
of Fort Sandusky.—Strength of the Besiegers.—Capture of Fort St.
Joseph.—Capture of Fort Michillimackinac.—Capture of Fort
Ouatanon.—Capture of Fort Miami.—Defence of Fort Presqu' Isle.
—Its Capture* .539

CHAPTER XIV.
1763.
THE INDIANS CONTINUE TO BLOCKADE DETROIT.

*Attack on the Armed Vessel.—News of the Treaty of Paris.—Pontiac
summons the Garrison.—Council at the Ottawa Camp.—Disappoint-*

ment of Pontiac. —He is joined by the Coureurs de Bois. —Sortie of the Garrison. —Death of Major Campbell. —Attack on Pontiac's Camp. — Fire Rafts. —The Wyandots and Pottawattamies beg for Peace . . .558

CHAPTER XV.
1763.
THE FIGHT OF BLOODY BRIDGE.

Dalzell's Detachment. —Dalzell reaches Detroit. —Stratagem of the Wyandots. —Night Attack on Pontiac's Camp. —Indian Ambuscade. —Retreat of the English. —Terror of Dalzell's Troops. —Death of Dalzell. — Defence of Campau's House. —Grant conducts the Retreat. —Exultation of the Indians. —Defence of the Schooner Gladwyn 570

CHAPTER XVI.
1763.
MICHILLIMACKINAC.

The Voyager on the Lakes. —Michillimackinac in 1763. —Green Bay and Ste. Marie. —The Northern Wilderness. —Tribes of the Lakes. —Adventures of a Trader. —Speech of Minavavana. —Arrival of English Troops. —Disposition of the Indians. —The Ojibwa War-chief. — Ambassadors from Pontiac. —Sinister Designs of the Ojibwas. —Warnings of Danger. —Wawatam. —Eve of the Massacre 582

CHAPTER XVII.
1763.
THE MASSACRE.

The King's Birthday. —Heedlessness of the Garrison. —Indian Ballplay. —The Stratagem. —Slaughter of the Soldiers. —Escape of Alexander Henry. —His appalling Situation. —His Hiding-place discovered. —Survivors of the Massacre. —Plan of retaking the Fort. —Adventures of Henry. —Unexpected Behavior of the Ottawas. —They take Possession of the Fort. —Their Council with the Ojibwas. —Henry and his Fellowprisoners. —He is rescued by Wawatam. —Cannibalism. —Panic among the Conquerors. —They retire to Mackinaw. —The Island of Mackinaw. —Indian Carouse. —Famine among the Indians. —They disperse to their Wintering Grounds. —Green Bay. The neighboring Tribes. —Gorell. His Address and Prudence. —He conciliates the Indians. —He abandons Green Bay. —The English driven from the Upper Lakes 593

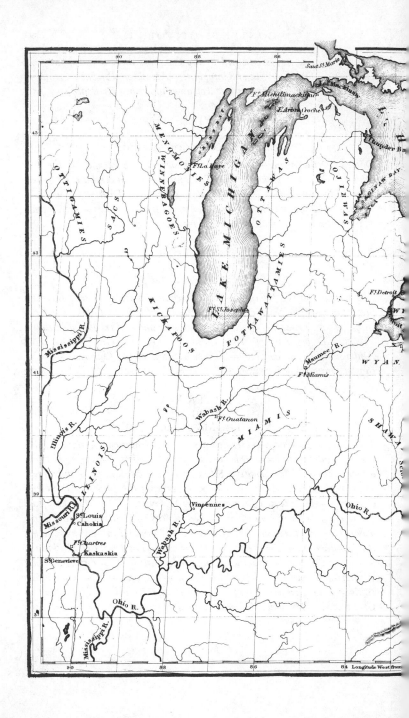

FORTS AND SETTLEMENTS
IN
AMERICA
A.D. 1763.

Ottowa R.

Montreal

St. Lawrence R.

Lake Champlain

45

L. ONTARIO

F.t Frontenac

Crown P.t

Ticonderoga

Oswego
F.t Brewerton

F.t George

Ft Niagara

Ft Stanwix

F.t Edward
Johnson Hall

43

Ft Schlosser

Mohawk R.

Schenectady

ALBANY

LAKE ERIE

SENECAS

CAYUGAS

ONONDAGAS

TUSCARORAS

ONEIDAS

MOHAWKS

NEW YORK

F.t Presqu'Isle

F.t Le Boeuf

F.t Venango

Susquehanna R.

Hudson R.

OTS &c.

OHIO R.

Beaver Cr.

DELAWARES

Allegheny R.

PENNSYLVANIA

Ft Augusta

New York

Muskingum R.

Ohio R.

Monongahela R.

F.t Pitt

F.t Ligonier

F.t Bedford

F.t Cumberland

Juniata R.

Carlisle

Susquehanna R.

Paxton

Lancaster

Conestoga

PHILADELPHIA

Schuylkill R.

NEW JERSEY

Delaware R.

DELAWARE

Kanawha R.

Allegheny Mts

MARYLAND

BALTIMORE

Potomack R.

39

VIRGINIA

Blue Ridge

Richmond

James R.

37

Norfolk

80

78

76

74

80

78

Chapter I.

INTRODUCTORY. — INDIAN TRIBES
EAST OF THE MISSISSIPPI.

THE INDIAN is a true child of the forest and the desert. The wastes and solitudes of nature are his congenial home. His haughty mind is imbued with the spirit of the wilderness, and the light of civilization falls on him with a blighting power. His unruly pride and untamed freedom are in harmony with the lonely mountains, cataracts, and rivers among which he dwells; and primitive America, with her savage scenery and savage men, opens to the imagination a boundless world, unmatched in wild sublimity.

The Indians east of the Mississippi may be divided into several great families, each distinguished by a radical peculiarity of language. In their moral and intellectual, their social and political state, these various families exhibit strong shades of distinction; but, before pointing them out, I shall indicate a few prominent characteristics, which, faintly or distinctly, mark the whole in common.

All are alike a race of hunters, sustaining life wholly, or in part, by the fruits of the chase. Each family is split into tribes; and these tribes, by the exigencies of the hunter life, are again divided into sub-tribes, bands, or villages, often scattered far asunder, over a wide extent of wilderness. Unhappily for the strength and harmony of the Indian race, each tribe is prone to regard itself, not as the member of a great whole, but as a sovereign and independent nation, often arrogating to itself an importance superior to all the rest of mankind;[1] and the warrior whose petty horde might muster a few scores of half-starved fighting men, strikes his hand upon his heart, and exclaims, in all the pride of patriotism, "I am a *Menomone*."

In an Indian community, each man is his own master. He abhors restraint, and owns no other authority than his own

[1] Many Indian tribes bear names which in their dialect signify *men*, indicating that the character belongs, *par excellence*, to them. Sometimes the word was used by itself, and sometimes an adjective was joined with it, as *original men, men surpassing all others*.

359

capricious will; and yet this wild notion of liberty is not inconsistent with certain gradations of rank and influence. Each tribe has its sachem, or civil chief, whose office is in a manner hereditary, and, among many, though by no means among all tribes, descends in the female line; so that the brother of the incumbent, or the son of his sister, and not his own son, is the rightful successor to his dignities.[1] If, however, in the opinion of the old men and subordinate chiefs, the heir should be disqualified for the exercise of the office by cowardice, incapacity, or any defect of character, they do not scruple to discard him, and elect another in his place, usually fixing their choice on one of his relatives. The office of the sachem is no enviable one. He has neither laws to administer nor power to enforce his commands. His counsellors are the inferior chiefs and principal men of the tribe; and he never sets himself in opposition to the popular will, which is the sovereign power of these savage democracies. His province is to advise, and not to dictate; but, should he be a man of energy, talent, and address, and especially should he be supported by numerous relatives and friends, he may often acquire no small measure of respect and power. A clear distinction is drawn between the civil and military authority, though both are often united in the same person. The functions of war-chief may, for the most part, be exercised by any one whose prowess and reputation are sufficient to induce the young men to follow him to battle; and he may, whenever he thinks proper, raise a band of volunteers, and go out against the common enemy.

We might imagine that a society so loosely framed would soon resolve itself into anarchy; yet this is not the case, and an Indian village is singularly free from wranglings and petty strife. Several causes conspire to this result. The necessities of the hunter life, preventing the accumulation of large communities, make more stringent organization needless; while a species of self-control, inculcated from childhood upon every

---

[1] The dread of female infidelity has been assigned, and with probable truth, as the origin of this custom. The sons of a chief's sister must necessarily be his kindred; though his own reputed son may be, in fact, the offspring of another.

individual, enforced by a sentiment of dignity and manhood, and greatly aided by the peculiar temperament of the race, tends strongly to the promotion of harmony. Though he owns no law, the Indian is inflexible in his adherence to ancient usages and customs; and the principle of hero-worship, which belongs to his nature, inspires him with deep respect for the sages and captains of his tribe. The very rudeness of his condition, and the absence of the passions which wealth, luxury, and the other incidents of civilization engender, are favorable to internal harmony; and to the same cause must likewise be ascribed too many of his virtues, which would quickly vanish, were he elevated from his savage state.

A peculiar social institution exists among the Indians, very curious in its character; and though I am not prepared to say that it may be traced through all the tribes east of the Mississippi, yet its prevalence is so general, and its influence on political relations so important, as to claim especial attention. Indian communities, independently of their local distribution into tribes, bands, and villages, are composed of several distinct clans. Each clan has its emblem, consisting of the figure of some bird, beast, or reptile; and each is distinguished by the name of the animal which it thus bears as its device; as, for example, the clan of the Wolf, the Deer, the Otter, or the Hawk. In the language of the Algonquins, these emblems are known by the name of *Totems*.[1] The members of the same clan, being connected, or supposed to be so, by ties of kindred, more or less remote, are prohibited from intermarriage. Thus Wolf cannot marry Wolf; but he may, if he chooses, take a wife from the clan of Hawks, or any other clan but his own. It follows that when this prohibition is rigidly observed, no

[1] Schoolcraft, *Oneota*, 172.

The extraordinary figures intended to represent tortoises, deer, snakes, and other animals, which are often seen appended to Indian treaties, are the totems of the chiefs, who employ these devices of their respective clans as their sign manual. The device of his clan is also sometimes tattoed on the body of the warrior.

The word *tribe* might, perhaps, have been employed with as much propriety as that of *clan*, to indicate the totemic division; but as the former is constantly employed to represent the local or political divisions of the Indian race, hopeless confusion would arise from using it in a double capacity.

single clan can live apart from the rest; but the whole must be mingled together, and in every family the husband and wife must be of different clans.

To different totems attach different degrees of rank and dignity; and those of the Bear, the Tortoise, and the Wolf are among the first in honor. Each man is proud of his badge, jealously asserting its claims to respect; and the members of the same clan, though they may, perhaps, speak different dialects, and dwell far asunder, are yet bound together by the closest ties of fraternity. If a man is killed, every member of the clan feels called upon to avenge him; and the wayfarer, the hunter, or the warrior is sure of a cordial welcome in the distant lodge of the clansman whose face perhaps he has never seen. It may be added that certain privileges, highly prized as hereditary rights, sometimes reside in particular clans; such as that of furnishing a sachem to the tribe, or of performing certain religious ceremonies or magic rites.

The Indians east of the Mississippi may be divided into three great families: the Iroquois, the Algonquin, and the Mobilian, each speaking a language of its own, varied by numerous dialectic forms. To these families must be added a few stragglers from the great western race of the Dahcotah, besides several distinct tribes of the south, each of which has been regarded as speaking a tongue peculiar to itself.[1] The Mobilian group embraces the motley confederacy of the Creeks, the crafty Choctaws, and the stanch and warlike Chickasaws. Of these, and of the distinct tribes dwelling in their vicinity, or within their limits, I shall only observe that they offer, with many modifications, and under different aspects, the same essential features which mark the Iroquois and the Algonquins, the two great families of the north.[2] The

---

[1] For an ample view of these divisions, see the *Synopsis* of Mr. Gallatin, *Trans. Am. Ant. Soc.* II.

[2] It appears from several passages in the writings of Adair, Hawkins, and others, that the totem prevailed among the southern tribes. In a conversation with the late Albert Gallatin, he informed me that he was told by the chiefs of a Choctaw deputation, at Washington, that in their tribe were eight totemic clans, divided into two classes, of four each. It is very remarkable that the same number of clans, and the same division into classes, were to be found among the Five Nations or Iroquois.

latter, who were the conspicuous actors in the events of the ensuing narrative, demand a closer attention.

THE IROQUOIS FAMILY.

Foremost in war, foremost in eloquence, foremost in their savage arts of policy, stood the fierce people called by themselves the *Hodenosaunee*, and by the French the *Iroquois*, a name which has since been applied to the entire family of which they formed the dominant member.[1] They extended their conquests and their depredations from Quebec to the Carolinas, and from the western prairies to the forests of Maine.[2] On the south, they forced tribute from the subjugated Delawares, and pierced the mountain fastnesses of the Cherokees with incessant forays.[3] On the north, they up-

[1] A great difficulty in the study of Indian history arises from a redundancy of names employed to designate the same tribe; yet this does not prevent the same name from being often used to designate two or more different tribes. The following are the chief of those which are applied to the Iroquois by different writers, French, English, and German: —

Iroquois, Five, and afterwards Six Nations; Confederates, Hodenosaunee, Aquanuscioni, Aggonnonshioni, Ongwe Honwe, Mengwe, Maquas, Mahaquase, Massawomecs, Palenachendchiesktajeet.

The name of Massawomecs has been applied to several tribes; and that of Mingoes is often restricted to a colony of the Iroquois which established itself near the Ohio.

[2] François, a well-known Indian belonging to the remnant of the Penobscots living at Old Town, in Maine, told me, in the summer of 1843, that a tradition was current, among his people, of their being attacked in ancient times by the Mohawks, or, as he called them, Mohogs, a tribe of the Iroquois, who destroyed one of their villages, killed the men and women, and roasted the small children on forked sticks, like apples, before the fire. When he began to tell his story, François was engaged in patching an old canoe, in preparation for a moose hunt; but soon growing warm with his recital, he gave over his work, and at the conclusion exclaimed with great wrath and earnestness, "Mohog all devil!"

[3] The tribute exacted from the Delawares consisted of wampum, or beads of shell, an article of inestimable value with the Indians. "Two old men commonly go about, every year or two, to receive this tribute; and I have often had opportunity to observe what anxiety the poor Indians were under, while these two old men remained in that part of the country where I was. An old Mohawk sachem, in a poor blanket and a dirty shirt, may be seen issuing his orders with as arbitrary an authority as a Roman dictator."—Colden, *Hist. Five Nations*, 4.

rooted the ancient settlements of the Wyandots; on the west they exterminated the Eries and the Andastes, and spread havoc and dismay among the tribes of the Illinois; and on the east, the Indians of New England fled at the first peal of the Mohawk war-cry. Nor was it the Indian race alone who quailed before their ferocious valor. All Canada shook with the fury of their onset; the people fled to the forts for refuge; the blood-besmeared conquerors roamed like wolves among the burning settlements, and the colony trembled on the brink of ruin.

The Iroquois in some measure owed their triumphs to the position of their country; for they dwelt within the present limits of the State of New York, whence several great rivers and the inland oceans of the northern lakes opened ready thoroughfares to their roving warriors through all the adjacent wilderness. But the true fountain of their success is to be sought in their own inherent energies, wrought to the most effective action under a political fabric well suited to the Indian life; in their mental and moral organization; in their insatiable ambition and restless ferocity.

In their scheme of government, as in their social customs and religious observances, the Iroquois displayed, in full symmetry and matured strength, the same characteristics which in other tribes are found distorted, withered, decayed to the root, or, perhaps, faintly visible in an imperfect germ. They consisted of five tribes or nations—the Mohawks, the Oneidas, the Onondagas, the Cayugas, and the Senecas, to whom a sixth, the Tuscaroras, was afterwards added.[1] To each of these tribes belonged an organization of its own. Each had several sachems, who, with the subordinate chiefs and principal men, regulated all its internal affairs; but, when foreign powers were to be treated with, or matters involving the whole con-

---

[1] The following are synonymous names, gathered from various writers:—

Mohawks, Anies, Agniers, Agnierrhonons, Sankhicans, Canungas, Mauguawogs, Ganeagaonoh.

Oneidas, Oneotas, Onoyats, Anoyints, Onneiouts, Oneyyotecaronoh, Onoiochrhonons.

Onondagas, Onnontagues, Onondagaonohs.

Cayugas, Caiyoquos, Goiogoens, Gweugwehonoh.

Senecas, Sinnikes, Chennessies, Genesees, Chenandoanes, Tsonnontouans, Jenontowanos, Nundawaronoh.

federacy required deliberation, all the sachems of the several tribes convened in general assembly at the great council-house, in the Valley of Onondaga. Here ambassadors were received, alliances were adjusted, and all subjects of general interest discussed with exemplary harmony.[1] The order of debate was prescribed by time-honored customs; and, in the fiercest heat of controversy, the assembly maintained its self-control.

But the main stay of Iroquois polity was the system of *totemship*. It was this which gave the structure its elastic strength; and but for this, a mere confederacy of jealous and warlike tribes must soon have been rent asunder by shocks from without or discord from within. At some early period, the Iroquois probably formed an individual nation; for the whole people, irrespective of their separation into tribes, consisted of eight totemic clans; and the members of each clan, to what nation soever they belonged, were mutually bound to one another by those close ties of fraternity which mark this singular institution. Thus the five nations of the confederacy were laced together by an eight-fold band; and to this hour their slender remnants cling to one another with invincible tenacity.

It was no small security to the liberties of the Iroquois— liberties which they valued beyond any other possession—

[1]"In the year 1745, August Gottlieb Spangenburg, a bishop of the United Brethren, spent several weeks in Onondaga, and frequently attended the great council. The council-house was built of bark. On each side six seats were placed, each containing six persons. No one was admitted besides the members of the council, except a few, who were particularly honored. If one rose to speak, all the rest sat in profound silence, smoking their pipes. The speaker uttered his words in a singing tone, always rising a few notes at the close of each sentence. Whatever was pleasing to the council was confirmed by all with the word Nee, or Yes. And, at the end of each speech, the whole company joined in applauding the speaker by calling Hoho. At noon, two men entered bearing a large kettle filled with meat, upon a pole across their shoulders, which was first presented to the guests. A large wooden ladle, as broad and deep as a common bowl, hung with a hook to the side of the kettle, with which every one might at once help himself to as much as he could eat. When the guests had eaten their fill, they begged the counsellors to do the same. The whole was conducted in a very decent and quiet manner. Indeed, now and then, one or the other would lie flat upon his back to rest himself, and sometimes they would stop, joke, and laugh heartily."—Loskiel, *Hist. Morav. Miss.* 138.

that by the Indian custom of descent in the female line, which among them was more rigidly adhered to than elsewhere, the office of the sachem must pass, not to his son, but to his brother, his sister's son, or some yet remoter kinsman. His power was constantly deflected into the collateral branches of his family; and thus one of the strongest temptations of ambition was cut off.[1] The Iroquois had no laws; but they had ancient customs which took the place of laws. Each man, or rather, each clan, was the avenger of its own wrongs; but the manner of the retaliation was fixed by established usage. The tribal sachems, and even the great council at Onondaga, had no power to compel the execution of their decrees; yet they were looked up to with a respect which the soldier's bayonet or the sheriff's staff would never have commanded; and it is highly to the honor of the Indian character that they could exert so great an authority where there was nothing to enforce it but the weight of moral power.[2]

[1]The descent of the sachemship in the female line was a custom universally prevalent among the Five Nations, or Iroquois proper. Since, among Indian tribes generally, the right of furnishing a sachem was vested in some particular totemic clan, it results of course that the descent of the sachemship must follow the descent of the totem; that is, if the totemship descend in the female line, the sachemship must do the same. This custom of descent in the female line prevailed not only among the Iroquois proper, but also among the Wyandots, and probably among the Andastes and the Eries, extinct members of the great Iroquois family. Thus, among any of these tribes, when a Wolf warrior married a Hawk squaw, their children were Hawks, and not Wolves. With the Creeks of the south, according to the observations of Hawkins (*Georgia Hist. Coll.* III. 69), the rule was the same; but among the Algonquins, on the contrary, or at least among the northern branches of this family, the reverse took place, the totemships, and consequently the chieftainships, descending in the male line, after the analogy of civilized nations. For this information concerning the northern Algonquins, I am indebted to Mr. Schoolcraft, whose opportunities of observation among these tribes have surpassed those of any other student of Indian customs and character.

[2]An account of the political institutions of the Iroquois will be found in Mr. Morgan's series of letters, published in the *American Review* for 1847. Valuable information may also be obtained from *Schoolcraft's Notes on the Iroquois*.

Mr. Morgan is of opinion that these institutions were the result of "a protracted effort of legislation." An examination of the customs prevailing among other Indian tribes makes it probable that the elements of the

The origin of the Iroquois is lost in hopeless obscurity. That they came from the west; that they came from the north; that they sprang from the soil of New York, are the testimonies of three conflicting traditions, all equally worthless as aids to historic inquiry.[1] It is at the era of their confederacy— the event to which the five tribes owed all their greatness and power, and to which we need assign no remoter date than that of a century before the first arrival of the Dutch in New York—that faint rays of light begin to pierce the gloom, and the chaotic traditions of the earlier epoch mould themselves into forms more palpable and distinct.

Taounyawatha, the God of the Waters—such is the belief of the Iroquois—descended to the earth to instruct his favorite people in the arts of savage life; and when he saw how they were tormented by giants, monsters, and evil spirits, he urged the divided tribes, for the common defence, to band themselves together in an everlasting league. While the injunction was as yet unfulfilled, the sacred messenger was recalled to the Great Spirit; but, before his departure, he promised that another should appear, empowered to instruct the people in all that pertained to their confederation. And accordingly, as a band of Mohawk warriors was threading the funereal labyrinth of an ancient pine forest, they heard, amid its blackest depths, a hoarse voice chanting in measured cadence; and, following the sound, they saw, seated among the trees, a monster so hideous, that they stood benumbed with terror. His features were wild and frightful. He was encompassed by hissing rattlesnakes, which, Medusa-like, hung writhing from his head; and on the ground around him were strewn im-

---

Iroquois polity existed among them from an indefinite antiquity; and the legislation of which Mr. Morgan speaks could only involve the arrangement and adjustment of already existing materials.

Since the above chapter was written, Mr. Morgan has published an elaborate and very able work on the institutions of the Iroquois. It forms an invaluable addition to this department of knowledge.

[1] Recorded by Heckewelder, Colden, and Schoolcraft. That the Iroquois had long dwelt on the spot where they were first discovered by the whites, is rendered probable by several circumstances. See Mr. Squier's work on the *Aborginal Monuments of New York*.

plements of incantation, and magic vessels formed of human skulls. Recovering from their amazement, the warriors could perceive that in the mystic words of the chant, which he still poured forth, were couched the laws and principles of the destined confederacy. The tradition further declares that the monster, being surrounded and captured, was presently transformed to human shape, that he became a chief of transcendent wisdom and prowess, and to the day of his death ruled the councils of the now united tribes. To this hour the presiding sachem of the council at Onondaga inherits from him the honored name of Atotarho.[1]

The traditional epoch which preceded the auspicious event of the confederacy, though wrapped in clouds and darkness, and defying historic scrutiny, has yet a character and meaning of its own. The gloom is peopled thick with phantoms; with monsters and prodigies, shapes of wild enormity, yet offering, in the Teutonic strength of their conception, the evidence of a robustness of mind unparalleled among tribes of a different lineage. In these evil days, the scattered and divided Iroquois were beset with every form of peril and disaster. Giants, cased in armor of stone, descended on them from the mountains of the north. Huge beasts trampled down their forests like fields of grass. Human heads, with streaming hair and glaring eyeballs, shot through the air like meteors, shedding pestilence and death throughout the land. A great horned serpent rose from Lake Ontario; and only the thunder-bolts of the skies could stay his ravages, and drive him back to his native deeps. The skeletons of men, victims of some monster of the forest, were seen swimming in the Lake of Teungktoo; and around the Seneca village on the Hill of Genundewah, a two-headed serpent coiled himself, of size so monstrous that the wretched people were unable to ascend his scaly sides, and perished in multitudes by his pestilential breath. Mortally wounded at length by the magic arrow of a child, he rolled down the steep, sweeping away the forest with his writhings, and plunging into the lake below, where he lashed the black waters till they boiled with blood and

[1] This preposterous legend was first briefly related in the pamphlet of Cusick, the Tuscarora, and after him by Mr. Schoolcraft, in his *Notes*. The curious work of Cusick will again be referred to.

foam, and at length, exhausted with his agony, sank, and perished at the bottom. Under the Falls of Niagara dwelt the Spirit of the Thunder, with his brood of giant sons; and the Iroquois trembled in their villages when, amid the blackening shadows of the storm, they heard his deep shout roll along the firmament.

The energy of fancy, whence these barbarous creations drew their birth, displayed itself, at a later period, in that peculiar eloquence which the wild democracy of the Iroquois tended to call forth, and to which the mountain and the forest, the torrent and the storm, lent their stores of noble imagery. That to this imaginative vigor was joined mental power of a different stamp, is witnessed by the caustic irony of Garangula and Sagoyewatha, and no less by the subtle policy, sagacious as it was treacherous, which marked the dealings of the Iroquois with surrounding tribes.[1]

With all this mental superiority, the arts of life among them had not emerged from their primitive rudeness; and their coarse pottery, their spear and arrow heads of stone, were in no way superior to those of many other tribes. Their agriculture deserves a higher praise. In 1696, the invading army of Count Frontenac found the maize fields extending a league and a half or two leagues from their villages; and, in 1779, the troops of General Sullivan were filled with amazement at their abundant stores of corn, beans, and squashes, and at the old apple orchards which grew around their settlements.

Their dwellings and works of defence were far from contemptible, either in their dimensions or in their structure; and though by the several attacks of the French, and especially by

---

[1]For traditions of the Iroquois see Schoolcraft, *Notes*, Chap. IX. Cusick, *History of the Five Nations*, and Clark, *Hist. Onondaga*, I.

Cusick was an old Tuscarora Indian, who, being disabled by an accident from active occupations, essayed to become the historian of his people, and produced a small pamphlet, written in a language almost unintelligible, and filled with a medley of traditions in which a few grains of truth are inextricably mingled with a tangled mass of absurdities. He relates the monstrous legends of his people with an air of implicit faith, and traces the presiding sachems of the confederacy in regular descent from the first Atotarho downwards. His work, which was printed at the Tuscarora village, near Lewiston, in 1828, is illustrated by several rude engravings representing the Stone Giants, the Flying Heads, and other traditional monsters.

the invasion of De Nonville, in 1687, and of Frontenac, nine years later, their fortified towns were levelled to the earth, never again to reappear; yet, in the works of Champlain and other early writers we find abundant evidence of their pristine condition. Along the banks of the Mohawk, among the hills and hollows of Onondaga, in the forests of Oneida and Cayuga, on the romantic shores of Seneca Lake and the rich borders of the Genessee, surrounded by waving maize fields, and encircled from afar by the green margin of the forest, stood the ancient strongholds of the confederacy. The clustering dwellings were encompassed by palisades, in single, double, or triple rows, pierced with loopholes, furnished with platforms within, for the convenience of the defenders, with magazines of stones to hurl upon the heads of the enemy, and with water conductors to extinguish any fire which might be kindled from without.[1]

The area which these defences enclosed was often several acres in extent, and the dwellings, ranged in order within, were sometimes more than a hundred feet in length. Posts, firmly driven into the ground, with an intervening framework of poles, formed the basis of the structure; and its sides and arched roof were closely covered with layers of elm bark. Each of the larger dwellings contained several distinct families, whose separate fires were built along the central space, while compartments on each side, like the stalls of a stable, afforded some degree of privacy. Here, rude couches were prepared, and bear and deer skins spread; while above, the ripened ears of maize, suspended in rows, formed a golden tapestry.[2]

---

[1]Lafitau, *Mœurs des Sauvages Ameriquains*, II. 4–10.

Frontenac, in his expedition against the Onondagas, in 1696 (see Official Journal, *Doc. Hist. New York*, I. 332), found one of their villages built in an oblong form, with four bastions. The wall was formed of three rows of palisades, those of the outer row being forty or fifty feet high. The usual figure of the Iroquois villages was circular or oval, and in this instance the bastions were no doubt the suggestion of some European adviser.

[2]Bartram gives the following account of the great council-house at Onondaga, which he visited in 1743: —

"We alighted at the council-house, where the chiefs were already assembled to receive us, which they did with a grave, cheerful complaisance, according to their custom; they shew'd us where to lay our baggage, and repose ourselves during our stay with them; which was in the two end apartments of

In the long evenings of midwinter, when in the wilderness without the trees cracked with biting cold, and the forest paths were clogged with snow, then, around the lodge-fires of the Iroquois, warriors, squaws, and restless naked children were clustered in social groups, each dark face brightening in the fickle firelight, while, with jest and laugh, the pipe passed round from hand to hand. Perhaps some shrivelled old warrior, the story-teller of the tribe, recounted to attentive ears the deeds of ancient heroism, legends of spirits and monsters, or tales of witches and vampires—superstitions not less rife among this all-believing race, than among the nations of the transatlantic world.

The life of the Iroquois, though void of those multiplying phases which vary the routine of civilized existence, was one of sharp excitement and sudden contrast. The chase, the war-path, the dance, the festival, the game of hazard, the race of political ambition, all had their votaries. When the assembled sachems had resolved on war against some foreign tribe, and when, from their great council-house of bark, in the Valley of Onondaga, their messengers had gone forth to invite the warriors to arms, then from east to west, through the farthest bounds of the confederacy, a thousand warlike hearts caught

---

this large house. The Indians that came with us were placed over against us. This cabin is about eighty feet long and seventeen broad, the common passage six feet wide, and the apartments on each side five feet, raised a foot above the passage by a long sapling, hewed square, and fitted with joists that go from it to the back of the house; on these joists they lay large pieces of bark, and on extraordinary occasions spread mats made of rushes: this favor we had; on these floors they set or lye down, every one as he will; the apartments are divided from each other by boards or bark, six or seven foot long, from the lower floor to the upper, on which they put their lumber; when they have eaten their homony, as they set in each apartment before the fire, they can put the bowl over head, having not above five foot to reach; they set on the floor sometimes at each end, but mostly at one; they have a shed to put their wood into in the winter, or in the summer to set to converse or play, that has a door to the south; all the sides and roof of the cabin are made of bark, bound fast to poles set in the ground, and bent round on the top, or set aflatt, for the roof, as we set our rafters; over each fireplace they leave a hole to let out the smoke, which, in rainy weather, they cover with a piece of bark, and this they can easily reach with a pole to push it on one side or quite over the hole; after this model are most of their cabins built."—Bartram, *Observations*, 40.

up the summons. With fasting and praying, and consulting dreams and omens; with invoking the war-god, and dancing the war-dance, the warriors sought to insure the triumph of their arms; and then, their rites concluded, they began their stealthy progress through the devious pathways of the forest. For days and weeks, in anxious expectation, the villagers awaited the result. And now, as evening closed, a shrill, wild cry, pealing from afar, over the darkening forest, proclaimed the return of the victorious warriors. The village was alive with sudden commotion; and snatching sticks and stones, knives and hatchets, men, women, and children, yelling like fiends let loose, swarmed out of the narrow portal, to visit upon the captives a foretaste of the deadlier torments in store for them. The black arches of the forest glowed with the fires of death; and with brandished torch and firebrand the frenzied multitude closed around their victim. The pen shrinks to write, the heart sickens to conceive, the fierceness of his agony; yet still, amid the din of his tormentors, rose his clear voice of scorn and defiance. The work was done; the blackened trunk was flung to the dogs, and, with clamorous shouts and hootings, the murderers sought to drive away the spirit of their victim.[1]

The Iroquois reckoned these barbarities among their most exquisite enjoyments; and yet they had other sources of pleasure, which made up in frequency and in innocence what they lacked in intensity. Each passing season had its feasts and dances, often mingling religion with social pastime. The young had their frolics and merry-makings; and the old had their no less frequent councils, where conversation and

---

[1]"Being at this place the 17 of June, there came fifty prisoners from the south-westward. They were of two nations, some whereof have few guns; the other none at all. One nation is about ten days' journey from any Christians, and trade onely with one greatt house, nott farr from the sea, and the other trade onely, as they say, with a black people. This day of them was burnt two women, and a man and a child killed with a stone. Att night we heard a great noyse as if ye houses had all fallen, butt itt was only ye inhabitants driving away ye ghosts of ye murthered.

"The 18th going to Canagorah, that day there were most cruelly burnt four men, four women and one boy. The cruelty lasted aboutt seven hours. When they were almost dead letting them loose to the mercy of ye boys, and taking the hearts of such as were dead to feast on."—Greenhalgh, *Journal*, 1677.

laughter alternated with grave deliberations for the public weal. There were also stated periods marked by the recurrence of momentous ceremonies, in which the whole community took part—the mystic sacrifice of the dogs, the orgies of the dream feast, and the loathsome festival of the exhumation of the dead. Yet in the intervals of war and hunting, these resources would often fail; and, while the women were toiling in the cornfields, the lazy warriors beguiled the hours with smoking or sleeping, with gambling or gallantry.[1]

If we seek for a single trait preëminently characteristic of the Iroquois, we shall find it in that boundless pride which impelled them to style themselves, not inaptly as regards their own race, "the men surpassing all others."[2] "Must I," exclaimed one of their great warriors, as he fell wounded among a crowd of Algonquins,—"must I, who have made the whole earth tremble, now die by the hands of children?" Their power kept pace with their pride. Their war-parties roamed over half America, and their name was a terror from the Atlantic to the Mississippi; but, when we ask the numerical strength of the dreaded confederacy, when we discover that, in the days of their greatest triumphs, their united cantons could not have mustered four thousand warriors, we stand amazed at the folly and dissension which left so vast a region the prey of a handful of bold marauders. Of the cities and villages now so thickly scattered over the lost domain of the Iroquois, a single one might boast a more numerous population than all the five united tribes.[3]

[1] For an account of the habits and customs of the Iroquois, the following works, besides those already cited, may be referred to:—

Charlevoix, *Letters to the Duchess of Lesdiguières*; Champlain, *Voyages de la Nouv. France*; Clark, *Hist. Onondaga*, I., and several volumes of the Jesuit *Relations*, especially those of 1656–1657 and 1659–1660.

[2] This is Colden's translation of the word Ongwehonwe, one of the names of the Iroquois.

[3] La Hontan estimated the Iroquois at from five thousand to seven thousand fighting men; but his means of information were very imperfect, and the same may be said of several other French writers, who have overrated the force of the confederacy. In 1677, the English sent one Greenhalgh to ascertain their numbers. He visited all their towns and villages, and reported their aggregate force at two thousand one hundred and fifty fighting men. The

From this remarkable people, who with all the ferocity of their race blended heroic virtues and marked endowments of intellect, I pass to other members of the same great family, whose different fortunes may perhaps be ascribed rather to the force of circumstance, than to any intrinsic inferiority.

The peninsula between the Lakes Huron, Erie, and Ontario was occupied by two distinct peoples, speaking dialects of the Iroquois tongue. The Hurons or Wyandots, including the tribe called by the French the Dionondadies, or Tobacco Nation,[1] dwelt among the forests which bordered the eastern shores of the fresh water sea, to which they have left their name; while the Neutral Nation, so called from their neutrality in the war between the Hurons and the Five Nations, inhabited the northern shores of Lake Erie, and even extended their eastern flank across the strait of Niagara.

The population of the Hurons has been variously stated at from ten thousand to thirty thousand souls, but probably did not exceed the former estimate. The Franciscans and the Jesuits were early among them, and from their descriptions it is apparent that, in legends and superstitions, manners and habits, religious observances and social customs, they were closely assimilated to their brethren of the Five Nations. Their capacious dwellings of bark, and their palisaded forts, seemed copied after the same model.[2] Like the Five Nations, they were divided into tribes, and cross-divided into totemic clans; and, as with them, the office of sachem descended in the female line. The same crude materials of a political fabric were to be

---

report of Colonel Coursey, agent from Virginia, at about the same period, closely corresponds with this statement. Greenhalgh's Journal will be found in Chalmers's *Political Annals*, and in the *Documentary History of New York*. Subsequent estimates, up to the period of the Revolution, when their strength had much declined, vary from twelve hundred to two thousand one hundred and twenty. Most of these estimates are given by Clinton, in his *Discourse on the Five Nations*, and several by Jefferson, in his *Notes on Virginia*.

[1] Hurons, Wyandots, Yendots, Ouendaets, Quatogies.

The Dionondadies are also designated by the following names: Tionontatez, Petuneux — Nation of Tobacco.

[2] See Sagard, *Hurons*, 115.

found in both; but, unlike the Iroquois, the Wyandots had not as yet wrought them into a system, and woven them into a harmonious whole.

Like the Five Nations, the Wyandots were in some measure an agricultural people; they bartered the surplus products of their maize fields to surrounding tribes, usually receiving fish in exchange; and this traffic was so considerable, that the Jesuits styled their country the Granary of the Algonquins.[1]

Their prosperity was rudely broken by the hostilities of the Five Nations; for though the conflicting parties were not ill matched in point of numbers, yet the united counsels and ferocious energies of the confederacy swept all before them. In the year 1649, in the depth of winter, their warriors invaded the country of the Wyandots, stormed their largest villages, and involved all within in indiscriminate slaughter.[2] The survivors fled in panic terror, and the whole nation was broken and dispersed.

Some found refuge among the French of Canada, where, at the village of Lorette, near Quebec, their descendants still remain; others were incorporated with their conquerors; while others again fled northward, beyond Lake Superior, and sought an asylum among the wastes which bordered on the north-eastern bands of the Dahcotah. Driven back by those fierce bison-hunters, they next established themselves about the outlet of Lake Superior, and the shores and islands in the northern parts of Lake Huron. Thence, about the year 1680, they descended to Detroit, where they formed a permanent settlement, and where, by their superior valor, capacity, and address, they soon acquired an ascendency over the surrounding Algonquins.

The ruin of the Neutral Nation followed close on that of the Wyandots, to whom, according to Jesuit authority, they bore

---

[1] Bancroft, in his chapter on the Indians east of the Mississippi, falls into a mistake when he says that no trade was carried on by any of the tribes. For an account of the traffic between the Hurons and Algonquins, see Mercier, *Relation des Hurons*, 1637, p. 171.

[2] See "Jesuits in North America."

an exact resemblance in character and manners.[1] The Senecas soon found means to pick a quarrel with them; they were assailed by all the strength of the insatiable confederacy, and within a few years their destruction as a nation was complete.

South of Lake Erie dwelt two members of the Iroquois family. The Andastes built their fortified villages along the valley of the Lower Susquehanna; while the Erigas, or Eries, occupied the borders of the lake which still retains their name. Of these two nations little is known, for the Jesuits had no missions among them, and few traces of them survive beyond their names and the record of their destruction. The war with the Wyandots was scarcely over, when the Five Nations turned their arms against their Erie brethren.

In the year 1655, using their canoes as scaling ladders, they stormed the Erie stronghold, leaped down like tigers among the defenders, and butchered them without mercy.[2] The greater part of the nation was involved in the massacre, and the remnant was incorporated with the conquerors, or with other tribes, to which they fled for refuge. The ruin of the Andastes came next in turn; but this brave people fought for twenty years against their inexorable assailants, and their destruction was not consummated until the year 1672, when they shared the fate of the rest.[3]

Thus, within less than a quarter of a century, four nations, the most brave and powerful of the North American savages, sank before the arms of the confederates. Nor did their triumphs end here. Within the same short space they subdued their southern neighbors the Lenape,[4] the leading members of the Algonquin family, and expelled the Ottawas, a numerous people of the same lineage, from the borders of the river which bears their name. In the north, the west, and the south,

[1] According to Lallemant, the population of the Neutral Nation amounted to at least twelve thousand; but the estimate is probably exaggerated.—*Relation des Hurons*, 1641, p. 50.

[2] The Iroquois traditions on this subject, as related to the writer by a chief of the Cayugas, do not agree with the narratives of the Jesuits. It is not certain that the Eries were of the Iroquois family. There is some reason to believe them Algonquins, and possibly identical with the Shawanoes.

[3] Charlevoix, *Nouvelle France*, I. 443.

[4] Gallatin places the final subjection of the Lenape at about the year 1750—a printer's error for 1650.—*Synopsis*, 48.

their conquests embraced every adjacent tribe; and meanwhile their war parties were harassing the French of Canada with reiterated inroads, and yelling the war-whoop under the walls of Quebec.

They were the worst of conquerors. Inordinate pride, the lust of blood and dominion, were the mainsprings of their warfare; and their victories were strained with every excess of savage passion. That their triumphs must have cost them dear; that, in spite of their cautious tactics, these multiplied conflicts must have greatly abridged their strength, would appear inevitable. Their losses were, in fact, considerable; but every breach was repaired by means of a practice to which they, in common with other tribes, constantly adhered. When their vengeance was glutted by the sacrifice of a sufficient number of captives, they spared the lives of the remainder, and adopted them as members of their confederated tribes, separating wives from husbands, and children from parents, and distributing them among different villages, in order that old ties and associations might be more completely broken up. This policy is said to have been designated among them by a name which signifies "flesh cut into pieces and scattered among the tribes."

In the years 1714—15, the confederacy received a great accession of strength. Southwards, about the headwaters of the rivers Neuse and Tar, and separated from their kindred tribes by intervening Algonquin communities, dwelt the Tuscaroras, a warlike people belonging to the generic stock of the Iroquois. The wrongs inflicted by white settlers, and their own undistinguishing vengeance, involved them in a war with the colonists, which resulted in their defeat and expulsion. They emigrated to the Five Nations, whose allies they had been in former wars with southern tribes, and who now gladly received them, admitting them as a sixth nation, into their confederacy.

It is a remark of Gallatin, that, in their career of conquest, the Five Nations encountered more stubborn resistance from the tribes of their own family, than from those of a different lineage. In truth, all the scions of this warlike stock seem endued with singular vitality and force, and among them we must seek for the best type of the Indian character. Few tribes could match them in prowess, constancy, moral energy, or intellectual vigor. The Jesuits remarked that they were more intelligent, yet less tractable, than other savages; and Charlevoix observes that, though the Algonquins were readily converted, they made but fickle proselytes; while the Hurons, though not easily won over to the church, were far more faithful in their adherence.[1] Of this tribe, the Hurons or Wyandots, a candid and experienced observer declares, that of all the Indians with whom he was conversant, they alone held it disgraceful to turn from the face of an enemy when the fortunes of the fight were adverse.[2]

Besides these inherent qualities, the tribes of the Iroquois race derived great advantages from their superior social organization. They were all, more or less, tillers of the soil, and were thus enabled to concentrate a more numerous population than the scattered tribes who live by the chase alone. In their well-peopled and well-constructed villages, they dwelt together the greater part of the year; and thence the religious rites and social and political usages, which elsewhere existed only in the germ, attained among them a full development. Yet these advantages were not without alloy, and the Jesuits were not slow to remark that the stationary and thriving Iroquois were more loose in their observance of social ties, than the wandering and starving savages of the north.[3]

THE ALGONQUIN FAMILY.

Except the detached nation of the Tuscaroras, and a few smaller tribes adhering to them, the Iroquois family was confined to the region south of the Lakes Erie and Ontario, and the peninsula east of Lake Huron. They formed, as it were, an island in the vast expanse of Algonquin population, extending from Hudson's Bay on the north to the Carolinas on the

[1] *Nouvelle France*, I. 196.

[2] William Henry Harrison, *Discourse on the Aborigines of the Ohio*. See *Ohio Hist. Trans. Part Second*, I. 257.

[3] "Here ye Indyans were very desirous to see us ride our horses, wch wee did: they made great feasts and dancing, and invited us y^t when all ye maides were together, both wee and our Indyans might choose such as lyked us to ly with."—Greenhalgh, *Journal*.

south; from the Atlantic on the east to the Mississippi and Lake Winnipeg on the west. They were Algonquins who greeted Jacques Cartier, as his ships ascended the St. Lawrence. The first British colonists found savages of the same race hunting and fishing along the coasts and inlets of Virginia; and it was the daughter of an Algonquin chief who interceded with her father for the life of the adventurous Englishman. They were Algonquins who, under Sassacus the Pequot, and Philip of Mount Hope, waged war against the Puritans of New England; who dwelt at Penacook, under the rule of the great magician, Passaconaway, and trembled before the evil spirits of the White Hills; and who sang *aves* and told their beads in the forest chapel of Father Rasles, by the banks of the Kennebec. They were Algonquins who, under the great tree at Kensington, made the covenant of peace with William Penn; and when French Jesuits and fur-traders explored the Wabash and the Ohio, they found their valleys tenanted by the same far-extended race. At the present day, the traveller, perchance, may find them pitching their bark lodges along the beach at Mackinaw, spearing fish among the rapids of St. Mary's, or skimming the waves of Lake Superior in their birch canoes.

Of all the members of the Algonquin family, those called by the English the Delawares, by the French the Loups, and by themselves Lenni Lenape, or Original Men, hold the first claim to attention; for their traditions declare them to be the parent stem whence other Algonquin tribes have sprung. The latter recognized the claim, and, at all solemn councils, accorded to the ancestral tribe the title of Grandfather.[1]

The first European colonists found the conical lodges of the Lenape clustered in frequent groups about the waters of the Delaware and its tributary streams, within the present limits of New Jersey, and Eastern Pennsylvania. The nation was separated into three divisions, and three sachems formed a

[1]The Lenape, on their part, call the other Algonquin tribes Children, Grandchildren, Nephews, or Younger Brothers; but they confess the superiority of the Wyandots and the Five Nations, by yielding them the title of Uncles. They, in return, call the Lenape Nephews, or more frequently Cousins.

triumvirate, who, with the council of old men, regulated all its affairs.[1] They were, in some small measure, an agricultural people; but fishing and the chase were their chief dependence, and through a great part of the year they were scattered abroad, among forests and streams, in search of sustenance.

When William Penn held his far-famed council with the sachems of the Lenape, he extended the hand of brotherhood to a people as unwarlike in their habits as his own pacific followers. This is by no means to be ascribed to any inborn love of peace. The Lenape were then in a state of degrading vassalage to the Five Nations, who, that they might drain to the dregs the cup of humiliation, had forced them to assume the name of Women, and forego the use of arms.[2] Dwelling under the shadow of the tyrannical confederacy, they were long unable to wipe out the blot; but at length, pushed from their ancient seats by the encroachments of white men, and removed westward, partially beyond the reach of their conquerors, their native spirit began to revive, and they assumed a tone of defiance. During the Old French War they resumed the use of arms, and while the Five Nations fought for the English, they espoused the cause of France. At the opening of the Revolution, they boldly asserted their freedom from the yoke of their conquerors; and a few years after, the Five Nations confessed, at a public council, that the Lenape were no longer women, but men.[3] Ever since that period, they have stood in high repute for bravery, generosity, and all the savage virtues; and the settlers of the frontier have often found, to their cost, that the *women* of the Iroquois have been transformed into a race of formidable warriors. At the present day, the small remnant settled beyond the Mississippi are among the bravest marauders of the west. Their war-parties pierce the farthest wilds of

[1] Loskiel, Part I. 130.

[2] The story told by the Lenape themselves, and recorded with the utmost good faith by Loskiel and Heckewelder, that the Five Nations had not conquered them, but, by a cunning artifice, had cheated them into subjection, is wholly unworthy of credit. It is not to be believed that a people so acute and suspicious could be the dupes of so palpable a trick; and it is equally incredible that a high-spirited tribe could be induced, by the most persuasive rhetoric, to assume the name of Women, which in Indian eyes is the last confession of abject abasement.

[3] Heckewelder, *Hist. Ind. Nat.* 53.

the Rocky Mountains; and the prairie traveller may sometimes meet the Delaware warrior returning from a successful foray, a gaudy handkerchief bound about his brows, his snake locks fluttering in the wind, and his rifle resting across his saddle-bow, while the tarnished and begrimed equipments of his half-wild horse bear witness that the rider has waylaid and plundered some Mexican cavalier.

Adjacent to the Lenape, and associated with them in some of the most notable passages of their history, dwelt the Shawanoes, the Chaouanons of the French, a tribe of bold, roving, and adventurous spirit. Their eccentric wanderings, their sudden appearances and disappearances, perplex the antiquary, and defy research; but from various scattered notices, we may gather that at an early period they occupied the valley of the Ohio; that, becoming embroiled with the Five Nations, they shared the defeat of the Andastes, and about the year 1672 fled to escape destruction. Some found an asylum in the country of the Lenape, where they lived tenants at will of the Five Nations; others sought refuge in the Carolinas and Florida, where, true to their native instincts, they soon came to blows with the owners of the soil. Again, turning northwards, they formed new settlements in the valley of the Ohio, where they were now suffered to dwell in peace, and where, at a later period, they were joined by such of their brethren as had found refuge among the Lenape.[1]

Of the tribes which, single and detached, or cohering in loose confederacies, dwelt within the limits of Lower Canada, Acadia, and New England, it is needless to speak; for they offered no distinctive traits demanding notice. Passing the country of the Lenape and the Shawanoes, and descending the Ohio, the traveller would have found its valley chiefly occupied by two nations, the Miamis or Twightwees, on the Wabash and its branches, and the Illinois, who dwelt in the neighborhood of the river to which they have given their name, while portions of them extended beyond the Mississippi. Though never subjugated, as were the Lenape, both the Miamis and the Illinois were reduced to the last extremity by

[1] The evidence concerning the movements of the Shawanoes is well summed up by Gallatin, *Synopsis*, 65. See also Drake, *Life of Tecumseh*, 10.

the repeated attacks of the Five Nations; and the Illinois, in particular, suffered so much by these and other wars, that the population of ten or twelve thousand, ascribed to them by the early French writers, had dwindled, during the first quarter of the eighteenth century, to a few small villages.[1] According to Marest, they were a people sunk in sloth and licentiousness; but that priestly father had suffered much at their hands, and viewed them with a jaundiced eye. Their agriculture was not contemptible; they had permanent dwellings as well as portable lodges; and though wandering through many months of the year among their broad prairies and forests, there were seasons when their whole population was gathered, with feastings and merry-making, within the limits of their villages.

Turning his course northward, traversing Lakes Michigan and Superior, and skirting the western margin of Lake Huron, the voyager would have found the solitudes of the wild waste around him broken by scattered lodges of the Ojibwas, Pottawattamies, and Ottawas. About the bays and rivers west of Lake Michigan, he would have seen the Sacs, the Foxes, and the Menomonies; and penetrating the frozen wilderness of the north, he would have been welcomed by the rude hospitality of the wandering Crees or Knisteneaux.

The Ojibwas, with their kindred, the Pottawattamies, and their friends the Ottawas,—the latter of whom were fugitives from the eastward, whence they had fled from the wrath of the Iroquois,—were banded into a sort of confederacy.[2] They were closely allied in blood, language, manners and character. The Ojibwas, by far the most numerous of the three, occupied the basin of Lake Superior, and extensive adjacent regions. In their boundaries, the career of Iroquois conquest found at length a check. The fugitive Wyandots sought refuge in the Ojibwa hunting-grounds; and tradition relates that, at the outlet of Lake Superior, an Iroquois war-party once encountered a disastrous repulse.

In their mode of life, they were far more rude than the Iroquois, or even the southern Algonquin tribes. The totemic system is found among them in its most imperfect state. The

---

[1] Father Rasles, 1723, says that there were eleven. Marest, in 1712, found only three.

[2] Morse, *Report, Appendix*, 141.

original clans have become broken into fragments, and indefinitely multiplied; and many of the ancient customs of the institution are but loosely regarded. Agriculture is little known, and, through summer and winter, they range the wilderness with restless wandering, now gorged to repletion, and now perishing with want. In the calm days of summer, the Ojibwa fisherman pushes out his birch canoe upon the great inland ocean of the north; and, as he gazes down into the pellucid depths, he seems like one balanced between earth and sky. The watchful fish-hawk circles above his head; and below, farther than his line will reach, he sees the trout glide shadowy and silent over the glimmering pebbles. The little islands on the verge of the horizon seem now starting into spires, now melting from the sight, now shaping themselves into a thousand fantastic forms, with the strange mirage of the waters; and he fancies that the evil spirits of the lake lie basking their serpent forms on those unhallowed shores. Again, he explores the watery labyrinths where the stream sweeps among pine-tufted islands, or runs, black and deep, beneath the shadows of moss-bearded firs; or he drags his canoe upon the sandy beach, and, while his camp-fire crackles on the grass-plat, reclines beneath the trees, and smokes and laughs away the sultry hours, in a lazy luxury of enjoyment.

But when winter descends upon the north, sealing up the fountains, fettering the streams, and turning the green-robed forests to shivering nakedness, then, bearing their frail dwellings on their backs, the Ojibwa family wander forth into the wilderness, cheered only on their dreary track by the whistling of the north wind, and the hungry howl of wolves. By the banks of some frozen stream, women and children, men and dogs, lie crouched together around the fire. They spread their benumbed fingers over the embers, while the wind shrieks through the fir-trees like the gale through the rigging of a frigate, and the narrow concave of the wigwam sparkles with the frost-work of their congealed breath. In vain they beat the magic drum, and call upon their guardian manitoes;—the wary moose keeps aloof, the bear lies close in his hollow tree, and famine stares them in the face. And now the hunter can fight no more against the nipping cold and blinding sleet. Stiff and stark, with haggard cheek and shrivelled lip, he lies among the snow drifts; till, with tooth and claw, the famished wildcat strives in vain to pierce the frigid marble of his limbs. Such harsh schooling is thrown away on the incorrigible mind of the northern Algonquin. He lives in misery, as his fathers lived before him. Still, in the brief hour of plenty he forgets the season of want; and still the sleet and the snow descend upon his houseless head.[1]

I have thus passed in brief review the more prominent of the Algonquin tribes; those whose struggles and sufferings form the theme of the ensuing History. In speaking of the Iroquois, some of the distinctive peculiarities of the Algonquins have already been hinted at. It must be admitted that, in moral stability and intellectual vigor, they are inferior to the former; though some of the most conspicuous offspring of the wilderness, Metacom, Tecumseh, and Pontiac himself, owned their blood and language.

The fireside stories of every primitive people are faithful reflections of the form and coloring of the national mind; and it is no proof of sound philosophy to turn with contempt from the study of a fairy tale. The legendary lore of the Iroquois, black as the midnight forests, awful in its gloomy strength, is but another manifestation of that spirit of mastery which uprooted whole tribes from the earth, and deluged the wilderness with blood. The traditionary tales of the Algonquins wear a different aspect. The credulous circle around an Ojibwa lodge-fire listened to wild recitals of necromancy and witchcraft—men transformed to beasts, and beasts transformed to men, animated trees, and birds who spoke with human tongue. They heard of malignant sorcerers dwelling among the lonely islands of spell-bound lakes; of grisly *ween-digoes*, and bloodless *geebi*; of evil *manitoes* lurking in the dens and fastnesses of the woods; of pygmy champions, diminutive in stature but mighty in soul, who, by the potency of charm and talisman, subdued the direst monsters of the waste; and of heroes, who, not by downright force and open onset, but by subtle strategy, tricks, or magic art, achieved marvellous

---

[1] See Tanner, Long, and Henry. A comparison of Tanner with the accounts of the Jesuit Le Jeune will show that Algonquin life in Lower Canada, two hundred years ago, was essentially the same with Algonquin life on the Upper Lakes within the last half century.

triumphs over the brute force of their assailants. Sometimes the tale will breathe a different spirit, and tell of orphan children abandoned in the heart of a hideous wilderness, beset with fiends and cannibals. Some enamored maiden, scornful of earthly suitors, plights her troth to the graceful manito of the grove; or bright aerial beings, dwellers of the sky, descend to tantalize the gaze of mortals with evanescent forms of loveliness.

The mighty giant, the God of the Thunder, who made his home among the caverns, beneath the cataract of Niagara, was a characteristic conception of Iroquois imagination. The Algonquins held a simpler faith, and maintained that the thunder was a bird who built his nest on the pinnacle of towering mountains. Two daring boys once scaled the height, and thrust sticks into the eyes of the portentous nestlings; which hereupon flashed forth such wrathful scintillations, that the sticks were shivered to atoms.[1]

The religious belief of the Algonquins—and the remark holds good, not of the Algonquins only, but of all the hunting tribes of America—is a cloudy bewilderment, where we seek in vain for system or coherency. Among a primitive and savage people, there were no poets to vivify its images, and no priests to give distinctness and harmony to its rites and symbols. To the Indian mind, all nature was instinct with deity. A spirit was embodied in every mountain, lake, and cataract; every bird, beast, or reptile, every tree, shrub, or grassblade, was endued with mystic influence; yet this untutored

[1]For Algonquin legends, see Schoolcraft, in *Algic Researches* and *Oneota*. Le Jeune early discovered these legends among the tribes of his mission. Two centuries ago, among the Algonquins of Lower Canada, a tale was related to him, which, in its principal incidents, is identical with the story of the "Boy who set a Snare for the Sun," recently found by Mr. Schoolcraft among the tribes of the Upper Lakes. Compare *Relation*, 1637, p. 172, and *Oneota*, p. 75. The coincidence affords a curious proof of the antiquity and wide diffusion of some of these tales.

The Dacotah, as well as the Algonquins, believe that the thunder is produced by a bird. A beautiful illustration of this idea will be found in Mrs. Eastman's *Legends of the Sioux*. An Indian propounded to Le Jeune a doctrine of his own. According to his theory, the thunder is produced by the eructations of a monstrous giant, who had unfortunately swallowed a quantity of snakes; and the latter falling to the earth, caused the appearance of lightning. "Voilà une philosophie bien nouvelle!" exclaims the astonished Jesuit.

pantheism did not exclude the conception of certain divinities, of incongruous and ever shifting attributes. The sun, too, was a god, and the moon was a goddess. Conflicting powers of good and evil divided the universe: but if, before the arrival of Europeans, the Indian recognized the existence of one, almighty, self-existent Being, the Great Spirit, the Lord of Heaven and Earth, the belief was so vague and dubious as scarcely to deserve the name. His perceptions of moral good and evil were perplexed and shadowy; and the belief in a state of future reward and punishment was by no means universal.[1]

Of the Indian character, much has been written foolishly, and credulously believed. By the rhapsodies of poets, the cant of sentimentalists, and the extravagance of some who should have known better, a counterfeit image has been tricked out, which might seek in vain for its likeness through every corner of the habitable earth; an image bearing no more resemblance to its original, than the monarch of the tragedy and the hero of the epic poem bear to their living prototypes in the palace and the camp. The shadows of his wilderness home, and the darker mantle of his own inscrutable reserve, have made the Indian warrior a wonder and a mystery. Yet to the eye of rational observation there is nothing unintelligible in him. He is full, it is true, of contradiction. He deems himself the centre of greatness and renown; his pride is proof against the fiercest torments of fire and steel; and yet the same man would beg for a dram of whiskey, or pick up a crust of bread thrown to him like a dog, from the tent door of the traveller. At one moment, he is wary and cautious to the verge of cowardice; at the next, he abandons himself to a very insanity of recklessness; and the habitual self-restraint which throws an impenetrable veil over emotion is joined to the unbridled passions of a madman or a beast.

Such inconsistencies, strange as they seem in our eyes, when viewed under a novel aspect, are but the ordinary incidents of humanity. The qualities of the mind are not uniform in their action through all the relations of life. With different

---

[1] Le Jeune, Schoolcraft, James, Jarvis, Charlevoix, Sagard, Brébeuf, Mercier, Vimont, Lallemant, Lafitau, De Smet, &c.

men, and different races of men, pride, valor, prudence, have different forms of manifestation, and where in one instance they lie dormant, in another they are keenly awake. The conjunction of greatness and littleness, meanness and pride, is older than the days of the patriarchs; and such antiquated phenomena, displayed under a new form in the unreflecting, undisciplined mind of a savage, call for no special wonder, but should rather be classed with the other enigmas of the fathomless human heart. The dissecting knife of a Rochefoucault might lay bare matters of no less curious observation in the breast of every man.

Nature has stamped the Indian with a hard and stern physiognomy. Ambition, revenge, envy, jealousy, are his ruling passions; and his cold temperament is little exposed to those effeminate vices which are the bane of milder races. With him revenge is an overpowering instinct; nay, more, it is a point of honor and a duty. His pride sets all language at defiance. He loathes the thought of coercion; and few of his race have ever stooped to discharge a menial office. A wild love of liberty, an utter intolerance of control, lie at the basis of his character, and fire his whole existence. Yet, in spite of this haughty independence, he is a devout hero-worshipper; and high achievement in war or policy touches a chord to which his nature never fails to respond. He looks up with admiring reverence to the sages and heroes of his tribe; and it is this principle, joined to the respect for age springing from the patriarchal element in his social system, which, beyond all others, contributes union and harmony to the erratic members of an Indian community. With him the love of glory kindles into a burning passion; and to allay its cravings, he will dare cold and famine, fire, tempest, torture, and death itself.

These generous traits are overcast by much that is dark, cold, and sinister, by sleepless distrust, and rankling jealousy. Treacherous himself, he is always suspicious of treachery in others. Brave as he is,—and few of mankind are braver,—he will vent his passion by a secret stab rather than an open blow. His warfare is full of ambuscade and stratagem; and he never rushes into battle with that joyous self-abandonment, with which the warriors of the Gothic races flung themselves into the ranks of their enemies. In his feasts and his drinking bouts we find none of that robust and full-toned mirth, which reigned at the rude carousals of our barbaric ancestry. He is never jovial in his cups, and maudlin sorrow or maniacal rage is the sole result of his potations.

Over all emotion he throws the veil of an iron self-control, originating in a peculiar form of pride, and fostered by rigorous discipline from childhood upward. He is trained to conceal passion, and not to subdue it. The inscrutable warrior is aptly imaged by the hackneyed figure of a volcano covered with snow; and no man can say when or where the wild-fire will burst forth. This shallow self-mastery serves to give dignity to public deliberation, and harmony to social life. Wrangling and quarrel are strangers to an Indian dwelling; and while an assembly of the ancient Gauls was garrulous as a convocation of magpies, a Roman senate might have taken a lesson from the grave solemnity of an Indian council. In the midst of his family and friends, he hides affections, by nature none of the most tender, under a mask of icy coldness; and in the torturing fires of his enemy, the haughty sufferer maintains to the last his look of grim defiance.

His intellect is as peculiar as his moral organization. Among all savages, the powers of perception preponderate over those of reason and analysis; but this is more especially the case with the Indian. An acute judge of character, at least of such parts of it as his experience enables him to comprehend; keen to a proverb in all exercises of war and the chase, he seldom traces effects to their causes, or follows out actions to their remote results. Though a close observer of external nature, he no sooner attempts to account for her phenomena than he involves himself in the most ridiculous absurdities; and quite content with these puerilities, he has not the least desire to push his inquiries further. His curiosity, abundantly active within its own narrow circle, is dead to all things else; and to attempt rousing it from its torpor is but a bootless task. He seldom takes cognizance of general or abstract ideas; and his language has scarcely the power to express them, except through the medium of figures drawn from the external world, and often highly picturesque and forcible. The absence of reflection makes him grossly improvident, and unfits him for pursuing any complicated scheme of war or policy.

Some races of men seem moulded in wax, soft and melting, at once plastic and feeble. Some races, like some metals, combine the greatest flexibility with the greatest strength. But the Indian is hewn out of a rock. You can rarely change the form without destruction of the substance. Races of inferior energy have possessed a power of expansion and assimilation to which he is a stranger; and it is this fixed and rigid quality which has proved his ruin. He will not learn the arts of civilization, and he and his forest must perish together. The stern, unchanging features of his mind excite our admiration from their very immutability; and we look with deep interest on the fate of this irreclaimable son of the wilderness, the child who will not be weaned from the breast of his rugged mother. And our interest increases when we discern in the unhappy wanderer the germs of heroic virtues mingled among his vices,—a hand bountiful to bestow as it is rapacious to seize, and even in extremest famine, imparting its last morsel to a fellow-sufferer; a heart which, strong in friendship as in hate, thinks it not too much to lay down life for its chosen comrade; a soul true to its own idea of honor, and burning with an unquenchable thirst for greatness and renown.

The imprisoned lion in the showman's cage differs not more widely from the lord of the desert, than the beggarly frequenter of frontier garrisons and dramshops differs from the proud denizen of the woods. It is in his native wilds alone that the Indian must be seen and studied. Thus to depict him is the aim of the ensuing History; and if, from the shades of rock and forest, the savage features should look too grimly forth, it is because the clouds of a tempestuous war have cast upon the picture their murky shadows and lurid fires.

Chapter II.

1608—1763.

FRANCE AND ENGLAND IN AMERICA.

THE AMERICAN COLONIES of France and England grew up to maturity under widely different auspices. Canada, the offspring of Church and State, nursed from infancy in the lap of power, its puny strength fed with artificial stimulants, its movements guided by rule and discipline, its limbs trained to martial exercise, languished, in spite of all, from the lack of vital sap and energy. The colonies of England, outcast and neglected, but strong in native vigor and self-confiding courage, grew yet more strong with conflict and with striving, and developed the rugged proportions and unwieldy strength of a youthful giant.

In the valley of the St. Lawrence, and along the coasts of the Atlantic, adverse principles contended for the mastery. Feudalism stood arrayed against Democracy; Popery against Protestantism; the sword against the ploughshare. The priest, the soldier, and the noble, ruled in Canada. The ignorant, light-hearted Canadian peasant knew nothing and cared nothing about popular rights and civil liberties. Born to obey, he lived in contented submission, without the wish or the capacity for self-rule. Power, centered in the heart of the system, left the masses inert. The settlements along the margin of the St. Lawrence were like a camp, where an army lay at rest, ready for the march or the battle, and where war and adventure, not trade and tillage, seemed the chief aims of life. The lords of the soil were petty nobles, for the most part soldiers, or the sons of soldiers, proud and ostentatious, thriftless and poor; and the people were their vassals. Over every cluster of small white houses glittered the sacred emblem of the cross. The church, the convent, and the roadside shrine were seen at every turn; and in the towns and villages, one met each moment the black robe of the Jesuit, the gray garb of the Recollet, and the formal habit of the Ursuline nun. The names of saints, St. Joseph, St. Ignatius, St. Francis, were perpetuated in the capes, rivers, and islands, the forts and villages of the land; and with every day, crowds of simple worshippers knelt in adoration before the countless altars of the Roman faith.

If we search the world for the sharpest contrast to the spiritual and temporal vassalage of Canada, we shall find it among her immediate neighbors, the Puritans of New England, where the spirit of non-conformity was sublimed to a fiery essence, and where the love of liberty and the hatred of power burned with sevenfold heat. The English colonist, with thoughtful brow and limbs hardened with toil; calling no man master, yet bowing reverently to the law which he himself had made; patient and laborious, and seeking for the solid comforts rather than the ornaments of life; no lover of war, yet, if need were, fighting with a stubborn, indomitable courage, and then bending once more with steadfast energy to his farm, or his merchandise,—such a man might well be deemed the very pith and marrow of a commonwealth.

In every quality of efficiency and strength, the Canadian fell miserably below his rival; but in all that pleases the eye and interests the imagination, he far surpassed him. Buoyant and gay, like his ancestry of France, he made the frozen wilderness ring with merriment, answered the surly howling of the pine forest with peals of laughter, and warmed with revelry the groaning ice of the St. Lawrence. Careless and thoughtless, he lived happy in the midst of poverty, content if he could but gain the means to fill his tobacco-pouch, and decorate the cap of his mistress with a ribbon. The example of a beggared nobility, who, proud and penniless, could only assert their rank by idleness and ostentation, was not lost upon him. A rightful heir to French bravery and French restlessness, he had an eager love of wandering and adventure; and this propensity found ample scope in the service of the fur-trade, the engrossing occupation and chief source of income to the colony. When the priest of St. Ann's had shrived him of his sins; when, after the parting carousal, he embarked with his comrades in the deep-laden canoe; when their oars kept time to the measured cadence of their song, and the blue, sunny bosom of the Ottawa opened before them; when their frail bark quivered among the milky foam and black rocks of the rapid; and when, around their camp-fire, they wasted half the night

with jests and laughter,—then the Canadian was in his element. His footsteps explored the farthest hiding-places of the
wilderness. In the evening dance, his red cap mingled with
the scalp-locks and feathers of the Indian braves; or, stretched
on a bear-skin by the side of his dusky mistress, he watched
the gambols of his hybrid offspring, in happy oblivion of the
partner whom he left unnumbered leagues behind.

The fur-trade engendered a peculiar class of restless bush-
rangers, more akin to Indians than to white men. Those who
had once felt the fascinations of the forest were unfitted ever
after for a life of quiet labor; and with this spirit the whole
colony was infected. From this cause, no less than from occasional wars with the English, and repeated attacks of the Iroquois, the agriculture of the country was sunk to a low ebb;
while feudal exactions, a ruinous system of monopoly, and
the intermeddlings of arbitrary power, cramped every branch
of industry.[1] Yet, by the zeal of priests and the daring enterprise of soldiers and explorers, Canada, though sapless and
infirm, spread forts and missions through all the western wilderness. Feebly rooted in the soil, she thrust out branches
which overshadowed half America; a magnificent object to
the eye, but one which the first whirlwind would prostrate in
the dust.

Such excursive enterprise was alien to the genius of the
British colonies. Daring activity was rife among them, but it
did not aim at the founding of military outposts and forest
missions. By the force of energetic industry, their population
swelled with an unheard-of rapidity, their wealth increased in
a yet greater ratio, and their promise of future greatness
opened with every advancing year. But it was a greatness
rather of peace than of war. The free institutions, the independence of authority, which were the source of their increase, were adverse to that unity of counsel and promptitude

[1]Raynal. *Hist. Indies*, VII. 87 (Lond. 1783).

Charlevoix, *Voyages, Letter* X.

The Swedish traveller Kalm gives an interesting account of manners in
Canada, about the middle of the eighteenth century. For the feudal tenure as
existing in Canada, see Bouchette, I. Chap. XIV. (Lond. 1831), and Garneau,
Hist. Canada, Book III. Chap. III.

of action which are the soul of war. It was far otherwise with their military rival. France had her Canadian forces well in hand. They had but one will, and that was the will of a mistress. Now here, now there, in sharp and rapid onset, they could assail the cumbrous masses and unwieldy strength of their antagonists, as the king-bird attacks the eagle, or the sword-fish the whale. Between two such combatants the strife must needs be a long one.

Canada was a true child of the Church, baptized in infancy and faithful to the last. Champlain, the founder of Quebec, a man of noble spirit, a statesman and a soldier, was deeply imbued with fervid piety. "The saving of a soul," he would often say, "is worth more than the conquest of an empire;"[1] and to forward the work of conversion, he brought with him four Franciscan monks from France. At a later period, the task of colonization would have been abandoned, but for the hope of casting the pure light of the faith over the gloomy wastes of heathendom.[2] All France was filled with the zeal of proselytism. Men and women of exalted rank lent their countenance to the holy work. From many an altar daily petitions were offered for the well-being of the mission; and in the Holy House of Mont-Martre, a nun lay prostrate day and night before the shrine, praying for the conversion of Canada.[3] In one convent, thirty nuns offered themselves for the labors of the wilderness; and priests flocked in crowds to the colony.[4] The powers of darkness took alarm; and when a ship, freighted with the apostles of the faith, was tempest-tost upon her voyage, the storm was ascribed to the malice of demons, trembling for the safety of their ancient empire.

The general enthusiasm was not without its fruits. The Church could pay back with usury all that she received of aid and encouragement from the temporal power; and the ambition of Richelieu could not have devised a more efficient enginery for the accomplishment of its schemes, than that

[1]Charlevoix, *Nouv. France*, I. 197.
[2]Charlevoix, I. 198.
[3]A. D. 1635. *Relation des Hurons*, 1636, p. 2.
[4]"Vivre en la Nouvelle France c'est à vray dire vivre dans le sein de Dieu." Such are the extravagant words of Le Jeune, in his report of the year 1635.

supplied by the zeal of the devoted propagandists. The priest and the soldier went hand in hand; and the cross and the *fleur de lis* were planted side by side.

Foremost among the envoys of the faith were the members of that mighty order, who, in another hemisphere, had already done so much to turn back the advancing tide of religious freedom, and strengthen the arm of Rome. To the Jesuits was assigned, for many years, the entire charge of the Canadian missions, to the exclusion of the Franciscans, early laborers in the same barren field. Inspired with a self-devoting zeal to snatch souls from perdition, and win new empires to the cross; casting from them every hope of earthly pleasure or earthly aggrandizement, the Jesuit fathers buried themselves in deserts, facing death with the courage of heroes, and enduring torments with the constancy of martyrs. Their story is replete with marvels—miracles of patient suffering and daring enterprise. They were the pioneers of Northern America.[1] We see them among the frozen forests of Acadia, struggling on snow-shoes, with some wandering Algonquin horde, or crouching in the crowded hunting-lodge, half stifled in the smoky den, and battling with troops of famished dogs for the last morsel of sustenance. Again we see the black-robed priest wading among the white rapids of the Ottawa, toiling with his savage comrades to drag the canoe against the headlong water. Again, radiant in the vestments of his priestly office, he administers the sacramental bread to kneeling crowds of plumed and painted proselytes in the forests of the Hurons; or, bearing his life in his hand, carries his sacred mission into the strongholds of the Iroquois, like one who invades unarmed a den of angry tigers. Jesuit explorers traced the St. Lawrence to its source, and said masses among the solitudes of Lake Superior, where the boldest fur-trader scarcely dared to follow. They planted missions at St. Mary's and at Michillimackinac; and one of their fraternity, the illustrious Marquette, discovered the Mississippi, and opened a new theatre to the boundless ambition of France.

The path of the missionary was a thorny and a bloody one;

---

[1] See Jesuit *Relations* and *Lettres Edifiantes*; also, Charlevoix, *passim*; Garneau, *Hist. Canada*, Book IV. Chap. II.; and Bancroft, *Hist. U. S.* Chap. XX.

and a life of weary apostleship was often crowned with a frightful martyrdom. Jean de Brebeuf and Gabriel Lallemant preached the faith among the villages of the Hurons, when their terror-stricken flock were overwhelmed by an irruption of the Iroquois. The missionaries might have fled; but, true to their sacred function, they remained behind to aid the wounded and baptize the dying. Both were made captive, and both were doomed to the fiery torture. Brebeuf, a veteran soldier of the cross, met his fate with an undaunted composure, which amazed his murderers. With unflinching constancy he endured torments too horrible to be recorded, and died calmly as a martyr of the early church, or a war-chief of the Mohawks.

The slender frame of Lallemant, a man younger in years and gentle in spirit, was enveloped in blazing savin-bark. Again and again the fire was extinguished; again and again it was kindled afresh; and with such fiendish ingenuity were his torments protracted, that he lingered for seventeen hours before death came to his relief.[1]

Isaac Jogues, taken captive by the Iroquois, was led from canton to canton, and village to village, enduring fresh torments and indignities at every stage of his progress.[2] Men, women, and children vied with each other in ingenious malignity. Redeemed, at length, by the humane exertions of a Dutch officer, he repaired to France, where his disfigured person and mutilated hands told the story of his sufferings. But the promptings of a sleepless conscience urged him to return and complete the work he had begun; to illumine the moral darkness upon which, during the months of his disastrous captivity, he fondly hoped that he had thrown some rays of light. Once more he bent his footsteps towards the scene of his living martyrdom, saddened with a deep presentiment that he was advancing to his death. Nor were his forebodings untrue. In a village of the Mohawks, the blow of a tomahawk closed his mission and his life.

Such intrepid self-devotion may well call forth our highest admiration; but when we seek for the results of these toils and

[1]Charlevoix, I. 292.
[2]*Ibid.* 238–276.

sacrifices, we shall seek in vain. Patience and zeal were thrown away upon lethargic minds and stubborn hearts. The reports of the Jesuits, it is true, display a copious list of conversions; but the zealous fathers reckoned the number of conversions by the number of baptisms; and, as Le Clercq observes, with no less truth than candor, an Indian would be baptized ten times a day for a pint of brandy or a pound of tobacco. Neither can more flattering conclusions be drawn from the alacrity which they showed to adorn their persons with crucifixes and medals. The glitter of the trinkets pleased the fancy of the warrior; and, with the emblem of man's salvation pendent from his neck, he was often at heart as thorough a heathen as when he wore in its place a necklace made of the dried forefingers of his enemies. At the present day, with the exception of a few insignificant bands of converted Indians in Lower Canada, not a vestige of early Jesuit influence can be found among the tribes. The seed was sown upon a rock.[1]

While the church was reaping but a scanty harvest, the labors of the missionaries were fruitful of profit to the monarch of France. The Jesuit led the van of French colonization; and at Detroit, Michillimackinac, St. Mary's, Green Bay, and other outposts of the west, the establishment of a mission was the precursor of military occupancy. In other respects no less, the labors of the wandering missionaries advanced the welfare of the colony. Sagacious and keen of sight, with faculties stimulated by zeal and sharpened by peril, they made faithful report of the temper and movements of the distant tribes among whom they were distributed. The influence which they often gained was exerted in behalf of the government under whose auspices their missions were carried on; and they strenuously labored to win over the tribes to the French alliance, and alienate them from the heretic English. In all things they approved themselves the stanch and steadfast auxiliaries of the imperial power; and the Marquis du Quesne observed of the missionary Picquet, that in his single person he was worth ten regiments.[2]

[1] For remarks on the futility of Jesuit missionary efforts, see Halkett, *Historical Notes*, Chap. IV.

[2] Picquet was a priest of St. Sulpice. For a sketch of his life, see *Lett. Edif.* XIV.

Among the English colonies, the pioneers of civilization were for the most part rude, yet vigorous men, impelled to enterprise by native restlessness, or lured by the hope of gain. Their range was limited, and seldom extended far beyond the outskirts of the settlements. With Canada it was far otherwise. There was no energy in the bulk of her people. The court and the army supplied the mainsprings of her vital action, and the hands which planted the lilies of France in the heart of the wilderness had never guided the ploughshare or wielded the spade. The love of adventure, the ambition of new discovery, the hope of military advancement, urged men of place and culture to embark on bold and comprehensive enterprise. Many a gallant gentleman, many a nobleman of France, trod the black mould and oozy mosses of the forest with feet that had pressed the carpets of Versailles. They whose youth had passed in camps and courts grew gray among the wigwams of savages; and the lives of Castine, Joncaire, and Priber[1] are invested with all the interest of romance.

Conspicuous in the annals of Canada stands the memorable name of Robert Cavelier de La Salle, the man who, beyond all his compeers, contributed to expand the boundary of French empire in the west. La Salle commanded at Fort Frontenac, erected near the outlet of Lake Ontario, on its northern shore, and then forming the most advanced military outpost of the colony. Here he dwelt among Indians, and half-breeds, traders, voyageurs, bush-rangers, and Franciscan monks, ruling his little empire with absolute sway, enforcing respect by his energy, but offending many by his rigor. Here he brooded upon the grand design which had long engaged his thoughts. He had resolved to complete the achievement of Father Marquette, to trace the unknown Mississippi to its mouth, to plant the standard of his king in the newly-discovered regions, and found colonies which should make good the sovereignty of France from the Frozen Ocean to Mexico. Ten years of his early life had passed, it is said, in connection with the Jesuits, and his strong mind had hardened to iron under

---

[1] For an account of Priber, see *Adair*, 240. I have seen mention of this man in contemporary provincial newspapers, where he is sometimes spoken of as a disguised Jesuit. He took up his residence among the Cherokees about the year 1736, and labored to gain them over to the French interest.

the discipline of that relentless school. To a sound judgment, and a penetrating sagacity, he joined a boundless enterprise and an adamantine constancy of purpose. But his nature was stern and austere; he was prone to rule by fear rather than by love; he took counsel of no man, and chilled all who approached him by his cold reserve.

At the close of the year 1678, his preparations were complete, and he despatched his attendants to the banks of the river Niagara, whither he soon followed in person. Here he began a little fort of palisades, and was the first military tenant of a spot destined to momentous consequence in future wars. Two leagues above the cataract, on the eastern bank of the river, he built the first vessel which ever explored the waters of the upper lakes.[1] Her name was the Griffin, and her burden was forty-five tons. On the seventh of August, 1679, she began her adventurous voyage amid the speechless wonder of the Indians, who stood amazed, alike at the unwonted size of the wooden canoe, at the flash and roar of the cannon from her decks, and at the carved figure of a griffin, which sat crouched upon her prow. She bore on her course along the virgin waters of Lake Erie, through the beautiful windings of the Detroit, and among the restless billows of Lake Huron, where a furious tempest had well nigh ingulphed her. La Salle pursued his voyage along Lake Michigan in birch canoes, and after protracted suffering from famine and exposure reached its southern extremity on the eighteenth of October.[2]

He led his followers to the banks of the river now called the St. Joseph. Here, again, he built a fort; and here, in after years, the Jesuits placed a mission and the government a garrison. Thence he pushed on into the unknown region of the Illinois; and now dangers and difficulties began to thicken about him. Indians threatened hostility; his men lost heart, clamored, grew mutinous, and repeatedly deserted; and worse than all, nothing was heard of the vessel which had been sent back to Canada for necessary supplies. Weeks wore on, and doubt ripened into certainty. She had foundered among the storms of these wilderness oceans; and her loss seemed to

[1] Sparks, *Life of La Salle*, 21.
[2] Hennepin, *New Discovery*, 98 (Lond. 1698.)

involve the ruin of the enterprise, since it was vain to proceed farther without the expected supplies. In this disastrous crisis, La Salle embraced a resolution characteristic of his intrepid temper. Leaving his men in charge of a subordinate at a fort which he had built on the river Illinois, he turned his face again towards Canada. He traversed on foot more than a thousand miles of frozen forest, crossing rivers, toiling through snow-drifts, wading ice-encumbered swamps, sustaining life by the fruits of the chase, and threatened day and night by lurking enemies. He gained his destination, but it was only to encounter a fresh storm of calamities. His enemies had been busy in his absence; a malicious report had gone abroad that he was dead; his creditors had seized his property; and the stores on which he most relied had been wrecked at sea, or lost among the rapids of the St. Lawrence. Still he battled against adversity with his wonted vigor, and in Count Frontenac, the governor of the province,—a spirit kindred to his own,—he found a firm friend. Every difficulty gave way before him; and with fresh supplies of men, stores, and ammunition, he again embarked for the Illinois. Rounding the vast circuit of the lakes, he reached the mouth of the St. Joseph, and hastened with anxious speed to the fort where he had left his followers. The place was empty. Not a man remained. Terrified, despondent, mutinous, and embroiled in Indian wars, they had fled to seek peace and safety, he knew not whither.

Once more the dauntless discoverer turned back towards Canada. Once more he stood before Count Frontenac, and once more bent all his resources and all his credit to gain means for the prosecution of his enterprise. He succeeded. With his little flotilla of canoes, he left his fort, at the outlet of Lake Ontario, and slowly retraced those interminable waters, and lines of forest-bounded shore, which had grown drearily familiar to his eyes. Fate at length seemed tired of the conflict with so stubborn an adversary. All went prosperously with the voyagers. They passed the lakes in safety, crossed the rough portage to the waters of the Illinois, followed its winding channel, and descended the turbid eddies of the Mississippi, received with various welcome by the scattered tribes who dwelt along its banks. Now the waters grew bitter to the taste; now the trampling of the surf was heard; and now the broad ocean opened upon their sight, and their goal was won. On the ninth of April, 1682, with his followers under arms, amid the firing of musketry, the chanting of the *Te Deum*, and shouts of "Vive le roi," La Salle took formal possession of the vast valley of the Mississippi, in the name of Louis the Great, King of France and Navarre.[1]

The first stage of his enterprise was accomplished, but labors no less arduous remained behind. Repairing to the court of France, he was welcomed with richly merited favor, and soon set sail for the mouth of the Mississippi, with a squadron of vessels freighted with men and material for the projected colony. But the folly and obstinacy of a jealous naval commander blighted his fairest hopes. The squadron missed the mouth of the river; and the wreck of one of the vessels, and the desertion of the commander, completed the ruin of the expedition. La Salle landed with a band of half-famished followers on the coast of Texas; and, while he was toiling with untired energy for their relief, a few vindictive miscreants conspired against him, and a shot from a traitor's musket closed the career of the iron-hearted discoverer.

It was left with another to complete the enterprise on which he had staked his life; and, in the year 1699, Lemoine d'Iberville planted the germ whence sprang the colony of Louisiana.[2]

Years passed on. In spite of a vicious plan of government, in spite of the bursting of the memorable Mississippi bubble, the new colony grew in wealth and strength. And now it remained for France to unite the two extremities of her broad American domain, to extend forts and settlements across the fertile solitudes between the valley of the St. Lawrence and the mouth of the Mississippi, and intrench herself among the forests which lie west of the Alleghanies, before the swelling tide of British colonization could overflow those mountain barriers. At the middle of the eighteenth century, her great project was fast advancing towards completion. The lakes and streams, the thoroughfares of the wilderness, were seized and

---

[1] *Procès Verbal*, in appendix to Sparks's *La Salle*.
[2] Du Pratz, *Hist. Louisiana*, 5. Charlevoix, II. 259.

guarded by a series of posts distributed with admirable skill. A fort on the strait of Niagara commanded the great entrance to the whole interior country. Another at Detroit controlled the passage from Lake Erie to the north. Another at St. Mary's debarred all hostile access to Lake Superior. Another at Michillimackinac secured the mouth of Lake Michigan. A post at Green Bay, and one at St. Joseph, guarded the two routes to the Mississippi, by way of the rivers Wisconsin and Illinois; while two posts on the Wabash, and one on the Maumee, made France the mistress of the great trading highway from Lake Erie to the Ohio. At Kaskaskia, Cahokia, and elsewhere in the Illinois, little French settlements had sprung up; and as the canoe of the voyager descended the Mississippi, he saw, at rare intervals, along its swampy margin, a few small stockade forts, half buried amid the redundancy of forest vegetation, until, as he approached Natchez, the dwellings of the *habitans* of Louisiana began to appear.

The forest posts of France were not exclusively of a military character. Adjacent to most of them, one would have found a little cluster of Canadian dwellings, whose tenants lived under the protection of the garrison, and obeyed the arbitrary will of the commandant; an authority which, however, was seldom exerted in a despotic spirit. In these detached settlements, there was no principle of increase. The character of the people, and of the government which ruled them, were alike unfavorable to it. Agriculture was neglected for the more congenial pursuits of the fur-trade, and the restless, roving Canadians, scattered abroad on their wild vocation, allied themselves to Indian women, and filled the woods with a mongrel race of bush-rangers.

Thus far secure in the west, France next essayed to gain foothold upon the sources of the Ohio; and about the year 1748, the sagacious Count Galissonnière proposed to bring over ten thousand peasants from France, and plant them in the valley of that beautiful river, and on the borders of the lakes.[1] But while at Quebec, in the Castle of St. Louis, soldiers and statesmen were revolving schemes like this, the slowly-moving power of England bore on with silent progress

[1] Smith, *Hist. Canada*, I. 208.

from the east. Already the British settlements were creeping along the valley of the Mohawk, and ascending the eastern slopes of the Alleghanies. Forests crashing to the axe, dark spires of smoke ascending from autumnal fires, were heralds of the advancing host; and while, on one side of the mountains, Celeron de Bienville was burying plates of lead, engraved with the arms of France, the ploughs and axes of Virginian woodsmen were enforcing a surer title on the other. The adverse powers were drawing near. The hour of collision was at hand.

Chapter III.

1608–1763.

THE FRENCH, THE ENGLISH, AND THE INDIANS.

THE FRENCH COLONISTS of Canada held, from the beginning, a peculiar intimacy of relation with the Indian tribes. With the English colonists it was far otherwise; and the difference sprang from several causes. The fur-trade was the life of Canada; agriculture and commerce were the chief sources of wealth to the British provinces. The Romish zealots of Canada burned for the conversion of the heathen; their heretic rivals were fired with no such ardor. And finally while the ambition of France grasped at empire over the farthest deserts of the west, the steady industry of the English colonists was contented to cultivate and improve a narrow strip of seaboard. Thus it happened that the farmer of Massachusetts and the Virginian planter were conversant with only a few bordering tribes, while the priests and emissaries of France were roaming the prairies with the buffalo-hunting Pawnees, or lodging in the winter cabins of the Dahcotah; and swarms of savages, whose uncouth names were strange to English ears, descended yearly from the north, to bring their beaver and otter skins to the market of Montreal.

The position of Canada invited intercourse with the interior, and eminently favored her schemes of commerce and policy. The river St. Lawrence, and the chain of the great lakes, opened a vast extent of inland navigation; while their tributary streams, interlocking with the branches of the Mississippi, afforded ready access to that mighty river, and gave the restless voyager free range over half the continent. But these advantages were well nigh neutralized. Nature opened the way, but a watchful and terrible enemy guarded the portal. The forests south of Lake Ontario gave harborage to the five tribes of the Iroquois, implacable foes of Canada. They waylaid her trading parties, routed her soldiers, murdered her missionaries, and spread havoc and woe through all her settlements.

It was an evil hour for Canada, when, on the twenty-eighth of May, 1609,[1] Samuel de Champlain, impelled by his own adventurous spirit, departed from the hamlet of Quebec to follow a war-party of Algonquins against their hated enemy, the Iroquois. Ascending the Sorel, and passing the rapids at Chambly, he embarked on the lake which bears his name, and with two French attendants, steered southward, with his savage associates, toward the rocky promontory of Ticonderoga. They moved with all the precaution of Indian warfare; when, at length, as night was closing in, they descried a band of the Iroquois in their large canoes of elm bark approaching through the gloom. Wild yells from either side announced the mutual discovery. The Iroquois hastened to the shore, and all night long the forest resounded with their discordant war-songs and fierce whoops of defiance. Day dawned, and the fight began. Bounding from tree to tree, the Iroquois pressed forward to the attack; but when Champlain advanced from among the Algonquins, and stood full in sight before them, with his strange attire, his shining breastplate, and features unlike their own,—when they saw the flash of his arquebuse, and beheld two of their chiefs fall dead,—they could not contain their terror, but fled for shelter into the depths of the wood. The Algonquins pursued, slaying many in the flight, and the victory was complete.

Such was the first collision between the white men and the Iroquois; and Champlain flattered himself that the latter had learned for the future to respect the arms of France. He was fatally deceived. The Iroquois recovered from their terrors, but they never forgave the injury; and yet it would be unjust to charge upon Champlain the origin of the desolating wars which were soon to scourge the colony. The Indians of Canada, friends and neighbors of the French, had long been harassed by inroads of the fierce confederates, and under any circumstances the French must soon have become parties to the quarrel.

Whatever may have been its origin, the war was fruitful of misery to the youthful colony. The passes were beset by ambushed war-parties. The routes between Quebec and

[1] Champlain, *Voyages*, 136 (Paris, 1632). Charlevoix, I. 142.

Montreal were watched with tiger-like vigilance. Bloodthirsty warriors prowled about the outskirts of the settlements. Again and again the miserable people, driven within the palisades of their forts, looked forth upon wasted harvests and blazing roofs. The Island of Montreal was swept with fire and steel. The fur-trade was interrupted, since for months together all communication was cut off with the friendly tribes of the west. Agriculture was checked; the fields lay fallow, and frequent famine was the necessary result.[1] The name of the Iroquois became a by-word of horror through the colony, and to the suffering Canadians they seemed troops of incarnate fiends. Revolting rites and monstrous superstitions were imputed to them; and, among the rest, it was currently believed that they cherished the custom of immolating young children, burning them, and drinking the ashes mixed with water to increase their bravery.[2] Yet the wildest imaginations could scarcely exceed the truth. At the attack of Montreal, they placed infants over the embers, and forced the wretched mothers to turn the spit;[3] and those who fell within their clutches endured torments too hideous for description. Their ferocity was equalled only by their courage and address.

At intervals, the afflicted colony found respite from its sufferings; and, through the efforts of the Jesuits, fair hopes began to rise of propitiating the terrible foe. At one time, the influence of the priests availed so far, that under their auspices a French colony was formed in the very heart of the Iroquois country; but the settlers were soon forced to a precipitate flight, and the war broke out afresh.[4] The French, on their part, were not idle; they faced their assailants with characteristic gallantry. Courcelles, Tracy, De la Barre, and De Nonville invaded by turns, with various success, the forest haunts of the confederates; and at length, in the year 1696, the veteran Count Frontenac marched upon their cantons with all the force of Canada. Stemming the surges of La Chine, gliding through the romantic channels of the Thousand Islands, and over the glimmering surface of Lake Ontario, and trailing

[1] Vimont, Colden, Charlevoix, *passim*.
[2] Vimont seems to believe the story.—*Rel. de la N. F.* 1640, 195.
[3] Charlevoix, I. 549.
[4] A. D. 1654–1658.—*Doc. Hist. N. Y.* I. 47.

in long array up the current of the Oswego, they disembarked on the margin of the Lake of Onondaga; and, startling the woodland echoes with the clangor of their trumpets, urged their march through the mazes of the forest. Never had those solitudes beheld so strange a pageantry. The Indian allies, naked to the waist and horribly painted, adorned with streaming scalp-locks and fluttering plumes, stole crouching among the thickets, or peered with lynx-eyed vision through the labyrinths of foliage. Scouts and forest-rangers scoured the woods in front and flank of the marching columns—men trained among the hardships of the fur-trade, thin, sinewy, and strong, arrayed in wild costume of beaded moccason, scarlet leggin, and frock of buck-skin, fantastically garnished with many-colored embroidery of porcupine. Then came the levies of the colony, in gray capotes and gaudy sashes, and the trained battalions from old France in cuirass and head-piece, veterans of European wars. Plumed cavaliers were there, who had followed the standards of Condé or Turenne, and who, even in the depths of a wilderness, scorned to lay aside the martial foppery which bedecked the camp and court of Louis the Magnificent. The stern commander was borne along upon a litter in the midst, his locks bleached with years, but his eye kindling with the quenchless fire which, like a furnace, burned hottest when its fuel was almost spent. Thus, beneath the sepulchral arches of the forest, through tangled thickets, and over prostrate trunks, the aged nobleman advanced to wreak his vengeance upon empty wigwams and deserted maize-fields.[1]

Even the fierce courage of the Iroquois began to quail before these repeated attacks, while the gradual growth of the colony, and the arrival of troops from France, at length convinced them that they could not destroy Canada. With the opening of the eighteenth century, their rancor showed signs of abating; and in the year 1726, by dint of skilful intrigue, the French succeeded in establishing a permanent military post at the important pass of Niagara, within the limits of the confederacy.[2] Meanwhile, in spite of every obstacle, the power of France had rapidly extended its boundaries in the

[1] Official Papers of the Expedition.—*Doc. Hist. N. Y.* I. 323.
[2] *Doc. Hist. N. Y.* I. 446.

west. French influence diffused itself through a thousand channels, among distant tribes, hostile, for the most part, to the domineering Iroquois. Forts, mission-houses, and armed trading stations secured the principal passes. Traders, and *coureurs de bois* pushed their adventurous traffic into the wildest deserts; and French guns and hatchets, French beads and cloth, French tobacco and brandy, were known from where the stunted Esquimaux burrowed in their snow caves, to where the Camanches scoured the plains of the south with their banditti cavalry. Still this far-extended commerce continued to advance westward. In 1738, La Verandrye essayed to reach those mysterious mountains which, as the Indians alleged, lay beyond the arid deserts of the Missouri and the Saskatchawan. Indian hostility defeated his enterprise, but not before he had struck far out into these unknown wilds, and formed a line of trading posts, one of which, Fort de la Reine, was planted on the Assinniboin, a hundred leagues beyond Lake Winnipeg. At that early period, France left her footsteps upon the dreary wastes which even now have no other tenants than the Indian buffalo-hunter or the roving trapper.

The fur-trade of the English colonists opposed but feeble rivalry to that of their hereditary foes. At an early period, favored by the friendship of the Iroquois, they attempted to open a traffic with the Algonquin tribes of the great lakes; and in the year 1687, Major McGregory ascended with a boat load of goods to Lake Huron, where his appearance excited great commotion, and where he was seized and imprisoned by the French.[1] From this time forward, the English fur-trade languished, until the year 1725, when Governor Burnet, of New York, established a post on Lake Ontario, at the mouth of the river Oswego; whither, lured by the cheapness and excellence of the English goods, crowds of savages soon congregated from every side, to the unspeakable annoyance of the French.[2] Meanwhile, a considerable commerce was springing up with the Cherokees and other tribes of the south; and during the first half of the century, the people of Pennsylvania

[1] La Hontan, *Voyages*, I. 74. Colden, *Memorial on the Fur-Trade*.
[2] *Doc. Hist. N. Y*. I. 444.

began to cross the Alleghanies, and carry on a lucrative traffic with the tribes of the Ohio. In 1749, La Jonquière, the Governor of Canada, learned, to his great indignation, that several English traders had reached Sandusky, and were exerting a bad influence upon the Indians of that quarter;[1] and two years later, he caused four of the intruders to be seized near the Ohio, and sent prisoners to Canada.[2]

These early efforts of the English, considerable as they were, can ill bear comparison with the vast extent of the French interior commerce. In respect also to missionary enterprise, and the political influence resulting from it, the French had every advantage over rivals whose zeal for conversion was neither kindled by fanaticism nor fostered by an ambitious government. Eliot labored within call of Boston, while the heroic Brebeuf faced the ghastly perils of the western wilderness; and the wanderings of Brainerd sink into insignificance compared with those of the devoted Rasles. Yet, in judging the relative merits of the Romish and Protestant missionaries, it must not be forgotten that while the former contented themselves with sprinkling a few drops of water on the forehead of the proselyte, the latter sought to wean him from his barbarism and penetrate his savage heart with the truths of Christianity.

In respect, also, to direct political influence, the advantage was wholly on the side of France. The English colonies, broken into separate governments, were incapable of exercising a vigorous and consistent Indian policy; and the measures of one government often clashed with those of another. Even in the separate provinces, the popular nature of the constitution and the quarrels of governors and assemblies were unfavorable to efficient action; and this was more especially the case in the province of New York, where the vicinity of the Iroquois rendered strenuous yet prudent measures of the utmost importance. The powerful confederates, hating the French with bitter enmity, naturally inclined to the English alliance; and a proper treatment would have secured their firm and lasting friendship. But, at the early periods of her history, the

[1] Smith, *Hist. Canada*, I. 214.
[2] *Précis des Faits*, 89.

assembly of New York was made up in great measure of narrow-minded men, more eager to consult their own petty interests than to pursue any far-sighted scheme of public welfare.[1] Other causes conspired to injure the British interest in this quarter. The annual present sent from England to the Iroquois was often embezzled by corrupt governors or their favorites.[2] The proud chiefs were disgusted by the cold and haughty bearing of the English officials, and a pernicious custom prevailed of conducting Indian negotiations through the medium of the fur-traders, a class of men held in contempt by the Iroquois, and known among them by the significant title of "rum carriers."[3] In short, through all the counsels of the province Indian affairs were grossly and madly neglected.[4]

With more or less emphasis, the same remark holds true of all the other English colonies.[5] With those of France, it was far otherwise; and this difference between the rival powers was naturally incident to their different forms of government, and different conditions of development. France labored with eager diligence to conciliate the Indians and win them to espouse her cause. Her agents were busy in every village, studying the language of the inmates, complying with their usages, flattering their prejudices, caressing them, cajoling them, and whispering friendly warnings in their ears against the wicked designs of the English. When a party of Indian chiefs visited a French fort, they were greeted with the firing of cannon and

[1] Smith, *Hist. N. Y. passim.*

[2] *Rev. Military Operations, Mass. Hist. Coll. 1st Series*, VII. 67.

[3] Colden, *Hist. Five Nat.* 161.

[4] *MS. Papers of Cadwallader Colden. MS. Papers of Sir William Johnson.*

"We find the Indians, as far back as the very confused manuscript records in my possession, repeatedly upbraiding this province for their negligence, their avarice, and their want of assisting them at a time when it was certainly in their power to destroy the infant colony of Canada, although supported by many nations; and this is likewise confessed by the writings of the managers of these times."—*MS. Letter—Johnson to the Board of Trade, May 24, 1765.*

[5] "I apprehend it will clearly appear to you, that the colonies had all along neglected to cultivate a proper understanding with the Indians, and from a mistaken notion have greatly despised them, without considering that it is in their power to lay waste and destroy the frontiers. This opinion arose from our confidence in our scattered numbers, and the parsimony of our people, who, from an error in politics, would not expend five pounds to save twenty."—*MS. Letter—Johnson to the Board of Trade, November 13, 1763.*

rolling of drums; they were regaled at the tables of the officers, and bribed with medals and decorations, scarlet uniforms and French flags. Far wiser than their rivals, the French never ruffled the self-complacent dignity of their guests, never insulted their religious notions, nor ridiculed their ancient customs. They met the savage half way, and showed an abundant readiness to mould their own features after his likeness.[1] Count Frontenac himself, plumed and painted like an Indian chief, danced the war-dance and yelled the war-song at the camp fires of his delighted allies. It would have been well had the French been less exact in their imitations, for at times they copied their model with infamous fidelity, and fell into excesses scarcely credible but for the concurrent testimony of their own writers. Frontenac caused an Iroquois prisoner to be burnt alive to strike terror into his countrymen; and Louvigny, French commandant at Michillimackinac, in 1695, tortured an Iroquois ambassador to death, that he might break off a negotiation between that people and the Wyandots.[2] Nor are these the only well-attested instances of such execrable inhumanity. But if the French were guilty of these cruelties against their Indian enemies, they were no less guilty of unworthy compliance with the demands of their Indian friends, in cases where Christianity and civilization would have dictated a prompt refusal. Even Montcalm stained his bright name by abandoning the hapless defenders of Oswego and William Henry to the tender mercies of an Indian mob.

In general, however, the Indian policy of the French cannot be charged with obsequiousness. Complaisance was tempered with dignity. At an early period, they discerned the peculiarities of the native character, and clearly saw that while on the one hand it was necessary to avoid giving offence, it was not less necessary on the other to assume a bold demeanor and a show of power; to caress with one hand, and grasp a drawn

---

[1] Adair, *Post's Journals*. Croghan's *Journal*, MSS. of Sir W. Johnson, etc., etc.
[2] La Hontan, I. 177. Potherie, *Hist. Am. Sept.* II. 298 (Paris, 1722).

These facts afford no ground for national reflections, when it is recollected that while Iroquois prisoners were tortured in the wilds of Canada, Elizabeth Gaunt was burned to death at Tyburn for yielding to the dictates of compassion, and giving shelter to a political offender.

sword with the other.[1] Every crime against a Frenchman was promptly chastised by the sharp agency of military law; while among the English, the offender could only be reached through the medium of the civil courts, whose delays, uncertainties and evasions excited the wonder and provoked the contempt of the Indians.

It was by observance of the course indicated above, that the French were enabled to maintain themselves in small detached posts, far aloof from the parent colony, and environed by barbarous tribes where an English garrison would have been cut off in a twelvemonth. They professed to hold these posts, not in their own right, but purely through the grace and condescension of the surrounding savages; and by this conciliating assurance they sought to make good their position, until, with their growing strength, conciliation should no more be needed.

In its efforts to win the friendship and alliance of the Indian tribes, the French government found every advantage in the peculiar character of its subjects—that pliant and plastic temper which forms so marked a contrast to the stubborn spirit of the Englishman. From the beginning, the French showed a tendency to amalgamate with the forest tribes. "The manners of the savages," writes the Baron La Hontan, "are perfectly agreeable to my palate;" and many a restless adventurer of high or low degree might have echoed the words of the erratic soldier. At first, great hopes were entertained that, by the mingling of French and Indians, the latter would be won over to civilization and the church; but the effect was precisely the reverse; for, as Charlevoix observes, the savages did not become French, but the French became savages. Hundreds betook themselves to the forest, never more to return. These outflowings of French civilization were merged in the waste of barbarism, as a river is lost in the sands of the desert. The wandering Frenchman chose a wife or a concubine among his Indian friends; and, in a few generations, scarcely a tribe of the west was free from an infusion of Celtic blood. The French empire in America could exhibit among its

[1] Le Jeune, *Rel. de la N. F.* 1636, 193.

subjects every shade of color from white to red, every grada-
tion of culture from the highest civilization of Paris to the
rudest barbarism of the wigwam.

The fur-trade engendered a peculiar class of men, known by
the appropriate name of bush-rangers, or *coureurs de bois*, half-
civilized vagrants, whose chief vocation was conducting the
canoes of the traders along the lakes and rivers of the interior;
many of them, however, shaking loose every tie of blood and
kindred, identified themselves with the Indians, and sank into
utter barbarism. In many a squalid camp among the plains
and forests of the west, the traveller would have encountered
men owning the blood and speaking the language of France,
yet, in their swarthy visages and barbarous costume, seeming
more akin to those with whom they had cast their lot. The
renegade of civilization caught the habits and imbibed the
prejudices of his chosen associates. He loved to decorate his
long hair with eagle feathers, to make his face hideous with
vermilion, ochre, and soot, and to adorn his greasy hunting
frock with horse-hair fringes. His dwelling, if he had one, was
a wigwam. He lounged on a bear-skin while his squaw boiled
his venison and lighted his pipe. In hunting, in dancing, in
singing, in taking a scalp, he rivalled the genuine Indian. His
mind was tinctured with the superstitions of the forest. He
had faith in the magic drum of the conjuror; he was not sure
that a thunder cloud could not be frightened away by whistling at it through the wing bone of an eagle; he carried the
tail of a rattlesnake in his bullet pouch by way of amulet; and
he placed implicit trust in his dreams. This class of men is not
yet extinct. In the cheerless wilds beyond the northern lakes,
or among the mountain solitudes of the distant west, they
may still be found, unchanged in life and character since the
day when Louis the Great claimed sovereignty over this
desert empire.

The borders of the English colonies displayed no such phenomena of mingling races; for here a thorny and impracticable barrier divided the white man from the red. The English
fur-traders, and the rude men in their employ, showed it is
true an ample alacrity to fling off the restraints of civilization;
but though they became barbarians, they did not become Indians; and scorn on the one side and hatred on the other still

marked the intercourse of the hostile races. With the settlers of the frontier it was much the same. Rude, fierce and contemptuous, they daily encroached upon the hunting-grounds of the Indians, and then paid them for the injury with curses and threats. Thus the native population shrank back from before the English, as from before an advancing pestilence; while, on the other hand, in the very heart of Canada, Indian communities sprang up, cherished by the government, and favored by the easy-tempered people. At Lorette, at Caughnawaga, at St. Francis, and elsewhere within the province, large bands were gathered together, consisting in part of fugitives from the borders of the hated English, and aiding in time of war to swell the forces of the French in repeated forays against the settlements of New York and New England.

There was one of the English provinces marked out from among the rest by the peculiar character of its founders, and by the course of conduct which was there pursued towards the Indian tribes. William Penn, his mind warmed with a broad philanthropy, and enlightened by liberal views of human government and human rights, planted on the banks of the Delaware the colony which, vivified by the principles it embodied, grew into the great commonwealth of Pennsylvania. Penn's treatment of the Indians was equally prudent and humane, and its results were of high advantage to the colony; but these results have been exaggerated, and the treatment which produced them made the theme of inordinate praise. It required no great benevolence to urge the Quakers to deal kindly with their savage neighbors. They were bound in common sense to propitiate them; since, by incurring their resentment, they would involve themselves in the dilemma of submitting their necks to the tomahawk, or wielding the carnal weapon, in glaring defiance of their pacific principles. In paying the Indians for the lands which his colonists occupied,—a piece of justice which has been greeted with a general clamor of applause,—Penn, as he himself confesses, acted on the prudent counsel of Compton, Bishop of London.[1] Nor is there any truth in the representations of Raynal and

[1] "I have exactly followed the Bishop of London's counsel, by buying, and not taking away, the natives' land."—*Penn's Letter to the Ministry, Aug. 14, 1683.* See Chalmer's *Polit. Ann.* 666.

other eulogists of the Quaker legislator, who hold him up to the world as the only European who ever acquired Indian lands by purchase, instead of seizing them by fraud or violence. The example of purchase had been set fifty years before by the Puritans of New England; and several of the other colonies had more recently pursued the same just and prudent course.[1]

With regard to the alleged results of the pacific conduct of the Quakers, our admiration will diminish on closely viewing the circumstances of the case. The position of the colony was a most fortunate one. Had the Quakers planted their colony on the banks of the St. Lawrence, or among the warlike tribes of New England, their shaking of hands and assurances of tender regard would not long have availed to save them from the visitations of the scalping-knife. But the Delawares, the people on whose territory they had settled, were like themselves debarred the use of arms. The Iroquois had conquered them, disarmed them, and forced them to adopt the opprobrious name of *women*. The humble Delawares were but too happy to receive the hand extended to them, and dwell in friendship with their pacific neighbors; since to have lifted the hatchet would have brought upon their heads the vengeance of their conquerors, whose good will Penn had taken pains to secure.[2]

The sons of Penn, his successors in the proprietorship of the province, did not evince the same kindly feeling towards the Indians which had distinguished their father. Earnest to acquire new lands, they commenced through their agents a series of unjust measures, which gradually alienated the Indians, and, after a peace of seventy years, produced a disastrous rupture. The Quaker population of the colony sympathized in the kindness which its founder had cherished towards

[1]"If any of the salvages pretend right of inheritance to all or any part of the lands granted in our patent, we pray you endeavor to purchase their tytle, that we may avoid the least scruple of intrusion."—*Instructions to Endicot*, 1629. See Hazard, *State Papers*, I. 263.

"The inhabitants of New England had never, except in the territory of the Pequods, taken possession of a foot of land without first obtaining a title from the Indians."—Bancroft, *Hist. U. S.* II. 98.

[2]He paid twice for his lands; once to the Iroquois, who claimed them by right of conquest, and once to their occupants, the Delawares.

the benighted race. This feeling was strengthened by years of friendly intercourse; and except where private interest was concerned, the Quakers made good their reiterated professions of attachment. Kindness to the Indian was the glory of their sect. As years wore on, this feeling was wonderfully reënforced by the influence of party spirit. The time arrived when, alienated by English encroachment on the one hand and French seduction on the other, the Indians began to assume a threatening attitude towards the province; and many voices urged the necessity of a resort to arms. This measure, repugnant alike to their pacific principles and to their love of the Indians, was strenuously opposed by the Quakers. Their affection for the injured race was now inflamed into a sort of benevolent fanaticism. The more rabid of the sect would scarcely confess that an Indian could ever do wrong. In their view, he was always sinned against, always the innocent victim of injury and abuse; and in the days of the final rupture, when the woods were full of furious war-parties, and the German and Irish settlers on the frontier were butchered by hundreds; when the western sky was darkened with the smoke of burning settlements, and the wretched fugitives were flying in crowds across the Susquehanna, a large party among the Quaker, secure by their Philadelphia firesides, could not see the necessity of waging even a defensive war against their favorite people.[1]

The encroachments on the part of the proprietors, which have been alluded to above, and which many of the Quakers viewed with disapproval, consisted in the fraudulent interpretation of Indian deeds of conveyance, and in the granting out of lands without any conveyance at all. The most notorious of these transactions, and the one most lamentable in its results, was commenced in the year 1737, and was known by the name of the *walking purchase*. An old, forgotten deed was raked out

---

[1]1755–1763. The feelings of the Quakers at this time may be gathered from the following sources: MS. *Account of the Rise and Progress of the Friendly Association for gaining and preserving Peace with the Indians by pacific Measures. Address of the Friendly Association to Governor Denny*. See Proud, *Hist. Pa., appendix*. Haz., *Pa. Reg*. VIII. 273, 293, 323. But a much livelier picture of the prevailing excitement will be found in a series of party pamphlets, published at Philadelphia in the year 1764.

of the dust of the previous century; a deed which was in itself of doubtful validity, and which had been virtually cancelled by a subsequent agreement. On this rotten title the proprietors laid claim to a valuable tract of land on the right bank of the Delaware. Its western boundary was to be defined by a line drawn from a certain point on Neshaminey Creek, in a north-westerly direction, as far as a man could walk in a day and a half. From the end of the walk, a line drawn eastward to the river Delaware was to form the northern limit of the purchase. The proprietors sought out the most active men who could be heard of, and put them in training for the walk; at the same time laying out a smooth road along the intended course, that no obstructions might mar their speed. By this means an incredible distance was accomplished within the limited time. And now it only remained to adjust the northern boundary. Instead of running the line directly to the Delaware, according to the evident meaning of the deed, the proprietors inclined it so far to the north as to form an acute angle with the river, and enclose many hundred thousand acres of valuable land, which would otherwise have remained in the hands of the Indians.[1] The land thus obtained lay in the Forks of the Delaware, above Easton, and was then occupied by a powerful branch of the Delawares, who, to their amazement, now heard the summons to quit for ever their populous village and fields of half-grown maize. In rage and distress they refused to obey, and the proprietors were in a perplexing dilemma. Force was necessary; but a Quaker legislature would never consent to fight, and especially to fight against Indians. An expedient was hit upon, at once safe and effectual. The Iroquois were sent for. A deputation of their chiefs appeared at Philadelphia, and having been well bribed, and deceived by

[1] *Causes of the Alienation of the Delaware and Shawanoe Indians from the British Interest*, 33, 68, (Lond. 1759). This work is a pamphlet written by Charles Thompson, afterwards secretary of Congress, and designed to explain the causes of the rupture which took place at the outbreak of the French war. The text is supported by copious references to treaties and documents. I have seen a copy in the possession of Francis Fisher, Esq., of Philadelphia, containing marginal notes in the handwriting of James Hamilton, who was twice governor of the province under the proprietary instructions. In these notes, though he cavils at several unimportant points of the relation, he suffers the essential matter to pass unchallenged.

false accounts of the transaction, they consented to remove the refractory Delawares. The delinquents were summoned before their conquerors, and the Iroquois orator, Canassatego, a man of tall stature and imposing presence,[1] looking with a grim countenance on his cowering auditors, addressed them in the following words:—

"You ought to be taken by the hair of the head and shaken soundly till you recover your senses. You don't know what you are doing. Our brother Onas's[2] cause is very just. On the other hand, your cause is bad, and you are bent to break the chain of friendship. How came you to take upon you to sell land at all? We conquered you; we made women of you; you know you are women, and can no more sell land than women. This land you claim is gone down your throats; you have been furnished with clothes, meat, and drink, by the goods paid you for it, and now you want it again, like children as you are. What makes you sell land in the dark? Did you ever tell us you had sold this land? Did we ever receive any part, even the value of a pipe-shank, from you for it? We charge you to remove instantly; we don't give you the liberty to think about it. You are women. Take the advice of a wise man and remove immediately. You may return to the other side of Delaware, where you came from; but we do not know whether, considering how you have demeaned yourselves, you will be permitted to live there; or whether you have not swallowed that land down your throats as well as the land on this side. We therefore assign you two places to go, either to Wyoming or Shamokin. We shall then have you more under our eye, and shall see how you behave. Don't deliberate, but take this belt of wampum, and go at once."[3]

The unhappy Delawares dared not disobey. They left their ancient homes, and removed, as they had been ordered, to the Susquehanna, where some settled at Shamokin, and some at Wyoming.[4] From an early period, the Indians had been annoyed by the unlicensed intrusion of settlers upon their lands,

[1] *Witham Marshe's Journal.*

[2] Onas was the name given by the Indians to William Penn and his successors.

[3] *Minutes of Indian council held at Philadelphia*, 1742.

[4] Chapman, *Hist. Wyoming*, 19.

and, in 1728, they had bitterly complained of the wrong.[1] The evil continued to increase. Many families, chiefly German and Irish, began to cross the Susquehanna and build their cabins along the valleys of the Juniata and its tributary waters. The Delawares sent frequent remonstrances from their new abodes, and the Iroquois themselves made angry complaints, declaring that the lands of the Juniata were theirs by right of conquest, and that they had given them to their cousins, the Delawares, for hunting-grounds. Some efforts at redress were made; but the remedy proved ineffectual, and the discontent of the Indians increased with every year. The Shawanoes, with many of the Delawares, removed westward, where for a time they would be safe from intrusion; and by the middle of the century, the Delaware tribe was separated into two divisions, one of which remained upon the Susquehanna, while the other, in conjunction with the Shawanoes, dwelt on the waters of the Alleghany and the Muskingum.

But now the French began to push their advanced posts into the valley of the Ohio. Unhappily for the English interest, they found the irritated minds of the Indians in a state which favored their efforts at seduction, and held forth a flattering promise that tribes so long faithful to the English might soon be won over to the cause of France.

While the English interests wore so inauspicious an aspect in this quarter, their prospects were not much better among the Iroquois. Since the peace of Utrecht, in 1713, these powerful tribes had so far forgotten their old malevolence against the French, that the latter were enabled to bring all their machinery of conciliation to bear upon them. They turned the opportunity to such good account, as not only to smooth away the asperity of the ancient grudge, but also to rouse in the minds of their former foes a growing jealousy against the English. Several accidental circumstances did much to aggravate this feeling. The Iroquois were in the habit of sending out frequent war-parties against their enemies, the Cherokees and Catawbas, who dwelt near the borders of Carolina and Virginia; and in these forays the invaders often became so

---

[1] *Colonial Records*, III. 340.

seriously embroiled with the white settlers, that sharp frays took place, and an open war seemed likely to ensue.[1]

It was with great difficulty that the irritation caused by these untoward accidents was allayed; and even then enough remained in the neglect of governments, the insults of traders, and the haughty bearing of officials, to disgust the proud confederates with their English allies. In the war of 1745, they yielded but cold and doubtful aid; and fears were entertained of their final estrangement.[2] This result became still more imminent, when, in the year 1749, the French priest Picquet established his mission of La Présentation on the St. Lawrence, at the site of Ogdensburg.[3] This pious father, like the martial churchmen of an earlier day, deemed it no scandal to gird on earthly armor against the enemies of the faith. He built a fort and founded a settlement; he mustered the Indians about him from far and near, organized their governments, and marshalled their war-parties. From the crenelled walls of his mission-house the warlike apostle could look forth upon a military colony of his own creating, upon farms and clearings, white Canadian cabins, and the bark lodges of Indian hordes which he had gathered under his protecting wing. A chief object of the settlement was to form a barrier against the English; but the purpose dearest to the missionary's heart was to gain over the Iroquois to the side of France; and in this he succeeded so well, that, as a writer of good authority declares, the number of their warriors within the circle of his influence surpassed the whole remaining force of the confederacy.[4]

Thoughtful men in the English colonies saw with anxiety the growing defection of the Iroquois, and dreaded lest, in the event of a war with France, her ancient foes might now be found her friends. But in this ominous conjuncture, one strong influence was at work to bind the confederates to their old alliance; and this influence was wielded by a man so re-

---

[1] Letter of Governor Spotswood, of Virginia, Jan. 25, 1720. See *Colonial Records of Pa.* III. 75.

[2] *Minutes of Indian Council*, 1746.

[3] *Doc. Hist. N. Y.* I. 423.

[4] MS. Letter—*Colden to Lord Halifax*, no date.

markable in his character, and so conspicuous an actor in the scenes of the ensuing history, as to demand at least some passing notice.

About the year 1734, in consequence it is said of the hapless issue of a love affair, William Johnson, a young Irishman, came over to America at the age of nineteen, where he assumed the charge of an extensive tract of wild land in the province of New York, belonging to his uncle, Admiral Sir Peter Warren. Settling in the valley of the Mohawk, he carried on a prosperous traffic with the Indians; and while he rapidly rose to wealth, he gained, at the same time, an extraordinary influence over the neighboring Iroquois. As his resources increased, he built two mansions in the valley, known respectively by the names of Johnson Castle and Johnson Hall, the latter of which, a well-constructed building of wood and stone, is still standing in the village of Johnstown. Johnson Castle was situated at some distance higher up the river. Both were fortified against attack, and the latter was surrounded with cabins built for the reception of the Indians, who often came in crowds to visit the proprietor, invading his dwelling at all unseasonable hours, loitering in the doorways, spreading their blankets in the passages, and infecting the air with the fumes of stale tobacco.

Johnson supplied the place of his former love by a young Dutch damsel, who bore him several children; and, in justice to them, he married her upon her death-bed. Soon afterwards he found another favorite in the person of Molly Brant, sister of the celebrated Mohawk war-chief, whose black eyes and laughing face caught his fancy, as, fluttering with ribbons, she galloped past him at a muster of the Tryon county militia.

Johnson's importance became so conspicuous, that when the French war broke out in 1755, he was made a major general; and, soon after, the colonial troops under his command gained the battle of Lake George against the French forces of Baron Dieskau. For this success, for which however he was entitled to little credit, he was raised to the rank of baronet, and rewarded with a gift of five thousand pounds from the king. About this time, he was appointed superintendent of Indian affairs for the northern tribes, a station in which he did signal service to the country. In 1759, when General Prideaux was killed by the bursting of a cohorn in the trenches before Niagara, Johnson succeeded to his command, routed the French in another pitched battle, and soon raised the red cross of England on the ramparts of the fort. After the peace of 1763, he lived for many years at Johnson Hall, constantly enriched by the increasing value of his vast estate, and surrounded by a hardy Highland tenantry, devoted to his interests; but when the tempest which had long been brewing seemed at length about to break, and signs of a speedy rupture with the mother country thickened with every day, he stood wavering in an agony of indecision, divided between his loyalty to the sovereign who was the source of all his honors, and his reluctance to become the agent of a murderous Indian warfare against his countrymen and friends. His final resolution was never taken. In the summer of 1774, he was attacked with a sudden illness, and died within a few hours, in the sixtieth year of his age, hurried to his grave by mental distress, or, as many believed, by the act of his own hand.

Nature had well fitted him for the position in which his propitious stars had cast his lot. His person was tall, erect, and strong; his features grave and manly. His direct and upright dealings, his courage, eloquence, and address, were sure passports to favor in Indian eyes. He had a singular facility of adaptation. In the camp, or at the council-board, in spite of his defective education, he bore himself as became his station; but at home he was seen drinking flip and smoking tobacco with the Dutch boors, his neighbors, and talking of improvements or the price of beaver-skins; while in the Indian villages he would feast on dog's flesh, dance with the warriors, and harangue his attentive auditors with all the dignity of an Iroquois sachem. His temper was genial; he encouraged rustic sports, and was respected and beloved alike by whites and Indians.

His good qualities, however, were alloyed with serious defects. His mind was as coarse as it was vigorous; he was vain of his rank and influence, and being quite free from any scruple of delicacy, he lost no opportunity of proclaiming them. His nature was eager and ambitious; and in pushing his own way, he was never distinguished by an anxious solicitude for the rights of others.[1]

At the time of which we speak, his fortunes had not reached their zenith; yet his influence was great; and during the war of 1745, when he held the chief control of Indian affairs in New York, it was exercised in a manner most beneficial to the province. After the peace of Aix la Chapelle, in 1748, finding his measures ill supported, he threw up his office in disgust. Still his mere personal influence sufficed to embarrass the intrigues of the busy priest at La Présentation; and a few years later, when the public exigency demanded his utmost efforts, he resumed, under better auspices, the official management of Indian affairs.

And now, when the blindest could see that between the rival claimants to the soil of America nothing was left but the arbitration of the sword, no man friendly to the cause of England could observe without alarm how France had strengthened herself in Indian alliances. The Iroquois, it is true, had not quite gone over to her side; nor had the Delawares wholly forgotten their ancient league with William Penn. The Miamis, too, in the valley of the Ohio, had lately taken umbrage at the conduct of the French, and betrayed a leaning to the side of England, while several tribes of the south showed a similar disposition. But, with few and slight exceptions, the numerous tribes of the great lakes and the Mississippi, besides a host of domiciliated savages in Canada itself, stood ready at the bidding of France to grind their tomahawks and turn loose their ravenous war-parties; while the British colonists had too much reason to fear that even those tribes which seemed most friendly to their cause, and which formed the sole barrier of their unprotected borders, might, at the first sound of the war-whoop, be found in arms against them.

[1] Allen, *Am. Biog. Dict.* and authorities there referred to. Campbell, *Annals of Tryon County, appendix*. Sabine, *Am. Loyalists*, 398. *Papers relating to Sir W. Johnson*. See *Doc. Hist. New York*, II. *MS. Papers of Sir W. Johnson*, etc., etc.

Chapter IV.

1700—1755.

COLLISION OF THE RIVAL COLONIES.

THE PEOPLE of the northern English colonies had learned to regard their Canadian neighbors with the bitterest enmity. With them, the very name of Canada called up horrible recollections and ghastly images: the midnight massacre of Schenectady, and the desolation of many a New England hamlet; blazing dwellings and reeking scalps; and children snatched from their mothers' arms, to be immured in convents and trained up in the abominations of Popery. To the sons of the Puritans, their enemy was doubly odious. They hated him as a Frenchman, and they hated him as a Papist. Hitherto he had waged his murderous warfare from a distance, wasting their settlements with rapid onsets, fierce and transient as a summer storm; but now, with enterprising audacity, he was intrenching himself on their very borders. The English hunter, in the lonely wilderness of Vermont, as by the warm glow of sunset he piled the spruce boughs for his woodland bed, started as a deep, low sound struck faintly on his ear, the evening gun of Fort Frederic, booming over lake and forest. The erection of this fort, better known among the English as Crown Point, was a piece of daring encroachment which justly kindled resentment in the northern colonies. But it was not here that the immediate occasion of a final rupture was to arise. By an article of the treaty of Utrecht, confirmed by that of Aix la Chapelle, Acadia had been ceded to England; but scarcely was the latter treaty signed, when debates sprang up touching the limits of the ceded province. Commissioners were named on either side to adjust the disputed boundary; but the claims of the rival powers proved utterly irreconcilable, and all negotiation was fruitless.[1] Meantime, the French and English forces in Acadia began to assume a belligerent attitude, and indulge their ill blood in mutual aggression and

---

[1]Garneau, Book VIII. Chap. III.

reprisal.[1] But while this game was played on the coasts of the Atlantic, interests of far greater moment were at stake in the west.

The people of the middle colonies, placed by their local position beyond reach of the French, had heard with great composure of the sufferings of their New England brethren, and felt little concern at a danger so doubtful and remote. There were those among them, however, who with greater foresight had been quick to perceive the ambitious projects of the rival nation; and, as early as 1716, Spotswood, governor of Virginia, had urged the expediency of securing the valley of the Ohio by a series of forts and settlements.[2] His proposal was coldly received, and his plan fell to the ground. The time at length was come when the danger was approaching too near to be slighted longer. In 1748, an association, called the Ohio Company, was formed with the view of making settlements in the region beyond the Alleghanies; and two years later, Gist, the company's surveyor, to the great disgust of the Indians, carried chain and compass down the Ohio as far as the falls at Louisville.[3] But so dilatory were the English, that before any effectual steps were taken, their agile enemies appeared upon the scene.

In the spring of 1753, the middle provinces were startled at the tidings that French troops had crossed Lake Erie, fortified themselves at the point of Presqu'-Isle, and pushed forward to the northern branches of the Ohio.[4] Upon this, Governor Dinwiddie, of Virginia, resolved to despatch a message requiring their removal from territories which he claimed as belonging to the British crown; and looking about him for the person best qualified to act as messenger, he made choice of George Washington, a young man twenty-one years of age, adjutant general of the Virginian militia.

Washington departed on his mission, crossed the mountains, descended to the bleak and leafless valley of the Ohio,

---

[1] Holmes, *Annals*, II. 183. *Mémoire contenant Le Précis des Faits, Pièces Justificatives*, Part I.

[2] Smollett, III. 370 (Edinburgh, 1805).

[3] Sparks's *Life and Writings of Washington*, II. 478. *Gist's Journal*.

[4] *Olden Time*, II. 9, 10. This excellent antiquarian publication contains documents relating to this period which are not to be found elsewhere.

and thence continued his journey up the banks of the Alleghany until the fourth of December. On that day he reached Venango, an Indian town on the Alleghany, at the mouth of French Creek. Here was the advanced post of the French; and here, among the Indian log-cabins and huts of bark, he saw their flag flying above the house of an English trader, whom the military intruders had unceremoniously ejected. They gave the young envoy a hospitable reception,[1] and referred him to the commanding officer, whose headquarters were at Le Bœuf, a fort which they had just built on French Creek, some distance above Venango. Thither Washington repaired, and on his arrival was received with stately courtesy by the officer, Legardeur de St. Pierre, whom he describes as an elderly gentleman of very soldier-like appearance. To the message of Dinwiddie, St. Pierre replied that he would forward it to the governor general of Canada; but that, in the mean time, his orders were to hold possession of the country, and this he should do to the best of his ability. With this answer Washington, through all the rigors of the midwinter forest, retraced his steps, with one attendant, to the English borders.

With the first opening of spring, a newly raised company of Virginian backwoodsmen, under Captain Trent, hastened across the mountains, and began to build a fort at the confluence of the Monongahela and Alleghany, where Pittsburg now stands; when suddenly they found themselves invested by a host of French and Indians, who, with sixty bateaux and three hundred canoes, had descended from Le Bœuf and Venango.[2] The English were ordered to evacuate the spot;

---

[1] "He invited us to sup with them, and treated us with the greatest complaisance. The wine, as they dosed themselves pretty plentifully with it, soon banished the restraint which at first appeared in their conversation, and gave a license to their tongues to reveal their sentiments more freely. They told me that it was their absolute design to take possession of the Ohio, and by G—d they would do it; for that, although they were sensible the English could raise two men for their one, yet they knew their motions were too slow and dilatory to prevent any undertaking of theirs. They pretend to have an undoubted right to the river from a discovery made by one La Salle, sixty years ago; and the rise of this expedition is, to prevent our settling on the river or waters of it, as they heard of some families moving out in order thereto."
—Washington, *Journal.*

[2] Sparks, *Life and Writings of Washington*, II. 6.

and, being quite unable to resist, they obeyed the summons, and withdrew in great discomfiture towards Virginia. Meanwhile Washington, with another party of backwoodsmen, was advancing from the borders; and, hearing of Trent's disaster, he resolved to fortify himself on the Monongahela, and hold his ground, if possible, until fresh troops could arrive to support him. The French sent out a scouting party under M. Jumonville, with the design, probably, of watching his movements; but, on a dark and stormy night, Washington surprised them, as they lay lurking in a rocky glen not far from his camp, killed the officer, and captured the whole detachment.[1] Learning that the French, enraged by this reverse, were about to attack him in great force, he thought it prudent to fall back, and retired accordingly to a spot called the Great Meadows, where he had before thrown up a slight intrenchment. Here he found himself assailed by nine hundred French and Indians, commanded by a brother of the slain Jumonville. From eleven in the morning till eight at night, the backwoodsmen, who were half famished from the failure of their stores, maintained a stubborn defence, some fighting within the intrenchment, and some on the plain without. In the evening, the French sounded a parley, and offered terms. They were accepted, and on the following day Washington and his men retired across the mountains, leaving the disputed territory in the hands of the French.[2]

While the rival nations were beginning to quarrel for a prize which belonged to neither of them, the unhappy Indians saw, with alarm and amazement, their lands becoming a bone of contention between rapacious strangers. The first appearance of the French on the Ohio excited the wildest fears in the tribes of that quarter, among whom were those who, disgusted by the encroachments of the Pennsylvanians, had fled to these remote retreats to escape the intrusions of the

[1] Sparks, II. 447. The conduct of Washington in this affair is regarded by French writers as a stain on his memory.

[2] For the French account of these operations, see *Mémoire contenant le Précis des Faits*. This volume, an official publication of the French court, contains numerous documents, among which are the papers of the unfortunate Braddock, left on the field of battle by his defeated army.

white men. Scarcely was their fancied asylum gained, when they saw themselves invaded by a host of armed men from Canada. Thus placed between two fires, they knew not which way to turn. There was no union in their counsels, and they seemed like a mob of bewildered children. Their native jealousy was roused to its utmost pitch. Many of them thought that the two white nations had conspired to destroy them, and then divide their lands. "You and the French," said one of them, a few years afterwards, to an English emissary, "are like the two edges of a pair of shears, and we are the cloth which is cut to pieces between them."[1]

The French labored hard to conciliate them, plying them with gifts and flatteries,[2] and proclaiming themselves their champions against the English. At first, these arts seemed in vain, but their effect soon began to declare itself; and this effect was greatly increased by a singular piece of infatuation on the part of the proprietors of Pennsylvania. During the summer of 1754, delegates of the several provinces met at Albany, to concert measures of defence in the war which now seemed inevitable. It was at this meeting that the memorable plan of a union of the colonies was brought forward; a plan, the fate of which was curious and significant, for the crown rejected it as giving too much power to the people, and the people as giving too much power to the crown.[3] A council was also held with the Iroquois, and though they were found but lukewarm in their attachment to the English, a treaty of friendship and alliance was concluded with their

[1]*First Journal* of C. F. Post.

[2]Letters of Robert Stobo, an English hostage at Fort du Quesne.

"Shamokin Daniel, who came with me, went over to the fort [du Quesne] by himself, and counselled with the governor, who presented him with a laced coat and hat, a blanket, shirts, ribbons, a new gun, powder, lead, &c. When he returned he was quite changed, and said, 'See here, you fools, what the French have given me. I was in Philadelphia, and never received a farthing;' and (directing himself to me) said, 'The English are fools, and so are you.'"—Post, *First Journal*.

Washington, while at Fort Le Bœuf, was much annoyed by the conduct of the French, who did their utmost to seduce his Indian escort by bribes and promises.

[3]Trumbull, *Hist. Conn.* II. 355. Holmes, *Annals*, II. 201.

deputies.[1] It would have been well if the matter had ended here; but, with ill-timed rapacity, the proprietary agents of Pennsylvania took advantage of this great assemblage of sachems to procure from them the grant of extensive tracts, including the lands inhabited by the very tribes whom the French were at that moment striving to seduce.[2] When they heard that, without their consent, their conquerors and tyrants, the Iroquois, had sold the soil from beneath their feet, their indignation was extreme; and, convinced that there was no limit to English encroachment, many of them from that hour became fast allies of the French.

The courts of London and Versailles still maintained a diplomatic intercourse, both protesting their earnest wish that their conflicting claims might be adjusted by friendly negotiation; but while each disclaimed the intention of hostility, both were hastening to prepare for war. Early in 1755, an English fleet sailed from Cork, having on board two regiments destined for Virginia, and commanded by General Braddock; and soon after, a French fleet put to sea from the port of Brest, freighted with munitions of war and a strong body of troops under Baron Dieskau, an officer who had distinguished himself in the campaigns of Marshal Saxe. The English fleet gained its destination, and landed its troops in safety. The French were less fortunate. Two of their ships, the Lys and the Alcide, became involved in the fogs of the banks of Newfoundland; and when the weather cleared, they found themselves under the guns of a superior British force, belonging to the squadron of Admiral Boscawen, sent out for the express purpose of intercepting them. "Are we at peace or war?" demanded the French commander. A broadside from the Englishman soon solved his doubts, and after a stout resistance the French struck their colors.[3] News of the capture caused great excitement in England, but the conduct of the

---

[1] At this council an Iroquois sachem upbraided the English, with great boldness, for their neglect of the Indians, their invasion of their lands, and their dilatory conduct with regard to the French, who, as the speaker averred, had behaved like men and warriors.—*Minutes of Conferences at Albany*, 1754.

[2] *Causes of the Alienation of the Delaware and Shawanoe Indians from the British Interest*, 77.

[3] Garneau, II. 551. *Gent. Mag.* XXV. 330.

aggressors was generally approved; and under pretence that the French had begun the war by their alleged encroachments in America, orders were issued for a general attack upon their marine. So successful were the British cruisers, that, before the end of the year, three hundred French vessels and nearly eight thousand sailors were captured and brought into port.[1] The French, unable to retort in kind, raised an outcry of indignation, and Mirepoix their ambassador withdrew from the court of London.

Thus began that memorable war which, kindling among the forests of America, scattered its fires over the kingdoms of Europe, and the sultry empire of the Great Mogul; the war made glorious by the heroic death of Wolfe, the victories of Frederic, and the exploits of Clive; the war which controlled the destinies of America, and was first in the chain of events which led on to her Revolution with all its vast and undeveloped consequences. On the old battle-ground of Europe, the contest bore the same familiar features of violence and horror which had marked the strife of former generations — fields ploughed by the cannon ball, and walls shattered by the exploding mine, sacked towns and blazing suburbs, the lamentations of women, and the license of a maddened soldiery. But in America, war assumed a new and striking aspect. A wilderness was its sublime arena. Army met army under the shadows of primeval woods; their cannon resounded over wastes unknown to civilized man. And before the hostile powers could join in battle, endless forests must be traversed, and morasses passed, and everywhere the axe of the pioneer must hew a path for the bayonet of the soldier.

Before the declaration of war, and before the breaking off of negotiations between the courts of France and England,

[1] Smollett, III. 436.

"The French inveighed against the capture of their ships, before any declaration of war, as flagrant acts of piracy; and some neutral powers of Europe seemed to consider them in the same point of view. It was certainly high time to check the insolence of the French by force of arms; and surely this might have been as effectually and expeditiously exerted under the usual sanction of a formal declaration, the omission of which exposed the administration to the censure of our neighbors, and fixed the imputation of fraud and freebooting on the beginning of the war."—Smollett, III. 481. See also Mahon, *Hist. England*, IV. 72.

the English ministry formed the plan of assailing the French in America on all sides at once, and repelling them, by one bold push, from all their encroachments.[1] A provincial army was to advance upon Acadia, a second was to attack Crown Point, and a third Niagara; while the two regiments which had lately arrived in Virginia under General Braddock, aided by a strong body of provincials, were to dislodge the French from their newly-built fort of Du Quesne. To Braddock was assigned the chief command of all the British forces in America; and a person worse fitted for the office could scarcely have been found. His experience had been ample, and none could doubt his courage; but he was profligate, arrogant, perverse, and a bigot to military rules.[2] On his first arrival in Virginia, he called together the governors of the several provinces, in order to explain his instructions and adjust the details of the projected operations. These arrangements complete, Braddock advanced to the borders of Virginia, and formed his camp at Fort Cumberland, where he spent several weeks in training the raw backwoodsmen, who joined him,

[1] Instructions of General Braddock. See *Précis des Faits*, 160, 168.

[2] The following is Horace Walpole's testimony, and writers of better authority have expressed themselves, with less liveliness and piquancy, to the same effect: —

"Braddock is a very Iroquois in disposition. He had a sister, who, having gamed away all her little fortune at Bath, hanged herself with a truly English deliberation, leaving only a note upon the table with those lines, 'To die is landing on some silent shore,' &c. When Braddock was told of it, he only said, 'Poor Fanny! I always thought she would play till she would be forced *to tuck herself up*.'"

Here follows a curious anecdote of Braddock's meanness and profligacy, which I omit. The next is more to his credit. "He once had a duel with Colonel Gumley, Lady Bath's brother, who had been his great friend. As they were going to engage, Gumley, who had good humor and wit (Braddock had the latter), said, 'Braddock, you are a poor dog! Here, take my purse. If you kill me, you will be forced to run away, and then you will not have a shilling to support you.' Braddock refused the purse, insisted on the duel, was disarmed, and would not even ask his life. However, with all his brutality, he has lately been governor of Gibraltar, where he made himself adored, and where scarce any governor was endured before."—*Letters to Sir H. Mann*, CCLXV. CCLXVI.

Washington's opinion of Braddock may be gathered from his Writings, II. 77.

into such discipline as they seemed capable of; in collecting horses and wagons, which could only be had with the utmost difficulty; in railing at the contractors, who scandalously cheated him; and in venting his spleen by copious abuse of the country and the people. All at length was ready, and early in June, 1755, the army left civilization behind, and struck into the broad wilderness as a squadron puts out to sea.

It was no easy task to force their way over that rugged ground, covered with an unbroken growth of forest; and the difficulty was increased by the needless load of baggage which encumbered their march. The crash of falling trees resounded in the front, where a hundred axemen labored with ceaseless toil to hew a passage for the army.[1] The horses strained their utmost strength to drag the ponderous wagons over roots and stumps, through gullies and quagmires; and the regular troops were daunted by the depth and gloom of the forest which hedged them in on either hand, and closed its leafy arches above their heads. So tedious was their progress, that, by the advice of Washington, twelve hundred chosen men moved on in advance with the lighter baggage and artillery, leaving the rest of the army to follow, by slower stages, with the heavy wagons. On the eighth of July, the advanced body reached the Monongahela, at a point not far distant from Fort du Quesne. The rocky and impracticable ground on the eastern side debarred their passage, and the general resolved to cross the river in search of a smoother path, and recross it a few miles lower down, in order to gain the fort. The first passage was easily made, and the troops moved, in glittering array, down the western margin of the water, rejoicing that their goal was well nigh reached, and the hour of their expected triumph close at hand.

Scouts and Indian runners had brought the tidings of Braddock's approach to the French at Fort du Quesne. Their dismay was great, and Contrecœur, the commander, thought only of retreat; when Beaujeu, a captain in the garrison, made the bold proposal of leading out a party of French and Indians to waylay the English in the woods, and harass or

---

[1] MS. *Diary of the Expedition*, in the British Museum.

interrupt their march. The offer was accepted, and Beaujeu hastened to the Indian camps.

Around the fort and beneath the adjacent forest were the bark lodges of savage hordes, whom the French had mustered from far and near; Ojibwas and Ottawas, Hurons and Caughnawagas, Abenakis and Delawares. Beaujeu called the warriors together, flung a hatchet on the ground before them, and invited them to follow him out to battle; but the boldest stood aghast at the peril, and none would accept the challenge. A second interview took place with no better success; but the Frenchman was resolved to carry his point. "I am determined to go," he exclaimed. "What, will you suffer your father to go alone?"[1] His daring proved contagious. The warriors hesitated no longer; and when, on the morning of the ninth of July, a scout ran in with the news that the English army was but a few miles distant, the Indian camps were at once astir with the turmoil of preparation. Chiefs harangued their yelling followers, braves bedaubed themselves with warpaint, smeared themselves with grease, hung feathers in their scalp-locks, and whooped and stamped till they had wrought themselves into a delirium of valor.

That morning, James Smith, an English prisoner recently captured on the frontier of Pennsylvania, stood on the rampart, and saw the half-frenzied multitude thronging about the gateway, where kegs of bullets and gunpowder were broken open, that each might help himself at will.[2] Then band after band hastened away towards the forest, followed and supported by nearly two hundred and fifty French and Canadians, commanded by Beaujeu. There were the Ottawas, led on, it is said, by the remarkable man whose name stands on the title-page of this history; there were the Hurons of Lorette under their chief, whom the French called Athanase,[3] and many more, all keen as hounds on the scent of blood. At

---

[1] Sparks's *Life and Writings of Washington*, II. 473. I am indebted to the kindness of President Sparks for copies of several French manuscripts, which throw much light on the incidents of the battle. These manuscripts are alluded to in the Life and Writings of Washington.

[2] *Smith's Narrative*. This interesting account has been several times published. It may be found in Drake's *Tragedies of the Wilderness*.

[3] "Went to Lorette, an Indian village about eight miles from Quebec. Saw

about nine miles from the fort, they reached a spot where the narrow road descended to the river through deep and gloomy woods, and where two ravines, concealed by trees and bushes, seemed formed by nature for an ambuscade. Beaujeu well knew the ground; and it was here that he had resolved to fight; but he and his followers were well nigh too late; for as they neared the ravines, the woods were resounding with the roll of the British drums.

It was past noon of a day brightened with the clear sunlight of an American midsummer, when the forces of Braddock began, for a second time, to cross the Monongahela, at the fording-place, which to this day bears the name of their ill-fated leader. The scarlet columns of the British regulars, complete in martial appointment, the rude backwoodsmen with shouldered rifles, the trains of artillery and the white-topped wagons, moved on in long procession through the shallow current, and slowly mounted the opposing bank.[1] Men were there whose names have become historic: Gage, who, twenty years later, saw his routed battalions recoil in disorder from before the breastwork on Bunker Hill; Gates, the future conqueror of Burgoyne; and one destined to a higher fame,— George Washington, a boy in years, a man in calm thought and self-ruling wisdom.

With steady and well ordered march, the troops advanced into the great labyrinth of woods which shadowed the eastern borders of the river. Rank after rank vanished from sight. The forest swallowed them up, and the silence of the wilderness

---

the Indians at mass, and heard them sing psalms tolerably well—a dance. Got well acquainted with Athanase, who was commander of the Indians who defeated General Braddock, in 1755—a very sensible fellow."—*MS. Journal of an English Gentleman on a Tour through Canada, in 1765.*

[1]"My feelings were heightened by the warm and glowing narration of that day's events, by Dr. Walker, who was an eye-witness. He pointed out the ford where the army crossed the Monongahela (below Turtle Creek, 800 yards). A finer sight could not have been beheld,—the shining barrels of the muskets, the excellent order of the men, the cleanliness of their appearance, the joy depicted on every face at being so near Fort du Quesne—the highest object of their wishes. The music re-echoed through the hills. How brilliant the morning—how melancholy the evening!"—*Letter of Judge Yeates, dated August, 1776.* See Haz., *Pa. Reg.*, VI. 104.

sank down once more on the shores and waters of the Monongahela.

Several engineers and guides and six light horsemen led the way; a body of grenadiers under Gage was close behind, and the army followed in such order as the rough ground would permit, along a narrow road, twelve feet wide, tunnelled through the dense and matted foliage. There were flanking parties on either side, but no scouts to scour the woods in front, and with an insane confidence Braddock pressed on to meet his fate. The van had passed the low grounds that bordered the river, and were now ascending a gently rising ground, where, on either hand, hidden by thick trees, by tangled undergrowth and rank grasses, lay the two fatal ravines. Suddenly, Gordon, an engineer in advance, saw the French and Indians bounding forward through the forest and along the narrow track, Beaujeu leading them on, dressed in a fringed hunting-shirt, and wearing a silver gorget on his breast. He stopped, turned, and waved his hat, and his French followers, crowding across the road, opened a murderous fire upon the head of the British column, while, screeching their war-cries, the Indians thronged into the ravines, or crouched behind rocks and trees on both flanks of the advancing troops. The astonished grenadiers returned the fire, and returned it with good effect; for a random shot struck down the brave Beaujeu, and the courage of the assailants was staggered by his fall. Dumas, second in command, rallied them to the attack; and while he, with the French and Canadians, made good the pass in front, the Indians from their lurking places opened a deadly fire on the right and left. In a few moments, all was confusion. The advance guard fell back on the main body, and every trace of subordination vanished. The fire soon extended along the whole length of the army, from front to rear. Scarce an enemy could be seen, though the forest resounded with their yells; though every bush and tree was alive with incessant flashes; though the lead flew like a hailstorm, and the men went down by scores. The regular troops seemed bereft of their senses. They huddled together in the road like flocks of sheep; and happy did he think himself who could wedge his way into the midst of the crowd, and place a barrier of human flesh between his life and the shot of the ambushed marksmen. Many were seen eagerly loading their muskets, and then firing them into the air, or shooting their own comrades in the insanity of their terror. The officers, for the most part, displayed a conspicuous gallantry; but threats and commands were wasted alike on the panic-stricken multitude. It is said that at the outset Braddock showed signs of fear; but he soon recovered his wonted intrepidity. Five horses were shot under him, and five times he mounted afresh.[1] He stormed and shouted, and, while the Virginians were fighting to good purpose, each man behind a tree, like the Indians themselves, he ordered them with furious menace to form in platoons, where the fire of the enemy mowed them down like grass. At length, a mortal shot silenced him, and two provincials bore him off the field. Washington rode through the tumult calm and undaunted. Two horses were killed under him, and four bullets pierced his clothes;[2] but his hour was not come, and he escaped without a wound. Gates was shot through the body, and Gage also was severely wounded. Of eighty-six officers, only twenty-three remained unhurt; and of twelve hundred soldiers who crossed the Monongahela, more than seven hundred were killed and wounded. None suffered more severely than the Virginians, who had displayed throughout a degree of courage and steadiness which put the cowardice of the regulars to shame. The havoc among them was terrible, for of their whole number scarcely one-fifth left the field alive.[3]

The slaughter lasted three hours; when, at length, the survivors, as if impelled by a general impulse, rushed tumultuously

[1] Letter—*Captain Orme, his aide-de-camp, to* ——, July 18.
[2] Sparks, I. 67.
[3] "The Virginia troops showed a good deal of bravery, and were nearly all killed; for I believe, out of three companies that were there, scarcely thirty men are left alive. Captain Peyrouny, and all his officers, down to a corporal, were killed. Captain Polson had nearly as hard a fate, for only one of his was left. In short, the dastardly behavior of those they call regulars exposed all others, that were inclined to do their duty, to almost certain death; and at last, in despite of all the efforts of the officers to the contrary, they ran, as sheep pursued by dogs, and it was impossible to rally them."—*Writings of Washington*, II. 87.

The English themselves bore reluctant testimony to the good conduct of the Virginians.—See Entick, *Hist. Late War*, 147.

from the place of carnage, and with dastardly precipitation fled across the Monongahela. The enemy did not pursue beyond the river, flocking back to the field to collect the plunder, and gather a rich harvest of scalps. The routed troops pursued their flight until they met the rear division of the army, under Colonel Dunbar; and even then their senseless terrors did not abate. Dunbar's soldiers caught the infection. Cannon, baggage, provisions and wagons were destroyed, and all fled together, eager to escape from the shadows of those awful woods, whose horrors haunted their imagination. They passed the defenceless settlements of the border, and hurried on to Philadelphia, leaving the unhappy people to defend themselves as they might against the tomahawk and scalping-knife.

The calamities of this disgraceful rout did not cease with the loss of a few hundred soldiers on the field of battle; for it brought upon the provinces all the miseries of an Indian war. Those among the tribes who had thus far stood neutral, wavering between the French and English, now hesitated no longer. Many of them had been disgusted by the contemptuous behavior of Braddock. All had learned to despise the courage of the English, and to regard their own prowess with unbounded complacency. It is not in Indian nature to stand quiet in the midst of war; and the defeat of Braddock was a signal for the western savages to snatch their tomahawks and assail the English settlements with one accord, murdering and pillaging with ruthless fury, and turning the frontier of Pennsylvania and Virginia into one wide scene of havoc and desolation.

The three remaining expeditions which the British ministry had planned for that year's campaign were attended with various results. Acadia was quickly reduced by the forces of Colonel Monkton; but the glories of this easy victory were tarnished by an act of cruelty. Seven thousand of the unfortunate people, refusing to take the prescribed oath of allegiance, were seized by the conquerors, torn from their homes, placed on shipboard like cargoes of negro slaves, and transported to the British provinces.[1] The expedition against Niagara was a

---

[1] Haliburton, *Hist. Nova Scotia*, I. Chap. IV.

total failure, for the troops did not even reach their destination. The movement against Crown Point met with no better success, as regards the main object of the enterprise. Owing to the lateness of the season, and other causes, the troops proceeded no farther than Lake George; but the attempt was marked by a feat of arms, which, in that day of failures, was greeted, both in England and America, as a signal victory.

General Johnson, afterwards Sir William Johnson, had been charged with the conduct of the Crown Point expedition; and his little army, a rude assemblage of hunters and farmers from New York and New England, officers and men alike ignorant of war, lay encamped at the southern extremity of Lake George. Here, while they languidly pursued their preparations, their active enemy anticipated them. Baron Dieskau, who, with a body of troops, had reached Quebec in the squadron which sailed from Brest in the spring, had intended to take forcible possession of the English fort of Oswego, erected upon ground claimed by the French as a part of Canada. Learning Johnson's movements, he changed his plan, crossed Lake Champlain, made a circuit by way of Wood Creek, and gained the rear of the English army, with a force of about two thousand French and Indians. At midnight, on the seventh of September, the tidings reached Johnson that the army of the French baron was but a few miles distant from his camp. A council of war was called, and the resolution formed of detaching a thousand men to reconnoitre. "If they are to be killed," said Hendrick, the Mohawk chief, "they are too many; if they are to fight, they are too few." His remonstrance was unheeded; and the brave old savage, unable from age and corpulence to fight on foot, mounted his horse, and joined the English detachment with two hundred of his warriors. At sunrise, the party defiled from the camp, and entering the forest disappeared from the eyes of their comrades.

Those who remained behind labored with all the energy of alarm to fortify their unprotected camp. An hour elapsed, when from the distance was heard a sudden explosion of musketry. The excited soldiers suspended their work to listen. A rattling fire succeeded, deadened among the woods, but growing louder and nearer, till none could doubt that their comrades had met the French, and were defeated.

This was indeed the case. Marching through thick woods, by the narrow and newly-cut road which led along the valley southward from Lake George, Williams, the English commander, had led his men full into an ambuscade, where all Dieskau's army lay in wait to receive them. From the woods on both sides rose an appalling shout, followed by a storm of bullets. Williams was soon shot down; Hendrick shared his fate; many officers fell, and the road was strewn with dead and wounded soldiers. The English gave way at once. Had they been regular troops, the result would have been worse; but every man was a woodsman and a hunter. Some retired in bodies along the road; while the greater part spread themselves through the forest, opposing a wide front to the enemy, fighting stubbornly as they retreated, and shooting back at the French from behind every tree or bush that could afford a cover. The Canadians and Indians pressed them closely, darting, with shrill cries, from tree to tree, while Dieskau's regulars, with steadier advance, bore all before them. Far and wide through the forest rang shout and shriek and Indian whoop, mingled with the deadly rattle of guns. Retreating and pursuing, the combatants passed northward towards the English camp, leaving the ground behind them strewn with dead and dying.

A fresh detachment from the camp came in aid of the English, and the pursuit was checked. Yet the retreating men were not the less rejoiced when they could discern, between the brown columns of the woods, the mountains and waters of Lake George, with the white tents of their encampments on its shore. The French followed no farther. The blast of their trumpets was heard recalling their scattered men for a final attack.

During the absence of Williams's detachment, the main body of the army had covered the front of their camp with a breastwork, — if that name can be applied to a row of logs, — behind which the marksmen lay flat on their faces. This preparation was not yet complete, when the defeated troops appeared issuing from the woods. Breathless and perturbed, they entered the camp, and lay down with the rest; and the army waited the attack in a frame of mind which boded ill for the result. Soon, at the edge of the woods which bordered the open space in front, painted Indians were seen, and bayonets glittered among the foliage, shining, in the homely comparison of a New-England soldier, like a row of icicles on a January morning. The French regulars marched in column to the edge of the clearing, and formed in line, confronting the English at the distance of a hundred and fifty yards. Their complete order, their white uniforms and bristling bayonets, were a new and startling sight to the eyes of Johnson's rustic soldiers, who raised but a feeble cheer in answer to the shouts of their enemies. Happily, Dieskau made no assault. The regulars opened a distant fire of musketry, throwing volley after volley against the English, while the Canadians and Indians, dispersing through the morasses on each flank of the camp, fired sharply, under cover of the trees and bushes. In the rear, the English were protected by the lake; but on the three remaining sides, they were hedged in by the flash and smoke of musketry.

The fire of the French had little effect. The English recovered from their first surprise, and every moment their confidence rose higher and their shouts grew louder. Levelling their long hunting guns with cool precision, they returned a fire which thinned the ranks of the French, and galled them beyond endurance. Two cannon were soon brought to bear upon the morasses which sheltered the Canadians and Indians; and though the pieces were served with little skill, the assailants were so terrified by the crashing of the balls among the trunks and branches, that they gave way at once. Dieskau still persisted in the attack. From noon until past four o'clock, the firing was scarcely abated, when at length the French, who had suffered extremely, showed signs of wavering. At this, with a general shout, the English broke from their camp, and rushed upon their enemies, striking them down with the buts of their guns, and driving them through the woods like deer. Dieskau was taken prisoner, dangerously wounded, and leaning for support against the stump of a tree. The slaughter would have been great, had not the English general recalled the pursuers, and suffered the French to continue their flight unmolested. Fresh disasters still awaited the fugitives; for, as they approached the scene of that morning's ambuscade, they were greeted by a volley of musketry. Two companies of New

York and New Hampshire rangers, who had come out from
Fort Edward as a scouting party, had lain in wait to receive
them. Favored by the darkness of the woods,—for night was
now approaching,—they made so sudden and vigorous an
attack, that the French, though far superior in number, were
totally routed and dispersed.[1]

This memorable conflict has cast its dark associations over
one of the most beautiful spots in America. Near the scene of
the evening fight, a pool, half overgrown by weeds and water
lilies, and darkened by the surrounding forest, is pointed out
to the tourist, and he is told that beneath its stagnant waters
lie the bones of three hundred Frenchmen, deep buried in
mud and slime.

The war thus begun was prosecuted for five succeeding
years with the full energy of both nations. The period was
one of suffering and anxiety to the colonists, who, knowing
the full extent of their danger, spared no exertion to avert it.
In the year 1758, Lord Abercrombie, who then commanded in
America, had at his disposal a force amounting to fifty thousand men, of whom the greater part were provincials.[2] The

---

[1]Holmes, II. 210. Trumbull, *Hist. Conn.* II. 368. Dwight, *Travels*, III. 361.
Hoyt, *Indian Wars*, 279. Entick, *Hist. Late War*, I. 153. *Review of Military
Operations in North America.* Johnson's *Letter to the Provincial Governors.*
Blodgett's *Prospective View of the Battle near Lake George.*

Blodgett's pamphlet is accompanied by a curious engraving, giving a bird's
eye view of the battle, including the surprise of Williams' detachment, and
the subsequent attack on the camp of Johnson. In the first half of the engraving, the French army is represented lying in ambuscade in the form of a
horseshoe. Hendrick is conspicuous among the English, from being mounted
on horseback, while all the others are on foot. In the view of the battle at the
lake, the English are represented lying flat on their faces, behind their breastwork, and busily firing at the French and Indians, who are seen skulking
among the woods and thickets.

I am again indebted to President Sparks for the opportunity of examining
several curious manuscripts relating to the battle of Lake George. Among
them is Dieskau's official account of the affair, and a curious paper, also written by the defeated general, and containing the story of his disaster, as related
by himself in an imaginary conversation with his old commander, Marshal
Saxe, in the Elysian Fields. Several writers have stated that Dieskau died of
his wounds. This, however, was not the case. He was carried prisoner to
England, where he lived for several years, but returned to France after the
peace of 1763.

[2]Holmes, II. 226.

operations of the war embraced a wide extent of country, from Cape Breton and Nova Scotia to the sources of the Ohio; but nowhere was the contest so actively carried on as in the neighborhood of Lake George, the waters of which, joined with those of Lake Champlain, formed the main avenue of communication between Canada and the British provinces. Lake George is more than thirty miles long, but of width so slight that it seems like some broad and placid river, enclosed between ranges of lofty mountains; now contracting into narrows, dotted with islands and shadowed by cliffs and crags, now spreading into a clear and open expanse. It had long been known to the French. The Jesuit Isaac Jogues, bound on a fatal mission to the ferocious Mohawks, had reached its banks on the eve of Corpus Christi Day, and named it Lac St. Sacrement. Its solitude was now rudely invaded. Armies passed and repassed upon its tranquil bosom. At its northern point the French planted their stronghold of Ticonderoga; at its southern stood the English fort William Henry, while the mountains and waters between were a scene of ceaseless ambuscades, surprises, and forest skirmishing. Through summer and winter, the crack of rifles and the cries of men gave no rest to their echoes; and at this day, on the field of many a forgotten fight, are dug up rusty tomahawks, corroded bullets, and human bones, to attest the struggles of the past.

The earlier years of the war were unpropitious to the English, whose commanders displayed no great degree of vigor or ability. In the summer of 1756, the French general Montcalm advanced upon Oswego, took it, and levelled it to the ground. In August of the following year, he struck a heavier blow. Passing Lake George with a force of eight thousand men, including about two thousand Indians, gathered from the farthest parts of Canada, he laid siege to Fort William Henry, close to the spot where Dieskau had been defeated two years before. Planting his batteries against it, he beat down its ramparts and dismounted its guns, until the garrison, after a brave defence, were forced to capitulate. They marched out with the honors of war; but scarcely had they done so, when Montcalm's Indians assailed them, cutting down and scalping them without mercy. Those who escaped came in to Fort Edward with exaggerated accounts of the horrors from which they had fled, and a general terror was spread through the country. The inhabitants were mustered from all parts to repel the advance of Montcalm; but the French general, satisfied with what he had done, repassed Lake George, and retired behind the walls of Ticonderoga.

In the year 1758, the war began to assume a different aspect, for Pitt was at the head of the government. Sir Jeffrey Amherst laid siege to the strong fortress of Louisburg, and at length reduced it; while in the south, General Forbes marched against Fort du Quesne, and, more fortunate than his predecessor, Braddock, drove the French from that important point. Another successful stroke was the destruction of Fort Frontenac, which was taken by a provincial army under Colonel Bradstreet. These achievements were counterbalanced by a great disaster. Lord Abercrombie, with an army of sixteen thousand men, advanced to the head of Lake George, the place made memorable by Dieskau's defeat and the loss of Fort William Henry. On a brilliant July morning, he embarked his whole force for an attack on Ticonderoga. Many of those present have recorded with admiration the beauty of the spectacle, the lines of boats filled with troops stretching far down the lake, the flashing of oars, the glitter of weapons, and the music ringing back from crags and rocks, or dying in mellowed strains among the distant mountains. At night, the army landed, and, driving in the French outposts, marched through the woods towards Ticonderoga. One of their columns, losing its way in the forest, fell in with a body of the retreating French; and in the conflict that ensued, Lord Howe, the favorite of the army, was shot dead. On the eighth of July, they prepared to storm the lines which Montcalm had drawn across the peninsula in front of the fortress. Advancing to the attack, they saw before them a breastwork of uncommon height and thickness. The French army were drawn up behind it, their heads alone visible, as they levelled their muskets against the assailants, while, for a hundred yards in front of the work, the ground was covered with felled trees, with sharpened branches pointing outward. The signal of assault was given. In vain the Highlanders, screaming with rage, hewed with their broadswords among the branches, struggling to get at the enemy. In vain the English, with their deep-toned shout, rushed on in heavy columns. A tempest of musket balls met them, and Montcalm's cannon swept the whole ground with terrible carnage. A few officers and men forced their way through the branches, passed the ditch, climbed the breastwork, and, leaping among the enemy, were instantly bayonetted. The English fought four hours with determined valor, but the position of the French was impregnable; and at length, having lost two thousand of their number, the army drew off, leaving many of their dead scattered upon the field. A sudden panic seized the defeated troops. They rushed in haste to their boats, and, though no pursuit was attempted, they did not regain their composure until Lake George was between them and the enemy. The fatal lines of Ticonderoga were not soon forgotten in the provinces; and marbles in Westminster Abbey preserve the memory of those who fell on that disastrous day.

This repulse, far from depressing the energies of the British commanders, seemed to stimulate them to new exertion; and the campaign of the next year, 1759, had for its object the immediate and total reduction of Canada. This unhappy country was full of misery and disorder. Peculation and every kind of corruption prevailed among its civil and military chiefs, a reckless licentiousness was increasing among the people, and a general famine seemed impending, for the population had of late years been drained away for military service, and the fields were left untilled. In spite of their sufferings, the Canadians, strong in rooted antipathy to the English, and highly excited by their priests, resolved on fighting to the last. Prayers were offered up in the churches, masses said, and penances enjoined, to avert the wrath of God from the colony, while every thing was done for its defence which the energies of a great and patriotic leader could effect.

By the plan of this summer's campaign, Canada was to be assailed on three sides at once. Upon the west, General Prideaux was to attack Niagara; upon the south, General Amherst was to advance upon Ticonderoga and Crown Point; while upon the east, General Wolfe was to besiege Quebec; and each of these armies, having accomplished its particular object, was directed to push forward, if possible, until all three had united in the heart of Canada. In pursuance of the plan,

General Prideaux moved up Lake Ontario and invested Niagara. This post was one of the greatest importance. Its capture would cut off the French from the whole interior country, and they therefore made every effort to raise the siege. An army of seventeen hundred French and Indians, collected at the distant garrisons of Detroit, Presqu' Isle, Le Bœuf, and Venango, suddenly appeared before Niagara.[1] Sir William Johnson was now in command of the English, Prideaux having been killed by the bursting of a cohorn. Advancing in order of battle, he met the French, charged, routed, and pursued them for five miles through the woods. This success was soon followed by the surrender of the fort.

In the mean time, Sir Jeffrey Amherst had crossed Lake George, and appeared before Ticonderoga; upon which the French blew up their works, and retired down Lake Champlain to Crown Point. Retreating from this position also, on the approach of the English army, they collected all their forces, amounting to little more than three thousand men, at Isle Aux Noix, where they intrenched themselves, and prepared to resist the farther progress of the invaders. The lateness of the season prevented Amherst from carrying out the plan of advancing into Canada, and compelled him to go into winter-quarters at Crown Point. The same cause had withheld Prideaux's army from descending the St. Lawrence.

While the outposts of Canada were thus successfully attacked, a blow was struck at a more vital part. Early in June, General Wolfe sailed up the St. Lawrence with a force of eight thousand men, and formed his camp immediately below Quebec, on the Island of Orleans.[2] From thence he could discern, at a single glance, how arduous was the task before him. Piles of lofty cliffs rose with sheer ascent on the northern border of the river; and from their summits the boasted citadel of Canada looked down in proud security, with its churches and convents of stone, its ramparts, bastions, and batteries; while over them all, from the brink of the precipice, towered the massive walls of the Castle of St. Louis. Above, for many a league, the bank was guarded by an unbroken range of steep

---

[1] *Annual Register*, 1759, p. 33.
[2] Mante, *Hist. Late War*, 238.

acclivities. Below, the River St. Charles, flowing into the St. Lawrence, washed the base of the rocky promontory on which the city stood. Lower yet lay an army of fourteen thousand men, under an able and renowned commander, the Marquis of Montcalm. His front was covered by intrenchments and batteries, which lined the bank of the St. Lawrence; his right wing rested on the city and the St. Charles; his left, on the cascade and deep gulf of Montmorenci; and thick forests extended along his rear. Opposite Quebec rose the high promontory of Point Levi; and the St. Lawrence, contracted to less than a mile in width, flowed between, with deep and powerful current. To a chief of less resolute temper, it might well have seemed that art and nature were in league to thwart his enterprise; but a mind like that of Wolfe could only have seen in this majestic combination of forest and cataract, mountain and river, a fitting theatre for the great drama about to be enacted there.

Yet nature did not seem to have formed the young English general for the conduct of a doubtful and almost desperate enterprise. His person was slight, and his features by no means of a martial cast. His feeble constitution had been undermined by years of protracted and painful disease.[1] His kind and genial disposition seemed better fitted for the quiet of domestic life than for the stern duties of military command; but to these gentler traits he joined a high enthusiasm, and an unconquerable spirit of daring and endurance, which made him the idol of his soldiers, and bore his slender frame through every hardship and exposure.

The work before him demanded all his courage. How to invest the city, or even bring the army of Montcalm to action, was a problem which might have perplexed a Hannibal. A French fleet lay in the river above, and the precipices along

[1] "I have this day signified to Mr. Pitt that he may dispose of my slight carcass as he pleases; and that I am ready for any undertaking within the reach and compass of my skill and cunning. I am in a very bad condition, both with the gravel and rheumatism; but I had much rather die than decline any kind of service that offers: if I followed my own taste, it would lead me into Germany; and if my poor talent was consulted, they should place me to the cavalry, because nature has given me good eyes, and a warmth of temper to follow the first impressions. However, it is not our part to choose, but to obey."—Letter—Wolfe to William Rickson, Salisbury, December 1, 1758.

the northern bank were guarded at every accessible point by sentinels and outposts. Wolfe would have crossed the Montmorenci by its upper ford, and attacked the French army on its left and rear; but the plan was thwarted by the nature of the ground and the vigilance of his adversaries. Thus baffled at every other point, he formed the bold design of storming Montcalm's position in front; and on the afternoon of the thirty-first of July, a strong body of troops was embarked in boats, and, covered by a furious cannonade from the English ships and batteries, landed on the beach just above the mouth of the Montmorenci. The grenadiers and Royal Americans were the first on shore, and their ill-timed impetuosity proved the ruin of the plan. Without waiting to receive their orders or form their ranks, they ran, pell-mell, across the level ground, and with loud shouts began, each man for himself, to scale the heights which rose in front, crested with intrenchments and bristling with hostile arms. The French at the top threw volley after volley among the hot-headed assailants. The slopes were soon covered with the fallen; and at that instant a storm, which had long been threatening, burst with sudden fury, drenched the combatants on both sides with a deluge of rain, extinguished for a moment the fire of the French, and at the same time made the steeps so slippery that the grenadiers fell repeatedly in their vain attempts to climb. Night was coming on with double darkness. The retreat was sounded, and, as the English re-embarked, troops of Indians came whooping down the heights, and hovered about their rear, to murder the stragglers and the wounded; while exulting cries of *Vive le roi*, from the crowded summits, proclaimed the triumph of the enemy.

With bitter agony of mind, Wolfe beheld the headlong folly of his men, and saw more than four hundred of the flower of his army fall a useless sacrifice.[1] The anxieties of the siege had told severely upon his slender constitution; and not long after this disaster, he felt the first symptoms of a fever, which soon confined him to his couch. Still his mind never wavered from its purpose; and it was while lying helpless in the chamber of a Canadian house, where he had fixed his headquarters, that

[1] Knox, *Journals*, I. 358.

he embraced the plan of the enterprise which robbed him of life, and gave him immortal fame.

This plan had been first proposed during the height of Wolfe's illness, at a council of his subordinate generals, Monkton, Townshend, and Murray. It was resolved to divide the little army; and, while one portion remained before Quebec to alarm the enemy by false attacks, and distract their attention from the scene of actual operation, the other was to pass above the town, land under cover of darkness on the northern shore, climb the guarded heights, gain the plains above, and force Montcalm to quit his vantage-ground, and perhaps to offer battle. The scheme was daring even to rashness; but its audacity was the secret of its success.

Early in September, a crowd of ships and transports, under Admiral Holmes, passed the city under the hot fire of its batteries; while the troops designed for the expedition, amounting to scarcely five thousand, marched upward along the southern bank, beyond reach of the cannonade. All were then embarked; and on the evening of the twelfth, Holmes's fleet, with the troops on board, lay safe at anchor in the river, several leagues above the town. These operations had not failed to awaken the suspicions of Montcalm; and he had detached M. Bougainville to watch the movements of the English, and prevent their landing on the northern shore.

The eventful night of the twelfth was clear and calm, with no light but that of the stars. Within two hours before daybreak, thirty boats, crowded with sixteen hundred soldiers, cast off from the vessels, and floated downward, in perfect order, with the current of the ebb tide. To the boundless joy of the army, Wolfe's malady had abated, and he was able to command in person. His ruined health, the gloomy prospects of the siege, and the disaster at Montmorenci, had oppressed him with the deepest melancholy, but never impaired for a moment the promptness of his decisions, or the impetuous energy of his action.[1] He sat in the stern of one of the boats,

---

[1] Entick, IV. III.

In his letter to the Ministry, dated Sept. 2, Wolfe writes in these desponding words: —

"By the nature of the river, the most formidable part of this armament is

pale and weak, but borne up to a calm height of resolution. Every order had been given, every arrangement made, and it only remained to face the issue. The ebbing tide sufficed to bear the boats along, and nothing broke the silence of the night but the gurgling of the river, and the low voice of Wolfe, as he repeated to the officers about him the stanzas of Gray's "Elegy in a Country Churchyard," which had recently appeared and which he had just received from England. Perhaps, as he uttered those strangely appropriate words, —

"The paths of glory lead but to the grave,"

the shadows of his own approaching fate stole with mournful prophecy across his mind. "Gentlemen," he said, as he closed his recital, "I would rather have written those lines than take Quebec tomorrow."[1]

As they approached the landing-place, the boats edged closer in towards the northern shore, and the woody precipices rose high on their left, like a wall of undistinguished blackness.

"*Qui vive?*" shouted a French sentinel, from out the impervious gloom.

---

deprived of the power of acting; yet we have almost the whole force of Canada to oppose. In this situation there is such a choice of difficulties, that I own myself at a loss how to determine. The affairs of Great Britain I know require the most vigorous measures, but then the courage of a handful of brave troops should be exerted only when there is some hope of a favorable event. However, you may be assured, that the small part of the campaign which remains shall be employed (as far as I am able) for the honor of his Majesty, and the interest of the nation; in which I am sure of being well seconded by the admiral and by the generals: happy if our efforts here can contribute to the success of his Majesty's arms in any other part of America."

[1]"This anecdote was related by the late celebrated John Robison, Professor of Natural Philosophy in the University of Edinburgh, who, in his youth, was a midshipman in the British navy, and was in the same boat with Wolfe. His son, my kinsman, Sir John Robison, communicated it to me, and it has since been recorded in the Transactions of the Royal Society of Edinburgh.

'The paths of glory lead but to the grave'

is one of the lines which Wolfe must have recited as he strikingly exemplified its application."—Grahame, *Hist. U. S.* IV. 50. See also *Playfair's Works*, IV. 126.

"La France!" answered a captain of Fraser's Highlanders, from the foremost boat.

"A quel régiment?" demanded the soldier.

"De la Reine!" promptly replied the Highland captain, who chanced to know that the regiment so designated formed part of Bougainville's command. As boats were frequently passing down the river with supplies for the garrison, and as a convoy from Bougainville was expected that very night, the sentinel was deceived, and allowed the English to proceed.

A few moments after, they were challenged again, and this time they could discern the soldier running close down to the water's edge, as if all his suspicions were aroused; but the skilful replies of the Highlander once more saved the party from discovery.[1]

They reached the landing-place in safety,—an indentation in the shore, about a league above the city, and now bearing the name of Wolfe's Cove. Here a narrow path led up the face of the heights, and a French guard was posted at the top to defend the pass. By the force of the current, the foremost boats, including that which carried Wolfe himself, were borne a little below the spot. The general was one of the first on shore. He looked upward at the rugged heights which towered above him in the gloom. "You can try it," he coolly observed to an officer near him; "but I don't think you'll get up."[2]

At the point where the Highlanders landed, one of their captains, Donald Macdonald, apparently the same whose presence of mind had just saved the enterprise from ruin, was climbing in advance of his men, when he was challenged by a sentinel. He replied in French, by declaring that he had been sent to relieve the guard, and ordering the soldier to withdraw.[3] Before the latter was undeceived, a crowd of Highlanders were close at hand, while the steeps below were

---

[1] Smollett, V. 56, *note* (Edinburgh, 1805). Mante simply mentions that the English were challenged by the sentinels, and escaped discovery by replying in French.

[2] This incident is mentioned in a manuscript journal of the siege of Quebec, by John Johnson, clerk and quartermaster in the 58th regiment. The journal is written with great care, and abounds in curious details.

[3] Knox, *Journal*, II. 68, note.

thronged with eager climbers, dragging themselves up by trees, roots, and bushes.[1] The guard turned out, and made a brief though brave resistance. In a moment, they were cut to pieces, dispersed, or made prisoners; while men after men came swarming up the height, and quickly formed upon the plains above. Meanwhile, the vessels had dropped downward with the current, and anchored opposite the landing-place. The remaining troops were disembarked, and, with the dawn of day, the whole were brought in safety to the shore.

The sun rose, and, from the ramparts of Quebec, the astonished people saw the Plains of Abraham glittering with arms, and the dark-red lines of the English forming in array of battle. Breathless messengers had borne the evil tidings to Montcalm, and far and near his wide-extended camp resounded with the rolling of alarm drums and the din of startled preparation. He, too, had had his struggles and his sorrows. The civil power had thwarted him; famine, discontent, and disaffection were rife among his soldiers; and no small portion of the Canadian militia had dispersed from sheer starvation. In spite of all, he had trusted to hold out till the winter frosts should drive the invaders from before the town; when, on that disastrous morning, the news of their successful temerity fell like a cannon shot upon his ear. Still he assumed a tone of confidence. "They have got to the weak side of us at last," he is reported to have said, "and we must crush them with our numbers." With headlong haste, his troops were pouring over the bridge of the St. Charles, and gathering in heavy masses under the western ramparts of the town. Could numbers give assurance of success, their triumph would have been secure; for five French battalions and the armed colonial peasantry amounted in all to more than seven thousand five hundred men. Full in sight before them stretched the long, thin lines of the British forces,—the half-wild Highlanders, the steady soldiery of England, and the hardy levies of the provinces,—less than five thousand in number, but all inured to battle, and strong in the full assurance of success. Yet, could the chiefs of that gallant army have pierced the secrets of the future, could they have foreseen that the victory which they

---

[1] Despatch of Admiral Saunders, Sept. 20, 1759.

burned to achieve would have robbed England of her proudest boast, that the conquest of Canada would pave the way for the independence of America, their swords would have dropped from their hands, and the heroic fire have gone out within their hearts.

It was nine o'clock, and the adverse armies stood motionless, each gazing on the other. The clouds hung low, and, at intervals, warm light showers descended, besprinkling both alike. The coppice and cornfields in front of the British troops were filled with French sharpshooters, who kept up a distant, spattering fire. Here and there a soldier fell in the ranks, and the gap was filled in silence.

At a little before ten, the British could see that Montcalm was preparing to advance, and, in a few moments, all his troops appeared in rapid motion. They came on in three divisions, shouting after the manner of their nation, and firing heavily as soon as they came within range. In the British ranks, not a trigger was pulled, not a soldier stirred; and their ominous composure seemed to damp the spirits of the assailants. It was not till the French were within forty yards that the fatal word was given, and the British muskets blazed forth at once in one crashing explosion. Like a ship at full career, arrested with sudden ruin on a sunken rock, the ranks of Montcalm staggered, shivered, and broke before that wasting storm of lead. The smoke, rolling along the field, for a moment shut out the view; but when the white wreaths were scattered on the wind, a wretched spectacle was disclosed; men and officers tumbled in heaps, battalions resolved into a mob, order and obedience gone; and when the British muskets were levelled for a second volley, the masses of the militia were seen to cower and shrink with uncontrollable panic. For a few minutes, the French regulars stood their ground, returning a sharp and not ineffectual fire. But now, echoing cheer on cheer, redoubling volley on volley, trampling the dying and the dead, and driving the fugitives in crowds, the British troops advanced and swept the field before them. The ardor of the men burst all restraint. They broke into a run, and with unsparing slaughter chased the flying multitude to the gates of Quebec. Foremost of all, the light-footed Highlanders dashed along in furious pursuit, hewing down the

Frenchmen with their broadswords, and slaying many in the very ditch of the fortifications. Never was victory more quick or more decisive.[1]

In the short action and pursuit, the French lost fifteen hundred men, killed, wounded, and taken. Of the remainder, some escaped within the city, and others fled across the St. Charles to rejoin their comrades who had been left to guard the camp. The pursuers were recalled by sound of trumpet; the broken ranks were formed afresh, and the English troops withdrawn beyond reach of the cannon of Quebec. Bougainville, with his corps, arrived from the upper country, and, hovering about their rear, threatened an attack; but when he saw what greeting was prepared for him, he abandoned his purpose and withdrew. Townshend and Murray, the only general officers who remained unhurt, passed to the head of every regiment in turn, and thanked the soldiers for the bravery they had shown; yet the triumph of the victors was mingled with sadness, as the tidings went from rank to rank that Wolfe had fallen.

In the heat of the action, as he advanced at the head of the grenadiers of Louisburg, a bullet shattered his wrist; but he wrapped his handkerchief about the wound, and showed no sign of pain. A moment more, and a ball pierced his side. Still he pressed forward, waving his sword and cheering his soldiers to the attack, when a third shot lodged deep within his breast. He paused, reeled, and, staggering to one side, fell to the earth. Brown, a lieutenant of the grenadiers, Henderson, a volunteer, an officer of artillery, and a private soldier, raised him together in their arms, and, bearing him to the rear, laid him softly on the grass. They asked if he would have a surgeon; but he shook his head, and answered that all was over with him. His eyes closed with the torpor of approaching death, and those around sustained his fainting form. Yet they could not withhold their gaze from the wild turmoil before them, and the charging ranks of their companions rushing through fire and smoke. "See how they run," one of the

[1]Despatch of General Townshend, Sept. 20. Gardiner, *Memoirs of the Siege of Quebec*, 28. *Journal of the Siege of Quebec, by a Gentleman in an Eminent Station on the Spot*, 40. *Letter to a Right Honorable Patriot on the Glorious Success of Quebec. Annual Register for 1759*, 40.

officers exclaimed, as the French fled in confusion before the levelled bayonets. "Who run?" demanded Wolfe, opening his eyes like a man aroused from sleep. "The enemy, sir," was the reply; "they give way everywhere." "Then," said the dying general, "tell Colonel Burton to march Webb's regiment down to Charles River, to cut off their retreat from the bridge. Now, God be praised, I will die in peace," he murmured; and, turning on his side, he calmly breathed his last.[1]

Almost at the same moment fell his great adversary, Montcalm, as he strove, with vain bravery, to rally his shattered ranks. Struck down with a mortal wound, he was placed upon a litter and borne to the General Hospital on the banks of the St. Charles. The surgeons told him that he could not recover. "I am glad of it," was his calm reply. He then asked how long he might survive, and was told that he had not many hours remaining. "So much the better," he said; "I am happy that I shall not live to see the surrender of Quebec." Officers from the garrison came to his bedside to ask his orders and instructions. "I will give no more orders," replied the defeated soldier; "I have much business that must be attended to, of greater moment than your ruined garrison and this wretched country. My time is very short; therefore, pray leave me." The officers withdrew, and none remained in the chamber but his confessor and the Bishop of Quebec. To the last, he expressed his contempt for his own mutinous and half-famished troops, and his admiration for the disciplined valor of his opponents.[2] He died before midnight, and was buried at his own desire in a cavity of the earth formed by the bursting of a bombshell.

The victorious army encamped before Quebec, and pushed their preparations for the siege with zealous energy; but before a single gun was brought to bear, the white flag was hung out, and the garrison surrendered. On the eighteenth of September, 1759, the rock-built citadel of Canada passed forever from the hands of its ancient masters.

The victory on the Plains of Abraham and the downfall of Quebec filled all England with pride and exultation. From north to south, the land blazed with illuminations, and re-

---

[1]Knox, II. 78. Knox derived his information from the person who supported Wolfe in his dying moments.

[2]Knox, II. 77.

sounded with the ringing of bells, the firing of guns, and the shouts of the multitude. In one village alone all was dark and silent amid the general joy; for here dwelt the widowed mother of Wolfe. The populace, with unwonted delicacy, respected her lonely sorrow, and forbore to obtrude the sound of their rejoicings upon her grief for one who had been through life her pride and solace, and repaid her love with a tender and constant devotion.[1]

Canada, crippled and dismembered by the disasters of this year's campaign, lay waiting, as it were, the final stroke which was to extinguish her last remains of life, and close the eventful story of French dominion in America. Her limbs and her head were lopped away, but life still fluttered at her heart. Quebec, Niagara, Frontenac, and Crown Point had fallen; but Montreal and the adjacent country still held out, and thither, with the opening season of 1760, the British commanders turned all their energies. Three armies were to enter Canada at three several points, and, conquering as they advanced, converge towards Montreal as a common centre. In accordance with this plan, Sir Jeffrey Amherst embarked at Oswego, crossed Lake Ontario, and descended the St. Lawrence with ten thousand men; while Colonel Haviland advanced by way of Lake Champlain and the River Sorel, and General Murray ascended from Quebec, with a body of the veterans who had fought on the Plains of Abraham.

By a singular concurrence of fortune and skill, the three armies reached the neighborhood of Montreal on the same day. The feeble and disheartened garrison could offer no resistance, and on the eighth of September, 1760, the Marquis de Vaudreuil surrendered Canada, with all its dependencies, to the British crown.

[1] *Annual Register for 1759*, 43.

Chapter V.

1755 – 1763.

THE WILDERNESS AND ITS TENANTS AT THE CLOSE OF THE FRENCH WAR.

WE HAVE already seen how, after the defeat of Braddock, the western tribes rose with one accord against the English. Then, for the first time, Pennsylvania felt the scourge of Indian war; and her neighbors, Maryland and Virginia, shared her misery. Through the autumn of 1755, the storm raged with devastating fury; but the following year brought some abatement of its violence. This may be ascribed partly to the interference of the Iroquois, who, at the instances of Sir William Johnson, urged the Delawares to lay down the hatchet, and partly to the persuasions of several prominent men among the Quakers, who, by kind and friendly treatment, had gained the confidence of the Indians.[1] By these means, that portion of the Delawares and their kindred tribes who dwelt upon the Susquehanna, were induced to send a deputation of chiefs to Easton, in the summer of 1757, to meet the provincial delegates; and here, after much delay and difficulty, a treaty of peace was concluded.

This treaty, however, did not embrace the Indians of the Ohio, who comprised the most formidable part of the Delawares and Shawanoes, and who still continued their murderous attacks. It was not till the summer of 1758, when General Forbes, with a considerable army, was advancing against Fort du Quesne, that these exasperated savages could be brought to reason. Well knowing that, should Forbes prove successful, they might expect a summary chastisement for their misdeeds, they began to waver in their attachment to the French; and the latter, in the hour of peril, found themselves threatened with desertion by allies who had shown an ample alacrity in the season of prosperity. This new tendency of the Ohio Indians was fostered by a wise step on the part of

---

[1]Gordon, *Hist. Penn.* 321. *Causes of the Alienation of the Delaware and Shawanese Indians from the British Interest*. MS. *Johnson Papers*.

the English. A man was found bold and hardy enough to venture into the midst of their villages, bearing the news of the treaty at Easton, and the approach of Forbes, coupled with proposals of peace from the governor of Pennsylvania.

This stout-hearted emissary was Christian Frederic Post, a Moravian missionary, who had long lived with the Indians, had twice married among them, and, by his upright dealings and plain good sense, had gained their confidence and esteem. His devout and conscientious spirit, his fidelity to what he deemed his duty, his imperturbable courage, his prudence and his address, well fitted him for the critical mission. His journals, written in a style of quaint simplicity, are full of lively details, and afford a curious picture of forest life and character. He left Philadelphia in July, attended by a party of friendly Indians, on whom he relied for protection. Reaching the Ohio, he found himself beset with perils from the jealousy and malevolence of the savage warriors, and the machinations of the French, who would gladly have destroyed him.[1] Yet he

---

[1] The following are extracts from his journals: —

"We set out from Kushkushkee for Sankonk; my company consisted of twenty-five horsemen and fifteen foot. We arrived at Sankonk in the afternoon. The people of the town were much disturbed at my coming, and received me in a very rough manner. They surrounded me with drawn knives in their hands, in such a manner that I could hardly get along; running up against me with their breasts open, as if they wanted some pretence to kill me. I saw by their countenances they sought my death. Their faces were quite distorted with rage, and they went so far as to say, I should not live long; but some Indians, with whom I was formerly acquainted, coming up and saluting me in a friendly manner, their behavior to me was quickly changed." . . .

"Some of my party desired me not to stir from the fire, for that the French had offered a great reward for my scalp, and that there were several parties out on that purpose. Accordingly I stuck constantly as close to the fire as if I had been chained there. . . .

"In the afternoon, all the captains gathered together in the middle town; they sent for us, and desired we should give them information of our message. Accordingly we did. We read the message with great satisfaction to them. It was a great pleasure both to them and us. The number of captains and counsellors were sixteen. In the evening, messengers arrived from Fort Duquesne, with a string of wampum from the commander; upon which they all came together in the house where we lodged. The messengers delivered their string, with these words from their father, the French king: —

" 'My children, come to me, and hear what I have to say. The English are coming with an army to destroy both you and me. I therefore desire you

found friends wherever he went, and finally succeeded in convincing the Indians that their true interest lay in a strict neutrality. When, therefore, Forbes appeared before Fort du Quesne, the French found themselves abandoned to their own resources; and, unable to hold their ground, they retreated down the Ohio, leaving the fort an easy conquest to the invaders. During the autumn, the Ohio Indians sent their deputies to Easton, where a great council was held, and a formal peace concluded with the provinces.[1]

While the friendship of these tribes was thus lost and regained, their ancient tyrants, the Iroquois, remained in a state of very doubtful attachment. At the outbreak of the war, they had shown, it is true, many signs of friendship;[2] but the disasters of the first campaign had given them a contemptible idea of British prowess. This impression was deepened, when, in the following year, they saw Oswego taken by the French, and the British general, Webb, retreat with dastardly haste from an enemy who did not dream of pursuing him. At this time, some of the confederates actually took up the hatchet on

---

immediately, my children, to hasten with all the young men; we will drive the English and destroy them. I, as a father, will tell you always what is best.' He laid the string before one of the captains. After a little conversation, the captain stood up, and said, 'I have just heard something of our brethren, the English, which pleaseth me much better. I will not go. Give it to the others; maybe they will go.' The messenger took up again the string, and said, 'He won't go; he has heard of the English.' Then all cried out, 'Yes, yes, we have heard from the English.' He then threw the string to the other fireplace, where the other captains were; but they kicked it from one to another, as if it was a snake. Captain Peter took a stick, and with it flung the string from one end of the room to the other, and said, 'Give it to the French captain, and let him go with his young men; he boasted much of his fighting; now let us see his fighting. We have often ventured our lives for him; and had hardly a loaf of bread when we came to him; and now he thinks we should jump to serve him.' Then we saw the French captain mortified to the uttermost; he looked as pale as death. The Indians discoursed and joked till midnight; and the French captain sent messengers at midnight to Fort Duquesne."

The kicking about of the wampum belt is the usual indication of contempt for the message of which the belt is the token. The uses of wampum will be described hereafter.

[1] *Minutes of Council at Easton*, 1758.

[2] *Account of Conferences between Major-General Sir W. Johnson and the Chief Sachems and Warriors of the Six Nations* (Lond. 1756).

the side of France, and there was danger that the rest might follow their example.[1] But now a new element was infused into the British counsels. The fortunes of the conflict began to change. Du Quesne and Louisburg were taken, and the Iroquois conceived a better opinion of the British arms. Their friendship was no longer a matter of doubt; and in 1760, when Amherst was preparing to advance on Montreal, the warriors flocked to his camp like vultures to the carcass. Yet there is little doubt, that, had their sachems and orators followed the dictates of their cooler judgment, they would not have aided in destroying Canada; for they could see that in the colonies of France lay the only barrier against the growing power and ambition of the English provinces.

The Hurons of Lorette, the Abenakis, and other domiciliated tribes of Canada, ranged themselves on the side of France throughout the war; and at its conclusion, they, in common with the Canadians, may be regarded in the light of a conquered people.

The numerous tribes of the remote west had, with few exceptions, played the part of active allies of the French; and warriors might be found on the farthest shores of Lake Superior who garnished their war-dress with the scalp-locks of murdered Englishmen. With the conquest of Canada, these tribes subsided into a state of inaction, which was not long to continue.

And now, before launching into the story of the sanguinary war which forms our proper and immediate theme, it will be well to survey the grand arena of the strife, the goodly heritage which the wretched tribes of the forest struggled to retrieve from the hands of the spoiler.

One vast, continuous forest shadowed the fertile soil, covering the land as the grass covers a garden lawn, sweeping over hill and hollow in endless undulation, burying mountains in verdure, and mantling brooks and rivers from the light of day. Green intervals dotted with browsing deer, and broad plains alive with buffalo, broke the sameness of the woodland scenery. Unnumbered rivers seamed the forest with their devious windings. Vast lakes washed its boundaries, where the Indian

[1]MS. *Johnson Papers.*

voyager, in his birch canoe, could descry no land beyond the world of waters. Yet this prolific wilderness, teeming with waste fertility, was but a hunting-ground and a battle-field to a few fierce hordes of savages. Here and there, in some rich meadow opened to the sun, the Indian squaws turned the black mould with their rude implements of bone or iron, and sowed their scanty stores of maize and beans. Human labor drew no other tribute from that exhaustless soil.

So thin and scattered was the native population, that, even in those parts which were thought well peopled, one might sometimes journey for days together through the twilight forest, and meet no human form. Broad tracts were left in solitude. All Kentucky was a vacant waste, a mere skirmishing ground for the hostile war-parties of the north and south. A great part of Upper Canada, of Michigan, and of Illinois, besides other portions of the west, were tenanted by wild beasts alone. To form a close estimate of the numbers of the erratic bands who roamed this wilderness would be impossible; but it may be affirmed that, between the Mississippi on the west and the ocean on the east, between the Ohio on the south and Lake Superior on the north, the whole Indian population, at the close of the French war, did not greatly exceed ten thousand fighting men. Of these, following the statement of Sir William Johnson, in 1763, the Iroquois had nineteen hundred and fifty, the Delawares about six hundred, the Shawanoes about three hundred, the Wyandots about four hundred and fifty, and the Miami tribes, with their neighbors the Kickapoos, eight hundred; while the Ottawas, the Ojibwas, and other wandering tribes of the north, defy all efforts at enumeration.[1]

A close survey of the condition of the tribes at this period will detect some signs of improvement, but many more of degeneracy and decay. To commence with the Iroquois, for to them with justice the priority belongs: Onondaga, the ancient capital of their confederacy, where their council-fire had burned from immemorial time, was now no longer what it had been in the days of its greatness, when Count Frontenac

[1] The estimates given by Croghan, Bouquet, and Hutchins, do not quite accord with that of Johnson. But the discrepancy is no greater than might have been expected from the difficulties of the case.

had mustered all Canada to assail it. The thickly clustered dwellings, with their triple rows of palisades, had vanished. A little stream, twisting along the valley, choked up with logs and driftwood, and half hidden by woods and thickets, some forty houses of bark, scattered along its banks, amid rank grass, neglected clumps of bushes, and ragged patches of corn and peas,—such was Onondaga when Bartram saw it, and such, no doubt, it remained at the time of which I write.[1] Conspicuous among the other structures, and distinguished only by its superior size, stood the great council-house, whose bark walls had often sheltered the congregated wisdom of the confederacy, and heard the highest efforts of forest eloquence. The other villages of the Iroquois resembled Onondaga; for though several were of larger size, yet none retained those defensive stockades which had once protected them.[2] From their European neighbors the Iroquois had borrowed many appliances of comfort and subsistence. Horses, swine, and in some instances cattle, were to be found among them. Guns and gunpowder aided them in the chase. Knives, hatchets, kettles, and hoes of iron, had supplanted their rude household utensils and implements of tillage; but with all this, English whiskey had more than cancelled every benefit which English civilization had conferred.

High up the Susquehanna were seated the Nanticokes, Conoys, and Mohicans, with a portion of the Delawares. Detached bands of the western Iroquois dwelt upon the head waters of the Alleghany, mingled with their neighbors, the Delawares, who had several villages upon this stream. The great body of the latter nation, however, lived upon the Beaver Creeks and the Muskingum, in numerous scattered towns and hamlets, whose barbarous names it is useless to record. Squalid log cabins and conical wigwams of bark were clustered at random, or ranged to form rude streets and squares. Starveling horses grazed on the neighboring meadows; girls and children bathed and laughed in the adjacent river;

[1] Bartram, *Observations*, 41.

[2] I am indebted to the kindness of Rev. S. K. Lothrop for a copy of the journal of Mr. Kirkland on his missionary tour among the Iroquois in 1765. The journal contains much information respecting their manners and condition at this period.

warriors smoked their pipes in haughty indolence; squaws labored in the cornfields, or brought fagots from the forest, and shrivelled hags screamed from lodge to lodge. In each village one large building stood prominent among the rest, devoted to purposes of public meeting, dances, festivals, and the entertainment of strangers. Thither the traveller would be conducted, seated on a bear-skin, and plentifully regaled with hominy and venison.

The Shawanoes had sixteen small villages upon the Scioto and its branches. Farther towards the west, on the waters of the Wabash and the Maumee, dwelt the Miamis, who, less exposed, from their position, to the poison of the whiskey-keg, and the example of debauched traders, retained their ancient character and customs in greater purity than their eastern neighbors. This cannot be said of the Illinois, who dwelt near the borders of the Mississippi, and who, having lived for more than half a century in close contact with the French, had become a corrupt and degenerate race. The Wyandots of Sandusky and Detroit far surpassed the surrounding tribes in energy of character and in social progress. Their log dwellings were strong and commodious, their agriculture was very considerable, their name stood high in war and policy, and they were regarded with deference by all the adjacent Indians. It is needless to pursue farther this catalogue of tribes, since the position of each will appear hereafter as they advance in turn upon the stage of action.

The English settlements lay like a narrow strip between the wilderness and the sea, and, as the sea had its ports, so also the forest had its places of rendezvous and outfit. Of these, by far the most important in the northern provinces was the frontier city of Albany. From thence it was that traders and soldiers, bound to the country of the Iroquois, or the more distant wilds of the interior, set out upon their arduous journey. Embarking in a bateau or a canoe, rowed by the hardy men who earned their livelihood in this service, the traveller would ascend the Mohawk, passing the old Dutch town of Schenectady, the two seats of Sir William Johnson, Fort Hunter at the mouth of the Scoharie, and Fort Herkimer at the German Flats, until he reached Fort Stanwix at the head of the river navigation. Then crossing over land to Wood Creek, he would follow its tortuous course, overshadowed by the dense forest on its banks, until he arrived at the little fortification called the Royal Blockhouse, and the waters of the Oneida Lake spread before him. Crossing to its western extremity, and passing under the wooden ramparts of Fort Brewerton, he would descend the River Oswego to Oswego,[1] on the banks of Lake Ontario. Here the vast navigation of the Great Lakes would be open before him, interrupted only by the difficult portage at the Cataract of Niagara.

The chief thoroughfare from the middle colonies to the Indian country was from Philadelphia westward, across the Alleghanies, to the valley of the Ohio. Peace was no sooner concluded with the hostile tribes, than the adventurous fur-traders, careless of risk to life and property, hastened over the mountains, each eager to be foremost in the wilderness market. Their merchandise was sometimes carried in wagons as far as the site of Fort du Quesne, which the English rebuilt after its capture, changing its name to Fort Pitt. From this point the goods were packed on the backs of horses, and thus distributed among the various Indian villages. More com-

---

[1]MS. *Journal of Lieutenant Gorell*, 1763. Anonymous MS. *Journal of a Tour to Niagara in 1765*. The following is an extract from the latter: —

"July 2d. Dined with Sir Wm. at Johnson Hall. The office of Superintendent very troublesome. Sir Wm. continually plagued with Indians about him—generally from 300 to 900 in number—spoil his garden, and keep his house always dirty. . . .

"10th. Punted and rowed up the Mohawk River against the stream, which, on account of the rapidity of the current, is very hard work for the poor soldiers. Encamped on the banks of the river, about 9 miles from Harkimer's.

"The inconveniences attending a married Subaltern strongly appear in this tour. What with the sickness of their wives, the squealing of their children, and the smallness of their pay, I think the gentlemen discover no common share of philosophy in keeping themselves from running mad. Officers and soldiers, with their wives and children, legitimate and illegitimate, make altogether a pretty compound oglio, which does not tend towards showing military matrimony off to any great advantage. . . .

"Monday, 14th. Went on horseback by the side of Wood Creek, 20 miles, to the Royal Blockhouse, a kind of wooden castle, proof against any Indian attacks. It is now abandoned by the troops, and a sutler lives there, who keeps rum, milk, rackoons, etc., which, though none of the most elegant, is comfortable to strangers passing that way. The Blockhouse is situated on the east end of the Oneida Lake, and is surrounded by the Oneida Indians, one of the Six Nations."

monly, however, the whole journey was performed by means of trains, or, as they were called, brigades of packhorses, which, leaving the frontier settlements, climbed the shadowy heights of the Alleghanies, and threaded the forests of the Ohio, diving through thickets, and wading over streams. The men employed in this perilous calling were a rough, bold, and intractable class, often as fierce and truculent as the Indians themselves. A blanket coat, or a frock of smoked deer-skin, a rifle on the shoulder, and a knife and tomahawk in the belt, formed their ordinary equipment. The principal trader, the owner of the merchandise, would fix his headquarters at some large Indian town, whence he would despatch his subordinates to the surrounding villages, with a suitable supply of blankets and red cloth, guns and hatchets, liquor, tobacco, paint, beads, and hawks' bells. This wild traffic was liable to every species of disorder; and it is not to be wondered at that, in a region where law was unknown, the jealousies of rival traders should become a fruitful source of broils, robberies, and murders.

In the backwoods, all land travelling was on foot, or on horseback. It was no easy matter for a novice, embarrassed with his cumbrous gun, to urge his horse through the thick trunks and undergrowth, or even to ride at speed along the narrow Indian trails, where at every yard the impending branches switched him across the face. At night, the camp would be formed by the side of some rivulet or spring; and, if the traveller was skilful in the use of his rifle, a haunch of venison would often form his evening meal. If it rained, a shed of elm or bass-wood bark was the ready work of an hour, a pile of evergreen boughs formed a bed, and the saddle or the knapsack a pillow. A party of Indian wayfarers would often be met journeying through the forest, a chief, or a warrior, perhaps, with his squaws and family. The Indians would usually make their camp in the neighborhood of the white men; and at meal-time the warrior would seldom fail to seat himself by the traveller's fire, and gaze with solemn gravity at the viands before him. If, when the repast was over, a fragment of bread or a cup of coffee should be handed to him, he would receive these highly prized rarities with an ejaculation of gratitude; for nothing is more remarkable in the character of this people than the union of inordinate pride and a generous love of glory with the mendicity of a beggar or a child.

He who wished to visit the remoter tribes of the Mississippi valley—an attempt, however, which, until several years after the conquest of Canada, no Englishman could have made without great risk of losing his scalp—would find no easier course than to descend the Ohio in a canoe or bateau. He might float for more than eleven hundred miles down this liquid highway of the wilderness, and, except the deserted cabins of Logstown, a little below Fort Pitt, the remnant of a Shawanoe village at the mouth of the Scioto, and an occasional hamlet or solitary wigwam along the deeply wooded banks, he would discern no trace of human habitation through all this vast extent. The body of the Indian population lay to the northward, about the waters of the tributary streams. It behooved the voyager to observe a sleepless caution and a hawk-eyed vigilance. Sometimes his anxious scrutiny would detect a faint blue smoke stealing upward above the green bosom of the forest, and betraying the encamping place of some lurking war-party. Then the canoe would be drawn in haste beneath the overhanging bushes which skirted the shore; nor would the voyage be resumed until darkness closed, when the little vessel would drift swiftly and safely by the point of danger.[1]

Within the nominal limits of the Illinois Indians, and towards the southern extremity of the present state of Illinois, were those isolated Canadian settlements, which had subsisted here since the latter part of the preceding century. Kaskaskia, Cahokia, and Vincennes were the centres of this scattered population. From Vincennes one might paddle his canoe northward up the Wabash, until he reached the little wooden fort of Ouatanon. Thence a path through the woods led to the banks of the Maumee. Two or three Canadians, or

---

[1] Mitchell, *Contest in America*. Pouchot, *Guerre de l'Amérique. Expedition against the Ohio Indians, appendix.* Hutchins, *Topographical Description of Virginia*, etc. Pownall, *Topographical Description of North America.* Evans, *Analysis of a Map of the Middle British Colonies.* Beatty, *Journal of a Tour in America.* Smith, *Narrative.* M'Cullough, *Narrative.* Jemmison, *Narrative.* Post, *Journals.* Washington, *Journals*, 1753–1770. Gist, *Journal*, 1750. Croghan, *Journal*, 1765, etc., etc.

half-breeds, of whom there were numbers about the fort, would carry the canoe on their shoulders, or, for a bottle of whiskey, a few Miami Indians might be bribed to undertake the task. On the Maumee, at the end of the path, stood Fort Miami, near the spot where Fort Wayne was afterwards built. From this point one might descend the Maumee to Lake Erie, and visit the neighboring fort of Sandusky, or, if he chose, steer through the Strait of Detroit, and explore the watery wastes of the northern lakes, finding occasional harborage at the little military posts which commanded their important points. Most of these western posts were transferred to the English, during the autumn of 1760; but the settlements of the Illinois remained several years longer under French control.

Eastward, on the waters of Lake Erie, and the Alleghany, stood three small forts, Presqu' Isle, Le Bœuf, and Venango, which had passed into the hands of the English soon after the capture of Fort du Quesne. The feeble garrisons of all these western posts, exiled from civilization, lived in the solitude of military hermits. Through the long, hot days of summer, and the protracted cold of winter, time hung heavy on their hands. Their resources of employment and recreation were few and meagre. They found partners in their loneliness among the young beauties of the Indian camps. They hunted and fished, shot at targets, and played at games of chance; and when, by good fortune, a traveller found his way among them, he was greeted with a hearty and open-handed welcome, and plied with eager questions touching the great world from which they were banished men. Yet, tedious as it was, their secluded life was seasoned with stirring danger. The surrounding forests were peopled with a race dark and subtle as their own sunless mazes. At any hour, those jealous tribes might raise the war-cry. No human foresight could predict the sallies of their fierce caprice, and in ceaseless watching lay the only safety.

When the European and the savage are brought in contact, both are gainers, and both are losers. The former loses the refinements of civilization, but he gains, in the rough schooling of the wilderness, a rugged independence, a self-sustaining energy, and powers of action and perception before unthought of. The savage gains new means of comfort and support, cloth, iron, and gunpowder; yet these apparent benefits have often proved but instruments of ruin. They soon become necessities, and the unhappy hunter, forgetting the weapons of his fathers, must thenceforth depend on the white man for ease, happiness, and life itself.

Those rude and hardy men, hunters and traders, scouts and guides, who ranged the woods beyond the English borders, and formed a connecting link between barbarism and civilization, have been touched upon already. They were a distinct, peculiar class, marked with striking contrasts of good and evil. Many, though by no means all, were coarse, audacious, and unscrupulous; yet, even in the worst, one might often have found a vigorous growth of warlike virtues, an iron endurance, an undespairing courage, a wondrous sagacity, and singular fertility of resource. In them was renewed, with all its ancient energy, that wild and daring spirit, that force and hardihood of mind, which marked our barbarous ancestors of Germany and Norway. These sons of the wilderness still survive. We may find them to this day, not in the valley of the Ohio, nor on the shores of the lakes, but far westward on the desert range of the buffalo, and among the solitudes of Oregon. Even now, while I write, some lonely trapper is climbing the perilous defiles of the Rocky Mountains, his strong frame cased in time-worn buck-skin, his rifle griped in his sinewy hand. Keenly he peers from side to side, lest Blackfoot or Arapahoe should ambuscade his path. The rough earth is his bed, a morsel of dried meat and a draught of water are his food and drink, and death and danger his companions. No anchorite could fare worse, no hero could dare more; yet his wild, hard life has resistless charms; and, while he can wield a rifle, he will never leave it. Go with him to the rendezvous, and he is a stoic no more. Here, rioting among his comrades, his native appetites break loose in mad excess, in deep carouse, and desperate gaming. Then follow close the quarrel, the challenge, the fight,—two rusty rifles and fifty yards of prairie.

The nursling of civilization, placed in the midst of the forest, and abandoned to his own resources, is helpless as an infant. There is no clew to the labyrinth. Bewildered and amazed, he circles round and round in hopeless wanderings. Despair and famine make him their prey, and unless the birds of heaven minister to his wants, he dies in misery. Not so the practised woodsman. To him, the forest is a home. It yields him food, shelter, and raiment, and he threads its trackless depths with undeviating foot. To lure the game, to circumvent the lurking foe, to guide his course by the stars, the wind, the streams, or the trees,—such are the arts which the white man has learned from the red. Often, indeed, the pupil has outstripped his master. He can hunt as well; he can fight better; and yet there are niceties of the woodsman's craft in which the white man must yield the palm to his savage rival. Seldom can he boast, in equal measure, that subtlety of sense, more akin to the instinct of brutes than to human reason, which reads the signs of the forest as the scholar reads the printed page, to which the whistle of a bird can speak clearly as the tongue of man, and the rustle of a leaf give knowledge of life or death.[1] With us the name of the savage is a byword of reproach. The Indian would look with equal scorn on those who, buried in useless lore, are blind and deaf to the great world of nature.

[1] A striking example of Indian acuteness once came under my observation. Travelling in company with a Canadian named Raymond, and an Ogillallah Indian, we came at nightfall to a small stream called Chugwater, a branch of Laramie Creek. As we prepared to encamp, we observed the ashes of a fire, the footprints of men and horses, and other indications that a party had been upon the spot not many days before. Having secured our horses for the night, Raymond and I sat down and lighted our pipes, my companion, who had spent his whole life in the Indian country, hazarding various conjectures as to the numbers and character of our predecessors. Soon after, we were joined by the Indian, who, meantime, had been prowling about the place. Raymond asked what discovery he had made. He answered, that the party were friendly, and that they consisted of eight men, both whites and Indians, several of whom he named, affirming that he knew them well. To an inquiry how he gained his information, he would make no intelligible reply. On the next day, reaching Fort Laramie, a post of the American Fur Company, we found that he was correct in every particular,—a circumstance the more remarkable, as he had been with us for three weeks, and could have had no other means of knowledge than we ourselves.

Chapter VI.

1760.

THE ENGLISH TAKE POSSESSION OF THE WESTERN POSTS.

THE WAR was over. The plains around Montreal were dotted with the white tents of three victorious armies, and the work of conquest was complete. Canada, with all her dependencies, had yielded to the British crown; but it still remained to carry into full effect the terms of the surrender, and take possession of those western outposts, where the lilies of France had not as yet descended from the flagstaff. The execution of this task, neither an easy nor a safe one, was assigned to a provincial officer, Major Robert Rogers.

Rogers was a native of New Hampshire. He commanded a body of provincial rangers, and stood in high repute as a partisan officer. Putnam and Stark were his associates; and it was in this woodland warfare that the former achieved many of those startling adventures and hair-breadth escapes which have made his name familiar at every New-England fireside. Rogers's Rangers, half hunters, half woodsmen, trained in a discipline of their own, and armed, like Indians, with hatchet, knife, and gun, were employed in a service of peculiar hardship. Their chief theatre of action was the mountainous region of Lake George, the debatable ground between the hostile forts of Ticonderoga and William Henry. The deepest recesses of these romantic solitudes had heard the French and Indian yell, and the answering shout of the hardy New-England men. In summer, they passed down the lake in whale boats or canoes, or threaded the pathways of the woods in single file, like the savages themselves. In winter, they journeyed through the swamps on snowshoes, skated along the frozen surface of the lake, and bivouacked at night among the snow-drifts. They intercepted French messengers, encountered French scouting parties, and carried off prisoners from under the very walls of Ticonderoga. Their hardships and adventures, their marches and countermarches, their frequent skirmishes and midwinter battles, had made them famous throughout America; and though it was the fashion of the day to sneer at the efforts of provincial troops, the name of Rogers's Rangers was never mentioned but with honor.

Their commander was a man tall and strong in person, and rough in feature. He was versed in all the arts of woodcraft, sagacious, prompt, and resolute, yet so cautious withal that he sometimes incurred the unjust charge of cowardice. His mind, naturally active, was by no means uncultivated; and his books and unpublished letters bear witness that his style as a writer was not contemptible. But his vain, restless, and grasping spirit, and more than doubtful honesty, proved the ruin of an enviable reputation. Six years after the expedition of which I am about to speak, he was tried by a court-martial for a meditated act of treason, the surrender of Fort Michilli-mackinac into the hands of the Spaniards, who were at that time masters of Upper Louisiana.[1] Not long after, if we may trust his own account, he passed over to the Barbary States, entered the service of the Dey of Algiers, and fought two battles under his banners. At the opening of the war of independence, he returned to his native country, where he made professions of patriotism, but was strongly suspected by many, including Washington himself, of acting the part of a spy. In fact, he soon openly espoused the British cause, and received a colonel's commission from the crown. His services, however, proved of little consequence. In 1778, he was proscribed and banished, under the act of New Hampshire, and the remainder of his life was passed in such obscurity that it is difficult to determine when and where he died.[2]

[1] MS. *Gage Papers*.

[2] Sabine, *American Loyalists*, 576. Sparks, *Writings of Washington*, III. 208, 244, 439; IV, 128, 520, 524.

Although Rogers, especially where his pecuniary interest was concerned, was far from scrupulous, I have no hesitation in following his account of the expedition up the lakes. The incidents of each day are minuted down in a dry, unambitious style, bearing the clear impress of truth. Extracts from the orderly books and other official papers are given, while portions of the narrative, verified by contemporary documents, may stand as earnests for the truth of the whole.

Rogers's published works consist of the *Journals* of his ranging service and his *Concise Account of North America*, a small volume containing much valuable information. Both appeared in London in 1765. To these may be added a

On the twelfth of September, 1760, Rogers, then at the height of his reputation, received orders from Sir Jeffrey Amherst to ascend the lakes with a detachment of rangers, and take possession, in the name of his Britannic Majesty, of Detroit, Michillimackinac, and other western posts included in the late capitulation. He left Montreal, on the following day, with two hundred rangers, in fifteen whale boats. Stemming the surges of La Chine and the Cedars, they left behind them the straggling hamlet which bore the latter name, and formed at that day the western limit of Canadian settlement.[1] They gained Lake Ontario, skirted its northern shore, amid rough and boisterous weather, and crossing at its western extremity, reached Fort Niagara on the first of October. Carrying their boats over the portage, they launched them once more above the cataract, and slowly pursued their voyage; while Rogers, with a few attendants, hastened on in advance to Fort Pitt, to deliver despatches, with which he was charged, to General Monkton. This errand accomplished, he rejoined his command at Presqu' Isle, about the end of the month, and the whole proceeded together along the southern margin of Lake Erie. The season was far advanced. The wind was chill, the lake was stormy, and the woods on shore were tinged with

---

curious drama, called *Ponteach, or the Savages of America*, which appears to have been written, in part, at least, by him. It is very rare, and besides the copy in my possession, I know of but one other, which may be found in the library of the British Museum. For an account of this curious production, see Appendix, B. An engraved full-length portrait of Rogers was published in London in 1776. He is represented as a tall, strong man, dressed in the costume of a ranger, with a powder-horn slung at his side, a gun resting in the hollow of his arm, and a countenance by no means prepossessing. Behind him, at a little distance, stand his Indian followers.

The steep mountain called Rogers' Slide, near the northern end of Lake George, derives its name from the tradition that, during the French war, being pursued by a party of Indians, he slid on snowshoes down its precipitous front, for more than a thousand feet, to the frozen lake below. On beholding the achievement, the Indians, as well they might, believed him under the protection of the Great Spirit, and gave over the chase. The story seems unfounded; yet it was not far from this mountain that the rangers fought one of their most desperate winter battles, against a force of many times their number.

[1]Henry, *Travels and Adventures*, 9.

the fading hues of autumn. On the seventh of November, they reached the mouth of a river called by Rogers the Chogage. No body of troops under the British flag had ever before penetrated so far. The day was dull and rainy, and, resolving to rest until the weather should improve, Rogers ordered his men to prepare their encampment in the neighboring forest.

Soon after the arrival of the rangers, a party of Indian chiefs and warriors entered the camp. They proclaimed themselves an embassy from Pontiac, ruler of all that country, and directed, in his name, that the English should advance no farther until they had had an interview with the great chief, who was already close at hand. In truth, before the day closed, Pontiac himself appeared; and it is here, for the first time, that this remarkable man stands forth distinctly on the page of history. He greeted Rogers with the haughty demand, what was his business in that country, and how he dared enter it without his permission. Rogers informed him that the French were defeated, that Canada had surrendered, and that he was on his way to take possession of Detroit, and restore a general peace to white men and Indians alike. Pontiac listened with attention, but only replied that he should stand in the path of the English until morning. Having inquired if the strangers were in need of any thing which his country could afford, he withdrew, with his chiefs, at nightfall, to his own encampment; while the English, ill at ease, and suspecting treachery, stood well on their guard throughout the night.[1]

In the morning, Pontiac returned to the camp with his attendant chiefs, and made his reply to Rogers's speech of the previous day. He was willing, he said, to live at peace with the English, and suffer them to remain in his country as long as they treated him with due respect and deference. The Indian chiefs and provincial officers smoked the calumet together, and perfect harmony seemed established between them.[2]

Up to this time, Pontiac had been, in word and deed, the

[1]There can be no reasonable doubt, that the interview with Pontiac, described by Rogers in his *Account of North America*, took place on the occasion indicated in his *Journals*, under date of the 7th of November. The Indians whom he afterwards met are stated to have been Hurons.

[2]Rogers, *Journals*, 214; *Account of North America*, 240, 243.

fast ally of the French; but it is easy to discern the motives
that impelled him to renounce his old adherence. The American forest never produced a man more shrewd, politic, and
ambitious. Ignorant as he was of what was passing in the
world, he could clearly see that the French power was on the
wane, and he knew his own interest too well to prop a falling
cause. By making friends of the English, he hoped to gain
powerful allies, who would aid his ambitious projects, and
give him an increased influence over the tribes; and he flattered himself that the new-comers would treat him with the
same respect which the French had always observed. In this,
and all his other expectations of advantage from the English,
he was doomed to disappointment.

A cold storm of rain set in, and the rangers were detained
several days in their encampment. During this time, Rogers
had several interviews with Pontiac, and was constrained to
admire the native vigor of his intellect, no less than the singular control which he exercised over those around him.

On the twelfth of November, the detachment was again in
motion, and within a few days they had reached the western
end of Lake Erie. Here they heard that the Indians of Detroit
were in arms against them, and that four hundred warriors lay
in ambush at the entrance of the river to cut them off. But the
powerful influence of Pontiac was exerted in behalf of his new
friends. The warriors abandoned their design, and the rangers
continued their progress towards Detroit, now within a short
distance.

In the mean time, Lieutenant Brehm had been sent forward
with a letter to Captain Belètre, the commandant at Detroit,
informing him that Canada had capitulated, that his garrison
was included in the capitulation, and that an English detachment was approaching to relieve it. The Frenchman, in great
wrath at the tidings, disregarded the message as an informal
communication, and resolved to keep a hostile attitude to the
last. He did his best to rouse the fury of the Indians. Among
other devices, he displayed upon a pole, before the yelling
multitude, the effigy of a crow pecking a man's head; the
crow representing himself, and the head, observes Rogers,
"being meant for my own." All his efforts were unavailing,

and his faithless allies showed unequivocal symptoms of defection in the hour of need.

Rogers had now entered the mouth of the River Detroit, whence he sent forward Captain Campbell with a copy of the capitulation, and a letter from the Marquis de Vaudreuil, directing that the place should be given up, in accordance with the terms agreed upon between him and General Amherst. Belètre was forced to yield, and with a very ill grace declared himself and his garrison at the disposal of the English commander.

The whale boats of the rangers moved slowly upwards between the low banks of the Detroit, until at length the green uniformity of marsh and forest was relieved by the Canadian houses, which began to appear on either bank, the outskirts of the secluded and isolated settlement. Before them, on the right side, they could see the village of the Wyandots, and on the left the clustered lodges of the Pottawattamies; while, a little beyond, the flag of France was flying for the last time above the bark roofs and weather-beaten palisades of the little fortified town.

The rangers landed on the opposite bank, and pitched their tents upon a meadow, while two officers, with a small detachment, went across the river to take possession of the place. In obedience to their summons, the French garrison defiled upon the plain, and laid down their arms. The *fleur de lis* was lowered from the flagstaff, and the cross of St. George rose aloft in its place, while seven hundred Indian warriors, lately the active allies of France, greeted the sight with a burst of triumphant yells. The Canadian militia were next called together and disarmed. The Indians looked on with amazement at their obsequious behavior, quite at a loss to understand why so many men should humble themselves before so few. Nothing is more effective in gaining the respect, or even attachment, of Indians than a display of power. The savage spectators conceived the loftiest idea of English prowess, and were astonished at the forbearance of the conquerors in not killing their vanquished enemies on the spot.

It was on the twenty-ninth of November, 1760, that Detroit fell into the hands of the English. The garrison were sent as prisoners down the lake, but the Canadian inhabitants were allowed to retain their farms and houses, on condition of swearing allegiance to the British crown. An officer was sent southward to take possession of the forts Miami and Ouatanon, which guarded the communication between Lake Erie and the Ohio; while Rogers himself, with a small party, proceeded northward to relieve the French garrison of Michillimackinac. The storms and gathering ice of Lake Huron forced him back without accomplishing his object; and Michillimackinac, with the three remoter posts of St. Marie, Green Bay, and St. Joseph, remained for a time in the hands of the French. During the next season, however, a detachment of the 60th regiment, then called the Royal Americans, took possession of them; and nothing now remained within the power of the French, except the few posts and settlements on the Mississippi and the Wabash, not included in the capitulation of Montreal.

The work of conquest was finished. The fertile wilderness beyond the Alleghanies, over which France had claimed sovereignty,—that boundless forest, with its tracery of interlacing streams, which, like veins and arteries, gave it life and nourishment,—had passed into the hands of her rival. It was by a few insignificant forts, separated by oceans of fresh water and uncounted leagues of forest, that the two great European powers, France first, and now England, endeavored to enforce their claims to this vast domain. There is something ludicrous in the disparity between the importance of the possession and the slenderness of the force employed to maintain it. A region embracing so many thousand miles of surface was consigned to the keeping of some five or six hundred men. Yet the force, small as it was, appeared adequate to its object, for there seemed no enemy to contend with. The hands of the French were tied by the capitulation, and little apprehension was felt from the red inhabitants of the woods. The lapse of two years sufficed to show how complete and fatal was the mistake.

Chapter VII.

ANGER OF THE INDIANS. — THE CONSPIRACY.

THE COUNTRY was scarcely transferred to the English, when smothered murmurs of discontent began to be audible among the Indian tribes. From the head of the Potomac to Lake Superior, and from the Alleghanies to the Mississippi, in every wigwam and hamlet of the forest, a deep-rooted hatred of the English increased with rapid growth. Nor is this to be wondered at. We have seen with what sagacious policy the French had labored to ingratiate themselves with the Indians; and the slaughter of the Monongahela, with the horrible devastation of the western frontier, the outrages perpetrated at Oswego, and the massacre at Fort William Henry, bore witness to the success of their efforts. Even the Delawares and Shawanoes, the faithful allies of William Penn, had at length been seduced by their blandishments; and the Iroquois, the ancient enemies of Canada, had half forgotten their former hostility, and well-nigh taken part against the British colonists. The remote nations of the west had also joined in the war, descending in their canoes for hundreds of miles, to fight against the enemies of France. All these tribes entertained towards the English that rancorous enmity which an Indian always feels against those to whom he has been opposed in war.

Under these circumstances, it behooved the English to use the utmost care in their conduct towards the tribes. But even when the conflict with France was impending, and the alliance with the Indians was of the last importance, they had treated them with indifference and neglect. They were not likely to adopt a different course now that their friendship seemed a matter of no consequence. In truth, the intentions of the English were soon apparent. In the zeal for retrenchment, which prevailed after the close of hostilities, the presents which it had always been customary to give the Indians, at stated intervals, were either withheld altogether, or doled out with a niggardly and reluctant hand; while, to make the matter worse, the agents and officers of government often appropriated the presents to themselves, and afterwards sold them at an exorbitant price to the Indians.[1] When the French had possession of the remote forts, they were accustomed, with a wise liberality, to supply the surrounding Indians with guns, ammunition, and clothing, until the latter had forgotten the weapons and garments of their forefathers, and depended on the white men for support. The sudden withholding of these supplies was, therefore, a grievous calamity. Want, suffering, and death, were the consequences; and this cause alone would have been enough to produce general discontent. But, unhappily, other grievances were superadded.[2]

[1] *MS. Johnson Papers.*

[2] Extract from a MS. letter—*Sir W. Johnson to Governor Colden*, Dec. 24, 1763.

"I shall not take upon me to point out the Originall Parsimony &c. to w^h the first defection of the Indians can with justice & certainty be attributed, but only observe, as I did in a former letter, that the Indians (whose friendship was never cultivated by the English with that attention, expense, & assiduity with w^h ye French obtained their favour) were for many years jealous of our growing power, were repeatedly assured by the French (who were at ye pains of having many proper emissaries among them) that so soon as we became masters of this country, we should immediately treat them with neglect, hem them in with Posts & Forts, encroach upon their Lands, and finally destroy them. All w^h after the reduction of Canada, seemed to appear too clearly to the Indians, who thereby lost the great advantages resulting from the possession w^h the French formerly had of Posts & Trade in their Country, neither of which they could have ever enjoyed but for the notice they took of the Indians, & the presents they bestowed so bountifully upon them, w^h however expensive, they wisely foresaw was infinitely cheaper, and much more effectual than the keeping of a large body of Regular Troops, in their several Countrys, . . . a Plan which has endeared their memory to most of the Indian Nations, who would I fear generally go over to them in case they ever got footing again in this Country, & who were repeatedly exhorted, & encouraged by the French (from motives of Interest & dislike w^h they will always possess) to fall upon us, by representing that their liberties & Country were in ye utmost danger." In January, 1763, Colonel Bouquet, commanding in Pennsylvania, writes to General Amherst, stating the discontent produced among the Indians by the suppression of presents. The commander-in-chief replies, "As to appropriating a particular sum to be laid out yearly to the warriors in presents, &c., that I can by no means agree to; nor can I think it necessary to give them any presents by way of *Bribes*, for if they do not behave properly they are to be punished." And again, in February, to the same officer, "As you are thoroughly acquainted with my sentiments

The English fur-trade had never been well regulated, and it was now in a worse condition than ever. Many of the traders, and those in their employ, were ruffians of the coarsest stamp, who vied with each other in rapacity, violence, and profligacy. They cheated, cursed, and plundered the Indians, and outraged their families; offering, when compared with the French traders, who were under better regulation, a most unfavorable example of the character of their nation.

The officers and soldiers of the garrisons did their full part in exciting the general resentment. Formerly, when the warriors came to the forts, they had been welcomed by the French with attention and respect. The inconvenience which their presence occasioned had been disregarded, and their peculiarities overlooked. But now they were received with cold looks and harsh words from the officers, and with oaths, menaces, and sometimes blows, from the reckless and brutal soldiers. When, after their troublesome and intrusive fashion, they were lounging everywhere about the fort, or lazily reclining in the shadow of the walls, they were met with muttered ejaculations of impatience, or abrupt orders to be gone, enforced, perhaps, by a touch from the butt of a sentinel's musket. These marks of contempt were unspeakably galling to their haughty spirit.[1]

But what most contributed to the growing discontent of the tribes was the intrusion of settlers upon their lands, at all times a fruitful source of Indian hostility. Its effects, it is true,

---

regarding the treatment of the Indians in general, you will of course order Cap. Ecuyer . . . not to give those who are able to provide for their families any encouragement to loiter away their time in idleness about the Fort."

[1] Some of the principal causes of the war are exhibited with spirit and truth in the old tragedy of *Ponteach*, written probably by Major Rogers. The portion of the play referred to is given in Appendix, B.

"The English treat us with much Disrespect, and we have the greatest Reason to believe, by their Behavior, they intend to Cut us off entirely; They have possessed themselves of our Country, it is now in our power to Dispossess them and Recover it, if we will but Embrace the opportunity before they have time to assemble together, and fortify themselves, there is no time to be lost, let us Strike immediately."—*Speech of a Seneca chief to the Wyandots and Ottawas of Detroit, July, 1761.*

could only be felt by those whose country bordered upon the English settlements; but among these were the most powerful and influential of the tribes. The Delawares and Shawanoes, in particular, had by this time been roused to the highest pitch of exasperation. Their best lands had been invaded, and all remonstrance had been fruitless. They viewed with wrath and fear the steady progress of the white man, whose settlements had passed the Susquehanna, and were fast extending to the Alleghanies, eating away the forest like a spreading canker. The anger of the Delawares was abundantly shared by their ancient conquerors, the Six Nations. The threatened occupation of Wyoming by settlers from Connecticut gave great umbrage to the confederacy.[1] The Senecas were more especially incensed at English intrusion, since, from their position, they were farthest removed from the soothing influence of Sir William Johnson, and most exposed to the seductions of the French; while the Mohawks, another member of the confederacy, were justly alarmed at seeing the better part of their lands patented out without their consent. Some Christian Indians of the Oneida tribe, in the simplicity of their hearts, sent an earnest petition to Sir William Johnson, that the English forts within the limits of the Six Nations might be removed, or, as the petition expresses it, *kicked out of the way.*[2]

The discontent of the Indians gave great satisfaction to the French, who saw in it an assurance of safe and bloody vengeance on their conquerors. Canada, it is true, was gone beyond hope of recovery; but they still might hope to revenge its loss. Interest, moreover, as well as passion, prompted them

---

[1] *Minutes of Conference with the Six Nations at Hartford*, 1763, MS. *Letter — Hamilton to Amherst*, May 10, 1761.

[2] "We are now left in Peace, and have nothing to do but to plant our Corn, Hunt the wild Beasts, smoke our Pipes, and mind Religion. But as these Forts, which are built among us, disturb our Peace, & are a great hurt to Religion, because some of our Warriors are foolish, & some of our Brother Soldiers don't fear God, we therefore desire that these Forts may be pull'd down, & kick'd out of the way."

At a conference at Philadelphia, in August, 1761, an Iroquois sachem said, "We, your Brethren of the several Nations, are penned up like Hoggs. There are Forts all around us, and therefore we are apprehensive that Death is coming upon us."

to inflame the resentment of the Indians; for most of the inhabitants of the French settlements upon the lakes and the Mississippi were engaged in the fur-trade, and, fearing the English as formidable rivals, they would gladly have seen them driven out of the country. Traders, *habitans*, *coureurs de bois*, and all classes of this singular population, accordingly dispersed themselves among the villages of the Indians, or held councils with them in the secret places of the woods, urging them to take up arms against the English. They exhibited the conduct of the latter in its worst light, and spared neither misrepresentation nor falsehood. They told their excited hearers that the English had formed a deliberate scheme to root out the whole Indian race, and, with that design, had already begun to hem them in with settlements on the one hand, and a chain of forts on the other. Among other atrocious plans for their destruction, they had instigated the Cherokees to attack and destroy the tribes of the Ohio valley.[1] These groundless calumnies found ready belief. The French declared, in addition, that the King of France had of late years fallen asleep; that, during his slumbers, the English had seized upon Canada; but that he was now awake again, and that his armies were advancing up the St. Lawrence and the Mississippi, to drive out the intruders from the country of his red children. To these fabrications was added the more substantial encouragement of arms, ammunition, clothing, and provisions, which the French trading companies, if not the officers of the crown, distributed with a liberal hand.[2]

The fierce passions of the Indians, excited by their wrongs,

---

[1]Croghan, *Journal*. See Hildreth, *Pioneer History*, 68. Also Butler, *Hist. Kentucky*, Appendix.

[2]Examination of Gershom Hicks, a spy. See *Pennsylvania Gazette*, No. 1846.

Many passages from contemporary letters and documents might be cited in support of the above. The following extract from a letter of Lieut. Edward Jenkins, commanding at Fort Ouatanon on the Wabash, to Major Gladwin commanding at Detroit, is a good example. The date is 28 March, 1763. "The Canadians here are eternally telling lies to the Indians. . . One La Pointe told the Indians a few days ago that we should all be prisoners in a short time (showing when the corn was about a foot high), that there was a great army to come from the Mississippi, and that they were to have a great number of Indians with them; therefore advised them not to help us. That they would

real or imagined, and exasperated by the representations of the French, were yet farther wrought upon by influences of another kind. A prophet rose among the Delawares. This man may serve as a counterpart to the famous Shawanoe prophet, who figured so conspicuously in the Indian outbreak, under Tecumseh, immediately before the war with England in 1812. Many other parallel instances might be shown, as the great susceptibility of the Indians to superstitious impressions renders the advent of a prophet among them no very rare occurrence. In the present instance, the inspired Delaware seems to have been rather an enthusiast than an impostor; or perhaps he combined both characters. The objects of his mission were not wholly political. By means of certain external observances, most of them sufficiently frivolous and absurd, his disciples were to strengthen and purify their natures, and make themselves acceptable to the Great Spirit, whose messenger he proclaimed himself to be. He also enjoined them to lay aside the weapons and clothing which they received from the white men, and return to the primitive life of their ancestors. By so doing, and by strictly observing his other precepts, the tribes would soon be restored to their ancient greatness and power, and be enabled to drive out the white men who infested their territory. The prophet had many followers. Indians came from far and near, and gathered together in large encampments to listen to his exhortations. His fame spread even to the nations of the northern lakes; but though his disciples followed most of his injunctions, flinging away flint and steel, and making copious use of emetics, with other observances equally troublesome, yet the requisition to abandon the use of fire-arms was too inconvenient to be complied with.[1]

---

soon take Detroit and these small posts, and then they would take Quebec, Montreal, &c., and go into our country. This, I am informed, they tell them from one end of the year to the other." He adds that the Indians will rather give six beaver-skins for a blanket to a Frenchman than three to an Englishman.

[1] *M'Cullough's Narrative.* See *Incidents of Border Life*, 98. M'Cullough was a prisoner among the Delawares, at the time of the prophet's appearance.

With so many causes to irritate their restless and warlike spirit, it could not be supposed that the Indians would long remain quiet. Accordingly, in the summer of the year 1761, Captain Campbell, then commanding at Detroit, received information that a deputation of Senecas had come to the neighboring village of the Wyandots for the purpose of instigating the latter to destroy him and his garrison.[1] On farther inquiry, the plot proved to be general; and Niagara, Fort Pitt, and other posts, were to share the fate of Detroit. Campbell instantly despatched messengers to Sir Jeffrey Amherst, and the commanding officers of the different forts; and, by this timely discovery, the conspiracy was nipped in the bud. During the following summer, 1762, another similar design was detected and suppressed. They proved to be the precursors of a tempest. When, early in 1763, it was announced to the tribes that the King of France had ceded all their country to the King of England, without even asking their leave, a ferment

[1]MS. *Minutes of a Council held by Deputies of the Six Nations, with the Wyandots, Ottawas, Ojibwas, and Pottawattamies, at the Wyandot town, near Detroit*, July 3, 1761.

Extract from a MS. Letter—*Captain Campbell, commanding at Detroit, to Major Walters, commanding at Niagara.*

"Sir: { "Detroit, June 17th. 1761, two o'clock in the morning.

"I had the favor of Yours, with General Amherst's Dispatches.

"I have sent You an Express with a very Important piece of Intelligence I have had the good fortune to Discover. I have been Lately alarmed with Reports of the bad Designs of the Indian Nations against this place and the English in General; I can now Inform You for certain it Comes from the Six Nations; and that they have Sent Belts of Wampum & Deputys to all the Nations, from Nova Scotia to the Illinois, to take up the hatchet against the English, and have employed the Messagues to send Belts of Wampum to the Northern Nations. . . .

"Their project is as follows: the Six Nations—at least the Senecas—are to Assemble at the head of French Creek, within five and twenty Leagues of Presqu' Isle, part of the Six Nations, the Delawares and Shanese, are to Assemble on the Ohio, and all at the same time, about the latter End of this Month, to surprise Niagara & Fort Pitt, and Cut off the Communication Every where; I hope this will Come time Enough to put You on Your Guard and to send to Oswego, and all the Posts on that communication, they Expect to be Joined by the Nations that are Come from the North by Toronto."

of indignation at once became apparent among them;[1] and, within a few weeks, a plot was matured, such as was never, before or since, conceived or executed by a North-American Indian. It was determined to attack all the English forts upon the same day; then, having destroyed their garrisons, to turn upon the defenceless frontier, and ravage and lay waste the settlements, until, as many of the Indians fondly believed, the English should all be driven into the sea, and the country restored to its primitive owners.

It is difficult to determine which tribe was first to raise the cry of war. There were many who might have done so, for all the savages in the backwoods were ripe for an outbreak, and the movement seemed almost simultaneous. The Delawares and Senecas were the most incensed, and Kiashuta, a chief of the latter, was perhaps foremost to apply the torch; but, if this was the case, he touched fire to materials already on the point of igniting. It belonged to a greater chief than he to give method and order to what would else have been a wild burst of fury, and convert desultory attacks into a formidable and protracted war. But for Pontiac, the whole might have ended in a few troublesome inroads upon the frontier, and a little whooping and yelling under the walls of Fort Pitt.

Pontiac, as already mentioned, was principal chief of the Ottawas. The Ottawas, Ojibwas, and Pottawattamies, had long been united in a loose kind of confederacy, of which he was the virtual head. Over those around him his authority was almost despotic, and his power extended far beyond the limits of the three united tribes. His influence was great among all the nations of the Illinois country; while, from the

---

[1]Letter, *Geo. Croghan to Sir J. Amherst, Fort Pitt, April 30, 1763,* MS. Amherst replies characteristically, "Whatever idle notions they may entertain in regard to the cessions made by the French Crown can be of very little consequence."

Croghan, Sir William Johnson's deputy, and a man of experience, had for some time been anxious as to the results of the arrogant policy of Amherst. On March 19th he wrote to Colonel Bouquet: "How they (*the Indians*) may behave I can't pretend to say, but I do not approve of Gen[l.] Amherst's plan of distressing them too much, as in my opinion they will not consider consequences if too much distrest, tho' Sir Jeffrey thinks they will."

Croghan urges the same views, with emphasis, in other letters; but Amherst was deaf to all persuasion.

sources of the Ohio to those of the Mississippi, and, indeed, to the farthest boundaries of the wide-spread Algonquin race, his name was known and respected.

The fact that Pontiac was born the son of a chief would in no degree account for the extent of his power; for, among Indians, many a chief's son sinks back into insignificance, while the offspring of a common warrior may succeed to his place. Among all the wild tribes of the continent, personal merit is indispensable to gaining or preserving dignity. Courage, resolution, address, and eloquence are sure passports to distinction. With all these Pontiac was pre-eminently endowed, and it was chiefly to them, urged to their highest activity by a vehement ambition, that he owed his greatness. He possessed a commanding energy and force of mind, and in subtlety and craft could match the best of his wily race. But, though capable of acts of magnanimity, he was a thorough savage, with a wider range of intellect than those around him, but sharing all their passions and prejudices, their fierceness and treachery. His faults were the faults of his race; and they cannot eclipse his nobler qualities. His memory is still cherished among the remnants of many Algonquin tribes, and the celebrated Tecumseh adopted him for his model, proving himself no unworthy imitator.[1]

Pontiac was now about fifty years old. Until Major Rogers came into the country, he had been, from motives probably both of interest and inclination, a firm friend of the French. Not long before the French war broke out, he had saved the garrison of Detroit from the imminent peril of an attack from some of the discontented tribes of the north. During the war, he had fought on the side of France. It is said that he commanded the Ottawas at the memorable defeat of Braddock;

[1]Drake, *Life of Tecumseh*, 138.

Several tribes, the Miamis, Sacs, and others, have claimed connection with the great chief; but it is certain that he was, by adoption at least, an Ottawa. Henry Conner, formerly government interpreter for the northern tribes, declared, on the faith of Indian tradition, that he was born among the Ottawas of an Ojibwa mother, a circumstance which proved an advantage to him by increasing his influence over both tribes. An Ojibwa Indian told the writer that some portion of his power was to be ascribed to his being a chief of the *Metai*, a magical association among the Indians of the lakes, in which character he exerted an influence on the superstition of his followers.

and it is certain that he was treated with much honor by the French officers, and received especial marks of esteem from the Marquis of Montcalm.[1]

We have seen how, when the tide of affairs changed, the subtle and ambitious chief trimmed his bark to the current, and gave the hand of friendship to the English. That he was disappointed in their treatment of him, and in all the hopes that he had formed from their alliance, is sufficiently evident from one of his speeches. A new light soon began to dawn upon his untaught but powerful mind, and he saw the altered posture of affairs under its true aspect.

It was a momentous and gloomy crisis for the Indian race, for never before had they been exposed to such imminent and pressing danger. With the downfall of Canada, the tribes had sunk at once from their position of importance. Hitherto the two rival European nations had kept each other in check upon the American continent, and the Indians had, in some measure, held the balance of power between them. To conciliate their good will and gain their alliance, to avoid offending them by injustice and encroachment, was the policy both of the French and English. But now the face of affairs was changed. The English had gained an undisputed ascendency, and the Indians, no longer important as allies, were treated as mere barbarians, who might be trampled upon with impunity. Abandoned to their own feeble resources and divided strength, they must fast recede, and dwindle away before the steady progress of the colonial power. Already their best hunting-grounds were invaded, and from the eastern ridges of the Alleghanies they might see, from far and near, the smoke of the settlers' clearings, rising in tall columns from the dark-green bosom of the forest. The doom of the race was sealed, and no human power could avert it; but they, in their ignorance, believed otherwise, and vainly thought that, by a desperate effort, they might yet uproot and overthrow the growing strength of their destroyers.

It would be idle to suppose that the great mass of the

---

[1]The venerable Pierre Chouteau, of St. Louis, remembered to have seen Pontiac, a few days before his death, attired in the complete uniform of a French officer, which had been given him by the Marquis of Montcalm not long before the battle on the Plains of Abraham.

Indians understood, in its full extent, the danger which threatened their race. With them, the war was a mere outbreak of fury, and they turned against their enemies with as little reason or forecast as a panther when he leaps at the throat of the hunter. Goaded by wrongs and indignities, they struck for revenge, and for relief from the evil of the moment. But the mind of Pontiac could embrace a wider and deeper view. The peril of the times was unfolded in its full extent before him, and he resolved to unite the tribes in one grand effort to avert it. He did not, like many of his people, entertain the absurd idea that the Indians, by their unaided strength, could drive the English into the sea. He adopted the only plan consistent with reason, that of restoring the French ascendency in the west, and once more opposing a check to British encroachment. With views like these, he lent a greedy ear to the plausible falsehoods of the Canadians, who assured him that the armies of King Louis were already advancing to recover Canada, and that the French and their red brethren, fighting side by side, would drive the English dogs back within their own narrow limits.

Revolving these thoughts, and remembering that his own ambitious views might be advanced by the hostilities he meditated, Pontiac no longer hesitated. Revenge, ambition, and patriotism wrought upon him alike, and he resolved on war. At the close of the year 1762, he sent ambassadors to the different nations. They visited the country of the Ohio and its tributaries, passed northward to the region of the upper lakes, and the borders of the river Ottawa; and far southward towards the mouth of the Mississippi.[1] Bearing with them the war-belt of wampum,[2] broad and long, as the importance of

---

[1]MS. Letter—*M. D'Abbadie to M. Neyon*, 1764.

[2]Wampum was an article much in use among many tribes, not only for ornament, but for the graver purposes of councils, treaties, and embassies. In ancient times it consisted of small shells, or fragments of shells, rudely perforated, and strung together; but more recently, it was manufactured by the white men, from the inner portions of certain marine and fresh water shells. In shape, the grains or beads resembled small pieces of broken pipe-stem, and were of various sizes and colors, black, purple, and white. When used for ornament, they were arranged fancifully in necklaces, collars, and embroidery; but when employed for public purposes, they were disposed in a great variety of patterns and devices, which, to the minds of the Indians, had all the

the message demanded, and the tomahawk stained red, in token of war, they went from camp to camp, and village to village. Wherever they appeared, the sachems and old men assembled, to hear the words of the great Pontiac. Then the chief of the embassy flung down the tomahawk on the ground before them, and holding the war-belt in his hand, delivered, with vehement gesture, word for word, the speech with which he was charged. It was heard everywhere with approval; the belt was accepted, the hatchet snatched up, and the assembled chiefs stood pledged to take part in the war. The blow was to be struck at a certain time in the month of May following, to be indicated by the changes of the moon. The tribes were to rise together, each destroying the English garrison in its neighborhood, and then, with a general rush, the whole were to turn against the settlements of the frontier.

The tribes, thus banded together against the English, comprised, with a few unimportant exceptions, the whole Algonquin stock, to whom were united the Wyandots, the Senecas, and several tribes of the lower Mississippi. The Senecas were the only members of the Iroquois confederacy who joined in the league, the rest being kept quiet by the influence

----

significance of hieroglyphics. An Indian orator, at every clause of his speech, delivered a belt or string of wampum, varying in size, according to the importance of what he had said, and, by its figures and coloring, so arranged as to perpetuate the remembrance of his words. These belts were carefully stored up like written documents, and it was generally the office of some old man to interpret their meaning.

When a wampum belt was sent to summon the tribes to join in war, its color was always red or black, while the prevailing color of a peace-belt was white. Tobacco was sometimes used on such occasions as a substitute for wampum, since in their councils the Indians are in the habit of constantly smoking, and tobacco is therefore taken as the emblem of deliberation. With the tobacco or the belt of wampum, presents are not unfrequently sent to conciliate the good will of the tribe whose alliance is sought. In the summer of the year 1846, when the western bands of the Dahcotah were preparing to go in concert against their enemies the Crows, the chief who was at the head of the design, and of whose village the writer was an inmate, impoverished himself by sending most of his horses as presents to the chiefs of the surrounding villages. On this occasion, tobacco was the token borne by the messengers, as wampum is not in use among the tribes of that region.

of Sir William Johnson, whose utmost exertions, however, were barely sufficient to allay their irritation.[1]

While thus on the very eve of an outbreak, the Indians concealed their designs with the dissimulation of their race. The warriors still lounged about the forts, with calm, impenetrable faces, begging, as usual, for tobacco, gunpowder, and whiskey. Now and then, some slight intimation of danger would startle the garrisons from their security. An English trader, coming in from the Indian villages, would report that, from their manner and behavior, he suspected them of brooding mischief; or some scoundrel half-breed would be heard boasting in his cups that before next summer he would have English hair to fringe his hunting-frock. On one occasion, the plot was nearly discovered. Early in March, 1763, Ensign Holmes, commanding at Fort Miami, was told by a friendly Indian that the warriors in the neighboring village had lately received a war-belt, with a message urging them to destroy him and his garrison, and that this they were preparing to do. Holmes called the Indians together, and boldly charged them with their design. They did as Indians on such occasions have often done, confessed their fault with much apparent contrition, laid the blame on a neighboring tribe, and professed eternal friendship to their brethren, the English. Holmes writes to report his discovery to Major Gladwyn, who, in his turn, sends the information to Sir Jeffrey Amherst, expressing his opinion that there has been a general irritation among the Indians, but that the affair will soon blow over, and that, in the neighborhood of his own post, the savages were perfectly tranquil.[2] Within cannon shot of the deluded officer's

[1] MS. *Johnson Papers.*
[2] MS. *Speech of a Miami Chief to Ensign Holmes.* MS. Letter—*Holmes to Gladwyn, March 16, 1763. Gladwyn to Amherst, March 21, 1763.*

Extract from a MS. Letter—*Ensign Holmes commanding at Miamis, to Major Gladwyn:* —

$\left\{ \begin{array}{l} \text{"Fort Miamis,} \\ \text{March 30th, 1763.} \end{array} \right.$

"Since my Last Letter to You, wherein I Acquainted You of the Bloody Belt being in this Village, I have made all the search I could about it, and have found it out to be True; Whereon I Assembled all the Chiefs of this Nation, & after a long and troublesome Spell with them, I Obtained the Belt, with a Speech, as You will Receive Enclosed; This Affair is very timely Stopt,

palisades, was the village of Pontiac himself, the arch enemy of the English, and prime mover in the plot.

With the approach of spring, the Indians, coming in from their wintering grounds, began to appear in small parties about the various forts; but now they seldom entered them, encamping at a little distance in the woods. They were fast pushing their preparations for the meditated blow, and waiting with stifled eagerness for the appointed hour.

---

and I hope the News of a Peace will put a Stop to any further Troubles with these Indians, who are the Principal Ones of Setting Mischief on Foot. I send you the Belt, with this Packet, which I hope You will Forward to the General."

Chapter VIII.

1763.

INDIAN PREPARATION.

I INTERRUPT the progress of the narrative to glance for a
moment at the Indians in their military capacity, and observe how far they were qualified to prosecute the formidable
war into which they were about to plunge.

A people living chiefly by the chase, and therefore, of
necessity, thinly and widely scattered; divided into numerous
tribes, held together by no strong principle of cohesion, and
with no central government to combine their strength, could
act with little efficiency against such an enemy as was now
opposed to them. Loose and disjointed as a whole, the government even of individual tribes, and of their smallest separate communities, was too feeble to deserve the name. There
were, it is true, chiefs whose office was in a manner hereditary; but their authority was wholly of a moral nature, and
enforced by no compulsory law. Their province was to advise,
and not to command. Their influence, such as it was, is chiefly
to be ascribed to the principle of hero-worship, natural to the
Indian character, and to the reverence for age, which belongs
to a state of society where a patriarchal element largely prevails. It was their office to declare war and make peace; but
when war was declared, they had no power to carry the declaration into effect. The warriors fought if they chose to do
so; but if, on the contrary, they preferred to remain quiet, no
man could force them to raise the hatchet. The war-chief,
whose part it was to lead them to battle, was a mere partisan,
whom his bravery and exploits had led to distinction. If he
thought proper, he sang his war-song and danced his war-
dance; and as many of the young men as were disposed to
follow him, gathered around and enlisted themselves under
him. Over these volunteers he had no legal authority, and
they could desert him at any moment, with no other penalty
than disgrace. When several war parties, of different bands
or tribes, were united in a common enterprise, their chiefs
elected a leader, who was nominally to command the whole;

but unless this leader was a man of uncommon reputation and ability, his commands were disregarded, and his authority was a cipher. Among his followers, every latent element of discord, pride, jealousy, and ancient half-smothered feuds, were ready at any moment to break out, and tear the whole asunder. His warriors would often desert in bodies; and many an Indian army, before reaching the enemy's country, has been known to dwindle away until it was reduced to a mere scalping party.

To twist a rope of sand would be as easy a task as to form a permanent and effective army of such materials. The wild love of freedom, and impatience of all control, which mark the Indian race, render them utterly intolerant of military discipline. Partly from their individual character, and partly from this absence of subordination, spring results highly unfavorable to continued and extended military operations. Indian warriors, when acting in large masses, are to the last degree wayward, capricious, and unstable; infirm of purpose as a mob of children, and devoid of providence and foresight. To provide supplies for a campaign forms no part of their system. Hence the blow must be struck at once, or not struck at all; and to postpone victory is to insure defeat. It is when acting in small, detached parties, that the Indian warrior puts forth his energies, and displays his admirable address, endurance, and intrepidity. It is then that he becomes a truly formidable enemy. Fired with the hope of winning scalps, he is stanch as a bloodhound. No hardship can divert him from his purpose, and no danger subdue his patient and cautious courage.

From their inveterate passion for war, the Indians are always prompt enough to engage in it; and on the present occasion, the prevailing irritation gave ample assurance that they would not remain idle. While there was little risk that they would capture any strong and well-defended fort, or carry any important position, there was, on the other hand, every reason to apprehend wide-spread havoc, and a destructive war of detail. That the war might be carried on with effect, it was the part of the Indian leaders to work upon the passions of their people, and keep alive their irritation; to whet their native appetite for blood and glory, and cheer them on to the attack; to guard against all that might quench their ardor, or cool their fierceness; to avoid pitched battles; never to fight except under advantage; and to avail themselves of all the aid which craft and treachery could afford. The very circumstances which unfitted the Indians for continued and concentrated attack were, in another view, highly advantageous, by preventing the enemy from assailing them with vital effect. It was no easy task to penetrate tangled woods in search of a foe, alert and active as a lynx, who would seldom stand and fight, whose deadly shot and triumphant whoop were the first and often the last tokens of his presence, and who, at the approach of a hostile force, would vanish into the black recesses of forests and pine swamps, only to renew his attacks with unabated ardor. There were no forts to capture, no magazines to destroy, and little property to seize upon. No warfare could be more perilous and harassing in its prosecution, or less satisfactory in its results.

The English colonies at this time were but ill fitted to bear the brunt of the impending war. The army which had conquered Canada was broken up and dissolved; the provincials were disbanded, and most of the regulars sent home. A few fragments of regiments, miserably wasted by war and sickness, had just arrived from the West Indies; and of these, several were already ordered to England, to be disbanded. There remained barely troops enough to furnish feeble garrisons for the various forts on the frontier and in the Indian country.[1] At the head of this dilapidated army was Sir Jeffrey Amherst, who had achieved the reduction of Canada, and clinched the nail which Wolfe had driven. In some respects he was well fitted for the emergency; but, on the other hand, he held the Indians in supreme contempt, and his arbitrary treatment of them and total want of every quality of conciliation where they were concerned, had had no little share in exciting them to war.

While the war was on the eve of breaking out, an event occurred which had afterwards an important effect upon its progress,—the signing of the treaty of peace at Paris, on the tenth of February, 1763. By this treaty France resigned her claims to the territories east of the Mississippi, and that great

[1] Mante, 485.

river now became the western boundary of the British colonial possessions. In portioning out her new acquisitions into separate governments, England left the valley of the Ohio and the adjacent regions as an Indian domain, and by the proclamation of the seventh of October following, the intrusion of settlers upon these lands was strictly prohibited. Could these just and necessary measures have been sooner adopted, it is probable that the Indian war might have been prevented, or, at all events, rendered less general and violent, for the treaty would have made it apparent that the French could never repossess themselves of Canada, and would have proved the futility of every hope which the Indians entertained of assistance from that quarter, while, at the same time, the royal proclamation would have tended to tranquillize their minds, by removing the chief cause of irritation. But the remedy came too late, and served only to inflame the evil. While the sovereigns of France, England, and Spain, were signing the treaty at Paris, countless Indian warriors in the American forests were singing the war-song, and whetting their scalping-knives.

Throughout the western wilderness, in a hundred camps and villages, were celebrated the savage rites of war. Warriors, women, and children were alike eager and excited; magicians consulted their oracles, and prepared charms to insure success; while the war-chief, his body painted black from head to foot, concealed himself in the solitude of rocks and caverns, or the dark recesses of the forest. Here, fasting and praying, he calls day and night upon the Great Spirit, consulting his dreams, to draw from them auguries of good or evil; and if, perchance, a vision of the great war-eagle seems to hover over him with expanded wings, he exults in the full conviction of triumph. When a few days have elapsed, he emerges from his retreat, and the people discover him descending from the woods, and approaching their camp, black as a demon of war, and shrunken with fasting and vigil. They flock around and listen to his wild harangue. He calls on them to avenge the blood of their slaughtered relatives; he assures them that the Great Spirit is on their side, and that victory is certain. With exulting cries they disperse to their wigwams, to array themselves in the savage decorations of the war-dress. An old man now passes through the camp, and invites the warriors to a feast in the name of the chief. They gather from all quarters to his wigwam, where they find him seated, no longer covered with black, but adorned with the startling and fantastic blazonry of the war-paint. Those who join in the feast pledge themselves, by so doing, to follow him against the enemy. The guests seat themselves on the ground, in a circle around the wigwam, and the flesh of dogs is placed in wooden dishes before them, while the chief, though goaded by the pangs of his long, unbroken fast, sits smoking his pipe with unmoved countenance, and takes no part in the feast.

Night has now closed in; and the rough clearing is illumined by the blaze of fires and burning pine-knots, casting their deep red glare upon the dusky boughs of the surrounding forest, and upon the wild multitude who, fluttering with feathers and bedaubed with paint, have gathered for the celebration of the war-dance. A painted post is driven into the ground, and the crowd form a wide circle around it. The chief leaps into the vacant space, brandishing his hatchet as if rushing upon an enemy, and, in a loud, vehement tone, chants his own exploits and those of his ancestors, enacting the deeds which he describes, yelling the war-whoop, throwing himself into all the postures of actual fight, striking the post as if it were an enemy, and tearing the scalp from the head of the imaginary victim. Warrior after warrior follows his example, until the whole assembly, as if fired with sudden frenzy, rush together into the ring, leaping, stamping, and whooping, brandishing knives and hatchets in the fire-light, hacking and stabbing the air, and breaking at intervals into a burst of ferocious yells, which sounds for miles away over the lonely, midnight forest.

In the morning, the warriors prepare to depart. They leave the camp in single file, still decorated with all their finery of paint, feathers, and scalp-locks; and, as they enter the woods, the chief fires his gun, the warrior behind follows his example, and the discharges pass in slow succession from front to rear, the salute concluding with a general whoop. They encamp at no great distance from the village, and divest themselves of their much-prized ornaments, which are carried back by the women, who have followed them for this purpose. The warriors pursue their journey, clad in the rough attire of hard service, and move silently and stealthily through the forest towards the hapless garrison, or defenceless settlement, which they have marked as their prey.

The woods were now filled with war-parties such as this, and soon the first tokens of the approaching tempest began to alarm the unhappy settlers of the frontier. At first, some trader or hunter, weak and emaciated, would come in from the forest, and relate that his companions had been butchered in the Indian villages, and that he alone had escaped. Next succeeded vague and uncertain rumors of forts attacked and garrisons slaughtered; and soon after, a report gained ground that every post throughout the Indian country had been taken, and every soldier killed. Close upon these tidings came the enemy himself. The Indian war-parties broke out of the woods like gangs of wolves, murdering, burning, and laying waste; while hundreds of terror-stricken families, abandoning their homes, fled for refuge towards the older settlements, and all was misery and ruin.

Passing over, for the present, this portion of the war, we will penetrate at once into the heart of the Indian country, and observe those passages of the conflict which took place under the auspices of Pontiac himself,—the siege of Detroit, and the capture of the interior posts and garrisons.

Chapter IX.

1763.

THE COUNCIL AT THE RIVER ECORCES.

To BEGIN the war was reserved by Pontiac as his own peculiar privilege. With the first opening of spring his preparations were complete. His light-footed messengers, with their wampum belts and gifts of tobacco, visited many a lonely hunting camp in the gloom of the northern woods, and called chiefs and warriors to attend the general meeting. The appointed spot was on the banks of the little River Ecorces, not far from Detroit. Thither went Pontiac himself, with his squaws and his children. Band after band came straggling in from every side, until the meadow was thickly dotted with their frail wigwams.[1] Here were idle warriors smoking and laughing in groups, or beguiling the lazy hours with gambling, feasting, or doubtful stories of their own martial exploits. Here were youthful gallants, bedizened with all the foppery of beads, feathers, and hawks' bells, but held as yet in light esteem, since they had slain no enemy, and taken no scalp. Here too were young damsels, radiant with bears' oil, ruddy with vermilion, and versed in all the arts of forest coquetry; shrivelled hags, with limbs of wire, and the voices of screech-owls; and troops of naked children, with small, black, mischievous eyes, roaming along the outskirts of the woods.

The great Roman historian observes of the ancient Germans, that when summoned to a public meeting, they would lag behind the appointed time in order to show their independence. The remark holds true, and perhaps with greater emphasis, of the American Indians; and thus it happened, that several days elapsed before the assembly was complete. In such a motley concourse of barbarians, where different bands and different tribes were mustered on one common camp ground, it would need all the art of a prudent leader to prevent their dormant jealousies from starting into open strife. No people are more prompt to quarrel, and none more

[1] *Pontiac*, MS. See Appendix, C.

prone, in the fierce excitement of the present, to forget the purpose of the future; yet, through good fortune, or the wisdom of Pontiac, no rupture occurred; and at length the last loiterer appeared, and farther delay was needless.

The council took place on the twenty-seventh of April. On that morning, several old men, the heralds of the camp, passed to and fro among the lodges, calling the warriors, in a loud voice, to attend the meeting.

In accordance with the summons, they issued from their cabins: the tall, naked figures of the wild Ojibwas, with quivers slung at their backs, and light war-clubs resting in the hollow of their arms; Ottawas, wrapped close in their gaudy blankets; Wyandots, fluttering in painted shirts, their heads adorned with feathers, and their leggins garnished with bells. All were soon seated in a wide circle upon the grass, row within row, a grave and silent assembly. Each savage countenance seemed carved in wood, and none could have detected the ferocious passions hidden beneath that immovable mask. Pipes with ornamented stems were lighted, and passed from hand to hand.

Then Pontiac rose, and walked forward into the midst of the council. According to Canadian tradition, he was not above the middle height, though his muscular figure was cast in a mould of remarkable symmetry and vigor. His complexion was darker than is usual with his race, and his features, though by no means regular, had a bold and stern expression; while his habitual bearing was imperious and peremptory, like that of a man accustomed to sweep away all opposition by the force of his impetuous will. His ordinary attire was that of the primitive savage,—a scanty cincture girt about his loins, and his long, black hair flowing loosely at his back; but on occasions like this he was wont to appear as befitted his power and character, and he stood doubtless before the council plumed and painted in the full costume of war.

Looking round upon his wild auditors he began to speak, with fierce gesture, and a loud, impassioned voice; and at every pause, deep, guttural ejaculations of assent and approval responded to his words. He inveighed against the arrogance, rapacity, and injustice, of the English, and contrasted them with the French, whom they had driven from the soil. He declared that the British commandant had treated him with neglect and contempt; that the soldiers of the garrison had abused the Indians; and that one of them had struck a follower of his own. He represented the danger that would arise from the supremacy of the English. They had expelled the French, and now they only waited for a pretext to turn upon the Indians and destroy them. Then, holding out a broad belt of wampum, he told the council that he had received it from their great father the King of France, in token that he had heard the voice of his red children; that his sleep was at an end; and that his great war canoes would soon sail up the St. Lawrence, to win back Canada, and wreak vengeance on his enemies. The Indians and their French brethren would fight once more side by side, as they had always fought; they would strike the English as they had struck them many moons ago, when their great army marched down the Monongahela, and they had shot them from their ambush, like a flock of pigeons in the woods.

Having roused in his warlike listeners their native thirst for blood and vengeance, he next addressed himself to their superstition, and told the following tale. Its precise origin is not easy to determine. It is possible that the Delaware prophet, mentioned in a former chapter, may have had some part in it; or it might have been the offspring of Pontiac's heated imagination, during his period of fasting and dreaming. That he deliberately invented it for the sake of the effect it would produce, is the least probable conclusion of all; for it evidently proceeds from the superstitious mind of an Indian, brooding upon the evil days in which his lot was cast, and turning for relief to the mysterious Author of his being. It is, at all events, a characteristic specimen of the Indian legendary tales, and, like many of them, bears an allegoric significancy. Yet he who endeavors to interpret an Indian allegory through all its erratic windings and puerile inconsistencies, has undertaken no enviable task.

"A Delaware Indian," said Pontiac, "conceived an eager desire to learn wisdom from the Master of Life; but, being ignorant where to find him, he had recourse to fasting, dreaming, and magical incantations. By these means it was revealed to him, that, by moving forward in a straight, undeviating course, he would reach the abode of the Great Spirit. He told his purpose to no one, and having provided the equipments of a hunter,—gun, powder-horn, ammunition, and a kettle for preparing his food,—he set out on his errand. For some time he journeyed on in high hope and confidence. On the evening of the eighth day, he stopped by the side of a brook at the edge of a meadow, where he began to make ready his evening meal, when, looking up, he saw three large openings in the woods before him, and three well-beaten paths which entered them. He was much surprised; but his wonder increased, when, after it had grown dark, the three paths were more clearly visible than ever. Remembering the important object of his journey, he could neither rest nor sleep; and, leaving his fire, he crossed the meadow, and entered the largest of the three openings. He had advanced but a short distance into the forest, when a bright flame sprang out of the ground before him, and arrested his steps. In great amazement, he turned back, and entered the second path, where the same wonderful phenomenon again encountered him; and now, in terror and bewilderment, yet still resolved to persevere, he took the last of the three paths. On this he journeyed a whole day without interruption, when at length, emerging from the forest, he saw before him a vast mountain, of dazzling whiteness. So precipitous was the ascent, that the Indian thought it hopeless to go farther, and looked around him in despair: at that moment, he saw, seated at some distance above, the figure of a beautiful woman arrayed in white, who arose as he looked upon her, and thus accosted him: 'How can you hope, encumbered as you are, to succeed in your design? Go down to the foot of the mountain, throw away your gun, your ammunition, your provisions, and your clothing; wash yourself in the stream which flows there, and you will then be prepared to stand before the Master of Life.' The Indian obeyed, and again began to ascend among the rocks, while the woman, seeing him still discouraged, laughed at his faintness of heart, and told him that, if he wished for success, he must climb by the aid of one hand and one foot only. After great toil and suffering, he at length found himself at the summit. The woman had disappeared, and he was left alone. A rich and beautiful plain lay before him, and at a little distance he saw three great villages, far superior to the squalid wigwams of the Delawares. As he approached the largest, and stood hesitating whether he should enter, a man gorgeously attired stepped forth, and, taking him by the hand, welcomed him to the celestial abode. He then conducted him into the presence of the Great Spirit, where the Indian stood confounded at the unspeakable splendor which surrounded him. The Great Spirit bade him be seated, and thus addressed him: —

"'I am the Maker of heaven and earth, the trees, lakes, rivers, and all things else. I am the Maker of mankind; and because I love you, you must do my will. The land on which you live I have made for you, and not for others. Why do you suffer the white men to dwell among you? My children, you have forgotten the customs and traditions of your fore-fathers. Why do you not clothe yourselves in skins, as they did, and use the bows and arrows, and the stone-pointed lances, which they used? You have bought guns, knives, kettles, and blankets, from the white men, until you can no longer do without them; and, what is worse, you have drunk the poison fire-water, which turns you into fools. Fling all these things away; live as your wise forefathers lived before you. And as for these English, — these dogs dressed in red, who have come to rob you of your hunting-grounds, and drive away the game, — you must lift the hatchet against them. Wipe them from the face of the earth, and then you will win my favor back again, and once more be happy and prosperous. The children of your great father, the King of France, are not like the English. Never forget that they are your brethren. They are very dear to me, for they love the red men, and understand the true mode of worship-ping me.' "

The Great Spirit next gave his hearer various precepts of morality and religion, such as the prohibition to marry more than one wife; and a warning against the practice of magic, which is worshipping the devil. A prayer, embodying the sub-stance of all that he had heard, was then presented to the Delaware. It was cut in hieroglyphics upon a wooden stick, after the custom of his people; and he was directed to send copies of it to all the Indian villages.[1]

The adventurer now departed, and, returning to the earth, reported all the wonders he had seen in the celestial regions.

Such was the tale told by Pontiac to the council; and it is worthy of notice, that not he alone, but many of the most notable men who have arisen among the Indians, have been opponents of civilization, and stanch advocates of primitive barbarism. Red Jacket and Tecumseh would gladly have brought back their people to the rude simplicity of their original condition. There is nothing progressive in the rigid, inflexible nature of an Indian. He will not open his mind to the idea of improvement; and nearly every change that has been forced upon him has been a change for the worse.

Many other speeches were doubtless made in the council, but no record of them has been preserved. All present were eager to attack the British fort; and Pontiac told them, in conclusion, that on the second of May he would gain admittance, with a party of his warriors, on pretence of dancing the calumet dance before the garrison; that they would take note of the strength of the fortification; and that he would then summon another council to determine the mode of attack.

The assembly now dissolved, and all the evening the women were employed in loading the canoes, which were drawn up on the bank of the stream. The encampments broke up at so early an hour, that when the sun rose, the savage swarm had melted away; the secluded scene was restored to its wonted silence and solitude, and nothing remained but the slender frame-work of several hundred cabins, with fragments of broken utensils, pieces of cloth, and scraps of hide, scattered over the trampled grass; while the smouldering embers of numberless fires mingled their dark smoke with the white mist which rose from the little river.

Every spring, after the winter hunt was over, the Indians were accustomed to return to their villages, or permanent encampments, in the vicinity of Detroit; and, accordingly, after the council had broken up, they made their appearance as

---

[1] *Pontiac*, MS.—*M'Dougal*, MSS. M'Dougal states that he derived his information from an Indian. The author of the *Pontiac* MS. probably writes on the authority of Canadians, some of whom were present at the council.

usual about the fort. On the first of May, Pontiac came to the gate with forty men of the Ottawa tribe, and asked permission to enter and dance the calumet dance, before the officers of the garrison. After some hesitation, he was admitted; and proceeding to the corner of the street, where stood the house of the commandant, Major Gladwyn, he and thirty of his warriors began their dance, each recounting his own exploits, and boasting himself the bravest of mankind. The officers and men gathered around them; while, in the mean time, the remaining ten of the Ottawas strolled about the fort, observing every thing it contained. When the dance was over, they all quietly withdrew, not a suspicion of their designs having arisen in the minds of the English.[1]

After a few days had elapsed, Pontiac's messengers again passed among the Indian cabins, calling the principal chiefs to another council, in the Pottawattamie village. Here there was a large structure of bark, erected for the public use on occasions like the present. A hundred chiefs were seated around this dusky council-house, the fire in the centre shedding its fitful light upon their dark, naked forms, while the pipe passed from hand to hand. To prevent interruption, Pontiac had stationed young men as sentinels, near the house. He once more addressed the chiefs; inciting them to hostility against the English, and concluding by the proposal of his plan for destroying Detroit. It was as follows: Pontiac would demand a council with the commandant concerning matters of great importance; and on this pretext he flattered himself that he and his principal chiefs would gain ready admittance within the fort. They were all to carry weapons concealed beneath their blankets. While in the act of addressing the commandant in the council-room, Pontiac was to make a certain signal, upon which the chiefs were to raise the war-whoop, rush upon the officers present, and strike them down. The other Indians, waiting meanwhile at the gate, or loitering among the houses, on hearing the yells and firing within the building, were to assail the astonished and half-armed soldiers; and thus Detroit would fall an easy prey.

In opening this plan of treachery, Pontiac spoke rather as a

[1] *Pontiac*, MS.

counsellor than as a commander. Haughty as he was, he had too much sagacity to wound the pride of a body of men over whom he had no other control than that derived from his personal character and influence. No one was hardy enough to venture opposition to the proposal of their great leader. His plan was eagerly adopted. Hoarse ejaculations of applause echoed his speech; and, gathering their blankets around them, the chiefs withdrew to their respective villages, to prepare for the destruction of the unsuspecting garrison.

Chapter X.

1763.

DETROIT.

To the credulity of mankind each great calamity has its dire prognostics. Signs and portents in the heavens, the vision of an Indian bow, and the figure of a scalp imprinted on the disk of the moon, warned the New England Puritans of impending war. The apparitions passed away, and Philip of Mount Hope burst from the forest with his Narragansett warriors. In October, 1762, thick clouds of inky blackness gathered above the fort and settlement of Detroit. The river darkened beneath the awful shadows, and the forest was wrapped in double gloom. Drops of rain began to fall, of strong, sulphurous odor, and so deeply colored that the people, it is said, collected them and used them for writing.[1] A literary and philosophical journal of the time seeks to explain this strange phenomenon on some principle of physical science; but the simple Canadians held a different faith. Throughout the winter, the shower of black rain was the foremost topic of their fireside talk; and forebodings of impending evil disturbed the breast of many a timorous matron.

La Motte-Cadillac was the founder of Detroit. In the year 1701, he planted the little military colony, which time has transformed into a thriving American city.[2] At an earlier date, some feeble efforts had been made to secure the possession of this important pass; and when La Hontan visited the lakes, a small post, called Fort St. Joseph, was standing near the present site of Fort Gratiot. The wandering Jesuits, too, made frequent sojourns upon the borders of the Detroit, and baptized the savage children whom they found there.

Fort St. Joseph was abandoned in the year 1688. The establishment of Cadillac was destined to a better fate, and soon rose to distinguished importance among the western outposts of Canada. Indeed, the site was formed by nature for pros-

[1]Carver, *Travels*, 153. *Gent. Mag.* XXXIV. 408.
[2]*Memorial of La Motte Cadillac.* See Schoolcraft, *Oneota*, 407.

perity; and a bad government and a thriftless people could not prevent the increase of the colony. At the close of the French war, as Major Rogers tells us, the place contained twenty-five hundred inhabitants.[1] The centre of the settlement was the fortified town, currently called the Fort, to distinguish it from the straggling dwellings along the river banks. It stood on the western margin of the river, covering a small part of the ground now occupied by the city of Detroit, and contained about a hundred houses, compactly pressed together, and surrounded by a palisade. Both above and below the fort, the banks of the stream were lined on both sides with small Canadian dwellings, extending at various intervals for nearly eight miles. Each had its garden and its orchard, and each was enclosed by a fence of rounded pickets. To the soldier or the trader, fresh from the harsh scenery and ambushed perils of the surrounding wilds, the secluded settlement was welcome as an oasis in the desert.

The Canadian is usually a happy man. Life sits lightly upon him; he laughs at its hardships, and soon forgets its sorrows. A lover of roving and adventure, of the frolic and the dance, he is little troubled with thoughts of the past or the future, and little plagued with avarice or ambition. At Detroit, all his propensities found ample scope. Aloof from the world, the simple colonists shared none of its pleasures and excitements, and were free from many of its cares. Nor were luxuries wanting which civilization might have envied them. The forests teemed with game, the marshes with wild fowl, and the rivers with fish. The apples and pears of the old Canadian orchards are even to this day held in esteem. The poorer inhabitants made wine from the fruit of the wild grape, which grew profusely in the woods, while the wealthier class procured a better quality from Montreal, in exchange for the canoe loads of furs which they sent down with every year. Here, as elsewhere in Canada, the long winter was a season of social enjoyment; and when, in summer and autumn, the traders and voyageurs, the *coureurs de bois*, and half-breeds, gathered from the distant forests of the north-west, the whole settlement was alive with dancing and feasting, drinking, gaming, and carousing.

[1]A high estimate. Compare Rameau, *Colonie du Detroit*, 28.

FORT AND SETTLEMENTS OF DETROIT A.D. 1763

Scale of Miles.

LAKE ERIE

Within the limits of the settlement were three large Indian villages. On the western shore, a little below the fort, were the lodges of the Pottawattamies; nearly opposite, on the eastern side, was the village of the Wyandots; and on the same side, five miles higher up, Pontiac's band of Ottawas had fixed their abode. The settlers had always maintained the best terms with their savage neighbors. In truth, there was much congeniality between the red man and the Canadian. Their harmony was seldom broken; and among the woods and wilds of the northern lakes roamed many a lawless half-breed, the mongrel offspring of the colonists of Detroit and the Indian squaws.

We have already seen how, in an evil hour for the Canadians, a party of British troops took possession of Detroit, towards the close of the year 1760. The British garrison, consisting partly of regulars and partly of provincial rangers, was now quartered in a well-built range of barracks within the town or fort. The latter, as already mentioned, contained about a hundred small houses. Its form was nearly square, and the palisade which surrounded it was about twenty-five feet high. At each corner was a wooden bastion, and a blockhouse was erected over each gateway. The houses were small, chiefly built of wood, and roofed with bark or a thatch of straw. The streets also were extremely narrow, though a wide passage way, known as the *chemin du ronde*, surrounded the town, between the houses and the palisade. Besides the barracks, the only public buildings were a council-house and a rude little church.

The garrison consisted of a hundred and twenty soldiers, with about forty fur-traders and *engagés*; but the latter, as well as the Canadian inhabitants of the place, could little be trusted, in the event of an Indian outbreak. Two small, armed schooners, the Beaver and the Gladwyn, lay anchored in the stream, and several light pieces of artillery were mounted on the bastions.

Such was Detroit,—a place whose defences could have opposed no resistance to a civilized enemy; and yet, far removed as it was from the hope of speedy succor, it could only rely, in the terrible struggles that awaited it, upon its own slight strength and feeble resources.[1]

[1]Croghan, *Journal*. Rogers, *Account of North America*, 168. Various MS. Journals, Letters, and Plans have also been consulted. The most remarkable of these is the *Plan Topographique du Detroit*, made by or for General Collot, in

Standing on the water bastion of Detroit, a pleasant landscape spread before the eye. The river, about half a mile wide, almost washed the foot of the stockade; and either bank was lined with the white Canadian cottages. The joyous sparkling of the bright blue water; the green luxuriance of the woods; the white dwellings, looking out from the foliage; and, in the distance, the Indian wigwams curling their smoke against the sky,—all were mingled in one broad scene of wild and rural beauty.

Pontiac, the Satan of this forest paradise, was accustomed to spend the early part of the summer upon a small island at the opening of the Lake St. Clair, hidden from view by the high woods that covered the intervening Isle au Cochon.[1] "The king and lord of all this country," as Rogers calls him, lived in no royal state. His cabin was a small, oven-shaped structure of bark and rushes. Here he dwelt, with his squaws and children; and here, doubtless, he might often have been seen, lounging, half-naked, on a rush mat, or a bear-skin, like any ordinary warrior. We may fancy the current of his thoughts, the turmoil of his uncurbed passions, as he revolved the treacheries which, to his savage mind, seemed fair and honorable. At one moment, his fierce heart would burn with the anticipation of vengeance on the detested English; at another, he would meditate how he best might turn the approaching tumults to the furtherance of his own ambitious schemes. Yet we may believe that Pontiac was not a stranger to the high emotion of the patriot hero, the champion not merely of his nation's rights, but of the very existence of his race. He did not dream how desperate a game he was about to play. He hourly flattered himself with the futile hope of aid from France, and thought in his ignorance that the British colonies must give way before the rush of his savage warriors;

1796. It is accompanied by a drawing in water-colors of the town as it appeared in that year. A fac-simile of this drawing is in my possession. The regular fortification, which, within the recollection of many now living, covered the ground in the rear of the old town of Detroit, was erected at a date subsequent to the period of this history.

[1]Tradition, communicated to H. R. Schoolcraft, Esq., by Henry Conner, formerly Indian interpreter at Detroit.

when, in truth, all the combined tribes of the forest might have chafed in vain rage against the rock-like strength of the Anglo-Saxon.

Looking across an intervening arm of the river, Pontiac could see on its eastern bank the numerous lodges of his Ottawa tribesmen, half hidden among the ragged growth of trees and bushes. On the afternoon of the fifth of May, a Canadian woman, the wife of St. Aubin, one of the principal settlers, crossed over from the western side, and visited the Ottawa village, to obtain from the Indians a supply of maple sugar and venison. She was surprised at finding several of the warriors engaged in filing off the muzzles of their guns, so as to reduce them, stock and all, to the length of about a yard. Returning home in the evening, she mentioned what she had seen to several of her neighbors. Upon this, one of them, the blacksmith of the village, remarked that many of the Indians had lately visited his shop, and attempted to borrow files and saws for a purpose which they would not explain.[1] These circumstances excited the suspicion of the experienced Canadians. Doubtless there were many in the settlement who might, had they chosen, have revealed the plot; but it is no less certain that the more numerous and respectable class in the little community had too deep an interest in the preservation of peace, to countenance the designs of Pontiac. M. Gouin, an old and wealthy settler, went to the commandant, and conjured him to stand upon his guard; but Gladwyn, a man of fearless temper, gave no heed to the friendly advice.[2]

In the Pottawattamie village, if there be truth in tradition, lived an Ojibwa girl, who could boast a larger share of beauty than is common in the wigwam. She had attracted the eye of Gladwyn. He had formed a connection with her, and she had become much attached to him. On the afternoon of the sixth, Catharine—for so the officers called her—came to the fort, and repaired to Gladwyn's quarters, bringing with her a pair of elk-skin moccasons, ornamented with porcupine work, which he had requested her to make. There was something unusual in her look and manner. Her face was sad and down-

---

[1] *St. Aubin's Account*, MS. See Appendix, C.
[2] *Gouin's Account*, MS.

cast. She said little, and soon left the room; but the sentinel at the door saw her still lingering at the street corner, though the hour for closing the gates was nearly come. At length she attracted the notice of Gladwyn himself; and calling her to him, he pressed her to declare what was weighing upon her mind. Still she remained for a long time silent, and it was only after much urgency and many promises not to betray her, that she revealed her momentous secret.

To-morrow, she said, Pontiac will come to the fort with sixty of his chiefs. Each will be armed with a gun, cut short, and hidden under his blanket. Pontiac will demand to hold a council; and after he has delivered his speech, he will offer a peace-belt of wampum, holding it in a reversed position. This will be the signal of attack. The chiefs will spring up and fire upon the officers, and the Indians in the street will fall upon the garrison. Every Englishman will be killed, but not the scalp of a single Frenchman will be touched.[1]

[1] Letter to the writer from H. R. Schoolcraft, Esq., containing the traditional account from the lips of the interpreter, Henry Conner. See, also, Carver, *Travels*, 155 (Lond. 1778).

Carver's account of the conspiracy and the siege is in several points inexact, which throws a shade of doubt on this story. Tradition, however, as related by the interpreter Conner, sustains him; with the addition that Catharine was the mistress of Gladwyn, and a few other points, including a very unromantic end of the heroine, who is said to have perished, by falling, when drunk, into a kettle of boiling maple-sap. This was many years after (see Appendix). Maxwell agrees in the main with Carver. There is another tradition, that the plot was disclosed by an old squaw. A third, current among the Ottawas, and sent to me in 1858 by Mr. Hosmer, of Toledo, declares that a young squaw told the plot to the commanding officer, but that he would not believe her, as she had a bad name, being a "straggler among the private soldiers." An Indian chief, pursues the same story, afterwards warned the officer. The Pontiac MS. says that Gladwyn was warned by an Ottawa warrior, though a woman was suspected by the Indians of having betrayed the secret. Peltier says that a woman named Catharine was accused of revealing the plot, and severely flogged by Pontiac in consequence. There is another story, that a soldier named Tucker, adopted by the Indians, was warned by his Indian sister. But the most distinct and satisfactory evidence is the following, from a letter written at Detroit on the twelfth of July, 1763, and signed James Macdonald. It is among the *Haldimand Papers* in the British Museum. There is also an imperfect copy, found among the papers of Colonel John Brodhead, in the library of the Historical Society of Pennsylvania: "About six o'clock that afternoon [May 7], six of their warriors returned and brought an old squaw prisoner, alleging that she had given us false information against them. The major

Such is the story told in 1768 to the traveller Carver at Detroit, and preserved in local tradition, but not sustained by contemporary letters or diaries. What is certain is, that Gladwyn received secret information, on the night of the sixth of May, that an attempt would be made on the morrow to capture the fort by treachery. He called some of his officers, and told them what he had heard. The defences of the place were feeble and extensive, and the garrison by far too weak to repel a general assault. The force of the Indians at this time is variously estimated at from six hundred to two thousand; and the commandant greatly feared that some wild impulse might precipitate their plan, and that they would storm the fort before the morning. Every preparation was made to meet the sudden emergency. Half the garrison were ordered under arms, and all the officers prepared to spend the night upon the ramparts.

The day closed, and the hues of sunset faded. Only a dusky redness lingered in the west, and the darkening earth seemed her dull self again. Then night descended, heavy and black, on the fierce Indians and the sleepless English. From sunset till dawn, an anxious watch was kept from the slender palisades of Detroit. The soldiers were still ignorant of the danger; and the sentinels did not know why their numbers were doubled, or why, with such unwonted vigilance, their officers repeatedly visited their posts. Again and again Gladwyn mounted his wooden ramparts, and looked forth into the gloom. There seemed nothing but repose and peace in the soft, moist air of

---

declared she had never given us any kind of advice. They then insisted on naming the author of what he had heard with regard to the Indians, which he declined to do, but told them that it was one of themselves, whose name he promised never to reveal; whereupon they went off, and carried the old woman prisoner with them. When they arrived at their camp, Pontiac, their greatest chief, seized on the prisoner, and gave her three strokes with a stick on the head, which laid her flat on the ground, and the whole nation assembled round her, and called repeated times, 'Kill her! kill her!' "

Thus it is clear that the story told by Carver must be taken with many grains of allowance. The greater part of the evidence given above has been gathered since the first edition of this book was published. It has been thought best to retain the original passage, with the necessary qualifications. The story is not without interest, and those may believe it who will.

the warm spring evening, with the piping of frogs along the river bank, just roused from their torpor by the genial influence of May. But, at intervals, as the night wind swept across the bastion, it bore sounds of fearful portent to the ear, the sullen booming of the Indian drum and the wild chorus of quavering yells, as the warriors, around their distant camp-fires, danced the war-dance, in preparation for the morrow's work.[1]

[1] *Maxwell's Account*, MS. See *Appendix*, C.

Chapter XI.

1763.

TREACHERY OF PONTIAC.

THE NIGHT passed without alarm. The sun rose upon fresh fields and newly budding woods, and scarcely had the morning mists dissolved, when the garrison could see a fleet of birch canoes crossing the river from the eastern shore, within range of cannon shot above the fort. Only two or three warriors appeared in each, but all moved slowly, and seemed deeply laden. In truth, they were full of savages, lying flat on their faces, that their numbers might not excite the suspicion of the English.[1]

At an early hour the open common behind the fort was thronged with squaws, children, and warriors, some naked, and others fantastically arrayed in their barbarous finery. All seemed restless and uneasy, moving hither and thither, in apparent preparation for a general game of ball. Many tall warriors, wrapped in their blankets, were seen stalking towards the fort, and casting malignant furtive glances upward at the palisades. Then, with an air of assumed indifference, they would move towards the gate. They were all admitted; for Gladwyn, who, in this instance at least, showed some knowledge of Indian character, chose to convince his crafty foe that, though their plot was detected, their hostility was despised.[2]

The whole garrison was ordered under arms. Sterling, and the other English fur-traders, closed their storehouses and armed their men, and all in cool confidence stood waiting the result.

Meanwhile, Pontiac, who had crossed with the canoes from the eastern shore, was approaching along the river road, at the head of his sixty chiefs, all gravely marching in Indian file. A Canadian settler, named Beaufait, had been that morning to the fort. He was now returning homewards, and as he reached the bridge which led over the stream then called

[1]*Meloche's Account*, MS.
[2]*Penn. Gaz.* No. 1808.

513

Parent's Creek, he saw the chiefs in the act of crossing from the farther bank. He stood aside to give them room. As the last Indian passed, Beaufait recognized him as an old friend and associate. The savage greeted him with the usual ejaculation, opened for an instant the folds of his blanket, disclosed the hidden gun, and, with an emphatic gesture towards the fort, indicated the purpose to which he meant to apply it.[1]

At ten o'clock, the great war-chief, with his treacherous followers, reached the fort, and the gateway was thronged with their savage faces. All were wrapped to the throat in colored blankets. Some were crested with hawk, eagle, or raven plumes; others had shaved their heads, leaving only the fluttering scalp-lock on the crown; while others, again, wore their long, black hair flowing loosely at their backs, or wildly hanging about their brows like a lion's mane. Their bold yet crafty features, their cheeks besmeared with ochre and vermilion, white lead and soot, their keen, deep-set eyes gleaming in their sockets, like those of rattlesnakes, gave them an aspect grim, uncouth, and horrible. For the most part, they were tall, strong men, and all had a gait and bearing of peculiar stateliness.

As Pontiac entered, it is said that he started, and that a deep ejaculation half escaped from his breast. Well might his stoicism fail, for at a glance he read the ruin of his plot. On either hand, within the gateway, stood ranks of soldiers and hedges of glittering steel. The swarthy *engagés* of the fur-traders, armed to the teeth, stood in groups at the street corners, and the measured tap of a drum fell ominously on the ear. Soon regaining his composure, Pontiac strode forward into the narrow street; and his chiefs filed after him in silence, while the scared faces of women and children looked out from the windows as they passed. Their rigid muscles betrayed no sign of emotion; yet, looking closely, one might have seen their small eyes glance from side to side with restless scrutiny.

Traversing the entire width of the little town, they reached

[1]This incident was related, by the son of Beaufait, to General Cass. See Cass, *Discourse before the Michigan Historical Society*, 30.

the door of the council-house, a large building standing near the margin of the river. On entering, they saw Gladwyn, with several of his officers, seated in readiness to receive them, and the observant chiefs did not fail to remark that every Englishman wore a sword at his side, and a pair of pistols in his belt. The conspirators eyed each other with uneasy glances. "Why," demanded Pontiac, "do I see so many of my father's young men standing in the street with their guns?" Gladwyn replied through his interpreter, La Butte, that he had ordered the soldiers under arms for the sake of exercise and discipline. With much delay and many signs of distrust, the chiefs at length sat down on the mats prepared for them; and, after the customary pause, Pontiac rose to speak. Holding in his hand the wampum belt which was to have given the fatal signal, he addressed the commandant, professing strong attachment to the English, and declaring, in Indian phrase, that he had come to smoke the pipe of peace, and brighten the chain of friendship. The officers watched him keenly as he uttered these hollow words, fearing lest, though conscious that his designs were suspected, he might still attempt to accomplish them. And once, it is said, he raised the wampum belt as if about to give the signal of attack. But at that instant Gladwyn signed slightly with his hand. The sudden clash of arms sounded from the passage without, and a drum rolling the charge filled the council-room with its stunning din. At this, Pontiac stood like one confounded. Some writers will have it, that Gladwyn, rising from his seat, drew the chief's blanket aside, exposed the hidden gun, and sternly rebuked him for his treachery. But the commandant wished only to prevent the consummation of the plot, without bringing on an open rupture. His own letters affirm that he and his officers remained seated as before. Pontiac, seeing his unruffled brow and his calm eye fixed steadfastly upon him, knew not what to think, and soon sat down in amazement and perplexity. Another pause ensued, and Gladwyn commenced a brief reply. He assured the chiefs that friendship and protection should be extended towards them as long as they continued to deserve it, but threatened ample vengeance for the first act of aggression. The council then broke up; but, before leaving the room, Pontiac told the officers that he would return in a few days, with his squaws and children, for he wished that they should all shake hands with their fathers the English. To this new piece of treachery Gladwyn deigned no reply. The gates of the fort, which had been closed during the conference, were again flung open, and the baffled savages were suffered to depart, rejoiced, no doubt, to breathe once more the free air of the open fields.[1]

Gladwyn has been censured, and perhaps with justice, for not detaining the chiefs as hostages for the good conduct of their followers. An entrapped wolf meets no quarter from the huntsman; and a savage, caught in his treachery, has no claim to forbearance. Perhaps the commandant feared lest, should he arrest the chiefs when gathered at a public council, and guiltless as yet of open violence, the act might be interpreted as cowardly and dishonorable. He was ignorant, moreover, of the true nature of the plot. In his view, the whole affair was one of those impulsive outbreaks so common among Indians; and he trusted that, could an immediate rupture be averted, the threatening clouds would soon blow over.

Here, and elsewhere, the conduct of Pontiac is marked with the blackest treachery; and one cannot but lament that a com-

---

[1] Carver, *Travels*, 159 (London, 1778). M'Kenney, *Tour to the Lakes*, 130. Cass, *Discourse*, 32. *Penn. Gaz.* Nos. 1807, 1808. *Pontiac* MS. *M'Dougal*, MSS. *Gouin's Account*, MS. *Meloche's Account*, MS. *St. Aubin's Account*, MS.

Extract from a MS. Letter—*Major Gladwyn to Sir J. Amherst*:

"Detroit, May 14, 1763.

"Sir:

"On the First Instant, Pontiac, the Chief of the Ottawa Nation, came here with about Fifty of his Men (forty, Pontiac MS.), and told me that in a few days, when the rest of his Nation came in, he Intended to Pay me a Formal Visit. The 7th he came, but I was luckily Informed, the Night before, that he was coming with an Intention to Surprize Us; Upon which I took such Precautions that when they Entered the Fort, (tho' they were, by the best Accounts, about Three Hundred, and Armed with Knives, Tomyhawks, and a great many with Guns cut short, and hid under their Blankets), they were so much surprized to see our Disposition, that they would scarcely sit down to Council: However in about Half an hour, after they saw their Designs were Discovered, they sat Down, and Pontiac made a speech which I Answered calmly, without Intimating my suspicion of their Intentions, and after receiving some Trifling Presents, they went away to their Camp."

manding and magnanimous nature should be stained with the odious vice of cowards and traitors. He could govern, with almost despotic sway, a race unruly as the winds. In generous thought and deed, he rivalled the heroes of ancient story; and craft and cunning might well seem alien to a mind like his. Yet Pontiac was a thorough savage, and in him stand forth, in strongest light and shadow, the native faults and virtues of the Indian race. All children, says Sir Walter Scott, are naturally liars; and truth and honor are developments of later education. Barbarism is to civilization what childhood is to maturity; and all savages, whatever may be their country, their color, or their lineage, are prone to treachery and deceit. The barbarous ancestors of our own frank and manly race are no less obnoxious to the charge than those of the cat-like Bengalee; for in this childhood of society brave men and cowards are treacherous alike.

The Indian differs widely from the European in his notion of military virtue. In his view, artifice is wisdom; and he honors the skill that can circumvent, no less than the valor that can subdue, an adversary. The object of war, he argues, is to destroy the enemy. To accomplish this end, all means are honorable; and it is folly, not bravery, to incur a needless risk. Had Pontiac ordered his followers to storm the palisades of Detroit, not one of them would have obeyed him. They might, indeed, after their strange superstition, have reverenced him as a madman; but, from that hour, his fame as a war-chief would have sunk forever.

Balked in his treachery, the great chief withdrew to his village, enraged and mortified, yet still resolved to persevere. That Gladwyn had suffered him to escape, was to his mind an ample proof either of cowardice or ignorance. The latter supposition seemed the more probable; and he resolved to visit the English once more, and convince them, if possible, that their suspicions against him were unfounded. Early on the following morning, he repaired to the fort with three of his chiefs, bearing in his hand the sacred calumet, or pipe of peace, its bowl carved in stone, and its stem adorned with feathers. Offering it to the commandant, he addressed him and his officers to the following effect: "My fathers, evil birds

have sung lies in your ear. We that stand before you are
friends of the English. We love them as our brothers; and, to
prove our love, we have come this day to smoke the pipe of
peace." At his departure, he gave the pipe to Captain Campbell, second in command, as a farther pledge of his sincerity.

That afternoon, the better to cover his designs, Pontiac
called the young men of all the tribes to a game of ball, which
took place, with great noise and shouting, on the neighboring
fields. At nightfall, the garrison were startled by a burst of
loud, shrill yells. The drums beat to arms, and the troops were
ordered to their posts; but the alarm was caused only by the
victors in the ball play, who were announcing their success by
these discordant outcries. Meanwhile, Pontiac was in the Pottawattamie village, consulting with the chiefs of that tribe,
and with the Wyandots, by what means they might compass
the ruin of the English.[1]

Early on the following morning, Monday, the ninth of
May, the French inhabitants went in procession to the principal church of the settlement, which stood near the river bank,
about half a mile above the fort. Having heard mass, they all
returned before eleven o'clock, without discovering any signs
that the Indians meditated an immediate act of hostility.
Scarcely, however, had they done so, when the common behind the fort was once more thronged with Indians of all the
four tribes; and Pontiac, advancing from among the multitude, approached the gate. It was closed and barred against
him. He shouted to the sentinels, and demanded why he was
refused admittance. Gladwyn himself replied, that the great
chief might enter, if he chose, but that the crowd he had
brought with him must remain outside. Pontiac rejoined, that
he wished all his warriors to enjoy the fragrance of the
friendly calumet. Gladwyn's answer was more concise than
courteous, and imported that he would have none of his rabble in the fort. Thus repulsed, Pontiac threw off the mask
which he had worn so long. With a grin of hate and rage, he
turned abruptly from the gate, and strode towards his followers, who, in great multitudes, lay flat upon the ground, just
beyond reach of gunshot. At his approach, they all leaped up

[1] *Pontiac* MS.

and ran off, "yelping," in the words of an eye-witness, "like so many devils."[1]

Looking out from the loopholes, the garrison could see them running in a body towards the house of an old English woman, who lived, with her family, on a distant part of the common. They beat down the doors, and rushed tumultuously in. A moment more, and the mournful scalp-yell told the fate of the wretched inmates. Another large body ran, yelling, to the river bank, and, leaping into their canoes, paddled with all speed to the Isle au Cochon, where dwelt an Englishman, named Fisher, formerly a sergeant of the regulars.

They soon dragged him from the hiding-place where he had sought refuge, murdered him on the spot, took his scalp, and made great rejoicings over this miserable trophy of brutal malice. On the following day, several Canadians crossed over to the island to inter the body, which they accomplished, as they thought, very effectually. Tradition, however, relates, as undoubted truth, that when, a few days after, some of the party returned to the spot, they beheld the pale hands of the dead man thrust above the ground, in an attitude of eager entreaty. Having once more covered the refractory members with earth, they departed, in great wonder and awe; but what was their amazement, when, on returning a second time, they saw the hands protruding as before. At this, they repaired in horror to the priest, who hastened to the spot, sprinkled the grave with holy water, and performed over it the neglected rites of burial. Thenceforth, says the tradition, the corpse of the murdered soldier slept in peace.[2]

Pontiac had borne no part in the wolfish deeds of his followers. When he saw his plan defeated, he turned towards the shore; and no man durst approach him, for he was terrible in his rage. Pushing a canoe from the bank, he urged it with vigorous strokes, against the current, towards the Ottawa village, on the farther side. As he drew near, he shouted to the inmates. None remained in the lodges but women, children, and old men, who all came flocking out at the sound of his

[1] MS. Letter—*Gladwyn to Amherst*, May 14. *Pontiac* MS., &c.
[2] *St. Aubin's Account*, MS.

imperious voice. Pointing across the water, he ordered that all should prepare to move the camp to the western shore, that the river might no longer interpose a barrier between his followers and the English. The squaws labored with eager alacrity to obey him. Provisions, utensils, weapons, and even the bark covering to the lodges, were carried to the shore; and before evening all was ready for embarkation. Meantime, the warriors had come dropping in from their bloody work, until, at nightfall, nearly all had returned. Then Pontiac, hideous in his war-paint, leaped into the central area of the village. Brandishing his tomahawk, and stamping on the ground, he recounted his former exploits, and denounced vengeance on the English. The Indians flocked about him. Warrior after warrior caught the fierce contagion, and soon the ring was filled with dancers, circling round and round with frantic gesture, and startling the distant garrison with unearthly yells.[1]

The war-dance over, the work of embarkation was commenced, and long before morning the transfer was complete. The whole Ottawa population crossed the river, and pitched their wigwams on the western side, just above the mouth of the little stream then known as Parent's Creek, but since named Bloody Run, from the scenes of terror which it witnessed.[2]

During the evening, fresh tidings of disaster reached the fort. A Canadian, named Desnoyers, came down the river in a birch canoe, and, landing at the water gate, brought news that two English officers, Sir Robert Davers and Captain Robertson, had been waylaid and murdered by the Indians, above Lake St. Clair.[3] The Canadian declared, moreover, that

---

[1] *Parent's Account*, MS. *Meloche's Account*, MS.

[2] *Gouin's Account*, MS.

[3] *Penn. Gaz*. Nos. 1807, 1808.

Extract from an anonymous letter — Detroit, July 9, 1763.

"You have long ago heard of our pleasant Situation, but the Storm is blown over. Was it not very agreeable to hear every Day, of their cutting, carving, boiling and eating our Companions? To see every Day dead Bodies floating down the River, mangled and disfigured? But Britons, you know, never shrink; we always appeared gay, to spite the Rascals. They boiled and eat Sir Robert Davers; and we are informed by Mr. Pauly, who escaped the

Pontiac had just been joined by a formidable band of Ojib-was, from the Bay of Saginaw.[1] These were a peculiarly fero-cious horde, and their wretched descendants still retain the character.

Every Englishman in the fort, whether trader or soldier, was now ordered under arms. No man lay down to sleep, and Gladwyn himself walked the ramparts throughout the night.

All was quiet till the approach of dawn. But as the first dim redness tinged the east, and fields and woods grew visible in the morning twilight, suddenly the war-whoop rose on every side at once. As wolves assail the wounded bison, howling their gathering cries across the wintry prairie, so the fierce Indians, pealing their terrific yells, came bounding naked to the assault. The men hastened to their posts. And truly it was time; for not the Ottawas alone, but the whole barbarian swarm—Wyandots, Pottawattamies, and Ojibwas—were upon them, and bullets rapped hard and fast against the pali-sades. The soldiers looked from the loopholes, thinking to see their assailants gathering for a rush against the feeble barrier. But, though their clamors filled the air, and their guns blazed thick and hot, yet very few were visible. Some were ensconced behind barns and fences, some skulked among bushes, and some lay flat in hollows of the ground; while those who could find no shelter were leaping about with the agility of mon-keys, to dodge the shot of the fort. Each had filled his mouth with bullets, for the convenience of loading, and each was charging and firing without suspending these agile gymnastics for a moment. There was one low hill, at no great distance from the fort, behind which countless black heads of Indians alternately appeared and vanished; while, all along the ridge, their guns emitted incessant white puffs of smoke. Every loophole was a target for their bullets; but the fire was re-turned with steadiness, and not without effect. The Canadian *engagés* of the fur-traders retorted the Indian war-whoops

---

other Day from one of the Stations surprised at the breaking out of the War, and commanded by himself, that he had seen an Indian have the Skin of Captain Robertson's Arm for a Tobacco-Pouch!"

[1] *Pontiac* MS.

with outcries not less discordant, while the British and provincials paid back the clamor of the enemy with musket and rifle balls. Within half gunshot of the palisades was a cluster of outbuildings, behind which a host of Indians found shelter. A cannon was brought to bear upon them, loaded with red-hot spikes. They were soon wrapped in flames, upon which the disconcerted savages broke away in a body, and ran off yelping, followed by a shout of laughter from the soldiers.[1]

For six hours, the attack was unabated; but as the day advanced, the assailants grew weary of their futile efforts. Their fire slackened, their clamors died away, and the garrison was left once more in peace, though from time to time a solitary shot, or lonely whoop, still showed the presence of some lingering savage, loath to be balked of his revenge. Among the garrison, only five men had been wounded, while the cautious enemy had suffered but trifling loss.

Gladwyn was still convinced that the whole affair was a sudden ebullition, which would soon subside; and being, moreover, in great want of provisions, he resolved to open negotiations with the Indians, under cover of which he might obtain the necessary supplies. The interpreter, La Butte, who, like most of his countrymen, might be said to hold a neutral position between the English and the Indians, was despatched to the camp of Pontiac, to demand the reasons of his conduct, and declare that the commandant was ready to redress any real grievance of which he might complain. Two old Canadians of Detroit, Chapeton and Godefroy, earnest to forward the negotiation, offered to accompany him. The gates were opened for their departure, and many other inhabitants of the place took this opportunity of leaving it, alleging as their motive, that they did not wish to see the approaching slaughter of the English.

Reaching the Indian Camp, the three ambassadors were received by Pontiac with great apparent kindness. La Butte delivered his message, and the two Canadians labored to dissuade the chief, for his own good and for theirs, from pur-

[1]*Pontiac MS. Penn. Gaz.* No. 1808. MS. Letter—*Gladwyn to Amherst*, May 14, etc.

suing his hostile purposes. Pontiac stood listening, armed with the true impenetrability of an Indian. At every proposal, he uttered an ejaculation of assent, partly from a strange notion of courtesy peculiar to his race, and partly from the deep dissimulation which seems native to their blood. Yet with all this seeming acquiescence, the heart of the savage was unmoved as a rock. The Canadians were completely deceived. Leaving Chapeton and Godefroy to continue the conference and push the fancied advantage, La Butte hastened back to the fort. He reported the happy issue of his mission, and added that peace might readily be had by making the Indians a few presents, for which they are always rapaciously eager. When, however, he returned to the Indian camp, he found, to his chagrin, that his companions had made no progress in the negotiation. Though still professing a strong desire for peace, Pontiac had evaded every definite proposal. At La Butte's appearance, all the chiefs withdrew to consult among themselves. They returned after a short debate, and Pontiac declared that, out of their earnest desire for firm and lasting peace, they wished to hold council with their English fathers themselves. With this view, they were especially desirous that Captain Campbell, second in command, should visit their camp. This veteran officer, from his just, upright, and manly character, had gained the confidence of the Indians. To the Canadians the proposal seemed a natural one, and returning to the fort, they laid it before the commandant. Gladwyn suspected treachery, but Captain Campbell urgently asked permission to comply with the request of Pontiac. He felt, he said, no fear of the Indians, with whom he had always maintained the most friendly terms. Gladwyn, with some hesitation, acceded; and Campbell left the fort, accompanied by a junior officer, Lieutenant M'Dougal, and attended by La Butte and several other Canadians.

In the mean time, M. Gouin, anxious to learn what was passing, had entered the Indian camp, and, moving from lodge to lodge, soon saw and heard enough to convince him that the two British officers were advancing into the lion's jaws.[1] He hastened to despatch two messengers to warn them

[1] *Gouin's Account*, MS.

of the peril. The party had scarcely left the gate when they were met by these men, breathless with running; but the warning came too late. Once embarked on the embassy, the officers would not be diverted from it; and passing up the river road, they approached the little wooden bridge that led over Parent's Creek. Crossing this bridge, and ascending a rising ground beyond, they saw before them the wide-spread camp of the Ottawas. A dark multitude gathered along its outskirts, and no sooner did they recognize the red uniform of the officers, than they all raised at once a horrible outcry of whoops and howlings. Indeed, they seemed disposed to give the ambassadors the reception usually accorded to captives taken in war; for the women seized sticks, stones, and clubs, and ran towards Campbell and his companion, as if to make them pass the cruel ordeal of running the gauntlet.[1] Pontiac came forward, and his voice allayed the tumult. He shook the officers by the hand, and, turning, led the way through the camp. It was a confused assemblage of huts, chiefly of a conical or half-spherical shape, and constructed of a slender framework covered with rush mats or sheets of birch-bark. Many of the graceful birch canoes, used by the Indians of the upper lakes, were lying here and there among paddles, fish-spears, and blackened kettles slung above the embers of the fires. The camp was full of lean, wolfish dogs, who, roused by the clamor of their owners, kept up a discordant baying as the strangers passed. Pontiac paused before the entrance of a large

[1]When a party returned with prisoners, the whole population of the village turned out to receive them, armed with sticks, clubs, or even deadlier weapons. The captive was ordered to run to a given point, usually some conspicuous lodge, or a post driven into the ground, while his tormentors, ranging themselves in two rows, inflicted on him a merciless flagellation, which only ceased when he had reached the goal. Among the Iroquois, prisoners were led through the whole confederacy, undergoing this martyrdom at every village, and seldom escaping without the loss of a hand, a finger, or an eye. Sometimes the sufferer was made to dance and sing, for the better entertainment of the crowd.

The story of General Stark is well known. Being captured, in his youth, by the Indians, and told to run the gauntlet, he instantly knocked down the nearest warrior, snatched a club from his hands, and wielded it with such good-will that no one dared approach him, and he reached the goal scot free, while his more timorous companion was nearly beaten to death.

lodge, and, entering, pointed to several mats placed on the ground, at the side opposite the opening. Here, obedient to his signal, the two officers sat down. Instantly the lodge was thronged with savages. Some, and these were for the most part chiefs, or old men, seated themselves on the ground before the strangers; while the remaining space was filled by a dense crowd, crouching or standing erect, and peering over each other's shoulders. At their first entrance, Pontiac had spoken a few words. A pause then ensued, broken at length by Campbell, who from his seat addressed the Indians in a short speech. It was heard in perfect silence, and no reply was made. For a full hour, the unfortunate officers saw before them the same concourse of dark, inscrutable faces, bending an unwavering gaze upon them. Some were passing out, and others coming in to supply their places, and indulge their curiosity by a sight of the Englishmen. At length, Captain Campbell, conscious, no doubt, of the danger in which he was placed, resolved fully to ascertain his true position, and, rising to his feet, declared his intention of returning to the fort. Pontiac made a sign that he should resume his seat. "My father," he said, "will sleep to-night in the lodges of his red children." The gray-haired soldier and his companion were betrayed into the hands of their enemies.

Many of the Indians were eager to kill the captives on the spot, but Pontiac would not carry his treachery so far. He protected them from injury and insult, and conducted them to the house of M. Meloche, near Parent's Creek, where good quarters were assigned them, and as much liberty allowed as was consistent with safe custody.[1] The peril of their situation was diminished by the circumstance that two Indians, who, several days before, had been detained at the fort for some

---

[1] *Meloche's Account*, MS. *Penn. Gaz*. No. 1808. In a letter of James MacDonald, Detroit, July 12, the circumstances of the detention of the officers are related somewhat differently. Singularly enough, this letter of MacDonald is identical with a report of the events of the siege sent by Major Robert Rogers to Sir William Johnson, on the eighth of August. Rogers, who was not an eye-witness, appears to have borrowed the whole of his brother officer's letter without acknowledgment.

slight offence, still remained prisoners in the power of the commandant.[1]

Late in the evening, La Butte, the interpreter, returned to the fort. His face wore a sad and downcast look, which sufficiently expressed the melancholy tidings that he brought. On hearing his account, some of the officers suspected, though probably without ground, that he was privy to the detention of the two ambassadors; and La Butte, feeling himself an object of distrust, lingered about the streets, sullen and silent, like the Indians among whom his rough life had been spent.

[1]Extract from a MS. Letter—*Sir J. Amherst to Major Gladwyn*.

"New York, 22nd June, 1763.

"The Precautions you took when the Perfidious Villains came to Pay you a Visit, were Indeed very wisely Concerted; And I Approve Entirely of the Steps you have since taken for the Defence of the Place, which, I hope, will have Enabled You to keep the Savages at Bay untill the Reinforcement, which Major Wilkins Writes me he had sent you, Arrives with you.

"I most sincerely Grieve for the Unfortunate Fate of Sir Robert Davers, Lieut. Robertson, and the Rest of the Poor People, who have fallen into the Hands of the Merciless Villains. I Trust you did not Know of the Murder of those Gentlemen, when Pontiac came with a Pipe of Peace, for if you had, you certainly would have put him, and Every Indian in your Power, to Death. Such Retaliation is the only Way of Treating such Miscreants.

"I cannot but Approve of your having Permitted Captain Campbell and Lieut. MacDougal to go to the Indians, as you had no other Method to Procure Provisions, by which means you may have been Enabled to Preserve the Garrison; for no Other Inducement should have prevailed on you to Allow those Gentlemen to Entrust themselves with the Savages. I am Nevertheless not without my Fears for them, and were it not that you have two Indians in your Hands, in Lieu of those Gentlemen, I should give them over for Lost.

"I shall Add no more at present; Capt. Dalzell will Inform you of the steps taken for Reinforcing you: and you may be assured—the utmost Expedition will be used for Collecting such a Force as may be Sufficient for bringing Ample Vengeance on the Treacherous and Bloody Villains who have so Perfidiously Attacked their Benefactors." MacDonald, and after him, Rogers, says that, after the detention of the two officers, Pontiac summoned the fort to surrender, threatening, in case of refusal, to put all within to the torture. The anonymous author of the *Diary of the Siege* adds that he sent word to Gladwyn that he kept the officers out of kindness, since, if they returned to the fort, he should be obliged to boil them with the rest of the garrison, the kettle being already on the fire.

Chapter XII.

1763.

PONTIAC AT THE SIEGE OF DETROIT.

O N THE MORNING after the detention of the officers, Pontiac crossed over, with several of his chiefs, to the Wyandot village. A part of this tribe, influenced by Father Pothier, their Jesuit priest, had refused to take up arms against the English; but, being now threatened with destruction if they should longer remain neutral, they were forced to join the rest. They stipulated, however, that they should be allowed time to hear mass, before dancing the war-dance.[1] To this condition Pontiac readily agreed, "although," observes the chronicler in the fulness of his horror and detestation, "he himself had no manner of worship, and cared not for festivals or Sundays." These nominal Christians of Father Pothier's flock, together with the other Wyandots, soon distinguished themselves in the war; fighting better, it was said, than all the other Indians,—an instance of the marked superiority of the Iroquois over the Algonquin stock.

Having secured these new allies, Pontiac prepared to resume his operations with fresh vigor; and to this intent, he made an improved disposition of his forces. Some of the Pottawattamies were ordered to lie in wait along the river bank, below the fort; while others concealed themselves in the woods, in order to intercept any Englishman who might approach by land or water. Another band of the same tribe were to conceal themselves in the neighborhood of the fort, when no general attack was going forward, in order to shoot down any soldier or trader who might chance to expose his person. On the eleventh of May, when these arrangements were complete, several Canadians came early in the morning to the fort, to offer what they called friendly advice. It was to the effect that the garrison should at once abandon the place, as it would be stormed within an hour by fifteen hundred Indians. Gladwyn refused, whereupon the Canadians departed; and

[1] *Pontiac* MS.

soon after some six hundred Indians began a brisk fusillade, which they kept up till seven o'clock in the evening. A Canadian then appeared, bearing a summons from Pontiac, demanding the surrender of the fort, and promising that the English should go unmolested on board their vessels, leaving all their arms and effects behind. Gladwyn again gave a flat refusal.[1]

On the evening of that day, the officers met to consider what course of conduct the emergency required; and, as one of them writes, the commandant was almost alone in the opinion that they ought still to defend the place.[2] It seemed to the rest that the only course remaining was to embark and sail for Niagara. Their condition appeared desperate; for, on the shortest allowance, they had scarcely provision enough to sustain the garrison three weeks, within which time there was little hope of succor. The houses being, moreover, of wood, and chiefly thatched with straw, might be set on fire with burning missiles. But the chief apprehensions of the officers arose from their dread that the enemy would make a general onset, and cut or burn their way through the pickets,—a mode of attack to which resistance would be unavailing. Their anxiety on this score was relieved by a Canadian in the fort, who had spent half his life among Indians, and who now assured the commandant that every maxim of their warfare was opposed to such a measure. Indeed, an Indian's idea of military honor widely differs, as before observed, from that of a white man; for he holds it to consist no less in a wary regard to his own life than in the courage and impetuosity with which he assails his enemy. His constant aim is to gain advantages without incurring loss. He sets an inestimable value on the lives of his own party, and deems a victory dearly purchased by the death of a single warrior. A war-chief attains the summit of his renown when he can boast that he has brought home a score of scalps without the loss of a man; and his reputation is wofully abridged if the mournful wailings of the women mingle with the exulting yells of the warriors. Yet, with all his

[1] MS. Letter—*James McDonald to* ——, Detroit, July 12.
[2] *Penn. Gaz.* No. 1808.

subtlety and caution, the Indian is not a coward, and, in his own way of fighting, often exhibits no ordinary courage. Stealing alone into the heart of an enemy's country, he prowls around the hostile village, watching every movement; and when night sets in, he enters a lodge, and calmly stirs the decaying embers, that, by their light, he may select his sleeping victims. With cool deliberation he deals the mortal thrust, kills foe after foe, and tears away scalp after scalp, until at length an alarm is given; then, with a wild yell, he bounds out into the darkness, and is gone.

Time passed on, and brought little change and no relief to the harassed and endangered garrison. Day after day the Indians continued their attacks, until their war-cries and the rattle of their guns became familiar sounds. For many weeks, no man lay down to sleep, except in his clothes, and with his weapons by his side.[1] Parties of volunteers sallied, from time to time, to burn the outbuildings which gave shelter to the enemy. They cut down orchard trees, and levelled fences, until the ground about the fort was clear and open, and the enemy had no cover left from whence to fire. The two vessels in the river, sweeping the northern and southern curtains of the works with their fire, deterred the Indians from approaching those points, and gave material aid to the garrison. Still, worming their way through the grass, sheltering themselves behind every rising ground, the pertinacious savages would crawl close to the palisade, and shoot arrows, tipped with burning tow, upon the roofs of

[1]MS. Letter from an officer at Detroit—no signature—July 31.

Extract from a letter dated Detroit, July 6.

"We have been besieged here two Months, by Six Hundred Indians. We have been upon the Watch Night and Day, from the Commanding Officer to the lowest soldier, from the 8th of May, and have not had our Cloaths off, nor slept all Night since it began; and shall continue so till we have a Reinforcement up. We then hope soon to give a good account of the Savages. Their Camp lies about a Mile and a half from the Fort; and that's the nearest they choose to come now. For the first two or three Days we were attacked by three or four Hundred of them, but we gave them so warm a Reception that now they don't care for coming to see us, tho' they now and then get behind a House or Garden, and fire at us about three or four Hundred yards' distance. The Day before Yesterday, we killed a Chief and three others, and wounded some more; yesterday went up with our Sloop, and battered their Cabins in such a Manner that they are glad to keep farther off."

the houses; but cisterns and tanks of water were everywhere provided against such an emergency, and these attempts proved abortive. The little church, which stood near the palisade, was particularly exposed, and would probably have been set on fire, had not the priest of the settlement threatened Pontiac with the vengeance of the Great Spirit, should he be guilty of such sacrilege. Pontiac, who was filled with eagerness to get possession of the garrison, neglected no expedient that his savage tactics could supply. He went farther, and begged the French inhabitants to teach him the European method of attacking a fortified place by regular approaches; but the rude Canadians knew as little of the matter as he; or if, by chance, a few were better informed, they wisely preferred to conceal their knowledge. Soon after the first attack, the Ottawa chief had sent in to Gladwyn a summons to surrender, assuring him that, if the place were at once given up, he might embark on board the vessels, with all his men; but that, if he persisted in his defence, he would treat him as Indians treat each other; that is, he would burn him alive. To this Gladwyn made answer that he cared nothing for his threats.[1] The attacks were now renewed with increased activity, and the assailants were soon after inspired with fresh ardor by the arrival of a hundred and twenty Ojibwa warriors from Grand River. Every man in the fort, officers, soldiers, traders, and *engagés*, now slept upon the ramparts; even in stormy weather none were allowed to withdraw to their quarters;[2] yet a spirit of confidence and cheerfulness still prevailed among the weary garrison.

Meanwhile, great efforts were made to procure a supply of provisions. Every house was examined, and all that could serve for food, even grease and tallow, was collected and placed in the public storehouse, compensation having first been made to the owners. Notwithstanding these precautions Detroit must have been abandoned or destroyed, but for the assistance of a few friendly Canadians, and especially of M. Baby, a prominent *habitant*, who lived on the opposite side of the river, and provided the garrison with

[1] *Pontiac* MS.
[2] *Penn. Gaz*. No. 1808.

cattle, hogs, and other supplies. These, under cover of night, were carried from his farm to the fort in boats, the Indians long remaining ignorant of what was going forward.[1]

They, on their part, began to suffer from hunger. Thinking to have taken Detroit at a single stroke, they had neglected, with their usual improvidence, to provide against the exigencies of a siege; and now, in small parties, they would visit the Canadian families along the river shore, passing from house to house, demanding provisions, and threatening violence in case of refusal. This was the more annoying, since the food thus obtained was wasted with characteristic recklessness. Unable to endure it longer, the Canadians appointed a deputation of fifteen of the eldest among them to wait upon Pontiac, and complain of his followers' conduct. The meeting took place at a Canadian house, probably that of M. Meloche, where the great chief had made his headquarters, and where the prisoners, Campbell and M'Dougal, were confined.

When Pontiac saw the deputation approaching along the river road, he was seized with an exceeding eagerness to know the purpose of their visit; for having long desired to gain the Canadians as allies against the English, and made several advances to that effect, he hoped that their present errand might relate to the object next his heart. So strong was his curiosity, that, forgetting the ordinary rule of Indian dignity and decorum, he asked the business on which they had come before

---

[1] Extract from a MS. Letter—*Major Gladwyn to Sir J. Amherst*.

"Detroit, July 8th, 1763.

"Since the Commencement of this Extraordinary Affair, I have been Informed, that many of the Inhabitants of this Place, seconded by some French Traders from Montreal, have made the Indians Believe that a French Army & Fleet were in the River St. Lawrence, and that Another Army would come from the Illinois; And that when I Published the cessation of Arms, they said it was a mere Invention of Mine, purposely Calculated to Keep the Indians Quiet, as We were Affraid of them; but they were not such Fools as to Believe me; Which, with a thousand other Lies, calculated to Stir up Mischief, have Induced the Indians to take up Arms; And I dare say it will Appear ere long, that One Half of the Settlement merit a Gibbet, and the Other Half ought to be Decimated; Nevertheless, there is some Honest Men among them, to whom I am Infinitely Obliged; I mean, Sir, Monsieur Navarre, the two Babys, & my Interpreters, St. Martin & La Bute."

they themselves had communicated it. The Canadians replied, that they wished the chiefs to be convened, for they were about to speak upon a matter of much importance. Pontiac instantly despatched messengers to the different camps and villages. The chiefs, soon arriving at his summons, entered the apartment, where they seated themselves upon the floor, having first gone through the necessary formality of shaking hands with the Canadian deputies. After a suitable pause, the eldest of the French rose, and heavily complained of the outrages which they had committed. "You pretend," he said, "to be friends of the French, and yet you plunder us of our hogs and cattle, you trample upon our fields of young corn, and when you enter our houses, you enter with tomahawk raised. When your French father comes from Montreal with his great army, he will hear of what you have done, and, instead of shaking hands with you as brethren, he will punish you as enemies."

Pontiac sat with his eyes riveted upon the ground, listening to every word that was spoken. When the speaker had concluded, he returned the following answer: —

"Brothers:

"We have never wished to do you harm, nor allow any to be done you; but among us there are many young men who, though strictly watched, find opportunities of mischief. It is not to revenge myself alone that I make war on the English. It is to revenge you, my Brothers. When the English insulted us, they insulted you also. I know that they have taken away your arms, and made you sign a paper which they have sent home to their country. Therefore you are left defenceless; and I mean now to revenge your cause and my own together. I mean to destroy the English, and leave not one upon our lands. You do not know the reasons from which I act. I have told you those only which concern yourselves; but you will learn all in time. You will cease then to think me a fool. I know, my brothers, that there are many among you who take part with the English. I am sorry for it, for their own sakes; for when our Father arrives, I shall point them out to him, and they will see whether they or I have most reason to be satisfied with the part we have acted.

"I do not doubt, my Brothers, that this war is very trouble-

some to you, for our warriors are continually passing and
repassing through your settlement. I am sorry for it. Do not
think that I approve of the damage that is done by them;
and, as a proof of this, remember the war with the Foxes,
and the part which I took in it. It is now seventeen years
since the Ojibwas of Michillimackinac, combined with the
Sacs and Foxes, came down to destroy you. Who then defended you? Was it not I and my young men? Mickinac, great
chief of all these nations, said in council that he would carry
to his village the head of your commandant—that he would
eat his heart and drink his blood. Did I not take your part?
Did I not go to his camp, and say to him, that if he wished
to kill the French, he must first kill me and my warriors?
Did I not assist you in routing them and driving them away?[1]
And now you think that I would turn my arms against you!
No, my Brothers; I am the same French Pontiac who assisted
you seventeen years ago. I am a Frenchman, and I wish to die
a Frenchman; and I now repeat to you that you and I are
one—that it is for both our interests that I should be
avenged. Let me alone. I do not ask you for aid, for it is
not in your power to give it. I only ask provisions for myself
and men. Yet, if you are inclined to assist me, I shall not
refuse you. It would please me, and you yourselves would be
sooner rid of your troubles; for I promise you, that, as soon

---

[1] The annals of these remote and gloomy regions are involved in such obscurity, that it is hard to discover the precise character of the events to which
Pontiac here refers. The only allusion to them, which the writer has met with,
is the following, inscribed on a tattered scrap of soiled paper, found among
the M'Dougal manuscripts:—

"Five miles below the mouth of Wolf River is the Great Death Ground.
This took its name from the circumstance, that some years before the Old
French War, a great battle was fought between the French troops, assisted by
the Menomonies and Ottaways on the one side, and the Sac and Fox Indians
on the other. The Sacs and Foxes were nearly all cut off; and this proved the
cause of their eventual expulsion from that country."

The M'Dougal manuscripts, above referred to, belonged to a son of the
Lieutenant M'Dougal who was the fellow-prisoner of Major Campbell. On
the death of the younger M'Dougal, the papers, which were very voluminous, and contained various notes concerning the Indian war, and the captivity of his father, came into the possession of a family at the town of St. Clair,
in Michigan, who permitted such of them as related to the subjects in question to be copied by the writer.

as the English are driven out, we will go back to our villages, and there await the arrival of our French Father. You have heard what I have to say; remain at peace, and I will watch that no harm shall be done to you, either by my men or by the other Indians."

This speech is reported by a writer whose chief characteristic is the scrupulous accuracy with which he has chronicled minute details without interest or importance. He neglects, moreover, no opportunity of casting ignominy and contempt upon the name of Pontiac. His mind is of so dull and commonplace an order as to exclude the supposition that he himself is author of the words which he ascribes to the Ottawa chief, and the speech may probably be taken as a literal translation of the original.

As soon as the council broke up, Pontiac took measures for bringing the disorders complained of to a close, while, at the same time, he provided sustenance for his warriors; and, in doing this, he displayed a policy and forecast scarcely paralleled in the history of his race. He first forbade the commission of farther outrage.[1] He next visited in turn the families of the Canadians, and, inspecting the property belonging to them, he assigned to each the share of provisions which it must furnish for the support of the Indians.[2] The contributions thus levied were all collected at the house of Meloche, near Parent's Creek, whence they were regularly issued, as the exigence required, to the savages of the different camps. As the character and habits of an Indian but ill qualify him to act the part of commissary, Pontiac in this matter availed himself of French assistance.

On the river bank, not far from the house of Meloche, lived an old Canadian, named Quilleriez, a man of exceeding vanity and self-conceit, and noted in the settlement for the gayety of his attire. He wore moccasons of the most elaborate pattern, and a sash plentifully garnished with beads and wampum. He was continually intermeddling in the affairs of the Indians, being anxious to be regarded as the

[1] *Peltier's Account*, MS.
[2] *Gouin's Account*, MS.

leader or director among them.[1] Of this man Pontiac evidently made a tool, employing him, together with several others, to discharge, beneath his eye, the duties of his novel commissariat. Anxious to avoid offending the French, yet unable to make compensation for the provisions he had exacted, Pontiac had recourse to a remarkable expedient, suggested, no doubt, by one of these European assistants. He issued promissory notes, drawn upon birch-bark, and signed with the figure of an otter, the totem to which he belonged; and we are told by a trustworthy authority that they were all faithfully redeemed.[2] In this, as in several other instances, he exhibits an openness of mind and a power of adaptation not a little extraordinary among a people whose intellect will rarely leave the narrow and deeply cut channels in which it has run for ages, who reject instruction, and adhere with rigid tenacity to ancient ideas and usages. Pontiac always exhibited an eager desire for knowledge. Rogers represents him as earnest to learn the military art as practised among Europeans, and as inquiring curiously into the mode of making cloth, knives, and the other articles of Indian trade. Of his keen and subtle genius we have the following singular testimony from the pen of General Gage: "From a paragraph of M. D'Abbadie's letter, there is reason to judge of Pontiac, not only as a savage possessed of the most refined cunning and treachery natural to the Indians, but as a person of extraordinary abilities. He says that he keeps two secretaries, one to write for him, and the other to read the letters

---

[1]Tradition related by M. Baby. The following is from the *Diary of the Siege*: "Mr. St. Martin said . . . that one Sibbold that came here last winter with his Wife from the Illinois had told at Mr. Cuellierry's (Quilleriez) that they might expect a French Army in this Spring, and that Report took rise from him. That the Day Capt. Campbell & Lt. McDougal was detained by the Indians, *Mr. Cuellierry accepted of their Offer of being made Commandant*, if this Place was taken, to which he spoke to Mr. Cuellierry about and ask'd him if he knew what he was doing, to which Mr. Cuellierry told him, I am almost distracted, they are like so many Dogs about me, to which Mr. St. Martin made him no Answer."

[2]Rogers, *Account of North America*, 244. The anonymous *Diary of the Siege* says that they bore the figure of a "coon."

he receives, and he manages them so as to keep each of them ignorant of what is transacted by the other."[1]

Major Rogers, a man familiar with the Indians, and an acute judge of mankind, speaks in the highest terms of Pontiac's character and talents. "He puts on," he says, "an air of majesty and princely grandeur, and is greatly honored and revered by his subjects."[2]

In the present instance, few durst infringe the command he had given, that the property of the Canadians should be respected; indeed, it is said that none of his followers would cross the cultivated fields, but always followed the beaten paths; in such awe did they stand of his displeasure.[3]

Pontiac's position was very different from that of an ordinary military leader. When we remember that his authority, little sanctioned by law or usage, was derived chiefly from the force of his own individual mind, and that it was exercised over a people singularly impatient of restraint, we may better appreciate the commanding energy that could hold control over spirits so intractable.

The glaring faults of Pontiac's character have already appeared too clearly. He was artful and treacherous, bold, fierce, ambitious, and revengeful; yet the following anecdotes will evince that noble and generous thought was no stranger to the savage hero of this dark forest tragedy. Some time after the period of which we have been speaking, Rogers came up to Detroit, with a detachment of troops, and, on landing, sent a bottle of brandy, by a friendly Indian, as a present to

[1]MS. Letter—*Gage to Lord Halifax, April 16, 1764.*
Extract from a MS. Letter—*William Smith, Jr., to ——.*
"New York, 22d Nov. 1763.
" 'Tis an old saying that the Devil is easier raised than laid. Sir Jeffrey has found it so, with these Indian Demons. They have cut his little Army to Pieces, & almost if not entirely obstructed the Communication to the Detroite, where the Enemy are grown very numerous; and from whence I fancy you'll soon hear, if any survive to relate them, very tragical Accounts. The Besiegers are led on by an enterprising Fellow called Pondiac. He is a Genius, for he possesses great Bravery, Art, & Oratory, & has had the Address to get himself not only at the Head of his Conquerors, but elected Generalissimo of all the confederate Forces now acting against us—Perhaps he may deserve to be called the Mithridates of the West."
[2]Rogers, *North America*, 240.
[3]*Gouin's Account*, MS.

Pontiac. The Indians had always been suspicious that the English meant to poison them. Those around the chief, endeavored to persuade him that the brandy was drugged. Pontiac listened to what they said, and, as soon as they had concluded, poured out a cup of the liquor, and immediately drank it, saying that the man whose life he had saved had no power to kill him. He referred to his having prevented the Indians from attacking Rogers and his party when on their way to demand the surrender of Detroit. The story may serve as a counterpart to the well-known anecdote of Alexander the Great and his physician.[1]

Pontiac had been an old friend of Baby; and one evening, at an early period of the siege, he entered his house, and, seating himself by the fire, looked for some time steadily at the embers. At length, raising his head, he said he had heard that the English had offered the Canadian a bushel of silver for the scalp of his friend. Baby declared that the story was false, and protested that he would never betray him. Pontiac for a moment keenly studied his features. "My brother has spoken the truth," he said, "and I will show that I believe him." He remained in the house through the evening, and, at its close, wrapped himself in his blanket, and lay down upon a bench, where he slept in full confidence till morning.[2]

Another anecdote, from the same source, will exhibit the power which he exercised over the minds of his followers. A few young Wyandots were in the habit of coming, night after night, to the house of Baby, to steal hogs and cattle. The latter complained of the theft to Pontiac, and desired his protection. Being at that time ignorant of the intercourse between Baby and the English, Pontiac hastened to the assistance of his friend, and, arriving about nightfall at the house, walked to and fro among the barns and enclosures. At a late hour, he distinguished the dark forms of the plunderers stealing through the gloom. "Go back to your village, you Wyandot dogs," said the Ottawa chief; "if you tread again on this man's land, you shall die." They slunk back abashed; and from that time forward the Canadian's property was safe. The

[1]Rogers, *North America*, 244.
[2]Tradition related by M. François Baby.

Ottawas had no political connection with the Wyandots, who speak a language radically distinct. Over them he could claim no legitimate authority; yet his powerful spirit forced respect and obedience from all who approached him.[1]

[1] Tradition related by M. François Baby, of Windsor, U. C., the son of Pontiac's friend, who lives opposite Detroit, upon nearly the same site formerly occupied by his father's house. Though Pontiac at this time assumed the attitude of a protector of the Canadians, he had previously, according to the anonymous *Diary of the Siege*, bullied them exceedingly, compelling them to plough land for him, and do other work. Once he forced them to carry him in a sedan chair from house to house, to look for provisions.

Chapter XIII.

1763.

ROUT OF CUYLER'S DETACHMENT. — FATE OF THE FOREST GARRISONS.

WHILE PERILS were thickening around the garrison of Detroit, the British commander-in-chief at New York remained ignorant of its danger. Indeed, an unwonted quiet had prevailed, of late, along the borders and about the neighboring forts. With the opening of spring, a strong detachment had been sent up the lakes, with a supply of provisions and ammunition for the use of Detroit and the other western posts. The boats of this convoy were now pursuing their course along the northern shore of Lake Erie; and Gladwyn's garrison, aware of their approach, awaited their arrival with an anxiety which every day increased.

Day after day passed on, and the red cross of St. George still floated above Detroit. The keen-eyed watchfulness of the Indians had never abated; and woe to the soldier who showed his head above the palisades, or exposed his person before a loophole. Strong in his delusive hope of French assistance, Pontiac had sent messengers to M. Neyon, commandant at the Illinois, earnestly requesting that a force of regular troops might be sent to his aid; and Gladwyn, on his side, had ordered one of the vessels to Niagara, to hasten forward the expected convoy. The schooner set sail; but on the next day, as she lay becalmed at the entrance of Lake Erie, a multitude of canoes suddenly darted out upon her from the neighboring shores. In the prow of the foremost the Indians had placed their prisoner, Captain Campbell, with the dastardly purpose of interposing him as a screen between themselves and the fire of the English. But the brave old man called out to the crew to do their duty, without regard to him. Happily, at that moment a fresh breeze sprang up; the flapping sails stretched to the wind, and the schooner bore prosperously on her course towards Niagara, leaving the savage flotilla far behind.[1]

The fort, or rather town, of Detroit had, by this time, lost its wonted vivacity and life. Its narrow streets were gloomy and silent. Here and there strolled a Canadian, in red cap and gaudy sash; the weary sentinel walked to and fro before the quarters of the commandant; an officer, perhaps, passed along with rapid step and anxious face; or an Indian girl, the mate of some soldier or trader, moved silently by, in her finery of beads and vermilion. Such an aspect as this the town must have presented on the morning of the thirtieth of May, when, at about nine o'clock, the voice of the sentinel sounded from the south-east bastion; and loud exclamations, in the direction of the river, roused Detroit from its lethargy. Instantly the place was astir. Soldiers, traders, and *habitants*, hurrying through the water-gate, thronged the canoe wharf and the narrow strand without. The half-wild *coureurs de bois*, the tall and sinewy provincials, and the stately British soldiers, stood crowded together, their uniforms soiled and worn, and their faces haggard with unremitted watching. Yet all alike wore an animated and joyous look. The long expected convoy was full in sight. On the farther side of the river, at some distance below the fort, a line of boats was rounding the woody projection, then called Montreal Point, their oars flashing in the sun, and the red flag of England flying from the stern of the foremost.[2] The toils and dangers of the garrison were

---

[1] *Penn. Gaz.* No. 1807. MS. Letter—*Wilkins to Amherst*, June 18.

This incident may have suggested the story told by Mrs. Grant, in her *Memoirs of an American Lady*. A young British officer, of noble birth, had been living for some time among the Indians, and having encountered many strange adventures, he was now returning in a canoe with a party of his late associates,—none of them, it appears, were aware that hostilities existed,— and approached the schooner just before the attack commenced, expecting a friendly reception. Sir Robert D——, the young officer, was in Indian costume, and, wishing to surprise his friends, he made no answer when hailed from the vessel, whereupon he was instantly fired at and killed.—The story is without confirmation, in any contemporary document, and, indeed, is impossible in itself. Sir Robert Davers was killed, as before mentioned, near Lake St. Clair; but neither in his character, nor in the mode of his death, did he at all resemble the romantic adventurer whose fate is commemorated by Mrs. Grant.

[2] *Pontiac* MS.

drawing to an end. With one accord, they broke into three hearty cheers, again and again repeated, while a cannon, glancing from the bastion, sent its loud voice of defiance to the enemy, and welcome to approaching friends. But suddenly every cheek grew pale with horror. Dark naked figures were seen rising, with wild gesture, in the boats, while, in place of the answering salute, the distant yell of the war-whoop fell faintly on their ears. The convoy was in the hands of the enemy. The boats had all been taken, and the troops of the detachment slain or made captive. Officers and men stood gazing in mournful silence, when an incident occurred which caused them to forget the general calamity in the absorbing interest of the moment.

Leaving the disappointed garrison, we will pass over to the principal victims of this deplorable misfortune. In each of the boats, of which there were eighteen, two or more of the captured soldiers, deprived of their weapons, were compelled to act as rowers, guarded by several armed savages, while many other Indians, for the sake of farther security, followed the boats along the shore.[1] In the foremost, as it happened, there were four soldiers and only three Indians. The larger of the two vessels still lay anchored in the stream, about a bow-shot from the fort, while her companion, as we have seen, had gone down to Niagara to hasten up this very re-enforcement. As the boat came opposite this vessel, the soldier who acted as steersman conceived a daring plan of escape. The principal Indian sat immediately in front of another of the soldiers. The steersman called, in English, to his comrade to seize the savage and throw him overboard. The man answered that he was not strong enough; on which the steersman directed him to change places with him, as if fatigued with rowing, a movement which would excite no suspicion on the part of their guard. As the bold soldier stepped forward, as if to take his companion's oar, he suddenly seized the Indian by the hair, and, griping with the other hand the girdle at his waist, lifted him by main force, and flung him into the river. The boat rocked till the water surged over her gunwale. The Indian held fast to his enemy's

[1] *Pontiac* MS.

clothes, and, drawing himself upward as he trailed alongside, stabbed him again and again with his knife, and then dragged him overboard. Both went down the swift current, rising and sinking; and, as some relate, perished, grappled in each other's arms.[1] The two remaining Indians leaped out of the boat. The prisoners turned, and pulled for the distant vessel, shouting aloud for aid. The Indians on shore opened a heavy fire upon them, and many canoes paddled swiftly in pursuit. The men strained with desperate strength. A fate inexpressibly horrible was the alternative. The bullets hissed thickly around their heads; one of them was soon wounded, and the light birch canoes gained on them with fearful rapidity. Escape seemed hopeless, when the report of a cannon burst from the side of the vessel. The ball flew close past the boat, beating the water in a line of foam, and narrowly missing the foremost canoe. At this, the pursuers drew back in dismay; and the Indians on shore, being farther saluted by a second shot, ceased firing, and scattered among the bushes. The prisoners soon reached the vessel, where they were greeted as men snatched from the jaws of fate; "a living monument," writes an officer of the garrison, "that Fortune favors the brave."[2]

They related many particulars of the catastrophe which had befallen them and their companions. Lieutenant Cuyler had left Fort Niagara as early as the thirteenth of May, and embarked from Fort Schlosser, just above the falls, with ninety-six men and a plentiful supply of provisions and ammunition. Day after day he had coasted the northern shore of Lake Erie, and seen neither friend nor foe amid those lonely forests and waters, until, on the twenty-eighth of the month, he landed at Point Pelée, not far from the mouth of the River Detroit. The boats were drawn on the beach, and the party prepared to encamp. A man and a boy went to gather firewood at a short distance from the spot, when an Indian leaped out of the woods, seized the boy by the hair, and tomahawked him. The man ran into camp with the

---

[1] Another witness, Gouin, affirms that the Indian freed himself from the dying grasp of the soldier, and swam ashore.

[2] *Penn. Gaz*. No. 1807. *St. Aubin's Account*, MS. *Peltier's Account*, MS.

alarm. Cuyler immediately formed his soldiers into a semi-circle before the boats. He had scarcely done so when the enemy opened their fire. For an instant, there was a hot blaze of musketry on both sides; then the Indians broke out of the woods in a body, and rushed fiercely upon the centre of the line, which gave way in every part; the men flinging down their guns, running in a blind panic to the boats, and struggling with ill-directed efforts to shove them into the water. Five were set afloat, and pushed off from the shore, crowded with the terrified soldiers. Cuyler, seeing himself, as he says, deserted by his men, waded up to his neck in the lake, and climbed into one of the retreating boats. The Indians, on their part, pushing two more afloat, went in pursuit of the fugitives, three boat-loads of whom allowed themselves to be recaptured without resistance; but the remaining two, in one of which was Cuyler himself, made their escape.[1] They rowed all night, and landed in the morning upon a small island. Between thirty and forty men, some of whom were wounded, were crowded in these two boats; the rest, about sixty in number, being killed or taken. Cuyler now made for Sandusky, which, on his arrival, he found burnt to the ground. Immediately leaving the spot, he rowed along the south shore to Presqu' Isle, from whence he proceeded to Niagara and reported his loss to Major Wilkins, the commanding officer.[2]

[1]"Being abandoned by my men, I was Forced to Retreat in the best manner I could. I was left with 6 men on the Beech, Endeavoring to get off a Boat, which not being able to Effect, was Obliged to Run up to my Neck, in the Lake, to get to a Boat that had pushed off, without my Knowledge.— When I was in the Lake I saw Five Boats manned, and the Indians having manned two Boats, pursued and Brought back Three of the Five, keeping a continual Fire from off the Shore, and from the two Boats that followed us, about a Mile on the Lake; the Wind springing up fair, I and the other Remaining Boat Hoisted sail and escaped."—*Cuyler's Report*, MS.

[2]*Cuyler's Report*, MS.

Extract from a MS. Letter—*Major Wilkins to Sir J. Amherst.*

"Niagara, 6th June, 1763.

"Just as I was sending off my Letter of Yesterday, Lieutenant Cuyler, of the Queen's Rangers, Arrived from his Intended Voyage to the Detroit. He has been very Unfortunate, Having been Defeated by Indians within 30 miles of the Detroit River; I observed that he was Wounded and Weak, and Desired

The actors in this bold and well-executed stroke were the Wyandots, who, for some days, had lain in ambush at the mouth of the river, to intercept trading boats or parties of troops. Seeing the fright and confusion of Cuyler's men, they had forgotten their usual caution, and rushed upon them in the manner described. The ammunition, provisions, and other articles, taken in this attack, formed a valuable prize; but, unfortunately, there was, among the rest, a great quantity of whiskey. This the Indians seized, and carried to their respective camps, which, throughout the night, presented a scene of savage revelry and riot. The liquor was poured into vessels of birch-bark, or any thing capable of containing it; and the Indians, crowding around, scooped it up in their cups and ladles, and quaffed the raw whiskey like water. While some sat apart, wailing and moaning in maudlin drunkenness, others were maddened to the ferocity of wild beasts. Dormant jealousies were awakened, old forgotten quarrels kindled afresh, and, had not the squaws taken the precaution of hiding all the weapons they could find before the debauch began, much blood would, no doubt, have been spilt. As it was, the savages were not entirely without means of indulging their drunken rage. Many were wounded, of whom two died in the morning; and several others had their noses bitten off,—a singular mode of revenge, much in vogue upon similar occasions, among the Indians of the upper lakes. The English were gainers by this scene of riot; for late in the evening, two Indians, in all the valor and vain-glory of drunkenness, came running directly towards the fort, boasting their prowess in a loud voice; but being greeted with two rifle

---

him to take the Surgeon's Assistance and some Rest, and Recollect the Particulars of the Affair, and let me have them in Writing, as perhaps I should find it Necessary to Transmit them to Your Excellency, which I have now Done.

"It is probable Your Excellency will have heard of what has Happened by way of Fort Pitt, as Ensign Christie, Commanding at Presqu' Isle, writes me he has sent an Express to Acquaint the Commanding Officer at that Place, of Sanduskie's being Destroyed, and of Lieut. Cuyler's Defeat.

"Some Indians of the Six Nations are now with me. They seem very Civil; The Interpreter has just told them I was writing to Your Excellency for Rum, and they are very glad."

bullets, they leaped into the air like a pair of wounded bucks, and fell dead on their tracks.

It will not be proper to pass over in silence the fate of the unfortunate men taken prisoners in this affair. After night had set in, several Canadians came to the fort, bringing vague and awful reports of the scenes that had been enacted at the Indian camp. The soldiers gathered round them, and, frozen with horror, listened to the appalling narrative. A cloud of deep gloom sank down upon the garrison, and none could help reflecting how thin and frail a barrier protected them from a similar fate. On the following day, and for several succeeding days, they beheld frightful confirmation of the rumors they had heard. Naked corpses, gashed with knives and scorched with fire, floated down on the pure waters of the Detroit, whose fish came up to nibble at the clotted blood that clung to their ghastly faces.[1]

[1]"The Indians, fearing that the other barges might escape as the first had done, changed their plan of going to the camp. They landed their prisoners, tied them, and conducted them by land to the Ottawas village, and then crossed them to Pondiac's camp, where they were all butchered. As soon as the canoes reached the shore, the barbarians landed their prisoners, one after the other, on the beach. They made them strip themselves, and then sent arrows into different parts of their bodies. These unfortunate men wished sometimes to throw themselves on the ground to avoid the arrows; but they were beaten with sticks and forced to stand up until they fell dead; after which those who had not fired fell upon their bodies, cut them in pieces, cooked, and ate them. On others they exercised different modes of torment by cutting their flesh with flints, and piercing them with lances. They would then cut their feet and hands off, and leave them weltering in their blood till they were dead. Others were fastened to stakes, and children employed in burning them with a slow fire. No kind of torment was left untried by these Indians. Some of the bodies were left on shore; others were thrown into the river. Even the women assisted their husbands in torturing their victims. They slitted them with their knives, and mangled them in various ways. There were, however, a few whose lives were saved, being adopted to serve as slaves."—*Pontiac* MS.

"The remaining barges proceeded up the river, and crossed to the house of Mr. Meloche, where Pontiac and his Ottawas were encamped. The barges were landed, and, the women having arranged themselves in two rows, with clubs and sticks, the prisoners were taken out, one by one, and told to run the gauntlet to Pontiac's lodge. Of sixty-six persons who were brought to the shore, sixty-four ran the gauntlet, and were all killed. One of the remaining two, who had had his thigh broken in the firing from the shore, and who was tied to his seat and compelled to row, had become by this time so much

Late one afternoon, at about this period of the siege, the garrison were again greeted with the dismal cry of death, and a line of naked warriors was seen issuing from the woods, which, like a wall of foliage, rose beyond the pastures in rear of the fort. Each savage was painted black, and each bore a scalp fluttering from the end of a pole. It was but too clear that some new disaster had befallen; and in truth, before nightfall, one La Brosse, a Canadian, came to the gate with the tidings that Fort Sandusky had been taken, and all its garrison slain or made captive.[1] This post had been attacked by the band of Wyandots living in its neighborhood, aided by a detachment of their brethren from Detroit. Among the few survivors of the slaughter was the commanding officer, Ensign Paully, who had been brought prisoner to Detroit, bound hand and foot, and solaced on the passage with the expectation of being burnt alive. On landing near the camp of Pontiac, he was surrounded by a crowd of Indians, chiefly squaws and children, who pelted him with stones, sticks, and gravel, forcing him to dance and sing, though by no means in a cheerful strain. A worse infliction seemed in store for him, when happily an old woman, whose husband had lately died, chose to adopt him in place of the deceased warrior. Seeing no alternative but the stake, Paully accepted the proposal; and, having been first plunged in the river, that the white blood might be washed from his veins, he was conducted to the lodge of the widow, and treated thenceforth with all the consideration due to an Ottawa warrior.

Gladwyn soon received a letter from him, through one of the Canadian inhabitants, giving a full account of the capture

---

exhausted that he could not help himself. He was thrown out of the boat and killed with clubs. The other, when directed to run for the lodge, suddenly fell upon his knees in the water, and having dipped his hand in the water, he made the sign of the cross on his forehead and breast, and darted out in the stream. An expert swimmer from the Indians followed him, and, having overtaken him, seized him by the hair, and crying out, 'You seem to love water; you shall have enough of it,' he stabbed the poor fellow, who sunk to rise no more."—*Gouin's Account*, MS.

[1] *Pontiac* MS.

of Fort Sandusky. On the sixteenth of May—such was the substance of the communication—Paully was informed that seven Indians were waiting at the gate to speak with him. As several of the number were well known to him, he ordered them, without hesitation, to be admitted. Arriving at his quarters, two of the treacherous visitors seated themselves on each side of the commandant, while the rest were disposed in various parts of the room. The pipes were lighted, and the conversation began, when an Indian, who stood in the door-way, suddenly made a signal by raising his head. Upon this, the astonished officer was instantly pounced upon and disarmed; while, at the same moment, a confused noise of shrieks and yells, the firing of guns, and the hurried tramp of feet, sounded from the area of the fort without. It soon ceased, however, and Paully, led by his captors from the room, saw the parade ground strown with the corpses of his murdered garrison. At nightfall, he was conducted to the margin of the lake, where several birch canoes lay in readiness; and as, amid thick darkness, the party pushed out from shore, the captive saw the fort, lately under his command, bursting on all sides into sheets of flame.[1]

Soon after these tidings of the loss of Sandusky, Gladwyn's garrison heard the scarcely less unwelcome news that the strength of their besiegers had been re-enforced by two strong bands of Ojibwas. Pontiac's forces in the vicinity of Detroit now amounted, according to Canadian computation, to about eight hundred and twenty warriors. Of these, two hundred and fifty were Ottawas, commanded by himself in person; one hundred and fifty were Pottawattamies, under Ninivay; fifty were Wyandots, under Takee; two hundred were Ojibwas, under Wasson; and added to these were a hundred and seventy of the same tribe, under their chief, Sekahos.[2] As the warriors brought their squaws and children with them, the whole number of savages congregated about Detroit no doubt exceeded three thousand; and the neigh-

[1]MS. Official Document—*Report of the Loss of the Posts in the Indian Country*, enclosed in a letter from Major Gladwyn to Sir Jeffrey Amherst, July 8, 1763.

[2]*Pontiac* MS.

boring fields and meadows must have presented a picturesque and stirring scene.

The sleepless garrison, worn by fatigue and ill fare, and harassed by constant petty attacks, were yet farther saddened by the news of disaster which thickened from every quarter. Of all the small posts scattered at intervals through the vast wilderness to the westward of Niagara and Fort Pitt, it soon appeared that Detroit alone had been able to sustain itself. For the rest, there was but one unvaried tale of calamity and ruin. On the fifteenth of June, a number of Pottawattamies were seen approaching the gate of the fort, bringing with them four English prisoners, who proved to be Ensign Schlosser, lately commanding at St. Joseph's, together with three private soldiers. The Indians wished to exchange them for several of their own tribe, who had been for nearly two months prisoners in the fort. After some delay, this was effected; and the garrison then learned the unhappy fate of their comrades at St. Joseph's. This post stood at the mouth of the River St. Joseph's, near the head of Lake Michigan, a spot which had long been the site of a Roman Catholic mission. Here, among the forests, swamps, and ocean-like waters, at an unmeasured distance from any abode of civilized man, the indefatigable Jesuits had labored more than half a century for the spiritual good of the Pottawattamies, who lived in great numbers near the margin of the lake. As early as the year 1712, as Father Marest informs us, the mission was in a thriving state, and around it had gathered a little colony of the forest-loving Canadians. Here, too, the French government had established a military post, whose garrison, at the period of our narrative, had been supplanted by Ensign Schlosser, with his command of fourteen men, a mere handful, in the heart of a wilderness swarming with insidious enemies. They seem, however, to have apprehended no danger, when, on the twenty-fifth of May, early in the morning, the officer was informed that a large party of the Pottawattamies of Detroit had come to pay a visit to their relatives at St. Joseph's. Presently, a chief, named Washashe, with three or four followers, came to his quarters, as if to hold a friendly "talk;" and immediately after a Canadian came in with intelligence that the fort was surrounded by Indians, who evidently had hostile intentions.

At this, Schlosser ran out of the apartment, and crossing the parade, which was full of Indians and Canadians, hastily entered the barracks. These were also crowded with savages, very insolent and disorderly. Calling upon his sergeant to get the men under arms, he hastened out again to the parade, and endeavored to muster the Canadians together; but while busying himself with these somewhat unwilling auxiliaries, he heard a wild cry from within the barracks. Instantly all the Indians in the fort rushed to the gate, tomahawked the sentinel, and opened a free passage to their comrades without. In less than two minutes, as the officer declares, the fort was plundered, eleven men were killed, and himself, with the three survivors, made prisoners, and bound fast. They then conducted him to Detroit, where he was exchanged as we have already seen.[1]

Three days after these tidings reached Detroit, Father Jonois, a Jesuit priest of the Ottawa mission near Michillimackinac, came to Pontiac's camp, together with the son of Minavavana, great chief of the Ojibwas, and several other Indians. On the following morning, he appeared at the gate of the fort, bringing a letter from Captain Etherington, commandant at Michillimackinac. The commencement of the letter was as follows: —

"Michillimackinac, 12 June, 1763.
"Sir:
"Notwithstanding what I wrote you in my last, that all the savages were arrived, and that every thing seemed in perfect tranquillity, yet on the second instant the Chippeways, who

---

[1] *Loss of the Posts in the Indian Country*, MS. Compare *Diary of the Siege*, 25.
The following is from a curious letter of one Richard Winston, a trader at St. Joseph's, to his fellow-traders at Detroit, dated 19 June, 1763: —
"Gentlemen, I address myself to you all, not knowing who is alive or who is dead. I have only to inform you that by the blessing of God and the help of M. Louison Chevalie, I escaped being killed when the unfortunate garrison was massacred, Mr. Hambough and me being hid in the house of the said Chevalie for 4 days and nights. Mr. Hambough is brought by the Savages to the Illinois, likewise Mr. Chim. Unfortunate me remains here Captive with the Savages. I must say that I met with no bad usage; however, I would that I was (with) some Christian or other. I am quite naked, & Mr. Castacrow, who is indebted to Mr. Cole, would not give me one inch to save me from death."

live in a plain near this fort, assembled to play ball, as they had done almost every day since their arrival. They played from morning till noon; then, throwing their ball close to the gate, and observing Lieutenant Lesley and me a few paces out of it, they came behind us, seized and carried us into the woods.

"In the mean time, the rest rushed into the fort, where they found their squaws, whom they had previously planted there, with their hatchets hid under their blankets, which they took, and in an instant killed Lieutenant Jamet, and fifteen rank and file, and a trader named Tracy. They wounded two, and took the rest of the garrison prisoners, five of whom they have since killed.

"They made prisoners all the English traders, and robbed them of every thing they had; but they offered no violence to the persons or property of any of the Frenchmen."

Captain Etherington next related some particulars of the massacre at Michillimackinac, sufficiently startling, as will soon appear. He spoke in high terms of the character and conduct of Father Jonois, and requested that Gladwyn would send all the troops he could spare up Lake Huron, that the post might be recaptured from the Indians, and garrisoned afresh. Gladwyn, being scarcely able to defend himself, could do nothing for the relief of his brother officer, and the Jesuit set out on his long and toilsome canoe voyage back to Michillimackinac.[1] The loss of this place was a very serious misfortune, for, next to Detroit, it was the most important post on the upper lakes.

The next news which came in was that of the loss of Oua-tanon, a fort situated upon the Wabash, a little below the site of the present town of La Fayette. Gladwyn received a letter from its commanding officer, Lieutenant Jenkins, informing him that, on the first of June, he and several of his men had been made prisoners by stratagem, on which the rest of the garrison had surrendered. The Indians, however, apologized for their conduct, declaring that they acted contrary to their own inclinations, and that the surrounding tribes compelled

[1] *Pontiac* MS.

them to take up the hatchet.[1] These excuses, so consolatory to the sufferers, might probably have been founded in truth, for these savages were of a character less ferocious than many of the others, and as they were farther removed from the settlements, they had not felt to an equal degree the effects of English insolence and encroachment.

Close upon these tidings came the news that Fort Miami was taken. This post, standing on the River Maumee, was commanded by Ensign Holmes. And here I cannot but remark on the forlorn situation of these officers, isolated in the wilderness, hundreds of miles, in some instances, from any congenial associates, separated from every human being except the rude soldiers under their command, and the white or red savages who ranged the surrounding woods. Holmes suspected the intention of the Indians, and was therefore on his

[1] "Ouatanon, June 1st, 1763.

"Sir:

"I have heard of your situation, which gives me great Pain; indeed, we are not in much better, for this morning the Indians sent for me, to speak to me, and Immediately bound me, when I got to their Cabbin, and I soon found some of my Soldiers in the same Condition: They told me Detroit, Miamis, and all them Posts were cut off, and that it was a Folly to make any Resistance, therefore desired me to make the few Soldiers, that were in the Fort, surrender, otherwise they would put us all to Death, in case one man was killed. They were to have fell on us and killed us all, last night, but Mr. Maisongville and Lorain gave them wampum not to kill us, & when they told the Interpreter that we were all to be killed, & he knowing the condition of the Fort, beg'd of them to make us prisoners. They have put us into French houses, & both Indians and French use us very well: All these Nations say they are very sorry, but that they were obliged to do it by the Other Nations. The Belt did not Arrive here 'till last night about Eight o'Clock. Mr. Lorain can inform you of all. Just now Received the News of St. Joseph's being taken, Eleven men killed and three taken Prisoners with the Officer: I have nothing more to say, but that I sincerely wish you a speedy succour, and that we may be able to Revenge ourselves on those that Deserve it.

"I Remain, with my Sincerest wishes for your safety,

"Your most humble servant,

"EDWᴰ JENKINS.

"N.B. We expect to set off in a day or two for the Illinois."

This expectation was not fulfilled, and Jenkins remained at Ouatanon. A letter from him is before me, written from thence to Gladwyn on the 29th July, in which he complains that the Canadians were secretly advising the Indians to murder all the English in the West.

guard, when, on the twenty-seventh of May, a young Indian girl, who lived with him, came to tell him that a squaw lay dangerously ill in a wigwam near the fort, and urged him to come to her relief. Having confidence in the girl, Holmes forgot his caution and followed her out of the fort. Pitched at the edge of a meadow, hidden from view by an intervening spur of the woodland, stood a great number of Indian wigwams. When Holmes came in sight of them, his treacherous conductress pointed out that in which the sick woman lay. He walked on without suspicion; but, as he drew near, two guns flashed from behind the hut, and stretched him lifeless on the grass. The shots were heard at the fort, and the sergeant rashly went out to learn the reason of the firing. He was immediately taken prisoner, amid exulting yells and whoopings. The soldiers in the fort climbed upon the palisades, to look out, when Godefroy, a Canadian, and two other white men, made their appearance, and summoned them to surrender; promising that, if they did so, their lives should be spared, but that otherwise they would all be killed without mercy. The men, being in great terror, and without a leader, soon threw open the gate, and gave themselves up as prisoners.[1]

Had detachments of Rogers's Rangers garrisoned these posts, or had they been held by such men as the Rocky Mountain trappers of the present day, wary, skilful, and almost ignorant of fear, some of them might, perhaps, have been saved; but the soldiers of the 60th Regiment, though many of them were of provincial birth, were not suited by habits and discipline for this kind of service.

The loss of Presqu' Isle will close this catalogue of calamity. Rumors of it first reached Detroit on the twentieth of June, and, two days after, the garrison heard those dismal cries

---

[1] *Loss of the Posts*, MS. Compare *Diary of the Siege*, 22, 26.

It appears by a deposition taken at Detroit on the 11th June, that Godefroy, mentioned above, left Detroit with four other Canadians three or four days after the siege began. Their professed object was to bring a French officer from the Illinois to induce Pontiac to abandon his hostile designs. At the mouth of the Maumee they met John Welsh, an English trader, with two canoes, bound for Detroit. They seized him, and divided his furs among themselves and a party of Indians who were with them. They then proceeded to Fort Miami, and aided the Indians to capture it. Welsh was afterwards carried to Detroit, where the Ottawas murdered him.

announcing scalps and prisoners, which, of late, had grown mournfully familiar to their ears. Indians were seen passing in numbers along the opposite bank of the river, leading several English prisoners, who proved to be Ensign Christie, the commanding officer at Presqu' Isle, with those of his soldiers who survived.

On the third of June, Christie, then safely ensconced in the fort which he commanded, had written as follows to his superior officer, Lieutenant Gordon, at Venango: "This morning Lieutenant Cuyler of Queen's Company of Rangers came here, and gave me the following melancholy account of his whole party being cut off by a large body of Indians at the mouth of the Detroit River." Here follows the story of Cuyler's disaster, and Christie closes as follows: "I have sent to Niagara a letter to the Major, desiring some more ammunition and provisions, and have kept six men of Lieutenant Cuyler's, as I expect a visit from the hell-hounds. I have ordered everybody here to move into the blockhouse, and shall be ready for them, come when they will."

Fort Presqu' Isle stood on the southern shore of Lake Erie, at the site of the present town of Erie. It was an important post to be commanded by an Ensign, for it controlled the communication between the lake and Fort Pitt; but the blockhouse, to which Christie alludes, was supposed to make it impregnable against Indians. This blockhouse, a very large and strong one, stood at an angle of the fort, and was built of massive logs, with the projecting upper story usual in such structures, by means of which a vertical fire could be had upon the heads of assailants, through openings in the projecting part of the floor, like the *machicoulis* of a mediæval castle. It had also a kind of bastion, from which one or more of its walls could be covered by a flank fire. The roof was of shingles, and might easily be set on fire; but at the top was a sentry-box or look-out, from which water could be thrown. On one side was the lake, and on the other a small stream which entered it. Unfortunately, the bank of this stream rose in a high steep ridge within forty yards of the blockhouse, thus affording a cover to assailants, while the bank of the lake offered them similar advantages on another side.

After his visit from Cuyler, Christie, whose garrison now

consisted of twenty-seven men, prepared for a stubborn defence. The doors of the block-house, and the sentry-box at the top, were lined to make them bullet-proof; the angles of the roof were covered with green turf as a protection against fire-arrows, and gutters of bark were laid in such a manner that streams of water could be sent to every part. His expectation of a "visit from the hell-hounds" proved to be perfectly well founded. About two hundred of them had left Detroit expressly for this object. At early dawn on the fifteenth of June, they were first discovered stealthily crossing the mouth of the little stream, where the bateaux were drawn up, and crawling under cover of the banks of the lake and of the adjacent saw-pits. When the sun rose, they showed themselves, and began their customary yelling. Christie, with a very unnecessary reluctance to begin the fray, ordered his men not to fire till the Indians had set the example. The consequence was, that they were close to the blockhouse before they received the fire of the garrison; and many of them sprang into the ditch, whence, being well sheltered, they fired at the loop-holes, and amused themselves by throwing stones and handfuls of gravel, or, what was more to the purpose, fire-balls of pitch. Some got into the fort and sheltered themselves behind the bakery and other buildings, whence they kept up a brisk fire; while others pulled down a small out-house of plank, of which they made a movable breastwork, and approached under cover of it by pushing it before them. At the same time, great numbers of them lay close behind the ridges by the stream, keeping up a rattling fire into every loophole, and shooting burning arrows against the roof and sides of the blockhouse. Some were extinguished with water, while many dropped out harmless after burning a small hole. The Indians now rolled logs to the top of the ridges, where they made three strong breastworks, from behind which they could discharge their shot and throw their fireworks with greater effect. Sometimes they would try to dart across the intervening space and shelter themselves with their companions in the ditch, but all who attempted it were killed or wounded. And now the hard-beset little garrison could see them throwing up earth and stones behind the nearest breastwork. Their implacable foes were undermining the blockhouse. There was little

time to reflect on this new danger; for another, more imminent, soon threatened them. The barrels of water, always kept
in the building, were nearly emptied in extinguishing the frequent fires; and though there was a well close at hand, in the
parade ground, it was death to approach it. The only resource
was to dig a subterranean passage to it. The floor was torn
up; and while some of the men fired their heated muskets
from the loopholes, the rest labored stoutly at this cheerless
task. Before it was half finished, the roof was on fire again,
and all the water that remained was poured down to extinguish it. In a few moments, the cry of fire was again raised,
when a soldier, at imminent risk of his life, tore off the burning shingles and averted the danger.

By this time it was evening. The garrison had had not a
moment's rest since the sun rose. Darkness brought little relief, for guns flashed all night from the Indian intrenchments.
In the morning, however, there was a respite. The Indians
were ominously quiet, being employed, it seems, in pushing
their subterranean approaches, and preparing fresh means for
firing the blockhouse. In the afternoon the attack began
again. They set fire to the house of the commanding officer,
which stood close at hand, and which they had reached by
means of their trenches. The pine logs blazed fiercely, and the
wind blew the flame against the bastion of the blockhouse,
which scorched, blackened, and at last took fire; but the garrison had by this time dug a passage to the well, and, half
stifled as they were, they plied their water-buckets with such
good will that the fire was subdued, while the blazing house
soon sank to a glowing pile of embers. The men, who had
behaved throughout with great spirit, were now, in the words
of their officer, "exhausted to the greatest extremity;" yet they
still kept up their forlorn defence, toiling and fighting without pause within the wooden walls of their dim prison, where
the close and heated air was thick with the smoke of gunpowder. The firing on both sides lasted through the rest of
the day, and did not cease till midnight, at which hour a voice
was heard to call out, in French, from the enemy's intrenchments, warning the garrison that farther resistance would be
useless, since preparations were made for setting the blockhouse on fire, above and below at once. Christie demanded if

there were any among them who spoke English; upon which, a man in the Indian dress came out from behind the breast-work. He was a soldier, who, having been made prisoner early in the French war, had since lived among the savages, and now espoused their cause, fighting with them against his own countrymen. He said that if they yielded, their lives should be spared; but if they fought longer, they must all be burnt alive. Christie told them to wait till morning for his answer. They assented, and suspended their fire. Christie now asked his men, if we may believe the testimony of two of them, "whether they chose to give up the blockhouse, or re-main in it and be burnt alive?" They replied that they would stay as long as they could bear the heat, and then fight their way through.[1] A third witness, Edward Smyth, apparently a corporal, testifies that all but two of them were for holding out. He says that when his opinion was asked, he replied that, having but one life to lose, he would be governed by the rest; but that at the same time he reminded them of the recent treachery at Detroit, and of the butchery at Fort William Henry, adding that, in his belief, they themselves could expect no better usage.

When morning came, Christie sent out two soldiers as if to treat with the enemy, but, in reality, as he says, to learn the truth of what they had told him respecting their preparations to burn the blockhouse. On reaching the breastwork, the sol-diers made a signal, by which their officer saw that his worst fears were well founded. In pursuance of their orders, they then demanded that two of the principal chiefs should meet with Christie midway between the breastwork and the block-house. The chiefs appeared accordingly; and Christie, going out, yielded up the blockhouse; having first stipulated that the lives of all the garrison should be spared, and that they might retire unmolested to the nearest post. The soldiers, pale and haggard, like men who had passed through a fiery ordeal, now issued from their scorched and bullet-pierced strong-

---

[1]*Evidence of Benjamin Gray, soldier in the* 1st *Battalion of the* 60th *Regiment, before a Court of Inquiry held at Fort Pitt,* 12th *Sept.* 1763. *Evidence of David Smart, soldier in the* 60th *Regiment, before a Court of Inquiry held at Fort Pitt,* 24th *Dec.,* 1763, *to take evidence relative to the loss of Presqu' Isle which did not appear when the last court sat.*

hold. A scene of plunder instantly began. Benjamin Gray, a Scotch soldier, who had just been employed, on Christie's order, in carrying presents to the Indians, seeing the confusion, and hearing a scream from a sergeant's wife, the only woman in the garrison, sprang off into the woods and succeeded in making his way to Fort Pitt with news of the disaster. It is needless to say that no faith was kept with the rest, and they had good cause to be thankful that they were not butchered on the spot. After being detained for some time in the neighborhood, they were carried prisoners to Detroit, where Christie soon after made his escape, and gained the fort in safety.[1]

After Presqu' Isle was taken, the neighboring posts of Le Bœuf and Venango shared its fate; while farther southward, at the forks of the Ohio, a host of Delaware and Shawanoe warriors were gathering around Fort Pitt, and blood and havoc reigned along the whole frontier.

[1] *Loss of the Posts*, MS. *Pontiac MS. Report of Ensign Christie*, MS. *Testimony of Edward Smyth*, MS. This last evidence was taken by order of Colonel Bouquet, commanding the battalion of the Royal American Regiment to which Christie belonged. Christie's surrender had been thought censurable both by General Amherst and by Bouquet. According to Christie's statements, it was unavoidable; but according to those of Smyth, and also of the two soldiers, Gray and Smart, the situation, though extremely critical, seems not to have been desperate. Smyth's testimony bears date 30 March, 1765, nearly two years after the event. Some allowance is therefore to be made for lapses of memory. He places the beginning of the attack on the twenty-first of June, instead of the fifteenth,—an evident mistake. The *Diary of the Siege of Detroit* says that Christie did not make his escape, but was brought in and surrendered by six Huron chiefs on the ninth of July. In a letter of Bouquet dated June 18th, 1760, is enclosed a small plan of Presqu' Isle.

Chapter XIV.
1763.

THE INDIANS CONTINUE TO BLOCKADE DETROIT.

WE RETURN once more to Detroit and its beleaguered garrison. On the nineteenth of June, a rumor reached them that one of the vessels had been seen near Turkey Island, some miles below the fort, but that, the wind failing her, she had dropped down with the current, to wait a more favorable opportunity. It may be remembered that this vessel had, several weeks before, gone down Lake Erie to hasten the advance of Cuyler's expected detachment. Passing these troops on her way, she had held her course to Niagara; and here she had remained until the return of Cuyler, with the remnant of his men, made known the catastrophe that had befallen him. This officer, and the survivors of his party, with a few other troops spared from the garrison of Niagara, were ordered to embark in her, and make the best of their way back to Detroit. They had done so, and now, as we have seen, were almost within sight of the fort; but the critical part of the undertaking yet remained. The river channel was in some places narrow, and more than eight hundred Indians were on the alert to intercept their passage.

For several days, the officers at Detroit heard nothing farther of the vessel, when, on the twenty-third, a great commotion was visible among the Indians, large parties of whom were seen to pass along the outskirts of the woods, behind the fort. The cause of these movements was unknown till evening, when M. Baby came in with intelligence that the vessel was again attempting to ascend the river, and that all the Indians had gone to attack her. Upon this, two cannon were fired, that those on board might know that the fort still held out. This done, all remained in much anxiety awaiting the result.

The schooner, late that afternoon, began to move slowly upward, with a gentle breeze, between the main shore and the long-extended margin of Fighting Island. About sixty men were crowded on board, of whom only ten or twelve were visible on deck; the officer having ordered the rest to lie hidden below, in hope that the Indians, encouraged by this apparent weakness, might make an open attack. Just before reaching the narrowest part of the channel, the wind died away, and the anchor was dropped. Immediately above, and within gunshot of the vessel, the Indians had made a breast-work of logs, carefully concealed by bushes, on the shore of Turkey Island. Here they lay in force, waiting for the schooner to pass. Ignorant of this, but still cautious and wary, the crew kept a strict watch from the moment the sun went down.

Hours wore on, and nothing had broken the deep repose of the night. The current gurgled with a monotonous sound around the bows of the schooner, and on either hand the wooded shores lay amid the obscurity, black and silent as the grave. At length, the sentinel could discern, in the distance, various moving objects upon the dark surface of the water. The men were ordered up from below, and all took their posts in perfect silence. The blow of a hammer on the mast was to be the signal to fire. The Indians, gliding stealthily over the water in their birch canoes, had, by this time, approached within a few rods of their fancied prize, when suddenly the dark side of the slumbering vessel burst into a blaze of cannon and musketry, which illumined the night like a flash of lightning. Grape and musket shot flew tearing among the canoes, destroying several of them, killing fourteen Indians, wounding as many more, and driving the rest in consternation to the shore.[1] Recovering from their surprise, they began to fire upon the vessel from behind their breastwork; upon which she weighed anchor, and dropped down once more beyond their reach, into the broad river below. Several days afterwards, she again attempted to ascend. This time, she met with better success; for, though the Indians fired at her constantly from the shore, no man was hurt, and at length she left behind her the perilous channels of the Islands. As she passed the Wyandot village, she sent a shower of grape among its yelping inhabitants, by which several were killed;

[1] *Pontiac* MS.

and then, furling her sails, lay peacefully at anchor by the side of her companion vessel, abreast of the fort.

The schooner brought to the garrison a much-needed supply of men, ammunition, and provisions. She brought, also, the important tidings that peace was at length concluded between France and England. The bloody and momentous struggle of the French war, which had shaken North America since the year 1755, had indeed been virtually closed by the victory on the Plains of Abraham, and the junction of the three British armies at Montreal. Yet up to this time, its embers had continued to burn, till at length peace was completely established by formal treaty between the hostile powers. France resigned her ambitious project of empire in America, and ceded Canada and the region of the lakes to her successful rival. By this treaty, the Canadians of Detroit were placed in a new position. Hitherto they had been, as it were, prisoners on capitulation, neutral spectators of the quarrel between their British conquerors and the Indians; but now their allegiance was transferred from the crown of France to that of Britain, and they were subjects of the English king. To many of them the change was extremely odious, for they cordially hated the British. They went about among the settlers and the Indians, declaring that the pretended news of peace was only an invention of Major Gladwyn; that the king of France would never abandon his children; and that a great French army was even then ascending the St. Lawrence, while another was approaching from the country of the Illinois.[1] This oft-repeated falsehood was implicitly believed by the Indians, who continued firm in the faith that their Great Father was about to awake from his sleep, and wreak his vengeance upon the insolent English, who had intruded on his domain.

Pontiac himself clung fast to this delusive hope; yet he was greatly vexed at the safe arrival of the vessel, and the assistance she had brought to the obstinate defenders of Detroit. He exerted himself with fresh zeal to gain possession of the place, and attempted to terrify Gladwyn into submission. He sent a message, in which he strongly urged him to surrender,

[1] MS. Letter—*Gladwyn to Amherst*, July 8.

adding, by way of stimulus, that eight hundred more Ojibwas were every day expected, and that, on their arrival, all his influence could not prevent them from taking the scalp of every Englishman in the fort. To this friendly advice Gladwyn returned a brief and contemptuous answer.

Pontiac, having long been anxious to gain the Canadians as auxiliaries in the war, now determined on a final effort to effect his object. For this purpose, he sent messages to the principal inhabitants, inviting them to meet him in council. In the Ottawa camp, there was a vacant spot, quite level, and encircled by the huts of the Indians. Here mats were spread for the reception of the deputies, who soon convened, and took their seats in a wide ring. One part was occupied by the Canadians, among whom were several whose withered, leathery features proclaimed them the patriarchs of the secluded little settlement. Opposite these sat the stern-visaged Pontiac, with his chiefs on either hand, while the intervening portions of the circle were filled by Canadians and Indians promiscuously mingled. Standing on the outside, and looking over the heads of this more dignified assemblage, was a motley throng of Indians and Canadians, half breeds, trappers, and voyageurs, in wild and picturesque, though very dirty attire. Conspicuous among them were numerous Indian dandies, a large class in every aboriginal community, where they hold about the same relative position as do their counterparts in civilized society. They were wrapped in the gayest blankets, their necks adorned with beads, their cheeks daubed with vermilion, and their ears hung with pendants. They stood sedately looking on, with evident self-complacency, yet ashamed and afraid to take their places among the aged chiefs and warriors of repute.

All was silent, and several pipes were passing round from hand to hand, when Pontiac rose, and threw down a war-belt at the feet of the Canadians.

"My brothers," he said, "how long will you suffer this bad flesh to remain upon your lands? I have told you before, and I now tell you again, that when I took up the hatchet, it was for your good. This year the English must all perish throughout Canada. The Master of Life commands it; and you, who know him better than we, wish to oppose his will. Until now

I have said nothing on this matter. I have not urged you to take part with us in the war. It would have been enough had you been content to sit quiet on your mats, looking on, while we were fighting for you. But you have not done so. You call yourselves our friends, and yet you assist the English with provisions, and go about as spies among our villages. This must not continue. You must be either wholly French or wholly English. If you are French, take up that war-belt, and lift the hatchet with us; but if you are English, then we declare war upon you. My brothers, I know this is a hard thing. We are all alike children of our Great Father the King of France, and it is hard to fight among brethren for the sake of dogs. But there is no choice. Look upon the belt, and let us hear your answer."[1]

One of the Canadians, having suspected the purpose of Pontiac, had brought with him, not the treaty of peace, but a copy of the capitulation of Montreal with its dependencies, including Detroit. Pride, or some other motive, restrained him from confessing that the Canadians were no longer children of the King of France, and he determined to keep up the old delusion that a French army was on its way to win back Canada, and chastise the English invaders. He began his speech in reply to Pontiac by professing great love for the Indians, and a strong desire to aid them in the war. "But, my brothers," he added, holding out the articles of capitulation, "you must first untie the knot with which our Great Father, the King, has bound us. In this paper, he tells all his Canadian children to sit quiet and obey the English until he comes, because he wishes to punish his enemies himself. We dare not disobey him, for he would then be angry with us. And you, my brothers, who speak of making war upon us if we do not do as you wish, do you think you could escape his wrath, if you should raise the hatchet against his French children? He would treat you as enemies, and not as friends, and you would have to fight both English and French at once. Tell us, my brothers, what can you reply to this?"

Pontiac for a moment sat silent, mortified, and perplexed;

[1] *Pontiac* MS.

but his purpose was not destined to be wholly defeated. "Among the French," says the writer of the diary, "were many infamous characters, who, having no property, cared nothing what became of them." Those mentioned in these opprobrious terms were a collection of trappers, voyageurs, and nondescript vagabonds of the forest, who were seated with the council, or stood looking on, variously attired in greasy shirts, Indian leggins, and red woollen caps. Not a few among them, however, had thought proper to adopt the style of dress and ornament peculiar to the red men, who were their usual associates, and appeared among their comrades with paint rubbed on their cheeks, and feathers dangling from their hair. Indeed, they aimed to identify themselves with the Indians, a transformation by which they gained nothing; for these renegade whites were held in light esteem, both by those of their own color and the savages themselves. They were for the most part a light and frivolous crew, little to be relied on for energy or stability; though among them were men of hard and ruffian features, the ringleaders and bullies of the voyageurs, and even a terror to the *Bourgeois*[1] himself. It

---

[1]This name is always applied, among the Canadians of the North-west, to the conductor of a trading party, the commander in a trading fort, or, indeed, to any person in a position of authority.

Extract from a Letter—*Detroit, July 9, 1763* (*Penn. Gaz. No. 1808*).

"Judge of the Conduct of the Canadians here, by the Behaviour of these few Sacres Bougres, I have mentioned; I can assure you, with much Certainty, that there are but very few in the Settlement who are not engaged with the Indians in their damn'd Design; in short, Monsieur is at the Bottom of it; we have not only convincing Proofs and Circumstances, but undeniable Proofs of it. There are four or five sensible, honest Frenchmen in the Place, who have been of a great deal of Service to us, in bringing us Intelligence and Provisions, even at the Risque of their own Lives; I hope they will be rewarded for their good Services; I hope also to see the others exalted on High, to reap the Fruits of their Labours, as soon as our Army arrives; the Discoveries we have made of their horrid villianies, are almost incredible. But to return to the Terms of Capitulation: Pondiac proposes that we should immediately give up the Garrison, lay down our Arms, as the French, their Fathers, were obliged to do, leave the Cannon, Magazines, Merchants' Goods, and the two Vessels, and be escorted in Battoes, by the Indians, to Niagara. The Major returned Answer, that the General had not sent him there to deliver up the Fort to Indians, or anybody else; and that he would defend it

was one of these who now took up the war-belt, and declared that he and his comrades were ready to raise the hatchet for Pontiac. The better class of Canadians were shocked at this proceeding, and vainly protested against it. Pontiac, on his part, was much pleased at such an accession to his forces, and he and his chiefs shook hands, in turn, with each of their new auxiliaries. The council had been protracted to a late hour. It was dark before the assembly dissolved, "so that," as the chronicler observes, "these new Indians had no opportunity of displaying their exploits that day." They remained in the Indian camp all night, being afraid of the reception they might meet among their fellow-whites in the settlement. The whole of the following morning was employed in giving them a feast of welcome. For this entertainment a large number of dogs were killed, and served up to the guests; none of whom, according to the Indian custom on such formal occasions, were permitted to take their leave until they had eaten the whole of the enormous portion placed before them.

Pontiac derived little advantage from his Canadian allies, most of whom, fearing the resentment of the English and the other inhabitants, fled, before the war was over, to the country of the Illinois.[1] On the night succeeding the feast, a party of the renegades, joined by about an equal number of Indians, approached the fort, and intrenched themselves, in order to fire upon the garrison. At daybreak, they were observed, the gate was thrown open, and a file of men, headed by Lieutenant Hay, sallied to dislodge them. This was effected without much difficulty. The Canadians fled with such despatch,

---

whilst he had a single man to fight alongside of him. Upon this, Hostilities recommenced, since which Time, being two months, the whole Garrison, Officers, Soldiers, Merchants, and Servants, have been upon the Ramparts every Night, not one having slept in a House, except the Sick and Wounded in the Hospital.

"Our Fort is extremely large, considering our Numbers, the Stockade being above 1000 Paces in Circumference; judge what a Figure we make on the Works."

The writer of the above letter is much too sweeping and indiscriminate in his denunciation of the French.

[1]Croghan, *Journal*. See Butler, *Hist. Kentucky*, 463.

that all of them escaped unhurt, though two of the Indians were shot.

It happened that among the English was a soldier who had been prisoner, for several years, among the Delawares, and who, while he had learned to hate the whole race, at the same time had acquired many of their habits and practices. He now ran forward, and, kneeling on the body of one of the dead savages, tore away the scalp, and shook it, with an exultant cry, towards the fugitives.[1] This act, as afterwards appeared, excited great rage among the Indians.

Lieutenant Hay and his party, after their successful sally, had retired to the fort; when, at about four o'clock in the afternoon, a man was seen running towards it, closely pursued by Indians. On his arriving within gunshot, they gave over the chase, and the fugitive came panting beneath the stockade, where a wicket was flung open to receive him. He proved to be the commandant of Sandusky, who, having, as before mentioned, been adopted by the Indians, and married to an old squaw, now seized the first opportunity of escaping from her embraces.

Through him, the garrison learned the unhappy tidings that Captain Campbell was killed. This gentleman, from his high personal character, no less than his merit as an officer, was held in general esteem; and his fate excited a feeling of anger and grief among all the English in Detroit. It appeared that the Indian killed and scalped, in the skirmish of that morning, was nephew to Wasson, chief of the Ojibwas. On hearing of his death, the enraged uncle had immediately blackened his face in sign of revenge, called together a party of his followers, and repairing to the house of Meloche, where Captain Campbell was kept prisoner, had seized upon him, and bound him fast to a neighboring fence, where they shot him to death with arrows. Others say that they tomahawked him on the spot; but all agree that his body was mutilated in a barbarous manner. His heart is said to have been eaten by his murderers, to make them courageous; a practice not uncommon among Indians, after killing an

[1] *Pontiac* MS.

enemy of acknowledged bravery. The corpse was thrown into the river, and afterwards brought to shore and buried by the Canadians. According to one authority, Pontiac was privy to this act; but a second, equally credible, represents him as ignorant of it, and declares that Wasson fled to Saginaw to escape his fury; while a third affirms that the Ojibwas carried off Campbell by force from before the eyes of the great chief.[1] The other captive, M'Dougal, had previously escaped.

The two armed schooners, anchored opposite the fort, were now become objects of awe and aversion to the Indians. This is not to be wondered at, for, besides aiding in the defence of the place, by sweeping two sides of it with their fire, they often caused great terror and annoyance to the besiegers. Several times they had left their anchorage, and, taking up a convenient position, had battered the Indian camps and villages with no little effect. Once in particular,—and this was the first attempt of the kind,—Gladwyn himself, with several of his officers, had embarked on board the smaller vessel, while a fresh breeze was blowing from the north-west. The Indians, on the banks, stood watching her as she tacked from shore to shore, and pressed their hands against their mouths in amazement, thinking that magic power alone could enable her thus to make her way against wind and current.[2] Making a long reach from the opposite shore, she came on directly towards the camp of Pontiac, her sails swelling, her masts leaning over till the black muzzles of her guns almost touched the river. The Indians watched her in astonishment. On she came, till their fierce hearts exulted in the idea that she would run ashore within their clutches, when suddenly a shout of command was heard on board, her progress was arrested, she

[1] *Gouin's Account*, MS. *St. Aubin's Account*, MS. *Diary of the Siege.*

James MacDonald writes from Detroit on the 12th of July. "Half an hour afterward the savages carried (the body of) the man they had lost before Capt. Campbell, stripped him naked, and directly murthered him in a cruel manner, which indeed gives me pain beyond expression, and I am sure cannot miss but to affect sensibly all his acquaintances. Although he is now out of the question, I must own I never had, nor never shall have, a Friend or Acquaintance that I valued more than he. My present comfort is, that if Charity, benevolence, innocence, and integrity are a sufficient dispensation for all mankind, that entitles him to happiness in the world to come."

[2] *Penn. Gaz.* No. 1808.

rose upright, and her sails flapped and fluttered as if tearing loose from their fastenings. Steadily she came round, broadside to the shore; then, leaning once more to the wind, bore away gallantly on the other tack. She did not go far. The wondering spectators, quite at a loss to understand her movements, soon heard the hoarse rattling of her cable, as the anchor dragged it out, and saw her furling her vast white wings. As they looked unsuspectingly on, a puff of smoke was emitted from her side; a loud report followed; then another and another; and the balls, rushing over their heads, flew through the midst of their camp, and tore wildly among the forest-trees beyond. All was terror and consternation. The startled warriors bounded away on all sides; the squaws snatched up their children, and fled screaming; and, with a general chorus of yells, the whole encampment scattered in such haste, that little damage was done, except knocking to pieces their frail cabins of bark.[1]

This attack was followed by others of a similar kind; and now the Indians seemed resolved to turn all their energies to the destruction of the vessel which caused them such annoyance. On the night of the tenth of July, they sent down a blazing raft, formed of two boats, secured together with a rope, and filled with pitch-pine, birch-bark, and other combustibles, which, by good fortune, missed the vessel, and floated down the stream without doing injury. All was quiet throughout the following night; but about two o'clock on the morning of the twelfth, the sentinel on duty saw a glowing spark of fire on the surface of the river, at some distance above. It grew larger and brighter; it rose in a forked flame, and at length burst forth into a broad conflagration. In this instance, too, fortune favored the vessel; for the raft, which was larger than the former, passed down between her and the fort, brightly gilding her tracery of ropes and spars, lighting up the old palisades and bastions of Detroit, disclosing the white Canadian farms and houses along the shore, and revealing the dusky margin of the forest behind. It showed, too, a dark group of naked spectators, who stood on the bank to watch the effect of their artifice, when a cannon flashed, a

[1] *Pontiac* MS.

loud report broke the stillness, and before the smoke of the gun had risen, these curious observers had vanished. The raft floated down, its flames crackling and glaring wide through the night, until it was burnt to the water's edge, and its last hissing embers were quenched in the river.

Though twice defeated, the Indians would not abandon their plan, but, soon after this second failure, began another raft, of different construction from the former, and so large that they thought it certain to take effect. Gladwyn, on his part, provided boats which were moored by chains at some distance above the vessels, and made other preparations of defence, so effectual that the Indians, after working four days upon the raft, gave over their undertaking as useless. About this time, a party of Shawanoe and Delaware Indians arrived at Detroit, and were received by the Wyandots with a salute of musketry, which occasioned some alarm among the English, who knew nothing of its cause. They reported the progress of the war in the south and east; and, a few days after, an Abenaki, from Lower Canada, also made his appearance, bringing to the Indians the flattering falsehood that their Great Father, the King of France, was at that moment advancing up the St. Lawrence with his army. It may here be observed, that the name of Father, given to the Kings of France and England, was a mere title of courtesy or policy; for, in his haughty independence, the Indian yields submission to no man.

It was now between two and three months since the siege began; and if one is disposed to think slightingly of the warriors whose numbers could avail so little against a handful of half-starved English and provincials, he has only to recollect, that where barbarism has been arrayed against civilization, disorder against discipline, and ungoverned fury against considerate valor, such has seldom failed to be the result.

At the siege of Detroit, the Indians displayed a high degree of comparative steadiness and perseverance; and their history cannot furnish another instance of so large a force persisting so long in the attack of a fortified place. Their good conduct may be ascribed to their deep rage against the English, to their hope of speedy aid from the French, and to the controlling spirit of Pontiac, which held them to their work. The

Indian is but ill qualified for such attempts, having too much caution for an assault by storm, and too little patience for a blockade. The Wyandots and Pottawattamies had shown, from the beginning, less zeal than the other nations; and now, like children, they began to tire of the task they had undertaken. A deputation of the Wyandots came to the fort, and begged for peace, which was granted them; but when the Pottawattamies came on the same errand, they insisted, as a preliminary, that some of their people, who were detained prisoners by the English, should first be given up. Gladwyn demanded, on his part, that the English captives known to be in their village should be brought to the fort, and three of them were accordingly produced. As these were but a small part of the whole, the deputies were sharply rebuked for their duplicity, and told to go back for the rest. They withdrew angry and mortified; but, on the following day, a fresh deputation of chiefs made their appearance, bringing with them six prisoners. Having repaired to the council-room, they were met by Gladwyn, attended only by one or two officers. The Indians detained in the fort were about to be given up, and a treaty concluded, when one of the prisoners declared that there were several others still remaining in the Pottawattamie village. Upon this, the conference was broken off, and the deputies ordered instantly to depart. On being thus a second time defeated, they were goaded to such a pitch of rage, that, as afterwards became known, they formed the desperate resolution of killing Gladwyn on the spot, and then making their escape in the best way they could; but, happily, at that moment the commandant observed an Ottawa among them, and, resolving to seize him, called upon the guard without to assist in doing so. A file of soldiers entered, and the chiefs, seeing it impossible to execute their design, withdrew from the fort, with black and sullen brows. A day or two afterwards, however, they returned with the rest of the prisoners, on which peace was granted them, and their people set at liberty.[1]

---

[1] Whatever may have been the case with the Pottawattamies, there were indications from the first that the Wyandots were lukewarm or even reluctant in taking part with Pontiac. As early as May 22, some of them complained that he had forced them into the war. *Diary of the Siege. Johnson* MSS.

Chapter XV.

1763.

THE FIGHT OF BLOODY BRIDGE.

F ROM THE TIME when peace was concluded with the Wyandots and Pottawattamies until the end of July, little worthy of notice took place at Detroit. The fort was still watched closely by the Ottawas and Ojibwas, who almost daily assailed it with petty attacks. In the mean time, unknown to the garrison, a strong re-enforcement was coming to their aid. Captain Dalzell had left Niagara with twenty-two barges, bearing two hundred and eighty men, with several small cannon, and a fresh supply of provisions and ammunition.[1]

Coasting the south shore of Lake Erie, they soon reached Presqu' Isle, where they found the scorched and battered blockhouse captured a few weeks before, and saw with surprise the mines and intrenchments made by the Indians in assailing it.[2] Thence, proceeding on their voyage, they reached Sandusky on the twenty-sixth of July; and here they marched inland to the neighboring village of the Wyandots, which they burnt to the ground, at the same time destroying the corn, which this tribe, more provident than most of the others, had planted there in the spring. Dalzell then steered

---

[1] Extract from a MS. Letter—*Sir J. Amherst to Sir W. Johnson.*

"New York, 16th June, 1763.

"Sir:

"I am to thank you for your Letter of the 6th Instant, which I have this moment Received, with some Advices from Niagara, concerning the Motions of the Indians that Way, they having attacked a Detachment under the Command of Lieut. Cuyler of Hopkins's Rangers, who were on their Route towards the Detroit, and Obliged him to Return to Niagara, with (I am sorry to say) too few of his Men.

"Upon this Intelligence, I have thought it Necessary to Dispatch Captain Dalyell, my Aid de Camp, with Orders to Carry with him all such Reinforcements as can possibly be collected (having, at the same time, a due Attention to the Safety of the Principal Forts), to Niagara, and to proceed to the Detroit, if Necessary, and Judged Proper."

[2] *Penn. Gaz.* No. 1811.

northward for the mouth of the Detroit, which he reached on the evening of the twenty-eighth, and cautiously ascended under cover of night. "It was fortunate," writes Gladwyn, "that they were not discovered, in which case they must have been destroyed or taken, as the Indians, being emboldened by their late successes, fight much better than we could have expected."

On the morning of the twenty-ninth, the whole country around Detroit was covered by a sea of fog, the precursor of a hot and sultry day; but at sunrise its surface began to heave and toss, and, parting at intervals, disclosed the dark and burnished surface of the river; then lightly rolling, fold upon fold, the mists melted rapidly away, the last remnant clinging sluggishly along the margin of the forests. Now, for the first time, the garrison could discern the approaching convoy.[1] Still they remained in suspense, fearing lest it might have met the fate of the former detachment; but a salute from the fort was answered by a swivel from the boats, and at once all apprehension passed away. The convoy soon reached a point in the river midway between the villages of the Wyandots and the Pottawattamies. About a fortnight before, as we have seen, these capricious savages had made a treaty of peace, which they now saw fit to break, opening a hot fire upon the boats from either bank.[2] It was answered by swivels and musketry; but before the short engagement was over, fifteen of the English were killed or wounded. This danger passed, boat after boat came to shore, and landed its men amid the cheers of the garrison. The detachment was composed of soldiers from the 55th and 80th Regiments, with twenty independent rangers, commanded by Major Rogers; and as the barracks in the place were too small to receive them, they were all quartered upon the inhabitants.

Scarcely were these arrangements made, when a great smoke was seen rising from the Wyandot village across the river, and the inhabitants, apparently in much consternation, were observed paddling down stream with their household utensils, and even their dogs. It was supposed that they had

[1] *Pontiac* MS.
[2] MS. Letter—*Major Rogers to* ——, Aug. 5.

abandoned and burned their huts; but in truth, it was only an artifice of these Indians, who had set fire to some old canoes and other refuse piled in front of their village, after which the warriors, having concealed the women and children, returned and lay in ambush among the bushes, hoping to lure some of the English within reach of their guns. None of them, however, fell into the snare.[1]

Captain Dalzell was the same officer who was the companion of Israel Putnam in some of the most adventurous passages of that rough veteran's life; but more recently he had acted as aide-de-camp to Sir Jeffrey Amherst. On the day of his arrival, he had a conference with Gladwyn, at the quarters of the latter, and strongly insisted that the time was come when an irrecoverable blow might be struck at Pontiac. He requested permission to march out on the following night, and attack the Indian camp. Gladwyn, better acquainted with the position of affairs, and perhaps more cautious by nature, was averse to the attempt; but Dalzell urged his request so strenuously that the commandant yielded to his representations, and gave a tardy consent.[2]

Pontiac had recently removed his camp from its old position near the mouth of Parent's Creek, and was now posted several miles above, behind a great marsh, which protected the Indian huts from the cannon of the vessel. On the afternoon of the thirtieth, orders were issued and preparations made for the meditated attack. Through the inexcusable carelessness of some of the officers, the design became known to a few Canadians, the bad result of which will appear in the sequel.

About two o'clock on the morning of the thirty-first of July, the gates were thrown open in silence, and the detach-

[1] *Pontiac* MS.
[2] Extract from a MS. Letter—*Major Gladwyn to Sir J. Amherst.*
"Detroit, Aug. 8th, 1763.
"On the 31st, Captain Dalyell Requested, as a particular favor, that I would give him the Command of a Party, in order to Attempt the Surprizal of Pontiac's Camp, under cover of the Night, to which I answered that I was of opinion he was too much on his Guard to Effect it; he then said he thought I had it in my power to give him a Stroke, and that if I did not Attempt it now, he would Run off, and I should never have another Opportunity; this induced me to give in to the Scheme, contrary to my Judgement."

ment, two hundred and fifty in number, passed noiselessly out. They filed two deep along the road, while two large bateaux, each bearing a swivel on the bow, rowed up the river abreast of them. Lieutenant Brown led the advance guard of twenty-five men; the centre was commanded by Captain Gray, and the rear by Captain Grant. The night was still, close, and sultry, and the men marched in light undress. On their right was the dark and gleaming surface of the river, with a margin of sand intervening, and on their left a succession of Canadian houses, with barns, orchards, and cornfields, from whence the clamorous barking of watch-dogs saluted them as they passed. The inhabitants, roused from sleep, looked from the windows in astonishment and alarm. An old man has told the writer how, when a child, he climbed on the roof of his father's house, to look down on the glimmering bayonets, and how, long after the troops had passed, their heavy and measured tramp sounded from afar, through the still night. Thus the English moved forward to the attack, little thinking that, behind houses and enclosures, Indian scouts watched every yard of their progress—little suspecting that Pontiac, apprised by the Canadians of their plan, had broken up his camp, and was coming against them with all his warriors, armed and painted for battle.

A mile and a half from the fort, Parent's Creek, ever since that night called Bloody Run, descended through a wild and rough hollow, and entered the Detroit amid a growth of rank grass and sedge. Only a few rods from its mouth, the road crossed it by a narrow wooden bridge, not existing at the present day. Just beyond this bridge, the land rose in abrupt ridges, parallel to the stream. Along their summits were rude intrenchments made by Pontiac to protect his camp, which had formerly occupied the ground immediately beyond. Here, too, were many piles of firewood belonging to the Canadians, besides strong picket fences, enclosing orchards and gardens connected with the neighboring houses. Behind fences, wood-piles, and intrenchments, crouched an unknown number of Indian warriors with levelled guns. They lay silent as snakes, for now they could hear the distant tramp of the approaching column.

The sky was overcast, and the night exceedingly dark. As

the English drew near the dangerous pass, they could discern the oft-mentioned house of Meloche upon a rising ground to the left, while in front the bridge was dimly visible, and the ridges beyond it seemed like a wall of undistinguished blackness. They pushed rapidly forward, not wholly unsuspicious of danger. The advance guard were half way over the bridge, and the main body just entering upon it, when a horrible burst of yells rose in their front, and the Indian guns blazed forth in a general discharge. Half the advanced party were shot down; the appalled survivors shrank back aghast. The confusion reached even the main body, and the whole recoiled together; but Dalzell raised his clear voice above the din, advanced to the front, rallied the men, and led them forward to the attack.[1] Again the Indians poured in their volley, and again the English hesitated; but Dalzell shouted from the van, and, in the madness of mingled rage and fear, they charged at a run across the bridge and up the heights beyond. Not an Indian was there to oppose them. In vain the furious soldiers sought their enemy behind fences and intrenchments. The active savages had fled; yet still their guns flashed thick through the gloom, and their war-cry rose with undiminished clamor. The English pushed forward amid the pitchy darkness, quite ignorant of their way, and soon became involved in a maze of out-houses and enclosures. At every pause they made, the retiring enemy would gather to renew the attack, firing back hotly upon the front and flanks. To advance farther would be useless, and the only alternative was to withdraw and wait for daylight. Captain Grant, with his company, recrossed the bridge, and took up his station on the road. The rest followed, a small party remaining to hold the enemy in check while the dead and wounded were placed on board the two bateaux which had rowed up to the bridge during the action. This task was commenced amid a sharp fire from both sides; and before it was completed, heavy volleys were heard from the rear, where Captain Grant was stationed. A great force of Indians had fired upon him from the house of Meloche and the neighboring orchards. Grant pushed up the hill, and drove them from the orchards at the point of the

[1] *Penn. Gaz.* No. 1811.

bayonet—drove them, also, from the house, and, entering it, found two Canadians within. These men told him that the Indians were bent on cutting off the English from the fort, and that they had gone in great numbers to occupy the houses which commanded the road below.[1] It was now evident that instant retreat was necessary; and the command being issued to that effect, the men fell back into marching order, and slowly began their retrograde movement. Grant was now in the van, and Dalzell at the rear. Some of the Indians followed, keeping up a scattering and distant fire; and from time to time the rear faced about, to throw back a volley of musketry at the pursuers. Having proceeded in this manner for half a mile, they reached a point where, close upon the right, were many barns and outhouses, with strong picket fences. Behind these, and in a newly dug cellar close at hand, lay concealed a great multitude of Indians. They suffered the advanced party to pass unmolested; but when the centre and rear came opposite their ambuscade, they raised a frightful yell, and poured a volley among them. The men had well-nigh fallen into a panic. The river ran close on their left, and the only avenue of escape lay along the road in front. Breaking their ranks, they crowded upon one another in blind eagerness to escape the storm of bullets; and but for the presence of Dalzell, the retreat would have been turned into a flight. "The enemy," writes an officer who was in the fight, "marked him for his extraordinary bravery;" and he had already received two severe wounds. Yet his exertions did not slacken for a moment. Some of the soldiers he rebuked, some he threatened, and some he beat with the flat of his sword; till at length order was partially restored, and the fire of the enemy returned with effect. Though it was near daybreak, the dawn was obscured by a thick fog, and little could be seen of the Indians, except the incessant flashes of their guns amid the mist, while hundreds of voices, mingled in one appalling yell, confused the faculties of the men, and drowned the shout of command. The enemy had taken possession of a house, from the windows of which they fired down upon the English. Major Rogers, with some of his provincial rangers, burst the

---

[1] *Detail of the Action of the 31st of July.* See *Gent. Mag.* XXXIII. 486.

door with an axe, rushed in, and expelled them. Captain Gray was ordered to dislodge a large party from behind some neighboring fences. He charged them with his company, but fell, mortally wounded, in the attempt.[1] They gave way, however; and now, the fire of the Indians being much diminished, the retreat was resumed. No sooner had the men faced about, than the savages came darting through the mist upon their flank and rear, cutting down stragglers, and scalping the fallen. At a little distance lay a sergeant of the 55th, helplessly wounded, raising himself on his hands, and gazing with a look of despair after his retiring comrades. The sight caught the eye of Dalzell. That gallant soldier, in the true spirit of heroism, ran out, amid the firing, to rescue the wounded man, when a shot struck him, and he fell dead. Few observed his fate, and none durst turn back to recover his body. The detachment pressed on, greatly harassed by the pursuing Indians. Their loss would have been much more severe, had not Major Rogers taken possession of another house, which commanded the road, and covered the retreat of the party.

He entered it with some of his own men, while many panic-stricken regulars broke in after him, in their eagerness to gain a temporary shelter. The house was a large and strong one, and the women of the neighborhood had crowded into the cellar for refuge. While some of the soldiers looked in blind terror for a place of concealment, others seized upon a keg of whiskey in one of the rooms and quaffed the liquor with eager thirst; while others, again, piled packs of furs, furniture, and all else within their reach, against the windows, to serve as a barricade. Panting and breathless, their faces moist with sweat and blackened with gunpowder, they thrust their muskets through the openings, and fired out upon the whooping assailants. At intervals, a bullet flew sharply whizzing through a crevice, striking down a man, perchance, or rapping harmlessly against the partitions. Old Campau, the master of the house, stood on a trap-door to prevent the frightened soldiers from seeking shelter among the women in the cellar. A ball grazed his gray head, and buried itself in the wall, where a few years since it might still have been seen. The

---

[1] *Penn. Gaz.* No. 1811.

screams of the half-stifled women below, the quavering war-whoops without, the shouts and curses of the soldiers, mingled in a scene of clamorous confusion, and it was long before the authority of Rogers could restore order.[1]

In the mean time, Captain Grant, with his advanced party, had moved forward about half a mile, where he found some orchards and enclosures, by means of which he could maintain himself until the centre and rear should arrive. From this point he detached all the men he could spare to occupy the houses below; and as soldiers soon began to come in from the rear, he was enabled to re-enforce these detachments, until a complete line of communication was established with the fort, and the retreat effectually secured. Within an hour, the whole party had arrived, with the exception of Rogers and his men, who were quite unable to come off, being besieged in the house of Campau, by full two hundred Indians. The two armed bateaux had gone down to the fort, laden with the dead and wounded. They now returned, and, in obedience to an order from Grant, proceeded up the river to a point opposite Campau's house, where they opened a fire of swivels, which swept the ground above and below it, and completely scattered the assailants. Rogers and his party now came out, and marched down the road, to unite themselves with Grant. The two bateaux accompanied them closely, and, by a constant fire, restrained the Indians from making an attack. Scarcely had Rogers left the house at one door, when the enemy entered it at another, to obtain the scalps from two or three corpses left behind. Foremost of them all, a withered old squaw rushed in, with a shrill scream, and, slashing open one of the dead bodies with her knife, scooped up the blood between her hands, and quaffed it with a ferocious ecstasy.

Grant resumed his retreat as soon as Rogers had arrived, falling back from house to house, joined in succession by the parties sent to garrison each. The Indians, in great numbers, stood whooping and yelling, at a vain distance, unable to make an attack, so well did Grant choose his positions, and so steadily and coolly conduct the retreat. About eight o'clock,

[1]Many particulars of the fight at the house of Campau were related to me, on the spot, by John R. Williams, Esq., of Detroit, a connection of the Campau family.

after six hours of marching and combat, the detachment entered once more within the sheltering palisades of Detroit.

In this action, the English lost fifty-nine men killed and wounded. The loss of the Indians could not be ascertained, but it certainly did not exceed fifteen or twenty. At the beginning of the fight, their numbers were probably much inferior to those of the English; but fresh parties were continually joining them, until seven or eight hundred warriors must have been present.

The Ojibwas and Ottawas alone formed the ambuscade at the bridge, under Pontiac's command; for the Wyandots and Pottawattamies came later to the scene of action, crossing the river in their canoes, or passing round through the woods behind the fort, to take part in the fray.[1]

In speaking of the fight of Bloody Bridge, an able writer in the Annual Register for the year 1763 observes, with justice, that although in European warfare it would be deemed a mere skirmish, yet in a conflict with the American savages, it rises to the importance of a pitched battle; since these people, being thinly scattered over a great extent of country, are accustomed to conduct their warfare by detail, and never take the field in any great force.

The Indians were greatly elated by their success. Runners were sent out for several hundred miles, through the surrounding woods, to spread tidings of the victory; and reenforcements soon began to come in to swell the force of Pontiac. "Fresh warriors," writes Gladwyn, "arrive almost every day, and I believe that I shall soon be besieged by upwards of a thousand." The English, on their part, were well prepared for resistance, since the garrison now comprised more than three hundred effective men; and no one entertained a doubt of their ultimate success in defending the

---

[1] MS. Letters—*MacDonald to Dr. Campbell*, Aug. 8. *Gage to Lord Halifax*, Oct. 12. *Amherst to Lord Egremont*, Sept. 3. *Meloche's Account*, MS. *Gouin's Account*, MS. *St. Aubin's Account*, MS. *Peltier's Account*, MS. *Maxwell's Account*, MS., etc. In the *Diary of the Siege* is the following, under date of August 1st: "Young Mr. Campo (Campau) brought in the Body of poor Capt. Dalyel (Dalzell) about three o'clock to-day, which was mangled in such a horrid Manner that it was shocking to human nature; the Indians wip'd his Heart about the Faces of our Prisoners."

place. Day after day passed on; a few skirmishes took place, and a few men were killed, but nothing worthy of notice occurred, until the night of the fourth of September, at which time was achieved one of the most memorable feats which the chronicles of that day can boast.

The schooner Gladwyn, the smaller of the two armed vessels so often mentioned, had been sent down to Niagara with letters and despatches. She was now returning, having on board Horst, her master, Jacobs, her mate, and a crew of ten men, all of whom were provincials, besides six Iroquois Indians, supposed to be friendly to the English. On the night of the third, she entered the River Detroit; and in the morning the six Indians asked to be set on shore, a request which was foolishly granted. They disappeared in the woods, and probably reported to Pontiac's warriors the small numbers of the crew. The vessel stood up the river until nightfall, when, the wind failing, she was compelled to anchor about nine miles below the fort. The men on board watched with anxious vigilance; and as night came on, they listened to every sound which broke the stillness, from the strange cry of the nighthawk, wheeling above their heads, to the bark of the fox from the woods on shore. The night set in with darkness so complete, that at the distance of a few rods nothing could be discerned. Meantime, three hundred and fifty Indians, in their birch canoes, glided silently down with the current, and were close upon the vessel before they were seen. There was only time to fire a single cannon-shot among them, before they were beneath her bows, and clambering up her sides, holding their knives clinched fast between their teeth. The crew gave them a close fire of musketry, without any effect; then, flinging down their guns, they seized the spears and hatchets with which they were all provided, and met the assailants with such furious energy and courage, that in the space of two or three minutes they had killed and wounded more than twice their own number. But the Indians were only checked for a moment. The master of the vessel was killed, several of the crew were disabled, and the assailants were leaping over the bulwarks, when Jacobs, the mate, called out to blow up the schooner. This desperate command saved her and her crew. Some Wyandots, who had gained the deck, caught the meaning of his words, and gave the alarm to their companions. Instantly every Indian leaped overboard in a panic, and the whole were seen diving and swimming off in all directions, to escape the threatened explosion. The schooner was cleared of her assailants, who did not dare to renew the attack; and on the following morning she sailed for the fort, which she reached without molestation. Six of her crew escaped unhurt. Of the remainder, two were killed, and four seriously wounded, while the Indians had seven men killed upon the spot, and nearly twenty wounded, of whom eight were known to have died within a few days after. As the action was very brief, the fierceness of the struggle is sufficiently apparent from the loss on both sides. "The appearance of the men," says an eye-witness who saw them on their arrival, "was enough to convince every one of their bravery; they being as bloody as butchers, and their bayonets, spears, and cutlasses, blood to the hilt." The survivors of the crew were afterwards rewarded as their courage deserved.[1]

---

[1]MS. Letter—*Gladwyn to Amherst*, Sept. 9. Carver, 164. *Relation of the Gallant Defence of the Schooner near Detroit*, published by order of General Amherst, in the New York papers. *Penn. Gaz.* No. 1816. MS. Letter—*Amherst to Lord Egremont*, Oct. 13. *St. Aubin's Account*, MS. *Peltier's Account*, MS. *Relation of some Transactions at the Detroit in Sept. and Oct. 1763*, MS.

The Commander-in-chief ordered a medal to be struck and presented to each of the men. Jacobs, the mate of the schooner, appears to have been as rash as he was brave; for Captain Carver says, that several years after, when in command of the same vessel, he was lost, with all his crew, in a storm on Lake Erie, in consequence of having obstinately refused to take in ballast enough.

As this affair savors somewhat of the marvellous, the following evidence is given touching the most remarkable features of the story. The document was copied from the archives of London.

Extract from "*A Relation of the Gallant Defence made by the Crew of the Schooner on Lake Erie, when Attacked by a Large Body of Indians; as Published by Order of Sir Jeffrey Amherst in the New York Papers.*"

"The Schooner Sailed from Niagara, loaded with Provisions, some time in August last: Her Crew consisted of the Master and Eleven Men, with Six Mohawk Indians, who were Intended for a particular Service. She entered the Detroit River, on the 3d September; And on the 4th in the Morning, the Mohawks seemed very Desirous of being put on Shore, which the Master, very Inconsiderately, agreed to. The Wind proved contrary all that Day; and in the Evening, the Vessell being at Anchor, about Nine o'Clock, the Boatswain discovered a Number of Canoes coming down the River, with about

And now, taking leave, for a time, of the garrison of Detroit, whose fortunes we have followed so long, we will turn to observe the progress of events in a quarter of the wilderness yet more wild and remote.

Three Hundred and Fifty Indians; Upon which the Bow Gun was Immediately Fired; but before the other Guns could be brought to Bear, the Enemy got under the Bow and Stern, in Spite of the Swivels & Small Arms, and Attempted to Board the Vessell; Whereupon the Men Abandoned their Small Arms, and took to their Spears, with which they were provided; And, with Amazing Resolution and Bravery, knocked the Savages in the Head; Killed many; and saved the Vessell. . . It is certain Seven of the Savages were Killed on the Spot, and Eight had Died of those that were Wounded, when the Accounts came away. The Master and One Man were Killed, and four Wounded, on Board the Schooner, and the other Six brought her Safe to the Detroit."

It is somewhat singular that no mention is here made of the command to blow up the vessel. The most explicit authorities on this point are Carver, who obtained his account at Detroit, three years after the war, and a letter published in the *Pennsylvania Gazette*, No. 1816. This letter is dated at Detroit, five days after the attack. The circumstance is also mentioned in several traditional accounts of the Canadians.

Chapter XVI.

1763.

MICHILLIMACKINAC.

IN THE SPRING of the year 1763, before the war broke out, several English traders went up to Michillimackinac, some adopting the old route of the Ottawa, and others that of Detroit and the lakes. We will follow one of the latter on his adventurous progress. Passing the fort and settlement of Detroit, he soon enters Lake St. Clair, which seems like a broad basin filled to overflowing, while, along its far distant verge, a faint line of forest separates the water from the sky. He crosses the lake, and his voyageurs next urge his canoe against the current of the great river above. At length, Lake Huron opens before him, stretching its liquid expanse, like an ocean, to the farthest horizon. His canoe skirts the eastern shore of Michigan, where the forest rises like a wall from the water's edge; and as he advances northward, an endless line of stiff and shaggy fir-trees, hung with long mosses, fringes the shore with an aspect of monotonous desolation. In the space of two or three weeks, if his Canadians labor well, and no accident occur, the trader approaches the end of his voyage. Passing on his right the extensive Island of Bois Blanc, he sees, nearly in front, the beautiful Mackinaw, rising, with its white cliffs and green foliage, from the broad breast of the waters. He does not steer towards it, for at that day the Indians were its only tenants, but keeps along the main shore to the left, while his voyageurs raise their song and chorus. Doubling a point, he sees before him the red flag of England swelling lazily in the wind, and the palisades and wooden bastions of Fort Michillimackinac standing close upon the margin of the lake. On the beach, canoes are drawn up, and Canadians and Indians are idly lounging. A little beyond the fort is a cluster of the white Canadian houses, roofed with bark, and protected by fences of strong round pickets.

The trader enters at the gate, and sees before him an extensive square area, surrounded by high palisades. Numerous houses, barracks, and other buildings, form a smaller square within, and in the vacant space which they enclose appear the red uniforms of British soldiers, the gray coats of Canadians, and the gaudy Indian blankets, mingled in picturesque confusion; while a multitude of squaws, with children of every hue, stroll restlessly about the place. Such was Fort Michillimackinac in 1763.[1] Its name, which, in the Algonquin tongue, signifies the Great Turtle, was first, from a fancied resemblance, applied to the neighboring island, and thence to the fort.

Though buried in a wilderness, Michillimackinac was still of no recent origin. As early as 1671, the Jesuits had established a mission near the place, and a military force was not long in following; for, under the French dominion, the priest and the soldier went hand in hand. Neither toil, nor suffering, nor all the terrors of the wilderness, could damp the zeal of the undaunted missionary; and the restless ambition of France was always on the alert to seize every point of vantage, and avail itself of every means to gain ascendency over the forest tribes. Besides Michillimackinac, there were two other posts in this northern region, Green Bay, and the Sault Ste. Marie. Both were founded at an early period, and both presented the same characteristic features—a mission-house, a fort, and a cluster of Canadian dwellings. They had been originally garrisoned by small parties of militia, who, bringing their families with them, settled on the spot, and were founders of these little colonies. Michillimackinac, much the largest of the three, contained thirty families within the palisades of the fort, and about as many more without. Besides its military value, it was important as a centre of the fur-trade; for it was here that the traders engaged their men, and sent out their goods in canoes, under the charge of subordinates, to the more distant regions of the Mississippi and the North-west.

During the greater part of the year, the garrison and the settlers were completely isolated—cut off from all connection with the world; and, indeed, so great was the distance, and so serious the perils, which separated the three sister posts of the

---

[1]This description is drawn from traditional accounts aided by a personal examination of the spot, where the stumps of the pickets and the foundations of the houses may still be traced.

northern lakes, that often, through the whole winter, all inter-course was stopped between them.[1]

It is difficult for the imagination adequately to conceive the extent of these fresh-water oceans, and vast regions of forest, which, at the date of our narrative, were the domain of na-ture, a mighty hunting and fishing ground, for the sustenance of a few wandering tribes. One might journey among them for days, and even weeks together, without beholding a hu-man face. The Indians near Michillimackinac were the Ojib-was and Ottawas, the former of whom claimed the eastern section of Michigan, and the latter the western, their respec-tive portions being separated by a line drawn southward from the fort itself.[2] The principal village of the Ojibwas contained about a hundred warriors, and stood upon the Island of Michillimackinac, now called Mackinaw. There was another smaller village near the head of Thunder Bay. The Ottawas, to the number of two hundred and fifty warriors, lived at the settlement of L'Arbre Croche, on the shores of Lake Michi-gan, some distance west of the fort. This place was then the seat of the old Jesuit mission of St. Ignace, originally placed, by Father Marquette, on the northern side of the straits. Many of the Ottawas were nominal Catholics. They were all somewhat improved from their original savage condition, living in log houses, and cultivating corn and vegetables to such an extent as to supply the fort with provisions, besides satisfying their own wants. The Ojibwas, on the other hand, were not in the least degree removed from their primitive barbarism.[3]

These two tribes, with most of the other neighboring Indi-ans, were strongly hostile to the English. Many of their war-riors had fought against them in the late war, for France had summoned allies from the farthest corners of the wilderness, to aid her in her struggle. This feeling of hostility was excited to a higher pitch by the influence of the Canadians, who dis-liked the English, not merely as national enemies, but also as rivals in the fur-trade, and were extremely jealous of their

[1]MS. *Journal of Lieutenant Gorell*, commanding at Green Bay, 1761–63.

[2]Carver, *Travels*, 29.

[3]Many of these particulars are derived from memoranda furnished by Henry R. Schoolcraft, Esq.

intrusion upon the lakes. The following incidents, which occurred in the autumn of the year 1761, will illustrate the state of feeling which prevailed:—

At that time, although Michillimackinac had been surrendered, and the French garrison removed, no English troops had yet arrived to supply their place, and the Canadians were the only tenants of the fort. An adventurous trader, Alexander Henry, who, with one or two others, was the pioneer of the English fur-trade in this region, came to Michillimackinac by the route of the Ottawa. On the way, he was several times warned to turn back, and assured of death if he proceeded; and, at length, was compelled for safety to assume the disguise of a Canadian voyageur. When his canoes, laden with goods, reached the fort, he was very coldly received by its inhabitants, who did all in their power to alarm and discourage him. Soon after his arrival, he received the very unwelcome information, that a large number of Ojibwas, from the neighboring villages, were coming, in their canoes, to call upon him. Under ordinary circumstances, such a visitation, though disagreeable enough, would excite neither anxiety nor surprise; for the Indians, when in their villages, lead so monotonous an existence, that they are ready to snatch at the least occasion of excitement, and the prospect of a few trifling presents, and a few pipes of tobacco, is often a sufficient inducement for a journey of several days. But in the present instance there was serious cause of apprehension, since Canadians and Frenchmen were alike hostile to the solitary trader. The story could not be better told than in his own words.

"At two o'clock in the afternoon, the Chippewas (Ojibwas) came to the house, about sixty in number, and headed by Minavavana, their chief. They walked in single file, each with his tomahawk in one hand and scalping-knife in the other. Their bodies were naked from the waist upward, except in a few examples, where blankets were thrown loosely over the shoulders. Their faces were painted with charcoal, worked up with grease, their bodies with white clay, in patterns of various fancies. Some had feathers thrust through their noses, and their heads decorated with the same. It is unnecessary to dwell on the sensations with which I beheld the approach of this uncouth, if not frightful assemblage.

"The chief entered first, and the rest followed without noise. On receiving a sign from the former, the latter seated themselves on the floor.

"Minavavana appeared to be about fifty years of age. He was six feet in height, and had in his countenance an indescribable mixture of good and evil. Looking steadfastly at me, where I sat in ceremony, with an interpreter on either hand, and several Canadians behind me, he entered, at the same time, into conversation with Campion, inquiring how long it was since I left Montreal, and observing that the English, as it would seem, were brave men, and not afraid of death, since they dared to come, as I had done, fearlessly among their enemies.

"The Indians now gravely smoked their pipes, while I inwardly endured the tortures of suspense. At length, the pipes being finished, as well as a long pause, by which they were succeeded, Minavavana, taking a few strings of wampum in his hand, began the following speech: —

" 'Englishman, it is to you that I speak, and I demand your attention.

" 'Englishman, you know that the French King is our father. He promised to be such; and we, in return, promised to be his children. This promise we have kept.

" 'Englishman, it is you that have made war with this our father. You are his enemy; and how, then, could you have the boldness to venture among us, his children? You know that his enemies are ours.

" 'Englishman, we are informed that our father, the King of France, is old and infirm; and that, being fatigued with making war upon your nation, he is fallen asleep. During his sleep you have taken advantage of him, and possessed yourselves of Canada. But his nap is almost at an end. I think I hear him already stirring, and inquiring for his children, the Indians; and when he does awake, what must become of you? He will destroy you utterly.

" 'Englishman, although you have conquered the French, you have not yet conquered us. We are not your slaves. These lakes, these woods and mountains, were left to us by our ancestors. They are our inheritance; and we will part with them to none. Your nation supposes that we, like the white people, cannot live without bread, and pork, and beef! But you ought to know that He, the Great Spirit and Master of Life, has provided food for us in these spacious lakes, and on these woody mountains.

" 'Englishman, our father, the King of France, employed our young men to make war upon your nation. In this warfare many of them have been killed; and it is our custom to retaliate until such time as the spirits of the slain are satisfied. But the spirits of the slain are to be satisfied in either of two ways; the first is by the spilling of the blood of the nation by which they fell; the other, by *covering the bodies of the dead*, and thus allaying the resentment of their relations. This is done by making presents.

" 'Englishman, your king has never sent us any presents, nor entered into any treaty with us; wherefore he and we are still at war; and, until he does these things, we must consider that we have no other father nor friend, among the white men, than the King of France; but for you, we have taken into consideration that you have ventured your life among us, in the expectation that we should not molest you. You do not come armed, with an intention to make war; you come in peace, to trade with us, and supply us with necessaries, of which we are in much want. We shall regard you, therefore, as a brother; and you may sleep tranquilly, without fear of the Chippewas. As a token of our friendship, we present you this pipe to smoke.'

"As Minavavana uttered these words, an Indian presented me with a pipe, which, after I had drawn the smoke three times, was carried to the chief, and after him to every person in the room. This ceremony ended, the chief arose, and gave me his hand, in which he was followed by all the rest."[1]

These tokens of friendship were suitably acknowledged by the trader, who made a formal reply to Minavavana's speech. To this succeeded a request for whiskey on the part of the Indians, with which Henry unwillingly complied; and, having distributed several small additional presents, he beheld, with profound satisfaction, the departure of his guests. Scarcely had he ceased to congratulate himself on having thus got rid

[1]Henry, *Travels*, 45.

of the Ojibwas, or, as he calls them, the Chippewas, when a more formidable invasion once more menaced him with destruction. Two hundred L'Arbre Croche Ottawas came in a body to the fort, and summoned Henry, together with Goddard and Solomons, two other traders, who had just arrived, to meet them in council. Here they informed their startled auditors that they must distribute their goods among the Indians, adding a worthless promise to pay them in the spring, and threatening force in case of a refusal. Being allowed until the next morning to reflect on what they had heard, the traders resolved on resistance, and, accordingly, arming about thirty of their men with muskets, they barricaded themselves in the house occupied by Henry, and kept strict watch all night. The Ottawas, however, did not venture an attack. On the following day, the Canadians, with pretended sympathy, strongly advised compliance with the demand; but the three traders resolutely held out, and kept possession of their stronghold till night, when, to their surprise and joy, the news arrived that the body of troops known to be on their way towards the fort were, at that moment, encamped within a few miles of it. Another night of watching and anxiety succeeded; but at sunrise, the Ottawas launched their canoes and departed, while, immediately after, the boats of the English detachment were seen to approach the landing-place. Michillimackinac received a strong garrison; and for a time, at least, the traders were safe.

Time passed on, and the hostile feelings of the Indians towards the English did not diminish. It necessarily follows, from the extremely loose character of Indian government,— if indeed the name government be applicable at all,— that the separate members of the same tribe have little political connection, and are often united merely by the social tie of totemship. Thus the Ottawas at L'Arbre Croche were quite independent of those at Detroit. They had a chief of their own, who by no means acknowledged the authority of Pontiac, though the high reputation of this great warrior everywhere attached respect and influence to his name. The same relations subsisted between the Ojibwas of Michillimackinac and their more southern tribesmen; and the latter might declare war and make peace without at all involving the former.

The name of the Ottawa chief at L'Arbre Croche has not survived in history or tradition. The chief of the Ojibwas, however, is still remembered by the remnants of his people, and was the same whom Henry calls Minavavana, or, as the Canadians entitled him, by way of distinction, *Le Grand Sauteur*, or the Great Ojibwa. He lived in the little village of Thunder Bay, though his power was acknowledged by the Indians of the neighboring islands. That his mind was of no common order is sufficiently evinced by his speech to Henry; but he had not the commanding spirit of Pontiac. His influence seems not to have extended beyond his own tribe. He could not, or at least he did not, control the erratic forces of an Indian community, and turn them into one broad current of steady and united energy. Hence, in the events about to be described, the natural instability of the Indian character was abundantly displayed.

In the spring of the year 1763, Pontiac, in compassing his grand scheme of hostility, sent, among the rest, to the Indians of Michillimackinac, inviting them to aid him in the war. His messengers, bearing in their hands the war-belt of black and purple wampum, appeared before the assembled warriors, flung at their feet a hatchet painted red, and delivered the speech with which they had been charged. The warlike auditory answered with ejaculations of applause, and, taking up the blood-red hatchet, pledged themselves to join in the contest. Before the end of May, news reached the Ojibwas that Pontiac had already struck the English at Detroit. This wrought them up to a high pitch of excitement and emulation, and they resolved that peace should last no longer. Their numbers were at this time more than doubled by several bands of their wandering people, who had gathered at Michillimackinac from far and near, attracted probably by rumors of impending war. Being, perhaps, jealous of the Ottawas, or willing to gain all the glory and plunder to themselves, they determined to attack the fort, without communicating the design to their neighbors of L'Arbre Croche.

At this time there were about thirty-five men, with their

officers, in garrison at Michillimackinac.[1] Warning of the tempest that impended had been clearly given; enough, had it been heeded, to have averted the fatal disaster. Several of the Canadians least hostile to the English had thrown out hints of approaching danger, and one of them had even told Captain Etherington, the commandant, that the Indians had formed a design to destroy, not only his garrison, but all the English on the lakes. With a folly, of which, at this period, there were several parallel instances among the British officers in America, Etherington not only turned a deaf ear to what he heard, but threatened to send prisoner to Detroit the next person who should disturb the fort with such tidings. Henry, the trader, who was at this time in the place, had also seen occasion to distrust the Indians; but on communicating his suspicions to the commandant, the latter treated them with total disregard. Henry accuses himself of sharing this officer's infatuation. That his person was in danger, had been plainly intimated to him, under the following curious circumstances: —

An Ojibwa chief, named Wawatam, had conceived for him one of those friendly attachments which often form so pleasing a feature in the Indian character. It was about a year since Henry had first met with this man. One morning, Wawatam had entered his house, and placing before him, on the ground, a large present of furs and dried meat, delivered a speech to the following effect: Early in life, he said, he had withdrawn, after the ancient usage of his people, to fast and pray in solitude, that he might propitiate the Great Spirit, and learn the future career marked out for him. In the course of his dreams and visions on this occasion, it was revealed to him that, in after years, he should meet a white man, who should be to him a friend and brother. No sooner had he seen Henry, than the irrepressible conviction rose up within him, that he was the man whom the Great Spirit had indicated, and that the dream was now fulfilled. Henry replied to the speech with suitable acknowledgments of gratitude, made a present in his turn, smoked a pipe with Wawatam, and, as the

---

[1] This appears from the letters of Captain Etherington. Henry states the number at ninety. It is not unlikely that he meant to include all the inhabitants of the fort, both soldiers and Canadians, in his enumeration.

latter soon after left the fort, speedily forgot his Indian friend and brother altogether. Many months had elapsed since the occurrence of this very characteristic incident, when, on the second of June, Henry's door was pushed open without ceremony, and the dark figure of Wawatam glided silently in. He said that he was just returned from his wintering ground. Henry, at length recollecting him, inquired after the success of his hunt; but the Indian, without replying, sat down with a dejected air, and expressed his surprise and regret at finding his brother still in the fort. He said that he was going on the next day to the Sault Ste. Marie, and that he wished Henry to go with him. He then asked if the English had heard no bad news, and said that through the winter he himself had been much disturbed by the singing of evil birds. Seeing that Henry gave little attention to what he said, he at length went away with a sad and mournful face. On the next morning he came again, together with his squaw, and, offering the trader a present of dried meat, again pressed him to go with him, in the afternoon, to the Sault Ste. Marie. When Henry demanded his reason for such urgency, he asked if his brother did not know that many bad Indians, who had never shown themselves at the fort, were encamped in the woods around it. To-morrow, he said, they are coming to ask for whiskey, and would all get drunk, so that it would be dangerous to remain. Wawatam let fall, in addition, various other hints, which, but for Henry's imperfect knowledge of the Algonquin language, could hardly have failed to draw his attention. As it was, however, his friend's words were spoken in vain; and at length, after long and persevering efforts, he and his squaw took their departure, but not, as Henry declares, before each had let fall some tears. Among the Indian women, the practice of weeping and wailing is universal upon all occasions of sorrowful emotion; and the kind-hearted squaw, as she took down her husband's lodge, and loaded his canoe for departure, did not cease to sob and moan aloud.

On this same afternoon, Henry remembers that the fort was full of Indians, moving about among the soldiers with a great appearance of friendship. Many of them came to his house, to purchase knives and small hatchets, often asking to see silver bracelets, and other ornaments, with the intention, as afterwards appeared, of learning their places of deposit, in order the more easily to lay hand on them at the moment of pillage. As the afternoon drew to a close, the visitors quietly went away; and many of the unhappy garrison saw for the last time the sun go down behind the waters of Lake Michigan.

Chapter XVII.

1763.

THE MASSACRE.

T HE FOLLOWING MORNING was warm and sultry. It was the fourth of June, the birthday of King George. The discipline of the garrison was relaxed, and some license allowed to the soldiers.[1] Encamped in the woods, not far off, were a large number of Ojibwas, lately arrived; while several bands of the Sac Indians, from the River Wisconsin, had also erected their lodges in the vicinity. Early in the morning, many Ojibwas came to the fort, inviting officers and soldiers to come out and see a grand game of ball, which was to be played between their nation and the Sacs. In consequence, the place was soon deserted by half its tenants. An outline of Michillimackinac, as far as tradition has preserved its general features, has already been given; and it is easy to conceive, with sufficient accuracy, the appearance it must have presented on this eventful morning. The houses and barracks were so ranged as to form a quadrangle, enclosing an extensive area, upon which their doors all opened, while behind rose the tall palisades, forming a large external square. The picturesque Canadian houses, with their rude porticoes, and projecting roofs of bark, sufficiently indicated the occupations of their inhabitants; for birch canoes were lying near many of them, and fishing-nets were stretched to dry in the sun. Women and children were moving about the doors; knots of Canadian voyageurs reclined on the ground, smoking and conversing; soldiers were lounging listlessly at the doors and windows of the barracks, or strolling in careless undress about the area.

Without the fort the scene was of a very different character. The gates were wide open, and soldiers were collected in groups under the shadow of the palisades, watching the Indian ball play. Most of them were without arms, and mingled among them were a great number of Canadians, while a

---

[1]The above is Henry's date. Etherington says, the second.

multitude of Indian squaws, wrapped in blankets, were conspicuous in the crowd.

Captain Etherington and Lieutenant Leslie stood near the gate, the former indulging his inveterate English propensity; for, as Henry informs us, he had promised the Ojibwas that he would bet on their side against the Sacs. Indian chiefs and warriors were also among the spectators, intent, apparently, on watching the game, but with thoughts, in fact, far otherwise employed.

The plain in front was covered by the ball-players. The game in which they were engaged, called *baggattaway* by the Ojibwas, is still, as it always has been, a favorite with many Indian tribes. At either extremity of the ground, a tall post was planted, marking the stations of the rival parties. The object of each was to defend its own post, and drive the ball to that of its adversary. Hundreds of lithe and agile figures were leaping and bounding upon the plain. Each was nearly naked, his loose black hair flying in the wind, and each bore in his hand a bat of a form peculiar to this game. At one moment the whole were crowded together, a dense throng of combatants, all struggling for the ball; at the next, they were scattered again, and running over the ground like hounds in full cry. Each, in his excitement, yelled and shouted at the height of his voice. Rushing and striking, tripping their adversaries, or hurling them to the ground, they pursued the animating contest amid the laughter and applause of the spectators. Suddenly, from the midst of the multitude, the ball soared into the air, and, descending in a wide curve, fell near the pickets of the fort. This was no chance stroke. It was part of a preconcerted stratagem to insure the surprise and destruction of the garrison. As if in pursuit of the ball, the players turned and came rushing, a maddened and tumultuous throng, towards the gate. In a moment they had reached it. The amazed English had no time to think or act. The shrill cries of the ball-players were changed to the ferocious war-whoop. The warriors snatched from the squaws the hatchets, which the latter, with this design, had concealed beneath their blankets. Some of the Indians assailed the spectators without, while others rushed into the fort, and all was carnage and confusion. At the outset, several strong hands had fastened their gripe upon Etherington and Leslie, and led them away from the scene of massacre towards the woods.[1] Within the area of the fort, the men were slaughtered without mercy. But here the task of description may well be resigned to the pen of the trader, Henry.

"I did not go myself to see the match which was now to be played without the fort, because, there being a canoe prepared to depart on the following day for Montreal, I employed myself in writing letters to my friends; and even when a fellow-trader, Mr. Tracy, happened to call upon me, saying that another canoe had just arrived from Detroit, and proposing that I should go with him to the beach, to inquire the news, it so happened that I still remained to finish my letters; promising to follow Mr. Tracy in the course of a few minutes. Mr. Tracy had not gone more than twenty paces from my door, when I heard an Indian war-cry, and a noise of general confusion.

"Going instantly to my window, I saw a crowd of Indians, within the fort, furiously cutting down and scalping every Englishman they found: in particular, I witnessed the fate of Lieutenant Jamette.

"I had, in the room in which I was, a fowling-piece, loaded with swan shot. This I immediately seized, and held it for a few minutes, waiting to hear the drum beat to arms. In this dreadful interval I saw several of my countrymen fall, and more than one struggling between the knees of an Indian, who, holding him in this manner, scalped him while yet living.

"At length, disappointed in the hope of seeing resistance made to the enemy, and sensible, of course, that no effort of my own unassisted arm could avail against four hundred Indians, I thought only of seeking shelter amid the slaughter which was raging. I observed many of the Canadian inhabitants of the fort calmly looking on, neither opposing the Indians nor suffering injury; and from this circumstance, I conceived a hope of finding security in their houses.

"Between the yard door of my own house and that of M. Langlade,[2] my next neighbor, there was only a low fence,

---

[1] MS. Letter—*Etherington to Gladwyn, June 12.* See Appendix, C.
[2] CHARLES LANGLADE, who is praised by Etherington, though spoken of

over which I easily climbed. At my entrance, I found the whole family at the windows, gazing at the scene of blood before them. I addressed myself immediately to M. Langlade, begging that he would put me into some place of safety until the heat of the affair should be over; an act of charity by which he might, perhaps, preserve me from the general massacre; but while I uttered my petition, M. Langlade, who had looked for a moment at me, turned again to the window, shrugging his shoulders, and intimating that he could do nothing for me—'*Que voudriez-vous que j'en ferais?*'

"This was a moment for despair; but the next a Pani[1] woman, a slave of M. Langlade's, beckoned me to follow her. She brought me to a door, which she opened, desiring me to enter, and telling me that it led to the garret, where I must go and conceal myself. I joyfully obeyed her directions; and she, having followed me up to the garret door, locked it after me, and, with great presence of mind, took away the key.

"This shelter obtained, if shelter I could hope to find it, I was naturally anxious to know what might still be passing without. Through an aperture, which afforded me a view of the area of the fort, I beheld, in shapes the foulest and most terrible, the ferocious triumphs of barbarian conquerors. The dead were scalped and mangled; the dying were writhing and shrieking under the unsatiated knife and tomahawk; and from the bodies of some, ripped open, their butchers were drinking the blood, scooped up in the hollow of joined hands, and quaffed amid shouts of rage and victory. I was shaken not only with horror, but with fear. The sufferings which I wit-

---

in equivocal terms by Henry, was the son of a Frenchman of good family and an Ottawa squaw. He was born at Mackinaw in 1724, and served with great reputation as a partisan officer in the old French war. He and his father, Augustin Langlade, were the first permanent settlers within the present State of Wisconsin. He is said to have saved Etherington and Leslie from the torture. See the *Recollections of Augustin Grignon*, his grandson, in *Collections of the Hist. Soc. of Wisconsin*, III. 197.

[1] This name is commonly written *Pawnee*. The tribe who bore it lived west of the Mississippi. They were at war with many surrounding nations, and, among the rest, with the Sacs and Foxes, who often brought their prisoners to the French settlements for sale. It thus happened that Pawnee slaves were to be found in the principal families of Detroit and Michillimackinac.

nessed I seemed on the point of experiencing. No long time elapsed before every one being destroyed who could be found, there was a general cry of 'All is finished.' At the same instant I heard some of the Indians enter the house where I was.

"The garret was separated from the room below only by a layer of single boards, at once the flooring of the one and the ceiling of the other. I could, therefore, hear every thing that passed; and the Indians no sooner came in than they inquired whether or not any Englishmen were in the house. M. Langlade replied, that 'he could not say, he did not know of any,' answers in which he did not exceed the truth; for the Pani woman had not only hidden me by stealth, but kept my secret and her own. M. Langlade was, therefore, as I presume, as far from a wish to destroy me as he was careless about saving me, when he added to these answers, that 'they might examine for themselves, and would soon be satisfied as to the object of their question.' Saying this, he brought them to the garret door.

"The state of my mind will be imagined. Arrived at the door, some delay was occasioned by the absence of the key; and a few moments were thus allowed me, in which to look around for a hiding-place. In one corner of the garret was a heap of those vessels of birch bark used in maple-sugar making.

"The door was unlocked and opening, and the Indians ascending the stairs, before I had completely crept into a small opening which presented itself at one end of the heap. An instant after, four Indians entered the room, all armed with tomahawks, and all besmeared with blood, upon every part of their bodies.

"The die appeared to be cast. I could scarcely breathe; but I thought the throbbing of my heart occasioned a noise loud enough to betray me. The Indians walked in every direction about the garret; and one of them approached me so closely, that, at a particular moment had he put forth his hand, he must have touched me. Still I remained undiscovered; a circumstance to which the dark color of my clothes, and the want of light, in a room which had no window in the corner in which I was, must have contributed. In a word, after taking several turns in the room, during which they told M. Langlade how many they had killed, and how many scalps they had taken, they returned downstairs; and I, with sensations not to be expressed, heard the door, which was the barrier between me and my fate, locked for the second time.

"There was a feather bed on the floor; and on this, exhausted as I was by the agitation of my mind, I threw myself down and fell asleep. In this state I remained till the dusk of the evening, when I was awakened by a second opening of the door. The person that now entered was M. Langlade's wife, who was much surprised at finding me, but advised me not to be uneasy, observing that the Indians had killed most of the English, but that she hoped I might myself escape. A shower of rain having begun to fall, she had come to stop a hole in the roof. On her going away, I begged her to send me a little water to drink, which she did.

"As night was now advancing, I continued to lie on the bed, ruminating on my condition, but unable to discover a resource from which I could hope for life. A flight to Detroit had no probable chance of success. The distance from Michillimackinac was four hundred miles; I was without provisions, and the whole length of the road lay through Indian countries, countries of an enemy in arms, where the first man whom I should meet would kill me. To stay where I was, threatened nearly the same issue. As before, fatigue of mind, and not tranquillity, suspended my cares, and procured me farther sleep.

"The respite which sleep afforded me during the night was put an end to by the return of morning. I was again on the rack of apprehension. At sunrise, I heard the family stirring; and, presently after, Indian voices, informing M. Langlade that they had not found my hapless self among the dead, and they supposed me to be somewhere concealed. M. Langlade appeared, from what followed, to be, by this time, acquainted with the place of my retreat; of which, no doubt, he had been informed by his wife. The poor woman, as soon as the Indians mentioned me, declared to her husband, in the French tongue, that he should no longer keep me in his house, but deliver me up to my pursuers; giving as a reason for this measure, that, should the Indians discover his instrumentality in my concealment, they might revenge it on her children, and that it was better that I should die than they. M. Langlade resisted, at first, this sentence of his wife, but soon suffered her to prevail, informing the Indians that he had been told I was in his house; that I had come there without his knowledge, and that he would put me into their hands. This was no sooner expressed than he began to ascend the stairs, the Indians following upon his heels.

"I now resigned myself to the fate with which I was menaced; and, regarding every effort at concealment as vain, I rose from the bed, and presented myself full in view to the Indians, who were entering the room. They were all in a state of intoxication, and entirely naked, except about the middle. One of them, named Wenniway, whom I had previously known, and who was upwards of six feet in height, had his entire face and body covered with charcoal and grease, only that a white spot, of two inches in diameter, encircled either eye. This man, walking up to me, seized me, with one hand, by the collar of the coat, while in the other he held a large carving-knife, as if to plunge it into my breast; his eyes, meanwhile, were fixed steadfastly on mine. At length, after some seconds of the most anxious suspense, he dropped his arm, saying, 'I won't kill you!' To this he added, that he had been frequently engaged in wars against the English, and had brought away many scalps; that, on a certain occasion, he had lost a brother, whose name was Musinigon, and that I should be called after him.

"A reprieve, upon any terms, placed me among the living, and gave me back the sustaining voice of hope; but Wenniway ordered me downstairs, and there informing me that I was to be taken to his cabin, where, and indeed everywhere else, the Indians were all mad with liquor, death again was threatened, and not as possible only, but as certain. I mentioned my fears on this subject to M. Langlade, begging him to represent the danger to my master. M. Langlade, in this instance, did not withhold his compassion; and Wenniway immediately consented that I should remain where I was, until he found another opportunity to take me away."

Scarcely, however, had he been gone an hour, when an Indian came to the house, and directed Henry to follow him to the Ojibwa camp. Henry knew this man, who was largely in his debt, and some time before, on the trader's asking him for payment, the Indian had declared, in a significant tone, that he would pay him soon. There seemed at present good ground to suspect his intention; but, having no choice, Henry was obliged to follow him. The Indian led the way out of the gate; but, instead of going towards the camp, he moved with a quick step in the direction of the bushes and sand-hills behind the fort. At this, Henry's suspicions were confirmed. He refused to proceed farther, and plainly told his conductor that he believed he meant to kill him. The Indian coolly replied that he was quite right in thinking so, and at the same time, seizing the prisoner by the arm, raised his knife to strike him in the breast. Henry parried the blow, flung the Indian from him, and ran for his life. He gained the gate of the fort, his enemy close at his heels, and, seeing Wenniway standing in the centre of the area, called upon him for protection. The chief ordered the Indian to desist; but the latter, who was foaming at the mouth with rage, still continued to pursue Henry, vainly striking at him with his knife. Seeing the door of Langlade's house wide open, the trader darted in, and at length found himself in safety. He retired once more to his garret, and lay down, feeling, as he declares, a sort of conviction that no Indian had power to harm him.

This confidence was somewhat shaken when, early in the night, he was startled from sleep by the opening of the door. A light gleamed in upon him, and he was summoned to descend. He did so, when, to his surprise and joy, he found, in the room below, Captain Etherington, Lieutenant Leslie, and Mr. Bostwick, a trader, together with Father Jonois, the Jesuit priest from L'Arbre Croche. The Indians were bent on enjoying that night a grand debauch upon the liquor they had seized; and the chiefs, well knowing the extreme danger to which the prisoners would be exposed during these revels, had conveyed them all into the fort, and placed them in charge of the Canadians.

Including officers, soldiers, and traders, they amounted to about twenty men, being nearly all who had escaped the massacre.

When Henry entered the room, he found his three companions in misfortune engaged in anxious debate. These men had supped full of horrors; yet they were almost on the point of risking a renewal of the bloodshed from which they had just escaped. The temptation was a strong one. The fort was this evening actually in the hands of the white men. The Indians, with their ordinary recklessness and improvidence, had neglected even to place a guard within the palisades. They were now, one and all, in their camp, mad with liquor, and the fort was occupied by twenty Englishmen, and about three hundred Canadians, principally voyageurs. To close the gates, and set the Indians at defiance, seemed no very difficult matter. It might have been attempted, but for the dissuasions of the Jesuit, who had acted throughout the part of a true friend of humanity, and who now strongly represented the probability that the Canadians would prove treacherous, and the certainty that a failure would involve destruction to every Englishman in the place. The idea was therefore abandoned, and Captain Etherington, with his companions, that night shared Henry's garret, where they passed the time in condoling with each other on their common misfortune.

A party of Indians came to the house in the morning, and ordered Henry to follow them out. The weather had changed, and a cold storm had set in. In the dreary and forlorn area of the fort were a few of the Indian conquerors, though the main body were still in their camp, not yet recovered from the effects of their last night's carouse. Henry's conductors led him to a house, where, in a room almost dark, he saw two traders and a soldier imprisoned. They were released, and directed to follow the party. The whole then proceeded together to the lake shore, where they were to embark for the Isles du Castor. A chilling wind blew strongly from the northeast, and the lake was covered with mists, and tossing angrily. Henry stood shivering on the beach, with no other upper garment than a shirt, drenched with the cold rain. He asked Langlade, who was near him, for a blanket, which the latter refused unless security were given for payment. Another Canadian proved more merciful, and Henry received a covering from the weather. With his three companions, guarded by seven Indians, he embarked in the canoe, the soldier being tied by his neck to one of the cross-bars of the vessel. The thick mists and the tempestuous weather compelled them to coast the shore, close beneath the wet dripping forests. In this manner they had proceeded about eighteen miles, and were approaching L'Arbre Croche, when an Ottawa Indian came out of the woods, and called to them from the beach, inquiring the news, and asking who were their prisoners. Some conversation followed, in the course of which the canoe approached the shore, where the water was very shallow. All at once, a loud yell was heard, and a hundred Ottawas, rising from among the trees and bushes, rushed into the water, and seized upon the canoe and prisoners. The astonished Ojibwas remonstrated in vain. The four Englishmen were taken from them, and led in safety to the shore. Good will to the prisoners, however, had by no means prompted the Ottawas to this very unexpected proceeding. They were jealous and angry that the Ojibwas should have taken the fort without giving them an opportunity to share in the plunder; and they now took this summary mode of asserting their rights.

The chiefs, however, shook Henry and his companions by the hand, professing great good will, assuring them, at the same time, that the Ojibwas were carrying them to the Isles du Castor merely to kill and eat them. The four prisoners, the sport of so many changing fortunes, soon found themselves embarked in an Ottawa canoe, and on their way back to Michillimackinac. They were not alone. A flotilla of canoes accompanied them, bearing a great number of Ottawa warriors; and before the day was over, the whole had arrived at the fort. At this time, the principal Ojibwa encampment was near the woods, in full sight of the landing-place. Its occupants, astonished at this singular movement on the part of their rivals, stood looking on in silent amazement, while the Ottawa warriors, well armed, filed into the fort, and took possession of it.

This conduct is not difficult to explain, when we take into consideration the peculiarities of the Indian character. Pride and jealousy are always strong and active elements in it. The Ottawas deemed themselves insulted because the Ojibwas had undertaken an enterprise of such importance without consulting them, or asking their assistance. It may be added, that the

Indians of L'Arbre Croche were somewhat less hostile to the English than the neighboring tribes; for the great influence of the priest Jonois seems always to have been exerted on the side of peace.

The English prisoners looked upon the new-comers as champions and protectors, and conceived hopes from their interference not destined to be fully realized. On the morning after their arrival, the Ojibwa chiefs invited the principal men of the Ottawas to hold a council with them, in a building within the fort. They placed upon the floor a valuable present of goods, which were part of the plunder they had taken; and their great war-chief, Minavavana, who had conducted the attack, rose and addressed the Ottawas.

Their conduct, he said, had greatly surprised him. They had betrayed the common cause, and opposed the will of the Great Spirit, who had decreed that every Englishman must die. Excepting them, all the Indians had raised the hatchet. Pontiac had taken Detroit, and every other fort had also been destroyed. The English were meeting with destruction throughout the whole world, and the King of France was awakened from his sleep. He exhorted them, in conclusion, no longer to espouse the cause of the English, but, like their brethren, to lift the hatchet against them.

When Minavavana had concluded his speech, the council adjourned until the next day; a custom common among Indians, in order that the auditors may have time to ponder with due deliberation upon what they have heard. At the next meeting, the Ottawas expressed a readiness to concur with the views of the Ojibwas. Thus the difference between the two tribes was at length amicably adjusted. The Ottawas returned to the Ojibwas some of the prisoners whom they had taken from them; still, however, retaining the officers and several of the soldiers. These they soon after carried to L'Arbre Croche, where they were treated with kindness, probably owing to the influence of Father Jonois.[1] The priest went down to Detroit with a letter from Captain Etherington, acquainting Major Gladwyn with the loss of Michillimackinac, and entreating

---

[1]MS. Letter—*Etherington to Gladwyn, June 28.*

that a force might be sent immediately to his aid. The letter, as we have seen, was safely delivered; but Gladwyn was, of course, unable to render the required assistance.

Though the Ottawas and Ojibwas had come to terms, they still looked on each other with distrust, and it is said that the former never forgot the slight that had been put upon them. The Ojibwas took the prisoners who had been returned to them from the fort, and carried them to one of their small villages, which stood near the shore, at no great distance to the south-east. Among the other lodges was a large one, of the kind often seen in Indian villages, erected for use on public occasions, such as dances, feasts, or councils. It was now to serve as a prison. The soldiers were bound together, two and two, and farther secured by long ropes tied round their necks, and fastened to the pole which supported the lodge in the centre. Henry and the other traders escaped this rigorous treatment. The spacious lodge was soon filled with Indians, who came to look at their captives, and gratify themselves by deriding and jeering at them. At the head of the lodge sat the great war-chief Minavavana, side by side with Henry's master, Wenniway. Things had remained for some time in this position, when Henry observed an Indian stooping to enter at the low aperture which served for a door, and, to his great joy, recognized his friend and brother, Wawatam, whom he had last seen on the day before the massacre. Wawatam said nothing; but, as he passed the trader, he shook him by the hand, in token of encouragement, and, proceeding to the head of the lodge, sat down with Wenniway and the war-chief. After he had smoked with them for a while in silence, he rose and went out again. Very soon he came back, followed by his squaw, who brought in her hands a valuable present, which she laid at the feet of the two chiefs. Wawatam then addressed them in the following speech:—

"Friends and relations, what is it that I shall say? You know what I feel. You all have friends, and brothers, and children, whom as yourselves you love; and you,—what would you experience, did you, like me, behold your dearest friend— your brother—in the condition of a slave; a slave, exposed every moment to insult, and to menaces of death? This case, as you all know, is mine. See there, [pointing to Henry,] my friend and brother among slaves,—himself a slave!

"You all well know that, long before the war began, I adopted him as my brother. From that moment he became one of my family, so that no change of circumstances could break the cord which fastened us together.

"He is my brother; and because I am your relation, he is therefore your relation too; and how, being your relation, can he be your slave?

"On the day on which the war began, you were fearful lest, on this very account, I should reveal your secret. You requested, therefore, that I would leave the fort, and even cross the lake. I did so; but I did it with reluctance. I did it with reluctance, notwithstanding that you, Minavavana, who had the command in this enterprise, gave me your promise that you would protect my friend, delivering him from all danger, and giving him safely to me.

"The performance of this promise I now claim. I come not with empty hands to ask it. You, Minavavana, best know whether or not, as it respects yourself, you have kept your word; but I bring these goods to buy off every claim which any man among you all may have on my brother as his prisoner."[1]

To this speech the war-chief returned a favorable answer. Wawatam's request was acceded to, the present was accepted, and the prisoner released. Henry soon found himself in the lodge of his friend, where furs were spread for him to lie upon, food and drink brought for his refreshment, and every thing done to promote his comfort that Indian hospitality could suggest. As he lay in the lodge, on the day after his release, he heard a loud noise from within the prison-house, which stood close at hand, and, looking through a crevice in the bark, he saw the dead bodies of seven soldiers dragged

---

[1]Henry, *Travels*, 102. The authenticity of this very interesting book has never been questioned. Henry was living at Montreal as late as the year 1809. In 1797 he, with others, claimed, in virtue of Indian grants, a large tract of land west of the River Cuyahoga, in the present State of Ohio. A letter from him is extant, dated in April of that year, in which he offers this land to the Connecticut Land Company, at one-sixth of a dollar an acre.

out. It appeared that a noted chief had just arrived from his wintering ground. Having come too late to take part in the grand achievement of his countrymen, he was anxious to manifest to all present his entire approval of what had been done, and with this design he had entered the lodge and despatched seven of the prisoners with his knife.

The Indians are not habitual cannibals. After a victory, however, it often happens that the bodies of their enemies are consumed at a formal war-feast—a superstitious rite, adapted, as they think, to increase their courage and hardihood. Such a feast took place on the present occasion, and most of the chiefs partook of it, though some of them, at least, did so with repugnance.

About a week had now elapsed since the massacre, and a revulsion of feeling began to take place among the Indians. Up to this time all had been triumph and exultation; but they now began to fear the consequences of their conduct. Indefinite and absurd rumors of an approaching attack from the English were afloat in the camp, and, in their growing uneasiness, they thought it expedient to shift their position to some point more capable of defence. Three hundred and fifty warriors, with their families and household effects, embarked in canoes for the Island of Michillimackinac, seven or eight miles distant. Wawatam, with his friend Henry, was of the number. Strong gusts of wind came from the north, and when the fleet of canoes was half way to the Island, it blew a gale, the waves pitching and tossing with such violence, that the frail and heavy-laden vessels were much endangered. Many voices were raised in prayer to the Great Spirit, and a dog was thrown into the lake, as a sacrifice to appease the angry manitou of the waters. The canoes weathered the storm, and soon drew near the island. Two squaws, in the same canoe with Henry, raised their voices in mournful wailing and lamentation. Late events had made him sensible to every impression of horror, and these dismal cries seemed ominous of some new disaster, until he learned that they were called forth by the recollection of dead relatives, whose graves were visible upon a neighboring point of the shore.

The Island of Michillimackinac, or Mackinaw, owing to its situation, its beauty, and the fish which the surrounding water supplied, had long been a favorite resort of Indians. It is about three miles wide. So clear are the waters of Lake Huron, which wash its shores, that one may count the pebbles at an incredible depth. The island is fenced round by white limestone cliffs, beautifully contrasting with the green foliage that half covers them, and in the centre the land rises in woody heights. The rock which forms its foundation assumes fantastic shapes—natural bridges, caverns, or sharp pinnacles, which at this day are pointed out as the curiosities of the region. In many of the caves have been found quantities of human bones, as if, at some period, the island had served as a grand depository for the dead; yet of these remains the present race of Indians can give no account. Legends and superstitions attached a mysterious celebrity to the place, and here, it was said, the fairies of Indian tradition might often be seen dancing upon the white rocks, or basking in the moonlight.[1]

The Indians landed at the margin of a little bay. Unlading their canoes, and lifting them high and dry upon the beach, they began to erect their lodges, and before night had completed the work. Messengers arrived on the next day from Pontiac, informing them that he was besieging Detroit, and urging them to come to his aid. But their warlike ardor had

---

[1]Tradition, preserved by Henry Conner. See also Schoolcraft, *Algic Researches*, II. 159.

"Their tradition concerning the name of this little island is curious. They say that Michapous, the chief of spirits, sojourned long in that vicinity. They believed that a mountain on the border of the lake was the place of his abode, and they called it by his name. It was here, say they, that he first instructed man to fabricate nets for taking fish, and where he has collected the greatest quantity of these finny inhabitants of the waters. On the island he left spirits, named Imakinakos; and from these aerial possessors it has received the appellation of Michillimakinac.

"When the savages, in those quarters, make a feast of fish, they invoke the spirits of the island, thank them for their bounty, and entreat them to continue their protection to their families. They demand of them to preserve their nets and canoes from the swelling and destructive billows, when the lakes are agitated by storms. All who assist in the ceremony lengthen their voices together, which is an act of gratitude. In the observance of this duty of their religion, they were formerly very punctual and scrupulous; but the French rallied them so much upon the subject, that they became ashamed to practise it openly."—Heriot, *Travels in Canada*, 185.

well-nigh died out. A senseless alarm prevailed among them, and they now thought more of securing their own safety than of injuring the enemy. A vigilant watch was kept up all day, and the unusual precaution taken of placing guards at night. Their fears, however, did not prevent them from seizing two English trading canoes, which had come from Montreal by way of the Ottawa. Among the booty found in them was a quantity of whiskey, and a general debauch was the immediate result. As night closed in, the dolorous chanting of drunken songs was heard from within the lodges, the prelude of a scene of riot; and Wawatam, knowing that his friend Henry's life would be in danger, privately led him out of the camp to a cavern in the hills, towards the interior of the island. Here the trader spent the night, in a solitude made doubly dreary by a sense of his forlorn and perilous situation. On waking in the morning, he found that he had been lying on human bones, which covered the floor of the cave. The place had anciently served as a charnel-house. Here he spent another solitary night, before his friend came to apprise him that he might return with safety to the camp.

Famine soon began among the Indians, who were sometimes without food for days together. No complaints were heard; but with faces blackened, in sign of sorrow, they patiently endured the privation with that resignation under inevitable suffering, which distinguishes the whole Indian race. They were at length compelled to cross over to the north shore of Lake Huron, where fish were more abundant; and here they remained until the end of summer, when they gradually dispersed, each family repairing to its winter hunting-grounds. Henry, painted and attired like an Indian, followed his friend Wawatam, and spent a lonely winter among the frozen forests, hunting the bear and moose for subsistence.[1]

---

[1] The following description of Minavavana, or the Grand Sauteur, who was the leader of the Ojibwas at the massacre of Michillimackinac, is drawn from Carver's *Travels*: —

"The first I accosted were Chipeways, inhabiting near the Ottowaw lakes; who received me with great cordiality, and shook me by the hand, in token of friendship. At some little distance behind these stood a chief remarkably tall and well made, but of so stern an aspect that the most undaunted person could not behold him without feeling some degree of terror. He seemed to

The posts of Green Bay and the Sault Ste. Marie did not share the fate of Michillimackinac. During the preceding winter, Ste. Marie had been partially destroyed by an accidental fire, and was therefore abandoned, the garrison withdrawing to Michillimackinac, where many of them perished in the massacre. The fort at Green Bay first received an English garrison in the year 1761, at the same time with the other posts of this region. The force consisted of seventeen men, of the 60th or Royal American regiment, commanded by Lieutenant Gorell. Though so few in number, their duties were of a very important character. In the neighborhood of Green Bay were numerous and powerful Indian tribes. The Menomonies lived at the mouth of Fox River, close to the fort. The Winnebagoes had several villages on the lake which bears their name, and the Sacs and Foxes were established on the River Wisconsin, in a large village composed of houses neatly built of logs and bark, and surrounded by fields of corn and vegetables.[1] West of the Mississippi was the powerful nation of the Dahcotah, whose strength was loosely estimated at thirty thousand fighting men, and who, in the excess of their haughtiness, styled the surrounding tribes their dogs and slaves.[2] The commandant of Green Bay was the representative of the British government, in communication with all these tribes. It devolved upon him to secure their friendship, and

---

have passed the meridian of life, and by the mode in which he was painted and tatowed, I discovered that he was of high rank. However, I approached him in a courteous manner, and expected to have met with the same reception I had done from the others; but, to my great surprise, he withheld his hand, and looking fiercely at me, said, in the Chipeway tongue, 'Cawin nishishin saganosh,' that is, 'The English are no good.' As he had his tomahawk in his hand, I expected that this laconick sentence would have been followed by a blow; to prevent which I drew a pistol from my belt, and, holding it in a careless position, passed close by him, to let him see I was not afraid of him. . . . Since I came to England, I have been informed, that the Grand Sautor, having rendered himself more and more disgustful to the English by his inveterate enmity towards them, was at length stabbed in his tent, as he encamped near Michillimackinac, by a trader."—Carver, 96.

[1] Carver, *Travels*, 47.

[2] Gorell, *Journal*, MS. The original manuscript is preserved in the library of the Maryland Historical Society, to which it was presented by Robert Gilmor, Esq.

keep them at peace; and he was also intrusted, in a great measure, with the power of regulating the fur-trade among them. In the course of each season, parties of Indians, from every quarter, would come to the fort, each expecting to be received with speeches and presents.

Gorell seems to have acquitted himself with great judgment and prudence. On first arriving at the fort, he had found its defences decayed and ruinous, the Canadian inhabitants unfriendly, and many of the Indians disposed to hostility. His good conduct contributed to allay their irritation, and he was particularly successful in conciliating his immediate neighbors, the Menomonies. They had taken an active part in the late war between France and England, and their spirits were humbled by the losses they had sustained, as well as by recent ravages of the small-pox. Gorell summoned them to a council, and delivered a speech, in which he avoided wounding their pride, but at the same time assumed a tone of firmness and decision, such as can alone command an Indian's respect. He told them that the King of England had heard of their ill conduct, but that he was ready to forget all that had passed. If, however, they should again give him cause of complaint, he would send an army, numerous as the trees of the forest, and utterly destroy them. Flattering expressions of confidence and esteem succeeded, and the whole was enforced by the distribution of a few presents. The Menomonies replied by assurances of friendship, more sincerely made and faithfully kept than could have been expected. As Indians of the other tribes came from time to time to the fort, they met with a similar reception; and, in his whole intercourse with them, the constant aim of the commandant was to gain their good will. The result was most happy for himself and his garrison.

On the fifteenth of June, 1763, an Ottawa Indian brought to Gorell the following letter from Captain Etherington: —

"Michillimackinac, June 11, 1763.
"Dear Sir:
"This place was taken by surprise, on the second instant, by the Chippeways, [Ojibwas,] at which time Lieutenant Jamet and twenty [fifteen] more were killed, and all the rest taken

prisoners; but our good friends, the Ottawas, have taken Lieutenant Lesley, me, and eleven men, out of their hands, and have promised to reinstate us again. You'll therefore, on the receipt of this, which I send by a canoe of Ottawas, set out with all your garrison, and what English traders you have with you, and come with the Indian who gives you this, who will conduct you safe to me. You must be sure to follow the instruction you receive from the bearer of this, as you are by no means to come to this post before you see me at the village, twenty miles from this. . . . I must once more beg you'll lose no time in coming to join me; at the same time, be very careful, and always be on your guard. I long much to see you, and am, dear sir,

    "Your most humble serv't.

       "GEO. ETHERINGTON.

 "J. GORELL,
"Royal Americans."

On receiving this letter, Gorell summoned the Menomonies to a council, told them what the Ojibwas had done, and said that he and his soldiers were going to Michillimackinac to restore order; adding, that during his absence he commended the fort to their care. Great numbers of the Winnebagoes and of the Sacs and Foxes afterwards arrived, and Gorell addressed them in nearly the same words. Presents were given them, and it soon appeared that the greater part were well disposed towards the English, though a few were inclined to prevent their departure, and even to threaten hostility. At this juncture, a fortunate incident occurred. A Dahcotah chief arrived with a message from his people to the following import: They had heard, he said, of the bad conduct of the Ojibwas. They hoped that the tribes of Green Bay would not follow their example, but, on the contrary, would protect the English garrison. Unless they did so, the Dahcotah would fall upon them, and take ample revenge. This auspicious interference must, no doubt, be ascribed to the hatred with which the Dahcotah had long regarded the Ojibwas. That the latter should espouse one side of the quarrel, was abundant reason to the Dahcotah for adopting the other.

Some of the Green Bay Indians were also at enmity with the Ojibwas, and all opposition to the departure of the English was now at an end. Indeed, some of the more friendly offered to escort the garrison on its way; and on the twenty-first of June, Gorell's party embarked in several bateaux, accompanied by ninety warriors in canoes. Approaching Isle du Castor, near the mouth of Green Bay, an alarm was given that the Ojibwas were lying there in ambush; on which the Menomonies raised the war-song, stripped themselves, and prepared to do battle in behalf of the English. The alarm, however, proved false; and, having crossed Lake Michigan in safety, the party arrived at the village of L'Arbre Croche on the thirtieth. The Ottawas came down to the beach, to salute them with a discharge of guns; and, on landing, they were presented with the pipe of peace. Captain Etherington and Lieutenant Leslie, with eleven men, were in the village, detained as prisoners, though treated with kindness. It was thought that the Ottawas intended to disarm the party of Gorell also; but the latter gave out that he would resist such an attempt, and his soldiers were permitted to retain their weapons.

Several succeeding days were occupied by the Indians in holding councils. Those from Green Bay requested the Ottawas to set their prisoners at liberty, and they at length assented. A difficulty still remained, as the Ojibwas had declared that they would prevent the English from passing down to Montreal. Their chiefs were therefore summoned; and being at this time, as we have seen, in a state of much alarm, they at length reluctantly yielded the point. On the eighteenth of July, the English, escorted by a fleet of Indian canoes, left L'Arbre Croche, and reaching, without interruption, the portage of the River Ottawa, descended to Montreal, where they all arrived in safety, on the thirteenth of August.[1] Except the garrison of Detroit, not a British soldier now remained in the region of the lakes.

[1]Gorell, *Journal*, MS.

END OF VOL. I.

CONSPIRACY OF PONTIAC

AND THE

INDIAN WAR

AFTER

THE CONQUEST OF CANADA

Vol. II.

Contents of Vol. II.

CHAPTER XVIII.
1763.
FRONTIER FORTS AND SETTLEMENTS.

Extent of British Settlements in 1763.—Forts and Military Routes.—Fort Pitt.—The Pennsylvania Frontier.—Alarms at Fort Pitt.—Escape of Calhoun.—Slaughter of Traders.—Fort Ligonier. Fort Bedford.—Situation of Fort Pitt.—Indian Advice.—Reply of Ecuyer.—News from Presqu' Isle.—Fate of Le Bœuf.—Fate of Venango.—Danger of Fort Pitt.—Council with the Delawares.—Threats of the Commandant.— General Attack 621

CHAPTER XIX.
1763.
THE WAR ON THE BORDERS.

Panic among the Settlers.—Embarrassments of Amherst.—Colonel Bouquet.—His Correspondence with the Commander-in-Chief.—Proposal to infect the hostile Indians with Small-pox.—Captain Ourry.—Lieutenant Blane.—Frontier War.—Alarm at Carlisle.—Scouting Parties.—Ambuscade on the Tuscarora.—The Dying Borderer.—Scenes at Carlisle 640

CHAPTER XX.
1763.
THE BATTLE OF BUSHY RUN.

The Army of Bouquet.—Dangers of his Enterprise.—Fort Ligonier relieved.—Bouquet at Fort Bedford.—March of his Troops.—Unexpected Attack.—The Night Encampment.—The Fight resumed.—Conflict of the second Day.—Successful Stratagem.—Rout of the Indians.—Bouquet reaches Fort Pitt.—Effects of the Victory 659

CHAPTER XXI.
1763.
THE IROQUOIS.—AMBUSCADE OF THE DEVIL'S HOLE.

Congress of Iroquois.—Effect of Johnson's Influence.—Incursions into New York.—False Alarm at Goshen.—The Niagara Portage.—The Convoy Attacked.—Second Attack.—Disaster on Lake Erie 671

CHAPTER XXII.
1763.
DESOLATION OF THE FRONTIERS.

Virginian Backwoodsmen. —Frontiers of Virginia. —Population of Penn-sylvania. —Distress of the Settlers. —Attack on Greenbrier. —A captive Amazon. —Attack on a School-house. —Sufferings of Captives. —The escaped Captive. —Feeble Measures of Defence. —John Elder. —Vir-ginian Militia. —Courage of the Borderers. —Encounter with a War-party. —Armstrong's Expedition. —Slaughter at Wyoming. —Quaker Prejudice. —Gage assumes the Command. —Political Disputes . . .677

CHAPTER XXIII.
1763.
THE INDIANS RAISE THE SIEGE OF DETROIT.

The Besiegers ask for Peace. —A Truce granted. —Letter from Neyon to Pontiac. —Autumn at Detroit. —Indians at their Wintering Grounds. —Iroquois War-parties. —The War in the South 695

CHAPTER XXIV.
1763.
THE PAXTON MEN.

Desperation of the Borderers. —Effects of Indian Hostilities. —The Con-estoga Band. —Paxton. —Matthew Smith and his Companions. — Massacre of the Conestogas. —Further Designs of the Rioters. — Remonstrance of Elder. —Massacre in Lancaster Jail. —State of Public Opinion. —Lazarus Stewart. —The Moravian Converts. —Their Re-treat to Philadelphia. —Their Reception by the Mob. 701

CHAPTER XXV.
1764.
THE RIOTERS MARCH ON PHILADELPHIA.

Excitement of the Borderers. —Their Designs. —Alarm of the Quakers. —The Converts sent to New York. —The Converts forced to Return. — Quakers and Presbyterians. —Warlike Preparation. —Excitement in the City. —False Alarm. —Paxton Men at Germantown. —Negotiations with the Rioters. —Frontiersmen in Philadelphia. —Paper Warfare. — Memorials of the Paxton Men 715

CHAPTER XXVI.

1764.

BRADSTREET'S ARMY ON THE LAKES.

Memorials on Indian Affairs. —Character of Bradstreet. —Departure of the Army. —Concourse of Indians at Niagara. —Indian Oracle. —Temper of the Indians. —Insolence of the Delawares and Shawanoes. —Treaty with the Senecas. —Ottawas and Menomonies. —Bradstreet leaves Niagara. —Henry's Indian Battalion. —Pretended Embassy. —Presumption of Bradstreet. —Indians of Sandusky. —Bradstreet at Detroit. —Council with the Chiefs of Detroit. —Terms of the Treaty. — Strange Conduct of Bradstreet. —Michillimackinac reoccupied. — Embassy of Morris. —Bradstreet at Sandusky. —Return of the Army. — Results of the Expedition 731

CHAPTER XXVII.

1764.

BOUQUET FORCES THE DELAWARES AND SHAWANOES TO SUE FOR PEACE.

Renewal of Indian Ravages. —David Owens, the White Savage. —Advance of Bouquet. —His Message to the Delawares. —The March of his Army. —He reaches the Muskingum. —Terror of the Enemy. —Council with the Indians. —Speech of the Delaware Orator. —Reply of Bouquet. —Its Effect. —The English Camp. —Letter from Bradstreet. — Desperate Purpose of the Shawanoes. —Peace Council. —Delivery of English Prisoners. —Situation of Captives among the Indians. —Their Reluctance to return to the Settlements. —The Forest Life. —Return of the Expedition .762

CHAPTER XXVIII.

1764.

THE ILLINOIS.

Boundaries of the Illinois. —The Missouri. The Mississippi. —Plants and Animals of the Illinois. —Its early Colonization. —Creoles of the Illinois. —Its Indian Population 796

CHAPTER XXIX.

1763–1765.

PONTIAC RALLIES THE WESTERN TRIBES.

Cession of French Territory in the West. —St. Louis. —St. Ange de Bellerive. —Designs of Pontiac. —His French Allies. —He visits the

Illinois.—His great War-belt.—Repulse of Loftus.—The English on the Mississippi.—New Orleans in 1765.—Pontiac's Embassy at New Orleans. .806

CHAPTER XXX.
1765.
RUIN OF THE INDIAN CAUSE.

Mission of Croghan.—Plunder of the Caravan.—Exploits of the Borderers.—Congress at Fort Pitt.—Fraser's Discomfiture.—Distress of the hostile Indians.—Pontiac. His desperate Position.—Croghan's Party attacked.—Croghan at Ouatanon.—His Meeting with Pontiac.—Pontiac offers Peace.—Croghan reaches Detroit.—Conferences at Detroit.— Peace Speech of Pontiac.—Results of Croghan's Mission.—The English take Possession of the Illinois 819

CHAPTER XXXI.
1766—1769
DEATH OF PONTIAC.

Effects of the Peace.—Pontiac repairs to Oswego.—Congress at Oswego.—Speech of Sir William Johnson.—Reply of Pontiac.—Prospects of the Indian Race.—Fresh Disturbances.—Pontiac visits St. Louis.—The Village of Cahokia.—Assassination of Pontiac.—Vengeance of his Followers .836

APPENDIX.

A.—THE IROQUOIS.—EXTENT OF THEIR CONQUESTS.—POLICY PURSUED TOWARDS THEM BY THE FRENCH AND THE ENGLISH. —MEASURES OF SIR WILLIAM JOHNSON.

1. Territory of the Iroquois 847
2. French and English Policy towards the Iroquois. Measures of Sir William Johnson. 848

B.—CAUSES OF THE INDIAN WAR.

1. Views of Sir William Johnson 851
2. Tragedy of Ponteach 853

C.—DETROIT AND MICHILLIMACKINAC.

1. The Siege of Detroit 860
2. Massacre of Michillimackinac 868

D.—The War on the Borders.

The Battle of Bushy Run 871

E.—The Paxton Riots.

1. Evidence against the Indians of Conestoga 875
2. Proceedings of the Rioters 876
3. Memorials of the Paxton Men 887

F.—The Campaign of 1764.

1. Bouquet's Expedition 895
2. Condition and Temper of the Western Indians. 897

Index 901

Chapter XVIII.

1763.

FRONTIER FORTS AND SETTLEMENTS.

WE HAVE FOLLOWED the war to its farthest confines, and watched it in its remotest operations; not because there is any thing especially worthy to be chronicled in the capture of a backwoods fort, and the slaughter of a few soldiers, but because these acts exhibit some of the characteristic traits of the actors. It was along the line of the British frontier that the war raged with its most destructive violence. To destroy the garrisons, and then turn upon the settlements, had been the original plan of the Indians; and while Pontiac was pushing the siege of Detroit, and the smaller interior posts were treacherously assailed, the tempest was gathering which was soon to burst along the whole frontier.

In 1763, the British settlements did not extend beyond the Alleghanies. In the province of New York, they reached no farther than the German Flats, on the Mohawk. In Pennsylvania, the town of Bedford might be regarded as the extreme verge of the frontier, while the settlements of Virginia extended to a corresponding distance. Through the adjacent wilderness ran various lines of military posts, to make good the communication from point to point. One of the most important among these passed through the country of the Six Nations, and guarded the route between the northern colonies and Lake Ontario. This communication was formed by the Hudson, the Mohawk, Wood Creek, the Oneida Lake, and the River Oswego. It was defended by Forts Stanwix, Brewerton, Oswego, and two or three smaller posts. Near the western extremity of Lake Ontario stood Fort Niagara, at the mouth of the river whence it derived its name. It was a strong and extensive work, guarding the access to the whole interior country, both by way of the Oswego communication just mentioned, and by that of Canada and the St. Lawrence. From Fort Niagara the route lay by a portage beside the great falls to Presqu' Isle, on Lake Erie, where the town of Erie now stands. Thence the traveller could pass, by a short overland passage, to Fort Le Bœuf, on a branch of the Alleghany; thence, by water, to Venango; and thence, down the Alleghany, to Fort Pitt. This last-mentioned post stood on the present site of Pittsburg—the point of land formed by the confluence of the Alleghany and the Monongahela. Its position was as captivating to the eye of an artist as it was commanding in a military point of view. On the left, the Monongahela descended through a woody valley of singular beauty; on the right, flowed the Alleghany, beneath steep and lofty banks; and both united, in front, to form the broad Ohio, which, flanked by picturesque hills and declivities, began at this point its progress towards the Mississippi. The place already had its historic associations, though, as yet, their roughness was unmellowed by the lapse of time. It was here that the French had erected Fort du Quesne. Within a few miles, Braddock encountered his disastrous overthrow; and on the hill behind the fort, Grant's Highlanders and Lewis's Virginians had been surrounded and captured, though not without a stout resistance on the part of the latter.

Fort Pitt was built by General Stanwix, in the year 1759, upon the ruins of Fort du Quesne, destroyed by General Forbes. It was a strong fortification, with ramparts of earth, faced with brick on the side looking down the Ohio. Its walls have long since been levelled to the ground, and over their ruins have risen warehouses, and forges with countless chimneys, rolling up their black volumes of smoke. Where once the bark canoe lay on the strand, a throng of steamers now lie moored along the crowded levee.

Fort Pitt stood far aloof in the forest, and one might journey eastward full two hundred miles, before the English settlements began to thicken. Behind it lay a broken and woody tract; then succeeded the great barrier of the Alleghanies, traversing the country in successive ridges; and beyond these lay vast woods, extending to the Susquehanna. Eastward of this river, cabins of settlers became more numerous, until, in the neighborhood of Lancaster, the country assumed an appearance of prosperity and cultivation. Two roads led from Fort Pitt to the settlements, one of which was cut by General Braddock in his disastrous march across the mountains, from Cumberland, in the year 1755. The other, which was the more frequented, passed by Carlisle and Bedford, and was made by General Forbes, in 1758. Leaving the fort by this latter route, the traveller would find himself, after a journey of fifty-six miles, at the little post of Ligonier, whence he would soon reach Fort Bedford, about a hundred miles from Fort Pitt. It was nestled among mountains, and surrounded by clearings and log cabins. Passing several small posts and settlements, he would arrive at Carlisle, nearly a hundred miles farther east, a place resembling Bedford in its general aspect, although of greater extent. After leaving Fort Bedford, numerous houses of settlers were scattered here and there among the valleys, on each side of the road from Fort Pitt, so that the number of families beyond the Susquehanna amounted to several hundreds, thinly distributed over a great space.[1] From Carlisle to Harris's Ferry, now Harrisburg, on the Susquehanna, was but a short distance; and from thence, the road led directly into the heart of the settlements. The frontiers of Virginia bore a general resemblance to those of Pennsylvania. It is not necessary at present to indicate minutely the position of their scattered settlements, and the small posts intended to protect them.[2] Along these borders all had remained quiet, and nothing occurred to excite alarm or uneasiness. Captain Simeon Ecuyer, a brave Swiss officer, who commanded at Fort Pitt, had indeed received warnings of danger. On the fourth of May, he wrote to Colonel Bouquet at Philadelphia: "Major Gladwyn writes to tell me that I am surrounded by rascals. He complains a great deal of the Delawares and Shawanoes. It is this *canaille* who stir up the rest to mischief." At length, on the twenty-seventh, at about dusk in the evening, a party of Indians was seen descending the banks of the Alleghany, with laden pack-horses. They built fires, and encamped on the shore till daybreak, when they all crossed over to the fort, bringing with them a great quantity of valuable furs. These they sold to the traders, demanding, in exchange, bullets,

---

[1] There was a cluster of log houses even around Fort Ligonier, and a trader named Byerly had a station at Bushy Run.

[2] The authorities for the foregoing topographical sketch are drawn from the Pennsylvania *Historical Collections*, and the *Olden Time*, an excellent antiquarian work, published at Pittsburg; together with various maps, plans, and contemporary papers.

hatchets, and gunpowder; but their conduct was so peculiar as to excite the just suspicion that they came either as spies or with some other insidious design.[1] Hardly were they gone, when tidings came in that Colonel Clapham, with several persons, both men and women, had been murdered and scalped near the fort; and it was soon after discovered that the inhabitants of an Indian town, a few miles up the Alleghany, had totally abandoned their cabins, as if bent on some plan of mischief. On the next day, two soldiers were shot within a mile of the fort. An express was hastily sent to Venango, to warn the little garrison of danger; but he returned almost immediately, having been twice fired at, and severely wounded.[2] A trader named Calhoun now came in from the Indian village of Tuscaroras, with intelligence of a yet more startling kind. At eleven o'clock on the night of the twenty-seventh, a chief named Shingas, with several of the principal warriors in the place, had come to Calhoun's cabin, and earnestly begged him to depart, declaring that they did not wish to see him killed before their eyes. The Ottawas and Ojibwas, they said, had

[1] Gordon, *Hist. Pa.* 622. MS. Letter—*Ecuyer to Bouquet*, 29 May, 1763.
[2] MS. Letter—*Bouquet to Amherst*, June 5.
Extract from a letter—*Fort Pitt, May 31* (*Penn. Gaz.* No. 1798).
"We have most melancholy Accounts here—The Indians have broke out in several Places, and murdered Colonel Clapham and his Family; also two of our Soldiers at the Saw-mill, near the Fort, and two Scalps are taken from each man. An Indian has brought a War-Belt to Tuscarora, and says Detroit is invested; and that St. Dusky is cut off, and Ensign Pawley made Prisoner—Levy's Goods are stopt at Tuscarora by the Indians—Last Night Eleven men were attacked at Beaver Creek, eight or nine of whom, it is said, were killed—And Twenty-five of Macrae's and Alison's Horses, loaded with Skins, are all taken."

Extract from a MS. Letter—*Ecuyer to Bouquet*.
"Fort Pitt, 29th May, 1763.
"Just as I had finished my Letter, Three men came in from Clapham's, with the Melancholy News, that Yesterday, at three O'clock in the Afternoon, the Indians Murdered Clapham, and Every Body in his House: These three men were out at work, & Escaped through the Woods. I Immediately Armed them, and sent them to Assist our People at Bushy Run. The Indians have told Byerly (at Bushy Run) to Leave his Place in Four Days, or he and his Family would all be murdered: I am Uneasy for the little Posts—As for this, I will answer for it."
The above is a contemporary translation. The original, which is before me, is in French, like all Ecuyer's letters to Bouquet.

taken up the hatchet, and captured Detroit, Sandusky, and all
the forts of the interior. The Delawares and Shawanoes of the
Ohio were following their example, and were murdering all
the traders among them. Calhoun and the thirteen men in his
employ lost no time in taking their departure. The Indians
forced them to leave their guns behind, promising that they
would give them three warriors to guide them in safety to
Fort Pitt; but the whole proved a piece of characteristic dissimulation and treachery. The three guides led them into an
ambuscade at the mouth of Beaver Creek. A volley of balls
showered upon them; eleven were killed on the spot, and Calhoun and two others alone made their escape.[1] "I see," writes
Ecuyer to his colonel, "that the affair is general. I tremble for
our outposts. I believe, from what I hear, that I am surrounded by Indians. I neglect nothing to give them a good
reception; and I expect to be attacked to-morrow morning.
Please God I may be. I am passably well prepared. Everybody
is at work, and I do not sleep; but I tremble lest my messenger should be cut off."

The intelligence concerning the fate of the traders in the
Indian villages proved but too true. They were slaughtered
everywhere, without mercy, and often under circumstances of
the foulest barbarity. A boy named M'Cullough, captured
during the French war, and at this time a prisoner among the
Indians, relates, in his published narrative, that he, with a
party of Indian children, went out, one evening, to gaze with
awe and wonder at the body of a trader, which lay by the side
of the path, mangled with tomahawks, and stuck full of
arrows.[2] It was stated in the journals of the day, that more
than a hundred traders fell victims, and that the property

[1] *Copy of intelligence brought to Fort Pitt by Mr. Calhoun*, MS.

[2] M'Cullough gives the following account of the murder of another of the
traders, named Green:—

"About sunrise, *Mussoughwhese* (an Indian, my adopted brother's nephew,
known by the name of Ben Dickson, among the white people), came to our
house; he had a pistol and a large scalping-knife, concealed under his blanket,
belted round his body. He informed *Kettoohhalend* (for that was my adopted
brother's name), that he came to kill Tom Green; but *Kettoohhalend* endeav-
oured to persuade him off it. They walked out together, and Green followed
them, endeavouring, as I suppose, to discover the cause of the alarm the
night before; in a short time they returned to the house, and immediately

taken from them, or seized at the capture of the interior posts, amounted to an incredible sum.[1]

The Moravian Loskiel relates that in the villages of the Hurons or Wyandots, meaning probably those of Sandusky, the traders were so numerous that the Indians were afraid to attack them openly, and had recourse to the following stratagem: They told their unsuspecting victims that the surrounding tribes had risen in arms, and were soon coming that way, bent on killing every Englishman they could find. The Wyandots averred that they would gladly protect their friends, the white men; but that it would be impossible to do so, unless the latter would consent, for the sake of appearances, to become their prisoners. In this case, they said, the hostile Indians would refrain from injuring them, and they should be set at liberty as soon as the danger was past. The traders fell into the snare. They gave up their arms, and, the better to carry out the deception, even consented to be

---

went out again. Green asked me to bring him his horse, as we heard the bell a short distance off; he then went after the Indians again, and I went for the horse. As I was returning, I observed them coming out of a house about two hundred yards from ours; *Kettoohhalend* was foremost, Green in the middle; I took but slight notice of them, until I heard the report of a pistol; I cast my eyes towards them, and observed the smoke, and saw Green standing on the side of the path, with his hands across his breast; I thought it had been him that shot; he stood a few minutes, then fell on his face across the path. I instantly got off the horse, and held him by the bridle,—*Kettoohhalend* sunk his pipe tomahawk into his skull; *Mussoughwhese* stabbed him under the arm-pit with his scalping-knife; he had shot him between the shoulders with his pistol. The squaws gathered about him and stripped him naked, trailed him down the bank, and plunged him into the creek; there was a freshet in the creek at the time, which carried him off. *Mussoughwhese* then came to me (where I was holding the horse, as I had not moved from the spot where I was when Green was shot), with the bloody knife in his hand; he told me that he was coming to kill me next; he reached out his hand and took hold of the bridle, telling me that that was his horse; I was glad to parley with him on the terms, and delivered the horse to him. All the Indians in the town immediately collected together, and started off to the Salt Licks, where the rest of the traders were, and murdered the whole of them, and divided their goods amongst them, and likewise their horses."

[1] *Gent. Mag.* XXXIII. 413. The loss is here stated at the greatly exaggerated amount of £500,000.

bound; but no sooner was this accomplished, than their treacherous counsellors murdered them all in cold blood.[1]

A curious incident, relating to this period, is given by the missionary Heckewelder. Strange as the story may appear, it is in strict accordance with Indian character and usage, and perhaps need not be rejected as wholly void of truth. The name of the person, to whom it relates, several times occurs in the manuscript journals and correspondence of officers in the Indian country. A trader named Chapman was made prisoner by the Indians near Detroit. For some time, he was protected by the humane interference of a Frenchman; but at length his captors resolved to burn him alive. He was tied to the stake, and the fire was kindled. As the heat grew intolerable, one of the Indians handed to him a bowl filled with broth. The wretched man, scorching with fiery thirst, eagerly snatched the vessel, and applied it to his lips; but the liquid was purposely made scalding hot. With a sudden burst of rage, he flung back the bowl and its contents into the face of the Indian. "He is mad! he is mad!" shouted the crowd; and though, the moment before, they had been keenly anticipating the delight of seeing him burn, they hastily put out the fire, released him from the stake, and set him at liberty.[2] Such is the superstitious respect which the Indians entertain for every form of insanity.

While the alarming incidents just mentioned were occurring at Fort Pitt, the garrison of Fort Ligonier received yet more unequivocal tokens of hostility; for one morning a volley of bullets was sent among them, with no other effect, however, than killing a few horses. In the vicinity of Fort Bedford, several men were killed; on which the inhabitants were mustered and organized, and the garrison kept constantly on the alert. A few of the best woodsmen were formed into a company, dressed and painted like Indians. A party of the enemy suddenly appeared, whooping and brandishing their tomahawks, at the skirts of the forest; on which these counterfeit savages dashed upon them at full gallop,

[1] Loskiel, 99.
[2] Heckewelder, *Hist. Ind. Nat.* 250.

routing them in an instant, and driving them far through the woods.[1]

At Fort Pitt every preparation was made for an attack. The houses and cabins outside the rampart were levelled to the ground, and every morning, at an hour before dawn, the drum beat, and the troops were ordered to their alarm posts.[2] The garrison consisted of three hundred and thirty soldiers, traders, and backwoodsmen; and there were also in the fort about one hundred women, and a still greater number of children, most of them belonging to the families of settlers who were preparing to build their cabins in the neighborhood.[3] "We are so crowded in the fort," writes Ecuyer to Colonel Bouquet, "that I fear disease; for, in spite of every care, I cannot keep the place as clean as I should like. Besides, the small-pox is among us; and I have therefore caused a hospital to be built under the drawbridge, out of range of musket-shot. . . . I am determined to hold my post, spare my men, and never expose them without necessity. This, I think, is what you require of me."[4] The desultory outrages with which the war began, and which only served to put the garrison on their guard, prove that among the neighboring Indians there was no chief of sufficient power to curb their wayward temper, and force them to conform to any preconcerted plan. The authors of the mischief were unruly young warriors, fevered with eagerness to win the first scalp, and setting at defiance

[1]*Pennsylvania Gazette*, No. 1799. I shall frequently refer to the columns of this journal, which are filled with letters, and extracts from letters, written at different parts of the frontier, and containing very minute and authentic details of the events which daily occurred.

[2]Extract from a Letter—*Fort Pitt*, June 16, 1763 (*Penn. Gaz*. No. 1801).

"We have Alarms from, and Skirmishes with, the Indians every Day; but they have done us little Harm as yet. Yesterday I was out with a Party of Men, when we were fired upon, and one of the Serjeants was killed; but we beat off the Indians, and brought the Man in with his Scalp on. Last Night the Bullock Guard was fired upon, when one Cow was killed. We are obliged to be on Duty Night and Day. The Indians have cut off above 100 of our Traders in the Woods, besides all our little Posts. We have Plenty of Provisions; and the Fort is in such a good Posture of Defence, that, with God's Assistance, we can defend it against 1000 Indians."

[3]MS. Letter—*Ecuyer to Bouquet*, June 5. *Ibid*. June 26.

[4]MS. Letter—*Ecuyer to Bouquet*, June 16 (Translation).

the authority of their elders. These petty annoyances, far from abating, continued for many successive days, and kept the garrison in a state of restless alarm. It was dangerous to venture outside the walls, and a few who attempted it were shot and scalped by lurking Indians. "They have the impudence," writes an officer, "to fire all night at our sentinels;" nor were these attacks confined to the night, for even during the day no man willingly exposed his head above the rampart. The surrounding woods were known to be full of prowling Indians, whose number seemed daily increasing, though as yet they had made no attempt at a general attack. At length, on the afternoon of the twenty-second of June, a party of them appeared at the farthest extremity of the cleared lands behind the fort, driving off the horses which were grazing there, and killing the cattle. No sooner was this accomplished than a general fire was opened upon the fort from every side at once, though at so great a distance that only two men were killed. The garrison replied by a discharge of howitzers, the shells of which, bursting in the midst of the Indians, greatly amazed and disconcerted them. As it grew dark, their fire slackened, though, throughout the night, the flash of guns was seen at frequent intervals, followed by the whooping of the invisible assailants.

At nine o'clock on the following morning, several Indians approached the fort with the utmost confidence, and took their stand at the outer edge of the ditch, where one of them, a Delaware, named the Turtle's Heart, addressed the garrison as follows:—

"My Brothers, we that stand here are your friends; but we have bad news to tell you. Six great nations of Indians have taken up the hatchet, and cut off all the English garrisons, excepting yours. They are now on their way to destroy you also.

"My Brothers, we are your friends, and we wish to save your lives. What we desire you to do is this: You must leave this fort, with all your women and children, and go down to the English settlements, where you will be safe. There are many bad Indians already here; but we will protect you from them. You must go at once, because if you wait till the six great nations arrive here, you will all be killed, and we can do nothing to protect you."

To this proposal, by which the Indians hoped to gain a safe and easy possession of the fort, Captain Ecuyer made the following reply. The vein of humor perceptible in it may serve to indicate that he was under no great apprehension for the safety of his garrison: —

"My Brothers, we are very grateful for your kindness, though we are convinced that you must be mistaken in what you have told us about the forts being captured. As for ourselves, we have plenty of provisions, and are able to keep the fort against all the nations of Indians that may dare to attack it. We are very well off in this place, and we mean to stay here.

"My Brothers, as you have shown yourselves such true friends, we feel bound in gratitude to inform you that an army of six thousand English will shortly arrive here, and that another army of three thousand is gone up the lakes, to punish the Ottawas and Ojibwas. A third has gone to the frontiers of Virginia, where they will be joined by your enemies, the Cherokees and Catawbas, who are coming here to destroy you. Therefore take pity on your women and children, and get out of the way as soon as possible. We have told you this in confidence, out of our great solicitude lest any of you should be hurt; and we hope that you will not tell the other Indians, lest they should escape from our vengeance."[1]

This politic invention of the three armies had an excellent effect, and so startled the Indians, that, on the next day, most of them withdrew from the neighborhood, and went to meet a great body of warriors, who were advancing from the westward to attack the fort. On the afternoon of the twenty-sixth, a soldier named Gray, belonging to the garrison of Presqu' Isle, came in with the report that, more than a week before, that little post had been furiously attacked by upwards of two hundred Indians from Detroit, that they had assailed it for three days, repeatedly setting it on fire, and had at length undermined it so completely, that the garrison was forced to capitulate, on condition of being allowed to retire in safety to

[1] MS. *Report of Alexander M'Kee, deputy agent for Indian affairs at Fort Pitt.*

Fort Pitt. No sooner, however, had they left their shelter, than the Indians fell upon them, and, as Gray declared, butchered them all, except himself and one other man, who darted into the woods, and escaped amid the confusion, hearing behind them, as they fled, the screams of their murdered comrades. This account proved erroneous, as the garrison were carried by their captors in safety to Detroit. Some time after this event, Captain Dalzell's detachment, on their way to Detroit, stopped at the place, and found, close to the ruined fort, the hair of several of the men, which had been shorn off, as a preliminary step in the process of painting and bedecking them like Indian warriors. From this it appears that some of the unfortunate soldiers were adopted on the spot into the tribes of their conquerors. In a previous chapter, a detailed account has been given of the defence of Presqu' Isle, and its capture.

Gray informed Captain Ecuyer that, a few days before the attack on the garrison, they had seen a schooner on the lake, approaching from the westward. She had sent a boat to shore with the tidings that Detroit had been beleaguered, for more than six weeks, by many hundred Indians, and that a detachment of ninety-six men had been attacked near that place, of whom only about thirty had escaped, the rest being either killed on the spot or put to death by slow torture. The panic-stricken soldier, in his flight from Presqu' Isle, had passed the spots where lately had stood the little forts of Le Bœuf and Venango. Both were burnt to the ground, and he surmised that the whole of their wretched garrisons had fallen victims.[1] The disaster proved less fatal than his fears led him to suspect; for, on the same day on which he arrived, Ensign Price, the officer commanding at Le Bœuf, was seen approaching along the bank of the Alleghany, followed by seven haggard and half-famished soldiers.[2] He and his men told the following story:—

[1] MS. Letter—*Ecuyer to Bouquet*, June 26.

[2] Extract from a Letter—*Fort Pitt*, June 26 (*Penn. Gaz.* No. 1802).

"This Morning, Ensign Price, of the Royal Americans, with Part of his Garrison, arrived here, being separated from the rest in the night.—The Enemy attacked his Post, and set it on Fire, and while they watched the Door of

The available defences of Fort Le Bœuf consisted, at the time, of a single ill-constructed blockhouse, occupied by the ensign, with two corporals and eleven privates. They had only about twenty rounds of ammunition each; and the powder, moreover, was in a damaged condition. At nine or ten o'clock, on the morning of the eighteenth of June, a soldier told Price that he saw Indians approaching from the direction of Presqu' Isle. Price ran to the door, and, looking out, saw one of his men, apparently much frightened, shaking hands with five Indians. He held open the door till the man had entered, the five Indians following close, after having, in obedience to a sign from Price, left their weapons behind. They declared that they were going to fight the Cherokees, and begged for powder and ball. This being refused, they asked leave to sleep on the ground before the blockhouse. Price assented, on which one of them went off, but very soon returned with thirty more, who crowded before the window of the blockhouse, and begged for a kettle to cook their food. Price tried to give them one through the window, but the aperture proved too narrow, and they grew clamorous that he should open the door again. This he refused. They then went to a neighboring storehouse, pulled out some of the founda-

---

the House, he got out on the other side, and the Indians continued firing a long Time afterwards, imagining that the Garrison was in it, and that they were consumed with the House.—He touched at Venango, found the Fort burnt to the Ground, and saw one of our Expresses lying killed on the Road.

"Four o'clock in the Afternoon. Just now came in one of the Soldiers from Presque Isle, who says, Mr. Christie fought two Days; that the Enemy Fifty times set Fire to the Blockhouse, but that they as often put it out: That they then undermined the House, and was ready to blow it up, when they offered Mr. Christie Terms, who accepted them, viz., That he, and his Garrison, was to be conducted to this Place.—The Soldier also says, he suspected they intended to put them all to Death; and that on hearing a Woman scream out, he supposed they were murdering her; upon which he and another Soldier came immediately off, but knows nothing of the rest: That the Vessel from Niagara was in Sight, but believes she had no Provisions, as the Indian told them they had cut off Little Niagara, and destroyed 800 Barrels: And that he thinks, by what he saw, Venango had capitulated."

The soldier here spoken of was no doubt Gray, who was mentioned above, though his story is somewhat differently given in the letter of Captain Ecuyer, just cited.

tion stones, and got into the cellar; whence, by knocking away one or two planks immediately above the sill of the building, they could fire on the garrison in perfect safety, being below the range of shot from the loopholes of the blockhouse, which was not ten yards distant. Here they remained some hours, making their preparations, while the garrison waited in suspense, cooped up in their wooden citadel. Towards evening, they opened fire, and shot such a number of burning arrows against the side and roof of the blockhouse, that three times it was in flames. But the men worked desperately, and each time the fire was extinguished. A fourth time the alarm was given; and now the men on the roof came down in despair, crying out that they could not extinguish it, and calling on their officer for God's sake to let them leave the building, or they should all be burnt alive. Price behaved with great spirit. "We must fight as long as we can, and then die together," was his answer to the entreaties of his disheartened men.[1] But he could not revive their drooping courage, and meanwhile the fire spread beyond all hope of mastering it. They implored him to let them go, and at length the brave young officer told them to save themselves if they could. It was time, for they were suffocating in their burning prison. There was a narrow window in the back of the blockhouse, through which, with the help of axes, they all got out; and, favored by the darkness,—for night had closed in,—escaped to the neighboring pine-swamp, while the Indians, to make assurance doubly sure, were still showering fire-arrows against the front of the blazing building. As the fugitives groped their way, in pitchy darkness, through the tangled intricacies of the swamp, they saw the sky behind them lurid with flames, and heard the reports of the Indians' guns, as these painted demons were leaping and yelling in front of the flaming blockhouse, firing into the loopholes, and exulting in the thought that their enemies were suffering the agonies of death within.

Presqu' Isle was but fifteen miles distant; but, from the direction in which his assailants had come, Price rightly judged

---

[1] *Record of Court of Inquiry, Evidence of Corporal Fisher*. The statement is supported by all the rest of the men examined.

that it had been captured, and therefore resolved to make
his way, if possible, to Venango, and reinforce Lieutenant
Gordon, who commanded there. A soldier named John Dortinger, who had been sixteen months at Le Bœuf, thought
that he could guide the party, but lost the way in the darkness; so that, after struggling all night through swamps and
forests, they found themselves at daybreak only two miles
from their point of departure. Just before dawn, several of the
men became separated from the rest. Price and those with
him waited for some time, whistling, coughing, and making
such other signals as they dared, to attract their attention, but
without success, and they were forced to proceed without
them. Their only provisions were three biscuits to a man.
They pushed on all day, and reached Venango at one o'clock
of the following night. Nothing remained but piles of smouldering embers, among which lay the half-burned bodies of its
hapless garrison. They now continued their journey down the
Alleghany. On the third night their last biscuit was consumed, and they were half dead with hunger and exhaustion
before their eyes were gladdened at length by the friendly
walls of Fort Pitt. Of those who had straggled from the party,
all eventually appeared but two, who, spent with starvation,
had been left behind, and no doubt perished.[1]

Not a man remained alive to tell the fate of Venango. An
Indian, who was present at its destruction, long afterwards
described the scene to Sir William Johnson. A large body of
Senecas gained entrance under pretence of friendship, then
closed the gates, fell upon the garrison, and butchered them
all except the commanding officer, Lieutenant Gordon, whom
they forced to write, from their dictation, a statement of the

---

[1]On the 27th of June, Price wrote to Colonel Bouquet from Fort Pitt,
announcing his escape; and again on the 28th, giving an account of the affair.
Both letters are before me; but the most satisfactory evidence is furnished by
the record of the court of inquiry held at Fort Pitt on the 12th of September,
to ascertain the circumstances of the loss of Presqu' Isle and Le Bœuf. This
embraces the testimony of most of the survivors; namely, Ensign George
Price, Corporals Jacob Fisher and John Nash, and privates John Dogood,
John Nigley, John Dortinger, and Uriah Trunk. All the men bear witness to
the resolution of their officer. One of them declared that it was with the
utmost difficulty that they could persuade him to leave the blockhouse with
them.

grievances which had driven them to arms, and then tortured over a slow fire for several successive nights, till he expired. This done, they burned the place to the ground, and departed.[1]

While Le Bœuf and Venango were thus assailed, Fort Ligonier was also attacked by a large body of Indians, who fired upon it with great fury and pertinacity, but were beaten off after a hard day's fighting. Fort Augusta, on the Susquehanna, was at the same time menaced; but the garrison being strengthened by a timely re-enforcement, the Indians abandoned their purpose. Carlisle, Bedford, and the small intermediate posts, all experienced some effects of savage hostility;[2] while among the settlers, whose houses were scattered throughout the adjacent valleys, outrages were perpetrated, and sufferings endured, which defy all attempt at description.

At Fort Pitt, every preparation was made to repel the attack which was hourly expected. A part of the rampart, undermined by the spring floods, had fallen into the ditch; but, by dint of great labor, this injury was repaired. A line of palisades was erected along the ramparts; the barracks were made

[1]MS. *Johnson Papers*. Not many years since, some traces of Fort Venango were yet visible. The following description of them is from the *Historical Collections of Pennsylvania*: —

"Its ruins plainly indicate its destruction by fire. Burnt stone, melted glass and iron, leave no doubt of this. All through the groundworks are to be found great quantities of mouldering bones. Amongst the ruins, knives, gunbarrels, locks, and musket-balls have been frequently found, and still continue to be found. About the centre of the area are seen the ruins of the magazine, in which, with what truth I cannot vouch, is said to be a well. The same tradition also adds, 'And in that well there is a cannon;' but no examination has been made for it."

[2]Extract from a Letter—*Fort Bedford, June 30, 1763* (*Penn. Gaz*. No. 1802).

"This Morning a Party of the Enemy attacked fifteen Persons, who were mowing in Mr. Croghan's Field, within a Mile of the Garrison; and News is brought in of two Men being killed.—Eight o'clock. Two Men are brought in, alive, tomahawked and scalped more than Half the Head over—Our Parade just now presents a Scene of bloody and savage Cruelty; three Men, two of which are in the Bloom of Life, the other an old man, lying scalped (two of them still alive) thereon: Any thing feigned in the most fabulous Romance, cannot parallel the horrid Sight now before me; the Gashes the poor People bear are most terrifying.—Ten o'clock. They are just expired—One of them, after being tomahawked and scalped, ran a little way, and got on a Loft in Mr. Croghan's House, where he lay till found by a Party of the Garrison."

shot-proof, to protect the women and children; and, as the interior buildings were all of wood, a rude fire-engine was constructed, to extinguish any flames which might be kindled by the burning arrows of the Indians. Several weeks, however, elapsed without any determined attack from the enemy, who were engaged in their bloody work among the settlements and smaller posts. From the beginning of July until towards its close, nothing occurred except a series of petty and futile attacks, by which the Indians abundantly exhibited their malicious intentions, without doing harm to the garrison. During the whole of this time, the communication with the settlements was completely cut off, so that no letters were written from the fort, or, at all events, none reached their destination; and we are therefore left to depend upon a few meagre official reports, as our only sources of information.

On the twenty-sixth of July, a small party of Indians was seen approaching the gate, displaying a flag, which one of them had some time before received as a present from the English commander. On the strength of this token, they were admitted, and proved to be chiefs of distinction; among whom were Shingas, Turtle's Heart, and others, who had hitherto maintained an appearance of friendship. Being admitted to a council, one of them addressed Captain Ecuyer and his officers to the following effect:—

"Brothers, what we are about to say comes from our hearts, and not from our lips.

"Brothers, we wish to hold fast the chain of friendship—that ancient chain which our forefathers held with their brethren the English. You have let your end of the chain fall to the ground, but ours is still fast within our hands. Why do you complain that our young men have fired at your soldiers, and killed your cattle and your horses? You yourselves are the cause of this. You marched your armies into our country, and built forts here, though we told you, again and again, that we wished you to remove. My Brothers, this land is ours, and not yours.

"My Brothers, two days ago we received a great belt of wampum from the Ottawas of Detroit, and the message they sent us was in these words:—

" 'Grandfathers the Delawares, by this belt we inform you

that in a short time we intend to pass, in a very great body, through your country, on our way to strike the English at the forks of the Ohio. Grandfathers, you know us to be a head-strong people. We are determined to stop at nothing; and as we expect to be very hungry, we will seize and eat up every thing that comes in our way.'[1]

"Brothers, you have heard the words of the Ottawas. If you leave this place immediately, and go home to your wives and children, no harm will come of it; but if you stay, you must blame yourselves alone for what may happen. Therefore we desire you to remove."

To the not wholly unreasonable statement of wrongs contained in this speech, Captain Ecuyer replied, by urging the shallow pretence that the forts were built for the purpose of supplying the Indians with clothes and ammunition. He then absolutely refused to leave the place. "I have," he said, "warriors, provisions, and ammunition, to defend it three years against all the Indians in the woods; and we shall never abandon it as long as a white man lives in America. I despise the Ottawas, and am very much surprised at our brothers the Delawares, for proposing to us to leave this place and go home. This is our home. You have attacked us without reason or provocation; you have murdered and plundered our warriors and traders; you have taken our horses and cattle; and at the same time you tell us your hearts are good towards your brethren the English. How can I have faith in you? Therefore, now, Brothers, I will advise you to go home to your towns, and take care of your wives and children. Moreover, I tell you that if any of you appear again about this fort, I will throw bombshells, which will burst and blow you to atoms, and fire cannon among you, loaded with a whole bag full of bullets. Therefore take care, for I don't want to hurt you."[2]

The chiefs departed, much displeased with their reception. Though nobody in his senses could blame the course pursued by Captain Ecuyer, and though the building of forts in the Indian country could not be charged as a crime, except by the most overstrained casuistry, yet we cannot refrain from

---

[1] This is a common Indian metaphor. To destroy an enemy is, in their phrase, to eat him.

[2] MS. *Report of Conference with the Indians at Fort Pitt*, July 26, 1763.

sympathizing with the intolerable hardship to which the progress of civilization subjected the unfortunate tenants of the wilderness, and which goes far to extenuate the perfidy and cruelty that marked their conduct throughout the whole course of the war.

Disappointed of gaining a bloodless possession of the fort, the Indians now, for the first time, began a general attack. On the night succeeding the conference, they approached in great numbers, under cover of the darkness, and completely surrounded it; many of them crawling under the banks of the two rivers, and, with incredible perseverance, digging, with their knives, holes in which they were completely sheltered from the fire of the fort. On one side, the whole bank was lined with these burrows, from each of which a bullet or an arrow was shot out whenever a soldier chanced to expose his head. At daybreak, a general fire was opened from every side, and continued without intermission until night, and through several succeeding days. No great harm was done, however. The soldiers lay close behind their parapet of logs, watching the movements of their subtle enemies, and paying back their shot with interest. The red uniforms of the Royal Americans mingled with the gray homespun of the border riflemen, or the fringed hunting-frocks of old Indian fighters, wary and adroit as the red-skinned warriors themselves. They liked the sport, and were eager to sally from behind their defences, and bring their assailants to close quarters; but Ecuyer was too wise to consent. He was among them, as well pleased as they, directing, encouraging, and applauding them in his broken English. An arrow flew over the rampart and wounded him in the leg; but, it seems, with no other result than to extort a passing execration. The Indians shot fire-arrows, too, from their burrows, but not one of them took effect. The yelling at times was terrific, and the women and children in the crowded barracks clung to each other in terror; but there was more noise than execution, and the assailants suffered more than the assailed. Three or four days after, Ecuyer wrote in French to his colonel, "They were all well under cover, and so were we. They did us no harm: nobody killed; seven wounded, and I myself slightly. Their attack lasted five days and five nights. We are certain of having killed and wounded twenty of them, without reckoning those we could not see. I let nobody fire till he had marked his man; and not an Indian could show his nose without being pricked with a bullet, for I have some good shots here. . . . Our men are doing admirably, regulars and the rest. All that they ask is to go out and fight. I am fortunate to have the honor of commanding such brave men. I only wish the Indians had ventured an assault. They would have remembered it to the thousandth generation! . . . I forgot to tell you that they threw fire-arrows to burn our works, but they could not reach the buildings, nor even the rampart. Only two arrows came into the fort, one of which had the insolence to make free with my left leg."

This letter was written on the second of August. On the day before the Indians had all decamped. An event, soon to be described, had put an end to the attack, and relieved the tired garrison of their presence.[1]

[1]Extract from a MS. Letter—*Colonel Bouquet to Sir J. Amherst:*—

"Fort Pitt, 11th Aug. 1763.

"Sir:

"We Arrived here Yesterday, without further Opposition than Scattered Shots along the Road.

"The Delawares, Shawnese, Wiandots, & Mingoes had closely Beset, and Attacked this Fort from the 27th July, to the First Instant, when they Quitted it to March against us.

"The Boldness of those Savages is hardly Credible; they had taken Post under the Banks of Both Rivers, Close to the Fort, where Digging Holes, they kept an Incessant Fire, and threw Fire Arrows: They are good Marksmen, and though our People were under Cover, they Killed one, & Wounded seven.—Captain Ecuyer is Wounded in the Leg by an Arrow.—I Would not Do Justice to that Officer, should I omit to Inform Your Excellency, that, without Engineer, or any other Artificers than a few Ship Wrights, he has Raised a Parapet of Logs round the Fort, above the Old One, which having not been Finished, was too Low, and Enfiladed; he has Fraised the Whole; Palisadoed the Inside of the Aria, Constructed a Fire Engine; and in short, has taken all Precautions, which Art and Judgment could suggest for the Preservation of this Post, open before on the three sides, which had suffered by the Floods."

Chapter XIX.

1763.

THE WAR ON THE BORDERS.

ALONG THE WESTERN frontiers of Pennsylvania, Maryland, and Virginia, terror reigned supreme. The Indian
scalping-parties were ranging everywhere, laying waste the
settlements, destroying the harvests, and butchering men,
women, and children, with ruthless fury. Many hundreds of
wretched fugitives flocked for refuge to Carlisle and the other
towns of the border, bringing tales of inconceivable horror.
Strong parties of armed men, who went out to reconnoitre
the country, found every habitation reduced to cinders, and
the half-burned bodies of the inmates lying among the smouldering ruins; while here and there was seen some miserable
wretch, scalped and tomahawked, but still alive and conscious. One writing from the midst of these scenes declares
that, in his opinion, a thousand families were driven from
their homes; that, on both sides of the Susquehanna, the
woods were filled with fugitives, without shelter and without
food; and that, unless the havoc were speedily checked, the
western part of Pennsylvania would be totally deserted, and
Lancaster become the frontier town.[1]

While these scenes were enacted on the borders of Pennsylvania and the more southern provinces, the settlers in the
valley of the Mohawk, and even along the Hudson, were
menaced with destruction. Had not the Six Nations been kept
tranquil by the exertions of Sir William Johnson, the most
disastrous results must have ensued. The Senecas and a few of
the Cayugas were the only members of the confederacy who
took part in the war. Venango, as we have seen, was destroyed by a party of Senecas, who soon after made a feeble
attack upon Niagara. They blockaded it for a few days, with
no other effect than that of confining the garrison within
the walls, and, soon despairing of success, abandoned the
attempt.

[1] *Penn. Gaz.* No. 1805–1809.

In the mean time, Sir Jeffrey Amherst, the Commander-in-chief, was in a position far from enviable. He had reaped laurels; but if he hoped to enjoy them in peace, he was doomed to disappointment. A miserable war was suddenly thrown on his hands, barren of honors and fruitful of troubles; and this, too, at a time when he was almost bereft of resources. The armies which had conquered Canada were, as we have seen, disbanded or sent home, and nothing remained but a few fragments and skeletons of regiments lately arrived from the West Indies, enfeebled by disease and hard service. In one particular, however, he had reason to congratulate himself,—the character of the officers who commanded under his orders in Pennsylvania, Virginia, and Maryland. Colonel Henry Bouquet was a Swiss, of the Canton of Berne, who had followed the trade of war from boyhood. He had served first the King of Sardinia, and afterwards the republic of Holland; and when the French war began in 1755, he accepted the commission of lieutenant-colonel, in a regiment newly organized, under the direction of the Duke of Cumberland, expressly for American service. The commissions were to be given to foreigners as well as to Englishmen and provincials; and the ranks were to be filled chiefly from the German emigrants in Pennsylvania and other provinces.[1] The men and officers of

---

[1] "The next object of the immediate attention of Parliament in this session was the raising of a new regiment of foot in North America, for which purpose the sum of £81,178 16s. was voted. This regiment, which was to consist of four battalions of 1000 men each, was intended to be raised chiefly out of the Germans and Swiss, who, for many years past, had annually transported themselves in great numbers to British plantations in America, where waste lands had been assigned them upon the frontiers of the provinces; but, very injudiciously, no care had been taken to intermix them with the English inhabitants of the place, so that very few of them, even of those who have been born there, have yet learned to speak or understand the English tongue. However, as they were all zealous Protestants, and in general strong, hardy men, accustomed to the climate, it was judged that a regiment of good and faithful soldiers might be raised out of them, particularly proper to oppose the French; but to this end it was necessary to appoint some officers, especially subalterns, who understood military discipline and could speak the German language; and as a sufficient number of such could not be found among the English officers, it was necessary to bring over and grant commissions to several German and Swiss officers and engineers. But as this step, by the Act of Settlement, could not be taken without the authority of Parliament, an act

this regiment, known as the "Royal American," had now, for more than six years, been engaged in the rough and lonely service of the frontiers and forests; and when the Indian war broke out, it was chiefly they, who, like military hermits, held the detached outposts of the West. Bouquet, however, who was at this time colonel of the first battalion, had his headquarters at Philadelphia, where he was held in great esteem. His person was fine, and his bearing composed and dignified; perhaps somewhat austere, for he is said to have been more respected than loved by his officers. Nevertheless, their letters to him are very far from indicating any want of cordial relations. He was fond of the society of men of science, and wrote English better than most British officers of the time. Here and there, however, a passage in his letters suggests the inference, that the character of the gallant mercenary was toned to his profession, and to the unideal epoch in which he lived. Yet he was not the less an excellent soldier; indefatigable, faithful, full of resource, and without those arrogant prejudices which had impaired the efficiency of many good British officers, in the recent war, and of which Sir Jeffrey Amherst was a conspicuous example. He had acquired a practical knowledge of Indian warfare; and it is said that, in the course of the hazardous partisan service in which he was often engaged, when it was necessary to penetrate dark defiles and narrow passes, he was sometimes known to advance before his men, armed with a rifle, and acting the part of a scout.[1]

Sir Jeffrey had long and persistently flattered himself that the Indian uprising was but a temporary ebullition, which would soon subside. Bouquet sent him, on the fourth of June,

---

was now passed for enabling his Majesty to grant commissions to a certain number of foreign Protestants, who had served abroad as officers or engineers, to act and rank as officers or engineers in America only."—Smollett, *England*, III. 475.

The Royal American Regiment is now the 60th Rifles. Its ranks, at the time of the Pontiac war, were filled by provincials of English as well as of German descent.

[1]There is a sketch of Bouquet's life prefixed to the French translation of the *Account of Bouquet's Expedition*. See also the reprint in the first volume of Clarke's "Ohio Valley Historical Series."

a copy of a letter from Captain Ecuyer,[1] at Fort Pitt, reporting the disturbances in that quarter. On the next day Bouquet wrote again, in a graver strain; and Amherst replied, from New York, on the sixth: "I gave immediate orders for completing the light infantry companies of the 17th, 42d, and 77th regiments. They are to assemble without loss of time, and to encamp on Staten Island, under Major Campbell, of the 42d. . . . Although I have thought proper to assemble this force, which I judge more than sufficient to quell any disturbances the whole Indian strength could raise, yet I am persuaded the alarm will end in nothing more than a rash attempt of what the Senecas have been threatening, and which we have heard of for some time past. As to their cutting off defenceless families, or even some of the small posts, it is certainly at all times in their power to effect such enterprises. . . . The post of Fort Pitt, or any of the others commanded by officers, can certainly never be in danger from such a wretched enemy. . . . I am only sorry that when such outrages are committed, the guilty should escape; for I am fully convinced the only true method of treating the savages is to keep them in proper subjection, and punish, without exception, the transgressors. . . . As I have no sort of dependence on the Assembly of Pennsylvania, I have taken such measures as will fully enable me to chastise any nation or tribe of Indians that dare to commit hostilities on his Majesty's subjects. I only wait to hear from you what farther steps the savages have taken; for I still think it cannot be any thing general, but the rash attempt of that turbulent tribe, the Senecas, who richly deserve a severe chastisement from our hands, for their treacherous behavior on many occasions."

On receiving this letter, Bouquet immediately wrote to Ecuyer at Fort Pitt: "The General has taken the necessary measures to chastise those infamous villains, and defers only to make them feel the weight of his resentment till he is better informed of their intentions." And having thus briefly despatched the business in hand, he proceeds to touch on the news of the day: "I give you joy of the success of our troops at the Manilla, where Captain George Ourry hath acquired

[1] An extract from this letter, which is dated May 30, is given on page 624.

the two best things in this world, glory and money. We hear of a great change in the ministry," etc. . . . . "P. S. I have lent three pounds to the express. Please to stop it for me. The General expects that Mr. Croghan will proceed directly to Fort Pitt, when he will soon discover the causes of this sudden rupture and the intentions of these rascals."

Scarcely had Bouquet sent off the express-rider with this letter, when another came from Ecuyer with worse reports from the west. He forwarded it to Amherst, who wrote on receiving it: "I find by the intelligence enclosed in your letter that the affair of the Indians appears to be more general than I had apprehended, although I believe nothing of what is mentioned regarding the garrison of the Detroit being cut off. It is extremely inconvenient at this time; . . . but I cannot defer sending you a reinforcement for the communication." Accordingly he ordered two companies of the 42d and 77th regiments to join Bouquet at Philadelphia. "If you think it necessary," he adds, "you will yourself proceed to Fort Pitt, that you may be the better enabled to put in execution the requisite orders for securing the communication and reducing the Indians to reason."

Amherst now bestirred himself to put such troops as he had into fighting order. The 80th regiment, Hopkins's company of Rangers, and a portion of the Royal Americans, were disbanded, and the men drafted to complete other broken corps. His plan was to push forward as many troops as possible to Niagara by way of Oswego, and to Presqu' Isle by way of Fort Pitt, and thence to send them up the lakes to take vengeance on the offending tribes.

Bouquet, recognizing at length the peril of the small outlying posts, like Venango and Le Bœuf, proposed to abandon them, and concentrate at Fort Pitt and Presqu' Isle; a movement which, could it have been executed in time, would have saved both blood and trouble. But Amherst would not consent. "I cannot think," he writes, "of giving them up at this time, if we can keep them, as such a step would give the Indians room to think themselves more formidable than they really are; and it would be much better we never attempted to take posts in what they call their country, if, upon every alarm, we abandon them. . . . It remains at present for us to take every precaution we can, by which we may put a stop, as soon as possible, to their committing any farther mischief, and to bring them to a proper subjection; for, without *that*, I never do expect that they will be quiet and orderly, as every act of kindness and generosity to those barbarians is looked upon as proceeding from our fears."

Bouquet next writes to report that, with the help of the two companies sent him, he has taken steps which he hopes will secure the communication to Fort Pitt and allay the fears of the country people, who are deserting their homes in a panic, though the enemy has not yet appeared east of the mountains. A few days later, on the twenty-third of June, Amherst writes, boiling with indignation. He had heard from Gladwyn of the investment of Detroit, and the murder of Sir Robert Davers and Lieutenant Robertson. "The villains after this," he says, "had the assurance to come with a *Pipe of Peace*, desiring admittance into the fort." He then commends the conduct of Gladwyn, but pursues: "I only regret that when the chief of the Ottawas and the other villains returned with the *Pipe of Peace*, they were not instantly put to *death*.[1] I conclude Major Gladwyn was not apprised of the murder of Sir Robert Davers, Lieutenant Robertson, etc., at that time, or he certainly would have revenged their deaths by that method; and, indeed, I cannot but wish that whenever we have any of the savages in our power, who have in so treacherous a way committed any barbarities on our people, a quick retaliation may be made without the least exception or hesitation. I am determined," he continues, "to take every measure in my power, not only for securing and keeping entire possession of the country, but for punishing those barbarians who have thus perfidiously massacred his Majesty's subjects. To effect this most essential service, I intend to collect, agreeable to what I wrote you in my last, all the force I can at Presqu' Isle and Niagara, that I may push them forwards as occasion may require. I have therefore ordered the remains of the 42d and 77th regiments—the first consisting of two hundred and fourteen men, including officers, and the latter of one hundred and thirty-three, officers included—to march this evening or

[1] The italics and capitals are Sir Jeffrey's.

early to-morrow morning, under the command of Major Campbell of the 42d, who has my orders to send an officer before to acquaint you of his being on the march, and to obey such further directions as he may receive from you. . . . You will observe that I have now forwarded from hence every man that was here; for the small remains of the 17th regiment are already on their march up the Mohawk, and I have sent such of the 42d and 77th as were not able to march, to Albany, to relieve the company of the 55th at present there, who are to march immediately to Oswego."

Two days after, the twenty-fifth of June, he writes again to Bouquet: "All the troops from hence that could be collected are sent you; so that should the whole race of Indians take arms against us, I can do no more."[1]

On the same day, Bouquet, who was on his way to the frontier, wrote to Amherst, from Lancaster: "I had this moment the honor of your Excellency's letter of the twenty-third instant, with the most welcome news of the preservation of the Detroit from the infernal treachery of the vilest of brutes. I regret sincerely the brave men they have so basely massacred, but hope that we shall soon take an adequate revenge on the barbarians. The reinforcement you have ordered this way, so considerable by the additional number of officers, will fully enable me to crush the little opposition they may dare to make along the road, and secure that part of the country against all their future attempts, till you think proper to order us to act in conjunction with the rest of your forces to extirpate that vermin from a country they have forfeited, and, with it, all claim to the rights of humanity."

Three days later the express-rider delivered the truculent letter, from which the above is taken, to Amherst at New York. He replied: "Last night I received your letter of the twenty-fifth, the contents of which please me very much,— your sentiments agreeing exactly with my own regarding the treatment the savages deserve from us. . . I need only add that I wish to hear of *no prisoners*, should any of the villains be met with in arms; and whoever of those who were concerned

---

[1] On the 29th of July following, the fragments of five more regiments arrived from Havana, numbering in all 982 men and officers fit for duty.— *Official Returns.*

in the murder of Sir Robert Davers, Lieutenant Robertson, etc., or were at the attack of the detachment going to the Detroit,[1] and that may be hereafter taken, shall certainly be put to *death*."[2]

Bouquet was now busy on the frontier in preparations for pushing forward to Fort Pitt with the troops sent him. After reaching the fort, with his wagon-trains of ammunition and supplies, he was to proceed to Venango and Le Bœuf, reinforce and provision them; and thence advance to Presqu' Isle to wait Amherst's orders for the despatch of his troops westward to Detroit, Michillimackinac, and the other distant garrisons, the fate of which was still unknown. He was encamped near Carlisle when, on the third of July, he heard what he styles the "fatal account of the loss of our posts at Presqu' Isle, Le Bœuf, and Venango." He at once sent the news to Amherst; who, though he persisted in his original plan of operations, became at length convinced of the formidable nature of the Indian outbreak, and felt bitterly the slenderness of his own resources. His correspondence, nevertheless, breathes a certain thick-headed, blustering arrogance, worthy of the successor of Braddock.[3] In his contempt for the Indians, he finds fault with Captain Ecuyer at Fort Pitt for

[1] *i.e.*, Cuyler's detachment.

[2] Amherst wrote again on the 16th of July: "My former orders for putting such of the Indians as are or have been in arms against us, and that fall in our power, to death, remain in full force; as the barbarities they have committed on the late commanding officer at Venango" (Gordon, whom they roasted alive during several nights) "and his unfortunate garrison fully prove that no punishment we can inflict is adequate to the crimes of those inhuman villains."

[3] The following is a characteristic example. He is writing to Johnson, 27 Aug. 1763: "I shall only say that it Behoves the Whole Race of Indians to Beware (for I Fear the best of them have in some Measure been privy to, and Concerned in the Late Mischief) of Carrying Matters much farther against the English, or Daring to form Conspiracys; as the Consequence will most Certainly occasion Measures to be taken, that, in the End, will put a most Effectual Stop to their Very Being."

The following is his view of the Indians, in a letter to Bouquet, 7 Aug. 1763: —

"I wish there was not an Indian Settlement within a thousand miles of our Country, for they are only fit to live with the Inhabitants of the woods: (i.e., *wild beasts*), being more allied to the *Brute* than the *human* Creation."

condescending to fire cannon at them, and with Lieutenant Blane at Fort Ligonier for burning some outhouses, under cover of which "so despicable an enemy" were firing at his garrison. This despicable enemy had, however, pushed him to such straits that he made, in a postscript to Bouquet, the following detestable suggestion:—

"Could it not be contrived to send the *Small Pox* among those disaffected tribes of Indians? We must on this occasion use every stratagem in our power to reduce them."

                         (Signed)   J. A.

Bouquet replied, also in postscript:—

"I will try to inoculate the —— with some blankets that may fall in their hands, and take care not to get the disease myself. As it is a pity to expose good men against them, I wish we could make use of the Spanish method, to hunt them with English dogs, supported by rangers and some light horse, who would, I think, effectually extirpate or remove that vermin."

Amherst rejoined: "You will do well to try to inoculate the Indians by means of blankets, as well as to try every other method that can serve to extirpate this execrable race. I should be very glad your scheme for hunting them down by dogs could take effect, but England is at too great a distance to think of that at present."

                         (Signed)   J. A.[1]

---

[1]This correspondence is among the manuscripts of the British Museum, *Bouquet and Haldimand Papers*, No. 21,634. The first postscript by Amherst is on a single leaf of foolscap, written at the top of the page and addressed on the back,—

    "On His Majesty's Service.
    "To Colonel BOUQUET,
                "etc."

"JEFF. AMHERST."

The postscript seems to belong to a letter written on the first leaf of the foolscap sheet, which is lost or destroyed. The other postscript by Amherst has neither indorsement nor address, but that of Bouquet is appended to a letter dated Carlisle, 13 July, 1763, and addressed to "His Excellency, Sir Jeffrey Amherst." It appears from a letter of Capt. Ecuyer that the small-pox had lately broken out at Fort Pitt, which would have favored the execution of the plan. We hear nothing more of it; but, in the following spring, Gershom

There is no direct evidence that Bouquet carried into effect the shameful plan of infecting the Indians though, a few months after, the small-pox was known to have made havoc among the tribes of the Ohio. Certain it is, that he was perfectly capable of dealing with them by other means, worthy of a man and a soldier; and it is equally certain, that in relations with civilized men he was in a high degree honorable, humane, and kind.

The scenes which daily met his eye might well have moved him to pity as well as indignation. When he reached Carlisle,

---

Hicks, who had been among the Indians, reported at Fort Pitt that the small-pox had been raging for some time among them, and that sixty or eighty Mingoes and Delawares, besides some Shawanoes, had died of it.

The suggestion of using dogs against the Indians did not originate with Bouquet. Just before he wrote, he received a letter from one John Hughes, dated Lancaster, July 11, in which an elaborate plan is laid down for conquering the Indians with the help of canine allies.

The following is the substance of the proposal, which is set forth under eight distinct heads: 1st, Each soldier to have a dog, which he is to lead on the march by a strap three feet long. 2d, All the dogs to be held fast by the straps, except one or two on each flank and as many in advance, to discover the enemy in ambush. 3d, When you are fired upon, let loose all the dogs, which will rush at the concealed Indians, and force them in self-defence to expose themselves and fire at their assailants, with so little chance of hitting them, that, in the words of the letter, "if 1000 Indians fired on 300 dogs, there would be at least 200 dogs left, besides all the soldiers' fires, which must put the Indians to flight very soon." 4th, If you come to a swamp, thicket, or the like, "only turn loose 3 or 4 dogs extraordinary, and you are immediately convinced what you have to fear." 5th, "No Indian can well conceal himself in a swamp or thicket as a spy, for y.ᵉ dogs will discover him, and may soon be learnt to destroy him too." 6th, "The leading the dogs makes them more fierce, and keeps them from being tired in running after wild beasts or fighting one another." 7th, Expatiates on the advantages of having the leading-straps short. 8th, "The greater the number of dogs, the more fierce they will be by a great deal, and the more terrible to the Indians; and if, when you get to Bedford, a few scouting parties were sent out with dogs, and one or two Indians killed and the dogs put at them to tear them to pieces, you would soon see the good effects of it; and I could almost venture my life that 500 men with 500 dogs would be much more dreadful to 2000 Indians than an army of some thousand of brave men in the regular way.

"Jⁿ HUGHES.

"COLONEL BOUQUET."

Probably there is no man who ever had occasion to fight Indians in the woods who would object to a dog as an ally.

at the end of June, he found every building in the fort, every house, barn, and hovel, in the little town, crowded with the families of settlers, driven from their homes by the terror of the tomahawk. Wives made widows, children made orphans, wailed and moaned in anguish and despair. On the thirteenth of July he wrote to Amherst: "The list of the people known to be killed increases very fast every hour. The desolation of so many families, reduced to the last extremity of want and misery; the despair of those who have lost their parents, relations, and friends, with the cries of distracted women and children, who fill the streets,—form a scene painful to humanity, and impossible to describe."[1] Rage alternated with grief. A Mohican and a Cayuga Indian, both well known as friendly and peaceable, came with their squaws and children to claim protection from the soldiers. "It was with the utmost difficulty," pursues Bouquet, "that I could prevail with the enraged multitude not to massacre them. I don't think them very safe in the gaol. They ought to be removed to Philadelphia."

Bouquet, on his part, was full of anxieties. On the road from Carlisle to Fort Pitt was a chain of four or five small forts, of which the most advanced and the most exposed were Fort Bedford and Fort Ligonier; the former commanded by Captain Lewis Ourry, and the latter by Lieutenant Archibald Blane. These officers kept up a precarious correspondence with him and each other, by means of express-riders, a service dangerous to the last degree and soon to become impracticable. It was of the utmost importance to hold these posts, which contained stores and munitions, the capture of which by the Indians would have led to the worst consequences. Ourry had no garrison worth the name; but at every Indian alarm the scared inhabitants would desert their farms, and gather for shelter around his fort, to disperse again when the alarm was over.

On the third of June, he writes to Bouquet: "No less than ninety-three families are now come in here for refuge, and

---

[1]This is the letter in which he accepts Amherst's proposal to infect the Indians. His just indignation at the atrocities which had caused so much misery is his best apology.

more hourly arriving. I expect ten more before night." He adds that he had formed the men into two militia companies. "My returns," he pursues, "amount already to a hundred and fifty-five men. My regulars are increased by expresses, etc., to three corporals and nine privates; no despicable garrison!"

On the seventh, he sent another letter. . . . "As to myself, I find I can bear a good deal. Since the alarm I never lie down till about twelve, and am walking about the fort between two and three in the morning, turning out the guards and sending out patrols, before I suffer the gates to remain open. . . . My greatest difficulty is to keep my militia from straggling by twos and threes to their dear plantations, thereby exposing themselves to be scalped, and weakening my garrison by such numbers absenting themselves. They are still in good spirits, but they don't know all the bad news. I shall use all means to prevail on them to stay till some troops come up. I long to see my Indian scouts come in with intelligence; but I long more to hear the Grenadiers' March, and see some more red-coats."

Ten days later, the face of affairs had changed. "I am now, as I foresaw, entirely deserted by the country people. No accident having happened here, they have gradually left me to return to their plantations; so that my whole force is reduced to twelve Royal Americans to guard the fort, and seven Indian prisoners. I should be very glad to see some troops come to my assistance. A fort with five bastions cannot be guarded, much less defended, by a dozen men; but I hope God will protect us."

On the next day, he writes again: "This moment I return from the parade. Some scalps taken up Dening's Creek yesterday, and to-day some families murdered and houses burnt, have restored me my militia. . . . Two or three other families are missing, and the houses are seen in flames. The people are all flocking in again."

Two days afterwards, he says that, while the countrymen were at drill on the parade, three Indians attempted to seize two little girls, close to the fort, but were driven off by a volley. "This," he pursues, "has added greatly to the panic of the people. With difficulty I can restrain them from murdering the Indian prisoners." And he concludes: "I can't help thinking that the enemy will collect, after cutting off the little posts one after another, leaving Fort Pitt as too tough a morsel, and bend their whole force upon the frontiers."

On the second of July, he describes an attack by about twenty Indians on a party of mowers, several of whom were killed. "This accident," he says, "has thrown the people into a great consternation, but such is their stupidity that they will do nothing right for their own preservation."

It was on the next day that he sent a mounted soldier to Bouquet with news of the loss of Presqu' Isle and its sister posts, which Blane, who had received it from Fort Pitt, had contrived to send him; though he himself, in his feeble little fort of Ligonier, buried in a sea of forests, hardly dared hope to maintain himself. Bouquet was greatly moved at the tidings, and his vexation betrayed him into injustice towards the defender of Presqu' Isle. "Humanity makes me hope that Christie is dead, as his scandalous capitulation, for a post of that consequence and so impregnable to savages, deserves the most severe punishment."[1] He is equally vehement in regard to Blane, who appears to have intimated, in writing to Ourry, that he had himself had thoughts of capitulating, like Christie. "I shivered when you hinted to me Lieutenant Bl——'s intentions. Death and infamy would have been the reward he would expect, instead of the honor he has obtained by his prudence, courage, and resolution. . . . This is a most trying time. . . . You may be sure that all the expedition possible will be used for the relief of the few remaining posts."[2]

As for Blane, the following extracts from his letters will show his position; though, when his affairs were at the worst, nothing was heard from him, as all his messengers were killed. On the fourth of June, he writes: "Thursday last my garrison was attacked by a body of Indians, about five in the morning; but as they only fired upon us from the skirts of the

---

[1] The blockhouse at Presqu' Isle had been built under the direction of Bouquet. Being of wood, it was not fire-proof; and he urged upon Amherst that it should be re-built of brick with a slate roof, thus making it absolutely proof against Indians.

[2] Bouquet had the strongest reasons for wishing that Fort Ligonier should hold out. As the event showed, its capture would probably have entailed the defeat and destruction of his entire command.

woods, I contented myself with giving them three cheers, without spending a single shot upon them. But as they still continued their popping upon the side next the town, I sent the sergeant of the Royal Americans, with a proper detachment, to fire the houses, which effectually disappointed them in their plan."

On the seventeenth, he writes to Bouquet: "I hope soon to see yourself, and live in daily hopes of a reinforcement. . . . Sunday last, a man straggling out was killed by the Indians; and Monday night three of them got under the n——house, but were discovered. The darkness secured them their retreat. . . . I believe the communication between Fort Pitt and this is entirely cut off, having heard nothing from them since the thirtieth of May, though two expresses have gone from Bedford by this post."

On the twenty-eighth, he explains that he has not been able to report for some time, the road having been completely closed by the enemy. "On the twenty-first," he continues, "the Indians made a second attempt in a very serious manner, for near two hours, but with the like success as the first. They began with attempting to cut off the retreat of a small party of fifteen men, who, from their impatience to come at four Indians who showed themselves, in a great measure forced me to let them out. In the evening, I think above a hundred lay in ambush by the side of the creek, about four hundred yards from the fort; and, just as the party was returning pretty near where they lay, they rushed out, when they undoubtedly must have succeeded, had it not been for a deep morass which intervened. Immediately after, they began their attack; and I dare say they fired upwards of one thousand shot. Nobody received any damage. So far, my good fortune in dangers still attends me."

And here one cannot but give a moment's thought to those whose desperate duty it was to be the bearers of this correspondence of the officers of the forest outposts with their commander. They were usually soldiers, sometimes backwoodsmen, and occasionally a friendly Indian, who, disguising his attachment to the whites, could pass when others would infallibly have perished. If white men, they were always mounted; and it may well be supposed that their horses did not lag by the way. The profound solitude; the silence, broken only by the moan of the wind, the caw of the crow, or the cry of some prowling tenant of the waste; the mystery of the verdant labyrinth, which the anxious wayfarer strained his eyes in vain to penetrate; the consciousness that in every thicket, behind every rock, might lurk a foe more fierce and subtle than the cougar or the lynx; and the long hours of darkness, when, stretched on the cold ground, his excited fancy roamed in nightmare visions of a horror but too real and imminent,—such was the experience of many an unfortunate who never lived to tell it. If the messenger was an Indian, his greatest danger was from those who should have been his friends. Friendly Indians were told, whenever they approached a fort, to make themselves known by carrying green branches thrust into the muzzles of their guns; and an order was issued that the token should be respected. This gave them tolerable security as regarded soldiers, but not as regarded the enraged backwoodsmen, who would shoot without distinction at any thing with a red skin.

To return to Bouquet, who lay encamped at Carlisle, urging on his preparations, but met by obstacles at every step. Wagons and horses had been promised, but promises were broken, and all was vexation and delay. The province of Pennsylvania, from causes to be shown hereafter, would do nothing to aid the troops who were defending it; and even the people of the frontier, partly from the apathy and confusion of terror, and partly, it seems, from dislike and jealousy of the regulars, were backward and sluggish in co-operating with them. "I hope," writes Bouquet to Sir Jeffrey Amherst, "that we shall be able to save that infatuated people from destruction, notwithstanding all their endeavors to defeat your vigorous measures. I meet everywhere with the same backwardness, even among the most exposed of the inhabitants, which makes every thing move on heavily, and is disgusting to the last degree." And again: "I find myself utterly abandoned by the very people I am ordered to protect. . . . I have borne very patiently the ill-usage of this province, having still hopes that they will do something for us; and therefore have avoided to quarrel with them."

While, vexed and exasperated, Bouquet labored at his

thankless task, remonstrated with provincial officials, or appealed to refractory farmers, the terror of the country people increased every day. When on Sunday, the third of July, Ourry's express rode into Carlisle with the disastrous news from Presqu' Isle and the other outposts, he stopped for a moment in the village street to water his horse. A crowd of countrymen were instantly about him, besieging him with questions. He told his ill-omened story; and added as, remounting, he rode towards Bouquet's tent, "The Indians will be here soon." All was now excitement and consternation. Messengers hastened out to spread the tidings; and every road and pathway leading into Carlisle was beset with the flying settlers, flocking thither for refuge. Soon rumors were heard that the Indians were come. Some of the fugitives had seen the smoke of burning houses rising from the valleys; and these reports were fearfully confirmed by the appearance of miserable wretches, who, half frantic with grief and dismay, had fled from blazing dwellings and slaughtered families. A party of the inhabitants armed themselves and went out, to warn the living and bury the dead. Reaching Shearman's Valley, they found fields laid waste, stacked wheat on fire, and the houses yet in flames; and they grew sick with horror at seeing a group of hogs tearing and devouring the bodies of the dead.[1] As they advanced up the valley, every thing betokened the recent presence of the enemy, while columns of smoke, rising among the surrounding mountains, showed how general was the work of destruction.

On the preceding day, six men, assembled for reaping the harvest, had been seated at dinner at the house of Campbell, a settler on the Juniata. Four or five Indians suddenly burst the door, fired among them, and then beat down the survivors with the butts of their rifles. One young man leaped from his seat, snatched a gun which stood in a corner, discharged it into the breast of the warrior who was rushing upon him, and, leaping through an open window, made his escape. He fled through the forest to a settlement at some distance, where he related his story. Upon this, twelve young men volunteered to cross the mountain, and warn the inhabitants of

[1] *Penn. Gaz.* No. 1804.

the neighboring Tuscarora valley. On entering it, they found that the enemy had been there before them. Some of the houses were on fire, while others were still standing, with no tenants but the dead. Under the shed of a farmer, the Indians had been feasting on the flesh of the cattle they had killed, and the meat had not yet grown cold. Pursuing their course, the white men found the spot where several detached parties of the enemy had united almost immediately before; and they boldly resolved to follow, in order to ascertain what direction the marauders had taken. The trail led them up a deep and woody pass of the Tuscarora. Here the yell of the war-whoop and the din of fire-arms suddenly greeted them, and five of their number were shot down. Thirty warriors rose from their ambuscade, and rushed upon them. They gave one discharge, scattered, and ran for their lives. One of them, a boy named Charles Eliot, as he fled, plunging through the thickets, heard an Indian tearing the boughs behind him, in furious pursuit. He seized his powder-horn, poured the contents at random down the muzzle of his gun, threw in a bullet after them, without using the ramrod, and, wheeling about, discharged the piece into the breast of his pursuer. He saw the Indian shrink back and roll over into the bushes. He continued his flight; but a moment after, a voice called his name. Turning to the spot, he saw one of his comrades stretched helpless upon the ground. This man had been mortally wounded at the first fire, but had fled a few rods from the scene of blood, before his strength gave out. Eliot approached him. "Take my gun," said the dying frontiersman. "Whenever you see an Indian, kill him with it, and then I shall be satisfied."[1] Eliot, with several others of the party, escaped, and finally reached Carlisle, where his story excited a spirit of uncontrollable wrath and vengeance among the fierce backwoodsmen. Several parties went out; and one of them, commanded by the sheriff of the place, encountered a band of Indians, routed them after a sharp fight, and brought in several scalps.[2]

[1] Robison, *Narrative*. Robison was one of the party, and his brother was mortally wounded at the first fire.

[2] Extract from a Letter—*Carlisle*, July 13 (*Penn. Gaz.* No. 1804):—

"Last Night Colonel Armstrong returned. He left the Party, who pursued further, and found several dead, whom they buried in the best manner they

The surrounding country was by this time completely abandoned by the settlers, many of whom, not content with seeking refuge at Carlisle, continued their flight to the eastward, and, headed by the clergyman of that place, pushed on to Lancaster, and even to Philadelphia.[1] Carlisle presented a most deplorable spectacle. A multitude of the refugees, unable to find shelter in the town, had encamped in the woods or on the adjacent fields, erecting huts of branches and bark, and living on such charity as the slender means of the townspeople could supply. Passing among them, one would have witnessed every form of human misery. In these wretched encampments were men, women, and children, bereft at one stroke of friends, of home, and the means of supporting life. Some stood aghast and bewildered at the sudden and fatal blow; others were sunk in the apathy of despair; others were weeping and moaning with irrepressible anguish. With not a few, the craven passion of fear drowned all other emotion, and day and night they were haunted with visions of the bloody knife and the reeking scalp; while in others, every faculty was absorbed by the burning thirst for vengeance, and mortal hatred against the whole Indian race.[2]

---

could, and are now all returned in.—From what appears, the Indians are travelling from one Place to another, along the Valley, burning the Farms, and destroying all the People they meet with.—This Day gives an Account of six more being killed in the Valley, so that since last Sunday Morning to this Day, Twelve o'clock, we have a pretty authentic Account of the Number slain, being Twenty-five, and four or five wounded.—The Colonel, Mr. Wilson, and Mr. Alricks, are now on the Parade, endeavouring to raise another Party, to go out and succour the Sheriff and his Party, consisting of Fifty Men, which marched Yesterday, and hope they will be able to send off immediately Twenty good Men.—The People here, I assure you, want nothing but a good Leader, and a little Encouragement, to make a very good Defence."

[1]Extract from a Letter—*Carlisle*, July 5 (*Haz. Pa. Reg.* IV. 390):—

"Nothing could exceed the terror which prevailed from house to house, from town to town. The road was near covered with women and children, flying to Lancaster and Philadelphia. The Rev.—— ——, Pastor of the Episcopal Church, went at the head of his congregation, to protect and encourage them on the way. A few retired to the Breast works for safety. The alarm once given could not be appeased. We have done all that men can do to prevent disorder. All our hopes are turned upon Bouquet."

[2]Extract from a Letter—*Carlisle*, July 12 (*Penn. Gaz.* No. 1804):—

"I embrace this first Leisure, since Yesterday Morning, to transmit you a brief Account of our present State of Affairs here, which indeed is very distressing; every Day, almost, affording some fresh Object to awaken the Compassion, alarm the Fears, or kindle into Resentment and Vengeance every sensible Breast, while flying Families, obliged to abandon House and Possession, to save their Lives by an hasty Escape; mourning Widows, bewailing their Husbands surprised and massacred by savage Rage; tender Parents, lamenting the Fruits of their own Bodies, cropt in the very Bloom of Life by a barbarous Hand; with Relations and Acquaintances, pouring out Sorrow for murdered Neighbours and Friends, present a varied Scene of mingled Distress.

"To-day a British Vengeance begins to rise in the Breasts of our Men.—One of them that fell from among the 12, as he was just expiring, said to one of his Fellows, Here, take my Gun, and kill the first Indian you see, and all shall be well."

Chapter XX.

1763.

THE BATTLE OF BUSHY RUN.

THE MISERABLE MULTITUDE were soon threatened with famine, and gathered in crowds around the tents of Bouquet, begging relief, which he had not the heart to refuse. After a delay of eighteen days, the chief obstacles were overcome. Wagons and draught animals had, little by little, been collected, and provisions gathered among the settlements to the eastward. At length all was ready, and Bouquet broke up his camp, and began his march. The force under his command did not exceed five hundred men, of whom the most effective were the Highlanders of the 42d regiment. The remnant of the 77th, which was also with him, was so enfeebled by West Indian exposures, that Amherst had at first pronounced it fit only for garrison duty, and nothing but necessity had induced him to employ it on this arduous service. As the heavy wagons of the convoy lumbered along the street of Carlisle, guarded by the bare-legged Highlanders, in kilts and plaids, the crowd gazed in anxious silence; for they knew that their all was at stake on the issue of this dubious enterprise. There was little to reassure them in the thin frames and haggard look of the worn-out veterans; still less in the sight of sixty invalid soldiers, who, unable to walk, were carried in wagons, to furnish a feeble reinforcement to the small garrisons along the route.[1] The desponding rustics watched the last gleam of the bayonets, the last flutter of the tartans, as the rear files vanished in the woods; then returned to their hovels, prepared for tidings of defeat, and ready, when they heard them, to abandon the country, and fly beyond the Susquehanna.

In truth, the adventure was no boy's play. In that gloomy wilderness lay the bones of Braddock and the hundreds that perished with him. The number of the slain on that bloody day exceeded Bouquet's whole force; while the strength of the assailants was inferior to that of the swarms who now

[1] *Account of Bouquet's Expedition*; *Introduction*, vi.

infested the forests. Bouquet's troops were, for the most part, as little accustomed to the backwoods as those of Braddock; but their commander had served seven years in America, and perfectly understood his work. He had attempted to engage a body of frontiersmen to join him on the march; but they preferred to remain for the defence of their families. He was therefore forced to employ the Highlanders as flankers, to protect his line of march and prevent surprise; but, singularly enough, these mountaineers were sure to lose themselves in the woods, and therefore proved useless.[1] For a few days, however, his progress would be tolerably secure, at least from serious attack. His anxieties centred on Fort Ligonier, and he resolved to hazard the attempt to throw a reinforcement into it. Thirty of the best Highlanders were chosen, furnished with guides, and ordered to push forward with the utmost speed, avoiding the road, travelling by night on unfrequented paths, and lying close by day. The attempt succeeded. After resting several days at Bedford, where Ourry was expecting an attack, they again set out, found Fort Ligonier beset by Indians, and received a volley as they made for the gate; but entered safely, to the unspeakable relief of Blane and his beleaguered men.

Meanwhile, Bouquet's little army crept on its slow way along the Cumberland valley. Passing here and there a few scattered cabins, deserted or burnt to the ground, they reached the hamlet of Shippensburg, somewhat more than twenty miles from their point of departure. Here, as at Carlisle, was gathered a starving multitude, who had fled from the knife and the tomahawk.[2] Beyond lay a solitude whence every settler had fled. They reached Fort Loudon, on the declivity of Cove Mountain, and climbed the wood-encumbered defiles beyond. Far on their right stretched the green ridges of

[1]"I cannot send a Highlander out of my sight without running the risk of losing the man, which exposes me to surprise from the skulking villains I have to deal with."—MS. Letter—*Bouquet to Amherst*, 26 July, 1763

[2]"Our Accounts from the westward are as follows, viz.:—

"On the 25th of July there were in Shippensburg 1384 of our poor distressed Back Inhabitants, viz. Men, 301; Women, 345; Children, 738; Many of whom were obliged to lie in Barns, Stables, Cellars, and under old leaky Sheds, the Dwelling-houses being all crowded."—*Penn. Gaz.* No. 1806.

the Tuscarora; and, in front, mountain beyond mountain was piled against the sky. Over rocky heights and through deep valleys, they reached at length Fort Littleton, a provincial post, in which, with incredible perversity, the government of Pennsylvania had refused to place a garrison.[1] Not far distant was the feeble little port of the Juniata, empty like the other; for the two or three men who held it had been withdrawn by Ourry.[2] On the twenty-fifth of July, they reached Bedford, hemmed in by encircling mountains. It was the frontier village and the centre of a scattered border population, the whole of which was now clustered in terror in and around the fort; for the neighboring woods were full of prowling savages. Ourry reported that for several weeks nothing had been heard from the westward, every messenger having been killed and the communication completely cut off. By the last intelligence Fort Pitt had been surrounded by Indians, and daily threatened with a general attack.

At Bedford, Bouquet had the good fortune to engage thirty backwoodsmen to accompany him.[3] He lay encamped three days to rest men and animals, and then, leaving his invalids to garrison the fort, put out again into the sea of savage verdure that stretched beyond. The troops and convoy defiled along the road made by General Forbes in 1758, if the name of road can be given to a rugged track, hewn out by axemen through forests and swamps and up the steep acclivities of rugged mountains; shut in between impervious walls of trunks, boughs, and matted thickets, and overarched by a canopy of

[1]"The government of Pennsylvania having repeatedly refused to garrison Fort Lyttleton (a provincial fort), even with the kind of troops they have raised, I have stationed some inhabitants of the neighborhood in it, with some provisions and ammunition, to prevent the savages burning it."—MS. Letter—*Bouquet to Amherst*, 26 July, 1763.

[2]MS. Letter—*Ourry to Bouquet*, 20 June, 1763.

[3]Extract from a *Letter of Bouquet to Amherst, Bedford*, July 26th, 1763:

"The troops & Convoy arrived here yesterday. . . . Three men have been massacred near Shippensburg since we left, but we have not perceived yet any of the Villains. . . . Having observed in our march that the Highlanders lose themselves in the woods as soon as they go out of the road, and cannot on that account be employed as Flankers, I have commissioned a person here to procure me about thirty woodsmen to march with us. . . . This is very irregular, but the circumstances render it so absolutely necessary that I hope you will approve it."

restless leaves. With difficulty and toil, the wagons dragged slowly on, by hill and hollow, through brook and quagmire, over roots, rocks, and stumps. Nature had formed the country for a war of ambuscades and surprises, and no pains were spared to guard against them. A band of backwoodsmen led the way, followed closely by the pioneers; the wagons and the cattle were in the centre, guarded by the regulars; and a rear guard of backwoodsmen closed the line of march. Frontier riflemen scoured the woods far in front and on either flank, and made surprise impossible. Thus they toiled heavily on till the main ridge of the Alleghanies, a mighty wall of green, rose up before them; and they began their zigzag progress up the woody heights amid the sweltering heats of July. The tongues of the panting oxen hung lolling from their jaws; while the pine-trees, scorching in the hot sun, diffused their resinous odors through the sultry air. At length from the windy summit the Highland soldiers could gaze around upon a boundless panorama of forest-covered mountains, wilder than their own native hills. Descending from the Alleghanies, they entered upon a country less rugged and formidable in itself, but beset with constantly increasing dangers. On the second of August, they reached Fort Ligonier, about fifty miles from Bedford, and a hundred and fifty from Carlisle. The Indians who were about the place vanished at their approach; but the garrison could furnish no intelligence of the motions and designs of the enemy, having been completely blockaded for weeks. In this uncertainty, Bouquet resolved to leave behind the oxen and wagons, which formed the most cumbrous part of the convoy, in order to advance with greater celerity, and oppose a better resistance in case of attack. Thus relieved, the army resumed its march on the fourth, taking with them three hundred and fifty pack horses and a few cattle, and at nightfall encamped at no great distance from Ligonier. Within less than a day's march in advance lay the dangerous defiles of Turtle Creek, a stream flowing at the bottom of a deep hollow, flanked by steep declivities, along the foot of which the road at that time ran for some distance. Fearing that the enemy would lay an ambuscade at this place, Bouquet resolved to march on the following day as far as a small stream called Bushy Run; to rest here until night, and then, by a forced march, to cross Turtle Creek under cover of the darkness.

On the morning of the fifth, the tents were struck at an early hour, and the troops began their march through a country broken with hills and deep hollows, covered with the tall, dense forest, which spread for countless leagues around. By one o'clock, they had advanced seventeen miles; and the guides assured them that they were within half a mile of Bushy Run, their proposed resting-place. The tired soldiers were pressing forward with renewed alacrity, when suddenly the report of rifles from the front sent a thrill along the ranks; and, as they listened, the firing thickened into a fierce, sharp rattle; while shouts and whoops, deadened by the intervening forest, showed that the advance guard was hotly engaged. The two foremost companies were at once ordered forward to support it; but, far from abating, the fire grew so rapid and furious as to argue the presence of an enemy at once numerous and resolute. At this, the convoy was halted, the troops formed into line, and a general charge ordered. Bearing down through the forest with fixed bayonets, they drove the yelping assailants before them, and swept the ground clear. But at the very moment of success, a fresh burst of whoops and firing was heard from either flank; while a confused noise from the rear showed that the convoy was attacked. It was necessary instantly to fall back for its support. Driving off the assailants, the troops formed in a circle around the crowded and terrified horses. Though they were new to the work, and though the numbers and movements of the enemy, whose yelling resounded on every side, were concealed by the thick forest, yet no man lost his composure; and all displayed a steadiness which nothing but implicit confidence in their commander could have inspired. And now ensued a combat of a nature most harassing and discouraging. Again and again, now on this side and now on that, a crowd of Indians rushed up, pouring in a heavy fire, and striving, with furious outcries, to break into the circle. A well-directed volley met them, followed by a steady charge of the bayonet. They never waited an instant to receive the attack, but, leaping backwards from tree to tree, soon vanished from sight, only to renew their attack with unabated ferocity in another quarter. Such was their activity, that very few of them were hurt; while the British, less expert in bush-fighting, suffered severely. Thus the fight went on, without intermission, for seven hours, until the forest grew dark with approaching night. Upon this, the Indians gradually slackened their fire, and the exhausted soldiers found time to rest.

It was impossible to change their ground in the enemy's presence, and the troops were obliged to encamp upon the hill where the combat had taken place, though not a drop of water was to be found there. Fearing a night attack, Bouquet stationed numerous sentinels and outposts to guard against it; while the men lay down upon their arms, preserving the order they had maintained during the fight. Having completed the necessary arrangements, Bouquet, doubtful of surviving the battle of the morrow, wrote to Sir Jeffrey Amherst, in a few clear, concise words, an account of the day's events. His letter concludes as follows: "Whatever our fate may be, I thought it necessary to give your Excellency this early information, that you may, at all events, take such measures as you will think proper with the provinces, for their own safety, and the effectual relief of Fort Pitt; as, in case of another engagement, I fear insurmountable difficulties in protecting and transporting our provisions, being already so much weakened by the losses of this day, in men and horses, besides the additional necessity of carrying the wounded, whose situation is truly deplorable."

The condition of these unhappy men might well awaken sympathy. About sixty soldiers, besides several officers, had been killed or disabled. A space in the centre of the camp was prepared for the reception of the wounded, and surrounded by a wall of flour-bags from the convoy, affording some protection against the bullets which flew from all sides during the fight. Here they lay upon the ground, enduring agonies of thirst, and waiting, passive and helpless, the issue of the battle. Deprived of the animating thought that their lives and safety depended on their own exertions; surrounded by a wilderness, and by scenes to the horror of which no degree of familiarity could render the imagination callous, they must have endured mental sufferings, compared to which the pain of their wounds was slight. In the probable event of defeat, a fate inexpressibly horrible awaited them; while even victory would not ensure their safety, since any great increase in their numbers would render it impossible for their comrades to transport them. Nor was the condition of those who had hitherto escaped an enviable one. Though they were about equal in number to their assailants, yet the dexterity and alertness of the Indians, joined to the nature of the country, gave all the advantages of a greatly superior force. The enemy were, moreover, exulting in the fullest confidence of success; for it was in these very forests that, eight years before, they had nearly destroyed twice their number of the best British troops. Throughout the earlier part of the night, they kept up a dropping fire upon the camp; while, at short intervals, a wild whoop from the thick surrounding gloom told with what fierce eagerness they waited to glut their vengeance on the morrow. The camp remained in darkness, for it would have been dangerous to build fires within its precincts, to direct the aim of the lurking marksmen. Surrounded by such terrors, the men snatched a disturbed and broken sleep, recruiting their exhausted strength for the renewed struggle of the morning.

With the earliest dawn of day, and while the damp, cool forest was still involved in twilight, there rose around the camp a general burst of those horrible cries which form the ordinary prelude of an Indian battle. Instantly, from every side at once, the enemy opened their fire, approaching under cover of the trees and bushes, and levelling with a close and deadly aim. Often, as on the previous day, they would rush up with furious impetuosity, striving to break into the ring of troops. They were repulsed at every point; but the British, though constantly victorious, were beset with undiminished perils, while the violence of the enemy seemed every moment on the increase. True to their favorite tactics, they would never stand their ground when attacked, but vanish at the first gleam of the levelled bayonet, only to appear again the moment the danger was past. The troops, fatigued by the long march and equally long battle of the previous day, were maddened by the torments of thirst, "more intolerable," says their commander, "than the enemy's fire." They were fully conscious of the peril in which they stood, of wasting away by slow degrees beneath the shot of assailants at once so daring, so cautious, and so active, and upon whom it was impossible to inflict any decisive injury. The Indians saw their distress, and pressed them closer and closer, redoubling their yells and howlings; while some of them, sheltered behind trees, assailed the troops, in bad English, with abuse and derision.

Meanwhile the interior of the camp was a scene of confusion. The horses, secured in a crowd near the wall of flour-bags which covered the wounded, were often struck by the bullets, and wrought to the height of terror by the mingled din of whoops, shrieks, and firing. They would break away by half scores at a time, burst through the ring of troops and the outer circle of assailants, and scour madly up and down the hill-sides; while many of the drivers, overcome by the terrors of a scene in which they could bear no active part, hid themselves among the bushes, and could neither hear nor obey orders.

It was now about ten o'clock. Oppressed with heat, fatigue, and thirst, the distressed troops still maintained a weary and wavering defence, encircling the convoy in a yet unbroken ring. They were fast falling in their ranks, and the strength and spirits of the survivors had begun to flag. If the fortunes of the day were to be retrieved, the effort must be made at once; and happily the mind of the commander was equal to the emergency. In the midst of the confusion he conceived a masterly stratagem. Could the Indians be brought together in a body, and made to stand their ground when attacked, there could be little doubt of the result; and, to effect this object, Bouquet determined to increase their confidence, which had already mounted to an audacious pitch. Two companies of infantry, forming a part of the ring which had been exposed to the hottest fire, were ordered to fall back into the interior of the camp; while the troops on either hand joined their files across the vacant space, as if to cover the retreat of their comrades. These orders, given at a favorable moment, were executed with great promptness. The thin line of troops who took possession of the deserted part of the circle were, from their small numbers, brought closer in towards the centre. The Indians mistook these movements for a retreat. Confident that their time was come, they leaped up on all sides, from behind the trees and bushes, and, with infernal screeches, rushed headlong towards the spot, pouring in a heavy and galling fire. The shock was too violent to be long endured. The men struggled to maintain their posts; but the Indians seemed on the point of breaking into the heart of the camp, when the aspect of affairs was suddenly reversed. The two companies, who had apparently abandoned their position, were in fact destined to begin the attack; and they now sallied out from the circle at a point where a depression in the ground, joined to the thick growth of trees, concealed them from the eyes of the Indians. Making a short *détour* through the woods, they came round upon the flank of the furious assailants, and fired a close volley into the midst of the crowd. Numbers were seen to fall; yet though completely surprised, and utterly at a loss to understand the nature of the attack, the Indians faced about with the greatest intrepidity, and returned the fire. But the Highlanders, with yells as wild as their own, fell on them with the bayonet. The shock was irresistible, and they fled before the charging ranks in a tumultuous throng. Orders had been given to two other companies, occupying a contiguous part of the circle, to support the attack whenever a favorable moment should occur; and they had therefore advanced a little from their position, and lay close crouched in ambush. The fugitives, pressed by the Highland bayonets, passed directly across their front; upon which they rose, and poured among them a second volley, no less destructive than the first. This completed the rout. The four companies, uniting, drove the flying savages through the woods, giving them no time to rally or reload their empty rifles, killing many, and scattering the rest in hopeless confusion.

While this took place at one part of the circle, the troops and the savages had still maintained their respective positions at the other; but when the latter perceived the total rout of their comrades, and saw the troops advancing to assail them, they also lost heart, and fled. The discordant outcries which had so long deafened the ears of the English soon ceased altogether, and not a living Indian remained near the spot. About sixty corpses lay scattered over the ground. Among them were found those of several prominent chiefs, while the blood which stained the leaves of the bushes showed that numbers had fled wounded from the field. The soldiers took but one prisoner, whom they shot to death like a captive wolf. The loss of the British in the two battles surpassed that of the enemy, amounting to eight officers and one hundred and fifteen men.[1]

Having been for some time detained by the necessity of making litters for the wounded, and destroying the stores which the flight of most of the horses made it impossible to transport, the army moved on, in the afternoon, to Bushy Run. Here they had scarcely formed their camp, when they were again fired upon by a body of Indians, who, however, were soon repulsed. On the next day they resumed their progress towards Fort Pitt, distant about twenty-five miles; and, though frequently annoyed on the march by petty

---

[1] MS. Letters—*Bouquet to Amherst*, Aug. 5, 6. *Penn Gaz.* 1809–1810. *Gent. Mag.* XXXIII. 487. *London Mag.* for 1763, 545. *Account of Bouquet's Expedition. Annual Register* for 1763, 28. Mante, 493.

The accounts of this action, published in the journals of the day, excited much attention, from the wild and novel character of this species of warfare. A well-written description of the battle, together with a journal of Bouquet's expedition of the succeeding year, was published in a thin quarto, with illustrations from the pencil of West. The writer was Dr. William Smith, of Philadelphia, and not, as has usually been thought, the geographer Thomas Hutchins. See the reprint, *Clarke's Historical Series*, Vol. I. A French translation of the narrative was published at Amsterdam in 1769.

Extract from a Letter—*Fort Pitt*, August 12 (*Penn. Gaz.* No. 1810): —

"We formed a Circle round our Convoy and Wounded; upon which the Savages collected themselves, and continued whooping and popping at us all the Evening. Next Morning, having mustered all their Force, they began the War-whoop, attacking us in Front, when the Colonel feigned a Retreat, which encouraged the Indians to an eager Pursuit, while the Light Infantry and Grenadiers rushed out on their Right and Left Flanks, attacking them where they little expected it; by which Means a great Number of them were killed; and among the rest, Keelyuskung, a Delaware Chief, who the Night before, and that Morning, had been Blackguarding us in English: We lost one Man in the Rear, on our March the Day after.

"In other Letters from Fort Pitt, it is mentioned that, to a Man, they were resolved to defend the Garrison (if the Troops had not arrived), as long as any Ammunition, and Provision to support them, were left; and that then they would have fought their Way through, or died in the Attempt, rather than have been made Prisoners by such perfidious, cruel, and Blood-thirsty Hell-hounds."

See Appendix, D.

attacks, they reached their destination, on the tenth, without serious loss. It was a joyful moment both to the troops and to the garrison. The latter, it will be remembered, were left surrounded and hotly pressed by the Indians, who had beleaguered the place from the twenty-eighth of July to the first of August, when, hearing of Bouquet's approach, they had abandoned the siege, and marched to attack him. From this time, the garrison had seen nothing of them until the morning of the tenth, when, shortly before the army appeared, they had passed the fort in a body, raising the scalp-yell, and displaying their disgusting trophies to the view of the English.[1]

The battle of Bushy Run was one of the best contested actions ever fought between white men and Indians. If there was any disparity of numbers, the advantage was on the side

[1] Extract from a Letter—*Fort Pitt*, August 12 (*Penn. Gaz.* No. 1810):

"As you will probably have the Accounts of these Engagements from the Gentlemen that were in them, I shall say no more than this, that it is the general Opinion, the Troops behaved with the utmost Intrepidity, and the Indians were never known to behave so fiercely. You may be sure the Sight of the Troops was very agreeable to our poor Garrison, being penned up in the Fort from the 27th of May to the 9th Instant, and the Barrack Rooms crammed with Men, Women, and Children, tho' providentially no other Disorder ensued than the Small-pox.—From the 16th of June to the 28th of July, we were pestered with the Enemy; sometimes with their Flags, demanding Conferences; at other Times threatening, then soothing, and offering their Cordial Advice, for us to evacuate the Place; for that they, the Delawares, tho' our dear Friends and Brothers, could no longer protect us from the Fury of Legions of other Nations, that were coming from the Lakes, &c., to destroy us. But, finding that neither had any Effect on us, they mustered their whole force, in Number about 400, and began a most furious Fire from all Quarters on the Fort, which they continued for four Days, and great Part of the Nights, viz., from the 28th of July to the last.—Our Commander was wounded by an Arrow in the Leg, and no other Person, of any Note, hurt, tho' the Balls were whistling very thick about our Ears. Nine Rank and File wounded, and one Hulings having his Leg broke, was the whole of our Loss during this hot Firing; tho' we have Reason to think that we killed several of our loving Brethren, notwithstanding their Alertness in skulking behind the Banks of the Rivers, &c.—These Gentry, seeing they could not take the Fort, sheered off and we heard no more of them till the Account of the above Engagements came to hand, when we were convinced that our good Brothers did us this second Act of Friendship.—What they intend next, God knows, but am afraid they will disperse in small Parties, among the Inhabitants, if not well defended."

of the troops; and the Indians had displayed throughout a fierceness and intrepidity matched only by the steady valor with which they were met. In the provinces, the victory excited equal joy and admiration, especially among those who knew the incalculable difficulties of an Indian campaign. The Assembly of Pennsylvania passed a vote expressing their sense of the merits of Bouquet, and of the service he had rendered to the province. He soon after received the additional honor of the formal thanks of the King.[1]

In many an Indian village, the women cut away their hair, gashed their limbs with knives, and uttered their dismal howlings of lamentation for the fallen. Yet, though surprised and dispirited, the rage of the Indians was too deep to be quenched, even by so signal a reverse; and their outrages upon the frontier were resumed with unabated ferocity. Fort Pitt, however, was effectually relieved; while the moral effect of the victory enabled the frontier settlers to encounter the enemy with a spirit which would have been wanting, had Bouquet sustained a defeat.

[1] Extract from a MS. Letter—*Sir J. Amherst to Colonel Bouquet*:—

"New York, 31st August, 1763.

"The Disposition you made for the Reception of the Indians, the Second Day, was indeed very wisely Concerted, and as happily Executed; I am pleased with Every part of your Conduct on the Occasion, which being so well seconded by the Officers and Soldiers under your Command, Enabled you not only to Protect your Large Convoy, but to rout a Body of Savages that would have been very formidable against any Troops but such as you had with you."

Chapter XXI.

1763.

THE IROQUOIS. — AMBUSCADE
OF THE DEVIL'S HOLE.

WHILE BOUQUET was fighting the battle of Bushy Run, and Dalzell making his fatal sortie against the camp of Pontiac, Sir William Johnson was engaged in the more pacific yet more important task of securing the friendship and alliance of the Six Nations. After several preliminary conferences, he sent runners throughout the whole confederacy to invite deputies of the several tribes to meet him in council at Johnson Hall. The request was not declined. From the banks of the Mohawk; from the Oneida, Cayuga, and Tuscarora villages; from the valley of Onondaga, where, from immemorial time, had burned the great council-fire of the confederacy,— came chiefs and warriors, gathering to the place of meeting. The Senecas alone, the warlike tenants of the Genesee valley, refused to attend; for they were already in arms against the English. Besides the Iroquois, deputies came from the tribes dwelling along the St. Lawrence, and within the settled parts of Canada.

The council opened on the seventh of September. Despite their fair words, their attachment was doubtful; but Sir William Johnson, by a dexterous mingling of reasoning, threats, and promises, allayed their discontent, and banished the thoughts of war. They winced, however, when he informed them that, during the next season, an English army must pass through their country, on its way to punish the refractory tribes of the West. "Your foot is broad and heavy," said the speaker from Onondaga; "take care that you do not tread on us." Seeing the improved temper of his auditory, Johnson was led to hope for some farther advantage than that of mere neutrality. He accordingly urged the Iroquois to take up arms against the hostile tribes, and concluded his final harangue with the following figurative words: "I now deliver you a good English axe, which I desire you will give to the warriors of all your nations, with directions to use it against these covenant-breakers, by cutting off the bad links which have sullied the chain of friendship."

These words were confirmed by the presentation of a black war-belt of wampum, and the offer of a hatchet, which the Iroquois did not refuse to accept. That they would take any very active and strenuous part in the war, could not be expected; yet their bearing arms at all would prove of great advantage, by discouraging the hostile Indians who had looked upon the Iroquois as friends and abettors. Some months after the council, several small parties actually took the field; and, being stimulated by the prospect of reward, brought in a considerable number of scalps and prisoners.[1]

Upon the persuasion of Sir William Johnson, the tribes of Canada were induced to send a message to the western Indians, exhorting them to bury the hatchet, while the Iroquois despatched an embassy of similar import to the Delawares on the Susquehanna. "Cousins the Delawares,"—thus ran the message,—"we have heard that many wild Indians in the West, who have tails like bears, have let fall the chain of friendship, and taken up the hatchet against our brethren the English. We desire you to hold fast the chain, and shut your ears against their words."[2]

In spite of the friendly disposition to which the Iroquois had been brought, the province of New York suffered not a little from the attacks of the hostile tribes who ravaged the borders of Ulster, Orange, and Albany counties, and threatened to destroy the upper settlements of the Mohawk.[3] Sir

---

[1] MS. *Minutes of Conference with the Six Nations and others, at Johnson Hall,* Sept. 1763. *Letters of Sir William Johnson.*

[2] MS. *Harrisburg Papers.*

[3] Extract from a MS. Letter—*Sir W. Johnson to Sir J. Amherst*: —

"Johnson Hall, July 8th, 1763.

"I Cannot Conclude without Representing to Your Excellency the great Panic and uneasiness into which the Inhabitants of these parts are cast, which I have endeavored to Remove by every Method in my power, to prevent their Abandoning their Settlements from their apprehensions of the Indians: As they in General Confide much in my Residence, they are hitherto Prevented from taking that hasty Measure, but should I be Obliged to retire (which I hope will not be the case), not only my Own Tenants, who are upwards of 120 Families, but all the Rest would Immediately follow the Example, which I am Determined against doing 'till the last Extremity, as I know it would prove of general bad Consequence."

William Johnson was the object of their especial enmity, and he several times received intimations that he was about to be attacked. He armed his tenantry, surrounded his seat of Johnson Hall with a stockade, and garrisoned it with a party of soldiers, which Sir Jeffrey Amherst had ordered thither for his protection.

About this time, a singular incident occurred near the town of Goshen. Four or five men went out among the hills to shoot partridges, and, chancing to raise a large covey, they all fired their guns at nearly the same moment. The timorous inhabitants, hearing the reports, supposed that they came from an Indian war-party, and instantly fled in dismay, spreading the alarm as they went. The neighboring country was soon in a panic. The farmers cut the harness of their horses, and, leaving their carts and ploughs behind, galloped for their lives. Others, snatching up their children and their most valuable property, made with all speed for New England, not daring to pause until they had crossed the Hudson. For several days the neighborhood was abandoned, five hundred families having left their habitations and fled.[1] Not long after this absurd affair, an event occurred of a widely different character. Allusion has before been made to the carrying-place of Niagara, which formed an essential link in the chain of communication between the province of New York and the interior country. Men and military stores were conveyed in boats up the River Niagara, as far as the present site of Lewiston. Thence a portage road, several miles in length, passed along the banks of the stream, and terminated at Fort Schlosser, above the cataract. This road traversed a region whose sublime features have gained for it a world-wide renown. The River Niagara, a short distance below the cataract, assumes an aspect scarcely less remarkable than that stupendous scene itself. Its channel is formed by a vast ravine, whose sides, now bare and weather-stained, now shaggy with forest-trees, rise in cliffs of appalling height and steepness. Along this chasm pour all the waters of the lakes, heaving their furious surges with the power of an ocean and the rage of a mountain torrent. About three miles below the cataract, the

[1] *Penn. Gaz.* No. 1809.

precipices which form the eastern wall of the ravine are broken by an abyss of awful depth and blackness, bearing at the present day the name of the Devil's Hole. In its shallowest part, the precipice sinks sheer down to the depth of eighty feet, where it meets a chaotic mass of rocks, descending with an abrupt declivity to unseen depths below. Within the cold and damp recesses of the gulf, a host of forest-trees have rooted themselves; and, standing on the perilous brink, one may look down upon the mingled foliage of ash, poplar, and maple, while, above them all, the spruce and fir shoot their sharp and rigid spires upward into sunlight. The roar of the convulsed river swells heavily on the ear; and, far below, its headlong waters, careering in foam, may be discerned through the openings of the matted foliage.

On the thirteenth of September, a numerous train of wagons and pack-horses proceeded from the lower landing to Fort Schlosser; and on the following morning set out on their return, guarded by an escort of twenty-four soldiers. They pursued their slow progress until they reached a point where the road passed along the brink of the Devil's Hole. The gulf yawned on their left, while on their right the road was skirted by low densely wooded hills. Suddenly they were greeted by the blaze and clatter of a hundred rifles. Then followed the startled cries of men, and the bounding of maddened horses. At the next instant, a host of Indians broke screeching from the woods, and rifle-butt and tomahawk finished the bloody work. All was over in a moment. Horses leaped the precipice; men were driven shrieking into the abyss; teams and wagons went over, crashing to atoms among the rocks below. Tradition relates that the drummer-boy of the detachment was caught, in his fall, among the branches of a tree, where he hung suspended by his drum-strap. Being but slightly injured, he disengaged himself, and, hiding in the recesses of the gulf, finally escaped. One of the teamsters also, who was wounded at the first fire, contrived to crawl into the woods, where he lay concealed till the Indians had left the place. Besides these two, the only survivor was Stedman, the conductor of the convoy; who, being well mounted, and seeing the whole party forced helpless towards the precipice, wheeled his horse, and resolutely spurred through the crowd of Indians. One of them, it is said, seized his bridle; but he freed himself by a dexterous use of his knife, and plunged into the woods, untouched by the bullets which whistled about his head. Flying at full speed through the forest, he reached Fort Schlosser in safety.

The distant sound of the Indian rifles had been heard by a party of soldiers, who occupied a small fortified camp near the lower landing. Forming in haste, they advanced eagerly to the rescue. In anticipation of this movement, the Indians, who were nearly five hundred in number, had separated into two parties, one of which had stationed itself at the Devil's Hole, to waylay the convoy, while the other formed an ambuscade upon the road, a mile nearer the landing-place. The soldiers, marching precipitately, and huddled in a close body, were suddenly assailed by a volley of rifles, which stretched half their number dead upon the road. Then, rushing from the forest, the Indians cut down the survivors with merciless ferocity. A small remnant only escaped the massacre, and fled to Fort Niagara with the tidings. Major Wilkins, who commanded at this post, lost no time in marching to the spot, with nearly the whole strength of his garrison. Not an Indian was to be found. At the two places of ambuscade, about seventy dead bodies were counted, naked, scalpless, and so horribly mangled that many of them could not be recognized. All the wagons had been broken to pieces, and such of the horses as were not driven over the precipice had been carried off, laden, doubtless, with the plunder. The ambuscade of the Devil's Hole has gained a traditionary immortality, adding fearful interest to a scene whose native horrors need no aid from the imagination.[1]

---

[1]MS. Letter—*Amherst to Egremont*, October 13. Two anonymous letters from officers at Fort Niagara, September 16 and 17. *Life of Mary Jemison*, Appendix. MS. *Johnson Papers*.

One of the actors in the tragedy, a Seneca warrior, named Blacksnake, was living a few years since at a very advanced age. He described the scene with great animation to a friend of the writer; and, as he related how the English were forced over the precipice, his small eyes glittered like those of the serpent whose name he bore.

Extract from a Letter—*Niagara,* September 16 (*Penn. Gaz.* No. 1815):

"On the first hearing of the Firing by the Convoy, Capt. Johnston, and three Subalterns, marched with about 80 Men, mostly of Gage's Light In-

The Seneca warriors, aided probably by some of the western Indians, were the authors of this unexpected attack. Their hostility did not end here. Several weeks afterwards, Major Wilkins, with a force of six hundred regulars, collected with great effort throughout the provinces, was advancing to the relief of Detroit. As the boats were slowly forcing their way upwards against the swift current above the falls of Niagara, they were assailed by a mere handful of Indians, thrown into confusion, and driven back to Fort Schlosser with serious loss. The next attempt was more fortunate, the boats reaching Lake Erie without farther attack; but the inauspicious opening of the expedition was followed by results yet more disastrous. As they approached their destination, a violent storm overtook them in the night. The frail bateaux, tossing upon the merciless waves of Lake Erie, were overset, driven ashore, and many of them dashed to pieces. About seventy men perished, all the ammunition and stores were destroyed, and the shattered flotilla was forced back to Niagara.[1]

---

fantry, who were in a little Camp adjacent; they had scarce Time to form when the Indians appeared at the above Pass; our People fired briskly upon them, but was instantly surrounded, and the Captain who commanded mortally wounded the first Fire; the 3 Subalterns also were soon after killed, on which a general Confusion ensued. The Indians rushed in on all Sides and cut about 60 or 70 Men in Pieces, including the Convoy: Ten of our Men are all we can yet learn have made their Escape; they came here through the Woods Yesterday. From many Circumstances, it is believed the Senecas have a chief Hand in this Affair."

Extract from a Letter—*Niagara,* September 17 (*Penn. Gaz.* No. 1815):

"Wednesday the 14th Inst. a large Body of Indians, some say 300, others 4 or 500, came down upon the Carrying-Place, attacked the Waggon Escort, which consisted of a Serjeant and 24 Men. This small Body immediately became a Sacrifice, only two Waggoners escaped. Two Companies of Light Infantry (the General's and La Hunt's), that were encamped at the Lower Landing, hearing the Fire, instantly rushed out to their Relief, headed by Lieuts. George Campbell, and Frazier, Lieutenant Rosco, of the Artillery, and Lieutenant Deaton, of the Provincials; this Party had not marched above a Mile and Half when they were attacked, surrounded, and almost every Man cut to Pieces; the Officers were all killed, it is reported, on the Enemy's first Fire; the Savages rushed down upon them in three Columns."

[1]MS. *Diary of an officer in Wilkins's Expedition against the Indians at Detroit.*

Chapter XXII.

1763.

DESOLATION OF THE FRONTIERS.

T HE ADVANCING FRONTIERS of American civilization have always nurtured a class of men of striking and peculiar character. The best examples of this character have, perhaps, been found among the settlers of Western Virginia, and the hardy progeny who have sprung from that generous stock. The Virginian frontiersman was, as occasion called, a farmer, a hunter, and a warrior, by turns. The well-beloved rifle was seldom out of his hand; and he never deigned to lay aside the fringed frock, moccasons, and Indian leggins, which formed the appropriate costume of the forest ranger. Concerning the business, pleasures, and refinements of cultivated life, he knew little, and cared nothing; and his manners were usually rough and obtrusive to the last degree. Aloof from mankind, he lived in a world of his own, which, in his view, contained all that was deserving of admiration and praise. He looked upon himself and his compeers as models of prowess and manhood, nay, of all that is elegant and polite; and the forest gallant regarded with peculiar complacency his own half-savage dress, his swaggering gait, and his backwoods jargon. He was wilful, headstrong, and quarrelsome; frank, straightforward, and generous; brave as the bravest, and utterly intolerant of arbitrary control. His self-confidence mounted to audacity. Eminently capable of heroism, both in action and endurance, he viewed every species of effeminacy with supreme contempt; and, accustomed as he was to entire self-reliance, the mutual dependence of conventional life excited his especial scorn. With all his ignorance, he had a mind by nature quick, vigorous, and penetrating; and his mode of life, while it developed the daring energy of his character, wrought some of his faculties to a high degree of acuteness. Many of his traits have been reproduced in his offspring. From him have sprung those hardy men whose struggles and sufferings on the bloody ground of Kentucky will always form a striking page in American history; and that band of adventurers before whose headlong charge, in the valley of Chihuahua, neither breastworks, nor batteries, nor fivefold odds could avail for a moment.

At the period of Pontiac's war, the settlements of Virginia had extended as far as the Alleghanies, and several small towns had already sprung up beyond the Blue Ridge. The population of these beautiful valleys was, for the most part, thin and scattered; and the progress of settlement had been greatly retarded by Indian hostilities, which, during the early years of the French war, had thrown these borders into total confusion. They had contributed, however, to enhance the martial temper of the people, and give a warlike aspect to the whole frontier. At intervals, small stockade forts, containing houses and cabins, had been erected by the joint labor of the inhabitants; and hither, on occasion of alarm, the settlers of the neighborhood congregated for refuge, remaining in tolerable security till the danger was past. Many of the inhabitants were engaged for a great part of the year in hunting; an occupation upon which they entered with the keenest relish.[1] Well versed in woodcraft, unsurpassed as marksmen, and practised in all the wiles of Indian war, they would have formed, under a more stringent organization, the best possible defence against a savage enemy; but each man came and went at his own sovereign will, and discipline and obedience were repugnant to all his habits.

The frontiers of Maryland and Virginia closely resembled each other; but those of Pennsylvania had peculiarities of their own. The population of this province was of a most motley complexion, being made up of members of various nations, and numerous religious sects: English, Irish, German, Swiss, Welsh, and Dutch; Quakers, Presbyterians, Lutherans,

---

[1]"I have often seen them get up early in the morning at this season, walk hastily out, and look anxiously to the woods, and snuff the autumnal winds with the highest rapture; then return into the house, and cast a quick and attentive look at the rifle, which was always suspended to a joist by a couple of buck's horns, or little forks. His hunting dog, understanding the intentions of his master, would wag his tail, and, by every blandishment in his power, express his readiness to accompany him to the woods."—Doddridge, *Notes on Western Va. and Pa.*, 124.

For a view of the state of the frontier, see also Kercheval, *Hist. of the Valley of Virginia*; and Smyth, *Travels in America*.

Dunkers, Mennonists, and Moravians. Nor is this catalogue by any means complete. The Quakers, to whose peaceful temper the rough frontier offered no attraction, were confined to the eastern parts of the province. Cumberland County, which lies west of the Susquehanna, and may be said to have formed the frontier, was then almost exclusively occupied by the Irish and their descendants; who, however, were neither of the Roman faith nor of Celtic origin, being emigrants from the colony of Scotch which forms a numerous and thrifty population in the north of Ireland. In religious faith, they were stanch and zealous Presbyterians. Long residence in the province had modified their national character, and imparted many of the peculiar traits of the American backwoodsman; yet the nature of their religious tenets produced a certain rigidity of temper and demeanor, from which the Virginian was wholly free. They were, nevertheless, hot-headed and turbulent, often setting law and authority at defiance. The counties east of the Susquehanna supported a mixed population, among which was conspicuous a swarm of German peasants; who had been inundating the country for many years past, and who for the most part were dull and ignorant boors, like some of their descendants. The Swiss and German sectaries called Mennonists, who were numerous in Lancaster County, professed, like the Quakers, principles of non-resistance, and refused to bear arms.[1]

It was upon this mingled population that the storm of Indian war was now descending with appalling fury,—a fury unparalleled through all past and succeeding years. For hundreds of miles from north to south, the country was wasted with fire and steel. It would be a task alike useless and revolting to explore, through all its details, this horrible monotony of blood and havoc.[2] The country was filled with the wildest

[1] For an account of the population of Pennsylvania, see Rupp's two histories of York and Lancaster, and of Lebanon and Berks Counties. See also the *History of Cumberland County*, and the *Penn. Hist. Coll.*

[2] "There are many Letters in Town, in which the Distresses of the Frontier Inhabitants are set forth in a most moving and striking Manner; but as these Letters are pretty much the same, and it would be endless to insert the whole, the following is the Substance of some of them, as near as we can recollect, viz.:—

"That the Indians had set Fire to Houses, Barns, Corn, Hay, and, in short,

dismay. The people of Virginia betook themselves to their forts for refuge. Those of Pennsylvania, ill supplied with such asylums, fled by thousands, and crowded in upon the older settlements. The ranging parties who visited the scene of devastation beheld, among the ruined farms and plantations, sights of unspeakable horror; and discovered, in the depths of the forest, the half-consumed bodies of men and women, still bound fast to the trees, where they had perished in the fiery torture.[1]

---

to every Thing that was combustible, so that the whole Country seemed to be in one general Blaze—That the Miseries and Distresses of the poor People were really shocking to Humanity, and beyond the Power of Language to describe—That Carlisle was become the Barrier, not a single Individual being beyond it—That every Stable and Hovel in the Town was crowded with miserable Refugees, who were reduced to a State of Beggary and Despair; their Houses, Cattle and Harvest destroyed; and from a plentiful, independent People, they were become real Objects of Charity and Commiseration— That it was most dismal to see the Streets filled with People, in whose Countenances might be discovered a Mixture of Grief, Madness and Despair; and to hear, now and then, the Sighs and Groans of Men, the disconsolate Lamentations of Women, and the Screams of Children, who had lost their nearest and dearest Relatives: And that on both Sides of the Susquehannah, for some Miles, the Woods were filled with poor Families, and their Cattle, who make Fires, and live like the Savages."—*Penn. Gaz.* No. 1805.

Extract from a MS. Letter, signature erased—*Staunton*, July 26:—

"Since the reduction of the Regiment, I have lived in the country, which enables me to enform yr Ho[nr] of some particulars, I think it is a duty incumbent on me to do. I can assert that in eight years' service, I never knew such a general consternation as the late irruption of Indians has occasioned. Should they make a second attempt, I am assured the country will be laid desolate, which I attribute to the following reasons. The sudden, great, and unexpected slaughter of the people; their being destitute of arms and ammunition; the country Lieut. being at a distance and not exerting himself, his orders are neglected; the most of the militia officers being unfit persons, or unwilling, not to say afraid to meet an Enemy; too busy with their harvest to run a risk in the field. The Inhabitants left without protection, without a person to stead them, have nothing to do but fly, as the Indians are saving and caressing all the negroes they take; should it produce an insurrection, it may be attended with the most serious consequences."

[1] "*To Col. Francis Lee, or, in his Absence, to the next Commanding Officer in Loudoun County.*" (*Penn. Gaz.* No. 1805).

"I examined the Express that brought this Letter from Winchester to Loudoun County, and he informed me that he was employed as an Express from Fort Cumberland to Winchester, which Place he left the 4th Instant, and that passing from the Fort to Winchester, he saw lying on the Road a Woman, who had been just scalped, and was then in the Agonies of Death,

Among the numerous war-parties which were now ravaging the borders, none was more destructive than a band, about sixty in number, which ascended the Kenawha, and pursued its desolating course among the settlements about the sources of that river. They passed valley after valley, sometimes attacking the inhabitants by surprise, and sometimes murdering them under the mask of friendship, until they came to the little settlement of Greenbrier, where nearly a hundred of the people were assembled at the fortified house of Archibald Glendenning. Seeing two or three Indians approach, whom they recognized as former acquaintances, they suffered them to enter without distrust; but the new-comers were soon joined by others, until the entire party were gathered in and around the buildings. Some suspicion was now awakened; and, in order to propitiate the dangerous guests, they were presented with the carcass of an elk lately brought in by the hunters. They immediately cut it up, and began to feast upon it. The backwoodsmen, with their families, were assembled in one large room; and finding themselves mingled among the Indians, and embarrassed by the presence of the women and children, they remained indecisive and irresolute. Meanwhile, an old woman, who sat in a corner of the room, and who had lately received some slight accidental injury, asked one of the warriors if he could cure the wound. He replied that he thought he could, and, to make good his words, killed her with his tomahawk. This was the signal for a scene of general butchery. A few persons made their escape; the rest were killed or captured. Glendenning snatched up one of his children, and rushed from the house, but was shot dead as he leaped the fence. A negro woman gained a place of concealment, whither she was followed by her screaming child; and, fearing lest the cries of the boy should betray her, she turned

---

with her Brains hanging over her Skull; his Companions made a Proposal to knock her on the Head, to put an End to her Agony, but this Express apprehending the Indians were near at Hand, and not thinking it safe to lose any Time, rode off, and left the poor Woman in the Situation they found her."

The circumstances referred to in the text are mentioned in several pamphlets of the day, on the authority of James Smith, a prominent leader of the rangers.

and killed him at a blow. Among the prisoners was the wife of Glendenning, a woman of a most masculine spirit, who, far from being overpowered by what she had seen, was excited to the extremity of rage, charged her captors with treachery, cowardice, and ingratitude, and assailed them with a tempest of abuse. Neither the tomahawk, which they brandished over her head, nor the scalp of her murdered husband, with which they struck her in the face, could silence the undaunted virago. When the party began their retreat, bearing with them a great quantity of plunder packed on the horses they had stolen, Glendenning's wife, with her infant child, was placed among a long train of captives guarded before and behind by the Indians. As they defiled along a narrow path which led through a gap in the mountains, she handed the child to the woman behind her, and, leaving it to its fate,[1] slipped into the bushes and escaped. Being well acquainted with the woods, she succeeded, before nightfall, in reaching the spot where the ruins of her dwelling had not yet ceased to burn. Here she sought out the body of her husband, and covered it with fence-rails, to protect it from the wolves. When her task was complete, and when night closed around her, the bold spirit which had hitherto borne her up suddenly gave way. The recollection of the horrors she had witnessed, the presence of the dead, the darkness, the solitude, and the gloom of the surrounding forest, wrought upon her till her terror rose to ecstasy; and she remained until daybreak, crouched among the bushes, haunted by the threatening apparition of an armed man, who, to her heated imagination, seemed constantly approaching to murder her.[2]

Some time after the butchery at Glendenning's house, an outrage was perpetrated, unmatched, in its fiend-like atrocity, through all the annals of the war. In a solitary place, deep within the settled limits of Pennsylvania, stood a small school-

---

[1]Her absence was soon perceived, on which one of the Indians remarked that he would bring the cow back to her calf, and, seizing the child, forced it to scream violently. This proving ineffectual, he dashed out its brains against a tree. This was related by one of the captives who was taken to the Indian villages and afterwards redeemed.

[2]Doddridge, *Notes*, 221. MS. *Narrative*, written by Colonel Stuart from the relation of Glendenning's wife.

house, one of those rude structures of logs which, to this day, may be seen in some of the remote northern districts of New England. A man chancing to pass by was struck by the un-wonted silence; and, pushing open the door, he looked in. In the centre lay the master, scalped and lifeless, with a Bible clasped in his hand; while around the room were strewn the bodies of his pupils, nine in number, miserably mangled, though one of them still retained a spark of life. It was after-wards known that the deed was committed by three or four warriors from a village near the Ohio; and it is but just to observe that, when they returned home, their conduct was disapproved by some of the tribe.[1]

Page after page might be filled with records like these, for the letters and journals of the day are replete with narratives no less tragical. Districts were depopulated, and the progress of the country put back for years. Those small and scattered settlements which formed the feeble van of advancing civiliza-tion were involved in general destruction, and the fate of one may stand for the fate of all. In many a woody valley of the Alleghanies, the axe and fire-brand of the settlers had laid a wide space open to the sun. Here and there, about the clear-ing, stood rough dwellings of logs, surrounded by enclosures and cornfields; while, farther out towards the verge of the woods, the fallen trees still cumbered the ground. From the clay-built chimneys the smoke rose in steady columns against the dark verge of the forest; and the afternoon sun, which brightened the tops of the mountains, had already left the

[1]Gordon, *Hist. Penn.* Appendix. Bard, *Narrative.*

"Several small parties went on to different parts of the settlements: it hap-pened that three of them, whom I was well acquainted with, came from the neighborhood of where I was taken from—they were young fellows, perhaps none of them more than twenty years of age,—they came to a school-house, where they murdered and scalped the master, and all the scholars, except one, who survived after he was scalped, a boy about ten years old, and a full cousin of mine. I saw the Indians when they returned home with the scalps; some of the old Indians were very much displeased at them for killing so many children, especially *Neeppaugh-whese*, or Night Walker, an old chief, or half king,—he ascribed it to cowardice, which was the greatest affront he could offer them."—M'Cullough, *Narrative.*

Extract from an anonymous Letter—*Philadelphia*, August 30, 1764:

"The Lad found alive in the School, and said to be since dead, is, I am informed, yet alive, and in a likely Way to recover."

valley in shadow. Before many hours elapsed, the night was lighted up with the glare of blazing dwellings, and the forest rang with the shrieks of the murdered inmates.[1]

Among the records of that day's sufferings and disasters, none are more striking than the narratives of those whose lives were spared that they might be borne captive to the Indian villages. Exposed to the extremity of hardship, they were urged forward with the assurance of being tomahawked or burnt in case their strength should fail them. Some made their escape from the clutches of their tormentors; but of these not a few found reason to repent their success, lost in a trackless wilderness, and perishing miserably from hunger and exposure. Such attempts could seldom be made in the neighborhood of the settlements. It was only when the party had penetrated deep into the forest that their vigilance began to relax, and their captives were bound and guarded with less rigorous severity. Then, perhaps, when encamped by the side of some mountain brook, and when the warriors lay lost in sleep around their fire, the prisoner would cut or burn asun-

---

[1] Extract from a MS. Letter—*Thomas Cresap to Governor Sharpe*:—

"Old Town, July 15th, 1763.

"May it please yr Excellency:

"I take this opportunity in the height of confusion to acquaint you with our unhappy and most wretched situation at this time, being in hourly expectation of being massacred by our barbarous and inhuman enemy the Indians, we having been three days successively attacked by them, viz. the 13th, 14th, and this instant. . . . I have enclosed a list of the desolate men and women, and children who have fled to my house, which is enclosed by a small stockade for safety, by which you see what a number of poor souls, destitute of every necessary of life, are here penned up, and likely to be butchered without immediate relief and assistance, and can expect none, unless from the province to which they belong. I shall submit to your wiser judgment the best and most effectual method for such relief, and shall conclude with hoping we shall have it in time."

Extract from a Letter—*Frederick Town,* July 19, 1763 (*Penn. Gaz.* No. 1807):—

"Every Day, for some Time past, has offered the melancholy Scene of poor distressed Families driving downwards, through this Town, with their Effects, who have deserted their Plantations, for Fear of falling into the cruel Hands of our Savage Enemies, now daily seen in the Woods. And never was Panic more general or forcible than that of the Back Inhabitants, whose Terrors, at this Time, exceed what followed on the Defeat of General Braddock, when the Frontiers lay open to the Incursions of both French and Indians."

der the cords that bound his wrists and ankles, and glide stealthily into the woods. With noiseless celerity he pursues his flight over the fallen trunks, through the dense undergrowth, and the thousand pitfalls and impediments of the forest; now striking the rough, hard trunk of a tree, now tripping among the insidious network of vines and brambles. All is darkness around him, and through the black masses of foliage above he can catch but dubious and uncertain glimpses of the dull sky. At length, he can hear the gurgle of a neighboring brook; and, turning towards it, he wades along its pebbly channel, fearing lest the soft mould and rotten wood of the forest might retain traces enough to direct the bloodhound instinct of his pursuers. With the dawn of the misty and cloudy morning, he is still pushing on his way, when his attention is caught by the spectral figure of an ancient birch-tree, which, with its white bark hanging about it in tatters, seems wofully familiar to his eye. Among the neighboring bushes, a blue smoke curls faintly upward; and, to his horror and amazement, he recognizes the very fire from which he had fled a few hours before, and the piles of spruce-boughs upon which the warriors had slept. They have gone, however, and are ranging the forest, in keen pursuit of the fugitive, who, in his blind flight amid the darkness, had circled round to the very point whence he set out; a mistake not uncommon with careless or inexperienced travellers in the woods. Almost in despair, he leaves the ill-omened spot, and directs his course eastward with greater care; the bark of the trees, rougher and thicker on the northern side, furnishing a precarious clew for his guidance. Around and above him nothing can be seen but the same endless monotony of brown trunks and green leaves, closing him in with an impervious screen. He reaches the foot of a mountain, and toils upwards against the rugged declivity; but when he stands on the summit, the view is still shut out by impenetrable thickets. High above them all shoots up the tall, gaunt stem of a blasted pine-tree; and, in his eager longing for a view of the surrounding objects, he strains every muscle to ascend. Dark, wild, and lonely, the wilderness stretches around him, half hidden in clouds, half open to the sight, mountain and valley, crag and glistening stream; but nowhere can he discern the trace of human hand or any hope of rest and harborage. Before he can look for relief, league upon league must be passed, without food to sustain or weapon to defend him. He descends the mountain, forcing his way through the undergrowth of laurel-bushes; while the clouds sink lower, and a storm of sleet and rain descends upon the waste. Through such scenes, and under such exposures, he presses onward, sustaining life with the aid of roots and berries or the flesh of reptiles. Perhaps, in the last extremity, some party of Rangers find him, and bring him to a place of refuge; perhaps, by his own efforts, he reaches some frontier post, where rough lodging and rough fare seem to him unheard-of luxury; or perhaps, spent with fatigue and famine, he perishes in despair, a meagre banquet for the wolves.

Within two or three weeks after the war had broken out, the older towns and settlements of Pennsylvania were crowded with refugees from the deserted frontier, reduced, in many cases, to the extremity of destitution.[1] Sermons were preached in their behalf at Philadelphia; the religious societies united for their relief, and liberal contributions were added by individuals. While private aid was thus generously bestowed upon the sufferers, the government showed no such promptness in arresting the public calamity. Early in July, Governor Hamilton had convoked the Assembly, and, representing the distress of the borders, had urged them to take measures of defence.[2] But the provincial government of Pennsylvania was more conducive to prosperity in time of peace than to effi-

---

[1] Extract from a Letter—*Winchester, Virginia*, June 22d (*Penn. Gaz.* No. 1801):—

"Last Night I reached this Place. I have been at Fort Cumberland several Days, but the Indians having killed nine People, and burnt several Houses near Fort Bedford, made me think it prudent to remove from those Parts, from which, I suppose, near 500 Families have run away within this week.—I assure you it was a most melancholy Sight, to see such Numbers of poor People, who had abandoned their Settlements in such Consternation and Hurry, that they had hardly any thing with them but their Children. And what is still worse, I dare say there is not Money enough amongst the whole Families to maintain a fifth Part of them till the Fall; and none of the poor Creatures can get a Hovel to shelter them from the Weather, but lie about scattered in the Woods."

[2] *Votes of Assembly*, V. 259.

ciency in time of war. The Quakers, who held a majority in the Assembly, were from principle and practice the reverse of warlike, and, regarding the Indians with a blind partiality, were reluctant to take measures against them. Proud, and with some reason, of the justice and humanity which had marked their conduct towards the Indian race, they had learned to regard themselves as its advocates and patrons, and their zeal was greatly sharpened by opposition and political prejudice. They now pretended that the accounts from the frontier were grossly exaggerated; and, finding this ground untenable, they alleged, with better show of reason, that the Indians were driven into hostility by the ill-treatment of the proprietaries and their partisans. They recognized, however, the necessity of defensive measures, and accordingly passed a bill for raising and equipping a force of seven hundred men, to be composed of frontier farmers, and to be kept in pay only during the time of harvest. They were not to leave the settled parts of the province to engage in offensive operations of any kind, nor even to perform garrison duty; their sole object being to enable the people to gather in their crops un-molested.

This force was divided into numerous small detached parties, who were stationed here and there at farm-houses and hamlets on both sides of the Susquehanna, with orders to range the woods daily from post to post, thus forming a feeble chain of defence across the whole frontier. The two companies assigned to Lancaster County were placed under the command of a clergyman, John Elder, pastor of the Presbyterian Church of Paxton; a man of worth and education, and held in great respect upon the borders. He discharged his military functions with address and judgment, drawing a cordon of troops across the front of the county, and preserving the inhabitants free from attack for a considerable time.[1]

---

[1]Extract from a MS. Letter—*John Elder to Governor Penn*:—

"Paxton, 4th August, 1763.

"Sir:

"The service your Hon^r was pleased to appoint me to, I have performed to the best of my power; tho' not with success equal to my desires. However, both companies will, I imagine, be complete in a few days: there are now

The feeble measures adopted by the Pennsylvania Assembly highly excited the wrath of Sir Jeffrey Amherst, and he did not hesitate to give his feelings an emphatic expression. "The conduct of the Pennsylvania legislature," he writes, "is altogether so infatuated and stupidly obstinate, that I want words to express my indignation thereat; but the colony of Virginia, I hope, will have the honor of not only driving the enemy from its own settlements, but that of protecting those of its neighbors who have not spirit to defend themselves."

Virginia did, in truth, exhibit a vigor and activity not unworthy of praise. Unlike Pennsylvania, she had the advantage of an existing militia law; and the House of Burgesses was neither embarrassed by scruples against the shedding of blood, nor by any peculiar tenderness towards the Indian race. The House, however, was not immediately summoned together; and the governor and council, without waiting to consult the Burgesses, called out a thousand of the militia, five hundred of whom were assigned to the command of Colonel Stephen, and an equal number to that of Major Lewis.[1] The presence of these men, most of whom were woodsmen and hunters, restored order and confidence to the distracted borders; and the inhabitants, before pent up in their forts, or flying before the enemy, now took the field, in conjunction with the militia. Many severe actions were fought, but it seldom happened that the Indians could stand their ground against the border riflemen. The latter were uniformly victorious until the end of the summer; when Captains Moffat and Phillips, with sixty men, were lured into an ambuscade, and routed, with the loss of half their number. A few weeks after, they took an ample revenge. Learning by their scouts that more than a hundred warriors were encamped near Jackson's River, preparing to attack the settlements, they

---

upwards of 30 men in each, exclusive of officers, who are now and have been employed since their enlistment in such service as is thought most safe and encouraging to the Frontier inhabitants, who are here and everywhere else in the back countries quite sunk and dispirited, so that it's to be feared that on any attack of the enemy, a considerable part of the country will be evacuated, as all seem inclinable to seek safety rather in flight than in opposing the Savage Foe."

[1] Sparks, *Writings of Washington*, II. 340.

advanced secretly to the spot, and set upon them with such fury that the whole party broke away and fled; leaving weapons, provisions, articles of dress, and implements of magic, in the hands of the victors.

Meanwhile the frontier people of Pennsylvania, finding that they could hope for little aid from government, bestirred themselves with admirable spirit in their own defence. The march of Bouquet, and the victory of Bushy Run, caused a temporary lull in the storm, thus enabling some of the bolder inhabitants, who had fled to Shippensburg, Carlisle, and other places of refuge, to return to their farms, where they determined, if possible, to remain. With this resolution, the people of the Great Cove, and the adjacent valleys beyond Shippensburg, raised among themselves a small body of riflemen, which they placed under the command of James Smith; a man whose resolute and daring character, no less than the native vigor of his intellect, gave him great popularity and influence with the borderers. Having been, for several years, a prisoner among the Indians, he was thoroughly acquainted with their mode of fighting. He trained his men in the Indian tactics and discipline, and directed them to assume the dress of warriors, and paint their faces red and black, so that, in appearance, they were hardly distinguishable from the enemy.[1] Thus equipped, they scoured the woods in front of the settlements, had various skirmishes with the enemy, and discharged their difficult task with such success that the inhabitants of the neighborhood were not again driven from their homes.

The attacks on the Pennsylvania frontier were known to proceed, in great measure, from several Indian villages, situated high up the west branch of the Susquehanna, and in-

---

[1] *Petition of the Inhabitants of the Great Cove*. Smith, *Narrative*. This is a highly interesting account of the writer's captivity among the Indians, and his adventures during several succeeding years. In the war of the Revolution, he acted the part of a zealous patriot. He lived until the year 1812, about which time, the western Indians having broken out into hostility, he gave his country the benefit of his ample experience, by publishing a treatise on the Indian mode of warfare. In Kentucky, where he spent the latter part of his life, he was much respected, and several times elected to the legislature. This narrative may be found in Drake's *Tragedies of the Wilderness*, and in several other similar collections.

habited by a debauched rabble composed of various tribes, of whom the most conspicuous were Delawares. To root out this nest of banditti would be the most effectual means of protecting the settlements, and a hundred and ten men offered themselves for the enterprise. They marched about the end of August; but on their way along the banks of the Susquehanna, they encountered fifty warriors, advancing against the borders. The Indians had the first fire, and drove in the vanguard of the white men. A hot fight ensued. The warriors fought naked, painted black from head to foot; so that, as they leaped among the trees, they seemed to their opponents like demons of the forest. They were driven back with heavy loss; and the volunteers returned in triumph, though without accomplishing the object of the expedition; for which, indeed, their numbers were scarcely adequate.[1]

Within a few weeks after their return, Colonel Armstrong, a veteran partisan of the French war, raised three hundred men, the best in Cumberland County, with a view to the effectual destruction of the Susquehanna villages. Leaving their rendezvous at the crossings of the Juniata, about the first of October, they arrived on the sixth at the Great Island, high up the west branch. On or near this island were situated the principal villages of the enemy. But the Indians had vanished, abandoning their houses, their cornfields, their stolen horses and cattle, and the accumulated spoil of the settlements. Leaving a detachment to burn the towns and lay waste the fields, Armstrong, with the main body of his men, followed close on the trail of the fugitives; and, pursuing them through a rugged and difficult country, soon arrived at another village, thirty miles above the former. His scouts informed him that the place was full of Indians; and his men, forming a circle around it, rushed in upon the cabins at a given signal. The Indians were gone, having stolen away in such haste that the hominy and bear's meat, prepared for their meal, were found smoking upon their dishes of birch-bark. Having burned the place to the ground, the party returned to the Great Island; and, rejoining their companions, descended the Susquehanna,

[1] *Penn. Gaz.* No. 1811.

reaching Fort Augusta in a wretched condition, fatigued, half famished, and quarrelling among themselves.[1]

Scarcely were they returned, when another expedition was set on foot, in which a portion of them were persuaded to take part. During the previous year, a body of settlers from Connecticut had possessed themselves of the valley of Wyoming, on the east branch of the Susquehanna, in defiance of the government of Pennsylvania, and to the great displeasure of the Indians. The object of the expedition was to remove these settlers, and destroy their corn and provisions, which might otherwise fall into the hands of the enemy. The party, composed chiefly of volunteers from Lancaster County, set out from Harris's Ferry, under the command of Major Clayton, and reached Wyoming on the seventeenth of October. They were too late. Two days before their arrival, a massacre had been perpetrated, the fitting precursor of that subsequent scene of blood which, embalmed in the poetic romance of Campbell, has made the name of Wyoming a household word. The settlement was a pile of ashes and cinders, and the bodies of its miserable inhabitants offered frightful proof of the cruelties inflicted upon them.[2] A large war-party had fallen upon the place, killed and carried off more than twenty of the people, and driven the rest, men, women, and children, in terror to the mountains. Gaining a point which commanded the whole expanse of the valley below, the fugitives looked back, and saw the smoke rolling up in volumes from their burning homes; while the Indians could be discerned roaming about in quest of plunder, or feasting in groups upon the slaughtered cattle. One of the principal settlers, a man named Hopkins, was separated from the rest, and driven into the woods. Finding himself closely pursued, he crept into the hollow trunk of a fallen tree, while the Indians passed without observing him. They soon returned to the spot, and ranged the surrounding woods like hounds at fault; two of

[1] *Penn. Gaz.* Nos. 1816–1818. MS. Letter—*Graydon to Bird*, October 12.

[2] Extract from a MS. Letter—*Paxton*, October 23:—

"The woman was roasted, and had two hinges in her hands, supposed to be put in red hot, and several of the men had awls thrust into their eyes, and spears, arrows, pitchforks, etc., sticking in their bodies."

them approaching so near, that, as Hopkins declared, he could hear the bullets rattle in their pouches. The search was unavailing; but the fugitive did not venture from his place of concealment until extreme hunger forced him to return to the ruined settlement in search of food. The Indians had abandoned it some time before; and, having found means to restore his exhausted strength, he directed his course towards the settlements of the Delaware, which he reached after many days of wandering.[1]

Having buried the dead bodies of those who had fallen in the massacre, Clayton and his party returned to the settlements. The Quakers, who seemed resolved that they would neither defend the people of the frontier nor allow them to defend themselves, vehemently inveighed against the several expeditions up the Susquehanna, and denounced them as seditious and murderous. Urged by their blind prejudice in favor of the Indians, they insisted that the bands of the Upper Susquehanna were friendly to the English; whereas, with the single exception of a few Moravian converts near Wyoming, who had not been molested by the whites, there could be no rational doubt that these savages nourished a rancorous and malignant hatred against the province. But the Quakers, removed by their situation from all fear of the tomahawk, securely vented their spite against the borderers, and doggedly closed their ears to the truth.[2] Meanwhile, the people of the frontier besieged the Assembly with petitions for relief; but little heed was given to their complaints.

Sir Jeffrey Amherst had recently resigned his office of commander-in-chief; and General Gage, a man of less efficiency than his predecessor, was appointed to succeed him. Immediately before his departure for England, Amherst had reluctantly condescended to ask the several provinces for

[1] MS. *Elder Papers*. Chapman, *Hist. Wyoming*, 70. Miner, *Hist. Wyoming*, 56.

[2] It has already been stated that the Quakers were confined to the eastern parts of the province. That their security was owing to their local situation, rather than to the kind feeling of the Indians towards them, is shown by the fact, that, of the very few of their number who lived in exposed positions, several were killed. One of them in particular, John Fincher, seeing his house about to be attacked, went out to meet the warriors, declared that he was a Quaker, and begged for mercy. The Indians laughed, and struck him dead with a tomahawk.

troops to march against the Indians early in the spring, and the first act of Gage was to confirm this requisition. New York was called upon to furnish fourteen hundred men, and New Jersey six hundred.[1] The demand was granted, on condition that the New England provinces should also contribute a just proportion to the general defence. This condition was complied with, and the troops were raised.

Pennsylvania had been required to furnish a thousand men; but in this quarter many difficulties intervened. The Assembly of the province, never prompt to vote supplies for military purposes, was now embroiled in that obstinate quarrel with the proprietors, which for years past had clogged all the wheels of government. The proprietors insisted on certain pretended rights, which the Assembly strenuously opposed; and the governors, who represented the proprietary interest, were bound by imperative instructions to assert these claims, in spite of all opposition. On the present occasion, the chief point of dispute related to the taxation of the proprietary estates; the governor, in conformity with his instructions, demanding that they should be assessed at a lower rate than other lands of equal value in the province. The Assembly stood their ground, and refused to remove the obnoxious clauses in the supply bill. Message after message passed between the House and the governor; mutual recrimination ensued, and ill blood was engendered. The frontiers might have been left to their misery but for certain events which, during

[1]MS. *Gage Papers.*
Extract from a MS. Letter—*William Smith, Jr., to* ——: —

"New York, 22d Nov. 1763.

"Is not Mr. Amherst the happiest of men to get out of this Trouble so seasonably? At last he was obliged to submit, to give the despised Indians so great a mark of his Consideration, as to confess he could not defend us, and to make a requisition of 1400 Provincials by the Spring—600 more he demands from New Jersey. Our People refused all but a few for immediate Defence, conceiving that all the Northern Colonies ought to contribute equally, and upon an apprehension that he has called for too insufficient an aid. . . .

"Is not Gage to be pitied? The war will be a tedious one, nor can it be glorious, even tho' attended with Success. Instead of decisive Battles, woodland skirmishes—instead of Colours and Cannon, our Trophies will be stinking scalps.—Heaven preserve you, my Friend, from a War conducted by a spirit of Murder rather than of brave and generous offence."

the winter, threw the whole province into disorder, and acted like magic on the minds of the stubborn legislators.

These events may be ascribed, in some degree, to the renewed activity of the enemy; who, during a great part of the autumn, had left the borders in comparative quiet. As the winter closed in, their attacks became more frequent; and districts, repeopled during the interval of calm, were again made desolate. Again the valleys were illumined by the flames of burning houses, and families fled shivering through the biting air of the winter night, while the fires behind them shed a ruddy glow upon the snow-covered mountains. The scouts, who on snowshoes explored the track of the marauders, found the bodies of their victims lying in the forest, stripped naked, and frozen to marble hardness. The distress, wrath, and terror of the borderers produced results sufficiently remarkable to deserve a separate examination.

Chapter XXIII.

1763—1764.

THE INDIANS RAISE THE SIEGE OF DETROIT.

I RETURN to the long-forgotten garrison of Detroit, which was left still beleaguered by an increasing multitude of savages, and disheartened by the defeat of Captain Dalzell's detachment. The schooner, so boldly defended by her crew against a force of more than twenty times their number, brought to the fort a much-needed supply of provisions. It was not, however, adequate to the wants of the garrison; and the whole were put upon the shortest possible allowance.

It was now the end of September. The Indians, with unexampled pertinacity, had pressed the siege since the beginning of May; but at length their constancy began to fail. The tidings had reached them that Major Wilkins, with a strong force, was on his way to Detroit. They feared the consequences of an attack, especially as their ammunition was almost exhausted; and, by this time, most of them were inclined to sue for peace, as the easiest mode of gaining safety for themselves, and at the same time lulling the English into security.[1] They thought that by this means they might retire unmolested to their wintering grounds, and renew the war with good hope of success in the spring.

Accordingly, on the twelfth of October, Wapocomoguth, great chief of the Mississaugas, a branch of the Ojibwas, living within the present limits of Upper Canada, came to the fort with a pipe of peace. He began his speech to Major Gladwyn, with the glaring falsehood that he and his people had always been friends of the English. They were now, he added, anxious to conclude a formal treaty of lasting peace and amity. He next declared that he had been sent as deputy by the Pottawattamies, Ojibwas, and Wyandots, who had instructed him to say that they sincerely repented of their bad conduct, asked forgiveness, and humbly begged for peace. Gladwyn perfectly understood the hollowness of these professions, but

---

[1] MS. Letter—*Gage to Johnson*, Dec. 25, 1763. *Penn. Gaz.* No. 1827.

the circumstances in which he was placed made it expedient to listen to their overtures. His garrison was threatened with famine, and it was impossible to procure provisions while completely surrounded by hostile Indians. He therefore replied, that, though he was not empowered to grant peace, he would still consent to a truce. The Mississauga deputy left the fort with this reply, and Gladwyn immediately took advantage of this lull in the storm to collect provisions among the Canadians; an attempt in which he succeeded so well that the fort was soon furnished with a tolerable supply for the winter.

The Ottawas alone, animated by Pontiac, had refused to ask for peace, and still persisted in a course of petty hostilities. They fired at intervals on the English foraging parties, until, on the thirty-first of October, an unexpected blow was given to the hopes of their great chief. French messengers came to Detroit with a letter from M. Neyon, commandant of Fort Chartres, the principal post in the Illinois country. This letter was one of those which, on demand of General Amherst, Neyon, with a very bad grace, had sent to the different Indian tribes. It assured Pontiac that he could expect no assistance from the French; that they and the English were now at peace, and regarded each other as brothers; and that the Indians had better abandon hostilities which could lead to no good result.[1] The emotions of Pontiac at receiving this message may be conceived. His long-cherished hopes of assistance from the French were swept away at once, and he saw himself and his people thrown back upon their own slender resources. His cause was lost. At least, there was no present hope for him but in dissimulation. True to his Indian nature, he would put on a mask of peace, and bide his time. On the day after the arrival of the message from Neyon, Gladwyn wrote as follows to Amherst: "This moment I received a message from Pondiac, telling me that he should send to all the nations concerned in the war to bury the hatchet; and he hopes your Excellency will forget what has passed."[2]

[1] MS. *Lettre de M. Neyon de la Vallière, à tous les nations de la Belle Rivière et du Lac,* etc.

[2] The following is Pontiac's message to Gladwyn, written for him by a Canadian: "Mon Frère,—La Parole que mon Père m'a envoyée, pour faire la paix, je l'ai acceptée, tous nos jeunes gens ont enterré leurs Casse-têtes. Je

Having soothed the English commander with these hollow overtures, Pontiac withdrew with some of his chiefs to the Maumee, to stir up the Indians in that quarter, and renew the war in the spring.

About the middle of November, not many days after Pontiac's departure, two friendly Wyandot Indians from the ancient settlement at Lorette, near Quebec, crossed the river, and asked admittance into the fort. One of them then unslung his powder-horn, and, taking out a false bottom, disclosed a closely folded letter, which he gave to Major Gladwyn. The letter was from Major Wilkins, and contained the disastrous news that the detachment under his command had been overtaken by a storm, that many of the boats had been wrecked, that seventy men had perished, that all the stores and ammunition had been destroyed, and the detachment forced to return to Niagara. This intelligence had an effect upon the garrison which rendered the prospect of the cold and cheerless winter yet more dreary and forlorn.

The summer had long since drawn to a close, and the verdant landscape around Detroit had undergone an ominous transformation. Touched by the first October frosts, the forest

---

pense que tu oublieras les mauvaises choses qui sont passées il y a long-temps; de même j'oublierai ce que tu peux m'avoir fait pour ne penser que de bonnes, moi, les Saulteurs (*Ojibwas*), les Hurons, nous devons t'aller parler quand tu nous demanderas. Fais moi la réponse. Je t'envoyes ce conseil (*Q. collier?*) afin que tu le voyes. Si tu es bien comme moi, tu me feras réponse. Je te souhaite le bonjour.

(Signé) "PONDIAC."

Gladwyn's answer is also in French. He says that he will communicate the message to the General; and doubts not that if he, Pontiac, is true to his words, all will be well.

The following is from the letter in which Gladwyn announces the overtures of peace to Amherst (Detroit, Nov. 1): "Yesterday M. Dequindre, a volunteer, arrived with despatches from the Commandant of the Illinois, copies of which I enclose you. . . . The Indians are pressing for peace. . . . I don't imagine there will be any danger of their breaking out again, provided some examples are made of our good subjects, the French, who set them on. . . . They have lost between 80 and 90 of their best warriors; but if yᵣ Excellency still intends to punish them further for their barbarities, *it may easily be done without any expense to the Crown, by permitting a free sale of rum, which will destroy them more effectually than fire and sword.*"

glowed like a bed of tulips; and, all along the river bank, the painted foliage, brightened by the autumnal sun, reflected its mingled colors upon the dark water below. The western wind was fraught with life and exhilaration; and in the clear, sharp air, the form of the fish-hawk, sailing over the distant head-land, seemed almost within range of the sportsman's gun.

A week or two elapsed, and then succeeded that gentler season which bears among us the name of the Indian sum-mer; when a light haze rests upon the morning landscape, and the many-colored woods seem wrapped in the thin drapery of a veil; when the air is mild and calm as that of early June, and at evening the sun goes down amid a warm, voluptuous beauty, that may well outrival the softest tints of Italy. But through all the still and breathless afternoon the leaves have fallen fast in the woods, like flakes of snow; and every thing betokens that the last melancholy change is at hand. And, in truth, on the morrow the sky is overspread with cold and stormy clouds; and a raw, piercing wind blows angrily from the north-east. The shivering sentinel quickens his step along the rampart, and the half-naked Indian folds his tattered blan-ket close around him. The shrivelled leaves are blown from the trees, and soon the gusts are whistling and howling amid gray, naked twigs and mossy branches. Here and there, in-deed, the beech-tree, as the wind sweeps among its rigid boughs, shakes its pale assemblage of crisp and rustling leaves. The pines and firs, with their rough tops of dark evergreen, bend and moan in the wind; and the crow caws sullenly, as, struggling against the gusts, he flaps his black wings above the denuded woods.

The vicinity of Detroit was now almost abandoned by its besiegers, who had scattered among the forests to seek suste-nance through the winter for themselves and their families. Unlike the buffalo-hunting tribes of the western plains, they could not at this season remain together in large bodies. The comparative scarcity of game forced them to separate into small bands, or even into single families. Some steered their canoes far northward, across Lake Huron; while others turned westward, and struck into the great wilderness of Michigan. Wandering among forests, bleak, cheerless, and choked with snow, now famishing with want, now cloyed with repletion, they passed the dull, cold winter. The chase yielded their only subsistence; and the slender lodges, borne on the backs of the squaws, were their only shelter. Encamped at intervals by the margin of some frozen lake, surrounded by all that is most stern and dreary in the aspects of nature, they were subjected to every hardship, and endured all with stubborn stoicism. Sometimes, during the frosty night, they were gathered in groups about the flickering lodge-fire, listening to traditions of their forefathers, and wild tales of magic and incantation. Perhaps, before the season was past, some bloody feud broke out among them; perhaps they were assailed by their ancient enemies the Dahcotah; or perhaps some sinister omen or evil dream spread more terror through the camp than the presence of an actual danger would have awakened. With the return of spring, the scattered parties once more united, and moved towards Detroit, to indulge their unforgotten hatred against the English.

Detroit had been the central point of the Indian operations; its capture had been their favorite project; around it they had concentrated their greatest force, and the failure of the attempt proved disastrous to their cause. Upon the Six Nations, more especially, it produced a marked effect. The friendly tribes of this confederacy were confirmed in their friendship, while the hostile Senecas began to lose heart. Availing himself of this state of things, Sir William Johnson, about the middle of the winter, persuaded a number of Six Nation warriors, by dint of gifts and promises, to go out against the enemy. He stimulated their zeal by offering rewards of fifty dollars for the heads of the two principal Delaware chiefs.[1] Two hundred of them, accompanied by a few

[1] Extract from a MS. Letter—*Sir W. Johnson to* ——: —

"For God's Sake exert yourselves like Men whose Honour & every thing dear to them is now at stake; the General has great Expectations from the success of your Party, & indeed so have all People here, & I hope they will not be mistaken,—in Order to Encourage your party I will, out of my own Pocket, pay to any of the Party 50 Dollars for the Head Men of the Delawares there, viz., Onuperaquedra, and 50 Dollars more for the Head of Long Coat, alias ——, in which case they must either bring them alive or their whole Heads; the Money shall be paid to the Man who takes or brings me them, or their Heads,—this I would have you tell to the Head men of the Party, as it will make them more eager."

provincials, left the Oneida country during the month of February, and directed their course southward. They had been out but a few days, when they found an encampment of forty Delawares, commanded by a formidable chief, known as Captain Bull, who, with his warriors, was on his way to attack the settlements. They surrounded the camp undiscovered, during the night, and at dawn of day raised the war-whoop and rushed in. The astonished Delawares had no time to snatch their arms. They were all made prisoners, taken to Albany, and thence sent down to New York, where they were conducted, under a strong guard, to the common jail; the mob crowding round them as they passed, and admiring the sullen ferocity of their countenances. Not long after this success, Captain Montour, with a party of provincials and Six Nation warriors, destroyed the town of Kanestio, and other hostile villages, on the upper branches of the Susquehanna. This blow, inflicted by supposed friends, produced more effect upon the enemy than greater reverses would have done, if encountered at the hands of the English alone.[1]

The calamities which overwhelmed the borders of the middle provinces were not unfelt at the south. It was happy for the people of the Carolinas that the Cherokees, who had broken out against them three years before, had at that time received a chastisement which they could never forget, and from which they had not yet begun to recover. They were thus compelled to remain comparatively quiet; while the ancient feud between them and the northern tribes would, under any circumstances, have prevented their uniting with the latter. The contagion of the war reached them, however, and they perpetrated numerous murders; while the neighboring nation of the Creeks rose in open hostility, and committed formidable ravages. Towards the north, the Indian tribes were compelled, by their position, to remain tranquil, yet they showed many signs of uneasiness; and those of Nova Scotia caused great alarm, by mustering in large bodies in the neighborhood of Halifax. The excitement among them was temporary, and they dispersed without attempting mischief.

[1] MS. *Johnson Papers.*

Chapter XXIV.

1763.

THE PAXTON MEN.

ALONG the thinly settled borders, two thousand persons had been killed, or carried off, and nearly an equal number of families driven from their homes.[1] The frontier people of Pennsylvania, goaded to desperation by long-continued suffering, were divided between rage against the Indians, and resentment against the Quakers, who had yielded them cold sympathy and inefficient aid. The horror and fear, grief and fury, with which these men looked upon the mangled remains of friends and relatives, set language at defiance. They were of a rude and hardy stamp, hunters, scouts, rangers, Indian traders, and backwoods farmers, who had grown up with arms in their hands, and been trained under all the influences of the warlike frontier. They fiercely complained that they were interposed as a barrier between the rest of the province and a ferocious enemy; and that they were sacrificed to the safety of men who looked with indifference on their miseries, and lost no opportunity to extenuate and smooth away the cruelties of their destroyers.[2] They declared that the Quakers would go farther to befriend a murdering Delaware

[1] Extract from a MS. Letter—*George Croghan to the Board of Trade*:

"They can with great ease enter our colonies, and cut off our frontier settlements, and thereby lay waste a large tract of country, which indeed they have effected in the space of four months, in Virginia, Maryland, Pennsylvania, and the Jerseys, on whose frontiers they have killed and captivated not less than two thousand of his Majesty's subjects, and drove some thousands to beggary and the greatest distress, besides burning to the ground nine forts or blockhouses in the country, and killing a number of his Majesty's troops and traders."

[2] Extract from the *Declaration of Lazarus Stewart*: —

"Did we not brave the summer's heat and the winter's cold, and the savage tomahawk, while the Inhabitants of Philadelphia, Philadelphia county, Bucks, and Chester, 'ate, drank, and were merry'?

"If a white man kill an Indian, it is a murder far exceeding any crime upon record; he must not be tried in the county where he lives, or where the offence was committed, but in Philadelphia, that he may be tried, convicted, sentenced and hung without delay. If an Indian kill a white man, it was the

701

than to succor a fellow-countryman; that they loved red blood better than white, and a pagan better than a Presbyterian. The Pennsylvania borderers were, as we have seen, chiefly the descendants of Presbyterian emigrants from the north of Ireland. They had inherited some portion of their forefathers' sectarian zeal, which, while it did nothing to soften the barbarity of their manners, served to inflame their animosity against the Quakers, and added bitterness to their just complaints. It supplied, moreover, a convenient sanction for the indulgence of their hatred and vengeance; for, in the general turmoil of their passions, fanaticism too was awakened, and they interpreted the command that Joshua should destroy the heathen[1] into an injunction that they should exterminate the Indians.

The prevailing excitement was not confined to the vulgar. Even the clergy and the chief magistrates shared it; and while they lamented the excess of the popular resentment, they maintained that the general complaints were founded in justice. Viewing all the circumstances, it is not greatly to be wondered at that some of the more violent class were inflamed to the commission of atrocities which bear no very favorable comparison with those of the Indians themselves.

It is not easy for those living in the tranquillity of polished life fully to conceive the depth and force of that unquenchable, indiscriminate hate, which Indian outrages can awaken in those who have suffered them. The chronicles of the American borders are filled with the deeds of men, who, having lost all by the merciless tomahawk, have lived for vengeance alone; and such men will never cease to exist so long as a hostile tribe remains within striking distance of an American settlement.[2] Never was this hatred more deep or more general than on the Pennsylvania frontier at this period; and never,

---

act of an ignorant Heathen, perhaps in liquor; alas, poor innocent! he is sent to the *friendly Indians* that he may be made a *Christian*."

[1]"And when the Lord thy God shall deliver them before thee, thou shalt smite them, and utterly destroy them; thou shalt make no covenant with them, nor show mercy unto them."—*Deuteronomy*, vii. 2.

[2]So promising a theme has not escaped the notice of novelists, and it has been adopted by Dr. Bird in his spirited story of *Nick of the Woods*.

perhaps, did so many collateral causes unite to inflame it to madness. It was not long in finding a vent.

Near the Susquehanna, and at no great distance from the town of Lancaster, was a spot known as the Manor of Conestoga; where a small band of Indians, speaking the Iroquois tongue, had been seated since the first settlement of the province. William Penn had visited and made a treaty with them, which had been confirmed by several succeeding governors, so that the band had always remained on terms of friendship with the English. Yet, like other Indian communities in the neighborhood of the whites, they had dwindled in numbers and prosperity, until they were reduced to twenty persons; who inhabited a cluster of squalid cabins, and lived by beggary and the sale of brooms, baskets, and wooden ladles, made by the women. The men spent a small part of their time in hunting, and lounged away the rest in idleness. In the immediate neighborhood, they were commonly regarded as harmless vagabonds; but elsewhere a more unfavorable opinion was entertained, and they were looked upon as secretly abetting the enemy, acting as spies, giving shelter to scalping-parties, and even aiding them in their depredations. That these suspicions were not wholly unfounded is shown by a conclusive mass of evidence, though it is probable that the treachery was confined to one or two individuals.[1] The exasperated frontiersmen were not in a mood to discriminate, and the innocent were destined to share the fate of the guilty.[2]

On the east bank of the Susquehanna, at some distance above Conestoga, stood the little town of Paxton; a place which, since the French war, had occupied a position of extreme exposure. In the year 1755 the Indians had burned it to the ground, killing many of the inhabitants, and reducing the rest to poverty. It had since been rebuilt; but its tenants were the relatives of those who had perished, and the bitterness of the recollection was enhanced by the sense of their own more

[1]See Appendix, E.

[2]For an account of the Conestoga Indians, see *Penn. Hist. Coll.* 390. It is extremely probable, as shown by Mr. Shea, that they were the remnant of the formidable people called Andastes, who spoke a dialect of the Iroquois, but were deadly enemies of the Iroquois proper, or Five Nations, by whom they were nearly destroyed about the year 1672.

recent sufferings. Mention has before been made of John Elder, the Presbyterian minister of this place; a man whose worth, good sense, and superior education gave him the character of counsellor and director throughout the neighborhood, and caused him to be known and esteemed even in Philadelphia. His position was a peculiar one. From the rough pulpit of his little church, he had often preached to an assembly of armed men, while scouts and sentinels were stationed without, to give warning of the enemy's approach.[1] The men of Paxton, under the auspices of their pastor, formed themselves into a body of rangers, who became noted for their zeal and efficiency in defending the borders. One of their principal leaders was Matthew Smith, a man who had influence and popularity among his associates, and was not without pretensions to education; while he shared a full proportion of the general hatred against Indians, and suspicion against the band of Conestoga.

Towards the middle of December, a scout came to the house of Smith, and reported that an Indian, known to have committed depredations in the neighborhood, had been traced to Conestoga. Smith's resolution was taken at once. He called five of his companions; and, having armed and mounted, they set out for the Indian settlement. They reached it early in the night; and Smith, leaving his horse in charge of the others, crawled forward, rifle in hand, to reconnoitre; when he saw, or fancied he saw, a number of armed warriors in the cabins. Upon this discovery he withdrew, and rejoined his associates. Believing themselves too weak for an attack, the party returned to Paxton. Their blood was up, and they determined to extirpate the Conestogas. Messengers went abroad through the neighborhood; and, on the following day, about fifty armed and mounted men, chiefly from the towns of Paxton and Donegal, assembled at the place agreed

[1] On one occasion, a body of Indians approached Paxton on Sunday, and sent forward one of their number, whom the English supposed to be a friend, to reconnoitre. The spy reported that every man in the church, including the preacher, had a rifle at his side; upon which the enemy withdrew, and satisfied themselves with burning a few houses in the neighborhood. The papers of Mr. Elder were submitted to the writer's examination by his son, an aged and esteemed citizen of Harrisburg.

upon. Led by Matthew Smith, they took the road to Conestoga, where they arrived a little before daybreak, on the morning of the fourteenth. As they drew near, they discerned the light of a fire in one of the cabins, gleaming across the snow. Leaving their horses in the forest, they separated into small parties, and advanced on several sides at once. Though they moved with some caution, the sound of their footsteps or their voices caught the ear of an Indian; and they saw him issue from one of the cabins, and walk forward in the direction of the noise. He came so near that one of the men fancied that he recognized him. "He is the one that killed my mother," he exclaimed with an oath; and, firing his rifle, brought the Indian down. With a general shout, the furious ruffians burst into the cabins, and shot, stabbed, and hacked to death all whom they found there. It happened that only six Indians were in the place; the rest, in accordance with their vagrant habits, being scattered about the neighborhood. Thus baulked of their complete vengeance, the murderers seized upon what little booty they could find, set the cabins on fire, and departed at dawn of day.[1]

The morning was cold and murky. Snow was falling, and already lay deep upon the ground; and, as they urged their horses through the drifts, they were met by one Thomas Wright, who, struck by their appearance, stopped to converse with them. They freely told him what they had done; and, on his expressing surprise and horror, one of them demanded if he believed in the Bible, and if the Scripture did not command that the heathen should be destroyed.

They soon after separated, dispersing among the farmhouses, to procure food for themselves and their horses.

---

[1]The above account of the massacre is chiefly drawn from the narrative of Matthew Smith himself. This singular paper was published by Mr. Redmond Conyngham, of Lancaster, in the *Lancaster Intelligencer* for 1843. Mr. Conyngham states that he procured it from the son of Smith, for whose information it had been written. The account is partially confirmed by incidental allusions, in a letter written by another of the Paxton men, and also published by Mr. Conyngham. This gentleman employed himself with most unwearied diligence in collecting a voluminous mass of documents, comprising, perhaps, every thing that could contribute to extenuate the conduct of the Paxton men; and to these papers, as published from time to time in the above-mentioned newspaper, reference will often be made.

Several rode to the house of Robert Barber, a prominent settler in the neighborhood; who, seeing the strangers stamping
their feet and shaking the snow from their blanket coats, invited them to enter, and offered them refreshment. Having
remained for a short time seated before his fire, they remounted and rode off through the snowstorm. A boy of the
family, who had gone to look at the horses of the visitors,
came in and declared that he had seen a tomahawk, covered
with blood, hanging from each man's saddle; and that a small
gun, belonging to one of the Indian children, had been leaning against the fence.[1] Barber at once guessed the truth, and,
with several of his neighbors, proceeded to the Indian settlement, where they found the solid log cabins still on fire. They
buried the remains of the victims, which Barber compared in
appearance to half-burnt logs. While they were thus engaged,
the sheriff of Lancaster, with a party of men, arrived on the
spot; and the first care of the officer was to send through the
neighborhood to collect the Indians, fourteen in number,
who had escaped the massacre. This was soon accomplished.
The unhappy survivors, learning the fate of their friends and
relatives, were in great terror for their own lives, and earnestly
begged protection. They were conducted to Lancaster, where,
amid great excitement, they were lodged in the county jail, a
strong stone building, which it was thought would afford the
surest refuge.

An express was despatched to Philadelphia with news of
the massacre; on hearing which, the governor issued a proclamation denouncing the act, and offering a reward for the discovery of the perpetrators. Undaunted by this measure, and
enraged that any of their victims should have escaped, the
Paxton men determined to continue the work they had begun.
In this resolution they were confirmed by the prevailing impression, that an Indian known to have murdered the relatives
of one of their number was among those who had received
the protection of the magistrates at Lancaster. They sent forward a spy to gain intelligence, and, on his return, once more
met at their rendezvous. On this occasion, their nominal
leader was Lazarus Stewart, who was esteemed upon the

[1] *Haz. Pa. Reg.* IX. 114.

borders as a brave and active young man; and who, there is strong reason to believe, entertained no worse design than that of seizing the obnoxious Indian, carrying him to Carlisle, and there putting him to death, in case he should be identified as the murderer.[1] Most of his followers, however, hardened amidst war and bloodshed, were bent on indiscriminate slaughter; a purpose which they concealed from their more moderate associates.

Early on the twenty-seventh of December, the party, about fifty in number, left Paxton on their desperate errand. Elder had used all his influence to divert them from their design; and now, seeing them depart, he mounted his horse, overtook them, and addressed them with the most earnest remonstrance. Finding his words unheeded, he drew up his horse across the narrow road in front, and charged them, on his authority as their pastor, to return. Upon this, Matthew Smith rode forward, and, pointing his rifle at the breast of Elder's horse, threatened to fire unless he drew him aside, and gave room to pass. The clergyman was forced to comply, and the party proceeded.[2]

At about three o'clock in the afternoon, the rioters, armed with rifle, knife, and tomahawk, rode at a gallop into Lancaster; turned their horses into the yard of the public house, ran to the jail, burst open the door, and rushed tumultuously in. The fourteen Indians were in a small yard adjacent to the building, surrounded by high stone walls. Hearing the shouts of the mob, and startled by the apparition of armed men in the doorway, two or three of them snatched up billets of wood in self-defence. Whatever may have been the purpose of the Paxton men, this show of resistance banished every thought of forbearance; and the foremost, rushing forward, fired their rifles among the crowd of Indians. In a moment more, the yard was filled with ruffians, shouting, cursing, and firing upon the cowering wretches; holding the muzzles of their pieces, in some instances, so near their victims' heads that the brains were scattered by the explosion. The work was soon finished. The bodies of men, women, and children,

---

[1] Papers published by Mr. Conyngham in the *Lancaster Intelligencer*.

[2] This anecdote was told to the writer by the son of Mr. Elder, and is also related by Mr. Conyngham.

mangled with outrageous brutality, lay scattered about the yard; and the murderers were gone.[1]

When the first alarm was given, the magistrates were in the church, attending the Christmas service, which had been postponed on the twenty-fifth. The door was flung open, and the voice of a man half breathless was heard in broken exclamations, "Murder—the jail—the Paxton Boys—the Indians."

The assembly broke up in disorder, and Shippen, the principal magistrate, hastened towards the scene of riot; but, before he could reach it, all was finished, and the murderers were galloping in a body from the town.[2] The sheriff and the coroner had mingled among the rioters, aiding and abetting them, as their enemies affirm, but, according to their own

[1]*Deposition of Felix Donolly*, keeper of Lancaster jail. *Declaration of Lazarus Stewart*, published by Mr. Conyngham. Rupp, *Hist. of York and Lancaster Counties*, 358. Heckewelder, *Narrative of Moravian Missions*, 79. See Appendix, E.

Soon after the massacre, Franklin published an account of it at Philadelphia, which, being intended to strengthen the hands of government by exciting a popular sentiment against the rioters, is more rhetorical than accurate. The following is his account of the consummation of the act:—

"When the poor wretches saw they had no protection nigh, nor could possibly escape, they divided into their little families, the children clinging to the parents; they fell on their knees, protested their innocence, declared their love to the English, and that, in their whole lives, they had never done them injury; and in this posture they all received the hatchet!"

This is a pure embellishment of the fancy. The only persons present were the jailer and the rioters themselves, who unite in testifying that the Indians died with the stoicism which their race usually exhibit under such circumstances; and indeed, so sudden was the act, that there was no time for enacting the scene described by Franklin.

[2]Extract from a MS. Letter—*Edward Shippen to Governor Penn*:—

"Lancaster, 27th Dec., 1763, P.M.

"Honoured Sir:—

"I am to acquaint your Honour that between two and three of the Clock this afternoon, upwards of a hundred armed men from the Westward rode very fast into Town, turned their Horses into Mr. Slough's (an Innkeeper's) yard, and proceeded with the greatest precipitation to the Work-House, stove open the door and killed all the Indians, and then took to their Horses and rode off: all their business was done, & they were returning to their Horses before I could get half way down to the Work-House. The Sheriff and Coroner however, and several others, got down as soon as the rioters, but could not prevail with them to stop their hands. Some people say they heard them declare they would proceed to the Province Island, & destroy the Indians there."

statement, vainly risking their lives to restore order.[1] A company of Highland soldiers, on their way from Fort Pitt to Philadelphia, were encamped near the town. Their commander, Captain Robertson, afterwards declared that he put himself in the way of the magistrates, expecting that they would call upon him to aid the civil authority; while, on the contrary, several of the inhabitants testify, that, when they urged him to interfere, he replied with an oath that his men had suffered enough from Indians already, and should not stir hand or foot to save them. Be this as it may, it seems certain that neither soldiers nor magistrates, with their best exertions, could have availed to prevent the massacre; for so well was the plan concerted, that, within ten or twelve minutes after the alarm, the Indians were dead, and the murderers mounted to depart.

The people crowded into the jail-yard to gaze upon the miserable spectacle; and, when their curiosity was sated, the bodies were gathered together, and buried not far from the town, where they reposed three quarters of a century; until, at length, the bones were disinterred in preparing the foundation for a railroad.

The tidings of this massacre threw the country into a ferment. Various opinions were expressed; but, in the border counties, even the most sober and moderate regarded it, not as a wilful and deliberate crime, but as the mistaken act of rash men, fevered to desperation by wrongs and sufferings.[2]

---

[1] Extract from a MS. Letter—*John Hay, the sheriff, to Governor Penn*:—
"They in a body left the town without offering any insults to the Inhabitants, & without putting it in the power of any one to take or molest any of them without danger of life to the person attempting it; of which both myself and the Coroner, by our opposition, were in great danger."

[2] Extract from a Letter—*Rev. Mr. Elder to Colonel Burd*:—

"Paxton, 1764.

"Lazarus Stewart is still threatened by the Philadelphia party; he and his friends talk of leaving—if they do, the province will lose some of their truest friends, and that by the faults of others, not their own; for if any cruelty was practised on the Indians at Conestogue or at Lancaster, it was not by his, or their hands. There is a great reason to believe that much injustice has been done to all concerned. In the contrariness of accounts, we must infer that much rests for support on the imagination or interest of the witness. The characters of Stewart and his friends were well established. Ruffians nor brutal they were not; humane, liberal and moral, nay, religious. It is evidently

When the news reached Philadelphia, a clamorous outcry rose from the Quakers, who could find no words to express their horror and detestation. They assailed not the rioters only, but the whole Presbyterian sect, with a tempest of abuse, not the less virulent for being vented in the name of philanthropy and religion. The governor again issued a proclamation, offering rewards for the detection and arrest of the murderers; but the latter, far from shrinking into concealment, proclaimed their deed in the face of day, boasted the achievement, and defended it by reason and Scripture. So great was the excitement in the frontier counties, and so deep the sympathy with the rioters, that to arrest them would have required the employment of a strong military force, an experiment far too dangerous to be tried. Nothing of the kind was attempted until nearly eight years afterwards, when Lazarus Stewart was apprehended on the charge of murdering the Indians of Conestoga. Learning that his trial was to take place, not in the county where the act was committed, but in Philadelphia, and thence judging that his condemnation was certain, he broke jail and escaped. Having written a declaration to justify his conduct, he called his old associates around him, set the provincial government of Pennsylvania at defiance, and withdrew to Wyoming with his band. Here he joined the settlers recently arrived from Connecticut, and thenceforth played a conspicuous part in the eventful history of that remarkable spot.[1]

---

not the wish of the party to give Stewart a fair hearing. All he desires, is to be put on trial, at Lancaster, near the scenes of the horrible butcheries, committed by the Indians at Tulpehocken, &c., when he can have the testimony of the Scouts or Rangers, men whose services can never be sufficiently rewarded."

[1]Papers published by Mr. Conyngham.

Extract from the *Declaration of Lazarus Stewart*: —

"What I have done was done for the security of hundreds of settlers on the frontiers. The blood of a thousand of my fellow-creatures called for vengeance. As a Ranger, I sought the post of danger, and now you ask my life. Let me be tried where prejudice has not prejudged my case. Let my brave Rangers, who have stemmed the blast nobly, and never flinched; let them have an equitable trial; they were my friends in the hour of danger — to desert them now were cowardice! What remains is to leave our cause with our God, and our guns."

After the massacre at Conestoga, the excitement in the frontier counties, far from subsiding, increased in violence daily; and various circumstances conspired to inflame it. The principal of these was the course pursued by the provincial government towards the Christian Indians attached to the Moravian missions. Many years had elapsed since the Moravians began the task of converting the Indians of Pennsylvania, and their steadfast energy and regulated zeal had been crowned with success. Several thriving settlements of their converts had sprung up in the valley of the Lehigh, when the opening of the French war, in 1755, involved them in unlooked-for calamities. These unhappy neutrals, between the French and Indians on the one side, and the English on the other, excited the enmity of both; and while from the west they were threatened by the hatchets of their own countrymen, they were menaced on the east by the no less formidable vengeance of the white settlers, who, in their distress and terror, never doubted that the Moravian converts were in league with the enemy. The popular rage against them at length grew so furious, that their destruction was resolved upon. The settlers assembled and advanced against the Moravian community of Gnadenhutten; but the French and Indians gained the first blow, and, descending upon the doomed settlement, utterly destroyed it. This disaster, deplorable as it was in itself, proved the safety of the other Moravian settlements, by making it fully apparent that their inhabitants were not in league with the enemy. They were suffered to remain unmolested for several years; but with the murders that ushered in Pontiac's war, in 1763, the former suspicion revived, and the expediency of destroying the Moravian Indians was openly debated. Towards the end of the summer, several outrages were committed upon the settlers in the neighborhood, and the Moravian Indians were loudly accused of taking part in them. These charges were never fully confuted; and, taking into view the harsh treatment which the converts had always experienced from the whites, it is highly probable that some of them were disposed to sympathize with their heathen countrymen, who are known to have courted their alliance. The Moravians had, however, excited in their converts a high degree of religious enthusiasm; which, directed as it was by the teachings of the missionaries, went farther than any thing else could have done to soften their national prejudices, and wean them from their warlike habits.

About three months before the massacre at Conestoga, a party of drunken Rangers, fired by the general resentment against the Moravian Indians, murdered several of them, both men and women, whom they found sleeping in a barn. Not long after, the same party of Rangers were, in their turn, surprised and killed, some peaceful settlers of the neighborhood sharing their fate. This act was at once ascribed, justly or unjustly, to the vengeance of the converted Indians, relatives of the murdered; and the frontier people, who, like the Paxton men, were chiefly Scotch and Irish Presbyterians, resolved that the objects of their suspicion should live no longer. At this time, the Moravian converts consisted of two communities, those of Nain and Wecquetank, near the Lehigh; and to these may be added a third, at Wyalusing, near Wyoming. The latter, from its distant situation, was, for the present, safe; but the two former were in imminent peril, and the inhabitants, in mortal terror for their lives, stood day and night on the watch.

At length, about the tenth of October, a gang of armed men approached Wecquetank, and encamped in the woods, at no great distance. They intended to make their attack under favor of the darkness; but before evening a storm, which to the missionaries seemed providential, descended with such violence, that the fires of the hostile camp were extinguished in a moment, the ammunition of the men wet, and the plan defeated.[1]

After so narrow an escape, it was apparent that flight was the only resource. The terrified congregation of Wecquetank broke up on the following day; and, under the charge of their missionary, Bernard Grube, removed to the Moravian town of Nazareth, where it was hoped they might remain in safety.[2]

In the mean time, the charges against the Moravian converts had been laid before the provincial Assembly; and, to secure the safety of the frontier people, it was judged expe-

---

[1] Loskiel, *Hist. Moravian Missions*, Part II. 211.
[2] MS. Letter—*Bernard Grube to Governor Hamilton*, Oct. 13.

dient to disarm the suspected Indians, and remove them to a part of the province where it would be beyond their power to do mischief.[1] The motion was passed in the Assembly with little dissent; the Quakers supporting it from regard to the safety of the Indians, and their opponents from regard to the safety of the whites. The order for removal reached its destination on the sixth of November; and the Indians, reluctantly yielding up their arms, prepared for departure. When a sermon had been preached before the united congregations, and a hymn sung in which all took part, the unfortunate exiles set out on their forlorn pilgrimage; the aged, the young, the sick, and the blind, borne in wagons, while the rest journeyed on foot.[2] Their total number, including the band from Wyalusing, which joined them after they reached Philadelphia, was about a hundred and forty. At every village and hamlet which they passed on their way, they were greeted with threats and curses; nor did the temper of the people improve as they advanced, for, when they came to Germantown, the mob could scarcely be restrained from attacking them. On reaching Philadelphia, they were conducted, amidst the yells and hootings of the rabble, to the barracks, which had been intended to receive them; but the soldiers, who outdid the mob in their hatred of Indians, refused to admit them, and set the orders of the governor at defiance. From ten o'clock in the morning until three in the afternoon, the persecuted exiles remained drawn up in the square before the barracks, surrounded by a multitude who never ceased to abuse and threaten them; but wherever the broad hat of a Quaker was seen in the crowd, there they felt the assurance of a friend,—a friend, who, both out of love for them, and aversion to their enemies, would spare no efforts in their behalf. The soldiers continued refractory, and the Indians were at length ordered to proceed. As they moved down the street, shrinking together in their terror, the mob about them grew so angry and clamorous, that to their missionaries they seemed like a flock of sheep in the midst of howling wolves.[3] A body-guard of Quakers gathered

[1] *Votes of Assembly*, V. 284.
[2] Loskiel, *Hist. Moravian Missions*, Part II. 214. Heckewelder, *Narrative of Missions*, 75.
[3] Loskiel, Part II. 216.

around, protecting them from the crowd, and speaking words of sympathy and encouragement. Thus they proceeded to Province Island, below the city, where they were lodged in waste buildings, prepared in haste for their reception, and where the Quakers still attended them, with every office of kindness and friendship.

Chapter XXV.

1764.

THE RIOTERS MARCH ON PHILADELPHIA.

THE CONESTOGA MURDERS did not take place until some weeks after the removal of the Moravian converts to Philadelphia; and the rioters, as they rode, flushed with success, out of Lancaster, after the achievement of their exploit, were heard to boast that they would soon visit the city and finish their work, by killing the Indians whom it had taken under its protection. It was soon but too apparent that this design was seriously entertained by the people of the frontier. They had tasted blood, and they craved more. It seemed to them intolerable, that, while their sufferings were unheeded, and their wounded and destitute friends uncared for, they should be taxed to support those whom they regarded as authors of their calamities, or, in their own angry words, "to maintain them through the winter, that they may scalp and butcher us in the spring."[1] In their blind rage, they would not see that the Moravian Indians had been removed to Philadelphia, in part, at least, with a view to the safety of the borders. To their enmity against Indians was added a resentment, scarcely less vehement, against the Quakers, whose sectarian principles they hated and despised. They complained, too, of political grievances, alleging that the five frontier counties were inadequately represented in the Assembly, and that from thence arose the undue influence of the Quakers in the councils of the province.

The excited people soon began to assemble at taverns and other places of resort, recounting their grievances, real or

[1] *Remonstrance* of the Frontier People to the Governor and Assembly. See *Votes of Assembly*, V. 313.

The "Declaration," which accompanied the "Remonstrance," contains the following passage: "To protect and maintain these Indians at the public expense, while our suffering brethren on the frontiers are almost destitute of the necessaries of life, and are neglected by the public, is sufficient to make us mad with rage, and tempt us to do what nothing but the most violent necessity can vindicate."

See Appendix, E.

imaginary; relating frightful stories of Indian atrocities, and launching fierce invectives against the Quakers.[1] Political agitators harangued them on their violated rights; self-constituted preachers urged the duty of destroying the heathen, forgetting that the Moravian Indians were Christians, and their exasperated hearers were soon ripe for any rash attempt. They resolved to assemble and march in arms to Philadelphia. On a former occasion, they had sent thither a wagon laden with the mangled corpses of their friends and relatives, who had fallen by Indian butchery; but the hideous spectacle had failed of the intended effect, and the Assembly had still turned a deaf ear to their entreaties for more effective aid.[2] Appeals to sympathy had been thrown away, and they now resolved to try the efficacy of their rifles.

They mustered under their popular leaders, prominent among whom was Matthew Smith, who had led the murderers

[1] MS. *Elder Papers.*
The following verses are extracted from a poem, published at Philadelphia, by a partisan of the Paxton men, entitled,

"The Cloven Foot Discovered.

"Go on, good Christians, never spare
  To give your Indians Clothes to wear;
  Send 'em good Beef, and Pork, and Bread,
  Guns, Powder, Flints, and Store of Lead,
  To Shoot your Neighbours through the Head;
  Devoutly then, make Affirmation,
  You're Friends to George and British Nation;
  Encourage ev'ry friendly Savage,
  To murder, burn, destroy, and ravage;
  Fathers and Mothers here maintain,
  Whose Sons add Numbers to the slain;
  Of Scotch and Irish let them kill
  As many Thousands as they will,
  That you may lord it o'er the Land,
  And have the whole and sole command."

[2] This incident occurred during the French war, and is thus described by a Quaker eye-witness: "Some of the dead bodies were brought to Philadelphia in a wagon, in the time of the General Meeting of Friends there in December, with intent to animate the people to unite in preparations for war on the Indians. They were carried along the streets—many people following—cursing the Indians, and also the Quakers, because they would not join in war for their destruction. The sight of the dead bodies, and the outcry of the people, were very afflicting and shocking."—Watson, *Annals of Phil.* 449 (Phil. 1830).

at Conestoga; and, towards the end of January, took the road to Philadelphia, in force variously estimated at from five hundred to fifteen hundred men. Their avowed purpose was to kill the Moravian Indians; but what vague designs they may have entertained to change the government, and eject the Quakers from a share in it, must remain a matter of uncertainty. Feeble as they were in numbers, their enterprise was not so hopeless as might at first appear, for they counted on aid from the mob of the city, while a numerous party, comprising the members of the Presbyterian sect, were expected to give them secret support, or at least to stand neutral in the quarrel. The Quakers, who were their most determined enemies, could not take arms against them without glaring violation of the principles which they had so often and loudly professed; and even should they thus fly in the face of conscience, the warlike borderers would stand in little fear of such unpractised warriors. They pursued their march in high confidence, applauded by the inhabitants, and hourly increasing in numbers.

Startling rumors of the danger soon reached Philadelphia, spreading alarm among the citizens. The Quakers, especially, had reason to fear, both for themselves and for the Indians, of whom it was their pride to be esteemed the champions. These pacific sectaries found themselves in a new and embarrassing position, for hitherto they had been able to assert their principles at no great risk to person or property. The appalling tempest, which, during the French war, had desolated the rest of the province, had been unfelt near Philadelphia; and while the inhabitants to the westward had been slaughtered by hundreds, scarcely a Quaker had been hurt. Under these circumstances, the aversion of the sect to warlike measures had been a fruitful source of difficulty. It is true that, on several occasions, they had voted supplies for the public defence; but unwilling to place on record such a testimony of inconsistency, they had granted the money, not for the avowed purpose of raising and arming soldiers, but under the title of a gift to the crown.[1] They were now to be deprived of even this poor subterfuge, and subjected to the dilemma of suffering their

[1] See Gordon, *Hist. Penn.* Chaps. XII.–XVIII.

friends to be slain and themselves to be plundered, or openly appealing to arms.

Their embarrassment was increased by the exaggerated ideas which prevailed among the ignorant and timorous respecting the size and strength of the borderers, their ferocity of temper, and their wonderful skill as marksmen. Quiet citizens, whose knowledge was confined to the narrow limits of their firesides and shops, listened horror-stricken to these reports; the prevalence of which is somewhat surprising, when it is considered that, at the present day, the district whence the dreaded rioters came may be reached from Philadelphia within a few hours.

Tidings of the massacre in Lancaster jail had arrived at Philadelphia on the twenty-ninth of December, and with them came the rumor that numerous armed mobs were already on their march to the city. Terror and confusion were universal; and, as the place was defenceless, no other expedient suggested itself than the pitiful one of removing the objects of popular resentment beyond reach of danger. Boats were sent to Province Island, and the Indians ordered to embark and proceed with all haste down the river; but, the rumor proving groundless, a messenger was despatched to recall the fugitives.[1] The assurance that, for a time at least, the city was safe, restored some measure of tranquillity; but, as intelligence of an alarming kind came in daily from the country, Governor Penn sent to General Gage an earnest request for a detachment of regulars to repel the rioters;[2] and, in the interval, means to avert the threatened danger were eagerly sought. A proposal was laid before the Assembly to embark the Indians and send them to England;[3] but the scheme was judged inexpedient, and another, of equal weakness, adopted in its place. It was determined to send the refugees to New York, and place them under the protection of the Indian Superintendent, Sir William Johnson; a plan as hastily executed as timidly conceived.[4] At

[1] Loskiel, Part II. 218.
[2] MS. Letter—*Penn to Gage*, Dec. 31.
[3] *Votes of Assembly*, V. 293.
[4] Extract from a MS. Letter—*Governor Penn to Governor Colden*:—

"Philadelphia, 5th January, 1764.

"Satisfied of the advantages arising from this measure, I have sent them

midnight, on the fourth of January, no measures having been taken to gain the consent of either the government of New York or Johnson himself, the Indians were ordered to leave the island and proceed to the city; where they arrived a little before daybreak, passing in mournful procession, thinly clad and shivering with cold, through the silent streets. The Moravian Brethren supplied them with food; and Fox, the commissary, with great humanity, distributed blankets among them. Before they could resume their progress, the city was astir; and as they passed the suburbs, they were pelted and hooted at by the mob. Captain Robertson's Highlanders, who had just arrived from Lancaster, were ordered to escort them. These soldiers, who had their own reasons for hating Indians, treated them at first with no less insolence and rudeness than the populace; but at length, overcome by the meekness and patience of the sufferers, they changed their conduct, and assumed a tone of sympathy and kindness.[1]

Thus escorted, the refugees pursued their dreary progress through the country, greeted on all sides by the threats and curses of the people. When they reached Trenton, they were received by Apty, the commissary at that place, under whose charge they continued their journey towards Amboy, where several small vessels had been provided to carry them to New York. Arriving at Amboy, however, Apty, to his great surprise, received a letter from Governor Colden of New York, forbidding him to bring the Indians within the limits of that province. A second letter, from General Gage to Captain Robertson, conveyed orders to prevent their advance; and a third, to the owners of the vessels, threatened heavy penalties if they should bring the Indians to the city.[2] The charges of

---

thro' Jersey and your Government to Sir W. Johnson, & desire you will favour them with your protection and countenance, & give them the proper passes for their journey to Sir William's Seat.

"I have recommended it, in the most pressing terms, to the Assembly, to form a Bill that shall enable me to apprehend these seditious and barbarous Murderers, & to quell the like insurrections for the future."

[1]Loskiel, Part II. 220. Heckewelder, *Narrative*, 81.

[2]Extract from a MS. Letter—*Thomas Apty to Governor Penn*:—
"Sir:—

"Agreeable to your Honour's orders, I passed on through the Province of

treachery against the Moravian Indians, the burden their presence would occasion, and the danger of popular disturbance, were the chief causes which induced the government of New York to adopt this course; a course that might have been foreseen from the beginning.[1]

Thus disappointed in their hopes of escape, the hapless Indians remained several days lodged in the barracks at Amboy, where they passed much of their time in religious services. A message, however, soon came from the Governor of New Jersey, requiring them to leave that province; and they were compelled reluctantly to retrace their steps to Philadelphia. A detachment of a hundred and seventy soldiers had arrived, sent by General Gage in compliance with the request of Governor Penn; and under the protection of these troops, the exiles began their backward journey. On the twenty-fourth of January, they reached Philadelphia, where they were lodged at the barracks within the city; the soldiers, forgetful of former prejudice, no longer refusing them entrance.

The return of the Indians, banishing the hope of repose with which the citizens had flattered themselves, and the tidings of danger coming in quick succession from the country, made it apparent that no time must be lost; and the Assembly, laying aside their scruples, unanimously passed a bill providing means for the public defence. The pacific city displayed a scene of unwonted bustle. All who held property, or regarded the public order, might, it should seem, have felt a deep interest in the issue; yet a numerous and highly respect-

---

New Jersey, in order to take the Indians under my care into New York; but no sooner was I ready to move from Amboy with the Indians under my care, than I was greatly surpriz'd & embarrass'd with express orders from the Governor of New York sent to Amboy, strictly forbidding the bringing of these poor Indians into his Province, & charging all his ferrymen not to let them pass."

[1] *Letters to Governor Penn from General Gage, Governor Franklin of New Jersey, and Governor Colden of New York.* See *Votes of Assembly,* V. 300–302. The plan was afterwards revived, at the height of the alarm caused by the march of the rioters on Philadelphia; and Penn wrote to Johnson, on the seventh of February, begging an asylum for the Indians. Johnson acquiesced, and wrote to Lieutenant-Governor Colden in favor of the measure, which, however, was never carried into effect. Johnson's letters express much sympathy with the sufferers.

able class stood idle spectators, or showed at best but a luke-warm zeal. These were the Presbyterians, who had naturally felt a strong sympathy with their suffering brethren of the frontier. To this they added a deep bitterness against the Quaker, greatly increased by a charge, most uncharitably brought by the latter against the whole Presbyterian sect, of conniving at and abetting the murders at Conestoga and Lancaster. They regarded the Paxton men as victims of Quaker neglect and injustice, and showed a strong disposition to palliate, or excuse altogether, the violence of which they had been guilty. Many of them, indeed, were secretly inclined to favor the designs of the advancing rioters; hoping that by their means the public grievances would be redressed, the Quaker faction put down, and the social and political balance of the state restored.[1]

Whatever may have been the sentiments of the Presbyterians and of the city mob, the rest of the inhabitants bestirred themselves for defence with all the alacrity of fright. The Quakers were especially conspicuous for their zeal. Nothing more was heard of the duty of non-resistance. The city was ransacked for arms, and the Assembly passed a vote, extending the English riot act to the province, the Quaker members heartily concurring in the measure. Franklin, whose energy and practical talents made his services invaluable, was the moving spirit of the day; and under his auspices the citizens were formed into military companies, six of which were of infantry, one of artillery, and two of horse. Besides this force, several thousands of the inhabitants, including many Quakers, held themselves ready to appear in arms at a moment's notice.[2]

These preparations were yet incomplete, when, on the fourth of February, couriers came in with the announcement that the Paxton men, horse and foot, were already within a short distance of the city. Proclamation was made through the streets, and the people were called to arms. A mob of citizen soldiers repaired in great excitement to the barracks, where the Indians were lodged, under protection of the handful of

[1] For indications of the state of feeling among the Presbyterians, see the numerous partisan pamphlets of the day. See also Appendix, E.

[2] Gordon, *Hist. Penn.* 406. *Penn. Gaz.* No. 1833.

regulars. Here the crowd remained all night, drenched with the rain, and in a dismal condition.[1]

On the following day, Sunday, a barricade was thrown up across the great square enclosed by the barracks; and eight cannon, to which four more were afterwards added, were planted to sweep the adjacent streets. These pieces were discharged, to convey to the rioters an idea of the reception prepared for them; but whatever effect the explosion may have produced on the ears for which it was intended, the new and appalling sounds struck the Indians in the barracks with speechless terror.[2] While the city assumed this martial attitude, its rulers thought proper to adopt the safer though less glorious course of conciliation; and a deputation of clergymen was sent out to meet the rioters, and pacify them by reason and Scripture. Towards night, as all remained quiet and nothing was heard from the enemy, the turmoil began to subside, the citizen soldiers dispersed, the regulars withdrew into quarters, and the city recovered something of the ordinary repose of a Sabbath evening.

Through the early part of the night, the quiet was undisturbed; but at about two o'clock in the morning, the clang of bells and the rolling of drums startled the people from their slumbers, and countless voices from the street echoed the alarm. Immediately, in obedience to the previous day's orders, lighted candles were placed in every window, till the streets seemed illuminated for a festival. The citizen soldiers, with more zeal than order, mustered under their officers. The governor, dreading an irruption of the mob, repaired to the house of Franklin; and the city was filled with the jangling of bells, and the no less vehement clamor of tongues. A great multitude gathered before the barracks, where it was supposed the attack would be made; and among them was seen many a Quaker, with musket in hand. Some of the more consistent of the sect, unwilling to take arms with their less scrupulous brethren, went into the barracks to console and reassure the Indians; who, however, showed much more composure than their comforters, and sat waiting the result with

[1] *Haz. Pa. Reg.* XII. 10.
[2] Loskiel, Part II. 223.

invincible calmness. Several hours of suspense and excitement passed, when it was recollected, that, though the other ferries of the Schuylkill had been secured, a crossing place, known as the Swedes' Ford, had been left open; and a party at once set out to correct this unlucky oversight.[1] Scarcely were they gone, when a cry rose among the crowd before the barracks, and a general exclamation was heard that the Paxton Boys were coming. In fact, a band of horsemen was seen advancing up Second Street. The people crowded to get out of the way; the troops fell into such order as they could; a cannon was pointed full at the horsemen, and the gunner was about to apply the match, when a man ran out from the crowd, and covered the touchhole with his hat. The cry of a false alarm was heard, and it was soon apparent to all that the supposed Paxton Boys were a troop of German butchers and carters, who had come to aid in defence of the city, and had nearly paid dear for their patriotic zeal.[2]

The tumult of this alarm was hardly over, when a fresh commotion was raised by the return of the men who had gone to secure the Swedes' Ford, and who reported that they had been too late; that the rioters had crossed the river, and were already at Germantown. Those who had crossed proved to be the van of the Paxton men, two hundred in number, and commanded by Matthew Smith; who, learning what welcome was prepared for them, thought it prudent to remain quietly at Germantown, instead of marching forward to certain destruction. In the afternoon, many of the inhabitants

[1] *Historical Account of the Late Disturbances*, 4.

[2] *Haz. Pa. Reg.* XII. 11. *Memoirs of a Life passed chiefly in Pennsylvania*, 39. Heckewelder, *Narrative*, 85. Loskiel, Part II., 223. Sparks, *Writings of Franklin*, VII. 293.

The best remaining account of these riots will be found under the first authority cited above. It consists of a long letter, written in a very animated strain, by a Quaker to his friend, containing a detailed account of what passed in the city from the first alarm of the rioters to the conclusion of the affair. The writer, though a Quaker, is free from the prejudices of his sect, nor does he hesitate to notice the inconsistency of his brethren appearing in arms. See Appendix, E.

The scene before the barracks, and the narrow escape of the German butchers, was made the subject of several poems and farces, written by members of the Presbyterian faction, to turn their opponents into ridicule; for which, indeed, the subject offered tempting facilities.

gathered courage, and went out to visit them. They found nothing very extraordinary in the aspect of the rioters, who, in the words of a writer of the day, were "a set of fellows in blanket coats and moccasons, like our Indian traders or back country wagoners, all armed with rifles and tomahawks, and some with pistols stuck in their belts."[1] They received their visitors with a courtesy which might doubtless be ascribed, in great measure, to their knowledge of the warlike preparations within the city; and the report made by the adventurers, on their return, greatly tended to allay the general excitement.

The alarm, however, was again raised on the following day; and the cry to arms once more resounded through the city of peace. The citizen soldiers mustered with exemplary despatch; but their ardor was quenched by a storm of rain, which drove them all under shelter. A neighboring Quaker meeting-house happened to be open, and a company of the volunteers betook themselves in haste to this convenient asylum. Forthwith, the place was bristling with bayonets; and the walls, which had listened so often to angry denunciations against war, now echoed the clang of weapons,—an unspeakable scandal to the elders of the sect, and an occasion of pitiless satire to the Presbyterians.[2]

This alarm proving groundless, like all the others, the governor and council proceeded to the execution of a design which they had formed the day before. They had resolved, in pursuance of their timid policy, to open negotiations with the rioters, and persuade them, if possible, to depart peacefully. Many of the citizens protested against the plan, and the soldiers volunteered to attack the Paxton men; but none were so vehement as the Quakers, who held that fire and steel were the only welcome that should be accorded to such violators of the public peace, and audacious blasphemers of the society of Friends.[3] The plan was nevertheless sustained; and Franklin, with three other citizens of character and influence, set out for Germantown. The rioters received them with marks of

[1] *Haz. Pa. Reg.* XII. 11.
[2] *Haz. Pa. Reg.* XII. 12.
[3] This statement is made in "The Quaker Unmasked," and other Presbyterian pamphlets of the day; and the Quakers, in their elaborate replies to these publications, do not attempt to deny the fact.

respect; and, after a long conference, the leaders of the mob were so far wrought upon as to give over their hostile designs, the futility of which was now sufficiently apparent.[1] An assurance was given, on the part of the government, that their complaints should have a hearing; and safety was guarantied to those of their number who should enter the city as their representatives and advocates. For this purpose, Matthew Smith and James Gibson were appointed by the general voice; and two papers, a "Declaration" and a "Remonstrance," were drawn up, addressed to the governor and Assembly. With this assurance that their cause should be represented, the rioters signified their willingness to return home, glad to escape so easily from an affair which had begun to threaten worse consequences.

Towards evening, the commissioners, returning to the city, reported the success of their negotiations. Upon this, the citizen soldiers were convened in front of the court house, and addressed by a member of the council. He thanked them for their zeal, and assured them there was no farther occasion for their services; since the Paxton men, though falsely represented as enemies of government, were in fact its friends, entertaining no worse design than that of gaining relief to their sufferings, without injury to the city or its inhabitants. The people, ill satisfied with what they heard, returned in no placid temper to their homes.[2] On the morrow, the good effect of the treaty was apparent in a general reopening of schools, shops, and warehouses, and a return to the usual activity of business, which had been wholly suspended for some days. The security was not of long duration. Before noon, an uproar more tumultuous than ever, a cry to arms, and a general exclamation that the Paxton Boys had broken the treaty and were entering the town, startled the indignant citizens. The streets were filled in an instant with a rabble of armed merchants and shopmen, who for once were fully bent on slaughter, and resolved to put an end to the long-protracted evil. Quiet was again restored; when it was found that the alarm was caused by about thirty of the frontiersmen, who,

---

[1] Sparks, *Writings of Franklin*, VII. 293.

[2] Barton, *Memoirs of Rittenhouse*, 148. Rupp, *Hist. York and Lancaster Counties*, 362.

with singular audacity, were riding into the city on a visit of curiosity. As their deportment was inoffensive, it was thought unwise to molest them. Several of these visitors had openly boasted of the part they had taken in the Conestoga murders, and a large reward had been offered for their apprehension; yet such was the state of factions in the city, and such the dread of the frontiersmen, that no man dared lay hand on the criminals. The party proceeded to the barracks, where they requested to see the Indians, declaring that they could point out several who had been in the battle against Colonel Bouquet, or engaged in other acts of open hostility. The request was granted, but no discovery made. Upon this, it was rumored abroad that the Quakers had removed the guilty individuals to screen them from just punishment; an accusation which, for a time, excited much ill blood between the rival factions.

The thirty frontiersmen withdrew from the city, and soon followed the example of their companions, who had begun to move homeward, leaving their leaders, Smith and Gibson, to adjust their differences with the government. Their departure gave great relief to the people of the neighborhood, to whom they had, at times, conducted themselves after a fashion somewhat uncivil and barbarous; uttering hideous outcries, in imitation of the war-whoop; knocking down peaceable citizens, and pretending to scalp them; thrusting their guns in at windows, and committing unheard-of ravages among hen-roosts and hog-pens.[1]

Though the city was now safe from all external danger, contentions sprang up within its precincts, which, though by no means as perilous, were not less clamorous and angry than those menaced from an irruption of the rioters.[2] The rival

[1] David Rittenhouse, in one of his letters, speaks with great horror of the enormities committed by the Paxton Boys, and enumerates various particulars of their conduct. See Barton, *Mem. of Rittenhouse*, 148.

[2] "Whether the Paxton men were 'more sinned against than sinning,' was a question which was agitated with so much ardor and acrimony, that even the schoolboys became warmly engaged in the contest. For my own part, though of the religious sect which had been long warring with the Quakers, I was entirely on the side of humanity and public duty, (or in this do I beg the question?) and perfectly recollect my indignation at the sentiments of one of the ushers who was on the opposite side. His name was Davis, and he was

factions turned savagely upon each other; while the more philosophic citizens stood laughing by, and ridiculed them both. The Presbyterians grew furious, the Quakers dogged and spiteful. Pamphlets, farces, dialogues, and poems came forth in quick succession. These sometimes exhibited a few traces of wit, and even of reasoning; but abuse was the favorite weapon, and it is difficult to say which of the combatants handled it with the greater freedom and dexterity.[1] The Quakers accused the Presbyterians of conniving at the act of

---

really a kind, good-natured man; yet from the dominion of his religious or political prejudices, he had been led to apologize for, if not to approve of an outrage, which was a disgrace to a civilized people. He had been among the riflemen on their coming into the city, and, talking with them upon the subject of the Lancaster massacre, and particularly of the killing of Will Sock, the most distinguished of the victims, related with an air of approbation, this rodomontade of the real or pretended murderer. 'I,' said he, 'am the man who killed Will Sock—this is the arm that stabbed him to the heart, and I glory in it.' "—*Memoirs of a Life chiefly passed in Pennsylvania*, 40.

[1] "Persons who were intimate now scarcely speak; or, if they happen to meet and converse, presently get to quarrelling. In short, harmony and love seem to be banished from amongst us."

The above is an extract from the letter so often referred to. A fragment of the "Paxtoniad," one of the poems of the day, is given in the Appendix. Few of the party pamphlets are worth quoting, but the titles of some of them will give an idea of their character: The Quaker Unmasked—A Looking-Glass for Presbyterians—A Battle of Squirt—Plain Truth—Plain Truth found to be Plain Falsehood—The Author of Plain Truth Stripped Stark Naked—Clothes for a Stark Naked Author—The Squabble, a Pastoral Eclogue—etc., etc.

The pamphlet called Plain Truth drew down the especial indignation of the Quakers, and the following extract from one of their replies to it may serve as a fair specimen of the temper of the combatants: "But how came you to give your piece the Title of Plain Truth; if you had called it downright Lies, it would have agreed better with the Contents; the Title therefore is a deception, and the contents manifestly false: in short, I have carefully examined it, and find in it no less than 17 Positive Lies, and 10 false Insinuations contained in 15 pages, Monstrous, and from what has been said must conclude that when you wrote it, Truth was banished entirely from you, and that you wrote it with a truly Pious Lying P——n Spirit, which appears in almost every Line!"

The peaceful society of Friends found among its ranks more than one such champion as the ingenious writer of the above. Two collections of these pamphlets have been examined, one preserved in the City Library of Philadelphia, and the other in that of the New York Historical Society.

murderers, of perverting Scripture for their defence, and of aiding the rioters with counsel and money in their audacious attempt against the public peace. The Presbyterians, on their part, with about equal justice, charged the Quakers with leaguing themselves with the common enemy and exciting them to war. They held up to scorn those accommodating principles which denied the aid of arms to suffering fellow-countrymen, but justified their use at the first call of self-interest. The Quaker warrior, in his sober garb of ostentatious simplicity, his prim person adorned with military trappings, and his hands grasping a musket which threatened more peril to himself than to his enemy, was a subject of ridicule too tempting to be overlooked.

While this paper warfare was raging in the city, the representatives of the frontiersmen, Smith and Gibson, had laid before the Assembly the memorial, entitled the Remonstrance; and to this a second paper, styled a Declaration, was soon afterwards added.[1] Various grievances were specified, for which redress was demanded. It was urged that those counties where the Quaker interest prevailed sent to the Assembly more than their due share of representatives. The memorialists bitterly complained of a law, then before the Assembly, by which those charged with murdering Indians were to be brought to trial, not in the district where the act was committed, but in one of the three eastern counties. They represented the Moravian converts as enemies in disguise, and denounced the policy which yielded them protection and support while the sick and wounded of the frontiers were cruelly abandoned to their misery. They begged that a suitable reward might be offered for scalps, since the want of such encouragement had "damped the spirits of many brave men." Angry invectives against the Quakers succeeded. To the "villany, infatuation, and influence of a certain faction, that have got the political reins in their hands, and tamely tyrannize over the other good subjects of the province," were to be ascribed, urged the memorialists, the intolerable evils which afflicted the people. The Quakers, they insisted, had held private treaties with the Indians, encouraged them to hostile acts, and excused their

[1] See Appendix, E.

cruelties on the charitable plea that this was their method of making war.

The memorials were laid before a committee, who recommended that a public conference should be held with Smith and Gibson, to consider the grounds of complaint. To this the governor, in view of the illegal position assumed by the frontiersmen, would not give his consent; an assertion of dignity that would have done him more honor had he made it when the rioters were in arms before the city, at which time he had shown an abundant alacrity to negotiate. It was intimated to Smith and Gibson that they might leave Philadelphia; and the Assembly soon after became involved in its inevitable quarrels with the governor, relative to the granting of supplies for the service of the ensuing campaign. The supply bill passed, as mentioned in a former chapter; and the consequent military preparations, together with a threatened renewal of the war on the part of the enemy, engrossed the minds of the frontier people, and caused the excitements of the winter to be forgotten. No action on the two memorials was ever taken by the Assembly; and the memorable Paxton riots had no other definite result than that of exposing the weakness and distraction of the provincial government, and demonstrating the folly and absurdity of all principles of non-resistance.

Yet to the student of human nature these events supply abundant food for reflection. In the frontiersman, goaded by the madness of his misery to deeds akin to those by which he suffered, and half believing that, in the perpetration of these atrocities, he was but the minister of divine vengeance; in the Quaker, absorbed by one narrow philanthropy, and closing his ears to the outcries of his wretched countrymen; in the Presbyterian, urged by party spirit and sectarian zeal to countenance the crimes of rioters and murderers,—in each and all of these lies an embodied satire, which may find its application in every age of the world, and every condition of society.

The Moravian Indians, the occasion—and, at least, as regards most of them, the innocent occasion—of the tumult, remained for a full year in the barracks of Philadelphia. There they endured frightful sufferings from the small-pox, which destroyed more than a third of their number. After the conclusion of peace, they were permitted to depart; and, having thanked the governor for his protection and care, they withdrew to the banks of the Susquehanna, where, under the direction of the missionaries, they once more formed a prosperous settlement.[1]

[1]Loskiel, Part II. 231.

Chapter XXVI.

1764.

BRADSTREET'S ARMY ON THE LAKES.

T HE CAMPAIGN of 1763, a year of disaster to the English
colonies, was throughout of a defensive nature, and no
important blow had been struck against the enemy. With the
opening of the following spring, preparations were made to
renew the war on a more decisive plan. Before the commencement of hostilities, Sir William Johnson and his deputy,
George Croghan, severally addressed to the lords of trade memorials, setting forth the character, temper, and resources of
the Indian tribes, and suggesting the course of conduct which
they judged it expedient to pursue. They represented that, before the conquest of Canada, all the tribes, jealous of French
encroachment, had looked to the English to befriend and protect them; but that now one general feeling of distrust and
hatred filled them all. They added that the neglect and injustice of the British government, the outrages of ruffian borderers and debauched traders, and the insolence of English
soldiers, had aggravated this feeling, and given double effect
to the restless machinations of the defeated French; who, to
revenge themselves on their conquerors, were constantly stirring up the Indians to war. A race so brave and tenacious of
liberty, so wild and erratic in their habits, dwelling in a country so savage and inaccessible, could not be exterminated or
reduced to subjection without an immoderate expenditure of
men, money, and time. The true policy of the British government was therefore to conciliate; to soothe their jealous pride,
galled by injuries and insults; to gratify them by presents, and
treat them with a respect and attention to which their
haughty spirit would not fail to respond. We ought, they said,
to make the Indians our friends; and, by a just, consistent,
and straightforward course, seek to gain their esteem, and
wean them from their partiality to the French. To remove the
constant irritation which arose from the intrusion of the
white inhabitants on their territory, Croghan urged the expediency of purchasing a large tract of land to the westward of

the English settlements; thus confining the tribes to remoter hunting-grounds. For a moderate sum the Indians would part with as much land as might be required. A little more, laid out in annual presents, would keep them in good temper; and by judicious management all hostile collision might be prevented, till, by the extension of the settlements, it should become expedient to make yet another purchase.[1]

This plan was afterwards carried into execution by the British government. Founded as it is upon the supposition that the Indian tribes must gradually dwindle and waste away, it might well have awakened the utmost fears of that unhappy people. Yet none but an enthusiast or fanatic could condemn it as iniquitous. To reclaim the Indians from their savage state has again and again been attempted, and each attempt has failed. Their intractable, unchanging character leaves no other alternative than their gradual extinction, or the abandonment of the western world to eternal barbarism; and of this and other similar plans, whether the offspring of British or American legislation, it may alike be said that sentimental philanthropy will find it easier to cavil at than to amend them.

Now, turning from the Indians, let us observe the temper of those whose present business it was to cudgel them into good behavior; that is to say, the British officers, of high and low degree. They seem to have been in a mood of universal discontent, not in the least surprising when one considers that they were forced to wage, with crippled resources, an arduous, profitless, and inglorious war; while perverse and jealous legislatures added gall to their bitterness, and taxed their patience to its utmost endurance. The impossible requirements of the commander-in-chief were sometimes joined to their other vexations. Sir Jeffrey Amherst, who had, as we have seen, but a slight opinion of Indians, and possibly of everybody else except a British nobleman and a British soldier, expected much of his officers; and was at times unreasonable in his anticipations of a prompt "vengeance on the barbarians." Thus he had no sooner heard of the loss of Michillimackinac, Miami, and other western outposts, than he sent orders to Gladwyn to re-establish them at once. Gladwyn, who had

[1] MS. *Johnson Papers*.

scarcely force enough to maintain himself at Detroit, thereupon writes to his friend Bouquet: "The last I received from the General is of the second July, in which I am ordered to establish the outposts immediately. At the time I received these orders, I knew it was impossible to comply with any part of them: the event shows I was right. I am heartily wearied of my command, and I have signified the same to Colonel Amherst (Sir Jeffrey's adjutant). I hope I shall be relieved soon; if not, I intend to quit the service, for I would not choose to be any longer exposed to the villany and treachery of the settlement and Indians."

Two or three weeks before the above was written, George Croghan, Sir William Johnson's deputy, who had long lived on the frontier, and was as well versed in Indian affairs as the commander-in-chief was ignorant of them, wrote to Colonel Bouquet:—"Seven tribes in Canada have offered their services to act with the King's troops; but the General seems determined to neither accept of Indians' services, nor provincials'. . . . I have resigned out of the service, and will start for England about the beginning of December. Sir Jeffrey Amherst would not give his consent; so I made my resignation in writing, and gave my reasons for so doing. Had I continued, I could be of no more service than I have been these eighteen months past; which was none at all, as no regard was had to any intelligence I sent, no more than to my opinion." Croghan, who could not be spared, was induced, on Gage's accession to the command, to withdraw his resignation and retain his post.

Next, we have a series of complaints from Lieutenant Blane of Fort Ligonier; who congratulates Bouquet on his recent victory at Bushy Run, and adds: "I have now to beg that I may not be left any longer in this forlorn way, for I can assure you the fatigue I have gone through begins to get the better of me. I must therefore beg that you will appoint me, by the return of the convoy, a proper garrison. . . . My present situation is fifty times worse than ever." And again, on the seventeenth of September: "I must beg leave to recommend to your particular attention the sick soldiers here; as there is neither surgeon nor medicine, it would really be charity to order them up. I must also beg leave to ask what you intend to do with the poor starved militia, who have neither shirts, shoes, nor any thing else. I am sorry you can do nothing for the poor inhabitants. . . . I really get heartily tired of this post." He endured it some two months more, and then breaks out again on the twenty-fourth of November: "I intend going home by the first opportunity, being pretty much tired of a service that's so little worth any man's time; and the more so, as I cannot but think I have been particularly unlucky in it."

Now follow the letters, written in French, of the gallant Swiss, Captain Ecuyer, always lively and entertaining even in his discontent. He writes to Bouquet from Bedford, on the thirteenth of November. Like other officers on the frontier, he complains of the settlers, who, notwithstanding their fear of the enemy, always did their best to shelter deserters; and he gives a list of eighteen soldiers who had deserted within five days:[1] "I have been twenty-two years in service, and I never in my life saw any thing equal to it,—a gang of mutineers, bandits, cut-throats, especially the grenadiers. I have been obliged, after all the patience imaginable, to have two of them whipped on the spot, without court-martial. One wanted to kill the sergeant and the other wanted to kill me. . . . For God's sake, let me go and raise cabbages. You can do it if you will, and I shall thank you eternally for it. Don't refuse, I beg you. Besides, my health is not very good; and I don't know if I can go up again to Fort Pitt with this convoy."

Bouquet himself was no better satisfied than his correspondents. On the twentieth of June, 1764, he wrote to Gage, Amherst's successor: "I flatter myself that you will do me the favor to have me relieved from this command, the burden and fatigues of which I begin to feel my strength very unequal to."

Gage knew better than to relieve him, and Bouquet was

[1]"The three companies of Royal Americans were reduced when I met them at Lancaster to 55 men, having lost 38 by desertion in my short absence. I look upon Sir Jeffrey Amherst's Orders forbidding me to continue to discharge as usual the men whose time of service was expired, and keeping us for seven years in the Woods,—as the occasion of this unprecedented desertion. The encouragement given everywhere in this Country to deserters, screened almost by every person, must in time ruin the Army, unless the Laws against Harbourers are better enforced by the American (*provincial*) government."— *Bouquet to Gage*, 20 June, 1764.

forced to resign himself to another year of bush-fighting. The plan of the summer's campaign had been settled; and he was to be the most important, if not the most conspicuous, actor in it. It had been resolved to march two armies from different points into the heart of the Indian country. The first, under Bouquet, was to advance from Fort Pitt into the midst of the Delaware and Shawanoe settlements of the valley of the Ohio. The other, under Colonel Bradstreet, was to pass up the lakes, and force the tribes of Detroit, and the regions beyond, to unconditional submission.

The name of Bradstreet was already well known in America. At a dark and ill-omened period of the French war, he had crossed Lake Ontario with a force of three thousand provincials, and captured Fort Frontenac, a formidable stronghold of the French, commanding the outlet of the lake. He had distinguished himself, moreover, by his gallant conduct in a skirmish with the French and Indians on the River Oswego. These exploits had gained for him a reputation beyond his merits. He was a man of more activity than judgment, self-willed, vain, and eager for notoriety; qualities which became sufficiently apparent before the end of the campaign.[1]

Several of the northern provinces furnished troops for the expedition; but these levies did not arrive until after the appointed time; and, as the service promised neither honor nor advantage, they were of very indifferent quality, looking, according to an officer of the expedition, more like candidates for a hospital than like men fit for the arduous duty before them. The rendezvous of the troops was at Albany, and thence they took their departure about the end of June. Adopting the usual military route to the westward, they passed up the Mohawk, crossed the Oneida Lake, and de-

---

[1] In the correspondence of General Wolfe, recently published in *Tait's Magazine*, this distinguished officer speaks in high terms of Bradstreet's military character. His remarks, however, have reference solely to the capture of Fort Frontenac; and he seems to have derived his impressions from the public prints, as he had no personal knowledge of Bradstreet. The view expressed above is derived from the letters of Bradstreet himself, from the correspondence of General Gage and Sir William Johnson, and from a MS. paper containing numerous details of his conduct during the campaign of 1764, and drawn up by the officers who served under him.

This paper is in the possession of Mrs. W. L. Stone.

scended the Onondaga. The boats and bateaux, crowded with men, passed between the war-worn defences of Oswego, which guarded the mouth of the river on either hand, and, issuing forth upon Lake Ontario, steered in long procession over its restless waters. A storm threw the flotilla into confusion; and several days elapsed before the ramparts of Fort Niagara rose in sight, breaking the tedious monotony of the forest-covered shores. The troops landed beneath its walls. The surrounding plains were soon dotted with the white tents of the little army, whose strength, far inferior to the original design, did not exceed twelve hundred men.

A striking spectacle greeted them on their landing. Hundreds of Indian cabins were clustered along the skirts of the forest, and a countless multitude of savages, in all the picturesque variety of their barbaric costume, were roaming over the fields, or lounging about the shores of the lake. Towards the close of the previous winter, Sir William Johnson had despatched Indian messengers to the tribes far and near, warning them of the impending blow; and urging all who were friendly to the English, or disposed to make peace while there was yet time, to meet him at Niagara, and listen to his words. Throughout the winter, the sufferings of the Indians had been great and general. The suspension of the fur-trade; the consequent want of ammunition, clothing, and other articles of necessity; the failure of expected aid from the French; and, above all, the knowledge that some of their own people had taken up arms for the English, combined to quench their thirst for war. Johnson's messengers had therefore been received with unexpected favor, and many had complied with his invitation. Some came to protest their friendship for the English; others hoped, by an early submission, to atone for past misconduct. Some came as spies; while others, again, were lured by the hope of receiving presents, and especially a draught of English milk, that is to say, a dram of whiskey.

The trader, Alexander Henry, the same who so narrowly escaped the massacre at Michillimackinac, was with a party of Ojibwas at the Sault Ste. Marie, when a canoe, filled with warriors, arrived, bringing the message of Sir William Johnson. A council was called; and the principal messenger, offering a belt of wampum, spoke as follows: "My friends and brothers, I am come with this belt from our great father, Sir William Johnson. He desired me to come to you, as his ambassador, and tell you that he is making a great feast at Fort Niagara; that his kettles are all ready, and his fires lighted. He invites you to partake of the feast, in common with your friends, the Six Nations, who have all made peace with the English. He advises you to seize this opportunity of doing the same, as you cannot otherwise fail of being destroyed; for the English are on their march with a great army, which will be joined by different nations of Indians. In a word, before the fall of the leaf they will be at Michillimackinac, and the Six Nations with them."

The Ojibwas had been debating whether they should go to Detroit, to the assistance of Pontiac, who had just sent them a message to that effect; but the speech of Johnson's messenger turned the current of their thoughts. Most of them were in favor of accepting the invitation; but, distrusting mere human wisdom in a crisis so important, they resolved, before taking a decisive step, to invoke the superior intelligence of the Great Turtle, the chief of all the spirits. A huge wigwam was erected, capable of containing the whole population of the little village. In the centre, a sort of tabernacle was constructed by driving posts into the ground, and closely covering them with hides. With the arrival of night, the propitious time for consulting their oracle, all the warriors assembled in the spacious wigwam, half lighted by the lurid glare of fires, and waited, in suspense and awe, the issue of the invocation. The medicine man, or magician, stripped almost naked, now entered the central tabernacle, which was barely large enough to receive him, and carefully closed the aperture. At once the whole structure began to shake with a violence which threatened its demolition; and a confusion of horrible sounds, shrieks, howls, yells, and moans of anguish, mingled with articulate words, sounded in hideous discord from within. This outrageous clamor, which announced to the horror-stricken spectators the presence of a host of evil spirits, ceased as suddenly as it had begun. A low, feeble sound, like the whine of a young puppy, was next heard within the recess; upon which the warriors raised a cry of joy, and hailed it as the voice of the Great Turtle—the spirit who never lied. The magician soon announced that the spirit was ready to answer any question which might be proposed. On this, the chief warrior stepped forward; and, having propitiated the Great Turtle by a present of tobacco thrust through a small hole in the tabernacle, inquired if the English were in reality preparing to attack the Indians, and if the troops were already come to Niagara. Once more the tabernacle was violently shaken, a loud yell was heard, and it was apparent to all that the spirit was gone. A pause of anxious expectation ensued; when, after the lapse of a quarter of an hour, the weak, puppy-like voice of the Great Turtle was again heard addressing the magician in a language unknown to the auditors. When the spirit ceased speaking, the magician interpreted his words. During the short interval of his departure, he had crossed Lake Huron, visited Niagara, and descended the St. Lawrence to Montreal. Few soldiers had as yet reached Niagara; but as he flew down the St. Lawrence, he had seen the water covered with boats, all filled with English warriors, coming to make war on the Indians. Having obtained this answer to his first question, the chief ventured to propose another; and inquired if he and his people, should they accept the invitation of Sir William Johnson, would be well received at Niagara. The answer was most satisfactory. "Sir William Johnson," said the spirit, "will fill your canoes with presents; with blankets, kettles, guns, gunpowder and shot; and large barrels of rum, such as the stoutest of the Indians will not be able to lift; and every man will return in safety to his family." This grateful response produced a general outburst of acclamations; and, with cries of joy, many voices were heard to exclaim, "I will go too! I will go too!"[1]

[1]Henry, *Travels and Adventures,* 171.

The method of invoking the spirits, described above, is a favorite species of imposture among the medicine men of most Algonquin tribes, and had been observed and described a century and a half before the period of this history. Champlain, the founder of Canada, witnessed one of these ceremonies; and the Jesuit Le Jeune gives an account of a sorcerer, who, having invoked a spirit in this manner, treacherously killed him with a hatchet; the mysterious visitant having assumed a visible and tangible form, which exposed him to the incidents of mortality. During these invocations, the lodge or tabernacle was always observed to shake violently to and fro, in a manner so remarkable as exceedingly to perplex the observers. The variety of discordant sounds,

They set out, accordingly, for Niagara; and thither also numerous bands of warriors were tending, urged by similar messages, and encouraged, it may be, by similar responses of their oracles. Crossing fresh-water oceans in their birch canoes, and threading the devious windings of solitary streams, they came flocking to the common centre of attraction. Such a concourse of savages has seldom been seen in America. Menomonies, Ottawas, Ojibwas, Mississaugas, from the north; Caughnawagas from Canada, even Wyandots from Detroit, together with a host of Iroquois, were congregated round Fort Niagara to the number of more than two thousand warriors; many of whom had brought with them their women and children.[1] Even the Sacs, the Foxes, and the Winnebagoes had sent their deputies; and the Osages, a tribe beyond the Mississippi, had their representative in this general meeting.

---

uttered by the medicine man, need not surprise us more than those accurate imitations of the cries of various animals, to which Indian hunters are accustomed to train their strong and flexible voices.

[1] MS. *Johnson Papers*.

The following extract from Henry's *Travels* will exhibit the feelings with which the Indians came to the conference at Niagara, besides illustrating a curious feature of their superstitions. Many tribes, including some widely differing in language and habits, regard the rattlesnake with superstitious veneration; looking upon him either as a manitou, or spirit, or as a creature endowed with mystic powers and attributes, giving him an influence over the fortunes of mankind. Henry accompanied his Indian companions to Niagara; and, on the way, he chanced to discover one of these snakes near their encampment: —

"The reptile was coiled, and its head raised considerably above its body. Had I advanced another step before my discovery, I must have trodden upon it.

"I no sooner saw the snake, than I hastened to the canoe, in order to procure my gun; but the Indians, observing what I was doing, inquired the occasion, and, being informed, begged me to desist. At the same time, they followed me to the spot, with their pipes and tobacco-pouches in their hands. On returning, I found the snake still coiled.

"The Indians, on their part, surrounded it, all addressing it by turns, and calling it their *grandfather*, but yet keeping at some distance. During this part of the ceremony, they filled their pipes; and now each blew the smoke toward the snake, who, as it appeared to me, really received it with pleasure. In a word, after remaining coiled, and receiving incense, for the space of half an hour, it stretched itself along the ground, in visible good humor. Its length was between four and five feet. Having remained outstretched for some time, at last it moved slowly away, the Indians following it, and still addressing it

Though the assembled multitude consisted, for the most part, of the more pacific members of the tribes represented, yet their friendly disposition was by no means certain. Several straggling soldiers were shot at in the neighborhood, and it

---

by the title of grandfather, beseeching it to take care of their families during their absence, and to be pleased to open the heart of Sir William Johnson, so that he might *show them charity*, and fill their canoe with rum.

"One of the chiefs added a petition, that the snake would take no notice of the insult which had been offered him by the Englishman, who would even have put him to death, but for the interference of the Indians, to whom it was hoped he would impute no part of the offence. They further requested, that he would remain, and not return among the English; that is, go eastward.

"After the rattlesnake was gone, I learned that this was the first time that an individual of the species had been seen so far to the northward and westward of the River Des Français; a circumstance, moreover, from which my companions were disposed to infer, that this *manito* had come, or been sent, on purpose to meet them; that his errand had been no other than to stop them on their way; and that consequently it would be most advisable to return to the point of departure. I was so fortunate, however, as to prevail with them to embark; and at six o'clock in the evening we again encamped.

"Early the next morning we proceeded. We had a serene sky and very little wind, and the Indians therefore determined on steering across the lake, to an island which just appeared in the horizon; saving, by this course, a distance of thirty miles, which would be lost in keeping the shore. At nine o'clock A.M. we had a light breeze, to enjoy the benefit of which we hoisted sail. Soon after, the wind increased, and the Indians, beginning to be alarmed, frequently called on the rattlesnake to come to their assistance. By degrees the waves grew high; and at eleven o'clock it blew a hurricane, and we expected every moment to be swallowed up. From prayers, the Indians proceeded now to sacrifices, both alike offered to the god-rattlesnake, or *manito-kinibic*. One of the chiefs took a dog, and after tying its fore legs together, threw it overboard, at the same time calling on the snake to preserve us from being drowned, and desiring him to satisfy his hunger with the carcass of the dog. The snake was unpropitious, and the wind increased. Another chief sacrificed another dog, with the addition of some tobacco. In the prayer which accompanied these gifts, he besought the snake, as before, not to avenge upon the Indians the insult which he had received from myself, in the conception of a design to put him to death. He assured the snake that I was absolutely an Englishman, and of kin neither to him nor to them.

"At the conclusion of this speech, an Indian, who sat near me, observed, that if we were drowned it would be for my fault alone, and that I ought myself to be sacrificed, to appease the angry manito; nor was I without apprehensions, that, in case of extremity, this would be my fate; but, happily for me, the storm at length abated, and we reached the island safely."— Henry, *Travels*, 175.

soon became apparent that the utmost precaution must be taken to avert a rupture. The troops were kept always on their guard; while the black muzzles of the cannon, thrust from the bastions of the fort, struck a wholesome awe into the savage throng below.

Although so many had attended the meeting, there were still numerous tribes, and portions of tribes, who maintained a rancorous, unwavering hostility. The Delawares and Shawanoes, however, against whom Bouquet, with the army of the south, was then in the act of advancing, sent a message to the effect, that, though they had no fear of the English, and though they regarded them as old women, and held them in contempt, yet, out of pity for their sufferings, they were willing to treat of peace. To this insolent missive Johnson made no answer; and, indeed, those who sent it were, at this very time, renewing the bloody work of the preceding year along the borders of Pennsylvania and Virginia. The Senecas, that numerous and warlike people, to whose savage enmity were to be ascribed the massacre at the Devil's Hole, and other disasters of the last summer, had recently made a preliminary treaty with Sir William Johnson, and at the same time pledged themselves to appear at Niagara to ratify and complete it. They broke their promise; and it soon became known that they had leagued themselves with a large band of hostile Delawares, who had visited their country. Upon this, a messenger was sent to them, threatening that, unless they instantly came to Niagara, the English would march upon them and burn their villages. The menace had full effect; and a large body of these formidable warriors appeared at the English camp, bringing fourteen prisoners, besides several deserters and runaway slaves. A peace was concluded, on condition that they should never again attack the English, and that they should cede to the British crown a strip of land, between the Lakes Erie and Ontario, four miles in width, on both sides of the River, or Strait, of Niagara.[1] A treaty was next made with a deputation of Wyandots from Detroit, on condition of the delivery of prisoners, and the preservation of friendship for the future.

[1] *Articles of Peace concluded with the Senecas, at Fort Niagara,* July 18, 1764, MS.

Councils were next held, in turn, with each of the various tribes assembled around the fort, some of whom craved forgiveness for the hostile acts they had committed, and deprecated the vengeance of the English; while others alleged their innocence, urged their extreme wants and necessities, and begged that English traders might once more be allowed to visit them. The council-room in the fort was crowded from morning till night; and the wearisome formalities of such occasions, the speeches made and replied to, and the final shaking of hands, smoking of pipes, and serving out of whiskey, engrossed the time of the superintendent for many successive days.

Among the Indians present were a band of Ottawas from Michillimackinac, and remoter settlements, beyond Lake Michigan, and a band of Menomonies from Green Bay. The former, it will be remembered, had done good service to the English, by rescuing the survivors of the garrison of Michillimackinac from the clutches of the Ojibwas; and the latter had deserved no less at their hands, by the protection they had extended to Lieutenant Gorell, and the garrison at Green Bay. Conscious of their merits, they had come to Niagara in full confidence of a favorable reception. Nor were they disappointed; for Johnson met them with a cordial welcome, and greeted them as friends and brothers. They, on their part, were not wanting in expressions of pleasure; and one of their orators exclaimed, in the figurative language of his people, "When our brother came to meet us, the storms ceased, the lake became smooth, and the whole face of nature was changed."

They disowned all connection or privity with the designs of Pontiac. "Brother," said one of the Ottawa chiefs, "you must not imagine I am acquainted with the cause of the war. I only heard a little bird whistle an account of it, and, on going to Michillimackinac, I found your people killed; upon which I sent our priest to inquire into the matter. On the priest's return, he brought me no favorable account, but a war-hatchet from Pontiac, which I scarcely looked on, and immediately threw away."

Another of the Ottawas, a chief of the remoter band of Lake Michigan, spoke to a similar effect, as follows: "We are not of the same people as those residing about Michillimackinac; we only heard at a distance that the enemy were killing your soldiers, on which we covered our heads, and I resolved not to suffer my people to engage in the war. I gathered them together, and made them sit still. In the spring, on uncovering my head, I perceived that they had again begun a war, and that the sky was all cloudy in that quarter."

The superintendent thanked them for their fidelity to the English; reminded them that their true interest lay in the preservation of peace, and concluded with a gift of food and clothing, and a permission, denied to all the rest, to open a traffic with the traders, who had already begun to assemble at the fort. "And now, my brother," said a warrior, as the council was about to break up, "we beg that you will tell us where we can find some rum to comfort us; for it is long since we have tasted any, and we are very thirsty." This honest request was not refused. The liquor was distributed, and a more copious supply promised for the future; upon which the deputation departed, and repaired to their encampment, much pleased with their reception.[1]

Throughout these conferences, one point of policy was constantly adhered to. No general council was held. Separate treaties were made, in order to promote mutual jealousies and rivalries, and discourage the feeling of union, and of a common cause among the widely scattered tribes. Johnson at length completed his task, and, on the sixth of August, set sail for Oswego. The march of the army had hitherto been delayed by rumors of hostile designs on the part of the Indians, who, it was said, had formed a scheme for attacking Fort Niagara, as soon as the troops should have left the ground. Now, however, when the concourse was melting away, and the tribes departing for their distant homes, it was thought that the danger was past, and that the army might safely resume its progress. They advanced, accordingly, to Fort Schlosser, above the cataract, whither their boats and bateaux had been sent before them, craned up the rocks at Lewiston, and dragged by oxen over the rough portage road. The troops had been joined by three hundred friendly Indians, and an

---

[1]MS. *Johnson Papers*. MS. *Minutes of Conference with the chiefs and warriors of the Ottawas and Menomonies at Fort Niagara*, July 20, 1764. The extracts given above are copied verbatim from the original record.

equal number of Canadians. The appearance of the latter in arms would, it was thought, have great effect on the minds of the enemy, who had always looked upon them as friends and supporters. Of the Indian allies, the greater part were Iroquois, and the remainder, about a hundred in number, Ojibwas and Mississaugas; the former being the same who had recently arrived from the Sault Ste. Marie, bringing with them their prisoner, Alexander Henry. Henry was easily persuaded to accompany the expedition; and the command of the Ojibwas and Mississaugas was assigned to him—"To me," writes the adventurous trader, "whose best hope it had lately been to live by their forbearance." His long-continued sufferings and dangers hardly deserved to be rewarded by so great a misfortune as that of commanding a body of Indian warriors; an evil from which, however, he was soon to be relieved. The army had hardly begun its march, when nearly all his followers ran off, judging it wiser to return home with the arms and clothing given them for the expedition, than to make war against their own countrymen and relatives. Fourteen warriors still remained; but on the following night, when the army lay at Fort Schlosser, having contrived by some means to obtain liquor, they created such a commotion in the camp, by yelling and firing their guns, as to excite the utmost indignation of the commander. They received from him, in consequence, a reproof so harsh and ill judged, that most of them went home in disgust; and Henry found his Indian battalion suddenly dwindled to four or five vagabond hunters.[1] A large number of Iroquois still followed the army, the strength of which, farther increased by a re-enforcement of Highlanders, was now very considerable.

The troops left Fort Schlosser on the eighth. Their boats and bateaux pushed out into the Niagara, whose expanded waters reposed in a serenity soon to be exchanged for the wild roar and tumultuous struggle of the rapids and the cataract. They coasted along the southern shore of Lake Erie until the twelfth, when, in the neighborhood of Presqu' Isle, they were overtaken by a storm of rain, which forced them to drag

[1] Henry, *Travels*, 183.

their boats on shore, and pitch their tents in the dripping forest. Before the day closed, word was brought that strange Indians were near the camp. They soon made their appearance, proclaiming themselves to be chiefs and deputies of the Delawares and Shawanoes, empowered to beg for peace in the name of their respective tribes. Various opinions were entertained of the visitors. The Indian allies wished to kill them, and many of the officers believed them to be spies. There was no proof of their pretended character of deputies; and, for all that appeared to the contrary, they might be a mere straggling party of warriors. Their professions of an earnest desire for peace were contradicted by the fact that they brought with them but one small belt of wampum; a pledge no less indispensable in a treaty with these tribes than seals and signatures in a convention of European sovereigns.[1] Bradstreet knew, or ought to have known, the character of the treacherous enemy with whom he had to deal. He knew that the Shawanoes and Delawares had shown, throughout the war, a ferocious and relentless hostility; that they had sent an insolent message to Niagara; and, finally, that in his own instructions he was enjoined to deal sternly with them, and not be duped by pretended overtures. Yet, in spite of the suspicious character of the self-styled deputies, in spite of the sullen wrath of his Indian allies, and the murmured dissent of his officers, he listened to their proposals, and entered into a preliminary treaty. He pledged himself to refrain from attacking the Delawares and Shawanoes, on condition that within twenty-five days the deputies should again meet him at Sandusky, in order to yield up their prisoners, and conclude a definite treaty of peace.[2] It afterwards ap-

---

[1] Every article in a treaty must be confirmed by a belt of wampum; otherwise it is void. Mante, the historian of the French war, asserts that they brought four belts. But this is contradicted in contemporary letters, including several of General Gage and Sir William Johnson. Mante accompanied Bradstreet's expedition with the rank of major; and he is a zealous advocate of his commander, whom he seeks to defend, at the expense both of Colonel Bouquet and General Gage.

[2] *Preliminary Treaty between Colonel Bradstreet and the Deputies of the Delawares and Shawanoes, concluded at L'Ance aux Feuilles, on Lake Erie*, August 12, 1764, MS.

peared—and this, indeed, might have been suspected at the time—that the sole object of the overtures was to retard the action of the army until the season should be too far advanced to prosecute the campaign. At this very moment, the Delaware and Shawanoe war-parties were murdering and scalping along the frontiers; and the work of havoc continued for weeks, until it was checked at length by the operations of Colonel Bouquet.

Bradstreet was not satisfied with the promise he had made to abandon his own hostile designs. He consummated his folly and presumption by despatching a messenger to his superior officer, Colonel Bouquet, informing him that the Delawares and Shawanoes had been reduced to submission without his aid, and that he might withdraw his troops, as there was no need of his advancing farther. Bouquet, astonished and indignant, paid no attention to this communication, but pursued his march as before.[1]

The course pursued by Bradstreet in this affair—a course which can only be ascribed to the vain ambition of finishing the war without the aid of others—drew upon him the severe censures of the commander-in-chief, who, on hearing of the treaty, at once annulled it.[2] Bradstreet has been accused of

---

[1] MS. Letter—*Bouquet to Gage*, Sept. 3.

[2] Extract from a MS. Letter—*Gage to Bradstreet*, Sept. 2:—

"I again repeat that I annul and disavow the peace you have made."

The following extracts will express the opinions of Gage with respect to this affair.

MS. Letter—*Gage to Bradstreet*, Oct. 15:—

"They have negotiated with you on Lake Erie, and cut our throats upon the frontiers. With your letters of peace I received others, giving accounts of murders, and these acts continue to this time. Had you only consulted Colonel Bouquet, before you agreed upon any thing with them (a deference he was certainly entitled to, instead of an order to stop his march), you would have been acquainted with the treachery of those people, and not have suffered yourself to be thus deceived, and you would have saved both Colonel Bouquet and myself from the dilemma you brought us into. You concluded a peace with people who were daily murdering us."

MS. Letter—*Gage to Johnson*, Sept. 4:—

"You will have received my letter of the 2d inst., enclosing you the unaccountable treaty betwixt Colonel Bradstreet and the Shawanese, Delawares, &c. On consideration of the treaty, it does not appear to me that the ten Indians therein mentioned were sent on an errand of peace. If they had, would they not have been at Niagara? or would the insolent and audacious

having exceeded his orders, in promising to conclude a definite treaty with the Indians, a power which was vested in Sir William Johnson alone; but as upon this point his instructions were not explicit, he may be spared the full weight of this additional charge.[1]

Having, as he thought, accomplished not only a great part of his own task, but also the whole of that which had been assigned to Colonel Bouquet, Bradstreet resumed his progress westward, and in a few days reached Sandusky. He had been ordered to attack the Wyandots, Ottawas, and Miamis, dwelling near this place; but at his approach, these Indians, hastening to avert the danger, sent a deputation to meet him, promising that, if he would refrain from attacking them, they would follow him to Detroit, and there conclude a treaty. Bradstreet thought proper to trust this slippery promise; though, with little loss of time, he might have reduced them, on the spot, to a much more effectual submission. He now bent his course for Detroit, leaving the Indians of Sandusky much delighted, and probably no less surprised, at the success of their embassy. Before his departure, however, he despatched Captain Morris, with several Canadians and friendly Indians, to the Illinois, in order to persuade the savages of that region to treat of peace with the English. The measure was in a high degree ill advised and rash, promising but doubtful advantage, and exposing the life of a valuable officer to imminent risk. The sequel of Morris's adventure will soon appear.

The English boats now entered the mouth of the Detroit, and on the twenty-sixth of August came within sight of the

---

message have been sent there in the lieu of offers of peace? Would not they have been better provided with belts on such an occasion? They give only one string of wampum. You will know this better, but it appears strange to me. They certainly came to watch the motions of the troops."

[1]MS. Letter—*Gage to Bradstreet*, Sept. 2: —

Bradstreet's instructions directed him to *offer peace* to such tribes as should make their submission. "*To offer peace*," writes Gage, "I think can never be construed a power to *conclude and dictate the articles of peace*, and you certainly know that no such power could with propriety be lodged in any person but in Sir William Johnson, his majesty's sole agent and superintendent for Indian affairs."

fort and adjacent settlements. The inhabitants of the Wyandot village on the right, who, it will be remembered, had recently made a treaty of peace at Niagara, ran down to the shore, shouting, whooping, and firing their guns,—a greeting more noisy than sincere,—while the cannon of the garrison echoed salutation from the opposite shore, and cheer on cheer, deep and heartfelt, pealed welcome from the crowded ramparts.

Well might Gladwyn's beleaguered soldiers rejoice at the approaching succor. They had been beset for more than fifteen months by their wily enemy; and though there were times when not an Indian could be seen, yet woe to the soldier who should wander into the forest in search of game, or stroll too far beyond range of the cannon. Throughout the preceding winter, they had been left in comparative quiet; but with the opening spring the Indians had resumed their pertinacious hostilities; not, however, with the same activity and vigor as during the preceding summer. The messages of Sir William Johnson, and the tidings of Bradstreet's intended expedition, had had great effect upon their minds, and some of them had begged abjectly for peace; but still the garrison were harassed by frequent alarms, and days and nights of watchfulness were their unvarying lot. Cut off for months together from all communication with their race; pent up in an irksome imprisonment; ill supplied with provisions, and with clothing worn threadbare, they hailed with delight the prospect of a return to the world from which they had been banished so long. The army had no sooner landed than the garrison was relieved, and fresh troops substituted in their place. Bradstreet's next care was to inquire into the conduct of the Canadian inhabitants of Detroit, and punish such of them as had given aid to the Indians. A few only were found guilty, the more culpable having fled to the Illinois on the approach of the army.

Pontiac too was gone. The great war-chief, his vengeance unslaked, and his purpose unshaken, had retired, as we have seen, to the banks of the Maumee, whence he sent a haughty defiance to the English commander. The Indian villages near Detroit were half emptied of their inhabitants, many of whom still followed the desperate fortunes of their indomitable leader. Those who remained were, for the most part, brought by famine and misery to a sincere desire for peace, and readily obeyed the summons of Bradstreet to meet him in council.

The council was held in the open air, on the morning of the seventh of September, with all the accompaniments of military display which could inspire awe and respect among the assembled savages. The tribes, or rather fragments of tribes, represented at this meeting, were the Ottawas, Ojibwas, Pottawattamies, Miamis, Sacs, and Wyandots. The Indians of Sandusky kept imperfectly the promise they had made, the Wyandots of that place alone sending a full deputation; while the other tribes were merely represented by the Ojibwa chief Wasson. This man, who was the principal chief of his tribe, and the most prominent orator on the present occasion, rose and opened the council.

"My brother," he said, addressing Bradstreet, "last year God forsook us. God has now opened our eyes, and we desire to be heard. It is God's will our hearts are altered. It was God's will you had such fine weather to come to us. It is God's will also there should be peace and tranquillity over the face of the earth and of the waters."

Having delivered this exordium, Wasson frankly confessed that the tribes which he represented were all justly chargeable with the war, and now deeply regretted their delinquency. It is common with Indians, when accused of acts of violence, to lay the blame upon the unbridled recklessness of their young warriors; and this excuse is often perfectly sound and valid; but since, in the case of a premeditated and long-continued war, it was glaringly inadmissible, they now reversed the usual course, and made scapegoats of the old chiefs and warriors, who, as they declared, had led the people astray by sinister counsel and bad example.[1]

Bradstreet would grant peace only on condition that they should become subjects of the King of England, and acknowledge that he held over their country a sovereignty as ample and complete as over any other part of his dominions. Nothing

[1]MS. *Minutes of Conference between Colonel Bradstreet and the Indians of Detroit*, Sept. 7, 1764. See, also, Mante, 517.

could be more impolitic and absurd than this demand. The smallest attempt at an invasion of their liberties has always been regarded by the Indians with extreme jealousy, and a prominent cause of the war had been an undue assumption of authority on the part of the English. This article of the treaty, could its purport have been fully understood, might have kindled afresh the quarrel which it sought to extinguish; but happily not a savage present was able to comprehend it. Subjection and sovereignty are ideas which never enter into the mind of an Indian, and therefore his language has no words to express them. Most of the western tribes, it is true, had been accustomed to call themselves children of the King of France; but the words were a mere compliment, conveying no sense of any political relation whatever. Yet it was solely by means of this harmless metaphor that the condition in question could be explained to the assembled chiefs. Thus interpreted, it met with a ready assent; since, in their eyes, it involved no concession beyond a mere unmeaning change of forms and words. They promised, in future, to call the English king father, instead of brother; unconscious of any obligation which so trifling a change could impose, and mentally reserving a full right to make war on him or his people, whenever it should suit their convenience. When Bradstreet returned from his expedition, he boasted that he had reduced the tribes of Detroit to terms of more complete submission than any other Indians had ever before yielded; but the truth was soon detected and exposed by those conversant with Indian affairs.[1]

At this council, Bradstreet was guilty of the bad policy and bad taste of speaking through the medium of a French interpreter; so that most of his own officers, as well as the Iroquois allies, who were strangers to the Algonquin language, remained in ignorance of all that passed. The latter were highly indignant, and refused to become parties to the treaty, or go through the usual ceremony of shaking hands with the chiefs of Detroit, insisting that they had not heard their speeches, and knew not whether they were friends or enemies. In another particular, also, Bradstreet gave great

[1] MS. Letter—*Johnson to the Board of Trade*, Oct. 30.

offence. From some unexplained impulse or motive, he cut to pieces, with a hatchet, a belt of wampum which was about to be used in the council; and all the Indians present, both friends and enemies, were alike incensed at this rude violation of the ancient pledge of faith, which, in their eyes, was invested with something of a sacred character.[1]

Having settled the affairs of Detroit, Bradstreet despatched Captain Howard, with a strong detachment, to take possession of Michillimackinac, which had remained unoccupied since its capture in the preceding summer. Howard effected his object without resistance, and, at the same time, sent parties of troops to reoccupy the deserted posts of Green Bay and Sault Ste. Marie. Thus, after the interval of more than a year, the flag of England was again displayed among the solitudes of the northern wilderness.[2]

While Bradstreet's army lay encamped on the fields near Detroit, Captain Morris, with a few Iroquois and Canadian attendants, was pursuing his adventurous embassy to the country of the Illinois. Morris, who has left us his portrait, prefixed to a little volume of prose and verse, was an officer of literary tastes, whose round English face did not indicate any especial degree of enterprise or resolution. He seems, however, to have had both; for, on a hint from the General, he had offered himself for the adventure, for which he was better fitted than most of his brother officers, inasmuch as he spoke French. He was dining, on the eve of his departure, in the tent of Bradstreet, when his host suddenly remarked, in the bluff way habitual to him, that he had a French fellow, a prisoner, whom he meant to hang; but that, if Morris would like him for an interpreter, he might have him. The prisoner in question was the Canadian Godefroy, who was presently led into the tent; and who, conscious of many misdemeanors, thought that his hour was come, and fell on his knees to beg his life. Bradstreet told him that he should be pardoned if he would promise to "go with this gentleman, and take good

---

[1] MS. *Remarks on the Conduct of Colonel Bradstreet*—found among the *Johnson Papers*.

See, also, an extract of a letter from Sandusky, published in several newspapers of the day.

[2] MS. *Report of Captain Howard*.

care of him," pointing to his guest. Godefroy promised; and, to the best of his power, he kept his word, for he imagined that Morris had saved his life.

Morris set out on the following afternoon with Godefroy, another Canadian, two servants, and a party of Indians, ascended the Maumee, and soon approached the camp of Pontiac; who, as already mentioned, had withdrawn to this river with his chosen warriors. The party disembarked from their canoes; and an Ottawa chief, who had joined them, lent them three horses. Morris and the Canadians mounted, and, preceded by their Indian attendants, displaying an English flag, advanced in state towards the camp, which was two leagues or more distant. As they drew near, they were met by a rabble of several hundred Indians, called by Morris "Pontiac's army." They surrounded him, beat his horse, and crowded between him and his followers, apparently trying to separate them. At the outskirts of the camp stood Pontiac himself, who met the ambassador with a scowling brow, and refused to offer his hand. Here, too, stood a man, in the uniform of a French officer, holding his gun with the butt resting on the ground, and assuming an air of great importance; while two Pawnee slaves stood close behind him. He proved to be a French drummer, calling himself St. Vincent, one of those renegades of civilization to be found in almost every Indian camp. He now took upon himself the office of a master of ceremonies; desired Morris to dismount, and seated himself at his side on a bearskin. Godefroy took his place near them; and the throng of savages, circle within circle, stood crowded around. "Presently," says Morris, "came Pontiac, and squatted himself, after his fashion, opposite to me." He opened the interview by observing that the English were liars, and demanding of the ambassador if he had come to lie to them, like the rest. "This Indian," pursues Morris, "has a more extensive power than ever was known among that people, for every chief used to command his own tribe; but eighteen nations, by French intrigue, had been brought to unite and choose this man for their commander."

Pontiac now produced a letter directed to himself, and sent from New Orleans, though purporting to be written by the

King of France. It contained, according to Morris, the grossest calumnies that the most ingenious malice could devise to incense the Indians against the English. The old falsehood was not forgotten: "Your French Father," said the writer, "is neither dead nor asleep; he is already on his way, with sixty great ships, to revenge himself on the English, and drive them out of America." Much excitement followed the reading of the letter, and Morris's situation became more than unpleasant; but St. Vincent befriended him, and hurried him off to his wigwam to keep him out of harm's way.

On the next day there was a grand council. Morris made a speech, in which he indiscreetly told the Indians that the King of France had given all the country to the King of England. Luckily, his auditors received the announcement with ridicule rather than anger. The chiefs, however, wished to kill him; but Pontiac interposed, on the ground that the life of an ambassador should be held sacred. "He made a speech," says Morris, "which does him honor, and shows that he was acquainted with the law of nations." He seemed in a mood more pacific than could have been expected, and said privately to Godefroy: "I will lead the nations to war no more. Let them be at peace if they choose; but I will never be a friend to the English. I shall be a wanderer in the woods; and, if they come there to seek me, I will shoot at them while I have an arrow left." Morris thinks that he said this in a fit of despair, and that, in fact, he was willing to come to terms.

The day following was an unlucky one. One of Morris's Indians, a Mohawk chief, ran off, having first stolen all he could lay hands on, and sold the ambassador's stack of rum, consisting of two barrels, to the Ottawas. A scene of frenzy ensued. A young Indian ran up to Morris, and stabbed at him savagely; but Godefroy caught the assassin's hand, and saved his patron's life. Morris escaped from the camp, and lay hidden in a corn-field till the howling and screeching subsided, and the Indians slept themselves sober. When he returned, an Indian, called the Little Chief, gave him a volume of Shakespeare,—the spoil of some slaughtered officer,—and then begged for gunpowder.

Having first gained Pontiac's consent, Morris now resumed

his journey to the Illinois. The river was extremely low, and it was with much ado that they pushed their canoe against the shallow current, or dragged it over stones and sandbars. On the fifth day, they met an Indian mounted on a handsome white horse, said to have belonged to General Braddock, and to have been captured at the defeat of his army, nine years before. On the morning of the seventh day, they reached the neighborhood of Fort Miami. This post, captured during the preceding year, had since remained without a garrison; and its only tenants were the Canadians, who had built their houses within its palisades, and a few Indians, who thought fit to make it their temporary abode. The meadows about the fort were dotted with the lodges of the Kickapoos, a large band of whom had recently arrived; but the great Miami village was on the opposite side of the stream, screened from sight by the forest which intervened.

The party landed a little below the fort; and, while his followers were making their way through the border of woods that skirted the river, Morris remained in the canoe, solacing himself by reading *Antony and Cleopatra* in the volume he had so oddly obtained. It was fortunate that he did so; for his attendants had scarcely reached the open meadow, which lay behind the woods, when they were encountered by a mob of savages, armed with spears, hatchets, and bows and arrows, and bent on killing the Englishman. Being, for the moment, unable to find him, the chiefs had time to address the excited rabble, and persuade them to postpone their intended vengeance. The ambassador, buffeted, threatened, and insulted, was conducted to the fort, where he was ordered to remain; though, at the same time, the Canadian inhabitants were forbidden to admit him into their houses. Morris soon discovered that this unexpected rough treatment was owing to the influence of a deputation of Delaware and Shawanoe chiefs, who had recently arrived, bringing fourteen war-belts of wampum, and exciting the Miamis to renew their hostilities against the common enemy. Thus it was fully apparent that while the Delawares and Shawanoes were sending one deputation to treat of peace with Bradstreet on Lake Erie, they were sending another to rouse the tribes of the Illinois to war.[1] From Fort Miami, the deputation had proceeded westward, spreading the contagion among all the tribes between the Mississippi and the Ohio; declaring that they would never make peace with the English, but would fight them as long as the sun should shine, and calling on their brethren of the Illinois to follow their example.

They had been aware of the approach of Morris, and had urged the Miamis to put him to death when he arrived. Accordingly, he had not been long at the fort when two warriors, with tomahawks in their hands, entered, seized him by the arms, and dragged him towards the river. Godefroy stood by, pale and motionless. *"Eh bien, vous m'abandonnez donc!"* said Morris. *"Non, mon capitaine,"* the Canadian answered, *"je ne vous abandonnerai jamais;"* and he followed, as the two savages dragged their captive into the water. Morris thought that they meant to drown and scalp him, but soon saw his mistake; for they led him through the stream, which was fordable, and thence towards the Miami village. As they drew near, they stopped, and began to strip him, but grew angry at the difficulty of the task; till, in rage and despair, he tore off his clothes himself. They then bound his arms behind him with his own sash, and drove him before them to the village, where they made him sit on a bench. A whooping, screeching mob of savages was instantly about him, and a hundred voices clamored together in dispute as to what should be done with him. Godefroy stood by him with a courageous fidelity that redeemed his past rascalities. He urged a nephew of Pontiac, who was present, to speak for the prisoner. The young Indian made a bold harangue to the crowd; and Godefroy added that, if Morris were killed, the English would take revenge on those who were in their power at Detroit. A Miami chief, called the Swan, now declared for the Englishman, untied his arms, and gave him a pipe to smoke; whereupon another chief, called the White Cat, snatched it from him, seized him, and bound him fast by the neck to a post. Naked, helpless,

[1] "About the end of next month," said the deputies to the Miamis, "we shall send you the war-hatchet." "Doubtless," remarks Morris, "their design was to amuse General Bradstreet with fair language, to cut off his army at Sandusky when least expected, and then to send the hatchet to the nations."

and despairing, he saw the crowd gathering around to torture him. "I had not the smallest hope of life," he says, "and I remember that I conceived myself as if going to plunge into a gulf, vast, immeasurable; and that, a few moments after, the thought of torture occasioned a sort of torpor and insensibility. I looked at Godefroy, and, seeing him exceedingly distressed, I said what I could to encourage him; but he desired me not to speak. I supposed it gave offence to the savages, and therefore was silent; when Pacanne, chief of the Miami nation, and just out of his minority, having mounted a horse and crossed the river, rode up to me. When I heard him calling to those about me, and felt his hand behind my neck, I thought he was going to strangle me, out of pity; but he untied me, saying, as it was afterwards interpreted to me: 'I give that man his life. If you want English meat, go to Detroit, or to the lake, and you'll find enough. What business have you with this man's flesh, who is come to speak with us?' I fixed my eyes steadfastly on this young man, and endeavored by looks to express my gratitude."

An Indian now offered him a pipe, and he was then pushed with abuse and blows out of the village. He succeeded in crossing the river and regaining the fort, after receiving a sharp cut of a switch from a mounted Indian whom he met on the way.

He found the Canadians in the fort disposed to befriend him. Godefroy and the metamorphosed drummer, St. Vincent, were always on the watch to warn him of danger; and one l'Esperance gave him an asylum in his garret. He seems to have found some consolation in the compassion of two handsome young squaws, sisters, he was told, of his deliverer, Pacanne; but the two warriors who had stripped and bound him were constantly lurking about the fort, watching an opportunity to kill him; and the Kickapoos, whose lodges were pitched on the meadow, sent him a message to the effect that, if the Miamis did not put him to death, they themselves would do so, whenever he should pass their camp. He was still on the threshold of his journey, and his final point of destination was several hundred miles distant; yet, with great resolution, he determined to persevere, and, if possible, fulfil his mission. His Indian and Canadian attendants used every means to dissuade him, and in the evening held a council with the Miami chiefs, the result of which was most discouraging. Morris received message after message, threatening his life, should he persist in his design; and word was brought him that several of the Shawanoe deputies were returning to the fort, expressly to kill him. Under these circumstances, it would have been madness to persevere; and, abandoning his mission, he set out for Detroit. The Indian attendants, whom he had brought from Sandusky, after behaving with the utmost insolence, abandoned him in the woods; their ringleader being a Christian Huron, of the Mission of Lorette, whom Morris pronounces the greatest rascal he ever knew. With Godefroy and two or three others who remained with him, he reached Detroit on the seventeenth of September, half dead with famine and fatigue. He had expected to find Bradstreet; but that agile commander had decamped, and returned to Sandusky. Morris, too ill and exhausted to follow, sent him his journal, together with a letter, in which he denounced the Delaware and Shawanoe ambassadors, whom he regarded, and no doubt with justice, as the occasion of his misfortunes. The following is his amiable conclusion:—

"The villains have nipped our fairest hopes in the bud. I tremble for you at Sandusky; though I was greatly pleased to find you have one of the vessels with you, and artillery. I wish the chiefs were assembled on board the vessel, and that she had a hole in her bottom. Treachery should be paid with treachery; and it is a more than ordinary pleasure to deceive those who would deceive us."[1]

Bradstreet had retraced his course to Sandusky, to keep his engagement with the Delaware and Shawanoe deputies, and

[1] MS. Letter—*Morris to Bradstreet*, 18 Sept. 1764.

The journal sent by Morris to Bradstreet is in the State Paper Office of London. This journal, and the record of an examination of Morris's Indian and Canadian attendants, made in Bradstreet's presence at Sandusky, were the authorities on which the account in the first edition of this work was based. Morris afterwards rewrote his journal, with many additions. Returning to England after the war, he lost his property by speculations, and re-solved, for the sake of his children, to solicit a pension, on the score of his embassy to the Illinois. With this view it was that the journal was rewritten; but failing to find a suitable person to lay it before the King, he resolved to print it, together with several original poems and a translation of the fourth

await the fulfilment of their worthless promise to surrender their prisoners, and conclude a definitive treaty of peace. His hopes were defeated. The appointed time expired, and not a chief was seen; though, a few days after, several warriors came to the camp, with a promise that, if Bradstreet would remain quiet, and refrain from attacking their villages, they would bring in the prisoners in the course of the following week. Bradstreet accepted their excuses; and, having removed his camp to the carrying-place of Sandusky, lay waiting in patient expectation. It was here that he received, for the first time, a communication from General Gage, respecting the preliminary treaty, concluded several weeks before. Gage condemned his conduct in severe terms, and ordered him to break the engagements he had made, and advance at once upon the enemy, choosing for his first objects of attack the Indians living upon the plains of the Scioto. The fury of Bradstreet was great on receiving this message; and it was not diminished when the journal of Captain Morris was placed in his hands, fully proving how signally he had been duped. He was in no temper to obey the orders of the commander-in-chief; and, to justify himself for his inaction, he alleged the impossibility of reaching the Scioto plains at that advanced season. Two routes thither were open to his choice, one by the River Sandusky, and the other by Cayahoga Creek. The water in the Sandusky was sunk low with the drought, and the carrying-place at the head of Cayahoga Creek was a few miles longer than had been represented; yet the army were ready for the attempt, and these difficulties could not have deterred a vigorous commander. Under cover of such excuses, Bradstreet remained idle at Sandusky for several days, while sickness and discontent were rife in his camp. The soldiers complained of his capricious, peremptory temper, his harshness to his

---

and fourteenth satires of Juvenal. The book appeared in 1791, under the title of *Miscellanies in Prose and Verse*. It is very scarce. I am indebted to the kindness of Mr. S. G. Drake for the opportunity of examining it.

The two journals and the evidence before Bradstreet's court of inquiry agree in essentials, but differ in some details. In this edition, I have followed chiefly the printed journal, borrowing some additional facts from the evidence taken before Bradstreet.

troops, and the unaccountable tenderness with which he treated the Sandusky Indians, some of whom had not yet made their submission; while he enraged his Iroquois allies by his frequent rebukes and curses.

At length, declaring that provisions were failing and the season growing late, he resolved to return home; and broke up his camp with such precipitancy that two soldiers, who had gone out in the morning to catch fish for his table, were inhumanly left behind;[1] the colonel remarking that they might stay and be damned. Soon after leaving Sandusky, he saw fit to encamp one evening on an open, exposed beach, on the south shore of Lake Erie, though there was in the neighborhood a large river, "wherein," say his critics, "a thousand boats could lie with safety." A storm came on: half his boats were dashed to pieces; and six pieces of cannon, with ammunition, provisions, arms, and baggage, were lost or abandoned. For three days the tempest raged unceasingly; and, when the angry lake began to resume its tranquillity, it was found that the remaining boats were insufficient to convey the troops. A body of Indians, together with a detachment of provincials, about a hundred and fifty in all, were therefore ordered to make their way to Niagara along the pathless borders of the lake. They accordingly set out, and, after many days of hardship, reached their destination; though such had been their sufferings, from fatigue, cold, and hunger; from wading swamps, swimming creeks and rivers, and pushing

---

[1] "8th. His going away, leaving at Sandusky Two Jersey Soldiers, who were sent out by his Orders to Catch Fish for his Table & Five Principal Inds. who were Hunting, notwithstanding several spoke to him abt. it & begged to allow a Boat to stay an hour or two for them; his Answer was, they might stay there & be damned, not a Boat should stay one Minute for them."— *Remarks on the Conduct*, etc., MS.

Another article of these charges is as follows: "His harsh treatment at Setting off to the Inds. and their officers & leaving some of them behind at every encampment from his flighty and unsettled disposition, telling them sometimes he intended encamping, on which some of the briskest Inds. went to kill some Game, on their return found the Army moved on, so were obliged to march along shore without any necessarys, and with difficulty got to Detroit half starved. At other times on being asked by the Ind^n officers (when the Boats were crowded) how they and ye Inds. should get along, His answer always verry ill natured, such as swim and be damned, or let them stay and be damned, &c.; all which was understood by many & gave great uneasiness."

their way through tangled thickets, that many of the provincials perished miserably in the woods. On the fourth of November, seventeen days after their departure from Sandusky, the main body of the little army arrived in safety at Niagara; and the whole, re-embarking on Lake Ontario, proceeded towards Oswego.[1] Fortune still seemed adverse; for a second tempest arose, and one of the schooners, crowded with troops, foundered in sight of Oswego, though most of the men were saved. The route to the settlements was now a short and easy one. On their arrival, the regulars went into quarters; while the troops levied for the campaign were sent home to their respective provinces.

This expedition, ill conducted as it was, produced some beneficial results. The Indians at Detroit had been brought to reason, and for the present, at least, would probably remain tranquil; while the re-establishment of the posts on the upper lakes must necessarily have great effect upon the natives of that region. At Sandusky, on the other hand, the work had been but half done. The tribes of that place felt no respect for the English; while those to the southward and westward had been left in a state of turbulence, which promised an abundant harvest of future mischief.[2] In one particular, at least, Bradstreet had occasioned serious detriment to the English interest. The Iroquois allies, who had joined his army, were disgusted by his treatment of them, while they were roused to contempt by the imbecility of his conduct towards the enemy; and thus the efforts of Sir William Johnson to secure the attachment of these powerful tribes were in no small degree counteracted and neutralized.[3]

[1] Mante, 535.

[2] MS. Letter—*Johnson to the Board of Trade*, December 26.

[3] The provincial officers, to whom the command of the Indian allies was assigned, drew up a paper containing complaints against Bradstreet, and particulars of his misconduct during the expedition. This curious document, from which a few extracts have been given, was found among the private papers of Sir William Johnson.

A curious discovery, in probable connection with Bradstreet's expedition, has lately been made public. At McMahon's Beach, on Lake Erie, eight or ten miles west of Cleveland, a considerable number of bayonets, bullets, musket-barrels, and fragments of boats, have from time to time been washed by storms from the sands, or dug up on the adjacent shore, as well as an English

While Bradstreet's troops were advancing upon the lakes, or lying idle in their camp at Sandusky, another expedition was in progress at the southward, with abler conduct and a more auspicious result.

---

silver-hilted sword, several silver spoons, and a few old French and English coins. A mound full of bones and skulls, apparently of Europeans hastily buried, has also been found at the same place. The probability is strong that these are the remains of Bradstreet's disaster. See a paper by Dr. J. P. Kirtland, in Whittlesey's *History of Cleveland*, 105.

Chapter XXVII.

1764.

BOUQUET FORCES THE DELAWARES AND SHAWANOES TO SUE FOR PEACE.

T HE WORK OF RAVAGE had begun afresh upon the borders. The Indians had taken the precaution to remove all their settlements to the western side of the River Muskingum, trusting that the impervious forests, with their unnumbered streams, would prove a sufficient barrier against invasion. Having thus, as they thought, placed their women and children in safety, they had flung themselves upon the settlements with all the rage and ferocity of the previous season. So fierce and active were the war-parties on the borders, that the English governor of Pennsylvania had recourse to a measure which the frontier inhabitants had long demanded, and issued a proclamation, offering a high bounty for Indian scalps, whether of men or women; a barbarous expedient, fruitful of butcheries and murders, but incapable of producing any decisive result.[1]

[1]The following is an extract from the proclamation: —

"I do hereby declare and promise, that there shall be paid out of the moneys lately granted for his Majesty's use, to all and every person and persons not in the pay of this province, the following several and respective premiums and bounties for the prisoners and scalps of the enemy Indians that shall be taken or killed within the bounds of this province, as limited by the royal charter, or in pursuit from within the said bounds; that is to say, for every male Indian enemy above ten years old, who shall be taken prisoner, and delivered at any forts garrisoned by the troops in the pay of this province, or at any of the county towns, to the keeper of the common jails there, the sum of one hundred and fifty Spanish dollars, or pieces of eight. For every female Indian enemy, taken prisoner and brought in as aforesaid, and for every male Indian enemy of ten years old or under, taken prisoner and delivered as aforesaid, the sum of one hundred and thirty pieces of eight. For the scalp of every male Indian enemy above the age of ten years, produced as evidence of their being killed, the sum of one hundred and thirty-four pieces of eight. And for the scalp of every female Indian enemy above the age of ten years, produced as evidence of their being killed, the sum of fifty pieces of eight."

The action of such measures has recently been illustrated in the instance of New Mexico before its conquest by the Americans. The inhabitants of that country, too timorous to defend themselves against the Apaches and other

762

Early in the season, a soldier named David Owens, who, several years before, had deserted and joined the Indians, came to one of the outposts, accompanied by a young provincial recently taken prisoner on the Delaware, and bringing five scalps. While living among the Indians, Owens had formed a connection with one of their women, who had borne him several children. Growing tired, at length, of the forest life, he had become anxious to return to the settlements, but feared to do so without first having made some atonement for his former desertion. One night, he had been encamped on the Susquehanna, with four Shawanoe warriors, a boy of the same tribe, his own wife and two children, and another Indian woman. The young provincial, who came with him to the settlements, was also of the party. In the middle of the night, Owens arose, and looking about him saw, by the dull glow of the camp-fire, that all were buried in deep sleep. Cautiously awakening the young provincial, he told him to leave the place, and lie quiet at a little distance, until he should call him. He next stealthily removed the weapons from beside the sleeping savages, and concealed them in the woods, reserving to himself two loaded rifles. Returning to the camp, he knelt on the ground between two of the yet unconscious warriors, and, pointing a rifle at the head of each, touched the triggers, and shot both dead at once. Startled by the reports, the survivors sprang to their feet in bewildered terror. The two remaining warriors bounded into the woods; but the women and children, benumbed with fright, had no power to escape, and one and all died shrieking under the hatchet of the miscreant. His devilish work complete, the wretch sat watching until daylight among the dead bodies of his children and comrades, undaunted by the awful

---

tribes, who descended upon them in frequent forays from the neighboring mountains, took into pay a band of foreigners, chiefly American trappers, for whom the Apache lances had no such terrors, and, to stimulate their exertions, proclaimed a bounty on scalps. The success of the measure was judged admirable, until it was found that the unscrupulous confederates were in the habit of shooting down any Indian, whether friend or enemy, who came within range of their rifles, and that the government had been paying rewards for the scalps of its own allies and dependants.

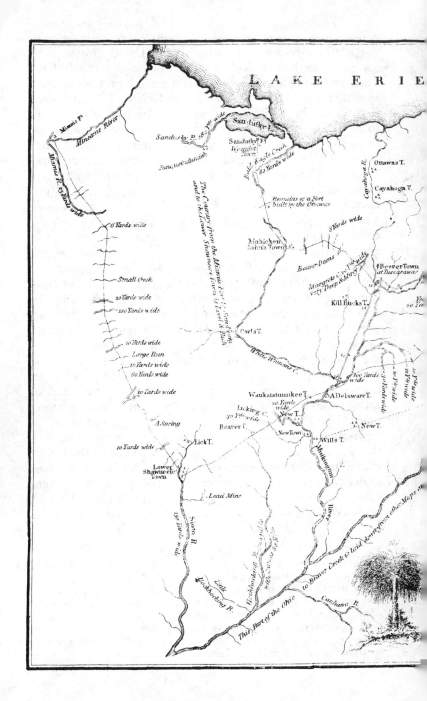

LAKE ERIE

Miamis Ft.

Mineame River

Miamis R. 45 Yards wide

Sandusky R. 18 yds wide

Sandusky L.

Sandusky Ft.

Wyandot Town

Junundatundih

Bald Eagle Creek

60 Yards wide

Cayahoga R.

Ottawas T.

Cayahoga T.

The Country from the Miamis Ford to Sandusky and to the Lower Shawnee Town is Level & Rich

Remains of a Fort built by the Ottawas

6 Yards wide

Mohicken John's Town

8 Yards wide

Beaver Dams

Margrets C. 50 Yds wide very Deep & Mirry

Beaver Town at Tuscgrawas

Small Creek

20 Yards wide

100 Yards wide

Kill Bucks T.

20 Ya

Owl's T.

White Womans C.

10 Yards wide

Large Run

10 Yards wide

60 Yards wide

100 Yards goYards wide

10 Yards wide

Waukatatunnkee T.

A Delaware T.

20 Yards wide

Licking C.

40 Yds wide

New T.

New T.

A Spring

Beaver I.

New Town

Wills T.

10 Yards wide

Lick T.

Muskingum River

Lower Shawnee Town

Lead Mine

Sioto R.

130 Yards wide

Hockhocking R. smaller with Cane at its Mouth

to Beaver Creek is laid down from other Maps

Little Hockhocking R.

Cachawa R.

This Part of the Ohio

Ft. Presq. Isle

Little Lake · Ft. Le Beeuf

Beef R.

Sugar Creek 10 Yards wide

The Allegheny R.

Venango Ft.

Salt Lick T.

Several Little Hills

Pematuning

Local Land A Spring

honing T.

Shaningo

Ohio Beaver R.

60 Y.ds wide

Allegheny R.

6 Yards wide

Kishkuke T.

30 Yards wide

Yards wide very Rapid & in a Mirey Swamp on each Side

12 Yards wide

Creek 20 Y.ds wide

Lit. Beavers 30 Yards wide

Several Little Ridges

Turtle C.

Bushy Run

Kiskemineta C.

Ft. Pitt

Coll Bouquets Field of Battle

G.l Braddocks Field

Genl Forbes

Monongahela R.

Ft. Ligonier

Road

Stony Creek

Shawanoe Cabbins

Juniata R.

Ft. Littleton

Yoxtio

Red Stone

Fort Bird

Genl

Allegheny Mountains

Sideling Hill

Wills Creek Gap

Ft. Bedford

Ft. Loudon

to Philadelphia

The Laurel Hill

Genl

Great Meadows

Braddocks

Little Road Meadows

PENSILVANIA

Ft. Cumberland

Potow mack R.

from a Silver

Savage R.

MARYLAND

FAC SIMILE

A MAP
of the COUNTRY on the
Ohio & Muskingum Rivers
Shewing the Situation
of the INDIAN TOWNS with
respect to the Army under the Command
of Colonel Bouquet
By
Tho.s Hutchins Ass.t Engineer.

VIRGINIA

Scale of Miles.
15   30   45

gloom and solitude of the darkened forest. In the morning, he scalped his victims, with the exception of the two children, and, followed by the young white man, directed his steps towards the settlements, with the bloody trophies of his atrocity. His desertion was pardoned; he was employed as an interpreter, and ordered to accompany the troops on the intended expedition. His example is one of many in which the worst acts of Indian ferocity have been thrown into shade by the enormities of white barbarians.[1]

Bouquet was now urging on his preparations for his march into the valley of the Ohio. We have seen how, in the preceding summer, he had been embarrassed by what he calls "the unnatural obstinacy of the government of Pennsylvania." "It disables us," he had written to the equally indignant Amherst, "from crushing the savages on this side of the lakes, and may draw us into a lingering war, which might have been terminated by another blow. . . . I see that the whole burden of this war will rest upon us; and while the few regular troops you have left can keep the enemy at a distance, the Provinces will let them fight it out without interfering."[2]

Amherst, after vainly hoping that the Assembly of Pennsylvania would "exert themselves like men,"[3] had, equally in

[1]Gordon, *Hist. Penn.* 625. Robison, *Narrative.*

Extract from a MS. Letter—*Sir W. Johnson to Governor Penn:*—

"Burnetsfield, June 18th, 1764.

"David Owens was a Corporal in Capt. McClean's Compy., and lay once in Garrison at my House. He deserted several times, as I am informed, & went to live among the Delaware & Shawanese, with whose language he was acquainted. His Father having been long a trader amongst them.

"The circumstances relating to his leaving the Indians have been told me by several Indians. That he went out a hunting with his Indian Wife and several of her relations, most of whom, with his Wife, be killed and scalped as they slept. As he was always much attached to Indians, I fancy he began to fear he was unsafe amongst them, & killed them rather to make his peace with the English, than from any dislike either to them or their principles."

[2]MS. Letter—*Bouquet to Amherst*, 15 Sept. 1763.

[3]"If the present situation of the poor families who have abandoned their settlements, and the danger that the whole province is threatened with, can have no effect in opening the hearts of your Assembly to exert themselves *like men*, I am sure no arguments I could urge will be regarded."—*Amherst to Governor Hamilton*, 7 July, 1763.

"The situation of this country is deplorable, and the infatuation of their government in taking the most dilatory and ineffectual measures for their

vain, sent Colonel James Robertson as a special messenger to the provincial commissioners. "I found all my pleading vain," the disappointed envoy had written, "and believe Cicero's would have been so. I never saw any men so determined in the right as these people are in this absurdly wrong resolve."[1] The resolve in question related to the seven hundred men whom the Assembly had voted to raise for protecting the gathering of the harvest, and whom the commissioners stiffly refused to place at the disposition of the military authorities.

It is apparent in all this that, at an early period of the war, a change had come over the spirit of the commander-in-chief, whose prejudices and pride had revolted, at the outset, against the asking of provincial aid to "chastise the savages," but who had soon been brought to reason by his own helplessness and the exigencies of the situation. In like manner, a change, though at the eleventh hour, had now come over the spirit of the Pennsylvania Assembly. The invasion of the Paxton borderers, during the past winter, had scared the Quaker faction into their senses. Their old quarrel with the governor and the proprietaries, their scruples about war, and their affection for Indians, were all postponed to the necessity of the hour. The Assembly voted to raise three hundred men to guard the frontiers, and a thousand to join Bouquet. Their commissioners went farther; for they promised to send to England for fifty couples of bloodhounds, to hunt Indian scalping-parties.[2]

In the preceding summer, half as many men would have sufficed; for, after the battle of Bushy Run, Bouquet wrote to Amherst from Fort Pitt, that, with a reinforcement of three hundred provincial rangers, he could destroy all the Delaware

---

protection, highly blamable. They have not paid the least regard to the plan I proposed to them on my arrival here, and will lose this and York counties if the savages push their attacks."—*Bouquet to Amherst*, 13 July, 1763.

[1] MS. Letter—*Robertson to Amherst*, 19 July, 1763.

[2] "They have at my recommendation agreed to send to Great Britain for 50 Couples of Blood Hounds to be employed with Rangers on horse back against Indian scalping parties, which will I hope deter more effectually the Savages from that sort of war than our troops can possibly do."—*Bouquet to Amherst*, 7 June, 1764.

towns, "and clear the country of that vermin between this fort and Lake Erie;"[1] but he added, with some bitterness, that the provinces would not even furnish escorts to convoys, so that his hands were completely tied.[2]

It was past midsummer before the thousand Pennsylvanians were ready to move; so that the season for navigating the Ohio and its branches was lost. As for Virginia and Maryland, they would do absolutely nothing. On the fifth of August, Bouquet was at Carlisle, with his new levies and such regulars as he had, chiefly the veterans of Bushy Run. Before the tenth, two hundred of the Pennsylvanians had deserted, sheltered, as usual, by the country people. His force, even with full ranks, was too small; and he now took the responsibility of writing to Colonel Lewis, of the Virginia militia, to send him two hundred volunteers, to take the place of the deserters.[3] A body of Virginians accordingly joined him at Fort Pitt, to his great satisfaction, for he set a high value on these backwoods riflemen; but the responsibility he had assumed proved afterwards a source of extreme annoyance to him.

The little army soon reached Fort Loudon, then in a decayed and ruinous condition, like all the wooden forts built during the French war. Here Bouquet received the strange communication from Bradstreet, informing him that he might return home with his troops, as a treaty had been concluded with the Delawares and Shawanoes. Bouquet's disgust found vent in a letter to the commander-in-chief: "I received this moment advice from Colonel Bradstreet. . . . The terms he gives them (the Indians) are such as fill me with astonishment. . . . Had Colonel Bradstreet been as well informed as

[1] MS. Letter—*Bouquet to Amherst*, 27 Aug. 1763.

[2] MS. Letter—*Bouquet to Amherst*, 24 Oct. 1763. In this letter, Bouquet enlarges, after a fashion which must have been singularly unpalatable to his commander, on the danger of employing regulars alone in forest warfare: "Without a certain number of woodsmen, I cannot think it advisable to employ regulars in the Woods against Savages, as they cannot procure any intelligence and are open to continual surprises, nor can they pursue to any distance their enemy when they have routed them; and should they have the misfortune to be defeated, the whole would be destroyed if above one day's march from a Fort. That is my opinion in wh. I hope to be deceived."

[3] MS. Letter—*Bouquet to Gage*, 10 Aug. 1764.

I am of the horrid perfidies of the Delawares and Shawanese, whose parties as late as the 22d instant killed six men . . . he never could have compromised the honor of the nation by such disgraceful conditions, and that at a time when two armies, after long struggles, are in full motion to penetrate into the heart of the enemy's country. Permit me likewise humbly to represent to your Excellency that I have not deserved the affront laid upon me by this treaty of peace, concluded by a younger officer, in the department where you have done me the honor to appoint me to command, without referring the deputies of the savages to me at Fort Pitt, but telling them that he shall send and prevent my proceeding against them. I can therefore take no notice of his peace, but (*shall*) proceed forthwith to the Ohio, where I shall wait till I receive your orders."[1]

After waiting for more than a week for his wrath to cool, he wrote to Bradstreet in terms which, though restrained and temperate, plainly showed his indignation.[2] He had now reached Fort Bedford, where more Pennsylvanians ran off, with their arms and horses, and where he vainly waited the arrival of a large reinforcement of friendly Indians, who had been promised by Sir William Johnson, but who never arrived. On reaching Fort Ligonier, he had the satisfaction of forwarding two letters, which the commander-in-chief had significantly sent through his hands, to Bradstreet, containing a peremptory disavowal of the treaty.[3] Continuing to advance, he passed in safety the scene of his desperate fight of

---

[1]MS. Letter—*Bouquet to Gage*, 27 Aug. 1764. He wrote to Governor Penn, as follows:—

"Fort Loudon, 27 Aug. 1764.

"Sir:

"I have the honor to transmit to you a letter from Colonel Bradstreet, who acquaints me that he has granted peace to all the Indians living between Lake Erie and the Ohio; but as no satisfaction is insisted on, I hope the General will not confirm it, and that I shall not be a witness to a transaction which would fix an indelible stain upon the Nation.

"I therefore take no notice of that pretended peace, & proceed forthwith on the expedition, fully determined to treat as enemies any Delawares or Shawanese I shall find in my way, till I receive contrary orders from the General."

[2]MS. Letter—*Bouquet to Bradstreet*, 5 Sept. 1764.

[3]See p. 746, *note*.

the last summer, and on the seventeenth of September arrived at Fort Pitt, with no other loss than that of a few men picked off from the flanks and rear by lurking Indian marksmen.[1]

The day before his arrival, ten Delaware chiefs and warriors appeared on the farther bank of the river, pretending to be deputies sent by their nation to confer with the English commander. Three of them, after much hesitation, came over to the fort, where, being closely questioned, and found unable to give any good account of their mission, they were detained as spies; while their companions, greatly disconcerted, fled back to their villages. Bouquet, on his arrival, released one of the three captives, and sent him home with the following message to his people: —

"I have received an account, from Colonel Bradstreet, that your nations had begged for peace, which he had consented to grant, upon assurance that you had recalled all your warriors from our frontiers; and, in consequence of this, I would not have proceeded against your towns, if I had not heard that, in open violation of your engagements, you have since murdered several of our people.

"I was therefore determined to have attacked you, as a

---

[1]Captain Grant, who had commanded during the spring at Fort Pitt, had sent bad accounts of the disposition of the neighboring Indians; but added, "At this Post we defy all the Savages in the Woods. I wish they would dare appear before us. . . . Repairing Batteaux, ploughing, gardening, making Fences, and fetching home fire Wood goes on constantly every day, from sun rise to the setting of the same." — *Grant to Bouquet*, 2 April, 1764. A small boy, captured with his mother the summer before, escaped to the fort about this time, and reported that the Indians meant to plant their corn and provide for their families, after which they would come to the fort and burn it. The youthful informant also declared that none of them had more than a pound of powder left. Soon after, a man named Hicks appeared, professing to have escaped from the Indians, though he was strongly suspected of being a renegade and a spy, and was therefore cross-questioned severely. He confirmed what the boy had said as to the want of ammunition among the Indians, and added that they had sent for a supply to the French at the Illinois, but that the reception they received from the commandant had not satisfied them. General Gage sent the following not very judicial instructions with regard to Hicks: "He is a great villain. I am glad he is secured. I must desire you will have him tried by a General Court-Martial for a Spy. Let the proceedings of the Court prove him a *Spy* as strong as they can, and if he does turn out a *spy*, he must be hanged." — *Gage to Bouquet*, 14 May, 1764. The court, however, could find no proof.

people whose promises can no more be relied on. But I will put it once more in your power to save yourselves and your families from total destruction, by giving us satisfaction for the hostilities committed against us. And, first, you are to leave the path open for my expresses from hence to Detroit; and as I am now to send two men with despatches to Colonel Bradstreet, who commands on the lakes, I desire to know whether you will send two of your people to bring them safe back with an answer. And if they receive any injury either in going or coming, or if the letters are taken from them, I will immediately put the Indians now in my power to death, and will show no mercy, for the future, to any of your nations that shall fall into my hands. I allow you ten days to have my letters delivered at Detroit, and ten days to bring me back an answer."[1]

The liberated spy faithfully discharged his mission; and the firm, decisive tone of the message had a profound effect upon the hostile warriors; clearly indicating, as it did, with what manner of man they had to deal. Many, who were before clamorous for battle, were now ready to sue for peace, as the only means to avert their ruin.

Before the army was ready to march, two Iroquois warriors came to the fort, pretending friendship, but anxious, in reality, to retard the expedition until the approaching winter should make it impossible to proceed. They represented the numbers of the enemy, and the extreme difficulty of penetrating so rough a country; and affirmed that, if the troops remained quiet, the hostile tribes, who were already collecting their prisoners, would soon arrive to make their submission. Bouquet turned a deaf ear to their advice, and sent them to inform the Delawares and Shawanoes that he was on his way to chastise them for their perfidy and cruelty, unless they should save themselves by an ample and speedy atonement.

Early in October, the troops left Fort Pitt, and began their westward march into a wilderness which no army had ever before sought to penetrate. Encumbered with their camp equipage, with droves of cattle and sheep for subsistence, and a long train of pack-horses laden with provisions, their progress

[1] *Account of Bouquet's Expedition*, 5.

was tedious and difficult, and seven or eight miles were the ordinary measure of a day's march. The woodsmen of Virginia, veteran hunters and Indian-fighters, were thrown far out in front and on either flank, scouring the forest to detect any sign of a lurking ambuscade. The pioneers toiled in the van, hewing their way through woods and thickets; while the army dragged its weary length behind them through the forest, like a serpent creeping through tall grass. The surrounding country, whenever a casual opening in the matted foliage gave a glimpse of its features, disclosed scenery of wild, primeval beauty. Sometimes the army defiled along the margin of the Ohio, by its broad eddying current and the bright landscape of its shores. Sometimes they descended into the thickest gloom of the woods, damp, still, and cool as the recesses of a cavern, where the black soil oozed beneath the tread, where the rough columns of the forest seemed to exude a clammy sweat, and the slimy mosses were trickling with moisture; while the carcasses of prostrate trees, green with the decay of a century, sank into pulp at the lightest pressure of the foot. More frequently, the forest was of a fresher growth; and the restless leaves of young maples and basswood shook down spots of sunlight on the marching columns. Sometimes they waded the clear current of a stream, with its vistas of arching foliage and sparkling water. There were intervals, but these were rare, when, escaping for a moment from the labyrinth of woods, they emerged into the light of an open meadow, rich with herbage, and girdled by a zone of forest; gladdened by the notes of birds, and enlivened, it may be, by grazing herds of deer. These spots, welcome to the forest traveller as an oasis to a wanderer in the desert, form the precursors of the prairies; which, growing wider and more frequent as one advances westward, expand at last into the boundless plains beyond the Mississippi.

On the tenth day after leaving Fort Pitt, the army reached the River Muskingum, and approached the objects of their march, the haunts of the barbarian warriors, who had turned whole districts into desolation. Their progress had met no interruption. A few skulking Indians had hovered about them, but, alarmed by their numbers, feared to venture an attack. The Indian cabins which they passed on their way were deserted by their tenants, who had joined their western brethren. When the troops crossed the Muskingum, they saw, a little below the fording-place, the abandoned wigwams of the village of Tuscaroras, recently the abode of more than a hundred families, who had fled in terror at the approach of the invaders.

Bouquet was in the heart of the enemy's country. Their villages, except some remoter settlements of the Shawanoes, all lay within a few days' march; and no other choice was left them than to sue for peace, or risk the desperate chances of battle against a commander who, a year before, with a third of his present force, had routed them at the fight of Bushy Run. The vigorous and active among them might, it is true, escape by flight; but, in doing so, they must abandon to the victors their dwellings, and their secret hordes of corn. They were confounded at the multitude of the invaders, exaggerated, doubtless, in the reports which reached their villages, and amazed that an army should force its way so deep into the forest fastnesses, which they had thought impregnable. They knew, on the other hand, that Colonel Bradstreet was still at Sandusky, in a position to assail them in the rear. Thus pressed on both sides, they saw that they must submit, and bend their stubborn pride to beg for peace; not alone with words, which cost nothing, and would have been worth nothing, but by the delivery of prisoners, and the surrender of chiefs and warriors as pledges of good faith. Bouquet had sent two soldiers from Fort Pitt with letters to Colonel Bradstreet; but these men had been detained, under specious pretexts, by the Delawares. They now appeared at his camp, sent back by their captors, with a message to the effect that, within a few days, the chiefs would arrive and hold a conference with him.

Bouquet continued his march down the valley of the Muskingum, until he reached a spot where the broad meadows, which bordered the river, would supply abundant grazing for the cattle and horses; while the terraces above, shaded by forest-trees, offered a convenient site for an encampment. Here he began to erect a small palisade work, as a depot for stores and baggage. Before the task was complete, a deputation of chiefs arrived, bringing word that their warriors were encamped, in great numbers, about eight miles from the spot, and desiring Bouquet to appoint the time and place for a council. He ordered them to meet him, on the next day, at a point near the margin of the river, a little below the camp; and thither a party of men was at once despatched, to erect a sort of rustic arbor of saplings and the boughs of trees, large enough to shelter the English officers and the Indian chiefs. With a host of warriors in the neighborhood, who would gladly break in upon them, could they hope that the attack would succeed, it behooved the English to use every precaution. A double guard was placed, and a stringent discipline enforced.

In the morning, the little army moved in battle order to the place of council. Here the principal officers assumed their seats under the canopy of branches, while the glittering array of the troops was drawn out on the meadow in front, in such a manner as to produce the most imposing effect on the minds of the Indians, in whose eyes the sight of fifteen hundred men under arms was a spectacle equally new and astounding. The perfect order and silence of the far-extended lines; the ridges of bayonets flashing in the sun; the fluttering tartans of the Highland regulars; the bright red uniform of the Royal Americans; the darker garb and duller trappings of the Pennsylvania troops, and the bands of Virginia backwoodsmen, who, in fringed hunting-frocks and Indian moccasons, stood leaning carelessly on their rifles,—all these combined to form a scene of military pomp and power not soon to be forgotten.

At the appointed hour, the deputation appeared. The most prominent among them were Kiashuta, chief of the band of Senecas who had deserted their ancient homes to form a colony on the Ohio; Custaloga, chief of the Delawares; and the head chief of the Shawanoes, whose name sets orthography at defiance. As they approached, painted and plumed in all their savage pomp, they looked neither to the right hand nor to the left, not deigning, under the eyes of their enemy, to cast even a glance at the military display around them. They seated themselves, with stern, impassive looks, and an air of sullen dignity; while their sombre brows betrayed the hatred still rankling in their hearts. After a few minutes had been consumed in the indispensable ceremony of smoking, Turtle Heart, a chief of the Delawares, and orator of the deputation, rose, bearing in his hand a bag containing the belts of wampum. Addressing himself to the English commander, he spoke as follows, delivering a belt for every clause of his speech:—

"Brother, I speak in behalf of the three nations whose chiefs are here present. With this belt I open your ears and your hearts, that you may listen to my words.

"Brother, this war was neither your fault nor ours. It was the work of the nations who live to the westward, and of our wild young men, who would have killed us if we had resisted them. We now put away all evil from our hearts; and we hope that your mind and ours will once more be united together.

"Brother, it is the will of the Great Spirit that there should be peace between us. We, on our side, now take fast hold of the chain of friendship; but, as we cannot hold it alone, we desire that you will take hold also, and we must look up to the Great Spirit, that he may make us strong, and not permit this chain to fall from our hands.

"Brother, these words come from our hearts, and not from our lips. You desire that we should deliver up your flesh and blood now captive among us; and, to show you that we are sincere, we now return you as many of them as we have at present been able to bring. [Here he delivered eighteen white prisoners, who had been brought by the deputation to the council.] You shall receive the rest as soon as we have time to collect them."[1]

In such figurative terms, not devoid of dignity, did the Indian orator sue for peace to his detested enemies. When he had concluded, the chiefs of every tribe rose in succession, to express concurrence in what he had said, each delivering a

---

[1] This speech is taken from the official journals of Colonel Bouquet, a copy of which is preserved in the archives of Pennsylvania, at Harrisburg, engrossed, if the writer's memory does not fail him, in one of the volumes of the *Provincial Records*. The published narrative, which has often been cited, is chiefly founded upon the authority of these documents; and the writer has used his materials with great skill and faithfulness, though occasionally it has been found advisable to have recourse to the original journals, to supply some omission or obscurity in the printed compilation.

belt of wampum and a bundle of small sticks; the latter designed to indicate the number of English prisoners whom his
followers retained, and whom he pledged himself to surrender. In an Indian council, when one of the speakers has advanced a matter of weight and urgency, the other party defers
his reply to the following day, that due time may be allowed
for deliberation. Accordingly, in the present instance, the
council adjourned to the next morning, each party retiring to
its respective camp. But, when day dawned, the weather had
changed. The valley of the Muskingum was filled with driving
mist and rain, and the meeting was in consequence postponed. On the third day, the landscape brightened afresh, the
troops marched once more to the place of council, and the
Indian chiefs convened to hear the reply of their triumphant
foe. It was not of a kind to please them. The opening words
gave an earnest of what was to come; for Bouquet discarded
the usual address of an Indian harangue: fathers, brothers, or
children,—terms which imply a relation of friendship, or a
desire to conciliate,—and adopted a sterner and more distant
form.

"Sachems, war-chiefs, and warriors,[1] the excuses you have
offered are frivolous and unavailing, and your conduct is
without defence or apology. You could not have acted as you
pretend to have done through fear of the western nations;
for, had you stood faithful to us, you knew that we would
have protected you against their anger; and as for your young
men, it was your duty to punish them, if they did amiss. You
have drawn down our just resentment by your violence and
perfidy. Last summer, in cold blood, and in a time of profound peace, you robbed and murdered the traders, who had
come among you at your own express desire. You attacked
Fort Pitt, which was built by your consent; and you de-

---

[1] The sachem is the civil chief, who directs the counsels of the tribe, and
governs in time of peace. His office, on certain conditions, is hereditary;
while the war-chief, or military leader, acquires his authority solely by personal merit, and seldom transmits it to his offspring. Sometimes the civil and
military functions are discharged by the same person, as in the instance of
Pontiac himself.

The speech of Bouquet, as given above, is taken, with some omission and
condensation, from the journals mentioned in the preceding note.

stroyed our outposts and garrisons, whenever treachery could place them in your power. You assailed our troops—the same who now stand before you—in the woods at Bushy Run; and, when we had routed and driven you off, you sent your scalping-parties to the frontier, and murdered many hundreds of our people. Last July, when the other nations came to ask for peace, at Niagara, you not only refused to attend, but sent an insolent message instead, in which you expressed a pretended contempt for the English; and, at the same time, told the surrounding nations that you would never lay down the hatchet. Afterwards, when Colonel Bradstreet came up Lake Erie, you sent a deputation of your chiefs, and concluded a treaty with him; but your engagements were no sooner made than broken; and, from that day to this, you have scalped and butchered us without ceasing. Nay, I am informed that, when you heard that this army was penetrating the woods, you mustered your warriors to attack us, and were only deterred from doing so when you found how greatly we outnumbered you. This is not the only instance of your bad faith; for, since the beginning of the last war, you have made repeated treaties with us, and promised to give up your prisoners; but you have never kept these engagements, nor any others. We shall endure this no longer; and I am now come among you to force you to make atonement for the injuries you have done us. I have brought with me the relatives of those you have murdered. They are eager for vengeance, and nothing restrains them from taking it but my assurance that this army shall not leave your country until you have given them an ample satisfaction.

"Your allies, the Ottawas, Ojibwas, and Wyandots, have begged for peace; the Six Nations have leagued themselves with us; the great lakes and rivers around you are all in our possession, and your friends the French are in subjection to us, and can do no more to aid you. You are all in our power, and, if we choose, we can exterminate you from the earth; but the English are a merciful and generous people, averse to shed the blood even of their greatest enemies; and if it were possible that you could convince us that you sincerely repent of your past perfidy, and that we could depend on your good behavior for the future, you might yet hope for mercy and peace. If I find that you faithfully execute the conditions which I shall prescribe, I will not treat you with the severity you deserve.

"I give you twelve days from this date to deliver into my hands all the prisoners in your possession, without exception: Englishmen, Frenchmen, women, and children; whether adopted into your tribes, married, or living among you under any denomination or pretence whatsoever. And you are to furnish these prisoners with clothing, provisions, and horses, to carry them to Fort Pitt. When you have fully complied with these conditions, you shall then know on what terms you may obtain the peace you sue for."

This speech, with the stern voice and countenance of the speaker, told with chilling effect upon the awe-stricken hearers. It quelled their native haughtiness, and sunk them to the depths of humiliation. Their speeches in reply were dull and insipid, void of that savage eloquence, which, springing from a wild spirit of independence, has so often distinguished the forest orators. Judging the temper of their enemies by their own insatiable thirst for vengeance, they hastened, with all the alacrity of terror, to fulfil the prescribed conditions, and avert the threatened ruin. They dispersed to their different villages, to collect and bring in the prisoners; while Bouquet, on his part, knowing that his best security for their good faith was to keep up the alarm which his decisive measures had created, determined to march yet nearer to their settlements. Still following the course of the Muskingum, he descended to a spot near its confluence with its main branch, which might be regarded as a central point with respect to the surrounding Indian villages. Here, with the exception of the distant Shawanoe settlements, they were all within reach of his hand, and he could readily chastise the first attempt at deceit or evasion. The principal chiefs of each tribe had been forced to accompany him as hostages.[1]

---

[1] The following is from a letter of Bouquet dated *Camp near Tuscarawas, 96 miles west of Fort Pitt*, 21st Oct. 1764: "They came accordingly on the 15th and met me here, to where I had moved the camp. Time does not permit me to send you all the messages which have passed since, and the conferences I have had with them, as we are going to march. I shall for the present inform you that they have behaved with the utmost submission, and have agreed to de-

For the space of a day, hundreds of axes were busy at their work. The trees were felled, the ground cleared, and, with marvellous rapidity, a town sprang up in the heart of the wilderness, martial in aspect and rigorous in discipline; with storehouses, hospitals, and works of defence, rude sylvan cabins mingled with white tents, and the forest rearing its sombre rampart around the whole. On one side of this singular encampment was a range of buildings, designed to receive the expected prisoners; and matrons, brought for this purpose with the army, were appointed to take charge of the women and children among them. At the opposite side, a canopy of branches, sustained on the upright trunks of young trees, formed a rude council-hall, in keeping with the savage assembly for whose reception it was designed.

And now, issuing from the forest, came warriors, conducting troops of prisoners, or leading captive children,—wild young barbarians, born perhaps among themselves, and scarcely to be distinguished from their own. Yet, seeing the sullen reluctance which the Indians soon betrayed in this ungrateful task, Bouquet thought it expedient to stimulate their efforts by sending detachments of soldiers to each of the villages, still retaining the chiefs in pledge for their safety. About this time, a Canadian officer, named Hertel, with a party of Caughnawaga Indians, arrived with a letter from Colonel Bradstreet, dated at Sandusky. The writer declared that he was unable to remain longer in the Indian country, and was on the point of retiring down Lake Erie with his army; a movement which, at the least, was of doubtful necessity, and which might have involved the most disastrous consequences. Had the tidings been received but a few days sooner, the whole effect of Bouquet's measures would probably have

---

liver into my hands all their prisoners, who appear to be very numerous, on the 1st of November; and, as I will not leave any thing undone, they have not only consented that I should march to their towns, but have given me four of their men to conduct the Army. This is the only point hitherto settled with them. Their excessive fear having nearly made them run away once more, that circumstance and the Treaty of Colonel Bradstreet, of which they produce the original, added to the total want of government among them, render the execution of my orders very intricate."

been destroyed, the Indians encouraged to resistance, and the war brought to the arbitration of a battle, which must needs have been a fierce and bloody one. But, happily for both parties, Bouquet now had his enemies firmly in his grasp, and the boldest warrior dared not violate the truce.

The messengers who brought the letter of Bradstreet brought also the tidings that peace was made with the northern Indians; but stated, at the same time, that these tribes had murdered many of their captives, and given up but few of the remainder, so that no small number were still within their power. The conduct of Bradstreet in this matter was the more disgraceful, since he had been encamped for weeks almost within gunshot of the Wyandot villages at Sandusky, where most of the prisoners were detained. Bouquet, on his part, though separated from this place by a journey of many days, resolved to take upon himself the duty which his brother officer had strangely neglected. He sent an embassy to Sandusky, demanding that the prisoners should be surrendered. This measure was in a great degree successful. He despatched messengers soon after to the principal Shawanoe village, on the Scioto, distant about eighty miles from his camp, to rouse the inhabitants to a greater activity than they seemed inclined to display. This was a fortunate step; for the Shawanoes of the Scioto, who had been guilty of atrocious cruelties during the war, had conceived the idea that they were excluded from the general amnesty, and marked out for destruction. This notion had been propagated, and perhaps suggested, by the French traders in their villages; and so thorough was the conviction of the Shawanoes, that they came to the desperate purpose of murdering their prisoners, and marching, with all the warriors they could muster, to attack the English. This plan was no sooner formed than the French traders opened their stores of bullets and gunpowder, and dealt them out freely to the Indians. Bouquet's messengers came in time to prevent the catastrophe, and relieve the terrors of the Shawanoes, by the assurance that peace would be granted to them on the same conditions as to the rest. Thus encouraged, they abandoned their design, and set out with lighter hearts for the English camp, bringing with them a portion of their prisoners. When about half-way on their journey, they were met by an Indian runner, who told them that a soldier had been killed in the woods, and their tribe charged with the crime. On hearing this, their fear revived, and with it their former purpose. Having collected their prisoners in a meadow, they surrounded the miserable wretches, armed with guns, war clubs, and bows and arrows, and prepared to put them to death. But another runner arrived before the butchery began, and, assuring them that what they had heard was false, prevailed on them once more to proceed. They pursued their journey without farther interruption, and, coming in safety to the camp, delivered the prisoners whom they had brought.

These by no means included all of their captives, for nearly a hundred were left behind, because they belonged to warriors who had gone to the Illinois to procure arms and ammunition from the French; and there is no authority in an Indian community powerful enough to deprive the meanest warrior of his property, even in circumstances of the greatest public exigency. This was clearly understood by the English commander, and he therefore received the submission of the Shawanoes, at the same time compelling them to deliver hostages for the future surrender of the remaining prisoners.

Band after band of captives had been daily arriving, until upwards of two hundred were now collected in the camp; including, as far as could be ascertained, all who had been in the hands of the Indians, excepting those belonging to the absent warriors of the Shawanoes. Up to this time, Bouquet had maintained a stern and rigorous demeanor; repressing his natural clemency and humanity, refusing all friendly intercourse with the Indians, and telling them that he should treat them as enemies until they had fully complied with all the required conditions. In this, he displayed his knowledge of their character; for, like all warlike savages, they are extremely prone to interpret lenity and moderation into timidity and indecision; and he who, from good-nature or mistaken philanthropy, is betrayed into yielding a point which he has before insisted on, may have deep cause to rue it. As their own dealings with their enemies are not leavened with such humanizing ingredients, they can seldom comprehend them; and to win over an Indian foe by kindness should only be attempted by one who has already proved clearly that he is able and ready to subdue him by force.

But now, when every condition was satisfied, such inexorable rigor was no longer demanded; and, having convoked the chiefs in the sylvan council-house, Bouquet signified his willingness to receive their offers of peace.

"Brother," began the Indian orator, "with this belt of wampum I dispel the black cloud that has hung so long over our heads, that the sunshine of peace may once more descend to warm and gladden us. I wipe the tears from your eyes, and condole with you on the loss of your brethren who have perished in this war. I gather their bones together, and cover them deep in the earth, that the sight of them may no longer bring sorrow to your hearts; and I scatter dry leaves over the spot, that it may depart for ever from memory.

"The path of peace, which once ran between your dwellings and mine, has of late been choked with thorns and briers, so that no one could pass that way; and we have both almost forgotten that such a path had ever been. I now clear away all such obstructions, and make a broad, smooth road, so that you and I may freely visit each other, as our fathers used to do. I kindle a great council-fire, whose smoke shall rise to heaven, in view of all the nations; while you and I sit together and smoke the peace-pipe at its blaze."[1]

---

[1]An Indian council, on solemn occasions, is always opened with preliminary forms, sufficiently wearisome and tedious, but made indispensable by immemorial custom; for this people are as much bound by their conventional usages as the most artificial children of civilization. The forms are varied to some extent, according to the imagination and taste of the speaker; but in all essential respects they are closely similar, throughout the tribes of Algonquin and Iroquois lineage. They run somewhat as follows, each sentence being pronounced with great solemnity, and confirmed by the delivery of a wampum belt: Brothers, with this belt I open your ears that you may hear—I remove grief and sorrow from your hearts—I draw from your feet the thorns which have pierced them as you journeyed thither—I clean the seats of the council-house, that you may sit at ease—I wash your head and body, that your spirits may be refreshed—I condole with you on the loss of the friends who have died since we last met—I wipe out any blood which may have been spilt between us. This ceremony, which, by the delivery of so many belts of wampum, entailed no small expense, was never used except on the most important occasions; and at the councils with Colonel Bouquet the angry warriors seem wholly to have dispensed with it.

In this strain, the orator of each tribe, in turn, expressed the purpose of his people to lay down their arms, and live for the future in friendship with the English. Every deputation received a separate audience, and the successive conferences were thus extended through several days. To each and all, Bouquet made a similar reply, in words to the following effect:—

"By your full compliance with the conditions which I imposed, you have satisfied me of your sincerity, and I now receive you once more as brethren. The King, my master, has commissioned me, not to make treaties for him, but to fight his battles; and though I now offer you peace, it is not in my power to settle its precise terms and conditions. For this, I refer you to Sir William Johnson, his Majesty's agent and superintendent for Indian affairs, who will settle with you the articles of peace, and determine every thing in relation to trade. Two things, however, I shall insist on. And, first, you are to give hostages, as security that you will preserve good faith, and send, without delay, a deputation of your chiefs to Sir William Johnson. In the next place, these chiefs are to be fully empowered to treat in behalf of your nation; and you will bind yourselves to adhere strictly to every thing they shall agree upon in your behalf."

An Indian orator is provided with a stock of metaphors, which he always makes use of for the expression of certain ideas. Thus, to make war is to raise the hatchet; to make peace is to take hold of the chain of friendship; to deliberate is to kindle the council-fire; to cover the bones of the dead is to make reparation and gain forgiveness for the act of killing them. A state of war and disaster is typified by a black cloud; a state of peace, by bright sunshine, or by an open path between the two nations.

The orator seldom speaks without careful premeditation of what he is about to say; and his memory is refreshed by the belts of wampum, which he delivers after every clause in his harangue, as a pledge of the sincerity and truth of his words. These belts are carefully preserved by the bearers, as a substitute for written records; a use for which they are the better adapted, as they are often worked with hieroglyphics expressing the meaning they are designed to preserve. Thus, at a treaty of peace, the principal belt often bears the figures of an Indian and a white man holding a chain between them.

For the nature and uses of wampum, see note, *ante*, p. 485, *note*.

Though a good memory is an essential qualification of an Indian orator, it would be unjust not to observe that striking outbursts of spontaneous eloquence have sometimes proceeded from their lips.

These demands were readily complied with. Hostages were given, and chiefs appointed for the embassy; and now, for the first time, Bouquet, to the great relief of the Indians,—for they doubted his intentions,—extended to them the hand of friendship, which he had so long withheld. A prominent chief of the Delawares, too proud to sue for peace, had refused to attend the council; on which Bouquet ordered him to be deposed, and a successor, of a less obdurate spirit, installed in his place. The Shawanoes were the last of the tribes admitted to a hearing; and the demeanor of their orator clearly evinced the haughty reluctance with which he stooped to ask peace of his mortal enemies.

"When you came among us," such were his concluding words, "you came with a hatchet raised to strike us. We now take it from your hand, and throw it up to the Great Spirit, that he may do with it what shall seem good in his sight. We hope that you, who are warriors, will take hold of the chain of friendship which we now extend to you. We, who are also warriors, will take hold as you do; and we will think no more of war, in pity for our women, children, and old men."[1]

On this occasion, the Shawanoe chiefs, expressing a hope for a renewal of the friendship which in former years had subsisted between their people and the English, displayed the dilapidated parchments of several treaties made between their ancestors and the descendants of William Penn,—documents, some of which had been preserved among them for more

[1] The Shawanoe speaker, in expressing his intention of disarming his enemy by laying aside his own designs of war, makes use of an unusual metaphor. To *bury the hatchet* is the figure in common use on such occasions, but he adopts a form of speech which he regards as more significant and emphatic,—that of throwing it up to the Great Spirit. Unwilling to confess that he yields through fear of the enemy, he professes to wish for peace merely for the sake of his women and children.

At the great council at Lancaster, in 1762, a chief of the Oneidas, anxious to express, in the strongest terms, the firmness of the peace which had been concluded, had recourse to the following singular figure: "In the country of the Oneidas there is a great pine-tree, so huge and old that half its branches are dead with time. I tear it up by the roots, and, looking down into the hole, I see a dark stream of water, flowing with a strong current, deep under ground. Into this stream I fling the hatchet, and the current sweeps it away, no man knows whither. Then I plant the tree again where it stood before, and thus this war will be ended for ever."

than half a century, with the scrupulous respect they are prone to exhibit for such ancestral records. They were told that, since they had not delivered all their prisoners, they could scarcely expect to meet the same indulgence which had been extended to their brethren; but that, nevertheless, in full belief of their sincerity, the English would grant them peace, on condition of their promising to surrender the remaining captives early in the following spring, and giving up six of their chiefs as hostages. These conditions were agreed to; and it may be added that, at the appointed time, all the prisoners who had been left in their hands, to the number of a hundred, were brought in to Fort Pitt, and delivered up to the commanding officer.[1]

From the hard formalities and rigid self-control of an Indian council-house, where the struggles of fear, rage, and hatred were deep buried beneath a surface of iron immobility, we turn to scenes of a widely different nature; an exhibition of mingled and contrasted passions, more worthy the pen of the dramatist than that of the historian; who, restricted to the meagre outline of recorded authority, can reflect but a feeble image of the truth. In the ranks of the Pennsylvania troops, and among the Virginia riflemen, were the fathers, brothers, and husbands of those whose rescue from captivity was a chief object of the march. Ignorant what had befallen them, and doubtful whether they were yet among the living, these men had joined the army, in the feverish hope of winning them back to home and civilization. Perhaps those whom they sought had perished by the slow torments of the stake;

---

[1] A party of the Virginia volunteers had been allowed by Bouquet to go to the remoter Shawanoe towns, in the hope of rescuing captive relatives. They returned to Fort Pitt at midwinter, bringing nine prisoners, all children or old women. The whole party was frost-bitten, and had endured the extremity of suffering on the way. They must have perished but for a Shawanoe chief, named Benewisica, to whose care Bouquet had confided them, and who remained with them both going and returning, hunting for them to keep them from famishing. — *Capt. Murray to Bouquet*, 31 Jan. 1765.

Besides the authorities before mentioned in relation to these transactions, the correspondence of Bouquet with the commander-in-chief, throughout the expedition, together with letters from some of the officers who accompanied him, have been examined. For General Gage's summary of the results of the campaign, see Appendix, F.

perhaps by the more merciful hatchet; or perhaps they still dragged out a wretched life in the midst of a savage horde. There were instances in which whole families had been carried off at once. The old, the sick, or the despairing, had been tomahawked, as useless encumbrances; while the rest, pitilessly forced asunder, were scattered through every quarter of the wilderness. It was a strange and moving sight, when troop after troop of prisoners arrived in succession—the meeting of husbands with wives, and fathers with children, the reunion of broken families, long separated in a disastrous captivity; and, on the other hand, the agonies of those who learned tidings of death and horror, or groaned under the torture of protracted suspense. Women, frantic between hope and fear, were rushing hither and thither, in search of those whose tender limbs had, perhaps, long since fattened the cubs of the she-wolf; or were pausing, in an agony of doubt, before some sunburnt young savage, who, startled at the haggard apparition, shrank from his forgotten parent, and clung to the tawny breast of his adopted mother. Others were divided between delight and anguish: on the one hand, the joy of an unexpected recognition; and, on the other, the misery of realized fears, or the more intolerable pangs of doubts not yet resolved. Of all the spectators of this tragic drama, few were obdurate enough to stand unmoved. The roughest soldiers felt the contagious sympathy, and softened into unwonted tenderness.

Among the children brought in for surrender, there were some, who, captured several years before, as early, perhaps, as the French war, had lost every recollection of friends and home. Terrified by the novel sights around them, the flash and glitter of arms, and the strange complexion of the pale-faced warriors, they screamed and struggled lustily when consigned to the hands of their relatives. There were young women, too, who had become the partners of Indian husbands; and who now, with all their hybrid offspring, were led reluctantly into the presence of fathers or brothers whose images were almost blotted from their memory. They stood agitated and bewildered; the revival of old affections, and the rush of dormant memories, painfully contending with more recent attachments, and the shame of their real or fancied disgrace; while their Indian lords looked on, scarcely less moved than they, yet hardening themselves with savage stoicism, and standing in the midst of their enemies, imperturbable as statues of bronze. These women were compelled to return with their children to the settlements; yet they all did so with reluctance, and several afterwards made their escape, eagerly hastening back to their warrior husbands, and the toils and vicissitudes of an Indian wigwam.[1]

Day after day brought renewals of these scenes, deepening in interest as they drew towards their close. A few individual incidents have been recorded. A young Virginian, robbed of his wife but a few months before, had volunteered in the expedition with the faint hope of recovering her; and, after long suspense, had recognized her among a troop of prisoners, bearing in her arms a child born during her captivity. But the joy of the meeting was bitterly alloyed by the loss of a former child, not two years old, captured with the mother, but soon taken from her, and carried, she could not tell whither. Days passed on; they could learn no tidings of its fate, and the mother, harrowed with terrible imaginations, was almost driven to despair; when, at length, she discovered her child in the arms of an Indian warrior, and snatched it with an irrepressible cry of transport.

When the army, on its homeward march, reached the town of Carlisle, those who had been unable to follow the expedition came thither in numbers, to inquire for the friends they had lost. Among the rest was an old woman, whose daughter had been carried off nine years before. In the crowd of female captives, she discovered one in whose wild and swarthy features she discerned the altered lineaments of her child; but the

[1] *Penn. Hist. Coll.* 267. *Haz. Pa. Reg.* IV. 390. M'Culloch, *Narrative*. M'Culloch was one of the prisoners surrendered to Bouquet. His narrative first appeared in a pamphlet form, and has since been republished in the *Incidents of Border Warfare*, and other similar collections. The autobiography of Mary Jemison, a woman captured by the Senecas during the French war, and twice married among them, contains an instance of attachment to Indian life similar to those mentioned above. After the conclusion of hostilities, learning that she was to be given up to the whites in accordance with a treaty, she escaped into the woods with her half-breed children, and remained hidden, in great dismay and agitation, until the search was over. She lived to an advanced age, but never lost her attachment to the Indian life.

girl, who had almost forgotten her native tongue, returned no sign of recognition to her eager words, and the old woman bitterly complained that the daughter, whom she had so often sung to sleep on her knee, had forgotten her in her old age. Bouquet suggested an expedient which proves him a man of feeling and perception. "Sing the song that you used to sing to her when a child." The old woman obeyed; and a sudden start, a look of bewilderment, and a passionate flood of tears, removed every doubt, and restored the long-lost daughter to her mother's arms.[1]

The tender affections by no means form a salient feature in the Indian character. They hold them in contempt, and scorn every manifestation of them; yet, on this occasion, they would not be repressed, and the human heart betrayed itself, though throbbing under a breastplate of ice. None of the ordinary signs of emotion, neither tears, words, nor looks, declared how greatly they were moved. It was by their kindness and solicitude, by their attention to the wants of the captives, by their offers of furs, garments, the choicest articles of food, and every thing which in their eyes seemed luxury, that they displayed their sorrow at parting from their adopted relatives and friends.[2] Some among them went much farther, and asked permission to follow the army on its homeward march, that they might hunt for the captives, and supply them with better food than the military stores could furnish. A young Seneca warrior had become deeply enamoured of a Virginian girl. At great risk of his life, he accompanied the troops far within the limits of the settlements; and, at every night's encampment, approaching the quarters of the captives as closely as the sentinels would permit, he sat watching, with patient vigilance, to catch a glimpse of his lost mistress.

The Indian women, whom no idea of honor compels to wear an iron mask, were far from emulating the frigid demeanor of their lords. All day they ran wailing through the

---

[1] *Ordinances of the Borough of Carlisle, Appendix. Penn. Hist. Coll.* 267.

[2] The author of *The Expedition against the Ohio Indians* speaks of the Indians "shedding torrents of tears." This is either a flourish of rhetoric, or is meant to apply solely to the squaws. A warrior, who, under the circumstances, should have displayed such emotion, would have been disgraced for ever.

camp; and, when night came, the hills and woods resounded with their dreary lamentations.[1]

The word *prisoner*, as applied to captives taken by the Indians, is a misnomer, and conveys a wholly false impression of their situation and treatment. When the vengeance of the conquerors is sated; when they have shot, stabbed, burned, or beaten to death, enough to satisfy the shades of their departed relatives, they usually treat those who survive their wrath with moderation and humanity; often adopting them to supply the place of lost brothers, husbands, or children, whose names are given to the successors thus substituted in their place. By a formal ceremony, the white blood is washed from their veins; and they are regarded thenceforth as members of the tribe, faring equally with the rest in prosperity or adversity, in famine or abundance. When children are adopted in this manner by Indian women, they nurture them with the same tenderness and indulgence which they extend, in a remarkable degree, to their own offspring; and such young women as will not marry an Indian husband are treated with a singular forbearance, in which superstition, natural temperament, and a sense of right and justice may all claim a share.[2] The captive, unless he excites suspicion by his conduct, or exhibits peculiar contumacy, is left with no other restraint than his own free will. The warrior who captured him, or to whom he was assigned in the division of the spoil, sometimes claims, it is true, a certain right of property in him, to the exclusion of others; but this claim is soon

---

[1] The outcries of the squaws, on such occasions, would put to shame an Irish death-howl. The writer was once attached to a large band of Indians, who, being on the march, arrived, a little after nightfall, at a spot where, not long before, a party of their young men had been killed by the enemy. The women instantly raised a most astounding clamor, some two hundred voices joining in a discord as wild and dismal as the shrieking of the damned in the *Inferno*; while some of the chief mourners gashed their bodies and limbs with knives, uttering meanwhile most piteous lamentations. A few days later, returning to the same encampment after darkness had closed in, a strange and startling effect was produced by the prolonged wailings of several women, who were pacing the neighboring hills, lamenting the death of a child, killed by the bite of a rattlesnake.

[2] This and what precedes is meant to apply only to tribes east of the Mississippi. Some of the western and south-western tribes treat prisoners merely as slaves, and habitually violate female captives.

forgotten, and is seldom exercised to the inconvenience of the captive, who has no other prison than the earth, the air, and the forest.[1] Five hundred miles of wilderness, beset with difficulty and danger, are the sole bars to his escape, should he desire to effect it; but, strange as it may appear, this wish is apt to expire in his heart, and he often remains to the end of his life a contented denizen of the woods.

Among the captives brought in for delivery were some bound fast to prevent their escape; and many others, who, amid the general tumult of joy and sorrow, sat sullen and scowling, angry that they were forced to abandon the wild license of the forest for the irksome restraints of society.[2] Thus to look back with a fond longing to inhospitable deserts, where men, beasts, and Nature herself, seem arrayed in arms, and where ease, security, and all that civilization reckons among the goods of life, are alike cut off, may appear to argue some strange perversity or moral malformation. Yet such has been the experience of many a sound and healthful mind. To him who has once tasted the reckless independence, the haughty self-reliance, the sense of irresponsible freedom, which the forest life engenders, civilization thenceforth seems flat and stale. Its pleasures are insipid, its pursuits wearisome, its conventionalities, duties, and mutual dependence alike tedious and disgusting. The entrapped wanderer grows fierce and restless, and pants for breathing-room. His path, it is true, was choked with difficulties, but his body and soul were hardened to meet them; it was beset with dangers, but these were the very spice of his life, gladdening his heart with exulting self-confidence, and sending the blood through his veins with a livelier current. The wilderness, rough, harsh, and inexorable, has charms more potent in their seductive influence than all the lures of luxury and sloth. And often he on whom it has cast its magic finds no heart to dissolve the spell, and

[1] The captives among the Shawanoes of the Scioto had most of them been recently taken; and only a small part had gone through the ceremony of adoption. Hence it was that the warriors, in their desperation, formed the design of putting them to death, fearing that, in the attack which they meditated, the captives would naturally take part with their countrymen.

[2] *Account of Bouquet's Expedition*, 29.

remains a wanderer and an Ishmaelite to the hour of his death.[1]

There is a chord, in the breasts of most men, prompt to answer loudly or faintly, as the case may be, to such rude appeals. But there is influence of another sort, strongest with minds of the finest texture, yet sometimes holding a controlling power over those who neither acknowledge nor suspect its workings. There are few so imbruted by vice, so perverted by art and luxury, as to dwell in the closest presence of Nature, deaf to her voice of melody and power, untouched by the ennobling influences which mould and penetrate the heart that has not hardened itself against them. Into the spirit of such an one the mountain wind breathes its own freshness, and the midsummer tempest, as it rends the forest, pours its own fierce energy. His thoughts flow with the placid stream of the broad, deep river, or dance in light with the sparkling current of the mountain brook. No passing mood or fancy of

---

[1]Colden, after describing the Indian wars of 1699, 1700, concludes in the following words:—

"I shall finish this Part by observing that notwithstanding the French Commissioners took all the Pains possible to carry Home the French that were Prisoners with the Five Nations, and they had full Liberty from the Indians, few of them could be persuaded to return. It may be thought that this was occasioned from the Hardships they had endured in their own Country, under a tyrannical Government and a barren Soil. But this certainly was not the Reason, for the English had as much Difficulty to persuade the People that had been taken Prisoners by the French Indians to leave the Indian Manner of living, though no People enjoy more Liberty, and live in greater Plenty than the common Inhabitants of New York do. No Arguments, no Intreaties, nor Tears of their Friends and Relations, could persuade many of them to leave their new Indian Friends and Acquaintance. Several of them that were by the Caressings of their Relations persuaded to come Home, in a little Time grew tired of our Manner of living, and ran away to the Indians, and ended their Days with them. On the other Hand, Indian Children have been carefully educated among the English, clothed and taught; yet, I think, there is not one Instance that any of these, after they had Liberty to go among their own People, and were come to Age, would remain with the English, but returned to their own Nations, and became as fond of the Indian Manner of Life as those that knew nothing of a civilized Manner of living. What I now tell of Christian Prisoners among Indians relates not only to what happened at the Conclusion of this War, but has been found true on many other Occasions."—Colden, 203.

his mind but has its image and its echo in the wild world around him. There is softness in the mellow air, the warm sunshine, and the budding leaves of spring; and in the forest flower, which, more delicate than the pampered offspring of gardens, lifts its tender head through the refuse and decay of the wilderness. But it is the grand and heroic in the hearts of men which finds its worthiest symbol and noblest inspiration amid these desert realms,—in the mountain, rearing its savage head through clouds and sleet, or basking its majestic strength in the radiance of the sinking sun; in the interminable forest, the thunder booming over its lonely waste, the whirlwind tearing through its inmost depths, or the sun at length setting in gorgeous majesty beyond its waves of verdure. To the sick, the wearied, or the sated spirit, nature opens a theatre of boundless life, and holds forth a cup brimming with redundant pleasure. In the other joys of existence, fear is balanced against hope, and satiety against delight; but here one may fearlessly drink, gaining, with every draught, new vigor and a heightened zest, and finding no dregs of bitterness at the bottom.

Having accomplished its work, the army left the Muskingum, and, retracing its former course, arrived at Fort Pitt on the twenty-eighth of November. The recovered captives were sent to their respective homes in Pennsylvania or Virginia; and the provincial troops disbanded, not without warm praises for the hardihood and steadiness with which they had met the difficulties of the campaign. The happy issue of the expedition spread joy throughout the country. At the next session of the Pennsylvania Assembly, one of its first acts was to pass a vote of thanks to Colonel Bouquet, expressing in earnest terms its sense of his services and personal merits, and conveying its acknowledgments for the regard which he had constantly shown to the civil rights of the inhabitants.[1] The Assembly of Virginia passed a similar vote; and both houses concurred in recommending Bouquet to the King for promotion.

Nevertheless, his position was far from being an easy or a pleasant one. It may be remembered that the desertion of his newly levied soldiers had forced him to ask Colonel Lewis to

[1] See Appendix, F.

raise for him one or two companies of Virginian volunteers. Virginia, which had profited by the campaign, though contributing nothing to it, refused to pay these troops; and its agents tried to throw the burden upon Bouquet in person. The Assembly of Pennsylvania, with a justice and a generosity which went far to redeem the past, came to his relief and assumed the debt, though not till he had suffered the most serious annoyance. Certain recent military regulations contributed at the same time to increase his vexation and his difficulties. He had asked in vain, the year before, to be relieved from his command. He now asked again, and the request was granted; on which he wrote to Gage: "The disgust I have conceived from the ill-nature and ingratitude of those individuals (*the Virginian officials*) makes me accept with great satisfaction your obliging offer to discharge me of this department, in which I never desire to serve again, nor, indeed, to be commanding officer in any other, since the new regulations you were pleased to communicate to me; being sensible of my inability to carry on the service upon the terms prescribed."[1]

He was preparing to return to Europe, when he received the announcement of his promotion to the rank of Brigadier General. He was taken completely by surprise; for he had supposed that the rigid prescriptions of the service had closed the path of advancement against him, as a foreigner. "I had, to-day," he wrote to Gage, "the honor of your Excellency's letter of the fifteenth instant. The unexpected honor, which his Majesty has condescended to confer upon me, fills my heart with the utmost gratitude. Permit me, sir, to express my sincere acknowledgments of my great obligation to you. . . . The flattering prospect of preferment, open to the other foreign officers by the removal of that dreadful barrier, gives me the highest satisfaction, being convinced that his Majesty has no subjects more devoted to his service."[2]

Among the letters of congratulation which he received from officers serving under him is the following, from Captain George Etherington, of the first battalion of the Royal

[1]MS. Letter—*Bouquet to Gage*, 4 March, 1765.
[2]*Ibid.*, 17 April, 1765.

American regiment, who commanded at Michillimackinac when it was captured: —

"Lancaster, Pa., 19 April, 1765.

"Sir:

"Though I almost despair of this reaching you before you sail for Europe, yet I cannot deny myself the pleasure of giving you joy on your promotion, and can with truth tell you that it gives great joy to all the gentlemen of the battalion, for two reasons: first, on your account; and, secondly, on our own, as by that means we may hope for the pleasure of continuing under your command.

"You can hardly imagine how this place rings with the news of your promotion, for the townsmen and boors (*i.e., German farmers*) stop us in the streets to ask if it is true that the King has made Colonel Bouquet a general; and, when they are told it is true, they march off with great joy; so you see the old proverb wrong for once, which says, he that prospers is envied; for sure I am that all the people here are more pleased with the news of your promotion than they would be if the government would take off the stamp duty. . . .

"GEO. ETHERINGTON.

"BRIGADIER GENERAL HENRY BOUQUET."

"And," concludes Dr. William Smith, the chronicler of the campaign, "as he is rendered as dear by his private virtues to those who have the honor of his more intimate acquaintance, as he is by his military services to the public, it is hoped he may long continue among us, where his experienced abilities will enable him, and his love of the English constitution entitle him, to fill any future trust to which his Majesty may be pleased to call him." This hope was not destined to fulfilment. Bouquet was assigned to the command of the southern military department; and, within three years after his return from the Muskingum, he was attacked with a fever at Pensacola, which closed the career of a gallant soldier and a generous man.

The Delawares and Shawanoes, mindful of their engagement and of the hostages which they had given to keep it, sent their deputies, within the appointed time, to Sir William

Johnson, who concluded a treaty with them; stipulating, among the other terms, that they should grant free passage through their country to English troops and travellers; that they should make full restitution for the goods taken from the traders at the breaking out of the war; and that they should aid their triumphant enemies in the difficult task which yet remained to be accomplished, — that of taking possession of the Illinois, and occupying its posts and settlements with British troops.[1]

[1] MS. *Johnson Papers.*

Chapter XXVIII.

1764.

THE ILLINOIS.

W E TURN to a region of which, as yet, we have caught but transient glimpses; a region which to our fore-fathers seemed remote and strange, as to us the mountain strongholds of the Apaches, or the wastes of farthest Oregon. The country of the Illinois was chiefly embraced within the boundaries of the state which now retains the name. Thither-ward, from the east, the west, and the north, three mighty rivers rolled their tributary waters; while countless smaller streams—small only in comparison—traversed the land with a watery network, impregnating the warm soil with exuberant fecundity. From the eastward, the Ohio—La Belle Rivière—pursued its windings for more than a thousand miles. The Mississippi descended from the distant north; while from its fountains in the west, three thousand miles away, the Mis-souri poured its torrent towards the same common centre. Born among mountains, trackless even now, except by the adventurous footstep of the trapper,—nurtured amid the howling of beasts and the war-cries of savages, never silent in that wilderness,—it holds its angry course through sun-scorched deserts, among towers and palaces, the architecture of no human hand, among lodges of barbarian hordes, and herds of bison blackening the prairie to the horizon. Fierce, reckless, headstrong, exulting in its tumultuous force, it plays a thousand freaks of wanton power; bearing away forests from its shores, and planting them, with roots uppermost, in its quicksands; sweeping off islands, and rebuilding them; frothing and raging in foam and whirlpool, and, again, glid-ing with dwindled current along its sandy channel. At length, dark with uncurbed fury, it pours its muddy tide into the reluctant Mississippi. That majestic river, drawing life from the pure fountains of the north, wandering among emerald prairies and wood-crowned bluffs, loses all its earlier charm with this unhallowed union. At first, it shrinks as with repug-nance; and along the same channel the two streams flow side

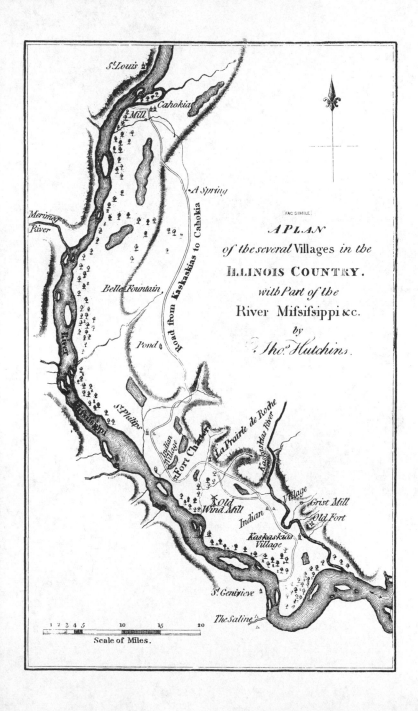

FAC SIMILE.

A PLAN

of the several Villages *in the*

ILLINOIS COUNTRY.

with Part of the

River Mifsifsippi &c.

by

Thoˢ Hutchins.

St Louis

Cahokia

Mill

A Spring

Merimeg River

Belle Fountain

Road from Kaskaskias to Cahokia

Pond

St Philips

Indian Village

Fort Chartres

La Prairie de Roche

Kaskaskias River

Old Wind Mill

Indian Village

Grist Mill

Old Fort

Kaskaskias Village

St Genivieve

The Saline

| 1 | 2 | 3 | 4 | 5 | 10 | 15 | 20 |

Scale of Miles.

by side, with unmingled waters. But the disturbing power prevails at length; and the united torrent bears onward in its might, boiling up from the bottom, whirling in many a vortex, flooding its shores with a malign deluge fraught with pestilence and fever, and burying forests in its depths, to insnare the heedless voyager. Mightiest among rivers, it is the connecting link of adverse climates and contrasted races; and, while at its northern source the fur-clad Indian shivers in the cold, where it mingles with the ocean, the growth of the tropics springs along its banks, and the panting negro cools his limbs in its refreshing waters.

To these great rivers and their tributary streams the country of the Illinois owed its wealth, its grassy prairies, and the stately woods that flourished on its deep, rich soil. This prolific land teemed with life. It was a hunter's paradise. Deer grazed on its meadows. The elk trooped in herds, like squadrons of cavalry. In the still morning, one might hear the clatter of their antlers for half a mile over the dewy prairie. Countless bison roamed the plains, filing in grave procession to drink at the rivers, plunging and snorting among the rapids and quicksands, rolling their huge bulk on the grass, rushing upon each other in hot encounter, like champions under shield. The wildcat glared from the thicket; the raccoon thrust his furry countenance from the hollow tree, and the opossum swung, head downwards, from the overhanging bough.

With the opening spring, when the forests are budding into leaf, and the prairies gemmed with flowers; when a warm, faint haze rests upon the landscape,—then heart and senses are inthralled with luxurious beauty. The shrubs and wild fruit-trees, flushed with pale red blossoms, and the small clustering flowers of grape-vines, which choke the gigantic trees with Laocoön writhings, fill the forest with their rich perfume. A few days later, and a cloud of verdure overshadows the land; while birds innumerable sing beneath its canopy, and brighten its shades with their glancing hues.

Yet this western paradise is not free from the primal curse. The beneficent sun, which kindles into life so many forms of loveliness and beauty, fails not to engender venom and death from the rank slime of pestilential swamp and marsh. In some stagnant pool, buried in the jungle-like depths of the forest, where the hot and lifeless water reeks with exhalations, the water-snake basks by the margin, or winds his checkered length of loathsome beauty across the sleepy surface. From beneath the rotten carcass of some fallen tree, the moccason thrusts out his broad flat head, ready to dart on the intruder. On the dry, sun-scorched prairie, the rattlesnake, a more generous enemy, reposes in his spiral coil. He scorns to shun the eye of day, as if conscious of the honor accorded to his name by the warlike race, who, jointly with him, claim lordship over the land.[1] But some intrusive footstep awakes him from his slumbers. His neck is arched; the white fangs gleam in his distended jaws; his small eyes dart rays of unutterable fierceness; and his rattles, invisible with their quick vibration, ring the sharp warning which no man will dare to contemn.

The land thus prodigal of good and evil, so remote from the sea, so primitive in its aspect, might well be deemed an undiscovered region, ignorant of European arts; yet it may boast a colonization as old as that of many a spot to which are accorded the scanty honors of an American antiquity. The earliest settlement of Pennsylvania was made in 1681; the first occupation of the Illinois took place in the previous year. La Salle may be called the father of the colony. That

[1] The superstitious veneration which the Indians entertain for the rattlesnake has been before alluded to. The Cherokees christened him by a name which, being interpreted, signifies *the bright old inhabitant*, a title of affectionate admiration of which his less partial acquaintance would hardly judge him worthy.

"Between the heads of the northern branch of the Lower Cheerake River, and the heads of that of Tuckaschchee, winding round in a long course by the late Fort Loudon, and afterwards into the Mississippi, there is, both in the nature and circumstances, a great phenomenon. Between two high mountains, nearly covered with old mossy rocks, lofty cedars and pines, in the valleys of which the beams of the sun reflect a powerful heat, there are, as the natives affirm, some bright old inhabitants, or rattlesnakes, of a more enormous size than is mentioned in history. They are so large and unwieldy, that they take a circle almost as wide as their length, to crawl round in their shortest orbit; but bountiful nature compensates the heavy motion of their bodies; for, as they say, no living creature moves within the reach of their sight, but they can draw it to them; which is agreeable to what we observe through the whole system of animated beings. Nature endues them with proper capacities to sustain life: as they cannot support themselves by their speed or cunning, to spring from an ambuscade, it is needful they should have the bewitching craft of their eyes and forked tongues."—Adair, 237.

remarkable man entered the country with a handful of followers, bent on his grand scheme of Mississippi discovery. A legion of enemies rose in his path; but neither delay, disappointment, sickness, famine, open force, nor secret conspiracy, could bend his soul of iron. Disasters accumulated upon him. He flung them off, and still pressed forward to his object. His victorious energy bore all before it; but the success on which he had staked his life served only to entail fresh calamity, and an untimely death; and his best reward is, that his name stands forth in history an imperishable monument of heroic constancy. When on his way to the Mississippi, in the year 1680, La Salle built a fort in the country of the Illinois; and, on his return from the mouth of the great river, some of his followers remained, and established themselves near the spot. Heroes of another stamp took up the work which the daring Norman had begun. Jesuit missionaries, among the best and purest of their order, burning with zeal for the salvation of souls, and the gaining of an immortal crown, here toiled and suffered, with a self-sacrificing devotion which extorts a tribute of admiration even from sectarian bigotry. While the colder apostles of Protestantism labored upon the outskirts of heathendom, these champions of the cross, the forlorn hope of the army of Rome, pierced to the heart of its dark and dreary domain, confronting death at every step, and well repaid for all, could they but sprinkle a few drops of water on the forehead of a dying child, or hang a gilded crucifix round the neck of some warrior, pleased with the glittering trinket. With the beginning of the eighteenth century, the black robe of the Jesuit was known in every village of the Illinois. Defying the wiles of Satan and the malice of his emissaries, the Indian sorcerers; exposed to the rage of the elements, and every casualty of forest life, they followed their wandering proselytes to war and to the chase; now wading through morasses, now dragging canoes over rapids and sand-bars; now scorched with heat on the sweltering prairie, and now shivering houseless in the blasts of January. At Kaskaskia and Cahokia they established missions, and built frail churches from the bark of trees, fit emblems of their own transient and futile labors. Morning and evening, the savage worshippers sang praises to the Virgin, and knelt in supplication before the shrine of St. Joseph.[1]

Soldiers and fur-traders followed where these pioneers of the church had led the way. Forts were built here and there throughout the country, and the cabins of settlers clustered about the mission-houses. The new colonists, emigrants from Canada or disbanded soldiers of French regiments, bore a close resemblance to the settlers of Detroit, or the primitive people of Acadia; whose simple life poetry has chosen as an appropriate theme, but who, nevertheless, are best contemplated from a distance. The Creole of the Illinois, contented, light-hearted, and thriftless, by no means fulfilled the injunction to increase and multiply; and the colony languished in spite of the fertile soil. The people labored long enough to gain a bare subsistence for each passing day, and spent the rest of their time in dancing and merry-making, smoking, gossiping, and hunting. Their native gayety was irrepressible, and they found means to stimulate it with wine made from the fruit of the wild grape-vines. Thus they passed their days, at peace with themselves, hand and glove with their Indian neighbors, and ignorant of all the world beside. Money was scarcely known among them. Skins and furs were the prevailing currency, and in every village a great portion of the land was held in common. The military commandant, whose station was at Fort Chartres, on the Mississippi, ruled the colony with a sway absolute as that of the Pacha of Egypt, and judged civil and criminal cases without right of appeal. Yet his power was exercised in a patriarchal spirit, and he usually commanded the respect and confidence of the people. Many years later, when, after the War of the Revolution, the Illinois came under the jurisdiction of the United States, the perplexed inhabitants, totally at a loss to understand the complicated machinery of republicanism, begged to be delivered from the intolerable burden of self-government, and to be once more subjected to a military commandant.[2]

---

[1] For an account of Jesuit labors in the Illinois, see the letters of Father Marest, in *Lett. Edif.* IV.

[2] The principal authorities for the above account of the Illinois colony are Hutchins, *Topographical Description*, 37. Volney, *View of the United States,* 370. Pitman, *Present State of the European Settlements on the Mississippi, passim.* Law,

The Creole is as unchanging in his nature and habits as the Indian himself. Even at this day, one may see, along the banks of the Mississippi, the same low-browed cottages, with their broad eaves and picturesque verandas, which, a century ago, were clustered around the mission-house at Kaskaskia; and, entering, one finds the inmate the same lively, story-telling, and pipe-smoking being that his ancestor was before him. Yet, with all his genial traits, the rough world deals hardly with him. He lives a mere drone in the busy hive of an American population. The living tide encroaches on his rest, as the muddy torrent of the great river chafes away the farm and homestead of his fathers. Yet he contrives to be happy, though looking back regretfully to the better ·days of old.

At the date of this history, the population of the colony, exclusive of negroes, who, in that simple community, were treated rather as humble friends than as slaves, did not exceed two thousand souls, distributed in several small settlements. There were about eighty houses at Kaskaskia, forty or fifty at Cahokia, a few at Vincennes and Fort Chartres, and a few more scattered in small clusters upon the various streams. The agricultural portion of the colonists were, as we have described them, marked with many weaknesses, and many amiable virtues; but their morals were not improved by a large admixture of fur-traders, — reckless, harebrained adventurers, who, happily for the peace of their relatives, were absent on their wandering vocation during the greater part of the year.[1]

Address before the Historical Society of Vincennes, 14. Brown, *Hist. Illinois*, 208. *Journal of Captain Harry Gordon*, in Appendix to Pownall's *Topographical Description*. Nicollet, *Report on the Hydrographical Basin of the Mississippi*, 75.

[1]Lieutenant Alexander Fraser visited the Illinois in 1765, as we shall see hereafter. He met extreme ill-treatment, and naturally takes a prejudiced view of the people. The following is from his MS. account of the country: —

"The Illinois Indians are about 650 able to bear arms. Nothing can equal their passion for drunkenness, but that of the French inhabitants, who are for the greatest part drunk every day, while they can get drink to buy in the Colony. They import more of this Article from New Orleans than they do of any other, and they never fail to meet a speedy and good market for it. They have a great many Negroes, who are obliged to labour very hard to support their Masters in their extravagant debaucheries; any one who has had any

Swarms of vagabond Indians infested the settlements; and, to people of any other character, they would have proved an intolerable annoyance. But the easy-tempered Creoles made friends and comrades of them; ate, drank, smoked, and often married with them. They were a debauched and drunken rabble, the remnants of that branch of the Algonquin stock known among the French as the Illinois, a people once numerous and powerful, but now miserably enfeebled, and corrupted by foreign wars, domestic dissensions, and their own licentious manners. They comprised the broken fragments of five tribes,—the Kaskaskias, Cahokias, Peorias, Mitchigamias, and Tamaronas. Some of their villages were in the close vicinity of the Creole settlements. On a hot summer morning, they might be seen lounging about the trading-house, basking in the sun, begging for a dram of whiskey, or chaffering with the hard-featured trader for beads, tobacco, gunpowder, and red paint.

About the Wabash and its branches, to the eastward of the Illinois, dwelt tribes of similar lineage, but more warlike in character, and less corrupt in manners. These were the Miamis, in their three divisions, their near kindred, the Piankishaws, and a portion of the Kickapoos. There was another settlement of the Miamis upon the River Maumee, still farther to the east; and it was here that Bradstreet's ambassador,

---

dealings with them must plainly see that they are for the most part transported Convicts, or people who have fled for some crimes; those who have not done it themselves are the offspring of such as those I just mentioned, inheriting their Forefathers' vices. They are cruel and treacherous to each other, and consequently so to Strangers; they are dishonest in every kind of business and lay themselves out to overreach Strangers, which they often do by a low cunning, peculiar to themselves; and their artful flatteries, with extravagant Entertainments (in which they affect the greatest hospitality) generally favor their schemes."

Of the traders, he says, "They are in general most unconscious (*unconscionable*) Rascals, whose interest it was to debauch from us such Indians as they found well disposed towards us, and to foment and increace the animosity of such as they found otherwise. To this we should alone impute our late war with the Indians."

He sets down the number of white inhabitants at about seven hundred able to bear arms, though he says that it is impossible to form a just estimate, as they are continually going and coming to and from the Indian nations.

Captain Morris, had met so rough a welcome. The strength of these combined tribes was very considerable; and, one and all, they looked with wrath and abhorrence on the threatened advent of the English.

Chapter XXIX.

PONTIAC RALLIES THE WESTERN TRIBES.

WHEN, by the treaty of Paris, in 1763, France ceded to England her territories east of the Mississippi, the Illinois was of course included in the cession. Scarcely were the articles signed, when France, as if eager to rob herself, at one stroke, of all her western domain, threw away upon Spain the vast and indefinite regions beyond the Mississippi, destined at a later day to return to her hands, and finally to swell the growing empire of the United States. This transfer to Spain was for some time kept secret; but orders were immediately sent to the officers commanding at the French posts within the territory ceded to England, to evacuate the country whenever British troops should appear to occupy it. These orders reached the Illinois towards the close of 1763. Some time, however, must necessarily elapse before the English could take possession; for the Indian war was then at its height, and the country was protected from access by a broad barrier of savage tribes, in the hottest ferment of hostility.

The colonists, hating the English with a more than national hatred, deeply imbittered by years of disastrous war, received the news of the treaty with disgust and execration. Many of them left the country, loath to dwell under the shadow of the British flag. Of these, some crossed the Mississippi to the little hamlet of St. Genevieve, on the western bank; others followed the commandant, Neyon de Villiers, to New Orleans; while others, taking with them all their possessions, even to the frames and clapboarding of their houses, passed the river a little above Cahokia, and established themselves at a beautiful spot on the opposite shore, where a settlement was just then on the point of commencement. Here a line of richly wooded bluffs rose with easy ascent from the margin of the water; while from their summits extended a wide plateau of fertile prairie, bordered by a framework of forest. In the shadow of the trees, which fringed the edge of the declivity, stood a newly built storehouse, with a few slight cabins and works of defence, belonging to a company of fur-traders. At their head was Pierre Laclede, who had left New Orleans with his followers in August, 1763; and, after toiling for three months against the impetuous stream of the Mississippi, had reached the Illinois in November, and selected the spot alluded to as the site of his first establishment. To this he gave the name of St. Louis.[1] Side by side with Laclede, in his adventurous enterprise, was a young man, slight in person, but endowed with a vigor and elasticity of frame which could resist heat or cold, fatigue, hunger, or the wasting hand of time. Not all the magic of a dream, nor the enchantments of an Arabian tale, could outmatch the waking realities which were to rise upon the vision of Pierre Chouteau. Where, in his youth, he had climbed the woody bluff, and looked abroad on prairies dotted with bison, he saw, with the dim eye of his old age, the land darkened for many a furlong with the clustered roofs of the western metropolis. For the silence of the wilderness, he heard the clang and turmoil of human labor, the din of congregated thousands; and where the great river rolled down through the forest, in lonely grandeur, he saw the waters lashed into foam beneath the prows of panting steamboats, flocking to the broad levee.[2]

---

[1] Nicollet, *Historical Sketch of St. Louis.* See *Report on the Hydrographical Basin of the Upper Mississippi River,* 75.

[2] Laclede, the founder of St. Louis, died before he had brought his grand fur-trading enterprise to a conclusion; but his young assistant lived to realize schemes still more bold and comprehensive; and to every trader, trapper, and voyageur, from the frontier of the United States to the Rocky Mountains, and from the British Possessions to the borders of New Mexico, the name of Pierre Chouteau is familiar as his own. I visited this venerable man in the spring of 1846, at his country seat, in a rural spot surrounded by woods, within a few miles of St. Louis. The building, in the picturesque architecture peculiar to the French dwellings of the Mississippi Valley, with its broad eaves and light verandas, and the surrounding negro houses filled with gay and contented inmates, was in singular harmony with the character of the patriarchal owner, who prided himself on his fidelity to the old French usages. Though in extreme old age, he still retained the vivacity of his nation. His memory, especially of the events of his youth, was clear and vivid; and he delighted to look back to the farthest extremity of the long vista of his life, and recall the acts and incidents of his earliest years. Of Pontiac, whom he had often seen, he had a clear recollection; and I am indebted to this interesting interview for several particulars regarding the chief and his coadjutors.

In the summer of 1764, the military commandant, Neyon, had abandoned the country in disgust, and gone down to New Orleans, followed by many of the inhabitants; a circumstance already mentioned. St. Ange de Bellerive remained behind to succeed him. St. Ange was a veteran Canadian officer, the same who, more than forty years before, had escorted Father Charlevoix through the country, and who is spoken of with high commendation by the Jesuit traveller and historian. He took command of about forty men, the remnant of the garrison of Fort Chartres; which, remote as it was, was then esteemed one of the best constructed military works in America. Its ramparts of stone, garnished with twenty cannon, scowled across the encroaching Mississippi, destined, before many years, to ingulf curtain and bastion in its ravenous abyss.

St. Ange's position was by no means an enviable one. He had a critical part to play. On the one hand, he had been advised of the cession to the English, and ordered to yield up the country whenever they should arrive to claim it. On the other, he was beset by embassies from Pontiac, from the Shawanoes, and from the Miamis, and plagued day and night by an importunate mob of Illinois Indians, demanding arms, ammunition, and assistance against the common enemy. Perhaps, in his secret heart, St. Ange would have rejoiced to see the scalps of all the Englishmen in the backwoods fluttering in the wind over the Illinois wigwams; but his situation forbade him to comply with the solicitations of his intrusive petitioners, and it is to be hoped that some sense of honor and humanity enforced the dictates of prudence. Accordingly, he cajoled them with flatteries and promises, and from time to time distributed a few presents to stay their importunity, still praying daily that the English might appear and relieve him from his uneasy dilemma.[1]

While Laclede was founding St. Louis, while the discontented settlers of the Illinois were deserting their homes, and while St. Ange was laboring to pacify his Indian neighbors, all the tribes from the Maumee to the Mississippi were in a turmoil of excitement. Pontiac was among them, furious as a

---

[1] MS. Letter—*St. Ange to D'Abbadie*, Sept. 9.

wild beast at bay. By the double campaign of 1764, his best hopes had been crushed to the earth; but he stood unshaken amidst the ruin, and still struggled with desperate energy to retrieve his broken cause. On the side of the northern lakes, the movements of Bradstreet had put down the insurrection of the tribes, and wrested back the military posts which cunning and treachery had placed within their grasp. In the south, Bouquet had forced to abject submission the warlike Delawares and Shawanoes, the warriors on whose courage and obstinacy Pontiac had grounded his strongest confidence. On every hand defeat and disaster were closing around him. One sanctuary alone remained, the country of the Illinois. Here the flag of France still floated on the banks of the Mississippi, and here no English foot had dared to penetrate. He resolved to invoke all his resources, and bend all his energies to defend this last citadel.[1]

He was not left to contend unaided. The fur-trading French, living at the settlements on the Mississippi, scattered about the forts of Ouatanon, Vincennes, and Miami, or domesticated among the Indians of the Rivers Illinois and Wabash, dreaded the English as dangerous competitors in their vocation, and were eager to bar them from the country. They

[1] By the following extract from an official paper, signed by Captain Grant, and forwarded from Detroit, it appears that Pontiac still retained, or professed to retain, his original designs against the garrison of Detroit. The paper has no date, but was apparently written in the autumn of 1764. By a note appended to it, we are told that the Baptiste Campau referred to was one of those who had acted as Pontiac's secretaries during the summer of 1763: —

"On Tuesday last Mr. Jadeau told me, in the presence of Col. Gladwin & Lieut. Hay of the 6th Regiment, that one Lesperance, a Frenchman, on his way to the Illinois, he saw a letter with the Ottawas, at the Miamee River, he is sure wrote by one Baptist Campau (a deserter from the settlement of Detroit), & signed by Pontiac, from the Illinois, setting forth that there were five hundred English coming to the Illinois, & that they, the Ottawas, must have patience; that he, Pontiac, was not to return until he had defeated the English, and then he would come with an army from the Illinois to take Detroit, which he desired they might publish to all the nations about. That powder & ball was in as great plenty as water. That the French Commissary La Cleff had sold above forty thousand weight of powder to the inhabitants, that the English if they came there might not have it.

"There was another letter on the subject sent to an inhabitant of Detroit, but he can't tell in whose hands it is."

lavished abuse and calumny on the objects of their jealousy, and spared no falsehood which ingenious malice and self-interest could suggest. They gave out that the English were bent on the ruin of the tribes, and to that end were stirring them up to mutual hostility. They insisted that, though the armies of France had been delayed so long, they were nevertheless on their way, and that the bayonets of the white-coated warriors would soon glitter among the forests of the Mississippi. Forged letters were sent to Pontiac, signed by the King of France, exhorting him to stand his ground but a few weeks longer, and all would then be well. To give the better coloring to their falsehoods, some of these incendiaries assumed the uniform of French officers, and palmed themselves off upon their credulous auditors as ambassadors from the king. Many of the principal traders distributed among the warriors supplies of arms and ammunition, in some instances given gratuitously, and in others sold on credit, with the understanding that payment should be made from the plunder of the English.[1]

Now that the insurrection in the east was quelled, and the Delawares and Shawanoes were beaten into submission, it was thought that the English would lose no time in taking

[1] MS. *Gage Papers*. MS. *Johnson Papers*. Croghan, *Journal*. Hildreth, *Pioneer History*, 68. *Examination of Gershom Hicks*, see *Penn. Gaz.* No. 1846.

Johnson's letters to the Board of Trade, in the early part of 1765, contain constant references to the sinister conduct of the Illinois French. The commander-in-chief is still more bitter in his invectives, and seems to think that French officers of the crown were concerned in these practices, as well as the traders. If we may judge, however, from the correspondence of St. Ange and his subordinates, they may be acquitted of the charge of any active interference in the matter.

"Sept. 14. I had a private meeting with the Grand Sauteur, when he told me he was well disposed for peace last fall, but was then sent for to the Illinois, where he met with Pondiac; and that then their fathers, the French, told them, if they would be strong, and keep the English out of the possession of that country but this summer, that the King of France would send over an army next spring, to assist his children, the Indians."—Croghan, *Journal*, 1765.

The *Diary of the Siege of Detroit*, under date May 17, 1765, says that Pontiac's nephew came that day from the Illinois, with news that Pontiac had caused six Englishmen and several disaffected Indians to be burned; and that he had seven large war-belts to raise the western tribes for another attack on Detroit, to be made in June of that year, without French assistance.

full possession of the country, which, by the peace of 1763, had been transferred into their hands. Two principal routes would give access to the Illinois. Troops might advance from the south up the great natural highway of the Mississippi, or they might descend from the east by way of Fort Pitt and the Ohio. In either case, to meet and repel them was the determined purpose of Pontiac.

In the spring, or early summer, he had come to the Illinois and visited the commandant, Neyon, who was then still at his post. Neyon's greeting was inauspicious. He told his visitor that he hoped he had returned at last to his senses. Pontiac laid before him a large belt of wampum. "My Father," he said, "I come to invite you and all your allies to go with me to war against the English." Neyon asked if he had not received his message of the last autumn, in which he told him that the French and English were thenceforth one people; but Pontiac persisted, and still urged him to take up the hatchet. Neyon at length grew angry, kicked away the wampum-belt, and demanded if he could not hear what was said to him. Thus repulsed, Pontiac asked for a keg of rum. Which being given him, he caused to be carried to a neighboring Illinois village; and, with the help of this potent auxiliary, made the assembled warriors join him in the war-song.[1]

It does not appear that, on this occasion, he had any farther success in firing the hearts of the Illinois. He presently returned to his camp on the Maumee, where, by a succession of ill-tidings, he learned the humiliation of his allies, and the triumph of his enemies. Towards the close of autumn, he again left the Maumee; and, followed by four hundred warriors, journeyed westward, to visit in succession the different tribes, and gain their co-operation in his plans of final defence. Crossing over to the Wabash, he passed from village to village, among the Kickapoos, the Piankishaws, and the three tribes of the Miamis, rousing them by his imperious eloquence, and breathing into them his own fierce spirit of resistance. Thence, by rapid marches through forests and over prairies, he reached the banks of the Mississippi, and summoned the four tribes of the Illinois to a general meeting. But

[1] *Diary of the Siege of Detroit*, under date June 9, 1764.

these degenerate savages, beaten by the surrounding tribes for many a generation past, had lost their warlike spirit; and, though abundantly noisy and boastful, showed no zeal for fight, and entered with no zest into the schemes of the Ottawa war-chief. Pontiac had his own way of dealing with such spirits. "If you hesitate," he exclaimed, frowning on the cowering assembly, "I will consume your tribes as the fire consumes the dry grass on the prairie." The doubts of the Illinois vanished like the mist, and with marvellous alacrity they declared their concurrence in the views of the orator. Having secured these allies, such as they were, Pontiac departed, and hastened to Fort Chartres. St. Ange, so long tormented with embassy after embassy, and mob after mob, thought that the crowning evil was come at last, when he saw the arch-demon Pontiac enter at the gate, with four hundred warriors at his back. Arrived at the council-house, Pontiac addressed the commandant in a tone of great courtesy: "Father, we have long wished to see you, to shake hands with you, and, whilst smoking the calumet of peace, to recall the battles in which we fought together against the misguided Indians and the English dogs. I love the French, and I have come hither with my warriors to avenge their wrongs."[1] Then followed a demand for arms, ammunition, and troops, to act in concert with the Indian warriors. St. Ange was forced to decline rendering the expected aid; but he sweetened his denial with soothing compliments, and added a few gifts, to remove any lingering bitterness. Pontiac would not be appeased. He angrily complained of such lukewarm friendship, where he had looked for ready sympathy and support. His warriors pitched their lodges about the fort, and threatening symptoms of an approaching rupture began to alarm the French.

In the mean time, Pontiac had caused his squaws to construct a belt of wampum of extraordinary size, six feet in length, and four inches wide. It was wrought from end to end with the symbols of the various tribes and villages, forty-seven in number, still leagued together in his alliance.[2] He con-

[1] Nicollet, *Report on the Basin of the Upper Mississippi*, 81. M. Nicollet's account is given on the authority of documents and oral narratives derived from Chouteau, Menard, and other patriarchs of the Illinois.

[2] MS. Letter—*St. Ange to D'Abbadie*, Sept. 9.

signed it to an embassy of chosen warriors, directing them to carry it down the Mississippi, displaying it, in turn, at every Indian village along its banks; and exhorting the inhabitants, in his name, to watch the movements of the English, and repel any attempt they might make to ascend the river. This done, they were to repair to New Orleans, and demand from the governor, M. D'Abbadie, the aid which St. Ange had refused. The bark canoes of the embassy put out from the shore, and whirled down the current like floating leaves in autumn.

Soon after their departure, tidings came to Fort Chartres, which caused a joyous excitement among the Indians, and relieved the French garrison from any danger of an immediate rupture. In our own day, the vast distance between the great city of New Orleans and the populous state of Illinois has dwindled into insignificance beneath the magic of science; but at the date of this history, three or four months were often consumed in the upward passage, and the settlers of the lonely forest colony were sometimes cut off from all communication with the world for half a year together. The above-mentioned tidings, interesting as they were, had occupied no less time in their passage. Their import was as follows:—

Very early in the preceding spring, an English officer, Major Loftus, having arrived at New Orleans with four hundred regulars, had attempted to ascend the Mississippi, to take possession of Fort Chartres and its dependent posts. His troops were embarked in large and heavy boats. Their progress was slow; and they had reached a point not more than eighty leagues above New Orleans, when, one morning, their ears were greeted with the crack of rifles from the thickets of the western shore; and a soldier in the foremost boat fell, with a mortal wound. The troops, in dismay, sheered over towards the eastern shore; but, when fairly within gunshot, a score of rifles obscured the forest edge with smoke, and filled the nearest boat with dead and wounded men. On this, they steered for the middle of the river, where they remained for a time, exposed to a dropping fire from either bank, too distant to take effect.

The river was high, and the shores so flooded, that nothing but an Indian could hope to find foothold in the miry labyrinth. Loftus was terrified; the troops were discouraged, and a council of officers determined that to advance was impossible. Accordingly, with their best despatch, they steered back for New Orleans, where they arrived without farther accident; and where the French, in great glee at their discomfiture, spared no ridicule at their expense. They alleged, and with much appearance of truth, that the English had been repulsed by no more than thirty warriors. Loftus charged D'Abbadie with having occasioned his disaster by stirring up the Indians to attack him. The governor called Heaven to witness his innocence; and, in truth, there is not the smallest reason to believe him guilty of such villany.[1] Loftus, who had not yet recovered from his fears, conceived an idea that the Indians below New Orleans were preparing an ambuscade to attack him on his way back to his station at Pensacola; and he petitioned D'Abbadie to interfere in his behalf. The latter, with an ill-dissembled sneer, offered to give him and his troops an escort of French soldiers to protect them. Loftus rejected the humiliating proposal, and declared that he only wished for a French interpreter, to confer with any Indians whom he might meet by the way. The interpreter was furnished; and Loftus returned in safety to Pensacola, his detachment not a little reduced by the few whom the Indians had shot, and by numbers who, disgusted by his overbearing treatment, had deserted to the French.[2]

The futile attempt of Loftus to ascend the Mississippi was followed, a few months after, by another equally abortive.

---

[1] D'Abbadie's correspondence with St. Ange goes far to exonerate him; and there is a letter addressed to him from General Gage, in which the latter thanks him very cordially for the efforts he had made in behalf of Major Loftus, aiding him to procure boats and guides, and make other preparations for ascending the river.

The correspondence alluded to forms part of a collection of papers preserved in the archives of the Department of the Marine and Colonies at Paris. These papers include the reports of various councils with the Indian tribes of the Illinois, and the whole official correspondence of the French officers in that region during the years 1763–5. They form the principal authorities for this part of the narrative, and throw great light on the character of the Indian war, from its commencement to its close.

[2] *London Mag.* XXXIII. 380. MS. *Detail de ce qui s'est passé à La Louisiane à l'occasion de la prise de possession des Illinois.*

Captain Pittman came to New Orleans with the design of proceeding to the Illinois, but was deterred by the reports which reached him concerning the temper of the Indians. The latter, elated beyond measure by their success against Loftus, and excited, moreover, by the messages and war-belt of Pontiac, were in a state of angry commotion, which made the passage too hazardous to be attempted. Pittman bethought himself of assuming the disguise of a Frenchman, joining a party of Creole traders, and thus reaching his destination by stealth; but, weighing the risk of detection, he abandoned this design also, and returned to Mobile.[1] Between the Illinois and the settlements around New Orleans, the Mississippi extended its enormous length through solitudes of marsh and forest, broken here and there by a squalid Indian village; or, at vast intervals, by one or two military posts, erected by the French, and forming the resting-places of the voyager. After the failure of Pittman, more than a year elapsed before an English detachment could succeed in passing this great thoroughfare of the wilderness, and running the gauntlet of the savage tribes who guarded its shores. It was not till the second of December, 1765, that Major Farmar, at the head of a strong body of troops, arrived, after an uninterrupted voyage, at Fort Chartres, where the flag of his country had already supplanted the standard of France.[2]

To return to our immediate theme. The ambassadors, whom Pontiac had sent from Fort Chartres in the autumn of 1764, faithfully acquitted themselves of their trust. They visited the Indian villages along the river banks, kindling the thirst for blood and massacre in the breasts of the inmates. They pushed their sanguinary mission even to the farthest tribes of Southern Louisiana, to whom the great name of Pontiac had long been known, and of late made familiar by repeated messages and embassies.[3] This portion of their task accomplished, they repaired to New Orleans, and demanded an audience of the governor.

[1]MS. *Correspondence of Pittman with M. D'Abbadie*, among the Paris Documents.

[2]MS. Letter—*Campbell to Gage*, Feb. 24, 1766.

[3]By the correspondence between the French officers of Upper and Lower Louisiana, it appears that Pontiac's messengers, in several instances, had

New Orleans was then a town of about seven thousand white inhabitants, guarded from the river floods by a levee extending for fifty miles along the banks. The small brick houses, one story in height, were arranged with geometrical symmetry, like the squares of a chess-board. Each house had its yard and garden, and the town was enlivened with the verdure of trees and grass. In front, a public square, or parade ground, opened upon the river, enclosed on three sides by the dilapidated church of St. Louis, a prison, a convent, government buildings, and a range of barracks. The place was surrounded by a defence of palisades strong enough to repel an attack of Indians, or insurgent slaves.[1]

When Pontiac's ambassadors entered New Orleans, they found the town in a state of confusion. It had long been known that the regions east of the Mississippi had been surrendered to England; a cession from which, however, New Orleans and its suburbs had been excepted by a special provision. But it was only within a few weeks that the dismayed inhabitants had learned that their mother country had transferred her remaining American possessions to the crown of Spain, whose government and people they cordially detested. With every day they might expect the arrival of a Spanish governor and garrison. The French officials, whose hour was drawing to its close, were making the best of their short-lived authority by every species of corruption and peculation; and the inhabitants were awaiting, in anger and repugnance, the approaching change, which was to place over their heads masters whom they hated. The governor, D'Abbadie, an ardent soldier and a zealous patriot, was so deeply chagrined at what he conceived to be the disgrace of his country, that his feeble health gave way, and he betrayed all the symptoms of a rapid decline.

Haggard with illness, and bowed down with shame, the

---

arrived in the vicinity of New Orleans, whither they had come, partly to beg for aid from the French, and partly to urge the Indians of the adjacent country to bar the mouth of the Mississippi against the English.

[1] Pittman, *European Settlements on the Mississippi*, 10. The author of this book is the officer mentioned in the text as having made an unsuccessful attempt to reach the Illinois.

dying governor received the Indian envoys in the council-hall of the province, where he was never again to assume his seat of office. Besides the French officials in attendance, several English officers, who chanced to be in the town, had been invited to the meeting, with the view of soothing the jealousy with which they regarded all intercourse between the French and the Indians. A Shawanoe chief, the orator of the embassy, displayed the great war-belt, and opened the council. "These red dogs," he said, alluding to the color of the British uniform, "have crowded upon us more and more; and when we ask them by what right they come, they tell us that you, our French fathers, have given them our lands. We know that they lie. These lands are neither yours nor theirs, and no man shall give or sell them without our consent. Fathers, we have always been your faithful children; and we now have come to ask that you will give us guns, powder, and lead, to aid us in this war."

D'Abbadie replied in a feeble voice, endeavoring to allay their vindictive jealousy of the English, and promising to give them all that should be necessary to supply their immediate wants. The council then adjourned until the following day; but, in the mean time, the wasted strength of the governor gave way beneath a renewed attack of his disorder; and, before the appointed hour arrived, he had breathed his last, hurried to a premature death by the anguish of mortified pride and patriotism. M. Aubry, his successor, presided in his place, and received the savage embassy. The orator, after the solemn custom of his people, addressed him in a speech of condolence, expressing his deep regret for D'Abbadie's untimely fate.[1] A chief of the Miamis then rose to speak, with a scowling brow, and words of bitterness and reproach. "Since we last sat on these seats, our ears have heard strange words. When the English told us that they had conquered you, we always thought that they lied; but now we have learned that they spoke the truth. We have learned that you, whom we

---

[1] At all friendly meetings with Indians, it was customary for the latter, when the other party had sustained any signal loss, to commence by a formal speech of condolence, offering, at the same time, a black belt of wampum, in token of mourning. This practice may be particularly observed in the records of early councils with the Iroquois.

have loved and served so well, have given the lands that we
dwell upon to your enemies and ours. We have learned that
the English have forbidden you to send traders to our villages
to supply our wants; and that you, whom we thought so
great and brave, have obeyed their commands like women,
leaving us to starve and die in misery. We now tell you, once
for all, that our lands are our own; and we tell you, moreover,
that we can live without your aid, and hunt, and fish, and
fight, as our fathers did before us. All that we ask of you is
this: that you give us back the guns, the powder, the hatchets,
and the knives which we have worn out in fighting your battles. As for you," he exclaimed, turning to the English officers, who were present as on the preceding day,—"as for
you, our hearts burn with rage when we think of the ruin you
have brought on us." Aubry returned but a weak answer to
the cutting attack of the Indian speaker. He assured the ambassadors that the French still retained their former love for
the Indians, that the English meant them no harm, and that,
as all the world were now at peace, it behooved them also to
take hold of the chain of friendship. A few presents were then
distributed, but with no apparent effect. The features of the
Indians still retained their sullen scowl; and on the morrow
their canoes were ascending the Mississippi on their homeward voyage.[1]

[1]MS. *Report of Conference with the Shawanoe and Miami delegates from Pontiac, held at New Orleans*, March, 1765. Paris Documents.

Chapter XXX.

1765.

RUIN OF THE INDIAN CAUSE.

THE REPULSE of Loftus, and rumors of the fierce temper of the Indians who guarded the Mississippi, convinced the commander-in-chief that to reach the Illinois by the southern route was an enterprise of no easy accomplishment. Yet, at the same time, he felt the strong necessity of a speedy military occupation of the country; since, while the *fleur de lis* floated over a single garrison in the ceded territory, it would be impossible to disabuse the Indians of the phantom hope of French assistance, to which they clung with infatuated tenacity. The embers of the Indian war would never be quenched until England had enforced all her claims over her defeated rival. Gage determined to despatch a force from the eastward, by way of Fort Pitt and the Ohio; a route now laid open by the late success of Bouquet, and the submission of the Delawares and Shawanoes.

To prepare a way for the passage of the troops, Sir William Johnson's deputy, George Croghan, was ordered to proceed in advance, to reason with the Indians as far as they were capable of reasoning; to soften their antipathy to the English, to expose the falsehoods of the French, and to distribute presents among the tribes by way of propitiation.[1] The mission was a critical one; but, so far as regarded the Indians, Croghan was well fitted to discharge it. He had been for years a trader among the western tribes, over whom he had gained much influence by a certain vigor of character, joined to a wary and sagacious policy, concealed beneath a bluff demeanor. Lieutenant Fraser, a young officer of education and intelligence, was associated with him. He spoke French, and, in other respects also, supplied qualifications in which his rugged colleague was wanting. They set out for Fort Pitt in February, 1765; and after traversing inhospitable mountains, and valleys clogged with snow, reached their destination at about

[1] MS. *Gage Papers*.

the same time that Pontiac's ambassadors were entering New Orleans, to hold their council with the French.

A few days later, an incident occurred, which afterwards, through the carousals of many a winter evening, supplied an absorbing topic of anecdote and boast to the braggadocio heroes of the border. A train of pack-horses, bearing the gifts which Croghan was to bestow upon the Indians, followed him towards Fort Pitt, a few days' journey in the rear of his party. Under the same escort came several companies of traders, who, believing that the long suspended commerce with the Indians was about to be reopened, were hastening to Fort Pitt with a great quantity of goods, eager to throw them into the market the moment the prohibition should be removed. There is reason to believe that Croghan had an interest in these goods, and that, under pretence of giving presents, he meant to open a clandestine trade.[1] The Paxton men, and their kindred spirits of the border, saw the proceeding with sinister eyes. In their view, the traders were about to make a barter of the blood of the people; to place in the hands of murdering savages the means of renewing the devastation to which the reeking frontier bore frightful witness. Once possessed with this idea, they troubled themselves with no more inquiries; and, having tried remonstrances in vain, they adopted a summary mode of doing themselves justice. At the head of the enterprise was a man whose name had been connected with more praiseworthy exploits, James Smith, already mentioned as leading a party of independent riflemen, for the defence of the borders, during the bloody autumn of 1763. He now mustered his old associates, made them resume their Indian disguise, and led them to their work with characteristic energy and address.

The government agents and traders were in the act of passing the verge of the frontiers. Their united trains amounted to seventy pack-horses, carrying goods to the value of more than four thousand pounds; while others, to the

[1]"The country people appear greatly incensed at the attempt they imagine has been made of opening a clandestine trade with the Savages under cover of presents; and, if it is not indiscreet in me, I would beg leave to ask whether Croghan had such extensive orders."—*Bouquet to Amherst*, 10 April, 1765, MS.

value of eleven thousand, were waiting transportation at Fort Loudon. Advancing deeper among the mountains, they began to descend the valley at the foot of Sidling Hill. The laden horses plodded knee-deep in snow. The mountains towered above the wayfarers in gray desolation; and the leaf-less forest, a mighty Æolian harp, howled dreary music to the wind of March. Suddenly, from behind snow-beplastered trunks and shaggy bushes of evergreen, uncouth apparitions started into view. Wild visages protruded, grotesquely horri-ble with vermilion and ochre, white lead and soot; stalwart limbs appeared, encased in buckskin; and rusty rifles thrust out their long muzzles. In front, and flank, and all around them, white puffs of smoke and sharp reports assailed the bewildered senses of the travellers, who were yet more confounded by the hum of bullets shot by unerring fingers within an inch of their ears. "Gentlemen," demanded the traders, in deprecating accents, "what would you have us do?" "Unpack your horses," roared a voice from the woods, "pile your goods in the road, and be off." The traders knew those with whom they had to deal. Hastening to obey the mandate, they departed with their utmost speed, happy that their scalps were not numbered with the booty. The spoilers appropriated to themselves such of the plunder as pleased them, made a bonfire of the rest, and went on their way rejoicing. The discomfited traders repaired to Fort Loudon, and laid their complaints before Lieutenant Grant, the com-mandant; who, inflamed with wrath and zealous for the cause of justice, despatched a party of soldiers, seized several innocent persons, and lodged them in the guard-house.[1] In high dudgeon at such an infraction of their liberties, the borderers sent messengers through the country, calling upon all good men to rise in arms. Three hundred obeyed the summons, and pitched their camp on a hill opposite Fort Loudon; a rare muster of desperadoes, yet observing a certain moderation in their wildest acts, and never at a loss for a plausible reason to justify any pranks which it might please them to exhibit. By some means, they contrived to waylay

---

[1] Before me is a curious letter from Grant, in which he expatiates on his troubles in language which is far from giving a flattering impression of the literary accomplishments of officers of the 42d Highlanders, at that time.

and capture a considerable number of the garrison, on which the commandant condescended to send them a flag of truce, and offer an exchange of prisoners. Their object thus accomplished, and their imprisoned comrades restored to them, the borderers dispersed for the present to their homes. Soon after, however, upon the occurrence of some fresh difficulty, the commandant, afraid or unable to apprehend the misdoers, endeavored to deprive them of the power of mischief by sending soldiers to their houses and carrying off their rifles. His triumph was short; for, as he rode out one afternoon, he fell into an ambuscade of countrymen, who, dispensing with all forms of respect, seized the incensed officer, and detained him in an uncomfortable captivity until the rifles were restored. From this time forward, ruptures were repeatedly occurring between the troops and the frontiersmen; and the Pennsylvania border retained its turbulent character until the outbreak of the Revolutionary War.[1]

[1]The account of the seizure of the Indian goods is derived chiefly from the narrative of the ringleader, Smith, published in Drake's *Tragedies of the Wilderness*, and elsewhere. The correspondence of Gage and Johnson is filled with allusions to this affair, and the subsequent proceedings of the freebooters. Gage spares no invectives against what he calls the licentious conduct of the frontier people. In the narrative is inserted a ballad, or lyrical effusion, written by some partisan of the frontier faction, and evidently regarded by Smith as a signal triumph of the poetic art. He is careful to inform the reader that the author received his education in the great city of Dublin. The following melodious stanzas embody the chief action of the piece:—

> "Astonished at the wild design,
>   Frontier inhabitants combin'd
>   With brave souls to stop their career;
>   Although some men apostatiz'd,
>   Who first the grand attempt advis'd,
>   The bold frontiers they bravely stood,
>   To act for their king and their country's good,
>   In joint league, and strangers to fear.

> "On March the fifth, in sixty-five,
>   The Indian presents did arrive,
>   In long pomp and cavalcade,
>   Near Sidelong Hill, where in disguise
>   Some patriots did their train surprise,
>   And quick as lightning tumbled their loads,
>   And kindled them bonfires in the woods,
>   And mostly burnt their whole brigade."

Whatever may have been Croghan's real attitude in this affair, the border robbers had wrought great injury to his mission; since the agency most potent to gain the affections of an Indian had been completely paralyzed in the destruction of the presents. Croghan found means, however, partially to repair his loss from the storehouse of Fort Pitt, where the rigor of the season and the great depth of the snow forced him to remain several weeks. This cause alone would have served to detain him; but he was yet farther retarded by the necessity of holding a meeting with the Delawares and Shawanoes, along whose southern borders he would be compelled to pass. An important object of the proposed meeting was to urge these tribes to fulfil the promise they had made, during the previous autumn, to Colonel Bouquet, to yield up their remaining prisoners, and send deputies to treat of peace with Sir

---

The following is an extract from Johnson's letter to the Board of Trade, dated July 10, 1765: —

"I have great cause to think that Mr. Croghan will succeed in his enterprise, unless circumvented by the artifices of the French, or through the late licentious conduct of our own people. Although His Excellency General Gage has written to the Ministry on that subject, yet I think I should not be silent thereupon, as it may be productive of very serious consequences.

"The frontier inhabitants of Pennsylvania, Maryland, and Virginia, after having attacked and destroyed the goods which were going to Fort Pitt (as in my last), did form themselves into parties, threatening to destroy all Indians they met, or all white people who dealt with them. They likewise marched to Fort Augusta, and from thence over the West branch of the Susquehanna, beyond the Bounds of the last purchase made by the Proprietaries, where they declare they will form a settlement, in defiance of Whites or Indians. They afterwards attacked a small party of His Majesty's troops upon the Road, but were happily obliged to retire with the loss of one or two men. However, from their conduct and threats since, there is reason to think they will not stop here. Neither is their licentiousness confined to the Provinces I have mentioned, the people of Carolina having cut off a party, coming down under a pass from Col. Lewis, of the particulars of which your Lordships have been doubtless informed.

"Your Lordships may easily conceive what effects this will have upon the Indians, who begin to be all acquainted therewith. I wish it may not have already gone too great a length to receive a timely check, or prevent the Indians' Resentment, who see themselves attacked, threatened, and their property invaded, by a set of ignorant, misled Rioters, who defy Government itself, and this at a time when we have just treated with some, and are in treaty with other Nations."

William Johnson; engagements which, when Croghan arrived at the fort, were as yet unfulfilled, though, as already mentioned, they were soon after complied with.

Immediately on his arrival, he had despatched messengers inviting the chiefs to a council; a summons which they obeyed with their usual reluctance and delay, dropping in, band after band, with such tardiness that a month was consumed before a sufficient number were assembled. Croghan then addressed them, showing the advantages of peace, and the peril which they would bring on their own heads by a renewal of the war; and urging them to stand true to their engagements, and send their deputies to Johnson as soon as the melting of the snows should leave the forest pathways open. Several replies, all of a pacific nature, were made by the principal chiefs; but the most remarkable personage who appeared at the council was the Delaware prophet mentioned in an early portion of the narrative, as having been strongly instrumental in urging the tribes to war by means of pretended or imaginary revelations from the Great Spirit.[1] He now delivered a speech by no means remarkable for eloquence, yet of most beneficial consequence; for he intimated that the Great Spirit had not only revoked his sanguinary mandates, but had commanded the Indians to lay down the hatchet, and smoke the pipe of peace.[2] In spite of this auspicious declaration, and in spite of the chastisement and humiliation of the previous autumn, Croghan was privately informed that a large party among the Indians still remained balanced between their anger and their fears; eager to take up the hatchet, yet dreading the consequences which the act might bring. Under this cloudy aspect of affairs, he was doubly gratified when a party of Shawanoe warriors arrived, bringing with them the prisoners whom they had promised Colonel Bouquet to surrender; and this faithful adherence to their word, contrary alike to Croghan's expectations, and to the prophecies of those best versed in Indian character, made it apparent that, whatever

[1] See *ante*, Vol. I. p. 480.

[2] MS. *Journal of the Transactions of George Croghan, Esq., deputy agent for Indian affairs, with different tribes of Indians, at Fort Pitt, from the 28th of February, 1765, to the 12th of May following*. In this journal the prophet's speech is given in full.

might be the sentiments of the turbulent among them, the more influential portion were determined on a pacific attitude.

These councils, and the previous delays, consumed so much time, that Croghan became fearful that the tribes of the Illinois might, meanwhile, commit themselves by some rash outbreak, which would increase the difficulty of reconciliation. In view of this danger, his colleague, Lieutenant Fraser, volunteered to proceed in advance, leaving Croghan to follow when he had settled affairs at Fort Pitt. Fraser departed, accordingly, with a few attendants. The rigor of the season had now begun to relent, and the ice-locked Ohio was flinging off its wintry fetters. Embarked in a birch canoe, and aided by the current, Fraser floated prosperously downwards for a thousand miles, and landed safely in the country of the Illinois. Here he found the Indians in great destitution, and in a frame of mind which would have inclined them to peace but for the secret encouragement they received from the French. A change, however, soon took place. Boats arrived from New Orleans, loaded with a great quantity of goods, which the French, at that place, being about to abandon it, had sent in haste to the Illinois. The traders' shops at Kaskaskia were suddenly filled again. The Indians were delighted; and the French, with a view to a prompt market for their guns, hatchets, and gunpowder, redoubled their incitements to war. Fraser found himself in a hornet's nest. His life was in great danger; but Pontiac, who was then at Kaskaskia, several times interposed to save him. The French traders picked a quarrel with him, and instigated the Indians to kill him; for it was their interest that the war should go on. A party of them invited Pontiac to dinner; plied him with whiskey; and, having made him drunk, incited him to have Fraser and his servant seized. They were brought to the house where the debauch was going on; and here, among a crowd of drunken Indians, their lives hung by a hair. Fraser writes, "He (Pontiac) and his men fought all night about us. They said we would get off next day if they should not prevent our flight by killing us. This Pontiac would not do. All night they did nothing else but sing the death song; but my servant and I, with the help of an Indian who was sober, defended ourselves till morning, when they thought proper to let us escape. When Pontiac was sober, he made me an apology for his behavior; and told me it was owing to bad counsel he had got that he had taken me; but that I need not fear being taken in that manner for the future."[1]

Fraser's situation was presently somewhat improved by a rumor that an English detachment was about to descend the Ohio. The French traders, before so busy with their falsehoods and calumnies, now held their peace, dreading the impending chastisement. They no longer gave arms and ammunition to the Indians; and when the latter questioned them concerning the fabrication of a French army advancing to the rescue, they treated the story as unfounded, or sought to evade the subject. St. Ange, too, and the other officers of the crown, confiding in the arrival of the English, assumed a more decisive tone; refusing to give the Indians presents, telling them that thenceforward they must trust to the English for supplies, reproving them for their designs against the latter, and advising them to remain at peace.[2]

Nevertheless, Fraser's position was neither safe nor pleasant. He could hear nothing of Croghan, and he was almost alone, having sent away all his men; except his servant, to save them from being abused and beaten by the Indians. He had discretionary orders to go down to Mobile and report to the English commandant there; and of these he was but too glad to avail himself. He descended the Mississippi in disguise, and safely reached New Orleans.[3]

[1] MS. Letter—*Fraser to Lieut. Col. Campbell*, 20 May, 1765.

[2] *Harangue faitte à la nation Illinoise et au Chef Pondiak par M. de St. Ange, Cap. Commandant au pais des Illinois pour S. M. T. C. au sujet de la guerre que Les Indiens font aux Anglois.*

[3] MS. Letter—*Aubry to the Minister*, July, 1765. Aubry makes himself merry with the fears of Fraser; who, however, had the best grounds for his apprehensions, as is sufficiently clear from the above as well as from the minutes of a council held by him with Pontiac and other Indians at the Illinois, during the month of April. The minutes referred to are among the Paris Documents.

Pontiac's first reception of Fraser was not auspicious, as appears from the following. Extract from a Letter—*Fort Pitt*, July 24 (*Pa. Gaz. Nos.* 1912, 1913):—

"Pondiac immediately collected all the Indians under his influence to the Illinois, and ordered the French commanding officer there to deliver up these Englishmen [Fraser and his party] to him, as he had prepared a large kettle in

Apparently, it was about this time that an incident took place, mentioned, with evident satisfaction, in a letter of the French commandant, Aubry. The English officers in the south, unable to send troops up the Mississippi, had employed a Frenchman, whom they had secured in their interest, to ascend the river with a boat-load of goods, which he was directed to distribute among the Indians, to remove their prejudice against the English and pave the way to reconciliation. Intelligence of this movement reached the ears of Pontiac, who, though much pleased with the approaching supplies, had no mind that they should be devoted to serve the interests of his enemies. He descended to the river bank with a body of his warriors; and as La Garantais, the Frenchman, landed, he seized him and his men, flogged them severely, robbed them of their cargo, and distributed the goods with exemplary impartiality among his delighted followers.[1]

Notwithstanding this good fortune, Pontiac daily saw his followers dropping off from their allegiance; for even the boldest had lost heart. Had any thing been wanting to convince him of the hopelessness of his cause, the report of his ambassadors returning from New Orleans would have banished every doubt. No record of his interview with them remains; but it is easy to conceive with what chagrin he must have learned that the officer of France first in rank in all America had refused to aid him, and urged the timid counsels of peace. The vanity of those expectations, which had been the mainspring of his enterprise, now rose clear and palpable before him; and, with rage and bitterness, he saw the rotten foundation of his hopes sinking into dust, and the whole structure of his plot crumbling in ruins about him.

All was lost. His allies were falling off, his followers de-

---

which he was determined to boil them and all other Englishmen that came that way. . . . Pondiac told the French that he had been informed of Mr. Croghan's coming that way to treat with the Indians, and that he would keep his kettle boiling over a large fire to receive him likewise."

Pontiac soon after relented as we have seen. Another letter, dated New Orleans, June 19, adds: "He [Fraser] says a Pondiac is a very clever fellow, and had it not been for him, he would never have got away alive."

[1]MS. Letter—*Aubry to the Minister*, 10 July, 1765.

serting him. To hold out longer would be destruction, and to fly was scarcely an easier task. In the south lay the Cherokees, hereditary enemies of his people. In the west were the Osages and Missouries, treacherous and uncertain friends, and the fierce and jealous Dahcotah. In the east the forests would soon be filled with English traders, and beset with English troops; while in the north his own village of Detroit lay beneath the guns of the victorious garrison. He might, indeed, have found a partial refuge in the remoter wilderness of the upper lakes; but those dreary wastes would have doomed him to a life of unambitious exile. His resolution was taken. He determined to accept the peace which he knew would be proffered, to smoke the calumet with his triumphant enemies, and patiently await his hour of vengeance.[1]

The conferences at Fort Pitt concluded, Croghan left that place on the fifteenth of May, and embarked on the Ohio, accompanied by several Delaware and Shawanoe deputies, whom he had persuaded those newly reconciled tribes to send with him, for the furtherance of his mission. At the mouth of the Scioto, he was met by a band of Shawanoe warriors, who, in compliance with a message previously sent to them, delivered into his hands seven intriguing Frenchmen, who for some time past had lived in their villages. Thence he pursued his voyage smoothly and prosperously, until, on the eighth of June, he reached a spot a little below the mouth of the Wabash. Here he landed with his party; when suddenly the hideous war-whoop, the explosion of musketry, and the whistling of arrows greeted him from the covert of the neighboring thickets. His men fell thick about him. Three Indians and two white men were shot dead on the spot; most of the remainder were wounded; and on the next instant the survivors found themselves prisoners in the hands of eighty yelling Kickapoos, who plundered them of all they had. No sooner, however, was their prey fairly within their clutches, than the cowardly assailants began to apologize for what they had done, saying it was all a mistake, and that the French had set them on by telling them that the Indians who accom-

---

[1] One of St. Ange's letters to Aubry contains views of the designs and motives of Pontiac similar to those expressed above.

panied Croghan were Cherokees, their mortal enemies; excuses utterly without foundation, for the Kickapoos had dogged the party for several days, and perfectly understood its character.[1]

It is superfluous to inquire into the causes of this attack. No man practically familiar with Indian character need be told the impossibility of foreseeing to what strange acts the wayward impulses of this murder-loving race may prompt them. Unstable as water, capricious as the winds, they seem in some of their moods like ungoverned children fired with the instincts of devils. In the present case, they knew that they hated the English,—knew that they wanted scalps; and thinking nothing of the consequences, they seized the first opportunity to gratify their rabid longing. This done, they thought it best to avert any probable effects of their misconduct by such falsehoods as might suggest themselves to their invention.

Still apologizing for what they had done, but by no means suffering their prisoners to escape, they proceeded up the Wabash, to the little French fort and settlement of Vincennes, where, to his great joy, Croghan found among the assembled Indians some of his former friends and acquaintance. They received him kindly, and sharply rebuked the Kickapoos, who, on their part, seemed much ashamed and crestfallen. From Vincennes the English were conducted, in a sort of honorable captivity, up the river to Ouatanon, where they arrived on the twenty-third, fifteen days after the attack, and where Croghan was fortunate enough to find a great number of his former Indian friends, who received him, to appearance at least, with much cordiality. He took up his quarters in the fort, where there was at this time no garrison, a mob of French traders and Indians being the only tenants of the place. For several days, his time was engrossed with receiving deputation after deputation from the various tribes and subtribes of the neighborhood, smoking pipes of peace, making

[1] A few days before, a boy belonging to Croghan's party had been lost, as was supposed, in the woods. It proved afterwards that he had been seized by the Kickapoo warriors, and was still prisoner among them at the time of the attack. They must have learned from him the true character of Croghan and his companions.—MS. *Gage Papers.*

and hearing speeches, and shaking hands with greasy warriors, who, one and all, were strong in their professions of good-will, promising not only to regard the English as their friends, but to aid them, if necessary, in taking possession of the Illinois.

While these amicable conferences were in progress, a miscreant Frenchman came from the Mississippi with a message from a chief of that region, urging the Indians of Ouatanon to burn the Englishman alive. Of this proposal the Indians signified their strong disapprobation, and assured the startled envoy that they would stand his friends,—professions the sincerity of which, happily for him, was confirmed by the strong guaranty of their fears.

The next arrival was that of Maisonville, a messenger from St. Ange, requesting Croghan to come to Fort Chartres, to adjust affairs in that quarter. The invitation was in accordance with Croghan's designs; and he left the fort on the following day, attended by Maisonville, and a concourse of the Ouatanon Indians, who, far from regarding him as their prisoner, were now studious to show him every mark of respect. He had advanced but a short distance into the forest when he met Pontiac himself, who was on his way to Ouatanon, followed by a numerous train of chiefs and warriors. He gave his hand to the English envoy, and both parties returned together to the fort. Its narrow precincts were now crowded with Indians, a perilous multitude, dark, malignant, inscrutable; and it behooved the Englishman to be wary, in his dealings with them, since a breath might kindle afresh the wildfire in their hearts.

At a meeting of the chiefs and warriors, Pontiac offered the calumet and belt of peace, and professed his concurrence with the chiefs of Ouatanon in the friendly sentiments which they expressed towards the English. The French, he added, had deceived him, telling him and his people that the English meant to enslave the Indians of the Illinois, and turn loose upon them their enemies the Cherokees. It was this which drove him to arms; and now that he knew the story to be false, he would no longer stand in the path of the English. Yet they must not imagine that, in taking possession of the French forts, they gained any right to the country; for the

French had never bought the land, and lived upon it by sufferance only.

As this meeting with Pontiac and the Illinois chiefs made it needless for Croghan to advance farther on his western journey, he now bent his footsteps towards Detroit, and, followed by Pontiac and many of the principal chiefs, crossed over to Fort Miami, and thence descended the Maumee, holding conferences at the several villages which he passed on his way. On the seventeenth of August, he reached Detroit, where he found a great gathering of Indians, Ottawas, Pottawattamies, and Ojibwas; some encamped about the fort, and others along the banks of the River Rouge. They obeyed his summons to a meeting with alacrity, partly from a desire to win the good graces of a victorious enemy, and partly from the importunate craving for liquor and presents, which never slumbers in an Indian breast. Numerous meetings were held; and the old council-hall where Pontiac had essayed his scheme of abortive treachery was now crowded with repentant warriors, anxious, by every form of submission, to appease the conqueror. Their ill success, their fears of chastisement, and the miseries they had endured from the long suspension of the fur-trade, had banished from their minds every thought of hostility. They were glad, they said, that the dark clouds were now dispersing, and the sunshine of peace once more returning; and since all the nations to the sunrising had taken their great father the King of England by the hand, they also wished to do the same. They now saw clearly that the French were indeed conquered; and thenceforth they would listen no more to the whistling of evil birds, but lay down the warhatchet, and sit quiet on their mats. Among those who appeared to make or renew their submission was the Grand Sauteur, who had led the massacre at Michillimackinac, and who, a few years after, expiated his evil deeds by a bloody death. He now pretended great regret for what he had done. "We red people," he said, "are a very jealous and foolish people; but, father, there are some among the white men worse than we are, and they have told us lies, and deceived us. Therefore we hope you will take pity on our women and children, and grant us peace." A band of Pottawattamies from St. Joseph's were also present, and, after excusing themselves for their past conduct by the stale plea of the uncontrollable temper of their young men, their orator proceeded as follows:—

"We are no more than wild creatures to you, fathers, in understanding; therefore we request you to forgive the past follies of our young people, and receive us for your children. Since you have thrown down our former father on his back, we have been wandering in the dark, like blind people. Now you have dispersed all this darkness, which hung over the heads of the several tribes, and have accepted them for your children, we hope you will let us partake with them the light, that our women and children may enjoy peace. We beg you to forget all that is past. By this belt we remove all evil thoughts from your hearts.

"Fathers, when we formerly came to visit our fathers the French, they always sent us home joyful; and we hope you, fathers, will have pity on our women and young men, who are in great want of necessaries, and not let us go home to our towns ashamed."

On the twenty-seventh of August, Croghan held a meeting with the Ottawas, and the other tribes of Detroit and Sandusky; when, adopting their own figurative language, he addressed them in the following speech, in which, as often happened when white men borrowed the tongue of the forest orator, he lavished a more unsparing profusion of imagery than the Indians themselves:—

"Children, we are very glad to see so many of you here present at your ancient council-fire, which has been neglected for some time past; since then, high winds have blown, and raised heavy clouds over your country. I now, by this belt, rekindle your ancient fire, and throw dry wood upon it, that the blaze may ascend to heaven, so that all nations may see it, and know that you live in peace and tranquillity with your fathers the English.

"By this belt I disperse all the black clouds from over your heads, that the sun may shine clear on your women and children, that those unborn may enjoy the blessings of this general peace, now so happily settled between your fathers the English and you, and all your younger brethren to the sun-setting.

"Children, by this belt I gather up all the bones of your

deceased friends, and bury them deep in the ground, that the buds and sweet flowers of the earth may grow over them, that we may not see them any more.

"Children, with this belt I take the hatchet out of your hands, and pluck up a large tree, and bury it deep, so that it may never be found any more; and I plant the tree of peace, which all our children may sit under, and smoke in peace with their fathers.

"Children, we have made a road from the sunrising to the sunsetting. I desire that you will preserve that road good and pleasant to travel upon, that we may all share the blessings of this happy union."

On the following day, Pontiac spoke in behalf of the several nations assembled at the council.

"Father, we have all smoked out of this pipe of peace. It is your children's pipe; and as the war is all over, and the Great Spirit and Giver of Light, who has made the earth and every thing therein, has brought us all together this day for our mutual good, I declare to all nations that I have settled my peace with you before I came here, and now deliver my pipe to be sent to Sir William Johnson, that he may know I have made peace, and taken the King of England for my father, in presence of all the nations now assembled; and whenever any of those nations go to visit him, they may smoke out of it with him in peace. Fathers, we are obliged to you for lighting up our old council-fire for us, and desiring us to return to it; but we are now settled on the Miami River, not far from hence: whenever you want us, you will find us there."[1]

---

[1] *Journal of George Croghan, on his journey to the Illinois*, 1765. This journal has been twice published—in the appendix to Butler's *History of Kentucky*, and in the *Pioneer History* of Dr. Hildreth. A manuscript copy also may be found in the office of the secretary of state at Albany. Dr. Hildreth omits the speech of Croghan to the Indians, which is given above as affording a better example of the forms of speech appropriate to an Indian peace harangue, than the genuine productions of the Indians themselves, who are less apt to indulge in such a redundancy of metaphor.

A language extremely deficient in words of general and abstract signification renders the use of figures indispensable; and it is from this cause, above all others, that the flowers of Indian rhetoric derive their origin. In the work of Heckewelder will be found a list of numerous figurative expressions appropriate to the various occasions of public and private intercourse,—forms

"Our people," he added, "love liquor, and if we dwelt near you in our old village of Detroit, our warriors would be always drunk, and quarrels would arise between us and you." Drunkenness was, in truth, the bane of the whole unhappy race; but Pontiac, too thoroughly an Indian in his virtues and his vices to be free from its destructive taint, concluded his speech with the common termination of an Indian harangue, and desired that the rum barrel might be opened, and his thirsty warriors allowed to drink.

At the end of September, having brought these protracted conferences to a close, Croghan left Detroit, and departed for Niagara, whence, after a short delay, he passed eastward, to report the results of his mission to the commander-in-chief. But before leaving the Indian country, he exacted from Pontiac a promise that in the spring he would descend to Oswego, and, in behalf of the tribes lately banded in his league, conclude a treaty of peace and amity with Sir William Johnson.[1]

Croghan's efforts had been attended with signal success. The tribes of the west, of late bristling in defiance, and hot for fight, had craved forgiveness, and proffered the calumet. The war was over; the last flickerings of that wide conflagration had died away; but the embers still glowed beneath the ashes, and fuel and a breath alone were wanting to rekindle those desolating fires.

---

which are seldom departed from, and which are often found identical among tribes speaking languages radically distinct. Thus, among both Iroquois and Algonquins, the "whistling of evil birds" is the invariable expression to denote evil tidings or bad advice.

The Indians are much pleased when white men whom they respect adopt their peculiar symbolical language,—a circumstance of which the Jesuit missionaries did not fail to avail themselves. "These people," says Father Le Jeune, "being great orators, and often using allegories and metaphors, our fathers, in order to attract them to God, adapt themselves to their custom of speaking, which delights them very much, seeing we succeed as well as they."

[1] In a letter to Gage, without a date, but sent in the same enclosure as his journal, Croghan gives his impression of Pontiac in the following words:—

"Pondiac is a shrewd, sensible Indian, of few words, and commands more respect among his own nation than any Indian I ever saw could do among his own tribe. He, and all the principal men of those nations, seem at present to be convinced that the French had a view of interest in stirring up the late differences between his Majesty's subjects and them, and call it a beaver war."

In the mean time, a hundred Highlanders of the 42d Regiment, those veterans whose battle-cry had echoed over the bloodiest fields of America, had left Fort Pitt under command of Captain Sterling, and, descending the Ohio, arrived at Fort Chartres just as the snows of early winter began to whiten the naked forests.[1] The flag of France descended from the rampart; and with the stern courtesies of war, St. Ange yielded up his post, the citadel of the Illinois, to its new masters. In that act was consummated the double triumph of British power in America. England had crushed her hereditary foe; and France, in her fall, had left to irretrievable ruin the savage tribes to whom her policy and self-interest had lent a transient support.

[1]MS. *Gage Papers*. M. Nicollet, in speaking of the arrival of the British troops, says, "At this news Pontiac raved." This is a mistake. Pontiac's reconciliation had already taken place, and he had abandoned all thoughts of resistance.

Chapter XXXI.
1766—1769.

DEATH OF PONTIAC.

THE WINTER passed quietly away. Already the Indians began to feel the blessings of returning peace in the partial reopening of the fur-trade; and the famine and nakedness, the misery and death, which through the previous season had been rife in their encampments, were exchanged for comparative comfort and abundance. With many precautions, and in meagre allowances, the traders had been permitted to throw their goods into the Indian markets; and the starving hunters were no longer left, as many of them had been, to gain precarious sustenance by the bow, the arrow, and the lance—the half-forgotten weapons of their fathers. Some troubles arose along the frontiers of Pennsylvania and Virginia. The reckless borderers, in contempt of common humanity and prudence, murdered several straggling Indians, and enraged others by abuse and insult; but these outrages could not obliterate the remembrance of recent chastisement, and, for the present at least, the injured warriors forbore to draw down the fresh vengeance of their destroyers.

Spring returned, and Pontiac remembered the promise he had made to visit Sir William Johnson at Oswego. He left his encampment on the Maumee, accompanied by his chiefs, and by an Englishman named Crawford, a man of vigor and resolution, who had been appointed, by the superintendent, to the troublesome office of attending the Indian deputation, and supplying their wants.[1]

We may well imagine with what bitterness of mood the defeated war-chief urged his canoe along the margin of Lake Erie, and gazed upon the horizon-bounded waters, and the lofty shores, green with primeval verdure. Little could he have dreamed, and little could the wisest of that day have imagined, that, within the space of a single human life, that lonely lake would be studded with the sails of commerce; that

[1]MS. *Johnson Papers.*

cities and villages would rise upon the ruins of the forest; and that the poor mementoes of his lost race—the wampum beads, the rusty tomahawk, and the arrowhead of stone, turned up by the ploughshare—would become the wonder of school-boys, and the prized relics of the antiquary's cabinet. Yet it needed no prophetic eye to foresee that, sooner or later, the doom must come. The star of his people's destiny was fading from the sky; and, to a mind like his, the black and withering future must have stood revealed in all its desolation.

The birchen flotilla gained the outlet of Lake Erie, and, shooting downwards with the stream, landed beneath the palisades of Fort Schlosser. The chiefs passed the portage, and, once more embarking, pushed out upon Lake Ontario. Soon their goal was reached, and the cannon boomed hollow salutation from the batteries of Oswego.

Here they found Sir William Johnson waiting to receive them, attended by the chief sachems of the Iroquois, whom he had invited to the spot, that their presence might give additional weight and solemnity to the meeting. As there was no building large enough to receive so numerous a concourse, a canopy of green boughs was erected to shade the assembly from the sun; and thither, on the twenty-third of July, repaired the chiefs and warriors of the several nations. Here stood the tall figure of Sir William Johnson, surrounded by civil and military officers, clerks, and interpreters; while before him reclined the painted sachems of the Iroquois, and the great Ottawa war-chief, with his dejected followers.

Johnson opened the meeting with the usual formalities, presenting his auditors with a belt of wampum to wipe the tears from their eyes, with another to cover the bones of their relatives, another to open their ears that they might hear, and another to clear their throats that they might speak with ease. Then, amid solemn silence, Pontiac's great peace-pipe was lighted and passed round the assembly, each man present inhaling a whiff of the sacred smoke. These tedious forms, together with a few speeches of compliment, consumed the whole morning; for this savage people, on whose supposed simplicity poets and rhetoricians have lavished their praises, may challenge the world to outmatch their bigoted adherence to usage and ceremonial.

On the following day, the council began in earnest, and Sir William Johnson addressed Pontiac and his attendant chiefs.

"Children, I bid you heartily welcome to this place; and I trust that the Great Spirit will permit us often to meet together in friendship, for I have now opened the door and cleared the road, that all nations may come hither from the sunsetting. This belt of wampum confirms my words.

"Children, it gave me much pleasure to find that you who are present behaved so well last year, and treated in so friendly a manner Mr. Croghan, one of my deputies; and that you expressed such concern for the bad behavior of those, who, in order to obstruct the good work of peace, assaulted and wounded him, and killed some of his party, both whites and Indians; a thing before unknown, and contrary to the laws and customs of all nations. This would have drawn down our strongest resentment upon those who were guilty of so heinous a crime, were it not for the great lenity and kindness of your English father, who does not delight in punishing those who repent sincerely of their faults.

"Children, I have now, with the approbation of General Gage (your father's chief warrior in this country), invited you here in order to confirm and strengthen your proceedings with Mr. Croghan last year. I hope that you will remember all that then passed, and I desire that you will often repeat it to your young people, and keep it fresh in your minds.

"Children, you begin already to see the fruits of peace, from the number of traders and plenty of goods at all the garrisoned posts; and our enjoying the peaceable possession of the Illinois will be found of great advantage to the Indians in that country. You likewise see that proper officers, men of honor and probity, are appointed to reside at the posts, to prevent abuses in trade, to hear your complaints, and to lay before me such of them as they cannot redress.[1] Interpreters

---

[1] The Lords of Trade had recently adopted a new plan for the management of Indian affairs, the principal feature of which was the confinement of the traders to the military posts, where they would conduct their traffic under the eye of proper officers, instead of ranging at will, without supervision or control, among the Indian villages. It was found extremely difficult to enforce this regulation.

are likewise sent for the assistance of each of them; and smiths are sent to the posts to repair your arms and implements. All this, which is attended with a great expense, is now done by the great King, your father, as a proof of his regard; so that, casting from you all jealousy and apprehension, you should now strive with each other who should show the most gratitude to this best of princes. I do now, therefore, confirm the assurances which I give you of his Majesty's good will, and do insist on your casting away all evil thoughts, and shutting your ears against all flying idle reports of bad people."

The rest of Johnson's speech was occupied in explaining to his hearers the new arrangements for the regulation of the fur-trade; in exhorting them to forbear from retaliating the injuries they might receive from reckless white men, who would meet with due punishment from their own countrymen; and in urging them to deliver up to justice those of their people who might be guilty of crimes against the English. "Children," he concluded, "I now, by this belt, turn your eyes to the sunrising, where you will always find me your sincere friend. From me you will always hear what is true and good; and I charge you never more to listen to those evil birds, who come, with lying tongues, to lead you astray, and to make you break the solemn engagements which you have entered into, in presence of the Great Spirit, with the King your father and the English people. Be strong, then, and keep fast hold of the chain of friendship, that your children, following your example, may live happy and prosperous lives."

Pontiac made a brief reply, and promised to return on the morrow an answer in full. The meeting then broke up.

The council of the next day was opened by the Wyandot chief, Teata, in a short and formal address; at the conclusion of which Pontiac himself arose, and addressed the superintendent in words, of which the following is a translation:

"Father, we thank the Great Spirit for giving us so fine a day to meet upon such great affairs. I speak in the name of all the nations to the westward, of whom I am the master. It is the will of the Great Spirit that we should meet here to-day; and before him I now take you by the hand. I call him to witness that I speak from my heart; for since I took Colonel

Croghan by the hand last year, I have never let go my hold, for I see that the Great Spirit will have us friends.

"Father, when our great father of France was in this country, I held him fast by the hand. Now that he is gone, I take you, my English father, by the hand, in the name of all the nations, and promise to keep this covenant as long as I shall live."

Here he delivered a large belt of wampum.

"Father, when you address me, it is the same as if you addressed all the nations of the west. Father, this belt is to cover and strengthen our chain of friendship, and to show you that, if any nation shall lift the hatchet against our English brethren, we shall be the first to feel it and resent it."

Pontiac next took up in succession the various points touched upon in the speech of the superintendent, expressing in all things a full compliance with his wishes. The succeeding days of the conference were occupied with matters of detail relating chiefly to the fur-trade, all of which were adjusted to the apparent satisfaction of the Indians, who, on their part, made reiterated professions of friendship. Pontiac promised to recall the war-belts which had been sent to the north and west, though, as he alleged, many of them had proceeded from the Senecas, and not from him; adding that, when all were gathered together, they would be more than a man could carry. The Iroquois sachems then addressed the western nations, exhorting them to stand true to their engagements, and hold fast the chain of friendship; and the councils closed on the thirty-first, with a bountiful distribution of presents to Pontiac and his followers.[1]

Thus ended this memorable meeting, in which Pontiac sealed his submission to the English, and renounced for ever the bold design by which he had trusted to avert or retard the ruin of his race. His hope of seeing the empire of France restored in America was scattered to the winds, and with it vanished every rational scheme of resistance to English en-

[1]MS. *Minutes of Proceedings at a Congress with Pontiac and Chiefs of the Ottawas, Pottawattamies, Hurons, and Chippewais; begun at Oswego, Tuesday*, July 23, 1766.

A copy of this document is preserved in the office of the secretary of state at Albany, among the papers procured in London by Mr. Brodhead.

croachment. Nothing now remained but to stand an idle spectator, while, in the north and in the south, the tide of British power rolled westward in resistless might; while the fragments of the rival empire, which he would fain have set up as a barrier against the flood, lay scattered a miserable wreck; and while the remnant of his people melted away or fled for refuge to remoter deserts. For them the prospects of the future were as clear as they were calamitous. Destruction or civilization—between these lay their choice; and few who knew them could doubt which alternative they would embrace.

Pontiac, his canoe laden with the gifts of his enemy, steered homeward for the Maumee; and in this vicinity he spent the following winter, pitching his lodge in the forest with his wives and children, and hunting like an ordinary warrior. With the succeeding spring, 1767, fresh murmurings of discontent arose among the Indian tribes, from the lakes to the Potomac, the first precursors of the disorders which, a few years later, ripened into a brief but bloody war along the borders of Virginia. These threatening symptoms might easily be traced to their source. The incorrigible frontiersmen had again let loose their murdering propensities; and a multitude of squatters had built their cabins on Indian lands beyond the limits of Pennsylvania, adding insult to aggression, and sparing neither oaths, curses, nor any form of abuse and maltreatment against the rightful owners of the soil.[1] The new regulations of the fur-trade could not prevent disorders among the reckless men engaged in it. This was particularly the case in the region of the Illinois, where the evil was aggravated by the renewed intrigues of the French, and especially of those who had fled from the English side of the Mississippi, and made their abode around the new settlement of St. Louis.[2] It is difficult to say how far Pontiac was involved in this agitation. It is certain that some of the English traders regarded him with jealousy and fear, as prime mover of the whole, and eagerly watched an opportunity to destroy him.

The discontent among the tribes did not diminish with the

[1]"It seems," writes Sir William Johnson to the lords of trade, "as if the people were determined to bring on a new war, though their own ruin may be the consequence."

[2]*Doc. Hist. N. Y.* II. 861–893, etc. MS. *Johnson Papers*. MS. *Gage Papers*.

lapse of time; yet for many months we can discern no trace of Pontiac. Records and traditions are silent concerning him. It is not until April, 1769, that he appears once more distinctly on the scene.[1] At about that time he came to the Illinois, with what design does not appear, though his movements excited much uneasiness among the few English in that quarter. Soon after his arrival, he repaired to St. Louis, to visit his former acquaintance, St. Ange, who was then in command at that post, having offered his services to the Spaniards after the cession of Louisiana. After leaving the fort, Pontiac proceeded to the house of which young Pierre Chouteau was an inmate; and to the last days of his protracted life, the latter could vividly recall the circumstances of the interview. The savage chief was arrayed in the full uniform of a French officer, which had been presented to him as a special mark of respect and favor by the Marquis of Montcalm, towards the close of the French war, and which Pontiac never had the bad taste to wear, except on occasions when he wished to appear with unusual dignity. St. Ange, Chouteau, and the other principal inhabitants of the infant settlement, whom he visited in turn, all received him cordially, and did their best to entertain him and his attendant chiefs. He remained at St. Louis for two or three days, when, hearing that a large number of Indians were assembled at Cahokia, on the opposite side of the river, and that some drinking bout or other social gathering was in progress, he told St. Ange that he would cross over to see what was going forward. St. Ange tried to dissuade him, and urged the risk to which he would expose himself; but Pontiac persisted, boasting that he was a match for the English, and had no fear for his life. He entered a canoe with some of his followers, and Chouteau never saw him again.

He who, at the present day, crosses from the city of St. Louis to the opposite shore of the Mississippi, and passes

---

[1]Carver says that Pontiac was killed in 1767. This may possibly be a mere printer's error. In the *Maryland Gazette*, and also in the *Pennsylvania Gazette*, were published during the month of August, 1769, several letters from the Indian country, in which Pontiac is mentioned as having been killed during the preceding April. M. Chouteau states that, to the best of his recollection, the chief was killed in 1768; but oral testimony is of little weight in regard to dates. The evidence of the Gazettes appears conclusive.

southward through a forest festooned with grape-vines, and fragrant with the scent of flowers, will soon emerge upon the ancient hamlet of Cahokia. To one fresh from the busy suburbs of the American city, the small French houses, scattered in picturesque disorder, the light-hearted, thriftless look of their inmates, and the woods which form the background of the picture, seem like the remnants of an earlier and simpler world. Strange changes have passed around that spot. Forests have fallen, cities have sprung up, and the lonely wilderness is thronged with human life. Nature herself has taken part in the general transformation; and the Mississippi has made a fearful inroad, robbing from the luckless Creoles a mile of rich meadow and woodland. Yet, in the midst of all, this relic of the lost empire of France has preserved its essential features through the lapse of a century, and offers at this day an aspect not widely different from that which met the eye of Pontiac, when he and his chiefs landed on its shore.

The place was full of Illinois Indians; such a scene as in our own time may often be met with in some squalid settlement of the border, where the vagabond guests, bedizened with dirty finery, tie their small horses in rows along the fences, and stroll idly among the houses, or lounge about the dram-shops. A chief so renowned as Pontiac could not remain long among the friendly Creoles of Cahokia without being summoned to a feast; and at such primitive entertainment the whiskey-bottle would not fail to play its part. This was in truth the case. Pontiac drank deeply, and, when the carousal was over, strode down the village street to the adjacent woods, where he was heard to sing the medicine songs, in whose magic power he trusted as the warrant of success in all his undertakings.

An English trader, named Williamson, was then in the village. He had looked on the movements of Pontiac with a jealousy probably not diminished by the visit of the chief to the French at St. Louis; and he now resolved not to lose so favorable an opportunity to despatch him. With this view, he gained the ear of a strolling Indian, belonging to the Kaskaskia tribe of the Illinois, bribed him with a barrel of liquor, and promised him a farther reward if he would kill the chief. The bargain was quickly made. When Pontiac entered the forest, the assassin stole close upon his track; and, watching his moment, glided behind him, and buried a tomahawk in his brain.

The dead body was soon discovered, and startled cries and wild howlings announced the event. The word was caught up from mouth to mouth, and the place resounded with infernal yells. The warriors snatched their weapons. The Illinois took part with their guilty countryman; and the few followers of Pontiac, driven from the village, fled to spread the tidings and call the nations to revenge. Meanwhile the murdered chief lay on the spot where he had fallen, until St. Ange, mindful of former friendship, sent to claim the body, and buried it with warlike honors, near his fort of St. Louis.[1]

Thus basely perished this champion of a ruined race. But could his shade have revisited the scene of murder, his savage spirit would have exulted in the vengeance which overwhelmed the abettors of the crime. Whole tribes were rooted out to expiate it. Chiefs and sachems, whose veins had thrilled

---

[1] Carver, *Travels*, 166, says that Pontiac was stabbed at a public council in the Illinois, by "a faithful Indian who was either commissioned by one of the English governors, or instigated by the love he bore the English nation." This account is without sufficient confirmation. Carver, who did not visit the Illinois, must have drawn his information from hearsay. The open manner of dealing with his victim, which he ascribes to the assassin, is wholly repugnant to Indian character and principles; while the gross charge, thrown out at random against an English governor, might of itself cast discredit on the story.

I have followed the account which I received from M. Pierre Chouteau, and from M. P. L. Cerré, another old inhabitant of the Illinois, whose father was well acquainted with Pontiac. The same account may be found, concisely stated, in Nicollet, p. 81. M. Nicollet states that he derived his information both from M. Chouteau and from the no less respectable authority of the aged Pierre Menard of Kaskaskia. The notices of Pontiac's death in the provincial journals of the day, to a certain extent, confirm this story. We gather from them, that he was killed at the Illinois, by one or more Kaskaskia Indians, during a drunken frolic, and in consequence of his hostility to the English. One letter, however, states on hearsay that he was killed near Fort Chartres; and Gouin's traditional account seems to support the statement. On this point, I have followed the distinct and circumstantial narrative of Chouteau, supported as it is by Cerré. An Ottawa tradition declares that Pontiac took a Kaskaskia wife, with whom he had a quarrel, and she persuaded her two brothers to kill him.

I am indebted to the kindness of my friend Mr. Lyman C. Draper for valuable assistance in my inquiries in relation to Pontiac's death.

with his eloquence; young warriors, whose aspiring hearts had caught the inspiration of his greatness, mustered to revenge his fate; and, from the north and the east, their united bands descended on the villages of the Illinois. Tradition has but faintly preserved the memory of the event; and its only annalists, men who held the intestine feuds of the savage tribes in no more account than the quarrels of panthers or wildcats, have left but a meagre record. Yet enough remains to tell us that over the grave of Pontiac more blood was poured out in atonement, than flowed from the veins of the slaughtered heroes on the corpse of Patroclus; and the remnant of the Illinois who survived the carnage remained for ever after sunk in utter insignificance.[1]

---

[1]"This murder, which roused the vengeance of all the Indian tribes friendly to Pontiac, brought about the successive wars, and almost total extermination, of the Illinois nation."—Nicollet, 82.

"The Kaskaskias, Peorias, Cahokias, and Illonese are nearly all destroyed by the Sacs and Foxes, for killing in cool blood, and in time of peace, the Sac's chief, Pontiac."—*Mass. Hist. Coll. Second Series*, II. 8.

The above extract exhibits the usual confusion of Indian names, the Kaskaskias, Peorias, and Cahokias being component tribes of the Illonese or Illinois nation. Pontiac is called a chief of the Sacs. This, with similar mistakes, may easily have arisen from the fact that he was accustomed to assume authority over the warriors of any tribe with whom he chanced to be in contact.

Morse says, in his *Report*, 1822: "In the war kindled against these tribes, [Peorias, Kaskaskias, and Cahokias,] by the Sauks and Foxes, in revenge for the death of their chief, Pontiac, these 3 tribes were nearly exterminated. Few of them now remain. About one hundred of the Peorias are settled on Current River, W. of the Mississippi; of the Kaskaskias 36 only remain in Illinois."—Morse, 363.

General Gage, in his letter to Sir William Johnson, dated July 10, 176–, says: "The death of Pontiac, committed by an Indian of the Illinois, believed to have been excited by the English to that action, had drawn many of the Ottawas and other northern nations towards their country to revenge his death."

"From Miami, Pontiac went to Fort Chartres on the Illinois. In a few years, the English, who had possession of the fort, procured an Indian of the Peoria [Kaskaskia] nation to kill him. The news spread like lightning through the country. The Indians assembled in great numbers, attacked and destroyed all the Peorias, except about thirty families, which were received into the fort. These soon began to increase. They removed to the Wabash, and were about to settle, when the Indians collected in the winter, surrounded their village, and killed the whole, excepting a few children, who were saved as prisoners.

Neither mound nor tablet marked the burial-place of Pontiac. For a mausoleum, a city has risen above the forest hero; and the race whom he hated with such burning rancor trample with unceasing footsteps over his forgotten grave.

Old Mr. Gouin was there at the time. He was a trader; and, when the attack commenced, was ordered by the Indians to shut his house and not suffer a Peoria to enter."—*Gouin's Account*, MS.

Pontiac left several children. A speech of his son Shegenaba, in 1775, is preserved in Force's *American Archives, 4th Series*, III. 1542. There was another son, named Otussa, whose grave is on the Maumee. In a letter to the writer, Mr. H. R. Schoolcraft says, "I knew *Atóka*, a descendant of Pontiac. He was the chief of an Ottawa village on the Maumee. A few years ago, he agreed to remove, with his people, to the west of the Mississippi."

Appendix A.

THE IROQUOIS. — EXTENT OF THEIR
CONQUESTS. — POLICY PURSUED TOWARDS
THEM BY THE FRENCH AND THE ENGLISH. —
MEASURES OF SIR WILLIAM JOHNSON.

1. TERRITORY OF THE IROQUOIS. (Vol. I. p. 363.)

Extract from a Letter — Sir W. Johnson to the Board of Trade, November 13, 1763: —

My Lords:

In obedience to your Lordships' commands of the 5th of August last, I am now to lay before you the claims of the Nations mentioned in the State of the Confederacies. The Five Nations have in the last century subdued the Shawanese, Delawares, Twighties, and Western Indians, so far as Lakes Michigan and Superior, received them into an alliance, allowed them the possession of the lands they occupied, and have ever since been in peace with the greatest part of them; and such was the prowess of the Five Nations' Confederacy, that had they been properly supported by us, they would have long since put a period to the Colony of Canada, which alone they were near effecting in the year 1688. Since that time, they have admitted the Tuscaroras from the Southward, beyond Oneida, and they have ever since formed a part of that Confederacy.

As original proprietors, this Confederacy claim the country of their residence, south of Lake Ontario to the great Ridge of the Blue Mountains, with all the Western Part of the Province of New York towards Hudson River, west of the Catskill, thence to Lake Champlain, and from Regioghne, a Rock at the East side of said Lake, to Oswegatche or La Gallette, on the River St. Lawrence, (having long since ceded their claim north of said line in favor of the Canada Indians, as Hunting-ground,) thence up the River St. Lawrence, and along the South side of Lake Ontario to Niagara.

In right of conquest, they claim all the country (comprehending the Ohio) along the great Ridge of Blue Mountains at the back of Virginia, thence to the head of Kentucky River, and down the same to the Ohio above the Rifts, thence Northerly to the South end of Lake Michigan, then along the Eastern shore of said lake to Michillimackinac, thence Easterly across the North end of Lake Huron to the great Ottawa River, (including the Chippewa or Mississagey County,) and down the said River to the Island of Montreal. However, these more distant claims being possessed by many powerful

847

nations, the Inhabitants have long begun to render themselves independent, by the assistance of the French, and the great decrease of the Six Nations; but their claim to the Ohio, and thence to the Lakes, is not in the least disputed by the Shawanese, Delawares, &c., who never transacted any sales of land or other matters without their consent, and who sent Deputies to the grand Council at Onondaga on all important occasions.

2. FRENCH AND ENGLISH POLICY TOWARDS THE IROQUOIS.— MEASURES OF SIR WILLIAM JOHNSON. (Vol. I. pp. 418–422.)

Extract from a Letter—Sir W. Johnson to the Board of Trade, May 24, 1765:—

The Indians of the Six Nations, after the arrival of the English, having conceived a desire for many articles they introduced among them, and thereby finding them of use to their necessities, or rather superfluities, cultivated an acquaintance with them, and lived in tolerable friendship with their Province for some time, to which they were rather inclined, for they were strangers to bribery, and at enmity with the French, who had espoused the cause of their enemies, supplied them with arms, and openly acted against them. This enmity increased in proportion as the desire of the French for subduing those people, who were a bar to their first projected schemes. However, we find the Indians, as far back as the very confused manuscript records in my possession, repeatedly upbraiding this province for their negligence, their avarice, and their want of assisting them at a time when it was certainly in their power to destroy the infant colony of Canada, although supported by many nations; and this is likewise confessed by the writings of the managers of these times. The French, after repeated losses discovering that the Six Nations were not to be subdued, but that they could without much difficulty effect their purpose (which I have good authority to show were . . . . standing) by favors and kindness, on a sudden, changed their conduct in the reign of Queen Anne, having first brought over many of their people to settle in Canada; and ever since, by the most endearing kindnesses and by a vast profusion of favors, have secured them to their interest; and, whilst they aggravated our frauds and designs, they covered those committed by themselves under a load of gifts, which obliterated the malpractices of . . . . among them, and enabled them to establish themselves wherever they pleased, without fomenting the Indians' jealousy. The able agents were made use of, and their unanimous indefatigable zeal for securing the Indian interest, were so much superior to any thing we had ever attempted, and to the futile transactions of the . . . . and trading Commissioners of Albany, that the latter became universally despised by the Indians, who daily withdrew from our interest, and conceived the most disadvantageous sentiments of our integrity and abilities. In this state of Indian affairs I was called to the management of these people, as my situation and opinion that it might become one day of service to the public, had induced me to cultivate a particular intimacy with these people, to accommodate myself to their manners, and even to their dress on many occasions. How I discharged this trust will best appear from the transactions of the war commenced in 1744, in which I was busily concerned. The steps I had then taken alarmed the jealousy of the French; rewards were offered for me, and I narrowly escaped assassination on more than one occasion. The French increased their munificence to the Indians, whose example not being at all followed at New York, I resigned the management of affairs on the ensuing peace, as I did not choose to continue in the name of an office which I was not empowered to discharge as its nature required. The Albany Commissioners (the men concerned in the clandestine trade to Canada, and frequently upbraided for it by the Indians) did then reassume their seats at that Board, and by their conduct so exasperated the Indians that several chiefs went to New York, 1753, when, after a severe speech to the Governor, Council, and Assembly, they broke the covenant chain of friendship, and withdrew in a rage. The consequences of which were then so much dreaded, that I was, by Governor, Council, and House of Assembly, the two latter then my enemies, earnestly entreated to effect a reconciliation with the Indians, as the only person equal to that task, as will appear by the Minutes of Council and resolves of the House. A commission being made out for me, I proceeded to Onondaga, and brought about the much wished for reconciliation, but declined having any further to say of Indian affairs, although the Indians afterwards refused to meet the Governor and Commissioners till I was sent for. At the arrival of General Braddock, I received his Commission with reluctance, at the same time assuring him that affairs had been so ill conducted, and the Indians so estranged from our interest, that I could not take upon me to hope for success. However, indefatigable labor, and (I hope I may say without vanity) personal interest, enabled me to exceed my own expectations; and my conduct since, if fully and truly known, would, I believe, testify that I have not been an unprofitable servant. 'Twas then that the Indians began to give public sign of their avaricious dispositions. The French had long taught them it; and the desire of some persons to carry a greater number of Indians into the field in 1755 than those who accompanied me, induced them to employ any agent at a high salary, who had the least interest with the Indians; and to grant the latter Captains' and Lieutenants' Commissions, (of which I have a number now by me,) with sterling pay, to induce them to desert me, but to little purpose, for tho' many of them received the Commissions, accompanied with large sums of money, they did not comply with the end proposed, but served with me; and this had not only served them with severe complaints against the English, as they were not afterwards all paid what had been promised, but has established a spirit of pride and avarice, which I have found it ever since impossible to subdue; whilst our extensive connections since the reduction of Canada, with so many powerful nations so long accustomed to partake largely of French bounty, has of course increased the expense, and rendered it in no small degree necessary for the preservation of our frontiers, outposts, and trade. . . .

Extract from a Letter—Cadwallader Colden to the Earl of Halifax, December 22, 1763:—

Before I proceed further, I think it proper to inform your Lordship of the different state of the Policy of the Five Nations in different periods of time. Before the peace of Utrecht, the Five Nations were at war with the French in Canada, and with all the Indian Nations who were in friendship with the French. This put the Five Nations under a necessity of depending on this province for a supply of every thing by which they could carry on the war or defend themselves, and their behavior towards us was accordingly.

After the peace of Utrecht, the French changed their measures. They took every method in their power to gain the friendship of the Five Nations, and succeeded so far with the Senecas, who are by far the most numerous, and at the greatest distance from us, that they were entirely brought over to the French interest. The French obtained the consent of the Senecas to the building of the Fort at Niagara, situated in their country.

When the French had too evidently, before the last war, got the ascendant among all the Indian Nations, we endeavored to make the Indians jealous of the French power, that they were thereby in danger of becoming slaves to the French, unless they were protected by the English. . . .

Appendix B.

CAUSES OF THE INDIAN WAR.

Extract from a Letter—Sir W. Johnson to the Board of Trade, November 13, 1763. (Chap. VII. Vol. I. p. 475.)

. . . The French, in order to reconcile them [the Indians] to their encroachments, loaded them with favors, and employed the most intelligent Agents of good influence, as well as artful Jesuits among the several Western and other Nations, who, by degrees, prevailed on them to admit of Forts, under the Notion of Trading houses, in their Country; and knowing that these posts could never be maintained contrary to the inclinations of the Indians, they supplied them thereat with ammunition and other necessaries in abundance, as also called them to frequent congresses, and dismissed them with handsome presents, by which they enjoyed an extensive commerce, obtained the assistance of these Indians, and possessed their frontiers in safety; and as without these measures the Indians would never have suffered them in their Country, so they expect that whatever European power possesses the same, they shall in some measure reap the like advantages. Now, as these advantages ceased on the Posts being possessed by the English, and especially as it was not thought prudent to indulge them with ammunition, they immediately concluded that we had designs against their liberties, which opinion had been first instilled into them by the French, and since promoted by Traders of that nation and others who retired among them on the surrender of Canada and are still there, as well as by Belts of Wampum and other exhortations, which I am confidently assured have been sent among them from the Illinois, Louisiana, and even Canada, for that purpose. The Shawanese and Delawares about the Ohio, who were never warmly attached to us since our neglects to defend them against the encroachments of the French, and refusing to erect a post at the Ohio, or assist them and the Six Nations with men or ammunition, when they requested both of us, as well as irritated at the loss of several of their people killed upon the communication of Fort Pitt, in the years 1759 and 1761, were easily induced to join with the Western Nations, and the Senecas, dissatisfied at many of our posts, jealous of our designs, and displeased at our neglect and contempt of them, soon followed their example.

These are the causes the Indians themselves assign, and which certainly occasioned the rupture between us, the consequence of which, in my opinion, will be that the Indians (who do not regard the distance) will be supplied with necessaries by the Wabache and several Rivers, which empty into the Mississippi, which it is by no means in our power to prevent, and in return the French will draw the valuable furs down that river to the advantage of their Colony and the destruction of our Trade; this will always induce the French to foment differences between us and the Indians, and the prospects many of them entertain, that they may hereafter become possessed of Canada, will incline them still more to cultivate a good understanding with the Indians, which, if ever attempted by the French, would, I am very apprehensive, be attended with a general defection of them from our interest, unless we are at great pains and expense to regain their friendship, and thereby satisfy them that we have no designs to their prejudice. . . .

The grand matter of concern to all the Six Nations (Mohawks excepted) is the occupying a chain of small Posts on the communication thro' their country to Lake Ontario, not to mention Fort Stanwix, exclusive of which there were erected in 1759 Fort Schuyler on the Mohawk River, and the Royal Blockhouse at the East end of Oneida Lake, in the Country of the Oneidas Fort Brewerton and a Post at Oswego Falls in the Onondagas Country; in order to obtain permission for erecting these posts, they were promised they should be demolished at the end of the war. General Shirley also made them a like promise for the posts he erected; and as about these posts are their fishing and hunting places, where they complain, that they are often obstructed by the troops and insulted, they request that they may not be kept up, the war with the French being now over.

In 1760, Sir Jeffrey Amherst sent a speech to the Indians in writing, which was to be communicated to the Nations about Fort Pitt, &c., by General Monkton, then commanding there, signifying his intentions to satisfy and content all Indians for the ground occupied by the posts, as also for any land about them, which might be found necessary for the use of the garrisons; but the same has not been performed, neither are the Indians in the several countries at all pleased at our occupying them, which they look upon as the first steps to enslave them and invade their properties.

And I beg leave to represent to your Lordships, that one very material advantage resulting from a continuance of good treatment and some favors to the Indians, will be the security and toleration thereby given to the Troops for cultivating lands about the garrisons, which the reduction of their Rations renders absolutely necessary. . . . .

PONTEACH: OR THE SAVAGES OF AMERICA. A Tragedy. London. Printed for the Author; and Sold by J. Millan, opposite the Admiralty, Whitehall. MDCCLXVI.

The author of this tragedy was evidently a person well acquainted with Indian affairs and Indian character. Various allusions contained in it, as well as several peculiar forms of expression, indicate that Major Rogers had a share in its composition. The first act exhibits in detail the causes which led to the Indian war. The rest of the play is of a different character. The plot is sufficiently extravagant, and has little or no historical foundation. Chekitan, the son of Ponteach, is in love with Monelia, the daughter of Hendrick, Emperor of the Mohawks. Monelia is murdered by Chekitan's brother Philip, partly out of revenge and jealousy, and partly in furtherance of a scheme of policy. Chekitan kills Philip, and then dies by his own hand; and Ponteach, whose warriors meanwhile have been defeated by the English, overwhelmed by this accumulation of public and private calamities, retires to the forests of the west to escape the memory of his griefs. The style of the drama is superior to the plot, and the writer displays at times no small insight into the workings of human nature.

The account of Indian wrongs and sufferings given in the first act accords so nearly with that conveyed in contemporary letters and documents, that two scenes from this part of the play are here given, with a few omissions, which good taste demands.

ACT I.

SCENE I.—AN INDIAN TRADING HOUSE.

Enter M'DOLE *and* MURPHEY, *Two Indian Traders, and their Servants.*

M'Dole. So, Murphey, you are come to try your Fortune
Among the Savages in this wild Desart?
Murphey. Ay, any thing to get an honest Living,
Which, faith, I find it hard enough to do;
Times are so dull, and Traders are so plenty,
That Gains are small, and Profits come but slow.
M'Dole. Are you experienced in this kind of Trade?
Know you the Principles by which it prospers,
And how to make it lucrative and safe?
If not, you're like a Ship without a Rudder,
That drives at random, and must surely sink.
Murphey. I'm unacquainted with your Indian Commerce

And gladly would I learn the arts from you,
Who're old, and practis'd in them many Years.
    M'Dole. That is the curst Misfortune of our Traders;
A thousand Fools attempt to live this Way,
Who might as well turn Ministers of State.
But, as you are a Friend, I will inform you
Of all the secret Arts by which we thrive,
Which if all practis'd, we might all grow rich,
Nor circumvent each other in our Gains.
What have you got to part with to the Indians?
    Murphey. I've Rum and Blankets, Wampum, Powder, Bells,
And such like Trifles as they're wont to prize.
    M'Dole. 'Tis very well: your Articles are good:
But now the Thing's to make a Profit from them,
Worth all your Toil and Pains of coming hither.
Our fundamental Maxim then is this,
That it's no Crime to cheat and gull an Indian.
    Murphey. How! Not a Sin to cheat an Indian, say you?
Are they not Men? hav'nt they a Right to Justice
As well as we, though savage in their Manners?
    M'Dole. Ah! If you boggle here, I say no more;
This is the very Quintessence of Trade,
And ev'ry Hope of Gain depends upon it;
None who neglect it ever did grow rich,
Or ever will, or can by Indian Commerce.
By this old Ogden built his stately House,
Purchased Estates, and grew a little King.
He, like an honest Man, bought all by weight,
And made the ign'rant Savages believe
That his Right Foot exactly weighed a Pound.
By this for many years he bought their Furs,
And died in Quiet like an honest Dealer.
    Murphey. Well, I'll not stick at what is necessary;
But his Devise is now grown old and stale,
Nor could I manage such a barefac'd Fraud.
    M'Dole. A thousand Opportunities present
To take Advantage of their Ignorance;
But the great Engine I employ is Rum,
More pow'rful made by certain strength'ning Drugs.
This I distribute with a lib'ral Hand,
Urge them to drink till they grow mad and valiant;
Which makes them think me generous and just,
And gives full Scope to practise all my Art.

I then begin my Trade with water'd Rum;
The cooling Draught well suits their scorching Throats.
Their Fur and Peltry come in quick Return:
My Scales are honest, but so well contriv'd,
That one small Slip will turn Three Pounds to One;
Which they, poor silly Souls! ignorant of Weights
And Rules of Balancing, do not perceive.
But here they come; you'll see how I proceed.
Jack, is the Rum prepar'd as I commanded?

    Jack. Yes, Sir, all's ready when you please to call.

    M'Dole. Bring here the Scales and Weights immediately;
You see the Trick is easy and conceal'd.

[Showing how to slip the Scale.

    Murphey. By Jupiter, it's artfully contriv'd;
And was I King, I swear I'd knight th' Inventor.
Tom, mind the Part that you will have to act.

    Tom. Ah, never fear; I'll do as well as Jack.
But then, you know, an honest Servant's Pain Deserves Reward.

    Murphey. O! I'll take care of that.

[Enter a Number of Indians with Packs of Fur.

    1st Indian. So, what you trade with Indians here to-day?

    M'Dole. Yes, if my Goods will suit, and we agree.

    2d Indian. 'Tis Rum we want; we're tired, hot, and thirsty.

    3d Indian. You, Mr. Englishman, have you got Rum?

    M'Dole. Jack, bring a Bottle, pour them each a Gill.
You know which Cask contains the Rum. The Rum?

    1st Indian. It's good strong Rum; I feel it very soon.

    M'Dole. Give me a Glass. Here's Honesty in Trade;
We English always drink before we deal.

    2d Indian. Good way enough; it makes one sharp and cunning.

    M'Dole. Hand round another Gill. You're very welcome.

    3d Indian. Some say you Englishmen are sometimes Rogues;
You make poor Indians drunk, and then you cheat.

    1st Indian. No, English good. The Frenchmen give no Rum.

    2d Indian. I think it's best to trade with Englishmen.

    M'Dole. What is your Price for Beaver Skins per Pound?

    1st Indian. How much you ask per Quart for this strong Rum?

    M'Dole. Five Pounds of Beaver for One Quart of Rum.

    1st Indian. Five Pounds? Too much. Which is't you call Five
      Pound?

    M'Dole. This little Weight. I cannot give you more.

    1st Indian. Well, take 'em; weigh 'em. Don't you cheat us now.

    M'Dole. No; He that cheats an Indian should be hanged.

[Weighing the Packs.

There's Thirty Pounds precisely of the Whole;
Five times Six is Thirty. Six Quarts of Rum.
Jack, measure it to them; you know the Cask.
This Rum is sold. You draw it off the best.

[Exeunt Indians to receive their Rum.

Murphey. By Jove, you've gained more in a single Hour
Than ever I have done in Half a Year:
Curse on my Honesty! I might have been
A *little King*, and lived without Concern,
Had I but known the proper Arts to thrive.

M'Dole. Ay, there's the Way, my honest Friend, to live.

[Clapping his shoulder.

There's Ninety Weight of Sterling Beaver for you,
Worth all the Rum and Trinkets in my Store;
And, would my Conscience let me do the Thing,
I might enhance my Price, and lessen theirs,
And raise my Profits to a higher Pitch.

Murphey. I can't but thank you for your kind Instructions,
As from them I expect to reap Advantage.
But should the Dogs detect me in the Fraud,
They are malicious, and would have Revenge.

M'Dole. Can't you avoid them? Let their Vengeance light
On others Heads, no matter whose, if you
Are but Secure, and have the Gain in Hand;
For they're indiff'rent where they take Revenge,
Whether on him that cheated, or his Friend,
Or on a Stranger whom they never saw,
Perhaps an honest Peasant, who ne'er dreamt
Of Fraud or Villainy in all his Life;
Such let them murder, if they will, a Score,
The Guilt is theirs, while we secure the Gain,
Nor shall we feel the bleeding Victim's Pain.

[Exeunt.

SCENE II.—A DESART.

Enter ORSBOURN *and* HONNYMAN, *Two English Hunters.*

Orsbourn. Long have we toil'd, and rang'd the woods in vain;
No Game, nor Track, nor Sign of any Kind
Is to be seen; I swear I am discourag'd
And weary'd out with this long fruitless Hunt.

No Life on Earth besides is half so hard,
So full of Disappointments, as a Hunter's:
Each Morn he wakes he views the destin'd Prey,
And counts the Profits of th' ensuing Day;
Each Ev'ning at his curs'd ill Fortune pines,
And till next Day his Hope of Gain resigns.
By Jove, I'll from these Desarts hasten home,
And swear that never more I'll touch a Gun.

    Honnyman. These hateful Indians kidnap all the Game.
Curse their black Heads! they fright the Deer and Bear,
And ev'ry Animal that haunts the Wood,
Or by their Witchcraft conjure them away.
No Englishman can get a single Shot,
While they go loaded home with Skins and Furs.
'Twere to be wish'd not one of them survived,
Thus to infest the World, and plague Mankind.
Curs'd Heathen Infidels! mere savage Beasts!
They don't deserve to breathe in Christian Air,
And should be hunted down like other Brutes.

    Orsbourn. I only wish the Laws permitted us
To hunt the savage Herd where-e'er they're found;
I'd never leave the Trade of Hunting then,
While one remain'd to tread and range the Wood.

    Honnyman. Curse on the Law, I say, that makes it Death
To kill an Indian, more than to kill a Snake.
What if 'tis Peace? these Dogs deserve no Mercy;
They kill'd my Father and my eldest Brother,
Since which I hate their very Looks and Name.

    Orsbourn. And I, since they betray'd and kill'd my Uncle;
Tho' these are not the same, 'twould ease my Heart
To cleave their painted Heads, and spill their Blood.
I do abhor, detest, and hate them all,
And now cou'd eat an Indian's Heart with Pleasure.

    Honnyman. I'd join you, and soop his savage Brains for Sauce;
I lose all Patience when I think of them,
And, if you will, we'll quickly have amends
For our long Travel and successless Hunt,
And the sweet Pleasure of Revenge to boot.

    Orsbourn. What will you do? Present, and pop one down?

    Honnyman. Yes, faith, the first we meet well fraught with Furs;
Or if there's Two, and we can make sure Work,
By Jove, we'll ease the Rascals of their Packs,
And send them empty home to their own Country.

But then observe, that what we do is secret,
Or the Hangman will come in for Snacks.
 Orsbourn. Trust me for that; I'll join with all my Heart;
Nor with a nicer Aim, or steadier Hand
Would shoot a Tyger than I would an Indian.
There is a Couple stalking now this way
With lusty Packs; Heav'n favor our Design.
Are you well charged?
 Honnyman. I am. Take you the nearest,
And mind to fire exactly when I do.
 Orsbourn. A charming Chance!
 Honnyman. Hush, let them still come nearer.
       [They shoot, and run to rifle the Indians.
They're down, old Boy, a Brace of noble Bucks!
 Orsbourn. Well tallow'd faith, and noble Hides upon 'em.
          [Taking up a Pack.
We might have hunted all the Season thro'
For Half this Game, and thought ourselves well paid.
 Honnyman. By Jove, we might, and been at great Expense
For Lead and Powder; here's a single Shot.
 Orsbourn. I swear, I have got as much as I can carry.
 Honnyman. And faith, I'm not behind; this Pack is heavy.
But stop; we must conceal the tawny Dogs,
Or their bloodthirsty Countrymen will find them,
And then we're bit. There'll be the Devil to pay;
They'll murder us, and cheat the Hangman too.
 Orsbourn. Right. We'll prevent all Mischief of this Kind.
Where shall we hide their Savage Carcases?
 Honnyman. There they will lie conceal'd and snug enough.
         [They cover them.
But stay—perhaps ere long there'll be a War,
And then their Scalps will sell for ready Cash,
Two Hundred Crowns at least, and that's worth saving.
 Orsbourn. Well! that is true; no sooner said than done—
         [Drawing his Knife.
I'll strip this Fellow's painted greasy Skull.
        [Strips off the Scalp.
 Honnyman. Now let them sleep to Night without their Caps,
        [Takes the other Scalp.
And pleasant Dreams attend their long Repose.
 Orsbourn. Their Guns and Hatchets now are lawful Prize,
For they'll not need them on their present Journey.

Honnyman. The Devil hates Arms, and dreads the Smell
      of Powder;
He'll not allow such Instruments about him;
They're free from training now, they're in his Clutches.
    Orsbourn. But, Honnyman, d'ye think this is not Murder?
I vow I'm shocked a little to see them scalp'd,
And fear their Ghosts will haunt us in the Dark.
    Honnyman. It's no more Murder than to crack a Louse,
That is, if you've the Wit to keep it private.
And as to Haunting, Indians have no Ghosts,
But as they live like Beasts, like Beasts they die.
I've killed a Dozen in this selfsame Way,
And never yet was troubled with their Spirits.
    Orsbourn. Then I'm content; my Scruples are removed.
And what I've done, my Conscience justifies.
But we must have these Guns and Hatchets alter'd,
Or they'll detect th' Affair, and hang us both.
    Honnyman. That's quickly done—Let us with Speed return,
And think no more of being hang'd or haunted;
But turn our Fur to Gold, our Gold to Wine,
Thus gaily spend what we've so slily won,
And Bless the first Inventor of a Gun.

                                                    [*Exeunt*.

The remaining scenes of this act exhibit the rudeness and insolence
of British officers and soldiers in their dealings with the Indians, and
the corruption of British government agents. Pontiac himself is
introduced and represented as indignantly complaining of the reception which he and his warriors meet with. These scenes are over-
charged with blasphemy and ribaldry, and it is needless to preserve
them here. The rest of the play is written in better taste, and contains
several vigorous passages.

Appendix C.

DETROIT AND MICHILLIMACKINAC.

I. THE SIEGE OF DETROIT. (Chap. IX.–XV.)

The authorities consulted respecting the siege of Detroit consist of numerous manuscript letters of officers in the fort, including the official correspondence of the commanding officer; of several journals and fragments of journals; of extracts from contemporary newspapers; and of traditions and recollections received from Indians or aged Canadians of Detroit.

THE PONTIAC MANUSCRIPT.

This curious diary was preserved in a Canadian family at Detroit, and afterwards deposited with the Historical Society of Michigan. It is conjectured to have been the work of a French priest. The original is written in bad French, and several important parts are defaced or torn away. As a literary composition, it is quite worthless, being very diffuse and encumbered with dull and trivial details; yet this very minuteness affords strong internal evidence of its authenticity. Its general exactness with respect to facts is fully proved by comparing it with contemporary documents. I am indebted to General Cass for the copy in my possession, as well as for other papers respecting the war in the neighborhood of Detroit.

The manuscript appears to have been elaborately written out from a rough journal kept during the progress of the events which it describes. It commences somewhat ambitiously, as follows: —

"Pondiac, great chief of all the Ottawas, Chippewas, and Pottawattamies, and of all the nations of the lakes and rivers of the North, a man proud, vindictive, warlike, and easily offended, under pretence of some insult which he thought he had received from Maj. Gladwin, Commander of the Fort, conceived that, being great chief of all the Northern nations, only himself and those of his nations were entitled to inhabit this portion of the earth, where for sixty and odd years the French had domiciliated for the purpose of trading, and where the English had governed during three years by right of the conquest of Canada. The Chief and all his nation, whose bravery consists in treachery, resolved within himself the entire destruction of the English nation, and perhaps the Canadians. In order to succeed in his undertaking, which he had not mentioned to any of his nation the Ottawas, he engaged their aid by a speech, and they, naturally inclined to evil, did not hesitate to obey him. But, as they found themselves too weak to undertake the enterprise alone, their chief endeavored to draw to his party the Chippewa nation by means of a council. This nation was governed by a chief named Ninevois. This man, who acknowledged Pondiac as his chief, whose mind was weak, and whose disposition cruel, listened to his advances, and joined him with all his band. These two nations consisted together of about four hundred men. This number did not appear to him sufficient. It became necessary to bring into their interests the Hurons. This nation, divided into two bands, was governed by two different chiefs of dissimilar character, and nevertheless both led by their spiritual father, a Jesuit. The two chiefs of this last nation were named, one Takee, of a temper similar to Pondiac's, and the other Teata, a man of cautious disposition and of perfect prudence. This last was not easily won, and having no disposition to do evil, he refused to listen to the deputies sent by Pondiac, and sent them back. They therefore addressed themselves to the first-mentioned of this nation, by whom they were listened to, and from whom they received the war-belt, with promise to join themselves to Pondiac and Ninevois, the Ottawas and Chippewas chiefs. It was settled by means of wampum belts, (a manner of making themselves understood amongst distant savages,) that they should hold a council on the 27th of April, when should be decided the day and hour of the attack, and the precautions necessary to take in order that their perfidy should not be discovered. The manner of counting used by the Indians is by the moon; and it was resolved in the way I have mentioned, that this council should be held on the 15th day of the moon, which corresponded with Wednesday the 27th of the month of April."

The writer next describes the council at the River Ecorces, and recounts at full length the story of the Delaware Indian who visited the Great Spirit. "The Chiefs," he says, "listened to Pondiac as to an oracle, and told him they were ready to do any thing he should require."

He relates with great minuteness how Pontiac, with his chosen warriors, came to the fort on the 1st of May, to dance the calumet dance, and observe the strength and disposition of the garrison, and describes the council subsequently held at the Pottawattamie village, in order to adjust the plan of attack.

"The day fixed upon having arrived, all the Ottawas, Pondiac at their head, and the bad band of the Hurons, Takee at their head, met at the Pottawattamie village, where the premeditated council was to be held. Care was taken to send all the women out of the village, that they might not discover what was decided upon. Pondiac then ordered sentinels to be placed around the village, to prevent any interruption to their council. These precautions taken, each seated himself in the circle, according to his rank, and Pondiac, as great chief of the league, thus addressed them:—

"It is important, my brothers, that we should exterminate from our land this nation, whose only object is our death. You must be all sensible, as well as myself, that we can no longer supply our wants in the way we were accustomed to do with our Fathers the French. They sell us their goods at double the price that the French made us pay, and yet their merchandise is good for nothing; for no sooner have we bought a blanket or other thing to cover us than it is necessary to procure others against the time of departing for our wintering ground. Neither will they let us have them on credit, as our brothers the French used to do. When I visit the English chief, and inform him of the death of any of our comrades, instead of lamenting, as our brothers the French used to do, they make game of us. If I ask him for any thing for our sick, he refuses, and tells us he does not want us, from which it is apparent he seeks our death. We must therefore, in return, destroy them without delay; there is nothing to prevent us: there are but few of them, and we shall easily overcome them,—why should we not attack them? Are we not men? Have I not shown you the belts I received from our Great Father the King of France? He tells us to strike,—why should we not listen to his words? What do you fear? The time has arrived. Do you fear that our brothers the French, who are now among us, will hinder us? They are not acquainted with our designs, and if they did know them, could they prevent them? You know, as well as myself, that when the English came upon our lands, to drive from them our father Bellestre, they took from the French all the guns that they have, so that they have now no guns to defend themselves with. Therefore now is the time: let us strike. Should there be any French to take their part, let us strike them as we do the English. Remember what the Giver of Life desired our brother the Delaware to do: this regards us as much as it does them. I have sent belts and speeches to our friends the Chippeways of Saginaw, and our brothers the Ottawas of Michillimacinac, and to those of the Rivière â la Tranche, (Thames River,) inviting them to join us, and they will not delay. In the mean time, let us strike. There is no longer any time to lose, and when the English shall be defeated, we will stop the way, so that no more shall return upon our lands.

"This discourse, which Pondiac delivered in a tone of much energy, had upon the whole council all the effect which he could have expected, and they all, with common accord, swore the entire destruction of the English nation.

"At the breaking up of the council, it was decided that Pondiac, with sixty chosen men, should go to the Fort to ask for a grand council from the English commander, and that they should have arms concealed under their blankets. That the remainder of the village should follow them armed with tomahawks, daggers, and knives, concealed under their blankets, and should enter the Fort, and walk about in such a manner as not to excite suspicion, whilst the others held council with the Commander. The Ottawa women were also to be furnished with short guns and other offensive weapons concealed under their blankets. They were to go into the back streets in the Fort. They were then to wait for the signal agreed upon, which was the cry of death, which the Grand Chief was to give, on which they should altogether strike upon the English, taking care not to hurt any of the French inhabiting the Fort."

The author of the diary, unlike other contemporary writers, states that the plot was disclosed to Gladwyn by a man of the Ottawa tribe, and not by an Ojibwa girl. He says, however, that on the day after the failure of the design Pontiac sent to the Pottawattamie village in order to seize an Ojibwa girl whom he suspected of having betrayed him.

"Pondiac ordered four Indians to take her and bring her before him; these men, naturally inclined to disorder, were not long in obeying their chief; they crossed the river immediately in front of their village, and passed into the Fort naked, having nothing but their breech-clouts on and their knives in their hands, and crying all the way that their plan had been defeated, which induced the French people of the Fort, who knew nothing of the designs of the Indians, to suspect that some bad design was going forward, either against themselves or the English. They arrived at the Pottawattamie village, and in fact found the woman, who was far from thinking of them; nevertheless they seized her, and obliged her to march before them, uttering cries of joy in the manner they do when they hold a victim in their clutches on whom they are going to exercise their cruelty: they made her enter the Fort, and took her before the Commandant, as if to confront her with him, and asked him if it was not from her he had learnt their design; but they were no better satisfied than if they had kept themselves quiet. They obtained from that Officer bread and beer for themselves, and for her. They then led her to their chief in the village."

The diary leaves us in the dark as to the treatment which the girl received; but there is a tradition among the Canadians that Pontiac, with his own hand, gave her a severe beating with a species of racket, such as the Indians use in their ball-play. An old Indian told Henry

Conner, formerly United States interpreter at Detroit, that she survived her punishment, and lived for many years; but at length, contracting intemperate habits, she fell, when intoxicated, into a kettle
of boiling maple sap, and was so severely scalded that she died in
consequence.

The outbreak of hostilities, the attack on the fort, and the detention of Campbell and McDougal are related at great length, and with
all the minuteness of an eye-witness. The substance of the narrative is
incorporated in the body of the work. The diary is very long, detail-
ing the incidents of every passing day, from the 7th of May to the
31st of July. Here it breaks off abruptly in the middle of a sentence,
the remaining part having been lost or torn away. The following
extracts, taken at random, will serve to indicate the general style and
character of the journal: —

"Saturday, June 4th. About 4 P. M. cries of death were heard from
the Indians. The cause was not known, but it was supposed they had
obtained some prize on the Lake.

"Sunday, June 5th. The Indians fired a few shots upon the Fort
to-day. About 2 P. M. cries of death were again heard on the opposite side of the River. A number of Indians were descried, part on
foot and part mounted. Others were taking up two trading boats,
which they had taken on the lake. The vessel fired several shots at
them, hoping they would abandon their prey, but they reached Pondiac's camp uninjured. . . .

"About 7 P. M. news came that a number of Indians had gone
down as far as Turkey Island, opposite the small vessel which was
anchored there, but that, on seeing them, she had dropped down
into the open Lake, to wait for a fair wind to come up the river.

"Monday, June 20th. The Indians fired some shots upon the fort.
About 4 P. M. news was brought that Presquisle and Beef River
Forts, which had been established by the French, and were now oc-
cupied by the English, had been destroyed by the Indians. . . .

"Wednesday, June 22d. The Indians, whose whole attention was
directed to the vessel, did not trouble the Fort. In the course of the
day, the news of the taking of Presquisle was confirmed, as a great
number of the Indians were seen coming along the shore with prisoners. The Commandant was among the number, and with him one
woman: both were presented to the Hurons. In the afternoon, the
Commandant received news of the lading of the vessel, and the
number of men on board. The Indians again visited the French for
provisions.

"Thursday, June 23d. Very early in the morning, a great number of
Indians were seen passing behind the Fort: they joined those below,

and all repaired to Turkey Island. The river at this place is very narrow. The Indians commenced making intrenchments of trees, &c., on the beach, where the vessel was to pass, whose arrival they awaited. About ten of the preceding night, the wind coming aft, the vessel weighed anchor, and came up the river. When opposite the Island the wind fell, and they were obliged to throw the anchor; as they knew they could not reach the Fort without being attacked by the Indians, they kept a strict watch. In order to deceive the Indians, the captain had hid in the hold sixty of his men, suspecting that the Indians, seeing only about a dozen men on deck, would try to take the vessel, which occurred as he expected. About 9 at night they got in their canoes, and made for the vessel, intending to board her. They were seen far off by one of the sentinels. The captain immediately ordered up all his men in the greatest silence, and placed them along the sides of the vessel, with their guns in their hands, loaded, with orders to wait the signal for firing, which was the rap of a hammer on the mast. The Indians were allowed to approach within less than gunshot, when the signal was given, and a discharge of cannon and small arms made upon them. They retreated to their intrenchment with the loss of fourteen killed and fourteen wounded; from which they fired during the night, and wounded two men. In the morning the vessel dropped down to the Lake for a more favorable wind.

"Friday, June 24th. The Indians were occupied with the vessel. Two Indians back of the Fort were pursued by twenty men, and escaped.

"Saturday, June 25th. Nothing occurred this day.

"Sunday, June 26th. Nothing of consequence.

"Monday, June 27th. Mr. Gamelin, who was in the practice of visiting Messrs. Campbell and McDougall, brought a letter to the Commandant from Mr. Campbell, dictated by Pondiac, in which he requested the Commandant to surrender the Fort, as in a few days he expected Kee-no-chameck, great chief of the Chippewas, with eight hundred men of his nation; that he (Pondiac) would not then be able to command them, and as soon as they arrived, they would scalp all the English in the Fort. The Commandant only answered that he cared as little for him as he did for them. . . .

"This evening, the Commandant was informed that the Ottawas and Chippewas had undertaken another raft, which might be more worthy of attention than the former ones: it was reported to be of pine boards, and intended to be long enough to go across the river. By setting fire to every part of it, it could not help, by its length, coming in contact with the vessel, which by this means they expected would certainly take fire. Some firing took place between the vessel and Indians, but without effect.

"Tuesday, July 19th. The Indians attempted to fire on the Fort, but being discovered, they were soon made to retreat by a few shot.

"Wednesday, July 20th. Confirmation came to the Fort of the report of the 18th, and that the Indians had been four days at work at their raft, and that it would take eight more to finish it. The Commandant ordered that two boats should be lined or clapboarded with oak plank, two inches thick, and the same defence to be raised above the gunnels of the boats of two feet high. A swivel was put on each of them, and placed in such a way that they could be pointed in three different directions.

"Thursday, July 21st. The Indians were too busily occupied to pay any attention to the Fort; so earnest were they in the work of the raft that they hardly allowed themselves time to eat. The Commandant farther availed himself of the time allowed him before the premeditated attack to put every thing in proper order to repulse it. He ordered that two strong graplins should be provided for each of the barges, a strong iron chain of fifteen feet was to be attached to the boat, and conducting a strong cable under water, fastened to the graplins, and the boats were intended to be so disposed as to cover the vessel, by mooring them, by the help of the above preparations, above her. The inhabitants of the S. W. ridge, or hill, again got a false alarm. It was said the Indians intended attacking them during the night: they kept on their guard till morning.

"Friday, July 22d. An Abenakee Indian arrived this day, saying that he came direct from Montreal, and gave out that a large fleet of French was on its way to Canada, full of troops, to dispossess the English of the country. However fallacious such a story might appear, it had the effect of rousing Pondiac from his inaction, and the Indians set about their raft with more energy than ever. They had left off working at it since yesterday." . . .

It is needless to continue these extracts farther. Those already given will convey a sufficient idea of the character of the diary.

REMINISCENSES OF AGED CANADIANS.

About the year 1824, General Cass, with the design of writing a narrative of the siege of Detroit by Pontiac, caused inquiry to be made among the aged Canadian inhabitants, many of whom could distinctly remember the events of 1763. The accounts received from them were committed to paper, and were placed by General Cass, with great liberality, in the writer's hands. They afford an interesting mass of evidence, as worthy of confidence as evidence of the kind can be. With but one exception,—the account of Maxwell,—they do not clash with the testimony of contemporary documents. Much caution has, however, been observed in their use; and no essential statement has been made on their unsupported authority. The most prominent of these accounts are those of Peltier, St. Aubin, Gouin, Meloche, Parent, and Maxwell.

PELTIER'S ACCOUNT.

M. Peltier was seventeen years old at the time of Pontiac's war. His narrative, though one of the longest of the collection, is imperfect, since, during a great part of the siege, he was absent from Detroit in search of runaway horses, belonging to his father. His recollection of the earlier part of the affair is, however, clear and minute. He relates, with apparent credulity, the story of the hand of the murdered Fisher protruding from the earth, as if in supplication for the neglected rites of burial. He remembers that, soon after the failure of Pontiac's attempt to surprise the garrison, he punished, by a severe flogging, a woman named Catharine, accused of having betrayed the plot. He was at Detroit during the several attacks on the armed vessels, and the attempts to set them on fire by means of blazing rafts.

ST. AUBIN'S ACCOUNT.

St. Aubin was fifteen years old at the time of the siege. It was his mother who crossed over to Pontiac's village shortly before the attempt on the garrison, and discovered the Indians in the act of sawing off the muzzles of their guns, as related in the narrative. He remembers Pontiac at his headquarters, at the house of Meloche; where his commissaries served out provision to the Indians. He himself was among those who conveyed cattle across the river to the English, at a time when they were threatened with starvation. One of his most vivid recollections is that of seeing the head of Captain Dalzell stuck on the picket of a garden fence, on the day after the battle of Bloody Bridge. His narrative is one of the most copious and authentic of the series.

GOUIN'S ACCOUNT.

M. Gouin was but eleven years old at the time of the war. His father was a prominent trader, and had great influence over the Indians. On several occasions, he acted as mediator between them and the English; and when Major Campbell was bent on visiting the camp of Pontiac, the elder Gouin strenuously endeavored to prevent the attempt. Pontiac often came to him for advice. His son bears emphatic testimony to the extraordinary control which the chief exercised over his followers, and to the address which he displayed in the management of his commissary department. This account contains many particulars not elsewhere mentioned, though bearing all the appearance of truth. It appears to have been composed partly from the recollections of the younger Gouin, and partly from information derived from his father.

Meloche's Account.

Mad. Meloche lived, when a child, on the borders of the Detroit, between the river and the camp of Pontiac. On one occasion, when the English were cannonading the camp from their armed schooner in the river, a shot struck her father's house, throwing down a part of the walls. After the death of Major Campbell, she picked up a pocket-book belonging to him, which the Indians had left on the ground. It was full of papers, and she carried it to the English in the fort.

Parent's Account.

M. Parent was twenty-two years old when the war broke out. His recollections of the siege are, however, less exact than those of some of the former witnesses, though his narrative preserves several interesting incidents.

Maxwell's Account.

Maxwell was an English provincial, and pretended to have been a soldier under Gladwyn. His story belies the statement. It has all the air of a narrative made up from hearsay, and largely embellished from imagination. It has been made use of only in a few instances, where it is amply supported by less questionable evidence. This account seems to have been committed to paper by Maxwell himself, as the style is very rude and illiterate.

The remaining manuscripts consulted with reference to the siege of Detroit have been obtained from the State Paper Office of London, and from a few private autograph collections. Some additional information has been derived from the columns of the New York Mercury, and the Pennsylvania Gazette for 1763, where various letters written by officers at Detroit are published.

2. THE MASSACRE OF MICHILLIMACKINAC.
(Chap. XVII.)

The following letter may be regarded with interest, as having been written by the commander of the unfortunate garrison a few days after the massacre. A copy of the original was procured from the State Paper Office of London.

Michillimackinac, 12 June, 1763.

Sir:

Notwithstanding that I wrote you in my last, that all the savages were arrived, and that every thing seemed in perfect tranquillity, yet, on the 2d instant, the Chippewas, who live in a plain near this fort, assembled to play ball, as they had done almost every day since their arrival. They played from morning till noon; then throwing their ball close to the gate, and observing Lieut. Lesley and me a few paces out of it, they came behind us, seized and carried us into the woods.

In the mean time the rest rushed into the Fort, where they found their squaws, whom they had previously planted there, with their hatchets hid under their blankets, which they took, and in an instant killed Lieut. Jamet and fifteen rank and file, and a trader named Tracy. They wounded two, and took the rest of the garrison prisoners, five [seven, Henry] of whom they have since killed.

They made prisoners all the English Traders, and robbed them of every thing they had; but they offered no violence to the persons or property of any of the Frenchmen.

When that massacre was over, Messrs. Langlade and Farli, the Interpreter, came down to the place where Lieut. Lesley and me were prisoners; and on their giving themselves as security to return us when demanded, they obtained leave for us to go to the Fort, under a guard of savages, which gave time, by the assistance of the gentlemen above-mentioned, to send for the Outaways, who came down on the first notice, and were very much displeased at what the Chippeways had done.

Since the arrival of the Outaways they have done every thing in their power to serve us, and with what prisoners the Chippeways had given them, and what they have bought, I have now with me Lieut. Lesley and eleven privates; and the other four of the Garrison, who are yet living, remain in the hands of the Chippeways.

The Chippeways, who are superior in number to the Ottaways, have declared in Council to them that if they do not remove us out of the Fort, they will cut off all communication to this Post, by which means all the Convoys of Merchants from Montreal, La Baye, St. Joseph, and the upper posts, would perish. But if the news of your posts being attacked (which they say was the reason why they took up the hatchet) be false, and you can send up a strong reinforcement, with provisions, &c., accompanied by some of your savages, I believe the post might be re-established again.

Since this affair happened, two canoes arrived from Montreal, which put in my power to make a present to the Ottaway nation, who very well deserve any thing that can be done for them.

I have been very much obliged to Messrs. Langlade and Farli, the Interpreter, as likewise to the Jesuit, for the many good offices they have done us on this occasion. The Priest seems inclinable to go down to your post for a day or two, which I am very glad of, as he is a very good man, and had a great deal to say with the savages, hereabout, who will believe every thing he tells them on his return, which I hope will be soon. The Outaways say they will take Lieut. Lesley, me, and the Eleven men which I mentioned before were in their hands, up to their village, and there keep us, till they hear what is doing at your Post. They have sent this canot for that purpose.

I refer you to the Priest for the particulars of this melancholy affair, and am, Dear Sir,

Yours very sincerely,

[Signed]   GEO. ETHERINGTON.

To MAJOR GLADWYN.

P. S. The Indians that are to carry the Priest to Detroit will not undertake to land him at the Fort, but at some of the Indian villages near it; so you must not take it amiss that he does not pay you the first visit. And once more I beg that nothing may stop your sending of him back, the next day after his arrival, if possible, as we shall be at a great loss for the want of him, and I make no doubt that you will do all in your power to make peace, as you see the situation we are in, and send up provision as soon as possible, and Ammunition, as what we had was pillaged by the savages.

Adieu.

GEO. ETHERINGTON.

Appendix D.

THE WAR ON THE BORDERS.

THE BATTLE OF BUSHY RUN. (Chap. XX.)

The despatches written by Colonel Bouquet, immediately after the two battles near Bushy Run, contain so full and clear an account of those engagements, that the collateral authorities consulted have served rather to decorate and enliven the narrative than to add to it any important facts. The first of these letters was written by Bouquet under the apprehension that he should not survive the expected conflict of the next day. Both were forwarded to the commander-in-chief by the same express, within a few days after the victory. The letters as here given were copied from the originals in the London offices.

Camp at Edge Hill, 26 Miles from⎱
Fort Pitt, 5th August, 1763. ⎰

Sir:

The Second Instant the Troops and Convoy Arrived at Ligonier, whence I could obtain no Intelligence of the Enemy; The Expresses Sent since the beginning of July, having been Either killed, or Obliged to Return, all the Passes being Occupied by the Enemy: In this uncertainty I Determined to Leave all the Waggons with the Powder, and a Quantity of Stores and Provisions, at Ligonier; And on the 4th proceeded with the Troops, and about 350 Horses Loaded with Flour.

I Intended to have Halted to Day at Bushy Run, (a Mile beyond this Camp,) and after having Refreshed the Men and Horses, to have Marched in the Night over Turtle Creek, a very Dangerous Defile of Several Miles, Commanded by High and Craggy Hills: But at one o'clock this Afternoon, after a march of 17 Miles, the Savages suddenly Attacked our Advanced Guard, which was immediately Supported by the two Light Infantry Companies of the 42d Regiment, Who Drove the Enemy from their Ambuscade, and pursued them a good Way. The Savages Returned to the Attack, and the Fire being Obstinate on our Front, and Extending along our Flanks, We made a General Charge, with the whole Line, to Dislodge the Savages from the Heights, in which attempt We succeeded without Obtaining by it any Decisive Advantage; for as soon as they were driven from One Post, they Appeared on Another, 'till, by continual Reinforcements, they were at last able to Surround Us, and attacked the Convoy left

871

in our Rear; This Obliged us to March Back to protect it; The Action then became General, and though we were attacked on Every Side, and the Savages Exerted themselves with Uncommon Resolution, they were constantly Repulsed with Loss.—We also Suffered Considerably: Capt. Lieut. Graham, and Lieut. James McIntosh of the 42d, are Killed, and Capt. Graham Wounded.

Of the Royal Amer'n Regt., Lieut. Dow, who acted as A. D. Q. M. G. is shot through the Body.

Of the 77th, Lieut. Donald Campbell, and Mr. Peebles, a Volunteer, are Wounded.

Our Loss in Men, Including Rangers, and Drivers, Exceeds Sixty, Killed or Wounded.

The Action has Lasted from One O'Clock 'till Night, And We Expect to Begin again at Day Break. Whatever Our Fate may be, I thought it necessary to Give Your Excellency this Early Information, that You may, at all Events, take such Measures as You will think proper with the Provinces, for their own Safety, and the Effectual Relief of Fort Pitt, as in Case of Another Engagement I Fear Insurmountable Difficulties in protecting and Transporting our Provisions, being already so much Weakened by the Losses of this Day, in Men and Horses; besides the Additional Necessity of Carrying the Wounded, Whose Situation is truly Deplorable.

I Cannot Sufficiently Acknowledge the Constant Assistance I have Received from Major Campbell, during this long Action; Nor Express my Admiration of the Cool and Steady Behavior of the Troops, Who Did not Fire a Shot, without Orders, and Drove the Enemy from their Posts with Fixed Bayonets.—The Conduct of the Officers is much above my Praises.

> I Have the
>> Honor to be, with great Respect,
>>> Sir,
>>>> &ca.
>>>>> HENRY BOUQUET.

His Excellency SIR JEFFREY AMHERST.

> Camp at Bushy Run, 6th August, 1763.

Sir:

I Had the Honor to Inform Your Excellency in my letter of Yesterday of our first Engagement with the Savages.

We Took Post last Night on the Hill, where Our Convoy Halted, when the Front was Attacked, (a commodious piece of Ground, and Just Spacious Enough for our Purpose.) There We Encircled the Whole, and Covered our Wounded with the Flour Bags.

In the Morning the Savages Surrounded our Camp, at the Distance of about 500 Yards, and by Shouting and Yelping, quite Round that Extensive Circumference, thought to have Terrified Us, with their Numbers. They Attacked Us Early, and, under Favour of an Incessant Fire, made Several Bold Efforts to Penetrate our Camp; And tho' they Failed in the Attempt, our Situation was not the Less Perplexing, having Experienced that Brisk Attacks had Little Effect upon an Enemy, who always gave Way when Pressed, & Appeared again Immediately; Our Troops were besides Extremely Fatigued with the Long March, and as long Action of the Preceding Day, and Distressed to the Last Degree, by a Total Want of Water, much more Intolerable than the Enemy's Fire.

Tied to our Convoy We could not Lose Sight of it, without Exposing it, and our Wounded, to Fall a prey to the Savages, who Pressed upon Us on Every Side; and to Move it was Impracticable, having lost many horses, and most of the Drivers, Stupified by Fear, hid themselves in the Bushes, or were Incapable of Hearing or Obeying Orders.

The Savages growing Every Moment more Audacious, it was thought proper still to increase their Confidence; by that means, if possible, to Entice them to Come Close upon Us, or to Stand their Ground when Attacked. With this View two Companies of Light Infantry were Ordered within the Circle, and the Troops on their Right and Left opened their Files, and Filled up the Space that it might seem they were intended to Cover the Retreat; The Third Light Infantry Company, and the Grenadiers of the 42d, were Ordered to Support the two First Companys. This Manœuvre Succeeded to Our Wish, for the Few Troops who Took possession of the Ground lately Occupied by the two Light Infantry Companys being Brought in Nearer to the Centre of the Circle, the Barbarians, mistaking these Motions for a Retreat, Hurried Headlong on, and Advancing upon Us, with the most Daring Intrepidity, Galled us Excessively with their Heavy Fire; But at the very moment that, Certain of Success, they thought themselves Masters of the Camp, Major Campbell, at the Head of the two First Companys, Sallied out from a part of the Hill they Could not Observe, and Fell upon their Right Flank; They Resolutely Returned the Fire, but could not Stand the Irresistible Shock of our Men, Who, Rushing in among them, Killed many of them, and Put the Rest to Flight. The Orders sent to the Other Two Companys were Delivered so timely by Captain Basset, and Executed with such Celerity and Spirit, that the Routed Savages, who happened to Run that Moment before their Front, Received their Full Fire, when Uncovered by the Trees: The

Four Companys Did not give them time to Load a Second time, nor Even to Look behind them, but Pursued them 'till they were Totally Dispersed. The Left of the Savages, which had not been Attacked, were kept in Awe by the Remains of our Troops, Posted on the Brow of the Hill, for that Purpose; Nor Durst they Attempt to Support, or Assist their Right, but being Witness to their Defeat, followed their Example and Fled. Our Brave Men Disdained so much to Touch the Dead Body of a Vanquished Enemy, that Scarce a Scalp was taken, Except by the Rangers, and Pack Horse Drivers.

The Woods being now Cleared and the Pursuit over, the Four Companys took possession of a Hill in our Front; and as soon as Litters could be made for the Wounded, and the Flour and Every thing Destroyed, which, for want of Horses, could not be Carried, We Marched without Molestation to this Camp. After the Severe Correction We had given the Savages a few hours before, it was Natural to Suppose We should Enjoy some Rest; but We had hardly Fixed our Camp, when they fired upon Us again: This was very Provoking! However, the Light Infantry Dispersed them, before they could Receive Orders for that purpose.—I Hope We shall be no more Disturbed, for, if We have another Action, We shall hardly be able to Carry our Wounded.

The Behavior of the Troops, on this Occasion, Speaks for itself so Strongly, that for me to Attempt their Eulogium, would but Detract from their merit.

I Have the Honor to be, most Respectfully,

Sir,

&ca.

Henry Bouquet.

P. S. I Have the Honor to Enclose the Return of the Killed, Wounded, and Missing in the two Engagements.

H. B.

His Excellency Sir Jeffrey Amherst.

Appendix E.

THE PAXTON RIOTS.

1. Evidence against the Indians of Conestoga.
(Chap. XXIV.)

Abraham Newcomer, a Mennonist, by trade a Gunsmith, upon his affirmation, declared that several times, within these few years, Bill Soc and Indian John, two of the Conestogue Indians, threatened to scalp him for refusing to mend their tomahawks, and swore they would as soon scalp him as they would a dog. A few days before Bill Soc was killed, he brought a tomahawk to be steeled. Bill said, "If you will not, I'll have it mended to your sorrow," from which expression I apprehended danger.

Mrs. Thompson, of the borough of Lancaster, personally appeared before the Chief Burgess, and upon her solemn oath, on the Holy Evangelists, said that in the summer of 1761, Bill Soc came to her apartment, and threatened her life, saying, "I kill you, all Lancaster can't catch me," which filled me with terror; and this lady further said, Bill Soc added, "Lancaster is mine, and I will have it yet."

Colonel John Hambright, gentleman, an eminent Brewer of the Borough of Lancaster, personally appeared before Robert Thompson, Esq., a justice for the county of Lancaster, and made oath on the Holy Evangelists, that, in August, 1757, he, an officer, was sent for provision from Fort Augusta to Fort Hunter, that on his way he rested at M'Kee's old place; a Sentinel was stationed behind a tree, to prevent surprise. The Sentry gave notice Indians were near; the deponent crawled up the bank and discovered two Indians; one was Bill Soc, lately killed at Lancaster. He called Bill Soc to come to him, but the Indians ran off. When the deponent came to Fort Hunter, he learnt that an old man had been killed the day before; Bill Soc and his companion were believed to be the perpetrators of the murder. He, the deponent, had frequently seen Bill Soc and some of the Conestogue Indians at Fort Augusta, trading with the Indians, but, after the murder of the old man, Bill Soc did not appear at that Garrison.

JOHN HAMBRIGHT.

Sworn and Subscribed the 28th of Feb., 1764, before me,

ROBERT THOMPSON, Justice.

Charles Cunningham, of the county of Lancaster, personally appeared before me, Thomas Foster, Esq., one of the Magistrates for said county, and being qualified according to law, doth depose and

875

say, that he, the deponent, heard Joshua James, an Indian, say, that he never killed a white man in his life, but six dutchmen that he killed in the Minisinks.

CHARLES CUNNINGHAM.

Sworn to, and Subscribed before THOMAS FOSTER, Justice.

Alexander Stephen, of the county of Lancaster, personally appeared before Thomas Foster, Esq., one of the Magistrates, and being duly qualified according to law, doth say, that Connayak Sally, an Indian woman, told him that the Conestogue Indians had killed Jegrea, an Indian, because he would not join the Conestogue Indians in destroying the English. James Cotter told the deponent that he was one of the three that killed old William Hamilton, on Sherman's Creek, and also another man, with seven of his family. James Cotter demanded of the deponent a canoe, which the murderers had left, as Cotter told him when the murder was committed.

ALEXANDER STEPHEN.

THOMAS FOSTER, Justice.

Note. — Jegrea was a Warrior Chief, friendly to the Whites, and he threatened the Conestogue Indians with his vengeance, if they harmed the English. Cotter was one of the Indians, killed in Lancaster county, in 1763.

Anne Mary Le Roy, of Lancaster, appeared before the Chief Burgess, and being sworn on the Holy Evangelists of Almighty God, did depose and say, that in the year 1755, when her Father, John Jacob Le Roy, and many others, were murdered by the Indians, at Mahoney, she, her brother, and some others were made prisoners, and taken to Kittanning; that stranger Indians visited them; the French told them they were Conestogue Indians, and that Isaac was the only Indian true to their interest; and that the Conestogue Indians, with the exception of Isaac, were ready to lift the hatchet when ordered by the French. She asked Bill Soc's mother whether she had ever been at Kittanning? she said "no, but her son, Bill Soc, had been there often; that he was good for nothing."

MARY LE ROY.

2. PROCEEDINGS OF THE RIOTERS. (Chap. XXIV., XXV.)

Deposition of Felix Donolly, keeper of Lancaster Jail.

This deposition is imperfect, a part of the manuscript having been defaced or torn away. The original, in the handwriting of Edward Shippen, the chief magistrate of Lancaster, was a few years since in the possession of Redmond Conyngham, Esq.

The breaking open the door alarmed me; armed men broke in; they demanded the strange Indian to be given up; they ran by me; the Indians guessed their intention; they seized billets of wood from the pile; but the three most active were shot; others came to their assistance; I was stupefied; before I could shake off my surprise, the Indians were killed and their murderers away.

Q. You say, "Indians armed themselves with wood;" did those Indians attack the rioters?

A. They did. If they had not been shot, they would have killed the men who entered, for they were the strongest.

Q. Could the murder have been prevented by you?

A. No: I nor no person here could have prevented it.

Q. What number were the rioters?

A. I should say fifty.

Q. Did you know any of them?

A. No; they were strangers.

Q. Do you now know who was in command?

A. I have been told, Lazarus Stewart of Donegal.

Q. If the Indians had not attempted resistance, would the men have fled? (fired?)

A. I couldn't tell; I do not know.

Q. Do you think or believe that the rioters came with the intent to murder?

A. I heard them say, when they broke in, they wanted a strange Indian.

Q. Was their object to murder him?

A. From what I have heard since, I think they meant to carry him off; that is my belief.

Q. What was their purpose?

A. I do not know.

Q. Were the Indians killed all friends of this province?

A. I have been told they were not. I cannot tell of myself; I do not know.

Donolly was suspected of a secret inclination in favor of the rioters. In private conversation he endeavored to place their conduct in as favorable a light as possible, and indeed such an intention is apparent in the above deposition.

Letter from Edward Shippen to Governor Hamilton.

Lancaster, ——, 1764.

Honoured Sir:

I furnish you with a full detail of all the particulars that could be gathered of the unhappy transactions of the fourteenth and twenty-seventh of December last, as painful for you to read as me to write. The Depositions can only state the fact that the Indians were killed. Be assured the Borough Authorities, when they placed the Indians in the Workhouse, thought it a place of security. I am sorry the Indians were not removed to Philadelphia, as recommended by us. It is too late to remedy. It is much to be regretted that there are evil-minded persons among us, who are trying to corrupt the minds of the people by idle tales and horrible butcheries—are injuring the character of many of our most respectable people. That printers should have lent their aid astonishes me when they are employed by the Assembly to print their laws. I can see no good in meeting their falsehoods by counter statements.

The Rev. Mr. Elder and Mr. Harris are determined to rely upon the reputation they have so well established.

For myself, I can only say that, possessing your confidence, and that of the Proprietaries, with a quiet conscience, I regard not the malignant pens of secret assailants—men who had not the courage to affix their names. Is it not strange that a too ready belief was at first given to the slanderous epistles? Resting on the favor I have enjoyed of the Government; on the confidence reposed in me, by you and the Proprietaries; by the esteem of my fellow-men in Lancaster, I silently remain passive.

Yours affectionately,

EDWARD SHIPPEN.

Extract from a letter of the Rev. Mr. Elder to Governor Penn, December 27, 1763.

The storm which had been so long gathering, has at length exploded. Had Government removed the Indians from Conestoga, which had frequently been urged, without success, this painful catastrophe might have been avoided. What could I do with men heated to madness? All that I could do, was done; I expostulated; but *life* and *reason* were set at defiance. And yet the men, in private life, are virtuous and respectable; not cruel, but mild and merciful.

The time will arrive when each palliating circumstance will be calmly weighed. This deed, magnified into the blackest of crimes, shall be considered one of those youthful ebullitions of wrath caused by momentary excitement, to which human infirmity is subjected.

Extract from "The Paxtoniade," a poem in imitation of Hudibras, published at Philadelphia, 1764, by a partisan of the Quaker faction:—

> O'Hara mounted on his Steed,
> (Descendant of that self-same Ass,

That bore his Grandsire Hudibras,)
And from that same exalted Station,
Pronounced an hortory Oration:
For he was cunning as a fox,
Had read o'er Calvin and Dan Nox;
A man of most profound Discerning,
Well versed in P——n Learning.
So after hemming thrice to clear
His Throat, and banish thoughts of fear,
And of the mob obtaining Silence,
He thus went on— "Dear Sirs, a while since
Ye know as how the Indian Rabble,
With practices unwarrantable,
Did come upon our quiet Borders,
And there commit most desperate murders;
Did tomahawk, butcher, wound and cripple,
With cruel Rage, the Lord's own People;
Did war most implacable wage
With God's own chosen heritage;
Did from our Brethren take their lives,
And kill our Children, kine and wives.
Now, Sirs, I ween it is but right,
That we upon these Canaanites,
Without delay, should Vengeance take,
Both for our own, and the K—k's sake;
Should totally destroy the heathen,
And never till we've killed 'em leave 'em;—
Destroy them quite frae out the Land;
And for it we have God's Command.
We should do him a muckle Pleasure,
As ye in your Books may read at leisure."
He paused, as Orators are used,
And from his pocket quick produced
A friendly Vase well stor'd and fill'd
With good old whiskey twice distill'd,
And having refresh'd his inward man,
Went on with his harangue again.
"Is't not, my Brethren, a pretty Story
That we who are the Land's chief Glory,
Who are i' the number of God's elected,
Should slighted thus be and neglected?
That we, who're the only Gospel Church,
Should thus be left here in the lurch;

Whilst our most antichristian foes,
Whose trade is war and hardy blows,
(At least while some of the same Colour,
With those who've caused us all this Dolor,)
In matchcoats warm and blankets drest,
Are by the Q——rs much caress'd,
And live in peace by good warm fires,
And have the extent of their desires?
Shall we put by such treatment base?
By Nox, we wont!"—And broke his Vase.
"Seeing then we've such good cause to hate 'em,
What I intend's to extirpate 'em;
To suffer them no more to thrive,
And leave nor Root nor Branch alive;
But would we madly leave our wives
And Children, and expose our lives
In search of these wh' infest our borders,
And perpetrate such cruel murders;
It is most likely, by King Harry,
That we should in the end miscarry.
I deem therefore the wisest course is,
That those who've beasts should mount their horses,
And those who've none should march on foot,
With as much quickness as will suit,
To where those heathen, nothing fearful,
That we will on their front and rear fall,
Enjoy Sweet Otium in their Cotts,
And dwell securely in their Hutts.
And as they've nothing to defend them,
We'll quickly to their own place send them!"

The following letter from Rev. John Elder to Colonel Shippen will serve to exhibit the state of feeling among the frontier inhabitants.

Paxton, Feb. 1, 1764.

Dear Sir:

Since I sealed the Governor's Letter, which you'll please to deliver to him, I suspect, from the frequent meetings I hear the people have had in divers parts of the Frontier Counties, that an Expedition is immediately designed against the Indians at Philadelphia. It's well known that I have always used my utmost endeavors to discourage these proceedings; but to little purpose: the minds of the Inhabitants are so exasperated against a particular set of men, deeply concerned in the government, for the singular regards they have always shown to savages, and the heavy burden by their means laid on the province in maintaining an expensive Trade and holding Treaties from time to time with the savages, without any prospect of advantage either to his Majesty or to the province, how beneficial soever it may have been to individuals, that it's in vain, nay even unsafe for any one to oppose their measures; for were Col. Shippen here, tho' a gentleman highly esteemed by the Frontier inhabitants, he would soon find it useless, if not dangerous, to act in opposition to an enraged multitude. At first there were but, as I think, few concerned in these riots, & nothing intended by some but to ease the province of part of its burden, and by others, who had suffered greatly in the late war, the gratifying a spirit of Revenge, yet the manner of the Quakers resenting these things has been, I think, very injurious and impolitick. The Presbyterians, who are the most numerous, I imagine, of any denomination in the province, are enraged at their being charged in bulk with these facts, under the name of Scotch-Irish, and other ill-natured titles, and that the killing the Conestogoe Indians is compared to the Irish Massacres, and reckoned the most barbarous of either, so that things are grown to that pitch now that the country seems determined that no Indian Treaties shall be held, or savages maintained at the expense of the province, unless his Majesty's pleasure on these heads is well known; for I understood to my great satisfaction that amid our great confusions, there are none, even of the most warm and furious tempers, but what are warmly attached to his Majesty, and would cheerfully risk their lives to promote his service. What the numbers are of those going on the above-mentioned Expedition, I can't possibly learn, as I'm informed they are collecting in all parts of the province; however, this much may be depended on, that they have the good wishes of the country in general, and that there are few but what are now either one way or other embarked in the affair, tho' some particular persons, I'm informed, are grossly misrepresented in Philadelphia; even my neighbor, Mr. Harris, it's said, is looked on there as the chief promoter of these riots, yet it's entirely false; he had aided as much in opposition to these measures as he could with any safety in his situation. Reports, however groundless, are spread by designing men on purpose to inflame matters, and enrage the parties against each other, and various methods used to accomplish their pernicious ends. As I am deeply concerned for the welfare of my country, I would do every thing in my power to promote its interests. I thought proper to give you these few hints; you'll please to make what use you think proper of them. I would heartily wish that some effectual measures might be taken to heal these growing evils, and this I judge may be yet done, and Col. Armstrong, who is now in town, may be usefully employed for this purpose.

Sir,

I am, etc.,

JOHN ELDER.

Extracts from a Quaker letter on the Paxton riots.

This letter is written with so much fidelity, and in so impartial a spirit, that it must always remain one of the best authorities in reference to these singular events. Although in general very accurate, its testimony has in a few instances been set aside in favor of the more direct evidence of eye-witnesses. It was published by Hazard in the twelfth volume of his Pennsylvania Register. I have, however, examined the original, which is still preserved by a family in Philadelphia. The extracts here given form but a small part of the entire letter.

Before I proceed further it may not be amiss to inform thee that a great number of the inhabitants here approved of killing the Indians, and declared that they would not offer to oppose the Paxtoneers, unless they attacked the citizens, that is to say, themselves—for, if any judgment was to be formed from countenances and behavior, those who depended upon them for defence and protection, would have found their confidence shockingly misplaced.

The number of persons in arms that morning was about six hundred, and as it was expected the insurgents would attempt to cross at the middle or upper ferry, orders were sent to bring the boats to this side, and to take away the ropes. Couriers were now seen continually coming in, their horses all of a foam, and people running with the greatest eagerness to ask them where the enemy were, and what were their numbers. The answers to these questions were various: sometimes they were at a distance, then near at hand—sometimes they were a thousand strong, then five hundred, then fifteen hundred; in short, all was doubt and uncertainty.

About eleven o'clock it was recollected the boat at the Sweed's ford was not secured, which, in the present case, was of the utmost consequence, for, as there was a considerable freshet in the Schuylkill, the securing that boat would oblige them to march some distance up the river, and thereby retard the execution of their scheme at least a day or two longer. Several persons therefore set off immediately to get it performed; but they had not been gone long, before there was a general uproar—They are coming! they are coming! Where? where? Down Second street! down Second street! Such of the company as had grounded their firelocks, flew to arms, and began to prime; the artillery-men threw themselves into order, and the people ran to get out of the way, for a troop of armed men, on horseback, appeared in reality coming down the street, and one of the artillery-men was just going to apply the fatal match, when a person, perceiving the mistake, clapped his hat upon the touch-hole of the piece he was going to fire. Dreadful would have been the consequence, had the cannon discharged; for the men that appeared proved to be a company of German butchers and porters, under the command of Captain Hoffman. They had just collected themselves, and being unsuspicious of danger, had neglected to give notice of their coming;—a false alarm was now called out, and all became quiet again in a few minutes. . . .

The weather being now very wet, Capt. Francis, Capt. Wood, and Capt. Mifflin, drew up their men under the market-house, which, not affording shelter for any more, they occupied Friends' meeting-house, and Capt. Joseph Wharton marched his company up stairs, into the monthly meeting room, as I have been told—the rest were stationed below. It happened to be the day appointed for holding of Youths' meeting, but never did the Quaker youth assemble in such a military manner—never was the sound of the drum heard before within those walls, nor ever till now was the Banner of War displayed in that rostrum, from whence the art has been so zealously declaimed against. Strange reverse of times, James—. Nothing of any consequence passed during the remainder of the day, except that Captain Coultas came into town at the head of a troop, which he had just raised in his own neighborhood. The Captain was one of those who had been marked out as victims by these devout conquerors, and word was sent to him from Lancaster to make his peace with Heaven, for that he had but about ten days to live.

In the evening our Negotiators came in from Germantown. They had conferred with the Chiefs of this illustrious—, and have prevailed with them to suspend all hostility till such time as they should receive an answer to their petition or manifesto, which had been sent down the day before. . . .

The weather now clearing, the City forces drew up near the Court House where a speech was made to them, informing them that matters had been misrepresented,—that the Paxtoneers were a set of very worthy men (or something to that purpose) who labored under great distress,—that Messrs. Smith, &c., were come (by their own authority) as representatives, from several counties, to lay their complaints before the Legislature, and that the reason for their arming themselves was for fear of being molested or abused. By whom?

Why, by the peaceable citizens of Philadelphia! Ha! ha! ha! Who can help laughing? The harangue concluded with thanks for the trouble and expense they had been at (about nothing), and each retired to their several homes. The next day, when all was quiet, and nobody dreamed of any further disturbance, we were alarmed again. The report now was, that the Paxtoneers had broke the Treaty, and were just entering the city. It is incredible to think with what alacrity the people flew to arms; in one quarter of an hour near a thousand of them were assembled, with a determination to bring the affair to a conclusion immediately, and not to suffer themselves to be harassed as they had been several days past. If the whole body of the enemy had come in, as was expected, the engagement would have been a bloody one, for the citizens were exasperated almost to madness; but happily those that appeared did not exceed thirty, (the rest having gone homewards), and as they behaved with decency, they were suffered to pass without opposition. Thus the storm blew over, and the Inhabitants dispersed themselves. . . .

The Pennsylvania Gazette, usually a faithful chronicler of the events of the day, preserves a discreet silence on the subject of the Paxton riots, and contains no other notice of them than the following condensed statement:—

On Saturday last, the City was alarmed with the News of Great Numbers of armed Men, from the Frontiers, being on the several Roads, and moving towards Philadelphia. As their designs were unknown, and there were various Reports concerning them, it was thought prudent to put the City in some Posture of Defence against any Outrages that might possibly be intended. The Inhabitants being accordingly called upon by the Governor, great numbers of them entered into an Association, and took Arms for the Support of Government, and Maintenance of good Order.

Six Companies of Foot, one of Artillery, and two Troops of Horse, were formed, and paraded, to which, it is said, some Thousands, who did not appear, were prepared to join themselves, in case any attempt should be made against the Town. The Barracks also, where the Indians are lodged, under Protection of the regular Troops, were put into a good Posture of Defence; several Works being thrown up about them, and eight Pieces of Cannon planted there.

The Insurgents, it seems, intended to rendezvous at Germantown; but the Precautions taken at the several Ferries over Schuylkill impeded their Junction; and those who assembled there, being made acquainted with the Force raised to oppose them, listened to the reasonable Discourses and Advice of some prudent Persons, who voluntarily went out to meet and admonish them; and of some Gentlemen sent by the Governor, to know the Reasons of their Insurrection; and promised to return peaceably to their Habitations, leaving only two of their Number to present a Petition to the Governor and Assembly; on which the Companies raised in Town were thanked by the Governor on Tuesday Evening, and dismissed, and the City restored to its former Quiet.

But on Wednesday Morning there was a fresh Alarm, occasioned by a false Report, that Four Hundred of the same People were on their March to Attack the Town. Immediately, on Beat of Drum, a much greater number of the Inhabitants, with the utmost Alacrity, put themselves under Arms; but as the Truth was soon known, they were again thanked by the Governor, and dismissed; the Country People being really dispersed, and gone home according to their Promise.—*Pennsylvania Gazette, No. 1833.*

The following extract from a letter of Rev. John Ewing to Joseph Reed affords a striking example of the excitement among the Presbyterians. (See Life and Correspondence of Joseph Reed, I. 34.)

Feb. —, 1764.

As to public affairs, our Province is greatly involved in intestine feuds, at a time, when we should rather unite, one and all, to manage the affairs of our several Governments, with prudence and discretion. A few designing men, having engrossed too much power into their hands, are pushing matters beyond all bounds. There are twenty-two Quakers in our Assembly, at present, who, although they won't absolutely refuse to grant money for the King's use, yet never fail to contrive matters in such a manner as to afford little or no assistance to the poor, distressed Frontiers; while our public money is lavishly squandered away in supporting a number of savages, who have been murdering and scalping us for many years past. This has so enraged some desperate young men, who had lost their nearest relations, by these very Indians, to cut off about twenty Indians that lived near Lancaster, who had, during the war, carried on a constant intercourse with our other enemies; and they came down to Germantown to inquire why Indians, known to be enemies, were supported, even in luxury, with the best that our markets afforded, at the public expense, while they were left in the utmost distress on the Frontiers, in want of the necessaries of life. Ample promises were made to them that their grievances should be redressed, upon which they immediately dispersed and went home. These persons have been unjustly represented as endeavoring to overturn Government, when nothing was more distant from their minds. However this matter may be looked upon in Britain, where you know very little of the matter, you may be assured that ninety-nine in an hundred of the Province are firmly persuaded, that they are maintaining our enemies, while our friends back are suffering the greatest extremities, neglected; and that few, but Quakers, think that the Lancaster Indians have suffered any thing but their just deserts. 'Tis not a little surprising to us here, that orders should be sent from the Crown, to apprehend and bring to justice those persons who have cut off that nest of enemies that lived near Lancaster. They never were subjects to his Majesty; were a free, independent state, retaining all the powers of a free state; sat in all our Treaties with the Indians, as one of the tribes belonging to the Six Nations, in alliance with us; they entertained the French and Indian spies—gave intelligence to them of the defenceless state of our Province—furnished them with Gazette every week, or fortnight—gave them intelligence of all the dispositions of the Province army against them—were frequently with the French and Indians at their forts and towns—supplied them with warlike stores—joined with the strange Indians in their war-dances, and in the parties that made incursions on our Frontiers—were ready to take up the hatchet against the English openly, when the French requested it—actually murdered and scalped some of the Frontier inhabitants—insolently boasted of the murders they had committed, when they saw our blood was cooled, after the last Treaty at Lancaster—confessed that they had been at war with us, and would soon be at war with us again (which accordingly happened), and even went so far as to put one of their own warriors, Jegarie, to death, because he refused to go to war with them against the English. All these things were known through the Frontier inhabitants, and are since proved upon oath. This occasioned them to be cut off by about forty or fifty persons, collected from all the Frontier counties, though they are called by the name of the little Township of Paxton, where, possibly, the smallest part of them resided. And what surprises us more than all the accounts we have from England, is, that our Assembly, in a petition they have drawn up, to the King, for a change of Government, should represent this Province in a state of uproar and riot, and when not a man in it has once resisted a single officer of the Government, nor a single act of violence committed, unless you call the Lancaster affair such, although it was no more than going to war with that tribe, as they had done before with others, without a formal proclamation of war by the

Government. I have not time, as you may guess by this scrawl, to write more at this time, but only that I am yours, &c.

JOHN EWING.

3. MEMORIALS OF THE PAXTON MEN. (Chap. XXV.)

5. To the Honorable John Penn, Esq., Governor of the Province of Pennsylvania, and of the Counties of New-Castle, Kent, and Sussex, upon Delaware; and to the Representatives of the Freemen of the said Province, in General Assembly met.

We, Matthew Smith and James Gibson, in Behalf of ourselves and his Majesty's faithful and loyal Subjects, the Inhabitants of the Frontier Counties of Lancaster, York, Cumberland, Berks, and Northampton, humbly beg Leave to remonstrate and lay before you the following Grievances, which we submit to your Wisdom for Redress.

First. We apprehend that, as Freemen and English Subjects, we have an indisputable Title to the same Privileges and immunities with his Majesty's other Subjects, who reside in the interior Counties of Philadelphia, Chester, and Bucks, and therefore ought not to be excluded from an equal Share with them in the very important Privilege of Legislation; — nevertheless, contrary to the Proprietor's Charter, and the acknowledged Principles of common Justice and Equity, our five Counties are restrained from electing more than ten Representatives, *viz.*, four for Lancaster, two for York, two for Cumberland, one for Berks, and one for Northampton, while the three Counties and City of Philadelphia, Chester, and Bucks elect Twenty-six. This we humbly conceive is oppressive, unequal and unjust, the Cause of many of our Grievances, and an Infringement of our natural Privileges of Freedom and Equality; wherefore we humbly pray that we may be no longer deprived of an equal Number with the three aforesaid Counties to represent us in Assembly.

Secondly. We understand that a Bill is now before the House of Assembly, wherein it is provided, that such Persons as shall be charged with killing any Indians in Lancaster County, shall not be tried in the County where the Fact was committed, but in the Counties of Philadelphia, Chester, or Bucks. This is manifestly to deprive British Subjects of their known Privileges, to cast an eternal Reproach upon whole Counties, as if they were unfit to serve their Country in the Quality of Jury-men, and to contradict the well known Laws of the British Nation, in a Point whereon Life, Liberty, and Security essentially depend; namely, that of being tried by their

Equals, in the Neighbourhood where their own, their Accusers, and the Witnesses Character and Credit, with the Circumstances of the Fact, are best known, and instead thereof putting their Lives in the Hands of Strangers, who may as justly be suspected of Partiality to, as the Frontier Counties can be of Prejudices against, Indians; and this too, in favour of Indians only, against his Majesty's faithful and loyal Subjects: Besides, it is well known, that the Design of it is to comprehend a Fact committed before such a Law was thought of. And if such Practices were tolerated, no Man could be secure in his most invaluable Interest.—We are also informed, to our great Surprise, that this Bill has actually received the Assent of a Majority of the House; which we are persuaded could not have been the Case, had our Frontier Counties been equally represented in Assembly.— However, we hope that the Legislature of this Province will never enact a Law of so dangerous a Tendency, or take away from his Majesty's good Subjects a Privilege so long esteemed sacred by Englishmen.

Thirdly. During the late and present Indian War, the Frontiers of this Province have been repeatedly attacked and ravaged by skulking Parties of the Indians, who have, with the most Savage Cruelty, murdered Men, Women, and Children, without Distinction, and have reduced near a Thousand Families to the most extreme Distress.—It grieves us to the very Heart to see such of our Frontier Inhabitants as have escaped Savage Fury, with the Loss of their Parents, their Children, their Wives or Relatives, left Destitute by the Public, and exposed to the most cruel Poverty and Wretchedness, while upwards of an Hundred and Twenty of these Savages, who are, with great Reason, suspected of being guilty of these horrid Barbarities, under the Mask of Friendship, have procured themselves to be taken under the Protection of the Government, with a View to elude the Fury of the brave Relatives of the Murdered, and are now maintained at the public Expense.—Some of these Indians, now in the Barracks of Philadelphia, are confessedly a Part of the Wyalusing Indians, which Tribe is now at War with us; and the others are the Moravian Indians, who, living with us, under the Cloak of Friendship, carried on a Correspondence with our known Enemies on the Great Island.—We cannot but observe, with Sorrow and Indignation, that some Persons in this Province are at Pains to extenuate the barbarous Cruelties practised by these Savages on our murdered Brethren and Relatives, which are shocking to human Nature, and must pierce every Heart, but that of the hardened Perpetrators or their Abettors. Nor is it less distressing to hear Others pleading, that although the Wyalusing Tribe is at War with us, yet that Part of it which is under the Protec-

tion of the Government, may be friendly to the English, and innocent:—In what Nation under the Sun was it ever the Custom, that
when a neighbouring Nation took up Arms, not an Individual
should be touched, but only the Persons that offered Hostilities?—
Who ever proclaimed War with a Part of a Nation and not with the
whole?—Had these Indians disapproved of the Perfidy of their
Tribe, and been willing to cultivate and preserve Friendship with us,
why did they not give Notice of the War before it happened, as it is
known to be the Result of long Deliberations, and a preconcerted
Combination among them?—Why did they not leave their Tribe immediately, and come among us, before there was Ground to suspect
them, or War was actually waged with their Tribe?—No, they stayed
amongst them, were privy to their Murders and Ravages, until we
had destroyed their provisions, and when they could no longer sub-
sist at Home, they come not as Deserters, but as Friends, to be
maintained through the Winter, that they may be able to scalp and
butcher us in the Spring.

And as to the Moravian Indians, there are strong Grounds at least
to suspect their Friendship, as it is known that they carried on a
Correspondence with our Enemies on the Great Island.—We killed
three Indians going from Bethlehem to the Great Island with Blankets, Ammunition, and Provisions, which is an undeniable Proof
that the Moravian Indians were in Confederacy with our open Enemies. And we cannot but be filled with Indignation to hear this Action of ours painted in the most odious and detestable Colours, as if
we had inhumanly murdered our Guides, who preserved us from
perishing in the Woods; when we only killed three of our known
Enemies, who attempted to shoot us when we surprised them.—
And, besides all this, we understand that one of these very Indians is
proved, by the Oath of Stinton's Widow, to be the very Person that
murdered her Husband.—How then comes it to pass, that he alone,
of all the Moravian Indians, should join the Enemy to murder that
family?—Or can it be supposed that any Enemy Indians, contrary to
their known Custom of making War, should penetrate into the Heart
of a settled Country, to burn, plunder, and murder the Inhabitants,
and not molest any Houses in their Return, or ever be seen or heard
of?—Or how can we account for it, that no Ravages have been
committed in Northampton County since the Removal of the Moravian Indians, when the Great Cove has been struck sir~e?—These
Things put it beyond Doubt with us that the Indians now at Philadelphia are his Majesty's perfidious Enemies, and therefore, to protect and maintain them at the public Expence, while our suffering
Brethren on the Frontiers are almost destitute of the Necessaries of

Life, and are neglected by the Public, is sufficient to make us mad with Rage, and tempt us to do what nothing but the most violent Necessity can vindicate.—We humbly and earnestly pray therefore, that those Enemies of his Majesty may be removed as soon as possible out of the Province.

Fourthly. We humbly conceive that it is contrary to the Maxims of good Policy and extremely dangerous to our Frontiers, to suffer any Indians, of what Tribe soever, to live within the inhabited Parts of this Province, while we are engaged in an Indian War, as Experience has taught us that they are all perfidious, and their Claim to Freedom and Independency, puts it in their Power to act as Spies, to entertain and give Intelligence to our Enemies, and to furnish them with Provisions and warlike Stores.—To this fatal Intercourse between our pretended Friends and open Enemies, we must ascribe the greatest Part of the Ravages and Murders that have been committed in the Course of this and the last Indian War.—We therefore pray that this Grievance be taken under Consideration, and remedied.

Fifthly. We cannot help lamenting that no Provision has been hitherto made, that such of our Frontier Inhabitants as have been wounded in Defence of the Province, their Lives and Liberties may be taken Care of, and cured of their Wounds, at the public Expence. —We therefore pray that this Grievance may be redressed.

Sixthly. In the late Indian War this Province, with others of his Majesty's Colonies, gave Rewards for Indian Scalps, to encourage the seeking them in their own Country, as the most likely Means of destroying or reducing them to Reason; but no such Encouragement has been given in this War, which has damped the Spirits of many brave Men, who are willing to venture their Lives in Parties against the Enemy.—We therefore pray that public Rewards may be proposed for Indian Scalps, which may be adequate to the Dangers attending Enterprises of this Nature.

Seventhly. We daily lament that Numbers of our nearest and dearest Relatives are still in Captivity among the savage Heathen, to be trained up in all their Ignorance and Barbarity, or to be tortured to Death with all the Contrivances of Indian Cruelty, for attempting to make their Escape from Bondage. We see they pay no Regard to the many solemn Promises which they have made to restore our Friends who are in Bondage amongst them.—We therefore earnestly pray that no Trade may hereafter be permitted to be carried on with them until our Brethren and Relatives are brought Home to us.

Eighthly. We complain that a certain Society of People in this Province in the late Indian War, and at several Treaties held by the King's Representatives, openly loaded the Indians with Presents;

and that F. P., a Leader of the said Society, in Defiance of all Government, not only abetted our Indian Enemies, but kept up a private Intelligence with them, and publickly received from them a Belt of Wampum, as if he had been our Governor, or authorized by the King to treat with his Enemies.—By this means the Indians have been taught to despise us as a weak and disunited People, and from this fatal Source have arose many of our Calamities under which we groan.—We humbly pray, therefore, that this Grievance may be redressed, and that no private Subject be hereafter permitted to treat with, or carry on a Correspondence with our Enemies.

Ninthly. We cannot but observe with Sorrow, that Fort Augusta, which has been very expensive to this Province, has afforded us but little Assistance during this or the last War. The Men that were stationed at that Place neither helped our distressed Inhabitants to save their Crops, nor did they attack our Enemies in their Towns, or patrol on our Frontiers.—We humbly request that proper Measures may be taken to make that Garrison more serviceable to us in our Distress, if it can be done.

N. B. We are far from intending any Reflection against the Commanding Officer stationed at Augusta, as we presume his Conduct was always directed by those from whom he received his Orders.

Signed on Behalf of ourselves, and by Appointment of a great Number of the Frontier Inhabitants,

MATTHEW SMITH.
JAMES GIBSON.

THE DECLARATION of the injured Frontier Inhabitants, together with a brief Sketch of Grievances the good Inhabitants of the Province labor under.

Inasmuch as the Killing those Indians at Conestogoe Manor and Lancaster has been, and may be, the Subject of much Conversation, and by invidious Representations of it, which some, we doubt not, will industriously spread, many, unacquainted with the true State of Affairs, may be led to pass a severe Censure on the Authors of those Facts, and any others of the like Nature which may hereafter happen, than we are persuaded they would, if Matters were duly understood and deliberated; we think it therefore proper thus openly to declare ourselves, and render some brief Hints of the Reasons of our Conduct, which we must, and frankly do, confess nothing but Necessity itself could induce us to, or justify us in, as it bears an Appearance of flying in the Face of Authority, and is attended with much Labour, Fatigue and Expence.

Ourselves then, to a Man, we profess to be loyal Subjects to the best of Kings, our rightful Sovereign George the Third, firmly attached to his Royal Person, Interest and Government, and of Consequence equally opposite to the Enemies of his Throne and Dignity, whether openly avowed, or more dangerously concealed under a Mask of falsely pretended Friendship, and chearfully willing to offer our Substance and Lives in his Cause.

These Indians, known to be firmly connected in Friendship with our openly avowed embittered Enemies, and some of whom have, by several Oaths, been proved to be Murderers, and who, by their better Acquaintance with the Situation and State of our Frontier, were more capable of doing us Mischief, we saw, with Indignation, cherished and caressed as dearest Friends;—But this, alas! is but a Part, a small Part, of that excessive Regard manifested to Indians, beyond his Majesty's loyal Subjects, whereof we complain, and which, together with various other Grievances, have not only inflamed with Resentment the Breasts of a Number, and urged them to the disagreeable Evidence of it, they have been constrained to give, but have heavily displeased, by far, the greatest Part of the good Inhabitants of this Province.

Should we here reflect to former Treaties, the exorbitant Presents, and great Servility therein paid to Indians, have long been oppressive Grievances we have groaned under; and when at the last Indian Treaty held at Lancaster, not only was the Blood of our many murdered Brethren tamely covered, but our poor unhappy captivated Friends abandoned to Slavery among the Savages, by concluding a Friendship with the Indians, and allowing them a plenteous trade of all kinds of Commodities, without those being restored, or any properly spirited Requisition made of them:—How general Dissatisfaction those Measures gave, the Murmurs of all good people (loud as they dare to utter them) to this Day declare. And had here infatuated Steps of Conduct, and a manifest Partiality in Favour of Indians, made a final Pause, happy had it been:—We perhaps had grieved in Silence for our abandoned enslaved Brethren among the Heathen, but Matters of a later Date are still more flagrant Reasons of Complaint.—When last Summer his Majesty's Forces, under the Command of Colonel Bouquet, marched through this Province, and a Demand was made by his Excellency, General Amherst, of Assistance, to escort Provisions, &c., to relieve that important Post, Fort Pitt, yet not one Man was granted, although never any Thing appeared more reasonable or necessary, as the Interest of the Province lay so much at Stake, and the Standing of the Frontier Settlements, in any Manner, evidently depended, under God, on the almost despaired of Success of his Majesty's little Army, whose Valour the whole Frontiers with Gratitude acknowledge, as the happy Means of having saved from Ruin great Part of the Province:—But when a Number of Indians, falsely pretended Friends and having among them some proved on Oath to have been guilty of Murder, since this War begun; when they, together with others, known to be his Majesty's Enemies, and who had been in the Battle against Colonel Bouquet, reduced to Distress by the Destruction of their Corn at the Great Island, and up the East Branch of Susquehanna, pretend themselves Friends, and desire a Subsistence, they are openly caressed, and the Public, that could not be indulged the Liberty of contributing to his Majesty's Assistance, obliged, as Tributaries to Savages, to Support these Villains, these Enemies to our King and our Country; nor only so, but the Hands that were closely shut, nor would grant his Majesty's General a single Farthing against a savage Foe, have been liberally opened, and the public Money basely prostituted, to hire, at an exorbitant Rate, a mercenary Guard to protect his Majesty's worst of Enemies, those falsely pretended Indian Friends, while, at the same Time, Hundreds of poor, distressed Families of his Majesty's Subjects, obliged to abandon their Possessions, and fly for their Lives at least, are left, except a small Relief at first, in the most distressing Circumstances to starve neglected, save what the friendly Hand of private Donations has contributed to their Support, wherein they who are most profuse towards Savages have carefully avoided having any Part.—When last Summer the Troops raised for Defence of the Province were limited to certain Bounds, nor suffered to attempt annoying our Enemies in their Habitations, and a Number of brave Volunteers, equipped at their own Expence, marched in September up the Susquehanna, met and defeated their Enemy, with the Loss of some of their Number, and having others dangerously wounded, not the least Thanks or Acknowledgment was made them from the Legislature for the confessed Service they had done, nor any the least Notice or Care taken of their Wounded; whereas, when a Seneca Indian, who, by the Information of many, as well as by his own Confession, had been, through the last War, our inveterate Enemy, had got a Cut in his Head last summer in a Quarrel he had with his own Cousin, and it was reported in Philadelphia that his Wound was dangerous, a Doctor was immediately employed, and sent to Fort Augusta to take Care of him, and cure him, if possible.—To these may be added, that though it was impossible to obtain through the Summer, or even yet, any Premium for Indian Scalps, or Encouragement to excite Volunteers to go forth against them, yet when a few of them, known to be the Fast Friends of our

Enemies, and some of them Murderers themselves, when these have been struck by a distressed, bereft, injured Frontier, a liberal Reward is offered for apprehending the Perpetrators of that horrible Crime of killing his Majesty's cloaked Enemies, and their Conduct painted in the most atrocious Colors; while the horrid Ravages, cruel Murders, and most shocking Barbarities, committed by Indians on his Majesty's Subjects, are covered over, and excused, under the charitable Term of this being their Method of making War.

But to recount the many repeated Grievances whereof we might justly complain, and Instances of a most violent Attachment to Indians, were tedious beyond the Patience of a Job to endure; nor can better be expected; nor need we be surprised at Indians Insolence and Villainy, when it is considered, and which can be proved from the public Records of a certain County, that some Time before Conrad Weiser died, some Indians belonging to the Great Island or Wyalousing, assured him that Israel Pemberton, (an ancient Leader of that Faction which, for so long a Time, have found Means to enslave the Province to Indians,) together with others of the Friends, had given them a Rod to scourge the white People that were settled on the purchased Lands; for that Onas had cheated them out of a great Deal of Land, or had not given near sufficient Price for what he had bought; and that the Traders ought also to be scourged, for that they defrauded the Indians, by selling Goods to them at too dear a Rate; and that this Relation is Matter of Fact, can easily be proved in the County of Berks.—Such is our unhappy Situation, under the Villainy, Infatuation and Influence of a certain Faction, that have got the political Reins in their Hands, and tamely tyrannize over the other good Subjects of the Province!—And can it be thought strange, that a Scene of such Treatment as this, and the now adding, in this critical Juncture, to all our former Distresses, that disagreeable Burden of supporting, in the very Heart of the Province, at so great an Expence, between One and Two hundred Indians, to the great Disquietude of the Majority of the good Inhabitants of this Province, should awaken the Resentment of a People grossly abused, unrighteously burdened, and made Dupes and Slaves to Indians?— And must not all well-disposed People entertain a charitable Sentiment of those who, at their own great Expence and Trouble, have attempted, or shall attempt, rescuing a laboring Land from a Weight so oppressive, unreasonable, and unjust?—It is this we design, it is this we are resolved to prosecute, though it is with great Reluctance we are obliged to adopt a Measure not so agreeable as could be desired, and to which Extremity alone compels.—God save the King.

Appendix F.

1. BOUQUET'S EXPEDITION.

Letter—General Gage to Lord Halifax, December 13, 1764. (Chap. XXVII.)

The Perfidy of the Shawanese and Delawares, and their having broken the ties, which even the Savage Nations hold sacred amongst each other, required vigorous measures to reduce them. We had experienced their treachery so often, that I determined to make no peace with them, but in the Heart of their Country, and upon such terms as should make it as secure as it was possible. This conduct has produced all the good effects which could be wished or expected from it. Those Indians have been humbled and reduced to accept of Peace upon the terms prescribed to them, in such a manner as will give reputation to His Majesty's Arms amongst the several Nations. The Regular and Provincial Troops under Colonel Bouquet, having been joined by a good body of Volunteers from Virginia, and others from Maryland and Pennsylvania, marched from Fort Pitt the Beginning of October, and got to Tuscaroras about the fifteenth. The March of the Troops into their Country threw the Savages into the greatest Consternation, as they had hoped their Woods would protect them, and had boasted of the Security of their Situation from our Attacks. The Indians hovered round the Troops during their March, but despairing of success in an Action, had recourse to Negotiations. They were told that they might have Peace, but every Prisoner in their possession must first be delivered up. They brought in near twenty, and promised to deliver the Rest; but as their promises were not regarded, they engaged to deliver the whole on the 1st of November, at the Forks of the Muskingham, about one hundred and fifty miles from Fort Pitt, the Centre of the Delaware Towns, and near to the most considerable settlement of the Shawanese. Colonel Bouquet kept them in sight, and moved his Camp to that Place. He soon obliged the Delawares and some broken tribes of Mohikons, Wiandots, and Mingoes, to bring in all their Prisoners, even to the Children born of White Women, and to tie those who were grown as Savage as themselves and unwilling to leave them, and bring them bound to the Camp. They were then told that they must appoint deputies to go to Sir William Johnson to receive such terms as should be imposed upon them, which the Nations should agree to ratify; and, for the security of their performance of this, and that no farther Hostilities should be committed, a number of their Chiefs must remain in our hands. The above Nations subscribed to these terms; but the Shawanese were more obstinate, and were particularly averse to the giving of Hostages. But finding their obstinacy had no effect, and would only tend to their destruction, the Troops having penetrated into the Heart of their Country, they at length became sensible that there was no safety but in Submission, and were obliged to stoop to the same Conditions as the other nations. They immediately gave up forty Prisoners, and promised the Rest should be sent to Fort Pitt in the Spring. This last not being admitted, the immediate Restitution of all the Prisoners being the *sine qua non* of peace, it was agreed, that parties should be sent from the Army into their towns, to collect the Prisoners, and conduct them to Fort Pitt. They delivered six of their principal Chiefs as hostages into our Hands, and appointed their deputies to go to Sir William Johnson, in the same manner as the Rest. The Number of Prisoners already delivered exceeds two hundred, and it was expected that our Parties would bring in near one hundred more from the Shawanese Towns. These Conditions seem sufficient Proofs of the Sincerity and Humiliation of those Nations, and in justice to Colonel Bouquet, I must testify the Obligations I have to him, and that nothing but the firm and steady conduct, which he observed in all his Transactions with those treacherous savages, would ever have brought them to a serious Peace.

I must flatter myself, that the Country is restored to its former Tranquillity, and that a general, and, it is hoped, lasting Peace is concluded with all the Indian Nations who have taken up Arms against his Majesty.

I remain,

etc.,

THOMAS GAGE.

IN ASSEMBLY, January 15, 1765, A. M.

To the Honourable Henry Bouquet, Esq., Commander in Chief of His Majesty's Forces in the Southern Department of America.

The Address of the Representatives of the Freemen of the Province of Pennsylvania, in General Assembly met

SIR:

The Representatives of the Freemen of the Province of Pennsylvania, in General Assembly met, being informed that you intend shortly to embark for England, and moved with a due Sense of the important Services you have rendered to his Majesty, his Northern Colonies in general, and to this Province in particular, during our late Wars with the French, and barbarous Indians, in the remarkable Victory over the savage Enemy, united to oppose you, near Bushy Run, in August, 1763, when on your March for the Relief of Pittsburg, owing, under God, to your Intrepidity and superior Skill in Command, together with the Bravery of your Officers and little Army; as also in your late March to the Country of the savage Nations, with the Troops under your Direction; thereby striking Terror through the numerous Indian Tribes around you; laying a Foundation for a lasting as well as honorable Peace, and rescuing, from savage Captivity, upwards of Two Hundred of our Christian Brethren, Prisoners among them. These eminent Services, and your constant Attention to the Civil Rights of his Majesty's Subjects in this Province, demand, Sir, the grateful Tribute of Thanks from all good Men; and therefore we, the Representatives of the Freemen of Pennsylvania, unanimously for ourselves, and in Behalf of all the People of this Province, do return you our most sincere and hearty Thanks for these your great Services, wishing you a safe and pleasant Voyage to England, with a kind and gracious Reception from his Majesty.

Signed, by Order of the House,

JOSEPH FOX, Speaker.

2. CONDITION AND TEMPER OF THE WESTERN INDIANS.

Extract from a letter of Sir William Johnson to the Board of Trade, 1764, December 26: —

Your Lordships will please to observe that for many months before the march of Colonel Bradstreet's army, several of the Western Nations had expressed a desire for peace, and had ceased to commit hostilities, that even Pontiac inclined that way, but did not choose to venture his person by coming into any of the posts. This was the state of affairs when I treated with the Indians at Niagara, in which number were fifteen hundred of the Western Nations, a number infinitely more considerable than those who were twice treated with at Detroit, many of whom are the same people, particularly the Hurons and Chippewas. In the mean time it now appears, from the very best authorities, and can be proved by the oath of several respectable persons, prisoners at the Illinois and amongst the Indians, as also from the accounts of the Indians themselves, that not only many French traders, but also French officers came amongst the Indians, as they said, fully authorized to assure them that the French King was determined to support them to the utmost, and not only invited them to the Illinois, where they were plentifully supplied with ammunition and other necessaries, but also sent several canoes at different times up the Illinois river, to the Miamis, and others, as well as up the Ohio to the Shawanese and Delawares, as by Major Smallman's account, and several others, (then prisoners), transmitted me by Colonel Bouquet, and one of my officers who accompanied him, will appear. That in an especial manner the French promoted the interest of Pontiac, whose influence is now become so considerable, as General Gage observes in a late letter to me, that it extends even to the Mouth of the Mississippi, and has been the principal occasion of our not as yet gaining the Illinois, which the French as well as Indians are interested in preventing. This Pontiac is not included in the late Treaty at Detroit, and is at the head of a great number of Indians privately supported by the French, an officer of whom was about three months ago at the Miamis Castle, at the Scioto Plains, Muskingum, and several other places. The Western Indians, who it seems ridicule the whole expedition, will be influenced to such a pitch, by the interested French on the one side, and the influence of Pontiac on the other, that we have great reason to apprehend a renewal of hostilities, or at least that they and the Twightees (Miamis) will strenuously oppose our possessing the Illinois, which can never be accomplished without their consent. And indeed it is not to be wondered that they should be concerned at our occupying that country, when we consider that the French (be their motive what it will) loaded them with favors, and continue to do so, accompanied with all outward marks of esteem, and an address peculiarly adapted to their manners, which infallibly gains upon all Indians, who judge by extremes only, and with all their acquaintance with us upon the frontiers, have never found any thing like it, but on the contrary, harsh treatment, angry words, and in short any thing which can be thought of to inspire them with a dislike to our manners and a jealousy of our views. I have seen so much of these matters, and I am so well convinced of the utter aversion that our people have for them in general, and of the imprudence with which they constantly express it, that I absolutely despair of our seeing tranquillity established, until your Lordships' plan is fully settled, so as I may have proper persons to reside at the Posts, whose business it shall be to remove their prejudices, and whose interest it becomes to obtain their esteem and friendship.

The importance of speedily possessing the Illinois, and thereby securing a considerable branch of trade, as well as cutting off the channel by which our enemies have been and will always be supplied, is a matter I have very much at heart, and what I think may be effected this winter by land by Mr. Croghan, in case matters can be so far settled with the Twightees, Shawanoes, and Pontiac, as to engage the latter, with some chiefs of the before-mentioned nations, to accompany him with a garrison. The expense attending this will be large, but the end to be obtained is too considerable to be neglected. I have accordingly recommended it to the consideration of General Gage, and shall, on the arrival of the Shawanoes, Delawares, &c., here, do all in my power to pave the way for effecting it. I shall also make such a peace with them, as will be most for the credit and advantage of the crown, and the security of the trade and frontiers, and tie them down to such conditions as Indians will most probably observe.

NOTE.

Of the accompanying maps, the first two were constructed for the illustration of this work. The others are fac-similes from the surveys of the engineer Thomas Hutchins. The original of the larger of these fac-similes is prefixed to the *Account of Bouquet's Expedition*. That of the smaller will be found in Hutchins's *Topographical Description of Virginia*, etc. Both of these works are rare.

Index.

A.

Abbadie. See *D'Abbadie*.

Abenakis, some of them present at the battle of the Monongahela, 432, 458.

Abercrombie, General James, has a force of 50,000 men, 440; fails in his attack on Ticonderoga, 442, 443.

Acadia ceded to the English crown, 423; disputes respecting its boundaries, *ib.*; reduced by Col. Monkton, 436; the inhabitants transported, *ib.*

Albany, meeting of colonial delegates there, 427; a rendezvous for Indian traders, 461.

Algonquin family of Indians, found over a vast extent of territory, 379; their inferiority to the Iroquois, 384; points of distinction, *ib.*; their legends, 384; and religious belief, 385; Algonquin life, 382, 383.

Allegory uttered by Pontiac, 497–499.

Ambuscade at the Devil's Hole, 674; a convoy lost there, 674; another ambuscade, 675.

Amherst, Sir Jeffrey, afterwards Lord Amherst, takes Louisburg, 442; also Ticonderoga and Crown Point, 444; captures Montreal, 454; sends a force to take possession of the western posts, 470; his contempt and careless treatment of the Indians, 482 *note*, 491; his letter to Major Gladwyn, 526 *note*; his uncomfortable position, 641; his inadequate comprehension of the Indian war, 642; takes measures to reinforce the frontier garrisons, 643, 644; hears of the murders near Detroit, 645; determines on "quick retaliation," 645; wishes to hear of no prisoners, 646; his blustering arrogance, 647 *note*; proposes to infect the Indians with small-pox, 648; his anger at the feeble conduct of the Pennsylvania Assembly, 688;

resigns his office as commander-in-chief, 690; his ignorance of Indian affairs, 732.

Andastes, swept away before the Iroquois, 376; a remnant of them at Conestoga, 703 *note*.

Armstrong, Colonel, his expedition against the Indians on the upper Susquehanna, 690.

Atotarho, name of the presiding sachem of the Iroquois: strange legend concerning the first of the name, 367, 368.

B.

Baby, a Canadian near Detroit, supplies food to the garrison, 530; scene between him and Pontiac, 537; befriends the garrison, 558.

Ball-play, Indian, described, 594; a prelude to the massacre at Michillimackinac, 594.

Barbarity, Indian, shocking instances of, 372, 405, 519, 520, 524 *note*, 545 *note*, 565, 596, 606, 634 *note*, 680, 681.

Bartram, John, the botanist, quoted, 370, 371 *note*.

Beaujeau, a French captain, leads a sortie of French and Indians against Braddock's army, 432; wounded in the fray, 434.

Bedford, Fort, repels an Indian attack, 627; crowded with fugitives, 650; reinforced, 661.

Belètre, captain, commandant at Detroit, 472; surrenders to Major Rogers, 473.

Bird, Dr. Robert M., his story of "Nick of the Woods," 702.

Blacksnake, a Seneca warrior, 675 *note*.

Blane, Lieutenant Archibald, commands at Fort Ligonier, 650; successfully defends the fort against an attack of the Indians, 652, 653;

vents his complaints of the service, 733.

Bloody Bridge fight, 573 et seq.; great loss of the English, 578.

Boscawen, Admiral Edward, captures a French squadron previous to a declaration of war, 428; and thus begins the war of 1755, 429; the act condemned by English writers, 429 note.

Bouquet, Colonel Henry, his history, 641; his letter to Sir Jeffrey Amherst, 639; an excellent officer, 642; his correspondence with Amherst and others about the war, 643 et seq.; his "truculent letter" to Amherst about extirpating the Indians, 646; hears of the destruction of the frontier garrisons, 646; he will try to send the small-pox among the Indians, and proposes to hunt them with English dogs, 648; is displeased with the surrender of Presqu' Isle, 652; complains of the negligence of the people of Pennsylvania, 654; his campaign against the Indians, 659 et seq.; difficulties and dangers of the march, 661; attacked by the Indians at Bushy Run, 663; his masterly stratagem, 666; and complete success, 667. See Appendix D. Arrives at Fort Pitt, 669; his dissatisfaction with the service, 734; severely blames the government of Pennsylvania, 766; sets out from Carlisle on an expedition against the Delawares and Shawanoes, 768; is displeased with Colonel Bradstreet, 768; arrives at Fort Pitt, 770; sends a message to the Delawares, 770; good effect of the message, 771; difficulties of the march through the woods, 771; the troops cross the Muskingum, 772; their number and fine appearance, 774; the commander holds a council with the Delawares, 774; his speech to them, 776–778; effect of the speech, 778; his decisive tone, 778; the Indians submit and give up their captives, 779, 780; number of the captives, 781; meeting of friends long separated, 785–787; some touching

incidents, 787; the troops, having accomplished their work, return home, 792; Bouquet made a brigadier-general, 793; his death, 794. See Appendix F.

Braddock, General Edward, sails in command of a military force for Virginia, 428; his character, 430; his duel with Gumley, 430 note; his march through the wilderness, 431; difficulties of the advance, ib.; the ambuscade, 433; the battle, 434; the utter defeat, 435; Braddock's insane behavior, 436; his death, ib.; the terrible carnage, ib.; the disgraceful rout, ib.; the unhappy results, 436, 437.

Bradstreet, Colonel John, captures Fort Frontenac, 422, 735; his expedition against the north-western Indians, 736 et seq.; the troops leave Niagara and embark on Lake Erie, 743, 744; he is shamefully duped by wily Indian foes, 745; he is reprimanded by General Gage, 746 note; arrives at Sandusky, 747; his imbecility, 747; reaches Detroit, 748; returns to Sandusky, 757.

Brebeuf, Jean de, a Jesuit missionary, his appalling fate, 395.

Bushy Run, severe battle there with the Indians, 663 et seq.; the enemy repulsed, 667; and totally routed, 667; the losses on both sides, 668. See Appendix D.

C.

Cadillac, La Motte, founds Detroit, 503.

Cahokia on the Illinois, a French settlement, 401, 464, 803; described, 843; Pontiac killed there, 843, 844.

Calhoun, a trader, betrayed by the Indians, but escapes, 624, 625.

Campbell, Lieutenant George, killed with all his command at Niagara, 676 note.

Campbell, Captain, commands at Detroit, 481; discovers an Indian plot, 481, 482; second in command, 518; treacherously detained in captivity by Pontiac, 523, 524; exposed by Indians to the fire of English guns, 539; cruelly murdered by the Indians, 565, 566.

Canada, a child of the church, 393; settled under religious impulses, 394; characteristics of the population, 391, 504; the fur-trade, 392; the true interest of the colony neglected, *ib.*; Jesuit missionaries in, 394; want of energy in the common people, 397, 401; advantages for intercourse with the Indian tribes, 403; the colony suffers from the hostility of the Iroquois, 405; Canada an object of the bitterest hatred to the English colonies, and why, 423; surrendered to the English arms, 453; Canadians excite the Indians to attack the English, 478, 479, 584.

Canadians compared with the people of New England, 391–393; their false representations of the English colonists, 485; their character, 506; unfriendly to the English after the conquest, 478, 479, 584.

Cannibalism of the Indians, 606.

Captives taken in war by the Indians, their treatment, 372, 405, 524 *note*, 789–792, 810 *note*; sometimes they prefer to remain with the Indians, 790.

Carlisle, Pa., a frontier town in 1760, 623; panic among the inhabitants, 655; deplorable scenes there, 656; many leave the place for Lancaster and Philadelphia, 657; it becomes the outer settlement, 680 *note*.

Carver, Capt. Jonathan, the traveller, 510; his account of the conspiracy of Pontiac, 510 *note*, 511; other statements made by him, 580, 581 *note*; his description of Minavavana, the Ojibwa chief, 608, 609 *note*; his account of the death of Pontiac, 844 *note*.

Cayugas, one of the Five Nations, 364. See *Iroquois*.

Champlain, Samuel de, attacks the Iroquois, 404; the baleful consequences, *ib.*.

Cherokees attacked by the Iroquois, 418;

remain quiet during the Pontiac war, 700.

Chippewa Indians. See *Ojibwa nation*.

Chouteau, Pierre, one of the first settlers of St. Louis, 807; surprising changes witnessed by him, *ib.*; the author visits him, *ib. note*; remembers seeing Pontiac, 807 *note*, 842.

Christie, Ensign, defends the fort at Presqu' Isle, 553–555; surrenders, 556; escapes and arrives at Detroit, 557; a further account of the matter, 632 *note*.

Church, Roman Catholic, its zeal for the conversion of the Indians, 390.

Clapham, Colonel, murdered by the Indians, 624 *note*.

Colden, Governor of New York, refuses to have the Moravian Indian converts brought within his province, 719.

Colonies of France and England, their distinctive traits, 390, 403.

Compton, Henry, bishop of London, advises William Penn to buy land of the Indians, 413.

Conestoga, a settlement of friendly Indians, 703; their manner of life, 704; suspected of hostile practices, *ib.*; a massacre there, 705. See *Appendix* E.

Conner, Henry, Indian interpreter, his statement respecting Pontiac's birth, 483 *note*; his account of the disclosure of the plans of Pontiac, 508–510.

Conference of Indians with Sir William Johnson at Niagara, 739; they ask forgiveness, 742.

Conspiracy of the Indians against the English after the French war, 475; its causes, 475; the English neglect to cultivate their friendship, 477; disorders of the English fur-trade, 477; intrusion of settlers on the Indian lands, 477; the arbitrary conduct of Sir Jeffrey Amherst, 491; the discontent of the Indians artfully increased by the French, 478; Indian plot to destroy the English, 481; a great crisis for the Indian race, 484; the conspiracy discovered, 509, 510; treachery of Pontiac, 513–518; the war begins, 519; attack on the fort at Detroit, 521, 522; negotiation, 523; comes to no good result, 524 *et seq.*

Conyngham, Redmond, publishes an account of the massacre at Conestoga, 705 *note.*

Council of Indians summoned by Pontiac, 495 *et seq.*; appearance of Pontiac, 496; his speech, 497 *et seq.*; council-house at Onondaga, 365 *note*, 370, 371.

"*Coureurs de bois,*" or bush-rangers, 412, 506; their degradation, *ib.*; and superstition, 412; excite the Indians against the English, 479.

Creek nation hostile to the English, 700.

Creoles along the Mississippi; their character and modes of life, 803.

Croghan, George, his representations to the Lords of Trade, 731; they are disregarded, 733; sent to negotiate with the western Indians, 819; his convoy seized by the Paxton men, 820, 821; at Fort Pitt he meets Indians in council, 824; finds them undecided in their plans, 824; descends the Ohio, 828; is attacked by the Kickapoos, 829; arrives at Vincennes, 829; meets with Pontiac, who offers the calumet of peace, 830; proceeds to Detroit, 831; holds a council there with the Indians, 831–834; his speech to the Ottawas, 832; outdoes the Indians in the use of figurative language, 832, 833 *note*; his complete success, 834.

Crown Point, a French fort erected there, 423; plan for its reduction, 430; the plan fails, 437; another attempt, 443; the fort evacuated, 444.

Cumberland County, Pa., settled by the Scotch-Irish, 679.

Cusick, a Tuscarora Indian, the historian of his tribe, 368, 369 *notes.*

Cuyler, Lieutenant, leaves Niagara with a reinforcement for Detroit, 542; is attacked by Indians, 543; fate of his detachment, 544.

D.

D'Abbadie, governor of the French, New Orleans, 816; gives audience to the messengers of Pontiac, 817; refuses aid, *ib.*; dies, *ib.*

Dahcotah, their estimated military strength, 609; their hatred of the Ojibwas, 612; their interference saves the English garrison at Green Bay, *ib.*

Dalzel, Captain, leaves Niagara with a reinforcement for Detroit, 570; attacked by the Indians, 571; arrives at Detroit, *ib.*; his night attack on the Indians, 572; his great bravery, 575; falls in the action, 576.

Davers, Sir Robert, murdered by Indians, 520; the transaction erroneously reported, 540.

Delaware tribe of Indians, a brave and generous people, 380; called also Lenni Lenape, 379; the parent stem of the Algonquin tribes, *ib.*; subjugated by the Iroquois, 363; recover their independence, 380; their treaty with William Penn, 380, 414; oppressed by his descendants, proprietors of Pennsylvania, 415–418, 428; driven from their homes, 417; some of them present at the battle of the Monongahela, 432; in alliance with the French, 455; attack the English settlements, 455; their number estimated, 459; where located in 1760, 460; found at present beyond the Mississippi, 380; incensed against the English, 478; a Delaware prophet, his wide influence, 480; the Delawares attack Fort Pitt, 628, 636; attack a body of British troops at Bushy Run, 663; are repulsed with great loss, 667; moral effect of the affair, 670; their hostile inroads in Pennsylvania, 689; a party of them brought prisoners to Albany, 700; their inveterate hostility, 754, 757; their worthless promises, 758; they sue for peace, 775–780.

Detroit founded, 503; description of, 503, 504, 507; held by a French garrison, 396, 401, 444, 470, 472; it capitulates to the English, 473, 474; its population at that time, 503; character of its inhabitants, 504; the fortifications, *ib.*; the British garrison in 1760, 507; plan of Pontiac to seize the fort, 509, 510; the plot revealed, 510; See *Appendix* C. Pontiac in Detroit, 513 *et seq.*; attack on the fort 514, 515; distress of the garrison, 529; Detroit alone of all the frontier posts escapes capture by the Indians, 548; the garrison reinforced, 560; Gladwyn holds a council with the Canadians, 560, 561; his speech to them, 561; Indian attempt to burn an armed schooner, 567; the garrison again reinforced, 571; their numbers, 578; a supply of provisions collected, 695; the Ojibwas and other tribes ask for peace, *ib.*; the siege of Detroit abandoned, 697; moral effect of the failure, 699; the garrison continue to be harassed by Indian hostility, 748; arrival of Bradstreet with a large military force, *ib.*; he meets the Indians in council, 749; his absurd demands, 750; gives great offence to the Indians, 751.

Devil's Hole, near Niagara, described, 674; a convoy attacked there by Indians, *ib.*; the fearful issue, 675.

Dieskau, Louis Auguste, Baron, sails from Brest with troops for Canada, 428; his defeat at Lake George, 438–439; wounded dangerously, but not mortally, 439, 440 *note*.

Dinwiddie, Robert, Lieutenant-Governor of Virginia, remonstrates against French encroachment, 424.

Dionondadies, or Tobacco Nation, 374.

Dogs, proposal to hunt the Indians with them, 648; the plan given in detail, 649 *note*.

E.

Easton, Pa., peace there made with the Indians, 455.

Ecuyer, Captain Simeon, commander at Fort Pitt, 623; his letters to Colonel Bouquet quoted, 623, 624 *note,* 626, 628, 637; his answer to the proposal to surrender, 629; his answer to a similar and subsequent demand, 636; his precautions for the safety of the fort, 639 *note*; his gallant conduct, 638; his discontent at the service, 734.

Elder, John, pastor at Paxton, Pa., his creditable military career, 687; his report to Governor Penn, 687 *note*; his character, 704; preaches to armed men, *ib.*; endeavors to divert the Paxton men from their murderous design, but in vain, 707; his letter to Colonel Burd, 709 *note*. See *Appendix* E.

Eliot, Charles, brave action of his, 656.

English colonies, their characteristics as contrasted with those of France, 390, 391, 392, 403, 408; neglect to cultivate the friendship of the Indians, 409, 475; plan for a union of these colonies, 427; its failure, and the reason why, 428; English colonies, their exposure to Indian hostility, in 1760, 491; how far they extended at that time, 621.

English treatment of the Indians, 409, 475, 484, 491; English parsimony towards them, 475. See *Appendix* B. English fur-trade badly conducted, 477; profligacy of the traders, *ib.*; treatment of the Indians by the soldiers in garrison, *ib.*

Eries, Indian tribe, destroyed by the Iroquois, 376.

Etherington, Captain George, commands at Michillimackinac, 590; is warned of danger, *ib.*; his disregard of the warning, *ib.*; his extreme carelessness, 594; the massacre of his men, 595; he is taken by the Indians, 550, 595; his letters quoted, 549, 610; how he passed the night after the massacre, 600, 601; his complimentary letter to Colonel Bouquet on his promotion, 794.

F.

Fire, torture by, inflicted by Indians, 372, 395, 405, 545 *note*, 634, 647 *note*.

Fisher, Sergeant, murdered by the Indians, 519; treatment of his body, *ib.*

Forbes, General John, drives the

French from Fort Du Quesne, 442, 455, 457.

Forest of the West, 458; routes and modes of travel through it, 461–464; the scattered Indian and French settlements, 459, 464; the forest garrisons, 465; hunters and trappers, 466.

Fort Du Quesne, built by the French, 430; Braddock's approach to it, 431; taken by General Forbes, 442, 457; the fort destroyed and rebuilt, 622; and the name changed to Fort Pitt, 462.

Fort Le Bœuf, taken by the Indians after a gallant defence, 631, 632.

Fort Ligonier, 623; attacked by Indians, 627, 652, 653; the fort is reinforced and holds out to the end, 660.

Fort Miami taken by the Indians, 551.

Fort Pitt, originally Fort Du Quesne, 462, 470; its commanding position, 622; built on the ruins of the old fort, 622; two roads from it to the English settlements, 622; exposed to danger from the Indians, 623, 629; strength of the garrison, 628; attacked by Indians, 629; the Indians frightened and withdraw, 630; the surrender of the fort twice demanded, 630, 636; a vigorous attack by the Indians, 638; the attack ineffectual, 639; the fort reinforced and secured from further danger, 668, 669; brief history of the siege by one of the garrison, 669 note.

Franklin, Benjamin, his account of the murder of Indians in Lancaster jail, 708 note; his energetic conduct in providing for the defence of Philadelphia, 721.

Fraser, Lieutenant Alexander, accompanies Croghan in an embassy to the Indians, 819; visits the country of the Illinois, 825; his account of that country, 803 note; is ill-treated and his life in danger, 825; Pontiac saves his life, 826; descends the Mississippi and arrives at New Orleans, ib.

French colonies, their distinctive characteristics, 390 et seq.; devotion to the Romish church, 391, 392; engaged in the fur-trade, 392; their lack of energy, 397; have an extended military frontier, 392, 400; French plan to exclude the Anglo-Saxon race from the valley of the Mississippi, 400; French expeditions against the Iroquois, 404–406; French influence among the Indians widely extended, 407, 409; instances of French inhumanity, 409, 410; complaisance towards the savages, 410; French blood mingles largely with Indian, 411, 507; the French in the Ohio valley, 418; obtain an influence over the Iroquois, 418, 419, and over the Indians on the Ohio, 426; occupation of Fort Du Quesne, 431; driven from all their possessions in North America, 453; French settlements in the Illinois valley, 464; French policy towards the Indians, 476 note. See Appendix B.

Frontenac, Count, Governor of Canada, aids the enterprises of La Salle, 399; his expedition against the Iroquois, 405, 406; cultivates the friendship of other Indians, 410; burns alive an Iroquois prisoner, ib.

Frontier of Virginia, 677; of Pennsylvania, 678; the frontiersman described, 677, 678.

Frontiers of the English provinces, 621; how guarded, 621; ravaged by the Indians, 640; sufferings of the settlers, 650; difficulties of communication between the outposts and the settled country, 653; the frontiers desolated, 679 et seq.; consternation of the settlers, 680; fearful scenes enacted, 681 et seq.; general distress, 686; the number slain or captivated during four months, 701; the frontier people make loud complaints of neglect, 701; their resentment against the Quakers, ib.; their intense hatred of the Indians, 702. See Appendix E.

Fur-trade as carried on from Canada, 392, 403, 407; from the English colonies, 407, 412; the coureurs de bois, renegades from civilization, 412; fur-trade, mode of operation, 462; equipment and character of the fur-trader, 463, 466; difficulties, hardships, and dangers of the way, 463, 464; the call for energy and courage, 465; character and habits of the existing trapper and hunter in the far west, 465, 466; the white savage compared with the red, 465; fur-trade as conducted by the English; its great faults, 477; bad character of the English traders, 477; French fur-traders inflame the resentment of the Indians, 478, 584.

G.

Gage, General Thomas, present at Braddock's defeat, 433; receives a severe wound, 435; his singular testimony concerning Pontiac, 535; succeeds Amherst as commander-in-chief, 692; sends a body of troops to Philadelphia, to protect it against the Paxton rioters, 720.

Galissonnière, Count, his plan of French colonization, 401.

Gallatin, Albert, quoted, 362, 376, 377.

Gates, General Horatio, present at Braddock's defeat, 433; severely wounded, 435.

Gladwyn, Major, commands at Detroit, 487, 501; the hostile plans of Pontiac disclosed to him, 509; his precautions, 511; scene between him and Pontiac, 514, 515; his letters to General Amherst, 516 note, 531 note; suffers Pontiac to escape, 515, 516, 518; refuses to abandon the fort, 528; Pontiac in vain endeavors to terrify him, 560; Gladwyn holds a council with the Canadians, 561–564; his speech to them, 561; obtains a supply of provisions, 695; proposes to exterminate the Indians by a free sale of RUM, 696, 697 note.

Gladwyn, schooner, on her return to Detroit from Niagara, is attacked by Indians, 579, 580; gallant defence by the crew, 579; saved by a desperate expedient, 580.

Glendenning, Archibald, killed by the Indians, 681; masculine spirit of his wife, 682.

Gnadenhutten, Pa., a Moravian missionary station, destroyed, 711.

Goddard, an English fur-trader, 588.

Godefroy, a Canadian, summons Fort Miami to surrender, 552; goes to Illinois as interpreter to an English embassy, 752; saves Morris's life, 753; stands firmly by his captain, 754–757.

Gordon, Lieutenant, commander at Fort Venango, 633; tortured to death by the Indians, 634; roasted alive during several nights, 647 note.

Gorell, Lieutenant J., extracts from his journal, 462; commands at Green Bay, 609; his important duties, ib.; his prudent conduct, 610; his speech to the Menomonies, 610, 611; embarks with his garrison, 612; arrives at Montreal, 612.

Goshen, N. Y., false alarm there; its singular cause, 673

Gouin, ——, a Canadian, cautions Gladwyn, 509; endeavors the security of British officers, 523; his account of transactions near Detroit, Appendix C., 545 note.

Grant, Mrs. Anne, her erroneous account of the murder of Sir Robert Davers, 540 note.

Grant, Captain, in the disastrous affair at Bloody Bridge, 573, 574, 577.

Gray, Captain, falls in the fight at Bloody Bridge, 576.

Gray, a soldier at Presqu' Isle, 630; escapes massacre, 631.

Gray, Thomas, his "Elegy in a Country Church-Yard," repeated by Wolfe, the night before his death, 448.

Green, Thomas, a trader, slain by the Indians, 625 note.

Green Bay, a French settlement, 396, 401; taken possession of by the English, 474; its early history, 583; an important post, 609; abandoned by its commander, but its garrison preserved 611, 612.

Greenbrier, Va., attack on, 681.

"Griffin," the first vessel built on the upper lakes, 398; her voyage on Lakes Erie and Huron, ib.

H.

Heckewelder, John, Moravian missionary, relates a curious story of the superstitious regard of Indians for insane persons, 627.

Hendrick, the Mohawk chief, slain at the battle of Lake George, 438.

Henry, Alexander, pioneer of the English fur-trade in the extreme Northwest, 585; his adventures, 585; his interview with an Ojibwa chief, 585–587; attacked by a party of Ottawas, 588; an Ojibwa chief takes a liking to him, 590; and warns him of danger, 591; escapes the massacre at Michillimackinac, 596; his account quoted, 595–599; his extreme danger, 597; his life spared, and the manner thereof, 596 et seq.; his further adventures, 600–602, 607; painted and attired like an Indian, 608; extract from Henry's Travels, 739, 740; he is delivered from captivity and brought safely to Niagara, 744.

Hodenosaunee, the Indian name for the Five Nations, 363.

Holmes, Ensign, commander of Fort Miami, discovers a plot of the Indians against the English, 487; the fort is taken, and he is killed by the Indians, 551.

Hopkins, Mr., of Wyoming, escapes the massacre there, 691, 692.

Howe, Lord, killed at Ticonderoga, 442.

Hughes, John, of Lancaster, Pa., details of his plan to hunt the Indians with dogs, 649 note.

Hurons or Wyandots, their population, 374; had characteristics in common with the Iroquois, 375; their utter ruin and dispersion, 376; present at Braddock's defeat, 432; their population estimated, 459; their energy, 461; a conquered people, 458.

I.

Iberville, Lemoine d', founds the colony of Louisiana, 400.

Illinois nation of Indians, 381; tribes of which that nation was composed, 845 note.

Illinois River, the region described, 796 et seq.; its early colonization, 800–802; character of the first settlers, 802; the population, its numbers and location, 803; the Indians of that country, 804, 805; the English take possession of Fort Chartres, and of the Illinois country, 815, 835.

Insanity, persons laboring under it, superstitious regard of Indians for, 627.

Indian summer described, 697, 698.

Indians, their general character, 357; all live by the chase, ib.; their pride and self-consciousness, 358; they cannot endure restraint, ib.; influence of the sachems, what, ib.; distinction between the civil and military authority, ib.; the Indian inflexibly adheres to ancient usages, 361; division into clans, ib.; the totems, or symbols of the clans, ib.; peculiar character of the clan, ib.; its privileges, 362; division of the Indian population into three great families, ib.; their dwellings and works of defence, 369; their mode of life, 371; their legendary lore, 384; and religious belief, 385; the unity of God unknown to them, 386; the Indian character often mistaken, ib.; the Indian strangely self-contradictory, ib.; his character summed up, 387–389; treatment of Indians by the French, 408–411; by the English, 407; by William Penn, 413; by his sons, 415; by the Quakers, 414, 415; attitude of the Indian tribes towards the English in 1755, 422; their alarm at the appearance of the French on the waters of the Ohio, 426; the French conciliate them, 427; effect on them of Braddock's defeat, 436; attached to the French interest, 458; estimate of the Indian population in 1760 in the present territory of the United States, 459; striking instance of Indian acuteness, 467 note; their feelings at the surrender of Detroit, 473; intense hatred of the English takes possession of the Indians, 475; its manifestations, *ib.*; treatment of the Indians by the English, 475, 476 *note*, 485; plot formed for the destruction of the English, 481, 482; their imperfect preparation for the war, 489; defects of their social system, *ib.*; without any central authority, *ib.*; their chiefs had no power but of advice and persuasion, 490; Indians will not submit to restraint or discipline, *ib.*; they are capricious and unstable, *ib.*; often desert their leaders, 490; they are formidable in small detached parties only, *ib.*; they are fond of war and ready to engage in it, *ib.*; they never fight but when sure to win, 491; alert and active, crafty and treacherous, they cause wide-spread havoc, but carefully avoid collision with a foe, *ib.*; Indians prone to quarrel, 495; Indian council, 495 *et seq.*; war-dance, 520; Indian attack on Detroit, 521 *et seq.*; idea of military honor, 528; courage, 529; sad effect of whiskey, 544; Indians fight from ambush, 542; Indian barbarity. See *Barbarity, Indian.* Indians attempt to destroy an armed schooner, 567; their prolonged blockade of Detroit, 568; a curious instance of Indian friendship, 590; Indian ball play, 594; fearful massacre by Indians at Michillimackinac, 595 *et seq.*; cannibalism, 606; revulsion of feeling, 606, 608; Indian faithlessness, 491, 594, 625, 626; Indians fight in ambuscade, 674, 688; cannot stand before border riflemen, 688; great conference of Indians at Niagara, 739 *et seq.*; veneration of Indians for the rattlesnake, 739 *note*; to some white people Indian life has charms, 790; Indians of the Illinois, 804; council of Indians meet Sir William Johnson at Johnson Hall, 671; again at Niagara, 739; council at Detroit, 831–834; Indians are pleased when white men adopt their figurative language, 833 *note*.

Iroquois, or Five Nations, afterwards Six Nations, 363; the term often applied to the entire family of which they were a part, *ib.*; their extended conquests, *ib.* See *Appendix* A. Causes of their success, 364; tribal organization, *ib.*; their manner of conducting public business, 365; divided into eight clans, *ib.*; great power of this system, *ib.*; descent of the sachemship in the female line, 366; extensive prevalence of this custom, *ib. note*; origin of the Iroquois, 367; Indian tradition concerning it, 367, 368; their fantastic legends, 368, 369; rude state of the arts among them, 369; their agriculture, *ib.*; their fortifications and strongholds, *ib.*; their dwellings, 370; their life of excitement, 371; preparation for war, 372; return from war, *ib.*; fiendish cruelty, *ib.*; their boundless pride, 373; military strength, *ib.*; destroy the Hurons, 375; and several other Indian nations, *ib.*; their cruel treatment of captives, 376; their licentiousness, 377; their god of thunder, 385; attack made on them by Champlain, 404; they become the irreconcilable foes of the French colonies, *ib.*; their attack on Montreal, 405; their extreme ferocity, *ib.*; expedition of Frontenac against them, 405, 406; their rancor abates, 406; irritated against the English and why, 418; influence over them gained by Sir William Johnson, 420. See *Appendix* A. They assume to dispose of lands in Pennsylvania, 416, 427; treaty of alliance with them, 428; they induce the Delawares to make peace with the English, 455; flock to the British standard, 458; estimate of their numbers, 459; what their approach to civilization, 460; meet Sir William Johnson in council, and are restrained by him from war against the English, 671; the Senecas already at war with them, 481, 486, 634, 640, 671; the Iroquois send a message to the Delawares, exhorting them to bury the hatchet, 672; a war-party of the Iroquois goes out to fight the Delawares, 700; their success, *ib.*

J.

Jacobs, mate of schooner Gladwyn, orders the vessel blown up, 579; lost in a storm, 580 *note*.

Jamet, Lieutenant, at Michillimackinac slain by the Indians, 595, 610.

Jenkins, Lieutenant Edward, taken prisoner by the Indians, 550; his letter, 551 *note*.

Jesuit missionaries in Canada, 394 *et seq.*; their religious zeal and enterprise, 395; their sufferings, 396; slender results, *ib.*; lead the van of French colonization, *ib.*; the firm auxiliaries of French power, *ib.*

Jogues, Isaac, a Jesuit missionary, a captive among the Iroquois, 395; tortured by them, *ib.*; his death, *ib.*

Johnson, Sir William, settles on the Mohawk River, 420; trades with the Indians, *ib.*; acquires great influence over them, *ib.* See *Appendix* A. Becomes a major-general and a baronet, 420; repeatedly defeats the French, 421, 437–440, 444; his death, 421; his good and bad qualities, *ib.*; his noble figure, 837; his estimate of the Indian population, 459; his annoyance from Indians, 462 *note*; his statement of the French policy toward the Indians and its results, 476 *note*; his letters quoted, 409 *note*, 672 *note*; his influence keeps the Indians around him quiet, 640; convokes a council of the Six Nations and persuades them not to attack the English, 671; arms his tenantry, 673; their numbers, 672 *note*; offers fifty dollars each for the heads of two noted Delaware chiefs, 699; sends messengers to the north-western tribes, 736; meets a conference of Indians at Niagara, 739 *note*; his interview with Pontiac at Oswego, 836 *et seq.*; his address, 838; his indecision at the outbreak of the Revolution, 421; his death, *ib.*

Johnston, Captain, cut off with nearly all his men, 675, 676 *note*.

Jonois, a Jesuit priest, 549; commended for humanity, 550, 600, 601, 603; visits Detroit, 549, 603.

K.

Kaskaskia, a French settlement, 401, 464.

Kickapoos attack George Croghan, 828, 829.

L.

L'Arbre Croche, a settlement of the Ottawa Indians, 588, 602, 603, 612.

La Butte, interpreter to Major Gladwyn at Detroit, 515; goes with a message to Pontiac, 522; his fidelity suspected, 526; Major Gladwyn confides in him, 531 *note*.

Laclede, Pierre, the founder of St. Louis, 807.

Lake George, called Lac St. Sacrement, 441; battle of, 437–440; the lake described, 441; the scene of active warfare, *ib.*

Lallemant, Gabriel, missionary among the Hurons, tortured with fire, 395; his lingering death, *ib.*

Lancaster, Pa., jail, Indians lodged there for safety, 706; the jail broken open and the Indians killed, 707, 708; an account of the affair by Franklin, 708 *note*.

Langlade, Charles, a resident at Mackinaw 595; a witness of the massacre and careless about it, 596, 597; kindness of his wife, 598; he surrenders Mr. Henry to his pursuers, 599; saves Henry's life, 600; his heartlessness, 601; he and his father the first white settlers in Wisconsin, 595 *note*.

La Salle, Robert Cavelier de, his great design, 397; his character, 398; builds his first vessel on the upper lakes, *ib.*; his voyage on Lakes Erie and Michigan, *ib.*; penetrates the region of the Illinois, 399; his difficulties and embarrassments, *ib.*; descends the Mississippi, *ib.*; reaches its mouth, and takes possession of the whole immense valley for Louis XIV., 400; ruin of his final expedition, *ib.*; his death, *ib.*; a further account of him, 800, 801.

La Verandrye attempts to reach the Rocky Mountains, 407; penetrates to the Assinniboin River, *ib.*

Legends of the Iroquois, their monstrous character, 368, 369, 384; of the Algonquins, 385, 386.

Lenni Lenape, see *Delawares*.

Leslie, Lieutenant, at Michillimackinac, 594; taken by the Indians, 595, 612.

Loftus, Major, his abortive attempt to ascend the Mississippi, 813, 814.

Loskiel, Moravian missionary, quoted, 626.

Louisiana colonized, 400.

M.

Macdonald, James, of Detroit, his account of the detention of two British officers, 525 *note*; his account of the death of Capt. Campbell, 566 *note*.

McDougal, Lieutenant, of Detroit, visits the Indian camp and is treacherously seized, 523; the McDougal MSS. quoted, 533; escapes, 566.

McGregory, Major, attempts the furtrade, but fails, 407.

Meloche, at his house two British officers are confined, 525, 531; further notice of the house, 574.

Menomonies, their location, 609; friends of the English in Pontiac's war, 612.

Miami nation of Indians, 381; friendly to the English, 422; retained their ancient character, 461.

Miami fort. See *Fort Miami*.

Michillimackinac, a French settlement and fort, 396, 401; taken possession of by the English, 474; captured by the Indians, 549; the approach to it described, 582; description of the place itself, 583, 593, 607; import of the name, 583; tradition concerning the name, 607 *note*; early history of the place, 583; its population in 1763, *ib.*; Indian tribes in the vicinity, 584;

they join in the conspiracy of Pontiac, 589; strength of the garrison at the time, 589; warnings of danger, 590; the evening before the massacre, 591; the morning of the massacre, ball-play, 593; the massacre, 595; shocking scenes, 596; followed by an Indian debauch, 600; the Indians leave the place, 608. See *Appendix* C.

Military honor, Indian idea of it, 490, 528.

Minavavana, the great Ojibwa chief, called also the Grand Sauteur, 585; his interview with Alexander Henry, 585–587; his character and influence, 589; leads the attack on Michillimackinac, 603; his speech to the Ottawas, *ib.*; releases Mr. Henry, 605; description of him from Carver's Travels, 608 *note*; comes to Detroit to ask for peace, 831.

Missionary labors among the Indians by the Jesuits, 394 *et seq.*, 408; by the English, 408.

Mohawks, attack the Penobscot Indians, 363 *note*.

"Mohog all devil!" 363 *note*.

Mongrel population, French and Indian, 412, 507.

Monkton, General, reduces Acadia, 436; commands under Wolfe in the expedition against Quebec, 447; in command at Fort Pitt, 470.

Monongahela River, passage of by Braddock's army, 431, 433; Battle of, 434–436.

Montcalm (Louis Joseph de St. Véran), Marquis of, takes Oswego, 441; captures Fort William Henry, *ib.*; repels the attack of General Abercrombie on Ticonderoga, 442, 443; commands the army in opposition to Wolfe, 445; his defeat and death, 453.

Montour, Captain, makes a successful inroad upon the Indians, 700.

Montreal, attack on it by the Iroquois, 405; surrenders to the English forces, 454.

Moravian missions in Pennsylvania, 711; the converts involved in danger from both the French and the English, *ib.*;

murder of some of them, 712; the mission broken up and the converts removed to Philadelphia, 713; sent thence to New York, 718, 719; insulted by the mob, 713; not allowed to enter New York or to stay in New Jersey, 719; brought back to Philadelphia, 720; remain there a whole year, 729.

Morris, Captain, goes on an embassy to the Illinois country, 751; his interview with Pontiac, 752; holds a council with the Indians, 753; encounters a band of savage warriors, 754; he is a captive among the Indians, 755; expects to be tortured, 756; is released, ib.; abandons his mission and returns to Detroit, 757; reference to his published journals, ib.; returns home, meeting with disaster on the way, 759, 760.

N.

Neutral Nation, why so named, 374; their destruction by the Iroquois, 375.

New England, population contrasted with that of Canada, 391 et seq.; their energy and patient industry, 392; did not obtain Indian lands but by purchase, 414 note.

New York, Province of, suffers from Indian hostilities, 672.

Niagara, French fort there, 390, 401, 406; attack on it by the English, 421; failure of the attack, 436; another attempt, 443; the fort surrenders, 444; great conference of Indians there, 739 et seq.

O.

Ohio River, no Indians dwelt on its banks, 464.

Ohio Company, formed, and for what purpose, 424.

Ohio Valley, proposal to secure it for the English, 424; French settlements there, 401; further encroachments, 418, 424 et seq.; alarm of the Indians of that vicinity, 426; Ohio Indians at war with the English, 455; estimate of their numbers, 459; the Ohio valley described as it was in 1760, 458 et seq.; its population, 458 et seq.; routes of travel, 461; modes of travel, 461–464.

Ojibwa nation of Indians, 382; check the career of Iroquois conquest, ib.; their modes of life, 383; sufferings in winter, ib.; some of them present at the battle of the Monongahela, 432; join Pontiac in his attack on the English, 521, 530; notice of their village on Mackinaw, 584; a party of them described, 585; interview with Alexander Henry, 585–587; their slaughter of the English garrison at Michillimackinac, 594 et seq.; hated by the Dahcotahs, 611; the Ojibwas ask for peace, 695; they consult their oracle, 737; the answer received, 738; peace concluded, 743.

Oneidas, a tribe united in confederacy with four others, 364. See Iroquois.

Onondaga, council-house at, 365 note; description of it, 370, 371 note, 459.

Onondagas, a tribe included in the Confederacy of the Five Nations, 364. See Iroquois.

Oswego, an English fort there, 407; taken by the French, 410, 441, 457.

Ottawas, 382; present at the battle of the Monongahela, 432; led by Pontiac, ib.; their village near Detroit, 507; their attack on Detroit, 521, 524; notice of their village near Mackinaw, 584; a party of them visit Mackinaw and threaten English fur-traders, 588; take English prisoners from the Ojibwas, 602; a party of them take possession of Michillimackinac, 602; collision with the Ojibwas, 602 et seq.; they incite the Delawares to war against the English, 629; the Ottawas refuse to bury the hatchet, 696; they meet Sir William Johnson at Niagara and make peace, 742; at Detroit they meet George Croghan for a like purpose, 832.

Ourry, Captain Lewis, commander at

Fort Bedford, 650; his slender force, 650, 651; his correspondence with Col. Bouquet, *ib.*

Owens, David, diabolically kills and scalps his own Indian wife and several of her relations, 765, 766.

P.

Paully, Ensign, a captive to the Indians, 546; adopted as one of them, 547; makes his escape, 565.

Paxton, in Pennsylvania, character of its inhabitants, 703; its worthy minister, John Elder, 704; a party of men proceed from this place and murder six friendly Indians, 704 *et seq.*; the survivors of the massacre lodged in Lancaster County jail, 706. See *Appendix* E. The act causes great excitement, 709; the deed justified from Scripture, 710; the rioters march on Philadelphia to kill the Moravian converts, 717; alarm of the citizens, 718, 722; measures for defence, 721; treaty with the rioters, 725; they withdraw, 726; a party of them make prize of Croghan's goods, 820, 821; they escape punishment and set the government at defiance, 822.

Pawnee woman saves the life of Alexander Henry, 596; the Pawnee tribe, 596 *note.*

Penn, William, his treatment of the Indians, 413; pays twice for his lands, 414 *note*; his sons pursue a contrary policy, 414.

Pennsylvania, treatment of the Indians in, 413 *et seq.*; the "walking purchase," 415; shameful conduct of the proprietors, 416, 427; Pennsylvania wasted by Indian war, 455; extent of its settlements in 1760, 622; the province refuses aid to its defenders, 654, 660; distress of the inhabitants on its frontier, 657; the frontier described, 678; origin and character of the inhabitants, *ib.*; the frontier settlers betake themselves to flight before Indian ravage, 680; general distress, 686; measures of defence opposed by the Quakers in the Assembly, 687; warfare along the Susquehanna, 690 *et seq.*; contests of the Assembly with the proprietary governors, 693; vigorous measures at length adopted, 720.

Penobscot Indians attacked by the Mohawks, 363 *note.*

Philadelphia, a place of outfit for the Indian trade, 462; the Moravian converts removed thither, 713; great alarm felt at the approach of the Paxton boys, 717; the people called to arms, 721; extreme excitement, 722; treaty with the rioters, 725. See *Appendix* E.

Picquet, a Jesuit missionary, 396; engages in military enterprises, 419.

Pittman, Captain, does not ascend the Mississippi, 814, 815.

Pittsburgh (Fort Du Quesne) occupied by the English, 425; by the French, 431; its capture by General Forbes, 442.

Pontiac, his origin, 483 *note*; leads the Ottawas out in the attack on Braddock's force, 432, 483; his interview with Rogers, 471; his haughty behavior, 472; his character, 472, 508, 517; submits to the English, 471, 472; his extensive influence among the Indians, 482; his commanding energy, 483; a fierce, wily savage, 483, 508, 517; his great qualities, 483, 536; his enduring fame, 537; in alliance with the French, 483; sends ambassadors to excite the Indians over all the West, 485; listens to the falsehoods of the Canadians, 485; resolves on war with the English, *ib.*; the proposal accepted, 486; he collects a multitude of Indians in a council, 495; his appearance, 496; his speech, 497 *et seq.*; allegory told by him, 497–499; his plan for an attack on Detroit, 500, 501; performs a calumet-dance within its walls, 501; Pontiac at home, 508; his plan to seize Detroit, 509, 510; the plot revealed, 510. See *Appendix* C. Pontiac admitted to the fort, 514, 518; finds that his designs are known, 515;

his treachery, 516, 517; scene between him and Gladwyn, 515, 516, 517; Gladwyn permits him to escape, 516, 517; Pontiac throws off the mask, 518; the war begins, 519; Pontiac enraged, 520; the war-dance, *ib.*; attack on the fort, 521, 522; his duplicity, 523; detains two British officers, 525; threatens to burn Gladwyn alive, 530; visited by a deputation of Canadians, 531–534; his speech to them, 532–534; provides supplies of food for his followers, 534; issues promissory notes for the payment, 535; is desirous of learning war from Europeans, *ib.*; General Gage's account of him, 535; Major Rogers's account, 536; account of him by William Smith, 536 *note*; his magnanimity illustrated by anecdotes, 537, 538; number of his followers, 547; tries to terrify Gladwyn into a surrender, 560; sends messengers to the Indians of Mackinaw, 589, 607; his long-cherished hopes of assistance from France come to an end, 696; his message to Gladwyn announcing this result, 696; abandons the siege of Detroit, 697; his interview with Captain Morris on the Maumee River, 752, 753; his hopes crushed, but his spirit whole, 809; goes to the Illinois country, *ib.*; is aided by the French settlers there, 810; they deceive him with hopes of aid from France, 810; Neyon, the French commandant, discourages him, 811; rouses the tribes of the Illinois to war, 812; sends messengers, with similar intent, to the Indians in Southern Louisiana, 815; and to New Orleans, 816; they return without success, 818; Pontiac saves the life of Lieutenant Fraser, 825; seizes a cargo of English goods, 827; his followers forsake him, and he finds that all is lost, 827; offers the English envoy, Croghan, the calumet of peace, 830; his speech to the Indian tribes assembled at Detroit, 833; meets Sir William Johnson at Oswego, 837; promises a full compliance with the English demands, 840; still supposed to cherish thoughts of vengeance, 841; visits St. Louis, 842; appears in French uniform, *ib.*; his assassination at Cahokia, 843, 844; buried near St. Louis, 844; his death avenged, 845. See *Appendix* B. and C.

Post, Christian Frederic, a Moravian missionary, visits the Ohio Indians to detach them from the French interest, 456; extracts from his journal, 456 *note*; succeeds in his errand, 457.

Pothier, a Jesuit priest, endeavors to restrain the Wyandots from hostilities, 527.

Pottawattamies, kindred of the Ojibwas, 382; located near Detroit, 473, 507; and near the head of Lake Michigan, 548.

Presbyterians of Pennsylvania, their stiffness of character, 679; hated by the Quakers, 710; the Quakers hated by them, 721; mutual recrimination, 728. See *Appendix* E.

Presqu' Isle, on Lake Erie, fortified by the French, 424, 465; occupied by the English, 470; taken by the Indians, 552; a false report respecting the capture, 630.

Price, Ensign George, commander at Fort Le Bœuf, 631; his gallant but unavailing defence, 632, 633; arrives at Fort Pitt, 631, 634.

Prideaux, General, killed at Niagara, 444.

Prophet, among the Delawares: his wide influence, 480; excites the Indians to war, *ib.*; exhorts them to bury the hatchet, 824.

Q.

Quakers of Pennsylvania: their treatment of the Indians, 413; anticipated in their policy by the Puritans of New England, 414; their love of the Indians runs to dangerous extremes, 415; persuade the Indians to cease their hostilities, 455; Quaker assemblymen oppose measures of defence, and justify the Indians in their raids on the settlements, 687, 692; their own security due to their remoteness from the scene of danger, 692; the Quakers alarmed at the approach of the Paxton men, 717; their dilemma, 717; they concur in measures for the defence of Philadelphia, 721; and thus abandon their favorite principle.

Quaker principles no security from the tomahawk, 692 *note*.

Quebec, strongly fortified, 444; surrenders to the English, 453.

R.

Rangers, description of this species of force, 468; their services, 468; their reputation, *ib.*; a body of them under Rogers sent to take possession of the western posts, 470.

Rattlesnake superstitiously venerated by the Indians, 739 *note, 800 note.*

Robertson, Captain, murdered by Indians, 520.

Rogers, Major Robert, commander of the Rangers, 468; described, 468; wanting in correct moral principle, 469; tried for meditated treason, *ib.*; his miserable end, *ib.*; his published works, 469, 470 *note. See Appendix* B. Sent to take possession of the Western posts, 470; passes up Lakes Ontario and Erie, *ib.*; his interview with Pontiac, 471; his statements respecting the detention of two British officers, 525, 526 *note*; his account of Pontiac, 536; Rogers and Pontiac, 537; comes to Detroit with a reinforcement, 571; engaged in the fight at Bloody Bridge, 575, 576, 577.

"Royal Americans," a regiment so denominated, 642; of what material composed, *ib.*

Rum: a proposal to exterminate the Indians by the free sale of this article, 697 *note*.

S.

Sacs and Foxes, their location, 609; defeated by the French near Detroit, 533 *note*; a party of Sacs visit Michillimackinac, 593.

Sandusky, fort, captured by the Indians, 547.

Sault Ste. Marie, a military post, 583; abandoned by the English, 609.

Schlosser, Ensign, taken prisoner by Indians, 548, 549.

School children, with their master, murdered and scalped by the Indians, 682, 683.

Schoolcraft, Henry R., quoted, 361, 366, 368, 508, 510.

Scotch-Irish in Pennsylvania, 679; their peculiarities, *ib.*

Seneca Indians join in the plot against the English, 481, 486; a party of them take and destroy Venango, 634, 640; destroy a convoy at the Devil's Hole, 675; make peace with the English, 741. See *Iroquois*.

Shawanoes, scattered widely after their defeat by the Iroquois, 381; driven again from their homes, 418; carry on hostilities against the English, 455; their number estimated, 459; their villages, 461; Colonel Bouquet compels them to sue for peace, 780.

Shippen, Edward, a magistrate of Lancaster, gives to Governor Penn an account of the massacre in Lanscaster jail, 708 *note*. See *Appendix* E.

Shippensburg, Pa., crowded with fugitives from the frontiers, 660 *note*.

Small-pox, proposal to infect the Indians with it, 648, 649; this disease found to exist among them, 648 *note*.

Smith, James, commands a body of border riflemen, 689; adopts the Indian costume and tactics, *ib.*; a further account of him, 689 *note*; heads a predatory expedition of Paxton men, 820; his narration of the affair, 822 *note*.

Smith, Matthew, a leader among the Paxton men, 704; conducts a party of men against the Indians at Conestoga, 705; the massacre, 705; Smith's narration of the affair, 705 *note*; he threatens to fire on his minister's horse if not allowed to pass, 707; leads in the massacre of Indians in Lancaster jail, *ib.*; conducts an armed rabble to Philadelphia, with a purpose to kill the Moravian Indians, 716; proceeds to Germantown, and there halts, 723; treaty with the rioters, 725. See *Appendix* E., pp. 887–891.

Smith, William, of New York, his account of Pontiac, 536 *note*.

Smollett's history of England, quoted in reference to the "Royal Americans," 641 *note*.

Solomons, an English fur-trader, 588.

Spangenburg, a Moravian bishop, attends the great Iroquois council at Onondaga, 365 *note*; his account of it, *ib.*

St. Ange de Bellerive, commander of the French fort Chartres, 808; keeps the Indians quiet, *ib.*; has a visit from Pontiac, 812; to whom he refuses aid, 812, 826.

St. Aubin, a Canadian, 509; his account of the siege of Detroit, *Appendix* C.

St. Ignace, mission of, 584.

St. Joseph River, a French fort there, 398, 401; taken possession of by the English, 474; the fort captured by Indians, 548.

St. Louis founded by Laclede, 807; surprising changes there in the memory of the living, 807.

St. Pierre, Legardeur de, French commandant on the waters of the Ohio, 425.

Stedman, conductor of a convoy, escapes from the Indians, 674.

Stewart, Lazarus, a leader of the Paxton men, 706; apprehended on a charge of murder, 710; escapes to Wyoming, *ib.*; issues a "declaration," *ib.*; the document quoted, 701 *note*; favorable character of him given by Rev. John Elder, 709 *note*.

Superstitious regard of Indians for insane persons illustrated by a curious story, 627; superstitious regard for rattlesnakes, 739 *note*, 800 *note*.

Susquehanna River, its banks a scene of Indian warfare, 689 *et seq.*

T.

Thunder, god of, 385.

Ticonderoga, its position, 441; repulse of the English there, 442, 443; taken by General Amherst, 444.

Totems, emblems of clans, 361, 362, 365; their influence, 365.

Tracy, a fur-trader, at Mackinaw, 595.

Traders among the Indians, their bad character, 407; many of them killed, 625, 626; treacherous conduct of the Indians towards them, 627.

Treacherous conduct of Indians, 490, 594, 625, 627, 632.

Treatment of captives taken in war, 372, 405, 524 *note*.

Treatment of Indians by the French, 408–411; by the English, 408, 475, 476 *note*, 485; by William Penn, 413; by his sons, 414, 415; by the Quakers, 413, 414; by the New England people, 414.

Treaty of 1763, its probable effect on the Indians had it been made sooner, 491, 492.

Trent, Captain, occupies the site of Pittsburg, 425; obliged to leave it, 426.

Tribute exacted by the Iroquois, what, 363 *note*.

Tuscaroras, a later member of the *Iroquois* confederacy, 364; removal from North Carolina, 377.

U.

Union of the colonies proposed, 427.

Union of the Mississippi and Missouri Rivers, 796.

V.

Venango, on the Alleghany River, 622; destroyed by the Indians and the garrison slaughtered, 634; the remains visible many years after, 635 *note*.

Vincennes, a French settlement, 464, 622.

Virginia troops, their good conduct at the time of Braddock's defeat, 435; Virginia wasted by Indian war, 455; character of the settlers of Western Virginia, 677; extent of settlement,

678; ravages of the Indians, 681, 682; energetic measures taken to protect the settlers, 688.

W.

"Walking Purchase," the, a fraudulent transaction, 415; its consequences, 416.

Walpole, Horace, his low opinion of General Braddock, 430.

Wampum, of what made, 485 *note*; its uses, 486 *note*; what the spurning of it denotes, 457 *note*; used in making a treaty, 745 *note*; black wampum and its use, 817.

Wapocomoguth, an Ojibwa chief, visits Detroit with proposals of peace, 695.

War, Indian appetite for it, 490; their mode of preparation for it, 371; wars of the Iroquois with other Indians, 375–377; with the French, 405, 406; war of 1755, 428–454; of the Indians of Ohio against the English, 455; war-parties of Indians, how formed, 489; Indian wars, how conducted, 490, 491; preparation for war, how made, 492–494; the war feast, 493; prognostics of the war, 503; the war dance, 520; the war instigated by Pontiac begins, 521; end of the war, its distresses, 840.

War of 1755, its beginning, 428; its peculiar character, 429; plan formed for 1755 by the English ministry, 430; plan for 1759, 443.

Washington, George, sent to remonstrate against French encroachment, 424; his interview with the French commandant on the waters of the Ohio, 425; surprises and captures a party of French on the Monongahela, 426; sustains the attack of a superior force of French and Indians, *ib.*; his calm behavior at the time of Braddock's defeat, 433.

Wawatam, an Ojibwa chief, his singular friendship for Alexander Henry, 590; warns Henry of danger, 591; the warning disregarded, *ib.*; procures the release of Henry from those who had him in their power, 604, 605;

again preserves the life of Henry, 608.

Webb, General, his dastardly conduct, 457.

Wilderness of the West described, 458; its vastness, its small and scattered Indian population, 459; estimate of the number, *ib.*; hunters and trappers, their character and habits, 466, 467.

Wilkins, Major, commands at Niagara, 675; conducts an expedition against the Indians, 676; meets with disaster, *ib.*; the failure of the expedition announced at Detroit, 697.

William Henry, Fort, its position, 441; taken by Montcalm, 441; massacre there, 410, 441.

Williams, Colonel Ephraim, slain at the battle of Lake George, 438.

Williamson, an English trader, procures the assassination of Pontiac, 843, 844.

Winnebagoes, their location, 609.

Winston, Richard, trader at St. Joseph's, his curious letter, 549 *note*.

Wisconsin, first white settlers in it, 596 *note*.

Wolfe, General James, arrives before Quebec, 444; his character, 445; difficulties of his situation, 445, 446; repeats Gray's "Elegy," 448; occupies the Plains of Abraham, 450; the battle, 451, 452; death of Wolfe in the arms of victory, 453.

Wyandots, or Hurons, where situated, 374; their early prosperity, 375; fiercely attacked and slaughtered by the Iroquois, 375; a fugitive remnant left, 375, 382; their energy of character, 377, 461; their steadiness in fight, 377, 378; their village near Detroit, 473, 507; they join in the conspiracy of Pontiac, 486; some of them do this under coercion, 527; a body of them surprise Cuyler's detachment, 544; a party of them capture Fort Sandusky, 546.

Wyoming Valley, settled from Connecticut, 691, 710; massacre of the settlers, 691.

Chronology

1823   Born September 16, on Beacon Hill, in Boston, and named Francis Parkman. First son of the Reverend Francis Parkman (b. 1788) and Caroline Hall Parkman (b. 1794). Family includes half-sister Sarah, by his father's first marriage. Father is Unitarian pastor of the New North Church and the son of a wealthy Boston merchant, Samuel Parkman. (Both parents come from old New England families: mother is a descendant of John Cotton and Edward Brooks, and father comes from a long line of ministers, including Indian fighter and diarist Ebenezer Parkman.)

1825   Sister Caroline ("Carrie") born.

1830   Sister Mary Brooks ("Moll") born.

1831–36   For reasons of health, lives on farm of maternal grandparents, Nathaniel and Joanna Cotton Brooks Hall, just outside of Medford, Massachusetts. Attends Mr. Angier's school in Medford and learns "a little Latin and Greek." Regularly plays and hunts in nearby woods (Middlesex Fells), and comes to love outdoor life. Sister Eliza ("Lizzie") born 1832. Brother John Eliot ("Elly" or "Jack") born 1834.

1836–40   Attends Gideon F. Thayer's Chauncy Place School in Boston. Family moves into mansion built by grandfather Samuel Parkman (d. 1824) on Bowdoin Square. Delights to see a group of Indians led by Black Hawk on Boston Common in 1837. Conducts chemical experiments in a shed behind the house which (he later wrote) "served little other purpose than injuring himself by confinement, poisoning him with noxious gases, and occasionally scorching him with some ill-starred explosion." Organizes amateur acting company, the "Star Theater," composed of cousins and neighborhood boys; performances are given regularly on Saturday afternoons. Studies Greek, Latin, English literature, and mathematics at school. Particularly likes class in English composition given by William Russell in which one of the exercises is to translate into idiomatic English passages from Virgil and Homer. Admires Sir Walter Scott, James Fenimore Cooper, and Lord Byron.

1840–41   Enters Harvard College. Rooms in Holworthy Hall with Benjamin Apthorp Gould, who becomes an astronomer and lifelong friend. During summer vacation, travels for one month with classmate Daniel D. Slade "to see the wilderness where it was as yet uninvaded by the hand of man." Keeps a journal of his travels. Almost falls to his death while climbing in the White Mountains. Decides to explore further in northern New Hampshire and Maine. Meets the State Geological Survey party led by Dr. Charles T. Jackson, and learns more about the country to the north. Hunts and fishes, and feels exhilarated by the adventure in spite of lack of proper equipment, but finds his companion less enthusiastic (though Slade never again accompanies Parkman on a wilderness trip, they remain lifelong friends).

1841–42   Takes room for himself in Cambridge. Begins independent historical research, consulting Jared Sparks, the first Harvard professor of modern history. Already showing "symptoms of 'Injuns' on the brain" and looking ahead to writing the history of the forest ("the whole course of the American conflict between France and England"), he spends much time horseback riding, boxing, and shooting. During summer vacation, goes again into wilderness, this time accompanied by Henry Orne White; explores Lake George and Lake Champlain in New York, the Green Mountains in Vermont, and the Eastern Townships along the Canadian border, returning south through northern New Hampshire and Maine and the White Mountains, the same route he had traveled the previous summer. Though Parkman again enjoys the adventure, he finds that White dislikes it even more than Slade had the summer before.

1842–43   Moves into Massachusetts Hall. Studies Latin, Greek, French, and Italian. Participates in many student clubs and enjoys debating. Is vice-president and then president of the Hasty Pudding Club. Trains intensely to perfect his shooting and riding, and learns to canoe. During summer vacation does historical research in Schenectady, Lake

George, Montreal, and Quebec, returning by way of White Mountains and visiting his favorite spots. Later accompanies sister Caroline to Gardiner, Maine, and goes alone to visit Penobscot Indian reservation north of Bangor.

1843–44   Suffers first breakdown in health because of "too violent exercise in the gymnasium" and leaves school in fall to travel in Europe. Sails as the only passenger on a small merchant ship to Gibraltar; from there goes on to Malta and then to Sicily. Tours Sicily on muleback accompanied by a guide. In Naples meets Unitarian minister and reformer Theodore Parker and his wife, and travels with them to Rome. Sees the Carnivals in both Naples and Rome. Meets his classmate and friend the painter William Morris Hunt in Rome and tours the Apennines on muleback with him. Closely observes the rites and practices of Roman Catholic priests and monks; stays at convent of Passionist Fathers for several days. Leaves Rome after Holy Week, traveling north through Florence, Bologna, Milan, and Lake Como, before crossing the Alps into Switzerland over the Splügen Pass. Tours Paris with divorced expatriated uncle, Samuel Parkman. Crosses the channel to London, and later tours Scotland; particularly enjoys the areas around Abbotsford and Edinburgh made famous by Sir Walter Scott. Sails from Liverpool and arrives in Boston in late June 1844. Spends a few weeks doing historical research in the Berkshires. Elected Phi Beta Kappa, and graduates from Harvard.

1844–45   Enters Dana Law School (later Harvard Law School). Rooms at Divinity Hall. Studies under judges Joseph Story and Simon Greenleaf. Publishes anonymously in *Knickerbocker Magazine* five tales and sketches using as background earlier wilderness excursions. Continues to do independent research, focusing on Ottawa Indian chief Pontiac. Travels in summer 1845 to New York, Philadelphia, and then along the old Alleghany frontier: Lancaster, Harrisburg, Williamsport, Tioga, Seneca Lake, and Buffalo. Goes by way of the Great Lakes to Detroit, Mackinaw, and Sault Ste. Marie. Meets Robert Stuart, once an important fur trader in Astor's fur company and now superintendent of Indian affairs for Michigan. Re-

turns to Boston via Niagara Falls, Syracuse, and Onondaga, the Mohawk Valley, and New York. Experiences difficulty reading at times and has sisters read to him.

1846 Graduates from law school in January. Does research on
Pontiac in New York, Philadelphia, and Baltimore, where
he meets Lyman C. Draper, historian, editor, and collector of early western American documents, and Brantz
Mayer, lawyer and collector of early colonial documents,
both of whom become long-time correspondents. Nervous and having trouble with eyes, decides to go with
cousin Quincy Adams Shaw, who is also having health
problems, on a western tour. Arranges to meet Shaw in
mid-April in St. Louis. After meeting with Indian expert
and translator Henry Rowe Schoolcraft and others in
New York, travels to Philadelphia and Pittsburgh. Takes a
steamboat down the Ohio and then up the Mississippi
River to St. Louis, where he meets Thomas Fitzpatrick,
important mountain man and expert on the western Indians, and old fur traders Pierre Louis Cerré and Pierre
Chouteau (who knew Pontiac). Visits the reported site of
Pontiac's assassination. Hires Henry Chatillon, trapper
and hunter married to daughter of Oglala chief Bull Bear,
as guide and Antoine Deslauriers as muleteer. Party travels
by steamboat on the Missouri River to Westport (now
part of Kansas City), and on to the Oregon Trail and Fort
Laramie. Continually records experiences in journal.
Hunts buffalo. Lives among the Sioux for several weeks,
and although weakened by dysentery and nervous disorder, joins their summer buffalo hunt and their preparations for war against rival Indians. Returns by way of old
Indian trails and the Santa Fe Trail to Westport. Soon after
return to Boston, health breaks down completely, and
Parkman goes to New York and Staten Island for treatment by eye specialist, Dr. S. M. Elliott. (Parkman remains in New York and Staten Island for the next two
years, making occasional visits home and taking trips for
treatment in the Catskills and at Brattleboro Spa in Vermont.) On Staten Island, spends time with cousins Francis
G. Shaw and family, including young Robert Gould
Shaw. Realizing that historical work is not yet possible,
begins dictating *The Oregon Trail*, based on journal notes,
to family members and friends.

1847   Continues work on *The Oregon Trail: Or a Summer's Journey Out of Bounds*, and publishes first installment in *Knickerbocker*, signed "A Bostonian" (later ones are signed with his own name; serial installments appear Feb. 1847 to Feb. 1849). Continues historical research on Pontiac, following historian William H. Prescott's method: has documents read aloud to him and writes in a box fitted with wire grids that guide his hand. Begins drafting manuscript on Pontiac.

1848   Though work goes very slowly, continues writing *The Conspiracy of Pontiac*, first of a series of volumes on Anglo-French wars in North America. Nervous ailment persists; symptoms include feeling of nervous exhaustion and an inability to bear sunlight or to write with eyes open, or to concentrate on any intellectual subject for more than a few minutes at a time. Develops close friendships with archeologist, traveler, and magazine writer Ephraim George Squier and Charles Eliot Norton, who helps in proofreading book version of *The Oregon Trail*.

1849   Publishes *The California and Oregon Trail* ("California" added by publisher Putnam to exploit gold-rush fever; subsequently issued as *The Oregon Trail*). To family's delight, announces engagement to Catherine Scollay Bigelow, daughter of well-known Boston doctor. Health improves somewhat, and with help from family members and readers, continues work on Pontiac. Begins long professional association with Buffalo attorney Orsamus Holmes Marshall, who shares Parkman's interest in original research. Uncle George Parkman, professor at Harvard Medical School, murdered by John White Webster, fellow professor who owed him money (hanged in 1850).

1850   Marries Catherine Scollay Bigelow. Takes house in Milton, Massachusetts, for summer. Makes great progress in writing *Conspiracy of Pontiac* with help of wife and her sister, Mary Bigelow, as amanuenses, and others who read aloud. Gives it to close friend George Ellis to read; Ellis acts as intermediary with publishers. Lives in father-in-law's house on Beacon Hill, Boston, in winter.

1851   Following practice of Prescott and George Ticknor, has book stereotyped at his own expense. Friends, including

Norton, help in proofreading. Moves to Brookline, four miles outside Boston (household includes wife and sister-in-law, Mary Bigelow). *The History of the Conspiracy of Pontiac* published by Little, Brown and Company, beginning his long association with that firm. Daughter Grace Parkman born. Suffers first symptoms of arthritis in knee.

1852   Publishes admiring essay-review of the works of James Fenimore Cooper, who had recently died, in *North American Review*. Goes to Northampton, Massachusetts, for water cure, again suffering from knee problem. Father dies.

1853–54 Illness stops historical work. Develops close friendship with cousin-in-law Mary Dwight Parkman, sister of classmate and close friend Edward Dwight. Francis Parkman III born 1854. Writes a novel for diversion.

1855–56 Resumes research. Writes old friend Henry Stevens, now a London bookseller and specialist in Americana, asking his help in finding rare books. Initiates correspondence with New York State historian Edmund B. O'Callaghan and John G. Shea, historian and former Jesuit novice. *Vassal Morton*, partly autobiographical novel, published; it emphasizes the protagonist's endurance through extreme physical and emotional hardship. Visits Montreal, Ottawa, and Quebec in October and November.

1857   Son Francis dies of scarlet fever. Begins professional correspondence with French archivist and historian Pierre Margry.

1858   Buys cottage and three acres on Jamaica Pond in Jamaica Plain, Boston, to stay in during summer months. Daughter Katherine Parkman born. Wife dies soon after of complications due to childbirth. Nervous illness worsens; feels as if "a steel band is tightening around his head." Puts daughters in care of sister-in-law, Mary Bigelow. Moves into house on Walnut Street, Boston, with mother and sisters Mary and Eliza. Goes to Paris to consult doctors; feels some improvement. Rides the omnibuses in Paris.

1859   Returns to Boston via Nice and Genoa. Daughters continue to live with sister-in-law. Joins Massachusetts Horticultural Society and pursues horticultural avocation at Jamaica Pond.

1860–61   Continues to cultivate and develop garden. When knee problem is severe, works in garden using a stool or wheelchair. Wins prizes for flowers. Writes a series of letters to the *Boston Daily Advertiser* on the national crisis brought on by the Civil War and the decline of political leadership (letters appear through 1863).

1862–63   Enters into business partnership to sell flowers, but firm dissolves within a year. Chagrined that poor health disqualifies him from service in the Civil War. Works on histories with help from sisters and outside readers. Publishes advance chapters from *Pioneers of France in the New World* in *Atlantic Monthly*. Tentatively courts Ida Agassiz, daughter of naturalist Louis Agassiz and sister-in-law of Quincy Adams Shaw, and is deeply disappointed when she decides to marry someone else.

1864   Publishes article, "Exploring the Magalloway," drawn from journals kept during wilderness vacations, in *Harper's Monthly*. Moves with mother and sisters to 50 Chestnut Street, Boston. Writes letter to *Boston Daily Advertiser* about harrowing experience of brother John Eliot, who is in the navy, during time he was a prisoner of war in the South.

1865   Travels to Richmond with friend Dr. Algernon Coolidge to collect Confederate imprints for Boston Athenaeum. Publication of *Pioneers of France in the New World* establishes reputation as a historian. Begins professional correspondence with ethnologist Lewis H. Morgan.

1866   Publishes horticultural work, *The Book of Roses*. Sister Mary dies. Starts lifelong correspondence and close friendship with Abbé Henri-Raymond Casgrain, romantic historian and leader of a movement to create a French-Canadian literature. Visits Quebec and Montreal for historical research. Stays with sister Caroline and her husband, the Reverend John Cordner, in Montreal.

1867   *The Jesuits in North America in the Seventeenth Century* published. Traces the routes of La Salle and Marquette on a five-week trip; goes down the Illinois River to the Mississippi, visits Henry Chatillon in St. Louis, then travels up the Mississippi River through Iowa to Fort Snelling in Minnesota. On return home stops at Madison, Wisconsin, to see the State Historical Society established there by his friend Lyman C. Draper.

1868   Elected to Board of Overseers at Harvard. Goes to Paris in December to recover from illness. Meets and begins warm friendship with archivist Pierre Margry, who helps in collection of material necessary to his research.

1869   Spends much time with Margry, who refuses Parkman access to La Salle materials but does agree to oversee copying of other documents that Parkman has uncovered. Meets the Marquis de Montcalm, great-grandson of the general, who allows Parkman to have family papers copied. Leaves Paris in March for England to search for collection of Montcalm papers there. *The Discovery of the Great West* published. Sends copies of *Pioneers*, *Jesuits*, and *The Discovery of the Great West* to Napoleon III.

1870   Publishes enlarged edition of *Pontiac* as *The Conspiracy of Pontiac and the Indian War after the Conquest of Canada*. Explores Mount Desert Island, Maine, staying with old Harvard classmate Judge Horace Gray.

1871   Has warm first meeting with Abbé Casgrain when he comes to visit in Boston. Introduces him to Henry Wadsworth Longfellow and Louis Agassiz. Resigns as member of Board of Overseers to accept professorship in horticulture at Bussey Institute, Harvard (resigns after a year). Mother dies. Continues to live at 50 Chestnut Street and Jamaica Pond with sister Eliza ("Lizzie"), who helps him with work, acts as amanuensis, reads current novels to him, and helps care for his daughters. Goes to Canada, stopping in Quebec, and then explores Acadian sites at Annapolis and the Minas Basin, Nova Scotia, and St. John and Fredericton, New Brunswick, returning by way of Bar Harbor, Maine. Brother John Eliot, a naval lieutenant, dies from accidental fall in San Francisco.

1872   Settles mother's estate. Goes to Europe in July and stays for three months, traveling on board ship with James

Russell Lowell and his wife, and Henry Adams and Marianne Hooper Adams, who are on their honeymoon. Joins sister Eliza, already in Paris, and introduces her to Pierre Margry. Meets historian Henry Harrisse. Revises *The Oregon Trail*. Returns to Boston and witnesses the great fire in November.

1873   After efforts fail to find a publisher for Margry's La Salle work, begins concentrated effort to get it subsidized; writes to forty congressmen, and involves historical associations all over the country to lobby for appropriation from Congress. (These efforts are later successful; Congress eventually gives $10,000.) Visits Abbé Casgrain at family home at Rivière-Ouelle on the lower St. Lawrence in August, going on from there to Annapolis, Nova Scotia, and St. John, New Brunswick, returning by way of Eastport and Portland, Maine. Elected to Saturday Club, which was founded by Emerson before the Civil War.

1874   Rebuilds home on Jamaica Pond. Visits Canada in July and sees many friends in Montreal and Quebec; continues historical research, hiring copyists as needed. *The Old Régime in Canada* published. William Dean Howells' review in the *Atlantic* introduces Parkman to wider public in America and England.

1875   Continuing Acadian studies, goes to Moosehead Lake in Maine with friend Judge Gray and climbs nearby mountain. Elected to the Harvard Corporation.

1876   Sells all the bulbs of *Lilium Parkmanni*, the hybrid lily he had developed, to an English horticulturist. Reviews first volume of Pierre Margry's *Découvertes et Etablissements des Français dans l'Ouest et dans le Sud de l'Amérique Septentrionale (1614–1754), Mémoirs et Documents originaux* in *The Nation* and reads for the first time the La Salle letters he was not allowed to see when composing *The Discovery of the Great West*. Elected to the Royal Historical Society in London. Visits Lake Champlain and Ottawa.

1877   Vacations in Maine. Publishes *Count Frontenac and New France under Louis XIV*.

1878   Upset over garbled French translations of *Pioneers* and *Jesuits* ("My name is put on the title page of a book which is not mine, either in form or substance"). In March, inspects the battlefields of Lake George. After twenty-year correspondence, meets historian George Bancroft. Articles on suffrage and democracy (1878–80) answered by feminists and reformers. In October, goes again to inspect battlefields around Lake George, Fort Ticonderoga, and Lake Champlain. Continuing research on *Montcalm*, travels to Quebec and Montreal in November. Laval University's proposal to award Parkman honorary degree blocked by Catholics offended by his anti-clericalism.

1879   Daughter Grace marries Charles P. Coffin in May. Publishes *La Salle and the Discovery of the Great West*, an enlarged and revised edition of *The Discovery of the Great West* (1869), based on documents in Margry's collection. Awarded honorary degree from McGill University. Returns in August to Quebec and Nova Scotia where he inspects Louisbourg fortress, Fort Lawrence, and Beauséjour, and then goes to Cape Breton. In September, daughter Katharine marries John Templeman Coolidge and accompanies him to Paris where he will study painting. Publishes "The Woman Question," which argues against women's suffrage, in the *North American Review*.

1880   Helps found St. Botolph Club in Boston (is its first president, 1880–86, and vice-president until 1893). Through position on executive committee of the Archeological Institute of America, and privately, helps Adolph Bandelier explore pueblo ruins of New Mexico. Travels to Europe during summer.

1881   Returns to Paris and England to continue work in archives and collect documents.

1882–83   Continues work on *Montcalm*; writes by hand rather than dictating to an amanuensis (will also write out *A Half-Century of Conflict*). In October 1882, visits the Adirondacks; in October 1883, rides on horseback through the White Mountains.

1884   Publishes *Montcalm and Wolfe* ahead of its chronological place in *France and England in North America* because he considers it the most important part of the history and wants it to appear before he dies.

1885   Travels in South Carolina and Florida to study the scenes of action described in *Pioneers of France*. (Parkman had not been able to visit them while writing *Pioneers* during the Civil War.) Receives letter of glowing praise from Henry James about *Montcalm*; responds by praising James's *The Bostonians*, which Eliza is reading aloud to him. Publishes revised edition of *Pioneers*, with new descriptions of Florida and some revisions of the section on Champlain. Awarded LL.D. by Williams College. Though health is improved in many ways, suffers increasingly from insomnia.

1886   Spends a month camping with friend and copyist (and future biographer) Charles H. Farnham, on the Batiscan River in Quebec Province. Goes canoeing and learns fly fishing. Stays seven weeks at camp on the Rangeley Lakes in Maine later in the summer; decides to build a cabin there that sister Eliza could also enjoy (his ill-health prevents using it). Writes long autobiographical letter to friend Martin Brimmer to be given to the Massachusetts Historical Society after his death.

1887   Publishes *Some of the Reasons Against Woman Suffrage*. Travels to Europe, part of the time in company with son-in-law J. T. Coolidge, intending to tour Spain, but in Madrid return of severe lameness in knee cuts trip short. Rows for an hour every day on Jamaica Pond for exercise and air, often accompanied by Eliza. Begins spending time at Old Wentworth House near Portsmouth, New Hampshire, bought by son-in-law Coolidge. Writes much of *A Half-Century* there. Enjoys playing with grandchildren.

1888   Lameness and insomnia persist. Often uses crutches. Resigns position on the Harvard Corporation.

1889   Awarded LL.D. by Harvard. Buys small island opposite the Old Wentworth House.

1890   Publishes *Our Common Schools* to defend the public schools against what he considers dangerous competition from parochial schools. Writes article, "A Convent in Rome," based on journal kept during stay in convent of Passionist Fathers in Rome in 1844.

1891   Though lameness and general ill-health persist, enjoys going to Portsmouth during summer.

1892   Publishes *A Half-Century of Conflict*, the last two volumes of *France and England in North America*.

1893   In June completes a new section to be added to the beginning of *The Old Régime in Canada* based on documents that were unavailable when he published the first edition. Suffers an attack of appendicitis which leads to peritonitis, and dies on November 8 at Jamaica Pond. Buried at Mt. Auburn Cemetery, Cambridge.

Note on the Texts

This volume presents *The Oregon Trail* and *The Conspiracy of Pontiac*, the first two works by Francis Parkman to appear in book form.

Parkman began work on *The Oregon Trail* in mid-October 1846 at the age of 23, soon after his return from his tour of the West. In February 1847 the first installment appeared in *Knickerbocker Magazine* under the title "The Oregon Trail: Or A Summer's Journey Out of Bounds: By A Bostonian." The series of 21 monthly installments ran through February 1849, with four breaks: there were no installments in March and November 1847 and September and November 1848. After his return from his strenuous western trip, Parkman's health, never very good, had broken down completely; among other difficulties, he was unable to use his eyes. Instead of writing the serial installments by hand, he dictated them to various family members and friends using as a guide the detailed journal he had kept during the trip. In September 1848, as the serial publication drew near its close, Parkman wrote his friend Charles Eliot Norton that he had not sent an installment in that month because he wanted "the book to be out before the appearance of the last chapter, for fear of piracy."

Parkman arranged for the book to be published by George P. Putnam early in the spring of 1849 and gratefully accepted Norton's offer to help with the proofreading (no one seems to have proofread the *Knickerbocker* installments before they were published). Parkman's health improved somewhat, and he was allowed to use his eyes for limited periods of time. With Norton's help, Parkman corrected errors, removed some extraneous adjectives, added a new Chapter X, "The War Parties," and created a new Chapter XXIV, "The Chase," from material that had originally appeared in Chapter XXV, "The Buffalo Camp," and in Chapter XXIII, "Indian Alarms." (The installments in the *Knickerbocker* were titled but not numbered.) The book was published by George P. Putnam in March 1849 under the unauthorized title of *The California and Oregon Trail: Being Sketches of Prairie and Rocky Mountain Life*.

Putnam reprinted the book in 1852 under a new title, *Prairie and Rocky Mountain Life; or, the California and Oregon Trail*, and with a "Preface to the Third Edition" written by Parkman. The text of the book, including the original engraved title, was printed from the same plates as the 1849 edition. A new edition (described as the "fourth"), extensively revised by Parkman, was brought out in 1872 by his Boston publishers, Little, Brown and Company, under the title *The Oregon Trail: Sketches of Prairie and Rocky-Mountain Life*. A note about the change of title is included in the 1872 edition: Parkman explains that the publisher had added "California" to the title without his permission and he was restoring it to its original form. The subtitle remained substantially the same, with only the word "Being" dropped. Parkman added a dedication to Quincy Adams Shaw and a new preface. The text itself was stylistically revised and shortened: colloquial expressions were made more formal; all of the epigraphs were dropped; some passages of personal biography were removed, as well as descriptions of other people, including Shaw, Chatillon, and the English travelers. By 1872, Parkman had established a reputation as an important historian and felt that his youthful work had been too outspoken. (Some examples of these revisions are indicated in the notes to this volume.) A new edition, illustrated by Frederic Remington, was brought out in 1892. Parkman made additional revisions for this edition, but they were not as extensive as those he had made in 1872. A new preface was added, some words were changed, and spelling and punctuation were modernized. Because *The Oregon Trail* is a personal narrative, the present volume prints the text of the 1849 Putnam edition, with the restored title, as the one that best represents the young Parkman who wrote it.

The Conspiracy of Pontiac, Parkman's first work of history, was the product of several years of research and travel devoted to collecting necessary documents and inspecting the sites of the events to be described. Because of persisting problems with his eyes, it was necessary to find people who would read documents to him. He made notes using a special box with wires strung across it to guide his hand so that he could write without using his eyes. The manuscript was then dictated to an amanuensis, usually his wife. On the advice of his friend, the historian Jared Sparks, Parkman decided to pay for the stereotyping of the book himself and then offer the plates to an American publisher for printing. Dr. George E. Ellis, Charles Eliot Norton, and other friends helped him with the proofreading. Little, Brown and Company of Boston, beginning a long association with Parkman, published *History of the Conspiracy of Pontiac, and the War of the North American Tribes Against the English Colonies After the Conquest of Canada* in September 1851. Richard Bentley agreed to publish an edition in London; but because the English edition had to appear simultaneously with the American for copyright reasons, the errors discovered by Norton at the last minute were not corrected in the English edition.

Immediately after the first printing, a correspondent, Samuel G. Drake, gave Parkman access to relevant material he had not seen before (Captain Thomas Morris's *Miscellanies in Prose and Verse*, containing a fuller account of his adventure than the journal Parkman had used). When a second printing (called a "second edition") was scheduled for 1852, Parkman added a few footnotes and a new section to Appendix F based on the new information. No changes were made in the next printing (called the "third edition") in 1863. (A small edition of 75 copies was made from type set by John Wilson in 1866, but no corrections were made in the text.) During the years after the 1852 printing, additional relevant material was discovered, in particular the anonymous *Diary of the Siege of Detroit*, now known to be by Lieutenant Jehu Hay, and a short journal kept during the siege by Major Robert Rogers. A fourth printing (called the "fourth edition") was made in 1868, for which Parkman wrote a new preface dated September 1867. For this printing Parkman added or expanded a number of notes and footnotes, occasionally shortening some lines of text to make room for the additions. A fifth printing (the "fifth edition") in 1869 contained no emendations.

In 1870, Little, Brown and Company decided to have new plates made to conform to the style of Parkman's other historical works. For this two-volume edition (called the "sixth edition") Parkman extensively revised the text, making changes on more than half of the original pages. His access to the

Bouquet papers deposited in the British Museum had furnished him with more information, and now for the first time he could rectify some of his earlier opinions, insert into the text some of the material he had previously placed in footnotes and in Appendix F, and add new information (examples of some of these changes are indicated in the notes to the present volume). He also wrote a new preface, added more firsthand corroborating material to the footnotes, and changed the title to *The Conspiracy of Pontiac and the Indian War After the Conquest of Canada*. Although there were many printings made from the plates of this edition, called the "seventh edition," "eighth," "ninth," and so on, no revisions or actual new editions were made until after Parkman's death. The 1870 edition thus contains Parkman's fullest and most accurate account, and the text of that edition is printed here.

This volume presents the texts of the original printings chosen for inclusion here but does not attempt to reproduce features of their typographic design, such as the display capitalization of chapter openings. The texts are printed without change, except for the correction of typographical errors. Spelling, punctuation, and capitalization are often expressive features, and they are not altered, even when inconsistent or irregular. The following is a list of typographical errors corrected, cited by page and line number: 9.3, Away,; 16.8, HAROLDE; 29.14, sorrow,' ; 30.21, Man; 36.3, Parkham; 50.21, 'Eothen?'; 53.30, deed; 57.31, you," said he; "it's; 58.4, a the; 61.37, persisting; 67.19, Dollar; 91.22, then; 91.26, pounds,; 96.3, alwless; 96.4, normild; 117.21, there.; 117.31, squaw?; 125.28, leisurly; 134.38, Objibwas; 137.15, hnng; 148.28, sbort; 151.20, sun-sorched; 151.26, loftly; 159.33, gallopping; 167.35–36, decending; 176.2, OGILLALAH; 176.3, as; 177.17, 'surround'; 177.25, Borgre; 179.29, It; 185.17, daybreak; 189.14, rick; 195.8, be.; 202.27, though; 217.40, meams; 226.17, theatening; 249.28, "Washtay!; 258.4, Gochè's; 264.6, thee; 276.23, there; 287.17, larga; 295.31, alway; 296.36, gallopped; 310.2, eyes; 313.10, sung; 322.11, *enfan de grace*; 323.37, Chattillon; 390.18, plougshare; 407.11, Verandye; 407.14, hostillty; 416.32, *Shaw-noe*; 433.4, Beajeau; 434.16, Beajeau; 434.25, Beajeau; 435.28, tumultously; 436.7, soldier's; 561.22, attire,; 633.10, three several times; 648.24, present.; 651.13, themeelves; 654.16, respe ted; 799.23, racoon; 886.41, unles; 907.42, Geeen; 911.6, Verendye.

Notes

In the notes that follow, the reference numbers denote page and line of this volume (the line count includes chapter headings). No note is made for information available in a standard desk-reference book. Quotations from Shakespeare have been keyed to *The Riverside Shakespeare*, ed. G. Blakemore Evans (Boston: Houghton Mifflin, 1974). Footnotes within the text are Parkman's own. For more detailed notes, references to other studies, and further biographical background than is included in the Chronology, see: Francis Parkman, *The Oregon Trail* (Madison: University of Wisconsin Press, 1969), edited by E. N. Feltskog; *The Journals of Francis Parkman*, two volumes (New York: Harper & Brothers, 1947), edited by Mason Wade; *Letters of Francis Parkman*, two volumes (Norman: University of Oklahoma Press, 1960), edited by Wilbur R. Jacobs; Howard Doughty, *Francis Parkman* (New York: Macmillan Co., 1962); Charles H. Farnham, *Life of Francis Parkman* (Boston: Little, Brown, and Company, 1900); Henry Dwight Sedgwick, *Francis Parkman*, (Boston: Houghton, Mifflin & Co., 1904); Mason Wade, *Francis Parkman: Heroic Historian*, (New York: The Viking Press, 1942).

THE OREGON TRAIL

1.4–8   "Let . . . Byron.]   *The Corsair* (1814), I.i.27–30.

6.1–17   *The journey . . . 1849.*]   Appears only in the first edition. In the 1852 printing of the first edition, Parkman added the following preface:

PREFACE TO THE THIRD EDITION.

"*This, too, shall pass away,*" were the words graven on the ring of the Persian despot, Nadir Shah, to remind him of the evanescence of all things earthly. *This, too, shall pass away,* was the doom long ago pronounced on all that is primitive in life or scenery within the limits of our national domain; but no one could have dreamed that the decree would find so swift an execution. Less than six years have passed since the incidents related in this volume took place, but that short interval has been the witness of changes almost incredible. The herds of buffalo which blackened the prairies of the Arkansas and the Platte have vanished before the increasing stream of emigrant caravans. Fort Laramie, which then was a mere trading post, occupied by a handful of Canadians, and overawed by surrounding savages, is now a military station of the United States, controlling and regulating the humbled tribes of the adjacent regions. The waste and lonely valley of the Great Salt Lake has become, as if by magic, the seat of a populous city, the hive of a fanatical multitude, whose movements are an object of national importance, and whose character and fortunes form a theme of the highest philosophic interest. Remote and barbarous California, rich in nothing but tallow and cowhides, is transformed into a modern Ophir, swarming with eager life, and threatening to revolutionize the financial system of the world with the outpourings of its wealth.

Primeval barbarism is assailed at last in front and rear, from the Mississippi and from the Pacific; and, thus brought between two fires, it cannot long sustain itself. With all respect to civilization, I cannot help regretting this final consummation; and such regret will not be misconstrued by any one who has tried the prairie and mountain life, who has learned to look with an affectionate interest on the rifle that was once his companion and protector, the belt that sustained his knife and pistol, and the pipe which beguiled the tedious hours of his midnight watch, while men and horses lay sunk in sleep around him.

The following narrative was written in great measure with the view of preserving, in my own mind, a clear memory of the scenes and adventures which it records. It therefore takes the form of a simple relation of facts, free, for the most part, from reflections or digressions of any kind; and in this circumstance of its origin, the reader will find good assurance of its entire authenticity.

February 1st, 1852.

In 1872, Parkman wrote the following dedication, note on the title, and preface (which replaced the 1852 preface):

TO

THE COMRADE OF A SUMMER

AND

THE FRIEND OF A LIFETIME,

QUINCY ADAMS SHAW.

The "Oregon Trail" is the title under which this book first appeared. It was afterwards changed by the publisher, and is now restored to the form in which it originally stood in the Knickerbocker Magazine. As the early editions were printed in my absence, I did not correct the proofs,—a process doubly necessary, since the book was written from dictation. The necessary corrections have been made in the present edition.

PREFACE TO THE FOURTH EDITION.

The following sketches first appeared in 1847. A summer's adventures of two youths just out of college might well enough be allowed to fall into oblivion, were it not that a certain interest will always attach to the record of that which has passed away never to return. This book is the reflection of forms and conditions of life which have ceased, in great measure, to exist. It mirrors the image of an irrevocable past.

I remember that, as we rode by the foot of Pike's Peak, when for a fortnight we met no face of man, my companion remarked, in a tone anything but complacent, that a time would come when those plains would be a grazing country, the buffalo give place to tame cattle, farmhouses be scattered along the water-courses, and wolves, bears, and Indians be numbered among the things that were. We condoled with each other on so melancholy a prospect, but we little thought what the future had in store. We knew that there was more or less gold in the seams of those untrodden mountains; but we did not foresee that it would build cities in the waste and plant hotels and gambling-houses among the haunts of the grizzly bear. We knew that a few fanatical outcasts were groping their way across the plains to seek an asylum from Gentile persecution; but we did not imagine that the polygamous hordes of Mormon would rear a swarming Jerusalem in the bosom of solitude itself. We knew that, more and more, year after year, the trains of emigrant wagons would creep in slow procession towards barbarous Oregon or wild and distant California; but we did not dream how Commerce and Gold would breed nations along the Pacific, the disenchanting shriek of the locomotive break the spell of weird mysterious mountains, woman's rights invade the fastnesses of the Arapahoes, and despairing savagery, assailed in front and rear, vail its scalp-locks and feathers before triumphant commonplace. We were no prophets to foresee all this; and, had we foreseen it, perhaps some perverse regrets might have tempered the ardor of our rejoicing.

The wild cavalcade that defiled with me down the gorges of the Black Hills, with its paint and war-plumes, fluttering trophies and savage embroidery, bows, arrows, lances, and shields, will never be seen again. Those who formed it have found bloody graves, or a ghastlier burial in the maws of wolves. The Indian of to-day, armed with a revolver and crowned with an old hat; cased, possibly, in trousers or muffled in a tawdry shirt,— is an Indian still, but an Indian shorn of the picturesqueness which was his most conspicuous merit.

The mountain trapper is no more, and the grim romance of his wild, hard life is a memory of the past.

As regards the motives which sent us to the mountains, our liking for them would have sufficed; but, in my case, another incentive was added. I went in great measure as a student, to prepare for a literary undertaking of which the plan was already formed, but which, from the force of inexorable circumstances, is still but half accomplished. It was this that prompted some proceedings on my part, which, without a fixed purpose in view, might be charged with youthful rashness. My business was observation, and I was willing to pay dearly for the opportunity of exercising it.

Two or three years ago, I made a visit to our guide, the brave and true-hearted Henry Chatillon, at the town of Carondelet, near St. Louis. It was more than twenty years since we had met. Time hung heavy on his hands, as usual with old mountain-men married and established; his hair was touched with gray, and his face and figure showed tokens of early hardship; but the manly simplicity of his character was unchanged. He told me that the Indians with whom I had been domesticated, a band of the hated Sioux, had nearly all been killed in fights with the white men.

The faithful Deslauriers is, I believe, still living on the frontier of Missouri. The hunter Raymond perished in the snow during Fremont's disastrous passage of the mountains in the winter of 1848.

BOSTON, March 30, 1872.

In the 1892 edition, which included drawings by Frederic Remington, Parkman kept the "Preface to the Fourth Edition" and added the following:

PREFACE TO THE ILLUSTRATED EDITION.

In the preface to the fourth edition of this book, printed in 1872, I spoke of the changes that had already come over the Far West. Since that time change has grown to metamorphosis. For Indian teepees, with their trophies of bow, lance, shield, and dangling scalplocks, we have towns and cities, resorts of health and pleasure seekers, with an agreeable society, Paris fashions, the magazines, the latest poem, and the last new novel. The sons of civilization, drawn by the fascinations of a fresher and bolder life, thronged to the western wilds in multitudes which blighted the charm that had lured them.

The buffalo is gone, and of all his millions nothing is left but bones. Tame cattle and fences of barbed wire have supplanted his vast herds and boundless grazing grounds. Those discordant serenaders, the wolves that howled at evening about the traveller's camp-fire, have succumbed to arsenic and hushed their savage music. The wild Indian is turned into an ugly caricature of his conqueror; and that which made him romantic, terrible, and hateful, is in large measure scourged out of him. The slow cavalcade of horsemen armed to the teeth has disappeared before parlor cars and the effeminate comforts of modern travel.

The rattlesnakes have grown bashful and retiring. The mountain lion shrinks from the face of man, and even grim "Old Ephraim,"[1] the grizzly bear, seeks the seclusion of his dens and caverns. It is said that he is no longer his former self, having found, by an intelligence not hitherto set to his credit, that his ferocious strength is no match for a repeating rifle; with which discovery he is reported to have grown diffident, and abated the truculence of his more prosperous days. One may be permitted to doubt if the blood-thirsty old savage has really experienced a change of heart; and before inviting him to single combat, the ambitious tenderfoot, though the proud possessor of a Winchester with sixteen cartridges in the magazine, would do well to consider not only the quality of his weapon, but also that of his own nerves.

He who dared neither bear, Indian, nor devil, the all-daring and all-enduring trapper, belongs to the past, or lives only in a few gray-bearded survivals. In his stead we have the cowboy, and even his star begins to wane.

The Wild West is tamed, and its savage charms have withered. If this book can help to keep their memory alive, it will have done its part. It has found a powerful helper in the pencil of Mr. Remington, whose pictures are as full of truth as of spirit, for they are the work of one who knew the prairies and the mountains before irresistible commonplace had subdued them.

BOSTON, 16 September, 1892.

[1] Alias "Old Caleb" and "Old Enoch."

3.13–14   *Uncas . . . Outalissi*] Uncas is a heroic young Indian in James Fenimore Cooper's *The Last of the Mohicans* (1826). Outalissi, a noble Oneida chief, appears in the narrative poem *Gertrude of Wyoming* (1809) by the Scottish poet Thomas Campbell.

9.3–5   "Away, . . . SHELLEY.] "To Jane: The Invitation" (1822), lines 21 and 23. Line 22 reads: "To the wild wood and the downs—."

9.10–12   Many . . . standing.] Omitted from the 1872 and 1892 editions.

9.18   'Radnor,' . . . lost,] The *Radnor*, carrying ammunition to Gen. Stephen Watts Kearny's Army of the West, hit the stump of a tree and sank around August 2, 1846.

12.4–5   Captain C. . . . Mr. R.] Captain William Chandler and his brother, John. "Mr. R." has been identified as William Govett Romaine (1815–93), a graduate of Trinity College, Cambridge, who later served in the Crimean War (1853–56) and held high positions in the Indian and Egyptian judiciaries. In a letter to his mother May 12, 1846, Parkman wrote that "Romain had been on this route before—in 1841." During that time he had traveled with the mission party of Pierre-Jean De Smet (1801–73), a Jesuit priest, and John Bidwell (1819–1900), who was leading a party of emigrants to California.

16.3–8   "Though . . . HAROLD.] *Childe Harold's Pilgrimage* (1812–18) by Lord Byron (1788–1824); Cf. I.xxx.5–9. In Byron, "weary" reads "toilsome" and "*prairie*" reads "mountain."

16.9–19   "BOTH . . . tribes.] Omitted from the 1872 and 1892 editions.

17.31   *"Sacre enfant de garce!"*] "Holy son of a bitch."

18.4   Jean Baptiste] Patron saint of French Canadians; colloquially, a French Canadian.

18.6   *bourgeois*] In *The Conspiracy of Pontiac*, Volume I, Chapter XIV, page 563.21–23 in this volume, Parkman wrote: "This name is always applied, among the Canadians of the North-west, to the conductor of a trading party, the commander in a trading fort, or, indeed, to any person in a position of authority."

21.40–22.4   Hendrick . . . Pontiac] Named for Indian leaders. Parkman wrote about the Mohawk chief Hendrick (d. 1755) in *Montcalm and Wolfe* (1884); also see *The Conspiracy of Pontiac* in this volume.

26.3–7   "I've . . . BRYANT.] Cf. *Hunter's Serenade*, lines 5–8, by William Cullen Bryant (1794–1878). In Bryant, "I've wandered wide" reads "I've wandered long," "but never" reads "and never," and "A spot more lovely" reads "A spot so lovely."

26.9–20   Colonel . . . Santa Fé] Stephen Watts Kearny (1794–1848) was placed in command of the Army of the West in May and made brigadier general on June 30, 1846. After organizing a force of about 1,660 men composed of the regular First Dragoons and units of Missouri volunteer cavalry and artillery, he marched into Mexican territory and captured Santa Fé without opposition on August 18, 1846.

29.3–15   'We . . . CORINTH.]   Introductory lines 6–17 of the poem (1816) by Lord Byron (the introduction was added to the poem posthumously in 1832).

29.16–19   THE . . . rule.]   Omitted from the 1872 and 1892 editions.

30.21–25   'Man . . . mute.']   Stanza xvii, lines 5–9 of Byron's *Mazeppa* (1819).

37.11–20   We . . . adopted.]   Omitted from the 1872 and 1892 editions.

39.3–9   "A man . . . DRYDEN.]   Cf. *Absalom and Achitophel* (1680), lines 545–50. In Dryden, "space" reads "course" in line 549, and line 550 reads: "Was chemist, fiddler, statesman, and buffoon."

39.14   Mormons]   Forced out of Nauvoo in Illinois, the first group of 1,600 Mormons started west in February 1846 but stopped for a while at Sugar Grove, Iowa. Small pioneering groups were then sent ahead to prepare the way for others, the first reaching the Missouri River in June 1846. By that autumn, 12,000 Mormons had established winter quarters not far from present-day Omaha.

43.9   'dor-bug;']   A kind of flying beetle.

45.23–24   'Voulez . . charette—]   "Would you like supper right away? . . . under the cart—."

47.5–51.32   'Good morning, Captain.' . . . ally.]   Omitted from the 1872 and 1892 editions.

50.21–24   "Eothen?" . . . Kinglake]   *Eōthen: or traces of travel brought home from the East*, published anonymously by Alexander Kinglake in 1844, recounts his reactions to places, events, and people encountered on a trip to the Near East ten years earlier. Richard Monckton Milnes' *Palm Leaves*, poetry written during a tour of Egypt and the Levant, was also published in 1844. His earlier works included *Memorials of a Tour in some Parts of Greece* (1833) and *Memorials of a Residence on the Continent* (1838).

50.35   Borrow . . . Spain,"]   The English writer George Borrow's travel narrative (1843) recounts his adventures as a distributor for the British and Foreign Bible Society in Spain from 1835 to 1840 during a period of civil strife.

50.38   Judge Story]   Joseph Story (1779–1845), with whom Parkman had studied, was associate justice of the Supreme Court (1811–45) and professor of law at Harvard (1829–45). His legal *Commentaries* appeared from 1832 to 1845.

51.39   'The livelong . . . spoke;'] *Marmion: A Tale of Flodden Field* (1808), III.xiii.17, by Walter Scott.

55.3–5   "Seest . . . LOST.] Milton; Book I, lines 180–81.

55.6–7   "Here . . . JOHN.] Shakespeare; I.i.19.

58.35–38   Having also . . . camp.] Omitted from the 1872 and 1892 editions.

65.21–32   The reader . . . West.] Omitted from the 1872 and 1892 editions.

67.3–7   "Twice . . . BRYANT.] *The Prairies*, lines 98–101.

67.11   *bois de vache*] Wood of the cow, i.e., dried buffalo dung

70.38–71.36   Nothing unusual . . . gallop.] Omitted from the 1872 and 1892 editions.

82.3–4   "Parting . . . JULIET.] Shakespeare; II.ii.184

87.10–11   *'Avance donc!'*] "Move!"

95.25–26   'At . . . saddle-bow.'] *Lay of the Last Minstrel* (1805), I.xxix.1–2, by Walter Scott.

96.3–5   " 'Tis . . . ABYDOS.] II.xx.1–2, from the poem (1813) by Byron.

106.1   *Meneaska*] *Mí-na-han-ska*, Dakota for "Long Knife."

108.6–109.33   One morning, . . . than ever.] Omitted from the 1872 and 1892 editions.

110.3–8   "By the . . . ROME.] "Horatius," stanza 1, lines 5–9, in the collection of poems (1842) by Thomas Babington Macaulay.

115.34–35   *par' fléche*] Rawhide.

118.23   Irving's 'Astoria.'] Washington Irving's history (1836) of John Jacob Astor's fur trade in the Northwest.

119.3   Jim Beckwith] James P. Beckwith (also spelled "Beckwourth"), (1798?–?1866), born in Virginia, the son of Sir Jennings Beckwith (a descendant of minor Irish aristocrats) and a mulatto slave.

121.14   Colonel R——] William Henry Russell (1802–73), "Colonel" by courtesy, was U.S. marshal in the District of Missouri from 1841 to 1845. He reached California in September 1846 and served as secretary of state in John C. Frémont's short-lived provisional government early in 1847.

121.27–31   Fearful . . . flesh!] A group of 87 emigrants (29 men, 15 women, and 43 children) under the leadership of Jacob and George Donner of Sangamon County, Illinois, broke away from the main California Trail in western Wyoming on July 20, 1846, to use the "Hastings Cutoff" advocated by Lansford W. Hastings in his *Emigrants' Guide to Oregon and California* (1845). The Donner party expected that Hastings would lead them, but discovered at Fort Bridger that he had gone ahead with another group; he later failed to keep a promised rendezvous with the emigrants in the Wasatch Mountains. Finding his route more arduous than anticipated, the Donner party spent three weeks crossing the mountains and six days traveling through the Great Salt Lake Desert, losing oxen along the way. Exhausted and suffering from dissension and indecision, the party lost five members before being trapped in the Sierra Nevadas at the end of October by an eight-day snowstorm and reached the brink of starvation in mid-December. On December 16 the "Forlorn Hope," 13 volunteers (eight men and five women) accompanied by two Indian guides who had brought supplies from California in October, left with six days' rations in an attempt to summon help, but were soon caught in a severe storm in which four men died. Their bodies were eaten by the other emigrants (the Indians refused to consume human flesh). Two more emigrants perished, and the Indians were shot and eaten before the seven survivors (including all five women) of the "Forlorn Hope" reached an Indian village on January 10, 1847. The first rescuers from Sutter's Fort (present-day Sacramento) reached the Donner party's camps through deep snow on February 18 and began bringing survivors down into the valley settlements; the last emigrant left camp on April 21. By that time many in the main party had died from exhaustion and malnutrition, and their flesh had been eaten by the others as a last resort. Of the original 87 emigrants, 47 survived.

128.4–5   ten . . . Israel.]   After the Assyrians destroyed the northern kingdom of Israel in 721 B.C., a number of Israelites were deported to Assyria (2 Kings 16–17). Although the deported Israelites and those who remained were eventually assimilated into other populations, legend held that the "ten lost tribes" continued to exist as a group in another part of the world. Among those sometimes conjectured to be their descendants were, variously, the American Indians, Nestorians, Afghans, Japanese, and English.

130.3–7   "Fierce . . . HAROLD.]   II.lxv.1–4.

135.39   'Parks,']   A chain of grassy plateaus surrounded by snow-capped mountains: North Park, about 50 miles north of present-day Denver, between the Medicine Bow Mountains and Park Range, Middle Park, near Denver, and South Park in central Colorado, the source of the South Platte River.

138.12–13   Le Borgne]   The One-Eyed.

143.35   *pommes blanches*]   Also known as *pomme de prairie* and prairie or Indian breadroot; a starchy, tuberous root eaten either raw or roasted and dried for use during the cold months.

144.34–39   and I do not exaggerate . . . noble attitude,]   Omitted from the 1872 and 1892 editions.

145.2–3   West . . . Vatican]   Benjamin West (1738–1820), American painter of historical scenes. The Apollo Belvedere, installed in the Belvedere Court in 1511, is a Roman copy in marble of a Greek bronze statue depicting Apollo as a vigorous, beautiful young man.

145.38–146.11   Medical . . . joke.]   Shortened and revised in the 1872 and 1892 editions.

146.19–26   No sooner . . . against it.]   Omitted from the 1872 and 1892 editions.

147.3–9   "One touch . . . MARMION.]   V.xii.37–42. See note 51.39.

151.32–37   All that . . . stimulant.]   Omitted from the 1872 and 1892 editions.

154.3–7   —"I tread, . . . GOLDSMITH.]   "The Hermit," stanza 2, by Oliver Goldsmith (?1728–74).

155.28–33   He would . . . resembled.]   Omitted from the 1872 and 1892 editions.

156.3–4   Leatherstocking]   Natty Bumppo, hero of James Fenimore Cooper's Leatherstocking Tales: *The Pioneers* (1823), *The Last of the Mohicans* (1826), *The Prairie* (1827), *The Pathfinder* (1840), and *The Deerslayer* (1841).

157.40–158.3   Shaw's limbs . . . morning.]   Omitted from the 1872 and 1892 editions.

172.16–37   While he was . . . the other.]   Omitted from the 1872 and 1892 editions.

172.26   Tom . . . Mountains]   Tom Crawford was the proprietor (1828–52) of Notch House, near what was later called Crawford Notch, New Hampshire.

176.3–7   "They waste us—. . . BRYANT.]   "An Indian at the Burial-Place of His Fathers," stanza 10.

183.12–16   for I . . . men.]   Omitted from the 1872 and 1892 editions.

187.21–24   "Et hæc . . . Virgil's line]   "Even this, moreover, may give pleasure to recall." Cf. *Aeneid*, Book I, line 203: "Forsam et haec olim meminisse iuvabit." "Perhaps even this will some day give pleasure to recall."

189.12   Mackenzie]   Kenneth Mackenzie (1797–1861), born in Scotland, emigrated to St. Louis in 1822. He established fortified posts throughout the

Upper Missouri region and by 1831 controlled its fur trade. In the 1840s he moved increasingly away from furs and into liquor importing and land speculation.

195.3–9   "The Persé . . . CHASE.]   *The Ballad of Chevy-Chase* (c. 15th century), Fytte I, stanza 1.

196.7   *pemmican*]   Made by drying strips of buffalo meat, pulverizing it, and mixing it with tallow and flavorings such as wild cherries. Pemmican was then stuffed, with more tallow, into rawhide or buffalo intestines.

205.10–11   ancient pastime . . . suffered]   *Don Quixote*, Book I, Part Three, Chapter XVII, regarding "misadventures at an inn."

206.1–2   'Fremont's Expedition,']   John Frémont, *Report of the Exploring Expedition to the Rocky Mountains in the Year 1842, and to Oregon and North California in the Years 1843–'44* (1845).

215.3–11   "Ours . . . CORSAIR.]   By Byron (1814); I.i.7–8, 15–18, and 25–26.

218.25–31   To some . . . death.]   Omitted from the 1872 and 1892 editions.

220.3–5   'if . . . laughter.']   Cf. Oliver Goldsmith, *The Vicar of Wakefield* (1766), Chapter XXXII: "I can't say whether we have more wit amongst us now than usual; but I am certain we had more laughing, which answered the end as well."

224.3–12   "To sit . . . HAROLD.]   II.xxv.1–9.

226.14–31   The objects . . . New England.]   Omitted from the 1872 and 1892 editions.

228.3–8   "Come, . . . LIKE IT.]   Shakespeare; II.i.21–25.

239.3–12   "Dear Nature . . . HAROLD.]   II.xxxvii.1–9.

243.17–245.2   Scenery . . . distance.]   Omitted from the 1872 and 1892 editions.

254.3–5   "Of antres . . . OTHELLO.]   Shakespeare; II.iii.140–41.

255.34–256.37   But I . . . bring forth.]   Omitted from the 1872 and 1892 editions.

261.23–25   General Kearney's . . . Matamoras.]   Kearny's Army of the West had marched up the Arkansas on its way to Santa Fé; see note 26.19–20. Mexico declared war on the United States on April 24, 1846, following the movement of American troops into territory between the Nueces and Rio Grande rivers claimed by both Mexico and Texas. Brigadier General Zachary Taylor defeated Mexican forces under General Mariano Arista north of the Rio Grande at Palo Alto on May 8 and at Resaca de la Palma on May 9, then crossed the river and occupied Matamoras, Mexico, on May 18; the United States, meanwhile, declared war on Mexico on May 13.

262.7 'to daff . . . pass.'] Cf. Shakespeare, 1 Henry IV, iv.i.96.

270.27–271.3 One could . . . against them.'] Omitted from the 1872 and 1892 editions.

270.28–37 stanza . . . closing year.'] II.xlii.1–9.

271.2–3 'Their hand . . . them.'] Cf. Genesis 16:12.

271.23–24 'La Fontaine qui Bouille,'] The Fountain that Boils.

272.3–7 "It came . . . HAROLD.] II.lxix.1–4.

273.12–13 battles . . . Palma.] See note 261.23–25.

277.29 United States yager] A U.S. army rifle named for the jäger (hunter) troops, the skirmishing and scouting riflemen in the German armies.

279.3–5 "Ah me! . . . HUDIBRAS.] By Samuel Butler; cf. Part I.iii.1–2 (1663). In Butler, line 1 reads: "Ay me! what perils do environ."

279.29 Tête Rouge] Redhead. Referred to as Hodgman in Parkman's *Journals*, he has been identified as H. C. Hodgman, an artilleryman from a St. Louis company serving in the West.

284.3–6 "To all . . . SCOTT.] The quotation, from Thomas Osbert Mordaunt's *Verses Written During the War* (1756–63), appeared above the signature *Anonymous* as an epigraph to Chapter XXXIV of *Old Mortality* (1816) by Walter Scott.

287.8–288.3 This story . . . another man.] Omitted from the 1872 and 1892 editions.

294.3–7 "Mightiest . . . CASTLE.] "Cadyow Castle, Addressed to the Right Honourable Lady Anne Hamilton," lines 57–60. Walter Scott's poem appeared in "Imitations of the Ancient Ballad" in *Minstrelsy of the Scottish Border* (1802–3), a collection compiled by Scott.

294.13–25 Indeed, . . . battlefield.] Omitted from the 1872 and 1892 editions.

298.31–32 'Oui, . . . fusil.'] "Yes, it's loaded for sure . . . — it's a good gun."

303.3–5 "In pastures . . . BRYANT.] "The Hunter of the Prairies," lines 13–14.

310.39–311.3 To borrow . . . etiquette.] Omitted from the 1872 and 1892 editions. Richard Porson (1759–1808), classical scholar and translator, was Regius Professor of Greek at Cambridge University. His elucidation of Greek idiom and usage, textual critiques, and studies of meter advanced Greek scholarship. The letters written by Philip Dormer Stanhope (1694–1773), 4th Earl of Chesterfield, to his son were published in 1774 and used as a handbook of good manners and deportment.

313.16–17   'preferring . . . night'] Cf. Shakespeare, *King Lear*, III.iv.2 ff.

317.3–11   "They quitted . . . MINSTREL.] I.iv.3– 10. See note 95.25–26.

320.38–321.6   No one . . . enterprise.] Omitted from the 1872 and 1892 editions.

322.11   *sacre . . . garce*] See note 17.31.

325.24–326.28   'Do you . . . congratulations.] Omitted from the 1872 and 1892 editions.

333.3–7   "And some . . . CORINTH.] Introductory lines 30–33. See note 29.3–15.

338.3–12   Some pigs . . . blood.] Omitted from the 1872 and 1892 editions.

339.15–18   For myself . . . visit them.] Omitted from the 1872 and 1892 editions.

340.29–341.13   After we had . . . vagabond again.] Omitted from the 1872 and 1892 editions.

341.30–39 and 342.7–16   *I cannot . . . reputation.] Omitted from the 1872 and 1892 editions.

THE CONSPIRACY OF PONTIAC

379.13   Father Rasles] Sébastien Rasles, or Râle, (1657?–1724), a Jesuit priest, arrived in Maine in 1689 and converted many of the Norridgewock, a leading tribe of the Abnaki confederacy, and compiled a dictionary of the Abnaki language. He was killed in a British raid on his settlement.

393.38   "Vivre . . . Dieu."] "To live in New France is truly to live in the bosom of God."

397.17   Castine, Joncaire, and Priber] Vincent, Baron de Castin, arrived in Canada in 1665 as colonel of the Carrignan regiment. He established a trading post at Penobscot (now Castine, Maine) in 1665, married the daughter of a Penobscot chief, and was a leader of the Penobscots during the French and Indian Wars; he died around 1722. Louis Thomas de Joncaire, seigneur de Chabert, (1670–1739), was captured by the Senecas soon after his arrival in New France in 1687, but earned their trust and lived among them for some time. He was appointed commander of Niagara by the French in 1720 and constructed the Magazin Royal, a storehouse for French traders made of bark and surrounded by a palisade, where he lived until his death. Christian

Priber, a Saxon whose utopian communitarian ideas were considered subversive, fled to England, then emigrated to Charlestown, South Carolina, in 1734 and two years later went to live among the Cherokee in the western mountains. He adopted their dress, learned their language, instructed them in his theories, and attempted to form a confederation of southern Indians that would maintain its neutrality by trading with both the British and the French. The colonists of South Carolina, believing Priber to be a French agent and possibly a Jesuit, twice attempted to arrest him, but he was protected by the Cherokee. He was finally captured in 1743 and sent to Frederica, Georgia, where he died a political prisoner.

421.2   cohorn]   Coehorns were small portable mortars named after their Dutch inventor, Baron Menno van Coehoorn (1641–1704).

429.12   empire . . . Mogul]   During the Seven Years War (1756–63) the British East India Company won control of Bengal and gained ascendancy over the French in their struggle for influence within the states of the declining Mogul empire.

433.4–8   Beaujeu . . . drums.]   In the 1851 edition, this read: Here the warriors ensconced themselves, and, levelling their guns over the edge, lay in fierce expectation, listening to the advancing drums of the English army.

434.3–29   Several . . . right and left.]   In the 1851 edition, this read: Several guides and six light horsemen led the way; a body of grenadiers was close behind, and the army followed in such order as the rough ground would permit. Their road was tunnelled through the forest; yet, deaf alike to the voice of common sense and to the counsel of his officers, Braddock had neglected to throw out scouts in advance, and pressed forward in blind security to meet his fate. Leaving behind the low grounds which bordered on the river, the van of the army was now ascending a gently-sloping hill; and here, well hidden by the thick standing columns of the forest, by mouldering prostrate trunks, by matted undergrowth, and low rank grasses, lay on either flank the two fatal ravines where the Indian allies of the French were crouched in breathless ambuscade. No man saw the danger, when suddenly a discordant cry arose in front, and a murderous fire blazed in the teeth of the astonished grenadiers. Instinctively as it were, the survivors returned the volley, and returned it with good effect; for a random shot struck down the brave Beaujeu, and the courage of the assailants was staggered by his fall. Dumas, second in command, rallied them to the attack; and while he, with the French and Canadians, made a good pass in front, the Indians opened a deadly fire on the right and left of the British column.

448.19–449.4   "Qui vive?" . . . Reine!"]   "Who goes there?" . . . "Of which regiment?" . . . "The Queen's!"

491.26–33   At the head . . . war.]   In the 1851 edition, this read: At the head of this dilapidated army was Sir Jeffrey Amherst, the able and resolute soldier who had achieved the reduction of Canada. He was a man well fitted for the emergency; cautious, bold, active, far-sighted, and endowed with a singular power of breathing his own energy and zeal into those who served under him. The command could not have been in better hands; and the results of the war, lamentable as they were, would have been much more disastrous, but for his promptness and vigor, and, above all, his judicious selection of those to whom he confided the execution of his orders.

495.25–26   Roman . . . Germans,]   Cornelius Tacitus (c. A.D. 56–120) in his treatise *De origine et situ Germanorum*.

527.30–528.7   On the eleventh . . . refusal.]   In the 1851 edition, this read: On the twelfth of May, when these arrangements were complete, the Indians once more surrounded the fort, firing upon it from morning till night.

537.10–11   anecdote . . . physician.]   The anecdote comes from Plutarch's *Lives*. After Alexander (356–23 B.C.) became seriously ill on his march through Asia Minor, he received a letter warning him that his friend and physician, Philip the Acarnanian, had been bribed by the king of Persia to poison him. When Philip brought in a cup of the medicine he had prepared, Alexander handed him the letter and, as his friend read it, calmly drank the contents of the cup. Within three days he had begun to regain his health.

553.7–557.31   On the third . . . Presqu' Isle.]   This is a revised and expanded version of the text that appeared in the 1851 edition.

563.26   Sacres Bougres]   Damned Blackguards.

596.10   'Que . . . ferais?']   "What would you want me to do about it?"

625.12–19   "I see," . . . cut off."]   Added in the 1870 edition.

628.12–19   "We are . . . of me."]   Added in the 1870 edition.

631.33–634.23   He and his . . . perished.]   Parkman revised and expanded this section, from the version that appeared in 1851, for the 1870 edition.

638.18–639.16   No great . . . presence.]   Revised and expanded for the 1870 edition, with Ecuyer's quote, pages 638.37–639.12, added.

641.1–658.14   In the mean . . . be well."]   Expanded to almost three times its original length for the 1870 edition.

691.17–18   scene . . . Campbell]   A raiding party of approximately 400 Tories and 500 Indians, commanded by Loyalist Colonel John Butler, entered the Wyoming Valley from the west on June 30, 1778, and defeated about 300 Continental regulars and militiamen under Colonel Zebulon Butler (no relation) on July 3. John Butler reported that the Indians took 227 scalps during and after the battle. Despite Butler's promises of protection, the raiders burned hundreds of buildings throughout the valley and carried many inhabitants into captivity, while the remainder of the population fled into the surrounding wilderness. The raid is described in the narrative poem *Gertrude of Wyoming* (1809) by the Scottish poet Thomas Campbell (1777–1844).

696.39–697.27   "Mon . . . bonjour.]   "My Brother,—The Word that my Father has sent to me, in order to make peace, I have accepted it, all our young people have buried their Tomahawks. I think that you will forget the bad things that happened long ago; likewise, I will also forget what you could have done to me in order to think only of good things, I, the Ojibwas, the Hurons, we must go to speak with you when you ask us to. Reply to me. I am sending you this counsel (*Q. necklace?*) so you will see it. If you are as I am, you will reply to me. I wish you good day."

732.21–735.10   Now, turning . . . submission.]   Added in the 1870 edition.

751.19–757.28   Morris, who . . . deceive us."]   This expanded section incorporated material that had appeared in Appendix F in the 1852 printing.

755.13–14   *"Eh bien, . . . jamais;"*]   "Well, then you are abandoning me after all!" . . . "No, my captain, . . . I will never abandon you."

766.10–770.3   Bouquet . . . marksmen.]   In the 1851 edition, this read: Colonel Bouquet was now pushing his preparations for the campaign with his utmost zeal; but August arrived before the provincial troops were in readiness. On the fifth of that month, the whole force was united at Carlisle, and consisted of five hundred regulars,—most of whom had fought in the battle of Bushy Run, of which that day was the anniversary,—a thousand Pennsylvanians, and a small but invaluable corps of Virginia riflemen. After remaining for a few days at Carlisle, the troops advanced to Fort Loudon, which they reached on the thirteenth. Here they were delayed for several weeks, and here Bouquet received the strange communication from Colonel Bradstreet, in which the latter informed him that he had made a preliminary treaty with the Delawares and Shawanoes, and that all operations against them might now be abandoned. We have already seen that Bouquet disregarded this message, thinking himself in no way called upon to lay aside his plans against an enemy who was suing for peace on one side, and butchering and scalping on another. Continuing therefore to advance, he passed in safety the scene of his desperate fight of the last summer, and on the seventeenth of September arrived at Fort Pitt, with no other loss than that of a few men picked off from the flanks and rear by lurking Indian marksmen.

811.8–23   In the spring, . . . war-song.]   Added in the 1870 edition.

814.40–41   *Detail . . . Illinois.*]   "Detailed account of that which occurred at The Louisiana on the occasion of the taking of the Illinois territory."

822.19–43   Smith . . . brigade."]   In *An Account of the Remarkable Occurrences in the Life and Travels of Colonel James Smith* (1799), Smith identifies the author of the ballad as "Mr. George Campbell, an Irish gentleman."

825.16–826.27   Here he found . . . New Orleans.]   This account of Fraser's mission is expanded from the earlier versions.

845.10–11   slaughtered . . . Patroclus;]   In Homer's *Iliad*, the death of the Achaian warrior Patroclus (in Book XVI) brings Achilles raging back to battle against the Trojans after other Achaians have fought without success to retrieve the corpse (Book XVII ff.).

878.38   "The Paxtoniade," . . . Hudibras,]   *The Paxtoniade by Christopher Gymnast, Esq., With the Prolegomena and Exercitations of Scriblerus* and *Hudibras* (1662–80), a satire by Samuel Butler.

CATALOGING INFORMATION

Parkman, Francis, 1823–1893.
   The Oregon trail; The conspiracy of Pontiac.
   Edited by William R. Taylor.

   (The Library of America; 53)
   1. West (U.S.)—Description and travel—To 1848.   2. Indians
of North America—West (U.S.)   3. Frontier and pioneer life—
West (U.S.)   4. Oregon Trail.   5. California Trail.   6. Pontiac's
Conspiracy, 1763–1765.   I. Title.   II. Title: Conspiracy of Pontiac.
III. Series.
F592.P284   1991   973.2'7—dc20   90–62264
ISBN 0–940450–54–2 (alk. paper)

*This book is set in 10 point Linotron Galliard,
a face designed for photocomposition by Matthew Carter
and based on the sixteenth-century face Granjon. The paper
is acid-free Ecusta Nyalite and meets the requirements for permanence of the American National Standards Institute. The binding
material is Brillianta, a 100% woven rayon cloth made by
Van Heek-Scholco Textielfabrieken, Holland. The composition is by Haddon Craftsmen, Inc., and The
Clarinda Company. Printing and binding
by R. R. Donnelley & Sons Company.
Designed by Bruce Campbell.*

THE LIBRARY OF AMERICA SERIES

1. Herman Melville, *Typee, Omoo, Mardi* (1982)
2. Nathaniel Hawthorne, *Tales and Sketches* (1982)
3. Walt Whitman, *Poetry and Prose* (1982)
4. Harriet Beecher Stowe, *Three Novels* (1982)
5. Mark Twain, *Mississippi Writings* (1982)
6. Jack London, *Novels and Stories* (1982)
7. Jack London, *Novels and Social Writings* (1982)
8. William Dean Howells, *Novels 1875–1886* (1982)
9. Herman Melville, *Redburn, White-Jacket, Moby-Dick* (1983)
10. Nathaniel Hawthorne, *Novels* (1983)
11. Francis Parkman, *France and England in North America* vol. I, (1983)
12. Francis Parkman, *France and England in North America* vol. II, (1983)
13. Henry James, *Novels 1871–1880* (1983)
14. Henry Adams, *Novels, Mont Saint Michel, The Education* (1983)
15. Ralph Waldo Emerson, *Essays and Lectures* (1983)
16. Washington Irving, *History, Tales and Sketches* (1983)
17. Thomas Jefferson, *Writings* (1984)
18. Stephen Crane, *Prose and Poetry* (1984)
19. Edgar Allan Poe, *Poetry and Tales* (1984)
20. Edgar Allan Poe, *Essays and Reviews* (1984)
21. Mark Twain, *The Innocents Abroad, Roughing It* (1984)
22. Henry James, *Essays, American & English Writers* (1984)
23. Henry James, *European Writers & The Prefaces* (1984)
24. Herman Melville, *Pierre, Israel Potter, The Confidence-Man, Tales & Billy Budd* (1985)
25. William Faulkner, *Novels 1930–1935* (1985)
26. James Fenimore Cooper, *The Leatherstocking Tales* vol. I, (1985)
27. James Fenimore Cooper, *The Leatherstocking Tales* vol. II, (1985)
28. Henry David Thoreau, *A Week, Walden, The Maine Woods, Cape Cod* (1985)
29. Henry James, *Novels 1881–1886* (1985)
30. Edith Wharton, *Novels* (1986)
31. Henry Adams, *History of the United States during the Administrations of Jefferson* (1986)
32. Henry Adams, *History of the United States during the Administrations of Madison* (1986)
33. Frank Norris, *Novels and Essays* (1986)
34. W. E. B. Du Bois, *Writings* (1986)
35. Willa Cather, *Early Novels and Stories* (1987)
36. Theodore Dreiser, *Sister Carrie, Jennie Gerhardt, Twelve Men* (1987)
37. Benjamin Franklin, *Writings* (1987)
38. William James, *Writings 1902–1910* (1987)
39. Flannery O'Connor, *Collected Works* (1988)
40. Eugene O'Neill, *Complete Plays 1913–1920* (1988)
41. Eugene O'Neill, *Complete Plays 1920–1931* (1988)
42. Eugene O'Neill, *Complete Plays 1932–1943* (1988)
43. Henry James, *Novels 1886–1890* (1989)
44. William Dean Howells, *Novels 1886–1888* (1989)
45. Abraham Lincoln, *Speeches and Writings 1832–1858* (1989)
46. Abraham Lincoln, *Speeches and Writings 1859–1865* (1989)
47. Edith Wharton, *Novellas and Other Writings* (1990)
48. William Faulkner, *Novels 1936–1940* (1990)
49. Willa Cather, *Later Novels* (1990)
50. Ulysses S. Grant, *Personal Memoirs and Selected Letters* (1990)
51. William Tecumseh Sherman, *Memoirs* (1990)
52. Washington Irving, *Bracebridge Hall, Tales of a Traveller, The Alhambra* (1991)
53. Francis Parkman, *The Oregon Trail, The Conspiracy of Pontiac*

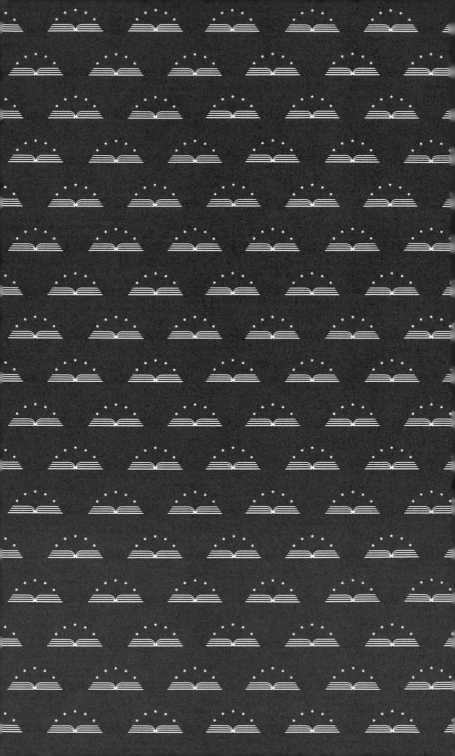